Cases and Materials on

Constitutional and Administrative Law

Tenth Edition

Michael J. Allen

LLB, LLM, Barrister

Brian Thompson

LLB, MLitt

OXFORD
UNIVERSITY PRESS

Great Clarendon Street, Oxford OX2 6DP

Oxford University Press is a department of the University of Oxford.
It furthers the University's objective of excellence in research, scholarship,
and education by publishing worldwide in

Oxford New York

Auckland Cape Town Dar es Salaam Hong Kong Karachi
Kuala Lumpur Madrid Melbourne Mexico City Nairobi
New Delhi Shanghai Taipei Toronto

With offices in

Argentina Austria Brazil Chile Czech Republic France Greece
Guatemala Hungary Italy Japan Poland Portugal Singapore
South Korea Switzerland Thailand Turkey Ukraine Vietnam

Oxford is a registered trade mark of Oxford University Press
in the UK and in certain other countries

Published in the United States
by Oxford University Press Inc., New York

Seventh edition 2002
Eighth edition 2005
Ninth edition 2008

British Library Cataloguing in Publication Data
Data available

Library of Congress Cataloging in Publication Data
Library of Congress Control Number: 2011904416

Typeset by Newgen Imaging Systems (P) Ltd, Chennai, India
Printed in Great Britain
on acid-free paper by
Ashford Colour Press Ltd, Gosport, Hampshire

ISBN 978–0–19–957904–4

3 5 7 9 10 8 6 4

OUTLINE CONTENTS

Public Law Online Resources from Oxford

Visit **www.oxfordtextbooks.co.uk/orc/publiclaw/** for access to a wealth of resources that accompany this book and have been designed to support your study of public law. These resources will help you to keep up-to-date with what is happening in the law and politics, as well as introducing you to key debates and providing a host of links to further material to help you direct your online study.

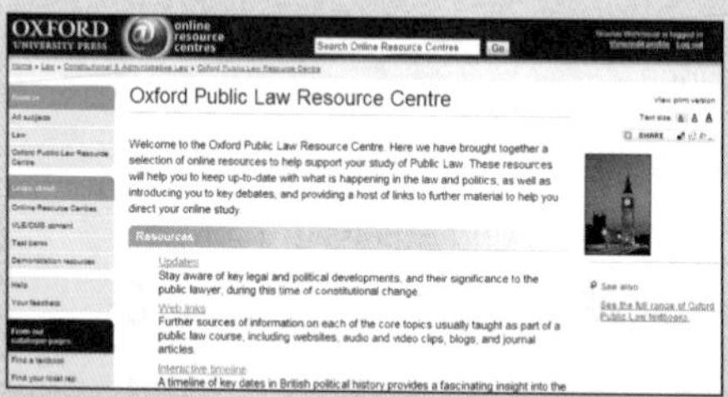

The following resources are all available on the site free of charge:

- **Regular updates** ensure that you are aware of key legal and political developments, and their significance to the public lawyer, during this time of constitutional change
- An extensive 'library' of **web links** is an invaluable resource that directs you immediately to further sources of information on each of the core topics usually taught as part of a public law course, including websites, audio and video clips, blogs, and journal articles
- A **timeline** of key dates in British political history provides a fascinating insight into the events that have influenced the development of constitutional and administrative law in the UK
- **'Oxford NewsNow' RSS feeds** provide constantly refreshed links to the latest relevant news stories
- **Audio podcasts** from expert Oxford authors discuss some key issues in public law and introduce you to their textbooks

www.oxfordtextbooks.co.uk/orc/publiclaw/

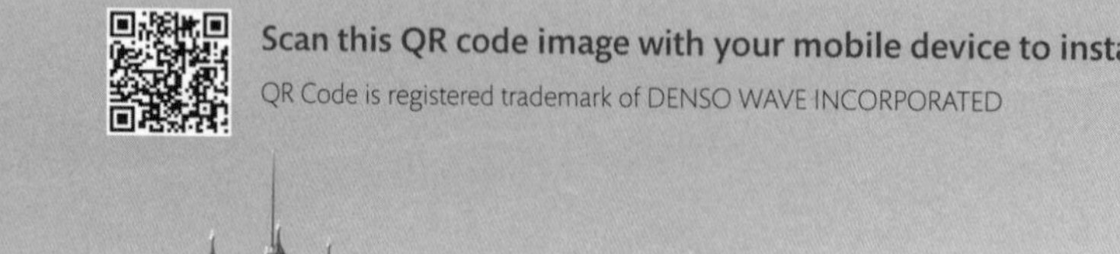

Scan this QR code image with your mobile device to instantly access this site.

QR Code is registered trademark of DENSO WAVE INCORPORATED

DETAILED CONTENTS

PREFACE

The publication of the 10th edition of a book is something of a landmark. There has been quite a lot of change in Constitutional and Administrative Law in the 21 years since the first edition appeared. What has not changed are the aims of the book. It is designed to supplement textbooks in Constitutional and Administrative or Public Law by collecting together legislation, cases, official papers, and scholarly literature and providing notes on them plus questions to stimulate understanding as well as promoting skills in handling primary sources. Not all topics are equally suited to this treatment, for example, devolution, but it is hoped that the coverage will satisfy academic and professional core requirements.

The preparation for this edition ended just over six months after the General Election of May 2010 and the formation of a coalition government between the Conservatives and the Liberal Democrats. Indeed I was just able to include a section of the draft *Cabinet Manual* on the formation of a government, which had been revised to take account of the experience of May 2010. This appears in Chapter 5 which has brought together the topics of the Royal Prerogative and Constitutional Conventions. The previous Labour government had embarked on a programme of reform which had included the possibility of significant changes to the royal prerogative. The outcome was more limited with the Constitutional Reform and Governance Act 2010 providing a statutory basis for the management of the civil service and the ratification of treaties. The link between the royal prerogative and constitutional conventions include debate over whether they can be codified or put on a statutory basis as well as constitutional convention acting as a means of regulating the exercise of the royal prerogative which includes the formation of a government.

Chapter 3 on the Rule of Law includes dicta from the both the High Court and House of Lords in *Corner House Research* v *Director of the Serious Fraud Office* on whether factors taken into account in discontinuing an investigation into allegations of bribery in arms contracts breached the rule of law.

New material on the separation of power and the appropriate checking role of the courts is added to the start of Chapter 4 on Judicial Independence, and other changes include extracts from the most recent reports of the Judicial Appointments Commission, the Office of Judicial Conduct, and the Judicial Appointments and Conduct Ombudsman, and extracts from the report of the Advisory Panel on Judicial Diversity.

The revision of the chapters dealing with Parliament includes updating of sessional information, the Wright reforms in the House of Commons in Chapter 6, and in Chapter 7 sessional information, and consideration of the regime for regulating standards including the registration of interests and the investigation of breaches of the Code of Conduct. Following the uproar over abuse by MPs of expenses and allowances, a new institution, the Independent Parliamentary Standard Authority, was established by the Parliamentary Standards Act 2009 which was amended by the Constitutional Reform and Governance Act 2010. Also included is the Supreme Court's decision in *R* v *Chaytor* which held that parliamentary privilege did not prevent prosecution of MPs for a breach of the criminal law in relation to claims for expenses and allowances.

The chapter on the European Union has been moved (Chapter 8) and it includes the Treaty of Lisbon's amendments to the Treaty on European Union and the renamed Treaty on the Functioning of the European Union.

Revisions to Chapter 9 on Human Rights include extracts from *London & Quadrant Housing Trust* v *Weaver* on what constitutes a public function for a 'hybrid' body, dicta from *Horncastle* on taking into account decisions of the European Court of Human Rights in Strasbourg, dicta from *Shayler* on the interpretation and application of the 'necessary in a democratic society' test for restricting a Convention right, and in the section on control orders, the adoption by the House of Lords in *Secretary of State for the Home Department* v *AF* of the test of the Strasbourg court in *A* v *United Kingdom,* for determining if the material disclosed to a controlee satisfies the requirements of a fair trial in accordance with Article 6.

Chapters 10 and 11 on Judicial Review have been updated in relation to statistics of cases in the Administrative Court, and amendments to Part 54 of the Civil Procedure Rules and Practice Direction 54D. This implements the regionalization of the Administrative Courts so that claims for judicial review can be heard in Birmingham, Cardiff, Leeds, and Manchester and some initial research on the first year of operation in those four centres is summarized.

In addition to the general updating of material taken from the Ombudsmen's annual reports, Chapter 10 also has extracts from all three of the Parliamentary and Health Service Ombudsman's sets of *Principles* as well as proposals from the Law Commission's consultation paper on Public Services Ombudsman, concerning abolition of the MP filter, on modifying the statutory bar on overlap with alternative remedies, and on making ombudsmen's findings binding.

The addition of new Immigration and Asylum Chambers in the two-tier structure is included in Chapter 13 on Tribunals along with an illustrative diagram and material on the approach of considering administrative justice as a system.

I am very grateful for the help and support provide by Tom Young, the commissioning editor at OUP, and his colleagues involved in the production of the book, both in-house and freelance.

Finally, when this book was first published, it was produced by three academics. Michael Allen is now a Member of the Criminal Cases Review Commission and Bernadette Walsh is now a Deputy Parliamentary Counsel. I hope they are not too unhappy with what I have done during my sole stewardship of the book.

Brian Thompson
December 2010

ACKNOWLEDGEMENTS

Grateful acknowledgement is made to all the authors and publishers of copyright material which appears in this book, and in particular to the following for permission to reprint material from the sources indicated:

Parliamentary copyright material is reproduced with the permission of the Controller of Her Majesty's Stationery Office on behalf of Parliament. Crown copyright material is reproduced under Class Licence Number C2006010631 with the permission of the Controller of OPSI and the Queen's Printer for Scotland.

Extracts from the reports of the European Court of Justice and Court of First Instance (ECR) are taken from www.curia.europa.eu. These are unauthenticated reports and are reproduced free of charge. The definitive versions are published in *Reports of Cases before the Court of Justice* or the *Official Journal of the European Union*.

Administrative Justice & Tribunals Council (which replaces the Council of Tribunals) and the authors for extracts from M Adler & J Gulland: *Tribunal Users' Experiences, Perceptions and Expectations: A Literature Review* (Council on Tribunals, 2003); the *AJTC Annual Report 2009/10*; *Principles for Administrative Justice 2009*; and a diagram from *The Developing Administrative Justice Landscape* (2009).

Ashgate Publishing and the authors for table from T Buck, R Kirkham and B Thompson: T*he Ombudsman Enterprise and Administrative Justice* (Ashgate Publishing, 2011).

Vernon Bogdanor for extract from V Bogdanor: *Introduction to Constitutions in Democratic Politics* (Ashgate Publishing, 1988).

Cambridge University Press and the editors for extract from introduction to J Elster and R Slagstad (eds.): *Constitutionalism and Democracy* (Cambridge University Press, 1988). © Cambridge University Press and Unversitetsforlaget (Norwegian University Press) 1988, reproduced with permission.

Cambridge Law Journal and the authors for extract from Ian Leigh and Laurence Lustgarten: 'Making rights real: The Courts, Remedies and Human Rights Act' in *Cambridge Law Journal* 58 (1999).

Commission for Local Administration in England (Local Government Ombudsman) for extract from *Annual Report 2009–10—Delivering Public Value.*

Cornell University Press for extract from Charles Howard McIlwain: *Constitutionalism Ancient and Modern*. Copyright © 1947 Cornell University; Renewed © 1975 by Charles Howard McIlwain. Used by permission of the publisher, Cornell University Press.

The Incorporated Council of Law Reporting for extracts from the *Appeal Cases Reports; Chancery Reports; Queen's Bench Reports;* and *Weekly Law Reports.*

The Right Honourable the Lord Irvine of Lairg for extracts from The Tom Sargant Memorial Lecture, 'The Development of Human Rights in Britain under an Incorporated Convention on Human Rights', 16 December 1997; and Address to the 3rd Clifford Chance Conference on the Impact of a Bill of Rights on English Law, 28 November 1997.

Sir Sydney Kentridge QC for extract from 'The Incorporation of the European Convention on Human Rights' in *Constitutional Reform of the United Kingdom: Practice and Principles* (Centre for Public Law, University of Cambridge, 1998).

Hart Publishing Limited for extract from *Kings College Law Journal:* Lord Bingham of Cornhill: 'The Courts and Constitution' 15 (1966/67).

MBA Literary Agents Ltd for extract from R Miliband: *The State in Capitalist Society* (Weidenfeld and Nicolson, 1969). Material from THE STATE OF CAPITALIST SOCIETY by Ralph Miliband is reproduced by kind permission of the author's Estate.

Oxford University Press for extracts from R Barker: *Political Legitimacy and the State* (OUP, 1990) and P Craig: 'Britain in the European Union' in Jeffrey Jowell and Dawn Oliver (eds.): *The Changing Constitution* (OUP, 2007); Peter Cane: *An Introduction to Administrative Law* (4e, OUP, 2004); Hazel Genn: 'Tribunal Review of Administrative Decision Making' in Generva Richardson and Hazel Genn: *Administrative Law and Government Action: The Courts and Alternative Mechanisms of Review* (OUP, 1994); H L A Hart: *The Concept of Law* (OUP, 1961); C B Macpherson: *The Real World of Democracy* (OUP, 1966); Geoffrey Marshall: *Conventions: The Rules and Forms of Political Accountability* (OUP, 1984); W F Murphy: 'Constitutions, Constitutionalism and Democracy' in D Greenberg, S N Katz, M B Oliveiro, and S C Wheatley (eds.): *Constitutionalism and Democracy: Transitions in the Contemporary World* (OUP, 1993);A Tomkins: *Public Law* (OUP, 2003);K C Wheare: *Modern Constitutions* (2e, OUP, 1966); and C R Munro, *Studies in Constitutional Law* 2e (OUP, 1999) .

Oxford University Press Journals for extracts from *Parliamentary Affairs*: A Abraham: 'The Ombudsman as Part of the UK Constitution: A Contested Role?' 61 PA 206 (2008); F F Ridley: 'There is no British Constitution: A Dangerous case of the Emperor's Clothes' 41 *Parliamentary Affairs* (1988); R Rose: 'Law as a Resource of Public Policy', 39 *Parliamentary Affairs* (1986); and Leslie Wolf-Phillips: 'A Long Look at the British Constitution', 37 *Parliamentary Affairs* (1984).

Parliamentary and Health Service Ombudsman for extracts from *Making an Impact: Annual Report 2009–10 (2010);* Principles of Good Administration (2009); Principles of Good Complaint Handling (2009); and Principles for Remedy (2009).

Pearson Education Inc, Upper Saddle River, NJ 07458, for extract from Carl Friedrich: *Limited Government: A Comparison* (Prentice Hall, 1974), copyright © 1974.

Sage Publications Ltd for extracts from David Beetham: 'Key Principles and Indices for a Democratic Audit' in David Beetham (ed.): *Defining and Measuring Democracy* (Sage, 1994), copyright © David Beetham 1994.

Scottish Council of Law Reporting for extract from *MacCormick v Lord Advocate* [1953] SC 396, *Reports of the Court of Sessions in Scotland* [SC].

SLS Legal Publications (NI) for extract from R Brazier: 'How near is a written Constitution?' in *Northern Ireland Legal Quarterly* 52 (2001).

Sweet & Maxwell Ltd for extracts from R. Blackburn and A. Kennon: *Griffith and Ryle on Parliament, Functions, Practices and Procedures* (Sweet & Maxwell, 2003); P McAuslan and J F McEldowney: 'Legitimacy and the Constitution: The Dissonance between Theory and Practice' in *Law, Legitimacy and the Constitution: Essays Marking the Centenary of Dicey's 'Law of the Constitution'* (Sweet & Maxwell, 1985); figure from R Rawlings: 'Parliamentary Redress of Grievance' in C Harlow (ed.): *Public Law and Policy* (Sweet & Maxwell, 1986); and extracts from *Civil Justice Quarterly*: K H Hendry: 'The Tasks of Tribunals: Some Thoughts' 1 CJQ 253 (1982); from *European Human Rights Law Review*: Lord Irvine of Lairg: 'Activism and Restraint: Human Rights and the Interpretative Process', ECHR (1999); from *Law Quarterly Review*: J Raz: 'The Rule of Law and its Virtue' 93 LQR (1977); 195–202and from *Public Law*: T R S Allan: 'The Limits of Parliamentary Sovereignty', *Public Law* (1985);R Baldwin and J Houghton: 'Circular Arguments: The Status and Legitimacy of Administrative Rules, *Public Law* (1986); Murray Hunt: 'The Horizontal Effect of the Human Rights Act', *Public Law* (1998); Sir John Laws: 'Law and Democracy', *Public Law* (1995); A Page: 'MPs and the Redress of Grievances', *Public Law* (1985); G Richardson and H Genn: 'Tribunals in Transition: Resolution or Adjudication?',

Public Law (2007); and The Rt Hon Lord Woolf of Barnes: 'Droit Public-English Style', *Public Law* (1995).

The Estate of Sir William Wade QC for Sir William Wade: 'The United Kingdom's Bill of Rights' in *Constitutional Reform in the United Kingdom: Practice and Principles* (Centre for Public Law, 1998).

Wiley-Blackwell Publishing Ltd for extracts from M Adler: 'Tribunal Reform: Proportionate Dispute Resolution and the Pursuit of Administrative Justice', 69 *Modern Law Review* 958 (2006); H F Rawlings: 'Judicial Review and the Control of Government', 64 *Public Administration* (1986);C Scott: 'Accountability in the Regulatory State', 27 *Journal of Law and Society* (2000);J Webber: 'Supreme Courts, Independence and Democratic Agency', 24 *Legal Studies* 55 (2004); and tables from A. Le Sueur, 'Developing Mechanisms for Judicial Accountability in the UK' (2004) *Legal Studies* 74.

Every effort has been made to trace and contact copyright holders prior to going to press but this has not been possible for material listed below this notice. Although we are continuing to seek the necessary permissions up to publication, if notified, the publisher will undertake to rectify any errors or omissions at the earliest opportunity.

TABLE OF CASES

References in **bold** indicate that the case is discussed significantly.

European Court of Human Rights

European Court of Justice—Alphabetical

European Court of Justice—Numerical

TABLE OF STATUTES

Page references in **bold** indicate the text is reproduced in full.

Statutory Instruments

TABLE OF EUROPEAN LEGISLATION

Page references in **bold** indicate the text is reproduced in full.

Treaties and Conventions

Directives

1

Constitutional Law in the United Kingdom

OVERVIEW

In this chapter we begin by introducing the idea of a constitution and then examine the key concepts of constitutionalism, legitimacy, democracy, limited government, and the state.

SECTION 1: INTRODUCTION

NOTE: Constitutional law is the law relating to the constitution. While this statement may be true, it is not particularly helpful. To study constitutional law we need to discover what a constitution is. There are many competing definitions. While many clubs, organizations and other groupings have constitutions, our concern is with the constitutions of nation-states.

Thomas Paine, *Rights of Man* in *The Complete Works of Thomas Paine*

pp. 302–303

A constitution is not the act of a government, but of a people constituting a government, and a government without a constitution is power without right.... A constitution is a thing antecedent to a government; and a government is only the creature of a constitution.

It was Paine's belief that England lacked a constitution, as he stated at p. 370 that 'the continual use of the word "constitution" in the English parliament shows there is none and the whole is merely a form of government without a constitution, and constituting itself with what power it pleases'. Paine admired, by contrast, the recent American Constitution.

C. H. McIlwain, *Constitutionalism Ancient and Modern*

(1947), pp. 8–10

...[T]he analysis Paine made of the early American constitution was remarkably acute. The significant points in that analysis are these:

That there is a fundamental difference between a people's government and that people's constitution, whether the government happens to be entrusted to a king or to a representative assembly.

That this constitution is 'antecedent' to the government.

That it defines the authority which the people commits to its government, and in so doing thereby limits it.

That any exercise of authority beyond these limits by any government is an exercise of 'power without right.'

That in any state in which the distinction is not actually observed between the constitution and the government there is in reality no constitution, because the will of the government has no check upon it, and that state is in fact a despotism.

One thing alone Paine fails to make fully clear. If a government exercises some 'power without right,' it seems to be necessarily implied that the people have a corresponding right to resist. But is this a legal or is it only a political right? Is such resistance a legalized rebellion or merely an extralegal revolution? Or, further, is it possible to incorporate in the framework of the state itself some provision or institution by which a governmental act or command *ultra vires* may be declared to be such, and subjects therefore exempted from its operation and released from any legal obligation to observe or obey it? In short, can government be limited legally and effectively by any method short of force? To these questions Paine gives no clear answer. It might be assumed that forcible resistance to power without right must itself be legal and not revolutionary; but in every case there seems no recourse except to force of some kind.

The one conspicuous element lacking in Paine's construction therefore seems to be the element of judicial review. Writing when he did, and as he did, to justify an actual rebellion, it is perhaps not strange that he was thinking primarily of politics rather than of law, that the 'rights' he had in mind were the rights of man rather than the rights of the citizen, or that the sanction for these rights should be extralegal action rather than any constitutional check. Paine, like many idealists in a hurry, was probably impatient of the slowness of legal remedies for existing abuses. But others, who were more constitutionally minded than he, had begun to feel that any such remedies, to be truly effective, must ultimately have the sanction of law. Years before, Lord Camden had insisted that the principles of the law of nature must be incorporated in the British Constitution if they were to be observed, and that they actually were so incorporated. The necessary inference from such a principle as his is that the interpreters of law should be the ones to define the rights of individuals and to trace the bounds of legitimate government over them. The protection of rights became for him, and for all who thought as he did, the enforcement of 'constitutional limitations.'

■ QUESTION

What did Paine mean by 'antecedent'? Did he mean that the constitution must exist prior in time to the Government or that the principles of the constitution should be superior in character, and binding in authority, to the actions of government? If the former is correct, does the United Kingdom have a constitution? (See the discussion which follows.) If the latter is correct, could the United Kingdom ever have constitutional government? (See Chapter 2.)

NOTE: Paine expressed a concept of constitutions which involved 'the conscious formulation by a people of its fundamental law' (McIlwain, *op. cit.*, p. 3). This would find expression in a written document or documents. The alternative view sees constitutions not as a conscious creation but rather as an evolutionary consequence made up of 'substantive principles to be deduced from a nation's actual institutions and their development' (McIlwain, *ibid.*). This could include an unwritten or uncodified constitution. This view was expressed by Bolingbroke.

Bolingbroke, *A Dissertation upon Parties (1733–34) in The Works of Lord Bolingbroke*

(1841), II, p. 88

By constitution we mean, whenever we speak with propriety and exactness, that assemblage of laws, institutions and customs, derived from certain fixed principles of reason, directed to certain fixed objects of public good, that compose the general system according to which the community hath agreed to be governed.... We call this a good government, when... the whole administration of public affairs is wisely pursued, and with a strict conformity to the principles and objects of the constitution.

■ QUESTION

When Paine stated that a governmental act contrary to the constitution is an act of 'power without right', did he thereby imply that such an act would be unconstitutional?

In Bolingbroke's terms such an act would warrant the conclusion that the Government is not a good one; is this the same thing?

NOTE: It can be argued that, according to Bolingbroke's definition, the United Kingdom has a constitution, as there are laws, institutions, and customs which combine to create a system of government to which the community agrees, or at least, from which it does not appear to dissent. This is the traditional view of most constitutional lawyers. Constitutional theorists have further refined their analysis of constitutions, creating other points of comparison. For example, K. C. Wheare, *Modern Constitutions* (1966), Chapter 2, proposed six classifications of constitutions: (1) written and unwritten; (2) rigid and flexible; (3) supreme and subordinate; (4) federal and unitary; (5) separated powers and fused powers; (6) republican and monarchical. If Wheare's definitions are applied to the United Kingdom, it may be said that there is an unwritten constitution in the sense that it is uncodified. There is no supreme or fundamental constitutional law, and the processes for changing the constitution are flexible. The state is a unitary (power has been devolved but can be reclaimed: see Scotland Act 1998, s. 28(7) at p. 82 *post*; perhaps the better term is union state which can accommodate the asymmetrical devolution in the United Kingdom), and monarchical one where powers are fused, there being a parliamentary Executive as opposed to a presidential Executive.

While most writers on the constitution are satisfied that, by comparison with the various definitions, the United Kingdom does have a constitution, some writers insist that there is no constitution.

F. F. Ridley, 'There is no British Constitution: A Dangerous Case of the Emperor's Clothes'

(1988) 41 *Parliamentary Affairs* 340–343, 359–360

Having a constitution seems to be a matter of self-respect: no state is properly dressed without. Every democracy except Britain, New Zealand and (with qualifications) Israel seems to have a written constitution, plainly labelled. Not to be left out of the world of constitutional democracies, British writers define constitution in a way which appears to give us one too, even though there is no document to prove it. The argument is that a constitution need not be embodied in a single document or, indeed, wholly written. We say instead that a country's constitution is a body of rules—some laws, some conventions—which regulate its system of government. Such a definition does not, however, bridge the gap between Britain and the rest of the world by providing us with a substitute for a documentary constitution: it simply shifts the ground, by using the word in an entirely different way.

We see this ambiguity in K. C. Wheare's now classic book on constitutions.

> The word constitution is commonly used in at least two senses in ordinary discussion of political affairs. First of all, it is used to describe the whole system of government, the collection of rules which establish and regulate it. These rules are partly legal and partly non-legal. When we speak of the British constitution that is the normal, if not the only possible meaning the word has. Everywhere else it is used in the sense of legal rules embodied in one document.

But that is not the real distinction. Foreign usage is not particularly concerned with the documentary character of a constitution. It appears in that form, but that is not its essential. Everywhere save Britain the constitution is defined as a special category of law. British usage dissolves the distinction between constitutional law and other laws because British courts recognise no such distinction. British political scientists, for their part, dissolve the distinction between law and other rules of behaviour because they are not much interested in law: for them, the constitution is practice.

Books of an old-fashioned sort with British Constitution in their title describe significant laws, conventions and institutions. This approach is now dismissed as formalistic by political scientists who regard such accounts as incomplete, if not misleading. They are right if their aim is to describe a system of government. In no country are all the important laws that shape the system of government embodied in a constitutional document. Nor can the operation of constitutional law be understood without reference to the practice of politics. Such arguments, however, miss the essential character of constitutions altogether. The wide focus of political scientists is right if their aim is to describe a system of government. Equating it with a study of the constitution, however, may owe less to a desire for realism than to a lack of concern about legal matters. This is often justified on the grounds that law is not a distinct and important element in understanding systems of government, but there are professional reasons too. Political studies did not originate in law faculties, as in continental Europe, and never subsequently developed any real interest in law. As a result, we get books called The British System of Government or, more fashionably, The British Political System, where politics is added to institutions. What such books include when they claim to describe the British 'constitution' depends on what their authors consider important to the framework of the system: what the 'constitution' consists of thus emerges from a survey of the system and is not determined by an independent, non-political definition that precedes it.

Much the same applies to books by lawyers. Works entitled Constitutional Law cover a selection of laws that appear important to the author, together with important conventions and often a reduced version of the topics treated by institutionally oriented political scientists. Since there appear to be no consequences in judicial practice if the label constitutional is applied to a particular law, it is in the end no more than a convenient way for textbook writers to organise their material, just as they produce books on industrial law or commercial law. That emerges clearly from one textbook definition of the study of constitutional law as 'that body of knowledge dealing with the law of the constitution in a broader sense... matters pertaining to the organisation of government and its relation to citizens'. That may cover almost anything, indeed F W Maitland said that 'there is hardly any department of law which does not, at one time or another, become of constitutional importance.'

Though there is broad agreement on the contents of such books on constitutional law, in the last resort it depends on what academic lawyers consider relevant—and a quick survey of standard textbooks will show that at the margins there are significant variations in what is brought into the orbit of the British 'constitution'. In the absence of legal criteria that distinguish constitutional law from other laws, the definition becomes so broad that it defines nothing at all. In the context of the British legal system, the term constitutional law is thus literally meaningless. Borrowing from political science for their definition of the British constitution, however, academic lawyers hardly even really address the question whether in legal, or indeed logical, terms Britain has a constitution at all.

Such accounts of the British 'constitution' are only superficially the result of the absence of a constitutional document. Because we feel uneasy about our difference from other democracies which do have labelled constitutions, we turn to what is now a peculiarly British usage of the word to prove that we are not really different at all. One purpose of this article is to show that Britain *is* different, and different in ways that are important politically as well as in law. It is to show that Britain does not really have a constitution at all, merely a system of government, even if some parts of it are more important to our democratic order than others or are treated (perhaps: were treated until Mrs Thatcher's time) with greater veneration. It may be embarrassing to explain that, as in the nursery tale, the Emperor has no clothes after all, that the constitutional attire his courtiers claim to see is empty words, but that is the essential of this article. Unless we face up to that fact, moreover, any discussion of how we can safeguard certain democratic arrangements that we regarded as part of the British 'constitution' in the past (e.g. the independence of local government) or entrench others (e.g. a Bill of Rights) against an 'elective dictatorship' will run into the sand.

Constitutions and their Characteristics

Use of the word constitution as the manner in which a polity is organised, the main characteristic of its governmental system, is undoubtedly the historic one. By the end of the eighteenth century, however, the word came to have another meaning. The American War of Independence and the French Revolution marked a turning point after which the new meaning became universal, Britain excepted. It applied to a special form of law embodied as a matter of convenience in a single document. As used elsewhere, it is now a term of law not politics. Constitutions there have certain essential characteristics, none of them found in Britain. Without these characteristics, it is impossible to distinguish a constitution from a description of the system of government in a way that is analytically precise. Without them, it is impossible to say that a country has a constitution in the current international sense of the word. More important, lest this be thought a linguistic quibble, without them a system of government lacks the legitimacy a constitution gives and a political system the protection it offers.

The characteristics of a constitution are as follows.

(1) It establishes, or constitutes, the system of government. Thus it is prior to the system of government, not part of it, and its rules can not be derived from that system.

(2) It therefore involves an authority outside and above the order it establishes. This is the notion of the constituent power ('pouvoir constituant'—because we do not think along these lines, the English translation sounds strange). In democracies that power is attributed to the people, on whose ratification the legitimacy of a constitution depends and, with it, the legitimacy of the governmental system.
(3) It is a form of law superior to other laws—because (i) it originates in an authority higher than the legislature which makes ordinary law and (ii) the authority of the legislature derives from it and is thus bound by it. The principle of hierarchy of law generally (but not always) leads to the possibility of judicial review of ordinary legislation.
(4) It is entrenched—(i) because its purpose is generally to limit the powers of government, but also (ii) again because of its origins in a higher authority outside the system. It can thus only be changed by special procedures, generally (and certainly for major change) requiring reference back to the constituent power.

James Bryce made all these points at the turn of the century. Defining a constitution as a framework of political society organised through law, he distinguished between 'statutory' and 'common law' types of constitutions. Of the former, he wrote: 'The instrument in which a constitution is embodied proceeds from a source different from that whence spring other laws, is regulated in a different way, and exerts a sovereign force. It is enacted not by the ordinary legislative authority but by some higher and specially empowered body. When any of its provisions conflict with a provision of the ordinary law, it prevails and the ordinary law must give way.' Bryce's alternative, the idea of a common-law constitution, is perhaps another way of saying that the British 'constitution' just grew, as the common law itself. His definition of a statutory constitution does, however, allow us to distinguish constitutional law from other law by clear criteria, thus giving the term not just a specific meaning, but a meaning with consequences. Though he, too, declared the distinction between written and unwritten constitutions old-fashioned, it is a pity that his summary has not served as a starting point for subsequent commentaries on the British 'constitution'.

... [T]he term British constitution is near meaningless even as used by British writers. It is impossible to isolate parts of the system of government to which the label may authoritatively be attached. There is no test to discriminate between constitutional and less than constitutional elements since labelling has no defined consequence, unlike countries where constitutions are a higher form of law. If used descriptively, as Wheare and others suggest, it is simply a fancy-dress way of saying the British system of government and at best redundant. More dangerous, those who talk of a British constitution may mislead themselves into thinking that there are parts of the system to which a special sanctity attaches. But in that normative sense the term is equally meaningless. When significant parts of the system are reformed, we have no test to tell us whether the outcome is an improper breach of the constitutional order, a proper amendment, or whether the reformed institutions were not part of the 'constitution' at all. I may be told that this is an academic quibble since our democratic politicians know what is of constitutional significance in our way of government, approach such matters differently from other reforms, and are politically if not legally constrained. That, however, is not the case. Our system of government is being changed, with increasing disregard for tradition, the only unwritten rules to which one might appeal as 'constitutional' principles.

There is cause for concern about the muddled way we think about the British 'constitution'; there is even greater cause for concern about the political consequences of its nature. It is sometimes said that our 'constitution' is now under stress as major changes occur far more rapidly than before in its written and unwritten parts. Is this due to changing ideas about how the British system of government should be organised, widely held, or is it simply that the government of the day is using its power to change the system in the pursuit of its own political goals? Is the constitutional order evolving or is it under attack? We have moved from consensus to conflict in politics: have we moved in that direction, too, as regards our constitutional order, taking that to mean the broad principles underlying the way government is organised and power exercised? Many old principles no longer command universal agreement and there are well-supported demands for new principles. We have had debates on the entrenchment of rights; on federalism or regional devolution as against the unitary state; on the case for consensus rather than majority as a basis for government, on the relative weight of national versus local mandates and the independence of local government; on the duty of civil servants; on electoral reform with all its implications for the operations of government; on who should define the national interest; on open government and official secrecy; on complementing representative democracy by referenda and other forms of participation—and much else. Political disagreement and disagreement on the proper constitutional order are linked. An ideologically-committed government, determined to implement its policies, will support different constitutional principles from those who want consensus policy-making; those concerned primarily with individual freedom and the rights of the public will support different principles from those who want strong government—and so on. Since opinion is now deeply divided on so many issues, one can probably no longer talk of the constitutional order as if it were a reflection of public opinion.

There are no grounds for complacency about British democracy.

NOTE: In the extract which follows, Brazier makes the point that the British constitution is largely written but remains uncodified.

R. Brazier, 'How Near is a Written Constitution?'

(2001) 52 *Northern Ireland Legal Quarterly* 3–5

As every schoolchild is supposed to know, the United Kingdom does not have a written constitution. A British citizen has to seek the rules of the constitution in a daunting number of places—legislation, judicial decisions, statements about constitutional conventions, the law and practice of Parliament, European Community law, and so on. It is hardly surprising that the interested citizen will normally leave those sources to one side and rely instead on books written by authoritative writers, and those who aspire to be authoritative. But just listing the primary materials which form the constitution demonstrates the extent to which the British constitution is largely a written one. Indeed, all the sources exist as official statements made by organs of the state, except for conventions, most of which have been reduced to writing only by the unofficial efforts of constitutional commentators. The British constitution is written, but it is not codified into a single official document, or limited number of such documents, setting out those legal rules which prescribe how the state is to be governed.

In implementing its range of reforms the Labour Government has caused Parliament to enact an additional and substantial corpus of statute law of a constitutional character. While, therefore, the United Kingdom still lacks a codified constitution, it has been given rather more of a written constitution by the addition of sixteen Acts of Parliament which, in whole or in part, add to the British constitution.[1] Perhaps most importantly towards that end, the United Kingdom now has the kind of Bill of Rights which features prominently in so many national constitutions, supplied by the Human Rights Act 1998. The lacuna which had existed in the enforcement of civil rights has now been filled. The devolution statutes have answered—at least for the time being—many long-standing queries about the appropriate relationships between the various parts of Great Britain, and with luck of the United Kingdom, and have redefined the juridical balance between them; the composition of the national legislature has been radically altered by the House of Lords Act 1999; and so on. There has been an exponential growth in the body of constitutional statute law since 1997, and because statute overrides case law and convention in the constitutional order the new laws represent some of the ground work which would be required for the production of a codified constitution. When it was still in opposition the Labour Party recognized that its legislative programme would have that effect in the narrower sense of the phrase constitution-making. In what was then its main constitutional policy document, *A New Agenda for Democracy*, adopted four years before coming to power, the party claimed that its changes would be a significant step in the direction of a written constitution, and the paper stated that the party would leave open the question of whether at a later stage progress should be made towards formal codification. Now that statement needs to be put into context. On the one hand, it was the first move—however tentative—by either of the two big political parties towards the idea of constitutional codification. On the other hand the statement did not

1. [Footnotes 10–12 omitted]

As in constitutional law generally, describing a statute as one of constitutional import can be a matter of choice. But the principal Acts are the Referendums (Scotland and Wales) Act 1997, the Data Protection Act 1997, the Scotland Act 1998, the Government of Wales Act 1998, the Northern Ireland Act 1998, the Greater London Authority (Referendum) Act 1998, the Human Rights Act 1998, the Regional Development Agencies Act 1998, the European Parliamentary Elections Act 1999, the Greater London Authority Act 1999, the House of Lords Act 1999, the Local Government Act 1999, the Regulation of Investigatory Powers Act 2000, the Political Parties, Elections and Referendums Act 2000, the Disqualifications Act 2000, and the Representation of the People Act 2000.

[Footnotes 14, 15 omitted]

really take account of all the other areas of the constitution which Labour's proposed changes would not affect but which would have to be reassessed and considered for inclusion in any constitutional code. For even after Labour's current reform programme has been fully implemented it would leave vital matters untouched, such as the monarchy, prerogative powers enjoyed by ministers, the powers of the House of Commons, and the judicial system. Clearly, too, that statement in the policy paper was over-terse, in that it ignored other important matters which would be crucial in any codification exercise, such as how and by whom it would be undertaken. Nor did the comments about codification find any place in Labour's 1997 General Election manifesto.

NOTE: The House of Lords Select Committee on the Constitution has the following terms of reference:

> To examine the constitutional implications of all public bills coming before the House; and to keep under review the operation of the constitution.

One of the first problems the Committee faced was to determine what the constitution was. It sought to address this question in its First Report.

First Report from the House of Lords Select Committee on the Constitution

HL 11 of 2001–02, paras. 17–21

17. . . . [T]he Committee could, if we so wished, look at any of a wide range of topics within our terms of reference. A glance at the contents page of any book on constitutional matters reveals the wide range of possible headings:

- Government
- the Royal Prerogative
- Parliament
- the Judiciary and judicial review
- the constitutional position of the Civil Service
- citizenship
- personal freedoms, liberties and free speech
- the EU
- devolution
- referendums
- electoral reform.

18. Many books have been written on, and many attempts have been made to consider, these and other topics which are thought to form the constitution of the United Kingdom. The constitution is said to be in flux, and the sense of what it is constantly evolving. The constitution is uncodified and although it is in part written there is no single, accepted and agreed list of statutes which form that part of the constitution which is indeed written down. While we would not wish, nor would we have the time, to write another such book ourselves, we nevertheless agreed that there was need to set for ourselves some kind of definition of what issues might fall within our remit. We do not see this as a dry academic exercise: our primary motive in doing so is as the first stage in determining which constitutional issues are in fact significant. There are many issues that are politically important both to individuals in the House and outside, and there are many issues which are matters of public debate. We would not wish to become a parliamentary magnet to which issues were attracted merely because the label 'constitutional' was attached to them by those who thought them important. A definitional exercise will, in our view, both help us to determine which issues are indeed of significance, and therefore form topics for our consideration, and assist us in working out the boundaries of our work in terms of overlap with that of other committees.

19. We accordingly asked all our witnesses what their definition was of the constitution. We are very grateful to those who responded and also to those who gave good reasons for not supplying a definition as such. We are very conscious that, given everything said in the preceding paragraphs, this was indeed something of a trick question. Lord Alexander of Weedon told us 'it is of the essence of our constitution that it is constitutional issues as they evolve. That seems to me largely to defy any attempt at a rigid definition' (Q 23). The Leader of the House, Baroness Jay of Paddington, said that it was 'quite difficult

to formulate a specific definition' but that the Government understood what was meant by the specifics of constitutional reform and that they did constitute a constitutional package (Q 175). Lord Strathclyde, Leader of the Conservative Peers offered us 'anything that affects the way we are governed, the balance between the different powers of Parliament and its associated repositories of powers. It is about the authorities under which we are governed' (Q 128). Lord Rodgers of Quarry Bank, Leader of the Liberal Democrat Peers, offered us 'the political and administrative structure, whether based on statute or convention, by which we are governed' (Q 63). Lord Craig of Radley, Convenor of the Cross Bench Peers, while not claiming to have any instant answer, referred to power, the exercise of power and the sharing of the exercising of power, a need for 'some form of checking balance' and 'a form of consensus or as near consensus as is reasonable to expect to be able to go ahead'. He referred to the balance between the various elements exercising authority and power (Q 154). Tony Wright MP, Chairman of the Commons Public Administration Committee, suggested that 'the constitution is.... whatever it is at any one time and we make it up as we go along... it is something to do with the relationship between citizens and the state and between the different parts of the state' (QQ 89, 91).

20. Against the background of these very helpful comments, which serve not least to illustrate the difficulties of any attempt to define a constitution we offer as our own working definition: 'the set of laws, rules and practices that create the basic institutions of the state, and its component and related parts, and stipulate the powers of those institutions and the relationship between the different institutions and between those institutions and the individual.'

21. We offer the following as the five basic tenets of the United Kingdom Constitution (phrases in italics indicate subjects falling within the remit of other parliamentary committees...):

- Sovereignty of the Crown in Parliament
- The Rule of Law, encompassing *the rights of the individual*
- Union State
- Representative Government
- Membership of the Commonwealth, *the European Union*, and other international organisations.

■ QUESTIONS

1. Does the provision of a list of tenets of the constitution amount to a definition of the constitution?
2. Is there any truth in the following statement by Sidney Low, in *The Governance of England* (1904), p. 12: 'British government is based upon a system of tacit understandings. But the understandings are not always understood'?
3. Colin Munro, *Studies in Constitutional Law* (1999), p. 3, states:

   The true distinction...is between states where some of the more important constitutional rules have been put in a document, or a set of associated documents, given special recognition, and states where the constitution has many sources, none of which enjoys such recognition.

   Is this an adequate explanation, or does the sanctity accorded to a constitution serve other important purposes such as helping to guarantee freedom and placing restraints on the exercise of power by government?
4. Is there some inherent virtue in a system of government derived from a constitution, which is lacking in a country which does not have such a codified constitution? Indeed, why are constitutions enacted? See Wheare, below.

K. C. Wheare, *Modern Constitutions*

(1966), pp. 4–8

[W]hat a Constitution says is one thing, and what actually happens in practice may be quite another. We must take account of this possible difference in considering the form and worth of Constitutions. What is more, we must be ready to admit that although almost all countries in the world have a Constitution, in many of them the Constitution is treated with neglect or contempt. Indeed in the middle of the twentieth century it can be said that the majority of the world's population lives under systems of government where the government itself and particularly the executive government are of more importance and are treated with more respect or fear than the Constitution. It is only in the states of Western Europe, in the countries of the British Commonwealth, in the United States of America, and in a few Latin-American states that government is carried on with due regard to the limitations imposed by a Constitution; it is only in these states that truly 'constitutional government' can be said to exist....

Since the Constitution of a country is only a part of that country's whole system of government, does it make any difference whether a country has a Constitution or not? The short answer is that in many countries the fact that there is a Constitution does make a difference. This brings to light a characteristic which most Constitutions exhibit. They are usually endowed with a higher status, in some degree, as a matter of law, than other legal rules in the system of government. At the least it is usually laid down that the amendment of the Constitution can take place only through a special process different from that by which the ordinary law is altered....

It is natural to ask... why it is that countries have Constitutions, why most of them make the Constitution superior to the ordinary law, and, further, why Britain, at any rate, has no Constitution, in this sense, at all.

If we investigate the origins of modern Constitutions, we find that, practically without exception, they were drawn up and adopted because people wished to make a fresh start, so far as the statement of their system of government was concerned. The desire or need for a fresh start arose either because, as in the United States, some neighbouring communities wished to unite together under a new government; or because, as in Austria or Hungary or Czechoslovakia after 1918, communities had been released from an Empire as the result of a war and were now free to govern themselves; or because, as in France in 1789 or the U.S.S.R. in 1917, a revolution had made a break with the past and a new form of government on new principles was desired; or because, as in Germany after 1918 or in France in 1875 or in 1946, defeat in war had broken the continuity of government and a fresh start was needed after the war. The circumstances in which a break with the past and the need for a fresh start come about vary from country to country, but in almost every case in modern times, countries have a Constitution for the very simple and elementary reason that they wanted, for some reason, to begin again and so they put down in writing the main outline, at least, of their proposed system of government. This has been the practice certainly since 1787 when the American Constitution was drafted, and as the years passed no doubt imitation and the force of example have led all countries to think it necessary to have a Constitution.

This does not explain, however, why many countries think it necessary to give the Constitution a higher status in law than other rules of law. The short explanation of this phenomenon is that in many countries a Constitution is thought of as an instrument by which government can be controlled. Constitutions spring from a belief in limited government. Countries differ however in the extent to which they wish to impose limitations. Sometimes the Constitution limits the executive or subordinate local bodies; sometimes it limits the legislature also, but only so far as amendment of the Constitution itself is concerned; and sometimes it imposes restrictions upon the legislature which go far beyond this point and forbid it to make laws upon certain subjects or in a certain way or with certain effects. Whatever the nature and extent of the restrictions, however, they are based upon a common belief in limited government and in the use of a Constitution to impose these limitations.

The nature of the limitations to be imposed on a government, and therefore the degree to which a Constitution will be supreme over a government, depends upon the objects which the framers of the Constitution wish to safeguard. In the first place they may want to do no more than ensure that the Constitution is not altered casually or carelessly or by subterfuge or implication; they may want to secure that this important document is not lightly tampered with, but solemnly, with due notice and deliberation, consciously amended. In that case it is legitimate to require some special process of constitutional amendment—say that the legislature may amend the Constitution only by a two-thirds majority or after a general election or perhaps upon three months' notice.

The framers of Constitutions often have more than this in mind. They may feel that a certain kind of relationship between the legislature and the executive is important; or that the judicature should have a certain guaranteed degree of independence of the legislature and executive. They may feel that there are certain rights which citizens have and which the legislature or the executive must not invade or remove. They may feel that certain laws should not be made at all....

In some countries only one of the considerations mentioned above may operate, in others some, and in some, all. Thus, in the Irish Constitution, the framers were anxious that amendment should be a deliberate process, that the rights of citizens should be safeguarded, and that certain types of laws should not be passed at all, and therefore they made the Constitution supreme and imposed restrictions upon the legislature to achieve these ends. The framers of the American Constitution also had these objects in mind, but on top of that they had to provide for the desire of the thirteen colonies to be united for some purposes only and to remain independent for others. This was an additional reason for giving supremacy to the Constitution and for introducing certain extra safeguards into it.

NOTE: As Ridley recognizes the framers of a constitution may have particular aims in mind. Constitutions may serve different functions in different countries or even within the same country at different times.

W. F. Murphy, 'Constitutions, Constitutionalism and Democracy' in D. Greenberg, S. N. Katz, M. B. Oliviero and S. C. Wheatley (eds), *Constitutionalism and Democracy*

(1993), pp. 8–10

What Are the Functions of a Constitution?

A Constitution as Sham, Cosmetic, or Reality. The principal function of a sham constitutional text is to deceive. Lest US citizens revel in righteousness, they might recall that Charles A. Beard charged the framers of the US text with hypocrisy, and the Conference of Critical Legal Studies still so accuses the entire American legal system. Whether Beard and the Critics have told the full story, they have reminded us that a constitutional document's representation of itself, its people, their values, and decisional processes is imperfect. Thus, even reasonably authoritative texts play a cosmetic role, allowing a nation to hide its failures behind idealistic rhetoric. But, insofar as a text is authoritative, its rhetoric also pushes a people to renew their better selves.

A Constitution as a Charter for Government. At minimum, an authoritative constitutional text must sketch the fundamental modes of legitimate governmental operations: who its officials are, how they are chosen, what their terms of office are, how authority is divided among them, what processes they must follow, and what rights, if any, are reserved to citizens. Such a text need not proclaim any substantive values, beyond obedience to itself; if it does proclaim values, they might be those of Naziism or Stalinism, anathema to constitutional democracy.

A Constitution as Guardian of Fundamental Rights. Thus the question immediately arises about the extent to which a constitutional text relies on or incorporates democratic and/or constitutional theories. Insofar as a text is authoritative and embodies democratic theory, it must protect rights to political participation. Insofar as it is authoritative and embodies constitutionalism, it must protect substantive rights by limiting the power of the people's freely chosen representatives.

The Constitution as Covenant, Symbol, and Aspiration. Insofar as a constitution is a covenant by which a group of people agree to (re)transform themselves into a nation, it may function for the founding generation like a marriage consummated through the pledging partners' positive, active consent to remain a nation for better or worse, through prosperity and poverty, in peace and war.

For later generations, a constitution may operate more as an arranged marriage in which consent is passive, for the degree of choice is then typically limited. Even where expatriation is a recognized right, exit from a society offers few citizens a viable alternative. Revolution becomes a legal right only if it succeeds and transforms revolutionaries into founders. And deeply reaching reform from within a constitutional framework tends to become progressively more difficult, for a system usually endures only by binding many groups to its terms.

The myth of a people's forming themselves into a nation presents a problem not unlike that between chicken and egg. To agree in their collective name to a political covenant, individuals must have already had some meaningful corporate identity *as a people*. Thus the notion of constitution as covenant must mean it formalizes or solidifies rather than invents an entity: it solemnizes a previous alliance into a more perfect union.

A constitution's formative force varies from country to country and time to time. The French, one can plausibly argue, have been the French under monarchies, military dictatorships, and assorted republics. It is also plausible, however, to contend that Germans have been a different people under the Kaiser, the Weimar Republic, the Third Reich, and the Federal Republic. In polyglotted societies such as Canada, India, and the United States or those riven by religious divisions and bleeding memories of civil war such as Ireland, 'there may be no other basis for uniting a nation of so many disparate groups.' A constitution may thus function as a uniting force, 'the only principle of order', for there may be 'no [other] shared moral or social vision that might bind together a nation.' [Sanford Levinson, *Constitutional Faith* (1988) p. 73.] It is difficult to imagine what has united the supposedly United States more than the political ideas of the Declaration of Independence and the text of 1787.

Reverence for the constitution may transform it into a holy symbol of the people themselves. The creature they created can become their own mythical creator. This symbolism might turn a constitutional text into a semisacred covenant, serving 'the unifying function of a civil religion.' [T. Grey, 'The Constitution as Scripture' (1984) 37 *Stanford Law Review* 1, 18.] In America, 'The Bible of verbal inspiration begat the constitution of unquestioned authority.'

Religious allusions remind us, however, that this symbolic role may also have a dark side. Long histories of bitter and often murderous struggles among Christians and among Muslims demonstrate that a sacred text may foster division rather than cohesion, conflict rather than harmony. The 'potential of a written constitution to serve as the source of fragmentation and disintegration' [Levinson] is nowhere more savagely illustrated than in the carnage of the US Civil War. For, ultimately, that fratricidal struggle was over two visions of one constitutional document. The result was a gory war that wiped out more than 600,000 lives. Complicating analysis is the fact that when the blood of battle dried, the document of 1787, duly amended, resumed its unifying role.

In a related fashion, a constitution may serve as a binding statement of a people's aspirations for themselves as a nation. A text may silhouette the sort of community its authors/subjects are or would like to become: not only their governmental structures, procedures, and basic rights, but also their goals, ideals, and the moral standards by which they want others, including their own posterity, to judge the community. In short, a constitutional text may guide as well as express a people's hopes for themselves as a society. The ideals the words enshrine, the processes they describe, and the actions they legitimize must either help to change the citizenry or at least reflect their current values. If a constitutional text is not 'congruent with' ideals that form or will reform its people and so express the political character they have or are willing to try to put on, it will quickly fade.

NOTE: While endless argument could be engaged upon on the question whether or not the United Kingdom has a constitution, perhaps a more profitable issue for consideration is whether the system of government in the United Kingdom displays congruence with certain values, principles, and concepts associated with constitutional government in a liberal democratic state. Wheare's remarks above should be noted, namely, that in many countries the constitution is 'treated with neglect or contempt'. Thus the existence of a (codified) constitution of itself may not be a guarantee against repressive or totalitarian governments which disregard individual liberty and abrogate human rights.

V. Bogdanor (ed.), Introduction to *Constitutions in Democratic Politics*

(1988), pp. 3–7

Constitutions are not, of course, confined to democratic states. Indeed, the vast majority of the 159 member states comprising the United Nations possess codified constitutions, although less than a third of these can fairly claim democratic credentials. The latter can, declares S E Finer with pardonable exaggeration, be counted on one's fingers and toes. Conversely, three countries which are indubitably democracies—Britain, Israel and New Zealand—lack...codified constitutions.

In the modern world, constitutions are almost ubiquitous and they are indeed part of the tribute which vice pays to virtue. For there *is* a conceptual connection, not so much between the constitution as a document and democracy, but between modern constitutionalism and the idea of a liberal democracy. Whether a country has a codified constitution is hardly something of great importance to the political scientist. Whether it achieves the aims which constitutions are intended to help achieve, is a matter of far greater moment. For codified constitutions are, after all, valued as a means to the end of limiting governmental power; and, in a democracy, limiting also the power of the people to whom government is responsible. The Founding Fathers in drawing up the American Constitution had, after all, two aims, not one. The first was to draw up a structure of government which could serve to protect the people from government, from the danger of a tyranny of the majority in the legislature; but the second aim was to protect the people from themselves.

Thus, the relationship between constitutionalism and liberalism...is by no means a simple or straightforward one. To live under an effectively working constitution is not the same as living under a regime of moral *laissez-faire*. Constitutional government presupposes a certain set of virtues amongst the ruled; and these virtues must include self-restraint, a willingness not to push the pursuit of one's aims beyond a certain point. In the 1930s, Mr Justice Stone declared that the United States Supreme Court ought not to see itself as the sole guardian of the constitution. While the other branches of the Constitution were limited by institutional restraints, by checks and balances, the only restraint which limited the Court was its sense of self-restraint. By analogy, one might argue that in a democracy in which the people are, in effect, sovereign, the only effective restraint in the last resort is likely to be that of the people over themselves. Constitutions thus both liberate and bind; they provide for a framework of ordered freedom within a set of rules which prevents both majorities and their elected representatives from doing what they might otherwise wish to do.

The term 'constitution', as S E Finer shows, is to be understood in positivistic terms as a code of rules which aspire to regulate the allocation of functions, powers and duties among the various agencies and officers of government, and defines the relationships between these and the public. Yet, even defined in these terms, the existence of a constitution, in so far as it is observed, serves to limit power. For, to allocate functions, powers and duties is also, *ipso facto*, to limit power. There must be some gain to the citizen, however minimal, in living under a constitution which regularises the way in which power is exercised; even where government is authoritarian, it matters that it is not arbitrary.

Yet, a number of democratic constitutions today contain more than a mere organisation chart of functions and powers; they contain Bills of Rights, which may also include a charter of social and economic rights, something characteristic of constitutions of the twentieth century, although generally honoured more in the breach than in the observance.

. . . [I]n the case of Britain and Israel, two countries without codified constitutions, such pressure as exists to adopt one is based less on the desire to possess a clear-cut organisational chart delimiting the institutions of government than on a feeling that rights would be better protected under a codified constitution than they are at present.

The concept of a constitution is closely bound up with the notion of the limitation of government by law, a source of authority higher than government and beyond its reach. An enacted constitution is a means—although, as the examples of Britain, Israel and New Zealand show, not an essential means—of securing this end. The law, it is suggested, is logically prior to government, and therefore constitutes a standard by which the actions of government are to be evaluated. It is . . . this 'appeal to a pre-existing law' which 'is the essence of constitutionalism'.

Yet analysis of constitutions cannot be restricted simply to the document called 'the Constitution', or to constitutional law. For a working constitution in a democracy implies reference to certain norms and standards which lie beyond and outside the document itself, and which cannot easily be inferred from it by someone who is not steeped in the history and culture of the country concerned. When conduct on the part of a government or some other public body is dubbed 'unconstitutional', what is often meant is not necessarily that the law has been broken, but rather that the action is out of keeping with the style or, more broadly, the 'way of life' of a country. . . .

This kind of appeal—to constitutional conventions—can, of course, also be raised in countries without codified constitutions. When, in Britain, it is suggested that the policies of the Conservative Government towards local authorities since 1979 raise constitutional questions, what is meant is not that these policies are in any sense illegal, but rather . . . that they breach hitherto accepted understandings, albeit tacit, as to how relationships between central government and local authorities should be ordered. These tacit understandings, which, in Sidney Low's graphic phrase, are so often misunderstood, may not be written down; yet they exert a normative influence upon those concerned with central/local relations comparable to, and perhaps greater than, the influence exerted by a constitutional document. What makes Britain together with Israel and New Zealand, constitutional democracies, despite the absence of codified constitutions, is this very fact that their governments in general feel under pressure to conform to such norms; when accused of unconstitutional action their defence is not that the term 'unconstitutional' is without meaning, but that their actions can, despite appearances, be defended in constitutional terms.

Thus, in addition to the basic meaning of 'constitution'—a document containing, at the very least, a code of rules setting out the allocation of functions, powers and duties among the various agencies and officers of government—there is a wider meaning of constitution, according to which every democratic state has a constitution. This wider meaning comprehends the normative attitudes held by the people towards government, their conception of how power ought to be regulated, of what it is proper to do and not to do. There are, as it were, pre-constitutional norms regulating government, and it is upon these that the health and viability of democratic systems will depend.

SECTION 2: CONSTITUTIONALISM

Governments wield considerable power. Constitutions, while they may create the institutions of government and allocate power to these institutions, also generally seek to control or restrain the exercise of power. The principle of constitutionalism rests on this idea of restraining the government in its exercise of power. Constitutionalism, therefore, is to be set in contradistinction to arbitrary power.

M. J. C. Vile, *Constitutionalism and the Separation of Powers*

(1967), p. 1

Western institutional theorists have concerned themselves with the problem of ensuring that the exercise of governmental power, which is essential to the realization of the values of their societies, should be controlled in order that it should not itself be destructive of the values it was intended to promote. The great theme of the advocates of constitutionalism, in contrast either to the theorists of utopianism, or of absolutism, of the right or of the left, has been the frank acknowledgment of the role of government in society, linked with the determination to bring that government under control and to place limits on the exercise of its power.

C. J. Friedrich, *Limited Government: A Comparison*

(1974), pp. 13–14

Constitutionalism by dividing power provides a system of effective restraints upon governmental action. In studying it, one has to explore the methods and techniques by which such restraints are established and maintained. Putting it another, more familiar, but less exact way, it is a body of rules ensuring fair play, thus rendering the government 'responsible.' There exist a considerable number of such techniques or methods.

The question confronts us: how did the idea of restraints arise? And who provided the support that made the idea victorious in many countries? There are two important roots to the idea of restraints. One is the medieval heritage of natural-law doctrine. For while the royal bureaucrats gained the upper hand in fact, the other classes in the community who had upheld the medieval constitutionalism—the barons and the free towns, and above all the church—developed secularized versions of natural law. At the same time, they clung to residual institutions, such as the *parlements* in France. After the task of unification had been accomplished, and the despotic methods of absolutism could no longer be justified, these elements came forward with the idea of a separation of power. Both the English and the French revolutions served to dramatize these events.

The other root of the idea of restraints is shared by medieval and modern constitutionalism and is peculiar to some extent to Western culture. It is Christianity, and more specifically the Christian doctrine of personality. The insistence upon the individual as the final value, the emphasis upon the transcendental importance of each man's soul, creates an insoluble conflict with any sort of absolutism. Here lies the core of the objection to all political conceptions derived from Aristotelian and other Greek sources. Since there exists a vital need for government just the same, this faith in the worth of each human being is bound to seek a balance of the two needs in some system of restraints which protects the individual, or at least minorities, against any despotic exercise of political authority. It is quite in keeping with this conflict that the apologists of unrestrained power have, in all ages of Western civilization, felt the necessity of *justifying* the exercise of such power, a necessity which was not felt elsewhere.

Nor was it felt by all in the West. Bacon and Hobbes, Bodin and Spinoza, and even Machiavelli insisted that some sort of inanimate force, such as reason, natural law, or enlightened self-interest would bring about a self-restraint. But a deep-seated distrust of power was part of the tradition that taught that 'my Kingdom is not of this world,' and that states are usually just 'great robber bands,' since they lack justice. Hence self-restraint of the ruler must be reinforced by effective institutions: restraints upon the arbitrary exercise of governmental power.

Modern constitutionalism then has always been linked with the problem of power, in theory as well as in practice. Historically, it constitutes a reaction against the concentration of power that accompanied the consolidation of modern states, dynastic and national. Its theorists have insisted on the importance of limiting and defining the power acquired by monarchs. Whilst Hobbes described the rational structure of such a concentration of power and developed it into a veritable philosophy of power, Locke, taking up the challenge, demanded that the exercise of this power, although it was derived from the ultimate and unified source of all power—the people—remain divided by virtue of a fundamental decision.

■ QUESTIONS

1. Which of the ideas of self-restraint or institutional restraint is the dominant one in the British system of government?
2. In the United Kingdom there is no codified constitution expressly imposing limits on governmental power. Is governmental power limited in other ways?

NOTE: In the United Kingdom, where Parliament is supreme and may enact, amend, or repeal any law it chooses, there is no distinction between 'ordinary' laws and 'constitutional' laws (but see Laws LJ at pp. 86–88, *post*). Laws of constitutional significance are not accredited 'fundamental' status—they have no special sanctity. No special procedures are required for amending or repealing such laws. Indeed, in the absence of a codified constitution, it is arguable that it is impossible to state what laws are of constitutional significance without reference to constitutions elsewhere to see what kinds of matters are dealt with therein. A further consequence is, as Bogdanor states in 'Britain: the Political Constitution' in Bogdanor, *Constitutions in Democratic Politics*, p. 56, that 'the term "unconstitutional" cannot in Britain mean contrary to law; instead it means contrary to convention, contrary to some understanding of what it is appropriate to do. But, unfortunately, there is by no means universal agreement on what the standards of appropriateness are or ought to be'. Should this be a matter of concern? Is it not sufficient to entrust Parliament with the task of ensuring that constitutionalism is respected in the United Kingdom?

J. Elster, 'Introduction' in J. Elster and R. Slagstad (eds), *Constitutionalism and Democracy*

(1988), pp. 8–9

Why would a political assembly want to abdicate from the full sovereignty which in principle it possesses, and set limits on its own future actions? In an intergenerational perspective, the question is what right one generation has to limit the freedom of action of its successors, and why the latter should feel bound by constraints laid down by their ancestors. A natural (although possibly misleading) point of departure is to consider individual analogies. Why, for instance, would two individuals want to form a legal marriage instead of simply cohabiting? What possible advantages could they derive from limiting their future freedom of action and by making it more difficult to separate should they form the wish to do so? One obvious answer is that they want to protect themselves against their own tendency to act rashly, in the heat of passion. By raising the costs of separation and imposing legal delays, marriage makes it less likely that the spouses will give way to strong but temporary impulses to separate. By increasing the expected duration of the relationship, legal marriage also enhances the incentive to have children, to invest in housing and make other long-term decisions. These decisions, in turn create bonds between the spouses and reinforce the marriage.

These answers have partial analogues in the constitutional domain. It is a truism that constitutional constraints make it more difficult for the assembly or the society to change its mind on important questions. Groups no less than individuals (although not in quite the same sense as individuals) are subject to fits of passion, self-deception and hysteria which may create a temporary majority for decisions which will later be regretted. But then, one may ask, why could the members of the assembly not simply undo the decisions if and when they come to regret them? The presumption must be, after all, that the assembly knows what it is doing, not that it needs to be protected against itself.

Part of the answer to this question is suggested by the marriage analogy. The expected stability and duration of political institutions is an important value in itself, since they allow for long-term planning.

Conversely, if all institutions are up for grabs all the time, individuals in power will be tempted to milk their positions for private purposes, and those outside power will hesitate to form projects which take time to bear fruit. Moreover, if nothing could ever be taken for granted, there would be large deadweight losses arising from bargaining and factionalism.

Another part of the answer is that not all unwise decisions can be undone. Imagine that a majority untrammelled by constitutional constraints decides that an external or internal threat justifies a suspension of civil liberties, or that retroactive legislation should be enacted against 'enemies of the people.' In the first place, such measures have victims whom one cannot always compensate at later times. Examples abound: the internment of the American Japanese during the Second World War, the excesses during the Chinese Cultural Revolution, the *Berufsverbot* against Communists in several countries. When society again comes to its senses, the victims may be dead or their lives destroyed. In the second place, the temporary suspension of rights easily leads to the permanent abolition of majority rule itself and to its replacement by dictatorship. It suffices to cite the years 1794 and 1933. This is possibly the central argument for constitutional constraints on democracy: without such constraints democracy itself becomes weaker, not stronger.

■ QUESTION

If Elster's analogy is not false, does it mean that the United Kingdom system of government lacks legitimacy?

SECTION 3: LEGITIMACY

Why, following a revolution, does a government which has effective power backed up with military force, seek to make a constitution? Friedrich, in *Limited Government: A Comparison*, p. 118, states that such a response is 'motivated by the belief that such a constitution, if popularly approved, would give them the right to rule, over and above the mere power to do so'. If a government has the right to rule it is regarded as legitimate, and this, in turn, provides it with authority. Legitimacy, therefore, is a quality which is valuable to government.

S. E. Finer, *Comparative Government*

(1970), pp. 30–31

The stable and effective exercise of a government's power is that which derives from its authority. By this I mean that the commands to do or to abstain proceed from persons who—no matter whether this is logical or reasonable or justifiable by any objective criterion—are *believed* to be persons who have the moral right to issue them: so that, correlatively, those to whom the commands are addressed feel a moral *duty* to *obey* them. Authority represents a two-way process: a claim to be obeyed, and a recognition that this claim is morally right. No public recognition of a claim means no authority.

Where a population recognizes a moral duty to obey, there is no need for the government to reason with it, persuade it, bribe it or threaten it, though all these exercises of power may be necessary for the marginal recalcitrants. The mere recognition of a duty to obey achieves for the government what an overwhelming application of violence would not satisfactorily achieve. As Rousseau said: 'The strongest is never strong enough unless he succeeds in turning might into right and obedience into duty.' As human nature goes, fear is certainly the father of power, but authority is its mother. To inculcate the population with the belief that their rulers have the right to demand obedience and they the corresponding duty to give it is the principal art of government.

■ QUESTION

What, then, is legitimacy, and how is it acquired?

D. Beetham, *The Legitimation of Power*

(1991), pp. 11–12, 15–20, 25–27 and 34–36

The different dimensions of legitimacy

The key to understanding the concept of legitimacy lies in the recognition that it is multi-dimensional in character. It embodies three distinct elements or levels, which are qualitatively different from one another. Power can be said to be legitimate to the extent that:

(i) it conforms to established rules
(ii) the rules can be justified by reference to beliefs shared by both dominant and subordinate, and
(iii) there is evidence of consent by the subordinate to the particular power relation....

(i) The first and most basic level of legitimacy is that of rules... Power can be said to be legitimate in the first instance if it is acquired and exercised in accordance with established rules. For convenience I shall call the rules governing the acquisition and exercise of power the 'rules of power'. These rules may be unwritten, as informal conventions, or they may be formalised in legal codes or judgments....

The opposite of legitimacy according to the rules is, simply, *illegitimacy*; power is illegitimate where it is either acquired in contravention of the rules (expropriation, usurpation, coup d'état), or exercised in a manner that contravenes or exceeds them. The illegal acquisition of power usually has more profound, because more all-pervasive, consequences for legitimacy than some breach or contravention in its exercise, though that depends upon the seriousness of the breach, and whether it is repeated. Where the rules of power are continually broken, we could speak of a condition of chronic illegitimacy.

(ii) On its own, legal validity is insufficient to secure legitimacy, since the rules through which power is acquired and exercised themselves stand in need of justification. This is the second level of legitimacy: power is legitimate to the extent that the rules of power can be justified in terms of beliefs shared by both dominant and subordinate. What kinds of justification and what kinds of belief are needed? To be justified, power has to be derived from a valid source of authority (this is particularly true of political power); the rules must provide that those who come to hold power have the qualities appropriate to its exercise; and the structure of power must be seen to serve a recognisably general interest, rather than simply the interests of the powerful. These justifications in turn depend upon beliefs current in a given society about what is the rightful source of authority; about what qualities are appropriate to the exercise of power and how individuals come to possess them; and some conception of a common interest, reciprocal benefit, or societal need that the system of power satisfies.

No society is characterised by a complete uniformity of beliefs. Indeed, one of the distinctive features of power relations is the difference of circumstances, opportunities and values between dominant and subordinate groups. Yet without a minimum of the appropriate beliefs defined above being shared between the dominant and the subordinate, and indeed among the subordinate themselves, there can be no basis on which justifications for the rules of power can find a purchase. Naturally what counts as an adequate or sufficient justification will be more open to dispute than what is legally valid, and there is no ultimate authority to settle such questions; nevertheless clear limits are set by logic and the beliefs of a given society to what justifications are plausible or credible within it.

This second level or dimension of legitimacy has its corresponding negative or opposite. Rules of power will lack legitimacy to the extent that they cannot be justified in terms of shared beliefs: either because no basis of shared belief exists in the first place (e.g. slavery, 'artificial' or divided communities); or because changes in belief have deprived the rules of their supporting basis (e.g. hereditary rule or male power, in face of a declining belief in the superior qualities supposedly ascribed by birth or sex); or because changing circumstances have made existing justifications for the rules implausible, despite beliefs remaining constant. [For example] it is argued that the British electoral system, with its first-past-the-post rules determining who shall be elected in each constituency, is losing its legitimacy, and to an extent therefore also weakening that of the governments elected under it. This is not because of any shift in people's beliefs, but because the rules have increasingly delivered results that diverge, both regionally and nationally, from the proportion of votes cast, and hence from accepted notions about the representative purpose of elections in a democracy. It is the increasingly unrepresentative character of the electoral system, and its consequent vulnerability to attack in a society that believes in representation, that is the basis for the weakening legitimacy of governments appointed under it. The vulnerability was there before it was exploited, and the weakening of legitimacy took place before people publicly acknowledged it. It may have taken the poll-tax legislation to bring the issue to the forefront of public attention. But the potential for doing so was already present in the growing discrepancy between the rules and the beliefs or values underpinning them....

These different situations clearly have widely differing significance, but they can all be described as examples, not so much of illegitimacy, as of *legitimacy deficit* or weakness.

(iii) The third level of legitimacy involves the demonstrable expression of consent on the part of the subordinate to the particular power relation in which they are involved, through actions which provide evidence of consent.... [T]he importance of actions such as concluding agreements with a superior, swearing allegiance, or taking part in an election, is the contribution they make *to* legitimacy. They do this in two ways. The first is that they have a subjectively binding force for those who have taken part in them, regardless of the motives for which they have done so. Actions expressive of consent, even if undertaken purely out of self-interest, will introduce a moral component into a relationship, and create a normative commitment on the part of those engaging in them. Secondly, such actions have a publicly symbolic or declaratory force, in that they constitute an express acknowledgement on the part of the subordinate of the position of the powerful, which the latter are able to use as confirmation of their legitimacy to third parties not involved in the relationship, or those who have not taken part in any expressions of consent. They are thus often associated with impressive forms of ceremonial....

What is common to legitimate power everywhere... is the need to 'bind in'... the subordinate, through actions or ceremonies publicly expressive of consent, so as to establish or reinforce their obligation to a superior authority, and to demonstrate to a wider audience the legitimacy of the powerful.

It is in the sense of the public actions of the subordinate, expressive of consent, that we can properly talk about the 'legitimation' of power, not the propaganda or public relations campaigns, the 'legitimations' generated by the powerful themselves. And if the public expression of consent contributes to the legitimacy of the powerful, then the withdrawal or refusal of consent will by the same token detract from it. Actions ranging from non-cooperation and passive resistance to open disobedience and militant opposition on the part of those qualified to give consent will in different measure erode legitimacy, and the larger the numbers involved, the greater this erosion will be. At this level, the opposite or negative of legitimacy can be called *delegitimation*.

For power to be fully legitimate, then, three conditions are required: its conformity to established rules; the justifiability of the rules by reference to shared beliefs; the express consent of the subordinate, or of the most significant among them, to the particular relations of power. All three components contribute to legitimacy, though the extent to which they are realised in a given context will be a matter of degree. Legitimacy is not an all-or-nothing affair.... Every power relation knows its breaches of the rules or conventions; in any society there will be some people who do not accept the norms underpinning the rules of power, and some who refuse to express their consent, or who do so only under manifest duress. What matters is how widespread these deviations are, and how substantial in relation to the underlying norms and conventions that determine the legitimacy of power in a given context. Legitimacy may be eroded, contested or incomplete; and judgements about it are usually judgements of degree, rather than all-or-nothing.

Above all, the analysis I have given above demonstrates that legitimacy is not a single quality that systems of power possess or not, but a set of distinct criteria, or multiple dimensions, operating at different levels, each of which provides moral grounds for compliance or cooperation on the part of those subordinate to a given power relation. By the same token, power can be non-legitimate in very different ways, which I have signalled by the different terms: illegitimacy, legitimacy deficit and delegitimation. The erosion of justificatory norms, slavery, conquest, dictatorship, coup d'état, separatist agitation, revolutionary mobilisation—all are examples where power lacks some element of legitimacy, but does so in very different ways. The accompanying diagram summarises in tabular form the different dimensions of legitimate and non-legitimate power that I have distinguished, to reinforce the argument of the text.

Table 1.1 The three dimensions of legitimacy

Criteria of Legitimacy	Form of Non-legitimate Power
i conformity to rules (legal validity)	illegitimacy (breach of rules)
ii justifiability of rules in terms of shared beliefs	legitimacy deficit (discrepancy between rules and supporting beliefs, absence of shared beliefs)
iii legitimation through expressed consent	delegitimation (withdrawal of consent)

The significance of legitimacy

Legitimacy, as we have seen, comprises the moral or normative aspect of power relationships; or, more correctly, the sum of these aspects. . . .

To consider first the behaviour of those subordinate within a power relationship; its legitimacy provides them with moral grounds for cooperation and obedience. Legitimate power or authority has the right to expect obedience from subordinates, even where they may disagree with the content of a particular law or instruction; and subordinates have a corresponding obligation to obey. This obligation is not absolute—hence the dilemmas that occur when people are required by a legitimate superior to do things that are morally objectionable to them, as opposed to inconvenient or merely stupid. But it is the right that legitimacy gives those in authority to require obedience in principle, regardless of the content of any particular law or instruction, that makes it so important to the coordination of people's behaviour in all spheres of social life.

The legitimacy or rightfulness of power, then, provides an explanation for obedience through the obligation it imposes on people to obey, and through the *grounds or reasons* it gives for their obedience.

However, normative grounds or reasons are not the only reasons people have for obedience. . . .

[P]ower relations are almost always constituted by a framework of incentives and sanctions, implicit if not always explicit, which align the behaviour of the subordinate with the wishes of the powerful. They do so by giving people good reasons of a different kind, those of self-interest or prudence, for not stepping out of line. Obedience is therefore to be explained by a complex of reasons, moral as well as prudential, normative as well as self-interested, that legitimate power provides for those who are subject to it. This complexity may make it difficult to determine the precise balance of reasons in any one situation; but it is important to distinguish them analytically, since each makes a very different kind of contribution to obedience. . . .

[What are the consequences of legitimacy for the behaviour of the dominant within a power relationship?]

If legitimacy, as I have argued, enhances the order, stability and effectiveness of a system of power, then we should expect that the powerful will seek to secure and maintain the legitimacy of their power, in view of its advantages to them. Here again, however, we must be careful to avoid drawing the wrong conclusions from a mistaken definition of legitimacy. If we reduce it to people's 'belief in legitimacy', then we are likely to conclude that the way in which the powerful maintain their legitimacy is primarily by means of ideological work, and through the influence they have over the beliefs and ideas of the subordinate. . . .

I do not wish to discount altogether the role of ideological work, particularly in reinforcing the basic norms that underpin a given system of power, though I shall want to argue later that the processes involved are complex ones, and have been oversimplified in much of the relevant literature. What I would emphasise at this point, however, is that we need to look quite elsewhere for the effect of legitimacy on the behaviour of the powerful. If legitimate power is, as I have argued, power that is valid according to rules, and where the rules themselves are justifiable by and in conformity with underlying norms and beliefs, then the main way in which the powerful will maintain their legitimacy is by respecting the intrinsic limits set to their power by the rules and the underlying principles on which they are grounded. Legitimate power, that is to say, is limited power; and one of the ways in which it loses legitimacy is when the powerful fail to observe its inherent limits.

What are these limits? I would draw attention to two different kinds. One kind of limit is set by the rules which determine what the powers of the powerful are, and what they can rightly expect those subordinate to them to do—which specify, in other words, the respective duties and obligations of those involved in a power relationship. These rules may be largely conventional, or they may be legally defined. A feature of the modern world is the increasingly precise legal specification of the respective powers, or 'sphere of competence', of each powerholder. Even today, however, there is still considerable room left for 'custom and practice', for conventional understandings built up over time through processes of struggle and compromise, which govern the expectations of the powerful and the subordinate about what is, and is not, required of them; what can, and cannot, legitimately be demanded.

For the powerful to breach these rules in a substantial way, say by imposing some new or additional obligation on subordinates without warning or consultation, is either to invite action for legal redress, or, where the law is silent, to provoke informal protests which may develop into a more widespread crisis of legitimacy for the system of power. Unless they are arrogant or stupid, powerholders will only take such action when it is essential to some important purpose, or if they are driven to it by a serious predicament of their own. The fact that mostly they do not do so, and that they mostly respect the rules and conventions governing their relations with those subordinate to them, makes it easy to overlook an essential feature of legitimacy: that it sets limits to the behaviour of the powerful as well as imposing obligations on the subordinate. Because we more readily notice what the powerful do than what they refrain from doing, this essential feature of legitimacy tends to go unremarked.

The other kind of constraint which their need to maintain legitimacy imposes on the powerful is a more fundamental one: to respect the basic principles that underpin the rules or system of power, and to protect them from challenge. Rulers who derive their legitimacy from a divine source must respect religious traditions and defer to religious authorities; they will regard any threat to religion or religious belief as among the most serious they face. Those who derive their authority from the people will ignore at their peril any insistent and widespread popular current of opinion; to be seen to favour foreign interests at the expense of national ones will do more damage to their standing than almost anything else. Those who claim a monopoly of representation of the working class by virtue of a privileged knowledge of their interests cannot afford to allow independent sources of working-class opinion to find expression, or alternative institutions of representation to develop, which might challenge their monopoly. The legitimating ideas and justificatory principles that underpin the given institutions of power define which challenges the ruler has to take most seriously, because they strike at the basis of the system of rule itself.

■ QUESTION

If a government, using its majority in Parliament, passes appropriate laws empowering it to do specified acts, are its activities thereby rendered legitimate because they are done in accordance with the law, regardless of how oppressive or repugnant those laws might be? See Chapter 3 and also the extract which follows.

P. McAuslan and J. F. McEldowney, 'Legitimacy and the Constitution: the Dissonance between Theory and Practice' in P. McAuslan and J. F. McEldowney (eds), *Law, Legitimacy and the Constitution*

(1985), pp. 11–14

Legitimacy...does not deal so much with whether activities of government are lawful as whether they accord with what are generally perceived to be or what have for long been held up to be, the fundamental principles of the constitution according to which government is or ought to be conducted. Lawfulness is clearly an issue in so far as one of the fundamental principles of the British, no less than most other constitutions, is that government action should take place under the authority of, and in accordance with law—the narrow literal meaning of the rule of law—so that repeated unlawful actions or a perceived casualness towards the duty to comply with the law would in itself begin to raise doubts about the legitimacy of governmental action. The rule of law is generally thought to have a broader 'political' meaning which covers the same ground as, if it is not quite synonymous with, the concept of limited government. This meaning embraces such matters as fair and equitable administrative practices; recognition of the rights of political opposition and dissent; complying with constitutional conventions; adequate means of redress of grievances about governmental action affecting one. Thus a government which while adhering to the rule of law narrowly defined, flouted all or most of the practices generally thought to be covered by the rule of law broadly defined would also give rise to doubts about its legitimacy. One of the clearest and best examples of a government on the whole scrupulous to comply with the rule of law narrowly defined yet consistently flouting it, as to the majority of its citizens, when broadly defined is the government of the Republic of South Africa, in relation to its non-white citizens.

What makes the issue of the legitimacy of our constitutional arrangements so problematic is the general open-endedness of those arrangements; that is, the difficulty of knowing whether a practice or non-practice is or is not constitutional.

Even where practices may not differ over time, or place, there may be an inconsistency about them or a lack of knowledge about them, or a long-standing dispute about them, which could make it equally difficult to argue that following or not following a practice was or was not constitutional or legitimate. Probably the best example of this is the use of the royal prerogative, and the extent to which the courts may pass judgment on any particular use. Notwithstanding that the royal prerogative as a source of power for the government antedates Acts of Parliament, has been at the root of a civil war and a revolution in England

and has been litigated about on countless major occasions in respect of its use both at home and overseas, its scope is still unclear as is the role of the courts in relation thereto. The use by the Prime Minister of powers under the royal prerogative to ban trade unions at the Government Communication Headquarters at Cheltenham in 1983 was contested both for its lawfulness—that is whether such powers could be used and if so whether they were used correctly—and also for its legitimacy—that is whether, even if the constitutional power existed, this was a proper and fair use of the power. It can be seen that questions of lawfulness and legitimacy shade into one another here though the answers do not: the lawfulness of the action taken, confirmed by the House of Lords in 1984 (*Council of Civil Service Unions* v *Minister for the Civil Service* [1984] 3 All ER 935) did not and does not dispose of its legitimacy.

The G.C.H.Q. case is valuable for another point. We have pointed out that lawfulness is not to be confused with legitimacy. No more is constitutionality. What the Prime Minister did was not merely lawful; she exercised the constitutional powers of her office in the way in which those powers had always been exercised. That is, the use of the royal prerogative as the legal backing for the management of the public service, the principle that a civil servant is a servant of the Crown and holds office at the pleasure of the Crown is one of the best known principles of constitutional law, hallowed by usage and sanctioned by the courts. What is in issue from the perspective of legitimacy is whether the particular use made of that undoubted constitutional power, the manner of its use, and the justification both for the use and manner of use—that considerations of national security required both a banning of trade unions and no consultation with affected officers before the ban was announced—was a fair and reasonable use of power? Did it accord with legitimate expectations of fair and reasonable persons or was it a high-handed exercise of power of a kind more to be expected of an authoritarian government than one guided by and subscribing to principles of limited government?

In considering the issue of legitimacy in relation to our constitutional arrangements and the exercise of governmental power, what has to be done is to examine a range of practices, decisions, actions (and non-practices, -decisions and -actions) statements and policies which between them can amount to a portrait of power, so that we can form a judgment or an assessment of that power set against the principles of limited government outlined and discussed so far. It is not every failure to comply with law or every constitutional and non-constitutional short cut which adds up to an approach to powers which give rise to questions of legitimacy. If that were so, there would scarcely be a government in the last 100 years which could be regarded as legitimate, but it is those uses of power and law which seem to betray or which can only be reasonably explained by a contempt for or at least an impatience with the principles of limited government and a belief that the rightness of the policies to be executed excuse or justify the methods whereby they are executed. If, as we believe to be the case, powers are being so exercised, then the issue of constitutional legitimacy which arises is quite simple: what is the value or use of a constitution based on and designed to ensure the maintenance of a system of limited government if it can, quite lawfully and even constitutionally, be set on one side? Have we not in such circumstances arrived at that 'elective dictatorship' of which Lord Hailsham gave warning in 1977:

> It is only now that men and women are beginning to realize that representative institutions are not necessarily guardians of freedom but can themselves become engines of tyranny. They can be manipulated by minorities, taken over by extremists, motivated by the self-interest of organised millions.

Occasionally the people from whom legitimacy ultimately derives, pass judgment on government.

McAuslan and McEldowney

ibid., p. 1

Mr Clive Ponting's acquittal by a jury in February 1985, after he had admitted to passing official Government papers to a person not authorised to receive them, the very essence of section 2 of the Official Secrets Act 1911, and despite the most explicit summing up by the trial judge that they should convict, raises the question of what motivated the jury. It would suggest that when faced with a choice between a case which rests on constitutional theories about limited government derived from a 'higher law' which controlled what government could legitimately do, and a case which rested on actual practices of government bolstered by actual law, the jury preferred the theory of what the constitution ought to be to the practice of what it is. Little wonder that, as one newspaper put it, ministers were aghast at the verdict. The *Concise Oxford Dictionary* defines 'aghast' as meaning terrified. This essay will seek to show ministers would indeed have good reason to be terrified if ordinary people began preferring constitutional theory to government practice and acted on their preferences in their judgment of politicians. More particularly the jury's verdict in the Ponting trial may be seen then as the response of ordinary people to trends in government practices which seem to them to be, in perhaps indefinable ways, wrong.

■ QUESTIONS

1. In this case it was a jury of 12 which, by its verdict, appeared to be commenting on the legitimacy of governmental action in attempting to mislead the Foreign Affairs Select Committee about the circumstances surrounding the sinking of the *General Belgrano*, an Argentinian warship, during the Falklands Campaign in 1982. These 12 jurors may, or may not, have been representative of the views of the public. Are there more representative ways in which public sentiments regarding governmental action may be expressed?
2. Is majority rule under a system of parliamentary democracy a sufficient guarantee of legitimacy? What does majority rule mean in the context of the United Kingdom?

SECTION 4: DEMOCRACY

In the opening sentences of *Le Contrat Social* (1762) Rousseau stated:

Man is born free and everywhere he is in chains. One thinks himself the master of others, and still remains the greater slave than they. How did this change come about? I do not know. What can make it legitimate? That question I think I can answer.

The answer he gave was that the only ground of legitimacy is to be found in the general will of the people, as only the people can say who has the right to rule them. Thus it is the people who give legitimacy to a constitution—sovereignty resides with the people and, in turn, where the constitution sets up a system of elected representative government, that government acquires its authority both from the constitution and the people who elect it.

Does the constitution in the United Kingdom (if there is one) have a democratic basis? Is the system of government democratic? A starting point is to examine what a liberal-democracy is.

C. B. Macpherson, *The Real World of Democracy*

(1966), pp. 4–11

[O]ur liberal-democracy, like any other system, is a system of power; that it is, indeed, again like any other, a double system of power. It is a system by which people can be *governed*, that is, made to do things they would not otherwise do, and made to refrain from doing things they otherwise might do. Democracy as a system of government is, then, a system by which power is exerted by the state over individuals and groups within it. But more than that, a democratic government, like any other, exists to uphold and enforce a certain kind of society, a certain set of relations between individuals, a certain set of rights and claims that people have on each other both directly, and indirectly through their rights to property. These relations themselves are relations of power—they give different people, in different capacities, power over others....

[L]iberal-democracy and capitalism go together. Liberal-democracy is found only in countries whose economic system is wholly or predominantly that of capitalist enterprise. And, with few and mostly temporary exceptions, every capitalist country has a liberal-democratic political system....

The claims of democracy would never have been admitted in the present liberal-democracies had those countries not got a solid basis of liberalism first. The liberal democracies that we know were liberal first and democratic later. To put this in another way, before democracy came in the Western world there came the society and the politics of choice, the society and politics of competition, the society and politics of the market. This was the liberal society and state. It will be obvious that I am using liberal here in a very broad sense. I use it in what I take to be its essential sense, to mean that both the society as a whole and the system of government were organized on a principle of freedom of choice....

To make this society work, or to allow it to operate, a non-arbitrary, or responsible, system of government was needed. And this was provided, by revolutionary action in England in the seventeenth century, in America in the eighteenth, in France in the eighteenth and nineteenth, and by a variety of methods in most other Western countries sometime within those centuries. What was established was a system whereby the government was put in a sort of market situation. The government was treated as the supplier of certain political goods—not just the political good of law and order in general, but the specific political goods demanded by those who had the upper hand in running that particular kind of society. What was needed was the kind of laws and regulations, and tax structure, that would make the market society work, or allow it to work, and the kind of state services—defence, and even military expansion, education, sanitation, and various sorts of assistance to industry, such as tariffs and grants for railway development—that were thought necessary to make the system run efficiently and profitably. These were the kinds of political goods that were wanted. But how was the demand to call forth the supply? How to make government responsive to the choices of those it was expected to cater to? The way was of course to put governmental power into the hands of men who were made subject to periodic elections at which there was a choice of candidates and parties. The electorate did not need to be a democratic one, and as a general rule was not; all that was needed was an electorate consisting of the men of substance, so that the government would be responsive to their choices.

To make this political choice an effective one, there had to be certain other liberties. There had to be freedom of association—that is, freedom to form political parties, and freedom to form the kind of associations we now know as pressure groups, whose purpose is to bring to bear on parties and on governments the combined pressure of the interests they represent. And there had to be freedom of speech and publication, for without these the freedom of association is of no use. These freedoms could not very well be limited to men of the directing classes. They had to be demanded in principle for everybody. The risk that the others would use them to get a political voice was a risk that had to be taken.

So came what I am calling the liberal state. Its essence was the system of alternate or multiple parties whereby governments could be held responsible to different sections of the class or classes that had a political voice. There was nothing necessarily democratic about the responsible party system. In the country of its origin, England, it was well established, and working well, half a century or a century before the franchise became at all democratic. This is not surprising, for the job of the liberal state was to maintain and promote the liberal society, which was not essentially a democratic or an equal society. The job of the competitive party system was to uphold the competitive market society, by keeping the government responsive to the shifting majority interests of those who were running the market society.

However, the market society did produce, after a time, a pressure for democracy which became irresistible....

So finally the democratic franchise was introduced into the liberal state. It did not come easily or quickly. In most of the present liberal-democratic countries it required many decades of agitation and organization, and in few countries was anything like it achieved until late in the nineteenth century. The female half of the population had to wait even longer for an equal political voice: not until substantial numbers of women had moved out from the shelter of the home to take an independent place in the labour market was women's claim to a voice in the political market allowed.

So democracy came as a late addition to the competitive market society and the liberal state. The point of recalling this is, of course, to emphasize that democracy came as an adjunct to the competitive liberal society and state. It is not simply that democracy came later. It is also that democracy in these societies, was demanded, and was admitted, on competitive liberal grounds. Democracy was demanded, and admitted, on the ground that it was unfair not to have it in a competitive society. It was something the competitive society logically needed....

What the addition of democracy to the liberal state did was simply to provide constitutional channels for popular pressures, pressures to which governments would have had to yield in about the same measure anyway, merely to maintain public order and avoid revolution. By admitting the mass of the people into the competitive party system, the liberal state did not abandon its fundamental nature; it simply opened the competitive political system to all the individuals who had been created by the competitive market society. The liberal state fulfilled its own logic. In so doing, it neither destroyed nor weakened itself; it strengthened both itself and the market society. It liberalized democracy while democratizing liberalism.

■ QUESTION

If this view is correct, did, or does, the 'constitution' in the United Kingdom have a democratic basis, i.e. was, or is, its legitimacy to be found in the general will of the people? See Ridley, below.

F. F. Ridley, 'There is no British Constitution: A Dangerous Case of the Emperor's Clothes'

(1988) 41 *Parliamentary Affairs* 340, 343–345

The first characteristic of a constitution . . . is that it constitutes—or reconstitutes—a system of government. . . . [I]n constitutional theory a governmental order derives its legitimacy from the constituent act which establishes it. . . .

Democratic constitutions universally state the principle of popular sovereignty and their legitimacy now rests on popular enactment. This follows the American tradition: 'We the people of the United States . . . do ordain and establish this constitution'. Similar words are found almost everywhere. Some may invoke a higher sanctity for parts of the constitution than the will of the people. Thus the American Bill of Rights is founded on the Declaration of Independence's self-evident truths that all men are endowed by their Creator with certain inalienable rights, but that does not alter the source of the constitution's authority. . . .

The people are generally called on to elect a special constituent assembly mandated to draft a constitution, though this may not always be the case—as in General de Gaulle's constitution for the Fifth Republic. Although the American constitution was ratified by state legislatures, in more recent times the people are almost universally called on to ratify it in a referendum. . . .

Britain never developed this idea of popular sovereignty in constitutional terms, even if we sometimes talk of the sovereignty of the electorate in political terms. Even if the latter were true, it would merely allow the people to choose their government: it does not base the governmental order, the British 'constitution', on their authority and thus only gives them only half their right. (Moreover, since a parliamentary majority can change that order, prolong its own life, alter the franchise or reform the electoral system, even the political rights of the electorate depend on Parliament.) What we have, instead, is the sovereignty of Parliament. Parliament determines—and alters—the country's system of government. If we ask where that power comes from, the answer is broadly that Parliament claimed it and the courts recognised it. The people never came into the picture. The liberal (middle-class) democracies established in Europe had, despite their generally limited franchise, to base their constitutions on the principle that ultimate authority was vested in the people. Britain seems to be the sole exception to this democratic path.

■ QUESTION

If, as it is argued, the 'constitution' of the United Kingdom had no democratic basis, is the system of government nevertheless democratic? See Finer, below.

S. E. Finer, *Comparative Government*

(1970), pp. 63–66

(1) The primary meaning of democracy is government which is derived from public opinion and is accountable to it. As to *accountability;* this implies that it is not sufficient for a government to justify its existence because at some time in the past it was representative of popular opinion; for the two may have diverged since then. 'Accountability' entails that a government must continuously test its representativeness, that is to say whether its claim that it is 'derived from public opinion' is still valid.

(2) This public opinion, it must therefore be presumed, is overtly and freely expressed. For if it is not, how can anybody *know* that the government is still 'derived from public opinion', i.e. is still representative? But 'overtly and freely to express opinion' implies some opportunity and machinery for making that opinion known, and therefore implies some kind of a suffrage, some kind of a voice or vote....

(3) In matters of contention between sections of public opinion it is the majority opinion that prevails.

These three characteristics must, it seems, form part of any definition of democracy....

Thus the first assumption of liberal-democracy is that it is a democracy in the sense expressed above. But liberal-democracy is a *qualified* democracy. In this type of government there are other presuppositions or assumptions beyond the one which we have already stated.

The first of these is that government is *limited*. This implies that the government is operating in a world of autonomous, spontaneously self-creating, voluntary associations. In such conditions the government operates only at the margin of social activity. That it ought to interfere and regulate or even suppress these autonomous, self-creating, voluntary associations is a matter for it to prove: it is not assumed.... The authority of government therefore is limited; and this can be expressed by saying that certain rights of the individual and of the private association are safeguarded. A kind of ring fence is drawn around them and the onus lies on the government to show whether, why and to what extent this ought to be breached.

The second qualification to democracy in this particular 'liberal' form is that society is recognized as being *pluralistic*.... To recognize society as being pluralistic, therefore, carries the additional assumption that the government sets out to rule, not in the interest of any one group or alliance of groups, but in the common interest of all....

This highlights the third qualification: the liberal-democratic type of government is one in which *it is denied that there is any objective science of society or of morals*. On the contrary, it is assumed that in the last resort truth is a matter of individual consciences where all consciences are held, by an act of faith, to be equal either in the sight of God or in the sight of man. Two working conclusions follow from this, namely, toleration and the qualification of majority rule.

Why toleration? Because if there is no objective science of society and morals, then clearly no group, not even the government, has any moral justification for imposing any creed, philosophy, religion or ideology upon the rest of society. Again, since it is assumed by this act of faith that all individuals are equal in the sight of God, man or both, then dissent must be tolerated and each has the right to put his own point of view. Again, since truth is held to be individual and also fallible, rulership will be both conditional and also temporary; because clearly the views as to what is true and therefore proper for government to act upon will change from time to time as opinion fluctuates amongst the body of the people. So, this qualified form of democracy entails that the government is representative of and responsive to public opinion; and that where this opinion is not unanimous it is representative of and responsive to the majority. But these majorities will usually be constantly changing....

But even majority rule is seriously qualified in the liberal-democracy.... But being a liberal-democracy also implies that the minorities must be given a chance to become a majority; and that means, therefore, that they must be given a chance status and a means to convert the majority. In order to make this possible, certain guarantees and machinery would have to be established.

NOTES

1. The ideas in the last paragraph of the extract from Finer, above, are taken further by Sir Stephen Sedley, 'The Common Law and the Constitution' in Lord Nolan and Sir Stephen Sedley, *The Making and Remaking of the British Constitution* (London, 1997), p. 5 where he states:

   > A democracy is more than a state in which power resides in the hands of a majority of elected representatives: it is a state in which individuals and minorities have an assurance of certain basic protections from the majoritarian interest, and in which independent courts of law hold the responsibility for interpreting, applying and—importantly—supplementing the law laid down by Parliament in the interests of every individual, not merely the represented majority.

   See further Chapter 9.
2. See further *United Communist Party of Turkey* v *Turkey* (1998) 26 EHRR 121, at p. 416, *post*.
3. Where there is a permanent majority, however, representative democracy may fail to provide legitimation either of a government or of the system of government. See Barker, below.

R. Barker, *Political Legitimacy and the State*

(1990), pp. 141–143

It is difficult to determine in any precise way the contribution of elections to the maintenance of legitimacy. By comparing the history of Northern Ireland with that of the rest of the United Kingdom it is clear that the mere fact of elections is not sufficient. If the result is never in any doubt, so that it is not 'the people' but always and only a section and that the same section of them which confers consent on government, then those who feel themselves permanently excluded will also feel no great obligations to the regime. No legitimacy without representation....

On the other hand, so long as the electoral system appears to give due weight to most parties, the fact that individual votes may often have little effect does not deter them from being cast. Voters turn out in large numbers in safe seats where their individual support or opposition to the sitting candidate can make no difference whatsoever to the result. Voting has a ritual aspect, whereby citizens formally and publicly show their preferences for one party over others, and hence their willingness to accept the result of the contest, and their legitimation of that result. It enables people to identify with those who lead or govern them, to see politicians and rulers as both special and, at the same time, exemplifying the character of their followers....

Thus two broad sanctioning functions can be identified in voting. First of the policies of particular governments, second of the governing system in general, of the state. These may of course in practice be confused or entangled with each other, as they are in Northern Ireland, or as they are in any state where the elections are largely or wholly a political ritual or a way of mobilizing mass support or approval for a regime in which party and state are indistinguishable, and electoral choice between contestants for office non-existent. Once this occurs the democratic process can have an important function in *failing* to legitimize the state, and in providing justification for a rejection by groups of subjects not only of particular governments, but of more general constitutional arrangements. The predictable ineffectiveness of the nationalist vote in Northern Ireland can be used to justify rejection not just of a particular government but of the whole constitutional structure which maintains the inclusion of Northern Ireland in the United Kingdom rather than in a new all-Ireland state. In a smaller way after 1987 the emergence of a Scottish electorate overwhelmingly hostile to a Conservative government in power on the basis of English electoral success can sustain nationalist arguments for the general illegitimacy of the constitutional arrangements of the United Kingdom.

NOTE: The theory of limited government appears to demand more than simple majority rule. It is important to examine whether the system of government in the United Kingdom has advanced beyond this idea of the 'rightness' of the majority. This involves an examination of how elections operate, how governments acquire power, and how they use that power. Do they claim authority simply on the basis of electoral victory to do as they please, including changing the constitutional framework, or do they find themselves restrained from so acting by certain fundamental principles?

Endeavouring to answer such questions has, in the past, involved largely value judgements. Political scientists are now attempting to develop indices to assist in informing such judgements. The extract which follows outlines some of the issues involved.

David Beetham, 'Key Principles and Indices for a Democratic Audit' in D. Beetham (ed.), *Defining and Measuring Democracy*

(1994), pp. 25–30

First, it is necessary to explain the idea of a 'democratic audit' itself. This is the simple but ambitious project of assessing the state of democracy in a single country. Like other Western countries, the UK calls itself a democracy, and claims to provide a model for others to follow. Yet how democratic is it actually? And how does it measure up to the standards that it uses to assess others, including the countries of the Third World? Such questions are not accidental, but are provoked by a widespread sense of disquiet within the UK at the state of its political institutions—a disquiet which runs deeper than the mere fact that a single party has been in power for so long...

The project of a democratic audit, then, not only requires a clear specification of what exactly is to be audited. It also requires a robust and defensible conception of democracy, from which can be derived specific criteria and standards of assessment. An account of this conception and these criteria is provided in the following section.

Principles and indices of democracy

...Democracy is a *political* concept, concerning the collectively binding decisions about the rules and policies of a group, association or society. It claims that such decision-making should be, and it is realized to the extent that such decision-making actually is, subject to the control of all members of the collectivity considered as equals. That is to say, democracy embraces the related principles of *popular control* and *political equality*. In small-scale and simple associations, people can control collective decision-making directly, through equal rights to vote on law and policy in person. In large and complex associations, they typically do so indirectly, for example through appointing representatives to act for them. Here popular control usually takes the form of control over decision-*makers*, rather than over decision-making itself; and typically it requires a complex set of institutions and practices to make the principle effective. Similarly political equality, rather than being realized in an equal say in decision-making directly, is realized to the extent that there exists an equality of votes between electors, an equal right to stand for public office, an equality in the conditions for making one's voice heard and in treatment at the hands of legislators, and so on.

These two principles, of popular control and political equality, form the guiding thread of a democratic audit. They are the principles which inform those institutions and practices of Western countries that are characteristically democratic; and they also provide a standard against which their level of democracy can be assessed. As they stand, however, they are too general. Like the indices developed by other political scientists, they need to be broken down into specific, and where possible, measurable, criteria for the purpose of assessment or audit.

To do this we have separated the process of popular control over government into four distinct, albeit overlapping, dimensions. First and most basic is the popular election of the parliament or legislature and the head of government. The degree or extent of popular control is here to be assessed by such criteria as: the *reach* of the electoral process (that is, which public offices are open to election, and what powers they have over non-elected officials); its *inclusiveness* (what exclusions apply, both formally and informally, to parties, candidates and voters, whether in respect of registration or voting itself); its *fairness* as between parties, candidates and voters, and the range of effective choice it offers the latter; its *independence* from the government of the day; and so on. These criteria can be summed up in the familiar phrase 'free and fair elections', though this phrase does not fully capture all the aspects needed for effective popular control.

The second dimension for analysis concerns what is known as 'open and accountable government'. Popular control requires, besides elections, the continuous accountability of government: directly, to the electorate, through the public justification for its policies; indirectly, to agents acting on the people's behalf. In respect of the latter, we can distinguish between the *political accountability* of government to the legislature or parliament for the content and execution of its policies; its *legal* accountability to the courts for ensuring that all state personnel, elected and non-elected, act within the laws and powers approved by the legislature; its *financial* accountability to both the legislature and the courts. Accountability in turn depends upon public knowledge of what government is up to, from sources that are independent of its own public relations machine. In all these aspects, a democratic audit will need to assess the respective powers and independence, both legal and actual, of different bodies: of the legislature and judiciary in relation to the executive; of the investigative capacity of the media; of an independent public statistical service; of the powers of individual citizens to seek redress in the event of maladministration or injustice.

Underpinning both the first two dimensions of popular control over government is a third: guaranteed civil and political rights or liberties. The freedoms of speech, association, assembly and movement, the right to due legal process, and so on, are not something specific to a particular *form* of democracy called 'liberal democracy'; they are essential to democracy as such, since without them no effective popular control over government is possible.... These rights or liberties are necessary if citizens are to communicate and associate with one another independently of government; if they are to express dissent from government or to influence it on an ongoing basis; if electoral choice and accountability is to be at all meaningful. A democratic audit will need to assess not only the legally prescribed content of these citizens' rights, but also the effectiveness of the institutions and procedures whereby they are guaranteed in practice.

A fourth dimension of popular control concerns the arena of what is called 'civil society': the nexus of associations through which people organize independently to manage their own affairs, and which can also act as a channel of influence upon government and a check on its powers. This is a more contestable dimension of democracy, not only because the criteria for its assessment are much less well formed than for the other three areas, but also because there is room for disagreement as to whether it should be seen as a necessary *condition for* democracy, or as an essential *part of* it. Our view is that a democratic society is a part of democracy, and goes beyond the concept of 'civil society', with its stress on the *independence* of societal self-organization, to include such features as: the representativeness of the media and their accessibility to different social groups and points of view; the public accountability and internal democracy of powerful private corporations; the degree of political awareness of the citizen body and the extent of its public participation; the democratic character of the political culture and of the education system.

The criteria or indices of popular control can thus be divided into four interrelated segments, which go to make up the major dimensions of democracy for contemporary societies.... A complete democratic audit should examine each segment in turn, to assess not only the effectiveness of popular control in practice, but also the degree of political equality in each area: under free and fair elections, how far each vote is of equal value, and how far there is equality of opportunity to stand for public office, regardless of which section of society a person comes from; under open and accountable government, whether any individuals or groups are systematically excluded from access to, or influence upon, government, or redress from it; under civil and political rights or liberties, whether these are effectively guaranteed to all sections of society; under democratic society, the degree of equal opportunity for self-organization, access to the media, redress from powerful corporations, and so on.

SECTION 5: LIMITED GOVERNMENT

A: Responsible government

The concept of limited government comprises two ideals, that of accountability of government for the exercise of its powers, and that of limits placed on the exercise of those powers. What, then, are the conditions for accountable or, as it is often termed, responsible government?

Jack Lively, *Democracy*

(1975), pp. 43–44

What then are the conditions necessary for the existence of responsible government? What is needed to ensure that some popular control can be exerted over political leadership, some governmental accountability can be enforced? Two main conditions can be suggested, that governments should be removable by electoral decisions and that some alternative can be substituted by electoral decision. The alternative, it should be stressed, must be more than an alternative governing group. It must comprehend alternatives in policy, since it is only if an electoral decision can alter the actions of government that popular control can be said to be established.... To borrow the economic analogy, competition is meaningless, or at any rate cannot create consumer sovereignty, unless there is some product differentiation.

In detail there might be a great deal of discussion about the institutional arrangements necessary to responsible government, but in general some are obvious. There must be free elections, in which neither the incumbent government nor any other group can determine the electoral result by means other than indications of how they will act if returned to power. Fraud, intimidation and bribery are thus incompatible with responsible government.... Another part of the institutional frame necessary to responsible government is freedom of association. Unless groups wishing to compete for leadership have the freedom to organize and formulate alternative programmes, the presentation of alternatives would be impossible.

Lastly, freedom of speech is necessary since silent alternatives can never be effective alternatives. In considering such arrangements, we cannot stick at simple legal considerations; we must move from questions of 'freedom from' to questions of 'ability to'. The absence of any legal bar to association will not, for example, create the ability to associate if there are heavy costs involved which only some groups can bear. Nor will the legal guarantee of freedom of speech be of much use if access to the mass media is severely restricted.

This could be summed up by saying that responsible government depends largely upon the existence of, and free competition between, political parties.

Whether the British system of government creates the conditions for responsible government is doubted in some quarters. Lord Hailsham spoke of 'elective dictatorship'.

Lord Hailsham, *The Dilemma of Democracy*

(1978), pp. 21–22

The old party structure, which for so long guaranteed the evolutionary character of our society, seems to me to have broken down....

[I]t seems to me that we are moving more and more in the direction of an elective dictatorship, not the less objectionable in principle because it is inefficient in practice, and not the less tyrannical in its nature because the opposed parties, becoming more and more polarized in their attitudes, seek with some prospects of success to seize the new levers of power and use them alternately to reverse the direction taken by their immediate predecessors. All the more unfortunate does this become in the presence of narrow majorities, each representing a minority of the electorate, sometimes a small minority, and when at least one of the parties believes that the prerogatives and rights conferred by electoral victory, however narrow, not merely entitle but compel it to impose on the helpless but unorganized majority irreversible changes for which it never consciously voted and to which most of its members are opposed.

It seems to me that this is a situation the reverse of liberal and even the reverse of democratic, in the sense in which the word has hitherto been understood. Fundamental and irreversible changes ought only to be imposed, if at all, in the light of an unmistakable national consensus. It follows that, if I am right, the overriding need of the moment is to pursue policies and enact legislation to ensure that a like situation to the present is never allowed to recur. It is true that the present nature of the threat can be seen to come from the left. But this need not necessarily be so, and almost certainly it will not always be so....

My thesis is that our institutions must be so structurally altered that, so far as regards permanent legislation, the will of the majority will always prevail against that of the party composing the executive for the time being, and that, whoever may form the government of the day will be compelled to follow procedures and policies compatible with the nature of Parliamentary democracy and the rule of freedom under law.

■ QUESTIONS

1. Lord Hailsham wrote in 1978; has anything changed since then to contradict his thesis, or have subsequent events confirmed his worst fears? See also Leslie Wolf-Phillips, below.
2. N. Johnson, 'Constitutional Reform: Some Dilemmas for a Conservative Philosophy' in *Conservative Party Politics* (Layton-Henry, ed., 1980), at p. 139, stated:

   A relative majority in the House of Commons may rest on a minority position in the country. Government on these terms is tolerable if the party in power recognises that there are limits to what it is entitled to do.

   Is there any evidence that such limits have been recognized in the last 20 years?

Leslie Wolf-Phillips, 'A Long Look at the British Constitution'

(1984) 37 *Parliamentary Affairs* 385, 398–401

The idealised view of the British system is that, under a head of State insulated from politics, generally admired, and with long and varied experience, the government of the day is led by a Prime Minister whose party has been given a parliamentary majority by a mature electorate which has participated in free and open elections. Parliament debates the great issues of the day, controls national expenditure and taxation, criticises government policy as an aid to its improvement, scrutinises the work of the central administration, and ensures the redress of collective and individual grievances. The Prime Minister heads a government composed of a Cabinet of her senior ministers and about eighty non-Cabinet ministers all bound to a policy implicitly approved by the electorate; the Prime Minister and all her colleagues must justify their actions and their policies before parliament, and if parliament withdraws its confidence, they must resign and face the stern judgment of the electorate upon their stewardship. Each minister has departmental responsibility and can be called to account for the working of his department before parliament; if incompetence or maladministration be proved then the minister will be called upon to resign either by the Prime Minister or by the direct action of parliament. The Queen as Head of State gives overall stability to the political system and the Prime Minister as Head of Government is one who has served a long apprenticeship in parliament in high office of state and who is the elected leader of a party which has the confidence of the nation. The 'Unwritten Constitution' has the virtue of flexibility and permits the wide use of constitutional conventions, both permitting and facilitating evolutionary consensual change. Finally, the House of Lords provides a forum removed from party ties and considerations, where the experienced and distinguished perform functions of assistance, advice, continuity and, when needed, a measure of restraint on the popularly-elected transient majority in the House of Commons.

What is the reality? The extension of the franchise, the growth of national mass parties and the development of the mass media have changed the nature of general elections, which have become largely personalised into a contest between party leaders. The majority of the electorate are only marginally politically conscious, and the personalisation of political issues and allegiances reflect this marginality. The voting pattern for the parties is so uniform throughout the country that the influence on a constituency of a particular candidate is insignificant; candidates without the support of a major party can expect to fail and minor or ad hoc or single-interest parties can expect to be swept aside.... Elections cannot be, and should not be regarded as, a means for approving the details of comprehensive manifestoes and the electors often seem to vote against a party rather than for the winning party....

The only mandate that most electors consider they have given to newly-elected Members of Parliament is to support the party and its leader; certainly, the Prime Minister expects, and usually gets, the support of the mass of the parliamentary majority party and the entire hundred or so members of the Government that is formed.

The supremacy of the Prime Minister is further enhanced by the authority to obtain (or threaten to obtain) a dissolution of parliament, the possibility of rebel Members being disowned and replaced by their constituency parties, the feelings of loyalty to one's party and the fear of giving aid and comfort to the opposition parties. Whatever the formal constitutional conventions and party rules, the Prime Minister is normally in effective control. Not only does he or she have the authority to appoint and dismiss or advance or relegate ministers, but there is also access to the patronage system for honours, awards and selection of candidates for high public office. The appointments and preferments policies of the present Prime Minister has shown the influence that can be borne in these matters. The former belief that the Prime Minister was primus inter pares (first among equals) has given way to the realisation that the office-holder is primum mobile (the first mover). The Prime Minister dominates the cabinet, its members wait upon a summons; there is control and prior approval of the agenda from the Prime Minister; the skilful exploitation of collective responsibility by the Prime Minister can neutralize and isolate a recalcitrant cabinet minority which has no choice but to 'shut up or get out'; the Prime Minister has wide access to a network of policy-making cabinet committees, and 'deals' can be made in inter-departmental committees, cabinet committees, or between the Prime Minister and individual ministers. Business laid before the full cabinet has often been the subject of previous informal agreement between the Prime Minister and certain colleagues in order that opposition may be outmanoeuvred....

In brief, the actual Westminster model is that of authoritarian single-party governments in a House of Commons dominated by the Prime Minister and composed largely of disciplined parties with most votes in the House of Commons being highly predictable; every three or four years there is a general election held under a crude simple majority electoral system with minimal participation by the electorate in the choice of who shall be their candidate, though they do have the choice between the candidates who are selected by the party activists; between 20% and 30% of the electorate do not vote at all. Governments rarely fall as a result of a vote in the House of Commons and resignations under ministerial responsibility are almost as rare. The vast majority of legislation proposed by the government of the day is passed; it is rare, indeed it is well-nigh impossible, for legislation to be passed of which the government does not approve. Orthodox constitutional theory bestows on individual members the right of independent action and does not regard them as the representative of the party without which they would not have been elected; over-solicitude for the wishes of their constituents would probably lead them into conflict with the party in parliament. The parties at large are not seen as the formers of policy for the government; that is a task reserved for the parliamentary members of the governing party.

B: Separation of powers

In what other ways may the powers of government be limited? At the outset it must be recognized that there are three institutions of government, each with specific functions. The legislature has the function of making new law or amending or repealing existing law. The executive has the administrative function of conducting government in accordance with the law. The judiciary has the function of interpreting the law and applying it to specific cases. In 1690 John Locke identified a danger arising from the possession of more than one power. In his *Second Treatise of Civil Government*, Chapter XII, para. 143, Locke stated:

It may be too great a temptation to human frailty, apt to grasp at power, for the same persons who have the power of making laws, to have also in their hands the power to execute them, whereby they may exempt themselves from obedience to the laws they make, and suit the law, both in its making and execution, to their own private advantage.

This idea was developed further by Montesquieu, the French philosopher, who expressed the view that it was the separation of powers of government which ensured the liberty of the English. He expressed the doctrine in *L'Esprit des Lois*, Book XI, Chapter VI (2nd edn, vol. 1, p. 220) as follows:

When the Legislative Power is united with the Executive Power in the same person or body of magistrates, there is no liberty because it is to be feared that the same Monarch or the same Senate will make tyrannical laws in order to execute them tyrannically. There is no liberty if the Judicial Power is not separated from the Legislative Power and from the Executive Power. If it were joined with the Legislative Power, the power over the life and liberty of citizens would be arbitrary, because the Judge would be Legislator. If it were joined to the Executive Power, the Judge would have the strength of an oppressor. All would be lost if the same man, or the same body of chief citizens, or the nobility, or the people, exercised these three powers, that of making laws, that of executing public decisions, and that of judging the crimes or the disputes of private persons.

This was a somewhat idealized view which did not truly reflect the political reality in England at the time. Montesquieu's views, however, were particularly influential in the eighteenth century as a reading of the Constitution of the United States of America reveals.

C. F. Strong, *Modern Political Constitutions*

(1972), pp. 211–212

Now, in no constitutional state is it true that the legislative and executive functions are in precisely the same hands, for...the executive must always be a smaller body than the legislature. But it is not to this distinction that the theory of the separation of powers points. The application of the theory means not only that the executive shall not be the same body as the legislature but that these two bodies shall be isolated from each other, so that the one shall not control the other. Any state which has adopted and maintained this doctrine in practice in its full force has an executive beyond the control of the legislature. Such an executive we call non-parliamentary or fixed. This type of executive still exists in the United States, whose Constitution has not been altered in this particular since its inception. But France, which, as we have said, applied the doctrine in its first constitutions born of the Revolution, later adopted the British executive system, and this feature appeared in the Constitutions of the Third and Fourth Republics, and again, though greatly modified, in that of the Fifth Republic. The system is one in which a cabinet of ministers is dependent for its existence on the legislature of which it is a part, the members of the executive being also members of the legislature.

This system, generally known as the Cabinet system, has been, in its broad features, adopted by most European constitutional states, and it matters not at all whether they are called monarchies or republics. It is also characteristic of the governments of British Commonwealth countries, old and new. The non-parliamentary system, on the other hand, is peculiar to the United States and those Latin American Republics which have founded their constitutions upon that of their great neighbour.

Lord Bingham of Cornhill, 'The Courts and the Constitution'

(1996/97), 7 *King's College Law Journal* 15–16

Every fourth-former knows that powers exercised on behalf of the state fall under three broad heads, the legislative, the executive and the judicial. The legislature makes the law, the executive carries it out and the judiciary, in case of doubt or dispute, interprets and applies it. Life in the fourth form is pleasantly simple.

But of course it is not quite as simple as that. True, Parliament does enact new laws—3,233 pages of it in 1985—but it also has important functions in debating policy, holding ministers to account and providing a forum for the redress of grievances. True, the executive does implement the laws made by Parliament, but it also plays a crucial role in initiating almost all new legislation; ministers exercise many powers which are not conferred by Parliament and ministers also, acting under legislative authority and usually subject to parliamentary control, make laws in the form of subordinate legislation—6,518 pages of it in 1985. True again, the judges interpret and apply the laws made by Parliament. But the cases which reach the courts are not usually cases in which Parliament has made its intention clear. In such cases there is nothing to litigate about. It is when the intention of parliament is unclear, or where Parliament has failed to provide for a particular eventuality at all, that litigation ensues. The essential function of the court is then to declare the law which it infers that Parliament intended to make, or would have made if it had addressed the point at all. This is not a legislative role, but nor is it a purely interpretative role, since the court may have to do a good deal more than elicit the meaning of what Parliament has enacted. In the great expanses of English law which are largely untouched by statute, the function of the courts is, I would suggest, even less interpretative, since the legal issues which fall to be decided rarely fall squarely within the ratio of an earlier decision, unless it is sought to challenge that decision. More often cases arise on the border between one decision and another, or at the confluence of two or more competing principles or in an area where there is virtually no relevant authority. The courts have then to decide, in the light of legal principle and such authority as there is, and having regard to the apprehended practical consequences of one decision as opposed to another, what the law should be. The courts also have a role in providing a forum for the redress of grievances and in holding the executive to account, if in either case (but only if) a breach of the law is shown. So the functions of legislature, executive and judiciary are not quite as distinct as one might suppose.

Nor, in contrast with many constitutions, notably the American, does our constitution provide for any rigid separation of powers. The fact that the cabinet, as the engine of the executive, and all other ministers, are necessarily members of one or other House of the legislature is indeed the clearest possible negation of the doctrine. But between the legislature and the executive on the one hand and the judiciary on the other the separation is all but total. . . .

G. Marshall, *Constitutional Theory*

(1971), pp. 103–104

A separation between the judicial and the legislative and executive branches obviously exists in both Britain and the United States in the sense that in practice the judges are secure in their offices and have an independent status. But whether the separation of powers doctrine implies the existence of that degree of checking or controlling which has come to be known as judicial review in the American sense is not easy to decide. The right to invalidate legislation obviously in one sense invades the principle that each department has an independent sphere of action and a right to take its own view on matters of constitutionality. On the other hand, the controlling or checking functions of the judicial branch can only consist in impartial application of the law, and where constitutional law places restrictions on legislative power, a duty to declare the law seems to imply a duty to declare when such restrictions have been violated, whether by the legislature or by anyone else.

NOTE: In the United States the Supreme Court in *Marbury* v *Madison* (1803) 1 Cranch 137, decided that it had the power to declare both the acts of Congress and of the President to be unconstitutional. In the United Kingdom courts have refused to adjudicate upon the validity of Acts of Parliament, but they have developed the doctrine of judicial review by which the exercise of power by other authorities may be reviewed in the courts.

R v *London Transport Executive, ex parte Greater London Council*

[1983] QB 484, Court of Appeal

KERR LJ: ... Authorities invested with discretionary powers by an Act of Parliament can only exercise such powers within the limits of the particular statute. So long as they do not transgress their statutory powers, their decisions are entirely a matter for them, and—in the case of local authorities—for the majority of the elected representatives; subject, however, to one important proviso. This is—again to put it broadly—that they must not exercise their powers arbitrarily or so unreasonably that the exercise of the discretion is clearly unjustifiable. This is an imperfect and generalised paraphrase of the well-known statement of Lord Greene MR in *Associated Provincial Picture Houses Ltd v Wednesbury Corporation* [1948] 1 KB 223, 229, which has come to be known as the *Wednesbury* principle and applied in countless cases.

If an authority misdirects itself in law, or acts arbitrarily on the basis of considerations which lie outside its statutory powers, or so unreasonably that its decisions cannot be justified by any objective standard of reasonableness, then it is the duty and function of the courts to pronounce that such decisions are invalid when these are challenged by anyone aggrieved by them and who has the necessary locus standi to do so.

The role of the courts in the constitution was further elucidated in the following cases.

Duport Steels Ltd v *Sirs*

[1980] 1 WLR 142, House of Lords

Private steel companies sought injunctions against the Iron and Steel Trades Confederation who were calling on workers in the private sector of the steel industry to come out on strike to support workers in the public sector who were striking over pay. The correct interpretation of s. 13(1) of the Trade Union and Labour Relations Act 1974 (as amended in 1976) was central to the case. Section 13(1) conferred immunity from liability in tort for an act done by a person 'in contemplation or furtherance of a trade dispute'. The Court of Appeal reversed the judge's decision to refuse the injunctions sought.

LORD DIPLOCK: ... My Lords, at a time when more and more cases involve the application of legislation which gives effect to policies that are the subject of bitter public and parliamentary controversy, it cannot be too strongly emphasised that the British constitution, though largely unwritten, is firmly based upon the separation of powers; Parliament makes the laws, the judiciary interpret them. When Parliament legislates to remedy what the majority of its members at the time perceive to be a defect or a lacuna in the existing law (whether it be the written law enacted by existing statutes or the unwritten common law as it has been expounded by the judges in decided cases), the role of the judiciary is confined to ascertaining from the words that Parliament has approved as expressing its intention what that intention was, and to giving effect to it. Where the meaning of the statutory words is plain and unambiguous it is not for the judges to invent fancied ambiguities as an excuse for failing to give effect to its plain meaning because they themselves consider that the consequences of doing so would be inexpedient, or even unjust or immoral. In controversial matters such as are involved in industrial relations there is room for difference of opinion as to what is expedient, what is just and what is morally justifiable. Under our constitution it is Parliament's opinion on these matters that is paramount.

A statute passed to remedy what is perceived by Parliament to be a defect in the existing law may in actual operation turn out to have injurious consequences that Parliament did not anticipate at the time the statute was passed; if it had, it would have made some provision in the Act in order to prevent them. It is at least possible that Parliament when the Acts of 1974 and 1976 were passed did not anticipate that so widespread and crippling use as has in fact occurred would be made of sympathetic withdrawals of labour and of secondary blacking and picketing in support of sectional interests able to exercise 'industrial muscle.' But if this be the case it is for Parliament, not for the judiciary, to decide whether any changes should be made to the law as stated in the Acts, and, if so, what are the precise limits that ought to be imposed upon the immunity from liability for torts committed in the course of taking industrial action. These are matters on which there is a wide legislative choice the exercise of which is likely to be influenced by the political complexion of the government and the state of public opinion at the time amending legislation is under consideration.

It endangers continued public confidence in the political impartiality of the judiciary, which is essential to the continuance of the rule of law, if judges, under the guise of interpretation, provide their own preferred amendments to statutes which experience of their operation has shown to have had consequences that members of the court before whom the matter comes consider to be injurious to the public interest. The frequency with which controversial legislation is amended by Parliament itself (as witness the Act of 1974 which was amended in 1975 as well as in 1976) indicates that legislation, after it has come into operation, may fail to have the beneficial effects which Parliament expected or may produce injurious results that Parliament did not anticipate. But, except by private or hybrid Bills, Parliament does not legislate for individual cases. Public Acts of Parliament are general in their application; they govern all cases falling within categories of which the definitions are to be found in the wording of the statute. So in relation to section 13(1) of the Acts of 1974 and 1976, for a judge (who is always dealing with an individual case) to pose himself the question: 'Can Parliament really have intended that the acts that were done in this particular case should have the benefit of the immunity?' is to risk straying beyond his constitutional role as interpreter of the enacted law and assuming a power to decide at his own discretion whether or not to apply the general law to a particular case. The legitimate questions for a judge in his role as interpreter of the enacted law are: 'How has Parliament, by the words that it has used in the statute to express its intentions, defined the category of acts that are entitled to the immunity? Do the acts done in this particular case fall within that description?'

LORD SCARMAN: . . . My basic criticism of all three judgments in the Court of Appeal is that in their desire to do justice the court failed to do justice according to law. When one is considering law in the hands of the judges, law means the body of rules and guidelines within which society requires its judges to administer justice. Legal systems differ in the width of the discretionary power granted to judges: but in developed societies limits are invariably set, beyond which the judges may not go. Justice in such societies is not left to the unguided, even if experienced, sage sitting under the spreading oak tree.

In our society the judges have in some aspects of their work a discretionary power to do justice so wide that they may be regarded as law-makers. The common law and equity, both of them in essence systems of private law, are fields where, subject to the increasing intrusion of statute law, society has been content to allow the judges to formulate and develop the law. The judges, even in this, their very own field of creative endeavour, have accepted, in the interests of certainty, the self-denying ordinance of 'stare decisis,' the doctrine of binding precedent: and no doubt this judicially imposed limitation on judicial law-making has helped to maintain confidence in the certainty and evenhandedness of the law.

But in the field of statute law the judge must be obedient to the will of Parliament as expressed in its enactments. In this field Parliament makes, and un-makes, the law: the judge's duty is to interpret and to apply the law, not to change it to meet the judge's idea of what justice requires. Interpretation does, of course, imply in the interpreter a power of choice where differing constructions are possible. But our law requires the judge to choose the construction which in his judgment best meets the legislative purpose of the enactment. If the result be unjust but inevitable, the judge may say so and invite Parliament to reconsider its provision. But he must not deny the statute. Unpalatable statute law may not be disregarded or rejected, merely because it is unpalatable. Only if a just result can be achieved without violating the legislative purpose of the statute may the judge select the construction which best suits his idea of what justice requires. Further, in our system the rule 'stare decisis' applies as firmly to statute law as it does to the formulation of common law and equitable principles. And the keystone of 'stare decisis' is loyalty throughout the system to the decisions of the Court of Appeal and this House. The Court of Appeal may not overrule a House of Lords decision: and only in the exceptional circumstances set out in the Practice Statement of July 1, 1966 (*Practice Statement (Judicial Precedent)* [1966] 1 WLR 1234), will this House refuse to follow its own previous decisions.

Within these limits, which cannot be said in a free society possessing elective legislative institutions to be narrow or constrained, judges, as the remarkable judicial career of Lord Denning himself shows, have a genuine creative role. Great judges are in their different ways judicial activists. But the constitution's separation of powers, or more accurately functions, must be observed if judicial independence is not to be put at risk. For, if people and Parliament come to think that the judicial power is to be confined by nothing other than the judge's sense of what is right (or, as Selden put it, by the length of the Chancellor's foot), confidence in the judicial system will be replaced by fear of it becoming uncertain and arbitrary in its application. Society will then be ready for Parliament to cut the power of the judges. Their power to do justice will become more restricted by law than it need be, or is today.

Appeal allowed.

R v Her Majesty's Treasury, ex parte Smedley

[1985] 1 QB 657, Court of Appeal

SIR JOHN DONALDSON MR: ... I think that I should say a word about the respective roles of Parliament and the courts. Although the United Kingdom has no written constitution, it is a constitutional convention of the highest importance that the legislature and the judicature are separate and independent of one another, subject to certain ultimate rights of Parliament over the judicature which are immaterial for present purposes. It therefore behoves the courts to be ever sensitive to the paramount need to refrain from trespassing upon the province of Parliament or, so far as this can be avoided, even appearing to do so. Although it is not a matter for me, I would hope and expect that Parliament would be similarly sensitive to the need to refrain from trespassing upon the province of the courts.

NOTE: In the long-running debate preceding the enactment of the Human Rights Act 1998 (see Chapter 9), the issue of separation of powers, particularly the relationship between Parliament and the courts, was a recurrent theme. The respective roles of Parliament and the courts following the Act coming into force in October 2000 have been articulated by Lord Irvine of Lairg, the Lord Chancellor, on a number of occasions.

Lord Irvine of Lairg LC, 'Constitutional Reform and a Bill of Rights'

[1997] *European Human Rights Law Review* 483

The British Constitution is firmly based on the separation of powers. It is essential that incorporation is achieved in a way which does nothing to disturb that balance. It is for Parliament to pass laws, not the judges. It is for the judges to interpret these laws and to develop the common law, not for Parliament or the executive. It is also for the courts to ensure that the powers conferred by Parliament on the executive and other bodies are neither exceeded nor abused but exercised lawfully. That will continue to be so after the European Convention becomes part of our domestic law.

Incorporation will enhance the judges' powers to protect the individual against the abuse of power by the State. We have a high quality of judicial review in this country. It has often rightly held the executive to account and improved the quality of administrative decision making. So the concept of judges protecting the citizen and holding the executive to account is nothing new. What is new is that the judges will be given a framework by Parliament within which to interpret the law.

Incorporating basic human rights into our domestic law will be a major new departure. It will offer new challenges. What is critical is that the form of incorporation sits comfortably with our United Kingdom institutions. It must not disturb the supremacy of Parliament. It should not put the judges in a position where they are seen as at odds with Parliament. That would be a recipe for conflict and mutual recrimination. It is vital that the courts should not become involved in a process of policy evaluation which goes far beyond its allotted constitutional role. In a democratic society, compromises between competing interests must be resolved by Parliament—or if Parliament so decides, by Ministers.

NOTES

1. The form of incorporation which has been adopted will not permit the courts to strike down or disapply legislation which is incompatible with the European Convention on Human Rights. This contrasts with the position arising from our membership of the European Community. As a result of s. 2(4) of the European Communities Act 1972, courts have acquired the power to disapply legislation which is inconsistent with EU law (see *R* v *Secretary of State for Transport, ex parte Factortame Ltd (No. 2)* [1991] 1 AC 603, at p. 86 below).
2. The Human Rights Act has, however, led to a greater separation of power by augmenting judicial independence through the Constitutional Reform Act 2005: see Chapter 4.

■ QUESTION

If separation of powers as expressed by Montesquieu does not exist, is there nevertheless sufficient separation of functions and a sufficient incidence of checks and balances to guarantee the maintenance of liberty?

SECTION 6: THE STATE

The next idea to consider in this chapter is the state. Bradley and Ewing in *Constitutional and Administrative Law* (2011), p. 3, state that 'constitutional law concerns the relationship between the individual and the state, seen from a particular viewpoint, namely the notion of law.... Law is not merely a matter of the rules which govern relations between private individuals.... Law also concerns the structure and powers of the state'. If we are to examine the ambit of constitutional law in the United Kingdom, we need to have some notion of what the state is.

C. F. Strong, *Modern Political Constitutions*

(1972), pp. 4–5

[T]he state is something more than a mere collection of families, or an agglomeration of occupational organisation, or a referee holding the ring between the conflicting interests of the voluntary associations which it permits to exist. In a properly organized political community the state exists for society and not society for the state; yet, however socially advanced a people may be, the society which it constitutes—made up of families, clubs, churches, trade unions, etc.—is not to be trusted to maintain itself without the ultimate arbitrament of force.

All associations make rules and regulations for their conduct, and when men are associated politically these rules and regulations are called laws, the power to make these being the prerogative of the state and of no other association. Thus, in the words of R M MacIver, a 'state is the fundamental association for the maintenance and development of social order, and to this end its central institution is endowed with the united power of the community.' But this definition might conceivably cover a pastoral or nomadic society which, indeed, found a bond of union in the patriarch or head of the family who, in some sort, discharged the powers of government. Such a society, however, lacks territoriality, an indispensable condition of true political organization, a condition emphasized by H J W Hetherington when he says: 'The state is the institution or set of institutions which, in order to secure certain elementary common purposes and conditions of life, unites under a single authority the inhabitants of a clearly-marked territorial area.' But what is this 'united power of the community' in the first, this 'single authority' in the second definition? It is the power or authority to make law. So we come to the definition given by Woodrow Wilson: 'A state is a people organized for law within a definite territory.'

S. E. Finer, *Comparative Government*

(1970), p. 24

The defining characteristics of a state . . . are: (1) It is a territorially defined association. (2) It embraces, compulsorily, all the persons in that territory. (3) It possesses the monopoly of violence throughout this area, by virtue of which it has the capacity, even if not the moral authority, to guarantee the finality of its decision in political disputes arising from the conflict of individuals or groups within its territory. (4) As a necessary accompaniment of all this, it has a body of persons who exercise this monopoly of violence in its name, namely, the common government.

R. Miliband, *The State in Capitalist Society*

(1969), pp. 49–54

There is one preliminary problem about the state which is very seldom considered, yet which requires attention if the discussion of its nature and role is to be properly focused. This is the fact that 'the state' is not a thing, that it does not, as such, exist. What 'the state' stands for is a number of particular institutions which, together, constitute its reality, and which interact as parts of what may be called the state system.

The point is by no means academic. For the treatment of one part of the state—usually the government—as the state itself introduces a major element of confusion in the discussion of the nature and incidence of state *power*; and that confusion can have large political consequences. Thus, if it is believed that the government is in fact the state, it may also be believed that the assumption of governmental power is equivalent to the acquisition of state power. Such a belief, resting as it does on vast assumptions about the nature of state power, is fraught with great risks and disappointments. To understand the nature of state power, it is necessary first of all to distinguish, and then to relate, the various elements which make up the state system.

It is not very surprising that government and state should often appear as synonymous for it is the government which speaks on the state's behalf. It was the state to which Weber was referring when he said, in a famous phrase, that, in order to be, it must 'successfully claim the monopoly of the legitimate use of physical force within a given territory'. But 'the state' cannot claim anything: only the government of the day, or its duly empowered agents, can. Men, it is often said, give their allegiance not to the government of the day but to the state. But the state, from this point of view, is a nebulous entity; and while men may choose to give their allegiance to it, it is to the government that they are required to give their obedience. A defiance of its orders is a defiance of the state, in whose name the government alone may speak and for whose actions it must assume ultimate responsibility. . . .

A second element of the state system which requires investigation is the administrative one, which now extends far beyond the traditional bureaucracy of the state, and which encompasses a large variety of bodies, often related to particular ministerial departments, or enjoying a greater or lesser degree of autonomy—public corporations, central banks, regulatory commissions, etc.—and concerned with the management of the economic, social, cultural and other activities in which the state is now directly or indirectly involved. The extraordinary growth of this administrative and bureaucratic element in all societies, including advanced capitalist ones, is of course one of the most obvious features of contemporary life; and the relation of its leading members to the government and to society is also crucial to the determination of the role of the state.

Formally, officialdom is at the service of the political executive, its obedient instrument, the tool of its will. In actual fact it is nothing of the kind. Everywhere and inevitably the administrative process is also part of the political process; administration is always political as well as executive, at least at the levels where policy-making is relevant, that is to say in the upper layers of administrative life. . . . Officials and administrators cannot divest themselves of all ideological clothing in the advice which they tender to their political masters, or in the independent decisions which they are in a position to take. The power which top civil servants and other state administrators possess no doubt varies from country to country, from department to department, and from individual to individual. But nowhere do these men *not* contribute directly and appreciably to the exercise of state power. . . .

Some of these considerations apply to all other elements of the state system. They apply for instance to a third such element, namely the military, to which may, for present purposes, be added the para-military, security and police forces of the state, and which together form that branch of it mainly concerned with the 'management of violence'.

In most capitalist countries, this coercive apparatus constitutes a vast, sprawling and resourceful establishment, whose professional leaders are men of high status and great influence, inside the state system and in society....

Whatever may be the case in practice, the formal constitutional position of the administrative and coercive elements is to serve the state by serving the government of the day. In contrast, it is not at all the formal constitutional duty of judges, at least in Western-type political systems, to serve the purposes of their governments. They are constitutionally independent of the political executive and protected from it by security of tenure and other guarantees. Indeed, the concept of judicial independence is deemed to entail not merely the freedom of judges from responsibility to the political executive, but their active duty to protect the citizen *against* the political executive or its agents, and to act, in the state's encounter with members of society, as the defenders of the latter's rights and liberties.... But in any case, the judiciary is an integral part of the state system, which affects, often profoundly, the exercise of state power.

So too, to a greater or lesser degree, does a fifth element of the state system, namely the various units of sub-central government. In one of its aspects, sub-central government constitutes an extension of central government and administration, the latter's antennae or tentacles. In some political systems it has indeed practically no other function. In the countries of advanced capitalism, on the other hand, sub-central government is rather more than an administrative device. In addition to being agents of the state these units of government have also traditionally performed another function. They have not only been the channels of communication and administration from the centre to the periphery, but also the voice of the periphery, or of particular interests at the periphery; they have been a means of overcoming local particularities, but also platforms for their expression, instruments of central control and obstacles to it. For all the centralisation of power, which is a major feature of government in these countries, sub-central organs of government... have remained power structures in their own right, and therefore able to affect very markedly the lives of the populations they have governed.

Much the same point may be made about the representative assemblies of advanced capitalism. Now more than ever their life revolves around the government; and even where, as in the United States, they are formally independent organs of constitutional and political power, their relationship with the political executive cannot be a purely critical or obstructive one. That relationship is one of conflict *and* cooperation.

Nor is this a matter of division between a pro-government side and an anti-government one. *Both* sides reflect this duality. For opposition parties cannot be wholly uncooperative. Merely by taking part in the work of the legislature, they help the government's business.

As for government parties, they are seldom if ever single-minded in their support of the political executive and altogether subservient to it. They include people who, by virtue of their position and influence must be persuaded, cajoled, threatened or bought off.

It is in the constitutionally-sanctioned performance of this cooperative and critical function that legislative assemblies have a share in the exercise of state power. That share is rather less extensive and exalted than is often claimed for these bodies. But... it is not, even in an epoch of executive dominance, an unimportant one.

■ QUESTION

Is the Government the State, or is it an institution or servant of the State? See the cases which follow.

D v *National Society for the Prevention of Cruelty to Children*

[1978] AC 171, House of Lords

The mother of a child (alleged by an informant to be the victim of ill-treatment) brought an action against the NSPCC for damages for nervous shock alleged to be the result of the society's investigation pursuant to the informant's complaint. The mother sought discovery of the identity of the informant. The NSPCC, an independent body incorporated by royal charter, claimed 'public interest immunity' as justifying its refusal to disclose the identity of its informants. The mother argued that the society could not rely on this defence as it was not part of the State.

LORD SIMON OF GLAISDALE: …'[T]he state' cannot on any sensible political theory be restricted to the Crown and the departments of central government (which are, indeed, part of the Crown in constitutional law). The state is the whole organisation of the body politic for supreme civil rule and government—the whole political organisation which is the basis of civil government. As such it certainly extends to local—and, as I think, also statutory—bodies in so far as they are exercising autonomous rule.

Chandler v *Director of Public Prosecutions*

[1964] AC 763, House of Lords

The appellants, in seeking to further the aims of the Campaign for Nuclear Disarmament, entered and sought to immobilize an airfield. The airfield was a 'prohibited place' under s. 3 of the Official Secrets Act 1911. The appellants were charged with conspiracy to commit a breach of s. 1 of the Act, whereby it is an offence to enter any prohibited place 'for any purpose prejudicial to the safety or interests of the State'. The appellants argued that their actions were not prejudicial to the safety or interests of the State, but rather it was their belief that their actions would be beneficial to the state. They further argued that 'State' means the numerical collection of inhabitants in the geographical area and not the Government or organs of government through which the State expresses its intentions.

LORD REID: …Next comes the question of what is meant by the safety or interests of the State. 'State' is not an easy word. It does not mean the Government or the Executive. 'L'Etat c'est moi' was a shrewd remark, but can hardly have been intended as a definition even in the France of the time. And I do not think that it means, as counsel argued, the individuals who inhabit these islands. The statute cannot be referring to the interests of all those individuals because they may differ and the interests of the majority are not necessarily the same as the interests of the State. Again we have seen only too clearly in some other countries what can happen if you personify and almost deify the State. Perhaps the country or the realm are as good synonyms as one can find and I would be prepared to accept the organised community as coming as near to a definition as one can get.

LORD DEVLIN: …What is meant by 'the State'? Is it the same thing as what I have just called 'the country'? Mr Foster, for the appellants, submits that it means the inhabitants of a particular geographical area. I doubt if it ever has as wide a meaning as that. I agree that in an appropriate context the safety and interests of the State might mean simply the public or national safety and interests. But the more precise use of the word 'State,' the use to be expected in a legal context, and the one which I am quite satisfied…was intended in this statute, is to denote the organs of government of a national community. In the United Kingdom, in relation at any rate to the armed forces and to the defence of the realm, that organ is the Crown. So long as the Crown maintains armed forces for the defence of the realm, it cannot be in its interest that any part of them should be immobilised.

LORD PEARCE: …I cannot accept the argument that the words 'the interests of the State' in this context mean the interests of the amorphous populace, without regard to the guiding policies of those in authority, and that proof of possible ultimate benefit to the populace may for the purposes of the Act justify an act of spying or sabotage. The protection covers certain specified places which are obviously vital to defence and other places to which the Secretary of State sees fit to extend the protection.…Parliament clearly intended to give stringent protection to such places. It is hard to believe that it intended to withhold that protection in all cases where a jury might think that the place in question was not necessary or desirable or where the authorities could not by evidence justify their policies to a jury's satisfaction. Questions of defence policy are vast, complicated, confidential, and wholly unsuited for ventilation before a jury. In such a context the interests of the State must in my judgment mean the interests of the State according to the policies laid down for it by its recognised organs of government and authority, the policies of the State as they are, not as they ought, in the opinion of a jury, to be. Anything which prejudices those policies is within the meaning of the Act 'prejudicial to the interests of the State.'

■ QUESTIONS

1. In the trial of Clive Ponting the judge directed the jury that the phrase 'in the interests of the State' in s. 2 of the Official Secrets Act 1911 means 'in the interests of the Government of the day'. This view was supported by the Attorney-General, Sir Michael Havers, in a speech in the House of Commons, but was contested by Lord Denning in a speech in the House of Lords. Who was correct? See Barker, below.
2. If the 'Government' is synonymous with the 'State', does this have any consequences for ideas such as constitutionalism and limited government? See Barker, below.
3. If the Government determines the interests of the State, does this harbour any threat to individual liberty?

R. Barker, *Political Legitimacy and the State*

(1990), pp. 183–184

The Ponting case also illustrates the ways in which the legitimacy of the state may be threatened if any of its various temporary governors act in a way which breaks down the distinction between state and government, and by wrapping the acts of particular governments in the flag of the state, make it impossible to attack one without assaulting the other. A distinction between the state, as the institution which carries on the function of government, and the government as the politicians currently in office, makes it possible to oppose policies without denying legitimacy, or even to challenge the legitimacy of particular ministerial procedures, without confronting the constitution as a whole. When that distinction is eroded, so is the possibility of loyal opposition. Thus a state whose institutions appear to be newly absorbed or influenced by the partisan considerations of government is likely to suffer erosion of legitimacy whenever it is challenged on a particular point. But so long as the distinction remains, disaffection in so far as it appeals to existing principles of legitimacy, can be both conservative and loyal. Vivienne Hart has pointed out how many actions, of which she takes populism as her example, which have been presented as subversive of government, are in fact defensive of the constitution in general against the constitutionally subversive, or supposed constitutionally subversive actions of particular governments and politicians.

The view that states imperil their own legitimacy when they offend their own subjects' conservative conceptions of constitutionality is found more amongst other academic students of politics than amongst political scientists themselves. Patrick McAuslan and John McEldowney write of the contribution to disaffection throughout western Europe of what they term the gap 'between on the one hand the rhetoric of democracy, of even-handed administration, and of equal opportunities for all, and on the other the increasing centralization and insensitivity of public administration'. Resistance to government can rest on support for the constitution. It is both 'the response of ordinary people to trends in government practices which seem to them to be, in perhaps indefinable ways, wrong' and a preference for 'the theory of what the constitution ought to be to the practice of what it is'. Much that appears as rejection of the legitimacy of the state is in fact quite the reverse. Moreover because the forms and principles of legitimacy present at any one time are likely to be varied, it is not simply a case of appealing to principles against practices, but can also be a matter of appealing against practices justified by one form of legitimacy to alternative practices justified by other principles.

■ QUESTIONS

The issues considered in this chapter have been, to a certain extent, theoretical. They are, however, issues of continuing relevance to any study of the constitution of the United Kingdom. Questions which it is worth keeping in mind when reading the remaining chapters in this book would be the following:

1. To what extent is the doctrine of constitutionalism respected in the United Kingdom?
2. To what extent does the principle of legitimacy inform constitutional debate?
3. Is the principle of limited government respected? To what extent is government made accountable by (i) Parliament, (ii) the electorate, and (iii) the courts?

4. Does the Human Rights Act 1998, or a possible British Bill of Rights, provide sufficient protection for fundamental rights in face of the competing claims of the 'majoritarian principle'?
5. Does the absence of a clear concept of the State, separate and distinguishable from government, prejudice individual rights?

2

The Legislative Supremacy of Parliament

OVERVIEW

In this chapter we deal with legislative supremacy, one of the key doctrines of constitutional law in the United Kingdom. First it is considered as a way of recognizing law, then we look at the political context, followed by an unpicking of its three main elements proposed by Dicey. We then examine the central proposition that Parliament cannot bind its successors and finally how the doctrine has been formally maintained yet modified.

NOTE: The doctrine of 'the legislative supremacy of Parliament' is often referred to as 'parliamentary sovereignty'. 'Sovereignty' is a word open to misunderstanding and one that is used in the sphere of international law (for example, the dispute with Argentina over the sovereignty of the Falkland Islands), and also in the political arena (for example, there is considerable rhetoric on sovereignty in the debates on the United Kingdom's membership of the European Union and on subsequent issues such as the treaties which have, and have sought to amend the founding treaties). To avoid confusion with these ideas, the terms 'legislative supremacy of Parliament' or 'parliamentary supremacy' will be used. These terms have the virtue that they express clearly the central legal concept of the doctrine—that is, that under our constitutional arrangements Parliament is legislatively supreme. In the extracts from cases and other materials which follow, where the term 'sovereignty' is used, the judges or writers are using it in the sense of 'supremacy'.

SECTION 1: THE LEGISLATIVE SUPREMACY OF PARLIAMENT AS A 'RULE OF RECOGNITION'

Part of the function of Parliament is to make laws, which it does by enacting statutes. These laws impose obligations on citizens, and obedience to these obligations is enforced by the courts. Why is a particular statute regarded as valid? Why do courts apply the law as declared in statutes and enforce their provisions? Whence does Parliament derive this power to make law?

H. L. A. Hart, *The Concept of Law*

(1961), pp. 89–107

The Elements of Law

It is, of course, possible to imagine a society without a legislature, courts or officials of any kind. Indeed, there are many studies of primitive communities which not only claim that this possibility is realized but depict in detail the life of a society where the only means of social control is that general attitude of the group towards its own standard modes of behaviour in terms of which we have characterized rules of obligation.... [W]e shall refer to such a social structure as one of primary rules of obligation. If a society is to live by such primary rules alone, there are certain conditions which, granted a few of the most obvious truisms about human nature and the world we live in, must clearly be satisfied. The first of these conditions is that the rules must contain in some form restrictions on the free use of violence, theft, and deception to which human beings are tempted but which they must, in general, repress, if they are to coexist in close proximity to each other.... Secondly, though such a society may exhibit the tension, already described, between those who accept the rules and those who reject the rules except where fear of social pressure induces them to conform, it is plain that the latter cannot be more than a minority, if so loosely organized a society of persons, approximately equal in physical strength, is to endure: for otherwise those who reject the rules would have too little social pressure to fear....

It is plain that only a small community closely knit by ties of kinship, common sentiment, and belief, and placed in a stable environment, could live successfully by such a régime of unofficial rules. In any other conditions such a simple form of social control must prove defective and will require supplementation in different ways. In the first place, the rules by which the group lives will not form a system, but will simply be a set of separate standards, without any identifying or common mark, except of course that they are the rules which a particular group of human beings accepts. They will in this respect resemble our own rules of etiquette. Hence if doubts arise as to what the rules are or as to the precise scope of some given rule, there will be no procedure for settling this doubt, either by reference to an authoritative text or to an official whose declarations on this point are authoritative. For, plainly, such a procedure and the acknowledgement of either authoritative text or persons involve the existence of rules of a type different from the rules of obligation or duty which *ex hypothesi* are all that the group has. This defect in the simple social structure of primary rules we may call its *uncertainty*.

A second defect is the *static* character of the rules. The only mode of change in the rules known to such a society will be the slow process of growth, whereby courses of conduct once thought optional become first habitual or usual, and then obligatory, and the converse process of decay, when deviations, once severely dealt with, are first tolerated and then pass unnoticed. There will be no means, in such a society, of deliberately adapting the rules to changing circumstances, either by eliminating old rules or introducing new ones: for, again, the possibility of doing this presupposes the existence of rules of a different type from the primary rules of obligation by which alone the society lives....

The third defect of this simple form of social life is the *inefficiency* of the diffuse social pressure by which the rules are maintained. Disputes as to whether an admitted rule has or has not been violated will always occur and will, in any but the smallest societies, continue interminably, if there is no agency specially empowered to ascertain finally, and authoritatively, the fact of violation....

The remedy for each of these three main defects in this simplest form of social structure consists in supplementing the *primary* rules of obligation with *secondary* rules which are rules of a different kind. The introduction of the remedy for each defect might, in itself, be considered a step from the pre-legal into the legal world; since each remedy brings with it many elements that permeate law: certainly all three remedies together are enough to convert the régime of primary rules into what is indisputably a legal system....

The simplest form of remedy for the *uncertainty* of the régime of primary rules is the introduction of what we shall call a 'rule of recognition'. This will specify some feature or features possession of which by a suggested rule is taken as a conclusive affirmative indication that it is a rule of the group to be supported by the social pressure it exerts. The existence of such a rule of recognition may take any of a huge variety of forms, simple or complex. It may, as in the early law of many societies, be no more than that an authoritative list or text of the rules is to be found in a written document or carved on some public monument....

In a developed legal system the rules of recognition are of course more complex; instead of identifying rules exclusively by reference to a text or list they do so by reference to some general characteristic possessed by the primary rules. This may be the fact of their having been enacted by a specific body, or their long customary practice, or their relation to judicial decisions. Moreover, where more than one of such general characteristics are treated as identifying criteria, provision may be made for their possible conflict by their arrangement in an order of superiority, as by the common subordination of custom or precedent to statute, the latter being a 'superior source' of law.... [E]ven in this simplest form, such a rule brings with it many elements distinctive of law. By providing an authoritative mark it introduces, although in embryonic form, the idea of a legal system: for the rules are now not just a discrete unconnected set but are, in a simple way, unified. Further, in the simple operation of identifying a given rule as possessing the required feature of being an item on an authoritative list of rules we have the germ of the idea of legal validity.

The remedy for the *static* quality of the régime of primary rules consists in the introduction of what we shall call 'rules of change'. The simplest form of such a rule is that which empowers an individual or body of persons to introduce new primary rules for the conduct of the life of the group, or of some class within it, and to eliminate old rules.... [I]t is in terms of such a rule, and not in terms of orders backed by threats, that the ideas of legislative enactment and repeal are to be understood. Such rules of change may be very simple or very complex: the powers conferred may be unrestricted or limited in various ways: and the rules may, besides specifying the persons who are to legislate, define in more or less rigid terms the procedure to be followed in legislation. Plainly, there will be a very close connexion between the rules of change and the rules of recognition: for where the former exists the latter will necessarily incorporate a reference to legislation as an identifying feature of the rules, though it need not refer to all the details of procedure involved in legislation. Usually some official certificate or official copy will, under the rules of recognition, be taken as a sufficient proof of due enactment. Of course if there is a social structure so simple that the only 'source of law' is legislation, the rule of recognition will simply specify enactment as the unique identifying mark or criterion of validity of the rules....

The third supplement to the simple régime of primary rules, intended to remedy the *inefficiency* of its diffused social pressure, consists of secondary rules empowering individuals to make authoritative determinations of the question whether, on a particular occasion, a primary rule has been broken. The minimal form of adjudication consists in such determinations, and we shall call the secondary rules which confer the power to make them 'rules of adjudication'. Besides identifying the individuals who are to adjudicate, such rules will also define the procedure to be followed. Like the other secondary rules these are on a different level from the primary rules: though they may be reinforced by further rules imposing duties on judges to adjudicate, they do not impose duties but confer judicial powers and a special status on judicial declarations about the breach of obligations. Again these rules, like the other secondary rules, define a group of important legal concepts: in this case the concepts of judge or court, jurisdiction and judgment. Besides these resemblances to the other secondary rules, rules of adjudication have intimate connexions with them. Indeed, a system which has rules of adjudication is necessarily also committed to a rule of recognition of an elementary and imperfect sort. This is so because, if courts are empowered to make authoritative determinations of the fact that a rule has been broken, these cannot avoid being taken as authoritative determinations of what the rules are. So the rule which confers jurisdiction will also be a rule of recognition, identifying the primary rules through the judgments of the courts and these judgments will become a 'source' of law....

If we stand back and consider the structure which has resulted from the combination of primary rules of obligation with the secondary rules of recognition, change and adjudication, it is plain that we have here not only the heart of a legal system, but a most powerful tool for the analysis of much that has puzzled both the jurist and the political theorist....

Rule of Recognition and Legal Validity

In a modern legal system where there are a variety of 'sources' of law, the rule of recognition is... complex: the criteria for identifying the law are multiple and commonly include a written constitution, enactment by a legislature, and judicial precedents. In most cases, provision is made for possible conflict by ranking these criteria in an order of relative subordination and primacy. It is in this way that in our system 'common law' is subordinate to 'statute'....

In the day-to-day life of a legal system its rule of recognition is very seldom expressly formulated as a rule; though occasionally, courts in England may announce in general terms the relative place of one criterion of law in relation to another, as when they assert the supremacy of Acts of Parliament over other sources or suggested sources of law. For the most part the rule of recognition is not stated, but its existence is *shown* in the way in which particular rules are identified, either by courts or other officials or private persons or their advisers....

The use of unstated rules of recognition, by courts and others, in identifying particular rules of the system is characteristic of the internal point of view. Those who use them in this way thereby manifest their own acceptance of them as guiding rules and with this attitude there goes a characteristic vocabulary different from the natural expressions of the external point of view. Perhaps the simplest of these is the expression, 'It is the law that...', which we may find on the lips not only of judges, but of ordinary men living under a legal system, when they identify a given rule of the system.... This attitude of shared acceptance of rules is to be contrasted with that of an observer who records *ab extra* the fact that a social group accepts such rules but does not himself accept them. The natural expression of this external point of view is not 'It is the law that...' but 'In England they recognize as law... whatever the Queen in Parliament enacts....' To say that a given rule is valid is to recognize it as passing all the tests provided by the rule of recognition and so as a rule of the system. We can indeed simply say that the statement that a particular rule is valid means that it satisfies all the criteria provided by the rule of recognition....

The rule of recognition providing the criteria by which the validity of other rules of the system is assessed is in an important sense, which we shall try to clarify, an *ultimate* rule: and where, as is usual, there are several criteria ranked in order of relative subordination and primacy one of them is *supreme*....

Of these two ideas, supreme criterion and ultimate rule, the first is the easiest to define. We may say that a criterion of legal validity or source of law is supreme if rules identified by reference to it are still recognized as rules of the system, even if they conflict with rules identified by reference to the other criteria, whereas rules identified by reference to the latter are not so recognized if they conflict with the rules identified by reference to the supreme criterion. A similar explanation in comparative terms can be given of the notions of 'superior' and 'subordinate' criteria which we have already used. It is plain that the notions of a superior and a supreme criterion merely refer to a *relative* place on a scale and do not import any notion of legally *unlimited* legislative power. Yet 'supreme' and 'unlimited' are easy to confuse—at least in legal theory. One reason for this is that in the simpler forms of legal system the ideas of ultimate rule of recognition, supreme criterion, and legally unlimited legislature seem to converge. For where there is a legislature subject to no constitutional limitations and competent by its enactment to deprive all other rules of law emanating from other sources of their status as law, it is part of the rule of recognition in such a system that enactment by that legislature is the supreme criterion of validity. This is, according to constitutional theory, the position in the United Kingdom. But even systems like that of the United States in which there is no such legally unlimited legislature may perfectly well contain an ultimate rule of recognition which provides a set of criteria of validity, one of which is supreme. This will be so, where the legislative competence of the ordinary legislature is limited by a constitution which contains no amending power, or places some classes outside the scope of that power. Here there is no legally unlimited legislature, even in the widest interpretation of 'legislature'; but the system of course contains an ultimate rule of recognition and, in the clauses of its constitution, a supreme criterion of validity....

Some writers, who have emphasized the legal ultimacy of the rule of recognition, have expressed this by saying that, whereas the legal validity of other rules of the system can be demonstrated by reference to it, its own validity cannot be demonstrated but is 'assumed' or 'postulated' or is a 'hypothesis'. This may, however, be seriously misleading. Statements of legal validity made about particular rules in the day-to-day life of a legal system whether by judges, lawyers, or ordinary citizens do indeed carry with them certain presuppositions. They are internal statements of law expressing the point of view of those who accept the rule of recognition of the system and, as such, leave unstated much that could be stated in external statements of fact about the system. What is thus left unstated forms the normal background or context of statements of legal validity and is thus said to be 'presupposed' by them. But it is important to see precisely what these presupposed matters are, and not to obscure their character. They consist of two things. First, a person who seriously asserts the validity of some given rule of law, say a particular statute, himself makes use of a rule of recognition which he accepts as appropriate for identifying the law. Secondly, it is the case that this rule of recognition, in terms of which he assesses the validity of a particular statute, is not only accepted by him but is the rule of recognition actually accepted and employed in the general operation of the system. If the truth of this presupposition were doubted, it could be established by reference to actual practice: to the way in which courts identify what is to count as law, and to the general acceptance of or acquiescence in these identifications....

Where...as in a mature legal system, we have a system of rules which includes a rule of recognition so that the status of a rule as a member of the system now depends on whether it satisfies certain criteria provided by the rule of recognition, this brings with it a new application of the word 'exist'. The statement that a rule exists may now no longer be what it was in the simple case of customary rules—an external statement of the *fact* that a certain mode of behaviour was generally accepted as a standard in practice. It may now be an internal statement applying an accepted but unstated rule of recognition and meaning (roughly) no more than 'valid given the systems criteria of validity'. In this respect, however, as in others a rule of recognition is unlike other rules of the system. The assertion that it exists can only be an external statement of fact. For whereas a subordinate rule of a system may be valid and in that sense 'exist' even if it is generally disregarded, the rule of recognition exists only as a complex, but normally concordant, practice of the courts, officials, and private persons in identifying the law by reference to certain criteria. Its existence is a matter of fact.

■ QUESTION

What is the Rule of Recognition in the United Kingdom?

A. V. Dicey, *An Introduction to the Study of the Law of the Constitution*

(10th edn, 1985), pp. 39–40

The principle of Parliamentary sovereignty means neither more nor less than this, namely, that Parliament thus defined has, under the English constitution, the right to make or unmake any law whatever; and, further, that no person or body is recognised by the law of England as having a right to override or set aside the legislation of Parliament.

A law may, for our present purpose, be defined as 'any rule which will be enforced by the courts.' The principle then of Parliamentary sovereignty may, looked at from its positive side, be thus described: Any Act of Parliament, or any part of an Act of Parliament, which makes a new law, or repeals or modifies an existing law, will be obeyed by the courts. The same principle, looked at from its negative side, may be thus stated: There is no person or body of persons who can, under the English constitution, make rules which override or derogate from an Act of Parliament, or which (to express the same thing in other words) will be enforced by the courts in contravention of an Act of Parliament.

NOTE: Parliament is the supreme law-maker, but what is Parliament? The words of enactment at the beginning of every statute are as follows:

> Be it enacted by the Queen's most Excellent Majesty, by and with the advice and consent of the Lords Spiritual and Temporal, and Commons, in this present Parliament assembled, and by the authority of the same, as follows:—

Thus it is the Queen in Parliament which enacts legislation. A measure having received the approval of a majority in both Houses and the Royal Assent is recognized by the common law as an Act of Parliament. This position has been modified, however, by the Parliament Acts 1911 and 1949, under which a Bill may be presented for the Royal Assent provided it has been passed by the House of Commons and other procedural requirements complied with, although it has not been passed by the House of Lords. If a Bill does not obtain the approval of a majority in each House, or if the Parliament Acts are not complied with, or if the Royal Assent is withheld, the product should not be regarded as an authentic Act of Parliament.

The courts, therefore, recognize as law and accord primacy to those measures which Parliament passes as Acts.

Why is Parliament legislatively supreme, and why are its enactments accorded primacy?

SECTION 2: THE POLITICAL CONTEXT

A common view is that the legal concept of the legislative supremacy of Parliament can, and indeed must, be distinguished from the political concept of sovereignty. This view, however, has been challenged. T. R. S. Allan suggests that political concepts should inform judicial decisions about the precise meaning of supremacy.

T. R. S. Allan, 'The Limits of Parliamentary Sovereignty'

[1985] *Public Law* 614

No greater testimony exists to the power and resilience of positivism in modern legal thought than the debate between constitutional lawyers about the nature of parliamentary sovereignty. At the root of almost all analyses of the nature and scope of the doctrine lies an unquestioned separation of legal from political principle. The political notion of the ultimate sovereignty of the electorate must be distinguished from the legal doctrine of legislative supremacy: the courts owe their allegiance to the latter and recognise no 'trust' between Parliament and people. Dicey was clear on the point, observing that

> 'the courts will take no notice of the will of the electors. The judges know nothing about any will of the people except in so far as that will is expressed by an Act of Parliament, and would never suffer the validity of a statute to be questioned on the ground of its having been passed or kept alive in opposition to the wishes of the electors.'

The extent of judicial loyalty to statute enjoined by the doctrine of parliamentary sovereignty therefore depends on the correct interpretation of the legal principle alone. It is a matter of accurately formulating the fundamental rule of the legal order. Its *existence* may be conceded to be a matter of political fact, but its normative content is a matter of law: the courts are required to enforce the terms of the most recent statement of Parliament's will, expressed in the usual form....

In short, the fundamental rule that accords legal validity to Acts of Parliament is not itself the foundation of the legal order, beyond which the lawyer is forbidden to look. The fundamental rule, however it should properly be characterised, derives its legal authority from the underlying moral or political theory of which it forms a part. The sterility and inconclusiveness of modern debate about the nature of sovereignty stems from Dicey's attempt to divorce legal doctrine from political principle. Legal questions which challenge the nature of our constitutional order can only be answered in terms of the political morality on which that order is based....

The legal doctrine of legislative supremacy articulates the courts' commitment to the current British scheme of parliamentary democracy. It ensures the effective expression of the political will of the electorate through the medium of its parliamentary representatives. If some conception of the nature and dimensions of the relevant political community provides the framework for the operation of the doctrine, equally some conception of democracy must provide its substantive political content. In other words, the courts' continuing adherence to the legal doctrine of sovereignty must entail commitment to some irreducible, minimum concept of the democratic principle. That political commitment will naturally demand respect for the legislative measures adopted by Parliament as the representative assembly, a respect for which the legal doctrine is in almost all likely circumstances a suitable expression. That respect cannot, however, be a limitless one. A parliamentary enactment whose effect would be the destruction of any recognisable form of democracy (for example, a measure purporting to deprive a substantial section of the population of the vote on the grounds of their hostility to Government policies) could not consistently be applied by the courts as law. Judicial obedience to the statute in such (extreme and unlikely) circumstances could not coherently be justified in terms of the doctrine of parliamentary sovereignty since the statute would plainly undermine the fundamental political principle which the doctrine serves to protect. The practice of judicial obedience to statute cannot itself be based on the authority of statute: it can only reflect a judicial choice based on an understanding of what (in contemporary conditions) political morality demands. The limits of that practice of obedience must therefore be constituted by the boundaries of that political morality. An enactment which threatened the essential elements of any plausible conception of democratic government would lie beyond those boundaries. It would forfeit, by the same token, any claim to be recognised as law.

Although, therefore, Dicey's sharp distinction between the application and interpretation of statute suffices for most practical purposes, it ultimately breaks down in the face of changing views of the contours of the political community or of serious threats to the central tenets of liberal democracy. Presumptions of legislative intent, which draw their strength from judicial perceptions of widely held notions of justice and fairness, cannot in normal circumstances override the explicit terms of an Act of Parliament. This is because a commitment to representative government and loyalty to democratic institutions are themselves fundamental constituents of our collective political morality. Judicial notions of justice must generally give way to those expressed by Parliament where they are inconsistent. The legal authority of statute depends in the final analysis, however, on its compatibility with the central core of that shared political morality. If Parliament ceased to be a representative assembly, in any plausible sense of the idea, or if it proceeded to enact legislation undermining the democratic basis of our institutions, political morality might direct judicial resistance rather than obedience. No neat distinction between legal doctrine and political principle can be sustained at this level of adjudication. Questions about the scope and limits of the doctrine of sovereignty are necessarily questions about the proper relations between the courts and Parliament. Such questions cannot be settled by resort to competing formulations of some supposed pre-existing legal rule: it is the scope and content of that rule which is itself in issue. Answers can only be supplied as a matter of political morality—and in terms of the values which the judges accept as fundamental to our constitutional order.

Dicey's insistence on distinguishing legal from political sovereignty entails an equivalent separation of law and convention. Neither distinction can be sustained when the courts are required to determine the limits of parliamentary sovereignty. The nature and limits of parliamentary sovereignty are constituted, in the same way that conventions are constituted, by the political morality which underlies the legal order. In this sense, the legal doctrine of sovereignty is the most fundamental of our constitutional conventions. I have argued that the limits of sovereignty are contained in the courts' central commitment to representative democracy: a purported statute which attempted to subvert democracy could derive no legal authority from the doctrine. Paradoxically, Dicey gives implicit support for this view when he considers the distinction between legal and political sovereignty in the context of conventions. He observes that, 'if Parliament be in the eye of the law a supreme legislature, the essence of representative government is, that the legislature should represent or give effect to the will of the political sovereign, *i.e.* of the electoral body, or of the nation.' His examination of a number of important constitutional conventions leads him to the conclusion that they are united in character by the possession of a single purpose—to secure that Parliament and government are ultimately subject to the wishes of the electorate. The right to demand a dissolution is the most striking example, since it represents an appeal from the legal to the political sovereign. 'The conventions of the constitution now consist of customs which (whatever their historical origin) are at the present day maintained for the sake of ensuring the supremacy of the House of Commons, and ultimately, through the elective House of Commons, of the nation. Our modern code of constitutional morality secures, though in a roundabout way, what is called abroad the 'sovereignty of the people'. Dicey presents conventions as a means of harmonising legal and political sovereignty, which remain conceptually distinct. A view of legal sovereignty as a component of political morality, however, locates its authority in the source from which the 'validity of constitutional maxims' is derived: it is equally 'subordinate and subservient to the fundamental principle of popular sovereignty.'

A residual judicial commitment to preserving the essentials of democracy does not provide the only constraint on parliamentary supremacy. The political morality which underlies the legal order is not exhausted by our attachment to democratic government. It consists also in attitudes about what justice and fairness require in the relations between government and governed, and some of these must be fundamental. If these attitudes authorise a restrictive approach to the interpretation of statutes which, more broadly construed, would threaten fundamental values, they might equally justify rejection of statutes whose infringement of such values was sufficiently grave. If an ambiguous penal provision should, as a matter of principle, be narrowly construed in the interests of liberty and fairness, a criminal statute which lacked all precision—authorising the punishment of whatever conduct officials deemed it expedient to punish—should, on the same principle, be denied any application at all. It would be sufficient for the court to deny its application to the particular circumstances of the case before it: there would in practice be no need to make a declaration of invalidity. The result, however, would be the same: the strength of the principle of interpretation, in effect denying the statute any application at all, would reflect the scale of the affront to the moral and political values we accept as fundamental....

The limits of sovereignty clearly cannot be stated with any precision. The scope of the legal doctrine, and its implications for constitutional change, cannot be settled except by analysis of the political morality which gives it its authority. The boundaries of sovereignty must be determined in the light of the prevailing moral and political climate when difficult questions of constitutional authority arise. No single characterisation or particular formulation of the rule enjoining judicial obedience to statute can supply answers in advance....

■ QUESTIONS

1. Allan states that a 'parliamentary enactment whose effect would be destruction of any recognisable form of democracy...could not consistently be applied by the courts as law'. This begs a question as to what is democracy? For example, what would the courts do if Party A obtaining 40 per cent of the vote gained 60 per cent of the seats in the legislature because the remaining 60 per cent of the vote was split between three other parties, and then it embarked on a legislative programme which was discriminatory, anti-libertarian and anti-democratic? What would political morality demand? How would the judges discover this political morality? Would it make any difference if Party A fought the election campaign on a manifesto which

openly outlined its policies, as opposed to the adoption of these policies after winning the election? If the judges refused to enforce the offensive legislation and an election was held with the same result followed by a reintroduction of the legislation, what would judges then do?

2. Is the 'shared political morality' of majoritarianism an adequate substitute for constitutionalism? Does Allan suggest that it is? What do you think he means when he states:

   The political morality which underlies the legal order is not exhausted by our attachment to democratic government. It consists also in attitudes about what justice and fairness require in the relations between government and the governed, and some of these must be fundamental.

   Who decides what justice and fairness require?

NOTE: What Allan is perhaps attempting to identify is a higher order of law which places a limit on the supremacy of Parliament. But this is, perhaps, to misstate the issue; the problem is not so much the supremacy of Parliament but the appropriation of that supremacy by the Executive which to all intents and purposes exercises a stranglehold over Parliament. Recent judicial appointees are showing a greater preparedness to challenge the Diceyan orthodoxy and to recognize the imperative of democracy—to recognize values more fundamental than a majority in Parliament.

The Rt. Hon. Lord Woolf of Barnes, 'Droit Public—English Style'

[1995] *Public Law* 57, 67–69

...But what happens if a party with a large majority in Parliament uses that majority to abolish the courts' entire power of judicial review in express terms? It is administratively expensive, absorbs far too large a proportion of the legal aid fund and results in the judiciary having misconceived notions of grandeur. Do the courts then accept that the legislation means what it says? I am sure this is in practice unthinkable. It will never happen. But if it did, for reasons I will now summarise, my own personal view is that they do not....

Our parliamentary democracy is based on the rule of law. One of the twin principles upon which the rule of law depends is the supremacy of the Parliament in its legislative capacity. The other principle is that the courts are the final arbiters as to the interpretation and application of the law. As both Parliament and the courts derive their authority from the rule of law so both are subject to it and can not act in manner which involves its repudiation. The respective roles do not give rise to conflict because the courts and Parliament each respects the role of the other. For example, Parliament is meticulous in upholding the *sub judice* rule so as to avoid interfering with the role of the courts. Equally the courts always respect the privileges of Parliament and will not become involved with the internal workings of Parliament. In addition the courts will seek to give effect wherever possible to both primary and subordinate legislation. The courts will for example where there is a conflict between Community and domestic legislation uphold the domestic legislation as far as possible. The courts will also readily accept legislation which controls how it exercises its jurisdiction or which confers or modifies its existing statutory jurisdiction. I however, see a distinction between such legislative action and that which seeks to undermine in a fundamental way the rule of law on which our unwritten constitution depends by removing or substantially impairing the entire reviewing role of the High Court on judicial review, a role which in its origin is as ancient as the common law, predates our present form of parliamentary democracy and the Bill of Rights.

My approach...does involve dispensing with fairy tales once and for all, but I would suggest this is healthy. It involves a proper recognition of both the pillars of the rule of law and the equal responsibility that Parliament and the courts are under to respect the other's burdens and to play their proper part in upholding the rule of law. I see the courts and Parliament as being partners both engaged in a common enterprise involving the upholding of the rule of law. It is reflected in the way that frequently the House of Lords in its judicial capacity will stress the desirability of legislation when faced with the new problems that contemporary society can create rather than creating a solution itself.

There are however situations where already, in upholding the rule of law, the courts have had to take a stand. The example that springs to mind is the *Anisminic* case [1969] 2 AC 147. In that case even the statement in an Act of Parliament that the Commission's decision 'shall not be called in question in any court of law' did not succeed in excluding the jurisdiction of the court. Since that case Parliament has not again mounted such a challenge to the reviewing power of the High Court. There has been, and I am confident there will continue to be, mutual respect for each other's roles.

However, if Parliament did the unthinkable, then I would say that the courts would also be required to act in a manner which would be without precedent. Some judges might chose to do so by saying that it was an unrebuttable presumption that Parliament could never intend such a result. I myself would consider there were advantages in making it clear that ultimately there are even limits on the supremacy of Parliament which it is the courts' inalienable responsibility to identify and uphold. They are limits of the most modest dimensions which I believe any democrat would accept. They are no more than are necessary to enable the rule of law to be preserved.

The Hon. Sir John Laws, 'Law and Democracy'

[1995] *Public Law* 72, 81–85, 87–88, 92–93

...

Democracy and fundamental rights

As a matter of fundamental principle, it is my opinion that the survival and flourishing of a democracy in which basic rights (of which freedom of expression may be taken as a paradigm) are not only respected but enshrined requires that those who exercise democratic, political power must have limits set to what they may do: limits which they are not allowed to overstep. If this is right, it is a function of democratic power itself that it be not absolute....

The government's constituency is the whole body of such citizens; and a democratic government can have no remit but to act in what it perceives to be their best interests. It may get it wrong, and let the people down. But it cannot *knowingly* do so, for that would be to act in bad faith; and no government can justify its own bad faith by pointing to the fact that it was elected by the people. That would be to assert that the electorate endorsed in advance the government's right deliberately to act against its interests, which is an impossible proposition.

Thus the free will of every citizen is a premise of all the government's dealings with the people, and so conditions its duty to act in good faith towards them. It cannot fulfil its duty without recognising this; but such a recognition entails the need to accord fundamental rights, high among them the right of freedom of expression...

Any but the crudest society will be ordered, will have, in whatever form, a government. Its citizens will make judgments about the government. The government can no more deny their right to do so, without also denying their nature as free and rational beings, than it can deny their right to make judgments upon each other. But more than this, the government cannot be *neutral* about free speech. If it is not to be denied, it must be permitted; there is no room for what the logicians would call an undisturbed middle; and if it must be permitted, it must be entrenched and protected, since its vindication is not a matter of legitimate political choice but an axiom of any community of free human beings. In the end the government's duty to good faith requires it to accord this fundamental freedom to the people.

The imperative of higher-order law

Now it is only by means of compulsory law that effective rights can be accorded, so that the medium of rights is not persuasion, but the power of rule: the very power which, if misused, could be deployed to subvert rights. We therefore arrive at this position: the constitution must guarantee by positive law such rights as that of freedom of expression, since otherwise its credentials as a medium of honest rule are fatally undermined. But this requires for its achievement what I may call a higher-order law: a law which cannot be abrogated as other laws can, by the passage of a statute promoted by a government with the necessary majority in Parliament. Otherwise the right is not in the keeping of the constitution at all; it is not a guaranteed right; it exists, in point of law at least, only because the government chooses to let it exist, whereas in truth no such choice should be open to any government.

The democratic credentials of an elected government cannot justify its enjoyment of a right to abolish fundamental freedoms. If its power in the state is in the last resort absolute, such fundamental rights as free expression are only privileges; no less so if the absolute power rests in an elected body. The byword of every tyrant is 'My word is law'; a democratic assembly having sovereign power beyond the reach of curtailment or review may make just such an assertion, and its elective base cannot immunise it from playing the tyrant's role....

Since in the last resort the government rules by consent, the source of public power is not the strong arm of the ruler, but the people themselves.

Even so, the fundamental sinews of the constitution, the cornerstones of democracy and of inalienable rights, ought not by law to be in the keeping of the government, because the only means by which these principles may be enshrined in the state is by their possessing a status which no government has the right to destroy. I have already argued this position in relation to fundamental individual rights; now I assert it also as regards democracy itself. It is a condition of democracy's preservation that the power of a democratically elected government—or Parliament—be not absolute. The institution of free and regular elections, like fundamental individual rights, has to be vindicated by a higher-order law: very obviously, no government can tamper with it, if it is to avoid the mantle of tyranny; no government, therefore, must be allowed to do so....

The thrust of this reasoning is that the doctrine of Parliamentary sovereignty cannot be vouched by Parliamentary legislation; a higher-order law confers it, and must of necessity limit it. Thus it is not, and cannot be, established by the measures which set in place the constitutional reforms of the late seventeenth century; nor by any legislation. Indeed Lord Browne-Wilkinson's construction of Article 9 of the Bill of Rights 1688, to which I have already referred, means only that no impediment may be placed on Parliamentary processes, such as, for instance, by a claim against an MP for defamation; it is no more nor less than a rule of absolute legal privilege. It has nothing to do with the question whether statutes in proper form are by law beyond challenge. Its effect is that no constraint of any kind is to be imposed on the freedom of Parliament to debate whatever it likes. That is of course a vital principle, and the courts have been at pains to respect what they regard as Parliament's rights. But it says nothing about the legal supremacy of legislation; the existence of a power in the courts to strike down a statute as inconsistent with a fundamental right or, were it to happen, with democracy itself, does not in any sense touch the freedom of members of either House, uninhibited by any law, to say whatever they choose during a Bill's passage.

So the rules which establish and vindicate a government's power are in a different category from laws which assume the existence of the framework, and are made under it, because they prescribe the framework itself. In states with written constitutions the rules are of course to be found in the text of the constitution, which, typically, will also contain provisions as to how they may be changed. Generally the mechanisms under which the framework may be changed are different from those by which ordinary laws, not part of the framework, may be repealed or amended; and the mechanisms will be stricter than those in place for the alteration of ordinary law.

But in Britain the rules establishing the framework possess, on the face of it, no different character from any other statute law. The requirement of elections at least every five years may in theory be altered by amending legislation almost as readily—though the 'almost' is important—as a provision defining dangerous dogs. The conventions under which cabinet government is carried on could in theory be changed with no special rules at all, as could any of the norms by which the government possesses the authority to govern. The rules by which the power of a government is conferred are in effect the same as the rules by which the government may legislate upon other matters after it has gained power. In the end the sanction for the maintenance of democracy is in point of law no greater than the sanction for the maintenance of the dangerous dogs definition....

Conclusion

We may now come full circle, and after this long discussion I can identify what seems to me to be the essence of the difference between judicial and elective power. The latter consists in the authority to make decisions of policy within the remit given by the electorate; this is a great power, with which neither the judges nor anyone else have any business to interfere. This is the place held by democracy in our constitution. It is the place of government. Within it, Parliament, even given its present unsatisfactory relationship with the Executive, is truly and totally supreme. It possesses what we may indeed call a political sovereignty. It is a sovereignty which cannot be objected to, save at the price of assaulting democracy itself. But it is not a constitutional sovereignty; it does not have the status of what earlier I called a sovereign text, of the kind found in states with written constitutions. Ultimate sovereignty rests, in every civilised constitution, not with those who wield governmental power, but in the conditions under which they are permitted to do so. The constitution, not the Parliament, is in this sense sovereign. In Britain these conditions should now be recognised as consisting in a framework of fundamental principles which include the imperative of democracy itself and those other rights, prime among them freedom of thought and expression, which cannot be denied save by a plea of guilty to totalitarianism.

For its part judicial power in the last resort rests in the guarantee that this framework will be vindicated. It consists in the assurance that, however great the democratic margin of appreciation (to use Strasbourg's language) that must be accorded to the elected arm of the state, the bedrock of pluralism will be maintained. We have no other choice. The dynamic settlement between the powers of the state requires, in the absence of a constitutional scripture, just such a distribution of authority. The judges are rightly and necessarily constrained not only by a prohibition against intrusion into what is Parliament's proper sphere, but by the requirement, and the truth, that they have in their duty no party political bias. Their interest and obligation in the context of this discussion is to protect values which no democratic politician could honestly contest: values which, therefore, may be described as apolitical, since they stand together above the rancorous but vital dissensions of party politicians. The judges are constrained also, and rightly, by the fact that their role is reactive; they cannot initiate; all they can do is to apply principle to what is brought before them by others. Nothing could be more distinct from the duty of political creativity owed to us by Members of Parliament.

Though our constitution is unwritten, it can and must be articulated. Though it changes, the principles by which it goes can and must be elaborated. They are not silent; they represent the aspirations of a free people. They must be spoken and explained and, indeed, argued over. Politicians, lawyers, scholars, and many others have to do this. Constitutional theory has, perhaps, occupied too modest a place here in Britain, so that the colour and reach of public power has not been exposed to a glare that is fierce enough. But the importance of these matters is so great that, whatever the merits or demerits of what I have had to say, we cannot turn our backs on the arguments. We cannot risk the future growth without challenge of new, perhaps darker, philosophies. We cannot fail to give principled answers to those who ask of the nature of state power by what legal alchemy, in any situation critical to the protection of our freedoms, the constitution measures the claims of the ruler and the ruled. The imperatives of democracy and fundamental rights do not only demand acceptance; they demand a vindication that survives any test of intellectual rigour.

NOTE: In *Jackson* v *Attorney General* [2005] UKHL 56, [206] 1 AC 262 (see p. 67, *post*) some of their Lordships offered some *obiter* observations on the limits of legislative supremacy of which the most striking was that of Lord Steyn. He said [102] that Dicey's account of a pure and absolute supremacy was out of place in the modern United Kingdom with its membership of the EU, devolution settlement and incorporation of the European Convention on Human Rights. He continued

> Nevertheless, the supremacy of Parliament is still the *general* principle of our constitution. It is a construct of the common law. The judges created this principle. If that is so, it is not unthinkable that circumstances could arise where the courts may have to qualify a principle established on a different hypothesis of constitutionalism. In exceptional circumstances involving an attempt to abolish judicial review or the ordinary role of the courts, the Appellate Committee of the House of Lords or a new Supreme Court may have to consider whether this is a constitutional fundamental which even a sovereign Parliament acting at the behest of a complaisant House of Commons cannot abolish.

Lord Hope said 'the rule of law enforced by the courts is the ultimate controlling factor on which our constitution is based' (para. 107). He stated that there are limits to the power to legislate as people must be prepared to recognize legislation as law and this 'depends upon the legislature maintaining the trust of the electorate' and that

> The principle of parliamentary sovereignty which, in the absence of higher authority, has been created by the common law is built upon the assumption that Parliament represents the people whom it exists to serve [126].

■ QUESTIONS

1. Has Sir John Laws successfully identified fundamental values arising from the notion of democracy which will be adequate to deal effectively with the worst excesses of

naked majoritarianism? Is it the role of a judge to identify such values and exalt them to a position superior to an Act of Parliament?

NOTE: What would happen if there was a revolution and the monarchy was overthrown, Parliament dissolved and all its members imprisoned, and new elections held to a Constitutional Convention which draws up a new constitution with a presidential system of government and a single chamber assembly? If this new order is accepted by the people and the courts, the currently accepted doctrine of the legislative supremacy of Parliament would become redundant (cf. *Madzimbamuto* v *Lardner-Burke* [1969] 1 AC 645, p. 77, *post*). It is power and politics which operate in such a situation, not legal theory. Under the old order the new regime would be regarded as illegal, but it will acquire its own legitimacy from the obedience shown to it. Sovereignty, as a political concept, ultimately resides in the people; if the people accept the new legal order they will thereby give to it validity and legitimacy. For example, while the Declaration of Independence in 1776 and the enactment of the United States Constitution in 1787 were illegal under the old legal order, they were validated by, and received their legitimacy and authority from, the People of the United States, who accepted them and agreed to abide by the new constitution.

Our constitutional order has evolved from the position where an absolute monarch was supreme, to the current position where Parliament is legislatively supreme. The biggest jump in this evolutionary process occurred in the seventeenth century with the Glorious Revolution of 1688, which led to the establishment of the doctrine of the legislative supremacy of Parliament. The ultimate authority for the doctrine stems from the acceptance by the people of William III as the new monarch, and the acceptance by the courts of the new legal order founded on this doctrine as expressed legally in the common law.

SECTION 3: THE NATURE OF THE LEGISLATIVE SUPREMACY OF PARLIAMENT

What are the implications of the legislative supremacy of Parliament? Dicey's statement of the doctrine (*ante*, p. 45) may be converted into three propositions which will be examined in more detail. They are:

A: Parliament is the supreme law-making authority.

B: The legislative powers of Parliament are unlimited.

C: No other body has authority to rule on the validity of its enactments.

Each of these propositions will be examined separately.

A: Parliament—the supreme law-making authority

In the fourteenth century Parliament emerged as an effective, if not supreme, law-making body. In the seventeenth century James I, by insisting on his right to rule by prerogative, created the conditions in which the battle between the Monarch and Parliament for supremacy was fought in the courts.

The Case of Proclamations

(1611) 12 Co Rep 74, 77 ER 1352

The King sought to check the overgrowth of the capital by issuing a proclamation to prohibit the building of new homes in London. He also sought to preserve wheat for human consumption and issued a proclamation prohibiting the manufacture of starch from wheat. The Commons complained that this was an abuse of proclamations, and the King sought the opinion of Chief Justice Coke who consulted with his fellow judges.

In the same term it was resolved by the two Chief Justices, Chief Baron, and Baron Altham, upon conference betwixt the Lords of the Privy Council and them, that the King by his proclamation cannot create any offence which was not an offence before, for then he may alter the law of the land by his proclamation in a high point; for if he may create an offence where none is, upon that ensues fine and imprisonment: also the law of England is divided into three parts, common law, statute law, and custom; but the King's proclamation is none of them: also *malum aut est malum in se, aut prohibitum*, that which is against common law is *malum in se, malum prohibitum* is such an offence as is prohibited by Act of Parliament, and not by proclamation.

Also, it was resolved, that the King hath no prerogative, but that which the law of the land allows him.

But the King for prevention of offences may by proclamation admonish his subjects that they keep the laws, and do not offend them; upon punishment to be inflicted by the law, &c.

Lastly, if the offence be not punishable in the Star-Chamber, the prohibition of it by proclamation cannot make it punishable there: and after this resolution, no proclamation imposing fine and imprisonment was afterwards made, &c.

NOTE: The Stuart kings also claimed to have other prerogative powers of considerable importance, namely a *suspending* power, which could be used to postpone the operation of a statute for an indefinite period, and a *dispensing* power, which could be used to relieve offenders from the statutory penalties they had incurred. It was James II's use of the suspending power in respect of penal laws relating to religion in the Declarations of Indulgence 1687 and 1688 which led to the revolution of 1688.

In the area of taxation it had been established by the time of Edward I that direct taxes could only be levied with the consent of Parliament. However, the Stuarts claimed they could raise money by means of the prerogative. First, the prerogative relating to foreign affairs was used to regulate trade by the imposition of duties (see *The Case of Impositions (Bate's Case)* (1606) 2 St Tr 371). Secondly, the prerogative power to defend the realm in face of an emergency was used to raise money for the navy. The King was found to be the sole judge of whether an emergency existed (see *The Case of Shipmoney (R* v *Hampden)* (1637) 3 St Tr 825).

The claims by the Stuart kings to rule by prerogative were resolved by the Bill of Rights 1689.

The Bill of Rights 1689

I Will & Mary Sess 2 ch 2

Whereas the late King James the second, by the Assistance of divers Evil Counsellors, Judges, and Ministers, imployed by him did endeavour to Subvert and extirpate the Protestant Religion, and the Lawes and Liberties of this Kingdome....

And whereas the said late King James the second having abdicated the Government and the throne being thereby vacant.

His Highnesse the Prince of Orange (whom it hath pleased Almighty God to make the glorious Instrument of delivering this Kingdom from Popery and Arbitrary Power) Did (by the advice of the Lords Spirituall and Temporall and divers principall persons of the Commons) Cause Letters to be written to the Lords Spirituall and Temporall being Protestants and other Letters to the several Countyes Citties Universities Burroughs and Cinqe Ports for the chuseing of such persons to represent them as were of right to be sent to Parliament to meet and sitt at Westminster upon the two and twentieth day of January in this Year 1688 in order to such an establishment as that their Religion Lawes and Libertyes might not againe be in danger of being subverted.

Upon which Letters Elections haveing been accordingly made.

And thereupon the said Lords Spirituall and Temporall and Commons pursuant to their respective letters and Elections being now assembled in a full and free representative of this nation taking into their most serious consideration the best meanes for atteyneing the ends aforesaid Doe in the first place (as their Ancestors in like Case have usually done) for the vindicating and asserting their antient rights and Liberties, Declare.

[1.] That the pretended power of suspending of Lawes or the execution of Lawes by Regall Authority without Consent of Parliament is illegall.

[2.] That the pretended power of dispensing with lawes or the Execution of lawes by regall authority as it has been assumed and exercised of late is illegall.

[3.] That the Commission for erecting the late Courte of Commissioners for Ecclesiasticall Causes and all other Commissions and Courts of like nature are illegall and pernicious.

[4.] That levying of money for or to the use of the Crowne by pretence of Prerogative without Grant of Parliament for longer time or in other manner, than the same is or shall be granted is illegall.

[5.] That it is the right of the Subjects to petition the King and all Committments and prosecutions for such petitioning are illegall.

[6.] That the raiseing or keeping a Standing Army within the Kingdom in time of Peace unlesse it be with consent of Parliament is against Law.

[7.] That the Subjects which are Protestants may have Armes for their defence Suitable to their Condition and as allowed by Law.

[8.] That Elections of Members of Parliament ought to be free.

[9.] That the freedome of Speech and debates or proceedings in Parliament ought not to be impeached or questioned in any Courte or place out of Parliament.

[10.] That excessive Bayle ought not to be required nor excessive fynes imposed nor cruel and unusuall Punishments inflicted.

[11.] That Jurors ought to be duely impannelled and returned and Jurors which passe upon men in tryalls for high Treason ought to be freeholders.

[12.] That all Grants and promises of fynes and forfeitures of particular persons before conviction are illegall and void.

[13.] And that for redress of all greivances and for the amending, strengthening and preserving of the Lawes, Parliaments ought to be held frequently.

And they do claime demand and insist upon all and singular the premises as their undoubted Rights and Liberties and that noe Declarations Judgements Doeings or proceedings to the prejudice of the People in any of the said premisses ought in any wise to bee drawne hereafter into Consequence or Example.

To which demand of their rights they are particularly Encouraged by the declaration of his Highnesse the Prince of Orange as being the only Meanes for obteyning a full redress and remedy therein.

Haveing therefore an intire Confidence that his said Highnesse the Prince of Orange will perfect the deliverance soe farr advanced by him and will still preserve them from the violation of their rights which they have here asserted and from all other attempts upon their Religion Rights and Liberties.

The said Lords Spirituall and Temporall and Commons Assembled at Westminster doe Resolve.

That William and Mary Prince and Princesse of Orange bee and bee declared, King and Queen of England France and Ireland and the Dominions thereunto belonging to hold the Crowne and Royall Dignity of the said Kingdom's and Dominions to them the said Prince and Princesss during their lives and the life of the Survivor of them and that the Sole and full exercise of the Regall Power be only in and executed by the said Prince of Orange in the Names of the said Prince and Princesse during their Joynt lives. And after their deceases the said Crowne and Royall Dignity of the said Kingdoms and Dominions to be to the heires of the body of the said Princesse: And for default of such Issue to the Princesse Anne of Denmarke and the heires of her body. And for default of such Issue to the heires of the body of the said Prince of Orange.

And the said Lords Spirituall and Temporall and Commons doe pray the said Prince and Princesse of Orange to accept the same accordingly. . . .

Upon which their said Majestyes did accept the crowne and royall dignitie of the kingdoms of England France and Ireland and the dominions thereunto belonging. . . . And thereupon their Majestyes were pleased that the said lords spirituall and temporall and commons being the two Houses of Parlyament should continue to sitt and with their Majesty's royall concurrence make effectuall provision for the settlement of the religion lawes and liberties of this kingdome soe that the same for the future might not be in danger againe of being subverted, to which the said lords spirituall and temporall and commons did agree and proceede to act accordingly. Now in pursuance of the premisses the said lords spirituall and temporall and commons in Parlyament assembled for the ratifying confirming and establishing the said declaration and the articles clauses matters and things therein contained by the force of a law made in due forme by authority of Parlyament doe pray that it may be declared and enacted that all and singular the rights and liberties asserted and claimed in the said declaration are the true auntient and indubitable rights and liberties of the people of this kingdome and soe shall be esteemed allowed adjudged deemed and taken to be and that all and every the particulars aforesaid shall be firmly and strictly holden and observed as they are expressed in the said declaration. And all officers and ministers whatsoever shall serve their Majestyes and their successors according to the same in all times to come....

D. Judge, *The Parliamentary State*

(1993), p. 20

The Constitutional Settlement of 1689 and the Rise of the Liberal State

The potency of the Constitutional Settlement of 1689 stems from its implicit principle of the supremacy of parliament in law. The acceptance by William and Mary of the gift of the crown was conditional upon the terms set by parliament. Henceforth, monarchical power was dependent upon parliament rather than *vice versa*. After 1689, as Munro points out:

> Parliament was to be its own master and free from interference... Parliaments were to be held frequently, and the election of their members was to be free. The Crown's power to levy taxes was made subject to parliamentary consent, its power to keep a standing army made subject to statute, and powers of suspending or dispensing with laws... were declared illegal. (1987: 80)

In other words, what was asserted and accepted in 1689 was the principle of *parliamentary sovereignty*, whereby parliament secured legal supremacy amongst the institutions of the state. Thus, not only was the monarchy subordinated to parliament, but, also, the last vestiges of the claim of the courts that parliament could not legislate in derogation of the principles of the common law were removed. Constitutional theory was at last reconciled to the legal practice that had been developing for nearly a century.

Above all, therefore, the Bill of Rights was a restraint upon arbitrary behaviour. Its passage confirmed the distinctiveness of English state development from its continental European counterparts. The concentration of power in the hands of the monarch and the exclusion of parliament from policy making—the political hallmarks of absolutism—were outlawed in England in 1689. The authority of statute was conferred upon the pre-existing principles—of consent and representation—so confirming the differences between the state-form in England and those in the absolutist regimes in France and Prussia for example....

B: The unlimited legislative powers of Parliament

Several cases have arisen where this idea has been tested.

There is a presumption used by the courts when construing statutes that Parliament does not intend to legislate contrary to the principles of international law, and, as far as possible, a statute will be interpreted in a way which avoids conflict. What do the courts do, however, when there is a clear conflict between a statute of the United Kingdom Parliament and the principles of international law? The answer is given in the following case.

Mortensen v Peters

(1906) 14 SLT 227, High Court of Justiciary

Mortensen was the captain of a Norwegian trawler charged with illegal trawl fishing in waters within the Moray Firth contrary to a bye-law made by the Fishery Board for Scotland under s. 7 of the Herring Fishery (Scotland) Act 1889. The Act defined the area for which bye-laws could be made, that is, all of the Moray Firth, although much of it comprised international waters. The trawler had been fishing five miles off the coast in international waters but within the prohibited area. Mortensen was convicted by the Sheriff's Court and appealed.

THE LORD JUSTICE GENERAL: My Lords, I apprehend that the question is one of construction and of construction only. In this Court we have nothing to do with the question of whether the legislature has or has not done what foreign powers may consider a usurpation in a question with them. Neither are we a tribunal sitting to decide whether an act of the legislature is *ultra vires* as in contravention of generally acknowledged principles of international law. For us an Act of Parliament duly passed by Lords and Commons and assented to by the King, is supreme, and we are bound to give effect to its terms....

It is said by the appellant...that International Law has firmly fixed that a locus such as this is beyond the limits of territorial sovereignty; and that consequently it is not to be thought that in such a place the legislature could seek to affect any but the King's subjects.

It is a trite observation that there is no such thing as a standard of International Law, extraneous to the domestic law of a kingdom, to which appeal may be made. International Law, so far as this Court is concerned, is the body of doctrine regarding the international rights and duties of States which has been adopted and made part of the Law of Scotland. Now can it be said to be clear by the law of Scotland that the locus here is beyond what the legislature may assert right to affect by legislation against all whomsoever for the purpose of regulating methods of fishing?

I do not think I need say anything about what is known as the three-mile limit. It may be assumed that within the three miles the territorial sovereignty would be sufficient to cover any such legislation as the present. It is enough to say that that is not a proof of the counter proposition that outside the three miles no such result could be looked for. The locus, although outside the three-mile limit, is within the bay known as the Moray Firth, and the Moray Firth, says the respondent, is *intra fauces terroe*. Now, I cannot say that there is any definition of what *fauces terroe* exactly are. But there are at least three points which go far to show that this spot might be considered as lying therein.

1st. The dicta of the Scottish Institutional Writers seem to show that it would be no usurpation, according to the law of Scotland, so to consider it.

Thus, Stair, II i. 5: 'The vast ocean is common to all mankind as to navigation and fishing, which are the only uses thereof, because it is not capable of bounds; but when the sea is inclosed in bays, creeks, *or otherwise is capable of any bounds or meiths as within the points of such lands*, or within the view of such shores, then it may become proper, but with the reservation of passage for commerce as in the land.' And Bell, Pr. S 639: 'The Sovereign...is proprietor of the narrow seas within cannon shot of the land, and the *firths*, gulfs, and bays around the Kingdom.'

2nd. The same statute puts forward claims to what are at least analogous places. If attention is paid to the Schedule appended to section 6, many places will be found far beyond the three-mile limit—e.g., the Firth of Clyde near its mouth. I am not ignoring that it may be said that this in one sense is proving *idem per idem*, but none the less I do not think the fact can be ignored.

3rd. There are many instances to be found in decided cases where the right of a nation to legislate for waters more or less landlocked or landembraced, although beyond the three-mile limit, has been admitted.

They will be found collected in the case of the *Direct United States Cable Company* v *Anglo-American Telegraph Company*, LR 2 App Cas 394, the bay there in question being Conception Bay, which has a width at the mouth of rather more than 20 miles.

It seems to me therefore, without laying down the proposition that the Moray Firth is for every purpose within the territorial sovereignty, it can at least be clearly said that the appellant cannot make out his proposition that it is inconceivable that the British legislature should attempt for fishery regulation to legislate against all and sundry in such a place. And if that is so, then I revert to the considerations already stated which as a matter of construction make me think that it did so legislate.

LORD KYLLACHY: ... A legislature may quite conceivably, by oversight or even design, exceed what an international tribunal (if such existed) might hold to be its international rights. Still, there is always a presumption against its intending to do so. I think that is acknowledged. But then it is only a presumption; and, as such, it must always give way to the language used if it is clear, and also to all counter presumptions which may legitimately be had in view in determining, on ordinary principles, the true meaning and intent of the legislation. Express words will, of course, be conclusive; and so also will plain implication.

Now it must, I think, be conceded that the language of the enactment here in question is fairly express—express, that is to say, to the effect of making an unlimited and unqualified prohibition, applying to the whole area specified, and affecting everybody—whether British subjects or foreigners.

LORD JOHNSTON: [delivered a concurring judgment]

Appeal dismissed

NOTE: In *Cheney* v *Conn* [1968] 1 All ER 779, a taxpayer challenged an assessment of income tax made under the Finance Act 1964 on the ground that part of the money raised would be used for the manufacture of nuclear weapons contrary to a treaty, the Geneva Convention, to which the United Kingdom was party. Ungoed-Thomas J stated:

> What the statute itself enacts cannot be unlawful, because what the statute says and provides is itself the law, and the highest form of law that is known to this country. It is the law which prevails over every other form of law, and it is not for the court to say that a parliamentary enactment, the highest law in this country, is illegal.

See also *R* v *Secretary of State for the Home Department, ex parte Thakrar* [1974] QB 684.

If international law can place no limitation on Parliament's powers, can time do so?

In *Burmah Oil Co* v *Lord Advocate* [1965] AC 75, HL, the company was successful in its claim for compensation against the Crown for the destruction of its installations in Burma during the Second World War, the destruction having been ordered by the commander of British forces to prevent the installations falling into the hands of the advancing Japanese forces. In response to this decision Parliament hastily passed the War Damage Act 1965 with retrospective effect to deny entitlement to compensation for damage for acts lawfully done by the Crown during a war in which the Sovereign was engaged.

C: Ruling on the validity of Parliament's enactments

The statement of Dicey above also suggests that no person or body has authority to rule on the validity of Parliament's enactments. Is it possible to challenge the validity of an Act of Parliament in the courts? In countries with a written constitution the ordinary courts or a constitutional court will have jurisdiction to determine whether the acts of the legislature are constitutional. In the United States the Supreme Court, in *Marbury* v *Madison* (1803) 1 Cranch 137, declared that it had power to decide whether or not the Acts of Congress conformed with the Constitution. In the United Kingdom the doctrine of legislative supremacy dictates that Parliament has power to legislate on constitutional matters. Thus Parliament may change the constitution by Act of Parliament. This being so, is it possible to challenge an Act on the ground that it is unconstitutional? Chief Justice Coke was of the opinion that the courts could intervene if Parliament enacted outrageous legislation. He stated in *Dr Bonham's Case* (1610) 8 Co Rep 114, at p. 118:

> In many cases, the common law will control Acts of Parliament, and sometimes adjudge them to be utterly void: for when an Act of Parliament is against common right and reason, or repugnant, or impossible to be performed, the common law will control it, and adjudge such an Act to be void.

However, this statement precedes the Glorious Revolution of 1688, since when the doctrine of the supremacy of Parliament has developed its modern meaning. In *Ex p. Canon Selwyn* (1872) 36 JP 54 a question arose regarding the validity of the Irish Church Act 1869. Cockburn CJ stated:

> [T]here is no judicial body in the country by which the validity of an act of parliament could be questioned. An act of the legislature is superior in authority to any court of law. We have only to administer the law as we find it, and no court could pronounce a judgment as to the validity of an act of Parliament.

In *Pickin* v *British Railways Board* [1974] AC 765, Lord Reid stated:

> In earlier times many learned lawyers seem to have believed that an Act of Parliament could be disregarded in so far as it was contrary to the law of God or the law of nature or natural justice, but since the supremacy of Parliament was finally demonstrated by the Revolution of 1688 any such idea has become obsolete.

In *Manuel* v *Attorney-General* [1983] Ch 77, Sir Robert Megarry VC stated, at p. 86:

> [T]he duty of the court is to obey and apply every Act of Parliament, and . . . the court cannot hold any such Act to be *ultra vires*. Of course there may be questions about what the Act means, and of course there is power to hold statutory instruments and other subordinate legislation *ultra vires*. But once an instrument is recognised as being an Act of Parliament, no English court can refuse to obey it or question its validity.

But what happens if there are two Acts on the statute books which conflict with one another? See the case which follows.

Ellen Street Estates Limited v Minister of Health

[1934] 1 KB 590, Court of Appeal

The Acquisition of Land (Assessment of Compensation) Act 1919 provided by s. 2 for the assessment of compensation in respect of land acquired compulsorily for public purposes according to certain rules. Section 7(1) stated 'The provisions of the Act or order by which the land is authorised to be acquired, or of any Act incorporated therewith, shall in relation to the matters dealt with in this Act, have effect subject to this Act, and so far as inconsistent with this Act those provisions shall cease to have or shall not have effect . . .'. The Housing Act 1925, s. 46 provided for the assessment of compensation for land acquired compulsorily under an improvement or reconstruction scheme made under that Act in a manner differing in certain respects from that prescribed by the Act of 1919. Section 7(1) could be construed as applying to previous enactments, but it was argued that it applied also to subsequent enactments. If this was so, inconsistent provisions in the 1925 Act would be of no effect.

> SCRUTTON LJ: . . . Such a contention involves this proposition, that no subsequent Parliament by enacting a provision inconsistent with the Act of 1919 can give any effect to the words it uses. Sect. 46, sub-s. 1, of the Housing Act, 1925, says this: 'Where land included in any improvement or reconstruction scheme . . . is acquired compulsorily,' certain provisions as to compensation shall apply. These are inconsistent with those contained in the Acquisition of Land (Assessment of Compensation) Act, 1919, and then s. 46, sub-s. 2, of the Act of 1925 provides: 'Subject as aforesaid, the compensation to be paid for such land shall be assessed in accordance with the Acquisition of Land (Assessment of Compensation) Act, 1919.' I asked Mr Hill [for the appellants] what these last quoted words mean, and he replied they mean nothing. That is absolutely contrary to the constitutional position that Parliament can alter an Act previously passed, and it can do so by repealing in terms the previous Act—Mr Hill agrees that it may do so—and it can do it also in another way—namely, by enacting a provision which is clearly inconsistent with the previous Act.
>
> MAUGHAM LJ: . . . The Legislature cannot, according to our constitution, bind itself as to the form of subsequent legislation, and it is impossible for Parliament to enact that in a subsequent statute dealing with

> the same subject-matter there can be no implied repeal. If in a subsequent Act Parliament chooses to make it plain that the earlier statute is being to some extent repealed, effect must be given to that intention just because it is the will of the Legislature.
>
> *Appeal dismissed.*

■ QUESTIONS

1. Was this case concerned with the *content* of the legislation or the *form* of the legislation?
2. When Maugham LJ stated that Parliament cannot bind itself as to the form of subsequent legislation, was this *obiter* or *ratio*?

NOTES AND QUESTIONS

1. The doctrine of implied repeal is a consequence of the traditional Diceyan view of supremacy: if Parliament cannot bind future Parliaments as to the content of legislation, subsequent legislation which is incompatible with a prior Act necessarily must be taken to have repealed the incompatible earlier provision. In New Zealand a Bill of Rights Act was passed in 1990 which sought to eliminate the possibility of judges declaring statutory provisions void for incompatibility with the Act. The Act expressly provided:

> 4. No courts shall, in relation to any enactment (whether passed or made before or after the commencement of this Bill of Rights):—
>
> (a) hold any provision of the enactment to be impliedly repealed or revoked, or to be in any way invalid or ineffective; or
>
> (b) decline to apply any provision of the enactment
>
> by reason only that the provision is inconsistent with any provision of this Bill of Rights.

Emmerson, 'Opinion: This Year's Model—The Options for Incorporation' [1997] EHRLR 313, at 325 states:

> It is important to scotch the notion that there is some sort of constitutional imperative for adopting a model with such obvious shortcomings. The New Zealand Act is not a faithful reflection of even the most orthodox view of parliamentary sovereignty. By expressly excluding the doctrine of implied repeal in relation to Acts passed before the Bill of Rights Act, it institutionalises a principle of legislative supremacy which is quite out of step with British constitutional theory, and which fails to acknowledge the constitutional character of human rights legislation.

The Human Rights Act 1998 provides:

> **3.**—(1) So far as it is possible to do so, primary legislation and subordinate legislation must be read and given effect in a way which is compatible with the Convention rights.
>
> (2) This section—
>
> (a) applies to primary legislation and subordinate legislation whenever enacted;
>
> (b) does not affect the validity, continuing operation or enforcement of any incompatible primary legislation; and
>
> (c) does not affect the validity, continuing operation or enforcement of any incompatible subordinate legislation if (disregarding any possibility of revocation) primary legislation prevents removal of the incompatibility.

Where it is not possible to construe a statute consistently with the Human Rights Act, the inconsistent statute takes precedence regardless of whether it was enacted before or after the Human Rights Act. In the White Paper, *Rights Brought Home: The Human Rights Bill*, Cm 3782, the Government stated:

> 2.13 The Government has reached the conclusion that courts should not have the power to set aside primary legislation, past or future, on the ground of incompatibility with the

> Convention. This conclusion arises from the importance which the Government attaches to Parliamentary sovereignty. In this context, Parliamentary sovereignty means that Parliament is competent to make any law on any matter of its choosing and no court may question the validity of any Act that it passes.... To make provision in the Bill for courts to set aside Acts of Parliament would confer on the judiciary a general power over the decisions of Parliament which under our present constitutional arrangements they do not possess, and would be likely on occasions to draw the judiciary into serious conflict with Parliament.

Does this passage misstate the traditional doctrine of supremacy? When a court applies the doctrine of implied repeal in respect of an earlier statutory provision which is incompatible with a later Act of Parliament, is it respecting the will of Parliament or is it setting itself above Parliament and adjudicating on the validity of legislation?

2. Has the Government in the White Paper confused implied repeal of earlier legislation with setting aside incompatible subsequent legislation?
3. While there may be a reluctance on the part of the courts to rule on the validity of Acts of Parliament, a related issue which has arisen is whether they may adjudicate upon the question whether something purporting to be an Act of Parliament actually is such. It is the Queen in Parliament which enacts legislation. Under the common law, for a Bill to become law it must be approved by the Lords and Commons and receive the Royal Assent. If an Act is challenged on the basis that there have been procedural defects during its passage through Parliament, will the courts look behind the formal words of enactment and inquire whether the requirements of the common law have been satisfied?

Pickin v British Railways Board

[1974] AC 765, House of Lords

Pickin was a railway enthusiast who, in 1969, purchased from the owner of a piece of land adjoining a disused railway line, all his estate and interest in the railway land and track. By s. 259 of a private Act of Parliament of 1836 setting up the railway line, it was provided that, if a line should be abandoned, the lands acquired for the track should vest in the owners for the time being of the adjoining lands. Pickin brought an action against the Board, claiming that by virtue of s. 259 he was the owner of that land to mid-track. The Board claimed that it owned the land by virtue of a private Act of Parliament, the British Railways Act 1968. Pickin claimed that the relevant provision (s. 18) of the 1968 Act was invalid and ineffective to deprive him of his title, as Parliament had been misled by the Board to obtain the passage of the Act. In particular the Bill was presented as being unopposed, but notice had not been given to affected landowners as required by Standing Orders. In addition, the preamble to the Bill contained a false recital that plans of the lands and a book of reference to such plans containing the names of the owners, lessees, and occupiers of the said land were duly deposited with the clerk of the county council. The Board sought to have these claims struck out as frivolous, vexatious, and an abuse of the process of the court.

> LORD REID: ...The idea that a court is entitled to disregard a provision in an Act of Parliament on any ground must seem strange and startling to anyone with any knowledge of the history and law of our constitution, but a detailed argument has been submitted to your Lordships and I must deal with it.
>
> I must make it plain that there has been no attempt to question the general supremacy of Parliament. In earlier times many learned lawyers seem to have believed that an Act of Parliament could be disregarded in so far as it was contrary to the law of God or the law of nature or natural justice, but since the supremacy of Parliament was finally demonstrated by the Revolution of 1688 any such idea has become obsolete.
>
> The respondent's contention is that there is a difference between a public and a private Act. There are of course great differences between the methods and procedures followed in dealing with public and private Bills, and there may be some differences in the methods of construing their provisions. But the respondent argues for a much more fundamental difference. There is little in modern authority that he can rely on. The mainstay of his argument is a decision of this House, *Mackenzie* v *Stewart* in 1754.

[In the Court of Appeal Pickin successfully argued that this case was authority for the House of Lords refusing to give effect to a private Act obtained by fraud.]

... It appears to me that far the most probable explanation of the decision is that it was a decision as to the true construction of the Act.... [I]t seems to me much more likely that Lord Hardwicke LC adopted [the construction argued for by Mackenzie] than that he laid down some new constitutional principle that the court had the power to give relief against the provision of a statute.

If the decision was only as to the construction of a statutory provision that would explain why the case has received little attention in later cases....

In my judgment the law is correctly stated by Lord Campbell in *Edinburgh and Dalkeith Railway Co.* v *Wauchope* (1842) 8 Cl & F 710, 1 Bell 252. Mr Wauchope claimed certain wayleaves. The matter was dealt with in a private Act. He appears to have maintained in the Court of Session that the provisions of that Act should not be applied because it had been passed without his having had notice as required by Standing Orders.... Lord Campbell [stated]:

> I must express some surprise that such a notion should have prevailed. It seems to me there is no foundation for it whatever; all that a court of justice can look to is the parliamentary roll; they see that an Act has passed both Houses of Parliament, and that it has received the royal assent, and no court of justice can inquire into the manner in which it was introduced into Parliament, what was done previously to its being introduced, or what passed in Parliament during the various stages of its progress through both Houses of Parliament. I therefore trust that no such inquiry will hereafter be entered into in Scotland, and that due effect will be given to every Act of Parliament, both private as well as public, upon the just construction which appears to arise upon it.

No doubt this was obiter but, so far as I am aware, no one since 1842 has doubted that it is a correct statement of the constitutional position.

The function of the court is to construe and apply the enactments of Parliament. The court has no concern with the manner in which Parliament or its officers carrying out its Standing Orders perform these functions. Any attempt to prove that they were misled by fraud or otherwise would necessarily involve an inquiry into the manner in which they had performed their functions in dealing with the Bill which became the British Railways Act 1968.

In whatever form the respondent's case is pleaded he must prove not only that the appellants acted fraudulently but also that their fraud caused damage to him by causing the enactment of section 18. He could not prove that without an examination of the manner in which the officers of Parliament dealt with the matter. So the court would, or at least might, have to adjudicate upon that.

For a century or more both Parliament and the courts have been careful not to act so as to cause conflict between them. Any such investigations as the respondent seeks could easily lead to such a conflict, and I would only support it if compelled to do so by clear authority. But it appears to me that the whole trend of authority for over a century is clearly against permitting any such investigation.

The respondent is entitled to argue that section 18 should be construed in a way favourable to him and for that reason I have refrained from pronouncing on that matter. But he is not entitled to go behind the Act to show that section 18 should not be enforced. Nor is he entitled to examine proceedings in Parliament in order to show that the appellants by fraudulently misleading Parliament caused him loss. I am therefore clearly of opinion that this appeal should be allowed....

LORD MORRIS OF BORTH-Y-GEST: ... The question of fundamental importance which arises is whether the court should entertain the proposition that an Act of Parliament can so be assailed in the courts that matters should proceed as though the Act or some part of it had never been passed. I consider that such doctrine would be dangerous and impermissible. It is the function of the courts to administer the laws which Parliament has enacted. In the processes of Parliament there will be much consideration whether a Bill should or should not in one form or another become an enactment. When an enactment is passed there is finality unless and until it is amended or repealed by Parliament. In the courts there may be argument as to the correct interpretation of the enactment: there must be none as to whether it should be on the Statute Book at all.

... The conclusion which I have reached results, in my view, not only from a settled and sustained line of authority which I see no reason to question and which I think should be endorsed but also from the view that any other conclusion would be constitutionally undesirable and impracticable. It must surely be for Parliament to lay down the procedures which are to be followed before a Bill can become an Act. It must be for Parliament to decide whether its decreed procedures have in fact been followed. It must be for Parliament to lay down and to construe its Standing Orders and further to decide whether they have been obeyed: it must be for Parliament to decide whether in any particular case to dispense with compliance with such orders. It must be for Parliament to decide whether it is satisfied that an Act should be passed in the form and with the wording set out in the Act. It must be for Parliament to decide what documentary material or testimony it requires and the extent to which Parliamentary privilege should attach. It would be impracticable and undesirable for the High Court of Justice to embark upon an inquiry concerning the effect or the effectiveness of the internal procedures in the High Court of Parliament or an inquiry whether in any particular case those procedures were effectively followed.

[His Lordship referred to *Edinburgh and Dalkeith Railway Co.* v *Wauchope* and several other cases and continued.]

Of equal clarity was the passage in the judgment of Willes J in 1871 when in *Lee* v *Bude and Torrington Junction Railway Co.* (1871) LR 6 CP 576 (in which case it was alleged that Parliament had been induced to pass an Act by fraudulent recitals) he said, at p. 582:

> 'Are we to act as regents over what is done by Parliament with the consent of the Queen, Lords, and Commons? I deny that any such authority exists. If an Act of Parliament has been obtained improperly, it is for the legislature to correct it by repealing it: but, so long as it exists as law, the courts are bound to obey it. The proceedings here are judicial, not autocratic, which they would be if we could make laws instead of administering them.'

...In the result I have not been persuaded that any doubt has been cast upon principles which are soundly directed as being both desirable and reasonable and which furthermore have for long been firmly established by authority.

I would allow the appeal....

Appeal allowed.

NOTE: See *Jackson* v *Attorney General* [2005] UKHL 56, [2006] 1 AC 262 p. 67 *post* on courts considering legislation.

■ QUESTION

When Lord Morris stated 'It must surely be for Parliament to lay down the procedures which are to be followed before a Bill can become an Act. It must be for Parliament to decide whether its decreed procedures have in fact been followed', was he referring to procedures laid down in Standing Orders or in Acts of Parliament?

SECTION 4: CAN PARLIAMENT LIMIT THE POWERS OF ITS SUCCESSORS?

The answer to this question depends upon the nature of parliamentary supremacy. There are differing theories. Hart recognized that there could be uncertainty regarding the nature of the rule of recognition.

H. L. A. Hart, *The Concept of Law*

(1961), pp. 145–146

In the overwhelming majority of cases the formula 'Whatever the Queen in Parliament enacts is law' is an adequate expression of the rule as to the legal competence of Parliament, and is accepted as an ultimate criterion for the identification of law, however open the rules thus identified may be at their periphery. But doubts can arise as to its meaning or scope; we can ask what is meant by 'enacted by Parliament' and when doubts arise they may be settled by the courts. What inference is to be drawn as to the place of courts within a legal system from the fact that the ultimate rule of a legal system may thus be in doubt and that courts may resolve the doubt. Does it require some qualification of the thesis that the foundation of a legal system is an accepted rule of recognition specifying the criteria of legal validity?

To answer these questions we shall consider here some aspects of the English doctrine of the sovereignty of Parliament, though, of course, similar doubts can arise in relation to ultimate criteria of legal validity in any system. Under the influence of the Austinian doctrine that law is essentially the product of a legally untrammelled will, older constitutional theorists wrote as if it was a logical necessity that there should be a legislature which was sovereign, in the sense that it is free, at every moment of its existence as a continuing body, not only from legal limitations imposed *ab extra*, but also from its own prior legislation. That Parliament is sovereign in this sense may now be regarded as established, and the principle that no earlier Parliament can preclude its 'successors' from repealing its legislation constitutes part of the ultimate rule of recognition used by the courts in identifying valid rules of law. It is, however, important to see that no necessity of logic, still less of nature, dictates that there should be such a Parliament; it is only one arrangement among others, equally conceivable, which has come to be accepted with us as the criterion of legal validity. Among these others is another principle which might equally well, perhaps better, deserve the name of 'sovereignty'. This is the principle that Parliament should *not* be incapable of limiting irrevocably the legislative competence of its successors but, on the contrary, should have this wider self-limiting power. Parliament would then at least once in its history be capable of exercising an even larger sphere of legislative competence than the accepted established doctrine allows to it. The requirement that at every moment of its existence Parliament should be free from legal limitations including even those imposed by itself is, after all, only one interpretation of the ambiguous idea of legal omnipotence. It in effect makes a choice between a *continuing* omnipotence in all matters not affecting the legislative competence of successive parliaments, and an unrestricted *self-embracing* omnipotence the exercise of which can only be enjoyed once. These two conceptions of omnipotence have their parallel in two conceptions of an omnipotent God: on the one hand, a God who at every moment of His existence enjoys the same powers and so is incapable of cutting down those powers, and, on the other, a God whose powers include the power to destroy for the future his omnipotence. Which form of omnipotence—continuing or self-embracing—our Parliament enjoys is an empirical question concerning the form of rule which is accepted as the ultimate criterion in identifying the law. Though it is a question about a rule lying at the base of a legal system, it is still a question of fact to which at any given moment of time, on some points at least, there may be a quite determinate answer. Thus it is clear that the presently accepted rule is one of continuing sovereignty, so that Parliament cannot protect its statutes from repeal.

NOTE: Dicey was a proponent of the 'continuing' theory of parliamentary supremacy, usually referred to as the 'traditional' theory. Others have tended towards the 'self-embracing' theory, or a variant of it. Proponents of this 'new' view would argue that Parliament may change the procedures governing law-making. The two extracts which follow summarize this view and point to its consequences.

R. F. V. Heuston, *Essays in Constitutional Law*

(2nd edn, 1964), Ch. 1, pp. 6–8

Summary of New View

It is suggested that the new view can be summarised thus:

(1) Sovereignty is a legal concept: the rules which identify the sovereign and prescribe its composition and functions are logically prior to it.
(2) There is a distinction between rules which govern, on the one hand, (a) the composition, and (b) the procedure, and, on the other hand, (c) the area of power, of a sovereign legislature.
(3) The courts have jurisdiction to question the validity of an alleged Act of Parliament on grounds 2 (a) and 2 (b), but not on ground 2 (c).
(4) This jurisdiction is exercisable either before or after the Royal Assent has been signified—in the former case by way of injunction, in the latter by way of declaratory judgment.

G. Marshall, *Constitutional Theory*

(1971), pp. 42–43

> Dicey simply implied, without examining, the proposition that authority in a 'sovereign' Parliament must be exercised at all times by a simple majority of legislators, who, since they are unrestricted in their powers, can always repeal any constitutional protections or restrictions on power enacted into law by their predecessors. To do Dicey justice, the Sovereign described in the *Law of the Constitution* is the British Parliament (though he did sometimes speak in terms of sovereigns in general). But even in relation to the British Parliament he did not fully examine the possibility that Parliament as at present constituted might conceivably bind the future or circumscribe the freedom of future legislators, not by laying down blanket prohibitions or attempting to enact a fundamental Bill of Rights, but by using their authority to provide different forms and procedures for legislation. A referendum or a joint sitting, for example, might be prescribed before certain things could be done. Or a two-thirds majority. Or a seventy-five per cent or eighty per cent majority. If it is also provided that any repeal of such provisions should not be by simple majority, the courts may be able to protect the arrangements laid down by declaring in suitable proceedings that any purported repeal by simple majority of a protected provision is *ultra vires* as being not, in the sense required by law, an 'Act of Parliament'. In this finding they would not be in any way derogating from parliamentary sovereignty but protecting Parliament's authority from usurpation by those not entitled for the purpose in hand to exercise it. Thus, for the English lawyer or political theorist, sovereignty may be purged of its dangerous absolutism. He can believe both in an ultimate Sovereign and in the possibility of restraint imposed by law upon the way in which legal power is used. He can believe in the possibility even of a modified Bill of Fundamental Rights grafted into the British constitution—or, to be more accurate, in a relatively fundamental set of provisions in which selected civil liberties are protected from attack in the future by, so to speak, taking out legislative insurance in the present, in the shape of requirements of special procedures or majorities. This would be to do rather more than is done in Canada's Bill of Rights, which declares certain rights and freedoms to be fundamental, but leaves them open to attack by any future legislation which specifically declares itself to apply, notwithstanding the Bill of Rights.

For the views of a proponent of the continuing theory of supremacy, see H. W. R. Wade, 'The Basis of Legal Sovereignty' [1955] *Cambridge Law Journal* 172.

A: Entrenchment and redefinition

The self-embracing theory would seem to allow Parliament to impose procedural requirements to make the passage of legislation more difficult, for example a requirement that a majority of voters vote in a referendum in favour of the proposed legislation, or a requirement of an enhanced majority in the Commons such as two-thirds instead of a simple majority. This issue has arisen in several Commonwealth cases.

Attorney-General for New South Wales v *Trethowan and Others*

[1932] AC 526, Privy Council

Under s. 5 of the Colonial Laws Validity Act 1865, the legislature of New South Wales had full power to legislate for its own constitution, powers, and procedure, provided that these laws were passed in 'the manner and form' required by the law in force at the time, whether it be imperial or colonial. In 1929 the Constitution (Legislative Council) Amendment Act was passed, which inserted a new s. 7A in the Constitution Act 1902, providing that no Bill for abolishing the Legislative Council should be presented to the Governor for His Majesty's assent until it had been approved by a majority of electors voting in a referendum and, further, that any Bill to repeal this referendum requirement must also be approved at a referendum. In 1930, following a change in government, both houses of the legislature passed two Bills, one to repeal s. 7A and the other to abolish the Legislative Council, both of which the Government intended to present for the Royal Assent without referenda being held. The plaintiffs were members of the Legislative Council and sought a declaration that the two Bills could not be presented for Royal Assent until approved by the electors in accordance with s. 7A, and injunctions restraining the presentation of the Bills.

LORD SANKEY LC: ... [T]he point involved in the case, ... is really a short one—namely, whether the legislature of the State of New South Wales has power to abolish the Legislative Council of the said State, or to repeal s. 7A of the Constitution Act, 1902, except in the manner provided by the said s. 7A. It will be sufficient for this Board to decide any other question if, and when, it arises.

[Section 5 of the Colonial Laws Validity Act 1865 provides:

> Section 5.—Every colonial legislature shall have and be deemed at all times to have had full power within its jurisdiction to establish Courts of Judicature, and to abolish and reconstitute the same, and to alter the constitution thereof, and to make provision for the administration of justice therein; and every representative legislature shall, in respect to the colony under its jurisdiction, have, and be deemed at all times to have had, full power to make laws respecting the constitution, power, and procedure of such legislature; provided that such laws shall have been passed in such manner and form as may from time to time be required by any Act of parliament, letters patent, Order in Council, or colonial law, for the time being in force in the said colony.]

... In their Lordships' opinion the legislature of New South Wales had power under s. 5 of the Act of 1865 to enact the Constitution (Legislative Council) Amendment Act, 1929, and thereby to introduce s. 7A into the Constitution Act, 1902. In other words, the legislature had power to alter the constitution of New South Wales by enacting that Bills relating to specified kind or kinds of legislation (e.g., abolishing the Legislative Council or altering its constitution or powers, or repealing or amending that enactment) should not be presented for the Royal assent until approved by the electors in a prescribed manner. There is here no question of repugnancy. The enactment of the Act of 1929 was simply an exercise by the legislature of New South Wales of its power (adopting the words of s. 5 of the Act of 1865) to make laws respecting the constitution, powers and procedure of the authority competent to make the laws for New South Wales.

The whole of s. 7A was competently enacted. It was intra vires s. 5 of the Act of 1865, and was (again adopting the words of s. 5) a colonial law for the time being in force when the Bill to repeal s. 7A was introduced in the Legislative Council.

The question then arises, could *that* Bill, a repealing Bill, after its passage through both chambers, be lawfully presented for the Royal assent without having first received the approval of the electors in the prescribed manner? In their Lordships' opinion, the Bill could not lawfully be so presented. The proviso in the second sentence of s. 5 of the Act of 1865 states a condition which must be fulfilled before the legislature can validly exercise its power to make the kind of laws which are referred to in that sentence. In order that s. 7A may be repealed (in other words, in order that *that* particular law 'respecting the constitution, powers and procedure' of the legislature may be validly made) the law for that purpose must have been passed in the manner required by s. 7A, a colonial law for the time being in force in New South Wales. An attempt was made to draw some distinction between a Bill to repeal a statute and a Bill for other purposes and between 'making' laws and the word in the proviso, 'passed.' Their Lordships feel unable to draw any such distinctions. As to the proviso they agree with the views expressed by Rich J [in the High Court of Australia] in the following words: 'I take the word "passed" to be equivalent to "enacted." The proviso is not dealing with narrow questions of parliamentary procedure'; and later in his judgment: 'In my opinion the proviso to s. 5 relates to the entire process of turning a proposed law into a legislative enactment, and was intended to enjoin fulfilment of every condition and compliance with every requirement which existing legislation imposed upon the process of law making.'

Again, no question of repugnancy here arises. It is only a question whether the proposed enactment is intra vires or *ultra vires* s. 5. A Bill, within the scope of sub-s. 6 of s. 7A, which received the Royal assent without having been approved by the electors in accordance with that section, would not be a valid Act of the legislature. It would be *ultra vires* s. 5 of the Act of 1865. Indeed, the presentation of the Bill to the Governor without such approval would be the commission of an unlawful act.

In the result, their Lordships are of opinion that s. 7A of the Constitution Act, 1902, was valid and was in force when the two Bills under consideration were passed through the Legislative Council and the Legislative Assembly. Therefore these Bills could not be presented to the Governor for His Majesty's assent unless and until a majority of the electors voting had approved them.

> For these reasons, their Lordships are of opinion that the judgment of the High Court dismissing the appeal from the decree of the Supreme Court of New South Wales was right....
>
> *Appeal dismissed.*

■ QUESTION

If the United Kingdom Parliament enacted a provision to the same effect as s. 7A, designed to protect the position of the House of Lords, would a subsequent Bill abolishing this provision and the House of Lords become an Act on receiving the Royal Assent, or would the referenda requirements be regarded by the courts as necessary prerequisites to the Bill becoming an Act?

NOTE: There is a division of view among constitutional theorists as to the relevance of the *Trethowan* case to the United Kingdom. Those who adhere to the traditional theory of supremacy argue that the decision is of no relevance as the New South Wales legislature was a subordinate legislature (see, e.g. Wade, 'The Basis of Legal Sovereignty' [1955] CLJ 172; Munro, *Studies in Constitutional Law* (2nd edn), Chapter 5). The proponents of this view rely on *Ellen St Estates Ltd* v *Minister of Health* (*supra*). Opponents of this view argue that the decision is applicable on the basis that at common law there is a rule that legislation may be enacted only in such manner and form as is prescribed by the law (see, e.g. Heuston, *Essays in Constitutional Law*, Chapter 1; Fazal, 'Entrenched Rights and Parliamentary Sovereignty' (1974) PL 295). If an Act lays down a specific procedure to be followed before it may be repealed, this is the law, and a measure passed in the normal way ignoring this procedure has not been passed in the manner and form prescribed by the law and therefore is not an Act of Parliament. Support for this view is found in *Harris* v *Minister of the Interior* 1952 (2) SA 428, and *Bribery Commissioner* v *Ranasinghe* [1965] AC 172. In the latter case the Privy Council held that the procedural requirement of the constitution of Ceylon regarding judicial appointments of a two-thirds majority of the legislature, was binding on the sovereign Parliament of Ceylon, which could not, therefore, set up the Bribery Commission by an ordinary Act of Parliament. The Privy Council held that the official copy of the statute was not conclusive of its validity if it appeared that the correct procedures had not been followed. Lord Pearce stated, at p. 197:

> [A] legislature has no power to ignore the conditions of law-making that are imposed by the instrument which itself regulates its power to make law. This restriction exists independently of the question whether the legislature is sovereign....

This statement would appear to lend support to Heuston and Fazal. However, the traditional theorists argue that *Harris* and *Ranasinghe* are not relevant to the United Kingdom because the legislatures of South Africa and Ceylon were subject to constituent instruments, whereas the United Kingdom has no written constitution. Latham in *The Law and the Commonwealth* (1949), p. 523, states:

> When the purported sovereign is anyone but a single actual person, the designation of him must include the statement of the rules for ascertainment of his will, and these rules, since their observance is a condition of the validity of his legislation are Rules of Law logically prior to him.

Is it crucial that these rules should be contained in a formal written constitution? Heuston believes not; he states (*supra*, at p. 26):

> It cannot make any difference whether the rules which identify the sovereign come entirely from the common law (as they did before 1911 in the United Kingdom) or entirely from statute (as they do in Ireland, New South Wales and South Africa) or partly from the common law and partly from statute (as they do in the United Kingdom since 1911). It is hard to see why those who argue thus should attach so much importance to the formal source of the complex set of rules identifying the location and composition of the sovereign.... The point here is the simple one that until these rules (whatever their source) have been changed in accordance with the manner which they themselves prescribe they must be obeyed.

■ QUESTIONS

1. Is it a necessary concomitant of supremacy that Parliament's powers to legislate be not subject to any procedural restraint? Marshall, 'Parliamentary sovereignty: the new horizons' [1997] *Public Law* 1, at p. 4, states:

> ...May a sovereign legislative body that acts by simple majority protect particularly important statutes of its own making...by providing for its repeal or amendment to require a specific majority, or possibly the backing of a referendum?...No UK enactment has ever attempted such a thing and in 1978 the House of Lords Select Committee on a Bill of Rights was advised that it was not possible. But of course it is possible if the courts believe that the power to change the law extends to a power to change the law about the way law is made. There is nothing in Dicey's concept of parliamentary sovereignty that is incompatible with this possibility. Procedurally and tactically it would be prudent for a special majority requirement to be applied not to an enacted Bill at the stage of a royal assent, but so as to prevent the further progress of any Bill of the prescribed kind that has not been carried by the required special majority at its second reading. Caution would suggest that an entrenching Act should also provide a judicial remedy to secure its enforcement, expressed to operate notwithstanding any existing rules as to standing or parliamentary privilege. If the remedy is effective, there would not then, on any view, be a later alleged Act of Parliament to rival the authority of the entrenchment statute or to threaten it with implicit repeal.

It is possible that entrenchment might be achieved by redefining Parliament, This point was discussed by some Law Lords in the following case.

Jackson v *Attorney General*

[2005] UHL 56, [2006] 1 AC 262, House of Lords

The Parliament Act 1911 removed the power of the House of Lords to veto legislation, replacing it with a two-year delaying power. This was enacted in accordance with the then existing law which required majorities in both Houses approving the Bill before it received the Royal Assent. The delaying power was reduced to one year by the Parliament Act 1949 which was itself passed without Lords' consent using the 1911 Act. The Hunting Act 2004 was enacted after one year using the Parliament Acts 1911, 1949 and its legality was unsuccessfully challenged in the High Court. The Court of Appeal dismissed the appeal. The appeal to the House of Lords was heard by a panel of nine of their Lordships.

LORD BINGHAM OF CORNHILL: ...7. Sir Sydney helpfully encapsulated the appellants' submissions in a series of key propositions, which he elaborated in written and oral argument. The propositions are these:

(1) Legislation made under the 1911 Act is delegated or subordinate, not primary.
(2) The legislative power conferred by section 2(1) of the 1911 Act is not unlimited in scope and must be read according to established principles of statutory interpretation.
(3) Among these is the principle that powers conferred on a body by an enabling Act may not be enlarged or modified by that body unless there are express words authorising such enlargement or modification.
(4) Accordingly, section 2(1) of the 1911 Act does not authorise the Commons to remove, attenuate or modify in any respect any of the conditions on which its law-making power is granted.
(5) Even if, contrary to the appellants' case, the Court of Appeal was right to regard section 2(1) of the 1911 Act as wide enough to authorise "modest" amendments of the Commons' law-making powers, the amendments in the 1949 Act were not "modest", but substantial and significant...

22. Sir Sydney submits that whereas legislation duly enacted by the Crown in Parliament commands general obedience and recognition as such, and is the ultimate political fact upon which the whole system of legislation hangs, legislation made under the 1911 Act is required to state on its face that it is made by the authority of the 1911 Act. Such legislation is not primary because it depends for its validity on a prior enactment, and legislation is not primary where that is so. Legislation under the 1911 Act is not similar to

other delegated or subordinate legislation, such as statutory instruments and bylaws made under the authority of statute, but it is delegated or subordinate or derivative in the sense that its validity is open to investigation in the courts, which would not be permissible in the case of primary legislation...

24. Despite the skill with which the argument is advanced and the respect properly due to the authorities relied on, I am of opinion that the Divisional Court was right to reject it, for two main reasons. First, sections 1(1) and 2(1) of the 1911 Act provide that legislation made in accordance with those provisions respectively shall "become an Act of Parliament on the Royal Assent being signified". The meaning of the expression "Act of Parliament" is not doubtful, ambiguous or obscure. It is as clear and well understood as any expression in the lexicon of the law. It is used, and used only, to denote primary legislation. If there were room for doubt, which to my mind there is not, it would be resolved by comparing the language of the second resolution, quoted in para. 15 above, with the language of section 2(1) as enacted. The resolution provided that a measure meeting the specified conditions "shall become Law without the consent of the House of Lords on the Royal Assent being declared". Section 2(1), as just noted, provides that a measure shall become an Act of Parliament. The change can only have been made to preclude just such an argument as the appellants are advancing. The 1911 Act did, of course, effect an important constitutional change, but the change lay not in authorising a new form of sub-primary parliamentary legislation but in creating a new way of enacting primary legislation.

25. I cannot, secondly, accept that the 1911 Act can be understood as a delegation of legislative power or authority by the House of Lords, or by Parliament, to the House of Commons...Section 1 of the 1911 Act involved no delegation of legislative power and authority to the Commons but a statutory recognition of where such power and authority in relation to supply had long been understood to lie. It would be hard to read the very similar language in section 2 as involving a delegation either, since the overall object of the Act was not to enlarge the powers of the Commons but to restrict those of the Lords. This is, in my opinion, clear from the historical context and from the Act itself. The first resolution (see para. 15 above) was that "it is expedient that the House of Lords be disabled by Law from"...The second resolution (para. 15 above) was that "it is expedient that the powers of the House of Lords, as respects Bills other than Money Bills, be restricted by Law"...The effect of section 1 of the 1911 Act is to restrict the power of the Lords to amend or reject money bills. The effect of section 2(1) is, despite the different conditions, the same, and is aptly summarised in the sidenote: "Restriction of the powers of the House of Lords as to Bills other than Money Bills". The certification of a money bill by the Speaker under section 1 and of a bill other than a money bill under section 2 is mandatory, and the presentation of a bill to the monarch for the royal assent to be signified under sections 1(1) and 2(1) is automatic, "unless the House of Commons direct to the contrary". If it be permissible to resort to the preamble of the 1911 Act, one finds reference to the expediency of making "such provision as in this Act appears for restricting the existing powers of the House of Lords". The overall object of the 1911 Act was not to delegate power: it was to restrict, subject to compliance with the specified statutory conditions, the power of the Lords to defeat measures supported by a majority of the Commons, and thereby obviate the need for the monarch to create (or for any threat to be made that the monarch would create) peers to carry the government's programme in the Lords.

(2) The scope of section 2(1)

28. Sir Sydney submits that, in accordance with long-established principles of statutory interpretation, the courts will often imply qualifications into the literal meaning of wide and general words in order to prevent them having some unreasonable consequence which Parliament could not have intended. He cites such compelling authority as *Stradling v Morgan* (1560) 1 Plow 199; *R (Edison First Power Limited) v Central Valuation Officer* [2003] UKHL 20, [2003] 4 All ER 209, para. 25; *R v Secretary of State for the Home Department, Ex p Pierson* [1998] AC 539, 573–575, 588; *R v Secretary of State for the Home Department, Ex p Simms* [2000] 2 AC 115, 131; and *R (Morgan Grenfell & Co Ltd) v Special Commissioner of Income Tax* [2003] 1 AC 563, paras 8, 44–45. He relies on these authorities as establishing (as it is put in the appellants' printed case)

> that general words such as section 2(1) should not be read as authorising the doing of acts which adversely affect the basic principles on which the law of the United Kingdom is based in the absence of clear words authorising such acts. There is no more fundamental principle of law in the UK than the identity of the sovereign body. Section 2(1) should not be read as modifying the identity of the sovereign body unless its language admits of no other interpretation.

The Divisional Court did not accept that the 1911 Act, properly construed, precluded use of the procedure laid down in that Act to amend the conditions specified in section 2: see Maurice Kay LJ in paras 17–19 of his judgment, and Collins J in paras 41–44 of his. The Court of Appeal took a different view (paras 40–41); it concluded that section 2(1) conferred powers which could be used for some purposes but not others (paras 42–45).

29. The Attorney General does not, I think, take issue with the general principles relied on by the appellants, which are indeed familiar and well-established. But he invites the House to focus on the language of the 1911 Act, and in this he is right, since a careful study of the statutory language, read in its statutory and historical context and with the benefit of permissible aids to interpretation, is the essential first step in any exercise of statutory interpretation. Here, section 2(1) makes provision, subject to three exceptions, for any public bill which satisfies the specified conditions to become an Act of Parliament without the consent of the Lords. The first exception relates to money bills, which are the subject of section 1 and to which different conditions apply. The second relates to bills containing any provision to extend the maximum duration of Parliament beyond five years. I consider this exception in detail below. The third relates to bills for confirming a provisional order, which do not fall within the expression "public bill" by virtue of section 5. Subject to these exceptions, section 2(1) applies to "any" public bill. I cannot think of any broader expression the draftsman could have used. Nor can I see any reason to infer that "any" is used in a sense other than its colloquial, and also its dictionary, sense of "no matter which, or what". The expression is repeatedly used in this sense in the 1911 Act, and it would be surprising if it were used in any other sense: see section 1(2) ("any of the following subjects", "any such charges", "any loan", "those subjects or any of them", "any taxation, money, or loan"); section 2(4) ("any amendments", "any further amendments", "any such suggested amendments"); section 3 ("Any certificate", "any court of law"); section 4(2) ("Any alteration"); section5 ("any Bill"). "Any" is an expression used to indicate that the user does not intend to discriminate, or does not intend to discriminate save to such extent as is indicated.

30. Sir Sydney is of course correct in submitting that the literal meaning of even a very familiar expression may have to be rejected if it leads to an interpretation or consequence which Parliament could not have intended. But in this case it is clear from the historical background that Parliament did intend the word "any", subject to the noted exceptions, to mean exactly what it said. Sir Henry Campbell-Bannerman's resolution of June 1907, adopted by the Commons before rejection of the 1909 Finance Bill, referred quite generally to "Bills passed by this House"... The second of the resolutions adopted on 14 April 1910... referred to "Bills other than Money Bills". Attempts to amend the resolution so as to enlarge the classes of bill to which the new procedure would not apply were all rejected (para. 15 above). During the constitutional Conference which followed the death of the King there was provisional agreement to exclude "the Act which is to embody this agreement" from application of the new procedure, but such a provision was never included in the Bill... During the passage of the Bill through Parliament, there were again repeated attempts to enlarge the classes of bill to which the new procedure would not apply, but save for the amendment related to bills extending the maximum duration of Parliament they were uniformly rejected... The suggestion that Parliament intended the conditions laid down in section 2(1) to be incapable of amendment by use of the Act is in my opinion contradicted both by the language of the section and by the historical record. This was certainly the understanding of Dicey, who was no friend of the 1911 Act. In the first edition of his *Introduction* after 1911 (the 8th edition, 1915), he wrote at p xxiii:

> "The simple truth is that the Parliament Act has given to the House of Commons, or, in plain language, to the majority thereof, the power of passing any Bill whatever, provided always that the conditions of the Parliament Act, section 2, are complied with."

31. The Court of Appeal concluded (in paras 98–100 of its judgment) that there was power under the 1911 Act to make a "relatively modest and straightforward amendment" of the Act, including the amendment made by the 1949 Act, but not to making "changes of a fundamentally different nature to the relationship between the House of Lords and the Commons from those which the 1911 Act had made". This was not, as I understand, a solution which any party advocated in the Court of Appeal, and none supported it in the House. I do not think, with respect, that it can be supported in principle. The known object of the Parliament Bill, strongly resisted by the Conservative party and the source of the bitterness and intransigence which characterised the struggle over the Bill, was to secure the grant of Home Rule to Ireland. This was, by any standards, a fundamental constitutional change. So was the disestablishment of the Anglican Church in Wales, also well known to be an objective of the government. Attempts to ensure

that the 1911 Act could not be used to achieve these objects were repeatedly made and repeatedly defeated... Whatever its practical merits, the Court of Appeal solution finds no support in the language of the Act, in principle or in the historical record. Had the government been willing to exclude changes of major constitutional significance from the operation of the new legislative scheme, it may very well be that the constitutional Conference of 1910 would not have broken down and the 1911 Act would never have been enacted.

32. It is unnecessary for resolution of the present case to decide whether the 1911 (and now the 1949) Act could be relied on to extend the maximum duration of Parliament beyond five years. It does not seem likely that such a proposal would command popular and parliamentary support (save in a national emergency such as led to extensions, by consent of both Houses, during both world wars), knowledge of parliamentary tyranny during the Long Parliament would weigh against such a proposal and article 3 of the First Protocol to the European Convention on Human Rights now requires elections at reasonable intervals. The Attorney General, however, submits that the 1911, and now the 1949, Act could in principle be used to amend or delete the reference to the maximum duration of Parliament in the parenthesis to section 2(1), and that a further measure could then be introduced to extend the maximum duration. Sir Sydney contends that this is a procedure which section 2(1) very clearly does not permit, stressing that the timetable in section 2(1) was very closely linked to the maximum duration of Parliament which the Act laid down. It is common ground that section 2(1) in its unamended form cannot without more be relied on to extend the maximum duration of Parliament, because a public bill to do so is outside the express terms of section 2(1). But there is nothing in the 1911 Act to provide that it cannot be amended, and even if there were such a provision it could not bind a successor Parliament. Once it is accepted, as I have accepted, that an Act passed pursuant to the procedures in section 2(1), as amended in 1949, is in every sense an Act of Parliament having effect and entitled to recognition as such, I see no basis in the language of section 2(1) or in principle for holding that the parenthesis in that subsection, or for that matter section 7 [which reduced the duration of a parliament from 7 to 5 years], are unamendable save with the consent of the Lords. It cannot have been contemplated that if, however improbably, the Houses found themselves in irreconcilable deadlock on this point, the government should have to resort to the creation of peers. However academic the point may be, I think the Attorney General is right.

(3) Enlargement of powers

33. Sir Sydney relies on what Hood Phillips and Jackson describe as the general principle of logic and law that delegates (the Queen and Commons) cannot enlarge the authority delegated to them: *Constitutional and Administrative Law*, 8th edn (2001), p 80. He also prays in aid the observations of Lord Donaldson of Lymington speaking extra-judicially in support of his Parliament Acts (Amendment) Bill (HL Hansard, 19 January 2001, cols 1308–1309): "As your Lordships well know, it is a fundamental tenet of constitutional law that, *prima facie*, where the sovereign Parliament—that is to say, the Monarch acting on the advice and with the consent of both Houses of Parliament—delegates power to legislate, whether to one House unilaterally, to the King or Queen in Council, to a Minister or to whomsoever, the delegate cannot use that power to enlarge or vary the powers delegated to him. The only exception is where the primary legislation, in this case the 1911 Act, expressly authorises the delegate to do so. In other words there has to be a Henry VIII clause." To support his argument Sir Sydney cites a number of cases relating to colonial and Dominion legislatures, the most significant of these cases perhaps being *R v Burah* (1878) 3 App Cas 889, 904–905; *Taylor v Attorney General of Queensland* (1917) 23 CLR 457; *McCawley v The King* [1920] AC 691, 703–704, 710–711; *Minister of the Interior v Harris* 1952 (4) SA 769, 790; *Clayton v Heffron* (1960) 105 CLR 214 and *Bribery Commissioner v Ranasinghe* [1965] AC 172, 196–198. In written submissions in reply this argument was elaborated and the authorities further analysed.

...

36. I cannot accept the appellants' submissions on this issue, for three main reasons. First, for reasons given in para. 25 above, the 1911 Act did not involve a delegation of power and the Commons, when invoking the 1911 Act, cannot be regarded as in any sense a subordinate body. Secondly, the historical context of the 1911 Act was unique. The situation was factually and constitutionally so remote from the grant of legislative authority to a colonial or Dominion legislature as to render analogies drawn from the latter situation of little if any value when considering the former. Thirdly, the Court of Appeal distilled from the authorities what is in my judgment the correct principle. The question is one of construction. There was nothing in the 1911 Act to preclude use of the procedure laid down by the Act to amend the Act. As explained in paras 29–32 above, the language of the Act was wide enough, as the Divisional Court and the Court of Appeal held, to permit the amendment made by the 1949 Act, and also (in my opinion) to make

much more far reaching changes. For the past half century it has been generally, even if not universally, believed that the 1949 Act had been validly enacted, as evidenced by the use made of it by governments of different political persuasions. In my opinion that belief was well-founded.

(4) The scope of the power to amend the conditions to which section 2(1) is subject

37. This submission is in essence a conclusion drawn from the propositions which precede it: see the summary in para. 7 above. It necessarily follows from the reasons I have given for rejecting those propositions that I cannot accept that section 2(1) of the 1911 Act "does not authorise the Commons to remove, attenuate or modify in any respect any of the conditions on which its law-making power is granted". As should be clear, I reject the premises on which that conclusion is founded. If the appellants were right, it would, I think, follow that the 1911 Act could not be invoked, for instance, to shorten (or even, perhaps, lengthen) the period allowed in section 1(1) for passing money bills, or to provide that a bill for confirming a provisional order should rank as a public bill: a government bent on achieving such an object with a clear and recent mandate to do so would have either to accept the veto of the Lords or resort to the creation of peers. That would seem an extravagant, and unhistorical, intention to attribute to Parliament.

(5) The significance of the 1949 Act

38. I agree with the appellants that the change made by the 1949 Act was not, as the Court of Appeal described it (para. 98), "relatively modest", but was substantial and significant. But I also agree with them and also the Attorney General that the breadth of the power to amend the 1911 Act in reliance on section 2(1) cannot depend on whether the amendment in question is or is not relatively modest. I have given my reasons for sharing that conclusion in paras 29–32 above. Such a test would be vague in the extreme, and impose on the Speaker a judgment which Parliament cannot have contemplated imposing.

Appeal disallowed

NOTES

1. Their Lordships held that despite the authority of *Pickin* it could entertain this challenge to the Hunting Act 2004. Lord Bingham said [27]

> I am, however, persuaded that the present proceedings are legitimate, for two reasons. First, in *Pickin*, unlike the present case, it was sought to investigate the internal workings and procedures of Parliament to demonstrate that it had been misled and so had proceeded on a false basis. This was held to be illegitimate [His Lordship quoted the passage by Lord Campbell in *Wauchope* see *Pickin* p. 60, *ante*]... Here, the court looks to the parliamentary roll and sees bills (the 1949 Act, and then the 2004 Act) which have not passed both Houses. The issue concerns no question of parliamentary procedure such as would, and could only, be the subject of parliamentary inquiry, but a question whether, in Lord Simon's language, these Acts are "enacted law". My second reason is more practical. The appellants have raised a question of law which cannot, as such, be resolved by Parliament. But it would not be satisfactory, or consistent with the rule of law, if it could not be resolved at all. So it seems to me necessary that the courts should resolve it, and that to do so involves no breach of constitutional propriety.

Lord Nichols said [49] that it was clear following *Pickin* and article 9 of the Bill of Rights [see p. 54, *ante*] that it was for each House of Parliament to judge the lawfulness of its own proceedings. He continued [51]

> Their challenge to the lawfulness of the 1949 Act is founded on a different and prior ground: the proper interpretation of section 2(1) of the 1911 Act. On this issue the court's jurisdiction cannot be doubted. This question of statutory interpretation is properly cognisable by a court of law even though it relates to the legislative process. Statutes create law. The proper interpretation of a statute is a matter for the courts, not Parliament. This principle is as fundamental in this country's constitution as the principle that Parliament has exclusive cognisance (jurisdiction) over its own affairs.

2. All of their Lordships rejected the delegated legislation argument and (most) accepted that Parliament had redefined itself for the making of primary legislation. All of them agreed that due to s. 2(1) extending the duration of a parliament was expressly excluded from the Parliament Act procedures. While there was an express exception in s. 2(1) as to what could be done using legislation made under the statute, they did not find implied exceptions. The speeches contain much

interesting *obiter* material. Only Lord Bingham, [32], thought that extending the duration of a parliament could be achieved without Lords' consent if it was done in two steps, the first step would be to remove the exception from s. 2(1) and the second would be to pass legislation extending the duration. A majority of their Lordships, Lord Nicholls, Steyn, Hope, and Carswell, and Baroness Hale, did not think that these two steps would be lawful, whereas Lords Rodger and Brown reserved their position, and Lord Walker did not consider the point. For Lord Nicholls [59]:

> 'That express exclusion carries with it, by necessary implication, a like exclusion in respect of legislation aimed at achieving the same result by two steps rather than one. If this were not so the express legislative intention could readily be defeated'

Lord Carswell agreed with Lord Nicholl's reasoning at [175]. Lord Steyn said [79]:

> In the context of a Parliamentary democracy the language of section 2(1) and section 7 supports the former interpretation. I would so rule.

Section 7 of the 1911 Act reduced the duration of a parliament from seven to five years. Lord Hope said [122]:

> '...there is an implied prohibition against the use of the section 2(1) procedure in such circumstances.

3. The redefinition of Parliament in the Parliament Acts 1911, 1949 to the Commons and sovereign may be said to have redefined Parliament downwards. From this Baroness Hale, [163] referred to the possibility of redefining upwards

> ...to require a particular Parliamentary majority or a popular referendum for particular types of measure. In each case, the courts would be respecting the will of the sovereign Parliament as constituted when that will had been expressed. But that is for another day.

Lord Steyn was more certain than Baroness Hale saying [81]

> The word Parliament involves both static and dynamic concepts. The static concept refers to the constituent elements which make up Parliament: the House of Commons, the House of Lords, and the Monarch. The dynamic concept involves the constituent elements functioning together as a law making body. The inquiry is: has Parliament spoken? The law and custom of Parliament regulates what the constituent elements must do to legislate: all three must signify consent to the measure. But, apart from the traditional method of law making, Parliament acting as ordinarily constituted may functionally redistribute legislative power in different ways. For example, Parliament could for specific purposes provide for a two-thirds majority in the House of Commons and the House of Lords. This would involve a redefinition of Parliament for a specific purpose. Such redefinition could not be disregarded. Owen Dixon neatly summarised this idea in 1935:
>
> "...The very power of constitutional alteration cannot be exercised except in the form and manner which the law for the time being prescribes. Unless the Legislature observes that manner and form, its attempt to alter its constitution is void. It may amend or abrogate for the future the law which prescribes that form or that manner. But, in doing so, it must comply with its very requirements."

See: 'The Law and the Constitution', 51 *LQR* 590, 601. This formulation can be traced to the majority judgment in *Attorney General for New South Wales* v *Trethowan* (1931) 44 CLR 394, and in particular to the judgment of Dixon J at 424.

Lord Hope was the only other Law Lord to comment on this point and he stated the traditional view [113]

> Nor does it seem to me to be helpful...to describe the 1911 Act as having remodelled or re-defined Parliament. The concept is not an easy one to grasp, because it is a fundamental aspect of the rule of sovereignty that no Parliament can bind its successors. There are no means by whereby, even with the assistance of the most skilful draftsman, it can entrench an Act of Parliament. It is impossible for Parliament to enact something which a subsequent statute dealing with the same subject matter cannot repeal. But there is no doubt that, in practice and as a matter of political reality, the 1911 Act did have that effect...It did what it was designed to do. It has limited the power of the House of Lords to legislate. In practice it has altered the balance of power between the two Houses.

■ QUESTIONS

1. Have their Lordships in *Jackson* not rejected *Pickin* and held that they can review legislation?
2. Imagine that in response to an outbreak of terrorism the Government introduced the Anti-Terrorism (Emergency Provisions) Bill which was rushed through all its parliamentary stages in a day receiving the Royal Assent the following day. The Home Secretary, who introduced the Bill, did not make a 'statement of compatibility' as required by s. 19(1)(a) of the Human Rights Act 1998 (see p. 434, *post*), nor did he make a statement that the Government wished the House to proceed with the Bill although he was unable to make a statement of compatibility. T is arrested by the police exercising new powers accorded them by the Anti-Terrorism (Emergency Provisions) Act. T applies to the Divisional Court for a writ of *habeas corpus* arguing that his arrest is unlawful as the Anti-Terrorism (Emergency Provisions) Act is not a duly enacted Act of Parliament. How might the court determine his application?

B: The Acts of Union

So far it has been assumed that Parliament is not subject to any constituent instrument. However, in 1707 the Parliaments of England and Scotland passed Acts of Union ratifying the Treaty of Union and creating the new Parliament of Great Britain. In 1800 a similar union took place between Great Britain and Ireland, creating the United Kingdom of Great Britain and Ireland. As these Acts of Union were antecedent to the new Parliaments they created, it is arguable that they were constituent Acts bringing into being a new state and a new Parliament (see Mitchell, *Constitutional Law* (2nd edn, 1968), pp. 69–74; Calvert, *Constitutional Law in Northern Ireland* (1968), Chapter 1; for a contrary view see Munro, *Studies in Constitutional Law* (1999), Chapter 5).

Certain provisions of the Treaties were declared to be fundamental and unalterable. The subsequent history reveals, however, that such provisions have been amended or repealed (see, e.g. the Universities (Scotland) Act 1853 and the Irish Church Act 1869); indeed the Union with Ireland was dissolved in 1922 when most of Ireland was given independence, with only Northern Ireland remaining in the United Kingdom. The issue of the nature of the Acts of Union has been argued in several Scottish cases but was not finally adjudicated upon.

MacCormick v *Lord Advocate*

[1953] SC 396, Court of Session, Inner House

Two members of the Scottish public petitioned the Court of Session for a declaration that a proclamation describing the Queen as 'Elizabeth the Second of the United Kingdom of Great Britain' was illegal, as being contrary to Article I of the Treaty and Acts of Union. The Lord Advocate argued that there was no conflict with Article I and that the number 'II' was authorized by the Royal Titles Act 1953. *Held*: The petition was dismissed, and the petitioners' appeal to the First Division of the Inner House was likewise dismissed on the grounds that there was nothing in Article I which forbade the use of the numeral, the petitioners had no title to sue, and the Royal Titles Act 1953 was irrelevant as it was enacted after the designation 'Elizabeth the Second' had been adopted and used. The President then went on to express his opinion on the Union legislation.

THE LORD PRESIDENT (COOPER): ...The principle of the unlimited sovereignty of Parliament is a distinctively English principle which has no counterpart in Scottish constitutional law.... Considering that the Union legislation extinguished the Parliaments of Scotland and England and replaced them by a new Parliament, I have difficulty in seeing why it should have been supposed that the new Parliament of Great Britain must inherit all the peculiar characteristics of the English Parliament but none of the Scottish Parliament, as if all that happened in 1707 was that Scottish representatives were admitted to the Parliament of England. That is not what was done. Further, the Treaty and the associated legislation, by which the Parliament of Great Britain was brought into being as the successor of the separate Parliaments of Scotland and England, contain some clauses which expressly reserve to the Parliament of Great Britain powers of subsequent modification, and other clauses which either contain no such power or emphatically exclude subsequent alteration by declarations that the provision shall be fundamental and unalterable in all time coming, or declarations of a like effect. I have never been able to understand how it is possible to reconcile with elementary canons of construction the adoption by the English constitutional theorists of the same attitude to these markedly different types of provisions.

The Lord Advocate conceded this point by admitting that the Parliament of Great Britain 'could not' repeal or alter such 'fundamental and essential' conditions.... I have not found in the Union legislation any provision that the Parliament of Great Britain should be 'absolutely sovereign' in the sense that that Parliament should be free to alter the Treaty at will....

But the petitioners have still a grave difficulty to overcome on this branch of their argument. Accepting that there are provisions in the Treaty of Union and associated legislation which are 'fundamental law,' and assuming for the moment that something is alleged to have been done—it matters not whether with legislative authority or not—in breach of that fundamental law, the question remains whether such a question is determinable as a justiciable issue in the Courts of either Scotland or England, in the same fashion as an issue of constitutional *vires* would be cognisable by the Supreme Courts of the United States, or of South Africa or Australia. I reserve my opinion with regard to the provisions relating expressly to this Court and to the laws 'which concern private right' which are administered here. This is not such a question, but a matter of 'public right' (articles 18 and 19). To put the matter in another way, it is of little avail to ask whether the Parliament of Great Britain 'can' do this thing or that, without going on to inquire who can stop them if they do. Any person 'can' repudiate his solemn engagement but he cannot normally do so with impunity. Only two answers have been suggested to this corollary to the main question. The first is the exceedingly cynical answer implied by Dicey (*Law of the Constitution*, (9th ed.) p. 82) in the statement that 'it would be rash of the Imperial Parliament to abolish the Scotch law courts, and assimilate the Law of Scotland to that of England. But no one can feel sure at what point Scottish resistance to such a change would become serious.' The other answer was that nowadays there may be room for the invocation of an 'advisory opinion' from the International Court of Justice. On these matters I express no view. This at least is plain, that there is neither precedent nor authority of any kind for the view that the domestic Courts of either Scotland or England have jurisdiction to determine whether a governmental act of the type here in controversy is or is not conform to the provisions of a Treaty, least of all when that Treaty is one under which both Scotland and England ceased to be independent states and merged their identity in an incorporating union. From the standpoint both of constitutional law and of international law the position appears to me to be unique, and I am constrained to hold that the action as laid is incompetent in respect that it has not been shown that the Court of Session has authority to entertain the issue sought to be raised....

NOTE: In *Gibson* v *Lord Advocate* 1975 SLT 134, a Scottish fisherman challenged an EEC Regulation which had become law by virtue of the European Communities Act 1972. The Regulation gave Member States equal access to fishing grounds. Gibson argued that this was invalid, being in breach of Article XVIII which forbade 'alteration...in the laws which concern private right except for the evident utility of the subjects within Scotland'. Lord Keith held that the control of fishing in territorial waters was not a matter of private right but of public law, and thus was not protected by Article XVIII. However, he went on to state obiter:

Like Lord President Cooper, I prefer to reserve my opinion on what the question would be if the United Kingdom Parliament passed an Act purporting to abolish the Court of Session or the Church of Scotland or to substitute English law for the whole body of Scots private law. I am, however, of opinion that the question whether a particular Act of the United Kingdom Parliament altering a particular aspect of Scots private law is or is not 'for the evident utility' of the subjects within

> Scotland is not a justiciable issue in this court. The making of decisions upon what must essentially be a political matter is no part of the function of the court, and it is highly undesirable that it should be.

By contrast, in *Stewart* v *Henry* 1989 SLT (Sh Ct) 34, Sheriff Stewart went so far as to say that he saw 'no absolute bar to a court's considering the question whether a particular change in the law is for the evident utility of the subjects in Scotland'. In the case of *Pringle* 1991 SLT 330, which, like *Stewart* v *Henry,* concerned the legislation which introduced the community charge in Scotland one year earlier than in England and Wales, it was argued that this contravened Art. IV of the Scots Act of Union which it was claimed required that there should be no difference in the rights, privileges and advantages enjoyed by citizens in Great Britain unless expressly provided for in the treaty. The petitioner did not seek to have the relevant statute (the Abolition of Domestic Rates Etc. (Scotland) Act 1987) declared invalid but rather sought relief from his own liability under the Act to pay the charge because of its alleged contravention of Art. IV. The First Division of the Inner House dismissed the petition on the basis that it did not have jurisdiction to grant the exceptional remedy sought. While this was sufficient to decide the case Lord Hope, the Lord President declined to accept the respondent registration officer's submission that the petitioner's arguments that the 1987 Act breached Art. IV raised a non-justiciable issue. Lord Hope stated (at p. 333):

> The fact that the methods of raising finance for local government in the two parts of the United Kingdom were different for the year in question would not be sufficient to persuade me, without a much more detailed inquiry into the overall effects of these differences, that there was a failure to do what this part of Art. IV intended should be done.

The inference to be drawn is that Lord Hope believed there might be circumstances in which a court could consider whether legislation was inconsistent with union legislation. The question of the constitutional effect of the Scots Articles of Union continues to remain unresolved.

In *Ex p. Canon Selwyn* (1872) 36 JP 54, the issue of the validity of the Irish Church Act 1869 was raised. This Act disestablished and disendowed the Episcopal Church in Ireland which Art. 5 of the Treaty of Union had established for ever. Mandamus was sought against the Lord President of the Council, commanding him to present to the Queen a petition asking her to refer for adjudication the question whether her assent to the Irish Church Act 1869 was contrary to the Coronation Oath and the Act of Settlement 1700. The application was refused by Cockburn CJ on the ground that 'there is no judicial body in the country by which the validity of an act of parliament could be questioned. An act of the legislature is superior in authority to any court of law'. Calvert takes issue with Cockburn CJ.

H. Calvert, *Constitutional Law in Northern Ireland*

(1968), p. 21

> These are strong words. But whilst the Coronation Oath did contain a solemn pledge to maintain the unified and established Church of England and Ireland, it is not here suggested that an Act can be challenged on this ground, or on grounds of contravention of the Act of Settlement. What it is suggested could have been, and what, surprisingly, was not argued in *Ex parte Canon Selwyn*, is that the severance and disestablishment of the Church of Ireland was a legal act power to effect which was withheld from the Parliament of the United Kingdom by its constituent Acts. It is all very well to speak of applying 'the law as we find it.' That begs the question of what we find. A judge appointed before 1800 and continuing in office after 1800 would find himself in a considerable dilemma. Sworn to uphold the laws of parliament, he would find two conflicting laws of two different parliaments, one purporting to disestablish the Irish Church and the other, which constituted the parliament enacting the first, having imposed upon it a statutory prohibition from disestablishing. It is, again, all very well to speak of 'an act of the legislature' being 'superior in authority to any court of law.' No doubt it is—but that is not the question. The question may be viewed as being whether 'an act of the legislature' is 'superior in authority' to a prior constituent Act of a predecessor parliament. There is a difference, which has been overlooked but which may well be crucial, between a parliament repealing its own Acts, and a parliament purporting to repeal the Acts of its constituent predecessor. English courts have never been faced, four square, with this question and English law has therefore never finally made up its mind—*a fortiori* Irish law.

■ QUESTIONS

1. Is Cockburn CJ's dictum reconcilable with the *obiter dicta* in *MacCormick* and *Gibson*?
2. Middleton, 'New Thoughts on the Union' 1954 JR 37, at p. 49, states that 'the fact that Parliament has done something cannot prove that it was entitled to do it'. Do the amendments to, and breaches and repeals of, provisions of the Acts of Union reveal that Parliament is supreme and unconstrained in its powers, or is it the case that Parliament is limited but there is no authority competent to rule on the validity of its Acts, that is, the amendments and repeals are invalid in legal theory but in political reality they exist and are acted upon?
3. Jennings, in *The Law and the Constitution* (5th edn, 1959), p. 170, argues that as the Acts of Union were passed to ratify two treaties, the amendments to these treaties were carried out in accordance with the maxim *nebus sic stantibus*, that is, it is a tacit condition attaching to all treaties that they shall cease to be obligatory so soon as the state of facts and conditions upon which they were founded has substantially changed. Is this a satisfactory explanation for the subsequent amendments to these treaties? If the conditions have not substantially changed in respect of a particular provision, would legislation in respect of it be illegal? If so, could or would any court declare it invalid?

C: Independence

One of the problems which constitutional lawyers have had to deal with is the granting of independence to many Commonwealth countries. This usually followed a two-stage process, with the colony being granted first Dominion status and subsequently being granted full independence. Section 4 of the Statute of Westminster provides:

> No Act of Parliament of the United Kingdom passed after the commencement of this Act shall extend, or be deemed to extend, to a Dominion as part of the law of that Dominion unless it is expressly declared in that Act that that Dominion has requested and consented to, the enactment thereof.

This gives rise to the question whether Parliament could ignore this provision and legislate directly for a Dominion without its request or consent? In *British Coal Corporation* v *The King* [1935] AC 500, at p. 520, Lord Sankey stated, regarding the application of s. 4 to Canada:

> It is doubtless true that the power of the Imperial Parliament to pass on its own initiative any legislation that it thought fit extending to Canada remains in theory unimpaired: indeed, the Imperial Parliament could, as a matter of abstract law, repeal or disregard s. 4 of the Statute.... But that is theory and has no relation to realities.

In *Blackburn* v *Attorney-General* [1971] 1 WLR 1037, at p. 1040, Lord Denning stated:

> We have all been brought up to believe that, in legal theory, one Parliament cannot bind another and that no Act is irreversible. But legal theory does not always march alongside political reality. Take the Statute of Westminster 1931, which takes away the power of Parliament to legislate for the Dominions. Can anyone imagine that Parliament could or would reverse that Statute? Take the Acts which have granted independence to the Dominions and territories overseas. Can anyone imagine that Parliament could or would reverse those laws and take away their independence? Most clearly not. Freedom once given cannot be taken away. Legal theory must give way to practical politics.

However, legal theory still dominates judicial reasoning. In 1965 when Rhodesia made a Unilateral Declaration of Independence, the Southern Rhodesia Act 1965 was rushed through Parliament. In terms of practical politics the Act had no effect in Rhodesia, where it was ignored. However, in *Madzimbamuto* v *Lardner-Burke* [1969] 1 AC 645, Lord Reid recited legal theory:

> It is often said that it would be unconstitutional for the United Kingdom Parliament to do certain things, meaning that the moral, political and other reasons against doing them are so strong that most people would regard it as highly improper if Parliament did these things. But that does not mean that it is beyond the power of Parliament to do these things. If Parliament chose to do any of them, the courts could not hold the Act of Parliament invalid.

Is it therefore impossible for Parliament to divest itself of the power to legislate for independent territories? Dicey's solution to the problem was the idea of abdication. He stated in *The Law of the Constitution* (1965), at p. 68:

> The impossibility of placing a limit on the exercise of sovereignty does not in any way prohibit either logically, or in matter of fact, the abdication of sovereignty. This is worth observation, because a strange dogma is sometimes put forward that a sovereign power, such as the Parliament of the United Kingdom, can never by its own act divest itself of sovereignty. This position is, however, clearly untenable.

■ QUESTION

In 1982 the United Kingdom Parliament enacted a new constitution for Canada by the Canada Act, and terminated its own legislative competence for Canada. Section 2 provides:

> No Act of the Parliament of the United Kingdom passed after the Constitution Act 1982 comes into force shall extend to Canada as part of its law.

If Parliament subsequently legislated for Canada would this legislation be *ultra vires*? Would a United Kingdom court be acting unconstitutionally in light of Dicey's doctrine of abdication, if it did not declare the offending statute invalid?

NOTE: The confusion which reigns in this area is evident in the following case.

Manuel v *Attorney-General*

[1983] Ch 77, Chancery Division

The Canada Act 1982 was enacted following the request of the Senate and House of Commons of Canada, and with the agreement of nine of the ten provincial governments. The claimants (previously called 'plaintiffs') were Aboriginal (Indian) Chiefs and sought declarations to the effect that the United Kingdom parliament had no power to amend the constitution of Canada so as to prejudice the Aboriginal nations without their consent, and that the Canada Act 1982 was *ultra vires*. The basis of their claim was that the enactment of the Canada Act 1982 was inconsistent with and a derogation from the constitutional safeguards provided for the Aboriginal peoples by the Statute of Westminster 1931 and the British North America Acts. The claimants' contention was that the consent of all the provincial legislatures, the Aboriginal nations of Canada and the federal Parliament were necessary before amendments to the Canadian Constitution (contained in the British North America Acts) could be enacted. The Attorney-General moved that the statement of claim be struck out as showing no reasonable cause of action.

MEGARRY VC: ...On the face of it, a contention that an Act of Parliament is *ultra vires* is bold in the extreme. It is contrary to one of the fundamentals of the British Constitution....

As was said by Lord Morris of Borth-y-Gest, at p. 789, it is not for the courts to proceed 'as though the Act or some part of it had never been passed'; there may be argument on the interpretation of the Act, but 'there must be none as to whether it should be on the Statute Book at all.' Any complaint on such matters is for Parliament to deal with and not the courts....

Mr Macdonald [counsel for the claimants] was, of course, concerned to restrict the ambit of the decision in *Pickin* v *British Railways Board*. He accepted that it was a binding decision for domestic legislation, but he said that it did not apply in relation to the Statute of Westminster 1931 or to the other countries of the Commonwealth. He also contended that it decided no more than that the courts would not inquire into what occurred in the course of the passage of a bill through Parliament, relying on what Lord Reid said at p. 787. This latter point is, I think, plainly wrong, since it ignores the words 'what was done previously to its being introduced' which Lord Reid cited with approval on that page. The wider point, however, is founded upon the theory that Parliament may surrender its sovereign power over some territory or area of land to another person or body....After such a surrender, any legislation which Parliament purports to enact for that territory is not merely ineffective there, but is totally void, in this country as elsewhere, since Parliament has surrendered the power to legislate; and the English courts have jurisdiction to declare such legislation *ultra vires* and void....

[The claimants argued that the United Kingdom Parliament had, by the Statute of Westminster 1931, transferred sovereignty to Canada and had deprived itself of all power to legislate for Canada subject only to s. 7 of that Act. Section 7 reserved to Parliament the power to repeal, amend or alter the British North America Acts. The claimants further argued that the true meaning of s. 4 of the 1931 Act dictated that these residuary legislative powers could only be exercised pursuant to the actual request and consent of the Dominion. For these purposes 'Dominion' meant not merely the Parliament of Canada but all the constituent constitutional factions of the Dominion, namely, Parliament, the provincial legislatures and the Aboriginal nations. As no such general consent had been given it was argued that the United Kingdom Parliament could not legislate for Canada. Megarry VC continued.] I am bound to say that from first to last I have heard nothing in this case to make me doubt the simple rule that the duty of the court is to obey and apply every Act of Parliament, and that the court cannot hold any such Act to be *ultra vires*. Of course there may be questions about what the Act means, and of course there is power to hold statutory instruments and other subordinate legislation *ultra vires*. But once an instrument is recognised as being an Act of Parliament, no English court can refuse to obey it or question its validity.

In the present case I have before me a copy of the Canada Act 1982 purporting to be published by Her Majesty's Stationery Office. After reciting the request and consent of Canada and the submission of an address to Her Majesty by the Senate and House of Commons of Canada, there are the words of enactment:

> 'Be it therefore enacted by the Queen's Most Excellent Majesty, by and with the advice and consent of the Lords Spiritual and Temporal, and Commons, in this present Parliament assembled, and by the authority of the same, as follows:...'

There has been no suggestion that the copy before me is not a true copy of the Act itself, or that it was not passed by the House of Commons and the House of Lords, or did not receive the Royal Assent....The Canada Act 1982 is an Act of Parliament, and sitting as a judge in an English court I owe full and dutiful obedience to that Act.

I do not think that, as a matter of law, it makes any difference if the Act in question purports to apply outside the United Kingdom. I speak not merely of statutes such as the Continental Shelf Act 1964 but also of statutes purporting to apply to other countries. If that other country is a colony, the English courts will apply the Act even if the colony is in a state of revolt against the Crown and direct enforcement of the decision may be impossible: see *Madzimbamuto* v *Lardner-Burke* [1969] 1 AC 645. It matters not if a convention had grown up that the United Kingdom Parliament would not legislate for that colony without the consent of the colony. Such a convention would not limit the powers of Parliament, and if Parliament legislated in breach of the convention, 'the courts could not hold the Act of Parliament invalid': see p. 723. Similarly if the other country is a foreign state which has never been British, I do not think that any English court would or could declare the Act *ultra vires* and void. No doubt the Act would normally be ignored by the foreign state and would not be enforced by it, but that would not invalidate the Act in this country. Those who infringed it could not claim that it was void if proceedings within the jurisdiction were taken against them. Legal validity is one thing, enforceability is another. Thus a marriage in Nevada may constitute statutory bigamy punishable in England (*Trial of Earl Russell* [1901] AC 446), just as acts in Germany may be punishable here as statutory treason: *Joyce* v *Director of Public Prosecutions* [1946] AC 347. Parliament in fact legislates only for British subjects in this way; but if it also legislated for others, I do not see how the English courts could hold the statute void, however impossible it was to enforce it, and no matter how strong the diplomatic protests.

I do not think that countries which were once colonies but have since been granted independence are in any different position. Plainly once statute has granted independence to a country, the repeal of the statute will not make the country dependent once more; what is done is done, and is not undone by revoking the authority do to it. Heligoland did not in 1953 again become British. But if Parliament then passes an Act applying to such a country, I cannot see why that Act should not be in the same position as an Act applying to what has always been a foreign country, namely, an Act which the English courts will recognise and apply but one which the other country will in all probability ignore....

For the reasons that I have given, I have come to the conclusion that the statement of claim in the Manuel action discloses no reasonable cause of action, and that, despite the persuasions of Mr Macdonald, this is plain and obvious enough to justify striking out the statement of claim....

Perhaps I may add this. I have grave doubts about the theory of the transfer of sovereignty as affecting the competence of Parliament. In my view, it is a fundamental of the English constitution that Parliament is supreme. As a matter of law the courts of England recognise Parliament as being omnipotent in all save the power to destroy its own omnipotence. Under the authority of Parliament the courts of a territory may be released from their legal duty to obey Parliament, but that does not trench on the acceptance by the English courts of all that Parliament does. Nor must validity in law be confused with practical enforceability.

The claimants appealed.

Court of Appeal

SLADE LJ: Mr Macdonald's argument will be seen to depend on a number of propositions, each one of which would be essential to its success at the trial of the action. Included among these essential propositions, though they are by no means the only ones, are the following three, each one of which must be established as arguable, if the plaintiffs are to succeed on this appeal: (1) that Parliament can effectively tie the hands of its successors, if it passes a statute which provides that any future legislation on a specified subject shall be enacted only with certain specified consents; (2) that section 7 (1) of the Statute of 1931 did not absolve the United Kingdom Parliament from the need to comply with the conditions of section 4 of the Statute of 1931 in enacting the Canada Act 1982, if the latter Act was to extend to Canada as an effective Act; (3) that the conditions of section 4 of the Statute of 1931 have not in fact been complied with in relation to the Canada Act 1982.

At least at first sight, the first of these propositions conflicts with the general statement of the law made by Maugham LJ in *Ellen Street Estates Ltd* v *Minister of Health* [1934] 1 KB 590, 597 [p. 58 *ante*].... For the purposes of this judgment we are content to assume in favour of the plaintiffs that the first of the three propositions to which we have referred is correct, though we would emphasise that we are not purporting to decide it....

As regards the second of them, Mr Macdonald submitted that the Canada Act 1982 does not fall within the exempting provisions of section 7 (1) of the Statute of 1931, on the grounds that its provisions go beyond a mere 'repeal, amendment or alteration of the British North America Acts.' We do not think it has been or could be disputed that at least a substantial part of the contents of the Constitution Act 1982, if regarded in isolation, would amount to no more than a mere 'repeal, amendment or alteration of the British North America Acts,' within those exempting provisions. Mr Macdonald, however, has submitted that at least some others of its contents (for example, the Charter of Rights and Freedoms) fall outside such exemption and accordingly make it necessary that the conditions of section 4 of the Statute of 1931 should be complied with in relation to the whole of the Canada Act 1982.

By far the greater part of the plaintiffs' argument on this appeal has been devoted to an attempt to show that the conditions of section 4 have not been complied with in this context.

In the circumstances we will proceed to consider the third of the propositions referred to above which relates to section 4 of the Statute of 1931. We will revert briefly to the second of them and to section 7 at the end of this judgment.

For the time being, therefore, let it be supposed that Parliament, in enacting the Canada Act 1982, had precisely to comply with the conditions of section 4 of the Statute of 1931, if that new Act was to be valid and effective. What then are the conditions which section 4 imposes? It is significant that, while the Preamble to the Statute of 1931 recites that

> it is in accord with the established constitutional position that no law hereafter made by the Parliament of the United Kingdom shall extend to any of the said Dominions as part of the law of that Dominion otherwise than at the request and with the consent of that Dominion:...

Section 4 itself does *not* provide that no Act of the United Kingdom Parliament shall extend to a Dominion as part of the law of that Dominion unless the Dominion has *in fact* requested and consented to the enactment thereof. The condition that must be satisfied is a quite different one, namely, that it must be 'expressly declared in that Act that that Dominion has requested, and consented to, the enactment thereof.' Though Mr Macdonald, as we have said, submitted that section 4 requires not only a declaration but a true declaration of a real request and consent, we are unable to read the section in that way. There is no ambiguity in the relevant words and the court would not in our opinion be justified in supplying additional words by a process of implication; it must construe and apply the words as they stand: see *Maxwell on Interpretation of Statutes*, 12th ed. (1969), p. 33 and the cases there cited. If an Act of Parliament contains an express declaration in the precise form required by section 4, such declaration is in our opinion conclusive so far as section 4 is concerned.

There was, we think, nothing unreasonable or illogical in this simple approach to the matter on the part of the legislature, in reserving to itself the sole function of deciding whether the requisite request and consent have been made and given. The present case itself provides a good illustration of the practical consequences that would have ensued, if section 4 had made an actual request and consent on the part of a Dominion a condition precedent to the validity of the relevant legislation, in such manner that the courts or anyone else would have had to look behind the relevant declaration in order to ascertain whether a statute of the United Kingdom Parliament, expressed to extend to that Dominion, was valid. There is obviously room for argument as to the identity of the representatives of the Dominion of Canada appropriate to express the relevant request and consent. Mr Macdonald, while firm in his submission that all legislatures of the Provinces of Canada had to join the Federal Parliament in expressing them, seemed less firm in his submission that all the Indian Nations had likewise to join. This is a point which might well involve difficult questions of Canadian constitutional law. Moreover, if all the Indian Nations did have to join, further questions might arise as to the manner in which the consents of these numerous persons and bodies had to be expressed and as to whether all of them had in fact been given. As we read the wording of section 4, it was designed to obviate the need for any further inquiries of this nature, once a statute, containing the requisite declaration, had been duly enacted by the United Kingdom Parliament. Parliament, having satisfied itself as to the request and consent, would make the declaration and that would be that.

Mr Macdonald submitted in the alternative that, even if section 4 on its proper construction does not itself bear the construction which he attributed to it, nevertheless, in view of the convention referred to in the third paragraph of the preamble, the actual request and consent of the Dominion is necessary before a law made by the United Kingdom Parliament can extend to that Dominion as part of its law. Whether or not an argument on these lines might find favour in the courts of a Dominion, it is in our opinion quite unsustainable in the courts of this country. The sole condition precedent which has to be satisfied if a law made by the United Kingdom Parliament is to extend to a Dominion as part of its law is to be found stated in the body of the Statute of 1931 itself (section 4). This court would run counter to all principles of statutory interpretation if it were to purport to vary or supplement the terms of this stated condition precedent by reference to some supposed convention, which, though referred to in the preamble, is not incorporated in the body of the Statute.

In the present instance, therefore, the only remaining question is whether it is arguable that the condition precedent specified in section 4 of the Statute of 1931 has not been complied with in relation to the Canada Act 1982. Is it arguable that it has not been 'expressly declared in that Act that that Dominion has requested, and consented to, the enactment thereof'? In our judgment this proposition is not arguable, inasmuch as the preamble to the Canada Act 1982 begins with the words 'Whereas Canada has requested and consented to the enactment of an Act of the Parliament of the United Kingdom to give effect to the provisions hereinafter set forth...'.

> ... [W]e conclude that, if and so far as the conditions of section 4 of the Statute of 1931 had to be complied with in relation to the Canada Act 1982, they were duly complied with by the declaration contained in the preamble to that Act.
>
> Consequently, it is unnecessary to consider further the second of the three propositions referred to earlier in this judgment. It is unnecessary to consider whether the Constitution Act 1982 contains provisions which go beyond 'the repeal, amendment or alteration of the British North America Acts' so as to fall outside the exempting provisions of section 7(1) of the Statute of 1931 and thus within section 4 of that Act. If it does contain such provisions, the express declaration of a request and consent required by section 4 is duly contained in the Canada Act 1982. If it contains no such provisions (as we understood Mr Mummery would have sought to submit on behalf of the Attorney-General, though we did not think it necessary to call on him), no declaration of request and consent was necessary.

■ QUESTIONS

1. Did the Court of Appeal decide whether Parliament can give up its sovereignty over a particular territory?
2. Did the Court of Appeal decide whether the validity of an Act of Parliament could be dependent upon the presence or absence of the consent of some other body?
3. How would Megarry VC answer the two questions above?
4. One of the fears of the proponents of the traditional theory of supremacy is that if Parliament could bind itself it could create a legislative vacuum. In cases of granting independence, a power to legislate is given to another body so there is no risk of a vacuum being created. The problem with the fully self-embracing theory of supremacy is that it does give rise to the possibility of Parliament binding its successors not to legislate on certain matters without transferring power to another body. In light of this and the above analysis, is it possible to argue that supremacy is a divisible concept: continuing with regard to the subject-matter of legislation; self-embracing with regard to territorial competence; and partly self-embracing with regard to the procedures to be followed and the manner and form in which legislation must be enacted?

SECTION 5: CONTINUITY AND CHANGE

In this section we consider the implications for supremacy following three major constitutional reforms in the last quarter of the twentieth century. Two of them also have their own have separate chapters, 8 and 9 for the United Kingdom's membership of the European Union and the partial incorporation of the European Convention on Human Rights, respectively. First we consider devolution to Scotland.

A: Scottish Devolution

Our focus will be on the provisions regarding legislative competence conferred on the Scottish Parliament by the Scotland Act 1998 as Scotland was devolved more legislative competence than Wales and Northern Ireland. The aim of devolution was to recognize and give effect to a Scottish identity within the United Kingdom. There would be a more democratic framework for accountability of government to be exercised by the Scottish Parliament. In relation to devolved matters the legislative competence of the Scottish Parliament would allow it to pass public and private statutes which could amend or repeal Westminster Acts which dealt with devolved matters. The scheme of the Scotland Act 1998 is that if a matter was not stated to be a reserved one, then it is devolved. Reserved matters include the constitution of the United Kingdom; UK foreign policy; UK defence and national security; the protection of borders and certain matters subject to border controls; the stability of the UK's fiscal, economic and monetary system; common markets for UK goods and services; employment legislation; social security policy and administration; regulation of certain professions; transport safety and regulation; equality legislation. The Scottish Parliament may not legislate incompatibly with EU law or European Convention rights.

It is expected that there will be good and timely liaison between Scottish departments and their Whitehall counterparts on policy and legislation. The Scotland Act 1998 seeks to ensure that the legislative process of the Scottish Parliament has various opportunities before introduction and between approval and presentation for Royal Assent to check that a measure is not outside its competence. The Judicial Committee of the Privy Council was given the jurisdiction to rule on the *vires* of Bills before Royal Assent. After Royal Assent such challenges to Acts and delegated legislation could be taken in the superior courts. The Judicial Committee is the final court of appeal but this jurisdiction was transferred to the Supreme Court of the United Kingdom when it was established in 2009. The Act makes it clear that Westminster's supremacy remains and so it can continue to legislate on matters which have been devolved, although there is a convention that the consent of the Scottish Parliament will be sought before Westminster legislates on such a matter (on this convention see p. 194, *post*). Note the instruction on how to interpret Scottish legislation. The proposals for devolution were approved in a 1997 referendum before the Bill which became the Scotland Act 1998 was introduced in Westminster.

SCOTLAND ACT 1998

...

28. Acts of the Scottish Parliament

(1) Subject to section 29, the Parliament may make laws, to be known as Acts of the Scottish Parliament.

...

(5) The validity of an Act of the Scottish Parliament is not affected by any invalidity in the proceedings of the Parliament leading to its enactment.

...

(7) This section does not affect the power of the Parliament of the United Kingdom to make laws for Scotland.

29. Legislative competence

(1) An Act of the Scottish Parliament is not law so far as any provision of the Act is outside the legislative competence of the Parliament.

(2) A provision is outside that competence so far as any of the following paragraphs apply—

(a) it would form part of the law of a country or territory other than Scotland, or confer or remove functions exercisable otherwise than in or as regards Scotland,
(b) it relates to reserved matters,
(c) it is in breach of the restrictions in Schedule 4,
(d) it is incompatible with any of the Convention rights or with Community law,
(e) it would remove the Lord Advocate from his position as head of the systems of criminal prosecution and investigation of deaths in Scotland.

(3) For the purposes of this section, the question whether a provision of an Act of the Scottish Parliament relates to a reserved matter is to be determined, subject to subsection (4), by reference to the purpose of the provision, having regard (among other things) to its effect in all the circumstances.

(4) A provision which—

(a) would otherwise not relate to reserved matters, but
(b) makes modifications of Scots private law, or Scots criminal law, as it applies to reserved matters,

is to be treated as relating to reserved matters unless the purpose of the provision is to make the law in question apply consistently to reserved matters and otherwise.

30. Legislative competence: supplementary

(1) Schedule 5 (which defines reserved matters) shall have effect.

(2) Her Majesty may by Order in Council make any modifications of Schedule 4 or 5 which She considers necessary or expedient.

...

31. Scrutiny of Bills before introduction

(1) A member of the Scottish Executive in charge of a Bill shall, on or before introduction of the Bill in the Parliament, state that in his view the provisions of the Bill would be within the legislative competence of the Parliament.

(2) The Presiding Officer shall, on or before the introduction of a Bill in the Parliament, decide whether or not in his view the provisions of the Bill would be within the legislative competence of the Parliament and state his decision.

...

32. Submission of Bills for Royal Assent

(1) It is for the Presiding Officer to submit Bills for Royal Assent.

(2) The Presiding Officer shall not submit a Bill for Royal Assent at any time when—

(a) the Advocate General, the Lord Advocate or the Attorney General is entitled to make a reference in relation to the Bill under section 33,
(b) any such reference has been made but has not been decided or otherwise disposed of by the Supreme Court, or
(c) an order may be made in relation to the Bill under section 35.

(3) The Presiding Officer shall not submit a Bill in its unamended form for Royal Assent if—

(a) the Supreme Court have decided that the Bill or any provision of it would not be within the legislative competence of the Parliament, or
(b) a reference made in relation to the Bill under section 33 has been withdrawn following a request for withdrawal of the reference under section 34(2)(b).

...

33. Scrutiny of Bills by the Supreme Court

(1) The Advocate General, the Lord Advocate or the Attorney General may refer the question of whether a Bill or any provision of a Bill would be within the legislative competence of the Parliament to the Supreme Court for decision.

(2) Subject to subsection (3), he may make a reference in relation to a Bill at any time during—

(a) the period of four weeks beginning with the passing of the Bill, and
(b) any period of four weeks beginning with any subsequent approval of the Bill in accordance with standing orders made by virtue of section 36(5).

(3) He shall not make a reference in relation to a Bill if he has notified the Presiding Officer that he does not intend to make a reference in relation to the Bill, unless the Bill has been approved as mentioned in subsection (2)(b) since the notification.

34. ECJ references

(1) This section applies where—

(a) a reference has been made in relation to a Bill under section 33,
(b) a reference for a preliminary ruling has been made by the Judicial Committee in connection with that reference, and
(c) neither of those references has been decided or otherwise disposed of.

(2) If the Parliament resolves that it wishes to reconsider the Bill—

(a) the Presiding Officer shall notify the Advocate General, the Lord Advocate and the Attorney General of that fact, and
(b) the person who made the reference in relation to the Bill under section 33 shall request the withdrawal of the reference.

(3) In this section 'a reference for a preliminary ruling' means a reference of a question to the European Court under Article 177 of the Treaty establishing the European Community, Article 41 of the Treaty establishing the European Coal and Steel Community or Article 150 of the Treaty establishing the European Atomic Energy Community.

35. Power to intervene in certain cases

(1) If a Bill contains provisions—

(a) which the Secretary of State has reasonable grounds to believe would be incompatible with any international obligations or the interests of defence or national security, or
(b) which make modifications of the law as it applies to reserved matters and which the Secretary of State has reasonable grounds to believe would have an adverse effect on the operation of the law as it applies to reserved matters,

he may make an order prohibiting the Presiding Officer from submitting the Bill for Royal Assent.

(2) The order must identify the Bill and the provisions in question and state the reasons for making the order.

(3) The order may be made at any time during—

(a) the period of four weeks beginning with the passing of the Bill,
(b) any period of four weeks beginning with any subsequent approval of the Bill in accordance with standing orders made by virtue of section 36(5),
(c) if a reference is made in relation to the Bill under section 33, the period of four weeks beginning with the reference being decided or otherwise disposed of by the Judicial Committee.

(4) The Secretary of State shall not make an order in relation to a Bill if he has notified the Presiding Officer that he does not intend to do so, unless the Bill has been approved as mentioned in subsection (3)(b) since the notification.

(5) An order in force under this section at a time when such approval is given shall cease to have effect.

...

37. Acts of Union

The Union with Scotland Act 1706 and the Union with England Act 1707 have effect subject to this Act.

...

101. Interpretation of Acts of the Scottish Parliament etc.

(1) This section applies to—

(a) any provision of an Act of the Scottish Parliament, or of a Bill for such an Act, and
(b) any provision of subordinate legislation made, confirmed or approved, or purporting to be made, confirmed or approved, by a member of the Scottish Executive, which could be read in such a way as to be outside competence.

(2) Such a provision is to be read as narrowly as is required for it to be within competence, if such a reading is possible, and is to have effect accordingly.

(3) In this section 'competence'—

(a) in relation to an Act of the Scottish Parliament, or a Bill for such an Act, means the legislative competence of the Parliament, and
(b) in relation to subordinate legislation, means the powers conferred by virtue of this Act.

102. Powers of courts or tribunals to vary retrospective decisions

(1) This section applies where any court or tribunal decides that—

(a) an Act of the Scottish Parliament or any provision of such an Act is not within the legislative competence of the Parliament, or
(b) a member of the Scottish Executive does not have the power to make, confirm or approve a provision of subordinate legislation that he has purported to make, confirm or approve.

(2) The court or tribunal may make an order—

(a) removing or limiting any retrospective effect of the decision, or
(b) suspending the effect of the decision for any period and on any conditions to allow the defect to be corrected.

(3) In deciding whether to make an order under this section, the court or tribunal shall (among other things) have regard to the extent to which persons who are not parties to the proceedings would otherwise be adversely affected.

(4) Where a court or tribunal is considering whether to make an order under this section, it shall order intimation of that fact to be given to—

(a) the Lord Advocate, and
(b) the appropriate law officer, where the decision mentioned in subsection (1) relates to a devolution issue (within the meaning of Schedule 6),

unless the person to whom the intimation would be given is a party to the proceedings.

(5) A person to whom intimation is given under subsection (4) may take part as a party in the proceedings so far as they relate to the making of the order.

NOTE: See further A. O'Neil, 'Parliamentary Sovereignty and the Judicial Review of Legislation' in A. McHarg and T. Mullen, (eds) *Public Law in Scotland*, (2006), p. 197.

■ QUESTION

If judicial review of Scottish legislation can be called judicial supremacy, and given the political fact of the approval of devolution in a referendum, might this be significant in challenging Westminster legislation which repealed the Scotland Act 1998 or dealt with a devolved matter without the Scottish Parliament's consent, and might this judicial supremacy spill-over elsewhere in constitutional law?

B: European Union

NOTE: In Chapter 8, the impact of the United Kingdom's membership of the European Union on the traditional view of the legislative supremacy of Parliament is explored. In *R* v *Secretary of State for Transport, ex parte Factortame (No. 2)* [1991] 1 AC 603, at 659, Lord Bridge stated that 'it was the duty of a United Kingdom court, when delivering final judgment, to override any rule of national law found to be in conflict with any directly enforceable rule of Community law'. In the context of EU law the effect of this decision is to abandon the traditional Diceyan view and to accept that Parliament has accorded priority to EU law over national law so long as the United Kingdom remains a member of the EU. The model for incorporation of EU law into domestic law in s. 2 of the European Communities Act 1972 (particularly s. 2(4)) has not been adopted in the Human Rights Act 1998 for incorporating the European Convention on Human Rights into United Kingdom law, which is premised on the traditional Diceyan view of legislative supremacy of Parliament. (See further Chapter 9.)

Thoburn v *Sunderland City Council*

[2002] EWHC (Admin) 195, [2003] QB 151, Divisional Court

A challenge to prosecutions for using imperial measurement units rather than metric units claimed that the regulations implementing directives and based on European Communities Act 1972, s. 2(2) (ECA) were invalid as the ECA provisions had been impliedly repealed by the Weights and Measures Act 1985. This argument was rejected. The court considered implied repeal more generally.

LAWS LJ: ...60. The common law has in recent years allowed, or rather created, exceptions to the doctrine of implied repeal: a doctrine which was always the common law's own creature. There are now classes or types of legislative provision which cannot be repealed by mere implication. These instances are given, and can only be given, by our own courts, to which the scope and nature of Parliamentary sovereignty are ultimately confided. The courts may say—have said—that there are certain circumstances in which the legislature may only enact what it desires to enact if it does so by express, or at any rate specific, provision. The courts have in effect so held in the field of European law itself, in the *Factortame* case, and this is critical for the present discussion. By this means, as I shall seek to explain, the courts have found their way through the *impasse* seemingly created by two supremacies, the supremacy of European law and the supremacy of Parliament.

61. The present state of our domestic law is such that substantive Community rights prevail over the express terms of any domestic law, including primary legislation, made or passed after the coming into force of the ECA, even in the face of plain inconsistency between the two. This is the effect of *Factortame (No 1)* [1990] 2 AC 85. To understand the critical passage in Lord Bridge's speech it is first convenient to repeat part of ECA s.2(4):

> 'The provision that may be made under subsection (2) above includes... any such provision (of any such extent) as might be made by Act of Parliament, and any enactment passed or to be passed, other than one contained in this Part of this Act, shall be construed and have effect subject to the foregoing provisions of the section.'

In *Factortame (No 1)* Lord Bridge said this at 140:

> 'By virtue of section 2(4) of the Act of 1972 Part II of the [Merchant Shipping] Act of 1988 is to be construed and take effect subject to directly enforceable Community rights... This has precisely the same effect as if a section were incorporated in Part II of the Act of 1988 which in terms enacted that the provisions with respect to registration of British fishing vessels were to be without prejudice to the directly enforceable Community rights of nationals of any member state of the EEC.'

So there was no question of an implied *pro tanto* repeal of the ECA of 1972 by the later Act of 1988; on the contrary the Act of 1988 took effect subject to Community rights incorporated into our law by the ECA. In *Factortame* no argument was advanced by the Crown in their Lordships' House to suggest that such an implied repeal might have been effected. It is easy to see what the argument might have been: Parliament in 1972 could not bind Parliament in 1988, and s. 2(4) was therefore ineffective to do so. It seems to me that there is no doubt but that in *Factortame (No 1)* the House of Lords effectively accepted that s. 2(4) could not be impliedly repealed, albeit the point was not argued.

62. Where does this leave the constitutional position which I have stated? Mr Shrimpton would say that *Factortame (No 1)* was wrongly decided; and since the point was not argued, there is scope, within the limits of our law of precedent, to depart from it and to hold that implied repeal may bite on the ECA as readily as upon any other statute. I think that would be a wrong turning. My reasons are these. In the present state of its maturity the common law has come to recognise that there exist rights which should properly be classified as constitutional or fundamental: see for example such cases as *Simms* [2000] 2 AC 115 *per* Lord Hoffmann at 131, *Pierson* v *Secretary of State* [1998] AC 539, *Leech* [1994] QB 198, *Derbyshire County Council* v *Times Newspapers Ltd.* [1993] AC 534, and *Witham* [1998] QB 575. And from this a further insight follows. We should recognise a hierarchy of Acts of Parliament: as it were 'ordinary' statutes and 'constitutional' statutes. The two categories must be distinguished on a principled basis. In my opinion a constitutional statute is one which (a) conditions the legal relationship between citizen and State in some general, overarching manner, or (b) enlarges or diminishes the scope of what we would now regard as fundamental constitutional rights. (a) and (b) are of necessity closely related: it is difficult to think of an instance of (a) that is not also an instance of (b). The special status of constitutional statutes follows the special status of constitutional rights. Examples are the Magna Carta, the Bill of Rights 1689, the Act of Union, the Reform Acts which distributed and enlarged the franchise, the HRA, the Scotland Act 1998 and the Government of Wales Act 1998. The ECA clearly belongs in this family. It incorporated the whole corpus of substantive Community rights and obligations, and gave overriding domestic effect to the judicial and administrative machinery of Community law. It may be there has never been a statute having such profound effects on so many dimensions of our daily lives. The ECA is, by force of the common law, a constitutional statute.

63. Ordinary statutes may be impliedly repealed. Constitutional statutes may not. For the repeal of a constitutional Act or the abrogation of a fundamental right to be effected by statute, the court would apply this test: is it shown that the legislature's *actual*—not imputed, constructive or presumed—intention was to effect the repeal or abrogation? I think the test could only be met by express words in the later statute, or by words so specific that the inference of an actual determination to effect the result contended for was irresistible. The ordinary rule of implied repeal does not satisfy this test. Accordingly, it has no application to constitutional statutes. I should add that in my judgment general words could not be supplemented, so as to effect a repeal or significant amendment to a constitutional statute, by reference to what was said in Parliament by the minister promoting the Bill pursuant to *Pepper* v *Hart* [1993] AC 593. A constitutional statute can only be repealed, or amended in a way which significantly affects its provisions touching fundamental rights or otherwise the relation between citizen and State, by unambiguous words on the face of the later statute.

64. This development of the common law regarding constitutional rights, and as I would say constitutional statutes, is highly beneficial. It gives us most of the benefits of a written constitution, in which fundamental rights are accorded special respect. But it preserves the sovereignty of the legislature and the flexibility of our uncodified constitution. It accepts the relation between legislative supremacy and fundamental rights is not fixed or brittle: rather the courts (in interpreting statutes, and now, applying the HRA) will pay more or less deference to the legislature, or other public decision-maker, according to the subject in hand. Nothing is plainer than that this benign development involves, as I have said, the recognition of the ECA as a constitutional statute.

...

68. On this part of the case, then, I would reject Miss Sharpston's submissions. At the same time I would recognise for reasons I have given that the common law has in effect stipulated that the principal executive measures of the ECA may only be repealed in the United Kingdom by specific provision, and not impliedly. It might be suggested that it matters little whether that result is given by the law of the EU (as Miss Sharpston submits) or by the law of England untouched by Community law (as I would hold). But the difference is vital to a proper understanding of the relationship between EU and domestic law.

69. In my judgment (as will by now be clear) the correct analysis of that relationship involves and requires these following four propositions. (1) All the specific rights and obligations which EU law creates are by the ECA incorporated into our domestic law and rank supreme: that is, anything in our substantive law inconsistent with any of these rights and obligations is abrogated or must be modified to avoid the inconsistency. This is true even where the inconsistent municipal provision is contained in primary legislation. (2) The ECA is a constitutional statute: that is, it cannot be impliedly repealed. (3) The truth of (2) is derived, not from EU law, but purely from the law of England: the common law recognises a category of constitutional statutes. (4) The fundamental legal basis of the United Kingdom's relationship with the EU rests with the domestic, not the European, legal powers. In the event, which no doubt would never happen in the real world, that a European measure was seen to be repugnant to a fundamental or constitutional right guaranteed by the law of England, a question would arise whether the general words of the ECA were sufficient to incorporate the measure and give it overriding effect in domestic law. But that is very far from this case.

70. I consider that the balance struck by these four propositions gives full weight both to the proper supremacy of Community law and to the proper supremacy of the United Kingdom Parliament. By the former, I mean the supremacy of *substantive* Community law. By the latter, I mean the supremacy of the legal *foundation* within which those substantive provisions enjoy their primacy. The former is guaranteed by propositions (1) and (2). The latter is guaranteed by propositions (3) and (4). If this balance is understood, it will be seen that these two supremacies are in harmony, and not in conflict...

Appeals dismissed.

NOTE: Craig suggests that there are three possible ways of understanding what the courts have done in following Community law over inconsistent national law. The first is statutory construction, that there is a modification of the traditional understanding to allow for the following of Community law unless Parliament clearly indicated a change. This is a significant change to the traditional understanding and interpretation could be a pretext, hiding the real position that there has been a technical revolution as suggested by Wade. Craig prefers the proposition that it is based on normative argument of legal principle the contents of which vary over time. In the following extract, Craig first instances some of these normative arguments by quoting from Lord Bridge's reasoning in *Factortame* [1991] 1 AC 603, 658–659, and then analyses them.

P. Craig, 'Britain in the European Union' in J. Jowell and D. Oliver (eds), *The Changing Constitution*

(2007) 84, at 94

Some public comments on the decision of the Court of Justice, affirming the jurisdiction of the courts of the member states to override national legislation if necessary to enable interim relief to be granted in protection of rights under Community law, have suggested that this was a novel and dangerous invasion by a Community institution of the sovereignty of the United Kingdom Parliament. But such comments are based on a misconception. If the supremacy within the European Community of Community law over the national law of member states was not always inherent in the EEC Treaty it was certainly well established in the jurisprudence of the Court of Justice long before the United Kingdom joined the Community. Thus, whatever limitation of its sovereignty Parliament accepted when it enacted the European Communities Act 1972 was entirely voluntary. Under the terms of the 1972 Act it has always been clear that it was the duty of a United Kingdom court, when delivering final judgment, to override any rule of national law found to be in conflict with any directly enforceable rule of Community law. Similarly, when decisions of the Court of Justice have exposed areas of United Kingdom statute law which failed to implement Council directives, Parliament has always loyally accepted the obligation to make appropriate and prompt amendments. Thus there is nothing in any way novel in according supremacy to rules of Community law in areas to which they apply and to insist that, in the protection of rights under Community law, national courts must not be prohibited by rules of national law from granting interim relief in appropriate cases is no more than a logical recognition of that supremacy.

There are three aspects of this reasoning that should be distinguished. One was essentially *contractarian*: the UK knew when it joined the EC that priority should be accorded to EC law, and it must be taken to have contracted on those terms. If, therefore, 'blame' was to be cast for a loss of sovereignty then this should be laid at the door of Parliament and not the courts. The second facet for Lord Bridge's reasoning was a priori and *functional*: it was always inherent in a regime such as the Community that it could only function adequately if EC law could take precedence in the event of a clash with domestic legal norms. The third factor at play was the existence of the European Communities Act 1972, which was said to impose a duty on national courts to override national law in the event of a clash with directly enforceable Community law.

NOTE: For an alternative view on first *Factortame* and secondly its implications for implied repeal and Laws LJ's distinction between ordinary and constitutional statutes, see below:

A. Tomkins, *Public Law*

(2003) pp. 118–119 and 123–124

As soon as the House of Lords (and all other courts in the United Kingdom) became empowered by section 3(1) of the ECA [see p. 372, *post*] to determine questions of Community law, it was clear from reading the text of the 1972 Act alongside the pre-existing jurisprudence of the Court of Justice that it was no longer true that nobody in England could set aside an Act of Parliament.

To clarify: it remains the case that under English law nobody has the power to override or to set aside a statute, but it is no longer the case that English law is the only law that is applicable in England. Since 1 January 1973 there have been two legal systems operating in this country, not one, and the doctrine of the legislative supremacy of statute is a doctrine known to only one of those two systems. This is not a revolution: it is rather the incorporation of a new legal order into a very old country. European Community law is, moreover, a new legal order that is to be enforced by the same courts as enforce domestic law. They may be the same courts, but they are not enforcing the same law. The House of Lords is one court with two jurisdictions, one in domestic law (which does not allow the court to set aside a statute) and one in Community law (which in certain circumstances does). Thus, as these legal systems currently stand, the doctrine of legislative supremacy may be stated as follows: Parliament may make or unmake any law whatsoever, and under English law nobody may override or set aside a statute. Even Dicey could surely have lived with that!

It is sometimes suggested that while the essentials of legislative supremacy are left intact by *Factortame*, the doctrine of implied repeal has been affected. That the House of Lords did not hold that the Merchant Shipping Act 1988 impliedly repealed the European Communities Act 1972 is taken by some commentators as evidence of the fact that the doctrine of implied repeal has been changed, or even abandoned. This view, while often repeated, is misconceived. There are two reasons for this. The first is that the provisions of the Merchant Shipping Act were not in conflict with those of the European Communities Act: rather, they were in conflict with certain Articles of the Treaty of Rome. The doctrine of implied repeal simply did not apply: it is concerned with conflicts between one statute and another, not with conflicts between statutes and other sources of law such as Treaty Articles.

The second reason is that even if there had been an allegation that the Merchant Shipping Act was in conflict with the European Communities Act (which there was not), the doctrine of implied repeal would still have been irrelevant to the case. This is because, as we saw above, implied repeal concerns incompatibilities between two statutes that both deal with the same subject-matter, as Maugham LJ made clear in his judgment in the leading case of *Ellen Street Estates* v *Minister of Health* [1934] 1 KB 590. The Merchant Shipping Act and the European Communities Act did not deal with the same subject-matter. The one concerned fishing and the other concerned the legal relationship between the United Kingdom and the European Community. It is frankly preposterous to suggest that there could have been an issue of implied repeal here...

What is of interest in the [*Thoburn*] case is not so much the outcome as the reasoning employed by Laws LJ. He offered a number of reasons why the implied repeal argument failed. His main reason was (correctly) that there was no inconsistency between the provisions of the 1972 Act and those of the 1985 Act. If he had stopped there, all would be well, but he continued to opine that even if there had been an irreducible inconsistency between the provisions of the ECA and those of a later Act there could in any event be no implied repeal of the ECA because it was 'by force of the common law, a constitutional statute' [para. 62]. While 'ordinary' statutes may be impliedly repealed, 'constitutional' statutes may not, according to Laws LJ. This previously unheard of category of constitutional statutes would include, in his opinion, Magna Carta, the Bill of Rights 1689, the Acts of Union, the Reform Acts (concerning the franchise), the Human Rights Act, and the devolution legislation of 1998, as well as the ECA.

The only authority Laws LJ cited in support of these—wholly novel—propositions was *Factortame I*, of which he stated that 'in *Factortame I* the House of Lords effectively accepted that section 2(4) [of the ECA] could not be impliedly repealed, albeit that the point was not argued' [para. 61]. Not only is it extremely unlikely that the House of Lords would ever accept a novel and controversial point that had not even been argued before it, but, as we have seen, this is emphatically not what the House of Lords held in *Factortame*. There was no issue of implied repeal in *Factortame*, as the two statutes (the ECA and the Merchant Shipping Act) each dealt with an entirely different subject-matter, such that there was no way the one could be held impliedly to have repealed the other. Only a statute that dealt with the same subject-matter as the ECA could impliedly repeal it. If Parliament were to re-legislate on the subject of the relationship between domestic and European Community law, and were to do so in a way that was inconsistent with the terms of the ECA 1972 without expressly repealing the 1972 provisions, then there is no reason why the courts would not hold that the later Act must be construed as having impliedly repealed the 1972 Act. All of this is very unlikely, of course. If Parliament were to re-legislate on the subject-matter of the ECA it would be absurd for it to do so without making express reference to the 1972 Act. Such a move would be exceptionally foolish, and extremely unlikely.

Acts can be impliedly repealed only by subsequent Acts that deal with the same subject-matter. Thus, Acts that deal with constitutional subjects can be impliedly repealed only by subsequent Acts that deal with the same, constitutional, subjects. An Act that concerns fishing, or weights and measures, cannot impliedly repeal statutes that concern constitutional law. But this is not to create a new and special category of constitutional statute that is different from ordinary statute. This is merely to restate the law of implied repeal, which has clearly been much misunderstood in recent years.

NOTE: Tomkins points out that Laws LJ's assumption that the Acts of Union have not been substantially amended is incorrect, citing C. Munro, *Studies in Constitutional Law* (1987), pp. 66–71. The first edition does give greater detail on this point than the treatment in the second edition (1999), at pp. 132–142.

C: The Human Rights Act

The Human Rights Act 1998 seeks to reconcile protecting human rights with preserving legislative supremacy by requiring courts to interpret where they can in conformity with convention rights (see s. 3 at p. 428, *post* and the dicta on what this requires the judges to do at pp. 459–469, *post*) but if that is not possible to make a declaration of incompatibility (see s. 4. at p. 428, *post*). This puts the ball in Parliament's court, it can use a fast track procedure to legislate so as to bring the law into conformity with Convention rights. (see s. 10 at p. 431, *post*).

Tomkins says, in *Public Law* (2003) p. 122, '…if Parliament decides not to amend or repeal a provision that has been declared by a court to be incompatible with a Convention right, so be it. Parliament continues to have the supreme legislative authority to legislate in contravention of convention rights if it so wishes, and no domestic court or tribunal may overturn or set aside such legislation notwithstanding the incomparability.' Whereas Ewing has remarked, 'As a matter of constitutional legality, Parliament may well be sovereign, but as a matter of constitutional practice it has transferred significant power to the judiciary ((1999) 62 MLR 79, 92). So far declarations of incompatibility have not been ignored (on anti-terrorism legislation and control orders cases see pp. 493–526 *post*).

A. Bradley, 'The Sovereignty of Parliament' in J. Jowell and D. Oliver (eds), *The Changing Constitution*

(2007) pp. 25, 56

One narrower question that may briefly be mentioned is whether the Human Rights Act has modified the doctrine of implied repeal. Certainly the Act does not rely upon the doctrine as a means by which it affects earlier legislation. Even if an earlier statute plainly infringes a Convention right, and cannot be given an interpretation consistent with the right, it remains in force but subject to a declaration of incompatibility. Conversely, later Acts that cannot be interpreted consistently with a Convention right do not themselves repeal by implication the effect of the Convention rights, since the Human Rights Act must be applied to the later Act. The operation of the later Act is not affected, save that either it can be interpreted in a manner consistently with Convention rights, or it is subject to a declaration of incompatibility. For a later Act to protect itself against the strong duty of interpretation in section 3 of the Human Rights Act and against the possibility of a declaration of incompatibility, it would seem necessary for the later Act to include a provision that expresses a plain intention to exclude operation of the Human Rights Act. Whether or not the doctrine of implied repeal is an indispensable facet of Parliamentary sovereignty, and earlier arguments in this chapter have suggested that it is not, the Human Rights Act has found a way of ensuring that in relation to Convention rights, there will be little space in which the doctrine can be applied.

NOTE: See further, N. Bamforth, 'Parliamentary Sovereignty and the Human Rights Act 1998 [1998] *Public Law* 572.

■ QUESTION

A. Bradley says in 'The Sovereignty of Parliament' in J. Jowell and D. Oliver (eds), *The Changing Constitution* (2007), p. 25, at 58:

> The place of parliamentary sovereignty in the government of the United Kingdom has changed in recent years and the process of change will continue during the present century. It may be as in the case of the Human Rights Act or the Scotland Act that ways can be found of retaining the form (or appearance) of parliamentary sovereignty; an emphasis on form may be expedient in facilitating the changes in substance that in reality are being made.

If this supposedly fundamental constitutional principle is unclear what should it be and how might it be identified and agreed?

3

The Rule of Law

OVERVIEW

In this chapter we consider another fundamental constitutional principle, the rule of law. First it is introduced and viewed as meaning government according to law, then as a broad political principle and finally we focus on Dicey's conception of it and criticism of it.

SECTION 1: INTRODUCTION

The rule of law is considered to be one of the fundamental doctrines of the Constitution of the United Kingdom. The constitution is said to be founded on the idea of the rule of law, and this is a concept favoured by politicians and lawyers, being imported into many debates. Despite its currency in political and constitutional discussion its meaning is far from precise, and it may mean different things to different people at different times.

Governments wield considerable power. Constitutions are concerned with the allocation of power and the control of its exercise. The doctrine of the rule of law is concerned with the latter. Aristotle stated that 'the rule of law is preferable to the rule of any individual'. This sentiment was echoed centuries later by English jurists.

Report of the Committee on Ministers' Powers

Cmd 4060, 1932, pp. 71–72

The supremacy or rule of law—Its history and meaning

1. The supremacy or rule of the law of the Land is a recognised principle of the English Constitution. The origin of the principle must be sought in the theory, universally held in the Middle Ages, that law of some kind—the law either of God or man—ought to rule the world. Bracton, in his famous book on English law, which was written in the first half of the thirteenth century, held this theory, and deduced from it the proposition that the king and other rulers were subject to law. He laid it down that the law bound all members of the state, whether rulers or subjects; and that justice according to law was due both to ruler and subject. This view was accepted by the common lawyers of the fourteenth and fifteenth centuries and is stated in the Year Books. In 1441, in the Year Book 19 Henry VI Pasch. pl. 1, it is said: 'the law is the highest inheritance which the king has; for by the law he and all his subjects are ruled, and if there was no law there would be no king and no inheritance.'

The rise of the power of Parliament in the fourteenth and fifteenth centuries both emphasized and modified this theory of the supremacy of the law. That the rise of the power of Parliament emphasized the theory is shown by the practical application given to it by Chief Justice Fortescue in Henry VI's reign. He used it as the premise, by means of which he justified the control which Parliament had gained over legislation and taxation. That the rise of the power of Parliament modified the theory is shown by the manner in which the theory of the supremacy of the law was combined with the doctrine of the supremacy of Parliament. The law was supreme, but Parliament could change and modify it...

The only period when this conception of the rule of law was seriously questioned was in the Stuart period. The Stuart Kings considered that the Royal prerogative was the sovereign power in the State, and so could override the law whenever they saw fit. Chief Justice Coke was dismissed from the bench because he asserted the supremacy of the law. But his views as to the supremacy of the law were accepted by Parliament when it passed the Petition of Right in 1628, and when it abolished the Court of the Star Chamber and the jurisdiction of the Privy Council in England in 1641. Those views finally triumphed as the result of the Great Rebellion, and the Revolution of 1688. In this, as in other matters, Coke's writings passed on the views of the medieval English lawyers into modern English law. But these views were passed on with one important addition, which was the result of the rise, in the sixteenth century, of the modern territorial state. The law which was thus supreme was the law of England; and this included the law, written and unwritten, administered by the Courts of Common Law, by the Courts of Equity, by the Court of Admiralty, and by the Ecclesiastical Courts. Thus the modern doctrine of the rule of law has come, as the result of this long historical development, to mean the supremacy of all parts of the law of England, both enacted and unenacted.

NOTE: Chief Justice Coke's assertion of the supremacy of law was stated clearly in the case which follows.

Prohibitions del Roy

(1607) 12 Co Rep 63, 77 ER 1342

Note, upon Sunday the 10th of November in this same term, the King, upon complaint made to him by Bancroft, Archbishop of Canterbury, concerning prohibitions, the King was informed, that when the question was made of what matters the Ecclesiastical judges have cognizance, either upon the exposition of the statutes concerning tithes, or any other thing ecclesiastical, or upon the statute 1 El. concerning the high commission or in any other case in which there is not express authority in law, the King himself may decide it in his Royal person; and that the Judges are but the delegates of the King, and that the King may take what causes he shall please to determine, from the determination of the Judges, and may determine them himself. And the Archbishop said, that this was clear in divinity, that such authority belongs to the King by the word of God in the Scripture. To which it was answered by me, in the presence, and with the clear consent of all the Judges of England, and Barons of the Exchequer, that the King in his own person cannot adjudge any case, either criminal, as treason, felony, &c. or betwixt party and party, concerning his inheritance, chattels, or goods, &c. but this ought to be determined and adjudged in some Court of Justice.... And the Judges informed the King, that no King after the Conquest assumed to himself to give any judgment in any cause whatsoever, which concerned the administration of justice within this realm, but these were solely determined in the Courts of Justice.

...[T]hen the King said, that he thought the law was founded upon reason, and that he and others had reason, as well as the Judges: to which it was answered by me, that true it was, that God had endowed His Majesty with excellent science, and great endowments of nature; but His Majesty was not learned in the laws of his realm of England, and causes which concern the life, or inheritance, or goods, or fortunes of his subjects, are not to be decided by natural reason but by the artificial reason and judgment of law, which law is an act which requires long study and experience, before that a man can attain to the cognizance of it: that the law was the golden met-wand and measure to try the causes of the subjects; and which protected His Majesty in safety and peace: with which the King was greatly offended, and said, that then he should be under the law, which was treason to affirm, as he said; to which I said, that Bracton saith, *quod Rex non debet esse sub homine, sed sub Deo et lege.*

NOTE: The law to which the Crown was subject was the common law as changed from time to time by Parliament. It is worth noting that at this time Parliament was not as active in legislating as it is now; the common law was the main source of law and legislation was very much a subsidiary source.

SECTION 2: GOVERNMENT ACCORDING TO THE LAW

Government according to the law means that the Executive or any civil authority or government official cannot exercise a power unless such exercise of it is authorized by some specific rule of law.

Entick v Carrington

(1765) 19 St Tr 1030, Court of Common Pleas

Two King's messengers, under the authority of a warrant issued by the Secretary of State, broke and entered Entick's house and took away his papers. Entick was alleged to be the author of seditious writings. When the messengers were sued by Entick for trespass to his house and goods, it was argued that the warrant was legal, as the power to issue such warrants was essential to government as 'the only means of quieting clamours and sedition'.

LORD CAMDEN CJ: ...This power, so claimed by the Secretary of State, is not supported by one single citation from any law book extant. It is claimed by no other magistrate in this kingdom but himself....

Before I state the question, it will be necessary to describe the power claimed by this warrant in its full extent. If honestly exerted, it is a power to seize that man's papers, who is charged upon oath to be the author or publisher of a seditious libel; if oppressively, it acts against every man, who is so described in the warrant, though he be innocent....

Such is the power, and therefore one should naturally expect that the law to warrant it should be clear in proportion as the power is exorbitant.

If it is law, it will be found in our books. If it is not to be found there, it is not law.

The great end, for which men entered into society, was to secure their property. That right is preserved sacred and incommunicable in all instances, where it has not been taken away or abridged by some public law for the good of the whole. The cases where this right of property is set aside by positive law, are various. Distresses, executions, forfeitures, taxes, etc. are all of this description; wherein every man by common consent gives up that right, for the sake of justice and the general good.

By the laws of England, every invasion of private property, be it ever so minute, is a trespass. No man can set his foot upon my ground without my licence, but he is liable to an action, though the damage be nothing.... If he admits the fact, he is bound to shew by way of justification, that some positive law has empowered or excused him. The justification is submitted to the judges, who are to look into the books; and see if such a justification can be maintained by the text of the statute law, or by the principles of common law. If no such excuse can be found or produced, the silence of the books is an authority against the defendant, and the plaintiff must have judgment.

According to this reasoning, it is now incumbent upon the defendants to shew the law, by which this seizure is warranted. If that cannot be done, it is a trespass.

Papers are the owner's goods and chattels: they are his dearest property; and are so far from enduring a seizure that they will hardly bear an inspection; and though the eye cannot by the laws of England be guilty of a trespass, yet where private papers are removed and carried away, the secret nature of those goods will be an aggravation of the trespass, and demand more considerable damages in that respect. Where is the written law that gives any magistrate such a power? I can safely answer, there is none, and therefore it is too much for us without such authority to pronounce a practice legal, which would be subversive of all the comforts of society....

I come now to the practice since the Revolution, which has been strongly urged, with this emphatical addition, that an usage tolerated from the area of liberty, and continued downwards to this time through the best ages of the constitution, must necessarily have a legal commencement. Now, though that pretence can have no place in the question made by this plea, because no such practice is there alleged; yet I will permit the defendant for the present to borrow a fact from the special verdict, for the sake of giving it an answer.

If the practice began then, it began too late to be law now. If it was more ancient, the Revolution is not to answer for it; and I could have wished, that upon this occasion the Revolution had not been considered as the only basis of our liberty....

With respect to the practice itself, if it goes no higher, every lawyer will tell you, it is much too modern to be evidence of the common law....

This is the first instance I have met with, where the ancient immemorable law of the land, in a public matter, was attempted to be proved by the practice of a private office. The names and rights of public magistrates, their power and forms of proceeding as they are settled by law, have been long since written, and are to be found in books and records. Private customs indeed are still to be sought from private tradition. But who ever conceived a notion, that any part of the public law could be buried in the obscure practice of a particular person?

To search, seize, and carry away all the papers of the subject upon the first warrant: that such a right should have existed from the time whereof the memory of man runneth not to the contrary, and never yet have found a place in any book of law; is incredible. But if so strange a thing could be supposed, I do not see, how we could declare the law upon such evidence.

But still it is insisted, that there has been a general submission, and no action brought to try the right.

I answer, there has been a submission of guilt and poverty to power and the terror of punishment. But it would be strange doctrine to assert that all the people of this land are bound to acknowledge that to be universal law, which a few criminal booksellers have been afraid to dispute....

It is then said, that it is necessary for the ends of government to lodge such a power with a state officer; and that it is better to prevent the publication before than to punish the offender afterwards.... [W]ith respect to the argument of State necessity, or a distinction that has been aimed at between State offences and others, the common law does not understand that kind of reasoning, nor do our books take notice of any such distinctions....

If the king himself has no power to declare when the law ought to be violated for reason of State, I am sure we his judges have no such prerogative.

Lastly, it is urged as an argument of utility, that such a search is a means of detecting offenders by discovering evidence....

In the criminal law such a proceeding was never heard of; and yet there are some crimes, such for instance as murder, rape, robbery, and house-breaking, to say nothing of forgery and perjury, that are more atrocious than libelling. But our law has provided no paper-search in these cases to help forward the conviction....

If, however, a right of search for the sake of discovering evidence ought in any case to be allowed, this crime above all others ought to be excepted, as wanting such a discovery less than any other. It is committed in open day-light, and in the face of the world; every act of publication makes new proof; and the solicitor of the treasury, if he pleases, may be the witness himself....

I have now taken notice of everything that has been urged upon the present point; and upon the whole we are all of opinion, that the warrant to seize and carry away the party's papers in the case of a seditious libel, is illegal and void.

■ QUESTION

Lord Camden CJ stated that 'by the laws of England every invasion of private property, be it ever so minute, is a trespass'. Is this still true? See, for example, s. 8 of the Police and Criminal Evidence Act 1984; s. 26(1) of the Theft Act 1968; s. 6(1) of the Criminal Damage Act 1971; ss. 7 and 24 of the Forgery and Counterfeiting Act 1981; s. 46 of the Firearms Act 1968; s. 23(3) of the Misuse of Drugs Act 1971; s. 3 of the Obscene Publications Act 1959; s. 27 of the Drug Trafficking Act 1994; s. 2(4) of the Criminal Justice Act 1987; and Sched. 5 to the Terrorism Act 2000.

NOTE: Views on the legality of official action, however, may differ. Lord Camden revealed an enthusiasm for liberty in a sweeping declaration when he stated:

> The great end for which men entered into society, was to secure their property. That right is preserved sacred and incommunicable in all instances, where it has not been taken away or abridged by some public law for the good of the whole.

In the extracts from the case which follows, echoes of Lord Camden's approach may be discerned in the judgment of Lord Denning in the Court of Appeal; whereas a much more restrictive approach was adopted in the House of Lords, having important consequences for the rights of the citizen, the power of Government, and the effectiveness of the rule of law in controlling the official exercise of power.

R* v *Inland Revenue Commissioners, ex parte Rossminster Ltd

[1980] AC 952, Court of Appeal

Section 20C of the Taxes Management Act 1970, as amended, provides:

(1) If the appropriate judicial authority'—and he is defined as the circuit judge—'is satisfied on information on oath given by an officer of the board that—(a) there is reasonable ground for suspecting that an offence involving any form of fraud in connection with, or in relation to, tax has been committed and that evidence of it is to be found on premises specified in the information; and (b) in applying under this section, the officer acts with the approval of the board given in relation to the particular case, the authority may issue a warrant in writing authorising an officer of the board to enter the premises, if necessary by force, at any time within 14 days from the time of issue of the warrant, and search them.... (3) On entering the premises with a warrant under this section, the officer may seize and remove any things whatsoever found there which he has reasonable cause to believe may be required as evidence for the purposes of proceedings in respect of such an offence as is mentioned in subsection (1) above....

Suspecting that some unspecified tax fraud had been committed by Rossminster Ltd, officers of the Inland Revenue obtained warrants to search Rossminster's premises. The officers seized anything which they believed might be required as evidence of a tax fraud, but they did not inform Rossminster Ltd of the offences suspected or of the persons suspected of having committed them. The warrants simply followed the wording in s. 20C without specifying what particular offences were suspected. The Court of Appeal, reversing the decision of the Divisional Court, granted, *inter alia*, an order of certiorari to quash the warrants.

LORD DENNING: ...Beyond all doubt this search and seizure was unlawful unless it was authorised by Parliament....The trouble is that the legislation is drawn so widely that in some hands it might be an instrument of oppression. It may be said that 'honest people need not fear: that it will never be used against them: that tax inspectors can be trusted, only to use it in the case of the big, bad frauds.' This is an attractive argument, but I would reject it. Once great power is granted, there is a danger of it being abused. Rather than risk such abuse, it is, as I see it, the duty of the courts so to construe the statute as to see that it encroaches as little as possible upon the liberties of the people of England....

The warrant is challenged on the ground that it does not specify any particular offence....The justification is: 'We do not wish to tell more to those we suspect because we do not want them to know too much about what we intend to do. Otherwise they will be on their guard.'

Is this a just excuse? The words 'an offence involving any form of fraud in connection with, or in relation to, tax' are very wide words. We were taken by Mr Davenport through a number of offences which might be comprised in them. There is no specific section in the Act itself. But there are a number of other offences which involve fraud....It seems to me that these words 'fraud...in relation to...tax' are so vague and so general that it must be exceedingly difficult for the officers of the Inland Revenue themselves to know what papers they can take or what they cannot take....The vice of a general warrant of this kind—which does not specify any particular offence—is two-fold. It gives no help to the officers when they have to exercise it. It means also that they can roam wide and large, seizing and taking pretty well all a man's documents and papers.

There is some assistance to be found in the cases. I refer to the law about arrest—when a man is arrested under a warrant for an offence. It is then established by a decision of the House of Lords that the warrant has to specify the particular offence with which the man is charged: see *Christie* v *Leachinsky* [1947] AC 573. I will read what Viscount Simon said, at p. 585:

> 'If the arrest was authorised by magisterial warrant, or if proceedings were instituted by the issue of a summons, it is clear law that the warrant or summons must specify the offence...it is a principle involved in our ancient jurisprudence. Moreover, the warrant must be founded on information in writing and on oath and, except where a particular statute provides otherwise, the information and the warrant must particularise the offence charged.'

Lord Simmonds put it more graphically when he said, at p. 592:

> 'Arrested with or without a warrant the subject is entitled to know why he is deprived of his freedom, if only in order that he may, without a moment's delay, take such steps as will enable him to regain it.'

So here. When the officers of the Inland Revenue come armed with a warrant to search a man's home or his office, it seems to me that he is entitled to say: 'Of what offence do you suspect me? You are claiming to enter my house and to seize my papers.' And when they look at the papers and seize them, he should be able to say: 'Why are you seizing these papers? Of what offence do you suspect me? What have these to do with your case?' Unless he knows the particular offence charged, he cannot take steps to secure himself or his property. So it seems to me, as a matter of construction of the statute and therefore of the warrant—in pursuance of our traditional role to protect the liberty of the individual—it is our duty to say that the warrant must particularise the specific offence which is charged as being fraud on the revenue.

If this be right, it follows necessarily that this warrant is bad. It should have specified the particular offence of which the man is suspected. On this ground I would hold that certiorari should go to quash the warrant.

House of Lords

LORD WILBERFORCE: ...The integrity and privacy of a man's home, and of his place of business, an important human right has, since the second world war, been eroded by a number of statutes passed by Parliament in the belief, presumably, that his right of privacy ought in some cases to be over-ridden by the interest which the public has in preventing evasions of the law. Some of these powers of search are reflections of dirigisme and of heavy taxation, others of changes in mores.... A formidable number of officials now have powers to enter people's premises, and to take property away, and these powers are frequently exercised, sometimes on a large scale. Many people, as well as the respondents, think that this process has gone too far; that is an issue to be debated in Parliament and in the press.

The courts have the duty to supervise, I would say critically, even jealously, the legality of any purported exercise of these powers. They are the guardians of the citizens' right to privacy. But they must do this in the context of the times, i.e. of increasing Parliamentary intervention, and of the modern power of judicial review. In my respectful opinion appeals to 18th century precedents of arbitrary action by Secretaries of State and references to general warrants do nothing to throw light on the issue. Furthermore, while the courts may look critically at legislation which impairs the rights of citizens and should resolve any doubt in interpretation in their favour, it is no part of their duty, or power, to restrict or impede the working of legislation, even of unpopular legislation; to do so would be to weaken rather than to advance the democratic process....

[On the question of the validity of the warrants his Lordship went on to state] I can understand very well the perplexity, and indeed indignation, of those present on the premises, when they were searched. Beyond knowing, as appears in the warrant, that the search is in connection with a 'tax fraud,' they were not told what the precise nature of the fraud was, when it was committed, or by whom it was committed. In the case of a concern with numerous clients, for example, a bank, without this knowledge the occupier of the premises is totally unable to protect his customers' confidential information from investigation and seizure. I cannot believe that this does not call for a fresh look by Parliament. But, on the plain words of the enactment, the officers are entitled if they can persuade the board and the judge, to enter and search *premises* regardless of whom they belong to: a warrant which confers this power is strictly and exactly within the parliamentary authority, and the occupier has no answer to it. I accept that some information as regards the person(s) who are alleged to have committed an offence and possibly as to the approximate dates of the offences must almost certainly have been laid before the board and the judge. But the occupier has no right to be told of this at this stage, nor has he the right to be informed of the 'reasonable grounds' of which the judge was satisfied....

The Court of Appeal took the view that the warrants were invalid because they did not sufficiently particularise the alleged offence(s). The court did not make clear exactly what particulars should have been given—and indeed I think that this cannot be done. The warrant followed the wording of the statute 'fraud in connection with or in relation to tax': a portmanteau description which covers a number of common law (cheating) and statutory offences (under the Theft Act 1968 et al.). To require specification at this investigatory stage would be impracticable given the complexity of 'tax frauds' and the different persons who may be involved (companies, officers of companies, accountants, tax consultants, taxpayers, wives of taxpayers etc.). Moreover, particularisation, if required, would no doubt take the form of a listing of one offence and/or another or others and so would be of little help to those concerned. Finally, there would clearly be power, on principles well accepted in the common law, after entry had been made in connection with one particular offence, to seize material bearing upon other offences within the portmanteau. So, particularisation, even if practicable, would not help the occupier.

I am unable, therefore, to escape the conclusion, that adherence to the statutory formula is sufficient.

LORD SCARMAN: ... My Lords, I agree that these appeals should be allowed and add some observations only because of the importance of the issues raised, and because I share the anxieties felt by the Court of Appeal. If power exists for officers of the Board of Inland Revenue to enter premises, if necessary by force, at any time of the day or night and then seize and remove any things whatsoever found there which they have reasonable cause to believe may be required as evidence for the purposes of proceedings in respect of any offence or offences involving any form of fraud in connection with, or in relation to, tax, it is the duty of the courts to see that it is not abused: for it is a breath-taking inroad upon the individual's right of privacy and right of property. Important as is the public interest in the detection and punishment of tax frauds, it is not to be compared with the public interest in the right of men and women to be secure in the privacy of their homes, their offices, and their papers. Yet if the law is that no particulars of the offence or offences suspected, other than that they are offences of tax fraud, need be given, how can the householder, or occupier of premises, hope to obtain an effective judicial review of the entry, search and seizure at the time of the events or shortly thereafter? And telling the victim that long after the event he may go to law and recover damages if he can prove the revenue acted unlawfully is cold comfort—even if he can afford it.

It is therefore with regret that I have to accept that, if the requirements of section 20C of the Taxes Management Act 1970, a section which entered the law as an amendment introduced by section 57 of the Finance Act 1976, are met, the power exists to enter, and search premises, and seize and remove things there found and that the prospect of an immediate judicial review of the exercise of the power is dim. Nevertheless, what Lord Camden CJ said in *Entick* v *Carrington* (1765) 19 State Tr 1029, 1066, remains good law today:

> 'No man can set his foot upon my ground without my licence, but he is liable to an action, though the damage be nothing... If he admits the fact, he is bound to show by way of justification, that some positive law has empowered or excused him.'

The positive law relied on in this case is the statute. If the requirements of the statute have been met, there is justification: but, if they have not, there is none...

Appeals allowed.

NOTE: But where courts are asked to determine the legality of the exercise of a discretionary power conferred by a statute they have shown a readiness to impose limits derived from common law principles as the following case discloses. (See further, *R* v *Lord Chancellor, ex parte Witham* [1998] QB 575; *Chesterfield Properties plc* v *Secretary of State for the Environment* [1998] JPL 568; *R* v *Lord Saville, ex parte A* [1999] 4 All ER 860, p. 409, *post*).

R v *Secretary of State for the Home Department, ex parte Pierson*

[1998] AC 539, House of Lords

In 1985, P was convicted of the murder of his parents and received two mandatory life sentences to be served concurrently. Under the system then in operation in 1988 (Criminal Justice Act 1961, s. 61, subsequently the Criminal Justice Act 1991, s. 35(2), and now the Crime (Sentences) Act 1997, s. 29) the Home Secretary, on the basis that P had committed a double premeditated murder, fixed the penal element of the sentence (or 'tariff' which represents the period to be served to satisfy the requirements of retribution and deterrence) at 20 years which represented the minimum period P should serve before he could be considered for release on licence. (The trial judge and Lord Chief Justice had recommended a tariff of 15 years.) In accordance with the then practice the judicial recommendations on tariff, and reasons for the Home Secretary's departure from them, were not communicated to P, neither was he asked to make representations thereon.

In June 1993 the House of Lords ruled in *R* v *Secretary of State for the Home Department, ex parte Doody and Others* [1994] 1 AC 531 (P being one of the 'others') that before fixing the 'tariff' the Home Secretary was required to disclose to a prisoner the recommendations of the judiciary and provide an opportunity for the prisoner to make written representations. In July 1993 the then Home Secretary announced that the tariff period would be reviewed before any mandatory life sentence prisoner would be considered for release, and in exceptional cases it might be increased. In August 1993, P was informed of the judicial recommendations in his case and the Home Secretary's reason for recommending 20 years, namely that 15 years would have been appropriate for a single premeditated murder but that this was a double murder. In response P's solicitors indicated that the murders were part of a single incident and were unpremeditated. The Home Secretary responded in May 1994, accepting that the murders were part of a single incident and unpremeditated, but indicating that he considered 20 years the appropriate tariff. P applied by way of judicial review for an order of certiorari to quash the Home Secretary's decision on the grounds that it was irrational, representing, in effect, an increase in the period.

The House of Lords (by a majority of three to two) quashed the Home Secretary's decision, so as to confirm a tariff of 20 years originally fixed on the basis of aggravating factors which did not exist amounted to an increase in the tariff.

LORD STEYN: ...In public law the emphasis should be on substance rather than form. This case should also not be decided on a semantic quibble about whether the Home Secretary's function is strictly 'a sentencing exercise.' The undeniable fact is that in fixing a tariff in an individual case the Home Secretary is making a decision about the punishment of the convicted man....

That brings me to the question whether any legal consequences flow from the characterisation of the Home Secretary's function as involving a decision on punishment. It is a general principle of the common law that a lawful sentence pronounced by a judge may not retrospectively be increased. In 1971 that principle was put on a statutory basis.... The general principle of our law is therefore that a convicted criminal is entitled to know where he stands so far as his punishment is concerned. He is entitled to legal certainty about his punishment. His rights will be enforced by the courts. Under English law a convicted prisoner, in spite of his imprisonment, retains all civil rights which are not taken away expressly or by necessary implication: *Raymond* v *Honey* [1983] 1 AC 1, 10H. The question must now be considered whether the Home Secretary, in making a decision on punishment, is free from the normal constraint applicable to a sentencing power. It is at this stage of the examination of the problem that it becomes necessary to consider where in the structure of public law it fits in. Parliament has not expressly authorised the Home Secretary to increase tariffs retrospectively. If Parliament had done so that would have been the end of the matter. Instead Parliament has by section 35(2) of the Act of 1991 entrusted the power to take decisions about the release of mandatory life sentence prisoners to the Home Secretary. The statutory power is wide enough to authorise the fixing of a tariff. But it does not follow that it is wide enough to permit a power retrospectively to increase the level of punishment.

The wording of section 35(2) of the Act of 1991 is wide and general. It provides that 'the Secretary of State may...release on licence a life prisoner who is not a discretionary life prisoner.' There is no ambiguity in the statutory language. The presumption that in the event of ambiguity legislation is presumed not to invade common law rights is inapplicable. A broader principle applies. Parliament does not legislate in a vacuum. Parliament legislates for a European liberal democracy founded on the principles and traditions of the common law. And the courts may approach legislation on this initial assumption. But this assumption only has prima facie force. It can be displaced by a clear and specific provision to the contrary...

In his *Law of the Constitution*, 10th ed. (1959), Dicey explained the context in which Parliament legislates, at p. 414:

> 'By every path we come round to the same conclusion, that Parliament sovereignty has favoured the rule of law, and that the supremacy of the law of the land both calls forth the exertion of Parliamentary sovereignty, and leads to its being exercised in a spirit of legality.

...

The operation of the principle of legality can further be illustrated by reference to the decision of the House of Lords in *Reg.* v *Secretary of State for the Home Department, Ex parte Doody* [1994] 1 AC 531.

In that case the House of Lords held that the common law principles of procedural fairness required disclosure to a prisoner of the advice to the Home Secretary of the trial judge and of the Lord Chief Justice in order to enable the prisoner to make effective representations before the Home Secretary fixed the tariff. The premise was that Parliament must be presumed to have intended that the Home Secretary would act in conformity with the common law principle of procedural fairness. And our public law is, of course, replete with other instances of the common law so supplementing statutes on the basis of the principle of legality....

Turning back to the circumstances of the present case, it was easy to conclude that the legislation authorises the policy of fixing a tariff. The wide statutory discretion of the Home Secretary justified that conclusion. But a general power to increase tariffs lawfully fixed is qualitatively in a different category. It contemplates a power unheard of in our criminal justice system until the 1993 policy statement of the Home Secretary (Mr Michael Howard) (Hansard (HC Debates), 27 July 1993, cols. 861–864: written answer). Such a power is not essential to the efficient working of the system: without a power to increase tariffs the system worked satisfactorily between 1983 and 1993. But I do not rest my judgment on this point. The critical factor is that a general power to increase tariffs duly fixed is in disharmony with the deep rooted principle of not retrospectively increasing lawfully pronounced sentences. In the absence of contrary indications it must be presumed that Parliament entrusted the wide power to make decisions on the release of mandatory life sentence prisoners on the supposition that the Home Secretary would not act contrary to such a fundamental principle of our law. There are no contrary indications. Certainly, there is not a shred of evidence that Parliament would have been prepared to vest a general power in the Home Secretary to increase retrospectively tariffs duly fixed. The evidence is to the contrary. When Parliament enacted section 35(2) of the Act of 1991—the foundation of the Home Secretary's present power—Parliament knew that since 1983 successive Home Secretaries had adopted a policy of fixing in each case a tariff period, following which risk is considered. Parliament also knew that it was the practice that a tariff, once fixed, would not be increased. That was clear from the assurance in the 1983 policy statement (Mr Leon Brittan (Hansard (HC Debates), 30 November 1983, cols. 505–507: written answer) that 'except where a prisoner has committed an offence for which he has received a further custodial sentence, the formal review date will not be put back.' What Parliament did not know in 1991 was that in 1993 a new Home Secretary would assert a general power to increase the punishment of prisoners convicted of murder whenever he considered it right to do so. It would be wrong to assume that Parliament would have been prepared to give to the Home Secretary such an unprecedented power, alien to the principles of our law....

The correct analysis of this case is in terms of the rule of law. The rule of law in its wider sense has procedural and substantive effect.... Unless there is the clearest provision to the contrary, Parliament must be presumed not to legislate contrary to the rule of law. And the rule of law enforces minimum standards of fairness, both substantive and procedural. I therefore approach the problem in the present case on this basis.

It is true that the principle of legality only has prima facie force. But in enacting section 35(2) of the Act of 1991, with its very wide power to release prisoners, Parliament left untouched the fundamental principle that a sentence lawfully passed should not retrospectively be increased. Parliament must therefore be presumed to have enacted legislation wide enough to enable the Home Secretary to make decisions on punishment on the basis that he would observe the normal constraint governing that function. Instead the Home Secretary has asserted a general power to increase tariffs duly fixed. Parliament did not confer such a power on the Home Secretary.

It follows that the Home Secretary did not have the power to increase a tariff lawfully fixed....

It was agreed before your Lordships' House that the Home Secretary's decision letter of 6 May 1994 did communicate a decision to Mr Pierson to increase the tariff in his case. That decision was in my judgment unlawful and ought to be quashed. My conclusion is based on the proposition that the Home Secretary has no general power to increase a tariff fixed and communicated.

R v *Horseferry Road Magistrates' Court, ex parte Bennett*

[1994] AC 42, House of Lords

Bennett, a New Zealand citizen, was wanted by United Kingdom police for a series of offences allegedly committed by him. He was arrested in South Africa but there was no extradition treaty between South Africa and the United Kingdom. The South African police, however, placed him on an aircraft bound for London where he was arrested by English police officers. The magistrates committed Bennett to the Crown Court for trial. He applied for judicial review of their decision alleging that he had been returned to the jurisdiction against his will as a result of kidnapping or quasi-extradition. He further alleged that this had occurred at the request of the English police and that the South African police had placed him on the plane on the pretext of deporting him to New Zealand via London, thereby enabling English police to arrest him. Bennett contended that in these circumstances it would be an abuse of the process of the court to permit the prosecution to proceed. The Divisional Court dismissed his application for judicial review of the magistrates' decision on the basis that, even if he had been kidnapped and illegally removed from South Africa with the collusion of English police officers, the court had no jurisdiction to inquire into these matters and prevent a prosecution as these were not relevant to the issue of whether he would have a fair trial. The House of Lords (Lord Oliver dissenting) reversed the decision of the Divisional Court.

LORD GRIFFITHS: . . . Your Lordships have been urged by the respondents to uphold the decision of the Divisional Court and the nub of its submission is that the role of the judge is confined to the forensic process. The judge, it is said, is concerned to see that the accused has a fair trial and that the process of the court is not manipulated to his disadvantage so that the trial itself is unfair; but the wider issues of the rule of law and the behaviour of those charged with its enforcement, be they police or prosecuting authority, are not the concern of the judiciary unless they impinge directly on the trial process. In support of this submission your Lordships have been referred to *R* v *Sang* [1979] 2 All ER 1222 esp at 1230, 1245–1246, [1980] AC 402 esp at 436–437, 454–455 where Lord Diplock and Lord Scarman emphasise that the role of the judge is confined to the forensic process and that it is no part of the judge's function to exercise disciplinary powers over the police or the prosecution. . . .

[After examining the cases on abuse of process his Lordship continued:]

Your Lordships are now invited to extend the concept of abuse of process a stage further. In the present case there is no suggestion that the appellant cannot have a fair trial, nor could it be suggested that it would have been unfair to try him if he had been returned to this country through extradition procedures. If the court is to have the power to interfere with the prosecution in the present circumstances it must be because the judiciary accept a responsibility for the maintenance of the rule of law that embraces a willingness to oversee executive action and to refuse to countenance behaviour that threatens either basic human rights or the rule of law.

My Lords, I have no doubt that the judiciary should accept this responsibility in the field of criminal law. The great growth of administrative law during the latter half of this century has occurred because of the recognition by the judiciary and Parliament alike that it is the function of the High Court to ensure that executive action is exercised responsibly and as Parliament intended. So also should it be in the field of criminal law and if it comes to the attention of the court that there has been a serious abuse of power it should, in my view, express its disapproval by refusing to act upon it.

. . .

The courts, of course, have no power to apply direct discipline to the police or the prosecuting authorities, but they can refuse to allow them to take advantage of abuse of power by regarding their behaviour as an abuse of process and thus preventing a prosecution.

LORD BRIDGE OF HARWICH: . . . There is, I think, no principle more basic to any proper system of law than the maintenance of the rule of law itself. When it is shown that the law enforcement agency responsible for bringing a prosecution has only been enabled to do so by participating in violations of international law and of the laws of another state in order to secure the presence of the accused within the territorial jurisdiction of the court, I think that respect for the rule of law demands that the court take cognisance of that circumstance. To hold that the court may turn a blind eye to executive lawlessness beyond the frontiers of its own jurisdiction is, to my mind, an insular and unacceptable view. Having then taken cognisance of the lawlessness it would again appear to be a wholly inadequate response for the court to hold that the only remedy lies in civil proceedings at the suit of the defendant or in disciplinary or criminal proceedings against the individual officers of the law enforcement agency who were concerned in the illegal action taken. Since the prosecution could never have been brought if the defendant had not been illegally abducted, the whole proceeding is tainted. If a resident in another country is properly extradited here, the time when the prosecution commences is the time when the authorities here set the extradition process in motion. By parity of reasoning, if the authorities, instead of proceeding by way of extradition, have resorted to abduction, that is the effective commencement of the prosecution process and is the illegal foundation on which it rests....

Appeal allowed. Case remitted to Divisional Court for further consideration.

NOTES

1. While *Entick* v *Carrington*, *ex parte Pierson* and *ex parte Bennett* demonstrate exemplary respect for the rule of law, the legality principle and the rejection of the ends justifying the means, it could be argued that there are circumstances in which utilitarian concerns of dealing with, for example, terrorist threats might justify increasing the scope of action afforded to the State and its agents in taking protective action. This has been particularly acute in the UK in countering terrorism, first in relation to Ireland and the IRA and currently Al Q'ueada and other Islamist extremists.
2. In Northern Ireland in 1971, powers granted under the Civil Authorities (Special Powers) Act (NI) 1922 were exercised by the Northern Ireland government to intern persons suspected of having acted or being about to act in a manner prejudicial to the preservation of peace or the maintenance of order. Some of those interned were interrogated by the security forces. The Crompton Report (Cmnd 4823, 1971) detailed the interrogation procedures as including keeping the detainees' heads covered with hoods; subjecting them to continuous monotonous noise; deprivation of sleep; deprivation of food and water, apart from meagre rations of bread and water at six-hourly intervals; and making the detainees stand facing a wall with legs apart and hands raised. Three Privy Councillors (Lord Parker of Waddington, a former Lord Chief Justice, J. A. Carpenter, a former Cabinet Minister, and Lord Gardiner, a former Lord Chancellor) were given the task of examining these procedures. They failed to agree and produced two conflicting reports. The majority, in *Report of the Committee of Privy Councillors Appointed to Consider Authorised Procedures or the Interrogation of Persons Suspected of Terrorism* (Cmnd 4901, 1972), recommended that the interrogation techniques were acceptable in the light of the prevailing conditions and subject to safeguards which would limit the number of incidences of use and the degree to which they can be applied. The authority of a UK government minister would be required to use them, and a doctor with psychiatric training should be present to observe and warn if the interrogation was being pressed too far, and there should be a procedure for the investigation of complaints. Lord Gardiner in his minority report found that the techniques were unlawful, morally repugnant and contrary to international developments in the protection of human rights. The Government eventually accepted Lord Gardiner's view, and the interrogation techniques were discontinued. The issue of interrogation of internees was taken in an inter-State application to the European Court of Human Rights. In *Ireland* v *United Kingdom* (1978) 2 EHRR 25, it was alleged that the techniques breached Art. 3. The Court held that they amounted to inhuman and degrading treatment contrary to Art. 3 but did not constitute torture.
3. More recently the House of Lords has ruled on the issue of whether evidence is admissible if it was produced by third parties not under the control of the British government using torture *A* v *Secretary of State for the Home Department (No. 2)* [2005] UKHL 71, [2006] 2 AC 221. Their Lordships ruled that such evidence was inadmissible but differed on the test to be used to decide admissibility where it was argued that torture had been used. The majority, Lords Hope, Carswell, Rodger and Brown of Eaton-Under-Heywood, followed the approach in the United Nations Convention Against Torture and Other Cruel Inhuman or Degrading Treatment or Punishment (1987), art. 15. The test for admissibility is, according to Lord Rodger [121]:

> Is it *established*, by means of such diligent inquiries into the sources that it is practicable to carry out and on a balance of probabilities, that the information relied on by the Secretary of State *was* obtained under torture?

For the minority of Lords Bingham, Nicholls and Hoffmann, the test expressed by Lord Bingham at [56] is that if after considering the particular facts and circumstance it

> is unable to conclude that there is not a real risk that the evidence has been obtained by torture, it should refuse to admit the evidence. Otherwise it should admit it.

4. As will be seen in Chapter 9, *post*, the United Kingdom has, through the Human Rights Act 1988, incorporated into domestic law many of the rights in the European Convention of Human Rights (ECHR) which includes in art 3 a prohibition on torture, inhuman and degrading treatment or punishment.
5. The idea of government according to law has been illustrated in a range of decisions by the courts developing the principles of *ultra vires* (Chapter 10, *post*) and natural justice (Chapter 10, *post*) which are the central doctrines in administrative law. By development of these doctrines the courts have sought to control the ways in which authorities exercise their powers and the procedures they adopt. Thus the exercise of a power by an authority will be struck down as *ultra vires* where the authority acts in excess of the power (see, e.g. *Laker Airways Ltd* v *Department of Trade* [1977] QB 643), or it abuses the power by exercising it ignoring relevant considerations or taking irrelevant considerations into account (see, e.g. *Associated Provincial Picture Houses Ltd* v *Wednesbury Corporation* [1948] 1 KB 223), or where it exercises the power for an improper purpose (see, e.g. *Roberts* v *Hopwood* [1925] AC 578), or it exercises the power unreasonably (*Wednesbury, ante*). Where powers are exercised courts may also impose procedural requirements upon the authority exercising the power to ensure that the decision to exercise the power was taken in accordance with the rules of natural justice or, more recently, that the decision respected the requirements of fairness. Thus the decision-maker should be unbiased and the subject of the decision should have had a fair hearing. What is fair may vary with the circumstances, but matters which will be taken into account are whether the subject received adequate notice of the hearing and the charges, was allowed to present his case in a written or oral form and call witnesses, and whether he was allowed legal representation.
6. In *R (Corner House Research)* v *Director of Serious Fraud Office* [2008] UKHL 60, [2008] 4 All ER 927 the House of Lords considered the legality of the decision by the Director of the Serious Fraud Office to discontinue an investigation into allegations of bribery by BAE Systems plc (BAE) in relation to the Al-Yamamah military aircraft contracts with the Kingdom of Saudi Arabia. Ministers had been informed by Saudi representatives that if the investigation did not stop, then there would be consequences which included ceasing Saudi co-operation with the United Kingdom over intelligence. The assessment of this threat recorded in a minute from the Prime Minister to the Attorney General and the Director was that it

> risks endangering UK national security, both directly in protecting citizens and service people, and indirectly through impeding our search for peace and stability in this critical part of the world.

The Director decided that it not in the public interest to continue the investigation. This was successfully challenged in the Divisional Court [2008] EWHC 714 (Admin) which concluded:

> 170. The claimants succeed on the ground that the Director and Government failed to recognise that the rule of law required the decision to discontinue to be reached as an exercise of independent judgment, in pursuance of the power conferred by statute. To preserve the integrity and independence of that judgment demanded resistance to the pressure exerted by means of a specific threat. That threat was intended to prevent the Director from pursuing the course of investigation he had chosen to adopt. It achieved its purpose.
>
> 171. The court has a responsibility to secure the rule of law. The Director was required to satisfy the court that all that could reasonably be done had been done to resist the threat. He has failed to do so. He submitted too readily because he, like the executive, concentrated on the effects which were feared should the threat be carried out and not on how the threat might be resisted. No-one, whether within this country or outside is entitled to interfere with the course of our justice. It is the failure of Government and the defendant to bear that essential principle in mind that justifies the intervention of this court. We shall hear further argument as to the nature of such intervention. But we intervene in fulfilment of our responsibility to protect the independence of the Director and of our criminal justice system from threat. On 11 December 2006, the Prime Minister said that this was the clearest case for intervention in the public interest he had seen. We agree.

Their Lordships disagreed with the Divisional court In the words of Lord Bingham:

> 41. The Director was confronted by an ugly and obviously unwelcome threat. He had to decide what, if anything, he should do. He did not surrender his discretionary power of decision to any

third party, although he did consult the most expert source available to him in the person of the Ambassador and he did, as he was entitled if not bound to do, consult the Attorney General who, however, properly left the decision to him. The issue in these proceedings is not whether his decision was right or wrong, nor whether the Divisional Court or the House agrees with it, but whether it was a decision which the Director was lawfully entitled to make. Such an approach involves no affront to the rule of law, to which the principles of judicial review give effect (see *R (Alconbury Developments Ltd)* v *Secretary of State for the Environment, Transport and the Regions* [2001] UKHL 23, [2003] 2 AC 295, para. 73, per Lord Hoffmann).

42. In the opinion of the House the Director's decision was one he was lawfully entitled to make. It may indeed be doubted whether a responsible decision-maker could, on the facts before the Director, have decided otherwise.

While these developments may help protect the citizen from the arbitrary exercise of power, do they have any effect on the legislature in controlling the laws it may pass and, therefore, the powers it may bestow upon government and other official agencies?

SECTION 3: THE RULE OF LAW AS A BROAD POLITICAL DOCTRINE

A. W. Bradley and K. D. Ewing, *Constitutional and Administrative Law* (15th edn, 2011), p. 97, state:

If the law is not to be merely a means of achieving whatever ends a particular government may favour, the rule of law must go beyond the principle of legality. The experience and values of the legal system are relevant not only to the question, 'What legal authority *does* the government have for its acts?' but also to the question, 'What legal powers *ought* the government to have?'

Several other writers have sought to specify certain minimum standards which laws should attain.

J. Raz, 'The Rule of Law and its Virtue'

(1977) 93 *Law Quarterly Review* 195–202

. . . The rule of law is a political ideal which a legal system may lack or may possess to a greater or lesser degree. That much is common ground. It is also to be insisted that the rule of law is just one of the virtues which a legal system may possess and by which it is to be judged. It is not to be confused with democracy, justice, equality (before the law or otherwise), human rights of any kind or respect for persons or for the dignity of man. A non-democratic legal system, based on the denial of human rights, on extensive poverty, on racial segregation, sexual inequalities and religious persecution may, in principle, conform to the requirements of the rule of law better than any of the legal systems of the more enlightened western democracies. This does not mean that it will be better than those western democracies. It will be an immeasurably worse legal system, but it will excel in one respect: in its conformity to the rule of law. . . .

1. The Basic Idea

'The rule of law' means literally what it says: The rule of the law. Taken in its broadest sense this means that people should obey the law and be ruled by it. But in political and legal theory it has come to be read in a narrower sense, that the government shall be ruled by the law and subject to it. The ideal of the rule of law in this sense is often expressed by the phrase 'government by law and not by men.' No sooner does one use these formulae than their obscurity becomes evident. Surely government must be both by law and by men. It is said that the rule of law means that all government action must have foundation in law, must be authorised by law. But is not that a tautology? Actions not authorised by law cannot be the actions of the government as a government. They would be without legal effect and often unlawful. . . . There is more to the rule of law than the law and order interpretation allows. It means more even than law and order applied to the government. I shall proceed on the assumption that we are concerned with government in the legal sense and with the conception of the rule of law which applies to government and to law and is no mere application of the law and order conception.

The problem is that now we are back with our initial puzzle. If the government is, by definition, government authorised by law the rule of law seems to amount to an empty tautology, not a political ideal.

The solution to this riddle is in the difference between the professional and the lay sense of law. For the lawyer anything is the law if it meets the conditions of validity laid down in the system's rules of recognition or in other rules of the system. This includes the constitution, parliamentary legislation, ministerial regulations, policeman's orders, the regulations of limited companies, conditions imposed in trading licences, etc. To the layman the law consists only of a subclass of these. To him the law is essentially a set of open, general and relatively stable laws. Government by law and not by men is not a tautology if 'law' means general, open and relatively stable law. In fact the danger of this interpretation is that the rule of law might set too strict a requirement, one which no legal system can meet and which embodies very little virtue. It is humanly inconceivable that law can consist only of general rules and it is very undesirable that it should. Just as we need government both by laws and by men, so we need both general and particular laws to carry out the jobs for which we need the law.

The doctrine of the rule of law does not deny that every legal system should consist of both general, open and stable rules (the popular conception of law) and particular laws (legal orders), an essential tool in the hands of the executive and the judiciary alike. As we shall see, what the doctrine requires is the subjection of particular laws to general, open and stable ones. It is one of the important principles of the doctrine that the *making of particular laws should be guided by open and relatively stable general rules*.

This principle shows how the slogan of the rule of law and not of men can be read as a meaningful political ideal. The principle does not, however, exhaust the meaning of the rule of law and does not by itself illuminate the reasons for its alleged importance. Let us, therefore, return to the literal sense of the 'rule of law.' It has two aspects: (1) that people should be ruled by the law and obey it, and (2) that the law should be such that people will be able to be guided by it. As was noted above, it is with the second aspect that we are concerned: the law must be capable of being obeyed. A person conforms with the law to the extent that he does not break the law. But he obeys the law only if part of his reason for conforming is his knowledge of the law. Therefore, if the law is to be obeyed it *must be capable of guiding the behaviour* of its subjects. It must be such that they can find out what it is and act on it.

This is the basic intuition from which the doctrine of the rule of law derives: the law must be capable of guiding the behaviour of its subjects. It is evident that this conception of the rule of law is a formal one. It says nothing about how the law is to be made: by tyrants, democratic majorities or any other way. It says nothing about fundamental rights, about equality or justice. It may even be thought that this version of the doctrine is formal to the extent that it is almost devoid of content. This is far from the truth. Most of the requirements which were associated with the rule of law before it came to signify all the virtues of the state can be derived from this one basic idea.

2. Some Principles

Many of the principles which can be derived from the basic idea of the rule of law depend for their validity or importance on the particular circumstances of different societies. There is little point in trying to enumerate them all, but some of the more important ones might be mentioned:

(1) *All laws should be prospective, open and clear.* One cannot be guided by a retroactive law. It does not exist at the time of action. Sometimes it is then known for certain that a retroactive law will be enacted. When this happens retroactivity does not conflict with the rule of law (though it may be objected to on other grounds). The law must be open and adequately publicised. If it is to guide people they must be able to find out what it is. For the same reason its meaning must be clear. An ambiguous, vague, obscure or imprecise law is likely to mislead or confuse at least some of those who desire to be guided by it.

(2) *Laws should be relatively stable.* They should not be changed too often. If they are frequently changed people will find it difficult to find out what the law is at any given moment and will be constantly in fear that the law has been changed since they last learnt what it is. But more important still is the fact that people need to know the law not only for short-term decisions (where to park one's car, how much alcohol is allowed in duty free, etc.) but also for long-term planning. Knowledge of at least the general outlines and sometimes even of details of tax law and company law are often important for business plans which will bear fruit only years later. Stability is essential if people are to be guided by law in their long-term decisions....

(3) *The making of particular laws (particular legal orders) should be guided by open, stable, clear and general rules*. It is sometimes assumed that the requirement of generality is of the essence of the rule of law. This notion derives (as noted above) from the literal interpretation of 'the rule of law' when 'law' is read in its lay connotations as being restricted to general, stable and open law. It is also reinforced by a belief that the rule of law is particularly relevant to the protection of equality and that equality is related to the generality of law. The last belief is, as has been often noted before, mistaken. Racial, religious and all manner of discrimination is not only compatible but often institutionalised by general rules.

The formal conception of the rule of law which I am defending does not object to particular legal orders as long as they are stable, clear, etc. But of course particular legal orders are mostly used by government agencies to introduce flexibility into the law. A police constable regulating traffic, a licensing authority granting a licence under certain conditions, all these and their like are among the more ephemeral parts of the law. As such they run counter to the basic idea of the rule of law. They make it difficult for people to plan ahead on the basis of their knowledge of the law. This difficulty is overcome to a large extent if particular laws of an ephemeral status are enacted only within a framework set by general laws which are more durable and which impose limits on the unpredictability introduced by the particular orders.

Two kinds of general rules create the framework for the enactment of particular laws: Those which confer the necessary powers for making valid orders and those which impose duties instructing the power-holders how to exercise their powers. Both have equal importance in creating a stable framework for the creation of particular legal orders.

Clearly, similar considerations apply to general legal regulations which do not meet the requirement of stability. They too should be circumscribed to conform to a stable framework. Hence the requirement that much of the subordinate administrative law-making should be made to conform to detailed ground rules laid down in framework laws. It is essential, however, not to confuse this argument with democratic arguments for the close supervision of popularly-elected bodies over law-making by non-elected ones. These further arguments may be valid but have nothing to do with the rule of law, and though sometimes they reinforce rule of law type arguments, on other occasions they support different and even conflicting conclusions.

(4) *The independence of the judiciary must be guaranteed*. It is of the essence of municipal legal systems that they institute judicial bodies charged, among other things, with the duty of applying the law to cases brought before them and whose judgments and conclusions as to the legal merits of those cases are final. Since just about any matter arising under any law can be subject to a conclusive court judgment it is obvious that it is futile to guide one's action on the basis of the law if when the matter comes to adjudication the courts will not apply the law and will act for some other reasons. The point can be put even more strongly. Since the court's judgment establishes conclusively what is the law in the case before it, the litigants can be guided by law only if the judges apply the law correctly. Otherwise people will only be able to be guided by their guesses as to what the courts are likely to do—but these guesses will not be based on the law but on other considerations.

The rules concerning the independence of the judiciary—the method of appointing judges, their security of tenure, the way of fixing their salaries and other conditions of service—are designed to guarantee that they will be free from extraneous pressures and independent of all authority save that of the law. They are, therefore, essential for the preservation of the rule of law.

(5) *The principles of natural justice must be observed*. Open and fair hearing, absence of bias and the like are obviously essential for the correct application of the law and thus, through the very same considerations mentioned above, to its ability to guide action.

(6) *The courts should have review powers over the implementation of the other principles*. This includes review of both subordinate and parliamentary legislation and of administrative action, but in itself it is a very limited review—merely to ensure conformity to the rule of law.

(7) *The courts should be easily accessible*. Given the central position of the courts in ensuring the rule of law (see principles 4 and 6) it is obvious that their accessibility is of paramount importance. Long delays, excessive costs, etc., may effectively turn the most enlightened law to a dead letter and frustrate one's ability effectively to guide oneself by the law.

(8) *The discretion of the crime preventing agencies should not be allowed to pervert the law*. Not only the courts but also the actions of the police and the prosecuting authorities can subvert the law. The

prosecution should not be allowed, e.g. to decide not to prosecute for commission of certain crimes, or for crimes committed by certain classes of offenders. The police should not be allowed to allocate its resources so as to avoid all effort to prevent and detect certain crimes or prosecute certain classes of criminals.

This list is very incomplete. Other principles could be mentioned and those which have been mentioned need further elaboration and further justification (why—as required by my sixth principle—should the courts and not some other body be in charge of reviewing conformity to the rule of law? etc.). My purpose in listing them was merely to illustrate the power and fruitfulness of the formal conception of the rule of law. It should, however, be remembered that in the final analysis the doctrine rests on its basic idea that the law should be capable of providing effective guidance. The principles do not stand on their own. They must be constantly interpreted in light of the basic idea.

The eight principles listed fall into two groups. Principles 1 to 3 require that the law should conform to standards designed to enable it effectively to guide action. Principles 4 to 8 are designed to ensure that the legal machinery of enforcing the law should not deprive it of its ability to guide through distorted enforcement and that it shall be capable of supervising conformity to the rule of law and provide effective remedies in cases of deviation from it. All the principles directly concern the system and method of government in matters directly relevant to the rule of law. Needlesss to say many other aspects in the life of a community may, in more indirect ways, either strengthen or weaken the rule of law. A free press run by people anxious to defend the rule of law is of great assistance in preserving it, just as a gagged press or one run by people wishing to undermine the rule of law is a threat to it. But we need not be concerned here with these more indirect influences.

NOTE: See also Lon. L. Fuller, *The Morality of Law* (2nd edn, 1969).

Some of the principles identified by Raz are given judicial expression in the cases which follow.

A: Laws should be clear

Merkur Island Shipping Corp. v *Laughton and Others*

[1983] 2 AC 570, Court of Appeal

In an action arising from a trade dispute between the owners and crew of a ship, members of the International Transport Workers' Federation were sued for damages for losses arising from secondary industrial action in which they had been involved. In deciding whether a trade union was immune from tortious liability, the court had to construe three statutes: the Trade Union and Labour Relations Act 1974, the Trade Union and Labour Relations (Amendment) Act 1976, and the Employment Act 1980.

LORD DONALDSON MR: ... At the beginning of this judgment I said that whilst I had reached the conclusion that the law was tolerably clear, the same could not be said of the way in which it was expressed. The efficacy and maintenance of the rule of law, which is the foundation of any parliamentary democracy, has at least two pre-requisites. First, people must understand that it is in their interests, as well as in that of the community as a whole, that they should live their lives in accordance with the rules and all the rules. Second, they must know what those rules are. Both are equally important and it is the second aspect of the rule of law which has caused me concern in the present case, the ITF having disavowed any intention to break the law.

In industrial relations it is of vital importance that the worker on the shop floor, the shop steward, the local union official, the district officer and the equivalent levels in management should know what is and what is not 'offside.' And they must be able to find this out for themselves by reading plain and simple words of guidance. The judges of this court are all skilled lawyers of very considerable experience, yet it has taken us hours to ascertain what is and what is not 'offside,' even with the assistance of highly experienced counsel. This cannot be right.

We have had to look at three Acts of Parliament, none intelligible without the other. We have had to consider section 17 of the Act of 1980, which adopts the 'flow' method of Parliamentary draftsmanship, without the benefit of a flow diagram. We have furthermore been faced with the additional complication that subsection (6) of section 17 contains definitions which distort the natural meaning of the words in the operative subsections. It was not always like this. If you doubt me, look at the comparative simplicity and clarity of Sir Mackenzie Chalmers's Sale of Goods Act 1893, his Bills of Exchange Act 1882, and his Marine Insurance Act 1906. But I do not criticise the draftsman. His instructions may well have left him no option. My plea is that Parliament, when legislating in respect of circumstances which directly affect the 'man or woman in the street' or the 'man or woman on the shop floor' should give as high a priority to clarity and simplicity of expression as to refinements of policy. Where possible, statutes, or complete parts of statutes, should not be amended but re-enacted in an amended form so that those concerned can read the rules in a single document. When formulating policy, ministers, of whatever political persuasion, should at all times be asking themselves and asking parliamentary counsel: 'Is this concept too refined to be capable of expression in basic English? If so, is there some way in which we can modify the policy so that it can be so expressed?' Having to ask such questions would no doubt be frustrating for ministers and the legislature generally, but in my judgment this is part of the price which has to be paid if the rule of law is to be maintained.

These sentiments were echoed by Lord Diplock in the House of Lords, at p. 612:

LORD DIPLOCK: ...I see no reason for doubting that those upon whom the responsibility for deciding whether and if so what industrial action shall be taken in any given circumstances wish to obey the law, even though it be a law which they themselves dislike and hope will be changed through the operation of this country's constitutional system of parliamentary democracy. But what the law is, particularly in the field of industrial relations, ought to be plain. It should be expressed in terms that can be easily understood by those who have to apply it even at shop floor level. I echo everything that the Master of the Rolls has said in the last three paragraphs of his judgment in this case. Absence of clarity is destructive of the rule of law; it is unfair to those who wish to preserve the rule of law; it encourages those who wish to undermine it. The statutory provisions which it became necessary to piece together into a coherent whole in order to decide the stage 3 point are drafted in a manner which, having regard to their subject matter and the persons who will be called upon to apply them, can, in my view, only be characterised as most regrettably lacking in the requisite degree of clarity.

B: Laws should be prospective

Phillips v Eyre

(1870) LR 6 QB 1, Exchequer Chamber

The legislature of Jamaica had passed an Indemnity Act following the suppression of a rebellion in the colony. If the Act was valid it would prevent the claimant suing for assault and false imprisonment.

WILLES J: ...Retrospective laws are, no doubt, prima facie of questionable policy, and contrary to the general principle that legislation by which the conduct of mankind is to be regulated ought, when introduced for the first time, to deal with future acts, and ought not to change the character of past transactions carried on upon the faith of the then existing law.... Accordingly, the Court will not ascribe retrospective force to new laws affecting rights, unless by express words or necessary implication it appears that such was the intention of the legislature....

In fine, allowing the general inexpediency of retrospective legislation, it cannot be pronounced naturally or necessarily unjust. There may be occasions and circumstances involving the safety of the state, or even the conduct of individual subjects, the justice of which, prospective laws made for ordinary occasions and the usual exigencies of society for want of prevision fails to meet, and in which the execution of the law as it stood at the time may involve practical public inconvenience and wrong, summum jus summa injuria. Whether the circumstances of the particular case are such as to call for special and exceptional remedy is a question which must in each case involve matter of policy and discretion fit for debate and decision in the parliament which would have had jurisdiction to deal with the subject-matter by preliminary legislation, and as to which a court of ordinary municipal law is not commissioned to inquire or adjudicate.

NOTE: See also *R v Secretary of State for the Home Department, ex parte Pierson* [1998] AC 539, p. 98, *ante*.

■ QUESTIONS

1. Can the doctrine of the rule of law prevent Parliament enacting retrospective laws? (See War Damage Act 1965, enacted pursuant to *Burmah Oil Co* v *Lord Advocate* [1965] AC 75, p. 57, *ante*.)
2. Is Lord Reid's confidence misplaced when he states in *Waddington* v *Miah* [1974] 2 All ER 377, at p. 379, that 'it is hardly credible that any government department would promote or that Parliament would pass retrospective criminal legislation'? See s. 1 of the War Crimes Act 1991, which provides:

'1. Jurisdiction over certain war crimes

(1) Subject to the provisions of this section, proceedings for murder, manslaughter or culpable homicide may be brought against a person in the United Kingdom irrespective of his nationality at the time of the alleged offence if that offence—

(a) was committed during the period beginning with 1st September 1939 and ending with 5th June 1945 in a place which at the time was part of Germany or under German occupation; and

(b) constituted a violation of the laws and customs of war.

(2) No proceedings shall by virtue of this section be brought against any person unless he was on 8th March 1990, or has subsequently become, a British citizen or resident in the United Kingdom, the Isle of Man or any of the Channel Islands.'

(Retrospective penal legislation contravenes Art. 7 of the European Convention on Human Rights.)

C: The independence of the judiciary must be guaranteed

The maintenance of the independence of the judiciary is essential if the rule of law is to be respected. In his presidential address to the Holdsworth Club in 1950, Lord Justice Denning, as he then was, stated:

> No member of the Government, no Member of Parliament and no official of any government department has any right whatever to direct or influence or to interfere with the decisions of any of the judges. It is the sure knowledge of this that gives the people their confidence in judges.... The critical test which they must pass if they are to receive the confidence of the people is that they must be independent of the executive.

NOTE: We will look more closely at this topic in Chapter 4 where we will consider the provisions of the Constitutional Reform Act 2005 which declares a continued guarantee of judicial independence (s. 1) and has changed the arrangements for the appointment and discipline of the judiciary and established after 2009 a new Supreme Court of the United Kingdom separating the final court of appeal and its judges from the legislature. It also declares that the statute does not adversely affect the rule of law (s. 3).

Our consideration of the rule of law will now switch focus from *formal* to *substantive* aspects.

P. Craig, The Rule of Law

Sixth Report from the House of Lords Select Committee on the Constitution, HL 151 of 2006–07, 97, 100–106

> The rule of law as presented thus far is not concerned with the actual content of the law, in the sense of whether the law is just or unjust, provided that the formal precepts of the rule of law are themselves met. To put the same point in another way, it is necessary on this view to consider the content of the law

in order to decide whether it complies with the precepts of the rule of law concerning clarity, generality, non-retrospectivity etc, but provided that it does so comply then that is the end of the inquiry.

The rationale for restricting the rule of law in this manner is as follows. [Raz, (1977) 93 *LQR* 195.] We may all agree that laws should be just, that their content should be morally sound and that rights should be protected within society. The problem is that if the rule of law is taken to encompass the necessity for 'good laws' in this sense then the concept ceases to have an independent function. There is a wealth of literature which should subsist therein, and the appropriate boundaries of governmental action. Political theory has tackled questions such as these from time immemorial. To bring these issues within the rubric of the rule of law would therefore rob this concept of an independent function. Laws would be condemned or upheld as being in conformity with, or contrary to, the rule of law when the condemnation or praise would simply be reflective of attachment to a particular conception of rights, democracy or the just society. The message is therefore that if you wish to argue about the justness of society do so by all means. If you wish to defend a particular type of individual right then present your argument. Draw upon the wealth of literature which addresses these matters directly. It is however on this view not necessary or desirable to cloak the conclusion in the mantle of the rule of law, since this will merely reflect the conclusion which has already been arrived at through reliance on a particular theory of rights or the just society.

(c) The Rule of Law, Justice and Accountable Government

The view presented above has however been challenged. Those who support the opposing view accept that the rule of law has the attributes mentioned in the previous section, but they argue that the concept has more far-reaching implications. Certain rights are said to be based on, or derived from, the rule of law. The concept is used as the foundation for these rights, which are then used to evaluate the quality of the laws produced by the legislature and courts.

It has also been argued that the rule of law provides the foundation for the controls exercised by the courts over governmental action through judicial review. In this sense the rule of law is expressive of how the state ought to behave towards individuals in society. The rule of law is said to demand that governmental action conforms to precepts of good administration developed through the courts, this being an essential facet of accountable government in a democratic society. The constraints imposed on government through judicial review are in part procedural and in part substantive. The range of these principles varies, but normally includes ideas such as: legality, procedural propriety, participation, fundamental rights, openness, rationality, relevancy, propriety of purpose, reasonableness, equality, legitimate expectations, legal certainty and proportionality. There has been a vibrant academic debate as to whether such principles must be legitimated by reference to legislative intent. There is nonetheless general agreement that it is the courts that have developed the principles of judicial review over the past 350 years.

This general view has been advanced by a number of writers and judges, although the precise detail of their analyses differ.

Thus Dworkin has argued forcefully that subject to questions of 'fit', the courts should decide legal questions according to the best theory of justice, which is central to the resolution of what rights people currently possess.[R. Dworkin, *Law's Empire* (1986)] According to this theory, 'propositions of law are true if they figure in or follow from the principles of justice, fairness and procedural due process that provide the best constructive interpretation of the community's legal practice'. It is integral to the Dworkinian approach that, subject to questions of fit, the court should choose between 'eligible interpretations by asking which shows the community's structure of institutions as a whole in a better light from the standpoint of political is forthcoming from the application of the above test.

Dworkin accepts the formal idea of the rule of law set out above, labelling this the 'rule book' conception. This requires that the government should never exercise power against individuals except in accordance with rules which have been set out in advance and made available to all. [R. Dworkin, *A Matter of Principle* (1985)] Such values feature in any serious theory of justice. However as Dworkin notes, this says little if anything about the content of the laws which exist within a legal system. Those who restrict the rule of law in this manner care about the content of the law, but regard this as a matter of substantive justice, which is 'an independent ideal, in no sense part of the ideal of the rule of law'.

Dworkin argues that we should however also recognise a rights-based conception of the rule of law. On this view citizens have moral rights and duties with respect to one another, and political rights against the state. These moral and political rights should be recognised in positive law, so that they can be enforced by citizens through the courts. The rule of law on this conception is the ideal of rule by an accurate public conception of individual rights. In the words of Dworkin, this view of the rule of law 'does not distinguish, as the rule book conception does, between the rule of law and substantive justice; on the contrary it requires, as part of the ideal of law, that the rules in the book capture and enforce moral rights'. It does not mean that this conception of the rule of law is consistent with only one theory of justice or freedom. There is no such argument. It does mean that it is not independent of the particular theory of justice, or vision of freedom, which constitutes its content at any point in time.

Similar themes have been advanced by Sir John Laws, writing extra-judicially. In an important series of articles he articulated the role of the courts in the protection of fundamental rights. [J. Laws, 'Is the High Court the Guardian of Fundamental Constitutional Rights' [1993] *Public Law* 59; 'Law and Democracy' [1995] *Public Law* 72; 'The Constitution: Morals and Rights' [1996] *Public Law* 622] The detailed nature of the argument is not of immediate concern to us here. Suffice it to say for the present that Sir John Laws presented an essentially rights-based conception of law and the role of the judge in cases involving fundamental rights. He posited a higher order law which was binding on the elected Parliament, with the courts as the guardian of both fundamental individual rights, and what may be termed structural constitutional rights. The thesis is premised on a particular conception of liberalism and individual autonomy, with a divide drawn between positive and negative rights. The rule of law is held to encompass an attachment to freedom, certainty and fairness. The first of these elements is the substantive component of the rule of law, while the second and the third bring in the more traditional attributes of the formal rule of law.

The important recent lecture by Lord Bingham on the rule of law is also relevant in this regard, more especially because it was given against the background of the Constitutional Reform Act 2005. [Lord Bingham, 'The Rule of Law' (2007) 68 *Cambridge Law Journal* 67] Lord Bingham articulates eight principles that comprise the rule of law. Certain of these principles address the more formal dimensions of the rule of law. These include the idea that the law must be accessible, and so far as possible, intelligible, clear and predictable; that questions of legal right and liability should ordinarily be resolved by application of the law and not the exercise of discretion; and that means should be provided for resolving without prohibitive cost or inordinate delay bona fide civil disputes which the parties themselves are unable to resolve.

It is however clear that Lord Bingham considers the rule of law as extending beyond these basic precepts. He regards it as including the central idea that the laws of the land should apply equally to all, save to the extent that objective differences justify differentiation, and that it demands that the law must afford adequate protection for fundamental rights. Lord Bingham expressly confronts the objection advanced by Raz to the inclusion of fundamental rights within the rubric of the rule of law, but disagrees with him in the following terms.

A state which savagely repressed or persecuted sections of its people could not in my view be regarded as observing the rule of law, even if the transport of the persecuted minority to the concentration camp or the compulsory exposure of the female children on the mountainside were the subject of detailed laws duly enacted and scrupulously observed. So to hold would, I think, be to strip the existing constitutional principle affirmed by section 1 of the 2005 Act of much of its virtue and infringe the fundamental compact which... underpins the rule of law. It is equally clear that Lord Bingham views the principles of judicial review as having their foundation in the rule of law. Thus he states that 'ministers and public officers at all levels must exercise the powers conferred on them reasonably, in good faith, for the purpose for which the powers were conferred and without exceeding the limits of such powers', and 'adjudicative procedures provided by the state should be fair'.

Jowell has also articulated a view of the rule of law, which has both a formal and a substantive dimension. [The Rule of Law Today', in Jowell and Oliver (eds.), *The Changing Constitution,* (6th ed., 2007)] He accepts that one must be careful about equating the rule of law with the substance of particular rules. He accepts also that a significant part of the rule of law is concerned with procedure or form as opposed to substance. Jowell does however believe that the rule of law has a substantive dimension. He perceives the rule of law as a principle of institutional morality and as a constraint on the uninhibited exercise of government power. The practical implementation of the rule of law takes place primarily through judicial review. Its substantive dimension is manifest in the judiciary's willingness to strike down administrative or executive action if it is unreasonable, arbitrary or capricious.

Allan's interpretation of the rule of law also contains an admixture of formal and substantive elements. [TRS Allan, Constitutional Justice, *A Liberal Theory of the Rule of Law* (2001)] He argues that we should go beyond the formal conception of the rule of law, but that we should stop short of regarding the rule of law as the expression of any particular theory of substantive justice. The rule of law on this view does not entail commitment to any particular vision of the public good or any specific conception of social justice, but does require that all legal obligations be justified by appeal to some such vision. The rule of law should embrace, in addition to its formal attributes, ideals of equality and rationality, proportionality and fairness, and certain substantive rights. These are said to constitute central components of any recognisably liberal theory of justice, while leaving the scope and content of the rights and duties which citizens should possess largely as a matter for independent debate and analysis. Formal equality is to be supplemented by a more substantive equality, which requires that relevant distinctions must be capable of reasoned justification in terms of some conception of the common good. Allan's theory also embraces certain substantive rights, namely freedoms of speech, conscience, association, and access to information. It is recognised that there will be other rights within a liberal polity, which should be faithfully applied, but these are not regarded as a constituent part of the rule of law.

It should be recognised that any approach of the kind under examination will require some choice as to what are to count as fundamental rights, and the more particular meaning ascribed to such rights. This choice will reflect assumptions as to the importance of differing interests in society. This is unavoidable. It is of course true that any democracy to be worthy of the name will have some attachment to particular liberty and equality interests. If, however, we delve beneath the surface of phrases such as liberty and equality then significant differences of view become apparent even amongst those who subscribe to one version or another of liberal belief. This leaves entirely out of account the issue as to how far social and economic interests ought to be protected. It also fails to take account of other visions of democracy, of a communitarian rather than liberal nature, which might well interpret the civil/political rights and the social/economic rights differently. It is therefore neither fortuitous, nor surprising, that in other common law systems which possess constitutionally enshrined rights, such as the United States and Canada, there is considerable diversity of opinion even amongst those who support a rights-based approach, as to whether this should be taken to mean some version of liberalism, a pluralist model, or a modified notion of republicanism.

This point is equally true of ideas such as legality, rationality, participation, openness, proportionality, procedural fairness and the like, which can be given interpreted differently depending upon the more general scheme into which they are to fit.

The consequences of breach of the rule of law in the sense considered within this section should also be addressed. It is important, as when discussing other versions of the concept, to distinguish between the consequences of breach of the rule of law in relation to primary statute and in relation to other measures.

The short answer in relation to a primary statute that violates the rule of law is as follows. The fact that a statute does not conform to this conception of the rule of law does not in itself lead to its invalidation. The UK courts have not traditionally exercised the power of constitutional review to annul primary statutes for failure to conform to fundamental rights, or other precepts of the rule of law that constitute the principles of judicial review. This proposition must nonetheless be qualified in three ways.

First, there are statements by judges countenancing the possibility that the courts might refuse to apply an Act of Parliament in certain extreme circumstances. The examples tend to be of (hypothetical) legislation that is morally repugnant, or of legislation through which Parliament seeks to re-order the constitutional structure by abolishing judicial review, by making illegitimate use of the Parliament Acts or by extending very considerably the life of a current Parliament. It should moreover be recognised that the case law authority for the traditional proposition that courts will not invalidate or refuse to apply statute is actually rather thin. There are to be sure many judicial statements extolling the sovereignty of Parliament, but they are principally just that, judicial statements rather than formal decisions. Insofar as there are formal decisions that could be said to be based on the traditional proposition, the facts of such cases were generally relatively innocuous. They were a very long way from the types of case where courts might consider it to be justified to refuse to apply a statute, which also means that such cases could be readily distinguished should a court feel minded to do so.

Secondly, one who subscribes to the version of the rule of law discussed in this section might well argue that courts should generally exercise the ultimate power to invalidate statute for failure to comply with constitutionally enshrined rights, or with rights that are regarded as fundamental or foundational even where they are not formally enshrined in a written constitution. Dworkin is a prominent exponent of this view. The literature on this topic is vast, with the debate for and against such judicial power being replayed in successive academic generations.

Thirdly, courts or judges who subscribe to the conception of the rule of law discussed in this section have in any event powerful interpretive tools at their disposal through which to read legislation so that it does not violate fundamental rights or other facets of the rule of law. Thus even prior to the Human Rights Act 1998, the courts made it clear through the principle of legality that statutes would be read so as to conform to such rights. If Parliament intended to infringe or limit fundamental rights then this would have to be stated expressly in the legislation, or be the only plausible reading of the statutory language. Legislation was therefore read subject to a principle of legality, which meant that fundamental rights could not be overridden by general or ambiguous words. This was, said Lord Hoffmann, because there was too great a risk that the full implications of their unqualified meaning might have passed unnoticed in the democratic process. In the absence of express language or necessary implication to the contrary, the courts would therefore presume that even the most general words were intended to be subject to the basic rights of the individual. Parliament had, therefore, to squarely confront what it was doing and accept the political cost. An interpretive approach is clearly evident once again in the Human Rights Act 1998, section 3, which provides that 'so far as it is possible to do so, primary legislation and subordinate legislation must be read and given effect in a way which is compatible with the Convention rights'. Section 3 does not, however, affect the validity, continuing operation or enforcement of any incompatible primary legislation. Where a court is satisfied that primary legislation is incompatible with a Convention right then it can, pursuant to section 4 of the HRA, make a declaration of that incompatibility.

The consequence of breach of the rule of law in relation to measures other than primary statute is more straightforward. Insofar as the rule of law is regarded as the foundation of the principles of judicial review then it follows that breach of the rule of law, manifested through breach of one of the more particular principles of judicial review, can lead to annulment of the measure. This says nothing about whether the judicial decision will be controversial or not. The great many judicial review decisions generate no political controversy, but there will inevitably be instances where Parliament, or more usually the relevant minister, feels that the court's judgment was 'wrong' in some way. There will more generally be wide ranging academic debate about the principles of judicial review and the way in which they are applied in particular cases.

It is fitting to conclude this paper by reverting to Lord Bingham's lecture, the catalyst for which was the statutory mention of the rule of law in the Constitutional Reform Act 2005, section 1. The importance of the interpretive tools used by courts is apparent once again in the following extract. Lord Bingham ['The Rule of Law' (2007) 68 *Camb LJ* 67, 69]

[T]he statutory affirmation of the rule of law as an existing constitutional principle and of the Lord Chancellor's existing role in relation to it does have an important consequence: that the judges, in their role as journeymen and judgment-makers, are not free to dismiss the rule of law as meaningless verbiage, the jurisprudential equivalent of motherhood and apple pie, even if they were inclined to do so. They would be bound to construe a statute so that it did not infringe an existing constitutional principle, if it were reasonably possible to do so. And the Lord Chancellor's conduct in relation to that principle would no doubt be susceptible, in principle, to judicial review.

■ QUESTION

If judges may adopt a substantive version of the rule of law in extreme situations, what are the criteria to identify such situations?

SECTION 4: DICEY AND THE RULE OF LAW

Dicey's views on the rule of law cannot be ignored because of the lasting influence he has had. His influence is all the more remarkable in light of the widespread criticisms which have been levelled against his views. In *An Introduction to the Study of the Law of the Constitution,* Dicey devoted a large part of the book to his exposition of the rule of law, to which he attributed three meanings, but we will not consider the third, about individual rights. The views of Dicey's critics will be stated after each.

A: The rule of law and discretionary powers

A. V. Dicey, *An Introduction to the Study of the Law of the Constitution*

(10th edn, 1985), pp. 188 and 202

We mean, in the first place, that no man is punishable or can be lawfully made to suffer in body or goods except for a distinct breach of law established in the ordinary legal manner before the ordinary courts of the land. In this sense the rule of law is contrasted with every system of government based on the exercise by persons in authority of wide, arbitrary, or discretionary powers of constraint. . . . It means . . . The absolute supremacy or predominance of regular law as opposed to the influence of arbitrary power, and excludes the existence of arbitrariness, of prerogative, or even of wide discretionary authority on the part of the government. Englishmen are ruled by the law, and by the law alone; a man may with us be punished for a breach of the law, but he can be punished for nothing else.

Sir Ivor Jennings, *The Law and the Constitution*

(5th edn, 1959), pp. 54–58

Dicey and the Rule of Law

The particular principle of the individualist or *laissez-faire* school was that any substantial discretionary power was a danger to liberty. The fact that he held such a principle was not explicitly avowed by Dicey, because he assumed that he was analysing not his own subjective notions (shared, of course, by many of his contemporaries), but the firm and unalterable principles of English constitutional law. . . . We need only contest the idea that the rule of law and discretionary powers are contradictory.

If we look around us we cannot fail to be aware that public authorities do in fact possess wide discretionary powers. Many of them formed part of the law even when Dicey wrote in 1885. Any court can punish me for contempt of court by imprisoning me for an indefinite period. If I am convicted of manslaughter, I may be released at once or imprisoned for life. If I am an alien, my naturalisation is entirely within the discretion of the Home Secretary. If the Queen declares war against the rest of the world, I am prohibited from having dealings abroad. If the country is in danger, my property can be taken, perhaps without compensation. If a public health authority wants to flood my land in order to build a reservoir, it can take it from me compulsorily. I can be compelled to leave my work for a month or more, in order to serve on a jury. All these powers, and many more, were possessed by public authorities in 1885, and can still be exercised.

Dicey did not mention all these, because nowhere in his book did he consider the *powers* of authorities. He seemed to think that the British Constitution was concerned almost entirely with the *rights of individuals*. He was imagining a constitution dominated by the doctrine of *laissez-faire*. The function of government, as he unconsciously assumed, was to protect the individual against internal and external aggression. Given such protection, each individual was allowed to live his life almost as he pleased, so long as he did not interfere with the similar liberty of others. He regarded this as desirable, and therefore tended to minimise the extent to which public authorities could interfere with private action. . . .

Nevertheless, the argument need not be placed entirely on this narrow ground. For the main discretionary power is placed in England not in the executive but in Parliament. Parliament, as has already been emphasised, can pass what legislation it pleases. It is not limited by any written constitution. Its powers are not only wide, but unlimited. In most countries, not only the administrative authorities but also the legislature have powers limited by the constitution. This, one would think, is the most effective rule of law. In England, the administration has powers limited by legislation, but the powers of the legislature are not limited at all. There is still, it may be argued, a rule of law, but the law is that the law may at any moment be changed.

Dicey attempts to meet this argument in two ways. 'The commands of Parliament,' he said, 'can be uttered only through the combined action of its three constituent parts, and must, therefore, always take the shape of formal and deliberate legislation.' Formal it may be; it may not be deliberate. We saw—Dicey saw before he died in 1922—how the Defence of the Realm Act was passed in 1914. The Cabinet decided that it wanted drastic powers. The majority which it commanded in the House of Commons supported its motion to suspend the Standing Orders. The Bill was passed through at one sitting. The House of Lords did the same. Thus at one stroke, without any long deliberation, the Cabinet acquired the powers it needed. The 'gold standard' was similarly swept away in 1931. The Cabinet ordered the Bank of England not to exchange notes into gold. The next day Parliament met and the necessary legislation was passed through not only to make paper currency inconvertible, but also to ratify the illegal acts of the Cabinet and of the Bank before the Act was passed. Here was arbitrary power indeed, but it was by no means as arbitrary as the powers exercised by Parliament in 1939 and 1940.

R. F. V. Heuston, 'The Rule of Law' in *Essays in Constitutional Law*

(2nd edn, 1964), pp. 40–42

The Rule of Law and Discretionary Powers

Two criticisms have, however, been made of this aspect of Dicey's definition. First, it is said that it is difficult to distinguish between regular law and arbitrary power. If the law gives the power, how can it be arbitrary or irregular? It may be very undesirable for such a power to have been given, but if it has been given, and validly given according to the legislative forms of that particular society, how, it is said, can it be criticised as being contrary to the Rule of Law?... What is authorised by the law cannot indeed be illegal within the framework of that particular system, but it may very well be contrary to the Rule of Law as a principle of constitutional government. The difficulty no doubt arises from the fact that Dicey described his doctrine as 'the Rule of Law,' thereby giving the impression that it was in some way a legal principle, whereas it is in truth only a constitutional principle based upon the practice of liberal democracies of the Western world. In this sense, the doctrine is still perfectly true today. Everyone, high or low, must be prepared to justify his acts by a reference to some statutory or common law power which authorises him to act precisely in the way in which he claims he can act. Superior orders or state necessity are no defence to an action otherwise illegal.

Secondly, it has been said that Dicey erred in saying that the doctrine of the Rule of Law 'excludes the existence even of wide discretionary authority on the part of the government.' This is certainly not true today. Modern government, as is well known, cannot be carried on at all without a host of wide discretionary powers, which are granted to the executive by the large number of statutes annually passed by Parliament. But it must be remembered, first of all, the kind of man Dicey was, and secondly, the times in which he wrote. First, Dicey was in politics an old-fashioned Whig. He was also a very typical example of the common lawyer who does not seriously believe in the existence of the Statute Book. To the true common lawyer the law is to be found in the law reports and books of authority. There are indeed statutes, but they can always be looked up if the opportunity arises. The judges, as has been well said, have never entered into the spirit of the Benthamite game and have always treated the statute as an interloper upon the rounded majesty of the common law. Secondly, it must be recalled that Dicey's great work was written in the early 1880s, a period when the *laissez-faire* state of the Victorians was only just beginning to give way to the welfare state of the modern world. Dicey was an acute, a marvellously acute, judge of public opinion and of the impact upon public opinion of legislative power, but even he hardly foresaw the extent to which statutory powers of government would change the nature of English constitutional law. Today the fundamental problem is that of the control of discretionary powers, and it is indeed a serious criticism of Dicey's doctrine that he suggests that discretionary powers are in some way undesirable or unnecessary.

Kenneth Culp Davis, *Discretionary Justice*

(1971), pp. 17 and 42

Even when rules can be written, discretion is often better. Rules without discretion cannot fully take into account the need for tailoring results to unique facts and circumstances of particular cases. The justification for discretion is often the need for individualized justice. This is so in the judicial process as well as in the administrative process.

Every governmental and legal system in world history has involved both rules and discretion. No government has ever been a government of laws and not of men in the sense of eliminating all discretionary power. Every government has always been *a government of laws and of men*. A close look at the meaning of Aristotle, the first user of the phrase 'government of laws and not of men,' shows quite clearly that he did not mean that governments could exist without discretionary power....

Elimination of all discretionary power is both impossible and undesirable. The sensible goal is development of a proper balance between rule and discretion. Some circumstances call for rules, some for discretion, some for mixtures of one proportion, and some for mixtures of another proportion. In today's American legal system, the special need is to eliminate *unnecessary* discretionary power, and to discover more successful ways to confine, to structure, and to check necessary discretionary power.

NOTE: Compare Heuston's first point with the contrasting views expressed in the Court of Appeal and the House of Lords in the *Rossminster* case, p. 96, *ante*.

B: The rule of law and equality

A. V. Dicey, *An Introduction to the Study of the Law of the Constitution*

(10th edn, 1985), pp. 202–203

It means... equality before the law, or the equal subjection of all classes to the ordinary law of the land administered by the ordinary law courts; the 'rule of law' in this sense excludes the idea of any exemption of officials or others from the duty of obedience to the law which governs other citizens or from the jurisdiction of the ordinary tribunals; there can be with us nothing really corresponding to the 'administrative law' (*droit administratif*) or the 'administrative tribunals' (*tribunaux administratifs)* of France. The notion which lies at the bottom of the 'administrative law' known to foreign countries is, that affairs or disputes in which the government or its servants are concerned are beyond the sphere of the civil courts and must be dealt with by special and more or less official bodies. This idea is utterly unknown to the law of England, and indeed is fundamentally inconsistent with our traditions and customs.

R. F. V. Heuston, 'The Rule of Law' in *Essays in Constitutional Law*

(2nd edn, 1964), pp. 44–48

...This exposition is still perfectly true in the sense that the social or political or economic status of an individual is by itself no answer to legal proceedings, civil or criminal. Everyone, whatever his position, must be ready to justify his actions by reference to some specific legal rule and be ready so to justify them in the ordinary courts...

This aspect of Dicey's doctrine has been criticised by Sir Ivor Jennings on the ground that it seems to suggest that officials have the same rights and duties as citizens. If Dicey did indeed mean that, then he was obviously wrong, for modern statutes have conferred wide powers on officials which the ordinary citizen has not got. Gas Board officials may enter my premises to collect the money from the meter, but my neighbours cannot. Officials of the Ministry of Supply can enter my rooms to see if I am conducting researches into nuclear fission, but the college porter cannot. Conversely, the Oxford City Council, as the local education authority, is under a duty to educate my children free although my employers, the University of Oxford and Pembroke College, are not. Many other examples could be produced. There is something in this criticism. We have already seen that Dicey was perhaps a little reluctant to read the Statute Book, and that if he had done so more regularly he might perhaps have altered some of his phrases. Nevertheless, I do not think that Sir Ivor Jennings' criticism touches the heart of the matter. This has been very well put by Lord Wright: 'all are equally subject to the law, though the law as to which some are subject may be different from the law to which others are subject.' In other words, however great the powers or the duties conferred upon the executive, all are equally responsible before the ordinary courts for the exercise of their powers, rights and duties. As was said in *R* v *Brixton Prison Governor, ex parte Soblen* [1963] 2 QB 243 at p. 273, *per* Stephenson J:

> I have no doubt that one of the court's most important duties is to see so far as possible that the great officers of State and those who act under their orders, no less than public bodies and private individuals, act lawfully in the exercise of their powers; and the greater the power which is exercised, and the higher the authority exercising it, the more important is the discharge by the court of this duty, and the more difficult.

A second criticism is much more serious. It arises from Dicey's assertion that the Rule of Law precludes anything corresponding to the administrative law (*droit administratif*) of France. This belief dominated English thinking for so long that not many years ago a Lord Chief Justice could refer to the phrase 'administrative law' as 'Continental jargon.' It is only within the last decade that it has become a respectable phrase. It is clear to us today that Dicey misunderstood the nature and functions of French administrative law, and especially the function of the *conseil d'état*, the chief court in the administrative hierarchy. This is not the time to go into detail; it is enough to say here that although the *conseil d'état* is not composed of professional judges, there are no grounds for supposing that it is in any way biased in favour of the administration. Indeed, there seems to be good reason to think that the liberties of the citizen are in many ways better protected by the *conseil d'état* than by the High Court of Justice. The mere fact that French officials are exempt from process in the ordinary civil courts does not necessarily mean that they are legally irresponsible. To Dicey, however, who had to the full the common lawyer's belief that it is the duty of the Queen's courts to control and supervise the activities of all other tribunals and persons within the realm, the notion that officials might be subject to a special system of rules administered in a special system of courts, was necessarily a very curious one.

NOTE: While it is accepted that, if the rule of law is to be adhered to, it is necessary that citizens be given legal protection against unlawful conduct on the part of officials, Dicey regarded it as necessary that such protection be afforded by the ordinary courts. He did not consider it possible to maintain the rule of law if there was a separate system of public law administered by separate courts, as occurred in France and many other continental countries. Dicey believed that this system was biased in favour of officials and that English law provided better protection. Dicey's influence was such that this view affected the development of administrative law for many years. It is only within the last 40 to 50 years that administrative law has come to be recognized as a separate branch of law, although the United Kingdom still lacks a separate system of administrative courts. There are, however, many tribunals dealing with administrative matters. In whatever way it is to be administered, the essential issue, if the rule of law is to be respected, is simply whether officials are subject to, and controlled by, the law.

Equality before the law should mean that no one is above the law. As with all rules, however, there are exceptions: for example, foreign sovereigns and diplomats, their staffs and families are immune from criminal prosecution or civil action; members of Parliament enjoy certain privileges; and judges enjoy the privilege of being immune from civil liability for anything said or done in the course of their office. These exceptions are limited and, in the case of judges and MPs, are designed to further the rule of law by giving protection to the institutions upon which a liberal democracy is founded, namely, an independent judiciary and an elected legislature.

In explaining his second proposition, Dicey stated that 'every man, whatever be his rank or condition, is subject to the ordinary law of the realm and amenable to the jurisdiction of the ordinary tribunals' (at p. 193). The accuracy of this statement came under challenge in the following case.

In re M

[1993] 3 WLR 433, House of Lords

M, a citizen of Zaire, arrived in the United Kingdom seeking political asylum. The Home Office rejected his application and ordered his removal from the United Kingdom, which was to take place by 6.30 pm on 1 May 1991. At 5.20 pm (after the Court of Appeal had refused an application for leave to apply for judicial review of the decision) a fresh application for leave to move for judicial review, alleging new grounds, was made to Garland J in chambers. Garland J indicated at about 5.30 pm that he wished M's departure to be postponed pending consideration of the application, and he understood from counsel for the Home Office that an undertaking to that effect had been given. (Counsel understood that he had only undertaken to *endeavour* to prevent M's removal.) Due to bungling and breakdown in lines of communication, M's departure was not prevented, nor was he removed from the onward flight to Zaire during a stopover at Paris. At 11.20 pm Garland J, being informed of M's removal from the jurisdiction, made a 'without notice' (formerly an '*ex parte* order') requiring the Home Secretary to procure the return of M to the jurisdiction and granting the Home Secretary liberty to apply for variation or discharge of the order on the morning of 2 May. Home Office officials then made arrangements for M's return. On the afternoon of 2 May, the Home Secretary, having taken advice from his officials and Treasury Counsel, concluded that the underlying asylum decision had been correct and that Garland J's 'without notice' order, being a mandatory interim injunction against a minister of the Crown, had been made without jurisdiction. Thereupon he cancelled the arrangements for M's return. On 3 May he applied to Garland J to set aside the order of 1 May, which Garland J did. Proceedings were then brought on behalf of M against the Home Office and the Home Secretary alleging contempt of court in respect of the breach of the undertaking and the order requiring M's return. Simon Brown J dismissed this motion on the basis that since the Crown's immunity from injunction was preserved by s. 21 of the Crown Proceedings Act 1947, neither it nor its departments, ministers, and officials acting in the course of their duties could be impleaded for contempt of court. The applicant appealed.

The Court of Appeal held that the original order by Garland J should not have been made, as injunctions could not be issued against the Crown. However, as the order was binding until set aside, failure to comply with it was a contempt. Further, while the Crown and Government Departments are not subject to the contempt jurisdiction of the High Court because they are 'non-persons', Mr Baker, the Home Secretary, was, however, personally guilty of contempt.

The Secretary of State appealed and the applicant cross-appealed in respect of his original application against the Home Office. The House of Lords considered two issues of constitutional import: first, could injunctions be issued against a government minister or department, and, secondly, could a government minister or department be found to be in contempt of court for failure to comply with an order of the court.

LORD TEMPLEMAN: My Lords, Parliament makes the law, the executive carry the law into effect and the judiciary enforce the law. The expression 'the Crown' has two meanings; namely the monarch and the executive. In the 17th century Parliament established its supremacy over the Crown as monarch, over the executive and over the judiciary. Parliamentary supremacy over the Crown as monarch stems from the fact that the monarch must accept the advice of a Prime Minister who is supported by a majority of Parliament. Parliamentary supremacy over the Crown as executive stems from the fact that Parliament maintains in office the Prime Minister who appoints the ministers in charge of the executive. Parliamentary supremacy over the judiciary is only exercisable by statute. The judiciary enforce the law against individuals, against institutions and against the executive. The judges cannot enforce the law against the Crown as monarch because the Crown as monarch can do no wrong but judges enforce the law against the Crown as executive and against the individuals who from time to time represent the Crown. A litigant complaining of a breach of the law by the executive can sue the Crown as executive bringing his action against the minister who is responsible for the department of state involved, in the present case the Secretary of State for Home Affairs. To enforce the law the courts have power to grant remedies including injunctions against a minister in his official capacity. If the minister has personally broken the law, the litigant can sue the minister, in this case Mr Kenneth Baker, in his personal capacity. For the purpose of enforcing the law against all persons and institutions, including ministers in their official capacity and in their personal capacity, the courts are armed with coercive powers exercisable in proceedings for contempt of court.

In the present case, counsel for the Secretary of State argued that the judge could not enforce the law by injunction or contempt proceedings against the minister in his official capacity. Counsel also argued that in his personal capacity Mr Kenneth Baker the Secretary of State for Home Affairs had not been guilty of contempt.

My Lords, the argument that there is no power to enforce the law by injunction or contempt proceedings against a minister in his official capacity would, if upheld, establish the proposition that the executive obey the law as a matter of grace and not as a matter of necessity, a proposition which would reverse the result of the Civil War. For the reasons given by my noble and learned friend, Lord Woolf, and on principle, I am satisfied that injunctions and contempt proceedings may be brought against the minister in his official capacity and that in the present case the Home Office for which the Secretary of State was responsible was in contempt. I am also satisfied that Mr Baker was throughout acting in his official capacity, on advice which he was entitled to accept and under a mistaken view as to the law. In these circumstances I do not consider that Mr Baker personally was guilty of contempt. I would therefore dismiss this appeal substituting the Secretary of State for Home Affairs as being the person against whom the finding of contempt was made.

LORD WOOLF: ... Mr Richards submits on behalf of the Home Office and on behalf of Mr Baker that neither the Crown in general, nor a department of state, nor a minister of the Crown, acting in his capacity as such, are amenable to proceedings in contempt. It is a necessary part of that submission that the courts also have no power to grant injunctions directed to such bodies and that the order which was made by Garland J, which it was held by Simon Brown J as well as the Court of Appeal that Mr Baker had contravened, was made without jurisdiction.

When advancing these submissions Mr Richards stressed that it was no part of his case that the Crown or ministers are above the law or that ministers are able to rely on their office so as to evade liability for wrongdoing. He argued that this was not a consequence of his submissions and he accepted that the Crown has a duty to obey the law as declared by the courts. He accepted that if a minister acted in disregard of the law as declared by the courts, or otherwise was engaged in wrongdoing, he would be acting outside his authority as a minister and so would expose himself to a personal liability for his wrongdoing.

The fact that these issues have only now arisen for decision by the courts is confirmation that in ordinary circumstances ministers of the Crown and government departments invariably scrupulously observe decisions of the courts. Because of this, it is normally unnecessary for the courts to make an executory order against a minister or a government department since they will comply with any declaratory judgment made by the courts and pending the decision of the courts will not take any precipitous action....

[His Lordship recounted the facts of the case.] What does appear to me to be clear from the events which occurred on 1 and 2 May 1991 is that, if there is no power in a court to make an order to prevent the Home Office moving a person in any circumstances, this would be a highly unsatisfactory situation. The facts of this case illustrate that circumstances can occur where it is in the interests both of a person who is subject to the powers of government and of the government itself that the courts should be in a position to make an order which clearly sets out either what should or what should not be done by the government. If there had been no confusion in this case as to the extent of the court's power, I have little doubt that Mr Baker would not find himself in his present position where he has been found guilty of contempt....

Injunctions and the Crown

Mr Kentridge [for the applicant M] placed at the forefront of his argument the issue as to whether the courts have jurisdiction to make coercive orders against the Crown or ministers of the Crown. It was appropriate for him to do so for at least two reasons. First, and more importantly, because whether the courts have or do not have such a coercive jurisdiction would be a strong indicator as to whether the courts had the jurisdiction to make a finding of contempt. If there were no power to make coercive orders, then the need to rely on the law of contempt for the purpose of enforcing the orders would rarely arise. The second reason is that, on the facts of this case, the issue is highly significant in determining the status of the order which Garland J made and which it is alleged Mr Baker breached. If that order was made without jurisdiction, then Mr Richards would rely on this in support of his contention that Mr Baker should not have been found guilty of contempt. As Mr Richards admitted, the issue is of constitutional importance since it goes to the heart of the relationship between the executive and the courts. Is the relationship based, as he submits, on trust and cooperation or ultimately on coercion?

Mr Richards submits that the answer to this question is provided by the decision of *R* v *Secretary for State for Transport, Ex parte Factortame Ltd* [1990] 2 AC 85 and in particular by the reasoning of Lord Bridge of Harwich who made the only speech in that case. This speech was highly influential in causing Simon Brown J and McCowan LJ to take a different view from the majority of the Court of Appeal as to the outcome of the present proceedings. That case was not, however, primarily concerned with the question as to whether injunctive relief was available against the Crown or its officers. It involved the allegedly discriminatory effect of the requirement of British ownership and the other requirements of Part II of the Merchant Shipping Act 1988 and the associated regulations, which prevented fishing vessels which were owned by Spanish nationals or managed in Spain being registered under the legislation. This it was said contravened Community law. It was an issue of difficulty which had accordingly been referred to the European Court under article 177 [now 234] of the EEC Treaty (Cmnd. 5179–II). The question then arose as to whether the applicants were entitled to interim relief pending the outcome of the reference. The primary contention of the applicants was that it was in the circumstances a requirement of Community law that interim relief should be available. This was an additional point as to which Community law was unclear so your Lordships' House decided that that issue should also not be determined until after a reference under article 177. This meant that pending the outcome of the second reference your Lordships had to determine whether interim relief should be granted under domestic law.

In deciding whether under domestic law interim relief should be granted Lord Bridge initially examined the position without reference to the involvement of a minister. He concluded that no relief could be granted since English law unassisted by Community law treated legislation as fully effective until it was set aside....

However, Lord Bridge went on to give a second reason for his decision which is directly relevant to the present appeal. The second reason is that injunctive relief is not available against the Crown or an officer of the Crown, when acting as such, in judicial review proceedings.... Since the decision in *Factortame* there has also been the important development that the European Court has determined the second reference against the Crown so that the unhappy situation now exists that while a citizen is entitled to obtain injunctive relief (including interim relief) against the Crown or an officer of the Crown to protect his interests under Community law he cannot do so in respect of his other interests which may be just as important.

Before examining the second reason that Lord Bridge gave for his conclusion I should point out that I was a party to the judgment of the majority in the *Smith Kline* case. In my judgment in that case I indicated that injunctive relief was available in judicial review proceedings not only against an officer of the Crown but also against the Crown. Although in reality the distinction between the Crown and an officer of the Crown is of no practical significance in judicial review proceedings, in the theory which clouds this subject the distinction is of the greatest importance. My judgment in the earlier case may have caused some confusion in *Factortame* by obscuring the important fact that, as was the position prior to the introduction of judicial review, while prerogative orders are made regularly against ministers in their official capacity, they are never made against the Crown.

Lord Bridge in determining the second issue acknowledged the importance of the relevant history in determining this issue and it is necessary for me to set out my understanding of that history.

His Lordship, starting from the premise that 'the fact that the Sovereign could do no wrong did not mean that a servant of the Crown could do no wrong', considered the history of civil proceedings against the Crown and the Crown Proceedings Act 1947, and the history of prerogative orders against Ministers of the Crown culminating in the introduction of judicial review in 1977 by RSC, Ord. 53 which was followed by primary legislation in s. 31 of the Senior Courts Act 1981, (p. 606, *post*). His Lordship considered in detail the speech of Lord Bridge in *Factortame* who, following the judgment of Upjohn J in *Merricks* v *Heathcoat-Amory* [1955] Ch 567, held that injunctions could not be issued against a Minister of the Crown in judicial review proceedings. His Lordship, while agreeing with the decision in the latter case, considered that the reasoning was mistaken. His Lordship further concluded that Lord Bridge had misunderstood the issue in *Factortame* due in part to the fact that the matter had not been fully argued before their Lordships.

I am, therefore, of the opinion that, the language of section 31 being unqualified in its terms, there is no warrant for restricting its application so that in respect of ministers and other officers of the Crown alone the remedy of an injunction, including an interim injunction, is not available. In my view the history of prerogative proceedings against officers of the Crown supports such a conclusion. So far as interim relief is concerned, which is the practical change which has been made, there is no justification for adopting a different approach to officers of the Crown from that adopted in relation to other respondents in the absence of clear language such as that contained in section 21(2) of the Act of 1947. The fact that in any event a stay could be granted against the Crown under Ord. 53. r. 3(10) emphasises the limits of the change in the situation which is involved. It would be most regrettable if an approach which is inconsistent with that which exists in Community law should be allowed to persist if this is not strictly necessary. The restriction provided for in section 21(2) of the Act of 1947 does, however, remain in relation to civil proceedings.

The fact that, in my view, the court should be regarded as having jurisdiction to grant interim and final injunctions against officers of the Crown does not mean that that jurisdiction should be exercised except in the most limited circumstances. In the majority of situations so far as final relief is concerned, a declaration will continue to be the appropriate remedy on an application for judicial review involving officers of the Crown. As has been the position in the past, the Crown can be relied upon to co-operate fully with such declarations. To avoid having to grant interim injunctions against officers of the Crown, I can see advantages in the courts being able to grant interim declarations. However, it is obviously not desirable to deal with this topic, if it is not necessary to do so, until the views of the Law Commission are known.

The validity of the injunction granted by Garland J

What has been said so far does not mean that Garland J was necessarily in order in granting the injunction. The injunction was granted before he had given the applicant leave to apply for judicial review. However, in a case of real urgency, which this was, the fact that leave had not been granted is a mere technicality. It would be undesirable if, in the situation with which Garland J was faced, he had been compelled to grant leave because he regarded the case as an appropriate one for an interim injunction. In the case of civil proceedings, there is recognition of the jurisdiction of the court to grant interim injunctions before the issue of a writ, etc. (see Ord. 29, r. 1(3)) and in an appropriate case there should be taken to be a similar jurisdiction to grant interim injunctions now under Order 53. The position is accurately set out in note 53/1–14/24 to *The Supreme Court Practice 1993* where it is stated that:

> Where the case is so urgent as to justify it, [the judge] could grant an interlocutory injunction or other interim relief pending the hearing of the application for leave to move for judicial review. But, if the judge has refused leave to move for judicial review he is functus officio and has no jurisdiction to grant any form of interim relief. The application for an interlocutory injunction or other interim relief could, however, be renewed before the Court of Appeal along with the renewal of the application for leave to move for judicial review.

There having been jurisdiction for Garland J to make the order which he did, it cannot be suggested that it was inappropriate for him to have made the order. On the view of the law which I now take, Garland J was therefore not required to set aside the order though his decision to do so was inevitable having regard to the state of the authorities at that time.

The effect of the advice received by Mr Baker

Having come to the conclusion that Garland J's order was properly made, the next question which has to be considered is the effect of the advice which was understandably given to Mr Baker that the order was made without jurisdiction. Here there are two important considerations. The first is that the order was made by the High Court and therefore has to be treated as a perfectly valid order and one which has to be obeyed until it is set aside: see the speeches of Lord Diplock in *In re Racal Communications*, [1981] AC 374, 384 and *Isaacs* v *Robertson* [1985] AC 97, 102. The second consideration is that it is undesirable to talk in the terms of technical contempt. The courts only make a finding of contempt if there is conduct by the person or body concerned which can, with justification, be categorised as contempt. If, therefore, there is a situation in which the view is properly taken (and usually this will only be possible when the action is taken in accordance with legal advice) that it is reasonable to defer complying with an order of the court until application is made to the court for further guidance then it will not be contempt to defer complying with the order until an application has been made to the court to discharge the order. However, this course can only be justified if the application is made at the first practicable opportunity and in the meantime all appropriate steps have been taken to ensure that the person in whose favour the order was made will not be disadvantaged pending the hearing of the application.

Mr Baker's difficulties in this case are that, while it was understandable that there should be delay before he could give the matter personal attention, Garland J was not kept informed of what was happening and totally inadequate steps were taken to protect the position of M, pending the application to the court. In addition Mr Baker has the problem that this House will not normally interfere with the assessment of the facts which was made by the Court of Appeal unless it can be shown that the assessment is flawed by some error of law.

Jurisdiction to make a finding of contempt

The Court of Appeal were of the opinion that a finding of contempt could not be made against the Crown, a government department or a minister of the Crown in his official capacity. Although it is to be expected that it will be rare indeed that the circumstances will exist in which such a finding would be justified, I do not believe there is any impediment to a court making such a finding, when it is appropriate to do so, not against the Crown directly, but against a government department or a minister of the Crown in his official capacity. Lord Donaldson of Lymington MR considered that a problem was created in making a finding of contempt because the Crown lacked a legal personality. However, at least for some purposes, the Crown has a legal personality. It can be appropriately described as a corporation sole or a corporation aggregate: *per* Lord Diplock and Lord Simon of Glaisdale respectively in *Town Investments Ltd* v *Department of the Environment* [1978] AC 359. The Crown can hold property and enter into contracts. On the other hand, even after the Act of 1947, it cannot conduct litigation except in the name of an authorised government department or, in the case of judicial review, in the name of a minister. In any event it is not in relation to the Crown that I differ from the Master of the Rolls, but as to a government department or a minister.

Nolan LJ, at p. 311, considered that the fact that proceedings for contempt are 'essentially personal and punitive' meant that it was not open to a court, as a matter of law, to make a finding of contempt against the Home Office or the Home Secretary. While contempt proceedings usually have these characteristics and contempt proceedings against a government department or a minister in an official capacity would not be either personal or punitive (it would clearly not be appropriate to fine or sequest the assets of the Crown or a government department or an officer of the Crown acting in his official capacity), this does not mean that a finding of contempt against a government department or minister would be pointless. The very fact of making such a finding would vindicate the requirements of justice. In addition an order for costs could be made to underline the significance of a contempt. A purpose of the courts' powers to make findings of contempt is to ensure that the orders of the court are obeyed. This jurisdiction is required to be coextensive with the courts' jurisdiction to make the orders which need the protection which the jurisdiction to make findings of contempt provides. In civil proceedings the court can now make orders (other than injunctions or for specific performance) against authorised government departments or the Attorney-General. On applications for judicial review orders can be made against ministers. In consequence of the developments identified already such orders must be taken not to offend the theory that the Crown can supposedly do no wrong. Equally, if such orders are made and not obeyed, the body against whom the orders were made can be found guilty of contempt without offending that theory, which would be the only justifiable impediment against making a finding of contempt.

In cases not involving a government department or a minister the ability to *punish* for contempt may be necessary. However, as is reflected in the restrictions on execution against the Crown, the Crown's relationship with the courts does not depend on coercion and in the exceptional situation when a government department's conduct justifies this, a finding of contempt should suffice. In that exceptional situation, the ability of the court to make a finding of contempt is of great importance. It would demonstrate that a government department has interfered with the administration of justice. It will then be for Parliament to determine what should be the consequences of that finding. In accord with tradition the finding should not be made against the 'Crown' by name but in the name of the authorised department (or the Attorney-General) or the minister so as to accord with the body against whom the order was made. If the order was made in civil proceedings against an authorised department, the department will be held to be in contempt. On judicial review the order will be against the minister and so normally should be any finding of contempt in respect of the order.

However, the finding under appeal is one made against Mr Baker personally in respect of an injunction addressed to him in his official capacity as the Secretary of State for the Home Department. It was appropriate to direct the injunction to the Secretary of State in his official capacity since, as previously indicated, remedies on an application for judicial review which involve the Crown are made against the appropriate officer in his official capacity. This does not mean that it cannot be appropriate to make a finding of contempt against a minister personally rather than against him in his official capacity provided that the contempt relates to his own default. Normally it will be more appropriate to make the order against the office which a minister holds where the order which has been breached has been made against that office since members of the department concerned will almost certainly be involved and investigation as to the part played by individuals is likely to be at least extremely difficult, if not impossible, unless privilege is waived (as commendably happened in this case). In addition the object of the exercise is not so much to punish an individual as to vindicate the rule of law by a finding of contempt. This can be achieved equally by a declaratory finding of the court as to the contempt against the minister as representing the department. By making the finding against the minister in his official capacity the court will be indicating that it is the department for which the minister is responsible which has been guilty of contempt. The minister himself may or may not have been personally guilty of contempt. The position so far as he is personally concerned would be the equivalent of that which needs to exist for the court to give relief against the minister in proceedings for judicial review. There would need to be default by the department for which the minister is responsible.

In addition Mr Richards argued that for a finding of contempt against Mr Baker personally it would not suffice to establish contempt to show that Mr Baker was aware of the order and had not complied with it. It would also be necessary to show an intention to interfere with or impede the administration of justice. If such an intent was shown to exist, then Mr Richards conceded that the conduct of the minister would fall outside his authority as a minister; it would be a personal act not the act of the Crown; and it would expose him to a personal liability for contempt. In support of the distinction which he relied upon, Mr Richards referred to the speech of Lord Oliver of Aylmerton in *Attorney-General* v *Times Newspapers Ltd* [1992] 1 AC 191, 217–218, where Lord Oliver stated:

> A distinction (which has been variously described as 'unhelpful' or 'largely meaningless') is sometimes drawn between what is described as 'civil contempt,' that is to say, contempt by a party to proceedings in a matter of procedure, and 'criminal contempt.' One particular form of contempt by a party to proceedings is that constituted by an intentional act which is in breach of the order of a competent court. Where this occurs as a result of the act of a party who is bound by the order or of others acting at his direction or on his instigation, it constitutes a civil contempt by him which is punishable by the court at the instance of the party for whose benefit the order was made and which can be waived by him. The intention with which the act was done will, of course, be of the highest relevance in the determination of the penalty (if any) to be imposed by the court, but the liability here is a strict one in the sense that all that requires to be proved is service of the order and the subsequent doing by the party bound of that which is prohibited. When, however, the prohibited act is done not by the party bound himself but by a third party, a stranger to the litigation, that person may also be liable for contempt. There is, however, this essential distinction that his liability is for criminal contempt and arises not because the contemnor is himself affected by the prohibition contained in the order but because his act constitutes a wilful interference with the administration of justice by the court in the proceedings in which the order was made. Here the liability is not strict in the sense referred to, for there has to be shown not only knowledge of the order but an intention to interfere with or impede the administration of justice—an intention which can of course be inferred from the circumstances.

I happily adopt the approach of Lord Oliver. It reflects the distinction which I have drawn between the finding of contempt and the punishment of the contempt. I also accept the distinction which Lord Oliver draws between the position of a person who is subject to an order and a third party. I also recognise the force of Mr Richards' submission that if Mr Baker was not under a strict liability to comply with the order it would not be possible to establish that he had the necessary intention to interfere with or impede the administration of justice to make him guilty of contempt as a third party. However, although the injunction was granted by Garland J against Mr Baker in his official capacity this does not mean that he is in the same position as a third party. To draw a distinction between his two personalities would be unduly technical. While he was Home Secretary the order was one binding upon him personally and one for the compliance with which he as the head of the department was personally responsible. He was, therefore, under a strict liability to comply with the order. However, on the facts of this case I have little doubt that if the Court of Appeal had appreciated that they could make a finding against Mr Baker in his official capacity this is what the court would have done. The conduct complained of in this case which justified the bringing of contempt proceedings was not that of Mr Baker alone and he was acting on advice. His error was understandable and I accept that there is an element of unfairness in the finding against him personally.

In addition, there are technical differences between the two findings because of the provisions of RSC, Ord. 77, r. 1 which define an 'order against the Crown' in a broad sense to include an order against the government department or against an officer of the Crown as such. Unlike the definition of 'civil proceedings by the Crown,' this definition expressly applies to proceedings 'on the Crown side of the Queen's Bench Division.' This means that the provisions of Orders 45 to 52 (which deal with execution and satisfaction of orders of the court) would not apply to an order against the Home Secretary while they would do so in the case of an order against Mr Baker personally.

It is for these reasons that I would dismiss this appeal and cross-appeal save for substituting the Secretary of State for Home Affairs as being the person against whom the finding of contempt was made. This was the alternative decision which was the subject of the cross-appeal, except that there the order was sought against the Home Office rather than the Home Secretary.

Order of Court of Appeal affirmed save for substitution of designation 'Secretary of State for Home Affairs' as proper object of finding of contempt.

Appeal and cross-appeal dismissed with costs.

■ QUESTIONS

1. Is the effect of this decision to give teeth to Dicey's second proposition regarding the rule of law?
2. Is it desirable that courts should seek to compel the Government to comply with their orders rather than leaving it to the electorate to condemn them in a future election for their failure to comply?
3. Bagehot in *The English Constitution* (1867) drew a distinction between what he referred to as the 'dignified' parts of the constitution and the 'efficient' parts. The former he claimed 'excite and preserve the reverence of the population'. One of the dignified institutions is the monarchy, i.e. the Crown, to whom loyalty is felt or allegiance is owed. The institutions of government are the efficient parts of the constitution wherein real power is vested. In the United Kingdom Government is conducted in the name of the Crown; thus it is referred to as Her Majesty's Government. When Lords Templeman and Woolf distinguished between the Crown as Monarch and the Crown as Executive, were they thereby adopting this distinction drawn by Bagehot?

NOTE: The position of members of the Security Service in relation to their criminal liability has given rise to some heated discussion in recent years. In *Francome and Another* v *Mirror Group Newspapers Ltd and Others* [1984] 2 All ER 408, at p. 412, Lord Donaldson MR stated:

Parliamentary democracy as we know it is based on the rule of law. That requires all citizens to obey the law, unless and until it can be changed by due process. There are no privileged classes to whom it does not apply. [If one person] can assert [a] right to act on the basis that the public interest, as he sees it, justifies breaches of the criminal law, so can any other citizen. This has only to be stated for it to be obvious that the result would be anarchy.... The right to break the law...is not obtainable at all in a parliamentary democracy, although different considerations arise under a totalitarian regime.

In one of the cases arising from the *Spycatcher* affair, *Attorney-General* v *Guardian Newspapers Ltd and Others (No. 2) and related appeals* [1988] 2 WLR 805, at p. 879, Lord Donaldson MR appeared to retreat somewhat from this position.

It would be a sad day for democracy and the rule of law if the service were ever to be considered to be above or exempt from the law of the land. And it is not. At any time any member of the service who breaks the law is liable to be prosecuted. But there is a need for some discretion and common sense. Let us suppose that the service has information which suggests that a spy may be operating from particular premises. It needs to have confirmation. It may well consider that, if he proves to be a spy, the interests of the nation are better served by letting him continue with his activities under surveillance and in ignorance that he has been detected rather than by arresting him. What is the service expected to do? A secret search of the premises is the obvious answer. Is this really 'wrongdoing'?

Let us test it in a mundane context known to us all. Prior to the passing of section 79 of the Road Traffic Regulation Act 1967, fire engines and ambulances, unlike police vehicles, had no exemption from the speed limits. Their drivers hurrying to an emergency broke the law. So far as I am aware that is still the position in relation to crossing traffic lights which are showing red and driving on the wrong side of the road to bypass a traffic jam. The responsible authorities in a very proper exercise of discretion simply do not prosecute them.

Even in the context of the work of the Security Service which, I must stress, is the defence of the realm, there must be stringent limits to what breaches of the law can be considered excusable. Thus I cannot conceive of physical violence ever coming within this category. Or physical restraint, other than in the powers of arrest enjoyed by every citizen or under the authority of a lawful warrant of arrest. But covert invasions of privacy, which I think is what Mr Wright means by 'burglary,' may in some circumstances be a different matter.

It may be that the time has come when Parliament should regularize the position of the service. It is certainly a tenable view. The alternative view, which is equally tenable, is that the public interest is better served by leaving the members of the service liable to prosecution for any breach of the law at the instance of a private individual or of a public prosecuting authority, but may expect that prosecuting authorities will exercise a wise discretion and that in an appropriate case the Attorney-General would enter a nolle prosequi, justifying his action to Parliament if necessary. In so acting, the Attorney-General is not acting as a political minister or as a colleague of ministers. He acts personally and in a quasi-judicial capacity as representing the Crown (see article entitled 'How the security services are bound by the rule of law' by Lord Hailsham in *The Independent*, 3 February 1988). It is not for me to form or express any view on which is the most appropriate course to adopt in the interests of the security of the nation and the maintenance of the rule of law. However that problem is resolved, it is absurd to contend that *any* breach of the law, whatever its character, will constitute such 'wrongdoing' as to deprive the service of the secrecy without which it cannot possibly operate.

■ QUESTIONS

1. Would the rule of law be supported or undermined by criminal activity by members of the Security Service?
2. Does the following provision from the Intelligence Services Act 1994 reaffirm the rule of law, or is it simply a shifting of 'the goalposts' by use of the legality principle? Who is left to decide what action is 'necessary'?
3. To what extent is it true to say that '[t]he section amounts to statutory authorization of ministerial general warrants for reasons of State necessity of the kind which the common law disapproved in the celebrated case of *Entick* v *Carrington*' (I. Leigh and L. Lustgarten, 'The Security Service Act 1989' (1989) 52 *Modern Law Review* 801, at p. 825)? Section 5 of the 1994 Act re-enacts with amendments s. 3 of the 1989 Act.

INTELLIGENCE SERVICES ACT 1994

5.—(1) No entry on or interference with property or with wireless telegraphy shall be unlawful if it is authorised by a warrant issued by the Secretary of State under this section.

(2) The Secretary of State may, on an application made by the Security Service, the Intelligence Service or GCHQ, issue a warrant under this section authorising the taking, subject to subsection (3) below, of such action as is specified in the warrant in respect of any property so specified or in respect of wireless telegraphy so specified if the Secretary of State—

(a) thinks it necessary for the action to be taken on the ground that it is likely to be of substantial value in assisting, as the case may be,—
   (i) the Security Service in carrying out any of its functions under the [Security Service Act] 1989...; or
   (ii) the Intelligence Service in carrying out any of its functions under section 1 above; or
   (iii) GCHQ in carrying out any function which falls within section 3(1)(a) above; and
(b) is satisfied that what the action seeks to achieve cannot reasonably be achieved by other means; and
(c) is satisfied that satisfactory arrangements are in force under section 2(2)(a) of the 1989 Act (duties of the Director-General of the Security Service), section 2(2)(a) above or section 4(2)(a) above with respect to the disclosure of information obtained by virtue of this section and that any information obtained under the warrant will be subject to those arrangements.

4

Judicial Independence

OVERVIEW

In this chapter we return to the separation of powers, focusing on the enhancement of judicial independence by the clearer separation between the judiciary and the other organs of government brought about by the Constitutional Reform Act 2005 and its changes to the office of Lord Chancellor, the arrangements for judicial appointment and discipline, and then we examine the judiciary's accountability to Parliament and the public.

SECTION 1: JUDICIAL INDEPENDENCE

A: Legal constitutionalism?

Before we examine how judicial independence has been enhanced, we consider first a case in which one senior judge is raising the question as to whether it is appropriate that we move to a conception of the separation of the powers where the courts are playing more of a checking role on the executive and legislature.

R v Secretary of State for the Home Department, ex parte Fire Brigades Union

[1995] 2 AC 513, House of Lords

LORD MUSTILL:.. This prompts one final observation. It is a feature of the peculiarly British conception of the separation of powers that Parliament, the executive and the courts each have their distinct and largely exclusive domain. Parliament has a legally unchallengeable right to make whatever laws it thinks right. The executive carries on the administration of the country in accordance with the powers conferred on it by law. The courts interpret the laws, and see that they are obeyed. This requires the courts on occasion to step into the territory which belongs to the executive, not only to verify that the powers asserted accord with the substantive law created by Parliament, but also, that the manner in which they are exercised conforms with the standards of fairness which Parliament must have intended. Concurrently with this judicial function Parliament has its own special means of ensuring that the executive, in the exercise of delegated functions, performs in a way which Parliament finds appropriate. Ideally, it is these latter methods which should be used to check executive errors and excesses; for it is the task of Parliament and the executive in tandem, not of the courts, to govern the country. In recent years, however, the employment in practice of these specifically Parliamentary remedies has on occasion been perceived as falling short, and sometimes well short, of what was needed to bring the performance of the executive into line with the law, and with the minimum standards of fairness implicit in every Parliamentary delegation of a decision-making function. To avoid a vacuum in which the citizen would be left without protection against a misuse of executive powers the courts have had no option but to occupy the dead ground in a manner, and in areas of public life, which could not have been foreseen thirty years ago. For myself, I am quite satisfied that this unprecedented judicial role has been greatly to the public benefit. Nevertheless, it has its risks, of which the courts are well aware. As the judges themselves constantly remark, it is not they who are appointed to administer the country. Absent a written constitution much sensitivity is required of the parliamentarian, administrator and judge if the delicate balance of the unwritten rules evolved (I believe successfully) in recent years is not to be disturbed, and all the recent advances undone. I do not for a moment suggest that the judges of the Court of Appeal in the present case overlooked this need. The judgments show clearly that they did not. Nevertheless some of the arguments addressed would have the court push to the very boundaries of the distinction between court and Parliament established in, and recognised ever since, the Bill of Rights 1688. Three hundred years have passed since then, and the political and social landscape has changed beyond recognition. But the boundaries remain; they are of crucial significance to our private and public lives; and the courts should I believe make sure that they are not overstepped.

NOTES

1. The dispute in the case concerned the action of the Home Secretary in using the royal prerogative to create a replacement for a criminal injuries scheme also established under the prerogative, instead of implementing a statutory scheme authorized by the Criminal Justice Act 1988 (see p. 326, *post*).
2. Tomkins in his book *Public Law* (2003), pp. 24–30 and Barendt in his article 'Constitutional Law and the Criminal Injuries Compensation Act [2005] *Public Law,* 357 make a similar point about the approach taken by Lord Mustill in contrast to the majority. Barendt argues that Lord Mustill adopted a constitutional law approach and the majority an administrative law approach. For Tomkins, Lord Mustill is adopting more of a political constitutional approach compared to the majority who are legal constitutionalists carrying out statutory interpretation. Lord Mustill wonders if the increasing resort to the courts and the expansion of their reach, which in this case enlarged the judicial control of the royal prerogative, is appropriate, although he does not doubt that in relation to the judiciary, the concept of separation of powers means that they must be guaranteed independence from the other two organs of government.

■ QUESTION

As you read the reasons underlying the desirability for the Constitutional Act reforms, are they driven by principle, by trying to keep in line with other countries, or a pragmatic approach to resolving problems in seeking to redress people's grievances?

B: The Constitutional Reform Act 2005

K. Malleson, 'The Effect of the Constitutional Reform Act 2005 on the Relationship Between the Judiciary, the Executive and Parliament', Sixth Report from the House of Lords Select Committee on the Constitution

HL 151 of 2006–07, pp. 60–61

The Background to the Constitutional Reform Act 2005

The origins of the Constitutional Reform Act lie in the expanding role played by the higher courts in the UK over the last thirty years. The combined effect of the growth of judicial review, the development of the EU and, most recently, the Human Rights Act and devolution has been to give the courts a more central place in the British constitution. The senior judges are now required to police constitutional boundaries and determine sensitive human rights issues in a way which would have been unthinkable forty years ago. This new judicial role is still developing, but it is clear that the effect of this trend will be to reshape the relationship between the judiciary and the other branches of government. In the light of these changes, the main provisions of the Constitutional Reform Act—reforming the office of Lord Chancellor, establishing a new Supreme Court and restructuring the judicial appointments process—were designed to bring the institutional relationships between the judiciary and the other branches of government into line with the changing substantive role of the courts. In particular, the reforms were intended to secure the independence of the judiciary by 'redrawing the relationship between the judiciary and the other branches of government' and putting it on a 'modern footing'.

Although the timing of the introduction of the Constitutional Reform Bill in 2003 took many by surprise, its content did not. Concerns about the relationship between the judiciary and the other branches of government had been building up over a number of years. Where once there had been a general consensus that the Lord Chancellor's three roles as member of cabinet, head of the judiciary and speaker of the House of Lords enhanced the functioning of the political system and strengthened judicial independence, they increasingly came to be regarded as a potential source of abuse of executive power. In particular, the Lord Chancellor's responsibility for appointing the judges became a source of growing concern as the senior judges' role in scrutinising government decision-making increased. Likewise, the presence of the top appellate court in Parliament had once been widely regarded as an effective means of drawing on the legal expertise of the top judges during the law-making process so enhancing the quality of legislation. By the 1990s, however, many Law Lords themselves had come to regard the lack of separation between the two as problematic as the same senior judges who participated in passing the laws were increasingly asked to decide on the conformity of those acts with basic human rights.

By the late 1990s, far fewer voices were heard in support of the argument that these overlaps between the branches of government were a source of its stability. Increasingly, the interconnection was seen as endangering judicial independence, breaching basic constitutional principles and out of step with the rest of Europe. By the start of the second term of the Labour Government in 2001, the long debate about these issues had slowly generated broad support across the political spectrum for a 'clearer and deeper' separation of the functions and powers of the judiciary from the other branches of government. The decision to embark upon extensive institutional reform was therefore anticipated, but the provisions set out in the Constitutional Reform Act were unusual in a number of respects. First, they ran counter to the trend of recent political developments in that they represented a conscious shift of power away from the executive. Second, they were forward looking, seeking to construct a new constitutional model which anticipated future needs rather than responding to an immediate perceived problem. In introducing the reforms the Government made clear that there was no suggestion that the overlapping constitutional roles of the Lord Chancellor or the presence of the Law Lords in the House of Lords had, in practice, undermined judicial independence but rather that the present system held inherent structural weaknesses which might give rise to such abuse in the future. The third surprising feature of the reforms is that they explicitly sought to promote constitutional principle above pragmatism. Whilst accepting that the previous arrangements had worked effectively, the changes were designed to restructure the relationship between the judiciary and the other branches of government so that it would conform more closely to the concept of the separation of powers. This elevation of principle above pragmatism is surprising given the traditional value ascribed to 'what works' in the British constitution.

NOTES

1. Various groups had been canvassing the creation of a judicial appointments commission and separating the Law Lords from Parliament and a restructuring to create a Ministry of Justice (see *Constitutional Innovation: the Creation of a Supreme Court for the United Kingdom; Domestic, Comparative and International Reflection* the special issue (2004) 24 *Legal Studies* 1–293). The Lord Chancellor, Lord Irvine of Lairg, was not in favour of reducing the roles and functions of the Lord Chancellor, and did not want to relinquish sitting as a judge, although he sat less frequently than many of his predecessors. When he left office unexpectedly in 2003, announcements were made about various reforms including the abolition of the post of Lord Chancellor and the renaming of the Lord Chancellor's Department as the Department for Constitutional Affairs. The abolition of the post of Lord Chancellor did not happen as it was realized that the reallocation of the Lord Chancellor's responsibilities was complicated and would require primary legislation. Consultation papers on Judicial Appointments and the creation of a Supreme Court followed a month later.

   The new Lord Chancellor, Lord Falconer, said that he would not sit as a judge. It is thought that this and the proposal to create a separate Supreme Court were partially attributable to the finding of a breach of Art. 6 of the European Convention in *McGonnell* v *UK* (2000) 30 EHRR 289. In this case the Bailiff of Guernsey determined a planning appeal having previously presided over proceedings in the legislature during which a development plan at issue in the planning appeal was adopted. The European Court of Human Rights ruled:

   1. The Court can agree with the [UK] Government that neither Article 6 nor any other provision of the Convention requires States to comply with any theoretical constitutional concepts as

such. The question is always whether, in a given case, the requirements of the Convention are met. The present case does not, therefore, require the application of any particular doctrine of constitutional law to the position in Guernsey: the Court is faced solely with the question whether the Bailiff had the required "appearance" of independence, or the required "objective" impartiality...

2. The Court thus considers that the mere fact that the Deputy Bailiff presided over the States of Deliberation when DDP6 was adopted in 1990 is capable of casting doubt on his impartiality when he subsequently determined, as the sole judge of the law in the case, the applicant's planning appeal. The applicant therefore had legitimate grounds for fearing that the Bailiff may have been influenced by his prior participation in the adoption of DDP6. That doubt in itself, however slight its justification, is sufficient to vitiate the impartiality of the Royal Court, and it is therefore unnecessary for the Court to look into the other aspects of the complaint.

Following the judgment Lord Irvine stated that he would 'never sit in any case concerning legislation in the passage of which he had been directly involved nor in any case where the interests of the executive were directly engaged' (HL Debs. Vol. 610, 23 February 2000, WA33). Contrast that reaction with a Scottish case about temporary sheriffs (judges) decided under the Human Rights Act 1998 which entered into force earlier in Scotland than England, which did lead to action to restore compatibility with convention rights on both sides of the border, and adjust the constitutional climate to a greater awareness of (potential) threats to judicial independence.

Starrs v *Ruxton* 2000 SLT 42

LORD REED: ...In my opinion, the most important of the three factors relied upon by the appellants is the absence of security of tenure. It was common ground before us that, as a matter of law, a temporary sheriff can be removed from office at any time for any reason. It was also common ground that a temporary sheriff can be appointed on an annual basis and that his allocation to courts, and the renewal of his appointment, are thereafter within the unfettered discretion of the Executive.... I am prepared to proceed on the basis that a temporary sheriff does not, as a matter of law, enjoy anything which constitutes security of tenure in the normally accepted sense of that term.

...

It is apparent that the system as operated depends on an assessment by the Scottish Executive, or in practice an assessment by the Lord Advocate, of what should be regarded as grounds for removal from office (or as grounds for not renewing the appointment or for deciding not to allocate work to a particular temporary sheriff, which are in substance equivalent to removal from office), and of what general policies should be followed (e.g. as to retiral age). The practice may alter from time to time, as in fact happened when the age limit of 65 was introduced. I do not doubt that the system has been operated by successive Lords Advocate with integrity and sound judgment, free from political considerations, and with a careful regard to the need to respect judicial independence. That is no doubt why it has operated for so long without occasioning any widespread expression of public concern, although disquiet has on occasion been expressed by members of the judiciary and others in Parliament and in academic or professional contexts. There is however no objective guarantee of security of tenure, such as can be found in section 12 of the 1971 Act; and I regard the absence of such a guarantee as fatal to the compatibility of the present system with Article 6.

The Solicitor General emphasised that it is inconceivable that the Lord Advocate would interfere with the performance of judicial functions. I readily accept that; but that is not the point. Judicial independence can be threatened not only by interference by the Executive, but also by a judge's being influenced, consciously or unconsciously, by his hopes and fears as to his possible treatment by the Executive. It is for that reason that a judge must not be dependent on the Executive, however well the Executive may behave: 'independence' connotes the absence of dependence. It also has to be borne in mind that judicial independence exists to protect the integrity of the judiciary and confidence in the administration of justice, and thus society as a whole, in bad times as well as good. The adequacy of judicial independence cannot appropriately be tested on the assumption that the Executive will always behave with appropriate restraint: as the European Court of Human Rights has emphasised in its interpretation of Article 6, it is important that there be 'guarantees' against outside pressures. In short, for the judiciary to be dependent on the Executive flies in the face of the principle of the separation of powers which is central to the requirement of judicial independence in Article 6…

Appeals allowed. Bills of Advocation passed.

NOTE: This decision led to no new business being allocated to temporary sheriffs. In the Bail, Judicial Appointments etc. (Scotland) Act 2000, s. 6 abolished the position of temporary sheriff and s. 7 created the new position of part-time sheriff to address the concerns about security of tenure raised in the High Court.

The Lord Chancellor carried out a review of the terms of service of part-time judicial office-holders in England and Wales, and Northern Ireland. On 12 April 2000 he announced that all Assistant Recorders would be appointed Recorders and that new arrangements to ensure independence would be brought in for part-time judicial appointments and certain part-time Tribunals appointments. Part-time appointments would be for a period of not less than five years.

A. Bradley, 'The New Constitutional Relationship Between the Judiciary, Government and Parliament'

Sixth Report from the House of Lords Select Committee on the Constitution, HL 151 of 2006–7, pp. 73–74

B The Constitutional Reform Act 2005

10. The principal structural changes made by the CRA may be very briefly summarised. They have provided for greater formal separation between government and judiciary (and, as regards the new Supreme Court, between Parliament and judiciary) and for a new statutory interface in England and Wales between government, in the person of the Lord Chancellor, and the judiciary, represented by the Lord Chief Justice.

(A) Contrary to the original intention of the Government, the Lord Chancellor remains in being, but he has lost his status as head of the judiciary in England and Wales and may not now sit as a judge. This greater separation between executive and judiciary made it essential for many functions of the Lord Chancellor to be reassigned, some being transferred to the Lord Chief Justice, others being exercisable jointly by the Lord Chancellor and the Lord Chief Justice. The Lord Chancellor retains many important executive functions relating to the judiciary (including funding the system of justice, making judicial appointments in accordance with new statutory rules, and approving procedural rules for the courts). Many of these functions are ring-fenced, to ensure that they are not transferred to another Minister by the Prime Minister without further primary legislation. Under the CRA, the Lord Chancellor is not required to have had a legal career, nor to be a member of the House of Lords.

(B) The Lord Chief Justice is now President of the Courts and Head of the Judiciary of England and Wales. He is responsible:

- (i) for representing the views of the judiciary to Parliament, to the Lord Chancellor and to other Ministers;
- (ii) for maintaining appropriate arrangements for the welfare, training and guidance of the judiciary within resources made available by the Lord Chancellor; and
- (iii) for maintaining appropriate arrangements for the deployment of the judiciary and the allocation of work within courts.

These broad duties are accompanied by many specific responsibilities, some of which are exercisable jointly with the Lord Chancellor, or with the concurrence of the Lord Chancellor.

(C) There will be a new Supreme Court for the United Kingdom, to take over the appellate functions now performed by the Appellate Committees of the House of Lords, together with the power to decide devolution issues transferred from the Judicial Committee of the Privy Council. This separation between the 'Law Lords' and the House does not mean any change in the extent of appellate jurisdiction. New provision has been made for funding and administering the Supreme Court. The CRA sets out in detail the procedure for the selection and appointment of judges to the Supreme Court, in place of the present practice by which the Prime Minister nominates to the Queen persons for appointment as Lords of Appeal in Ordinary.

(D) Judicial appointments in general are entrusted to the Judicial Appointments Commission, and are no longer a matter primarily for decision by Ministers. Within the framework of the CRA, it will be for the Commission to give substance to the statutory rule that selection must be solely on merit (section 63(2)); and the Commission must have regard to the need to encourage diversity in the range of persons available for selection (section 64(1)).

(E) A new post of Judicial Appointments and Conduct Ombudsman is created to deal with two rather different classes of complaint: (a) in relation to the observance of proper procedure in judicial appointments, and (b) in respect of the conduct of judges.

(F) While the historic tenure of senior judges derived from the Act of Settlement continues (subject to a new power to suspend a judge while parliamentary proceedings for removal are pending: section 108(6)), the removal of other judges by the Lord Chancellor is now subject to statutory procedures; in general, disciplinary powers in respect of the judiciary (including power to suspend) may be exercised by the Lord Chief Justice, acting with the agreement of the Lord Chancellor.

11. The cumulative effect of the changes made by the CRA is very extensive. Alongside the statutory provisions has to be read a document known as the Concordat, entitled *Constitutional Reform: the Lord Chancellor's judiciary-related functions*, prepared in January 2004 while the Constitutional Reform Bill was before the House of Lords, at a time when the Government was proposing to abolish the office of Lord Chancellor and it was not known what the attitude of the judiciary would be to the proposals. The Concordat represented an agreement between the Lord Chancellor and the Lord Chief Justice (then Lord Woolf) regarding the future exercise of the Lord Chancellor's judiciary-related functions, and as such it facilitated the passage of the Constitutional Reform Bill through Parliament.

C: The Lord Chancellor

The Constitutional Reform Act did not, as the government had originally intended, abolish the office of Lord Chancellor, rather it made it possible for future holders of the office to be MPs and not to be legally qualified. Jack Straw MP was the first MP to hold the office, although he did qualify as a barrister as did his successor Ken Clarke QC, MP. There had been substantial opposition to these changes, not least amongst the judges who felt that the Lord Chancellor was both a link and a protecting barrier between the executive and the judiciary. The Constitutional Reform Act 2005 provides:

3 Guarantee of continued judicial independence

(1) The Lord Chancellor, other Ministers of the Crown and all with responsibility for matters relating to the judiciary or otherwise to the administration of justice must uphold the continued independence of the judiciary...

(4) The following particular duties are imposed for the purpose of upholding that independence.

(5) The Lord Chancellor and other Ministers of the Crown must not seek to influence particular judicial decisions through any special access to the judiciary.

(6) The Lord Chancellor must have regard to—

- (a) the need to defend that independence;
- (b) the need for the judiciary to have the support necessary to enable them to exercise their functions;
- (c) the need for the public interest in regard to matters relating to the judiciary or otherwise to the administration of justice to be properly represented in decisions affecting those matters.

(7) In this section "the judiciary" includes the judiciary of any of the following—

- (a) the Supreme Court;
- (b) any other court established under the law of any part of the United Kingdom;
- (c) any international court.

Thus all Ministers and those with administration of justice responsibilities must uphold judicial independence. During the passage of the bill some wanted the provision to be strengthened so as to be capable of enforcement and to be protected against implied repeal. In evidence to the House of Lords Select Committee which examined the Constitutional Reform Bill. Lord Woolf compared it to declaratory provisions that had been included in education and National Health Service legislation, and told the Committee that it was not intended that such declaratory provisions should be enforceable in the courts and that a minister failing to fulfil the responsibilities set out in the Clause 'would be answerable to Parliament and the public for the failure to do so' (HL 125 of 2003–4, para. 76).

The fears of those who were concerned about Ministers not upholding judicial independence have been realized.

Sixth Report from the House of Lords Select Committee on the Constitution

HL 151 of 2006–07, paras 42–43, 45–49, 51

42. It seems there is widespread agreement on the limits of what ministers should and should not say about individual cases, but this does not mean that ministers will always behave accordingly. The Lord Chancellor's duty, as the defender of judicial independence in the Cabinet, is both to ensure that ministers are aware of the need to avoid attacking individual judges and to reprimand them if they breach this principle. As Lord Falconer told us, "the effect of the Constitutional Reform Act is that I have got an obligation to speak out both privately and, if necessary, publicly to defend the independence of the judges". As to whether his performance of this role had been adversely affected by the fact that he was no longer a judge or head of the judiciary, he insisted "emphatically not".

43. The Lord Chief Justice has emphasised that this kind of intervention by the Lord Chancellor is "a most valuable constitutional protection of judicial independence", because the only alternative would be for the Lord Chief Justice himself to intervene publicly, which would risk a high-profile dispute that would not be "in the interests of the administration of justice". Lord Mackay of Clashfern added that "the sooner a response is made [by the Lord Chancellor] the better"...

45. There has moreover been one case since the CRA was enacted where the then Lord Chancellor, Lord Falconer, was forced to speak out publicly. The case concerned the convicted paedophile Craig Sweeney, who was given a life sentence with a minimum tariff of five years and 108 days. When passing sentence in the Crown Court at Cardiff in June 2003, Judge Griffith Williams, the Recorder of Cardiff, explained very clearly how he reached this tariff and emphasised that Sweeney would only be released "when and if there is no risk of you re-offending". Nonetheless, the then Home Secretary (John Reid MP) attacked the sentence as "unduly lenient" and asked the then Attorney General (Lord Goldsmith) to examine the case as the tariff "does not reflect the seriousness of the crime", thereby inappropriately casting aspersions on the competence of Judge Williams. Lord Goldsmith's spokesman responded sharply to Dr Reid's comments, pledging that "the Attorney will make a decision [on whether to appeal] purely on the merits of the case and not in response to political or public pressure".

46 ...In short, Lord Falconer did not publicly defend Judge Williams until appearing on the BBC's *Question Time* programme three days after the sentence was handed down. Even then, he defended Dr Reid's intervention. Lord Falconer subsequently had to rebuke and extract an apology from his junior minister, Vera Baird MP, for directly criticising the judge when appearing on a radio programme. The Lord Chief Justice later labelled the attacks "intemperate, offensive and unfair", whilst the Secretary of the Council of Circuit Judges, Judge Keith Cutler, told the BBC that "some of the judges felt that there was quite a silence, and there was no-one actually speaking on behalf of the judges... We are thinking that we must perhaps change that". Ultimately, Judge Williams was vindicated when Lord Goldsmith decided not to appeal.

47. When we asked the panel of legal editors about this case, they were highly critical of the then Lord Chancellor. Frances Gibb, Legal Editor of *The Times*, told us that "the Lord Chancellor should have stepped

in much more quickly to defend judges in the face of some of his colleagues' comments", and Joshua Rozenberg, Legal Editor of *The Daily Telegraph*, said that the Lord Chancellor had left the judges "to swing in the wind". Astonishingly, Mr Rozenberg had been told by a DCA press officer that it was for the Lord Chief Justice rather than the Lord Chancellor to speak out on these matters.

48. Although the Lord Chief Justice could have publicly criticised Dr Reid, this would probably have exacerbated tensions between the executive and the judiciary at a sensitive time. In fact, the Lord Chief Justice was in Poland at the time and the responsibility for dealing with the controversy fell to Sir Igor Judge. He did not speak to Lord Falconer until two days after the sentence was handed down, and in retrospect admitted that he should have contacted him "more quickly". The Lord Chief Justice should also have been more proactive in ensuring that the matter was being dealt with promptly.

49. The Sweeney case was the first big test of whether the new relationship between the Lord Chancellor and the judiciary was working properly, and it is clear that there was a systemic failure. Ensuring that ministers do not impugn individual judges, and restraining and reprimanding those who do, is one of the most important duties of the Lord Chancellor. In this case, Lord Falconer did not fulfil this duty in a satisfactory manner. The senior judiciary could also have acted more quickly to head off the inflammatory and unfair press coverage which followed the sentencing decision...

51. The key to harmonious relations between the judiciary and the executive is ensuring that ministers do not violate the independence of the judiciary in the first place. To this end, we recommend that when the Ministerial Code is next revised the Prime Minister should insert strongly worded guidelines setting out the principles governing public comment by ministers on individual judges.

■ QUESTIONS

1. If the Lord Chancellor is a junior member of the cabinet might that play a part in the speed and robustness of action under the s. 3 duty taken against a more senior cabinet colleague?
2. What would be the appropriate sanction for a Minister who breached this duty if it was included in the Ministerial Code?

D: The Supreme Court

The point made by Malleson is that the creation of a Supreme Court was seemingly and unusually in the UK, more driven by principle than pragmatism. The Government's case for the creation of a Supreme Court was that 'The Government believes that in so doing they will reflect and enhance the independence of the Judiciary from both the legislature and the executive'. How real were the threats to judicial independence by having judges who were also members of the legislature? Judicial independence assists the impartiality of the judges.

J. Webber, Supreme Courts, Independence and Democratic Agency

(2004) 24 *Legal Studies* 55, 63, 67–68

...the law of bias has always required definite indication of extraneous influence or predetermination. Cases of bias tend to fall into one of three categories: 1) where the decision-maker has declared his or her opinion on the specific case in issue—where he or she has literally prejudged the issue on these facts; 2) where the judge has a strong antipathy or a close connection to a party—a connection that goes beyond mere sympathy, so that the judge might be seen to have an extraneous interest in the outcome (for example, the existence of family relationship, business association, professional partnership, or close friendship between the judge and a party); or 3) where the judge may obtain a direct personal benefit from the outcome. The disqualification of Lord Hoffmann in the Pinochet extradition case met this higher test: Lord Hoffmann was at the time a director of a charity that was closely aligned to Amnesty International and that shared Amnesty's objects; Amnesty itself had become a party to the Pinochet case precisely in order to argue for a particular outcome... All that is left, in the great run of cases, is whether simple membership in the House of Lords is sufficient to generate bias in the same way that being an officer of a company might do so in a private dispute. Might the position of the Law Lords, when viewed in this light, be analogous to that of Lord Hoffmann? The arguments have not generally been posed in this form. They have focused instead on the possibility of bias on a specific issue, for good reason. The Parliament of the United Kingdom is not characterised by a unified commitment to a set of objects. It is a deliberative body in which individuals representing a wide range of interests come together to debate matters for society as a whole. It does not make sense, then, to presume bias on the basis of mere membership, but rather to focus on the specific impairment of decision-making...

The constraints that the Law Lords have voluntarily assumed deal effectively, in substance, with both impartiality and judicial independence. The remaining concerns seem highly abstract and formal. Of course, problems of impartiality and substantive independence may still arise in particular cases—they arise even in courts that enjoy full institutional separation—but those can be addressed by the individual judges withdrawing from those cases. In fact, this remedy is more easily available in the Appellate Committee than it is in most supreme courts. Most such courts have a set membership, combined with a strong ethic that each case should be heard by the full bench. In contrast, less than half the full-time membership of the Appellate Committee sits on any given case, and there remain a number of additional judges who may be called upon if necessary. There is therefore much greater scope for avoiding situations of conflict.

It is true that the Appellate Committee's independence and impartiality depends on the Law Lords' own good sense—on their judgment in restricting their activities in the legislative business of the House, on maintaining their relative freedom from party entanglements, and on recusing themselves when their engagements have compromised their ability to judge, in fact or in appearance. The current structure does not provide the peremptory barriers to legislative entanglement that institutional separation would create. There might be some reason to remove the judges from the House in order to erect such barriers, if the presence of the Law Lords offered no substantial benefits (although it is important to realise that barriers could supplement but not replace the role of a strong judicial ethic; in matters like this, structure can never do all the work). In weighing that balance, one would want to assess carefully the contributions made by the Law Lords to the legislative business of the House—a task I leave to others. But one would also want to weigh the symbolic implications of the change, implications that (I believe) speak to the important subtext that runs throughout the present debate.

NOTES

1. The argument was put that it was useful for the Law Lords to participate in the legislative proceedings of the House of Lords as they could contribute legal expertise but also they would gain knowledge and understanding from their involvement. The Royal Commission on Reform of the House of Lords in its 2000 report *A House for the Future* (Cm 4183) thought the Law Lords should be retained for their expertise and recommended that they issue a statement on the principles which would regulate their involvement in the legislature (para. 9.10). Lord Bingham as Senior Law Lord made a statement on behalf of the Law Lords (HL Debs. Vol. 610, col 419, 22 June 2000):

> ...first, the Lords of Appeal in Ordinary do not think it appropriate to engage in matters where there is a strong element of party political controversy; and secondly the Lords of Appeal in Ordinary bear in mind that they might render themselves ineligible to sit judicially if they were to express an opinion on a matter which might later be relevant to an appeal to the House.

The consequence of this was that only four Law Lords subsequently intervened in proceedings, Lords Nicholls and Hoffmann on one occasion each, Lord Hope on five occasions and Lord Scott on 11 occasions, seven of which were debates on reports of the Lord's European Affairs Select Committee and he was the chairman of its sub-committee on Law and Institutions (Appendix 8, HL 124 of 2003–04).

A majority of the Law Lords in their response to the Government's consultation paper on the Supreme Court took the view that, 'on pragmatic grounds, the proposed change is unnecessary and will be harmful' (Lords Nicholls of Birkenhead, Hoffmann, Hope of Craighead, Hutton, Millett, Rodger of Earlsferry) and a minority 'regard the functional separation of the judiciary at all levels from the legislature and the executive as a cardinal feature of a modern, liberal, democratic state governed by the rule of law' (Lords Bingham of Cornhill, Steyn, Saville of Newdigate, Walker of Gestingthorpe).

2. Another area of concern about Law Lords (and other judges too) is their chairing of inquiries which are politically controversial. The arguments for and against the involvement of judges were considered by the House of Commons Public Administration Select Committee report on the proposed legislation on inquiries. The committee endorsed Lord Woolf's wish that the legislation should not only require consultation by Ministers with the relevant Chief Justice or Senior Law Lord (now President of the Supreme Court) when proposing to appoint a judge but that the decision should be taken co-equally. The Government resisted this and when the Lords amended the bill to give, in effect, the Chief Justice a veto, they were overturned in the Commons and the Lords did not press the matter. Mr Leslie MP, the Minister who moved the amendment to restore consultation said:

> It is important to emphasise that we are talking about inviting a judge to chair an inquiry, not forcing them. The sense that Ministers are somehow able to undermine the independence of a judge is slightly peculiar, to say the least. All our judges are of the highest standing and repute and would not take on inquiries if they felt that they were being used, as some would suggest. Judges will be able to decide for themselves whether to chair inquiries and neither the Lord Chief Justice nor the Minister should be able to force a judge to do so or have a veto on a judge's involvement (Standing Committee B 22 March col 67).

Earlier at col. 62 he had said:

> The matter reaches further than consideration of just the impact on the judiciary and the administration of justice because, when appointing an inquiry panel, Ministers should be able to weigh up what is in the wider public interest. That depends on many factors, including the nature of the problem and the level of public concern. To be blunt, public inquiries can be more important than the judicial business demands that apply from time to time in the courts. For instance, the appointment of Lord Phillips as chairman of the BSE inquiry is an example of a case in which the wider public interest of investigating that crisis outweighed the loss of the Lord to the courts.

See the Public Administration Committee report HC 51 of 2005–06 and Sir J. Beatson 'Should Judges Conduct Public Inquiries?' (2005) 121 *Law Quarterly Review* 221.

■ QUESTION

If the principle of judicial independence requires the separation of senior judges from the legislature, does it not apply with as much, or even more force to government invitations to conduct inquiries?

E: Judicial appointments

The judicial appointments process established under the CRA is somewhat complex with variations for different judges in (a) the Supreme Court, (b) for the Court of Appeal and for Heads of Division and the Lord Chief Justice and (c) the High Court and below. In the consultation paper there were three models of judicial appointments commission suggested: the appointing, the recommending and the hybrid and the Government's preference was for a recommending commission with a single candidate being put forward which the Minister could select for appointment by the Sovereign.

The first justices of the Supreme Court were the current Law Lords but future appointments will involve a Commission which is different from that used for High Court judges. In part this can be justified by the fact that the Supreme Court is a United Kingdom body and that there are judicial appointments bodies throughout the three jurisdictions. In Scotland a non-statutory Judicial Appointments Board (five legal and five lay members chaired by a lay member), in Northern Ireland the Northern Ireland Judicial Appointments Commission (chaired by the Lord Chief Justice with five other judicial members, five lay members and a practising solicitor and barrister) and in England and Wales the Judicial Appointments Commission (JAC, see its composition at p. 138, *post*). The members of the selection commission for the Supreme Court are the Supreme Court President and Deputy President, with one member each from the three judicial appointments bodies nominated by the Lord Chancellor on the recommendation of those bodies. One of these three members is not to be legally qualified. The statute specifies those judges who may take the place of the President or Deputy President on the selection commission. Such judges must indicate that they are not candidates for the post for which they are selecting. Under s. 26, it will be the Prime Minister who nominates to the Sovereign the candidate for appointment to the Supreme Court. The process which notifies that nomination is as follows.

Constitutional Reform Act 2005

27 Selection process

(1) The commission must—

(a) determine the selection process to be applied,
(b) apply the selection process, and
(c) make a selection accordingly.

(2) As part of the selection process the commission must consult each of the following—

(a) such of the senior judges as are not members of the commission and are not willing to be considered for selection;
(b) the Lord Chancellor;
(c) the First Minister in Scotland;
(d) the First Minister for Wales;
(e) the Secretary of State for Northern Ireland.

(3) If for any part of the United Kingdom no judge of the courts of that part is to be consulted under subsection (2)(a), the commission must consult as part of the selection process the most senior judge of the courts of that part who is not a member of the commission and is not willing to be considered for selection.

(4) Subsections (5) to (10) apply to any selection under this section or section 31.

(5) Selection must be on merit.

(6) A person may be selected only if he meets the requirements of section 25.

(7) A person may not be selected if he is a member of the commission.

(8) In making selections for the appointment of judges of the Court the commission must ensure that between them the judges will have knowledge of, and experience of practice in, the law of each part of the United Kingdom.

(9) The commission must have regard to any guidance given by the Lord Chancellor as to matters to be taken into account (subject to any other provision of this Act) in making a selection.

(10) Any selection must be of one person only.

28 Report

(1) After complying with section 27 the commission must submit a report to the Lord Chancellor.

(2) The report must—

(a) state who has been selected;
(b) state the senior judges consulted under section 27(2)(a) and any judge consulted under section 27(3);
(c) contain any other information required by the Lord Chancellor.

(3) The report must be in a form approved by the Lord Chancellor.

(4) After submitting the report the commission must provide any further information the Lord Chancellor may require.

(5) When he receives the report the Lord Chancellor must consult each of the following—

(a) the senior judges consulted under section 27(2)(a);
(b) any judge consulted under section 27(3);
(e) the First Minister in Scotland;
(f) the First Minister for Wales;
(g) the Secretary of State for Northern Ireland.

29 The Lord Chancellor's options

(1) This section refers to the following stages—
Stage 1: where a person has been selected under section 27
Stage 2: where a person has been selected following a rejection or reconsideration at stage 1
Stage 3: where a person has been selected following a rejection or reconsideration at stage 2.

(2) At stage 1 the Lord Chancellor must do one of the following—

(a) notify the selection;
(b) reject the selection;
(c) require the commission to reconsider the selection.

(3) At stage 2 the Lord Chancellor must do one of the following—

(a) notify the selection;
(b) reject the selection, but only if it was made following a reconsideration at stage 1;
(c) require the commission to reconsider the selection, but only if it was made following a rejection at stage 1.

(4) At stage 3 the Lord Chancellor must notify the selection, unless subsection (5) applies and he makes a notification under it.

(5) If a person whose selection the Lord Chancellor required to be reconsidered at stage 1 or 2 was not selected again at the next stage, the Lord Chancellor may at stage 3 notify that person's name to the Prime Minister.

(6) In this Part references to the Lord Chancellor notifying a selection are references to his notifying to the Prime Minister the name of the person selected.

30 Exercise of powers to reject or require reconsideration

(1) The power of the Lord Chancellor under section 29 to reject a selection at stage 1 or 2 is exercisable only on the grounds that, in the Lord Chancellor's opinion, the person selected is not suitable for the office concerned.

(2) The power of the Lord Chancellor under section 29 to require the commission to reconsider a selection at stage 1 or 2 is exercisable only on the grounds that, in the Lord Chancellor's opinion—

there is not enough evidence that the person is suitable for the office concerned,
there is evidence that the person is not the best candidate on merit, or
there is not enough evidence that if the person were appointed the judges of the Court would between them have knowledge of, and experience of practice in, the law of each part of the United Kingdom.

(3) The Lord Chancellor must give the commission reasons in writing for rejecting or requiring reconsideration of a selection.

31 Selection following rejection or requirement to reconsider

(1) If under section 29 the Lord Chancellor rejects or requires reconsideration of a selection at stage 1 or 2, the commission must select a person in accordance with this section.

(2) If the Lord Chancellor rejects a selection, the commission—
may not select the person rejected, and
where the rejection is following reconsideration of a selection, may not select the person (if different) whose selection it reconsidered.

(3) If the Lord Chancellor requires a selection to be reconsidered, the commission—

may select the same person or a different person, but
where the requirement is following a rejection, may not select the person rejected.

(4) The commission must inform the Lord Chancellor of the person selected following a rejection or requirement to reconsider.

NOTE: For appointments in England and Wales to the High Court and to salaried judicial posts, including High Court Masters and Registrars, Circuit Judges, Tribunal Presidents, Tribunal Chairman and Tribunal Judges, District Judges, District Judges (Magistrates' Court) and to fee paid posts including tribunal appointments (including many non-legal appointments), Recorders, Deputy District Judges, Deputy District Judges (Magistrates' Courts) and, Deputy Masters and Registrars, the JAC will conduct the selection exercise and make a recommendation to the Lord Chancellor. As with recommendations for the Supreme Court, the Lord Chancellor has a three-stage options process which allows for one rejection and/or one reconsideration, however, the JAC can state that the selection process did not identify a candidate of sufficient merit to make a selection (s. 92), and the Lord Chancellor may require the JAC to reconsider that decision not to select and they must inform him of any person then selected. If they make a selection on reconsideration, the Lord Chancellor will have the same options in relation to the appointment as in ordinary cases (s. 93).

Constitutional Reform Act 2005

Schedule 12

1 The Commission consists of—

(a) a chairman, and
(b) 14 other Commissioners, appointed by Her Majesty on the recommendation of the Lord Chancellor.

2 (1) The chairman must be a lay member.
(2) Of the other Commissioners—

(a) 5 must be judicial members,
(b) 2 must be professional members,
(c) 5 must be lay members,
(d) 1 other must be the holder of an office listed in Part 3 of Schedule 14, and
(e) 1 other must be a lay justice member.

(3) Of the Commissioners appointed as judicial members—

(a) 1 must be a Lord Justice of Appeal;
(b) 1 must be a puisne judge of the High Court;
(c) 1 other must be either a Lord Justice of Appeal or a puisne judge of the High Court;
(d) 1 must be a circuit judge;
(e) 1 must be a district judge of a county court, a District Judge (Magistrates' Courts) or a person appointed to an office under section 89 of the Supreme Court Act 1981 (c. 54).

(4) Of the Commissioners appointed as professional members—

(a) 1 must be a practising barrister in England and Wales;
(b) 1 must be a practising solicitor of the Senior Courts of England and Wales.

(5) A Commissioner is not to be taken into account for the purposes of any paragraph of sub-paragraph (2) unless he was appointed for the purposes of that paragraph. 3 A person must not be appointed as a Commissioner if he is employed in the civil service of the State.

4 (1) A judicial member is a person who holds an office listed in paragraph 2(3) and who is not a practising lawyer.

[Paragraph 7 provides that a person may recommended for appointment by the Queen to the JAC on the recommendation of a panel]

Panels

8 (1) A panel appointed under paragraph 7(2) must have four members (subject to sub-paragraph (7)).

(2) The first member must be a person selected by the Lord Chancellor with the agreement of the Lord Chief Justice (or, if the office of Lord Chief Justice is vacant, with the agreement of the senior Head of Division).

(3) That member is to be chairman of the panel.

(4) The second member must be the Lord Chief Justice or his nominee, unless the office of Lord Chief Justice is vacant.

(5) If that office is vacant, the second member must be the senior Head of Division or his nominee.

(6) The third member must be a person nominated by the first member.

(7) The chairman of the Commission must also be a member of the panel unless his office is vacant or is the office for which a recommendation is to be made.

(8) A person must not be a member of the panel if he is employed in the civil service of the State.

(9) A person must not be the first member if he is one of the following—

(a) a Commissioner;
(b) a member of the staff of the Commission;
(c) a practising lawyer;
(d) the holder of a listed judicial office;
(e) a member of the House of Commons.

(10) A person must not be the third member if he is a member of the House of Commons.

(11) The Lord Chancellor before selecting a person to be appointed as the first member, and the Lord Chief Justice or Head of Division before agreeing to the selection, must consider these questions—

(a) whether the person has exercised functions that appear to him to be of a judicial nature and such as to make the person inappropriate for the appointment;
(b) whether any past service in a capacity listed in sub-paragraph (8) or (9) appears to him to make the person inappropriate for the appointment;
(c) whether the extent of any present or past party political activity or affiliations appears to him to make the person inappropriate for the appointment.

(12) The first member must consider the same questions before nominating a person to be appointed as the third member.

9 The Lord Chancellor may pay to a member of a panel appointed under paragraph 7(2) such remuneration, fees or expenses as he may determine.

NOTES

1. In its fourth annual report the JAC explained the appointments process and how it has been modified.

Judicial Appointments Commission, *Annual Report 2009–10*, pp. 14, 15–17

OVERVIEW OF THE SELECTION PROCESS

The JAC selects candidates for judicial office on merit, through fair and open competition, from the widest range of eligible candidates.

Prior to October 2006 selections were made on the basis of the definition of merit applied by the former Department for Constitutional Affairs. The JAC made it an early priority to devise its own merit criteria and, since 31 October 2006, all selection exercises up to and including High Court level, have been based on the JAC's definition of merit. The JAC defines merit in terms of qualities and related abilities. A core set was agreed following discussion with key interested parties and these are used as the basis on which recommendations are made. The JAC's core qualities and abilities are set out below, these are adjusted as appropriate for different appointments.

Qualities and abilities

Intellectual capacity:

- High level of expertise in a chosen area or profession
- Ability to absorb and analyse information quickly

Appropriate knowledge of the law and its underlying principles, or the ability to acquire this knowledge where necessary

Personal qualities:

- Integrity and independence of mind
- Sound judgement
- Decisiveness
- Objectivity
- Ability and willingness to learn and develop professionally

An ability to understand and deal fairly:

- Ability to treat everyone with respect and sensitivity, whatever their background
- Willingness to listen with patience and courtesy

Authority and communication skills:

- Ability to explain the procedure and any decisions reached clearly and succinctly
- to everyone involved
- Ability to inspire respect and confidence
- Ability to maintain authority when challenged

Efficiency:

- Ability to work at speed and under pressure
- Ability to organise time effectively and produce clear, reasoned judgements
- quickly and efficiently
- Ability to work constructively with others (including leadership and managerial skills where appropriate)...

What is the process for selecting candidates?

Early stages

The selection process typically starts when a vacancy request is received from the Lord Chancellor who must have consulted the Lord Chief Justice or the Senior President of Tribunals. This includes minimum eligibility requirements for appointment laid down by statute and any non-statutory criteria applied additionally by the Lord Chancellor. The JAC ensures the application form and accompanying information pack provide all that is required for each selection exercise. Prospective candidates can obtain a copy of the application form and information pack, which includes guidance on the selection process, by downloading them from the website or contacting the JAC. Candidates can now submit their application forms online, as well as by email and in hardcopy. Each application is checked to see whether the candidate meets the eligibility requirements.

Shortlisting

A shortlist of candidates who will go forward to the next stage of the selection process is made. Shortlists are created following either a qualifying test or a paper-based sift. Qualifying tests provide objective evidence of candidates' abilities, whatever their specialism. The JAC uses qualifying tests for most selection exercises below the level of Senior Circuit Judge. Processes are tailored to each post, so a paper-based sift may be used if the number of vacancies or expected applicants is small, or in other limited circumstances. For appointments made above Circuit Bench level, shortlisting is normally carried out by a paper sift based on self assessments and references.

- Qualifying test – this consists of a written paper which tests a number of the qualities and abilities required for judicial office, such as intellectual capacity and efficiency. Shortlisting is a competitive process, so the tests are designed to be challenging and include an element of time pressure. Qualifying tests do not have a pass mark; rather they identify those people to be invited to selection day. The JAC normally invites candidates to selection day in a ratio of between two and three candidates per vacancy.

- Paper-based sift – a panel typically consisting of a panel chair, judicial member and independent member assesses written evidence supplied by the candidate, and their references. The information is assessed against the qualities and abilities framework, and the candidates who best demonstrate these are invited to the next stage of the application process. Experienced judges generally prepare, mark and moderate qualifying tests to ensure appropriateness and consistency. Tests are usually piloted both with people recently appointed to the role and people representative of likely suitable applicants. Before they are used in a live exercise, tests are equality proofed by independent experts and diversity representatives from the Law Society, Bar Council and the Institute of Legal Executives, to ensure that they are fair for all candidates.

References

The JAC uses references to gain a view of a candidate's past performance, experience, track record and suitability for appointment. The JAC uses two types of reference: JAC nominated and candidate nominated. The JAC nominated referees are tailored for each selection exercise. The generic title of the JAC nominated referee (either judicial or professional) is listed and the candidate is asked to supply the name and contact details. For example, if existing tribunal members apply, the JAC may ask the Chair or President of the relevant tribunal for a reference for those candidates. Candidate nominated referees are expected to have direct knowledge of either the professional or voluntary work of the candidate. If a paper sift is used to shortlist candidates, references are normally taken up before the sift and are used in deciding the shortlist. If qualifying tests are used references are normally taken up after the test but before the selection day; they do not form a part of the shortlisting process.

Selection day

Shortlisted candidates are invited to a selection day, which may consist of an interview only (possibly including a presentation), or an interview and role-plays. These are conducted and assessed by a panel usually consisting of a panel chair, judicial member and independent member. The role-plays, which are usually devised by judges or tribunal members, typically simulate a court or tribunal environment. The candidate is asked to take on the role of the judicial office-holder. This gives candidates the opportunity to demonstrate that they have the required qualities and abilities, and whether they can perform under pressure.

Panel assessment

The panel members consider all the information about each candidate (their performance in the interview and roleplays, the candidate's self-assessment and references) and assess them against the qualities and abilities. The panel chair then completes a summary report, providing an overall panel assessment. This forms part of the information presented to Commissioners when they make their selection.

Statutory consultation

For all candidates likely to be considered for selection, the summary reports are sent to the Lord Chief Justice and to one other person who has held the post or has relevant experience – this is a requirement under the CRA. These 'statutory consultees' are asked to give a view on the suitability of each candidate so referred. When they consider candidates to recommend for appointment, Commissioners take into account the responses from statutory consultees with all the other information about a candidate. They may decide not to follow the views expressed by the consultees but if this happens, when making recommendations to the Lord Chancellor, Commissioners must give reasons.

Selection

Commissioners make the final decision on which candidates to recommend to the Lord Chancellor for appointment. In doing so, they consider those candidates that selection panels have assessed as best meeting the requirements of the role, having been provided with information gathered on those individuals during the whole process.

Checks

In accordance with the JAC's statutory duty the good character of the candidates is also assessed. Guidance to enable candidates to decide whether there is anything in their past conduct or present circumstances that would affect their application for judicial appointment is on the JAC website. If the recommended candidate is an existing judicial office holder, the Office for Judicial Complaints is asked to check whether there are complaints outstanding against them. For other recommended candidates financial, criminal and professional background checks are carried out.

Quality assurance

Quality assurance measures are applied throughout the process to ensure that the proper procedures are applied and the highest standards are maintained. The quality checks include:

- assigning a Commissioner to each exercise, who works closely with the JAC selection exercise team to ensure standards are met. The Assigned Commissioner will, for example:
- oversee development of tests and roleplays;
- review results to check for anomalies or signs of bias; and
- help brief panel members to ensure they are fully prepared.
- reviewing the progression of candidates through each stage of the process for any
- possible unfairness;
- observing interviews to share good practice across panels; and
- overseeing moderation in the marking of tests and the results of panel assessments to ensure consistency (because of the number of candidates, many exercises will use a number of test markers and more than one panel).

Developments in the selection process

The development of the selection process included wide consultation with representatives of the legal profession, partners in the judiciary and the Ministry of Justice, including HM Courts Service and the Tribunals Service. During 2009/10, the JAC has continued to improve the selection process, ensuring that the vast majority of exercises are completed to schedule. For example, it now undertakes an assessment of good character following selection day in parallel with the statutory consultation, rather than at the beginning of the process. This change was piloted on a number of exercises, before being introduced for all exercises during 2009/10.

Feedback report on the qualifying test

The JAC has responded to the comments it received from candidates following qualifying tests and, in particular, that they would welcome feedback on the tests. While the number of applications received means that individual feedback cannot be provided to all those who sat a qualifying test, an overall feedback report has been published for candidates in the Recorder (Civil) qualifying test and the Deputy District Judge (Civil) qualifying test taken in December 2009 and January 2010, respectively. This report is designed to help candidates understand what characterised a successful paper, and to consider that against their experience. The report provides general comment on how candidates performed. It includes identification and analysis of common problems and comment on each question as well as giving a broad indication of the general standard of test papers and the range and distribution of marks awarded. The reports produced so far have been well received and in future will be produced for all qualifying tests.

2. There are too many appointments for the Commissioners to be involved in all of them so the JAC appoints people to the panels. Commissioners, however, will be members of panels in the selection exercises for senior appointments. The panels will have three members, a chair, an independent member and a judicial member.
3. The JAC in 2009–10 ran 25 selection exercises for posts at High Court level and below for which there were 3,084 applications and 446 recommendations were made. At the more senior level three Lord Justices of Appeal were appointed and two Heads of Division.
4. The JAC in consultation with the Ministry of Justice now present, on their website, an outline of the main selection exercises which will run in a three-year period beyond the current year. The aim is to help candidates plan their application for a judicial appointment with more certainty.
5. Selection is on merit and good character (s. 63) but the JAC has a duty 'to have regard to the need to encourage diversity in the range of persons available for selection for appointments' (s. 64). The Advisory Panel On Judicial Diversity reported in February 2010. Its analysis and recommendations included:

> 1. There is a strong case for a more diverse judiciary. Not only should there be equality of opportunity for those eligible to apply, but in a democratic society the judiciary should reflect the diversity of society and the legal profession as a whole. Judges drawn from a wide range of backgrounds and

life experiences will bring varying perspectives to bear on critical legal issues. A judiciary which is visibly more reflective of society will enhance public confidence.

2. We have concluded that there is no quick fix to moving towards a more diverse judiciary. This will come as no surprise to those who have worked to promote diversity over recent years...
4. The message from our research and consultations is consistent with research and experience in other jurisdictions: we will achieve significant transformation if, and only if, diversity is addressed systematically – not only within the appointments process, but throughout a legal and judicial career, from first consideration of the possibility of joining the judiciary to promotion at the most senior level...
5. Delivering a more diverse judiciary is not just about recruiting talent wherever it may be found, important though that is, but about retaining talent and enabling capable individuals to reach the top...
7. Sustained progress on judicial diversity requires a fundamental shift in approach from a focus on selection processes towards a judicial career that addresses diversity at every stage.
8. This approach requires:
   - ensuring that lawyers from all backgrounds recognise early on in their career that becoming a judge could be a possibility for them.
   - more effort by the legal professions to promote diversity at all levels and to support applications from talented candidates from all backgrounds.
   - better information on the career paths available. These career paths must promote opportunities across the courts and tribunals as one judiciary.
   - providing a variety of means for potential applicants for judicial office to understand what the role involves and to gain practical experience and
   - build confidence.
   - open and transparent selection processes that promote diversity and recognise potential, not just at the entry points to the judiciary but also for progression within it to the most senior levels...
9. To deliver the fundamental change that is needed will also require new ways of working together, from an approach that co-ordinates activity to one that actively drives change. In particular:
   - Change must be implemented as a comprehensive package of reform.
   - the existing tripartite judicial diversity strategy between the Lord Chancellor, the Lord Chief Justice and the Chairman of the Judicial Appointments Commission needs refocusing and extending to include the leaders of the legal profession (Bar Council, Law Society, and Institute of Legal Executives (ILEX)) and the Senior President of Tribunals. This Judicial Diversity Taskforce should oversee an agreed action plan for change as a result of this Panel's findings and publish an annual report that demonstrates where progress has been made and where it has not. It must measure its success, acting as a group that delivers change and holds its members to account.
   - this group also needs to ensure that we learn from experience. That means systematic, consistent monitoring and evaluation of what works and what does not, so that resources can be allocated where they are most effective.
   - there needs to be proactive campaign of mythbusting to dispel the widespread misconceptions that are deterring good candidates from under-represented groups from coming forward.
   - there must be a new form of engagement. The legal profession must actively promote judicial office among those who are currently not coming forward - the work of the Solicitors in Judicial Office Working Group outlined in this report represents a significant and welcome change. The Judicial Appointments Commission needs to be more responsive to the experience of its customers. The judiciary needs to support and encourage new entrants more actively.

6. The JAC's outreach activities include speaking engagements; taking part in conferences; undertaking and hosting visits; producing articles and items for the media and its own website and organizing regular candidate seminars. All of these activities are designed to demystify the judicial selection process, to encourage eligible candidates to apply and to explain how the JAC can make a difference and what part they can all play in implementing lasting change.

7. While the annual report refers to some delays in selection which are attributed to 'problems in the timing and accuracy of vacancy requests' it does not refer to the first Circuit Judge selection exercise the JAC ran in which there was confusion about the stage at which references were read and initially rejected people were reconsidered, delaying the procedure. This was the subject of strong questioning by the Select Committee (see Constitutional Affairs Select Committee uncorrected transcript of evidence 20 March 2007, HC 416i of 2006–07). The Chair of the JAC was also firmly pressed on how they would measure success in diversity if they were not using targets, to which the response was that they were seeking comparators to establish benchmarking as they can only consider candidates who meet the eligibility requirements whatever their gender, ethnicity and whether disabled or not.
8. Complaints about the appointments process may be made within 28 days of the events complained by a person as a candidate for selection or a person selected as claiming to have been adversely affected by (a) the JAC or one of its committees, or (b) by the Lord Chancellor or his department (s. 99). The JAC and the department (Ministry of Justice) must arrange for such complaints to be investigated. Following the outcome of such an investigation the person affected may complain to the Judicial Appointments and Conduct Ombudsman (s. 101). See p. 145, *post* for consideration of both the appointments and conduct aspects of the ombudsman's work.

■ QUESTIONS

1. Why should there be two members of the Supreme Court on the commission for appointments to that court?
2. What advantages might there be in allowing the Lord Chancellor the three-stage option response to the recommendation of a single candidate over a recommendation of two candidates, either ranked or not?
3. Why is the JAC's need to encourage diversity related to the range of persons available for selection to appointments?

F: Discipline

Constitutional Reform Act 2005

108 Disciplinary powers

(1) Any power of the Lord Chancellor to remove a person from an office listed in Schedule 14 is exercisable only after the Lord Chancellor has complied with prescribed procedures (as well as any other requirements to which the power is subject).

(2) The Lord Chief Justice may exercise any of the following powers but only with the agreement of the Lord Chancellor and only after complying with prescribed procedures.

(3) The Lord Chief Justice may give a judicial office holder formal advice, or a formal warning or reprimand, for disciplinary purposes (but this section does not restrict what he may do informally or for other purposes or where any advice or warning is not addressed to a particular office holder).

(4) He may suspend a person from a judicial office for any period during which any of the following applies—

(a) the person is subject to criminal proceedings;
(b) the person is serving a sentence imposed in criminal proceedings;
(c) the person has been convicted of an offence and is subject to prescribed procedures in relation to the conduct constituting the offence.

(5) He may suspend a person from a judicial office for any period if—

(a) the person has been convicted of a criminal offence,
(b) it has been determined under prescribed procedures that the person should not be removed from office, and
(c) it appears to the Lord Chief Justice with the agreement of the Lord Chancellor that the suspension is necessary for maintaining confidence in the judiciary.

(6) He may suspend a person from office as a senior judge for any period during which the person is subject to proceedings for an Address.

(7) He may suspend the holder of an office listed in Schedule 14 for any period during which the person—

(a) is under investigation for an offence, or
(b) is subject to prescribed procedures.

(8) While a person is suspended under this section from any office he may not perform any of the functions of the office (but his other rights as holder of the office are not affected).

NOTES

1. The position in relation to judges in the High Court and above is that under the Act of Settlement 1701 and the Supreme Court Act 1981, they hold office 'during good behaviour' and may only be removed following an address to the Sovereign by both Houses of Parliament.
2. Where previously the Lord Chancellor as Head of the Judiciary would have exercised other disciplinary powers they are now exercised concurrently with the Lord Chief Justice, who may be said to operate as a check upon each other. Complaints about the conduct of judges, tribunal judges and members and lay magistrates will be investigated by the Office of Judicial Conduct (OJC) under the Judicial Discipline (Prescribed Procedures) Regulations 2006. Complaints against Tribunal Judicial Office Holders and Magistrates are handled locally in the first instance by Tribunal Presidents and Advisory Committees respectively. The OJC's fourth Annual Report, 2009–10, records that 59 per cent of the complaints received were out of jurisdiction as they were about judicial decisions. The OJC seeks to redirect them to those who may be able to help them appeal a judicial decision.

Nature of Complaint	Number of Complaints	Action						Total
		Guidance Issued	Formal Advice/ Warning	Reprimand	Removed from Office	Resignation	Suspension	
Inappropriate Behaviour or Comments	422	9	6	4	6	4	0	29
Discrimination	83	0	0	0	0	0	0	0
Miscellaneous	33	0	0	0	0	0	0	0
Not Fulfilling Judicial Duty	27	2	5	1	12	3	0	23
Conflict of Interest	19	0	0	0	1	0	0	1
Not Specified	19	0	0	0	0	0	0	0
Criminal or Other Court Proceedings / Convictions	14	1	0	1	5	6	1	14
Professional Conduct	10	0	0	1	3	1	0	5
Motoring Offences	9	6	0	1	1	2	0	10
Misuse of Judicial Status	9	0	0	3	0	2	0	5
Not related to Judicial Office Holder	2	0	0	0	0	0	0	0
Total	647	18	11	11	28	18	1	87

Judicial Office Held	Number of Complaints
None Defined	391
Magistrate	70
Tribunals	7
Coroner	36
Court of Protection	5
District Bench	620
Circuit Bench	334
High Court	84
Court of Appeal	24

3. The Judicial Appointments and Conduct Ombudsman can only investigate conduct cases which have been considered by the OJC, Tribunal President or Magistrates Local Advisory Committee, or if referred by the Lord Chancellor or Lord Chief Justice. Appointments cases can be raised by the person adversely affected or on referral by the Lord Chancellor or Lord Chief Justice. The Ombudsman's fourth Annual Report 2009–10 records:

Financial year	2006–07	2007–08	2008–09	2009–10
Cases received	304	314	278	379
Cases determined	37	101	103	70
Conduct (OJC, Tribunal, Advisory Committee)	4 upheld or partial	10 upheld or partial	44 upheld or partial	21 upheld or partial
	10 not upheld	63 not upheld	47 not upheld	33 not upheld
Appointments (JAC)	5 upheld or partial upheld	1 upheld or partial upheld	1 upheld or partial upheld	0 upheld or partial upheld
	18 not upheld	27 not upheld	11 not upheld	16 not upheld

The Judicial Appointments and Conduct Ombudsman's office operate a three-track system. The first level, 'initial check' determines if cases are within remit and that a conduct complaint had first been made to the first-tier organisation. The second level 'fast track' provides a more detailed evaluation of eligibility and the third level is the 'full investigation'. In 2009–10, 150 cases were found ineligible at the first level, and at the second level, 85 out of 229 were deemed not to move on to the third level, where 72 cases received (19 per cent) required a full investigation resulting in 70 determinations. Around 80 per cent of cases are disposed of at the first two levels, with the majority of them being processed within six weeks.

The Ombudsman reported on some recurrent themes. Two appointments examples:

- some candidates have high expectations of the written explanation (or feedback) that the JAC provides to unsuccessful candidates. I do not consider it proportionate for the JAC to respond in the level of detail requested by some, and I do not find it unreasonable that the JAC has reduced the level of detail in the explanations it provides to unsuccessful candidates; and
- an increasing number of complainants expect, unreasonably in my view, to be told of their precise scores, or to be given sight of their marked papers, as part of their feedback. It is not JAC policy to disclose this information and, whilst I will have sight of this information as required for my investigations, it is not for me to disclose it to candidates.

Examples of recurring themes in conduct cases include:

- failing to make sufficient enquiries or to obtain independent verification;
- not keeping complainants informed of the progress of their complaint;
- insufficient care with dismissal letters to ensure that the investigation process is clearly explained, and that letters are appropriate and unambiguous.

■ QUESTION

Why should judges in the High Court and above have greater security of tenure than circuit judges?

G: Accountability of the judiciary to Parliament

The House of Lords Select Committee on the Constitution in its report on *Relations Between the Executive, the Judiciary and Parliament* stated that it was an interesting argument put forward by Professor Bogdanor that

judges should not be "answerable" to Parliament in terms of justifying their decisions, but should "answer" to Parliament through committee appearances—in other words, they should be accountable to Parliament not in the "sacrificial" sense, but in the "explanatory" sense (HL 151 of 2006–7, para. 122).

As the Lord Chancellor could no longer answer on behalf of the judiciary, the report considered other ways in which Parliament could hold the judiciary accountable.

The Question of Accountability

The Role of Select Committees

186. We believe that select committees can play a central part in enabling the role and proper concerns of the judiciary to be better understood by the public at large, and in helping the judiciary to remain accountable to the people via their representatives in Parliament. Not only should senior judges be questioned on the administration of the justice system, they might also be encouraged to discuss their views on key legal issues in the cause of transparency and better understanding of such issues amongst both parliamentarians and the public. However, under no circumstances must committees ask judges to comment on the pros and cons of individual judgments....

A Parliamentary Committee on the Judiciary

187. We are not currently convinced of the need for a joint committee on the judiciary, but we shall keep the situation under review, not least in evaluating our Committee's effectiveness in providing the necessary oversight and contact. The Constitutional Affairs Select Committee in the House of Commons also has an important role to play...

Post-legislative Scrutiny

188. We repeat our earlier conclusion that post-legislative scrutiny is highly desirable and should be undertaken far more generally. This would boost the level of constructive dialogue between Parliament and the courts.

The Judiciary of England and Wales, *Response from the Judiciary to the House of Lords Select Committee on the Constitution report on relations between the executive, the judiciary and Parliament*

(2007) <www.judiciary.gov.uk/docs/const_committee_response.pdf>

... 'sacrificial'... accountability would be incompatible with the principle of the independence of the judiciary. It is right, however, that if the judiciary is to have the input we would like into all aspects of the administration of justice, then we should account for the way in which we have discharged our administrative responsibilities. The question is how to do this in a way which is not incompatible with the judiciary's core responsibility as the branch of the State responsible for providing the fair and impartial resolution of disputes between citizens and the State, in accordance with the prevailing rules of law.

Your Report suggests that Select Committees "can play an important role in holding the judiciary to account by questioning in public"...we see merit in the suggestion that Select Committees can represent an appropriate and helpful forum for the Lord Chief Justice, after publication of his annual report, to explain his views on aspects of the administration of justice that are of general interest or concern and upon which it is appropriate for the judiciary to comment. There may, of course, be other circumstances in which the judiciary consider it appropriate to express views to Parliament on other issues...we are cautious about your suggestion that this should include their views on "key legal issues". There are difficulties in judges giving views on new legislative proposals or the operation of the law. Although, as our guidance recognises, it is appropriate for a judge to comment on the operation and procedures of his or her jurisdiction and the implications of any Bill or Act in these respects we need to be particularly aware of the fact that a senior judge might, at some stage in the future, be asked to adjudicate on an issue they had commented on in the past. An awareness and appreciation of the guidelines, from both the judiciary and the Committee, should ensure that we avoid any such pitfalls.

We are concerned, however, that the appearance of judges and magistrates before Select Committees should not become routine for fear of stepping beyond the proper boundary between the judiciary and Parliament. We have already seen an increase in the number of invitations to appear in the 18 months since the implementation of the constitutional reforms. Therefore, while we welcome the indication that Committees would be open to additional appearances from the judiciary, such appearances need, we believe, to be truly necessary and appropriate.

Guidance for Judges Appearing Before or Providing Written Evidence to Parliamentary Committees

(2006) <www.judiciary.gov.uk/docs/accountability.pdf para. 21>

There are well established and longstanding rules that prevent Judges from commenting on certain matters. Parliamentary Committees can be expected to understand and respect these. Judges will therefore need to consider carefully whether they can answer questions about the matters listed below, and, if so, the extent to which they can. The matters are:

- the merits of individual cases or decisions where cases are pending or ongoing, and generally also where they have been finally concluded (including collapsed trials), although particular trials may be used as examples of practice when discussing general policy issues or lessons to be learnt; the general principles of law, etc, arising from existing case law would not be inappropriate.
- cases over which they have presided (in view of the longstanding convention that judges do not comment publicly on such cases, and Select Committees would be no exception to this general rule),
- the merits or personalities of particular serving judicial office-holders, politicians and other public figures or more generally on the quality of appointments,
- the merits, meaning or likely effect of provisions in any Bill or other prospective legislation in such a way as could be seen to call into question his or her judicial impartiality in the event of subsequently being called upon to apply or interpret those provisions judicially,
- the merits of Government policy, save where the policy in question affects the administration of justice within his or her area of judicial responsibility, so that it is legitimate and appropriate for example to answer questions relating to the operation and the procedures of his or her jurisdiction and the implications of any Bill or Act in these respects, and
- the administration of justice which fall outside his or her area of judicial responsibility or previous responsibility.

NOTE: Section 5 of the Constitutional Reform Act 2005 allows the Lord Chief Justice to lay written representations before Parliament 'on matters that appear to him to be matters of importance relating to the judiciary, or otherwise to the administration of justice, in that part of the United Kingdom'.

This is regarded as being exceptional and the Lords Select Committee on the Constitution suggested at para. 119 that if such representations are laid that they

> ...should be published in Hansard; that the business managers should find time for the issue to be debated in the House at the earliest possible opportunity; and that the Government should respond to such representations in good time before either House has finished considering the bill or initiative in question. Further, this Committee will endeavour to scrutinise any such representations in time to inform deliberations in the House.

The judiciary's response to this was that

> We welcome the proposed handling arrangements for any such representations made by the Lord Chief Justice; the opportunity for an early debate and a timely response from the Government will be essential to ensure that there can be full and proper consideration of issues that are raised.

In fact the Lord Chief Justice had told the Constitutional Affairs Select Committee that he had been wondering if he should lay written representations on the issue of the negotiations with the Ministry of Justice over the implications of the creation of the Ministry in respect of a possible conflict between the Lord Chancellor's responsibilities to resource the court system and to operate the prison which had been transferred from the Home Office. The then Senior Presiding Judge, Thomas LJ had referred to the situation in Ireland, the Netherlands and Denmark where 'an "autonomous court administration with a greater degree of judicial participation" had been "very successful", and concluding that new structure akin to these models is, in the view of the judiciary, a constitutional safeguard made necessary by the Ministry of Justice' (HL 151 of 2006–07, para. 85). The Lords' committee, however, were not persuaded that the creation of the new ministry 'lends any additional urgency to their desire for an autonomous court administration'.

If such a development occurred, then the judiciary would have to submit not only to full and rigorous accountability to Parliament over their running of the courts but they would have to engage in the budget bidding and allocation process in the public spending round.

H: The judiciary, media, and the public

Sixth Report from the House of Lords Select Committee on the Constitution,

HL 151 of 2006–07, paras 191–194

> *Public Perceptions*
>
> 191. We believe that the media, especially the popular tabloid press, all too often indulge in distorted and irresponsible coverage of the judiciary, treating judges as "fair game". A responsible press should show greater restraint and desist from blaming judges for their interpretation of legislation which has been promulgated by politicians. If the media object to a judgment or sentencing decision, we suggest they focus their efforts on persuading the Government to rectify the legal and policy framework. In order to ensure more responsible reporting, we recommend that the Editors' Code of Practice, which is enforced by the Press Complaints Commission, be regularly updated to reflect these principles...
>
> *The Role of Individual Judges*
>
> 192. Whilst judges should never be asked to justify their decisions outside the courtroom, it is desirable for them to communicate with the public and the media on appropriate issues. We therefore strongly encourage the occasional use of media releases alongside judgments, as for example in the Charlotte Wyatt case. Further, we cannot see any reason why judges should not co-operate with the media on features about their activities outside the courtroom, if they so wish. However, we are strongly of the opinion that whatever the media pressure, judges should not give off-the-record briefings...
>
> *The Role of the Lord Chief Justice*
>
> 193. It is wholly within the discretion of the Lord Chief Justice to determine how he can most effectively communicate with the media and the public. However, we suggest that he may from time to time need to re-appraise his strategy in light of the new constitutional relationship between the judiciary, the executive and Parliament. We believe that, in these days of greater separation of powers, it is highly desirable for him to ensure that the views of the judiciary are effectively conveyed to the public...

The Role of the Judicial Communications Office

194. We conclude that the judges should consider making the Judicial Communications Office more active and assertive in its dealings with the media in order to represent the judiciary effectively. We suggest that consideration be given to appointing one or more spokesmen with appropriate qualifications and legal experience who would be permitted to speak to the media with the aim of securing coverage which accurately reflects the judgment or sentencing decision. However, under no circumstances should such spokesmen seek to justify decisions as opposed to explaining them.

The Judiciary of England and Wales, *Response from the Judiciary to the House of Lords Select Committee on the Constitution report on relations between the executive, the judiciary and Parliament* (2007) <http://www.judiciary.gov.uk/Resources/JCO/Documents/const_committee_response.pdf>

We agree. Judges have their own part to play in maintaining public confidence in the judiciary and the justice system.

Public perceptions

We agree with the Committee's view on the public position Government Ministers should take in relation to judicial decisions.

Role of individual judges

It is a cardinal principle that a judge should give his decision and the reasons for it in public. It has, for some time, been the practice that where a judgment is long and complex a judge will, where practicable, incorporate into his judgment a short summary to assist public understanding. When making sentencing remarks in shorter judgments a judge will always endeavour to explain the reasons for his decisions in a way that can be understood by the public who may not be familiar with the details of the case. Where reasons are given orally, as is almost always the case when sentencing, judges are encouraged to consider preparing a written note of their sentencing remarks to be given by hand to reporters in court. It is inappropriate for a judge outside of his decision to seek to amplify or explain his decision—his public judgment speaks for itself. It follows from this principle and the nature of judicial office that we endorse the Committee's views that judges should not give media briefings.

The Role of the Lord Chief Justice

The Lord Chief Justice has been Head of the Judiciary for 18 months. As the Committee acknowledges, there will always be a gap between the level of activity the media would like to see from the Lord Chief Justice and what is wise or even appropriate for the Lord Chief Justice to undertake. In fact, as the Committee advocates, this is kept under constant review, not least as interview bids and other requests arrive for him on a daily basis.

It is important to bear in mind that the Lord Chief Justice has now a direct means of communication with the public through the judicial website (www.judiciary.gov.uk): an illustration of this is the publication on the website of his two interviews with Marcel Berlins (there have been 8840 downloads since April 2006), as well as the publication of speeches and statements by him and other senior judges.

The Role of the Judicial Communications Office

The JCO is, in government terms, a small and relatively new unit responsible for providing communications support to more than 40,000 judicial office-holders. It provides support to the judiciary and to the media when questions arise about judicial issues and keeps up to date the judicial website which, as we have said, is an important means of external communication.

It is accepted there may be occasions, such as the media's reporting following the Sweeney judgment in June 2006, when the timely use of a judicial spokesperson, rather than a JCO press officer, to explain sentencing *process* might help provide a balance in the reportage. The Judges' Council is, therefore, considering the best means of developing a proposal, that whilst ensuring adherence to the principle that judicial decisions must speak for themselves, to provide in certain circumstances information through certain serving judges that will assist public understanding and debate.

Along with the judicial website, the JCO is actively involved in producing educational material for schools and the public generally about the work of judges within the operation of the justice system.

NOTES

1. A mapping exercise of different types of judicial accountability can aid an analysis of the select committee's and the judiciary's views.

A. Le Sueur, Developing Mechanisms for Judicial Accountability in the UK

(2004) *Legal Studies* 74, 79–81

Individual (personal) accountability—examples	Institutional (court) accountability—examples
• discipline for personal misconduct (in serious cases resulting in dismissal/an expectation of resignation); • writing individual reasoned judgments in a multi-judge court • explanations of personal views on law and the constitution delivered in public lectures, interviews with the press or scholarly academic publications	• publication of annual reports about the work of a court; • consultation over proposed changes to court rules and practice; • financial audit requirements; • the requirement for a court to sit in public • the existence of rights of appeal to a higher court • for courts of EU members states/Council of Europe, responding to judgments of the ECJ and ECtHR • parliamentary debates on the judicial function (e.g. HL Debs., Vol.648, col. 876, 21 May 2003)

Accountability via formal processes—examples	Accountability via civil society—examples
• publishing written reasons for a court's decisions • rights of appeal to higher courts against alleged errors; publication of annual reports by a court • scrutiny of individual judicial appointments and the appointments process generally	• robust and accurate reporting on judgments in the news media; • academic commentary on particular judgments and the conduct of courts generally; • public education by the Bar and other legal professional organisations.

Content accountability—examples	Process accountability—examples	Performance accountability	Probity accountability—examples
Written, reasoned judgments	methods for selecting which cases to hear	Explanations for time taken to determine cases	basic financial audit of court's annual expenditure
Contributions of individual judges to law reviews and public speeches	selection of panels of judges (in courts which do not sit en banc)		systems for judges registering or disclosing pecuniary and other interests

2. The first two sets of tables showing individual and institutional aspects, and the formal and via civil society processes are more self-explanatory than the final table. It seems that the judiciary accept a linkage between the first two tables that they should engage with the media through the JCO to reach the public. Le Sueur suggested that more might be done with the format of law reports which would make then easier to understand and he referred to the practice of the Supreme Court of the US which issues a 'prefatory syllabus' a summary of multiple judgments prepared by the court reporter but officially sanctioned. Would it not be possible for the format of judgments to include explanatory material. Surely that is just as important as the neutral citation system and numbered paragraphs which belatedly accommodated electronic publication and retrieval of law reports?
3. Le Sueur says that performance accountability is rather more intrusive than probity accountability. It can involve the setting of targets, one type of which are key performance indicators. The fashion for target-setting in public and private management ebbs and flows, and an inappropriate target may skew performance but in the court setting it can be a useful tool and would have to be adopted if the judiciary were to play a greater role in managing the court which they appear to want.
4. Process accountability, it is suggested encompasses the explanation and justification of the decision-making process a body uses for its job. Le Sueur points out that it was not until 2003 that the Appellate Committee of the House of Lords began to give reasons where they had refused permission to appeal. He suggests that explaining how panels will be composed to hear appeals in the House of Lords and Supreme Court is important. He referred to a point made by Lord Lester that political concern could arise in Edinburgh, Cardiff or Belfast in devolution cases previously before the Judicial Committee of the Privy Council if criteria on panel composition were not published. The Senior President of Tribunals will be under a duty to publish a policy on how judges and members will be assigned to chambers in the First-tier and Upper Tribunals (see *post*, p. 701).
5. The issue with content accountability is the extent to which judges may render an account of the legal and constitutional values which their judgments promote, beyond lectures and articles at the request of Parliament. The judiciary accept this with limitations on what they say and a concern about the frequency upon which they may be asked to do it. One problematic aspect of the tension between accountability and judicial independence was raised by Mr Charles Clarke MP, a former Home Secretary. He was concerned that after delivering their declaration of incompatibility with the European Convention on Human Rights and the Anti-Terrorism Crime and Security Act 2001 provisions on detention without trial provisions in *A v Secretary of State for the Home Department* [20004] 56 UKHL, [2005] 2 AC 68, he was left with little guidance on what measures would be Convention compatible and also meet the security threat to the nation. He would have liked a meeting with the Law Lords to discuss what might be and what might not be lawful in devising the control orders. He thought that 'the idea that their independence would be corrupted by such discussions is risible' (HL 151 of 2006–07, paras 93–95). The Lords select committee did have sympathy with the difficulties outlined by Mr Clarke but accepted the views of Lord Bingham, the Senior Law Lord, and Lord Woolf, the former Lord Chief Justice and a member of the committee, who pointed out respectively, that the Law Lords cannot appear to collude with the executive when they may have to determine challenges to actions taken by the executive, and that the Law Lords are 'the final arbiters of law on particular facts' (paras 96–97).
6. In the Green Paper *The Governance of Britain* (Cm 7170) the Government indicated it would review the arrangements for judicial appointments with the possibility of involving Parliament. The response to the consultation proposals below, indicated that while some feel that there may be a role for Parliament in overseeing the JAC and the appointments process, there is a very tiny amount of support for Parliament holding confirmation hearings.

The Governance of Britain: Judicial Appointments

Cm 7210, paras 4.30–4.53

Accountability and a check on the process

4.30 Currently, the executive acts as a check on JAC appointments. If the role of the executive is reduced or removed, there is a risk that the accountability to Parliament which exists under the existing arrangements would be reduced as the Lord Chancellor could not be held to answer to Parliament for the process to the same degree. In addition, despite the rigour of the JAC processes and the statutory requirement to select solely on merit, confidence in the appointments system may require that there should be at least the possibility of some other check on the process. Ideally, this would be before appointments are made. An unintended consequence of a change in this direction could be to put the JAC under more pressure from Parliament and over time call its independence into question.

4.31 At present, the JAC is required to consult the Lord Chief Justice and other members of the judiciary, although it is not obliged to follow consultees' views. The Judicial Appointments and Conduct Ombudsman is also able to investigate the JAC's processes, but any investigation would usually take place after a decision had been made. The Lord Chancellor can also withdraw a request to the JAC if he considers there to have been problems with the selection process.

4.32 If a check on the JAC's operation of the selection process is thought to be of value, consideration needs to be given to who would be best placed to act as that check, other than the Lord Chancellor. It might be possible to create a role for the Lord Chief Justice, as head of the judiciary, in acting as a final check on the JAC's decision. On the other hand, the judiciary is already involved in the process at various stages, and it might be argued that further involvement would be perceived as concentrating too much influence in their hands. In addition, an enhanced role for the judiciary would reduce accountability to Parliament, unless the Lord Chief Justice could be held to account in some way for his role in appointments.

A role for Parliament?

4.33 Some have argued that there might be benefits in Parliament exercising a greater role in relation to judicial appointments. Parliament already has the power to call for evidence and witnesses, and is able to question the JAC, including on any issues arising out of the JAC's annual report, and the Judicial Appointments and Conduct Ombudsman (JACO), in relation to the investigation of complaints about the process. In comparison with other countries' appointments systems, however, Parliamentary involvement in our system of judicial appointments is minimal, so arguably we would not want to *reduce* Parliamentary involvement.

4.34 As we have seen, the judiciary is not accountable to Parliament in the same way as the executive is, and although the Lord Chief Justice and Heads of Division now sometimes appear before the Constitutional Affairs Select Committee, they do so as representatives of the judiciary as a whole rather than as individuals, accountable for their decisions. Any move towards focusing on the individuals and their individual views would undoubtedly be highly controversial.

4.35 This is in contrast to the position in some other jurisdictions, most notably the United States, where appointments by the President to the Supreme Court are subject to the "advice and consent" of the Senate and where the political views of appointees are the focus of the discussion at confirmation hearings.

4.36 To adopt such an approach in this country could lead to the strong perception that judicial appointments were being politicised, and such a perception could have an impact on confidence in the independence of the judiciary. Even though it would not be open to Parliament to substitute its own candidate, and it would have to rely on those candidates selected by the JAC, there would nonetheless be the risk that the decision to confirm or reject could be based on factors other than the candidate's ability to do the job effectively. The questioning during the hearing could stray away from the candidate's experience into matters of a more political nature.

4.37 There are other difficulties with a Parliamentary veto over appointments. If a Select Committee chose to reject a candidate, there would be a potentially significant delay in the appointments process and posts could be left vacant for long periods of time. One further likely side-effect of pre-appointment hearings is that the prospect of having to appear before a Parliamentary committee may discourage potential candidates from applying, particularly at the lower levels. This could have a severe impact on the ability of the JAC to select the best candidates for posts and could reduce the numbers of high-quality applicants from diverse backgrounds who were willing to put themselves forward. But it may be that once the process bedded in, and firm ground rules were set, the number of applications would regularise.

4.38 In addition, although Select Committees aim to work by consensus, it is possible that any voting to confirm or reject an appointment would be along party lines. Given the executive's inbuilt majority on Commons Committees, this would not in practice remove the executive from the decision-making process on appointments.

4.39 Finally, there is the practical question of Parliamentary time and resources. It does not seem possible that hearings could be held for the thousands of Magistrates, Tribunals, Recorder, and District bench appointments made each year. Even the Circuit Bench, usually with over 50 appointments in any year, and the High Court, with 10 or more per year, would be problematic. One solution might be to restrict hearings to only the most senior appointments (Court of Appeal and above), and to make the decision to hold a hearing discretionary.

4.40 The Government recognises that pre-appointment hearings could be a way of giving Parliament a real and meaningful say in appointments. However, for the reasons outlined above, the Government has serious reservations about adopting this approach. The Government considers that the independent selection process provided by the JAC is the best way to identify the best candidates on merit, and with no political input into the decision making.

4.41 An alternative option would be to allow Parliament, perhaps through a Select Committee, to hold non-binding hearings on appointments before they were confirmed. This approach would allow for a similar level of scrutiny of the JAC's selection as the model outlined above, but without some of the difficulties posed by a formal power of veto.

4.42 However, the Government's view is that the risk of politicisation, or perception of politicisation, would still remain even under this option. If the issue under consideration at the hearing was whether or not the selected candidate was right for the post, it is difficult to see how the committee would perform that role and what factors it would base its advice on. In the case of judges, the qualities needed—intellectual capacity, sound judgement, integrity and merit—are specifically tested through the JAC's selection process in an open and transparent manner. It is difficult to see what questions the committee could ask to add to that process.

4.43 In addition, the non-binding nature of the hearings could lead to a situation in which Parliament had publicly cast doubt on an appointee's capabilities or suitability for office. This would potentially be very damaging for the candidate in question once confirmed in post.

Post-appointment hearings

4.44 A further possible option might be for Parliament to hold Select Committee hearings for candidates after they have been appointed but before they take up post. This is similar to the approach the Treasury Select Committee takes in relation to new Governors and Deputy Governors of the Bank of England, and other members of the Bank's Monetary Policy Committee.

4.45 Such an approach would allow for a degree of Parliamentary oversight of the JAC's decisions in relation to individual appointments, but without influencing the appointments themselves. This approach is therefore less likely to lead to the perception of politicisation of the appointments process than other models, such as the binding pre-appointment confirmation hearing that take place in the United States. However, some risk of perceived politicisation could remain, since MPs would be able to question judges on an individual basis in a way that does not currently happen.

4.46 An added advantage is that this approach would be unlikely to result in additional delay to the appointments process, since hearings could take place once the appointment had been made, and taking up the post would not be contingent on a hearing having taken place.

4.47 The issue of Parliamentary resources remains, however, and unless such hearings were restricted to the most senior posts, it is difficult to see how Parliament could cope with such numbers of hearings.

4.48 Aside from perceived politicisation, there appear to be two other significant disadvantages to this approach. Firstly, it is likely that there would still be a reduction in the number of candidates applying for posts. Secondly, it is not immediately clear what benefits post-appointment hearings would add to the process. It could be argued that they would create a stronger link between Parliament and the judiciary by allowing MPs the opportunity to get to know senior judges before they take up office. But if a stronger link between Parliament and the judiciary and greater accountability of the judiciary is what is sought, there are other ways to achieve that, for example the presentation by the Lord Chief Justice of an annual report to Parliament on judicial matters. If the objective of hearings is to ensure effective scrutiny of the JAC's selection, the fact that they would take place after appointments had been made would mean that if, as a result of a hearing, the Select Committee casts doubt on an appointee's suitability for office, there would in reality be very little, if anything, that could be done to remedy the position. This would also put the judge in a very difficult position.

4.49 There is one set of senior judges for which post-appointment hearings of a specific kind might be considered to be more suitable. Certain senior judges—the Lord Chief Justice and the Heads of Division (the Master of the Rolls, President of the Queen's Bench Division, President of the Family Division and the Chancellor of the High Court)—have specific leadership roles within the judiciary and are responsible for the deployment of judges and judicial work and for representing the judiciary within their area. It might be deemed appropriate for Parliament to hold post-appointment hearings in relation to those administrative roles, rather than in relation to the appointees' role as sitting judges. This could be partly as a familiarisation exercise with those key judicial members before they take up post, and partly with a view to questioning the appointees on how they intend to approach the challenges of office (in relation to their "nonjudicial" functions). The Lord Chief Justice commented in a recent speech that, in his view, Select Committees do provide an appropriate forum for the senior judiciary to discuss issues relating to the administration of justice, albeit not in the specific context of post-appointment hearings.

4.50 At that most senior level, it may be much less likely that the prospect of a Parliamentary hearing, especially if post-appointment, would have an impact on candidates' willingness to put themselves forward for posts. Equally, if hearings were restricted to only those most senior judicial appointments, it is unlikely that hearings would have a significant impact on Parliamentary resources. Finally, since such hearings would not address the appointees' roles as judges in individual cases, it is arguable that such hearings would not adversely affect judicial independence.

Parliamentary scrutiny of the judicial appointments process

4.51 As an alternative to, or possibly in addition to, a formal Parliamentary role in relation to individual appointments, there might be benefit in Parliament taking a more active role in scrutinising the procedure used by the JAC to select judges. While Parliament already has the power to call for evidence and witnesses, there might be merit in encouraging a greater Parliamentary role, especially if the Lord Chancellor's current role is to be reduced. Such an approach would ensure that there was proper scrutiny of the processes used, but without straying into the territory of politicisation.

4.52 To assist in this function, the existing powers of the JACO in investigating JAC selection processes could be used. Parliament might be encouraged to make more use of existing methods to draw specific concerns to the attention of the Lord Chancellor, who could then require JACO to investigate. This would ensure that the scrutiny and investigation function could be performed making use of JACO's expertise as an independent Ombudsman.

4.53 A further variation on this would be to enable Parliament to call on the JACO directly at any time: this would arguably necessitate a transfer of responsibility for the JACO from the Lord Chancellor to Parliament, along with responsibility for resources. Unless the executive were to play no role at all in respect of appointments, it would be necessary to consider whether the Lord Chancellor should retain the existing power to call on the JACO to carry out an investigation (albeit with the JACO still, ultimately, being responsible to Parliament).

■ QUESTIONS

1. If the risk of politicization is too great to permit parliamentary involvement in appointments, is there a case for parliamentary involvement in appointment of judges as judicial managers, the Lord Chief Justice and Heads of Division and, if so, what would be the appropriate types of question which parliamentarians could pose?

2. Why should such parliamentary involvement be post-appointment and not pre-appointment? (see the views of the Public Administration committee on parliamentary hearings for non-judicial public appointments at p. 274 *post*).
3. Would it be a constitutionally proper exchange if senior judges were no longer to chair inquiries but were required to channel some of their law review article writing and lecturing activities into appearances before select committees?

5

The Royal Prerogative and Constitutional Conventions

OVERVIEW

In this chapter we consider the royal prerogative, a particular source of legislative and executive power most of which is now exercised by ministers rather than by the Queen. There are personal prerogatives of the Queen, which are regulated by conventions. In the section on the prerogative we identify the various types and consider recent reform which includes putting two prerogatives on a statutory basis, and an attempt to codify constitutional practice including the personal prerogative of appointment of the Prime Minister. This involves looking at convention and so bridges into the second section and consideration of constitutional conventions, first as a source of the constitution; then we look at what they are, their relationship with law, their nature as rules of political behaviour, and the example of a convention at Westminster in relation to Scottish devolution. We then ask if conventions can crystallize into law and consider more generally the treatment of conventions in the courts, and end with the feasibility and desirability of codifying conventions.

SECTION 1: ROYAL PREROGATIVE

A: What is the Royal Prerogative?

The Governance of Britain, Review of the Executive Royal Prerogative Powers: Final Report

(2009), pp. 7, 31–34

25. Originally the prerogative would have been exercised by the reigning Monarch. However, over time a distinction was drawn between the Monarch acting in his or her individual capacity and the powers possessed by the Monarch as an embodiment of the State. As the governance of the realm became more complex, power was devolved from the Monarch and exercised by his or her advisers. In modern times Government Ministers exercise the bulk of the prerogative powers, either in their own right or through the advice they provide to The Queen which she is constitutionally bound to follow.

26. A V Dicey defines the Royal prerogative as 'The residue of discretionary or arbitrary authority, which at any given time is legally left in the hands of the Crown' [*Introduction to the Study of the Law of the Constitution*, 10th edn., 1959, p. 424]. William Blackstone however describes the prerogative more tightly, as those powers that 'the King enjoys alone, in contradistinction to others, and not to those he enjoys in common with any of his subjects' *Commentaries on the Laws of England, a facsimile of the first edition of 1765-1769* (University of Chicago Press, 1979, p111) . Blackstone's notion of the prerogative being those

powers of an exclusive nature was favoured by Lord Parmoor in the *De Keyser's Royal Hotel* case [1920 AC 508, p571. But Lord Reid in the *Burmah Oil* case [1965] AC 75, p105. expressed some difficulty with this idea. Case law exists to support both views, and a clear distinction has not been necessary in any relevant cases. The question may never need to be settled by the courts as there are few cases that deal directly with the prerogative itself.

27. The scope of the Royal prerogative power is notoriously difficult to determine. It is clear that the existence and extent of the power is a matter of common law, making the courts the final arbiter of whether or not a particular type of prerogative power exists ["The King hath no prerogative, but that which the law of the land allows him"; see the *Proclamations Case* (1610) 12 Co Rep 74, 76]. The difficulty is that there are many prerogative powers for which there is no recent judicial authority and sometimes no judicial authority at all. In such circumstances, the Government, Parliament and the wider public are left relying on statements of previous Government practice and legal textbooks, the most comprehensive of which is now nearly 200 years old [Joseph Chitty *A Treatise on the Law of the Prerogatives of the Crown* (1820)].

28. This uncertainty has been criticised. Professor Rodney Brazier has written '….the demand for a statement of what may be done by virtue of [the Royal prerogative] is of practical importance ['Constitutional Reform and the Crown' in M Sunkin and S Payne (eds), *The Nature of the Crown* (Oxford, OUP, 1999) p339]. Yet it has been said judicially that such a statement cannot be arrived at, because only through a process of piecemeal judicial decisions over the centuries have particular powers been seen to exist, or not to exist, as the case maybe *R v Secretary of State for the Home Department, ex parte Northumbria Police Authority* [1989] QB26, (CA) p56 (Nourse LJ)]. . . .

MINISTERIAL PREROGATIVE POWERS

(a) Government and the Civil Service

- Powers concerning the machinery of Government including the power to set up a department or a non-departmental public body
- Powers concerning the civil service, including the power to appoint and regulate most civil servants
- Power to prohibit civil servants and certain other crown servants from issuing election addresses or announcing themselves, or being announced as, a Parliamentary candidate or a Prospective Parliamentary candidate
- Power to set nationality rules for 'non-aliens'—British, Irish and Commonwealth citizens—concerning eligibility for employment in the civil service
- Power to require security vetting of contractors working alongside civil servants on sensitive projects
- Powers concerning the Office of the Civil Service Commissioners, the Security Vetting Appeals Panel, the Office of the Commissioner for Public Appointments, the Advisory Committee on Business, the Civil Service Appeal Board and the House of Lords Appointments Commission, including the power to establish those bodies, to appoint members of those bodies and the powers of those bodies

(b) Justice system and law and order

- Powers to appoint Queen's Counsel
- Power to make provisional and full order extradition requests to countries not covered by Part 1 of the Extradition Act 2003
- Prerogative of mercy
- Power to keep the peace

(c) Powers relating to foreign affairs

- Power to send ambassadors abroad and receive and accredit ambassadors from foreign states
- Recognition of states

- Governance of British Overseas Territories
- Power to make and ratify treaties
- Power to conduct diplomacy
- Power to acquire and cede territory
- Power to issue, refuse or withdraw passport facilities
- Responsibility for the Channel Islands and Isle of Man
- Granting diplomatic protection to British citizens abroad

(d) Powers relating to armed forces, war and times of emergency

- Right to make war or peace or institute hostilities falling short of war
- Deployment and use of armed forces overseas
- Maintenance of the Royal Navy
- Use of the armed forces within the United Kingdom to maintain the peace in support of the police or otherwise in support of civilian authorities (e.g. to maintain essential services during a strike)
- The government and command of the armed forces is vested in Her Majesty
- Control, organisation and disposition of armed forces
- Requisition of British ships in times of urgent national necessity
- Commissioning of officers in all three armed forces
- Armed forces pay
- Certain armed forces pensions which are now closed to new members
- War pensions for death or disablement due to service before 6 April 2005 (s. 12 of the Social Security (Miscellaneous Provisions) Act 1977 provides that the prerogative may be exercised by Order in Council
- Crown's right to claim Prize (enemy ships or goods captured at sea)
- Regulation of trade with the enemy
- Crown's right of angary, in time of war, to appropriate the property of a neutral which is within the realm, where necessity requires
- Powers in the event of a grave national emergency, including those to enter upon, take and destroy private property

(e) Miscellaneous

- Power to establish corporations by Royal Charter and to amend existing Charters (for example that of the British Broadcasting Corporation, last amended in July 2006)
- The right of the Crown to ownership of treasure trove (replaced for finds made on or after 24 September 1997 by a statutory scheme for treasure under the Treasure Act 1996)
- Power to hold public inquiries (where not covered by the Inquiries Act)
- Controller of Her Majesty's Stationery Office as Queen's Printer:
- Power to appoint the Controller
- Power to hold and exercise all rights and privileges in connection with prerogative copyright
- Sole right of printing or licensing the printing of the Authorised Version of the Bible, the Book of Common Prayer, state papers and Acts of Parliament
- Power to issue certificates of eligibility in respect of prospective inter-country adopters (in non-Hague Convention cases)
- Powers connected with prepaid postage stamps
- Powers concerning the visitorial function of the Crown

OTHER PREROGATIVE POWERS

In the Governance of Britain Green Paper, the Government confirmed that no changes would be proposed to the majority of either the legal prerogatives of the Crown or the Monarch's constitutional or personal prerogatives. In some areas the Government proposes to change the mechanism by which Ministers arrive at their recommendations for the Monarch's exercise of the power. These prerogatives are listed below. Also listed are certain prerogatives of a largely historical nature.

Constitutional/personal prerogatives

Powers within the constitutional/personal prerogative category of powers include:

- Appointment and removal of Ministers
- Appointment of Prime Minister
- Power to dismiss government
- Power to summon, prorogue and dissolve Parliament
- Assent to legislation
- The appointment of privy counsellors
- Granting of honours, decorations, arms and regulating matters of precedence.
- Queen's honours—Order of the Garter, Order of the Thistle, Royal Victorian Order and the Order of Merit
- A power to appoint judges in a residual category of posts which are not statutory and other holders of public office where that office is non-statutory
- A power to legislate under the prerogative by Order in Council or by letters patent in a few residual areas, such as Orders in Council for British Overseas Territories
- Grant of special leave to appeal from certain non-UK courts to the Privy Council
- May require the personal services of subjects in case of imminent danger
- Grant of civic honours and civic dignities
- Grant of approval for certain uses of Royal names and titles

Powers exercised by the Attorney General

The Attorney General's Office consulted on the role of the Attorney General in 2007. That consultation set out the functions of the Attorney General. A number of those functions are non-statutory and have been described as prerogative powers. These functions include:

- Functions in relation to charities
- Functions in relation to criminal proceedings—including the power to enter a *nolle prosequi*
- Functions in relation to civil proceedings—including the ability to institute legal proceedings to protect a public right at the relation of a person who would otherwise lack standing (relator proceedings)

Archaic prerogative powers

The nature of the prerogative has changed overtime. Historically the Royal prerogative has been described as residual powers of the Crown. In particular there are some powers which can be described as residual powers relating to small, specific issues or which are a legacy of a time before legislation was enacted in that area. It is unclear whether some of these prerogative powers continue to exist.

- Guardianship of infants and those suffering certain mental disorders
- Right to *bona vacantia*
- Right to sturgeon, (wild and unmarked) swans and whales as casual revenue
- Right to wreck as casual revenue
- Right to construct and supervise harbours

- By prerogative right the Crown is *prima facie* the owner of all land covered by the narrow seas adjoining the coast, or by arms of the sea or public navigable rivers, and also of the foreshore, or land between high and low water mark
- Right to waifs & strays
- Right to impress men into the Royal Navy
- Right to mint coinage
- Right to mine precious metals (Royal Mines); also to dig for saltpetre
- Grant of franchises, e.g. for markets, ferries and fisheries; pontage & murage.
- Restraining a person from leaving the realm when the interests of state demand it by means of the writ *ne exeat regno*
- The power of the Crown in time of war to intern, expel or otherwise control an enemy alien

Legal Prerogatives of the Crown

The legal prerogatives of the Crown are powers that the Monarch possesses as an embodiment of the Crown. Sometimes described as Crown "privileges or immunities", these prerogatives have been significantly affected by statute—in particular, the Crown Proceedings Act 1947.

- Crown is not bound by statute save by express words or necessary implication
- Crown immunities in litigation, including that the Crown is not directly subject to the contempt jurisdiction and the Sovereign has personal immunity from prosecution or being sued for a wrongful act
- Tax not payable on income received by the Sovereign
- Crown is a preferred creditor in a debtors insolvency
- Time does not run against the Crown (ie no prescriptive rights run)
- Priority of property rights of the Crown in certain circumstances

B: Putting the prerogative on a statutory basis

NOTES

1. This Review followed on from a programme of work on the prerogative announced in the 2007 Green Paper *The Governance of Britain* (Cm 7170) paras. 15, 24:

> 15. The flow of power from the people to government should be balanced by the ability of Parliament to hold government to account. However, then the executive relies on the powers of the royal prerogative... it is difficult for Parliament to scrutinise and challenge government's actions. If voters do not believe that government wields power appropriately or that it is properly accountable then public confidence in the accountability of decision-making risks being lost...
>
> 24. The Government believes that in general the prerogative powers should be put onto a statutory basis and brought under stronger parliamentary scrutiny and control. This will ensure that government is more clearly subject to the mandate of the people's representatives. Proposals in relation to certain specific powers are set out below and these can be addressed now. The Government also intends to undertake a wider review of the remaining prerogative powers and will consider whether in the longer term, all these powers should be codified or put on a statutory basis.
>
> [In a footnote it was made clear that]
>
> 'No changes are proposed to either the legal prerogatives of the Crown on the Monarch's constitutional or personal prerogatives, although in some areas the Government proposes to change the mechanism by which Ministers arrive at their recommendations on the Monarch's exercise of those powers.'

2. Subsequently Consultation Papers were published on the Role of the Attorney-General (Cm 7192), Judicial Appointment (Cm 7210), War Powers and Treaties (Cm 7239). A White Paper, *The Governance of Britain – Constitutional Renewal,* Cm 7342, and draft Constitutional Renewal Bill were produced in 2008 and these were considered by select committees. A major new area was placing the civil service on a statutory basis.
3. The Constitutional Reform and Governance Bill was introduced in the 2008–09 session and carried over into the 2009–10 session. It was passed but a large part of the Bill was lost in the negotiations to deal with legislation in the 'wash-up', the period between the calling of a general election and the dissolution of Parliament. Two prerogatives were thereby placed on a statutory footing, the management of the civil service and the ratification of treaties.

Constitutional Reform and Governance Act 2010

PART 1

THE CIVIL SERVICE

CHAPTER 1

STATUTORY BASIS FOR MANAGEMENT OF THE CIVIL SERVICE

1 Application of Chapter

(1) Subject to subsections (2) and (3), this Chapter applies to the civil service of the State.

(2) This Chapter does not apply to the following parts of the civil service of the State—

(a) the Secret Intelligence Service;
(b) the Security Service;
(c) the Government Communications Headquarters;
(d) the Northern Ireland Civil Service;
(e) the Northern Ireland Court Service.

(3) Further, this Chapter—

(a) does not apply in relation to the making, outside the United Kingdom, of selections of persons who are not members of the civil service of the State for appointment to that service for the purpose only of duties to be carried out wholly outside the United Kingdom;
(b) does not apply in relation to the appointment of a person to the civil service of the State who was selected for the appointment as mentioned in paragraph (a);
(c) does not apply to the civil service of the State so far as it consists of persons—
  (i) who were appointed to the civil service of the State as mentioned in paragraph (b), and
  (ii) all of whose duties are carried out wholly outside the United Kingdom.

(4) In this Chapter references to the civil service—

(a) are to the civil service of the State excluding the parts mentioned in subsections (2) and (3)(c);
(b) are to be read subject to subsection (3)(a) and (b); and references to civil servants are to be read accordingly.

Civil Service Commission

2 Establishment of the Civil Service Commission

(1) There is to be a body corporate called the Civil Service Commission ("the Commission").

(2) Schedule 1 (which is about the Commission) has effect.

(3) The Commission has the role in relation to selections for appointments to the civil service set out in sections 11 to 14.

(4) See also—

(a) section 9 (which sets out the Commission's role in dealing with conduct that conflicts with civil service codes of conduct);

(b) section 17 (under which the Commission may be given additional functions).

Power to manage the civil service

3 Management of the civil service

(1) The Minister for the Civil Service has the power to manage the civil service (excluding the diplomatic service).

(2) The Secretary of State has the power to manage the diplomatic service.

(3) The powers in subsections (1) and (2) include (among other things) power to make appointments.

(4) But they do not cover national security vetting (and, accordingly, subsections (1) and (2) do not affect any power relating to national security vetting).

(5) The agreement of the Minister for the Civil Service is required for any exercise of the power in subsection (2) in relation to—

(a) remuneration of civil servants (including compensation payable on leaving the civil service), or
(b) the conditions on which a civil servant may retire.

(6) In exercising his power to manage the civil service, the Minister for the Civil Service shall have regard to the need to ensure that civil servants who advise Ministers are aware of the constitutional significance of Parliament and of the conventions governing the relationship between Parliament and Her Majesty's Government.

4 Other statutory management powers

(1) All statutory management powers in effect when section 3 comes into force continue to have effect.

(2) But those and all other statutory management powers are exercisable subject to section 3.

(3) "Statutory management power" means a power in relation to the management of any part of the civil service conferred by an Act (whenever passed) or an instrument under an Act (whenever made).

(4) "Act" includes—

(a) an Act of the Scottish Parliament;
(b) an Act or Measure of the National Assembly for Wales; but excludes this Part of this Act.

(5) Subsection (2) does not apply to a statutory management power conferred by the Superannuation Act 1965 or the Superannuation Act 1972 or an instrument under any of those Acts.

Codes of conduct

5 Civil service code

(1) The Minister for the Civil Service must publish a code of conduct for the civil service (excluding the diplomatic service).

(2) For this purpose, the Minister may publish separate codes of conduct covering civil servants who serve the Scottish Executive or the Welsh Assembly Government.

(3) Before publishing a code (or any revision of a code) under subsection (2), the Minister must consult the First Minister for Scotland or the First Minister for Wales (as the case may be).

(4) In this Chapter "civil service code" means a code of conduct published under this section as it is in force for the time being.

(5) The Minister for the Civil Service must lay any civil service code before Parliament.

(6) The First Minister for Scotland must lay before the Scottish Parliament any civil service code under subsection (2) that covers civil servants who serve the Scottish Executive.

(7) The First Minister for Wales must lay before the National Assembly for Wales any civil service code under subsection (2) that covers civil servants who serve the Welsh Assembly Government.

(8) A civil service code forms part of the terms and conditions of service of any civil servant covered by the code.

6 Diplomatic service code

(1) he Secretary of State must publish a code of conduct for the diplomatic service.

(2) In this Chapter "diplomatic service code" means the code of conduct published under this section as it is in force for the time being.

(3) The Secretary of State must lay the diplomatic service code before Parliament.

(4) The diplomatic service code forms part of the terms and conditions of service of any civil servant covered by the code.

7 Minimum requirements for civil service and diplomatic service codes

(1) This section sets out the provision that must be included in a civil service code or the diplomatic service code in relation to the civil servants covered by the code.

(The code may include other provision as well.)

(2) The code must require civil servants who serve an administration mentioned in subsection (3) to carry out their duties for the assistance of the administration as it is duly constituted for the time being, whatever its political complexion.

(3) The administrations are—

(a) Her Majesty's Government in the United Kingdom;
(b) the Scottish Executive;
(c) the Welsh Assembly Government.

(4) The code must require civil servants to carry out their duties—

(a) with integrity and honesty, and
(b) with objectivity and impartiality.

(5) But the code need not require special advisers (see section 15) to carry out their duties with objectivity or impartiality.

8 Special advisers code

(1) The Minister for the Civil Service must publish a code of conduct for special advisers (see section 15).

(2) For this purpose, the Minister may publish separate codes of conduct covering special advisers who serve the Scottish Executive or the Welsh Assembly Government.

(3) Before publishing a code (or any revision of a code) under subsection (2), the Minister must consult the First Minister for Scotland or the First Minister for Wales (as the case may be).

(4) In this Chapter "special advisers code" means a code of conduct published under this section as it is in force for the time being.

(5) Subject to subsection (6), a special advisers code must provide that a special adviser may not—

(a) authorise the expenditure of public funds;

(b) exercise any power in relation to the management of any part of the civil service of the State;

(c) otherwise exercise any power conferred by or under this or any other Act or any power under Her Majesty's prerogative.

(6) A special advisers code may permit a special adviser to exercise any power within subsection (5)(b) in relation to another special adviser.

(7) In subsection (5)(c) "Act" includes—

(a) an Act of the Scottish Parliament;

(b) an Act or Measure of the National Assembly for Wales;

(c) Northern Ireland legislation.

(8) The Minister for the Civil Service must lay any special advisers code before Parliament.

(9) The First Minister for Scotland must lay before the Scottish Parliament any special advisers code under subsection (2) that covers special advisers who serve the Scottish Executive.

(10) The First Minister for Wales must lay before the National Assembly for Wales any special advisers code under subsection (2) that covers special advisers who serve the Welsh Assembly Government.

(11) A special advisers code forms part of the terms and conditions of service of any special adviser covered by the code.

9 Conduct that conflicts with a code of conduct: complaints by civil servants

(1) This section applies in relation to any civil service code and the diplomatic service code; and "code" is to be read accordingly.

(2) Subsection (3) applies if a civil servant ("P") covered by a code has reason to believe—

(a) that P is being, or has been, required to act in a way that conflicts with the code, or

(b) that another civil servant covered by the code is acting, or has acted, in a way that conflicts with the code.

(3) P may complain to the Commission about the matter.

(4) A code may include provision about the steps that must be taken by a civil servant before making a complaint (and P must take the steps accordingly).

(5) The Commission—

(a) must determine procedures for the making of complaints and for the investigation and consideration of complaints by the Commission;

(b) after considering a complaint, may make recommendations about how the matter should be resolved.

(6) For the purposes of the investigation or consideration of a complaint, the following must provide the Commission with any information it reasonably requires—

(a) civil service management authorities;

(b) the complainant;

(c) any civil servant whose conduct is covered by the complaint.

(7) The revision of a code does not affect the application of this section in relation to anything occurring before the revision.

Appointment

10 Selections for appointments to the civil service

(1) This section applies to the selection of persons who are not civil servants for appointment to the civil service.

(2) A person's selection must be on merit on the basis of fair and open competition.

(3) The following selections are excepted from this requirement—

(a) a person's selection for an appointment to the diplomatic service either as head of mission or in connection with the person's appointment (or selection for appointment) as Governor of an overseas territory;
(b) selection for an appointment as special adviser (see section 15);
(c) a selection excepted by the recruitment principles (see sections 11 and 12(1)(b)).

(4) In determining for the purposes of subsection (1) whether or not a person is a civil servant, ignore any appointment for which the person was selected in reliance on subsection (3).

(5) But, in relation to persons selected in reliance on subsection (3)(c), the recruitment principles may disapply subsection (4) in specified cases.

11 Recruitment principles

(1) The Commission must publish a set of principles to be applied for the purposes of the requirement in section 10(2).

(2) Before publishing the set of principles (or any revision of it), the Commission must consult the Minister for the Civil Service.

(3) In this Chapter "recruitment principles" means the set of principles published under this section as it is in force for the time being.

(4) Civil service management authorities must comply with the recruitment principles.

12 Approvals for selections and exceptions

(1) The recruitment principles may include provision—

(a) requiring the Commission's approval to be obtained for a selection which is subject to the requirement in section 10(2);
(b) excepting a selection from that requirement for the purposes of section 10(3)(c).

(2) The Commission may participate in the process for a selection for which its approval is required by provision within subsection (1)(a).

(3) It is up to the Commission to decide how it will participate.

(4) Provision within subsection (1)(b) may be included only if the Commission is satisfied—

(a) that the provision is justified by the needs of the civil service, or
(b) that the provision is needed to enable the civil service to participate in a government employment initiative that major employers in the United Kingdom (or a part of the United Kingdom) have been asked to participate in.

(5) Provision within subsection (1)(a) or (b) may be made in any way, including (for example) by reference to—

(a) particular appointments or descriptions of appointments;
(b) the circumstances in which a selection is made;
(c) the circumstances of the person to be selected;
(d) the purpose of the requirement to obtain approval or the purpose of the exception.

(6) Provision within subsection (1)(b) may also (for example)—

(a) deal with the way in which selections made in reliance on section 10(3)(c) are to be made;
(b) specify terms and conditions that must be included in the terms and conditions of an appointment resulting from a selection made in reliance on section 10(3)(c).

(7) Provision within subsection (1)(a) or (b) may confer discretions on the Commission or civil service management authorities.

13 Complaints about competitions

(1) Subsection (2) applies if a person has reason to believe that a selection for an appointment has been made in contravention of the requirement in section 10(2).

(2) The person may complain to the Commission about the matter.

(3) The Commission—

(a) may determine steps that must be taken by a person before making a complaint (and those steps must be taken accordingly);
(b) must determine procedures for the making of complaints and for the investigation and consideration of complaints by the Commission;
(c) after considering a complaint, may make recommendations about how the matter should be resolved.

(4) For the purposes of the investigation or consideration of a complaint, the following must provide the Commission with any information it reasonably requires—

(a) civil service management authorities;
(b) the complainant.

14 Monitoring by the Commission

(1) The Commission must carry out whatever reviews of recruitment policies and practices it thinks are necessary to establish—

(a) that the principle of selection on merit on the basis of fair and open competition is being upheld in accordance with the requirement in section 10(2) and the recruitment principles, and
(b) that the requirement in section 10(2) and the recruitment principles are not being undermined in any way (apart from non-compliance).

(2) For this purpose, civil service management authorities must provide the Commission with any information it reasonably requires.

Special advisers

15 Definition of "special adviser"

(1) In this Chapter "special adviser" means a person ("P") who holds a position in the civil service serving an administration mentioned below and whose appointment to that position meets the applicable requirements set out below.

Her Majesty's Government in the United Kingdom

The requirements are—

(a) P is appointed to assist a Minister of the Crown after being selected for the appointment by that Minister personally;
(b) the appointment is approved by the Prime Minister;
(c) the terms and conditions of the appointment (apart from those by virtue of section 8(11)) are approved by the Minister for the Civil Service;
(d) those terms and conditions provide for the appointment to end not later than—
  (i) when the person who selected P ceases to hold the ministerial office in relation to which P was appointed to assist that person, or
  (ii) if earlier, the end of the day after the day of the poll at the first parliamentary general election following the appointment.

Scottish Executive

The requirements are—

(a) P is appointed to assist the Scottish Ministers (or one or more of the ministers mentioned in section 44(1)(a) and (b) of the Scotland Act 1998) after being selected for the appointment by the First Minister for Scotland personally;

(b) the terms and conditions of the appointment (apart from those by virtue of section 8(11)) are approved by the Minister for the Civil Service;
(c) those terms and conditions provide for the appointment to end not later than when the person who selected P ceases to hold office as First Minister.

The reference above to the Scottish Ministers excludes the Lord Advocate and the Solicitor General for Scotland.

Welsh Assembly Government

The requirements are—
(a) P is appointed to assist the Welsh Ministers (or one or more of the ministers mentioned in section 45(1)(a) and (b) of the Government of Wales Act 2006) after being selected for the appointment by the First Minister for Wales personally;
(b) the terms and conditions of the appointment (apart from those by virtue of section 8(11)) are approved by the Minister for the Civil Service;
(c) those terms and conditions provide for the appointment to end not later than when the person who selected P ceases to hold office as First Minister.

(2) In subsection (1), in relation to an appointment for which the selection is made personally by a person designated under section 45(4) of the Scotland Act 1998 or section 46(5) of the Government of Wales Act 2006, the reference to the person who selected P ceasing to hold office as First Minister for Scotland or Wales (as the case may be) is to be read as a reference to the designated person ceasing to be able to exercise the functions of the First Minister by virtue of the designation.

16 Annual reports about special advisers

(1) The Minister for the Civil Service must—

(a) prepare an annual report about special advisers serving Her Majesty's Government in the United Kingdom, and
(b) lay the report before Parliament.

(2) The First Minister for Scotland must—

(a) prepare an annual report about special advisers serving the Scottish Executive, and
(b) lay the report before the Scottish Parliament.

(3) The First Minister for Wales must—

(a) prepare an annual report about special advisers serving the Welsh Assembly Government, and
(b) lay the report before the National Assembly for Wales.

(4) A report under this section must contain information about the number and cost of the special advisers.

Additional functions of the Commission

17 Agreements for the Commission to carry out additional functions

(1) The Minister for the Civil Service and the Commission may agree that the Commission is to carry out functions in relation to the civil service in addition to those given to it under the other provisions of this Chapter.

(2) The Commission is to carry out those additional functions accordingly.

(3) For the purposes of any additional function, civil service management authorities must provide the Commission with any information it reasonably requires.

Final provisions

18 Definitions etc

(1) In this Chapter—

"civil servant" is read as stated in section 1(4);

"civil service" is read as stated in section 1(4);

"civil service code" is defined in section 5(4);

"civil service management authority" means any person involved in the management of any part of the civil service;

"the Commission" is defined in section 2(1);

"diplomatic service" means Her Majesty's diplomatic service;

"diplomatic service code" is defined in section 6(2);

"function" includes power or duty;

"information" means information recorded in any form;

"recruitment principles" is defined in section 11(3);

"special adviser" is defined in section 15;

"special advisers code" is defined in section 8(4).

(2) Subsection (3) applies for the purposes of sections 9(6), 13(4), 14(2) and 17(3).

(3) No person may be required to provide information which the person could not be compelled to provide in civil proceedings before the High Court or the Court of Session.

Ratification of treaties

20 Treaties to be laid before Parliament before ratification

(1) Subject to what follows, a treaty is not to be ratified unless—

(a) a Minister of the Crown has laid before Parliament a copy of the treaty,
(b) the treaty has been published in a way that a Minister of the Crown thinks appropriate, and
(c) period A has expired without either House having resolved, within period A, that the treaty should not be ratified.

(2) Period A is the period of 21 sitting days beginning with the first sitting day after the date on which the requirement in subsection (1)(a) is met.

(3) Subsections (4) to (6) apply if the House of Commons resolved as mentioned in subsection (1)(c) (whether or not the House of Lords also did so).

(4) The treaty may be ratified if—

(a) a Minister of the Crown has laid before Parliament a statement indicating that the Minister is of the opinion that the treaty should nevertheless be ratified and explaining why, and
(b) period B has expired without the House of Commons having resolved, within period B, that the treaty should not be ratified.

(5) Period B is the period of 21 sitting days beginning with the first sitting day after the date on which the requirement in subsection (4)(a) is met.

(6) A statement may be laid under subsection (4)(a) in relation to the treaty on more than one occasion.

(7) Subsection (8) applies if—

(a) the House of Lords resolved as mentioned in subsection (1)(c), but
(b) the House of Commons did not.

(8) The treaty may be ratified if a Minister of the Crown has laid before Parliament a statement indicating that the Minister is of the opinion that the treaty should nevertheless be ratified and explaining why.

(9) "Sitting day" means a day on which both Houses of Parliament sit.

21 Extension of 21 sitting day period

(1) A Minister of the Crown may, in relation to a treaty, extend the period mentioned in section 20(1)(c) by 21 sitting days or less.

(2) The Minister does that by laying before Parliament a statement—

(a) indicating that the period is to be extended, and
(b) setting out the length of the extension.

(3) The statement must be laid before the period would have expired without the extension.

(4) The Minister must publish the statement in a way the Minister thinks appropriate.

(5) The period may be extended more than once.

22 Section 20 not to apply in exceptional cases

(1) Section 20 does not apply to a treaty if a Minister of the Crown is of the opinion that, exceptionally, the treaty should be ratified without the requirements of that section having been met.

(2) But a treaty may not be ratified by virtue of subsection (1) after either House has resolved, as mentioned in section 20(1)(c), that the treaty should not be ratified.

(3) If a Minister determines that a treaty is to be ratified by virtue of subsection (1), the Minister must, either before or as soon as practicable after the treaty is ratified—

(a) lay before Parliament a copy of the treaty,
(b) arrange for the treaty to be published in a way that the Minister thinks appropriate, and
(c) lay before Parliament a statement indicating that the Minister is of the opinion mentioned in subsection (1) and explaining why.

23 Section 20 not to apply to certain descriptions of treaties

(1) Section 20 does not apply to—

(a) a treaty covered by section 12 of the European Parliamentary Elections Act 2002 (treaty providing for increase in European Parliament's powers not to be ratified unless approved by Act of Parliament);
(b) a treaty covered by section 5 of the European Union (Amendment) Act 2008 (treaty amending founding Treaties not to be ratified unless approved by Act of Parliament).

(2) Section 20 does not apply to a treaty in relation to which an Order in Council may be made under one or more of the following—

(a) section 158 of the Inheritance Tax Act 1984 (double taxation conventions);
(b) section 2 of the Taxation (International and Other Provisions) Act 2010 (double taxation arrangements);
(c) section 173 of the Finance Act 2006 (international tax enforcement arrangements).

(3) Section 20 does not apply to a treaty concluded (under authority given by the government of the United Kingdom) by the government of a British overseas territory, of any of the Channel Islands or of the Isle of Man.

(4) Section 20 does not apply to a treaty a copy of which is presented to Parliament by command of Her Majesty before that section comes into force.

24 Explanatory memoranda

In laying a treaty before Parliament under this Part, a Minister shall accompany the treaty with an explanatory memorandum explaining the provisions of the treaty, the reasons for Her Majesty's Government seeking ratification of the treaty, and such other matters as the Minister considers appropriate.

25 Meaning of "treaty" and "ratification"

(1) In this Part "treaty" means a written agreement—
(a) between States or between States and international organisations, and
(b) binding under international law.

(2) But "treaty" does not include a regulation, rule, measure, decision or similar instrument made under a treaty (other than one that amends or replaces the treaty (in whole or in part)).

(3) In this Part a reference to ratification of a treaty is a reference to an act of a kind specified in subsection (4) which establishes as a matter of international law the United Kingdom's consent to be bound by the treaty.

(4) The acts are—
(a) deposit or delivery of an instrument of ratification, accession, approval or acceptance;
(b) deposit or delivery of a notification of completion of domestic procedures.

NOTE: These provisions present, more or less, in statutory form the pre-existing situation. Thus the current Civil Service Commissioners will become members of the new statutory Civil Service Commission and will continue to have responsibility for ensuring that appointments are made on merit on the basis of fair and open competition. In relation to ratification of treaties, the House of Commons can resolve against ratification and thus make it unlawful for the Government to ratify a treaty. The House of Lords will not be able to prevent the Government from ratifying a treaty, but if they resolve against ratification the Government will have to produce a further explanatory statement explaining its belief that the agreement should be ratified. Part 2 concerns scrutiny of the ratification of agreements entered into by the Government under international law. It does not change the current position that an Act of Parliament would be required if it were intended to give effect in domestic law to matters embodied in such an agreement.

C: Codification?

House of Commons Library, The Royal Prerogative

2009, Standard Note SN/PC/03862, p. 5

The Crown's personal prerogative powers

There are three main prerogative powers recognised under the common law which still reside in the jurisdiction of the Crown.

Firstly, the appointment of a Prime Minister; the sovereign must appoint that person who is in the best position to receive the support of the majority in the House of Commons. However, this does not involve the sovereign in making a personal assessment of leading politicians since no major party could fight a general election without a recognised leader.

However, if after an election no one party has an absolute majority in the House (as in 1923, 1929 and February 1974) then the Queen will send for the leader of the party with the largest number of seats (as in 1929 and 1974) or with the next largest number of seats (as in January 1924). Alternatively, the sovereign would have to initiate discussions with and between the parties to discover, for example, whether a government could be formed by a politician who was not a party leader or whether a coalition government could be formed.

Secondly, the dissolution of Parliament, in the absence of a regular term for the life of Parliament fixed by statute, the Sovereign may by the prerogative dissolve Parliament and cause a general election to be held. The sovereign normally accepts the advice of the Prime Minister and grants dissolution when it is requested; a refusal would probably be treated by the Prime Minister as tantamount to a dismissal. These areas of the prerogative are the subject of continuing academic debate.

Thirdly, the giving of royal assent to legislation, in 1708 Queen Anne was the last sovereign to refuse royal assent to a bill passed by Parliament. Additionally, no monarchs since the sixteenth century have signed Bills themselves and Queen Victoria was the last to give the Royal Assent in person in 1854.

NOTES

1. *Review of the Executive Royal Prerogative Powers: Final Report* noted at para. 39:

> In other areas, also, work is under way to increase Parliamentary input into Ministerial recommendations on the Monarch's exercise of prerogative powers. The House of Commons Modernisation Committee is currently examining the conventions governing the dissolution and recall of Parliament. The Government has proposed that the Prime Minister should be required to seek the approval of the House of Commons before asking the Monarch for a dissolution. The Government's proposal in relation to recall is that the Standing Orders of the House be amended to provide for the Speaker to recall the House if he or she receives requests from over half of its membership.

2. The Cabinet Secretary has been engaged in compiling a Cabinet Manual a draft version of which was published in December 2010 to undergo a consultation exercise. Its Chapters are as follows:
Chapter 1 The Sovereign
Chapter 2 Elections and government formation
Chapter 3 The Executive—the Prime Minister, ministers and the structure of government
Chapter 4 Collective Cabinet decision-making
Chapter 5 Ministers and Parliament
Chapter 6 Ministers and the law
Chapter 7 Ministers and the Civil Service
Chapter 8 Relations with the Devolved Administrations and local government
Chapter 9 Relations with the European Union and other international institutions Chapter 10 Government finance and expenditure
Chapter 11 Official information
Annex A Election timetable
Annex B Statutory limits on ministerial salaries
Annex C Detail on devolution settlements

The first public unveiling of a part of an earlier draft of the Cabinet Manual was Chapter 2 when it was considered by the House of Commons Justice Select Committee and was reproduced in the report, *Constitutional Processes Following a General Election,* Fifth Report from the House of Commons Justice Committee (2010, HC 396 of 2009–10). This chapter was of interest due to the fact that in the run-up to the general election in May 2010, the opinion polls were indicating that a 'hung' Parliament was a possibility. The extracts below deal with the purpose of the Cabinet Manual and Chapter 2.

The Cabinet Manual – Draft: A guide to laws, conventions, and rules on the operation of government

Cabinet Office, December 2010, pp, 2,3 23-29

> While some parts of the way in which the Government operates are governed by statute law – for example limits on the number of ministerial salaries – many other aspects, such as the existence of Cabinet itself, are matters of convention or precedent. These conventions have evolved over time and in some cases have been the subject of uncertainty.
>
> In recent years, more and more information has been made available on how government operates. For example, *Questions of Procedure for Ministers* was first made public in 1992, and its successor, the *Ministerial Code*, was first published in 1997 (with the most recent version published following the 2010 General Election). Information on other issues, such as the operation of Cabinet and its committees, is already available on the Cabinet Office website.
>
> However, there has never been a single source of information on how the Government works and interacts with the Sovereign, Parliament, the judiciary, international organisations, the Devolved Administrations and local government.
>
> Other countries with a "Westminster-style" system similar to the UK have faced the same issue and consolidated their guidance. In particular, over the past 20 years, New Zealand has gradually developed its own Cabinet Manual, which, as the New Zealand Prime Minister said in the foreword to the latest edition, is now seen as "an authoritative guide to central government decision making for Minsters, their offices, and those working within government".

The role and content of the Cabinet Manual

The Cabinet Manual is intended to be a source of information on the UK"s laws, conventions and rules, including those of a constitutional nature, that affect the operation and procedures of government. It is written from the perspective of the Executive branch of government. It is not intended to have any legal effect or set issues in stone. It is intended to guide, not to direct.

The Cabinet Manual is a statement of the arrangements as they are on the date of publication. Some areas of the Manual continue to be subject to public debate. The Manual, however, does not seek to resolve or move forward those debates, but is instead a factual description of the situation today. In other words, it will be a record of incremental changes rather than a driver of change...

Meeting of the new Parliament

40. Recent practice had been for Parliament to meet on the Wednesday following the election. In 2007, the Select Committee on the Modernisation of the House of Commons recommended a reversion to the previous practice of 12 days between polling day and the first meeting of Parliament. This was adopted in 2010, when there was an interval of 12 days.

41. The first business of the House of Commons when it meets is to elect or re-elect a Speaker and for Members to take the oath. The first business of the House of Lords is for its Members also to take the oath. Normally the Queen's Speech outlining the Government's legislative programme will take place in the second week of Parliament's sitting and is followed by four or five days of debate. This is when the business of the new Parliament properly begins.

42. The election of the Lord Speaker is not dependent on a general election: it takes place no more than five years after the previous election of the Lord Speaker, the last having taken place on 28 June 2006. Where a dissolution of Parliament has been announced and coincides with the very limited circumstances that consideration is likely to be given to the exercise of the reserve power to refuse it, for example when such a request is made very soon after a previous dissolution. In those circumstances, the Sovereign would normally wish to know before granting a second dissolution that those involved in the political process had ascertained that there was no alternative potential government that would be likely to command the confidence of the House of Commons. *This paragraph will be substantially affected if Parliament agrees the proposals in the Fixed- term Parliaments Bill, which will provide for five-year fixed-term Parliaments.*

Confidence

43. The ability of a government to command the confidence of the elected House of Commons is central to its authority to govern. It is tested by votes on motions of confidence, or no confidence. Confidence votes can take three broad forms:

a vote on a motion "that this House has no confidence in Her Majesty's Government", tabled by the Opposition, or "that this House has confidence in Her Majesty's Government", tabled by the Government. By convention, the Government will make parliamentary time available for a debate on a no-confidence motion tabled by the Opposition at an early opportunity. A Government defeat on a confidence motion which it has tabled would be treated the same as the passing of a no-confidence motion tabled by the Opposition

a vote on a matter which the Government has publicly declared that it regards as a matter of confidence. This may be any proposal which allows the House to reach a clear decision, such as the second reading of a specified bill, a substantive motion expressing a view on the Government's policies, or a motion for the adjournment of the House

a vote on any matter which is so fundamental to the Government's position that its rejection by the House (or, in the case of a non-Government proposal, its acceptance) constitutes a fatal objection to the Government's continuation in office.

44. Votes on the Address in reply to the Queen's Speech have traditionally been regarded as votes of confidence (other than votes on minor amendments). Following an election, once the Government has secured the support of the Commons for the Queen's Speech programme it is considered to have the confidence of the Commons unless and until it loses a confidence vote.

45. Commanding the confidence of the House of Commons is not the same as having a majority or winning every vote. Minority government is possible; and governments with a majority have lost votes on particular issues.

The principles of government formation

46. Governments hold office unless and until they resign. If the Prime Minister resigns, the Sovereign will invite the person who it appears is most likely to be able to command the confidence of the House to serve as Prime Minister and to form a government. It is the responsibility of those involved in the political process, and in particular the parties represented in Parliament, to seek to determine and communicate clearly who that person should be. At the time of his or her resignation, the incumbent Prime Minister may also be asked by the Sovereign for a recommendation on who can best command the confidence of the House of Commons in his or her place.

Parliaments with an overall majority in the House of Commons

47. After an election, if an incumbent government retains an overall majority in the new Parliament, it will normally continue in office and resume normal business. There is no need for the Sovereign to ask the Prime Minister to continue. If the election results in an overall majority for a different party, the incumbent Prime Minister and government will immediately resign and the Sovereign will invite the leader of the party that has won the election to form a government. Details on the appointment of the Prime Minister and Ministers can be found in Chapter 3.

Parliaments with no overall majority in the House of Commons

48. Where an election does not result in an overall majority for a single party, the incumbent government remains in office unless and until the Prime Minister tenders his or her resignation and the Government's resignation to the Sovereign. An incumbent government is entitled to wait until the new Parliament has met to see if it can command the confidence of the House of Commons, but is expected to resign if it becomes clear that it is unlikely to be able to command that confidence and there is a clear alternative.

49. Where a range of different administrations could potentially be formed, discussions will take place between political parties on who should form the next government. The Sovereign would not expect to become involved in such negotiations, although the political parties and the Cabinet Secretary would have responsibilities in ensuring that the Palace is provided with information on the progress of discussions and their conclusion. The Principal Private Secretary to the Prime Minister may also have a role.

50. The incumbent Prime Minister is not expected to resign until it is clear that there is someone else who should be asked to form a government because they are better placed to command the confidence of the House of Commons and that information has been communicated to the Sovereign.

51. Any negotiations between political parties over the formation of a stable government need to be as well informed as possible, and the leaders of the political parties involved may therefore seek the support of the Civil Service. Such support may be organised by the Cabinet Secretary, with the authorisation of the Prime Minister.

52. Civil Service support may be provided for negotiations between the Government and opposition parties and/or between opposition parties themselves, and would normally be made available to parties with a realistic prospect of forming, joining or formally supporting the Government. Support would be focused and provided on an equal basis to all the parties involved, including the party that was currently in government. The incumbent government would also continue to be supported by the Civil Service in the usual way.

53. The support provided by the Civil Service to the parties could include: advice on the constitutional processes of government formation; provisions of factual information in relation to specific policy proposals; and facilitation of discussions and negotiations (including the provision of facilities, such as meeting rooms). Support would only commence following the election and support for opposition parties would normally cease once a stable government had been formed, although it could continue, with the authorisation of the Prime Minister, for any party formally supporting the Government. Following the election in May 2010, where there was no overall majority, the Civil Service provided

support to negotiations between political parties. Further information on the nature of that support can be found at:

www.cabinetoffice.gov.uk/resource-library/civil-service-support-coalition-negotiations

54. As long as there is significant doubt following an election over the Government's ability to command the confidence of the House of Commons, certain restrictions on government activity apply; see paragraphs 67 to 73.

55. The nature of the government formed will be dependent on discussions between political parties and any resulting agreement. Where there is no overall majority, there are essentially three broad types of government that could be formed:

single-party, minority government, where the party may (although not necessarily) be supported by a series of ad hoc agreements based on common interests

formal inter-party agreement, for example the Liberal–Labour pact from 1977 to 1978, or formal coalition government, which generally consists of ministers from more than one political party, and typically commands a majority in the House of Commons.

Change of Prime Minister or government during the life of a Parliament

56. If a government is defeated on a motion of confidence in the House of Commons, the Prime Minister is expected to tender the Government"s resignation, unless circumstances allow him or her to opt instead to request dissolution. If it is clear who should form an alternative administration, such a resignation should take effect immediately.

57. Where a range of different administrations could potentially be formed, discussions will take place between political parties on who should form the next government. In these circumstances the processes and considerations described in paragraphs 48 to 55 would apply.

58. At present, the Prime Minister may request that the Sovereign dissolves Parliament so that an early election takes place. The Sovereign is not bound to accept such a request, although in practice it would only be in very limited circumstances that consideration is likely to be given to the exercise of the reserve power to refuse it, for example when such a request is made very soon after a previous dissolution. In those circumstances, the Sovereign would normally wish to know before granting a second dissolution that those involved in the political process had ascertained that there was no alternative potential government that would be likely to command the confidence of the House of Commons. *This paragraph will be substantially affected if Parliament agrees the proposals in the Fixed- term Parliaments Bill, which will provide for five-year fixed-term Parliaments.*

59. Although they have not been exercised in modern times, the Sovereign retains reserve powers to dismiss the Prime Minister or make a personal choice of successor, and to withhold consent to a request for dissolution. However, there is a duty on the Prime Minister to act in a way that prevents the Sovereign being drawn into political controversy by having to exercise those reserve powers.

NOTES

1. This consultation version of the chapter has been amended in the light of the experience of the negotiations which led to the formation of the Conservative–Liberal Democrat coalition government. In particular, para. 50 was added because of the concern that Gordon Brown wished to resign before the other two parties had successfully concluded their coalition agreement.
2. The Justice Committee's report did raise questions about understanding elements of the draft chapter, and this issue of codification presenting problems about the interpretation of, rather than the existence of, conventions which is related to the discussion about problems of definition and the need for adjudication in the report of the Joint Committee on Conventions: see pp. 201–203, *post* on the codification of constitutional conventions. The next section deals with constitutional conventions. In reading it, notice the similarities in some aspects of the royal prerogative and convention: their nature, as well as codification and the differences as in their status as law and possible conversion into statute.

SECTION 2: CONSTITUTIONAL CONVENTIONS

A: Sources of the constitution

As the United Kingdom does not have a written constitution, the sources of our constitutional arrangements must be sought elsewhere. Most textbooks contain sections outlining the sources of the constitution. In these sections they highlight legislation and judicial precedent as the source of the legal rules of the constitution. The source of the non-legal rules is provided by conventions.

A. V. Dicey, *An Introduction to the Study of The Law of the Constitution*

(10th edn, 1985), pp. 23–24

[T]he rules which make up constitutional law, as the term is used in England, include two sets of principles or maxims of a totally distinct character.

The one set of rules are in the strictest sense 'laws,' since they are rules which (whether written or unwritten, whether enacted by statute or derived from the mass of custom, tradition, or judge-made maxims known as the common law) are enforced by the courts; these rules constitute 'constitutional law' in the proper sense of that term, and may for the sake of distinction be called collectively 'the law of the constitution.'

The other set of rules consist of conventions, understandings, habits, or practices which, though they may regulate the conduct of the several members of the sovereign power, of the Ministry, or of other officials, are not in reality laws at all since they are not enforced by the courts. This portion of constitutional law may, for the sake of distinction, be termed the 'conventions of the constitution,' or constitutional morality.

To put the same thing in a somewhat different shape, 'constitutional law,' as the expression is used in England, both by the public and by authoritative writers, consists of two elements. The one element, here called the 'law of the constitution,' is a body of undoubted law; the other element, here called the 'conventions of the constitution,' consists of maxims or practices which, though they regulate the ordinary conduct of the Crown, of Ministers, and of other persons under the constitution, are not in strictness laws at all.

E. C. S. Wade, 'Introduction' in A. V. Dicey, *An Introduction to the Study of The Law of the Constitution*

(10th edn, 1985), pp. cli–clvii

The Widened Sphere of Constitutional Conventions.—It is largely through the influence of Dicey that the term, convention, has been accepted to describe a constitutional obligation, obedience to which is secured despite the absence of the ordinary means of enforcing the obligation in a court of law. Dicey defined conventions as 'rules for determining the mode in which the discretionary powers of the Crown (or of the Ministers as servants of the Crown) ought to be exercised.' He was concerned to establish that conventions were 'intended to secure the ultimate supremacy of the electorate as the true political sovereign of the State.'

In discussing conventions as a source of constitutional law it must be noted that the obligation does not necessarily, or indeed usually, derive from express agreement. It is more likely to take its origin from custom or from practice arising out of sheer expediency. . . .

Dicey discusses mainly the rules governing the exercise of the royal prerogative by Ministers of the Crown and that part of the 'law and custom' of Parliament which rests upon custom alone. In both these cases the rules are based on custom or expediency rather than as a result of formal agreement. Conventions, however, have a wider application and have, during the present century, played an important part in building up the political relationship between the various member States of the British Commonwealth. Some of these conventions, in particular the rules governing the full competence of Commonwealth Parliaments to legislate, were made statutory by the Statute of Westminster, 1931, and later enactments.

But much of the relationship is still conventional and has been based on agreement reached by Prime Ministers at Imperial Conferences. Constitutional matters no longer figure prominently on the agenda of the periodic meetings of Prime Ministers or other Ministers of Commonwealth Governments which are less formal than the earlier Imperial Conferences. But this is because constitutional issues have now been settled and in no way minimises the important part which conventions have in the past played in this sphere of constitutional development.

Dicey concentrated attention upon the conventional rules which precedent showed were fundamental to the working of the Cabinet....

It is the prerogative of the Sovereign to appoint the Prime Minister. Convention limits the range of choice to that of a party leader who can command a majority in the House of Commons. This convention to some extent lacks the binding force which conventions in other fields possess. This does not mean that the rules can normally be disregarded, but that unforeseen circumstances may deprive them of their force on a particular occasion; any departure from the normal would have to conform to recognising the supremacy of the electorate and not to serve autocratic ends. Some writers would not include a practice or usage which is not regarded as obligatory, though none the less usually followed, in the category of constitutional conventions. It is, however, very difficult to draw the line between an obligatory and a non-obligatory practice. The characteristic of conventions, namely, that they supplement the laws which are enforced by the courts, would seem to preclude their precise definition. On the whole it seems preferable to regard the political practices of Sovereigns in choice of Prime Ministers as within the category of conventional rules, even though those rules are still somewhat inconclusive and therefore sufficiently flexible to meet unforeseen circumstances. For they are clearly rules of conduct referable to the requirements of constitutional government and are aimed at reflecting the supremacy of the electorate. The same is true of the practices and precepts which surround the prerogative of dissolution of Parliament. But in this case there is the fundamental understanding that the power may only be exercised on the advice of Ministers. That advice may not be available to the Sovereign in the choice of a Prime Minister, where his predecessor has been removed by death or his own resignation.

Perhaps the relationship between law and convention is best illustrated by contrasting the legal and conventional position of Ministers. They, like civil servants and members of the armed forces, are in law the servants of the Crown. By convention they, unlike all other servants of the Crown, are responsible directly to Parliament both for their own activities and those of civil servants, their subordinates, who by custom are never referred to by name in Parliament. This responsibility of Ministers is designed to make them answerable through Parliament to the electorate. To rely solely on their legal responsibility to their master, the Sovereign, would entirely fail to secure their responsibility to the public in general and indeed might make them the agents of a Sovereign who disregarded the public will, as in the days before the prerogative powers were restricted by Parliament.

Conventions relating to internal government go much further than the examples which were chosen by Dicey from the exercise of the royal prerogative and the relationship between the two Houses of Parliament. They nowadays provide for the working of the whole complicated governmental machine. A Cabinet in deciding upon policy will require to know whether it already has the power in law to take the action which it proposes. It is certainly not limited to exercising those prerogative powers of the Sovereign which are entrusted to it by convention. Through its command of a majority in the House of Commons it is normally in a position to take legal powers if they do not already exist. Moreover it is the responsibility of the Cabinet to ensure unity in the constitutional system and in particular to avoid or, if need be, to settle conflicts of policy and of action by the various departments. In all these activities rules and practices develop in order to secure the desired end. The growth of the committee system within the Cabinet organisation is an extra-legal development which has introduced important changes in Cabinet government since Dicey formulated his views on the place of conventions in the working of the constitution. One can properly describe this development as conventional. It is in no sense an obligation imposed by law upon Ministers that they should consult an elaborate system of committees. Yet no one supposes that a modern government could be conducted without some such machinery. So we have the position that the Cabinet itself is to all intents and purposes the creation of convention designed to secure political harmony between the Crown and its subjects. From this conventional institution there have grown up in the present century such devices as formal committees, like the Defence Committee, and *ad hoc* committees, appointed for a particular purpose but often remaining in being after their original purpose has been fulfilled.... In addition there are royal commissions, select committees of either House of Parliament, committees appointed by departmental Ministers, all of which play an important part in the formulation of policy. For none of these is there any legal requirement. But no appreciation of the working of the governmental machine would be complete without their inclusion. And since their purpose is to focus public opinion on a particular problem, they are designed to secure that harmony between the Ministers of the Crown and the public which is the principal justification for supplementing the law of the constitution with conventions.

■ QUESTION

What are the various ways in which conventions may arise?

B: What are conventions?

Conventions represent important rules of political behaviour which are necessary for the smooth running of the constitution. It is not only in the constitutional arrangements of the United Kingdom that conventions are important; K. C. Wheare, in *Modern Constitutions* (1966), p. 122, states that 'in all countries usage and convention are important and ... in many countries which have Constitutions usage and convention play as important a part as they do in England'. Conventions facilitate evolution and change within the constitution while the legal form remains unchanged.

G. Marshall and G. C. Moodie, *Some Problems of the Constitution*

(5th edn, 1971), pp. 23–25

What then are the conventions of the British Constitution? One way of answering the question is to point to particular examples. Thus, among them are such rules as that the Monarch should normally on the resignation of a government, ask the Leader of the Opposition to form the new one; or (before 1911) that the House of Lords should not oppose a money bill duly passed by the House of Commons; or (to quote from the Preamble to the Statute of Westminster of 1931) 'that any alteration in the law touching the Succession to the Throne or the Royal Style and Titles shall hereafter require the assent as well of the Parliaments of all the Dominions as of the Parliament of the United Kingdom'. An alternative approach is to put forward a formal definition. By the conventions of the Constitution, then, we mean certain rules of constitutional behaviour which are considered to be binding by and upon those who operate the Constitution, but which are not enforced by the law courts (although the courts may recognise their existence), nor by the presiding officers in the Houses of Parliament. Not all writers would agree to the inclusion of this last phrase. But it seems best to exclude from the category of convention 'the law and custom of Parliament' which define much of its procedure, and which are applied and interpreted by, for example, the Speaker of the House of Commons. On the other hand, certain important rules of procedure—for example, resort to the usual channels through which, among other things, important decisions about the agenda of the House of Commons are reached—are 'unknown' both to the courts and to the Speaker and must clearly be counted as conventions.

Such conventions are to be found in all established constitutions, and soon develop even in the newest. One reason for this is that no general rule of law is self-applying, but must be applied according to the terms of additional rules. These additional rules may be concerned with the interpretation of the general rule, or with the exact circumstances in which it should apply, about either of which uncertainty may exist, and the greater the generality the greater will the uncertainty tend to be. Many constitutions include a large number of additional legal rules to clarify the meaning and application of their main provisions, but in a changing world it is rarely possible to eradicate or prevent all doubts on these points by enactment or even by adjudication. The result often is to leave a significant degree of discretion to those exercising the rights or wielding the powers legally conferred, defined, or permitted. As Dicey pointed out, it is to regulate the use of such discretionary power that conventions develop. Thus the rules prescribing the procedure to be followed by the Monarch in the selection of a Prime Minister regulate the way in which she should exercise her prerogative power to appoint advisers. The legal prerogative remains intact, and appointments to the office of Prime Minister (itself a conventional position) can still be made only by the

Monarch. Similarly, it remains true that no bill can become a statute until it receives the Royal Assent; but the Monarch's discretion in deciding whether or not to assent is governed by a rule that she should always assent to a bill which has duly passed both Houses. In this case the royal discretion is so limited as virtually to have been abolished. But the legal position remains untouched and thus, it is sometimes argued, may still be exercised under certain circumstances.

The definition of 'conventions' may thus be amplified by saying that their purpose is to define the use of constitutional discretion. To put this in slightly different words, it may be said that conventions are non-legal rules regulating the way in which legal rules shall be applied. Sometimes, of course, they do so only indirectly, in that they relate primarily to already existing conventions. Not all discretionary powers are so limited, but the most important ones usually are in some degree. In Britain it has been the growth of conventional limitations of the royal prerogative, in conjunction with changes in the legal rules contained in such statutes as the Act of Settlement and the various Acts extending the suffrage (as well as those changes brought about by judicial interpretation), which has largely created our modern system of government. As Sir Kenneth Wheare has said, it is 'the association of law with convention within the constitutional structure which is the essential characteristic'. This is why it is impossible to settle constitutional disputes merely by reference to the state of the law.

G. Wilson, 'Postscript: The Courts, Law and Convention' in Nolan and Sedley, *The Making and Remaking of the British Constitution*

(1997), pp. 97–98

In spite of the use of the law for some of the changes it still remains the case that important parts of the constitution are regulated not by law but by convention, and this remains one of its major distinguishing features. There are, it is said, legal rules and there are conventional rules, each with the same binding force but with many of the conventions not supported by legal rule and therefore not falling within the jurisdiction of the courts. What might be called the grand conventions still lie at the heart of the constitution. They underpinned the gradual transfer of powers from the monarch to her ministers, the limitation of her freedom to choose who should be her ministers, in particular the prime minister, the person who was entitled to form a government, and to dismiss ministers or dissolve Parliament, and the virtual extinction of her power to refuse assent to legislation. But it does not stop there. Conventions reach into every part of the constitution. The rules of procedure and practice of the House of Commons, which help to shape the ground rules of political debate and include provisions as regards the legislative process, the curtailment of debate, the rights of the opposition to choose the subject matter of debate, and which strike the current balance between the need for governments to be able to implement their plans and policies and the opportunities granted to the opposition not only to express their public criticism of them, but also to present themselves to the electorate as a future alternative government—all these rest on convention. It is convention which protects them from arbitrary change and gives them their fundamental character. With none of these do the courts have any direct involvement.

C: Laws and conventions

In the passage by Dicey (p. 176, *ante*), he distinguished between laws and conventions, stating that laws are enforced by the courts whereas conventions are not. Sir Ivor Jennings in *The Law and the Constitution* (5th edn, 1959), at pp. 103–136, takes issue with Dicey. Much of the argument is semantic, being centred on the issue whether all laws are enforced by the courts. Jennings chose to interpret this to mean that Dicey was suggesting that courts would apply sanctions for the breach of any and every law. Many laws are not enforced by the application of sanctions; but they are given effect to by the courts, in that they are adhered to and applied. In this sense they are enforced, whereas conventions are treated differently. Other contrasts between laws and conventions have been noted by Munro.

C. R. Munro, *Studies in Constitutional Law*

(2nd edn, 1999), pp. 69–71

For example, instead of being concerned with the practical effects of breaches of rules, we might consider how the rules come into being. In a legal system, a certain number of sources are recognised as law-constitutive. So there are rules specifying what counts as law (or what, by implication, does not). In England, for instance, the courts accept as law only legislation made or authorised by Parliament and the body of rules evolved by the courts called common law. There are formal signs, such as the words of enactment used for Acts of Parliament, denoting that rules have passed a test for being laws. The point here is not merely to reiterate that conventions fall outside the categories recognised as law (which it has been the object of this section so far to show). Rather, what is significant is that conventions do not share the same qualities as laws. They do not come from a 'certain' number of sources: their origins are amorphous, and there are any number of dramatis personae whose behaviour may later be taken as evidence for the existence of a constitutional rule or practice. No body has the function of deciding whether conventions exist. There is no formal sign of their entitlement to be so regarded, and there are no agreed rules for deciding.

These points are related to a larger contrast which may be drawn. Rules of law form parts of a system. Included in the system are rules about the rules: there are provisions about entry to, and exit from, the system, and procedures for the determination and application of the rules. We cannot conceive of a single legal rule, in isolation from a system. However, conventions do not form a system. There is no unifying feature which they possess, and no apparatus of secondary rules. They merely evolve in isolation from each other.

Here, incidentally, lies the answer to Jennings' specious argument that laws and conventions are the same because both 'rest essentially upon general acquiescence'. That is quite misleading. Conventions rest entirely on acquiescence, but individually. If a supposed convention is not accepted as binding by those to whom it would apply, then there could not be said to be a convention, and this is a test on which each must be separately assessed. Laws do not depend upon acquiescence. Individual laws may be unpopular or widely disobeyed, but it does not mean that they are not laws. No doubt the system as a whole must possess some measure of de facto effectiveness for us to recognise it as valid, although it might be stretching language to describe the citizens of any country occupied by enemy forces or ruled by a brutal dictatorship as 'acquiescing' in the laws which govern them. In any event, it is obvious that the comparison is inapt.

When 'acquiescence' is properly analysed, another means of distinguishing emerges. Breaches of a legal rule do not bring into question the existence or validity of the rule; for example, however frequently motorists might exceed the speed limits, the road traffic laws are no less laws for that. However, according to a generally accepted definition, conventions are supposed to be 'rules of political practice which are regarded as binding by those to whom they apply.' If such rules are broken, it becomes appropriate to ask whether they are still 'regarded as binding', and if they are broken often, surely one cannot say that any obligatory rule exists? In other words, the breach of a convention carries a destructive effect, which is absent with laws. The reason for this is that 'feeling obliged' is a necessary condition for the existence of a convention, whereas it is neither a necessary nor a sufficient condition for the existence of laws.

■ QUESTION

If the courts do not apply sanctions for failure to observe a convention, why are conventions observed?

D: The nature of conventions

The nature of conventions received considerable attention in a Canadian case *Reference Re Amendment of the Constitution of Canada* (1982) 125 DLR (3d) 1. This case arose because of a special procedure in Canada whereby an issue may be referred to court for an advisory opinion; there is no such procedure in the United Kingdom.

The Dominion of Canada was created by the British North America Act 1867 which divided legislative and executive powers between the federal and provincial legislatures. As the 1867 Act was a Westminster statute, further amendment of it could only be carried out through legislation passed at Westminster. The British North America (No. 2) Act 1949 transferred powers of amendment of the constitution to the Canadian Federal Parliament, with the exception of amendments affecting the distribution of powers between the provincial and federal governments. Conventions developed in relation to the procedure for amendment. These were stated as four principles in a White Paper issued by the Canadian Government in 1965, entitled 'The Amendment of the Constitution of Canada'. The four principles were agreed by all the Provinces before the White Paper was published.

The Amendment of the Constitution of Canada

(1965), p. 15

The first general principle that emerges in the foregoing resumé is that although an enactment by the United Kingdom is necessary to amend the British North America Act, such action is taken only upon formal request from Canada. No Act of the United Kingdom Parliament affecting Canada is therefore passed unless it is requested and consented to by Canada. Conversely, every amendment requested by Canada in the past has been enacted.

The second general principle is that the sanction of Parliament is required for a request to the British Parliament for an amendment to the British North America Act. This principle was established early in the history of Canada's constitutional amendments, and has not been violated since 1895. The procedure invariably is to seek amendments by a joint Address of the Canadian House of Commons and Senate to the Crown.

The third general principle is that no amendment to Canada's Constitution will be made by the British Parliament merely upon the request of a Canadian province. A number of attempts to secure such amendments have been made, but none has been successful. The first such attempt was made as early as 1868, by a province which was at that time dissatisfied with the terms of Confederation. This was followed by other attempts in 1869, 1874 and 1887. The British Government refused in all cases to act on provincial government representations on the grounds that it should not intervene in the affairs of Canada except at the request of the federal government representing all of Canada.

The fourth general principle is that the Canadian Parliament will not request an amendment directly affecting federal-provincial relationships without prior consultation and agreement with the provinces. This principle did not emerge as early as others but since 1907, and particularly since 1930, has gained increasing recognition and acceptance. The nature and the degree of provincial participation in the amending process, however, have not lent themselves to easy definition.

In 1980, after numerous attempts by the Federal Government to reach agreement with the provinces on constitutional reform, the federal government decided to press ahead with a scheme which would patriate the Canadian Constitution by ending the link with Westminster and establish a new procedure for constitutional amendment, and create a new Charter of Rights which would be binding on both federal and provincial legislatures. Eight of the ten provinces opposed the scheme. The question arose whether the federal authorities were entitled to request Westminster to enact the proposed scheme in the absence of unanimous approval from the provinces. The issue ended up in the Canadian Supreme Court when Manitoba, Newfoundland, and Quebec (three of the dissenting provinces) instituted proceedings to obtain a ruling on the constitutionality of the action being taken by the Federal Government. Several important questions arose for determination. Was there a convention that the Federal Parliament would not request an amendment to the constitution affecting federal–provincial relationships without prior consultation and agreement with the provinces? Could the Federal Government *legally* request such amendment despite the absence of such agreement (in other words, could the convention, if it existed, be enforced by the courts)? Another question related to whether a convention could crystallize into law. The case is important because of the examination of the nature of conventions and how they may be recognized.

Reference Re Amendment of the Constitution of Canada

(1982) 125 DLR (3d) 1, Supreme Court of Canada

The essential questions for determination, and the answers of the majority, were as follows:

ON THE APPEAL FROM THE MANITOBA AND NEWFOUNDLAND COURTS OF APPEAL

1. If the amendments to the Constitution of Canada sought in the 'Proposed Resolution for a Joint Address to Her Majesty the Queen respecting the Constitution of Canada', or any of them, were enacted, would federal-provincial relationships or the powers, rights or privileges granted or secured by the Constitution of Canada to the provinces, their legislatures or governments be affected and if so, in what respect or respects?
Answer by all members of the Court: Yes.

2. Is it a constitutional convention that the House of Commons and Senate of Canada will not request Her Majesty the Queen to lay before the Parliament of the United Kingdom ... a measure to amend the Constitution of Canada affecting federal-provincial relationships or the powers, rights or privileges granted or secured by the Constitution of Canada to the provinces, their legislatures or governments without first obtaining the agreement of the provinces?
Answer by the majority: Yes.

3. Is the agreement of the provinces of Canada constitutionally required for amendment to the Constitution of Canada where such amendment affects federal-provincial relationships or alters the powers, rights or privileges granted or secured by the Constitution of Canada to the provinces, their legislatures or governments?
Answer by the majority: No.

ON THE APPEAL FROM THE QUEBEC COURT OF APPEAL

A. If the Canada Act and the Constitution Act 1981 should come into force and if they should be valid in all respects in Canada would they affect:

(i) the legislative competence of the provincial legislatures in virtue of the Canadian Constitution?
(ii) the status or role of the provincial legislatures or governments within the Canadian Federation?

Answer by all members of the Court: Yes.

B. Does the Canadian Constitution empower, whether by statute, convention or otherwise, the Senate and the House of Commons of Canada to cause the Canadian Constitution to be amended without the consent of the provinces and in spite of the objection of several of them, in such a manner as to affect:

(i) the legislative competence of the provincial legislatures in virtue of the Canadian Constitution?
(ii) the status or role of the provincial legislatures or governments within the Canadian Federation?

Answer by the majority: As a matter of law, Yes. As a matter of convention, No.

THE MAJORITY—The Law: ... The proposition was advanced on behalf of the Attorney-General of Manitoba that a convention may crystallize into law and that the requirement of provincial consent to the kind of Resolution that we have here, although in origin political, has become a rule of law....

In our view, this is not so. No instance of an explicit recognition of a convention as having matured into a rule of law was produced. The very nature of a convention, as political in inception and as depending on a consistent course of political recognition by those for whose benefit and to whose detriment (if any) the convention developed over a considerable period of time is inconsistent with its legal enforcement.

The attempted assimilation of the growth of a convention to the growth of the common law is misconceived. The latter is the product of judicial effort, based on justiciable issues which have attained legal formulation and are subject to modification and even reversal by the Courts which gave them birth when acting within their role in the State in obedience to statutes or constitutional directives. No such parental role is played by the Courts with respect to conventions.

It was urged before us that a host of cases have given legal force to conventions. This is an overdrawn proposition. One case in which direct recognition and enforcement of a convention was sought is *Madzimbamuto* v *Lardner-Burke et al.*, [1969] 1 AC 645. There the Privy Council rejected the assertion that a convention formally recognized by the United Kingdom as established, namely, that it would not legislate for Southern Rhodesia on matters within the competence of the latter's Legislature without its Government's consent, could not be overridden by British legislation made applicable to Southern Rhodesia after the unilateral declaration of independence by the latter's Government. Speaking for the Privy Council, Lord Reid pointed out that although the convention was a very important one, 'it had no legal effect in limiting the legal power of Parliament' (at p. 723). And, again (at the same page):

> It is often said that it would be unconstitutional for the United Kingdom Parliament to do certain things, meaning that the moral, political and other reasons against doing them are so strong that most people would regard it as highly improper if Parliament did these things. But that does not mean that it is beyond the power of Parliament to do such things. If Parliament chose to do any of them the courts could not hold the Act of Parliament invalid. It may be that it would be unconstitutional to disregard this convention. But it may also be that the unilateral Declaration of Independence released the United Kingdom from any obligation to observe the convention. Their Lordships in declaring the law are not concerned with these matters. They are only concerned with the legal powers of Parliament.

Counsel for Manitoba sought to distinguish this case on the ground that the *Statute of Westminster, 1931* did not embrace Southern Rhodesia, a point to which the Privy Council adverted. The *Statute of Westminster*... if it had been in force in Southern Rhodesia it would be only under its terms and not through any conventional rule *per se* that the Parliament of the United Kingdom would have desisted from legislating for Southern Rhodesia.

Having examined various Canadian, United Kingdom and Commonwealth cases without finding any support for the crystallization argument, the Majority continued:

We were invited to consider academic writings on the matter under discussion. There is no consensus among the author-scholars, but the better and prevailing view is that expressed in an article by Munro, 'Laws and Conventions Distinguished', 91 Law Q Rev 218 (1975), where he says (at p. 228):

> The validity of conventions cannot be the subject of proceedings in a court of law. Reparation for breach of such rules will not be effected by any legal sanction. There are no cases which contradict these propositions. In fact, the idea of a court enforcing a mere convention is so strange that the question hardly arises.

Another passage from this article deserves mention, as follows (at p. 224):

> If in fact laws and conventions are different in kind, as is my argument, then an accurate and meaningful picture of the constitution may only be obtained if this distinction is made. If the distinction is blurred, analysis of the constitution is less complete; this is not only dangerous for the lawyer, but less than helpful to the political scientist.

There is no difference in approach whether the issue arises in a unitary State or in a federal State: see Hogg, *Constitutional Law of Canada* (1977), at pp. 7–11.

A contrary view relied on by the provincial appellants is that expressed by Professor W. R. Lederman in two published articles, one entitled 'Process of Constitutional Amendment in Canada', 12 McGill LJ 371 (1967), and the second entitled 'Constitutional Amendment and Canadian Unity', Law Soc UC Lectures 17 (1978). As a respected scholar, Professor Lederman's views deserve more than cursory consideration. He himself recognizes that there are contrary views, including those of an equally distinguished scholar, Professor F. R. Scott: see Scott, *Essays on the Constitution* (1977), pp. 144, 169, 204–5, 245, 370–1, 402. There is also the contrary view of Professor Hogg, already cited.

Professor Lederman relies in part on a line of cases that has already been considered, especially the reasons of Sir Lyman P. Duff in the *Labour Conventions* case. The leap from convention to law is explained almost as if there was a common law of constitutional law, but originating in political practice. That is simply not so. What is desirable as a political limitation does not translate into a legal limitation, without expression in imperative constitutional text or statute. The position advocated is all the more unacceptable when substantial provincial compliance or consent is by him said to be sufficient. Although Professor Lederman would not give a veto to Prince Edward Island, he would to Ontario or Quebec or British Columbia or Alberta. This is an impossible position for a Court to manage.

Turning now to the authority or power of the two federal Houses to proceed by Resolution to forward the address and appended draft statutes to Her Majesty the Queen for enactment by the Parliament of the United Kingdom. There is no limit anywhere in law, either in Canada or in the United Kingdom... to the power of the Houses to pass resolutions. Under s. 18 of the *British North America Act, 1867*, the federal Parliament may by statute define those privileges, immunities and powers, so long as they do not exceed those held and enjoyed by the British House of Commons at the time of the passing of the federal statute....

It is said, however, that where the Resolution touches provincial powers, as the one in question here does, there is a limitation on federal authority to pass it on to Her Majesty the Queen unless there is provincial consent. If there is such a limitation, it arises not from any limitation on the power to adopt Resolutions but from an external limitation based on other considerations.... [I]t is relevant to point out that even in those cases where an amendment to the *British North America Act, 1867* was founded on a Resolution of the federal Houses after having received provincial consent, there is no instance, save in the *British North America Act, 1930* where such consent was recited in the Resolution. The matter remained, in short, a conventional one within Canada, without effect on the validity of the Resolution in respect of United Kingdom action....

This Court is being asked, in effect, to enshrine as a legal imperative a principle of unanimity for constitutional amendment to overcome the anomaly—more of an anomaly today than it was in 1867—that the *British North America Act, 1867* contained no provision for effecting amendments by Canadian action alone....

The stark legal question is whether this Court can enact by what would be judicial legislation a formula of unanimity to initiate the amending process which would be binding not only in Canada but also on the Parliament of the United Kingdom with which amending authority would still remain. It would be anomalous indeed, overshadowing the anomaly of a Constitution which contains no provision for its amendment, for this Court to say retroactively that in law we have had an amending formula all along, even if we have not hitherto known it; or, to say, that we have had in law one amending formula, say from 1867 to 1931, and a second amending formula that has emerged after 1931. No one can gainsay the desirability of federal-provincial accord of acceptable compromise. That does not, however, go to legality....

The provincial contentions asserted a legal incapacity in the federal Houses to proceed with the Resolution which is the subject of the References and of the appeals here. Joined to this assertion was a claim that the United Kingdom Parliament had, in effect, relinquished its legal power to act on a Resolution such as the one before this Court, and that it could only act in relation to Canada if a request was made by 'the proper authorities'. The federal Houses would be such authorities if provincial powers or interests would not be affected; if they would be, then the proper authorities would include the Provinces. It is not that the Provinces must be joined in the federal address to Her Majesty the Queen; that was not argued. Rather their consent (or, as in the Saskatchewan submission, substantial provincial compliance or approval) was required as a condition of the validity of the process by address and Resolution and, equally, as a condition of valid action thereon by the United Kingdom Parliament....

[T]he *Statute of Westminster, 1931* ... is put forward not only as signifying an equality of status as between the Dominion and the Provinces vis-à-vis the United Kingdom Parliament, but also as attenuating the theretofore untrammelled legislative authority of that Parliament in relation to Canada where provincial interests are involved.... What s. 7(1), reinforced by s. 7(3), appeared to do was to maintain the *status quo ante*; that is, to leave any changes in the *British North America Act, 1867* (that is, such changes which, under its terms, could not be carried out by legislation of the Provinces or of the Dominion) to the prevailing situation, namely, with the legislative authority of the United Kingdom Parliament being left untouched. As Sir William Jowitt put it ... 'the old machinery' remained in place as a result of the *Statute of Westminster, 1931*. No other conclusion is supportable on any fair reading of the terms of the *Statute of Westminster, 1931*....

It was argued that the 'request and consent' which must be declared in a British statute to make it applicable to Canada, is the request and consent of the Dominion and the Provinces if the statute is one affecting provincial interests or powers, for example, an amendment of the *British North America Act, 1867* as envisaged by the Resolution herein. The word 'Dominion' in s. 4, it is said, must be read in what may be called a conjoint or collective sense as including both the Dominion and the Provinces; otherwise, it is submitted, the purpose of the *Statute of Westminster, 1931* would be defeated....

Nothing in the language of the *Statute of Westminster, 1931* supports the provincial position yet it is on this interpretation that it is contended that the Parliament of the United Kingdom has relinquished or yielded its previous omnipotent legal authority in relation to the *British North America Act, 1867*, one of its own statutes. As an argument... it asserts a legal diminution of United Kingdom legislative supremacy. The short answer to this ramified submission is that it distorts both history and ordinary principles of statutory or constitutional interpretation. The plain fact is that s. 7(1) was enacted to obviate any inference of direct unilateral federal power to amend the *British North America Act, 1867*....

[T]he challenge to the competency in law of the federal Houses to seek enactment by the Parliament of the United Kingdom of the statutes embodied in the Resolution is based on the recognized supremacy of provincial Legislatures in relation to the powers conferred upon them under the *British North America Act, 1867*, a supremacy vis-à-vis the federal Parliament. Reinforcement, or perhaps the foundation of this supremacy is said to lie in the nature or character of Canadian federalism.

The supremacy position, taken alone, needs no further justification than that found in the respective formulations of the powers of Parliament and the provincial Legislatures in ss. 91 and 92 of the *British North America Act, 1867*. Federal paramountcy is, however, the general rule in the actual exercise of these powers. This notwithstanding, the exclusiveness of the provincial powers (another way of expressing supremacy and more consonant with the terms of the *British North America Act, 1867*) cannot be gainsaid....

What is put forward by the Provinces which oppose the forwarding of the address without provincial consent is that external relations with Great Britain in this respect must take account of the nature and character of Canadian federalism. It is contended that a legal underpinning of their position is to be found in the Canadian federal system as reflected in historical antecedents, in the pronouncements of leading political figures and in the preamble to the *British North America Act, 1867*.

The arguments from history do not lead to any consistent view or any single view of the nature of the *British North America Act, 1867*.... History cannot alter the fact that in law there is a British statute to construe and apply in relation to a matter, fundamental as it is, that is not provided for by the statute....

So too, with pronouncements by political figures or persons in other branches of public life. There is little profit in parading them.

Support for a legal requirement of provincial consent to the Resolution that is before this Court, consent which is also alleged to condition United Kingdom response to the Resolution, is, finally, asserted to lie in the preamble of the *British North America Act, 1867* itself, and in the reflection, in the substantive terms of the Act, of what are said to be fundamental presuppositions in the preamble as to the nature of Canadian federalism. The preamble recites (and the whole of it is reproduced) the following:

> Whereas the Provinces of Canada, Nova Scotia, and New Brunswick have expressed their Desire to be federally united into One Dominion under the Crown of the United Kingdom of Great Britain and Ireland, with a Constitution similar in Principle to that of the United Kingdom:
>
> And whereas such a Union would conduce to the Welfare of the Provinces and promote the Interests of the British Empire:
>
> And whereas on the Establishment of the Union by Authority of Parliament it is expedient, not only that the Constitution of the Legislative Authority in the Dominion be provided for, but also that the Nature of the Executive Government therein be declared:
>
> And whereas it is expedient that Provision be made for the eventual Admission into the Union of other Parts of the British North America:...

What is stressed is the desire of the named Provinces 'to be federally united ... with a Constitution similar in principle to that of the United Kingdom'. The preamble speaks also of union into 'one Dominion' and of the establishment of the Union 'by authority of Parliament', that is the United Kingdom Parliament. What, then, is to be drawn from the preamble as a matter of law? A preamble, needless to say, has no enacting force but, certainly, it can be called in aid to illuminate provisions of the statute in which it appears. Federal union 'with a constitution similar in principle to that of the United Kingdom' may well embrace responsible government and some common law aspects of the United Kingdom's unitary constitutionalism, such as the rule of law and Crown prerogatives and immunities.... There is also an internal contradiction in speaking of federalism in the light of the invariable principle of British parliamentary supremacy. Of course, the resolution of this contradiction lies in the scheme of distribution of legislative power, but this owes nothing to the preamble, resting rather on its own exposition in the substantive terms of the *British North America Act, 1867*....

...[I]t is the allocation of legislative power as between the central Parliament and the provincial Legislatures that the Provinces rely on as precluding unilateral federal action to seek amendments to the *British North America Act, 1867* that affect, whether by limitation or extension, provincial legislative authority. The Attorney-General of Canada was pushed to the extreme by being forced to answer affirmatively the theoretical question whether in law the federal Government could procure an amendment to the *British North America Act, 1867* that would turn Canada into a unitary State. That is not what the present Resolution envisages because the essential federal character of the country is preserved under the enactments proposed by the Resolution.

That, it is argued, is no reason for conceding unilateral federal authority to accomplish, through invocation of legislation by the United Kingdom Parliament, the purposes of the Resolution. There is here, however, an unprecedented situation in which the one constant since the enactment of the *British North America Act* in 1867 has been the legal authority of the United Kingdom Parliament to amend it. The law knows nothing of any requirement of provincial consent, either to a resolution of the federal Houses or as a condition of the exercise of United Kingdom legislative power.

THE MAJORITY—Convention:... [M]any Canadians would perhaps be surprised to learn that important parts of the Constitution of Canada, with which they are the most familiar because they are directly involved when they exercise their right to vote at federal and provincial elections, are nowhere to be found in the law of the Constitution. For instance it is a fundamental requirement of the Constitution that if the Opposition obtains the majority at the polls, the Government must tender its resignation forthwith. But fundamental as it is, this requirement of the Constitution does not form part of the law of the Constitution.

It is also a constitutional requirement that the person who is appointed Prime Minister or Premier by the Crown and who is the effective head of the Government should have the support of the elected branch of the Legislature; in practice this means in most cases the leader of the political party which has won a majority of seats at a general election. Other ministers are appointed by the Crown on the advice of the Prime Minister or Premier when he forms or reshuffles his cabinet. Ministers must continuously have the confidence of the elected branch of the Legislature, individually and collectively. Should they lose it, they must either resign or ask the Crown for a dissolution of the Legislature and the holding of a general election. Most of the powers of the Crown under the prerogative are exercised only upon the advice of the Prime Minister or the Cabinet which means that they are effectively exercised by the latter, together with the innumerable statutory powers delegated to the Crown in council.

Yet none of these essential rules of the Constitution can be said to be a law of the Constitution. It was apparently Dicey who, in the first edition of his *Law of the Constitution*, in 1885, called them 'the conventions of the constitution' (W. S. Holdsworth, 'The Conventions of the Eighteenth Century Constitution', 17 Iowa Law Rev 161 (1932)), an expression which quickly became current. What Dicey described under these terms are the principles and rules of responsible government, several of which are stated above and which regulate the relations between the Crown, the Prime Minister, the Cabinet and the two Houses of Parliament. These rules developed in Great Britain by way of custom and precedent during the nineteenth century and were exported to such British colonies as were granted self-government.

Dicey first gave the impression that constitutional conventions are a peculiarly British and modern phenomenon. But he recognized in later editions that different conventions are found in other constitutions. As Sir William Holdsworth wrote (W. S. Holdsworth, *op. cit.*, p. 162):

> In fact conventions must grow up at all times and in all places where the powers of government are vested in different persons or bodies—where in other words there is a mixed constitution. 'The constituent parts of a state,' said Burje, [French Revolution, 28] 'are we obliged to hold their public faith with each other, and with all those who derive any serious interest under their engagements, as much as the whole state is bound to keep its faith with separate communities.' Necessarily conventional rules spring up to regulate the working of the various parts of the constitution, their relations to one another, and to the subject.

Within the British Empire, powers of government were vested in different bodies which provided a fertile ground for the growth of new constitutional conventions unknown to Dicey whereby self-governing colonies acquired equal and independent status within the Commonwealth. Many of these culminated in the *Statute of Westminster*, 1931, 22 Geo. V, c. 4 (U.K.)....

The main purpose of constitutional conventions is to ensure that the legal framework of the Constitution will be operated in accordance with the prevailing constitutional values or principles of the period. For example, the constitutional value which is the pivot of the conventions stated above and relating to responsible government is the democratic principle: the powers of the State must be exercised in accordance with the wishes of the electorate; and the constitutional value or principle which anchors the conventions regulating the relationship between the members of the Commonwealth is the independence of the former British colonies.

Being based on custom and precedent, constitutional conventions are usually unwritten rules. Some of them, however, may be reduced to writing and expressed in the proceedings and documents of Imperial conferences, or in the preamble of statutes such as the *Statute of Westminster, 1931*, or in the proceedings and documents of federal-provincial conferences. They are often referred to and recognized in statements made by members of governments.

The conventional rules of the Constitution present one striking peculiarity. In contradistinction to the laws of the Constitution, they are not enforced by the Courts. One reason for this situation is that, unlike common law rules, conventions are not judge-made rules. They are not based on judicial precedents but on precedents established by the institutions of government themselves. Nor are they in the nature of statutory commands which it is the function and duty of the Courts to obey and enforce. Furthermore, to enforce them would mean to administer some formal sanction when they are breached. But the legal system from which they are distinct does not contemplate formal sanctions for their breach.

Perhaps the main reason why conventional rules cannot be enforced by the Courts is that they are generally in conflict with the legal rules which they postulate and the Courts are bound to enforce the legal rules. The conflict is not of a type which would entail the commission of any illegality. It results from the fact that legal rules create wide powers, discretions and rights which conventions prescribe should be exercised only in a certain limited manner, if at all.

[An] example will illustrate this point.

As a matter of law, the Queen, or the Governor General or the Lieutenant Governor could refuse assent to every bill passed by both Houses of Parliament or by a Legislative Assembly as the case may be. But by convention they cannot of their own motion refuse to assent to any such bill on any ground, for instance because they disapprove of the policy of the bill. We have here a conflict between a legal rule which creates a complete discretion and a conventional rule which completely neutralizes it. But conventions, like laws, are sometimes violated. And if this particular convention were violated and assent were improperly withheld, the Courts would be bound to enforce the law, not the convention. They would refuse to recognize the validity of a vetoed bill. This is what happened in *Gallant* v *The King*, [1949] 2 DLR 425 ... a case in keeping with the classic case of *Stockdale* v *Hansard* (1839), 9 Ad & E 1, 112 ER 1112, where the English Court of Queen's Bench held that only the Queen and both Houses of Parliament could make or unmake laws. The Lieutenant-Governor who had withheld assent in *Gallant* apparently did so towards the end of his term of office. Had it been otherwise, it is not inconceivable that his withholding of assent might have produced a political crisis leading to his removal from office which shows that if the remedy for a breach of a convention does not lie with the Courts, still the breach is not necessarily without a remedy. The remedy lies with some other institutions of Government; furthermore, it is not a formal remedy and it may be administered with less certainty or regularity than it would be by a Court.

This conflict between convention and law which prevents the Courts from enforcing conventions also prevents conventions from crystallizing into laws, unless it be by statutory adoption.

It is because the sanctions of convention rest with institutions of government other than Courts, such as the Governor General or the Lieutenant-Governor, or the Houses of Parliament, or with public opinion and ultimately, with the electorate that it is generally said that they are political. . . .

It should be borne in mind, however, that, while they are not laws, some conventions may be more important than some laws. Their importance depends on that of the value or principle which they are meant to safeguard. Also they form an integral part of the Constitution and of the constitutional system. . . .

That is why it is perfectly appropriate to say that to violate a convention is to do something which is unconstitutional although it entails no direct legal consequence. But the words 'constitutional' and 'unconstitutional' may also be used in a strict legal sense, for instance with respect to a statute which is found *ultra vires* or unconstitutional. The foregoing may perhaps be summarized in an equation: constitutional conventions plus constitutional law equal the total Constitution of the country.

The Majority next addressed the issue whether a particular convention exists or not is purely a political question or one upon which a court may adjudicate. They concluded that this was a constitutional question which it is proper for a court to decide and they cited various cases in which courts had recognised the existence of conventions.

In so recognizing conventional rules, the Courts have described them, sometimes commented upon them and given them such precision as is derived from the written form of a judgment. They did not shrink from doing so on account of the political aspects of conventions, nor because of their supposed vagueness, uncertainty or flexibility.

In our view, we should not, in a constitutional reference, decline to accomplish a type of exercise that Courts have been doing of their own motion for years....

The requirements for establishing a convention bear some resemblance with those which apply to customary law. Precedents and usage are necessary but do not suffice. They must be normative. We adopt the following passage of Sir W. Ivor Jennings in *The Law and the Constitution*, 5th edn. (1959), p. 136:

> We have to ask ourselves three questions: first, what are the precedents; secondly, did the actors in the precedents believe that they were bound by a rule; and thirdly, is there a reason for the rule? A single precedent with a good reason may be enough to establish the rule. A whole string of precedents without such a reason will be of no avail, unless it is perfectly certain that the persons concerned regarded them as bound by it.

(i) The precedents

An account of the statutes enacted by the Parliament of Westminster to modify the Constitution of Canada is found in a White Paper published in 1965 under the authority of the Honourable Guy Favreau, then Minister of Justice for Canada, under the title of 'The Amendment of the Constitution of Canada' (the White Paper)....

The Majority listed the 22 amendments noting that five of these directly affected federal-provincial relationships in the sense of changing provincial legislative powers.

Every one of these five amendments was agreed upon by each Province whose legislative authority was affected.

In negative terms, no amendment changing provincial legislative powers has been made since Confederation when agreement of a Province whose legislative powers would have been changed was withheld.

There are no exceptions.

Furthermore, in even more telling negative terms, in 1951, an amendment was proposed to give the Provinces a limited power of indirect taxation. Ontario and Quebec did not agree and the amendment was not proceeded with....

The accumulation of these precedents, positive and negative, concurrent and without exception, does not of itself suffice in establishing the existence of the convention; but it unmistakedly points in its direction. Indeed, if the precedents stood alone, it might be argued that unanimity is required....

Finally, it was noted in the course of argument that in the case of four of the five amendments mentioned above where provincial consent effectively had been obtained, the statutes enacted by the Parliament of Westminster did not refer to this consent. This does not alter the fact that consent was obtained.

(ii) The actors treating the rule as binding

The Majority referred next to the White Paper of 1965 and the four principles it stated (pp. 195–196, *ante*).

The text which precedes the four general principles makes it clear that it deals with conventions. It refers to the laws and conventions by which a country is governed and to constitutional rules which are not binding in any strict sense (that is in a legal sense) but which have come to be recognized and accepted in practice as part of the amendment process in Canada. The first three general principles are statements of well-known constitutional conventions governing the relationships between Canada and the United Kingdom with respect to constitutional amendments.

In our view, the fourth general principle equally and unmistakedly states and recognizes as a rule of the Canadian Constitution the convention referred to in the second question of the Manitoba and Newfoundland References as well as in Question B of the Quebec Reference, namely, that there is a requirement for provincial agreement to amendments which change provincial legislative powers....

It seems clear that while the precedents taken alone point at unanimity, the unanimity principle cannot be said to have been accepted by all the actors in the precedents....

The Majority quoted statements of former Prime Ministers in various Commons Debates.

In 1965, the White Paper had stated that: 'The nature and the degree of provincial participation in the amending process ... have not lent themselves to easy definition.'

Nothing has occurred since then which would permit us to conclude in a more precise manner.

Nor can it be said that this lack of precision is such as to prevent the principle from acquiring the constitutional *status* of a conventional rule. If a consensus had emerged on the measure of provincial agreement, an amending formula would quickly have been enacted and we would no longer be in the realm of conventions. To demand as much precision as if this were the case and as if the rule were a legal one is tantamount to denying that this area of the Canadian Constitution is capable of being governed by conventional rules.

Furthermore, the Government of Canada and the Governments of the Provinces have attempted to reach a consensus on a constitutional amending formula in the course of ten federal-provincial conferences held in 1927, 1931, 1935, 1950, 1960, 1964, 1971, 1978, 1979 and 1980. (Gérald A. Beaudoin, *op. cit.*, at p. 346.) A major issue at these conferences was the quantification of provincial consent. No consensus was reached on this issue. But the discussion of this very issue for more than fifty years postulates a clear recognition by all the Governments concerned of the principle that a substantial degree of provincial consent is required.

It would not be appropriate for the Court to devise in the abstract a specific formula which would indicate in positive terms what measure of provincial agreement is required for the convention to be complied with. Conventions by their nature develop in the political field and it will be for the political actors, not this Court, to determine the degree of provincial consent required.

It is sufficient for the Court to decide that at least a substantial measure of provincial consent is required and to decide further whether the situation before the Court meets with this requirement. The situation is one where Ontario and New Brunswick agree with the proposed amendments whereas the eight other Provinces oppose it. By no conceivable standard could this situation be thought to pass muster. It clearly does not disclose a sufficient measure of provincial agreement. Nothing more should be said about this.

(iii) A reason for the rule

The reason for the rule is the federal principle. Canada is a federal union. The preamble of the *BNA Act* states that 'the Provinces of Canada, Nova Scotia, and New Brunswick have expressed their Desire to be federally united ...'.

The federal character of the Canadian Constitution was recognized in innumerable judicial pronouncements. We will quote only one, that of Lord Watson in *Liquidators of Maritime Bank* v *Receiver-General of New Brunswick* [1982] AC 437 at pp. 441–2:

> The object of the Act was neither to weld the provinces into one, nor to subordinate provincial governments to a central authority, but to create a federal government in which they should all be represented, entrusted with the exclusive administration of affairs in which they had a common interest, each province retaining its independence and autonomy.

The federal principle cannot be reconciled with a state of affairs where the modification of provincial legislative powers could be obtained by the unilateral action of the federal authorities. It would indeed offend the federal principle that 'a radical change to [the] constitution [be] taken at the request of a bare majority of the members of the Canadian House of Commons and Senate'. (Report of Dominion-Provincial Conference, 1931, p. 3.) ...

Furthermore, as was stated in the fourth general principle of the White Paper, the requirement of provincial consent did not emerge as easily as other principles, but it has gained increasing recognition and acceptance since 1907 and particularly since 1930. This is clearly demonstrated by the proceedings of the Dominion-Provincial Conference of 1931.

Then followed the positive precedents of 1940, 1951 and 1964 as well as the abortive ones of 1951, 1960 and 1964, all discussed above. By 1965, the rule had become recognized as a binding constitutional one formulated in the fourth general principle of the White Paper already quoted reading in part as follows:

> *The fourth general principle* is that the Canadian Parliament will not request an amendment directly affecting federal-provincial relationships without prior consultation and agreement with the provinces.

The purpose of this conventional rule is to protect the federal character of the Canadian Constitution and prevent the anomaly that the House of Commons and Senate could obtain by simple resolutions what they could not validly accomplish by statute....

We have reached the conclusion that the agreement of the Provinces of Canada, no views being expressed as to its quantification, is constitutionally required for the passing of the 'Proposed Resolution for a joint Address to Her Majesty respecting the Constitution of Canada' and that the passing of this Resolution without such agreement would be unconstitutional in the conventional sense.

■ QUESTIONS

1. If conventions will not be enforced by the courts, what is the sanction for failure to observe a convention?
2. Is it possible to state and define conventions with precision?
3. Is Jenning's test for recognizing conventions, approved by the Supreme Court, a satisfactory and precise test?
4. Should the courts in the United Kingdom be asked to give advisory opinions on the constitution?

NOTE: What would have happened if the Federal Government had pressed ahead with the request in the absence of a 'substantial degree of provincial consent'? Would Westminster have passed the necessary legislation? Was it a convention that any amendment requested by Canada be automatically enacted by Westminster, regardless of the degree of support in Canada for the requested amendment? Certainly there was no example of such a request being refused in the past; but was this sufficient to establish a convention? This matter was examined by the House of Commons Select Committee on Foreign Affairs which reported before the Supreme Court's decision.

First Report from the Foreign Affairs Committee (Kershaw Report)

HC 42 of 1980–81

The purpose of our inquiry

4. The Canadian Government have been vigorously arguing, since the beginning of October 1980, that

> the British Parliament or government *may not look behind any federal request* for amendment, including a request for patriation of the Canadian constitution. Whatever role the Canadian provinces might play in constitutional amendments is a matter of *no consequence as far as the UK Government and Parliament are concerned.*

But the same Canadian Government document, in the preceding sentence, also said: 'The British Parliament is bound to act in accordance with a *proper* request from the federal government...'. So our first question was, and remains: Under what conditions is a request from the Canadian Government a proper request?

5. At the same time, our attention was directed by the FCO to a series of Ministerial statements in the UK Parliament. These have, as their common thread, the formula:

> If a request to effect such a change were to be received from the Parliament of Canada it would be *in accordance with precedent* for the United Kingdom Government to introduce in Parliament, and for Parliament to enact, appropriate legislation in compliance with the request.

So we were led to ask: What are the precedents, in relation to requests from Canada? Is there a significant difference between the UK Ministers' references to requests from the Canadian *Parliament* and the Canadian Government's references to requests from the Canadian *Government*? If there is a significant difference, does it reflect a convention, requiring that requests, to be 'proper', must have the support of the Parliament (Senate as well as House of Commons) of Canada? If that is a convention recognised by the UK Government, are there other conventions defining what counts as a proper request from Canada? How and when did such conventions arise? If a convention or principle is created, or becomes recognised, by action and opinion in Canada, is it to be taken into account by the UK Government and Parliament? And, even if it is to be taken into account in the UK, does such a principle of the Canadian constitution *determine* the responsibilities of (or 'bind') the UK Parliament?

6. The fundamental question we had to consider is the subject of Chapter VI of this Report: Is the UK Parliament bound, by convention or principle, to act automatically on any request from the Canadian Parliament for amendment or patriation of the BNA Acts? In view of the weight of evidence against an affirmative answer to that question, it became necessary to consider the further question, discussed in Chapter VII: Is it correct to say that the UK Parliament, when requested to enact constitutional changes which would directly affect Canadian Federal—Provincial relations, should not accede to the request unless it is concurred in by all the Provinces directly affected?...

A requirement of automatic action?

56. In this Chapter, we consider the question whether there is a rule, principle or convention that the UK Parliament, when requested by the Canadian Government and Parliament to amend (or patriate) the BNA Acts, should accede to the request 'automatically', ie regardless of the way that amendment would affect Federal-Provincial relations and of the concurrence or lack of concurrence of the Provinces in an amendment directly affecting the powers or rights of the Provincial legislatures or governments.

Proper requests should be enacted without delay

57. There can be no doubt that if a request by the Canadian Government and Parliament is a proper request, it is the responsibility of the UK Government and Parliament to secure the enactment of the request with all the urgency or priority which the Canadian Government may reasonably desire. That, indeed, is the practice of the UK Parliament, and it should be adhered to. But it is one thing to treat all proper requests as matters of priority, and quite another to consider oneself bound to regard all requests as proper requests....

UK practice since 1931

68. There is nothing in UK *practice* (as distinct from Ministerial statements ...) that should be regarded as creating a convention of automatic action in the sense specified in para. 56 above. For the Canadian Government and Parliament, from 1931 to this day, have been careful not to make any request for UK action, in any matter clearly and 'directly affecting federal-provincial relations' in the sense of the 'fourth general principle' set out and explained by the 1965 White Paper ... except with the concurrence of all the Provinces. The amendments of 1940, 1951, 1960 and 1964 directly affected the powers or rights of Provincial authorities as such. All these were requested only with the agreement of all Provinces. The amendments of 1943, 1946 and 1949 (twice), which were requested without Provincial concurrence, did not affect the powers or rights of Provincial authorities as such....

The central issue of principle: Canada's federal character

82. Canada's constitutional system is federal. This federal character is stressed again and again in the authoritative Canadian judicial and political pronouncements which we analysed in paras 32–37 and 47–55 above. Those pronouncements have all underlined the way in which the federal nature of Canada's constitutional system affects the law, convention and practice relating to amendment of that system.

83. All the evidence and advice which we received from UK constitutional lawyers and UK academic authorities learned in Commonwealth constitutions was to the same effect: *it would be in accord with the established constitutional position for the UK Government and Parliament*—particularly Parliament—*to take account of the federal nature of Canada's constitutional system*, when considering how to respond to a request by the Canadian Government and Parliament for amendment and/or patriation of the BNA Acts. For when it acts or declines to act, on such a request, the UK Parliament is exercising its powers and responsibilities as ... 'part of the process of Canadian constitutional amendment'. It would *not* be in accord with the established constitutional position for the UK Parliament to regard itself as in any way the subject of a rule, principle or convention that it should accede to such requests automatically, ie regardless of whether the request was made in a manner contrary to the principles of Canada's federal system and/or to the conventions regulating the making of such requests. If the UK Parliament were to proceed

on the basis that it ought to accede to such requests automatically (subject only to the requirements of correct legislative form), it would be treating itself as for all relevant purposes the agent of the Canadian Government and Parliament. It would thus be treating the Canadian Government and Parliament as having, in constitutional reality, a substantially unilateral power of amending or abolishing Canada's federal system. For any one Government and Parliament to have such a unilateral power is inconsistent with the federal character of that system; nor is it in accord with the 'rules and principles relating to amendment procedures' which have 'emerged from the practices and procedures employed in securing various amendments to the British North American Act since 1867'.

84. Such is the gist of all the evidence and advice from UK experts.... We accept it as an accurate delineation of the role and responsibility of the UK Parliament in relation to the amendment and/or patriation of the BNA Acts. The precedents, consisting of actions by the UK Government and Parliament and statements in Parliament by UK Ministers, seem to us not to involve any acknowledgement of a requirement of automatic action. Those precedents all relate to requests made by the Canadian Government and Parliament in apparent conformity with the established Canadian constitutional position regarding the making of requests. They leave the UK Government and Parliament *constitutionally (not merely legally or technically) free to decide that the making of a request is so out of line with the established constitutional position that the UK Government can rightly decline to act on that request*. There is *no precedent* for the UK Government and Parliament receiving and acting upon a request, the making of which was clearly and substantially not in accord with the established Canadian constitutional position....

Conclusions

111. The considerations set out in this Chapter, taken with the preceding Chapter, lead us to the conclusion that the UK Parliament is not bound, even conventionally, either by the supposed requirement of automatic action on Federal requests, or by the supposed requirement of unanimous Provincial consent to amendments altering Provincial powers. Instead the UK Parliament retains the role of deciding whether or not a request for amendment or patriation of the BNA Acts conveys the clearly expressed wish of Canada as a whole, bearing in mind the federal nature of that community's constitutional system. In all ordinary circumstances, the request of the Canadian Government and Parliament will suffice to convey that wish. But where the requested amendment or patriation directly affects the *federal* structure of Canada, and the opposition of Provincial governments and legislatures is officially represented to the UK authorities, something more is required.

112. We recognise that that conclusion involves an unpalatable and thankless role for the UK Government and Parliament....

113. The role involves a responsibility in relation to Canada as a federally structured whole. It is not a *general* responsibility for the welfare of Canada or of its Provinces and peoples. It is simply the responsibility of exercising the UK Parliament's residual powers in a manner consistent with the federal character of Canada's constitutional system, *inasmuch as that federal character affects the way in which the wishes of Canada, on the subject of constitutional change, are to be expressed. It would be quite improper for the UK Parliament to deliberate about the suitability of requested amendments or methods of patriation*, or about the effects of those amendments on the welfare of Canada or any of its communities or peoples.

114. Is there any available criterion for measuring whether a request accords with the wishes of the Canadian people as a federally structured community? We do not think the UK Parliament should invent a criterion of its own; what is needed is a criterion with a basis in the constitutional history and politics of Canada. Such a criterion seems to us to be available. We think that it would not be inappropriate for the UK Parliament to expect that a request for patriation by an enactment significantly affecting the federal structure of Canada should be conveyed to it with *at least that degree of Provincial concurrence* (expressed by governments, legislatures or referendum majorities) *which would be required for a post-patriation amendment* affecting the federal structure in a similar way. For example a federal request that had the support of the two largest Provinces and of Provinces containing 50 per cent of the Western and 50 per cent of the Atlantic populations would be one that could be said to correspond to the wishes of the Canadian peoples on a whole. This criterion has roots in the historic structure of Canadian federalism as reflected in the Divisions of Canada for the purposes of the Provincial representation in the Senate of Canada; and it broadly accords both with the last (if not the only) clear consensus of Canadian

Federal and Provincial governments (at Victoria in 1971) and with the present proposals... of the Canadian Government in relation to post-patriation amendment.

115. Some forms or modes of patriation would affect the federal structure of Canada less than would some amendments of the BNA Acts. So one further possibility arises for consideration. The UK Government and Parliament might receive from the Canadian Government and Parliament, without the concurrence of the Provinces, a request for patriation/amendment involving *only* (i) termination of the UK's legislative powers and (ii) a post-patriation amendment formula providing for amendment only with at least such a degree of provincial support as is required to initiate an amendment procedure in Part IV of the proposed 'Canada Constitution Act, 1980'. It might well be proper for the UK Parliament to accede to such a request. For such action by the UK Parliament, while arguably not strictly pursuant to the clearly expressed wishes of Canada as a federally structured whole, would give effect, for the future, to those constitutional changes, and only those changes, which corresponded with such wishes. Since the UK Parliament's action would involve no other substantial constitutional change, it would not substantially affect the federal character of Canada's constitutional system and would not be out of accord with the UK's role in the established constitutional position as we have tried to explain it.

NOTE: The decision of the Supreme Court that the convention required a substantial degree of provincial consent was in line with the view expressed by the Kershaw Committee. The convention was designed to protect the federal character of the Canadian Constitution and prevent the Federal Parliament achieving by means of a resolution addressed to Westminster what it could not achieve domestically by means of legislation.

■ QUESTION

In a Memorandum to the Kershaw Committee, Professor H. W. R. Wade stated:

> Conventions are the rules of the game of politics, and it may be necessary to correct one infringement by another. If for example a British government were to refuse to resign after being defeated on a motion of no confidence, the Queen would be justified in dismissing the ministers against their will. The fact that the UK Parliament does not in practice look behind amendments requested by Canada is entirely dependent upon those requests being in conformity with Canadian conventions. If those conventions are infringed, the duty of the UK Parliament is to take corrective action.

Is it desirable that the sanction for breach of one convention is the breach of another—a principle of constitutional tit-for-tat?

NOTE: In response to the Supreme Court's decision the Federal Government decided not to press on with the request to Westminster to enact legislation. Further discussions were held with the provinces and concessions were offered. In response, nine provinces agreed to the revised proposals. A new request was made, and the Canada Act 1982 was duly enacted at Westminster following a recommendation from the Kershaw Committee that consent from nine out of ten provinces constituted a substantial measure of support for the proposals.

First Report from the Foreign Affairs Committee (Kershaw Report)

HC 128 of 1981–82

6. The criteria suggested in our First Report for assessing the appropriate level of Provincial support were put forward, not as minima required by any existing constitutional rule or convention, but rather as indications of what 'Parliament would be justified in regarding as sufficient' or of what 'it would not be inappropriate for the UK Parliament to expect'. Since then, the Supreme Court of Canada has determined that what is constitutionally required is 'at least a substantial measure of Provincial consent'. The Court decided that unanimity is not required, but did not define or quantify 'a substantial measure'. The Government of Quebec have, we understand, commenced litigation to establish whether their concurrence is constitutionally required. So it is important to observe that the Supreme Court has stated, 'It will be for the political actors, not this Court, to determine the degree of provincial consent required'. The Federal-Provincial Agreement of 5 November 1981, made in the wake of the Supreme Court's judgement

and accepted by nine of the ten Provinces, appears to us to amount to a determination by the political actors in Canada that the concurrence of nine Provinces is constitutionally sufficient, albeit the dissenting Province be Quebec.

7. In this situation, what we said in our First Report seems applicable: 'the UK Parliament is bound to exercise its best judgement in deciding whether the request, in all the circumstances, conveys the clearly expressed wishes of Canada as a federally structured whole'. In our view, the present request does this.

E: Devolution and the Sewel Convention

Under the arrangements for devolution to Scotland the Westminster Parliament retains the right to make laws for Scotland (Scotland Act 1998, s. 28(7)). (There is a similar provision in the Northern Ireland Act 1998 (s. 5(6)).) The power to legislate for Scotland could, if used too regularly, undermine the devolution process. When the Scotland Bill was being debated in the House of Lords, Lord Sewel announced on behalf of the Government (HL Debates, 21 July 1998, col. 791) that the Government:

would expect a convention to be established that Westminster would not normally legislate with regard to devolved matters in Scotland without the consent of the Scottish Parliament.

Such a convention governed legislation by Westminster for former dependent territories which had become independent members of the Commonwealth (see the preamble to and s. 4 of the Statute of Westminster 1931). In the *Memorandum of Understanding and Supplementary Agreements Between the United Kingdom Government Scottish Ministers the Cabinet of the National Assembly for Wales and the Northern Ireland Executive Committee* (2001), Cm 5240, the principle of not legislating for Scotland without its consent is reiterated. The *Memorandum of Understanding* provides as follows:

2. This memorandum is a statement of political intent, and should not be interpreted as a binding agreement. It does not create legal obligations between the parties. . . .

Parliamentary Business

13. The United Kingdom Parliament retains authority to legislate on any issue, whether devolved or not. It is ultimately for Parliament to decide what use to make of that power. However the UK Government will proceed in accordance with the convention that the UK Parliament would not normally legislate with regard to devolved matters except with the agreement of the devolved legislature. The devolved administrations will be responsible for seeking such agreement as may be required for this purpose on an approach from the UK Government.

14. The United Kingdom Parliament retains the absolute right to debate, enquire into or make representations about devolved matters. It is ultimately for Parliament to decide what use to make of that power, but the UK Government will encourage the UK Parliament to bear in mind the primary responsibility of devolved legislatures and administrations in these fields and to recognise that it is a consequence of Parliament's decision to devolve certain matters that Parliament itself will in future be more restricted in its field of operation.

The Office of the Deputy Prime Minister in Devolution Guidance No. 10, *Post Devolution Primary Legislation Affecting Scotland*, October 2002, states that the convention applies only where the Westminster Bill:

makes provision specifically for a devolved purpose.

The position in relation to legislative consent motions (called Sewel motions until 30 November 2005) is as follows:

Legislative Consent Memorandums and Motions

<http://www.scottish.parliament.uk/business/legConMem/LCM-Stats.htm>

Statistics by session				
	Legislative Consent Memorandums Lodged	**Supplementary Memorandums Published/Lodged**	**Legislative Consent Motions Lodged**	**Legislative Consent Motions Passed**
Session 3 9 May 2007 –	29	3	25	25
	Sewel Memorandums Published/ Legislative Consent Memorandums Lodged	**Supplementary Memorandums Published/Lodged**	**Legislative Consent/Sewel Motions Lodged**	**Legislative Consent/ Sewel Motions Passed**
Session 2 7 May 2003 – 2 April 2007	41	3	38	38
	Sewel Memorandums Published	**Supplementary Memorandums Published**	**Sewel Motions Lodged**	**Sewel Motions Passed**
Session 1 12 May 1999– 31 March 2003	38	1	39	39

See N. Burrows (2002) *Juridical Review* 213 and A. Page & A. Batey [2002] *Public Law* 501.

F: Can conventions crystallize into law?

This question was answered in the negative by the Supreme Court in *Reference Re Amendment of the Constitution of Canada* (p. 182, *ante*). It also arose before a United Kingdom court in *Manuel* v *Attorney-General* [1983] 1 Ch 77. The suggestion in this case was that the convention that Westminster would not enact legislation for a dominion except at its request and with its consent had crystallized into law so that actual consent had to be established. The action had been brought by Aboriginal chiefs seeking a declaration that the Canada Act 1982 was *ultra vires*, as the consent of the Aboriginal people did not exist. Section 4 of the Statute of Westminster 1931 provides:

> No Act of Parliament of the United Kingdom passed after the commencement of this Act shall extend, or be deemed to extend, to a Dominion as part of the law of that Dominion, unless it is expressly declared in that Act that that Dominion has requested, and consented to, the enactment thereof.

This section did not enact the convention but incorporated it in a modified form. The issues involved are clearly stated in the judgment of Slade LJ, pp. 79–81, *ante*.

G: Conventions in the courts

It is clear that courts will not enforce conventions by imposing sanctions for their breach. Recognition of the existence of a convention by a court, however, can be significant in the court's decision of the issues before it. Conventions may be used as an aid to statutory interpretation or to support judicial decisions not to review discretionary powers of the executive because of the Minister's accountability to Parliament (see *Liversidge* v *Anderson* [1942] AC 206). In *Carltona* v *Commissioners of Works* [1943] 2 All ER 560, Lord Greene MR placed considerable emphasis on the convention of ministerial responsibility in reaching his decision. He stated (at p. 563):

> In the administration of government in this country the functions which are given to ministers (and constitutionally properly given to ministers because they are constitutionally responsible) are functions so multifarious that no minister could ever personally attend to them. To take the example of the present case no doubt there have been thousands of requisitions in this country by individual ministries. It cannot be supposed that this regulation meant that, in each case, the minister in person should direct his mind to the matter. The duties imposed upon ministers and the powers given to ministers are normally exercised under the authority of the ministers by responsible officials of the department. Public business could not be carried on if that were not the case. Constitutionally, the decision of such an official is, of course, the decision of the minister. The minister is responsible. It is he who must answer before Parliament for anything that his officials have done under this authority, and, if for an important matter he selected an official of such junior standing that he could not be expected competently to perform the work, the minister would have to answer for that in Parliament. The whole system of departmental organisation and administration is based on the view that ministers, being responsible to Parliament, will see that important duties are committed to experienced officials. If they do not do that, Parliament is the place where complaint must be made against them.

One of the best examples of judicial consideration of conventions in a United Kingdom court is the case which follows.

Attorney-General v *Jonathan Cape Ltd*

[1976] QB 752, High Court

Between 1964 and 1970 Richard Crossman was a Cabinet Minister, and he kept a political diary. Following his death in 1974, his diary for 1964–66 was edited for publication. A copy was sent to the Secretary to the Cabinet for his approval but was rejected on the ground that publication was against the public interest, in that the doctrine of collective responsibility would be harmed by the disclosure of details of Cabinet decisions, the revelation of differences between members of the Cabinet, and the disclosure of advice given by, and discussions regarding the appointment of, civil servants. When Crossman's literary executors decided to publish extracts of the diary in the *Sunday Times*, the Attorney-General sought injunctions against the publishers, literary executors, and the *Sunday Times* to restrain publication of the book or extracts from it.

> LORD WIDGERY CJ: ... It has always been assumed by lawyers and, I suspect, by politicians, and the Civil Service, that Cabinet proceedings and Cabinet papers are secret, and cannot be publicly disclosed until they have passed into history. It is quite clear that no court will compel the production of Cabinet papers in the course of discovery in an action, and the Attorney-General contends that not only will the court refuse to compel the production of such matters, but it will go further and positively forbid the disclosure of such papers and proceedings if publication will be contrary to the public interest.
>
> The basis of this contention is the confidential character of these papers and proceedings, derived from the convention of joint Cabinet responsibility whereby any policy decision reached by the Cabinet has to be supported thereafter by all members of the Cabinet whether they approve of it or not, unless they feel compelled to resign. It is contended that Cabinet decisions and papers are confidential for a period to

the extent at least that they must not be referred to outside the Cabinet in such a way as to disclose the attitude of individual Ministers in the argument which preceded the decision....

There is no doubt that Mr Crossman's manuscripts contain frequent references to individual opinions of Cabinet Ministers.... There have, as far as I know, been no previous attempts in any court to define the extent to which Cabinet proceedings should be treated as secret or confidential, and it is not surprising that different views on this subject are contained in the evidence before me....

The Attorney-General contends that all Cabinet papers and discussions are prima facie confidential, and that the court should restrain any disclosure thereof if the public interest in concealment outweighs the public interest in a right to free publication. The Attorney-General further contends that, if it is shown that the public interest is involved, he has the right and duty to bring the matter before the court. In this contention he is well supported by Lord Salmon in *Reg v Lewes Justices, Ex parte Secretary of State for the Home Department* [1973] AC 388, 412, where Lord Salmon said:

> when it is in the public interest that confidentiality shall be safeguarded, then the party from whom the confidential document or the confidential information is being sought may lawfully refuse it. In such a case the Crown may also intervene to prevent production or disclosure of that which in the public interest ought to be protected.

I do not understand Lord Salmon to be saying, or the Attorney-General to be contending, that it is only necessary for him to evoke the public interest to obtain an order of the court. On the contrary, it must be for the court in every case to be satisfied that the public interest is involved, and that, after balancing all the factors which tell for or against publication, to decide whether suppression is necessary.

The defendants' main contention is that whatever the limits of the convention of joint Cabinet responsibility may be, there is no obligation enforceable at law to prevent the publication of Cabinet papers and proceedings, except in extreme cases where national security is involved. In other words, the defendants submit that the confidential character of Cabinet papers and discussions is based on a true convention as defined in the evidence of Professor Henry Wade, namely, an obligation founded in conscience only. Accordingly, the defendants contend that publication of these Diaries is not capable of control by any order of this court.

If the Attorney-General were restricted in his argument to the general proposition that Cabinet papers and discussion are all under the seal of secrecy at all times, he would be in difficulty. It is true that he has called evidence from eminent former holders of office to the effect that the public interest requires a continuing secrecy, and he cites a powerful passage from the late Viscount Hailsham to this effect. The extract comes from a copy of the Official Report (House of Lords) for December 21, 1932, in the course of a debate on Cabinet secrecy. Lord Hailsham said; col. 527:

> But, my Lords, I am very glad that the question has been raised because it has seemed to me that there is a tendency in some quarters at least to ignore or to forget the nature and extent of the obligations of secrecy and the limitations which rigidly hedge round the position of a Cabinet Minister. My noble friend has read to your Lordships what in fact I was proposing to read—that is, the oath which every Privy Councillor takes when he is sworn of His Majesty's Privy Council. Your Lordships will remember that one reason at least why a Cabinet Minister must of necessity be a member of the Privy Council is that it involves the taking of that oath. Having heard that oath read your Lordships will appreciate what a complete misconception it is to suppose, as some people seem inclined to suppose, that the only obligation that rests upon a Cabinet Minister is not to disclose what are described as the Cabinet's minutes. He is sworn to keep secret all matters committed and revealed unto him or that shall be treated secretly in Council.

Lord Hailsham then goes on to point out that there are three distinct classes to which the obligation of secrecy applies. He describes them as so-called Cabinet minutes; secondly, a series of documents, memoranda, telegrams and despatches and documents circulated from one Cabinet Minister to his colleagues to bring before them a particular problem and to discuss the arguments for and against a particular course of conduct; and, thirdly, apart from those two classes of documents, he says there is the recollection of the individual Minister of what happens in the Cabinet. Then the extract from Lord Hailsham's speech in the House of Lord's report continues in these words:

> I have stressed that because, as my noble and learned friend Lord Halsbury suggested and the noble Marquis, Lord Salisbury, confirmed, Cabinet conclusions did not exist until 16 years ago. The old practice is set out in a book which bears the name of the noble earl's father, Halsbury's Laws of England, with which I have had the honour to be associated in the present edition.

Then the last extract from Lord Hailsham's speech is found in col. 532, and is in these words:

> It is absolutely essential in the public interest that discussions which take place between Cabinet Ministers shall take place in the full certainty of all of them that they are speaking their minds with absolute freedom to colleagues on whom they can explicitly rely, upon matters on which it is their sworn duty to express their opinions with complete frankness and to give all information, without any haunting fear that what happens may hereafter by publication create difficulties for themselves or, what is far more grave, may create complications for the King and country that they are trying to serve. For those reasons I hope that the inflexible rule which has hitherto prevailed will be maintained in its integrity, and that if there has been any relaxation or misunderstanding, of which I say nothing, the debate in this House will have done something to clarify the position and restate the old rule in all its rigour and all its inflexibility.

The defendants, however, in the present action, have also called distinguished former Cabinet Ministers who do not support this view of Lord Hailsham, and it seems to me that the degree of protection afforded to Cabinet papers and discussion cannot be determined by a single rule of thumb. Some secrets require a high standard of protection for a short time. Others require protection until a new political generation has taken over. In the present action against the literary executors, the Attorney-General asks for a perpetual injunction to restrain further publication of the Diaries in whole or in part. I am far from convinced that he has made out a case that the public interest requires such a Draconian remedy when due regard is had to other public interests, such as the freedom of speech: see Lord Denning MR in *In re X (A Minor) (Wardship: Jurisdiction)* [1975] Fam 47. ... It seems to me ... that the Attorney-General must first show that whatever obligation of secrecy or discretion attaches to former Cabinet Ministers, that obligation is binding in law and not merely in morals.

I have read affidavits from a large number of leading politicians, and the facts, so far as relevant, appear to be these. In 1964, 1966 and 1969 the Prime Minister (who was in each case Mr Harold Wilson) issued a confidential document to Cabinet Ministers containing guidance on certain questions of procedure. Paragraph 72 of the 1969 edition provides:

> The principle of collective responsibility and the obligation not to disclose information acquired whilst holding Ministerial office apply to former Ministers who are contemplating the publication of material based upon their recollections of the conduct of Cabinet and Cabinet committee business in which they took part.

The general understanding of Ministers while in office was that information obtained from Cabinet sources was secret and not to be disclosed to outsiders.

There is not much evidence of the understanding of Ministers as to the protection of such information after the Minister retires. It seems probable to me that those not desirous of publishing memoirs assumed that the protection went on until the incident was 30 years old, whereas those interested in memoirs would discover on inquiry at the Cabinet Office that draft memoirs were normally submitted to the Secretary of the Cabinet for his advice on their contents before publication. Manuscripts were almost always submitted to the Secretary of the Cabinet in accordance with the last-mentioned procedure. Sir Winston Churchill submitted the whole of his manuscripts concerned with the war years, and accepted the advice given by the Secretary of the Cabinet as to publication....

The main framework of the defence is to be found in eight submissions from Mr Comyn. The first two have already been referred to, the allegation being that there is no power in law for the court to interfere with publication of these diaries or extracts, and that the Attorney-General's proper remedy lies in obtaining a change of the statute law.

I have already indicated some of the difficulties which face the Attorney-General when he relied simply on the public interest as a ground for his actions. That such ground is enough in extreme cases is shown by the universal agreement that publication affecting national security can be restrained in this way. It may be that in the short run (for example, over a period of weeks or months) the public interest is equally compelling to maintain joint Cabinet responsibility and the protection of advice given by civil servants, but I would not accept without close investigation that such matters must, as a matter of course, retain protection after a period of years.

However, the Attorney-General has a powerful reinforcement for his argument in the developing equitable doctrine that a man shall not profit from the wrongful publication of information received by him in confidence. This doctrine, said to have its origin in *Prince Albert* v *Strange* (1849) 1 H & T 1, has been frequently recognised as a ground for restraining the unfair use of commercial secrets transmitted in confidence. Sometimes in these cases there is a contract which may be said to have been breached by the breach of confidence, but it is clear that the doctrine applies independently of contract: see *Saltman Engineering Co. Ltd* v *Campbell Engineering Co. Ltd* (1948) 65 RPC 203. Again in *Coco* v *A. N. Clark (Engineers) Ltd* [1969] RPC 41 Megarry J, reviewing the authorities, set out the requirements necessary for an action based on breach of confidence to succeed. He said, at p. 47:

> In my judgment three elements are normally required if, apart from contract, a case of breach of confidence is to succeed. First, the information itself, in the words of Lord Greene MR ... must 'have the necessary quality of confidence about it.' Secondly, that information must have been imparted in circumstances importing an obligation of confidence. Thirdly, there must be an unauthorised use of that information to the detriment of the party communicating it.

It is not until the decision in *Duchess of Argyll* v *Duke of Argyll* [1967] Ch 302, that the same principle was applied to domestic secrets such as those passing between husband and wife during the marriage. It was there held by Ungoed-Thomas J that the plaintiff wife could obtain an order to restrain the defendant husband from communicating such secrets, and the principle is well expressed in the headnote in these terms, at p. 304:

> A contract or obligation of confidence need not be expressed but could be implied, and a breach of contract or trust or faith could arise independently of any right of property or contract ... and that the court, in the exercise of its equitable jurisdiction, would restrain a breach of confidence independently of any right at law.

This extension of the doctrine of confidence beyond commercial secrets has never been directly challenged, and was noted without criticism by Lord Denning MR in *Fraser* v *Evans* [1969] 1 QB 349, 361. I am sure that I ought to regard myself, sitting here, as bound by the decision of Ungoed-Thomas J.

Even so, these defendants argue that an extension of the principle of the *Argyll* case to the present dispute involves another large and unjustified leap forward, because in the present case the Attorney-General is seeking to apply the principle to public secrets made confidential in the interests of good government. I cannot see why the courts should be powerless to restrain the publication of public secrets, while enjoying the *Argyll* powers in regard to domestic secrets. Indeed, as already pointed out, the court must have power to deal with publication which threatens national security, and the difference between such a case and the present case is one of degree rather than kind. I conclude, therefore, that when a Cabinet Minister receives information in confidence the improper publication of such information can be restrained by the court, and his obligation is not merely to observe a gentleman's agreement to refrain from publication.

It is convenient next to deal with Mr Comyn's third submission, namely, that the evidence does not prove the existence of a convention as to collective responsibility, or adequately define a sphere of secrecy. I find overwhelming evidence that the doctrine of joint responsibility is generally understood and practised and equally strong evidence that it is on occasion ignored. The general effect of the evidence is that the doctrine is an established feature of the English form of government, and it follows that some matters leading up to a Cabinet decision may be regarded as confidential. Furthermore, I am persuaded that the nature of the confidence is that spoken for by the Attorney-General, namely, that since the confidence is imposed to enable the efficient conduct of the Queen's business, the confidence is owed to the Queen and cannot be released by the members of Cabinet themselves. I have been told that a resigning Minister who wishes to make a personal statement in the House, and to disclose matters which are confidential under the doctrine obtains the consent of the Queen for this purpose. Such consent is obtained through the Prime Minister. I have not been told what happened when the Cabinet disclosed divided opinions during the European Economic Community referendum. But even if there was here a breach of confidence (which I doubt) this is no ground for denying the existence of the general rule. I cannot accept the suggestion that a Minister owes no duty of confidence in respect of his own views expressed in Cabinet. It would only need one or two Ministers to describe their own views to enable experienced observers to identify the views of the others.

The other defence submissions are either variants of those dealt with, or submissions with regard to relief.

The Cabinet is at the very centre of national affairs, and must be in possession at all times of information which is secret or confidential. Secrets relating to national security may require to be preserved indefinitely. Secrets relating to new taxation proposals may be of the highest importance until Budget day, but public knowledge thereafter. To leak a Cabinet decision a day or so before it is officially announced is an accepted exercise in public relations, but to identify the Ministers who voted one way or another is objectionable because it undermines the doctrine of joint responsibility.

It is evident that there cannot be a single rule governing the publication of such a variety of matters. In these actions we are concerned with the publication of diaries at a time when 11 years have expired since the first recorded events. The Attorney-General must show (a) that such publication would be a breach of confidence; (b) that the public interest requires that the publication be restrained, and (c) that there are no other facts of the public interest contradictory of and more compelling than that relied upon. Moreover, the court, when asked to restrain such a publication, must closely examine the extent to which relief is necessary to ensure that restrictions are not imposed beyond the strict requirement of public need.

Applying those principles to the present case, what do we find? In my judgment, the Attorney-General has made out his claim that the expression of individual opinions by Cabinet Ministers in the course of Cabinet discussion are matters of confidence, the publication of which can be restrained by the court when this is clearly necessary in the public interest.

The maintenance of the doctrine of joint responsibility within the Cabinet is in the public interest, and the application of that doctrine might be prejudiced by premature disclosure of the views of individual Ministers.

There must, however, be a limit in time after which the confidential character of the information, and the duty of the court to restrain publication, will lapse. Since the conclusion of the hearing in this case I have had the opportunity to read the whole of volume one of the Diaries, and my considered view is that I cannot believe that the publication at this interval of anything in volume one would inhibit free discussion in the Cabinet of today, even though the individuals involved are the same, and the national problems have a distressing similarity with those of a decade ago. It is unnecessary to elaborate the evils which might flow if at the close of a Cabinet meeting a Minister proceeded to give the press an analysis of the voting, but we are dealing in this case with a disclosure of information nearly 10 years later.

It may, of course, be intensely difficult in a particular case, to say at what point the material loses its confidential character, on the ground that publication will no longer undermine the doctrine of joint Cabinet responsibility. It is this difficulty which prompts some to argue that Cabinet discussions should retain their confidential character for a longer and arbitrary period such as 30 years, or even for all time, but this seems to me to be excessively restrictive. The court should intervene only in the clearest of cases where the continuing confidentiality of the material can be demonstrated. In less clear cases—and this, in my view, is certainly one—reliance must be placed on the good sense and good taste of the Minister or ex-Minister concerned.

In the present case there is nothing in Mr Crossman's work to suggest that he did not support the doctrine of joint Cabinet responsibility. The question for the court is whether it is shown that publication now might damage the doctrine notwithstanding that much of the action is up to 10 years old and three general elections have been held meanwhile. So far as the Attorney-General relies in his argument on the disclosure of individual ministerial opinions, he has not satisfied me that publication would in any way inhibit free and open discussion in Cabinet hereafter.

It remains to deal with the Attorney-General's two further arguments, namely, (a) that the Diaries disclose advice given by senior civil servants who cannot be expected to advise frankly if their advice is not treated as confidential; (b) the Diaries disclose observations made by Ministers on the capacity of individual senior civil servants and their suitability for specific appointments. I can see no ground in law which entitles the court to restrain publication of these matters. A Minister is, no doubt, responsible for his department and accountable for its errors even though the individual fault is to be found in his subordinates. In these circumstances, to disclose the fault of the subordinate may amount to cowardice or bad taste, but I can find no ground for saying that either the Crown or the individual civil servant has an enforceable right to have the advice which he gives treated as confidential for all time.

For these reasons I do not think that the court should interfere with the publication of volume one of the Diaries, and I propose, therefore, to refuse the injunction sought but to grant liberty to apply in regard to material other than volume one if it is alleged that different considerations may there have to be applied.

Injunction refused.

NOTE: Following the decision in the case, a committee of privy councillors considered the problem of memoirs of former Cabinet Ministers (Cmnd 6386, 1976). The Committee drew a distinction between secret information relating to national security and international relations, and other confidential material about relationships between Ministers or between Ministers and civil servants. In the former case the Minister must accept the decision of the Cabinet Secretary, while in the latter case there should be no publication within 15 years except with approval of the Cabinet Secretary but, in the event of a dispute, the final decision would lie with the former Minister as to what to publish. The Committee did not consider that legislation would be appropriate.

■ QUESTIONS

1. What role did the convention of collective responsibility play in Lord Widgery CJ's decision? (See further on collective responsibility, pp. 207–209, *post*.)
2. Do conventions, to use Dicey's words, 'secure the ultimate supremacy of the electorate as the true political sovereign of the State'?

H: Codification of conventions

As part of the process of reform of the House of Lords a Joint Lords Commons select committee was created and asked to codify the conventions regulating the relations between the two Houses of Parliament.

Report of the Joint Committee on Conventions

HL 265/ HC1212 of 2005–06, paras. 253–256, 263–269, 272–279

253. "Codification" may be taken in at least two senses: (i) the broad sense of an authoritative statement, and (ii) the narrow sense of reduction to a literal code or system. In the context of Parliament, an authoritative statement could take any of the following forms:

a) a statement made anywhere, e.g. in a book
b) some form of concordat or memorandum of understanding
c) a statement made in Parliament, e.g. in Hansard or in evidence to a Committee
d) a Committee report
e) a report agreed to by one or both Houses of Parliament
f) a resolution of one or both Houses of Parliament
g) a literal Code, such as each House's Code of Conduct for Members
h) a statement in the House of Lords' *Companion to Standing Orders*
i) words in *Erskine May*
j) a Standing Order
k) an Act of Parliament

254. It might be felt that only the most formal of these–a Code, a Standing Order or an Act–would really constitute codification. But the Leader of the House of Commons appeared to have a broader definition in mind when he noted, in the Commons debate on setting up this Committee, that "[t]he manner in which the conventions could be codified ranges from a codification in the body of the Committee's report, to a code that has been negotiated by both Houses and which we endorse in resolutions, through to its inclusion in Standing Orders or its enshrinement in law. That is a subsequent matter". He later said that, in his opinion, "it would be a grave error to put any description of the convention[s] into legislation".

255. We are aware that our remit is to an extent self-fulfilling. The authoritative statements about conventions, by our witnesses and in this report, will be cited in future, even if the report leads to no further action.

256. As well as the end product of codification, there is the question of process. Some of the items in the above list have their own process (e.g. a resolution is preceded by debate), but additional steps are possible, e.g. a Speakers' Conference...

263. The Clerk of the Parliaments distinguishes conventions from rules. Conventions evolve; rules are fixed. Rules require enforcement and sanctions; conventions have no sanctions. Conventions may evolve

into fixed rules; those under consideration are "too new to have become fixed". If they were codified and fixed, they would cease to be conventions and become rules.

264. He gives examples of conventions described as such and set out in the *Companion*. One of them, the target rising time of 10pm, was substantially breached 53 times between its introduction in 2002 and the Whitsun recess 2006, showing that recording a convention in an agreed form may introduce clarity without ensuring observance.

265. The Clerk of the Parliaments draws attention to the question of who is bound by a convention and is in a position to deliver observance. For the Salisbury-Addison Convention, his answer is, the Leader of the Opposition. But for the reasonable time and delegated legislation conventions it is less clear, and in a self-regulating House any backbencher could provoke a breach.

266. If it were intended to embody a convention in a Standing Order or an Act, new clarity would be needed, e.g. in defining a manifesto Bill for the purposes of the Salisbury-Addison Convention. Formally defined powers might be used to the limit, rather than with restraint–though, as he pointed out, the Parliament Acts give the Lords a month to pass a Money Bill but they often do so within days. And legislation would raise the possibility of intervention by the courts, which would be undesirable and "uncomfortable for both sides".

267. In oral evidence, the Clerk of the Parliaments canvassed the more acceptable option of a unanimous report from this Committee endorsed by resolutions of both Houses. "It does not mean to say that one cannot depart from the norm, but the clearer the norm is the more the House would have to justify, in the forum of public opinion, taking a different line". Peer pressure would also operate. He denied that doing this would inhibit evolution.

268. The Clerk of the House of Commons, Sir Roger Sands, observed first that "conventions must be understood in the context of the constitutional and political circumstances in which they have been forged... The 'practicality' of codification... is not merely a matter of reviewing the technical options; it is a matter of considering whether the settled and predictable constitutional circumstances exist which would provide the necessary context for codification".

269. He gave his own list of arguments against turning conventions into rules. This would involve difficulties of definition, and lead to loss of flexibility. It would imply a need for adjudication; for conventions governing relations between the Houses, this would have to be by either an extraparliamentary body or some kind of Conference of the two Houses. Paradoxically, codifying the conventions could lead to increased delay, while awaiting adjudication. And if codification took the form of statute law, it would create a possibility of court intervention, which in his opinion could not be excluded, and which might be more likely with the creation of the new Supreme Court in 2009. Sir Roger agreed that this would be a "substantial constitutional change". Commenting on the notion of embodying an agreed description of the conventions in resolutions, the Clerk of the House of Commons confirmed that this would be a weak form of codification. It would warrant entries in *Erskine May* and the *Companion*, "but no more; and so the Speaker would find it very difficult to give rulings just on the basis of a codification in that form". This is the process proposed by the Hunt report for codifying the Salisbury-Addison Convention, and the Hunt report envisaged eliminating "any doubt or ambiguity as to their [the conventions'] application in all circumstances". The Clerk of the House of Commons did not think that was "a viable proposition"...

272. According to Lord Norton of Louth "'codifying conventions' is a contradiction in terms... If conventions are codified, they cease to be conventions". This is because in his view codification by definition involves enforceability and a convention is by definition unenforceable. He admits however that one could adopt "a soft definition of codification", i.e. "simply listing what are agreed to be conventions"; but in his view this exercise would be "nugatory". He also admits that "strong" codification, i.e. turning the conventions into enforceable rules, would be possible; but he argues against it. It would change the relationship between the Houses by taking from the Lords the leverage derived from reserve powers; it would require an enforcement mechanism; and in any case the present system works "reasonably well". Also it would reduce the capacity of the constitution to evolve in response to political reality.

273. Dr Russell observed that there is "nowhere comparable" to this Parliament for reliance on conventions as opposed to written rules. Likewise Professor Bogdanor observed, "Conventions are bound to play a most important role in an uncodified constitution such as that of the United Kingdom".

274. Professor Bradley likewise sees two possible forms of codification: "merely summarising past practice or an exercise in formulating rules for future conduct". He argues against the rule-making approach. "The British system is dynamic and flexible, rather than rigid". Its lack of clarity may sometimes seem a nuisance, but it enables it to evolve as circumstances change. A convention may be the practical expression of a principle; in a certain situation it may be possible, even necessary, to appear to breach the convention while upholding the principle. The sovereignty of Parliament means that exceptions must be expected: "a bill may raise a fundamental constitutional question such that it is not possible in advance to predict how the Lords should respond". In the absence of rules, all this can "come out in the political wash".

275. Professor Bogdanor agrees with Professor Bradley in seeing the conventions as defined by, and changing in response to, the political situation, in which he includes public opinion. He agrees with Sir Roger Sands that now, "when the constitution is in ferment", is a bad time to try to pin conventions down.

276. According to the Clerk of the Australian Senate, relations between the Houses in Canberra are governed entirely by the constitution and by standing orders. "Various participants in the parliamentary processes have attempted at various times to invent conventions to suit their purposes, but no conventions have been established". The Acting Clerk of the Australian House of Representatives provides an interesting illustration of the fact that a written constitution may still leave room for doubt and disagreement on important matters.

277. In Australia, a Constitutional Convention met in 1983–85 to "recognise and declare" constitutional conventions previously unwritten. But this concerned the relationship between the Governor-General and the Prime Minister (and in particular the power of the Governor-General to call an Election), not relations between the Houses. Professor Bogdanor commented, "It declared that 'the following principles and practices shall be observed in Australia'. It is not clear what authority the Commission had for making such a statement".

278. The Clerk of the Canadian Senate says, "In many respects, the relations between the contemporary Senate and the House of Commons, as in the UK Parliament, have followed certain recognisable practices. These practices have never been codified and are not usually identified as conventions"...

279. In our view the word "codification" is unhelpful, since to most people it implies rule-making, with definitions and enforcement mechanisms. Conventions, by their very nature, are unenforceable. In this sense, therefore, codifying conventions is a contradiction in terms. It would raise issues of definition, reduce flexibility, and inhibit the capacity to evolve. It might create a need for adjudication, and the presence of an adjudicator, whether the courts or some new body, is incompatible with parliamentary sovereignty. Even if an adjudicator could be found, the possibility of adjudication would introduce uncertainty and delay into the business of Parliament. In these ways, far from reducing the risk of conflict, codification might actually damage the relationship between the two Houses, making it more confrontational and less capable of moderation through the usual channels. This would benefit neither the Government nor Parliament.

NOTE: The report was approved in resolutions in identical terms in both Houses. See C. J. G Sampford 'Recognise and Declare: An Australian Experiment in Codifying Constitutional Conventions' (1987) 7 *Oxford Journal of Legal Studies* 369.

■ QUESTION

If the committee did not codify the conventions of the United Kingdom Parliament, what did they do and was it worthwhile?

6

Parliament: Scrutiny of Policy and Administration

OVERVIEW

In this chapter, which examines the operation of our parliamentary style of government, we focus on the House of Commons with an emphasis upon the responsibility and accountability of the Government. The most important constitutional convention is that of responsible government, the idea that the Executive will be responsible for its exercise of power and be accountable to Parliament and thence to the electorate. Having set the theory we look at the practice and the various procedures in select committees, on the floor of the Commons and in correspondence, ending with some recent reforms.

SECTION 1: THE ROLE OF PARLIAMENT

Philip Norton (ed.), *Parliament in the 1980s*

(1985), pp. 4–6, 8

Some observers identify a variety of functions, others list only two or three. An analysis of writings on Parliament, of constitutional practice and of parliamentary behaviour would suggest three primary ones: those of providing the personnel of government, of legitimization, and of subjecting measures of public policy to scrutiny and influence. This is to identify them in rather bald terms. Each is in need of qualification and amplification.

Providing the personnel of government

This is the least problematic of the functions. By convention, ministers are drawn from and remain within Parliament. Again by convention, most ministers—including the Prime Minister and most members of the Cabinet—are drawn from the elected chamber. (No less than two but rarely more than four peers are appointed now to the Cabinet.) There is no formal prohibition on a Prime Minister appointing as a minister someone who is neither an MP or a peer; such occasions are rare but not unknown. However, those given office are normally then elevated to the peerage or (more riskily) seek a Commons seat through the medium of a by-election. In practice, most ministers have served a parliamentary apprenticeship of several years before their appointments. Parliament provides both the personnel of government and the forum in which those seeking office can make their mark. Though there are occasional calls for non-parliamentarians (businessmen, industrialists and the like) to be brought into government, this function of Parliament arouses no serious debate or controversy.

Legitimization

Most national assemblies exist for the purpose of giving assent to measures of public policy. Indeed, this constitutes the primary purpose for which representatives of the local English communities (*communes*) were first summoned in the thirteenth century. Today, the broad rubric of legitimization encompasses different elements. The most obvious and the most significant is that of manifest legitimization. This constitutes the formal giving of assent to measures, enabling them to be designated Acts of Parliament; such Acts are accepted as having general and binding applicability by virtue of having been passed by the country's elected or part-elected national assembly (the elected chamber now having dominance within that assembly). A second element is that of latent legitimization. The government derives its primary political legitimacy from being elected through (if no longer by) the House of Commons. The collectivity of ministers that form the government enjoy enhanced legitimacy also by being drawn from and remaining in Parliament. For Parliament as an institution, this of course constitutes an essentially passive function.

There are two other sub-functions that fall under the heading of legitimization: those of tension-release and support-mobilization. By meeting and debating issues, Parliament provides an outlet, an authoritative outlet, for the expression of different views within society. Thus it plays an important part in the dissipation of tension. For example, during the Falklands crisis in 1982, Parliament provided the authoritative forum for the expression of public feelings on the issue. In Argentina, by contrast, citizens enjoyed no such body through which their views could be expressed and were forced instead to take to the streets to make their feelings known. Parliament also seeks to mobilize public support for measures which it has approved. In essence, these two sub-functions constitute a two-way process between electors and the elected, the views of citizens being channelled through Parliament (tension-release) and Parliament then mobilizing support for those measures which it has approved (support-mobilization). In practice, the extent to which Parliament is capable of fulfilling these functions has been much overlooked and, when considered by writers, has often been found wanting.

Scrutiny and influence

Parliament ceased to be a policy-making legislature in the nineteenth century. Instead it acquired the characteristics of what I have elsewhere termed a policy-influencing legislature. It ceased to be involved in the making of public policy, but it was expected to subject such policy to a process of scrutiny and influence. Scrutiny and influence are analytically separable terms, but scrutiny without any consequent sanction to effect influence is of little worth; and influence is best and most confidently attempted when derived from prior scrutiny. Hence, scrutiny and influence may be conjoined as a single function of Parliament. It is, in practice, its most debated and contentious function.

The exercise of scrutiny and influence can be seen to operate at two levels. These, in simple terms, may be characterized as being at the macro and the micro level of public policy. At the macro level, Parliament is expected to subject measures of public policy, embodied in legislative bills or in executive actions, to scrutiny and influence prior to giving assent to them. It is essentially a reactive function, exercised at a moderately late stage in the policy cycle... It is one which is most often carried out through the party elements in both Houses, the official Opposition or, nowadays, opposition parties seeking to exert the most sustained scrutiny of government measures. However, Parliament is but one of many influences at work in the policy cycle and, by virtue of what is usually an assured government majority at the end of the scrutinizing process, is rarely deemed to be the most important. Indeed, in some analyses, it is of no great importance at all.

At the micro level, Parliament is expected to scrutinize and respond to the effects of policy on the community. In practice, this task is exercised less through the party elements and Parliament as a collective entity, and more through Members of Parliament as Constituency representatives. Members represent territorially designated areas (constituencies) and seek to defend and pursue the interests of their constituents and groups within their constituencies. Whereas at the macro level MPs will be concerned to debate the principle of public policy, usually within the context of party ideology, at the micro level they are much more concerned with the policy's practical implications for their constituents.

In terms of the working life of Parliament, scrutiny and influence constitute its most demanding function. Seeking to subject government actions and legislative measures to scrutiny and a degree of influence occupies most of Parliament's time and energies. It is also the function that attracts the most debate and criticism. At best, effective fulfilment of the function allows Parliament to set the broad limits within which government can govern. (At the end of the day, it retains the formal sanction to deny assent to the government's legislative proposals and its request for supply.) At worst, the function may be fulfilled in the most superficial of ways, providing no effective check upon the executive.

NOTE: Norton does not say that the House of Commons controls the Executive. Michael Ryle in *The Commons Today* (1981) says that it is a popular misapprehension to regard the Commons as a governmental rather than a critical body. As he puts it, 'Parliament is the forum where the exercise of government is publicly displayed and is open to scrutiny and criticism'.

■ QUESTIONS

1. Does what Norton refers to as 'micro level' scrutiny by MPs include constituency work where the public can come to MPs' surgeries to complain about various matters? Is the redress of citizens' grievances against officialdom not a very important part of MPs' work? (See pp. 264–266, *post*.)
2. What exactly is meant by legitimization? Is legitimization real if Parliament approves the actions of the executive in the manner of a rubber stamp?

SECTION 2: POLICY AND ADMINISTRATION

A: Ministerial responsibility

C. Turpin, 'Ministerial Responsibility: Myth or Reality?' in J. Jowell & D. Oliver (eds), *The Changing Constitution*

(2nd edn, 1989), pp. 55–57

When it is said that ministers are collectively and individually responsible to Parliament, what is meant by 'responsible'? It may help us find the answer if we compare the idea of ministerial responsibility to Parliament with that of *control* by Parliament of the executive. Much contemporary discussion of the relations between Parliament and government is concerned with the reassertion of parliamentary control, and by this is generally meant a power to influence the decisions of government. Control, that is to say, is exercised a priori. On the other hand, when it is said that ministers are 'responsible' or 'answerable' or 'accountable'—terms not generally distinguished in meaning—to Parliament, reference is usually being made to the obligation of ministers to respond or answer or account for actions already performed (or left unperformed): responsibility is retrospective or a posteriori. There is, of course, an overlap between the parliamentary functions of 'controlling' and 'holding responsible' ('calling to account'). Some techniques, such as parliamentary questions and scrutiny by selected committees, are directed both to control and to the assertion of responsibility. An a posteriori investigation or check may have the aim of influencing future policy-making. The notion of 'responsible government' implies both acceptance of responsibility for things done and 'responsiveness' to influence, persuasion, and pressure for modifications of policy. Activist parliamentarians of our day aim to 'redress the balance' of the constitution in favour of Parliament by strengthening both control and responsibility of the executive, without making a fine discrimination between these concepts. This is not to say that equal progress is to be expected in establishing control and in extending responsibility.... A posteriori responsibility implies that certain obligations are owed by ministers to Parliament. What are these obligations?

It is demanded of ministers, in the first place, that they should *answer* or give account, discharging the essential 'obligation of Ministers, collectively and individually, to meet Parliament and provide information about their policies'. This includes a duty to provide financial accounts attesting to the regularity of government expenditure, as one element of a fuller 'explanatory accountability' which requires the giving of reasons and explanations for action taken, whether or not involving expenditure. That this is not a negligible aspect of responsibility was recognized by H. J. Laski: 'A Government that is compelled to explain itself under cross-examination will do its best to avoid the grounds of complaint. Nothing makes responsible government so sure.' The requirement to answer goes further: it imports an obligation to submit to scrutiny—to provide opportunities for Parliament to question, challenge, probe, and criticize. A duty to answer is something hollow if there are not apt procedures, respected by government, for such 'calling to account'.

The obligation to answer and submit to scrutiny is ancillary to what we may see as government's traditional obligation to redress grievances, which here means to take remedial action for revealed errors or defects of policy or administration, whether by compensating individuals, reversing or modifying policies or decisions, disciplining Civil Servants, or altering departmental procedures. This may be called 'amendatory accountability'; it presupposes an acknowledgement by ministers that they 'bear responsibility' to Parliament for what is shown to have gone wrong, whether or not they accept personal blame for the failure.

The obligations to answer, to submit to scrutiny, and to redress grievances may seem in practice to lack the support of any coercive rule or sanction. Undoubtedly these obligations are imperfect, resting as they do upon conventions, practices, and procedures which are liable to change and to be variously interpreted and applied, and which depend ultimately upon the political culture. But this is far from saying that the obligations in question lack substance, or that they can be flouted with impunity.

(a) Collective ministerial responsibility

Ministerial responsibility comprises both collective and individual responsibility. In his book on constitutional conventions, Marshall classifies the branches of collective ministerial responsibility as the confidence rule, the unanimity rule, and the confidentiality rule.

(1) Confidence

G. Marshall, *Constitutional Conventions*

(1984), pp. 55–56

It sometimes used to be said that a prime non-legal rule of the Constitution was that governments defeated by the House on central issues of policy were obliged to resign. But only one Prime Minister has resigned as the result of a defeat in the House in the twentieth century and that was immediately after being deprived of his majority by a General Election (Baldwin in January 1924). MacDonald was defeated on a confidence issue in 1924 and Callaghan in 1979, but neither resigned. Both fought the subsequent General Elections as leader of a government, having advised dissolution.

So the rule about a government that loses the confidence of the House seems to be that it must *either* resign *or* advise dissolution. Its right is only to advise, not to have, dissolution; since dissolution can, as we have seen, in some circumstances be refused. Resignation might therefore follow as the result of such a refusal (by the Queen), but that has not happened. As to what constitutes a loss of confidence there seems also to have been a development in doctrine. The books used to say that defeat on major legislative measures or policy proposals as well as on specifically worded confidence motions was fatal to the continuance of the government. But this no longer seems to be believed or acted on. In 1977 *The Times* propounded the view that 'there is no constitutional principle that requires a government to regard any specific policy defeat as evidence that it no longer possesses the necessary confidence of the House of Commons'. Some were greatly shocked by this doctrine and Professor Max Beloff wrote to *The Times* to say that it was inconsistent with the principles of the Constitution as hitherto understood. Sir Ivor Jennings, he pointed out, had said in *Cabinet Government* that the government must go if the House failed to approve its policy. What provoked the disagreement was that the Labour Government had just failed to carry a budget proposal about the rate of income tax and was proposing to remain in office in defiance of Sir Ivor Jennings's view of the established convention. Sir Ivor Jennings was of course dead, which is supposed to augment the authority of a textbook writer by allowing his views to be cited more freely in the course of litigation. Unfortunately there is a countervailing disadvantage in that his works may go out of print and are no longer constantly perused by Ministers, who are thereby enabled to fall into lax habits and disregard established constitutional conventions. In the 1960s and 1970s, in any event, governments seem to have been following a new rule, according to which only votes specifically stated by the Government to be matters of confidence, or votes of no confidence by the Opposition are allowed to count. Just conceivably one can imagine amongst recent Prime Ministers those who might have felt it their duty to soldier on in the general interest even in the face of such a vote.

(2) Unanimity

House of Lords, HL Deb

Vol. 239, cols 833–34, 8 April 1878

THE MARQUESS OF SALISBURY: ... My Lords, my noble Friend [the Earl of Derby] pointed out several measures of the Government to which in the public eye he was an assenting party. He did not, he said, in reality assent to all; one was a compromise, while to another, he was persuaded by some observations which fell from the Chancellor of the Exchequer, which appeared to be founded on a mistake. Now, my Lords, am I not defending a great Constitutional principle, when I say that, for all that passes in Cabinet, each member of it who does not resign is absolutely and irretrievably responsible, and that he has no right afterwards to say that he agreed in one case to a compromise, while in another he was persuaded by one of his Colleagues. Consider the inconvenience which will arise if such a great Constitutional law is not respected. ... It is, I maintain, only on the principle that absolute responsibility is undertaken by every Member of a Cabinet who, after a decision is arrived at, remains a Member of it, that the joint responsibility of Ministers to Parliament can be upheld, and one of the most essential conditions of Parliamentary responsibility established.

House of Commons, HC Deb

Vol. 889, Written Answers, Mr H. Wilson, col. 351, 7 April 1975

THE PRIME MINISTER: In accordance with my statement in the House on 23rd January last, those Ministers who do not agree with the Government's recommendation in favour of continued membership of the European Community are, in the unique circumstances of the referendum, now free to advocate a different view during the referendum campaign in the country.

This freedom does not extend to parliamentary proceedings and official business. Government business in Parliament will continue to be handled by all Ministers in accordance with Government policy. Ministers responsible for European aspects of Government business who themselves differ from the Government's recommendation on membership of the European Community will state the Government's position and will not be drawn into making points against the Government recommendation. Wherever necessary Questions will be transferred to other Ministers. At meetings of the Council of Ministers of the European Community and at other Community meetings, the United Kingdom position in all fields will continue to reflect Government policy.

I have asked all Ministers to make their contributions to the public campaign in terms of issues, to avoid personalising or trivialising the argument, and not to allow themselves to appear in direct confrontation, on the same platform or programme, with another Minister who takes a different view on the Government recommendation.

NOTE: This breach or suspension of unanimity or Cabinet solidarity was criticized as being simply a device to keep the Labour Party together. The United Kingdom's membership of the European Communities has caused problems for the Labour Party. In 1977 the point at issue was the use of proportional representation as the method of voting in the direct elections to the European Parliament. As unanimity in Cabinet could not be achieved, collective responsibility was, once again, suspended. The then Prime Minister, Mr Callaghan, answering a question in the House of Commons about collective responsibility, said: 'I think the doctrine should apply except in cases where I announce that it does not.' (HC Deb, Vol. 993, col. 552, 16 June 1977.)

The occasions on which it has been formally announced that unanimity in a government would be suspended have been few. Ministers have resigned because they could not agree with their colleagues on governmental policy. Mr Ian Gow resigned as Junior Minister in the Treasury because he did not agree with the Anglo-Irish Agreement 1985. Mr Michael Heseltine resigned as Secretary of State for Defence in the Westland Affair because he could not accept the requirement that all Ministers should clear speeches about Westland with the Cabinet Office.

■ QUESTION

What purpose does Cabinet solidarity serve, and whom does it (and its suspension) benefit?

(3) Confidentiality

The confidentiality of Cabinet proceedings is, of course, related to unanimity in that body. Disclosures of what happened in Cabinet do occur. Ministers may 'leak', i.e. brief journalists, on the basis that they do not name their source, or they may publish their memoirs. The publication of the Crossman Diaries has changed the practice, if not the convention, of confidentiality. (See *Attorney-General* v *Jonathan Cape Ltd* [1976] QB 752 and Lord Widgery CJ's judgment at p. 196, *ante*.)

Subsequently the Report of the Radcliffe Committee of Privy Councillors on Ministerial Memoirs (Cmnd. 6386) was published. According to its guidelines, Ministers should not disclose what happened in Cabinet until 15 years have passed where the material concerns national security; or where foreign relations would be adversely affected; or where it would reveal relationships between Ministers and (a) officials, or (b) Ministers' outside advisers.

(b) Individual ministerial responsibility

The confusion which was seen over when a government should resign when defeated in the House of Commons is also present in the issue of what should prompt the resignation of an individual Minister. In 1982 Lord Carrington, the Secretary of State, and two of his junior ministers resigned from the Foreign and Commonwealth Office after Argentinean troops had invaded the Falkland Islands. Lord Carrington wrote in his letter of resignation:

> The Argentine invasion of the Falkland Islands has led to strong criticism in Parliament and in the press on the Government's policy. In my view, much of the criticism is unfounded. But I have been responsible for the conduct of that policy and I think it right that I should resign ... [T]he invasion of the Falkland Islands has been a humiliating affront to this country.

This is an example of a classic case of a Minister accepting that the faults in a Department were his responsibility and then resigning. As such it is unusual.

In the following year there was a mass break-out from the Maze Prison in County Down, Northern Ireland. There was an inquiry into the circumstances of the escape by Her Majesty's Chief Inspector of Prisons (HC 203 of 1983–84), which found that the prison governor must be held accountable for a major failure in the prison's security arrangements. This report, the Hennessy Report, was debated in the House of Commons.

House of Commons, HC Deb

Vol. 53, cols 1042, 1060–61, 9 February 1984

> THE SECRETARY OF STATE FOR NORTHERN IRELAND (MR J. PRIOR): There are those who, while they accept this policy, have nevertheless suggested that the circumstances of the escape demand ministerial resignation. I take that view seriously and have given it the most careful consideration. I share hon. Members' concern about the honour of public life and the maintenance of the highest standards. I said at the time of my statement to the House on 24 October, without any pre-knowledge of what Hennessy would find:
>
> > It would be a matter for resignation if the report of the Hennessy inquiry showed that what happened was the result of some act of policy that was my responsibility, or that I failed to implement something that I had been asked to implement, or should have implemented. In that case, I should resign.—[*Official Report*, 24 October 1983, Vol. 47, c. 23–24.]
>
> In putting the emphasis that I did on the issue of 'policy', I was not seeking to map out some new doctrine of ministerial responsibility. I was responding to the accusations made at the time that it was policy decisions, reached at the end of the hunger strike, that made the escape possible.
>
> Since the report was published, the nature of the charges levelled at my hon. Friend and myself has changed. It is now argued in some quarters that Ministers are responsible for everything that happens in their Departments and should resign if anything goes wrong. My position has not changed, and I want to make it quite clear that if there were any evidence in the Hennessy report that Ministers were to blame for the escape, I would not hesitate to accept that blame and act accordingly, and so I know, would my hon.

Friend. However, I do not accept—and I do not think it right for the House to accept—that there is any constitutional or other principle that requires ministerial resignations in the face of failure, either by others to carry out orders or procedures or by their supervisors to ensure that staff carried out those orders. Let the House be clear: the Hennessy report finds that the escape would not have succeeded if orders and procedures had been properly carried out that Sunday afternoon.

Of course, I have looked carefully at the precedents. There are those who quote the Crichel Down case. I do not believe that it is a precedent or that it establishes a firm convention. It is the only case of its sort in the past 50 years, and constitutional lawyers have concluded that the resignation was not required by convention and was exceptional.

Whatever some may wish, there is no clear rule and no established convention. Rightly, it is a matter of judgment in the light of individual circumstances. I do not intend to review the judgments made by Ministers faced with the question whether to resign following failures in their Departments. Nor do I seek to justify my decision on the ground that there are many difficulties in Northern Ireland. There are, but that adds to rather than subtracts from the argument. The question that I have asked myself is whether on Sunday afternoon, 25 September, I was to blame for those prisoners escaping. The Hennessy report is quite explicit in its conclusion that, although there may have been weaknesses in the physical security of the prison and in the prisons department, the escape could not have taken place if the procedures laid down for the running of the prison had been followed. ...

MR J. ENOCH POWELL (Down, South): The Secretary of State, from the beginning of his speech, recognised the central issue in this debate, that of ministerial responsibility, without which the House scarcely has a real function or any real service that it can perform for the people whom it represents. We are concerned with the nature of the responsibility, the ministerial responsibility, for an event which, even in isolation from its actual context, was a major disaster.

I want to begin by eliminating from this consideration the Under-Secretary of State for Northern Ireland, the hon. Member for Chelsea (Mr Scott), because references to him in this context have shown a gross misconception. There has been argument about how long the hon. Member has been in the branch of the Northern Ireland Office concerned with the prison service, as though that were in the least degree relevant. The fact is that the entire responsibility, whether or not it is delegated to a junior Minister, rests with the Secretary of State. The Secretary of State has confirmed this to me in the past 24 hours, in another context, when I drew his attention to the reports to the fact that the Minister in charge of the environment had himself taken the decision to re-name the district of Londonderry. The right hon. Gentleman quite correctly said:

> In discharging his duties, my hon. Friend acts on my behalf.—[*Official Report*, 8 February 1984; Vol. 53, c. 623.]

There is a responsibility, of a different kind, obviously, on the part of every junior Minister towards his Ministry, but the responsibility for everything that he does or says or fails to do or say rests irrevocably with the Minister—the Secretary of State—and he alone is responsible to the House.

It is, therefore, a total misconception to imagine that any of the responsibility can be devolved to a junior Minister. A junior Minister may choose, if his chief resigns, to resign in solidarity with him; he may choose himself to resign for a variety of reasons. But there is no constitutional significance in acceptance by him of a responsibility which is not his. The locus of the responsibility is beyond challenge. It lies with the Secretary of State and, through him, with the Government as a whole.

As the Secretary of State reminded us this afternoon, even before the publication of the report he drew a distinction, which I believe to be invalid, between responsibility for policy and responsibility for administration. I believe that this is a wholly fallacious view of the nature of ministerial responsibility. I shall argue presently that there is a policy element in the event that we are considering and that it cannot be understood fully except in its policy framework. But even if all considerations of policy could be eliminated, the responsibility for the administration of a Department remains irrevocably with the Minister in charge. It is impossible for him to say to the House or to the country, 'The policy was excellent and that was mine, but the execution was defective or disastrous and that has nothing to do with me.' If that were to be the accepted position, there would be no political source to which the public could complain about administration or from which it could seek redress for failings of administration.

What happened was an immense administrative disaster. It was not a disaster in a peripheral area of the responsibilities of the Northern Ireland Department. It was a disaster that occurred in an area which was quite clearly central to the Department's responsibilities. If the responsibility for administration so central to a Department can be abjured by a Minister, a great deal of our proceedings in the House is a beating of the air because we are talking to people who, in the last resort, disclaim the responsibility for the administration.

NOTE: Mr Powell's view is not one, it would appear, which is shared by Ministers. The classic statement about the circumstances in which a Minister will be responsible for the action of his officials was given in 1954 by Sir David Maxwell-Fyfe, who was Home Secretary at the time. He made his statement on the occasion of the debate of the report into the Crichel Down affair. Some land had been compulsorily acquired by the Air Ministry. It was later transferred to the Ministry of Agriculture, which then leased the land to a tenant in breach of promises made about the way in which such a disposal of the land would be carried out. The Minister for Agriculture, Sir Thomas Dugdale, resigned.

House of Commons, HC Deb

Vol. 530, cols 1285–88, 10 July 1954

THE SECRETARY OF STATE FOR THE HOME DEPARTMENT (SIR DAVID MAXWELL-FYFE): ... There has been criticism that the principle [of Ministerial responsibility] operates so as to oblige Ministers to extend total protection to their officials and to endorse their acts, and to cause the position that civil servants cannot be called to account and are effectively responsible to no one. That is a position which I believe is quite wrong. ... It is quite untrue that well-justified public criticism of the actions of civil servants cannot be made on a suitable occasion. The position of the civil servant is that he is wholly and directly responsible to his Minister. It is worth stating again that he holds his office 'at pleasure' and can be dismissed at any time by the Minister; and that power is none the less real because it is seldom used. The only exception relates to a small number of senior posts, like permanent secretary, deputy secretary, and principal financial officer, where, since 1920, it has been necessary for the Minister to consult the Prime Minister, as he does on appointment.

I would like to put the different categories where different considerations apply ... [I]n the case where there is an explicit order by a Minister, the Minister must protect the civil servant who has carried out his order. Equally, where the civil servant acts properly in accordance with the policy laid down by the Minister, the Minister must protect and defend him.

I come to the third category, which is different. ... Where an official makes a mistake or causes some delay, but not on an important issue of policy and not where a claim to individual rights is seriously involved, the Minister acknowledges the mistake and he accepts the responsibility, although he is not personally involved. He states that he will take corrective action in the Department. I agree with the right hon. Gentleman that he would not, in those circumstances, expose the official to public criticism. ...

But when one comes to the fourth category, where action has been taken by a civil servant of which the Minister disapproves and has no prior knowledge, and the conduct of the official is reprehensible, then there is no obligation on the part of the Minister to endorse what he believes to be wrong, or to defend what are clearly shown to be errors of his officers. The Minister is not bound to defend action of which he did not know, or of which he disapproves. But, of course, he remains constitutionally responsible to Parliament for the fact that something has gone wrong, and he alone can tell Parliament what has occurred and render an account of his stewardship. The fact that a Minister has to do that does not affect his power to control and discipline his staff. One could sum it up by saying that it is part of a Minister's responsibility to Parliament to take necessary action to ensure efficiency and the proper discharge of the duties of his Department. On that, only the Minister can decide what it is right and just to do, and he alone can hear all sides, including the defence.

It has been suggested in this debate, and has been canvassed in the Press, that there is another aspect which adds to our difficulties, and that is that today the work and the tasks of Government permeate so many spheres of our national life that it is impossible for the Minister to keep track of all these matters. I believe that that is a matter which can be dealt with by the instructions which the Minister gives in his Department. He can lay down standing instructions to see that his policy is carried out. He can lay down rules by which it is ensured that matters of importance, of difficulty or of political danger are brought to his attention. Thirdly, there is the control of this House, and it is one of the duties of this House to see that that control is always put into effect.

... As I have said, it is a matter for the Minister to decide when civil servants are guilty of shortcomings in their official conduct. Normally, the Civil Service has no procedure equivalent to a court-martial, or anything of that kind. There have in the past been a few inquiries to establish the facts and the degree of culpability of individuals, but the decision as to the disciplinary action to be taken has been left to the Minister....

NOTE: It has been held by some that Sir Thomas's resignation was one in which he accepted responsibility for the wrongdoing of his officials. However, the current view seems to be that the resignation occurred because Sir Thomas had lost the support of his ministerial and party colleagues. See, for example, I. F. Nicolson, *The Mystery of Crichel Down* (1986), and J. A. G. Griffith, 'Crichel Down: The Most Famous Farm in British Constitutional History' (1987) 1 *Contemporary Record* 35. Perhaps this explains Lord Prior's view that Crichel Down did not set a precedent for resignation.

(c) Ministerial responsibility and accountability

Ministerial responsibility and accountability were considered by the Public Administration Select Committee in an inquiry which had initially focused upon fears that the civil service was politicized, by which they meant the political involvement in appointment and promotion of civil servants, but they widened it out to explore aspects of the governing relationship between ministers and officials. Between the beginning of the inquiry and the report there was a series of political and administrative failures, and arguments about where responsibility lies. The Department for the Environment, Food and Rural Affairs failed to implement the new system of farm payments; the Home Office failed to keep track of foreign prisoners who should have been considered for deportation and the National Health Service failed to make its budget balance. The committee quoted from a speech by William Waldegrave in the Government's response to the Public Service Select Committee's report on *Ministerial Responsibility and Accountability* in HC of 1996–07, Appendix, para. 4:

There is a clear democratic line of accountability which runs from the electorate through MPs to the Government which commands the confidence of a majority of those MPs in Parliament. The duly constituted government—whatever its political complexion—is assisted by the Civil Service which is permanent and politically impartial. Hence, Ministers are accountable to Parliament; civil servants are accountable to Ministers. That is the system we have in this country.

Third Report from the Public Administration Select Committee

HC 122 of 2006–07, paras 21–69

The Accountability Gap

21. The tradition of civil service impartiality in the United Kingdom runs so strong that the rationale for such impartiality is rarely questioned. It can seem an end in itself rather than a means to good governance. Yet the Northcote Trevelyan report that ended patronage and opened up appointment on merit to the civil service was clear that a system in which posts were obtained by patronage would deter "able young men" from the civil service as a career. In other words, the argument for an impartial civil service was one of operational effectiveness.

22. Recent events have suggested that permanence, independence and impartiality do not necessarily secure an operationally effective civil service. In fact, it is possible to go further. Some have suggested that the current arrangements actively militate against effectiveness by blurring the division of ministerial and civil service accountability. It has been held that they create a system in which politicians and civil servants can hide behind each other, so that no one is really held to account. Ministers are politically accountable to Parliament, but although civil servants are theoretically accountable to ministers, the doctrine of independence makes it difficult for this accountability to be exercised effectively, and may prevent a minister from dismissing or disciplining individual civil servants.

23. There is no consensus about the respective responsibilities of ministers and civil servants. Indeed, Janet Paraskeva, the First Civil Service Commissioner told us "I believe that the doctrine of ministerial responsibility needs to be reviewed.... We no longer understand what it means...". It has been possible to reconcile a doctrine of ministerial accountability which holds that ministers are ultimately accountable for everything done on their behalf (whether by civil servants or other public employees) with the doctrine of civil service independence for over a century. Why has it now become more problematic? There are many reasons for this, but it is likely that the new attention to transparency, accountability and performance has played a major part. Indeed, the development of scrutiny by Parliamentary Committees has exposed the difficulties of assigning responsibilities. Senior civil servants have been made more visible by their regular appearances before Committees, supposedly on ministers' behalf. At the same time, Permanent Secretaries continue to appear before the Public Accounts Committee in their role as Accounting Officers, where they are individually responsible.

24. If ideas about ministerial and civil service responsibilities are varied and inconsistent, it is no wonder that the public service bargain is no longer as straightforward as once it seemed. We try here to tease out some of the theory and reality of civil service and ministerial responsibility. This is a complex area, where different kinds of responsibility and accountability are closely interrelated, and where assumptions about the proper roles of ministers and civil servants are contested. We look at:

- the doctrine of ministerial accountability to Parliament;
- the extent to which civil servants are responsible to ministers and to what extent they have wider responsibilities;
- the effect of civil service independence on ministers' ability to run their departments;
- where authority and accountability should lie;
- the extent to which clear division between political and administrative responsibilities is possible; and
- the benefits of impartiality and the extent to which they are effectively secured.

This brief survey will give some idea of the muddle that is reality. We then consider whether there are ways in which the muddle could at least be tidied up.

Ministerial accountability to Parliament

25. The last Parliamentary examination of ministerial accountability was our predecessor Public Service Committee's report on *Ministerial Accountability and Responsibility,* [HC 313 of 1995–96] which gives a detailed historical analysis. As that Report says, government has attempted to draw a distinction between actions for which ministers are *responsible*, where their acts and omissions have contributed to a policy or operational failure; and those for which they are *accountable* where, although they are not directly culpable, they have a duty to explain to Parliament what happened. That formulation has influenced debate on the issue, but has not been entirely accepted.

26. The Public Service Committee recommended the following as a working definition of Ministerial Accountability:

> Ministers owe a fundamental duty to account to Parliament. This has, essentially, two meanings. First, that the executive is obliged to give an account—to provide full information about and explain its actions in Parliament so that they are subject to proper democratic scrutiny....
>
> Second, a Minister's duty to account to Parliament means that the executive is liable to be held to account: it must respond to concerns and criticisms raised in Parliament about its actions because Members of Parliament are democratically elected representatives of the people. A Minister's effective performance of his functions depends on his having the confidence of the House of Commons...

27. The Committee also considered that, as part of ministers' obligation to explain their actions to Parliament, they should make civil servants available to committees. The Government accepted the broad principles set out by the Select Committee, but was concerned that giving civil servants the responsibility to give information to Parliament on their own behalf would muddle their accountability.

28. On 19 March 1997 the House agreed a resolution on ministerial accountability in the following terms:

> Ministers have a duty to Parliament to account, and be held to account, for the policies, decisions and actions of their Department and Next Steps Agencies;
>
> It is of paramount importance that Ministers give accurate and truthful information to Parliament, correcting any inadvertent error at the earliest opportunity. Ministers who knowingly mislead Parliament will be expected to offer their resignation to the Prime Minister.
>
> Ministers should be as open as possible with Parliament, refusing to provide information only when disclosure would not be in the public interest, which should be decided in accordance with relevant statute and the Government's Code of Practice on Access to Government Information (Second Edition, January 1997);
>
> Similarly, Ministers should require civil servants who give evidence before Parliamentary Committees on their behalf and under their directions to be as helpful as possible in providing accurate, truthful and full information in accordance with the duties and responsibilities of civil servants as set out in the Civil Service Code (January 1996).

It can be seen that the resolution gives civil servants duties toward Parliament only in carrying out the requirements of their ministers. The existing responsibility of Accounting Officers to give an account to the Commons of their handling of public funds was not changed.

29. The Public Service Committee did a great deal to clarify the nature of ministerial responsibility, and the Resolution of 1997 set out the best compromise which could be reached on the matter. Nonetheless, the Committee did not wholly accept the Government's attempts to distinguish between matters for which ministers were directly *responsible* and those for which they were merely *accountable*. As the Committee concluded "it is not possible absolutely to distinguish an area in which a minister is personally responsible, and liable to take blame, from one in which he is constitutionally accountable. Ministerial responsibility is not composed of two elements which have a clear break between the two". We agree that under our current constitutional arrangements there will never be precise clarity about the boundaries of ministerial accountability. That in itself suggests that we should be wary of constitutional changes which reduce ministerial responsibility without clearly transferring responsibility and accountability elsewhere. The question is, whether it is possible to clarify matters further in a way that would improve the effectiveness and accountability of our governing arrangements.

Civil service accountability to ministers

30. Just as it is impossible to be definitive about the boundaries of ministerial accountability, so civil service accountability is far from clear. The doctrine enunciated at the time of the Crichel Down affair was that civil servants were accountable to ministers. Sir David Maxwell Fyfe asserted confidently that:

> The position of the civil servant is that he is wholly and directly responsible to his minister. It is worth stating again that he holds his office "at pleasure" and can be dismissed at any time by the Minister; and that power is nonetheless real because it is seldom used. The only exception relates to a small number of senior posts, like a permanent secretary, deputy secretary or principal finance officer, where since 1920, it has been necessary for the Minister to consult the Prime Minister, as he does on appointment.

It is clear from more recent cases, including the attempt by a former Home Secretary to dismiss the Director of the Prison Service, that matters are much less straightforward than that. In 1996 the Employment Rights Act extended many employment rights to civil servants. When we pressed on the current constitutional position, we were told that employment law "applies to civil servants in the same way as it does to employees" and that the "Civil Service Management Code assumes that it is civil servants who take the actual decision to dismiss". Yet successive governments have stressed that civil servants are responsible to ministers, not Parliament.

31. Some of our witnesses felt that civil service independence had a political function, in balancing the strong executive power of British governments. This concern with the wider responsibility of the civil service is not new. When the Armstrong Memorandum famously asserted that "civil servants are

servants of the Crown ... for all practical purposes the Crown in this context is represented by the government of the day", the [First Division Association- senior civil servants' trade union] expressed concern that this approach ignored the wider responsibilities civil servants had to Parliament.

32. The importance of those wider responsibilities was endorsed by our predecessors. Successive Committee Reports have made it clear that elected accountability does not mean that ministers should have the ability to act without any checks on their behaviour, or that the civil service should be considered as wholly the creature of a current administration. The Treasury and Civil Service Committee supported the introduction of a code which would clarify the duties and responsibilities of civil servants. The Code drafted by that Committee formed the basis of the Code issued by the Government, which noted "that civil servants owe their loyalty to the duly constituted Government", subject to the provisions of this Code. In other words, loyalty to the Government was fundamental but not unconditional.

33. Thus the civil service's relationship with government has long been recognised as more complex than simply being the enthusiastic instrument of government policies. As Dr Matthew Flinders of Sheffield University put it: "In practice, it is quite clear that the bureaucracy has its own implicit values, wants and desires and these may on occasion conflict with the instructions of ministers". Yet the only explicit acknowledgement of this potential for conflict within the current system is when civil servants act in the role of Accounting Officers. In that context, they have a clearly defined role as the guardians of propriety in public expenditure. If they believe a particular expenditure would be a misuse of public funds, they may formally note the fact. The minister may override their objections, but the note is sent to the Treasury and the Comptroller and Auditor General. Such a note will inevitably come to the attention of the Public Accounts Committee.

34. The civil service is responsible to ministers, but, as the role of Accounting Officer shows, that responsibility is complex, and not limited simply to implementing government policies.

Ministers and departments

35. Until now, we have been able to manage with the twin principles that ministers were accountable for everything, and that the civil service was independently appointed; but recent events have led some to question whether that remains possible. The problems of civil service capability do not come from the confusion of political and administrative accountability alone. However, it is clear that the lack of agreement about who should be accountable for what, to whom, and what that accountability and its consequences might mean, contributes to the difficulties.

36. Former Home Secretaries who gave evidence to us had very different views about the extent to which politicians could in practice control departments. Michael Howard was very clear that:

> I believe that it is a delusion to suppose that there is some different kind of structure which will make everything easy and solve the problems. What one needs in any department, including the Home Office, is strong political leadership and a clear expression of determination by the Secretary of State as to what he wants to do and a determination to get it done.

Although David Blunkett agreed that strong political leadership was central, his memorandum suggested that Cabinet Ministers could feel the machine worked against them, and that they were excluded from managerial decisions:

> Senior Civil Servants frequently tell Ministers, "Departmental Policy is this". Good Ministers say, "Departmental Policy is what I, on behalf of the Government, say it is, so long as it is in line with the legislation available to me, the administrative or executive powers which have been accorded to me, or in line with the stated Policy of the Government and the Prime Minister and/or the Party's own Manifesto when elected to Government". However, there will inevitably be a large number of occasions where policy recommendations are made by the Civil Service and therefore the role of the civil service in policy making as well as in policy delivery is inevitably blurred.

Mr Blunkett went on to argue that part of ministers' problems in making sure their policies were implemented came from the structures which were intended to protect civil service impartiality:

> What also makes this difficult is that Ministers are precluded from a direct role in ensuring that the structure to deliver the policies that Parliament has voted on or Ministers have executive power to implement, are capable or appropriate to do so.

37. It is clear that there is no consensus currently about the proper constitutional relationship between ministers and their permanent officials. The Treasury has attempted to clarify the responsibilities of the Boards which assist Permanent Secretaries in running departments by producing a *Code of Practice for Corporate Governance*. This should, in principle, make the division of responsibilities clearer by setting out board members' roles. But Sir Nicholas Montagu was concerned that the Code muddled ministerial and civil service responsibilities, and:

> would extend the power of Ministers—and therefore ultimately political control— into areas previously the preserve of Permanent Heads of Department. In very broad terms the traditional split of responsibilities between Ministerial and Permanent Head is that the Minister sets the policy objectives and parameters within which the Department is to work; and the Permanent Secretary organises the Department and its management processes to see that those objectives are delivered.

In his view:

> corporate governance is the whole apparatus that we have to protect the Head of Department in the role of Accounting Officer. It is the totality of the systems and frameworks that ensure that Departments are run properly. That means ... planning processes are in place with a "clear line of sight" through the organisation, so that everyone knows where (s)he fits in to the delivery of the department's strategic objectives: those objectives themselves will be shaped by the priorities of the government of the day and the minister in charge of the department. Perhaps above all, the culture of accountability permeates throughout the organisation, so that people know just what their responsibilities are and are equipped with the appropriate skills to exercise them.

38. However, this view was challenged not only by the Code itself, which considers that the Board of a Department works for, and may properly be chaired by, a minister, but by Sir Michael Quinlan, a distinguished former Permanent Secretary, who supported the assumptions implicit in the Treasury code:

> I dissent from Sir Nicholas Montagu's view that ... Ministers and Permanent secretaries have in some sense parallel responsibilities. The Permanent Secretary's responsibilities run to the Minister and are included within his/hers; they do not run separately, aside from the special category of Accounting Officer responsibilities. And these latter are, I believe, narrower than Sir Nicholas conveys; they are not "for the running of the Department". I think it incorrect, unrealistic and undesirable to suppose that Ministers "should not [in the sense of ought not] get involved in the actual running of Departments".

39. It is clear that there is no consensus, either among politicians or officials, about the way in which ministerial and civil service responsibilities are divided. This means there can be no consensus about where accountability should lie.

Authority and Accountability

40. The relationship between the government and the civil service is complex and shifting. We do not believe that it could ever be otherwise. But nor do we believe that complexity means that we cannot have guiding principles about accountability and authority, or make sensible suggestions for improvement. In deciding where authority should rest, we need to focus on accountability. Accountability to Parliament is a key constituent of general ministerial responsibility. It is Parliament which holds ministers to account and Parliamentary pressure can, in the end, force their removal. Discussions about ministerial accountability often end here, as if accountability to the House was the final point. But in fact ministers are in the electoral as well as the political firing line. Elected politicians, backbenchers and ministers alike, are accountable to the electorate. Election is a great leveller. The permanent executive will be open to influence, quite properly, from a wide range of groups with direct interests who know how to work the system. Elections enable everyone to participate. They are the foundation of the key democratic relationship between governors and governed. Ultimately, therefore, ministerial accountability means accountability to the electorate.

41. We consider that the relationship between government and civil service, and civil service and Parliament, should be structured to ensure the ultimate accountability of the government to the electorate. The corollary of this is that elected ministers should have freedom to perform their functions as they see fit, within any framework set by Parliament.

International Comparisons

42. In Britain the balance between independent appointment on merit and ministers' ability to give political direction through staffing decisions is struck in a way that sits at one end of an international spectrum. Sir Christopher Foster drew a parallel between civil service independence and independence of the judiciary. However Ed Straw, a partner at PricewaterhouseCoopers, who appeared in a private capacity, was concerned about this:

> No-one that I am aware of holds the independence of the Civil Service on the same state as the independence of the judiciary, which is what we have here in fact.

Sir Robin Young considered "we are the least politicised civil service probably in the whole world".

43. The sharpest contrast to the United Kingdom is the United States, where large numbers of appointments are made by the political executive. Yet even in very different political traditions, some political influence on the civil service is considered unexceptionable, and not incompatible with merit. For example in Finland, often ranked as the leader in good governance, Permanent Secretaries may themselves have political affiliations, and we were told that when there were a number of vacancies it was felt desirable to have some party balance in the appointments made. Nor is Britain unique in having concerns about the extent to which the civil service is, or should be, responsive to political direction. Both Sweden and Finland have introduced the "State Secretary" system, in which departments are headed by political appointees, as well as by Permanent Secretaries, and in both there is some concern about this development. Some of the pressure for State Secretaries comes from the fact that there is no provision for appointing junior ministers, but it is worth noting that the State Secretaries have precisely the combination of political and administrative functions which has caused concern in the United Kingdom.

44. Comparisons with other countries are far from straightforward. Much depends on history and political culture. Nonetheless, in relation to ministerial accountability and politicisation of bureaucracy, it is useful to be reminded that the British system is extreme in the division it makes between the administrative and the political world, and that this division is, in some respects, increasing. This at least provides a context for a discussion which tends to be very parochial.

A more independent civil service?

45. As we have seen, previous governments have resisted giving civil servants direct duties to Parliament, except in their role as Accounting Officers. On the other hand, it has long been clear that ministers cannot be expected to be responsible for everything which occurs within a department. Reforms such as the introduction of Next Steps Agencies have sought to give explicit responsibilities to Agency Chief Executives. When an agency has been successful, this has worked well; in the case of high profile and politically embarrassing failures, clarity has soon been lost.

46. The Institute for Public Policy Research (IPPR) has recently suggested a radical extension of mechanisms to separate political and administrative responsibilities. It proposes that, while ministers would be responsible for setting policy, civil servants should be governed and managed by independent bodies, and should be accountable internally to a civil service executive and externally to a new statutory governing body for the civil service. The IPPR report cites the New Zealand system as a precedent for such a separation between ministerial and civil service responsibilities, although its proposals go further than the current New Zealand system.

47. The IPPR claims that its proposals would not lead to a loss of ministerial authority as it would be for the Government to decide the shape, configuration and size of the civil service, and how it should be funded. The powers delegated to the civil service would be defined, but ministers would still be free to make operational decisions provided that they did so explicitly. If that were the case though, it might be thought that a substantial infrastructure would have been erected for little more than might be gained through the establishment of a few more agencies, or even internal agreements like those currently published for the Home Office.

48. If such a scheme was to be effective, it would radically change the terms of trade between the Government and the civil service. The new Civil Service Governors would be charged with "defining and redefining" the values and role of the civil service. Unlike the New Zealand States Services Commission, they would also be charged with demarcating roles and assigning responsibility. If disputes arose about

whether a failure occurred because the policy was unworkable, or because it had been badly implemented, it would be for the Civil Service Governors to adjudicate, "investigating cases of administrative failure and, where required, laying out, as far as possible, where responsibility for the failure lies".

49. Not only is that a huge amount of political power, it would be extremely difficult to challenge such a body. It would not be directly or indirectly accountable to the electorate. Parliament would appoint its members, who would have to be approved by the Prime Minister, but it is hard to see how the Board of Governors could be effectively held to account. Once "operations" had come to be the sphere of a professional civil service, under control of a professional governing body, ministers would find it difficult to argue against that body's recommendations. New governments may have new priorities, and may wish to do things in new ways. Political philosophy may not simply be about the distribution of resources, but about the ways in which the state engages with the citizen. In extreme cases, such a system could mean that ministers were only able to make policies approved by their officials. Nor does it seem desirable to increase the accountability of civil servants if this also means reducing the accountability of ministers.

50. There is the further question of what would become of the *Carltona doctrine*, the legal principle that civil servants act on behalf of ministers, and can exercise powers on their behalf. The doctrine has survived the introduction of the Executive Agencies, and might survive more extreme delegation, but would surely come under strain in an arrangement where a statutory body was responsible for so much policy on the civil service.

51. There are some roles where the need for independence overrides the need for accountability. We do not believe this is one of them. The purpose of civil service reform should be to ensure that the civil service is effective in carrying out its functions, and is responsive to the government of the day. A system in which the civil service was itself beyond political accountability would not be effective.

52. Leaving aside the constitutional difficulties in such a proposal, we have serious doubts about whether it would in fact improve the performance of the civil service or of government as a whole. Reviews of the New Zealand experience have noted that the emphasis on defined agreements between ministers and officials have led to departments taking a narrow view of their responsibilities, and have reduced the extent to which there is a sense of what the Government as a whole is trying to achieve. Most of our witnesses felt that the separation of policy from operations was fraught with problems. Sir David Omand called it a "gigantic category error". Professor Christopher Hood and Dr Martin Lodge point out that "in the real world of politicking and blame-avoidance, the pressures for each side to cheat on such a deal, exploiting the ragged edges between policy and administration, are very strong". Giving control of interest rates to the Monetary Policy Committee (MPC) of the Bank of England, the most commonly used example of such separation, was felt to be exceptional, rather than a model with wider application. It is also notable that the Chancellor may have given responsibility to the MPC, but it is a body that he appoints directly. Ed Straw was in no doubt that the Chancellor was ultimately responsible for its performance.

53. This is not an argument against trying to clarify administrative and political responsibilities. As we have said, there are evident difficulties and confusions in the present arrangements. If the answer is not to be found by an inflexible and unrealistic separation of policy and administration, this does not mean that nothing can be done. Further defined delegation may well be possible, but in our view it should be tailored to particular functions and organisations. A single division between a monolithic, self-governing civil service and the elected government would not be conducive to effective government.

Accounting to Parliament

54. The doctrine of accountability described above by Michael Howard, in which "Ministers should be responsible for decisions which they have taken; civil servants should be responsible for decisions which they have taken", can only work if there is transparency about what decisions were taken, and who took them. The current conventions about civil service relationship to Parliament prevent that transparency, and therefore inhibit accountability. The one exception is in the extremely rare cases when an Accounting Officer has formally advised against expenditure (see paragraph 33).

55. In the past Committees have called for civil servants to have some direct accountability to Parliament. This has been resisted, on the grounds that it would produce a division of loyalties for civil servants. Yet it is clear that in other jurisdictions civil servants have far more freedom to account for themselves, while ministers remain accountable for policy.

56. The doctrine of ministerial accountability means that when civil servants appear before Parliament it is as ministers' proxies. They get neither credit nor blame. By contrast, in both Finland and Sweden, civil servants operate under legal frameworks which give them a considerable degree of autonomy and accountability. As we have already noted, political and constitutional systems are complex, and must be considered in their entirety. In the United Kingdom, the legal assumption is that civil servants act on ministers' behalf, and exercise ministers' powers. In contrast, in Sweden and Finland civil servants are legally accountable themselves for the decisions they take, and will personally be held to account for those decisions. We have argued against the feasibility or desirability of a formal separation of accountability of this kind. Nonetheless, we believe that civil servants could be considerably more open with Parliament without threatening the doctrine of ministerial responsibility.

57. Times are changing. We now have a Freedom of Information Act. Recent major inquiries have illuminated the inner workings of government. The Leader of the House has undertaken that select committees will have access to the civil servants they consider best able to help them. Witnesses before this committee have been remarkably frank about the policy making process. These are welcome changes, but the formal position has not altered since the 1997 Resolution on ministerial responsibility. We consider it is time for it to do so. We consider that increasing the expectation that civil servants will account honestly to Parliament does not undermine the principle of ministerial responsibility, but strengthens accountability as a whole.

A new Public Service Bargain

58. There are good reasons for having an independent and impartial civil service. Sir Robin Mountfield set these out succinctly:

> It is a defence against corruption: 'jobs for the boys' or the 'spoils system' invite abuse.
>
> It provides continuity, especially after a change of government.
>
> It maintains deep expertise and 'institutional memory' of the background to policy issues.
>
> It provides real knowledge of how the machinery of government works, making it possible for a government to achieve the results it wants.
>
> It provides a loyal and supportive, but detached and politically-neutral, analytical challenge to political enthusiasm: an essential health-check in a democratic process.
>
> It entrenches a deeply-rooted and distinctive ethical base to the public service.

We agree with this analysis. However, we heard evidence that these claimed benefits might not always be achieved in practice.

59. For example, some former ministers told us that, although individuals might be excellent, the service as a whole was not good at retaining collective memory. This is made worse where there is a rapid turnover of ministers themselves. The administrative structures deliberately encouraged circulation of staff, but this could be at the expense of experience and expertise. In other words, one of the key advantages of a permanent and impartial civil service was not in fact secured.

60. Similarly, impartiality does not seem to have fostered the ability to "speak truth unto power" to the extent that is sometimes claimed. Sir Christopher Foster told us that ministers should not influence civil service appointment and promotion because "it is impossible to get honest, independent but particularly challenging views from people, when, rightly or wrongly, they believe that those to whom they have given such views might use such power to influence their future and future careers". The Civil Service Commissioners feared that political appointees would tell ministers what they wished to hear. Lord Butler also considered political appointments would undermine the professionalism and objectivity of the civil service.

61. Whatever the theoretical arguments, it is notable that the skills civil servants were found to lack in open competitions included "self-confidence, presentational skills... putting your head above the parapet"—exactly the qualities needed for speaking truth unto power. We also note that if the need to please an employer meant that objectivity and challenge were impossible, few businesses would ever succeed.

62. A high degree of independence has not prevented accusations that the civil service has neglected its traditional skills, and failed in its duty to ensure that ministers are properly briefed. The Butler and Hutton Reports have been cited as revealing the way in which good government is undermined by inadequate procedures. The ability to speak truth unto power seems to have been lacking, together with a willingness or ability to hold a constitutional line. Clearly, there can be pressures which prevent the full advantages of independence from being secured. There is no easy answer to the division of responsibility between ministers and officials, but the relationship between ministers and their senior civil servants, particularly their Permanent Secretaries, is crucial to effective government. That relationship will necessarily be complex. It will depend on political context, personal styles, and different approaches to the job. Sir Gus O'Donnell told us that even principles of accountability were worked out in different ways with different ministers and civil servants. Some ministers will want (as Baroness Shephard told us she had wanted) to be more administratively active than others. Above all, it will depend on the current understanding of what has been described as the "public service bargain".

63. As we have seen, there is no clear understanding of this at present. Delegating responsibility may help, but it is not as straightforward as is sometimes suggested. As Professor Hood and Dr Lodge point out, the attempt to demarcate accountability can bring with it damaging behavioural consequences for good government:

> If civil servants can routinely expect to be fired for Government mistakes, they will not be disposed to help ministers out of political holes ... they will have every incentive to act defensively to make sure Ministers are formally committed on paper (or more likely through killer emails) to all potentially blameworthy courses of action ...

The task is to get ministers and civil servants working together effectively, not to lock them into potentially antagonistic bunkers.

64. Yet there is no doubt that the traditional public service bargain is under strain. Former ministers are heard to complain that civil servants lack the delivery skills, managerial competence and commitment to policy success that are demanded of them; while former civil servants are heard to complain that ministers do not take their advice, fail to provide consistent leadership and are obsessed with new initiatives of doubtful practicality. Such complaints are not new; but what is new is that they are now expressed (on both sides) so publicly. This suggests that it is time to consider whether a new public service bargain is needed.

65. What this means for civil service and ministerial skills we discuss in a separate inquiry that will report shortly. Here we confine ourselves to underlying principles. Without introducing artificial and unhelpful demarcation lines, it should be possible to be more explicit about the legitimate expectations and duties of both parties to this key governing relationship. That is what we mean by a new public service bargain. There is a code for ministers; and a code for civil servants. What is lacking is a code for ministers *and* civil servants, a good governance code that incorporates the operating principles of British central government. Unlike the code of this name produced by the Treasury, which excludes the relationship between ministers and civil servants, it would have this relationship at its centre.

66. Under its provisions, civil servants would expect to have their access to ministers safeguarded and their right to give advice, however unpalatable, protected. Their role in procedural and propriety matters should be made explicit. Just as Accounting Officers have a right to give clear advice about expenditure, and to be absolved from responsibility if it is overridden, so Permanent Secretaries should have a right to advise on procedure and propriety. Civil servants have a right to expect clear and consistent political leadership and that programmes will be matched by resources, and a right not to be made public scapegoats when things go wrong for which they are not responsible. For their part, ministers should expect professional and committed service to their governing objectives, along with good advice. They have a right to expect that poor performance will be dealt with effectively, that there is a robust system of performance management, and that civil servants will have the skills and experience to enable them to support ministers efficiently. It should be accepted that ministers may have a role in organising departments if they wish.

67. The compact that the Home Office has recently produced goes some way toward this, although it also demonstrates the difficulty of clear demarcation of responsibilities. It states that ministers are responsible for "accounting to Parliament and the public for the policy and delivery of the Home Office",

while officials are responsible for "increasingly answering externally for operational matters for which they are responsible". It is still far from clear who is accountable when "operational matters" affect delivery as a whole. Moreover, while ministers are enjoined to ensure their decisions reflect an understanding of resource constraints and officials are responsible for delivery of strategy and policy "within a clear performance framework and allocated resources", the compact is silent about who is responsible for resource allocation, and for determining whether resources are appropriate. Even so, the compact may be helpful, since it increases pressure on each side to communicate properly with the other, and to clarify responsibilities in particular cases. We also note the increased emphasis on the performance of individual officials and the department as a whole, and the explicit involvement of ministers in performance review. We are similarly encouraged by the development of the Capability Reviews, which offer greater transparency about civil service performance. This is an important initiative, which we examine in more detail in our forthcoming report on *Skills for Government*.

68. A clearer understanding of the public service bargain should be accompanied by an increased willingness to give a full account of operational errors to Parliament, and an acceptance that civil servants do have some direct accountability to Parliament. That will only be possible if Committees accept that a blame culture will not lead to good administration. There will be circumstances in which individual responsibility cannot be overlooked, and ministers need to be held to account, but investigations of policy should not routinely become a political blame game. If that happens we will have swapped a culture in which ministers and civil servants can hide behind each other for one in which they push the other into the firing line.

69. For all its ambiguities, a revised and fuller version of the Home Office compact might form the basis of a clearer division of responsibilities between ministers and officials. There have been suggestions that such a governance code might also be extended to include wider requirements about how government should be conducted. Sir Christopher Foster and Sir Nicholas Monck have proposed such a broader code of good governance, spelling out precise steps in policy making and consultation, to ensure that policy proposals are sound, and well tested. This is certainly worth discussing. Former Cabinet secretaries are on record as deploring the decline of proper government process—Lord Butler told us "There are elements of our government that need improvement and it has got worse". Parliament has a legitimate interest in the quality of the governing process that provides it with its core business. It is essential to get the key governing relationship between ministers and civil servants on to a clearer footing. That is why we propose a new public service bargain, underpinned by a good governance code.

NOTES

1. The wording of the resolution on ministerial accountability reported at para. 28 differed from that proposed at para. 60 in the Public Service Committee's report (HC 313 of 1995–96). The resolution has been incorporated into the guidance given to Ministers, *Ministerial Code*, the current version was revised in 2010 (Cabinet Office, para. 1.6).
2. The Public Administration committee at para. 68 seem to have taken a view similar to that of D. Woodhouse in 'The Reconstruction of Constitutional Accountability' [2002] PL 72, which suggested that attention should be moved away from 'causal' responsibility, with its focus upon direct ministerial involvement, towards 'role' responsibility which concentrates upon the requirements of the job of a Minister including supervision of a department, explaining actions carried out in its name, and correcting any deficiencies. This would avoid the confusion introduced by managerial accountability with its 'responsibility/accountability' and 'policy/operations' distinctions. Woodhouse suggests that the actions of some Ministers seem to be based upon this 'role' conception: the setting up of an inquiry and the implementation of reform following allegations that Foreign Office officials had sanctioned the supply of military equipment to Sierra Leone and the Home Secretary apologizing for the backlog in processing and issuing passports by the executive agency, the Passport Office.
3. The concern about identifying responsibility and accountability when things go wrong was addressed in the Environment, Food and Rural Affairs select committee report on the Rural Payments Agency and the implementation of the single payment scheme. In its thorough report (HC 107 of 2006–07) the committee highlighted problems and suggested improvements, and expressed the view that it was odd that the only the Chief Executive of the agency was removed from his post. The committee pointed out that another official was specified in the

governance arrangements as sharing responsibility and suggested that in a company the chairman and senior executives would face dismissal over such an operational failure so that they were surprised that the Permanent Secretary was still in place and they noted the Secretary of State had been promoted (HC of 2006–07). The committee was very unimpressed with the delay in the Government's response to its report, and called its content 'shoddy'. On accountability, the Government response regretted that the committee had criticized named officials, as select committees in the Government's view are not concerned with discipline inside departments (see Government guidance on this p. 234, *post*) and stated on the publication of the report that the Prime Minister and Head of the Civil Service had expressed their confidence in the Permanent Secretary and that the guidance on ministerial responsibilities in the Ministerial Code did not require any supplement (HC 956 of 2006–07).

■ QUESTIONS

1. Will it be possible to draft clearly the respective duties of Ministers and Chief Executives, thus ending the current ambiguity about policy and operations which seems to enable Ministers to choose what is and is not policy and therefore those things for which they can be held responsible?
2. How different is Woodhouse's 'role' responsibility from Enoch Powell's conception of ministerial responsibility, at p. 210, *ante*?

Second Report from the Public Service Committee

HC 313 of 1995–96, paras 170–174

IX. DIFFERENT SORTS OF ACCOUNTABILITY

170. In this Report, we have been mainly concerned with Parliamentary accountability. But we are well aware that government are not accountable only through Parliament. Mr David Faulkner of St John's College, Oxford, put this point in his evidence to us: Accountability

> can also take different forms—political, financial, managerial, operational, legal, professional. It can be to different authorities, institutions or individuals—Parliament, Ministers, managers, the courts, auditors, inspectors, regulators, users, customers or the general public. ... Accountability can operate through direct supervision or contact, through formal arrangements for reporting or consultation (in public or in private), through procedures (such as complaints) which can be activated when required, and in various other ways ... accountability—or responsibility—should lie, not just to central government and Parliament, but also to the organisations with which they work and on which they may depend; to local communities; to users; and to the wider public. Accountability should take multiple forms and operate through multiple, and often reciprocal, channels.

171. In recent years, three institutions or developments have tended to increase the extent to which the public is able to ensure that public services are properly accountable. The growth of judicial review is one of them. The Treasury and Civil Service Committee noted in 1994, the accountability of the executive through the Courts has been enhanced in recent years by the growth of judicial review. That Committee also noted the Government's observation that 'existence of judicial review has clearly and substantially increased the work of both lawyers and administrators, in effect to "judicial review-proof" departmental decisions, but it has also improved the quality of decision-making by making it more structured and consistent'. Judicial review was 'a contribution to upholding the values of fairness, reasonableness and objectivity in the conduct of public business'. in addition to judicial review, statutory right of appeal against many types of administrative decision—such as on asylum applications, or planning applications—is now provided. Many of these are on essentially the same grounds as might be claimed in an application for judicial review.

172. Another is the role of the Parliamentary Commissioner for Administration (the Ombudsman) in investigating complaints from persons or organisations who contend that there is prima facie evidence of maladministration, by a body within his jurisdiction (generally speaking, government departments

and bodies), which has led to hardship or injustice. A number of those who sent us memoranda referred to the powers of the Ombudsman and the possibility of their extension. Dr Diana Woodhouse wrote that 'whether supplementary mechanisms for accountability need to be strengthened and new ones established' should be considered. In particular, she thought that the Ombudsman should have powers to investigate cases referred to him directly by individuals (rather than having to go through a Member of Parliament) and have a mechanism for enforcing the conclusions of his reports. Professors Gavin Drewry and Dawn Oliver of the University of London felt that 'an extension of the jurisdiction of the PCA to embrace illegality ... could help to counter the problems experienced by the High Court in dealing with applications for judicial review': this would also 'greatly enhance the effectiveness of provisions for redress of grievance'. They also argued that the PCA could be given an explicit role in developing 'best practice' guidance, and thereby have 'a substantial and recognised input into improving the quality of administration as well as providing redress after the event'. These matters are the province of the Select Committee on the Parliamentary Commissioner for Administration, they are rather beyond the scope of the current inquiry and are not ones on which this Committee is qualified to comment. We note that that Committee has recently considered a number of them in their reports on the 'Powers, Work and Jurisdiction of the Ombudsman' and 'Maladministration and Redress'. In the former inquiry the Committee concluded that what it referred to as 'the MP filter' be retained, but 'coupled with concerted attention to the means whereby access to the Ombudsman can be strengthened and enlarged', and also recommended that the Ombudsman be given the power to conduct audits of the operation of administrative procedures in bodies within his jurisdiction.

173. A third facet of the recent growth in different types of accountability is the introduction of the Citizen's Charter. The initiative was launched in 1991. It is, according to the White Paper introducing it, 'the most comprehensive programme ever to raise quality, increase choice, secure better value, and extend accountability'. The White Paper set out 'principles of public service' which 'every citizen is entitled to expect': explicit standards, published and prominently displayed at the point of delivery; openness—'no secrecy about how public services are run, how much they cost, who is in charge, and whether or not they are meeting their standards'; full, accurate information, readily available, about what services are being provided, with published targets; choice; non-discrimination; accessibility; and proper procedures to put right things that have gone wrong. Those that meet a certain standard for the delivery of quality in public services—the Charter standard—become entitled to use the Chartermark. The Citizen's Charter has had an important impact in improving the delivery of the public services and in making them more responsive to the public. The initiative will form the subject of our next inquiry.

174. Recent changes in the management of the public service have had an impact, in many ways, on the extent to which it is effectively publicly accountable. Delegation and privatisation are reducing the extent to which effective political accountability can be provided through Parliament. Accountability might be provided by some other mechanism, by Charters, through the Ombudsman, through the courts, even; and we welcome that. Accountability, however, should be a broad obligation, to many different bodies. Accountability to Parliament should not preclude accountability to the public; and *vice versa*. Parliament needs to retain and protect its role; and to do so, it has to be more effective in fulfilling it. A number of our recommendations involve changes to (or implications for) the House's practices and procedures. We hope that these will be further considered by the appropriate Committees of the House, particularly the Procedure Committee and the Liaison Committee. We have considered, in this Report, mainly what government does to comply with its obligation of accountability to Parliament; we hope that others will carry this forward by considering what Parliament can do to enforce it.

■ QUESTION

Would the imposition of legal liability upon Chief Executives improve their accountability?

C. Scott, 'Accountability in the Regulatory State'

(2000) 27 *Journal of Law and Society* 38, 41–43, 50–54, 57–60

... It is helpful to keep distinct the three sets of accountability questions: 'who is accountable?'; 'to whom?'; and 'for what?' With the 'who is accountable'? question, the courts have been willing to

For what?	Economic Values	Social/Procedural Values	Continuity/ Security Values
To whom?			
'Upwards' accountability	Of departments to treasury for expenditure	Of administrative decision-makers to courts/tribunals	Of utility companies to regulators
'Horizontal' accountability	Of public bodies to external and internal audit for probity and VFM	Review of decisions by grievance-handlers	Third-party accreditation of safety standards
'Downwards' accountability	Of utility companies to financial markets	Of public/privatized service providers to users	Consultation requirements re: universal service requirements

Figure 1 Examples of linkages between values and accountability institutions

review all decisions involving the exercise of public power, even where exercised by bodies in private ownership. In the utilities sectors the exercise of public privileges, such as monopoly rights, by private companies carry with them responsibilities to account for their activities, both in domestic fora and EC law. In some instances, the receipt of public funds by private bodies renders recipients liable to public accountability through audit mechanisms. Considerable attention has been paid to this issue in the literature, with a consensus for the view that simple distinctions between private actors (not publicly accountable) and public actors (subject to full public accountability) are thus not sustainable.

The 'to whom?' question has often been mingled with the 'for what?' question, for example in the distinction between legal accountability (to the courts in respect of the juridical values of fairness, rationality and legality) and political accountability (to ministers and to Parliament or other elected bodies such as local authorities and via these institutions ultimately to the electorate). Furthermore, while it might be helpful to think of 'administrative accountability' as accountability to administrative bodies such as grievance [handlers] and auditors, in fact these mechanisms for accountability have conventionally been distinguished, with administrative accountability only indicating the former, while financial accountability is used for the latter.

Separating the 'to whom?' and 'for what?' we find three broad classes within each category. Thus accountability may be rendered to a higher authority ('upwards accountability'), to a broadly parallel institution ('horizontal accountability') or to lower level institutions and groups (such as consumers) ('downwards accountability'). The range of values for which accountability is rendered can be placed in three categories: economic values (including financial probity and value for money (VFM)); social and procedural values (such as fairness, equality, and legality); continuity/security values (such as social cohesion, universal service, and safety). Figure 1 sets out the possible configurations of the 'to whom?' and 'for what?' questions, producing nine possible pairs of co-ordinates.

...If we think of traditional accountability as encompassing the 'upwards' mechanisms of accountability to ministers, Parliament, and courts, with some recognition of the more formal horizontal mechanisms (such as grievance-handlers and auditors) then it is possible to conceive of a concept of 'extended accountability' within which traditional accountability is only part of a cluster of mechanisms through which public bodies are in fact held to account.

...Close exploration of the structures of extended accountability in the United Kingdom reveals at least two different models which have developed which feature overlapping and fuzzy responsibility and accountability: interdependence and redundancy. No domain is likely to precisely correspond to one or other of these models. There are likely to be elements of both identifiable in many policy domains but, for reasons of clarity, the examples used in the following sections are presented in somewhat simplified and ideal-type form.

1. Interdependence

The identification and mapping out of relationships of interdependence within policy domains has been one of the key contributions of the recent pluralist literature in public policy. The identification of interdependence has important implications for accountability structures. Interdependence provides a model of accountability in which the formal parliamentary, judicial, and administrative methods of traditional accountability are supplemented by an extended accountability. Interdependent actors are dependent on each other in their actions because of the dispersal of key resources of authority (formal and informal), information, expertise, and capacity to bestow legitimacy such that each of the principal actors has constantly to account for at least some of its actions to others within the space, as a precondition to action. The executive generally, and the Treasury in particular, has long had a central role in calling public bodies to account over a range of values, in a way that is often less transparent in the case of the more dignified, but arguably less efficient parliamentary mechanisms of accountability. But these less formal and more hidden accountability mechanisms extend well beyond the capacities of central government, extending potentially to any actors, public or private, within a domain with the practical capacity to make another actor, public or private, account for its actions. Within the pluralist political science literature this conception is sometimes referred to as 'constituency relations' or 'mutual accountability'. Indeed it may be that the simple monolithic structures presented as the welfare state model are too simple, that they disguise intricate internal and opaque webs of control and accountability that are functionally equivalent to the new instruments of the regulatory state, but are less formal and transparent. Among the more obvious examples were the consumer committees established for the nationalized industries with a brief to hold those public corporations to account from a collective consumer viewpoint.

This model is exemplified by the United Kingdom telecommunications sector (Figure 4). Figure 4 shows that though BT is subject to diminished upwards accountability to parliament and courts (noted above), it has a new forms of accountability in each dimension—upwards to a new regulator, horizontally to the mechanisms of corporate governance, and downwards to shareholders (and possibly also the market for corporate control) and users. The financial markets arguably provide a more rigorous form of financial accountability than applies to public bodies because there are so many individual and institutional actors with a stake in scrutinizing BT's financial performance. The accountability of BT to the regulator, OFTEL, is also more focused, in the sense that OFTEL has a considerable stake in getting its regulatory scrutiny right, being itself scrutinized closely by BT, by other licensees, and by ministers, in addition to the more traditional scrutiny by the courts and by public audit institutions. OFTEL's quest for legitimacy has caused it to develop novel consultative procedures, and to publish a very wide range of documents on such matters as competition investigations and enforcement practices. Each of these other actors has powers or capacities which constrain the capacities of the others and require a day-to-day accounting for actions, more intense in character than the accountability typically applied within traditional upwards accountability mechanisms. This form of accountability, premised upon interdependence, is not linear, but more like a servo-mechanism holding the regime in a broadly acceptable place through the opposing tensions and forces generated. Such a model creates the potential to use the shifting of balances in order to change the way the model works in any particular case.

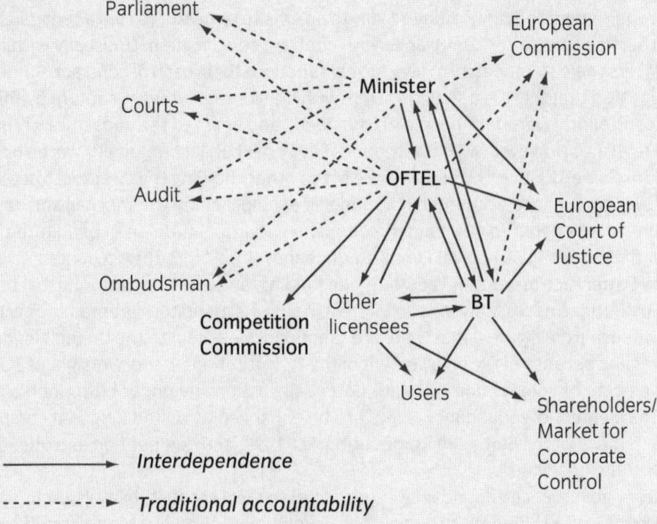

Figure 4 Accountability for provision of telecoms services 2: Interdependence model

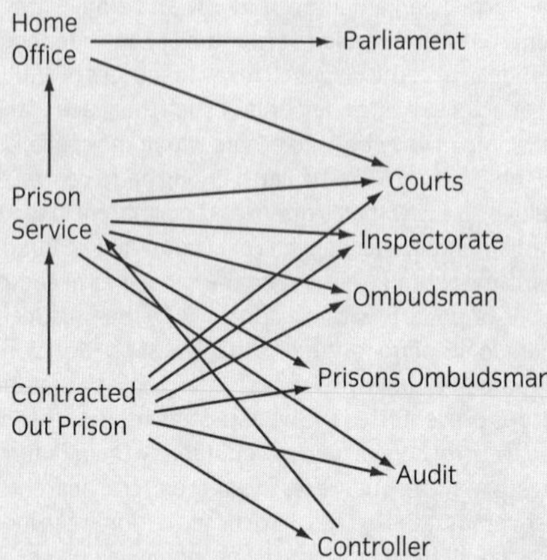

Figure 5 Accountability for prisons provision: redundancy model

2. Redundancy

A second extended accountability model is that of redundancy, in which overlapping (and ostensibly superfluous) accountability mechanisms reduce the centrality of any one of them. In common parlance, redundancy is represented by the 'belt and braces' approach, within which two independent mechanisms are deployed to ensure the system does not fail, both of which are capable of working on their own. Where one fails the other will still prevent disaster. Redundancy in failsafe mechanisms is a common characteristic of public sector activities generally, and can be threatened by privatization. Equally explicit concern about risks associated with change may cause redundancy to be built in to oversight structures. Redundancy can be an unintended effect of certain institutional configurations. In practice, examples of redundancy in accountability regimes appear to be a product of a mixture of design and contingency.

There are at least two forms to the redundancy model: traditional and multi-level governance. The traditional redundancy model is exemplified by the accountability mechanisms for contracted-out prisons in the United Kingdom (Figure 5). Directors of contracted-out prisons are subject to all the forms of accountability directed at publicly operated prisons: upwards (legal, to the courts); financial (to the National Audit Office); and horizontal (to the Prisons Inspectorate, the Prisons Ombudsman, and prison visitors). But, contracted-out prisons are additionally subject to a further form of horizontal accountability with a requirement to account, day-to-day to an on-site regulator (called a controller), appointed by the Prison Service to monitor compliance with contract specification. Unusually within the prisons sector, controllers wield the capacity to levy formal sanctions for breach of contract. Some commentators have suggested that there is a structural risk with on-site regulators of capture by the director, in the sense of controllers over-identifying with the needs and limits to the capacities of those they are supposed to regulate. However, with the redundancy model of accountability were such capture to occur it would likely be identified by one or more of the others holding the director to account.

The multi-level governance accountability model is exemplified by the mechanisms for accounting for expenditures made under jointly funded national and European Union expenditure programmes, notably under the European Structural Funds. Redundancy is built into the accountability mechanisms deliberately by EU decision makers, by requiring joint funding, and therefore ensuring that both domestic and EU audit institutions necessarily take an interest in single expenditure programmes within member states. It will be seen from Figure 4 that there is a redundancy element to the United Kingdom telecommunications regime because of the involvement of the EC institutions in the oversight of EC competition policy. Infringements of competition rules are potentially actionable under both United Kingdom and EC regimes. The element of redundancy is likely to be enhanced as United Kingdom competition rules are aligned with those of the EC by the Competition Act 1998, and competition and utilities regulators exercise concurrent jurisdiction.

The multi-level governance redundancy model of extended accountability is likely to see further development in the United Kingdom arising out the devolution of considerable powers to a new Scottish

Parliament and Northern Irish and Welsh Assemblies. In each of these jurisdictions new executives and parliamentary/assembly committees have the potential to develop and reinvent the parliamentary oversight already exercised over United Kingdom-wide or multi-jurisdiction public functions.

...

The challenge for public lawyers is to know when, where, and how to make appropriate strategic interventions in complex accountability networks to secure appropriate normative structures and outcomes. What I have in mind here is something like process of 'collibration' described by Andrew Dunsire. Dunsire sees collibration as a stratagem common to a wide variety of processes by which balances are shifted to change the nature of the way that control systems (such as accountability mechanisms) work ['Tipping the Balance: Autopoiesis and Governance' (1996) 28 *Administration and Society* 299, 312–4]. Such interventions may be applied to any of the three accountability parameters: who is accountable? for what? to whom? This offers the possibility of meeting Martin Loughlin's challenge for public law to 'adopt as its principal focus the examination of the manner in which the normative structures of law can contribute to the guidance, control and evaluation in government'. The value of such changes may lie not directly in the development of a single accountability mechanism, but rather in the effects on the overall balance within the regime. The logic of the argument presented here is that conflict and tension are inevitable within the complex accountability webs within any particular domain, and that the objective should not be to iron out conflict, but to exploit it to hold regimes in appropriate tension.

To take an example, within a redundancy model of accountability for contracted-out prisons, how do we ensure proper accountability for the range of values, such as humanity, efficiency, and security which might be deemed appropriate desiderata for a prisons regime? The orthodox answer would be to say that we have an inspector with a specific mandate to check on the humanity of prison regimes, and auditors to assess efficiency, and security people overseeing security. But this is only a partial answer. Within the redundancy model we have other mechanisms which directly or indirectly check on each of these values—the controller, company management, the Prisons Ombudsman, the European Committee for the Prevention of Torture, and the courts. These mechanisms are in tension with another, in the sense of having different concerns, powers, procedures, and culture which generate competing agendas and capacities. Within contracted-out prisons, corporate governance structures will hold directors to account for the expenditure of money, so that within an efficient redundancy system enough money but no more than is necessary to provide a humane regime will he spent. We might expect periodically that value for money norms or security norms might inhibit the achievement of humanity norms. The solution would not necessarily be to crank up the humanity regime, but rather to apply techniques of selective inhibition to the other norm structures so that their pull on the overall system was diminished somewhat. This might, for example, be through changing financial incentives or oversight structures, or through enhancing access of prisoners to grievance-handlers or judicial review.

...

The transformation of public administration in the United Kingdom has made more transparent the dense networks of accountability within which public power is exercised. The constitutional significance of this observation is to suggest that there is a potential to harness these networks for the purposes of achieving effective accountability or control, even as public power continues to be exercised in more fragmented ways. Outstanding questions for this analysis are whether there are other models of accountability in the regulatory state not captured by the interdependence and redundancy models, and whether it is possible to capture the complete set within an overall theory of extended accountability. Areas requiring further exploration are the role of voluntary organizations (such as prisons campaigners and consumer groups) and the media in rendering public and quasi-public bodies accountable.

Each of the two models of extended accountability discussed in this article presents difficulties for public lawyers and more generally. Neither model is directly 'programmable' with the public law norms (fairness, legality, rationality, and so on). Interventions to secure appropriate normative outcomes must necessarily be indirect and unpredictable in their effects. The interdependence model carries with it the risk that special interests, such as those of a particular firm or group of firms, may capture the regime through their overall weighting of power within it. The redundancy model presents particular problems. If redundancy *per se* is a good characteristic for an accountability regime, it is difficult to calculate how much redundancy is sufficient and how to know when an additional layer of accountability is inefficient and to be removed. Equally, there is also the risk within a redundancy model of simultaneous failure of different parts of the system for the same reason. Where, for example, information is successfully hidden from more than one part of the accountability network, there is a risk of complete failure in respect of the matters for which that information is relevant.

Close observation of the structures of accountability in the regulatory state suggests that the public lawyer's concerns, premised upon an over-formal conception of accountability, if not unfounded are then neglectful of the complex webs of extended accountability which spring up in practice. Indeed, these extended accountability mechanisms already evidence a capacity to hold not only public but also private actors accountable for the exercise of power which is broadly public in character. Whilst not agreeing with Wilks and Freeman that it is possible to conceive of the accountability of a regulatory regime, it is nevertheless helpful to think in terms of the *aggregate* accountability of each of the actors exercising power within a regime.

NOTES

1. Scott points out some of the deficiencies in his two models of extended accountability, and it would seem that the situation is improved if the different mechanisms are all operating. This ideal may not happen in practice. In 'Accountability, New Public Management, and the Problems of the Child Support Agency' (1999) 26 JLS 150, Carol Harlow concluded that while the external accountability provided by the Social Security Committee, the Select Committee on the Parliamentary Commissioner for Administration, and the Public Accounts Committee was very good, many of the operational problems they dealt with had their roots in policy which was not given a sufficiently rigorous scrutiny by Parliament during the passage of legislation. This fault of inadequate consultation is known; see the Hansard Society, p. 290, *post*, and the Modernisation Committee, p. 296, *post*. Thus it seems unfair that the only resignation was that of the Agency's first chief executive who arrived after the policy had been formulated by Ministers. Internal accountability procedures associated with the New Public Management, such as business plans and performance indicators, were of no assistance to clients when things went wrong. Harlow also points out that judicial review in child support was like the 'dog which never barked'. She wonders if an explanation may be found in the fact that the child support cases were heard by judges in the family law division rather than the public law division.
2. The Hansard Society's report *The Challenge for Parliament: Making Government Accountable* (2001) agrees with Harlow's analysis of Parliament and the Child Support Agency about the partial success of Parliament's dealing with the Child Support Agency. The vast majority of the report's case studies show inadequacies in Parliament's oversight, e.g., despite the availability of early warning about problems in the Passport Office in spring 1999, the Public Accounts Committee's report in summer 2000 was full but, as is usual, the relevant departmental select committee (Home Affairs) had not conducted a watching brief and the debating opportunities tend to be used for party political matters rather than one of public interest. It was noted that Parliament is unclear about its relationship with regulators, inspectorates, and other outside bodies. Parliament should use the information about individual cases which they can provide by drawing out the lessons from this work and giving greater worth to their investigations by using it as the basis for holding Government to account. The report recommends that Parliament should be at the apex of a network of regulatory bodies and alternative scrutiny mechanisms. A culture of scrutiny should be developed and improvements made to work done in committee and the chamber in the House of Commons with more emphasis given to financial scrutiny. The House of Lords should complement the Commons and there should be better communication between Parliament and the public.

(d) The Royal Prerogative

See Chapter 5 Section 1 pp. 157–175 *ante*, on the Royal Prerogative. While some reform has been carried out, one of the areas also considered was going to war.

The Governance of Britain

Cm 7170, paras 25–30

Deploying the Armed Forces abroad

25. There are few political decisions more important than the deployment of the Armed Forces into armed conflict. The Government can currently exercise the prerogative power to deploy the Armed Forces for armed conflict overseas without requiring any formal parliamentary agreement.

26. The Government believes that this is now an outdated state of affairs in a modern democracy. On an issue of such fundamental importance to the nation, the Government should seek the approval of the representatives of the people in the House of Commons for significant, non-routine deployments of the Armed Forces into armed conflict, to the greatest extent possible. This needs to be done without prejudicing the Government's ability to take swift action to protect our national security, or undermining operational security or effectiveness. The Government will therefore consult Parliament and the public on how best to achieve this.

27. There have been several attempts in recent years to introduce legislation which would set out the conditions under which the Government could not proceed with a deployment without the approval of the House of Commons. The House of Commons Public Administration Select Committee in its report *Taming the Prerogative* [HC 422 of 2003–04] thought that this was an area in which the Government should consider introducing legislation. The House of Lords Constitution Committee undertook an extensive inquiry in 2005–6 into this subject. [HL 236 of 2005–06] Its report concluded, conversely, that legislation is not the best route. Instead, it favoured the development of a parliamentary convention. Such a convention could be formalised by a resolution of the House of Commons with the same status as Standing Orders of the House.

28. Both reports recognised that there were difficult issues which would need to be addressed to ensure that the mechanism put in place would provide sufficient flexibility for deployments which need to be made without prior parliamentary approval for reasons of urgency or necessary operational secrecy. We would want to avoid any risk that members of the Armed Forces could be subject to legal liability for actions taken in good faith while protecting the national interest in such deployments.

29. The Government will propose that the House of Commons develop a parliamentary convention that could be formalised by a resolution. In parallel, it will give further consideration to the option of legislation, taking account of the need to preserve the flexibility and security of the Armed Forces. It will be important to strike a balance between providing Parliament with enough information to make an informed decision while restricting the disclosure of information to maintain operational security.

30. As set out in the motion approved by the House of Commons when it debated this issue on 15 May 2007, the Government will undertake further consultation on this issue before bringing forward more detailed proposals for Parliament to consider.

The Governance of Britain—War powers and treaties: Limiting Executive powers

Cm 7239, paras 1–13

1. The power to commit the country to international obligations through the conclusion of treaties, and the power to send armed forces into conflict situations, are two of the most important powers a government can wield. But there is presently no legal requirement for the people's representatives in the House of Commons in Parliament, which sustains the Government and which is the supreme body in our constitution, to have any particular role in either decision. In practice, no government these days would seek to commit troops to a substantial overseas deployment without giving Parliament the opportunity to debate it. But the terms of that debate are very much set by the Government. In particular, it has been rare in the past for Parliament to have a substantive vote on a proposed deployment before the troops are committed.

2. The position on treaties is different. There are mechanisms that may give Parliament a voice. When any treaty requires changes to the UK's domestic law before the UK can comply with it, the debate on the legislative provisions gives Parliament the power to decide. There is a long-standing convention that many treaties have to be laid before Parliament for a minimum length of time before ratification so that Parliament has the opportunity to demand a vote if it wishes. In considering ways of putting this convention onto a statutory footing, we need to strike a balance between the right of Parliament to consider and where it thinks it appropriate decide on treaty ratification on the one hand, and what will be both practical and workable for Parliament on the other.

War powers

3. In his statement to the House of Commons on 3 July 2007, the Prime Minister gave a clear commitment that "the Government will now consult on a resolution to guarantee that on the grave issue of peace

and war it is ultimately this House of Commons that will make the decision." In seeking to give Parliament the final say in decisions to commit UK troops to armed conflict overseas, it is nevertheless essential that we do not undermine the ability of the executive to carry out its proper functions. The responsibility to execute such operations with minimum loss of British lives has to remain with the executive.

4. There are a number of important issues which need to be taken into account in determining what will be the best way to enhance Parliament's role. Key considerations are:

- The need to ensure that the UK can continue to be able to fulfil its international obligations;
- The need to ensure that we do not undermine our reputation as a helpful and willing participant in multinational operations;
- The need to respect the views and information of any coalition partners;
- The need to ensure that any mechanism does not undermine the operational flexibility and freedom of the commanders in the field. The mechanism must provide sufficient flexibility for deployments which need to be made without prior Parliamentary approval for reasons of urgency or secrecy. Commanders should not be fearful that Parliament was trying to 'second guess' their decisions;
- The need not to impact on the morale of the armed forces. One objective of a more structured role for Parliament is to show the troops that Parliament, and through them the nation, is fully behind them and supports them in the difficult and dangerous task they are undertaking. The procedures put into place must not undermine that objective;
- The need to ensure that if, for whatever reason, the Government is not able (or indeed, in an exceptional case, willing) to respect the mechanism that is put into place, there are no consequences for individual soldiers, for example finding themselves accused of having acted illegally through taking part in a deployment which Parliament has not approved.

5. Against this background, the paper looks at the key questions which need to be answered in drawing up a mechanism for seeking the approval of Parliament, in particular the House of Commons.

- What should fall within the scope of the new mechanism? If linked to armed conflict how should the term 'armed conflict' be defined? Is it necessary to have a definition at all? Would it be possible to provide a detailed list of 'armed conflict situations', or alternatively a list of situations which would not be covered by the definition for the purposes of the Parliamentary approval mechanism? There is certainly a case for ensuring that the provisions do not have to apply to every deployment, however small or uncontroversial. Would a better approach be to take some general and existing definition such as those in the Geneva Conventions? On balance, the Government thinks the approach of a general definition with some exclusions is the best one.
- Is it necessary to define armed forces? If so, what should fall within or outside that definition? There is a definition in the Armed Forces Act 2006; is this the best one to use? What should be the position of either the reserve forces or the special forces? On balance, the Government favours including the reserve forces.
- Should any procedure allow for deployments to occur without the prior approval of Parliament for exceptional (urgent or secret) operations? Under what circumstances should it be possible for the Government to engage troops in a conflict which falls within the definition agreed without prior Parliamentary approval? Two immediate circumstances which are discussed in the paper are where there is an emergency situation, and where it is necessary to keep the operation secret. The Government favours a broad definition of both terms; by their very nature, they are unlikely to be easily predictable in advance.
- What should be the consequences of a decision by the Government to deploy forces without Parliamentary approval (for reasons of urgency, national security etc)? Should the Government be obliged to seek retrospective approval, or should it just inform Parliament? What should the consequences be if an approval was sought for a deployment retrospectively and denied? There might be significant difficulties in such a situation if Parliament were ever to withhold its approval. The paper therefore canvasses the option that the Government, in those circumstances, should simply be required to inform Parliament when such deployments have taken place.
- Should the recall of Parliament be required if under an emergency procedure a deployment has taken place? How long a period should be allowed to elapse before Parliament is recalled? Should there be a special procedure for when Parliament is dissolved? It is obviously always open to the Government to seek a recall of Parliament if it is simply adjourned or prorogued. The situation is more difficult

when Parliament is dissolved. Should the Government in those circumstances be required to seek Parliamentary approval as soon as the new Parliament is assembled, or should it be sufficient that Parliament is then informed of what has taken place (bearing in mind that there may be a new government after the election)?

- What information should be provided to Parliament? Should it go beyond the objectives, locations and an indication of the legal basis for the operation? Who should decide what information should be disclosed? How might requirements to disclose information be adapted to the particular circumstances of different deployments? A course has to be steered between giving Parliament as much information as it requires to make a decision and not compromising or endangering the operation itself by revealing information which might be of use to opponents. The Government favours, on balance, limiting the requirement to an indication of the objectives and location of a deployment and the legal basis for the operation, but that the Prime Minister maintain some discretion over the level of information released.
- At what point during the preparations for deployment should Parliament's approval be sought? Should the exact timing be left to the discretion of the Prime Minister? Should there be a Parliamentary role in deciding the best timing? Should Parliament be asked to approve an operation well in advance of the troops being committed, or should approval be sought only when it is possible to provide the maximum amount of relevant information? Or should this be left to the Prime Minister to decide according to the circumstances. The Government favours the latter.
- How is legal protection best afforded to Service Personnel deployed under the different possible mechanisms? The Government will wish to ensure the highest degree of protection.
- How should Parliamentary support be maintained throughout a deployment? How frequently should the Government be required to report to Parliament on the continued conduct of the deployment? Is there a case for asking the Government to seek a renewal of Parliament's approval at regular intervals? There would be significant difficulties in the last if, at any time, Parliament were to decide not to renew its approval, given the logistical difficulties of any disengagement in the middle of a conflict, and the impact on the UK's international obligations. For these reasons, the Government does not favour specifically requiring Parliament to renew its approval at regular intervals, but it is prepared to look at whether the Government should be required to make a formal report to Parliament at regular intervals. The other mechanisms by which Parliament regularly holds the government to account would also continue to be available.
- The UK has a bicameral Parliament. This raises the issue of the role of the House of Lords. Should the role of the House of Lords be to inform the debates of the House of Commons but not to take a vote? If it too were given the formal right to approve a deployment, there would be problems if the two Houses were to disagree on the issue. It is the Government's view that it is entirely appropriate that the matter should be aired by the House of Lords, where possible *before* the House of Commons decided whether or not to approve a deployment so that the Lords' opinion could be properly taken into account. The decision, however, should be for the Commons alone.
- Is there a need for a new Parliamentary committee? How would a new regime governing decisions about deployments affect other parts of the system, eg, the Defence and Foreign Affairs Select Committees and the Intelligence and Security Committee? What role might these committees play? For example could they receive in confidence information which could never be sensibly revealed in open debate, which would enable them to guide the House in its response to a request from the Government for approval of a deployment?

6. The final question asked in the consultation is whether any mechanism for obtaining Parliamentary approval should take the form of a Parliamentary convention, perhaps embodied in a resolution of the House of Commons, or whether it should be made statutory.

7. A Parliamentary convention in the form of a resolution has the advantages of being more flexible and adaptable. The interpretation of the resolution would lie clearly in the hands of Parliament rather than the courts. It could be framed in more general terms than is possible with statute. It is therefore less likely to interfere with the operational freedoms and responsibilities of commanders in the field.

8. Legislation might be seen as providing a stronger incentive for the government of the day to comply with an approval requirement as the need to obtain approval could only be resolved by further primary legislation. Legislation would also allow Parliament to make clear that failure to comply with the procedure was not intended to make the conflict unlawful nor expose any individuals to civil or criminal liability.

It might be possible to combine the respective advantages of convention and legislation in a "hybrid" approach in the form of a short Act which requires the approval of Parliament or the House of Commons to deploying armed forces into armed conflict abroad, and provides very clear legal protection for individuals, while leaving the detailed Resolution arrangements to procedures that would be determined later.

NOTE: The consultation period ran from October 2007 to January 2008 but no proposed legislation has been produced.

■ QUESTION

Even if there is no agreement on the issues raised in the consultation, how likely is it that the armed forces will be deployed without first seeking Parliamentary approval?

B: Select Committees

An account of the genesis of the reforms of the Select Committee system can be found in Chapter 1 of G. Drewry (ed.), *The New Select Committees* (2nd edn, 1989).

First Report from the Liaison Committee

HC 323 of 1996–97, paras 8–16

Powers to summon persons, papers and records

8. When the Departmental Select Committee system was established in 1979, it was acknowledged that committees' general powers to send for persons, papers and records did not extend to ordering the attendance of Ministers nor to the production of specific Government papers. In rejecting a recommendation of the Procedure Committee, that committees should be able to take the failure to provide papers automatically to the floor of the House, the then Leader of the House committed the Government to making available to committees as much information as possible and to giving the House an early opportunity to debate a matter on the floor of the House if the Government refused to provide information and that refusal was of serious concern to the House as a whole. These undertakings have been amplified in the intervening period.

9. The Public Service and Trade and Industry Committees in their recent Reports have made a number of specific recommendations about the powers of committees in this respect. In particular they called

- for committees to be given the power to order the attendance of Members of the House as witnesses in the same way as other witnesses can be summoned;
- for there to be 'a presumption that Ministers accept requests by committees that individual named civil servants give evidence to them'; and,
- in relation to papers, for the House to agree to a 1978 recommendation by the Procedure Committee for a procedure which would 'restore to select committees in certain specified circumstances the right, which formerly belonged to any backbencher, to move for an Address or an Order for a Return of Papers'.

10. The reports from individual Chairmen indicate that, with a few exceptions, there have not been any real difficulties in the current Parliament. Nonetheless there remains concern that the lack of specific powers leaves committees at a disadvantage in obtaining the fullest cooperation from Government.

Members

11. There have been a number of instances since 1979 when Members who are former Ministers have been unwilling or reluctant to appear before select committees to assist inquiries into matters for which they had previously been responsible. The Foreign Affairs Committee failed to persuade the former Prime Minister (Baroness Thatcher) to give evidence to its inquiry into the contract for the Pergau Dam. The Hon Member for Derbyshire South (Mrs Currie) initially refused to appear before the Agriculture Committee when it was investigating salmonella in eggs (although eventually she was prevailed upon

to appear). While it is the practice that Cabinet Ministers currently in post accept invitations to appear before committees, it has been suggested that Prime Ministers or former Prime Ministers should not be invited to give evidence in relation to their current or former responsibilities. We see no justification for any Minister or former Minister to decline to appear before a select committee undertaking an inquiry within its remit.

12. The House has recently decided that all of its Members are bound to give evidence to the Committee on Standards and Privileges. Its Standing Order provides that the Committee has power to order the attendance of any Member—and indeed to require that specific documents or records in the possession of a Member relating to its inquiries be laid before the Committee. We see a case for consistency in this regard although we doubt whether use of the power will be necessary. Its availability should be sufficient encouragement. Accordingly we recommend that all select committees should be given the powers contained in paragraph 6 of the orders of reference of the Committee on Standards and Privileges.

Civil Servants

13. Few cases have been documented of named officials being prevented from giving evidence to a select committee when invited to do so. In the present Parliament, the Foreign Affairs Committee was unable to procure evidence from the intelligence services in its inquiry into UK policy on weapons proliferation and arms control. There is also a reluctance on the part of Government concerning former civil servants giving evidence about their erstwhile responsibilities. In its inquiry into Arms to Iraq (the Supergun), the Trade and Industry Committee had difficulty in contacting former civil servants whom they would have wished to examine. The Head of the Civil Service has affirmed that when named civil servants are *summoned* to appear, they have a duty to attend although Ministers reserve the right to suggest that other civil servants also give evidence or to attend themselves in place of civil servants. We consider that, except where their personal conduct may be at issue and they may be subject to disciplinary proceedings, all civil servants should attend upon committees when invited and that Departments should assist in identifying their former staff where requested to do so to enable them to be called. It is unacceptable that committees should be denied access to civil servants whose knowledge of and involvement in Government activity is essential to a committee inquiry. We therefore endorse the recommendation of the Public Service Committee that there should be a presumption that Ministers accept requests by committees that individual named civil servants give evidence to them.

Provision of Documents

14. It is in the area of provision of documents that most difficulties have arisen. There is a basic problem facing committees in so far as they are not always aware of the information and documents available in Departments which are germane to their inquiries. Some Committees have complained of the difficulties in discerning the existence of documents. We conclude as the Procedure Committee did in its 1990 Report, that it should be the duty of Departments to ensure that select committees are furnished with any important information which appears to be relevant to their inquiries without waiting to be asked for it specifically.

15. In most but not all cases where specific problems have arisen it has been because papers were, or were alleged to be, sensitive, either politically, militarily or commercially. Frequently it has been possible to reach a reasonable compromise but this was not always the case. There are established arrangements under which committees may receive classified evidence—and indeed publish that evidence subject to agreement on sidelining (that is, excising the particularly sensitive passages from the published evidence). On occasions it has been helpful for committees to see particularly sensitive material under the 'crown jewels' procedure although some committees have misgivings about the restrictions thereby placed on their freedom to comment upon the evidence. There is evidence that Government is using outside experts more frequently to consider specialist subjects such as 'efficiency'. Such advice has been claimed as 'advice to Ministers' and thus denied to select committees. We believe this is unacceptable.

16. Since 1979, the Government has given a series of undertakings that time would be provided for debate in the fairly rare cases where there is disagreement about the provision of information or papers. It is clear that these undertakings are not entirely satisfactory in the rare cases where a committee needs access to a specific document but the Department concerned will not release it. There have been a significant number of cases where committees have been refused specific documents but the Government has not provided time for the subject to be debated. The onus should be shifted onto

the Government to defend in the House its refusal to disclose information to a select committee. A committee should be able to table and have debated a motion for the return of a specific document. A debate for an hour or so would enable the committee and the Government to set out their points of view and the House could decide the matter on a division. This procedure would be analogous to the one hour debate provided for in Standing Orders if nominations to select committees are opposed on the floor of the House. In practice we believe the existence of such a fall-back procedure would encourage a compromise to be reached before the matter had to be taken to the floor of the House. We recommend that Standing Orders be amended to provide that if the Chairman of a departmental select committee tables a motion on behalf of the committee that a specific document be laid before the committee the motion should be debated on the floor of the House within ten sitting days and brought to a conclusion after one hour.

NOTE: See the House of Commons' resolution p. 214, *ante*, which is incorporated in the *Ministerial Code*. Ministers should be open with Parliament, including its Select Committees, and should authorize their officials to attend as witnesses. The rules below, formerly known as the 'Osmotherly Rules', regulate what officials may say.

Departmental Evidence and Response to Select Committees

Cabinet Office (2005), paras 1–2, 9, 40–61, 65, 67–74, 79–92

1. INTRODUCTION

Status of the Guidance

1. This memorandum gives guidance to officials from Departments, their Agencies and NDPBs who may be called upon to give evidence before, or prepare memoranda for submission to, Parliamentary Select Committees. It replaces the January 1997 edition.

2. In providing guidance, the memorandum attempts to summarise a number of long-standing conventions that have developed in the relationship between Parliament, in the form of its Select Committees, and successive Governments. As a matter of practice, Parliament has generally recognised these conventions. It is important to note, however, that this memorandum is a Government document. Although Select Committees will be familiar with its contents, it has no formal Parliamentary standing or approval, nor does it claim to have.

...

Central Principles

9. Select Committees have a crucial role in ensuring the full and proper accountability of the Executive to Parliament. Ministers have emphasised that, when officials represent them before Select Committees, they should be as forthcoming and helpful as they can in providing information relevant to Committee inquiries. In giving evidence to Select Committees, as elsewhere, officials should be guided by the Government's Code of Practice on Access to Government Information and the Freedom of Information Act from January 2005. This point is reinforced in the Ministerial Code.

...

SECTION 3: ROLE OF OFFICIALS GIVING EVIDENCE TO SELECT COMMITTEES

General

40. Civil servants who give evidence to Select Committees do so on behalf of their Ministers and under their directions.

41. This is in accordance with the principle that it is Ministers who are accountable to Parliament for the policies and actions of their Departments. Civil servants are accountable to Ministers and are subject to their instruction; but they are not directly accountable to Parliament in the same way. It is for this reason that when civil servants appear before Select Committees they do so on behalf of their Ministers and under their directions because it is the Minister, not the civil servant, who is accountable to Parliament for the evidence given to the Committee. This does not mean, of course, that officials may not be called upon

to give a full account of Government policies, or indeed of their own actions or recollections of particular events, but their purpose in doing so is to contribute to the central process of Ministerial accountability, not to offer personal views or judgements on matters of political controversy (see paragraphs 54–55), or to become involved in what would amount to disciplinary investigations which are for Departments to undertake (see paragraphs 72–77).

42. This Guidance should therefore be seen as representing standing instructions to officials appearing before Select Committees. These instructions may be supplemented by specific Ministerial instructions on specific matters.

Summoning of Named Officials

43. The line of ministerial accountability means that it is for Ministers to decide which official or officials should represent them.

44. Where a Select Committee indicates that it wishes to take evidence from a particular named official, including special advisers, the presumption should be that Ministers will agree to meet such a request. However, the final decision on who is best able to represent the Minister rests with the Minister concerned and it remains the right of a Minister to suggest an alternative civil servant to that named by the Committee if he or she feels that the former is better placed to represent them. In the unlikely event of there being no agreement about which official should most appropriately give evidence, it is open to the Minister to offer to appear personally before the Committee.

45. Where a civil servant is giving evidence to a Select Committee for the first time, Departments will wish to ensure that they provide appropriate guidance and support. Committees may be willing to consider requests for individuals to be supported in oral evidence sessions by more experienced civil servants.

46. It has also been agreed that it is not the role of Select Committees to act as disciplinary tribunals (see paragraphs 73–78). A Minister will therefore wish to consider carefully a Committee's request to take evidence from a named official where this is likely to expose the individual concerned to questioning about their personal responsibility or the allocation of blame as between them and others. This will be particularly so where the official concerned has been subject to, or may be subject to, an internal departmental inquiry or disciplinary proceedings. Ministers may, in such circumstances, wish to suggest either that he or she give evidence personally to the Committee or that a designated senior official do so on their behalf. This policy was set out in the then Government's response to a report from the Public Service Committee on Ministerial Accountability and Responsibility (First Report, Session 1996–97, HC 67).

47. If a Committee nonetheless insists on a particular official appearing before them, contrary to the Minister's wishes, the formal position remains that it could issue an order for attendance, and request the House to enforce it. In such an event the official, as any other citizen, would have to appear before the Committee but, in all circumstances, would remain subject to Ministerial instruction under the terms of this Guidance, the Civil Service Code ...

Agency Chief Executives

50. Where a Select Committee wishes to take evidence on matters assigned to an Agency in its Framework Document. Ministers will, normally, wish to nominate the Chief Executive as being the official best placed to represent them. While Agency Chief Executives have managerial authority to the extent set out in their Framework Documents, like other officials they give evidence on behalf of the Minister to whom they are accountable and are subject to that Minister's instruction.

NDPBs

51. Departmental Select Committees have an important role in examining the expenditure, administration and policies of NDPBs. Members of NDPBs invited to give evidence should be as helpful as possible in providing accurate, truthful and full information, taking care to ensure that no information is withheld which would not be exempted if a parallel request were made under the FOI Act. Further guidance for members of NDPBs invited to give evidence to select Committees is set out in the Cabinet Office publication *Guidance on Codes of Practice for Board Members of Public Bodies*.

Parliamentary Privilege

52. Parliamentary proceedings are subject to absolute privilege, to ensure that those participating in them, including witnesses before select committees, can do so without fear of external consequences. This protection, enshrined in the Bill of Rights, is an essential element in ensuring that Parliament can exercise its powers freely on behalf of its electors. There must be no disciplinary action taken against civil servants or members of NDPBs (or anyone else) as a consequence of them giving evidence to a Select Committee. Any such action might be regarded as contempt of the House, with potentially serious consequences for those involved. [See Sixth Report of the Committee on Standards and Privileges, Session 2003–04, HC1055.]

SECTION 4: EVIDENCE TO SELECT COMMITTEES

4A. PROVISION OF EVIDENCE BY OFFICIALS: CENTRAL PRINCIPLES

General

53. The central principle to be followed is that it is the duty of officials to be as helpful as possible to Select Committees. Officials should be as forthcoming as they can in providing information, whether in writing or in oral evidence, to a Select Committee. Any withholding of information should be decided in accordance with the law and care should be taken to ensure that no information is withheld which would not be exempted if a parallel request were made under the FOI Act.

Accuracy of Evidence

54. Officials appearing before Select Committees are responsible for ensuring that the evidence they give is accurate. They will therefore need to be fully briefed on the main facts of the matters on which they expect to be examined. This can be a major exercise as a Committee's questions can range widely and can be expected to be testing. Should it nevertheless be discovered subsequently that the evidence unwittingly contained factual errors, these should be made known to the Committee, usually via the Clerk, at the earliest opportunity. Where appropriate, a correcting footnote will appear in the published transcript of the evidence.

Discussion of Government policy

55. Officials should as far as possible confine their evidence to questions of fact and explanation relating to government policies and actions. They should be ready to explain what those policies are; the justification and objectives of those policies as the Government sees them; the extent to which those objectives have been met; and also to explain how administrative factors may have affected both the choice of policy measures and the manner of their implementation. Any comment by officials on government policies and actions should always be consistent with the principle of civil service political impartiality. Officials should as far as possible avoid being drawn into discussion of the merits of alternative policies where this is politically contentious. If official witnesses are pressed by the Committee to go beyond these limits, they should suggest that the questioning should be referred to Ministers.

56. A Select Committee may invite specialist (as opposed to administrative) officials to comment on the professional or technical issues underlying government policies or decisions, This can require careful handling where Committees wish to take evidence from, for example, government economists or statisticians on issues which bear on controversial policy questions and which are also matters of controversy within the respective profession. Such specialists may find themselves in some difficulty if their own judgement on the professional issues has, or appears to have, implications that are critical of Government policies. It is not generally open to such witnesses to describe or comment upon the advice which they have given to Departments, or would give if asked. They should not therefore go beyond explaining the reasoning which, in the Government's judgement, supports its policy. The status of such evidence should, if necessary, be made clear to the Committee. If pressed for a professional judgement on the question the witness should, if necessary, refer to the political nature of the issue and, as above, suggest that the line of questioning be referred to Ministers.

NAO and PAC Reports

57. In those areas where the National Audit Office (NAO) and the Parliamentary Commissioner for Administration (the Parliamentary Ombudsman) have direct access to departmental papers, this does not itself confer a similar right of access on the Committees which they serve. In considering any request

from the Committee of Public Accounts (PAC) for such access, the Treasury should be consulted. Where the Public Administration Select Committee is taking evidence on Ombudsman issues, it may be necessary to quote from departmental papers in connection with particular Parliamentary or Health Service Commissioner cases. It is not however the practice of the Committee to require evidence which would amount to the 'retrial' of individual cases.

58. A departmentally-related Select Committee may, on occasion and with the agreement of the PAC, take up a NAO report and invite departmental evidence on it. The Government has confirmed that it has no objection to such an arrangement provided that it is not taken as implying any alteration in the Comptroller and Auditor General's remit or programme of work in support of the PAC, or in the procedures for consulting Departments on draft NAO reports. The conventions relating to departmentally-related Select Committee business, for example governing the choice of witnesses to represent Ministers and the form of the response to the Committee's report, should continue to apply in such cases. A full statement of these provisos is set out in the Government's response (Cm 1532) to recommendation (xlvi) of the Procedure Committee's 1990 Report on the Working of the Select Committee System.

Consulting Ministers on Evidence

59. Because officials appear on behalf of their Ministers, written evidence and briefing material should be cleared with them as necessary. It may only be necessary for Ministers to be consulted if there is any doubt among officials on the detail of the policy to be explained to the Committee, or on what information should be disclosed. However, as Ministers are ultimately accountable for deciding what information is to be given and for defending those decisions as necessary, their views should be sought if a question arises of withholding information which a Committee has asked for.

Inter-departmental Liaison

60. The subjects of inquiry by Select Committees may on occasion go beyond the responsibilities of the Department which they are responsible for monitoring. It is important in these cases that the Department with the predominant role should take the lead to ensure that the evidence given is co-ordinated and consistent. This will usually, but not invariably, be the Department which the Committee in question has a remit to 'shadow'. If the subject under inquiry is one under which no Department can be said to have a predominant role, it may be necessary for a central co-ordinating office, such as the Cabinet Office, to act as lead Department and, for example, to submit the Government's written evidence; that will, however, be the exception rather than the rule.

61. In such cases it is clearly desirable for all the Departments concerned, in accordance with normal working practice, to be kept in touch on the preparation of evidence and on the subsequent response to the Committee's Report. Very often there will be co-ordinating machinery in place for the subject already but Liaison Officers also have an important role here and should always be informed of requests for evidence involving other Departments.

...

Ministerial Statements

65. Wherever possible, Committees should be given advance notice of impending Ministerial statements on matters which are relevant to their current inquiries. A convenient method if the Minister is making the statement in Parliament is by way of notification to the Clerk at the same time as the Whips inform the Opposition, which is normally at noon on the day of the statement. This notification to the Clerk should be of the fact that the statement is to be made but should not include the text of the statement itself. If the statement is to be made other than in the House, similar arrangements should apply, and should continue to be observed during the Parliamentary Recess or after dissolution of Parliament (see paragraph 39).

...

4B. PROVISION OF INFORMATION

General

67. Although the powers of Select Committees to send for 'persons, papers and records' relating to their field of enquiry are unqualified, there are certain long-standing conventions on the provision of information which have been observed in practice by successive administrations on grounds of public policy.

68. The Government is committed to being as open and as helpful as possible with Select Committees. The presumption is that requests for information from Select Committees will be agreed to. Where a Department feels that it cannot meet a Committee's request for information, it should make clear its reasons for doing so, if appropriate in terms similar to those in the Freedom of Information Act (without resorting to explicit reference to the Act itself or to section numbers). Where a department feels it cannot disclose information in open evidence sessions or in memoranda submitted for publication, Departments will wish to consider whether the information requested could be provided on a confidential basis. These procedures are described in paragraphs 85 to 92 below.

Excessive Cost

69. Although the provisions under the Code for charging applicants do not apply in the case of Select Committees, it may occasionally prove necessary to decline requests for information which would involve the Department in excessive cost or diversion of effort. Ministers should always be consulted on their priorities in such cases.

70. Requests for named officials who are serving overseas to attend to give evidence should not be refused on cost grounds alone if the official concerned is the person best placed to represent the Minister. Committees will generally be willing to arrange for such witnesses to give evidence on a mutually acceptable date. Evidence by video link is an alternative that should also be explored with the Committee.

Matters which may be *sub judice*

71. Committees are subject to the same rules by which the House regulates its conduct in relation to matters awaiting the adjudication of the courts (although the bar on debating such matters may be lifted if a Committee is meeting in closed session). If a matter already before the courts is likely to come up for discussion before a Committee at a public session, the Clerk will usually be aware of this and will draw the attention of the Chairman to the relevant rules of the House. Nonetheless, if a Department has reason to believe that such matters may arise, the Liaison Officer may wish to check with the Clerk that the Committee is also aware. It should be noted, however, that the Committee Chairman has an overriding discretion to determine what is appropriate in the hearing of evidence.

72. Officials should take care in discussing or giving written evidence on matters which may become the subject of litigation but which, at the time, do not strictly come under the rules precluding public discussion of sub judice questions. Such caution should be exercised whether or not the Crown is likely to be a party to such litigation. If such matters seem likely to be raised, officials should first consult their departmental legal advisers or the Treasury Solicitor on how to handle questions which might arise. In any case of doubt about the extent to which details may be disclosed of criminal cases, not currently sub judice, the Law Officers are available for consultation. Similar considerations apply in cases where a Minister has or may have a quasi-judicial or appellate function, for example in relation to planning applications and appeals.

Conduct of Individual Officials

73. Occasionally questions from a Select Committee may appear to be directed to the conduct of individual officials, not just in the sense of establishing the facts about what occurred in making decisions or implementing Government policies, but with the implication of allocating individual criticism or blame.

74. In such circumstances, and in accordance with the principles of Ministerial accountability, it is for the Minister to look into the matter and if necessary to institute a formal inquiry. Such an inquiry into the conduct and behaviour of individual officials and consideration of disciplinary action is properly carried out within the Department according to established procedures designed and agreed for the purpose, and with appropriate safeguards for the individual. It is then the Minister's responsibility to inform the Committee of what has happened, and of what has been done to put the matter right and to

prevent a recurrence. Evidence to a Select Committee on this should be given not by the official or officials concerned, but by the Minister or by a senior official designated by the Minister to give such evidence on the Minister's behalf.

...

Papers of a Previous Administration

79. There are well established conventions which govern the withholding of policy papers of a previous Administration from an Administration of a different political complexion. These were set out in a Parliamentary answer from the Prime Minister on 24 January 1980 (Official Report, Columns 305–307). Since officials appear before Select Committees as representatives of their Ministers, and since Select Committees are themselves composed on a bipartisan basis, it follows that officials should not provide a Committee with evidence from papers of a previous Administration which they are not in a position to show to their present Ministers. If such evidence is sought, Ministers should be consulted. Where Ministers propose to make an exception, it would be necessary to consult a representative of the previous Administration before either showing the papers to present Ministers or, with Ministers' authority, releasing information from them to a Committee.

4C. STATUS AND HANDLING OF EVIDENCE

Status of Evidence

House of Commons

80. Once information has been supplied to a Committee it becomes 'evidence' and, subject to any agreement with the Committee on the non-publication of protectively marked information (paragraphs 85–92), it is entirely up to the Committee whether or not to publish it and report it to the House. Certain rules apply to the further public use of such evidence by the Government prior to its publication by the Committee. Departments should be careful to observe these rules as failure to do so could amount to a breach of Parliamentary privilege. Committees are usually helpfully flexible in applying the rules but, in cases of doubt, Departments should consult the relevant Committee Clerk for guidance.

81. The basic rule is a Commons resolution of 1837 which states that '... the evidence taken by any Select Committee of this House, and Documents presented to such Committee, and which have not been reported to the House, ought not to be published by any Member of such Committee or any person'. This Resolution still stands but is now subject to important modifications which give Committees power to authorise witnesses to publish the memoranda of evidence they have submitted (Commons Standing Order No. 135) and which permit the publication of evidence given in public session before it is formally reported to the House (Commons Standing Order No. 136). Many Committees now agree to a resolution giving permission to witnesses to publish their evidence, either generally or in respect of a specific inquiry.

82. The practical implications of these rules for Departments are as follows:

Oral evidence given in public session. There is no constraint on Departments using or repeating the substance of material given in public evidence sessions but verbatim transcripts of oral evidence (advance proof copies of which will be sent by the Clerk to Departments for checking) should not be copied to third parties until they have been published by the Committee. Uncorrected transcripts are now normally published on the Parliament website within a few days of the evidence session.

Oral evidence given in closed session. Evidence given in closed sessions should not be disclosed by Departments before the evidence (sidelined as appropriate) has been published by the Committee. Departments will not, of course, want to disclose the sidelined passages of their evidence to third parties in any event.

Unclassified memoranda. Memoranda provided in advance of an oral evidence session are usually published on the internet with the transcript of the oral evidence, and in due course with the Committee's report. Once they have been published, Departments are free to make copies available to third parties. If a Department wishes to make copies of their submitted memoranda available to third parties in advance of this, they must first obtain the permission of the Committee. The Committee itself will usually make copies available to the media at the time of the evidence session but Liaison Officers may wish to check this with the Clerk and brief their Press Office accordingly.

Classified (protectively marked) memoranda. Similar rules apply, but naturally with the same caveat as for oral evidence given in closed session.

House of Lords

83. House of Lords Committees treat evidence in a quite different way. Once received by the Committee, it is treated as being in the public domain unless other arrangements have been made. It may be reproduced freely, provided the fact that it was originally prepared for the Committee is acknowledged.

Comment on Evidence from other Witnesses

84. Evidence critical of a Department may be given in public session by witnesses outside the Department. This may prompt questions to the department by the media or others. Departments can of course respond to such questions. Departments may also wish to explore with the Clerk whether it would be appropriate to submit further evidence setting out the Department's position.

Providing Sensitive Information in Confidence

85. It is to the benefit of Committees in carrying out their task of scrutinising Government activities, and to Government in explaining its actions and policies, for sensitive information, including that carrying a protective security marking, to be provided from time to time on the basis that it will not be published and will be treated in confidence. Procedures have been developed to accommodate this.

86. When this arises, the Department should inform the Clerk that the information in question can be made available only on this basis, explaining the reasons in general terms. Such information should not be made available until the Committee has agreed to handle it appropriately, either by treating it wholly in confidence or by agreeing to publish it with a reasonable degree of sidelining (i.e. with the relevant passages omitted but with the location of the omissions indicated). It is important when submitting such information to make clear that the papers are provided in confidence and are not for publication. Information provided to Committees in confidence will be covered by Parliamentary privilege, and therefore will be exempt from release under FOI, but they will eventually be considered for release under the 30 year rule. In cases of particular sensitivity, Departments may wish to register a wish to be consulted before release. It should be appreciated, however, that once evidence is given to a Committee, whether in confidence or not, it becomes the property of the Committee, to deal with as it thinks fit.

Handling of Sensitive Information in Oral Evidence

87. It would clearly be inappropriate for any evidence which a Department wished to be treated as confidential to be given at a public session of the Committee. If it appears likely, therefore, that subjects to be discussed at a forthcoming public session are such that the witnesses would only be able to give substantive answers in confidence, the Department should write to the Chairman or the Clerk explaining why this is so. The Committee may then agree to take that part of the Department's evidence in closed session.

88. If, despite such an approach, a Committee questions an official witness in public session on confidential matters, or if such matters are raised unexpectedly, the official should inform the Committee that the questions could only be answered on a confidential basis. The Committee may then decide to go into closed session or request a confidential memorandum. It is not for the witness to suggest that the Committee should go into closed session as this is wholly a matter for the Committee to decide.

89. Where confidential evidence has been given in a closed session the witness should, at the end of the session, let the Clerk know which parts of the evidence these are. Pending the Committee's final decision on what they will agree to omit from the published version, the Clerk will send two copies of a full transcript to the Department. One copy is for retention; the other should be returned to the Clerk with those passages sidelined which contain sensitive information which, in the Department's judgment, it would not be in the public interest to publish.

90. Although Committees usually respect such requests for sidelining, they may occasionally challenge a particular request. Witnesses should therefore bear in mind when providing confidential memoranda,

or in giving evidence in private, that their evidence may be published unless there is a clear justification for sidelining. The final decision on publication rests with the Committee.

Handling of Sensitive Information in Written Evidence

91. Where information is submitted to a Committee on the understanding that it will be kept confidential, this understanding should be recorded in the covering letter forwarding the evidence to the Clerk. The letter should make clear whether the whole memorandum or, as is often the case, particular sections are to be kept confidential. The confidentiality of the papers will also be taken into account when the information is being considered for disposal in future years.

92. An agreement was reached with the Liaison Committee in 1975 on the conditions under which classified information may be disclosed to Select Committees. This agreement still stands, the key points are as follows:

(a) Information marked TOP SECRET or SECRET will be restricted to those persons (in addition to the Clerk) to whom the Department has agreed to release it. In practice this will usually mean only the members of the Select Committee or of the Sub-Committee concerned and, in the case of a Sub-Committee, the Chairman of the main Committee in addition. The disclosure of information marked RESTRICTED or CONFIDENTIAL will be similarly limited except that, where it has been disclosed to members of Sub-Committees, it may also be made available to members of the main Committee concerned.
(b) The release of TOP SECRET information under these arrangements is subject to the personal approval of the responsible Minister in each case.
(c) Protectively marked information may also be disclosed to a Committee's Specialist Advisers provided they have security clearance in accordance with arrangements agreed with the Clerk of the House.
(d) Protectively marked memoranda (and the full transcripts of oral evidence containing classified information) will be made available to those authorised to see it only during Committee or Sub-Committee meetings and on request in the Committee Office. Members may not take protectively marked documents away with them.

NOTE: Occasionally witnesses may refuse to answer questions. The Social Security Select Committee had begun a general investigation into pension funds when the death of Mr Robert Maxwell led to disclosures about malpractice concerning the management of the Mirror Group Newspapers and the Maxwell Corporation pension funds. The Committee ordered the attendance of his sons Messrs Ian and Kevin Maxwell to question them in their capacity as trustees of the pension funds. When the Maxwells appeared before the Committee on 13 January 1992, each was accompanied by Queen's Counsel. The Maxwells declined to answer questions. The Committee reported on this matter to the House of Commons in HC 353 of 1991–92. However, their recommendation that the Maxwells be brought before the House for their refusal to answer the Committee's questions was not acted upon. It is likely that this was, in part, because of subsequent events.

The Maxwell brothers were arrested and charged with fraud on 18 June 1992. They were tried and, in early 1996, acquitted. Further charges were brought unsuccessfully against Kevin Maxwell.

■ QUESTION

Was the Committee's investigation of these particular pension funds appropriate given the inquiries conducted by the Serious Fraud Office?

NOTES

1. These rules have not been formally agreed to by Parliament.
2. Some witnesses do not attend when requested. Whilst committees have powers to call persons, backed by resolution of the House, there is a convention that MPs and Peers are not summoned to appear. The select committee dealing with transport has complained about occasions when they were not able to see witnesses despite having requested that they attend the committee. The committee issued two special reports on this in 2002. The first (HC 655 of 2001–02) concerned

Lord Birt who was acting as a special advisor to the Prime Minister. The Government made a general case against committees seeing advisors:

- If they had to appear before Select Committees and answer questions, advisers would be unwilling to take on the job.
- They are unpaid.
- If the Prime Minister's advisers were to appear before Select Committees the system of Cabinet Government would be undermined.
- The advice given by advisers to Ministers should be confidential.

But the Committee pointed out that in the past other advisors had given evidence. They could not compel Lord Birt's attendance because of the convention against compelling Peers to attend a select committee, and so they wished that the convention be modified as it was inappropriate for advisors to the Prime Minister and other Ministers to be able to avoid the committee. In the end the committee did not think Lord Birt was a significant advisor on the particular matter, but they were concerned about advisors in general and those advising the Prime Minister in particular, a point taken up by the Liaison Committee (HC 446 of 2003–04, para. 90).

The second report (HC 771 of 2001–02) concerned the failure of a Treasury Minister to appear before the committee during its inquiry into the London Underground to give evidence on the Public–Private Partnership financial arrangements. The committee felt that the Treasury was pushing this particular policy and so wished the House to make an order requiring a Treasury minister to give evidence to them on this matter.

The Government response to the report on Treasury ministers (HC 1241 of 2001–02) argued that it was inappropriate for the House to make the requested order as the Secretary of State for Transport speaks for the Government on transport matters and it is he who should appear before the committee on this matter. Treasury Ministers would appear on matters where they have responsibility and a Treasury Minister had appeared to give evidence on taxation policy in the transport committee's inquiry into the Ten-Year Plan for Transport in March 2002.

3. Prime Minister Blair had declined to attend committees, claiming precedent, but agreed in May 2002 to meet the Liaison Committee twice a year.

■ QUESTION

Which is more surprising, committees with a government majority seeking to compel a Minister to appear before them to give evidence, or the Government, despite its commitment to co-operation, resisting that particular claim with an argument founded on ministerial responsibility?

NOTE: An assessment of the first ten years of the working of the select committee system was carried out by the Procedure Committee, which judged it to be a success. A further ten years of experience led the Liaison Committee to repeat the verdict of success, but to make recommendations for reform in HC 300 of 1999–2000 (entitled *Shifting the Balance: Select Committees and the Executive*). One idea was to remove appointments to select committees from party political control through the whips or 'usual channels'. This particular proposal was rejected by the Government in its response (Cm 4734) and the reaction of the Leader of the House of Commons angered the Liaison Committee which subsequently took evidence from her and then issued a further report (HC 748 of 1999–2000, *Independence or Control?*). The report of the Hansard Society's Commission on Parliamentary Scrutiny (*The Challenge for Parliament: Making Government Accountable*) was published some 12 months later and the role of select committees was crucial in the extensive recommendations for reform to improve the holding of the Government to account. The issue became more topical when the Labour Party Chief Whip did not propose two Labour MPs to the select committees which they had chaired in the two previous Parliaments. It was perceived that these MPs were regarded as too independent and their committees had been robust in holding Labour Ministers to account in the 1997–2001 Parliament. When the nominations to select committees were voted upon in the Commons, the two MPs were restored to the committees and subsequently re-elected by their fellow committee members to chair them again.

When he was Leader of the House of Commons, Robin Cook was perceived as being sympathetic to reform and he chaired the select committee on Modernisation of the House of Commons. He published a memorandum to that committee outlining some ideas on reform of the Commons in general (HC 440 of 2001–02). This committee then produced some proposals on reform of the select committees.

First Report from the Select Committee on Modernisation of the House of Commons

HC 224 of 2001–02, pp. 1–2

List of recommendations

1. [Paragraph 15]—We recommend that at the start of each Parliament the Committee of Nomination should be set up under the Chairman of Ways and Means. The Chairman of Ways and Means should chair proceedings, but in order to preserve the impartiality of his office have no vote.

2. [Paragraph 16]—We recommend that appointment to the Chairmen's Panel must remain firmly in the hands of the Speaker and not subject to any party interest or lobbying.

3. [Paragraph 17]—We recommend that membership of the Committee of Nomination should be prescribed in Standing Orders. We recommend that the Committee of Nomination should consist of the Chairman of Ways and Means and nine other members:

Seven Members of the Chairmen's Panel chosen with broad regard to the party balance, reflecting gender balance and based on length of service as Members of the Panel. Those seven would consist of:

- the four most senior Members of the Government party on the Panel including the most senior woman Member of that party;
- the two most senior Members of the official Opposition on the Panel, including the most senior woman Member of that party; and
- the most senior Member of the second largest opposition party on the Panel;
- the most senior back-bencher on the Government side of the House; and the most senior back-bencher on the opposition benches.

The quorum of the Committee when nominating committees afresh at the start of a Parliament should be six, and three when filling subsequent vacancies, not including the Chairman of Ways and Means. In the unavoidable absence of the Chairman of Ways and Means the First Deputy Chairman or in his or her absence the Second Deputy Chairman shall act as chairman.

4. [Paragraph 25]—We recommend that the proposed allocation between parties of the posts of chairmen of select committees should be reported to the Committee of Nomination.

5. [Paragraph 28]—We recommend that the House of Commons Commission should make available the necessary funds for a central unit of specialist support staff to be in place in the next financial year.

6. [Paragraph 29]—We recommend that the National Audit Office be invited to help assess the need for specialist and other support staff for select committees and to advise on how this could best be provided, and that the House of Commons Commission should look favourably on funding for staffing increases which may be proposed.

7. [Paragraph 30]—We recommend that within the Committee Office there should be sufficient staff to assist with the function of supporting the administrative workload of the select committee chairmen.

8. [Paragraph 33]—We recommend that there should be an agreed statement of the core tasks of the departmental select committees.

9. [Paragraph 34]—We recommend the following model as an illustration of what we would regard as the principal objectives of departmental select committees:

'It shall be the duty, where appropriate, of each select committee:

to consider major policy initiatives

to consider the Government's response to major emerging issues

to propose changes where evidence persuades the Committee that present policy requires amendment

to conduct pre-legislative scrutiny of draft bills

to examine and report on main Estimates, annual expenditure plans and annual resource accounts

to monitor performance against targets in the public service agreements
to take evidence from each Minister at least annually
to take evidence from independent regulators and inspectorates
to consider the reports of Executive Agencies
to consider, and if appropriate report on, major appointments by a Secretary of State or other senior ministers
to examine treaties within their subject areas.'

10. [Paragraph 34]—We recommend that select committees should experiment with appointing one of their number as a rapporteur on a specific task, such as for example financial scrutiny.

11. [Paragraph 35]—We recommend that as part of the process of producing an annual report each departmental select committee should submit to the Liaison Committee a statement of how it has met each core task in the scrutiny of its department.

12. [Paragraph 36]—We recommend that, in the light of the recommendations of the Joint Committee on Parliamentary Privilege, this limitation on the power to require witnesses to give evidence should be reviewed by the appropriate committees of both Houses.

13. [Paragraph 37]—We recommend that the investigative select committees should be named 'scrutiny committees'.

14. [Paragraph 39]—We recommend that there should be a Scrutiny Liaison Committee including the chairmen of the scrutiny committees, and also the chairmen of those committees which have a legislative or procedural role such as Deregulation and Regulatory Reform, Procedure, and Standards and Privileges.

15. [Paragraph 41]—We recommend that the value of a parliamentary career devoted to scrutiny should be recognised by an additional salary to the chairmen of the principal investigative committees.

16. [Paragraph 43]—We recommend that the House should impose an indicative upper limit of two consecutive Parliaments on service as chairman. We recognise that the House may wish to make special provision in the case of short Parliaments.

17. [Paragraph 47]—We recommend that the standard size of departmental scrutiny committees should be fifteen.

18. [Paragraph 49]—We recommend that the scrutiny committees should have the right to report to the Committee of Nomination any member who has a record of poor attendance without good cause and that the Committee of Nomination should have the right to replace that member.

19. [Paragraph 50]—We recommend a reduction in size of the membership and of the quorum of select committees where there has been a persistent problem securing attendance.

20. [Paragraph 53]—We recommend that the Committee Office procures the services, either on a consultancy or a salaried basis, of experts in design and layout to ensure that reports benefit from the most modern technology and the most attractive design.

21. [Paragraph 56]—We recommend that Notes for Visitors should be prepared, setting out in plain language the nature of the proceedings, and that where practical this should be supplemented on the day with guidance on the topics under discussion.

22. [Paragraph 57]—We recommend that all reports of select committees should be eligible for debate in Westminster Hall after the closure of the two month period within which Government is expected to publish its response, whether or not such a response has been tabled.

NOTES

1. The Liaison Committee has commented on these proposals and, on the whole, given them strong support (HC 692 of 2001–02). The Liaison Committee was pleased that the Modernisation Committee had adopted its ideas of giving better resources, including the creation of a group of

officials with specialist skills who could be called upon by select committees, and that the role of chairing committees be recognized as important to the extent that it could be regarded as an alternative career to that of Government Minister gaining the administrative support and additional salary which Ministers enjoy. On a free vote the House of Commons did not accept the proposal to reduce the influence of the whips in determining the membership of select committees (see HC Deb, Vol. 385, cols 648–730, 14 May 2002).

2. It is clear that the Hansard Society's report *The Challenge for Parliament: Making Government Accountable* has influenced the Modernisation Committee's proposals. The Hansard Society, which was chaired by a former Conservative Minister, whose posts included being Leader of the House of Commons, wanted all backbench MPs to serve on a committee but the Modernisation Committee proposed an increase of the standard membership from 11 to 15. The Liaison Committee did not think that there were enough members willing to serve on committees, that there could be problems in maintaining the party ratios in the expanded committees, that it would militate against the cohesiveness of the committees, and that there could be accommodation problems.
3. The Liaison Committee approved the idea of core tasks but wished to see included the systematic follow-up of previous reports. These ideas were also suggested by the Hansard Society: *The Challenge for Parliament: Making Government Accountable* (2001).

New core tasks were agreed for select committees as follows.

First Report from the Liaison Committee

HC 558 of 2002–03, pp. 34–36

ANNEX 1

Departmental Select Committee Objectives And Tasks: An Illustrative Template

OBJECTIVE A: TO EXAMINE AND COMMENT ON THE POLICY OF THE DEPARTMENT

Task 1: To examine policy proposals from the UK Government and the European Commission in Green Papers, White Papers, draft Guidance etc, and to inquire further where the Committee considers it appropriate

This calls for more systematic scrutiny of proposals made. It is not intended to involve formal written or oral evidence as a matter of course, but to ensure that a Committee is at least apprised of proposals and has the opportunity to consider whether detailed scrutiny of them should form part of their programme of work.

Departments must ensure that Committees are informed directly of policy proposals and provided with the necessary documentation, rather than waiting to be asked.

****

Task 2: To identify and examine areas of emerging policy, or where existing policy is deficient, and make proposals

This calls for Committees to identify areas where, based on judgement of Members, views of others etc, a Committee inquiry would be worthwhile.

Ministers must be prepared to give proper consideration to policy proposals from committees. This may involve revision of the practice on instant reaction/rebuttal.

****

Task 3: To conduct scrutiny of any published draft bill within the Committee's responsibilities

This calls for Committees to commit time for necessary oral evidence and reporting, subject to its timetable for other inquiries.

Ministers must ensure that committees are warned early on the likely appearance of draft bills: must consult with committee chairmen on how they are to be handled: and must allow a decent time for committee consideration.

****

Task 4: To examine specific output from the department expressed in documents or other decisions

This calls for a formal framework for being informed of secondary legislation, circulars and guidance, treaties and previously identified casework decisions, so that they can if needed be drawn to a Committee's attention.

Departments will have to engage in co-operative discussions with committee staff on the best means of ensuring that committees are kept abreast of such outputs.

****

OBJECTIVE B: TO EXAMINE THE EXPENDITURE OF THE DEPARTMENT

Task 5: To examine the expenditure plans and out-turn of the department, its agencies and principal NDPBs

This calls for a systematic framework for committee scrutiny of the Department's Main and Supplementary Estimates: its expenditure plans; and its annual accounts.

Departments will as a matter of course have to produce more explanatory material on financial matters, eg on Supplementary Estimates, underspends etc

****

OBJECTIVE C: TO EXAMINE THE ADMINISTRATION OF THE DEPARTMENT

Task 6: To examine the department's Public Service Agreements, the associated targets and the statistical measurements employed, and report if appropriate

This calls for an established cycle of written scrutiny and annual reporting of results.

Ministers must be prepared to be genuinely responsive to committee concerns on PSAs etc

****

Task 7: To monitor the work of the department's Executive Agencies, NDPBs, regulators and other associated public bodies

This calls for a systematic cycle of scrutiny of annual reports. It does not require either written or oral evidence except where a Committee judges it to be necessary.

The bodies concerned must ensure that their accountability to Parliament is recognised by full and regular provision of information, including annual reports and other publications.

****

Task 8: To scrutinise major appointments made by the department

This would call for scrutiny of all major appointments made.

Departments would have to systematically notify committees in advance of all major appointments pending and/or made.

****

Task 9: To examine the implementation of legislation and major policy initiatives

This would call for a framework of detailed annual progress reports from departments on Acts and major policy initiatives so that committees could decide whether to undertake inquiry.

Ministers must be more willing to provide for annual reports on particular pieces of legislation, and departments to provide detailed annual reports on identified policy areas or initiatives.

OBJECTIVE D: TO ASSIST THE HOUSE IN DEBATE AND DECISION

Task 10: To produce Reports which are suitable for debate in the House, including Westminster Hall, or debating committees.

This could call for committees to come to an explicit view when deciding on an inquiry as to whether a debate was in due course envisaged.

****

4. The Liaison Committee report for 2003 (HC 446 of 2003–04) shows how the select committees have worked in the first full calendar year since the 2002 reforms in relation to their tasks, working practices, and resources. Amongst the core tasks they were enthusiastic about the scrutiny of draft bills recommending at para. 29:

> While expressing pleasure in the step change towards greater pre-legislative scrutiny, we call on the Government to continue to produce an increasing number of bills in draft form; to have a working assumption that existing departmental select committees are usually the most appropriate means by which draft bills can be scrutinised, unless there are compelling reasons for an alternative approach, such as reluctance by the committee because of its existing programme, or the wish to include a wider range of Members from both Houses; to provide realistic timescales for the scrutiny of draft bills; and to co-operate fully with chairmen and committee secretariats.

In terms of working practices the report details examples of innovation, including the creation of sub-committees, the gathering of information using video-links and on-line consultation, the holding of a special conference, and the seeking out of the views of young people. On resources the report notes that in January 2004 the Scrutiny Unit reached its full staffing complement of seven core staff and ten specialists (accountants, statisticians, lawyers, audit and policy experts). The unit provides specialist assistance to committees on expenditure matters and the consideration of draft bills, and provides some extra capacity to cope with surges of work or periods of staffing shortages. There had also been a review of select committee resources and the House of Commons Commission had agreed that resources should be increased to match the committees' greater workload. Some additional specialists had been appointed and each departmental select committee should get 1.5 extra members of staff to assist with inquiry management and administrative functions.

The report also pointed out that the co-operation which government gave to select committees could still be improved. The Hutton Inquiry had greater access to papers and persons than committees. The committee reiterated concern about:

- access to No. 10 policy advisers;
- availability of current policy reviews and reports;
- evidence on 'joined-up' policies from Government departments involved, including HM Treasury.

The Prime Minister and the Leader of the House of Commons both undertook that the Government would review the 'Osmotherly rules' (see pp. 234–241, *ante*).

The committee reiterated its concern that whilst there had been an improvement the Government was not meeting its commitment to respond to committees' reports within 60 days.

■ QUESTION

Is the proposed de-politicization of the arrangements, through the reduction of the influence of the Whips and the promotion of committee chairmanship as an alternative to a ministerial career, and the reforms in resources and working practices of select committees, out of keeping with the traditional 'government through and not by Parliament' culture?

C: The floor of the House of Commons

The passage of legislation, which is considered, *post*, at p. 276, is the activity which takes up a significant amount of time for business in the House of Commons. In the 2007–08, 2008–09 and 2009–10 sessions it accounted for 40 per cent, 36 per cent, and 30 per cent of time in the Commons. In the following table we can see how the rest of the time was spent.

Public Information Office, House of Commons Sessional Information Digest 2007–2008, 2008–2009, 2009–2010, pp. 1–2

Analysis of the time of the session			
Types of Business	Total time spent (hours:minutes)		
	2007–08	2008–09	2009–10
1. Addresses, other than Prayers (including debate on Queen's Speech)	37:42	31:35	37:57
4. Government motions			
a) European Community Documents	5:35	5:32	0:14
b) Business Motions	10:36	1:55	3:55
c) General	64:35	39:00	21:52
5. Opposition Motions			
a) Opposition Days	125:22	127:18	36:17
6. Private Members' Motions (substantive)	2:54	8:12	0.46
7. Adjournment			
a) Government debates on motions for the Adjournment	99:16	100:01	24:13
b) Topical Debates	35:42	16:12	7:43
c) Daily (at end of business)	82:40	69:17	34:54
d) Emergency debates (SO No. 24)	3:14	00:00	00:00
e) Last day before Recesses	16:12	15:55	5:37
Estimates	19.21	13:41	11:10
Oral Questions	112:57	91:37	46:52
Topical Questions	1:16	21:45	12:19
Urgent Questions		4:05	5:03
Statements	75:37	65:08	24:52
Business statements	30:6	24:59	11:57
SO No. 24 Applications	00:09	0:07	0:00
Points of Order and Speaker's Rulings	6:50	10:48	5:22
Presentation of Public Petitions	4:24	3:02	3:04
Daily Prayers	13:25	10:54	5:38
Miscellaneous (including suspension of proceedings of the House)	21:06	12:19	5:03

NOTES

1. The General Election in May 2010 meant that the 2009–10 session was shorter than average.
2. SO No. 24 refers to Standing Order No. 24 (previously SO 20) which is a procedure under which there is an adjournment of the House in order to discuss an urgent and important matter. It is considered, *post*, at pp. 260–261.

(i) Debate

R. Blackburn and A. Kennon, *Griffith & Ryle on Parliament Functions, Practice and Procedures*

(2003), p. 286

...The process of debate, as established by basic procedures... is the main process used for most of the House's business—but not all; it is not used in questions or ministerial statements, or in select committee proceedings, for example. The process is essentially simple: a motion is made ('That this House approves...'); a question is proposed by the Chair in the same form; debate arises; the question is put; it is agreed to or negatived; if agreed a resolution (expressing an opinion) or an order (requiring action by the House, or a committee or individual Members or officers) results. There are all sorts of variations or modern qualifications of this basic process; amendments may be moved on which a question is again proposed and each amendment must be disposed of separately, before the main question (as amended if it has been) is put; there may be amendments to amendments; some motions may not, by standing order, be amended or others may not be debated; debate on motions or amendments may be adjourned; debate may be closured; and motions or amendments may be withdrawn. But the essentials are plain; only one motion is considered at a time and in the end all motions (and amendments) must either be agreed to, negatived, or withdrawn.

The logic of this procedure is binary. Decisions are taken in sequence, singly, and each decision on each motion and each amendment is a simple 'yes' or 'no.' With a few exceptions there are no qualified majorities:

(i) 100 members must vote in the majority for a closure to be effective.
(ii) If a division shows that fewer than 40 Members are present, the business concerned stands over until another day.
(iii) 20 or more Members can block a motion to refer a bill to a second reading committee (and thereby insist on second reading on the floor of the House).

There is no requirement on any question for an absolute majority, and, as we will see, there are not even any procedures for registering abstentions in a division. This binary process is mirrored in—or is a reflection of—the two-sided, confrontational nature of the House's proceedings.... The systematic logic of these procedures protects the clarity of decision taking.

P. Norton, *The Commons in Perspective*

(1981), p. 119

[G]eneral debates are nevertheless not without some uses in helping to ensure a measure of scrutiny and influence, however limited. A debate prevents a Government from remaining mute. Ministers have to explain and justify the Government's position. They may want to reveal as little as possible, but the Government cannot afford to hold back too much for fear of letting the Opposition appear to have the better argument. The involvement of Opposition spokesman and backbenchers ensures that any perceived cracks in the Government's position will be exploited. If it has failed to carry its own side privately, the Government may suffer the embarrassment of the publicly expressed dissent of some of its own supporters, dissent which provides good copy for the press. On some occasions, Ministers may even be influenced by comments made in debate. They will not necessarily approach an issue with closed minds, and will normally not wish to be totally unreceptive to the comments of the Opposition (whose co-operation they need for the efficient despatch of business) or of their own Members (whose support they need in the lobbies, and among whom morale needs to be maintained); a Minister who creates a good impression by listening attentively to views expressed by Members may enhance his own prospects of advancement. The likelihood of a Minister's being influenced may be greatest when he is at the despatch box. Though the House may be nearly empty for much of a debate, it fills up during the front-bench speeches, and this is when the atmosphere of the House becomes important. A Minister faced by a baying Opposition and silence behind him may be unnerved and realise that he is not carrying Members on either side with him, and in consequence may moderate or even, in extreme cases, reverse his position. On such an occasion, the debate-vote relationship may become important, the fear of defeat concentrating the minds of Ministers. A recent example of such a debate was that on Members' pay in 1979, when the Leader of the House, Norman St John-Stevas, received such a rough reception at the despatch box that the Cabinet realised it did not have the support of the House and changed its previous decision.

In addition, debates may act as useful channels for the expression of views held by the general interests and specific bodies represented by Members. If a Member with a known constituency interest in a certain subject rises to speak, he will invariably be listened to with greater respect than one who seeks solely to score party political points, and may even have some influence on the Minister's thinking; all MPs—Ministers and backbenchers—represent constituencies, and will normally have at least a degree of empathy for a Member seeking conscientiously to defend the interests of his constituents.

NOTE: Debates may be on motions proposed by the Government, the Opposition and the various committees of the House. The following extracts are taken from the debate on the second reading of the Bill when general principles are usually discussed.

House of Commons, HC Deb

Vol. 375, cols 21–29, 19 November 2001

Orders of the Day

Anti-terrorism, Crime and Security Bill

[Relevant documents: First Report from the Home Affairs Committee, Session 2001–02, on the Anti-terrorism, Crime and Security Bill, HC351.

Second Report from the Joint Committee on Human Rights, Session 2001–02, on the Anti-terrorism, Crime and Security Bill, HL Paper 37/HC 372.]

Order for Second Reading read.

3.30 pm

MR DOUGLAS HOGG (SLEAFORD AND NORTH HYKEHAM): On a point of order, Mr Speaker. As you know, a timetable motion has been tabled on which we shall vote later, at least under the deferred procedure. So many hon. Members wish to speak that you have felt it necessary to impose a 10-minute limit on Back-Bench speeches. There is genuine anxiety about the timetable. Will you consider not putting the Question on the timetable motion unless and until the Home Secretary makes a statement to explain why two days are deemed sufficient?

MR SPEAKER: If the motion is on the Order Paper and is moved, I must put the Question.

SIMON HUGHES (SOUTHWARK, NORTH AND BERMONDSEY): On a point of order, Mr Speaker. After the Second Reading debate and the vote on the timetable, we will consider a motion, which has an hour and a half for debate, on whether to support and agree to this country's derogation from article 5 of the European convention on human rights.

Last week, my hon. Friend the Member for North Cornwall (Mr Tyler) wrote to the Leader of the House to ask whether discussion of the derogation could wait until we had completed our consideration of the Bill. That would enable us properly to consider the need for the derogation. This afternoon, there is a debate in the House of Lords about whether such consideration should happen at the end of the Bill's passage through both Houses.

May I, through you, ask a Minister to explain whether the Government are willing to accept that logical proposal? If they are, we would not have to spend a lot of time today arguing about whether to pull out of an article of the human rights convention when it may be rendered unnecessary by Parliament amending the Bill.

MR SPEAKER: That matter could be explained during the debate that we are about to hold.

Before we proceed, I point out that the right hon. and learned Member for Sleaford and North Hykeham (Mr Hogg) was right to say that there is a 10-minute limit on Back-Bench speeches ...

THE SECRETARY OF STATE FOR THE HOME DEPARTMENT (MR DAVID BLUNKETT): I beg to move, That the Bill be now read a Second time.

I thank all those—my advisers, officials and hon. Members, including my ministerial team—who have worked so diligently with me on the Bill. I should also like to put on record my thanks to the members of the Joint Committee on Human Rights and of the Select Committee on Home affairs for their speedy and diligent work.

It would be useful to deal with the question that the hon. Member for Southwark, North and Bermondsey (Simon Hughes) asked about the derogation from article 5 of the European convention on human rights. We believe that it is sensible to seek the consent of the House of Commons and the House of Lords because unless Parliament agrees to clauses 21 to 23 and associated provisions, which relate to detention, the need to seek a derogation from article 5 under article 15 will not arise. It is therefore sensible to have the provision in place. It will fall automatically if Parliament does not consent to the clauses that I mentioned.

SIMON HUGHES: Will the Home Secretary give way?

MR BLUNKETT: I shall, but I want to make a little progress afterwards. Obviously, I shall then give way to hon. Members.

SIMON HUGHES: I thank the Home Secretary for being as courteous on this matter as he has been throughout the proceedings so far. Will he reconsider the issue that he heard me raise earlier, and with which he has partially dealt? Does he accept that, by virtue of the order that the Government laid last week, there is a 40-day period within which the order is the law. At the end of the 40 days, it will lapse if Parliament does not agree to the proposal in both Houses. Given that the Government have the cover that they seek, is it not, in a sense, an abuse of the judgment of both Houses to assume that they will agree that the Bill should remain as it is, when there may be ways—following the Human Rights Committee's proposal—in which it could be amended to avoid derogation? In that case, the Government would not need the decisions of both Houses, the 40-day period would lapse in the normal way and the Government would not, to put it crudely, be putting the cart before the horse on a hugely important national and international legal obligation.

MR BLUNKETT: The 40-day period stands, but we do not agree that there is an alternative way of proceeding that would be acceptable to the Government; if there were, we would propose it. This issue will be the subject of the debate today, and of subsequent debates here and in the House of Lords. On that basis, we are seeking the consent of the House on derogation.

Circumstances and public opinion demanded urgent and appropriate action after the 11 September attacks on the World Trade Centre and the Pentagon. Many parliamentarians understandably demanded caution, proportionality and a response that would last for the future. Over the five weeks following the attacks, in which thousands of men and women lost their lives, it was the Government's task to appraise the measures that would be necessary to close loopholes and set aside anomalies that had developed over many years in existing legislation. We therefore took our time in preparing the statement of 15 October, which laid out precisely the kind of measures that I am proposing this afternoon. I make no apology for having taken another five weeks to come to the House with these measures, which required consideration. Given the need to put in place safeguards that could be required any day and at any time.

I do not believe that 10 weeks is a hurried period. It is important to recognise that, in the first few weeks after 11 September, the emotional response to what had happened—the sight that people beheld and the hundreds of public service workers and volunteers who lost their lives trying to save the lives of others—could have evoked an immediate and, I would have thought, universal call for even more draconian measures than those that I am accused of introducing. It would have been wrong to do that. [*Interruption.*]

Conservative Members laugh, but it was understandable that the United States Government sought to pass their Patriot Act by 26 October, which they did and it has now received the signature of the President. It was appropriate for us to be more circumspect, and to bring to the House what we consider to be proportionate and reasonable measures.

MR HOGG: The right hon. Gentleman made the point that he has taken 10 weeks to contemplate the contents of the Bill. That was indeed right. Given that it was necessary for him to take 10 weeks, does he understand the anxiety in this place that we are being asked to pass the Bill—all 114 pages and 125 clauses of it—in two days beyond today? Surely that cannot be right.

MR BLUNKETT: I am not absolutely certain that the length of the debate and the scrutiny given to a Bill are one and the same thing. The length of the debate and our scrutiny of it depend on the availability of time to deal with the aspects of the Bill on which there is genuine disagreement. Disagreeing with something on which there is general approbation is entirely different. It seems to me that the time available in this House and the House of Lords will be used effectively and rightly to scrutinise those proposals that have already received public attention and on which there has been considerable comment.

MR KEVIN MCNAMARA (HULL, NORTH): My right hon. Friend will be aware that the time set aside for consideration in Committee, on Report and on Third Reading is roughly equivalent to four Committee sittings. Is that a proper way to deal with this most important legislation, the significance of which he has underlined, given that terrorism and other such Bills were considered for much longer? The Bill contains the embryo of five Bills.

MR BLUNKETT: I do not accept that it contains the embryo of five Bills. The measures are coherent, they deal with a threat of a particular nature, they were laid out on 15 October with one or two exceptions—Opposition Members pressed us on those, including that in respect of corruption—and they are before the House for agreement. If there were no emergency, if there had not been a terrorist attack and if there were no danger that not passing the Bill by the end of the year would put us at risk, I would not be introducing it in the first place.

MR EDWARD GARNIER (HARBOROUGH) rose—

MR ELFYN LLWYD (MEIRIONNYDD NANT CONWY) rose—

MR BLUNKETT: I shall give way once more, but then I must make progress so that we do not lose time for the debate that Members want. We must get on to arguing about the content.

MR GARNIER: I am most grateful to the Home Secretary for giving way a fourth time so early in his speech.

My right hon. and learned Friend the Member for Sleaford and North Hykeham (Mr Hogg) complained about the lack of parliamentary time to discuss the Bill following the 10-week gestation period. It was published only towards the end of last week, but it will complete its Commons stages by the beginning of next. That allows only a week for outside bodies to concentrate on its terms and lobby those in the House who are interested in its content and implications. Although the Home Secretary may be right that he spent 10 hard weeks drafting the Bill, surely those outside the House should have rather longer than a week to lobby Members and the Government on its content and effect.

MR BLUNKETT: But the debate has been going on for 10 weeks, and the detail was laid out on 15 October.

MR MARK FISHER (STOKE-ON-TRENT, CENTRAL): Not the detail of the Bill.

MR BLUNKETT: I am being substantially heckled by my hon. Friend. Does he want to intervene?

MR FISHER: I am most grateful to the Home Secretary. Surely he appreciates the distinction between the principles that he laid out on 15 October and the detail of the Bill. We are expected to scrutinise and pass law, and that law is based on the wording of the Bill. As the hon. and learned Member for Harborough (Mr. Garnier) said, outside bodies have only a week in which to consider the Bill and advise us. Surely the Home Secretary accepts the historical precedent that when the House acts quickly, it seldom acts wisely.

MR BLUNKETT: I have no intention of getting into conflict this afternoon, but, if I might say so, I had not noticed that the past 10 weeks were free of detailed comment by a range of lobbying organisations and individuals. [*Interruption.*] Yes, about the Bill, the nature of its content, the statement of 15 October and the work undertaken by the Human Rights Committee and the Home Affairs Committee over the past week, including detailed evidence given to them by the very groups to which my hon. Friend the Member for Stoke-on-Trent, Central (Mr Fisher) referred. Those groups clearly had a handle on the principle and the detailed substance of the Bill, and the Under-Secretary, my hon. Friend the Member for Stretford and Urmston (Beverley Hughes), and I were questioned in detail in those Committees on that content. The idea that people have been deprived of knowledge of the details or implications of the Bill does not bear thinking about.

I have certainly learned one thing. I believed that lobby groups and those connected with the law understood the existing provisions more fully than proves to be the case. I shall try to deal with that this afternoon, because what the Bill seeks to do is build on what is already there rather than transform or overturn it. If there is any confusion in the minds of those giving advice or lobbying Members, I hope that we shall be able to end it during the days ahead.

MR LLWYD: As a legal challenge to the Bill is highly likely, will the Home Secretary elaborate on his definition of a public emergency, and also explain why the United Kingdom is the only country subscribing to the European convention that considers such an emergency to exist?

MR BLUNKETT: I shall deal with the second point during my speech. I am well aware of the differences that exist not merely within countries that are signatories to the convention, but across the world. However, the definition of terrorism in the Terrorism Act 2000 and the article 15 provisions gave us precisely the power to act in circumstances envisaged by those who drew up both the European convention on human rights, as approved in 1953, and the European convention on refugees, as approved in 1951. They foresaw circumstances in which it would be necessary to take action to derogate—to suspend temporarily—a particular article or clause, in order to be able to act in a particular way to respond to what was happening. I am positing that the circumstances of 11 September and its aftermath are such that they warrant immediate action. An article in *The Times* on 15 September stated:

> 'Despite fine promises and emergency legislation, Britain is still home to hundreds of extremists who have made this country one of the centres for the violent transnational network that inspired and encouraged the barbarism in New York and Washington.'

That is just one of hundreds of statements that have been made over the past 10 weeks about what people perceive to be the situation in our country. Again and again, people—including people in the United States—have illustrated the real dangers that exist, and it is on that basis that I shall spell out today why we felt it necessary to act.

Let us recall for a moment not just what happened on 11 September, but what has happened since. Let us recall the interviews given and the video recordings made by bin Laden and the al-Qaeda group, which have spelt out their determination not simply to threaten once, but to threaten the civilian populations of the United States and those working with it. It is for that reason that we are proposing measures allowing us to take rational, reasonable and proportionate steps to deal with an internal threat and an external, organised terrorist group that could threaten at any time not just our population, but the populations of other friendly countries.

JEREMY CORBYN (ISLINGTON, NORTH): Does the Home Secretary accept that many people who are obviously appalled at what happened on 11 September believe that the answer is not to suspend traditional legal rights such as the right of access to courts in this country, but to use the criminal law against those planning or perpetrating criminal acts? Many people are deeply disturbed about this piece of emergency legislation, and believe that it will be no more effective than the Prevention of Terrorism (Temporary Provisions) Act 1974. Peace eventually came to Ireland through a political process, not a legal process.

MR BLUNKETT: I would take my hon. Friend's appeal more to heart if it were not for the fact that we are debating use of the very machinery that the House agreed, in 1997, to ensure that the legal process is followed and legal rights exist. I think that fundamental misunderstandings have arisen among lobby groups and others because of that point. In 1997, the House unanimously passed the Special Immigration Appeals Commission Act 1997, which established the commission. I would be interested to know whether any hon. Member would like to use their comments in debates on that legislation to contradict me now on this legislation. Does anyone wish to intervene? No hon. Member from either side of the House voted against that legislation, which was subsequently approved by the other place. It was approved not only because previous practice had been judged not to accord with the level of human rights that was needed and accepted at the end of the 20th century, but because, in November 1996, the then Government had lost the Chahal case, which considered the acceptability of the process being used to eject people from the United Kingdom. It was adjudged in the Chahal case that there had been improvements in the process, such as use of the three wise men and women, but it was also held that the process for ratifying the Home Secretary's power of certification for removal was not acceptable because the power infringed article 3 of the European convention on human rights. That is the nub of the issue. There is also no disagreement that the previous Government would have introduced the 1997 Act.

After the Chahal judgment, therefore, the House passed a measure that effectively provided judicial review of the Home Secretary's right to certificate the removal of an individual who is not a British national, but who is judged to be endangering national security or whose presence is not conducive to the public good.

MR HOGG: Will the right hon. Gentleman give way?

MR BLUNKETT: I shall give way in a moment, but I should like first to deal with what I consider to be a fundamental misunderstanding of our proposals. The question for hon. Members is, what did they think that the Special Immigration Appeals Commission and the judicial process would do? What cases was the commission to hear? Was it to hear cases in which there was judged to be a risk, or cases in which the presence of an individual was not conducive to the public good and the Home Secretary had heard evidence from the security and intelligence services and was prepared to act? The answer is yes; the commission was established to consider precisely those types of case. Nevertheless, the very judgment that led to the commission's establishment was the one that held that article 3 precluded us from sending people back to their death, to torture or to degrading treatment.

The current situation, therefore, is that evidence may be adduced by the security and intelligence services, the Home Secretary may believe that he or she is correct to issue a certificate and the Special Immigration Appeals Commission—SIAC—may judge that that belief is correct, but the Home Secretary cannot deport that person because of the risk to the person's life. That is, and has been, the situation. The difference now is that we want to ensure that people cannot continue to conduct or organise terrorism from this country.

MR HOGG: Will the right hon. Gentleman give way?

MR BLUNKETT: I shall give way in a moment, when I have finished making this point.

The issue for me to decide is whether I should seek an opt-out from the European convention, and then to opt-in again by using, I think, article 58; to say that individuals should be released although we have evidence which SIAC is prepared to uphold that warrants detention; or to seek to hold those individuals. It is the third choice that we are putting before the House this afternoon. If we were prepared to derogate, or if I were prepared to sign a certificate to send someone to their death because no third safe country was available, we would not be introducing the measure in this form. We are doing so precisely to avoid that eventuality. That is why—you will forgive me for mentioning this, Mr Speaker—I have been slightly depressed over the past day or two about how the case has been put, and how some in the media who know better have sought to mislead those who have no reason to know better because they were not present, did not see and could not read about the steps that led to the establishment of SIAC precisely to deal with the circumstances that I described.

MR HOGG: The right hon. Gentleman places great weight on the Special Immigration Appeals Commission. Surely he should remind the House that under the Act that established that commission, it is entitled to withhold from the detained person particulars of the reason why he is detained. Furthermore, the Law Officers of the Crown can appoint a representative for that person who is expressly stated not to be responsible to the persons whose interests he is appointed to represent. That is not a very good safeguard of rights.

MR BLUNKETT: The right hon. and learned Gentleman may make a judgment about whether that is acceptable to him, but it was acceptable to the whole House in 1997. Following a challenge in the courts in the case of Mullah Rehman, the Lords judged five weeks ago that both the process and the threshold of evidential base were acceptable and in line with what the House intended when it passed the Act unanimously in the first place.

DAVID WINNICK: Will my right hon. Friend give way?

MR BLUNKETT: I shall in two seconds—but first I shall answer the second element of the question.

The person who is adjudged to be a risk has the right to take on a legal advocate of his own. When the case reaches the point at which evidence is presented by the security and intelligence services the delivery of which—this is why SIAC was established—would put at risk the operation of the security services, and those working with them and for them, often covertly, an advocate from a list of advocates is provided, as in 1997 the House judged should happen, to allow evidence to be presented and the case on behalf of the person charged to be heard and properly dealt with legally. Then a right of appeal on a point of law to both the Court of Appeal and the House of Lords is provided in similar circumstances and with similar rights.

DAVID WINNICK: I take the view that in all circumstances the powers that my right hon. Friend is taking are necessary. I am not happy—no one could be—about what is happening, and I work on the assumption that several people have been allowed in who should never have been allowed in. Does my right hon. Friend accept that some of us who take that view are, despite his comments, worried about the lack of judicial review? If we introduce measures that no one likes, and people are to be locked up for reasons that we believe are justified, some form of judicial review—apart from what my right hon. Friend—has been explaining, is all the more necessary, and its existence would make me much happier.

MR BLUNKETT: We would have to return to anything that the House decides about extradition or asylum issues more generally. All that we seek to do in the Bill is to make clear what SIAC and the Lords believe to be the case. In the cases that have gone to SIAC since the Act was passed four years ago, judicial review has not been sought, because the operation of SIAC has been judged to constitute a judicial review of the Home Secretary's certification. That is the issue that we are dealing with and that is why SIAC was seen as a substantial improvement on what existed previously.

The issue this afternoon is whether it is right that we should hold people in circumstances where we cannot transfer them to a third safe country, where the country to which we originally sought to transfer them does not have extradition agreements and therefore where their lives would be at risk, or whether we should release them into the community. At issue is an enhanced risk, post-11 September, which we believe warrants our taking that difficult but balanced and proportionate step. In doing so, we will ensure that the House will annually reaffirm or otherwise the measure on detention. In any case, the derogation has a five-year life and is automatically a sunset clause.

I also wish to make it clear that we do not think that a debate of one and a half hours would be adequate should we have to seek reaffirmation of the provision under the affirmative procedure and, with the agreement of the Leader of the House, we would seek to provide a more extensive opportunity for debate.

MR ROBERT MARSHALL-ANDREWS (MEDWAY): My question is not intended to be pejorative, because I am genuinely interested in the answer. Does the Home Secretary accept that there is a sea of difference between SIAC being used to deal with issues of deportation—with all the problems that SIAC has as a review body—and its being used to review decisions to incarcerate and imprison, indefinitely, without trial and, indeed, without charge? If evidence exists against the people about whom we have heard, why are they not being charged and tried in this country?

MR BLUNKETT: If the evidence that would be adduced and presented in a normal court were available, of course we would use it, as we have done in the past. We are talking today about those who are adjudged to have committed, organised and supported and helped those involved in terrorism worldwide in the circumstances of 11 September. Those who drew up the European convention and the refugee convention could not have dreamt of the act that took place on 11 September, but they did envisage some act of that kind that would at some point require us to be able to take the necessary steps. That is why I am using article 15 to derogate from article 5, rather than seeking to withdraw altogether. If evidence could be presented that is not subject to the parameters that I laid out a moment ago, it would be used. I know that my hon. and learned Friend is a barrister and, as a non-lawyer, I always listen carefully to those who are—[Hon. Members: 'Airy-fairy ones?'] I listen carefully whether they are airy-fairy or not.

MR MARSHALL-ANDREWS: What about SIAC?

MR BLUNKETT: I am coming to SIAC. It was the establishment of SIAC and the judgment in the Rehman case that upheld the threshold required and the nature of the way in which the evidence should be presented that answer my hon. and learned Friend's question. The House accepted, and the House of Lords agreed, that in some cases the nature of the evidence from the security and intelligence services will be such that it would put at risk the operation of those services and the lives of those who act clandestinely to help them if that evidence were presented in normal open court. That is the measure of the proposals this afternoon.

NOTES

1. The major point in these extracts from the Second Reading debate on the Bill was the derogation from Art. 5(1) EHCR required because of the power conferred on the Home Secretary to detain those suspected of being international terrorists (*Chahal* v *UK* (1996) 23 EHRR 413, *Secretary of State for the Home Department* v *Rehman* [2001] UKHL 47, [2001] 3 WLR 877). The Human Rights (Designated Derogation) Order 2001 (SI 2001 No. 3644) was passed before the Act. See *A and Others* v *Secretary of State for the Home Department* (p. 495, *post*) for the quashing of the derogation order.
2. The Act does not exclude the SIAC from judicial review. An amendment made the SIAC a superior court of record, part of the High Court and therefore subject to the Court of Appeal which is the only body which can deal with a challenge to SIAC decisions.
3. MPs were concerned about the speed with which Parliament was required to consider the Bill. The House of Lords did reject some clauses and in order to get the Bill on to the statute book the Government (with its clear majority in the Commons) accepted some of the changes made in the Lords.

The Hansard Society, *The Challenge for Parliament: Making Government Accountable*

(2001), pp. 58–59

Principle 4—Restoring the centrality of the Commons' chamber

The floor of the House of Commons is the main public focus for activity at Westminster. However, attendance by MPs and the extent to which it dominates political debate has declined.

Recommendations

20. To improve the attendance and influence of the chamber its core tasks need to be refined and clarified. It should become the plenary session of the Parliament. (para. 4.27)

21. In order to reflect the importance attached to the select committee system, and not take MPs away from the chamber, one day each week should be devoted to committee activity. To reflect the importance of this work other parliamentary business should be arranged around the committees so that the chamber would not meet on this day. (para. 4.28)

22. In general, the chamber should have fewer lengthy debates. Opportunities for MPs to initiate short debates on substantive issues should be increased. Opposition parties should be able to trade some of their Opposition Days for the chance to call for a statement on a topical issue. (paras 4.30–4.32)

23. In addition, the Speaker should grant a greater number of Private Notice Questions each session. (para. 4.33)

24. MPs should have the ability to call for 'public interest debates' on issues of public concern on a cross-party basis. (para. 4.34)

25. Prime Minister's Questions (PMQs) displays many of the worst aspects of Westminster. Open-ended questions should be banned at PMQs (although the leaders of the main opposition parties should retain this ability); instead Members should give notice of their intention to ask a question ten days in advance and should table their (substantive) question by noon two days before PMQs. (para. 4.40)

26. However, even a reformed PMQs is unlikely to ensure the necessary scrutiny of the Prime Minister's expanding role and office. The Prime Minister should appear before a select committee on an annual basis to account for the work of the Government. The most appropriate opportunity would be once a year to give evidence on the Government's Annual Report. (para. 4.42)

27. Question time for other departments and ministers should also be reformed to improve its topicality, substance and relevance. No more than ten questions should appear on the Order Paper for each Question Time and no duplicate questions should be allowed. The period of notice for oral questions should be reduced from ten working days to five. (paras 4.44–4.45)

28. In cases where the Government does not produce a response to a written question the reasons for not answering must be made clearer. A denial of information should be accompanied by a reference to the relevant section of the Code of Practice on Open Government or the Freedom of Information Act. (para. 4.46)

(ii) Parliamentary questions

Questions may be divided into those to be answered orally, or in writing. Written answers to Parliamentary Questions, or PQs, will be dealt with *post*, at p. 266.

In its report on PQs the Procedure Committee put forward the following objectives of PQs:

(a) a vehicle for individual backbenchers to raise their constituents' grievances;
(b) an opportunity for the House of Commons to probe the detailed actions of the Executive;
(c) a means of illuminating differences of policy on major issues between the various political parties or of judging the Parliamentary skills of individual MPs on both sides of the House;
(d) a combination of these or any other purposes, for example a way of enabling the Government to disseminate information about particular policy decisions; and
(e) the obtaining of information by the House from the Government and its subsequent publication (HC 178 of 1990–91, para. 26).

PQs for oral answer must be tabled in advance by at least ten sitting days. In fact, to have any chance of being answered orally the PQ must be tabled on the first day for which PQs to a particular minister may be accepted and then the order of questions is decided by ballot. The Prime Minister answers PQs now on Wednesdays, previously on Tuesdays and Thursdays, whereas question time for other Ministers is determined by a rota.

There are quite detailed rules on the form and content of PQs. These rules have derived from the rulings of the Speaker and are collected in *Erskine May's Treatise on the Law, Privileges, Proceedings and Usage of Parliament* (24th edn, 2011). PQs which deal with matters under consideration by Royal Commissions, parliamentary committees, or which are *sub judice* are inadmissible. Ministers only answer PQs on matters for which they are responsible.

This can create a problem as Ministers vary in their practice in answering questions which relate to other public bodies. The rule in *Erskine May* is that PQs 'should relate to the public affairs with which they are officially concerned, to proceedings in Parliament or to matters for which they are responsible (p. 295)'. The Committee recommended that the Table Office, which receives PQs, should give the benefit of the doubt to MPs when they want to ask a PQ about one of these public bodies which operates at 'arm's length' from the Minister.

Where the Chief Executive of a Next Steps Executive Agency answers a PQ on an operational matter, the answer is now published in *Hansard*, as would be the case with a ministerial answer.

The aim of most MPs tabling a PQ for an oral answer is to be able to pose a supplementary question for which no notice is necessary. Thus the tabled question may be quite general, or open, in nature. This is particularly so of PQs directed at the Prime Minister. A typical open PQ to the Prime Minister will inquire about the Prime Minister's engagements for that day. The Leader of Her Majesty's Opposition does not table PQs but is called by the Speaker to ask at least one supplementary, and possibly up to four supplementary, questions.

R. Blackburn and A. Kennon, *Griffith & Ryle on Parliament Functions, Practice and Procedures*

(2003), p. 370

...The formula which is nowadays almost uniformly adopted is 'To ask the Prime Minister if he will list his official engagements for [the day of answer.]' Every Wednesday some 200 questions of this kind are tabled but only the top 20 appear on the Order Paper, with only one or two on specific topics and a few questions 'To ask the Prime Minister if he will pay an official visit to [somewhere in the Member's constituency]' (which is a geographically narrowed form of open question). Despite the change in May 1997, there is usually no more than one substantive question to the Prime Minister in the top 20 listed on the Order Paper each Wednesday. Those who, by the luck of the shuffle, come in the first eight on the list will have an opportunity to fire a supplementary at the Prime Minister on a subject of their own choosing; but the Prime Minister only reads out a standard answer about his engagements in reply to the first question—he no longer refers 'the Hon. Member to the reply I gave some moments ago'. Those who have tabled 'engagements' questions are called by the Speaker and proceed at once to ask their substantive question, *e.g.* 'will the Prime Minister give consideration to the rising unemployment caused by the shut down of factories in any constituency, and what is he doing about it...?'. Any Member who has tabled a substantive question simply calls the number of the question, to which the Prime Minister replies, before the Member asks a supplementary and receives a reply to that. This underlines the difference between substantive and open questions to the Prime Minister.

6-201 Again the Speaker controls the calling of additional Members to ask supplementaries, but here he has further factors to take into account. First, very many Members want to join in and this causes considerable pressure on the Chair. The Speaker calls Members, in turn, from either side. Records are kept showing how many times back-benchers have been called, so as to be as fair as possible...

Secondly, the leader of the opposition is allowed up to six questions to the Prime Minister; and the leader of the second largest opposition party (recently the Liberal Democrats) has been allowed two questions; no-one else has more than one. The leader of the opposition sometimes takes his questions in two separate batches of three at the start and towards the end of Prime Minister's Questions. This is a prime opportunity for the leader of the opposition to put on the political agenda the issue of the day.

NOTE: Political points are also made in PQs directed to other Ministers, as this extract from *Hansard* shows on a day when it was the turn of ministers at the Ministry of Justice to answer questions. The extracts are taken from the end of the session in an innovation which was adopted after a trial, see further at p. 271 *post*.

House of Commons, HC Deb

cols 161–139, 23 November 2010

Topical Questions

T1. [25585] **Mrs Jenny Chapman (Darlington) (Lab):** If he will make a statement on his departmental responsibilities.

The Lord Chancellor and Secretary of State for Justice (Mr Kenneth Clarke): Following the conviction of Jon Venables on 23 July for possessing and distributing indecent images of children, I commissioned Sir David Omand to undertake an independent review into the management of Jon Venables from his release from local authority detention in June 2001 until his recall to custody on 24 February 2010. Today, I have placed a copy of Sir David's report in the Library. Sir David has concluded that Jon Venables was effectively and properly supervised at an appropriate level and frequency of contact, having regard to the particular circumstances of his case. Sir David also concludes that no reasonable supervisory regime would have been expected to detect his use of the computer to download indecent images. The report contains a number of recommendations on the future management of this and similar cases that will be taken forward by the National Offender Management Service.

Mrs Chapman: Nineteen-year-old Scots Guardsman Andrew Gibson was killed in a Darlington night-club. Yesterday, the Attorney-General said that he was unable to refer what many view as an excessively lenient sentence of just two and a half years to the Court of Appeal. Will the Secretary of State undertake to investigate the awarding of lenient sentences in which alcohol is an aggravating factor?

Mr Clarke: The Attorney-General has a power to exercise in these cases and he has to exercise it in his quasi-judicial role by making a proper judgment and not just reacting politically. I understand the hon. Lady's concern about that case, but sentences are normally imposed by the court that has had the opportunity to hear all the evidence, facts and information about the accused person. The Attorney-General takes seriously his responsibility to step in where a mistake seems to have been made and ask a higher court to consider imposing a more serious sentence. I cannot claim to exercise any control over him in that regard; it is his difficult judgment to take in each case.

T2. [25586] **Andrew Rosindell (Romford) (Con):** The Lord Chancellor will be only too aware that one of his key responsibilities is looking after the Crown dependencies of Jersey, Guernsey, the Isle of Man, Alderney and Sark. Will he explain to the House why the Crown dependencies were yet again refused the right to lay a wreath on Remembrance Sunday this year? Will he address this issue to ensure that next year they can do so like other countries in the Commonwealth?

Mr Clarke: My right hon. Friend Lord McNally has the responsibility and the honour to lead on matters concerning Crown dependencies, which I assure my hon. Friend he takes very seriously. I keep discovering that he has made visits to the Crown dependencies to discuss these matters. I was quite unaware of this problem and I shall make inquiries of Lord McNally and those responsible for the ceremony about the background to this issue of laying a wreath on behalf of the Channel Islands and the Isle of Man.

Sadiq Khan (Tooting) (Lab): The Secretary of State announced in the House last week—a day after ITN—that significant sums of money were to be paid to British residents and citizens who were detained at Guantanamo Bay, and he explained the factors behind the decision. Does he agree that there is an urgent need to resolve the claims of British victims of terrorist attacks overseas and will he commit today to such compensation being paid as a matter of urgency?

Mr Clarke: The right hon. Gentleman rightly expresses irritation about leaks to newspapers and the television, and I assure him that I share all that irritation. *[Interruption.]* If I were indulging in the kind of masterful spin-doctoring of the previous Administration, I would have trailed them better than occurred either in the newspapers or ITN. I made the statement when I did because I was told that ITN had carried the news the night before. I assure the right hon. Gentleman that, if he helps me to find out where the information is coming from, I will take appropriate steps. On compensation for victims of terrorism and crimes, we are having to review the criminal injuries compensation scheme. We are having to look at the prospects for the compensation for terrorism scheme. The fact is that we were left with a system of criminal injuries compensation which was not working. We have enormous liabilities piling up for which the previous Government had not made any adequate funds available, so we have hundreds of millions of pounds-worth of arrears of claims.

Sadiq Khan: That is a different issue.

Mr Clarke: It is not a different issue. They are related issues and we will give our conclusions in due course.

Several hon. Members rose—

Mr Speaker: Order. There is a lot of interest and little time. From now on, we need short questions and short answers.

T3. [25587] **Andrew George (St Ives) (LD):** What assurance can Ministers give my constituents in west Cornwall that the legal aid reforms published last week will not adversely affect the coverage of, or reduce access to, legal aid, particularly in civil and family proceedings?

The Parliamentary Under-Secretary of State for Justice (Mr Jonathan Djanogly): The hard facts are that the amount of legal aid being paid out in civil cases will be reduced. As part of the Government's savings of £2 billion, £350 million is subject to be taken out of legal aid by 2014–15. That means that we will focus legal aid on the most vulnerable who need legal representation.

T4. [25588] **Toby Perkins (Chesterfield) (Lab):** A number of professionals have contacted me about their worries that, once the Youth Justice Board disappears, there will be a lack of co-ordination and an increase in reoffending by young people. Can the Secretary of State give any reassurance to those professionals that when their work disappears inside the Ministry of Justice, that co-ordination work will still be taken seriously?

The Parliamentary Under-Secretary of State for Justice (Mr Crispin Blunt): Yes, I can give the hon. Gentleman that assurance. As the Minister with responsibility for youth justice, I will make sure that those functions carried out by the Youth Justice Board will be properly executed within the Ministry of Justice. The Youth Justice Board has done good work, but now it is time for Ministers to take direct responsibility for the work.

T5. [25589] **Priti Patel (Witham) (Con):** Families in Witham town are concerned about the presence of paedophiles and sex offenders, and the risk that they pose to children in our local community. What steps is the Secretary of State taking, in conjunction with other Government agencies, to ensure that my constituents are protected from those dangerous individuals?

The Minister for Policing and Criminal Justice (Nick Herbert): My hon. Friend might know about the child sex offender disclosure scheme, which is being extended to 24 police forces, having been successfully piloted in 11 police force areas. It allows members of the public to ask the police to check whether people have contact with their children at risk. They have already successfully protected children and provided considerable reassurance to parents.

T6. [25590] **Luciana Berger (Liverpool, Wavertree) (Lab/Co-op):** It is clearly inappropriate for convicted criminals to celebrate Christmas with raucous parties in prison. Is the Secretary of State certain that present Ministry of Justice guidance will prohibit such activity this Christmastime?

Mr Kenneth Clarke: I hate to tell the hon. Lady that there are no good parties going on in prisons to which I can invite her over Christmas. The whole story about parties was faintly ridiculous. The announcement by the Under-Secretary of State for Justice, my hon. Friend the Member for Reigate (Mr Blunt) did not mention parties and had very little to do with parties. Time was-I can remember from my youth-when a popular song began with

"The warden threw a party in the county jail,"

but we do not approve of that kind of thing nowadays.

(iii) Urgent questions

These are questions which refer to points which are urgent matters of public importance, or which relate to the arrangement of business in the House. Application is made to the Speaker on the day on which the MP wishes to ask the question, and, if granted, the urgent notice question will be asked at the conclusion of the normal Question Time.

In the sessions 2007–08, 2008–09, and 2009–10 the numbers of urgent questions (excluding business questions) asked were 4,12 and 12. Session 2009–10 was shorter than average because of the General Election in May 2010.

(iv) Adjournment debates

There are four types of adjournment debate, but only two will be covered here. These are the daily adjournment debate and the emergency adjournment debate.

Adjournment debates do not involve a division as they are a method by which an MP may raise a matter for a Minister who has responsibility. There is a ballot for the daily adjournment debate. The emergency adjournment debate is a relatively rare event which deals with an urgent matter not otherwise covered in the current business of the House. The tables below give an indication of the incidence of, and topics discussed in, emergency adjournment debates.

R. Blackburn and A. Kennon, *Griffith & Ryle on Parliament Functions, Practice and Procedures*

(2003), pp. 494, 496

Applications for emergency adjournment debates

Session	Total number of applications*	Number of applications by opposition front bench and leaders of smaller parties	Number granted	Number granted to opposition front bench
1974–75	33	0	1	0
1975–76	58	1	3	1
1976–77	44	0	3	0
1977–78	38	0	2	0
1978–79 (a)	66	0	3	0
1979–80 (b)	89	4	2	0
1980–81	48	3	1	1
1981–82	61	9	2	1
1982–83 (a)	50	5	2	2
1983–84 (b)	84	11	3	2
1984–85	61	13	1	1
1985–86	87	10	1	1
1986–87 (a)	48	8	2	2
1987–88 (b)	88	16	1	1
1988–89	43	6	1	1
1989–90	31	3	0	0
1990–91	13	1	0	0

1991–92 (a)	8	0	0	0
1992–93 (b)	18	4	1	1
1993–94	3	1	0	0
1994–95	5	0	0	0
1995–96	3	0	0	0
1996–97 (a)	6	1	0	0
1997–98 (b)	4	1	0	0
1998–99	3	0	0	0
1999–2000	2	0	0	0
2000–01 (a)	4	0	0	0

Notes:
* This includes some multiple applications
(a) Unusually short session.
(b) Unusually long session.

Emergency debates: successful applications by opposition front-bench

Date of debate	Topic	Member moving
January 27, 1981	Proposed purchase of *The Times*	John Smith
December 22, 1981	The Greater London Council	Albert Booth
December 15, 1982	NATO Council meeting	Denis Healey
February 14, 1983	Dispute in the water industry	Gerald Kaufman
October 26, 1983	Invasion of Grenada by USA	Denis Healey
May 24, 1984	Closures at British Leyland	Peter Shore
December 19, 1984	Local authorities capital expenditure	John Cunningham
January 27, 1986	Westland plc	Neil Kinnock
December 18, 1986	Airborne early warning system	Denzil Davies
February 3, 1987	Official Secrets Act: activities of Special Branch	Gerald Kaufman
April 13, 1988	Changes in the social security system	Robin Cook
November 9, 1989	Ambulance dispute	Robin Cook
June 24, 1993	Trident re-fit and the Scottish economy	George Foulkes
March 20, 2002	Troops being sent to Afghanistan	*

NOTE: In sessions 2007–08, 2008–09 and 2009–10 there were four, three and no applications for emergency debates. The subject of the only successful application, in 2007–08, was on the Pre-Budget Report.

(v) Early day motion

Public Information Office, *House of Commons Factsheet Series P, No. 3*

(2010), pp. 1, 3–5

Early day motion (EDM) is a colloquial term for a notice of motion given by a Member for which no date has been fixed for debate. EDMs exist to allow Members to put on record their opinion on a subject and canvass support for it from fellow Members. In effect, the primary function of an EDM is to form a kind of petition that MPs can sign and there is very little prospect of these motions being debated on the floor of the House.

...

Types of EDMs

EDMs tend to fall into several distinct groups. First, the Opposition may put down an EDM to pray against statutory instruments. Many appear in the name of the Leader of the Opposition or of another opposition party. This is how the Opposition gives public notice that it may seek to secure a debate on an SI; this type of EDM is generally the only one which can lead to a debate. Under Standing Order No. 118, the Government may refer a statutory instrument subject to negative procedure [see **Factsheet** L7] for debate in a standing committee once a motion for its annulment has been tabled. Motions of Censure are also put down as EDMs; the motion eventually approved by the House which led to the fall of the 1974–79 Labour Government started out as an EDM (see Appendix C).

Second, a group within a party might put down an EDM. This may express a view different from the official position of the party concerned. For example, motions put down by Government backbenchers may seek to accelerate or otherwise change Government action.

Another type frequently found is the all-party motion, which expresses a view across party divides. This type of EDM might raise for example, a social issue or a subject which has been promoted by one party but will also attract signatures from MPs of a different political allegiance.

It is generally only all-party motions that can obtain large numbers of signatures. The titles of the motions given in Appendix B will give an idea of the subjects which have regularly commanded wide support. When looking at an EDM, scrutiny of the names of the six sponsors will usually provide a clue as to its type. Certain motions, especially of the all-party category, are suggested to Members by pressure groups outside the House, and such organisations often go to much trouble in trying to persuade Members to sign 'their' motion.

Some EDMs are completely ephemeral in character, for example those offering congratulations to a particular football or cricket club (it has been known for separate but virtually identical EDMs of this type to be tabled). Other EDMs relate to local issues, for instance criticising the decision to close a post office or hospital, or purely personal matters (eg a deportation or similar case).

Members often seek to draw up an EDM if they have been debarred from putting down questions on a subject because of the rules of the House.

Occasionally EDMs are tabled criticising another Member of the House, or a member of the House of Lords. These EDMs will usually have a title beginning 'Conduct of ...'. It is unacceptable to criticise the conduct of honourable Members by innuendo, so such an EDM must state clearly what the allegation is, in a form that would allow the House to take a clear decision if the matter were ever debated.

Signatures

Additional Members can sign Early Day Motions. Commonly, Members do this by tearing out pages from their copy of the 'Blues' and signing below the chosen Motion or Motions. The pages are then handed to the Table Office, and the EDM (together with its top six sponsors, but not others who have previously signed the Motion) will be reprinted in the next Notice Paper with the new names added. Members often simply give the Table Office the relevant number and ask for their name to be added. A running total of the number of signatures to date is also printed each time the EDM appears in the 'Blues'. Signatures given in when the House is not sitting will be added on the next sitting day.

Members may give the Table Office the names of other Members to be added to the list of those supporting the EDM. Any Member doing so is personally responsible for the accuracy of the names of other Members appended by them to EDMs and they ought to have those Members' authority for the addition of their names. Members may not assume that because other Members have agreed to support an EDM in one session that they will automatically support an identical motion tabled in a subsequent parliamentary session.

Members themselves sometimes accidentally sign EDMs which they have already signed. Any such duplication is filtered out by the Table Office computer system, and only the original signature is printed or counted towards the total number of signatures.

...

Amendments

A Member may put down an amendment or amendments to another Member's EDM. If a Member wishes to table an amendment to an EDM which they have already signed, they first have to withdraw their name from the main motion.

Some amendments advance a view contrary to that offered by the main Motion and may advocate the replacement of the whole text from 'that' with an alternative proposition on the same subject, whilst others may seek additional or strengthening provisions. The Table Office can advise whether amendments which amount to total opposition to the EDM (in the form of an 'expanded negative') would be in order.

Members sign amendments in the same way as main motions, and the Notice Paper counts and records these in exactly the same way. Members can therefore solicit support for amendments and it is by no means unknown for an amendment to attract more support than the original motion.

Some examples taken from the on-line data base for November 2007: <http://edmi.parliament.uk/EDMi>. The proposer and the first subsequent four names are listed and the total of signatories is given beside the *.

189 FAREPAK
Clark, Katy
Devine, Jim
Brake, Tom
Hancock, Mike
Spink, Bob
*235

That this House notes that over a year has passed since the Christmas saving company Farepak collapsed; further notes that the collapse forced many families into the arms of debt lenders who charge extortionate rates of interest; believes that the victims of Farepak are entitled to justice and that those responsible for the Farepak collapse should be held accountable for their actions; notes that many of the innocent victims of the Farepak collapse have not received any compensation; believes that compensation must now be made available; and calls on the Government to introduce legislation to ensure that a Farepak-style collapse cannot happen again and for the Government to publish the report into the collapse of Farepak.

71 STANDING AREAS AT FOOTBALL GROUNDS
Hancock, Mike
Sanders, Adrian
Stringer, Graham
Taylor, David
MacNeil, Angus
*96

That this House urges the Government to accept the case for introducing small, limited sections of safe standing areas at football grounds; further urges the Government to recognise that there is widespread support for such areas and that improvements in stadium design and technology mean that with rigorous safety specifications, standing areas could be safely re-introduced; and calls on the Government to convene a meeting of representatives of the police, supporters, Premier League clubs and the Football Licensing Authority to find a way forward.

127 FAMILY COURTS
Hemming, John
Davies, Dai
Breed, Colin
Gidley, Sandra
Hoey, Kate
*25

That this House regrets the Government's proposals to retain secrecy within the family courts; believes that this secrecy permeates bad practice throughout the whole system of children services; feels that it is possible to protect the identity of the child while allowing parents to talk and seek advice publicly about their treatment in the family courts, and that professional witnesses should be uniquely identified to monitor consistency; further believes that every case should have an anonymised judgement handed to the parents that they can discuss publicly; and calls on the Government to recognise that there are very serious problems in the system that have been postponed rather than resolved by the limited proposals contained within the consultation document.

NOTE: In sessions 2007–08, 2008–09 and 2009–10, 2,727, 2,272, and 1,248 EDMs were tabled.

(vi) Westminster Hall

Following a report made by the Select Committee on the Modernisation of the House of Commons (HC 194 of 1998–99), an experiment was agreed for the 1999–2000 session in which a parallel chamber would be established, to be known as, and to take place in, Westminster Hall. The idea behind this initiative, which is modelled on the Main Committee in the House of Representatives in Canberra, is to allow for the House of Commons to deal with business which currently cannot be conducted on the floor of the House because of lack of time, and with business which is not currently taken. Westminster Hall will be chaired by Deputy Speakers and the layout of the room will be a wide hemi-cycle. The business which will be conducted in the Westminster Hall will differ from the Chamber in that there will not be any divisions. If there is to be a decision made in a sitting in Westminster Hall then it must be unanimous. There will be sittings on Tuesday and Wednesday mornings which will deal with private Members' business, and a third sitting on Thursday afternoon which will deal with business agreed through the usual channels (the Whips). The business which can be taken in Westminster Hall will include additional opportunities for adjournment debates, debates on the reports of select committees and new business such as opportunities for regular debates on (a) different regions of the world to augment the annual adjournment debate on foreign affairs, and (b) Green Papers and other consultative documents.

The experiment was a success and was made permanent.

D: Correspondence

(a) Constituents' grievances

Much of the correspondence conducted by MPs is concerned with their role as the persons who attempt to remedy the grievances of their constituents.

R. Rawlings, 'Parliamentary Redress of Grievance' in C. Harlow (ed.), *Public Law and Politics*

(1986), p. 120

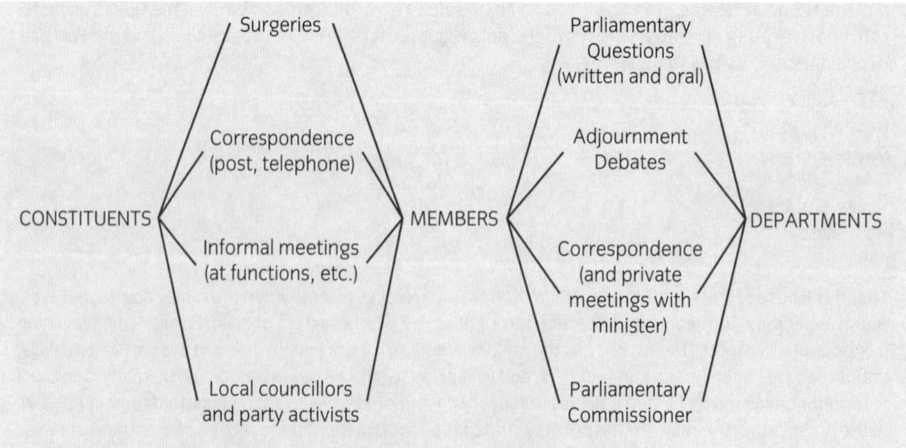

Parliamentary Redress and Central Departments: the Grievance Chain

NOTE: Rawlings (at pp. 128–129) points out that MPs as intermediaries can act in different ways in chasing grievances on behalf of constituents. They may act as *gatekeepers*, which means that they filter out some kinds of complaint; or they may be *letterboxes*, simply passing on complaints; or they may perform the role of *advocate*, actively taking up the complaint and using whatever means they wish in order to have it resolved in the constituent's favour. An MP can, of course, act in all of these roles, depending upon expertise in the matter, availability of time, sympathy for the complainant, and party political/electoral considerations.

Some studies have attempted to gauge the number of letters which MPs write to public authorities, including Ministers, on their constituents' behalf. Ridley's conservative estimate was that public authorities receive more than half a million letters from MPs annually (F. Ridley (1984) 37 *Parliamentary Affairs* 24). Norton projected that between 156,000 and 830,000 were written to Ministers by MPs each year (P. Norton (1982) 35 *Parliamentary Affairs* 60).

A. Page, 'MPs and the Redress of Grievances'

[1985] *Public Law* 1, 6–9

That MPs through their intervention do succeed in getting decisions changed there is no doubt. The impression, however, is that this is a relatively infrequent outcome: '... most letters do not result in a changed decision or new course of action being pursued.' Moreover, even where a decision is changed, it is by no means clear that the same result could not have been achieved without the intervention of the MP. Indeed, the

> strict tradition is that the Member's letter does not call forth a different decision from that which would be given to any other analogous case, unless very rarely it induces a Minister to initiate a change in policy.

The only advantage of an MP's intervention which can be pointed to is that because MPs' letters are normally considered at a higher level within departments, the chances of an inappropriate routine response being made to a case are reduced.

Comment

If it is the case that MPs' intervention normally makes little difference, then it would seem legitimate to ask whether the emphasis which is placed on MPs' role in the redress of grievances is altogether justified or indeed in the best interests of their constituents. Their status in relation to many of the agencies which are the subject of complaint is uncertain, how well or badly they perform their role can normally be only guessed at, and they suffer from all of the disadvantages of being 'unspecialised, ill-equipped, amateurish and over-worked.'

In reply, a number of arguments can be put forward. Undoubtedly the strongest is that, in handling the number of cases which they do, MPs are meeting a need which is not being met by anyone else. Moreover, they are doing something which is expected of them, although, as we have seen, MPs themselves have been partly responsible for generating this expectation. Their involvement in personal cases, therefore, helps MPs to keep their constituents satisfied, a concern which although understandable does create the risk of an unspoken conspiracy between MPs and Ministers to keep aggrieved individuals happy rather than genuinely to pursue their grievances, as well as themselves informed of local problems and difficulties. It has also been argued that MPs' constituency work is an important part of the legitimation not only of MPs but also Parliament in the eyes of the electorate. On the basis of these arguments, the only question which arises is whether MPs are sufficiently well-equipped in terms of secretarial and research facilities to fulfil their constituents' expectations of them. Accepting that they are not, additional assistance might conceivably increase their effectiveness in the redress of grievances.

It is at this point that one comes back to the fact that the PCA was intended to help MPs to carry out more effectively their role in the protection of the individual against government. However, MPs are supposed to regard the PCA as of only limited value and as the least effective of the available means of pursuing their constituents' grievances. This is no doubt partly attributable to the restrictions on his jurisdiction, but MPs' views are less than disinterested. Thus, a condition of the acceptance of the PCA by MPs was the insertion of the 'MP filter' to allay their fears that the PCA might come to supplant their own role in the redress of grievances, and the fact that MPs continue to oppose removal of the filter suggests that they remain extremely jealous of their own perceived primacy in the redress of grievances.

MPs' welfare role, however, is not without its costs. It represents a substantial burden for MPs themselves and for the administration. In the view of the Fulton Committee, Parliament should 'take fully into account the cumulative cost (not only in time but in the quality of the administration) that the raising of minutiae imposes ...' Whether MPs' insistence on their primacy in the redress of grievances is in the best interests of aggrieved individuals is also questionable. Certainly in his most recent Annual Report, the PCA questions whether it always is:

> I have often employed the familiar arguments in defence of our system, chief of which is that every Member of Parliament is an ombudsman for his constituents and that the body of Members makes a natural and valuable filter for discriminating between simple and complex cases, the worthy and the unworthy. But five years' experience has led me to doubt the validity of these arguments, at any rate in opposition to some modification of our arrangements. At present the Member may, and often does, ask the Minister for the appropriate Department to let him have, in the familiar phrase, 'an answer which I can send to my constituent' about his grievance. But on receipt of that reply, the Member has neither the time, nor the resources, nor the powers to verify by examination of departmental papers or witnesses the explanations offered, which must of necessity be composed on the basis of facts and opinions advanced by those against whom the complaint is laid. When Members do send me their files, it sometimes happens that the Minister's letter of response is the starting point of an investigation which shows that there is more to the case than the letter might be thought to suggest. [HC 322, 1983–84, para. 7.]

The PCA went on to recommend that an individual who had first asked his MP to take up his case but who was dissatisfied with the ultimate response should have the right to invite the PCA to examine the progress made. Whether this recommendation will be acted upon remains to be seen. If MPs, rather than the Government, were to oppose its implementation, their motives would be open to question, for the point which emerges from this survey is not that MPs should not act on behalf of their constituents, but that what they do should be kept firmly in perspective, and inflated claims, such as 'the primary responsibility for defending the citizen against the executive rests with the Member of Parliament,' should not be allowed to stifle the development of other forms of redress. As Mitchell observed:

The problem of finding a place in the sun for the backbench MP is essentially different from the problem of finding effective means of redress for the individual who has suffered injustice.

NOTE: See Chapter 12 on Ombudsmen, *post*, at p. 651–653.

■ QUESTIONS

1. Is there competition between the Ombudsman and MPs in remedying citizens' grievances? Should they not work together? See Rawlings, at pp. 137–141, for a proposal which seeks to use the casework of MPs as a means of external oversight, and therefore adding to the House of Commons function of scrutiny and influence.
2. Is writing a letter to a Minister more effective than asking a PQ or seeking an adjournment debate, or does an MP have resort to these parliamentary procedures if a letter does not satisfactorily resolve the situation?

(b) Parliamentary Questions for Written Answer

Public Information Office, *House of Commons Sessional Information Digest*
2007–2008, 2008–2009, and 2009–2010, p. 2

PARLIAMENTARY QUESTIONS

Statistics of Parliamentary Questions are available in two forms. The figures for each, which for various reasons (mainly owing to methods of counting and recording) are not exactly comparable, are as follows:

Questions appearing on the Order Paper calculated by the Journal Office

	2007–08	2008–09	2009–10
Appearing on the Order Paper for Oral Answer	5,151	4,113	1,924
Put down for priority Written Answer	12,351	8,907	4,307
Put down for non-priority Written Answer	61,006	47,285	21,160
Total	78,508	60,305	27,391

(Not more than about half of all questions put down for Oral Answer will receive such an answer—the rest are answered in writing.)

Questions appearing in Hansard are indexed in the Parliamentary Information Management Service (PIMS)

	2007–08	2008–09	2009–10
Oral replies (including supplementaries)	6,760	4,658	2,685
Oral replies (excluding supplementaries)	2,648	1,293	942
Written replies	73,495	56,387	23,916
Total	80,255	61,045	26,601

NOTE: The General Election in May 2010 meant that the 2009–10 session was shorter than average.

Questions for Written Answer are used mainly to seek information and are usually more specific than the 'open' PQ for Oral Answer.

House of Commons, HC Deb

Written Answers, cols 169W–171W, 23 November2010

Home Department

Departmental Public Expenditure

Ed Balls: To ask the Secretary of State for the Home Department what the *(a)* resource and *(b)* capital funding for her Department will be in (i) 2011–12, (ii) 2012–13, (iii) 2013–14 and (iv) 2014–15; and for each such year what the real terms change will be compared to 2010–11. [24005]

Mrs May *[holding answer 15 November 2010]:* The following table sets out the Home Office's resource and capital funding and the real-terms change compared to 2010–11.

	2010–11	2011–12	2012–13	2013–14	2014–15
Resource non ring-fence (£ billion)	9.3	8.9	8.5	8.1	7.8
Resource ring-fence[(1)] (£ billion)	0.2	0.3	0.3	0.2	0.2
Total resource budget (£ billion)	9.5	9.2	8.8	8.3	[(2)]8.1
Real terms change compared to 2010–11 (percentage)	–	-5	–11	–18	23
Capital DEL (£ billion)	0.8	0.5	0.5	0.4	0.5
Real terms change compared to 2010–11 (percentage)	–	–41	–42	–59	–49

[(1)] The headline resource figures in the spending review announcement excluded a technical accounting element of Department's budgets referred to as the resource ring-fence that mostly covers costs for depreciation. For completeness both the headline resource numbers and resource ring-fence figures have been included in the table. [(2)] Total resource is higher than the sum of resource non ring-fence and resource ring-fence due to rounding to one decimal point.

Deportation: Offenders

Mr Bone: To ask the Secretary of State for the Home Department how many foreign nationals who have been convicted and imprisoned for offences relating to human trafficking were deported to their country of origin in the last five years. [25660]

Damian Green *[holding answer 22 November 2010]:* Between January 2008 and June 2010, the UK Border Agency have removed or deported approximately 13,350 foreign nationals referred by the Prison Service. Of these less than 1% had a recorded latest primary offence of human trafficking (or similar). This figure is based on internal management information and should therefore be treated as provisional and subject to change. Reliable data on offence types is not available prior to 2008.

Data on the total number of foreign nationals convicted or imprisoned for offences relating to human trafficking is held by the Ministry of Justice and not the UK Border Agency.

23 Nov 2010 : Column 170W

Human Trafficking

Alex Cunningham: To ask the Secretary of State for the Home Department when the inter-departmental ministerial group on trafficking will next meet; and what will be discussed at that meeting. [25618]

Damian Green: The Government recognise the importance of monitoring the progress of anti-trafficking efforts in the UK and our international obligations.

A date is being sought for the next meeting of the Inter-Departmental Ministerial Group in the near future. Discussions at the Group will reflect ongoing developments in trafficking policy.

Fiona Bruce: To ask the Secretary of State for the Home Department when she expects to publish her Department's strategy on human trafficking. [25730]

Damian Green: We plan to publish the strategy on tackling human trafficking in spring 2011 alongside the strategy on organised crime.

Fiona Bruce: To ask the Secretary of State for the Home Department whether the UK Human Trafficking Centre has a business plan. [25798]

Damian Green: The UK Human Trafficking Centre (UKHTC) became part of the Serious Organised Crime Agency (SOCA) on 1 April 2010.

All of SOCA's activities, including on human trafficking, are covered in its annual plan which is published at the start of each financial year.

Illegal Immigrants

Dr Huppert: To ask the Secretary of State for the Home Department how many raids for immigration purposes have been conducted *(a)* in total and *(b)* between the hours of 3.00 am and 7.00 am in each of the last 24 months. [25396]

Damian Green *[holding answer 19 November 2010]:* The following table shows the total number of enforcement visits to business premises and private addresses conducted by the UK Border Agency in each month from November 2008 to October 2010, the number of those visits conducted between 03.00 hrs and 07.00 hrs, and the percentage of the overall number that the latter represent (the majority of such operations in fact take place between 06.00 hrs and 07.00 hrs). All data are sourced from management information tools and are not quality assured under national statistics protocols. The figures provided do not constitute part of national statistics and should be treated as provisional.

The timing of each enforcement visit will be dependent upon the type of visit to be conducted. For example, visits to private addresses will not normally be conducted either very late at night or very early in the morning; however, visits to business premises are approached with more flexibility. All visits are subject to prior risk assessment and required to be proportionate to the legitimate aims of the UK Border [Agency]

23 Nov 2010 : Column 171W

Month	(a) All visits	(b) Visits between 03.00 and 07.00	%
November 2008	1,084	343	32
December 2008	778	213	27
January 2009	1,101	368	33
February 2009	1,020	330	32

March 2009	1,125	296	26
April 2009	668	204	31
May 2009	747	230	31
June 2009	915	263	29
July 2009	947	313	33
August 2009	878	287	33
September 2009	1,057	361	34
October 2009	1,119	459	41
November 2009	1,217	470	39
December 2009	843	313	37
January 2010	1,067	405	38
February 2010	1,172	428	37
March 2010	1,254	514	41
April 2010	892	330	37
May 2010	1,143	455	40
June 2010	1,221	461	38
July 2010	1,210	407	34
August 2010	1,219	438	36
September 2010	1,351	465	34
October 2010	1,266	471	37
Totals	25,294	8,824	35

Notes: 1. All data are sourced from management information tools and are not quality assured under National Statistics protocols. The figures provided do not constitute part of National Statistics and should be treated as provisional.

2. The timing of each enforcement visit will be dependent upon the type of visit to be conducted. For example, visits to private addresses will not normally be conducted either very late at night or very early in the morning; however, visits to business premises are approached with more flexibility. All visits are subject to prior risk assessment and required to be proportionate to the legitimate aims of the UK Border Agency's operations.

Immigration Controls

Ed Balls: To ask the Secretary of State for the Home Department (1) on what dates Ministers in her Department have met representatives from the *(a)* CBI, *(b)* British Chambers of Commerce and *(c)* Federation of Small Businesses to discuss the Government's proposed immigration cap since 11 May 2010; [24603]

(2) on what dates Ministers in her Department have met the Secretary of State for Business, Innovation and Skills to discuss the Government's proposed immigration cap. [24604]

Mrs May *[holding answer 16 November 2010]:* I met representatives from the CBI on 21 September 2010 and 10 November 2010, and the Minister for Immigration met a representative of the British Chambers of Commerce on 26 May 2010 to discuss our proposals for limiting non-EU economic migration. My officials have met the CBI, the British Chambers of Commerce and the Federation of Small Businesses to discuss these proposals.

I have met with the Secretary of State for Business, Innovation and Skills, the right hon. Member for Twickenham (Vince Cable) on several occasions to discuss proposals for limiting non-EU economic migration.

In addition to this, the Minister for Immigration, the hon. Member for Ashford (Damian Green) has met with the Minister for Universities and Science, the right hon. Member for Havant (Mr Willetts) to discuss these proposals on a number of occasions.

NOTES

1. The Freedom of Information Act 2000 provides for a right to recorded information held by public authorities. The duty covers confirming or denying that the requested information is held by the public authority, and if the requested information is held to communicate it to the applicant. A request for information may be subject to a fee and can be refused if the cost of providing it is disproportionate. There are time limits within which compliance with a request must be carried out. Public authorities have a duty to advise and assist applicants and to publish publication schemes which outline the information which they publish or intend to publish and which information will be free or subject to a fee. Public authorities must give the basis for their refusal to provide information and this may be challenged by the applicant before the Information Commissioner who, on finding that the public authority has not met its duty, may issue an enforcement notice which requires steps to be taken in order to comply with the statute. There are various types of information which are exempt and may not be provided. Some exemptions are absolute:
   - information accessible by other means—s. 21,
   - supplied by, or relating to bodies dealing with security—s. 23;
   - court records—s. 32;
   - Parliamentary privilege—s. 34;
   - prejudice to the conduct of public affairs—s. 36;
   - personal information—s. 40(1)(2),
   - information provided in confidence—s. 41;
   - disclosure is prohibited by another statute, Community law obligation, or would be a contempt of court—s. 44.

   Other categories of information will be exempt if the public interest in maintaining the exemption outweighs disclosure:
   - information intended for future publication—s. 22;
   - national security—s. 24;
   - defence—s. 26;
   - international relations—s. 27;
   - relations within the UK—s. 28;
   - the economy—s. 29;
   - investigations and proceedings conducted by public authorities—s. 30;
   - law enforcement—s. 31;
   - audit functions—s. 33;
   - formulation of government policy—s. 35;
   - communications with Her Majesty, etc. and honours—s. 37;
   - health and safety—s. 38;
   - legal professional privilege—s. 42;
   - commercial interests—s. 43.

   Notices issued by the Information Commissioner may be appealed to the Information Tribunal. An accountable officer may issue a certificate which excepts the public authority from compliance with those notices. The accountable officer is the First and Deputy First Minister acting together in relation to a Northern Ireland Assembly department of public authority; the First Minister in relation to National Assembly for Wales department of public authority in Wales or, for any other public authority, a Cabinet Minister or Attorney General or Advocate General for Scotland or Northern Ireland.
2. The general principles to be adopted by departments are in the central guidance on drafting answers to Parliamentary Questions which was revised for the full implementation of the Freedom of Information Act 2000 in January 2005.

Handling Correspondence from Members of Parliament: Guidance on Drafting Answers to Parliamentary Questions

Cabinet Office, 2005

> 1. Never forget Ministers' obligations to Parliament which are set out in the Ministerial Code:
>
> 'It is of paramount importance that Ministers give accurate and truthful information to Parliament, correcting any inadvertent error at the earliest opportunity. Ministers who knowingly mislead

Parliament will be expected to offer their resignation to the Prime Minister. Ministers should be as open as possible with Parliament and the public, refusing to provide information only when disclosure would not be in the public interest, which should be decided in accordance with the relevant statutes and the Government's Code of Practice on Access to Government Information'.

2. It is a civil servant's responsibility to Ministers to help them fulfil those obligations. It is the Minister's right and responsibility to decide how to do so. Ministers want to explain and present Government policy and actions in a positive light. They will rightly expect a draft answer that does full justice to the Government's position.

3. Approach every question predisposed to give relevant information fully, as concisely as possible and in accordance with guidance on disproportionate cost. If there appears to be a conflict between the requirement to be as open as possible and the requirement to protect information whose disclosure would not be in the public interest, you should consult your FOI liaison officer if necessary.

4. Where information is being refused on the grounds of disproportionate cost, there should be a presumption that any of the requested information which is readily available should be provided.

5. Do not omit information sought merely because disclosure could lead to political embarrassment or administrative inconvenience.

6. Where there is a particularly fine balance between openness and non-disclosure, and when the draft answer takes the latter course, this should be explicitly drawn to the Minister's attention. Similarly, if it is proposed to reveal information of a sort which is not normally disclosed, this should be explicitly drawn to Ministers' attention. The Minister should also be advised of any relevant FOI cases which are under consideration which could impact on the way the PQ should be answered.

7. If you conclude that material information must be withheld and the PQ cannot be fully answered as a result, draft an answer which makes this clear and explains the reasons, such as disproportionate cost or the information not being available, or explains in terms similar to those in the Freedom of Information Act (without resorting to explicit reference to the Act itself or to section numbers) the reason for the refusal. For example, 'The release of this information would prejudice commercial interests'. Take care to avoid draft answers which are literally true but likely to give rise to misleading inferences.

■ QUESTION

How real is the commitment to openness given the rules and practice on answering PQs and on officials' evidence to select committees (see pp. 234–241, *ante*), and will the Freedom of Information Act and its exceptions, improve matters?

E: Recent reforms

The Select Committee on Modernisation of the House of Commons produced a report *Revitalising the Chamber: the role of the Back-Bench MP* (HC 337 of 2005–06) which combined its inquiries into making better use of non-legislative time and strengthening the role of the back-bencher. The committee noted that MPs were interested in participating in the work of the House despite the 'tidal wave' of constituency work. The committee's recommendations may be grouped into those dealing with improving the topicality of the House; improving engagement and the opportunities to initiate business.

(a) Improving topicality

There was a perception that proceedings in the House did not manage to keep up with topical events and so recommendations were made in relation to questions, and debates. The period between the tabling and answering of PQ for oral answer has reduced and that it was agreed that the final 10–15 minutes of each Departmental Question Time could be reserved for 'Topical Questions', from Members who had been successful in a ballot, in a process similar to that of Prime Minister's Questions. (see the extracts at p. 258 *ante*).

This change did not require revision of Standing Orders whereas implementing changes on Topical Debates did. There was agreement on a weekly 90-minute debate on matters of regional, national or international importance but there was concern about who would choose the topics and if they would be taken from Opposition Time. In the 2007–08 session there is an experiment and Members can suggest topics for these debates to the Leader of the House who will announce the date and topic. This has been done by amending Standing Order No. 24, other changes include trying to give the Speaker some leeway when dealing with requests for what are now renamed, for session 2007–08, as Emergency Debates. It was felt that Members needed more advice on the criteria which the Speaker uses in determining requests both for these debates and urgent questions as most applications are unsuccessful (see p. 260–261 *ante*).

(b) Improving engagement

Standing Orders have been amended for session 2007–08 to provide for general debates on motions which may not be amended. Such a motion will note that the House has considered a matter and not end in with a defined outcome which some had urged should be the case; however it seems that maintaining flexibility was preferred. The Government agreed to rebalance the mix and duration of some set piece debates on the Queens' Speech, the Budget and Defence, thus allowing for more topical matters to be debated. The Government also accepted the case for having some shorter debates, including the possibility of dividing some full-day debates into half-day debates on different topics. The Government did not accept the recommendation that weekly half-hour debates on Select Committee reports should take place in Westminster Hall during which a Minister could make a brief response to the report, preferring that the House has an opportunity to debate such reports when the Government's response has been made. Agreement was reached for the 2007–08 session on changes to Standing Orders that there could be time limits on speeches so as to try to give more time to back-benchers. The Speaker would have the possibility of varying the time limits imposed on back-benchers during the debate so as to maximize participation in accordance with the available time. There would be mandatory time limits for front-benchers in the new topical debates.

(c) Opportunities to initiate business

Whilst it was agreed that it was desirable to make the best use of opportunities which backbenchers have to initiate business: Private Members' bills; motions for leave to introduce bills (ten minute rule motions); debates on the adjournment, requiring a minister to account for his policy or actions; amendments to bills at Report stage, as in Committee; and questions to ministers, the suggestion to reintroduce Private Member's Motions was felt to cause difficulties as if there were substantive motions, then there would voting and the Leader of the House wondered if Members wanted to increase the amount of time spent in divisions.

(d) Departmental debates

The Green Paper *The Governance of Britain* (Cm 7170) was produced in July 2007 shortly after Mr Brown succeeded Mr Blair as Prime Minister in June. In the chapter on making the executive more accountable it was noted that while select committees had the opportunity to scrutinize department, there were some opportunities to debate issues concerning departments in Westminster Hall but as the debate is on a motion for the adjournment, this limits Parliament's ability to challenge government policy. The Government has asked the Modernisation Select committee to consider ways the House of Commons could have guaranteed opportunities to debate, in the chamber, the annual objective and plans of the major Government departments, thus strengthening Parliament's scrutiny of the executive.

(e) Wright committee report

In the aftermath of the scandal over MPs' expenses, a Select Committee on Reform of the House of Commons was established, chaired by Dr Tony Wright MP, who was chair of the Public Administration Committee. The report *Rebuilding the House* (HC 1117 of 2008–09 outlined the principles which guided their work:

> (a) We should seek to enhance the House of Commons' control over its own agenda, timetable and procedures, in consultation with Government and Opposition, whilst doing nothing to reduce or compromise such powers where they already exist;
> (b) We should seek to enhance the collective power of the Chamber as a whole, and to promote non-adversarial ways of working, without impeding the ability of the parties to debate key issues of their choosing; and to give individual Members greater opportunities;
> (c) We should seek to enhance the transparency of the House's decision making to Members and to the public, and to increase the ability of the public to influence and understand parliamentary proceedings;
> (d) We should recognise that the Government is entitled to a guarantee of having its own business, and in particular Ministerial legislation, considered at a time of its own choosing, and concluded by a set date;
> (e) We should recognise that time in the Chamber, Westminster Hall and committees is necessarily limited, and therefore should work broadly within the existing framework of sitting days and sitting hours;
> (f) Changes should be devised with sensitivity to real-world political constraints, and in a way which maximises the likelihood of achieving majority support in the House.

Their recommendations dealt with select committees, business in the House, and greater involvement of the public through petitions. In relation to select committees, their proposals about electing chairs and members, rather than having them selected by the party whips, and establishing them quickly after the a beginning of a new Parliament were accepted and implemented. The major innovation in their proposals on the conduct of business in the House was a Backbench Business Committee which would schedule a specified amount of backbench business. Standing Orders were amended, and under SO 14(3A) 35 days were allocated in each session to backbench business in the House and Westminster Hall with at least 27 days to be in the House. Topical debates would be decided by this new Committee and it would also schedule business in Westminster Hall on Thursdays.

(f) Public appointments

The Governance of Britain

(Cm 7170) paras 72–79

> **Improving current processes and strengthening the House of Commons' role**
>
> 72. Public bodies at arm's-length from Ministers play an important role in public life across a range of areas ranging from the regulation of key utilities to health service bodies and from the boards of museums and galleries to those who can investigate complaints about the way key public services are provided. All in all there are some 21,000 such appointments and ultimately they are the responsibility of Ministers, who are accountable to Parliament for these appointments.

73. Lord Nolan's report in 1995 recommended a number of measures designed to bolster public confidence in such appointments. The independent Office of the Commissioner for Public Appointments was created, which oversees and audits a wide range of public appointments in line with core principles of appointment on merit, probity and transparency.

74. Building on these improvements, the Government believes the time is now right to go further and seek to involve Parliament in the appointment of key public officials. The role of Parliament, and specifically the issue of Committee hearings with those nominated for office, has been the subject of considerable debate over the past decade. Some, including the Commissioner for Public Appointments, have drawn attention to potential risks about deterring suitable candidates and the need for confidentiality in appointments processes, because, for example, a number of key appointments could impact on the financial markets.

75. However, there are a number of positions in which Parliament has a particularly strong interest because the officeholder exercises statutory or other powers in relation to protecting the public's rights and interests. Some of these appointments are not subject to oversight by the Commissioner for Public Appointments or other form of independent scrutiny.

76. The Government therefore believes that Parliament, through its select committees, should play this role. It therefore proposes that the Government nominee for key positions such as those listed below should be subject to a pre-appointment hearing with the relevant select committee. The hearing would be non-binding, but in the light of the report from the committee, Ministers would decide whether to proceed. The hearings would cover issues such as the candidate's suitability for the role, his or her key priorities, and the process used in selection.

77. The Government, in consultation with the Liaison Committee, will prepare a list of such appointments for which these hearings will apply. Where responsibility is devolved, it will be for the respective administration to consider the appointment. Examples might include:

- The First Civil Service Commissioner (following the announcement by the Government that it is to legislate to place the Civil Service and its independent Commissioners on a statutory footing, it is right that Parliament should have a role in this appointment);
- The Commissioner for Public Appointments (who is responsible for ensuring public confidence in several thousand other appointments);
- The Parliamentary Commissioner for Administration and Health Service Commissioner for England (who is responsible for investigating maladministration in central government and the NHS);
- The Local Government Ombudsman for England; and
- Independent inspectors such as the Chief Inspector of Prisons and the Chief Inspector of Probation for England and Wales.

78. This list will be kept under review and discussed with the Liaison Committee, and, where appropriate, the Commissioner for Public Appointments.

79. For market-sensitive and certain other appointments, including the Governor and the two Deputy Governors of the Bank of England, the Chairman of the Financial Services Authority, and some utility regulators, there is a particular set of issues around confirmation hearings. But the Government does believe that it is important to ensure greater accountability than currently exists. So, for these positions, once the appointment has been approved, the relevant select committee will be invited to convene a hearing with the nominee before he or she takes up post. The relevant department will consult with the select committee as to what such hearings might usefully cover.

NOTE: The Public Administration Select Committee has reported on this proposal. In its conclusions it said the pre-appointment hearings cannot be about accountability, so they must be about selection.

Third Report from the Public Administration Committee

HC 152 of 2007–08 pp 16–18

5. The proper role for select committees in the selection of candidates for public appointments is in informing the final ministerial decision, not in influencing the impartial process that precedes that decision. Select committees should only become involved once every part of the interview and selection process has been completed except for this final decision. (Paragraph 13)

6. The value that committees can add over and above that provided by a rigorous selection process is to expose a candidate to parliamentary and public scrutiny. (Paragraph 14)

7. Hearings should normally apply only to posts for which accountability to Parliament and the public are an important part of the role. A positive outcome of holding pre-appointment hearings for such posts is the likelihood that appointees will perform this accountability function more effectively. (Paragraph 14)

8. Hearings might also be appropriate where a ministerial appointment might otherwise appear to be improperly partisan, particularly where there had been no transparent process of appointment on merit. There also needs to be clarity and consistency about which appointments are made with cross-party agreement and are put to Parliament for approval. (Paragraph 16)

9. We would expect pre-appointment hearings to apply to major auditors, ombudsmen, regulators and inspectors, as well as to those responsible for the appointments system itself. (Paragraph 17) ...

12. We understand why the Government might be cautious about adding a public scrutiny element to the appointments process if this might affect markets or dissuade private-sector candidates from putting themselves forward. However, it is not clear what the value would be of a hearing which was able neither to influence the appointment of a candidate nor to allow an office-holder to account for their performance. (Paragraph 21) ...

18. We recommend that the Government should ensure that a Minister, when coming to a decision on an appointment, will not be dissuaded by the risk of legal challenge from taking committee proceedings into account. If committee involvement in an appointment led a Minister to change his or her mind on the suitability of candidate, it would be absurd if the Minister felt required for legal reasons to proceed with the appointment against his or her better judgement. (Paragraph 36)

19. It is not intended that pre-appointment hearings will be binding, and Ministers will therefore retain the right to disagree with a committee's views on an appointee. Pre-appointment hearings will only be of any significance, however, if there is the possibility that Ministers might change their minds, and that a candidate's appointment might not be approved. We expect that it will be only in very exceptional cases that committees will recommend against the appointment of a candidate; but the test of the Government's commitment to pre-appointment hearings will be how Ministers react in such cases. (Paragraph 38)

20. Clear procedures are needed to avoid protracted media speculation about a candidate's fate following a pre-appointment hearing, particularly where a committee is minded to recommend against an appointment. We invite the Liaison Committee to ensure that these procedures are in place. (Paragraph 39)

■ QUESTIONS

1. Will making procedures more amenable to topical issues bring public attention back to Parliament from the radio and television studios?
2. Should there be more or less effort made in increasing topicality as opposed to improving Parliament's accountability mechanisms?
3. Will the reforms relating to backbench business encourage a more independent approach or simply contain it within the allocated periods?
4. Is it preferable that select committees hold persons in public office to account rather than seeking to influence in their appointment?

7

Parliament: Law-making and Standards Self-regulation

OVERVIEW

In this chapter we first consider the different types of legislative measures, then the methods of control used before and during their consideration by Parliament and finally judicial review of delegated legislation. In the section on standards self-regulation, we consider the arrangements for the MPs' Code of Conduct which requires registration of interests and provides for their investigation by an independent officer and for enforcement within parliamentary privilege. A parallel system relating to the claiming of allowances following the 2009 expenses' scandal is also considered and finally the relationship between parliamentary privilege and the ordinary criminal law.

SECTION 1: LAW-MAKING

There are many varieties of legislation: statutes, delegated legislation, and what may be called quasi-legislation which can encompass administrative rules and guidance. Quasi-legislation can take the form, for example, of circulars from central departments, or codes of practice. The Americans refer to legislative activity carried out by administrative bodies as rule-making, and this includes what the British call delegated and quasi-legislation. It is important to realize that not all legislation will be made by Parliament. Our consideration of law-making will focus, first, on the assorted types of legislative measures and their rationale, and then on the methods for, and issues concerning, control of these legislative measures.

One of the characteristics of legislation is that it is empowering, that is it gives a public body the power to carry out tasks which the legislation also imposes upon the public body.

A: Types of legislative measure

(a) Statute

R. Rose, 'Law as a Resource of Public Policy'

(1986) 39 *Parliamentary Affairs* 297, 302–305

LAWS are a fundamental and unique resource of government. Without Acts of Parliament, force, personal preferences or momentary whim would justify the actions of government. Without laws, citizens would have no protection against arbitrary authority, no entitlements to social benefits, and no obligation to pay taxes. Without laws, civil servants would have no authority to act, or procedures to follow. Without laws, elections could not be held, for there would be no rules about who could vote, how votes should be counted, and who should be elected as MPs. In order to understand government, we must understand the uses of laws.

Until the growth of the twentieth-century welfare state, MPs viewed law as the principal resource of government. The characteristic concern of Parliament was not with public expenditure issues, but with the principles to be embodied in Acts of Parliament that involved questions of civil and political rights such as the franchise...

Once the importance of laws is recognised, the next question to address is: In what ways are laws important? The distinctive feature of law is that it is an expression of authority. It is not coercive in the sense that actions by the police may be coercive. Nor does the law consist of cash incentives to actions, as do the wages paid civil servants.

Statute laws establish parameters within which individuals and organisations may carry out their activities. Since the activities of society are heterogeneous, the parameters of laws are multiple. In order to understand the broad effect of laws, we need to understand the nature of laws as parameters; the extent of discretion that can be exercised within legal parameters; and then, whose activities have bounds set upon them by the statute book.

Parameters: more route maps than tethers. The traditional idea of laws as a set of commands and prohibitions ('Thou shalt...' or 'Thou shalt not...') presents a misleading picture of the uses of laws in the contemporary state. While there are some compelling and forbidding laws about crime, public health and safety, nine-tenths of statutes concern ways in which individuals or organisations may proceed of their own volition.

When a law sets parameters upon behaviour in society, it neither commands nor compels. Rules are promulgated which remain constant while the facts of specific circumstances vary. For example, laws governing marriage are hardly affected by characteristics of the partners of the marriage. Nor does the existence of such laws compel everyone to get married. Procedures are laid down which describe the actions that a pair of individuals should take if they want their union to be legally valid. There are few prohibitions, e.g. a minimum age, but these constrain the behaviour of a very, very small proportion of the population.

Most laws about the everyday activities of citizens are virtually unnoticed. For example, laws affecting property rights in a house; the content of foods; the conditions of driving a motor car or being a passenger on public transport; conditions of employment; or laws concerning broadcasting. This is not to say that such laws are unnecessary. Instead of involving the compulsion and prohibition of acts, most laws give guidance about ways to maintain a well ordered society.

Most contemporary laws are best conceived as a route map, laying down conditions by which one may proceed. Their relevance is contingent, taking the form of 'If...then' propositions. For example, 'If you want to drive a car, then you must have a driver's licence, the car must be licensed and insured, and you must drive within the traffic code'. Most laws do not tether behaviour in the sense of confining a person to act within narrowly circumscribed limits.

Scope for discretion. Both jurisprudential and sociological analyses emphasise that even the most carefully stated statute cannot control 100 per cent of behaviour. Violations of the law occur in every society. Yet violations are only a small proportion of total social activity, e.g. fraud arises in only a very small percentage of market transactions, and violent assault or murder in an infinitesimal proportion of social interactions.

The most significant limitation upon law is the existence of 'gaps' that give some latitude for discretion, i.e. choice within the parameters of the statute book. In the real world, the statute book is subject to multiple imperfections—vagueness of language, omissions, and the incapacity to anticipate every possible concatenation of events. In falling short of the perfection of an ideal-type, it is no different from administration, markets, or democracy itself. Discretion can be found in four main areas.

(a) *Judges* inevitably are faced with 'hard' cases, that is, circumstances in which lawyers dispute how the law is to be interpreted and applied to the facts of a particular case. Bell describes judges as acting as interstitial lesiglators: 'There are situations where the legal audience would recognise that there is no single clear solution to a case and that several possible solutions are at least arguable. At the same time, it must be recognised that, in presenting his decision, the judge has to justify himself within the legal materials, showing how the solution fits within existing legal prescriptions and standards. It is thus somewhat misleading to suggest that the law in such situations 'runs out', as if anything at all could be used to fill the 'gap'.'

(b) *Executive lawmaking* occurs through the issuance of a variety of rules and regulations that can be made pursuant to Acts of Parliament; in Britain these measures can conveniently be described as Statutory Instruments. Acts of Parliament establish the parameters within which executive rule-making may be done; these are necessarily more confined than those of the Act itself. Statutory instruments typically affect procedures for putting an Act into effect, or fill out details that may be negotiated with subjects of regulation, or are likely to vary from time to time in relation to changing economic or social conditions. The limited political significance of this form of executive rule-making is shown by the fact that less than one per cent of Statutory Instruments are deemed worthy of careful scrutiny by the parliamentary committee exercising oversight of them. The chief reason is that these regulations are likely to be agreed with affected parties in advance of their promulgation.

British membership of the European Community has created procedures authorised by Act of Parliament that enable Community laws and regulations to be put into effect by actions of the British government, without recourse to conventional procedures for a bill becoming a law. This too has led to the establishment of select committees in Parliament to monitor actions thus taken. Notwithstanding the significance of the principle, the practical political effect has been slight.

(c) *Administrative discretion* is an element in the implementation of a new Act of Parliament, and in the routine operation of many acts. The degree of discretion depends upon the extent to which laws and regulations can prescribe the parameters of action. The extent is variable: pensions officials, postal clerks and airline pilots have much less discretion than public employees who deliver services to citizens in conditions in which the services provided cannot be tightly circumscribed nor their behaviour closely monitored, for example policemen, teachers, doctors and social workers.

Lipsky argues that 'street-level' public employees are not rule-bound bureaucrats but individuals with a significant degree of discretion to decide how to treat individuals seeking their services. Just as the law sets parameters upon what officials may do, so the informal norms and routines of low-level officials may reciprocally constrain what the law can achieve. While awareness of an element of discretion is an important caution against excessive legalism, it does not justify Lipsky writing as if public policies could be carried out by ignoring or flouting the parameters of the law.

(d) *Adaptive behaviour* can be undertaken by citizens in ways that recognise the parameters of the law, but may not be what was anticipated by lawmakers. Within the parameters of any Act of Parliament citizens are free to behave in many ways. Adaptive behaviour is most familiar in tax avoidance, that is, the alteration of behaviour to lessen the legal liability to taxation. By definition, tax avoidance (e.g. working a limited number of hours a week to avoid national insurance tax, or converting income subject to a high marginal income tax rate into a capital gain subject to a lower rate) is within the law. But it is also action taken to avoid what would otherwise be undesirable consequences.

In a mixed society the role of law is not so much that of telling people what they must and must not do; it is to establish rules and regulations under which individuals and organisations can carry out their everyday affairs in ways that are orderly, predictable and recognised and accepted by all concerned. Only in a totalitarian society could the law claim to be all-powerful. A major contribution of law to public policy in a free society is that it establishes parameters within which individuals and organisations can then be free to pursue what they regard as their own wellbeing and interests. This liberal idea of the limits of laws poses problems for democratic socialists who want certain outcomes, for example, equality of educational opportunity, but do not want to use laws to prohibit private education or compel everyone to have their children educated at state schools.

NOTE: Legislation can be divided into public and private. Rose discussed public statutes, which are normally initiated by the Government but may be introduced by MPs as a Private Member's Bill. Private legislation may confer powers or benefits on particular individuals or bodies, which may be in addition to, or in conflict with, the general law. Such measures will be promoted by the relevant individuals or bodies such as local authorities, universities, or companies. A hybrid bill is one, usually initiated by the Government, which is public in nature but will affect private rights. As, for example, with the Channel Tunnel, where power may be given to a Minister to acquire specified land.

(b) Delegated legislation

Report of the Committee on Ministers' Powers

Cmd 4046, pp. 51–52

Necessity for Delegation

We have already expressed the view that the system of delegated legislation is both legitimate and constitutionally desirable for certain purposes, within certain limits, and under certain safeguards. We proceed to set out briefly—mostly by way of recapitulation—the reasons which have led us to this conclusion:—

(1) Pressure upon Parliamentary time is great. The more procedure and subordinate matters can be withdrawn from detailed Parliamentary discussion, the greater will be the time which Parliament can devote to the consideration of essential principles in legislation.

(2) The subject matter of modern legislation is very often of a technical nature. Apart from the broad principles involved, technical matters are difficult to include in a Bill, since they cannot be effectively discussed in Parliament....

(3) If large and complex schemes of reform are to be given technical shape, it is difficult to work out the administrative machinery in time to insert in the Bill all the provisions required; it is impossible to foresee all the contingencies and local conditions for which provision must eventually be made....

(4) The practice, further, is valuable because it provides for a power of constant adaptation to unknown future conditions without the necessity of amending legislation. Flexibility is essential. The method of delegated legislation permits of the rapid utilisation of experience, and enables the results of consultation with interests affected by the operation of new Acts to be translated into practice....

(5) The practice, again, permits of experiment being made and thus affords an opportunity, otherwise difficult to ensure, of utilising the lessons of experience. The advantage of this in matters, for instance, like town planning, is... obvious....

(6) In a modern State there are many occasions when there is a sudden need of legislative action. For many such needs delegated legislation is the only convenient or even possible remedy. No doubt, where there is time, on legislative issues of great magnitude, it is right that Parliament itself should either decide what the broad outlines of the legislation shall be, or at least indicate the general scope of the delegated powers which it considers are called for by the occasion.

But emergency and urgency are matters of degree; and the type of need may be of greater or less national importance. It may be not only prudent but vital for Parliament to arm the executive Government in advance with almost plenary power to meet occasions of emergency, which affect the whole nation—as in the extreme case of the Defence of the Realm Acts in the Great War, where the exigency had arisen; or in the less extreme case of the Emergency Powers Act, 1920, where the exigency had not arisen but power was conferred to meet emergencies that might arise in future....

But the measure of the need should be the measure alike of the power and of its limitation. It is of the essence of constitutional Government that the normal control of Parliament should not be suspended either to a greater degree, or for a longer time, than the exigency demands....

NOTE: Delegated legislation may take several forms—regulations, Orders in Council, rules, and orders. Parliament usually makes delegated legislation as statutory instruments, the passage of which is governed by the Statutory Instruments Act 1946. The more important pieces of delegated legislation are Orders in Council. Legislative measures which would have been passed as Acts of the Northern Ireland Assembly and its predecessor were passed as Orders in Council when the devolved institutions were suspended.

There is an overlap between delegated legislation and administrative rules of quasi-legislation, even though the legal forms of these measures differ. The following extract suggests a classification of administrative rules based on function.

(c) Quasi-legislation

R. Baldwin and J. Houghton, 'Circular Arguments: The Status and Legitimacy of Administrative Rules'

[1986] *Public Law* 239, 241–245

(1) Procedural Rules

Most bodies that distribute licences or money publish documents describing the procedures to be adopted. Thus, the Gaming Board and the Independent Broadcasting Authority instruct applicants for licences to follow set procedures. The Prison Rules lay down disciplinary procedures for prisoners and new police codes lay down practices to be followed in dealing with suspects and arrested persons. A principal issue is whether such rules are mandatory or directory.

(2) Interpretative Guides

This heading covers all official statements of departmental or agency policy, explanations of how terms or rules will be interpreted or applied, expressions of criteria to be followed, standards to be enforced or considerations to be taken into account. In Gifford's terms, this would include all 'decisional referents' where of general applicability.

(3) Instructions to Officials

Although resembling interpretative guides in some respects, these instructions are principally aimed not at offering guidance to parties outside a bureaucracy but at controlling the exercise of powers within that bureaucracy. They aim not to inform citizens but to impose internal order—usually so as to facilitate planning or to encourage consistency. Strong arguments have been made for the publication of all such rules but secrecy is sustained by the desire to avoid having to justify them in public. Examples of low-visibility instructions are Prison Department Circulars, Standing Orders and Regulations and Home Office Circulars to Chief Constables.

A principal worry about secret codes is that they may conflict with published law. Thus, there was concern in 1984 when *The Observer* and the Legal Action Group exposed the operation of the Department of Health and Social Security's secret 'L' Code, a provision of which instructed legal aid assessment officers to pass on information to other officials in breach of the confidentiality provisions of section 22 of the Legal Aid Act 1974.

(4) Prescriptive/Evidential Rules

In some cases, regulatory bodies may want to do more than describe their policies or instruct their officials as to how to act: they may want to tell people what to do. It is of course possible to influence the behaviour of a regulated group by issuing a strong interpretative guide. ('We will only take action as provided for in the statute if conditions A, B, and C are met') or by publishing similarly formulated instructions to officials. Matters can be taken a step further, however, by prescribing courses of action on the understanding that a sanction exists at law (in primary or delegated legislation) or administratively (e.g. through non-allocation of a licence or other item of largesse). A common posture for such a 'prescriptive' rule is that of 'guide to compliance' with other legislation. Sanctions are usually indirect; thus, breach of the rule or code might not in itself lead to legal liability under a parent or associate rule.

A well-known example is the Highway Code. Breach of this is not an offence in itself but it may be taken into account in judging civil or criminal liability. Under the Health and Safety at Work Act 1974, 'approved codes of practice' may be issued by the Health and Safety Commission so as to 'provide practical guidance' in relation to the requirements of the parent Act or regulations. In the employment field, a number of codes offer 'practical guidance' but have an evidential role also. The Employment Act 1980 states that any provisions of the Secretary of State's Code of Practice on Picketing (1980) may be taken into account in proceedings before a court or tribunal. It is this code which advises that pickets should in general not exceed six at any entrance to a workplace. As has been clear from the miners' dispute of 1984, the 'guidance' offered by such a code may take a most compelling form. It may be treated by enforcement officials as if it were primary legislation.

Less contentious, perhaps, are the codes of practice on industrial relations. Power to issue these is given to the Advisory, Conciliation and Arbitration Service (ACAS), the Equal Opportunities Commission and the Commission for Racial Equality. Under the Employment Protection Act 1975, section 6, the ACAS codes again have evidential status: they are admissible in evidence and a tribunal or arbitration committee is specifically empowered to take relevant codes into account in determining issues.

Prescriptive rules may be backed up with sanctions other than the civil or criminal law such as disciplinary action. This is the case with the Codes of Practice that replace the Judges' Rules under the terms of the Police and Criminal Evidence Act. The Secretary of State issues codes on detention, treatment, questioning, identification of suspects, searches of premises, seizure and stops and searches. Failure to observe the terms of these codes may render police officers liable to disciplinary sanctions but will not give rise to criminal or civil liability or to the automatic exclusion of evidence.

(5) Commendatory Rules

The prescriptive model of rule involves instruction plus some variety of (often indirect) sanction. Commendation, on the other hand, has as its principal function the recommending of some course of action. Failure to adhere will not involve direct or indirect legal liability. A good example of commendations within a hierarchy of rules is provided in health and safety regulation. Primary duties are *statutory* and are set out in the Health and Safety at Work Act 1974 (see sections 2–9). These are made more specific in the Secretary of State's *regulations*, breach of which involves criminal liability and may be admissible in evidence in civil proceedings. *Codes of practice*, we have noted, offer 'practical guidance', are of evidential value and may reverse the onus of proof. *Guidance notes* constitute the lowest tier of the system. These are issued by the Health and Safety Commission and Executive: they advise on how safety objectives may be achieved, they encourage and recommend courses of action but they deal with issues beyond the area of legal sanction and lack legal force.

Commendatory rules thus do not accord with Austinian notions of threat plus sanction: they are more attuned to a facilitative role. Some rules of evidential significance might be considered commendations (e.g. the ACAS industrial relations codes) and here is the main overlap with prescriptive rules.

(6) Voluntary Codes

Self-regulatory codes differ from externally-imposed prescriptions in their origins and sanctions. Usually employed to stave off government regulation by upholding standards within a defined interest group, they may nevertheless carry considerable force: expulsion from the group for breach of a code may close down a business. The City Code on Takeovers and Mergers is a prime example of a voluntary code. It is issued by the Council for the Securities Industry (CSI) and offers a codification of good standards of commercial behaviour. The code has a governmental role insofar as breaches stand to be investigated by the Department of Trade.

Instances of such codes are to be found in many industries, such as advertising and housebuilding. In recent years, business self-regulation has blossomed, especially where relations with consumers are affected and deviant members of associations may be fined. Many businesses indulge in voluntary labelling, publish codes of ethics and good practice and some of these are stamped with the approval of the Office of Fair Trading. Indeed, section 124 (3) of the Fair Trading Act 1973 imposes a duty on the Director-General of Fair Trading to encourage trade associations to prepare codes of practice for guidance in promoting consumer interests and over 20 codes were approved in the period 1974–84.

The rules of domestic and professional bodies may have legal effects deriving from the law of contract, but the governmental role of many associations has led a leading text to liken such rules more to delegated legislation than to the terms of a contract.

(7) Rules of Practice, Management or Operation

Some rules have considerable effect without being directly normative. These are what Megarry called 'subject-and-subject' rules, 'consisting of arrangements made by administrative bodies which affect the operation of the law between one subject and another'. Thus, a new policy or enforcement practice would come under this heading.

The extra-statutory concessions made by the Commissioners for Inland Revenue are in point. Sometimes the Commissioners will act according to a stated policy, at others they will exercise discretion *ad hoc*. The courts have been uncertain in their responses. In *IRC* v *Korner* [1979] 1 All ER 679, Lord Upjohn described an unpublished concession as conducive to 'great justice between the Crown and the subject'. On the other hand, Lord Parker CJ has talked of 'the word of the Minister outweighing the law of the land'

and Lord Radcliffe of 'opening the door of Parliament'. More recently in the Court of Appeal, Lawton LJ described the IRC's decision to cancel a tax advantage as 'a managerial discretion' which was reviewable only where there was an abuse of power.

(8) Consultative Devices and Administrative Pronouncements

There is no distinct line between legal and administrative rules or, indeed, between rules and other forms of pronouncement such as decisions. It is clear, however, that a statement may have normative effects in certain circumstances or from some perspectives and it may lack them in a different context. To adhere to rigid definitions or conceptual distinctions is therefore to fall into a trap.

Our final group is thus something of a safety-net. It covers those pronouncements which fit into none of the other groups but which have a significance that goes beyond the individual case. Principal amongst these are consultative statements. These often involve draft outlines of agency or departmental policy and invite comments. As such, they form a halfway house in the rule-making or adjudicative processes. They allow an expression of policy views without undertaking a rigid commitment.

NOTE: See also G. Ganz, *Quasi-Legislation: Some Recent Developments in Secondary Legislation* (1987) and R. Baldwin, *Rules and Government* (1995).

(d) Prerogative

According to Blackstone, the Royal Prerogative is 'singular and eccentrical', something which applies to rights and capacities only enjoyed by the Monarch. The *Case of Proclamations* (1611) 12 Co Rep 74 and the Bill of Rights 1689 (see p. 53, *ante*) have made it clear that the prerogative cannot be used as a means to bypass Parliament in order to change the general law of the land. Today the prerogative is restricted to the conduct of foreign affairs; the declaration of war, and the disposition of the armed forces; the appointment of civil servants and Ministers, Privy Councillors, judges, and bishops; the conferral of peerages and honours; the dissolution of Parliament: see pp. 157–161, *ante*.

What is the status of the prerogative where legislation has been passed concerning an area within the scope of the prerogative?

Attorney-General v De Keyser's Royal Hotel Ltd

[1920] AC 508, House of Lords

During the First World War the Crown took possession of the respondents' hotel in order to house staff of the Royal Flying Corps. The Crown purported to do this under the authority of the Defence of the Realm Regulations. The Crown contended that compensation was not payable to the respondents because there still existed a residue of the prerogative which permitted temporary occupation of a subject's property in time of war. This residue of the prerogative was exercised under the regulations. The respondents contended that the Defence Act 1842 required that compensation should be paid.

LORD ATKINSON: ...It is quite obvious that it would be useless and meaningless for the Legislature to impose restrictions and limitations upon, and to attach conditions to, the exercise by the Crown of the powers conferred by a statute, if the Crown were free at its pleasure to disregard these provisions, and by virtue of its prerogative do the very thing the statutes empowered it to do. One cannot in the construction of a statute attribute to the Legislature (in the absence of compelling words) an intention so absurd. It was suggested that when a statute is passed empowering the Crown to do a certain thing which it might theretofore have done by virtue of its prerogative, the prerogative is merged in the statute. I confess I do not think the word 'merged' is happily chosen. I should prefer to say that when such a statute, expressing the will and intention of the King and of the three estates of the realm, is passed, it abridges the Royal Prerogative while it is in force to this extent: that the Crown can only do the particular thing under and in accordance with the statutory provisions, and that its prerogative power to do that thing is in abeyance. Whichever mode of expression be used, the result intended to be indicated is, I think, the same—namely, that after the statute has been passed, and while it is in force, the thing it empowers the Crown to do can thenceforth only be done by and under the statute, and subject to all the limitations, restrictions and conditions by it imposed, however unrestricted the Royal Prerogative may theretofore have been.

[Lord Atkinson found that the proper construction of the regulations meant that the 1842 statute governed the occupation and that compensation under that statute was payable. Lords Dunedin, Moulton, Sumner and Parmoor delivered concurring speeches.]

Appeal dismissed.

NOTE: In *Studies in Constitutional Law* (1999), at pp. 274–275, Munro argues that if a statute which overlapped with the prerogative was repealed, then the prerogative would be restored to the position it had before that statute was enacted. Thus only express statutory provision can abolish the prerogative.

(e) European Union legislation

The legislative powers of the EU are laid down in Art. 288 (ex 249) of the TFEU Treaty (see p. 368, *post*). Regulations, directives, and decisions are binding, but recommendations and opinions are not. The procedural requirements specified in Art. 296 (ex 253 TEC) (see p. 370, *post*) must be carried out otherwise the measure could be annulled under Arts 19 TEU (see p. 371, *post*) and 263, 264 TFEU (ex 230 and 231 TEC). Although Art. 297 TFEU (ex 254 TEC) only requires publication of regulations and some directives, other directives are also published, as are many decisions.

Some legislation implementing EU measures will be passed by Parliament in the form of Orders in Council or rules and regulations. This is provided for in s. 2(2) of the European Communities Act 1972 (see p. 379, *post*).

Statutes are enacted to ratify treaty amendments, such as the Single European Act which was effected by the European Communities (Amendment) Act 1986.

B: Control

(a) Consultation

D. R. Miers and A. C. Page, *Legislation*

(2nd edn, 1990), pp. 39–43

Once it has been decided that legislation is desirable, a detailed legislative proposal must be formulated. This will be undertaken within the responsible department, and the proposal will normally go through a number of drafts. Achieving a measure of coherence in government policy requires that views of other affected departments be taken into account in the preparation of proposals. For example, the Treasury must be consulted if public resources are involved, as must the Scottish, Welsh and Northern Ireland Offices if their interests are affected. Where Cabinet approval for the introduction of the measure has been obtained, consultations between the responsible department and interested departments take place on the basis of a draft memorandum. In addition, the formulation of major proposals will be supervised by the appropriate Cabinet policy committee. Where the approval of the Cabinet has not been previously obtained, it will be sought on the basis of the memorandum as revised in the light of such preliminary consultations as have taken place.

Whereas consultation within government is mandatory, consultation with outside interests takes place at the discretion of government. The extent of such consultation varies: some proposals are the subject of extensive consultation, others very little. The extent to which affected interests are consulted also varies. On major issues of party policy the government may choose not to consult affected interests (particularly those traditionally opposed to it), though even here it may do so if only to minimise disagreement. In general, however, sectional and in particular producer groups are consulted to a much greater extent than other groups. In the absence of the direct and permanent access to government enjoyed by sectional groups, cause groups' efforts are more visibly directed towards influencing the media and lobbying MPs.

How can we account for the greater likelihood of sectional group involvement in the preparation of legislation? Most commonly it is attributed to a shared pluralist conception of authority on the part of government and outside interests. Thus, Beer attributes their greater involvement to 'the widespread acceptance of functional representation in British political culture.' Acceptance of functional representation has in turn meant that: 'It has now almost become a convention of the constitution that the interests likely to be affected by developments in public policy have, through their representative associations, a right to be consulted by policy makers,' and that governments 'are regarded as having a corresponding duty to consult before taking final decisions.' Whether these expectations as to the way in which public, including legislative, power will be examined are as widely shared today as they were 10 to 20 years ago is doubtful. But even if they are not, there remain strong incentives for government to consult. A failure to consult may make the passage of the legislation more difficult; more importantly, it may prejudice its successful implementation and thereby the attainment of the government's objectives. The brute fact is that these groups possess the capacity to 'limit, deflect and even frustrate government initiatives.' For this reason, if no other, government seeks through consultation to arrive at an understanding with them beforehand.

Commentators rightly emphasise the benefits derived from the involvement of these groups by both the groups themselves and government. For the groups, their involvement constitutes a procedural guarantee that their interests and views will be given a hearing if not reflected in the content of proposals. For government, on the other hand, the groups' expertise and advice may be crucial to the formulation of workable proposals and their acquiescence, if not active co-operation, may be equally vital to the successful implementation of proposals. These groups are thus seen as important and necessary channels of communication which parallel representation through the electoral system. Without their activity, Finer observes, party rule would be 'a rigid and ignorant tyranny,' and public administration 'a rigid and stupid bureaucracy.' Their privileged position in relation to government does, however, carry with it the danger that interests other than those immediately involved will be ignored.

The consultative process itself varies in its formality. Consultation may take place on the basis of a Green Paper published with Cabinet approval on which the views of interested parties are sought. Publication of the government's proposals in the form of a White Paper implies, instead, that the government is committed to at least the main principles of the policy outlined and the scope for consultation is correspondingly reduced. More commonly, however, consultation takes place on the basis of informal and private communications between departments and affected interests.

Consultation need not of course be confined to any single stage in the preparation of a proposal. A group's influence on a proposal cannot be determined therefore solely by reference to the extent to which it is formally consulted during its preparation. Thus it may, for example, have been the prime mover in the identification of an issue, or its views may have been canvassed and reflected in the report of a committee upon which legislation is ultimately based. Where the group has not had the opportunity of expressing its views previously, its influence will depend, in part, on the stage of the preparatory process at which it is consulted and, in particular, on whether it is consulted before the principles of the legislation have been settled.

The most effective time for groups to operate is after a decision to legislate has been taken, but before a Bill has actually been drafted and published. Once the government has publicly committed itself to the main lines of a Bill, disagreement and opposition by interested parties can only usually be manifested by public or parliamentary campaigns, which groups are not well-fitted to undertake. Given the structure of public decision-making in Britain, in which Parliament plays a distinctly subordinate role, this line of action is usually far less likely to be successful than attempting to persuade the Minister.

A group's influence will also depend on whether or not there is any scope for negotiation: there is a fundamental distinction between consultation involving simply an expression of views (for example, on a Green Paper or in response to specific requests) and consultation involving negotiation or actual bargaining between the parties. Whereas the views expressed in consultation of the former type may or may not be taken into account by the government, the latter implies a much greater involvement of groups in the formulation of the proposal and the effective renunciation by government of unilateral decision-making. As Hartley and Griffith point out:

The Department will tell those whom it chooses to consult...what are the broad intentions of the Government, what is sought to be achieved by the Bill then being put together, and what means are proposed. On particular matters, or when asked by affected interests, the department may go into more detail, sometimes putting forward alternatives and seeking the opinion of those interested on the various merits of the alternatives. Where, as is often the case, the co-operation of the affected interests is highly desirable in order to make the Bill most effective in practice, something very like a bargain may be struck and undertakings may be given on both sides.

NOTE: The courts have distinguished between 'legislative' and 'administrative' activity in respect of consultation.

Bates v *Lord Hailsham of St Marylebone*

[1972] 1 WLR 1373, Chancery Division

Under s. 56(3) of the Solicitors Act 1957, drafts of orders prescribing solicitors' remuneration in respect of non-contentious business were required to be sent to the Council of the Law Society by the Lord Chancellor. The committee which had the power to make the orders had to consider any written observations from the Council of the Law Society before making such orders.

The committee proposed an order which was sent in draft to the Law Society. The claimant was a member of the British Legal Association which objected to the proposed order. This body, which had some 2,900 members, wished to delay the making of the order so that there might be more consultation with the legal profession. The claimant sought a declaration that, if an order was made without the British Legal Association first being consulted, then this would be *ultra vires*.

MEGARRY J: ...Mr Nicholls relied on *Reg.* v *Liverpool Corporation, Ex parte Liverpool Taxi Fleet Operators' Association* [1972] 2 QB 299; and he read me some passages from the judgments of Lord Denning MR and Roskill LJ. It cannot often happen that words uttered by a judge in his judicial capacity will, within six months, be cited against him in his personal capacity as defendant; yet that is the position here. The case was far removed from the present case. It concerned the exercise by a city council of its powers to licence hackney carriages, and a public undertaking given by the chairman of the relevant committee which the council soon proceeded to ignore. The case supports propositions relating to the duty of a body to act fairly when exercising administrative functions under a statutory power: see at pp. 307, 308 and 310. Accordingly, in deciding the policy to be applied as to the number of licences to grant, there was a duty to hear those who would be likely to be affected. It is plain that no legislation was involved: the question was one of the policy to be adopted in the exercise of a statutory power to grant licences.

In the present case, the committee in question has an entirely different function: it is legislative rather than administrative or executive. The function of the committee is to make or refuse to make a legislative instrument under delegated powers. The order, when made, will lay down the remuneration for solicitors generally; and the terms of the order will have to be considered and construed and applied in numberless cases in the future. Let me accept that in the sphere of the so-called quasi-judicial the rules of natural justice run, and that in the administrative or executive field there is a general duty of fairness. Nevertheless, these considerations do not seem to me to affect the process of legislation, whether primary or delegated. Many of those affected by delegated legislation, and affected very substantially, are never consulted in the process of enacting that legislation: and yet they have no remedy. Of course, the informal consultation of representative bodies by the legislative authority is a commonplace; but although a few statutes have specifically provided for a general process of publishing draft delegated legislation and considering objections (see, for example, the Factories Act 1961, Schedule 4), I do not know of any implied right to be consulted or make objections, or any principle upon which the courts may enjoin the legislative process at the suit of those who contend that insufficient time for consultation and consideration has been given. I accept that the fact that the order will take the form of a statutory instrument does not per se make it immune from attack, whether by injunction or otherwise; but what is important is not its form but its nature, which is plainly legislative....

Order accordingly.

NOTE: The distinction between 'administrative' and 'legislative' is a fine one. In *R* v *Secretary of State for the Environment, ex parte Brent LBC* [1982] QB 593, local authorities successfully argued that the Minister was under a duty to hear their representations before exercising powers under delegated legislation to reduce their rate support grant.

In another case, concerning lawyers' remuneration, representatives of the Bar argued that they had a legitimate expectation of being consulted about regulations to be made under the Legal Aid Act 1974. The point was not decided because the case was settled.

Sometimes there is a statutory requirement to consult. Such a requirement may be derogated from, as in social security, where the Minister need not consult the Social Security Advisory Committee about draft regulations if it is inexpedient to do so by reason of urgency (Social Security Administration Act 1992, s. 173(1)(a)).

Where a consultation obligation is imposed in respect of legislation, what will be considered to be sufficient consultation?

R v Secretary of State for Social Services, ex parte Association of Metropolitan Authorities

[1986] 1 WLR 1, Queen's Bench Division

Before making regulations constituting the housing benefits scheme, the Minister was required, by s. 36(1) of the Social Security and Housing Benefits Act 1982, to consult with organizations which appeared to him to be representative of the housing authorities concerned. The applicant was such an organization whose views had been sought by the Minister's officials on proposed amendments to the 1982 regulations. The consultative letter was written on 16 November 1984 and received by the applicant on 22 November. A response was requested by 30 November. The applicant complained about the shortness of time and asked for an extension so that its advisers could be consulted. On 4 December officials wrote to the applicant seeking its views on further proposed amendments. No draft of the proposals was forwarded and no mention was made of a material feature which required local authorities to investigate whether housing benefit claimants had created joint tenancies so as to gain from the housing benefit scheme. A response was requested by 12 December. The applicant answered the first letter on 7 December and sent brief comments about the second letter on 13 December. The Housing Benefits Amendment (No. 4) Order Regulations 1984 were made on 17 December and came into effect on 19 December. The applicant sought, *inter alia*, a declaration that the Minister had not exercised his duty under s. 36(1) of the Act of 1982, and an order of *certiorari* to quash the regulations because of the failure to consult.

WEBSTER J: ... There is no general principle to be extracted from the case law as to what kind or amount of consultation is required before delegated legislation, of which consultation is a precondition, can validly be made. But in any context the essence of consultation is the communication of a genuine invitation to give advice and a genuine receipt of that advice. In my view it must go without saying that to achieve consultation sufficient information must be supplied by the consulting to the consulted party to enable it to tender helpful advice. Sufficient time must be given by the consulting to the consulted party to enable it to do that, and sufficient time must be available for such advice to be considered by the consulting party. Sufficient, in that context, does not mean ample, but at least enough to enable the relevant purpose to be fulfilled. By helpful advice, in this context, I mean sufficiently informed and considered information or advice about aspects of the form or substance of the proposals, or their implications for the consulted party, being aspects material to the implementation of the proposal as to which the Secretary of State might not be fully informed or advised and as to which the party consulted might have relevant information or advice to offer.

These propositions, as it seems to me, can partly be derived from, and are wholly consistent with, the decisions and various dicta, which I need not enumerate, in *Rollo* v *Minister of Town and Country Planning* [1948] 1 All ER 13 and *Port Louis Corporation* v *Attorney-General of Mauritius* [1965] AC 1111.

...In the present case, looking at the 'whole scope and purpose' of the Act of 1982, one matter which stands out is that its day-to-day administration is in the hands of local housing authorities who bear 10 per cent of the cost of the scheme. It is common ground that in them resides the direct expertise necessary to administer schemes made under the Act on a day-to-day basis. For these reasons, if for no other, I conclude that the obligation laid on the Secretary of State to consult organisations representative of those authorities is mandatory, not directory.

The last question of principle to be decided before turning to the facts is the test to be applied to the facts as I find them for the purposes of judicial review....[T]o what extent is it for the Secretary of State, not the court, to judge how much consultation is necessary and how long is to be given for it? The answer to that question may qualify the word 'sufficient' in the requirements of consultation which I have set out above....

....[T]he first point to note is that the power to make the regulations is conferred on the Secretary of State and that his is the duty to consult. Save for those consulted, no one else is involved in the making of the regulations. Secondly, both the form or substance of new regulations and the time allowed for consulting, before making them, may well depend in whole or in part on matters of a political nature, as to the force and implications of which it would be reasonable to expect the Secretary of State, rather than the court, to be the best judge. Thirdly, issues may well be raised after the making of the regulations as to the detailed merits of one or other reason for making them, or as to the precise degree of urgency required in their making, issues which have been raised on this application. Those issues cannot be said to be wholly irrelevant to a challenge to the vires of the regulations, and Mr Beloff has not submitted that they are irrelevant; but at the same time it would seem to me to be inherently improbable that the question of the vires of the regulations should depend upon precise findings of fact on issues such as those. In my view, therefore, the court, when considering the question whether the consultation required by section 36(1) was in substance carried out, should have regard not so much to the actual facts which preceded the making of the regulations as to the material before the Secretary of State when he made the regulations, that material including facts or information as it appeared or must have appeared to him acting in good faith, and any judgments made or opinions expressed to him before the making of the regulations about those facts which appear or could have appeared to him to be reasonable. The department's good faith is not challenged on this application.

The effect of treating as material the facts as they appeared to the Secretary of State, and not necessarily as they were, is to give a certain flexibility to the notions of sufficiency, sufficient information, sufficient time and sufficiently informed and considered information and advice in my homespun attempt to define proper consultation. Thus, it can have the effect that what would be sufficient information or time in one case might be more or less than sufficient in another, depending on the relative degrees of urgency and the nature of the proposed regulation. There is no degree of urgency, however, which absolves the Secretary of State from the obligation to consult at all.

Upon consideration of the facts, his Lordship said that the Minister's view on the urgency of the need for the amending regulations and the nature of the proposed amendments justified requiring comments to be expressed quickly, but not in so short a period that the comments would be insufficiently informed or insufficiently considered. When account was also taken of the fact that the applicant had no notice of a material feature until after the regulations were made, his Lordship concluded that the Minister had not discharged his duty to consult before making the regulations.

Having decided that the provisions of section 36(1) are mandatory and that they were not complied with before the regulations were made, I now have to consider the relief which I should give to the association. They ask me to quash the regulations. I do not think that I should do so.

I acknowledge, with respect, that in the ordinary case a decision—I emphasize the word 'decision'—made ultra vires is likely to be set aside in accordance with the dictum of Lord Diplock in *Grunwick Processing Laboratories Ltd* v *Advisory, Conciliation and Arbitration Service* [1978] AC 655, 695, where he said:

> My Lords, where a statutory authority has acted ultra vires any person who would be affected by its act if it were valid is normally entitled ex debito justiciae to have it set aside...

But whereas the ordinary case is that of a ministerial departmental decision, which adversely affects the rights of one person or of a class of persons, and which can be struck down without, usually, more than individual or local implications, in this case the association seeks to strike down regulations which have become part of the public law of the land. Although I have been shown and have found no authority to support the proposition, I suspect that it is not necessarily to be regarded as the normal practice, where delegated legislation is held to be ultra vires, to revoke the instrument, but that the inclination would be the other way, in the absence of special circumstances making it desirable to revoke that instrument. But in principle I treat the matter as one of pure discretion and so treating it decline to revoke the instrument for the following reasons, no particular significance being attached to the order in which I state them.

Although six organisations were and are habitually consulted in this context, only one of them has applied for revocation of the instrument and that one applies only on the ground that it was not properly consulted. It makes no formal complaint that the other organisations were not consulted. Although the association complains about the substance of the regulations, it is apparent that its principal complaint throughout is, and has been, the absence of proper consultation and it and other organisations were able to express some, albeit in a sense piecemeal, views about the proposal which apparently the department took into account before making the regulations, but without, be it noted, any effort whatsoever on the November or December amendments. The regulations have been in force for about six months and, although their implementation creates difficulties for some at least of the housing authorities who have to administer them, those authorities must by now have adapted themselves as best they can to those difficulties. If, however, the regulations were to be revoked all applicants who had been refused benefit because of the new regulations would be entitled to make fresh claims, and all authorities would be required to consider each such claim.

Finally, the Housing Benefits Amendment (No. 4) Regulations 1984 have been consolidated into the Housing Benefits Regulations 1985 (S.I. 1985 No. 677), which were made on 29 April 1985, laid before Parliament on 30 April and came into operation and indeed have come into operation for the most part, today, 21 May. Those regulations are not at present challenged. If, therefore, the Housing Benefits Amendment (No. 4) Regulations 1984 were to be revoked, and so long as the Regulations of 1985 remain valid, any person entitled to reconsideration of his claim to benefit would, if successful, at best be entitled to benefits for about six months. For all these reasons, I refuse, in the exercise of my discretion, to revoke the Housing Benefits Amendment (No. 4) Regulations 1984.

I can see no reason whatsoever, however, for refusing the association the declaration for which they ask....

Declaration accordingly. Application for order of certiorari refused.

■ QUESTIONS

1. Consultation is not generally required for legislation, although central governmental practice is usually to conduct consultation amongst interested bodies and consultation exercises are regulated by the following:

HM Government, Code of Practice on Consultation

(3rd edn, 2008), pp. 5–6

The seven consultation criteria are as follows:

(1) When to consult: formal consultations should take place at a stage where there is scope to influence the policy outcome.
(2) Duration of consultation exercises: consultations should normally last for at least 12 weeks with consideration given to longer timescales where feasible and sensible.
(3) Clarity of scope and impact: consultation documents should be clear about the consultation process, what is being proposed, the scope to influence the proposals and the expected costs and benefits of the proposals.
(4) Accessibility of consultation exercises: consultation exercises should be designed to be accessible to, and clearly targeted at, those people the exercise is intended to reach.
(5) The burden of consultation: keeping the burden of consultation to a minimum is essential if consultations are to be effective and if consultees' buy-in to the process is to be obtained.
(6) Responsiveness of consultation exercises: consultation responses should be analysed carefully and clear feedback should be provided to participants following the consultation.
(7) Capacity to consult: officials running consultations should seek guidance in how to run an effective consultation exercise and share what they have learned from the experience.

The Code states that it 'does not have legal force' but it further states that 'the Code and the criteria within it apply to all UK public consultations by government departments and agencies'. In the following case the challenge to the consultation was that there was a failure: (see also: *R (Greenpeace)* v *Secretary of State for Trade and Industry* [2007] EWHC 311 (Admin), at p. 577, *post*). In *Bhatt Murphy* the argument concerned a change in policy (a) to cease a discretionary compensation scheme which was more generous than a statutory one, and (b) to use different a different and less generous assessment for fees, the Court of Appeal ruled on the general applicability of legitimate expectations and dismissed the appeal contending that the consultation was unlawful:

R (Bhatt Murphy) v *The Independent Assessor*

[2008] EWCA Civ 755

50. A very broad summary of the place of legitimate expectations in public law might be expressed as follows. The power of public authorities to change policy is constrained by the legal duty to be fair (and other constraints which the law imposes). A change of policy which would otherwise be legally unexceptionable may be held unfair by reason of prior action, or inaction, by the authority. If it has distinctly promised to consult those affected or potentially affected, then ordinarily it must consult (the paradigm case of procedural expectation). If it has distinctly promised to preserve existing policy for a specific person or group who would be substantially affected by the change, then ordinarily it must keep its promise (substantive expectation). If, without any promise, it has established a policy distinctly and substantially affecting a specific person or group who in the circumstances was in reason entitled to rely on its continuance and did so, then ordinarily it must consult before effecting any change (the secondary case of procedural expectation). To do otherwise, in any of these instances, would be to act so unfairly as to perpetrate an abuse of power...

54 As regards the Code of Practice I agree entirely with the Divisional Court. May LJ said:

> 23 ...The Introduction states that the Code and the criteria apply to all public consultations by government departments and agencies. Mr Swift submits, correctly in my view, that this means that the Code is to apply whenever it is decided as a matter of policy to have a public consultation; not that public consultation is a required prelude to every policy change. The Code states that it does not have legal force but should generally be regarded as binding on United Kingdom departments and their agencies unless Ministers conclude that exceptional circumstances require a departure from it. Ministers retain their existing discretion not to conduct a formal written consultation exercise under the terms of the Code, for example where the issue is very specialised and where there is a very limited number of so-called stakeholders who have been directly involved in the policy development process.
>
> 24 For the reasons given by Mr Swift, I do not consider that it is possible to read this document as any form of governmental promise or undertaking that policy changes will never be made without consultation. It would be very surprising if it could be so read, not least because a decision in a particular case whether to consult is itself a policy decision. Rather the Code prescribes how generally public consultation should be conducted if there is to be public consultation.

This leaves the area of quasi-legislation produced by other public authorities and agencies. Bearing in mind that the courts seem to have regard to the distinctions between legislative, executive, and administrative action, should there be a general statutory obligation imposed on all public bodies who make any measures, whether they take the form of primary, delegated, or quasi-legislation?

2. What are the benefits and disadvantages of consultation, and would the benefits outweigh the disadvantages:
    (a) generally;
    (b) only for some types of quasi-legislation?

3. If such a general duty of consultation were required, would it be in conflict with the representative nature of our parliamentary democratic constitution?
4. For the purposes of a duty to consult, should we make a distinction between those measures which are subject to parliamentary oversight and those which are not?

NOTE: The Hansard Society produced a report on the legislative process. In this they proposed guiding principles which underpinned their recommendations for reform. The evidence which they received indicated that the current arrangements for consultation were unsatisfactory.

The Hansard Society, *Making the Law*

(1993), pp. 14, 15, 139–41

...[W]e have agreed five central principles which guide and govern all the recommendations we make:

- Laws are made for the benefit of the citizens of the state. All citizens directly affected should be involved as fully and openly as possible in the process by which statute law is prepared.
- Statute law should be as certain as possible and as intelligible and clear as possible, for the benefit of the citizens to whom it applies.
- Statute law must be rooted in the authority of Parliament and thoroughly exposed to open democratic scrutiny by the representatives of the people in Parliament.
- Ignorance of the law is no excuse, therefore the current statute law must be as accessible as possible to all who need to know it.
- The Government needs to be able to secure the passage of its legislation, but to get the law right and intelligible, for the benefit of citizens, is as important as to get it passed quickly.

[Recommendations on consultation]

Primary Legislation

4. The overwhelming impression from the evidence is that many of those most directly affected are deeply dissatisfied with the extent, nature, timing and conduct of consultation on bills as at present practised...the Government must heed this criticism and seek to meet it....

5. The Government should always seek the fullest advice from those affected on the problems of implementing and enforcing proposed legislation....

6. Although some bills are inevitably required in a hurry, getting a bill right should always have priority over passing it quickly, and we recommend that the Government should publicly endorse this policy....

7. The Government should make every effort to get bills in a form fit for enactment, without major alteration, before they are presented to Parliament; in the Government's review of the legislative process, this should be a first and overriding objective....

8. Proper consultation should play a central part in the preparation of bills, and we recommend that all Government departments should act accordingly....

9. Good consultation practice requires that when a bill is being prepared, bodies with relevant experience or interests—particularly those directly affected—should be given all the relevant information and an opportunity to make their views known or to give information or advice, at each level of decision-taking....

10. Consultation should be as open as possible....

11. Secrecy regarding the content and results of consultations should be minimised and feedback maximised....

12. When major reviews are required of how the current law is operating and of the need for reform, we would welcome more frequent appointment of independent inquiries, including Royal Commissions. If the Government is not prepared to accept the advice of such inquiries, it would be expected to publish its reasons....

13. Consultative documents should be as clear and precise as possible. They should be specific about the questions on which departments want responses, while leaving opportunity for bodies to put forward further ideas of their own on relevant points. Green Papers should set out the facts fully and, as far as possible, the options being considered. White Papers should normally be preceded by Green Papers. White Papers should, where possible, systematically detail changes from Green Papers, indicating why these changes had been made....

14. Departments should offer more consultations on draft texts, especially in so far as they relate to practical questions of the implementation and enforcement of legislation....

15. The experience of the Inland Revenue in consulting on individual draft clauses of the Finance Bill should be studied by other departments and adopted in other fields....

16. Where there is no great urgency for a bill, the whole bill might sometimes be published in draft in a Green Paper, as the basis for further consultation and possibly parliamentary scrutiny....

17. Government departments should consult the main bodies concerned in each case and seek to agree how much time should be allowed for their responses to a consultation document....

18. Consultation should not be delayed....

19. Bodies invited by Government departments to respond to consultative documents on proposed legislation, and other bodies with a *bona fide* interest, should be given, free of charge, as many copies of those documents as they can show they need....

20. Bodies which have contributed to consultation on proposed legislation should be supplied, free of charge, with copies of the resulting bills, Acts and statutory instruments....

21. The Government should, drawing on best practice, prepare consultation guidelines which would be applicable to all Government departments when preparing legislation....

22. We recommend that—

(a) the Government's guidelines on consultation should be published;
(b) each department when applying to the Future Legislation Committee for inclusion of a bill in the Government's legislative programme should submit a check-list indicating how far it has been able to comply with the guidelines, and give details of the consultations it has already carried out or proposes to conduct; and
(c) an up-dated version of the check-list and this information should be submitted with the draft bill to the Legislation Committee and published with the bill....

Delegated legislation

23. There should be consultation where appropriate at the formative stage of delegated legislation, but wherever possible departments should also consult outside experts and affected bodies on drafts of the actual instruments that they propose to lay before Parliament....

24. The Government's guidelines that we have recommended regarding consultation on bills, should be applied with appropriate modifications to consultation on delegated legislation....

NOTE: In a subsequent Hansard Society report, A. Brazier et al, *Law in the Making: Influence and Change in the Legislative Process* (2008), p. 179, there was criticism by some groups that some consultation exercises were simply 'going through the motions', and that they were designed to produce a particular outcome or only the views of certain 'trusted' groups were really considered.

■ QUESTIONS

1. Does consultation operate more as an attempt to legitimise rather than control legislation?
2. Do the Hansard Society's proposals focus more on the workability of legislation when made, whereas the government concentrates more on the processes and politics of making legislation?

(b) Publicity

All statutes are published, as is delegated legislation governed by the Statutory Instruments Act 1946, but this does leave open the possibility of other legislative measures not being readily available or known about.

STATUTORY INSTRUMENTS ACT 1946

1.—(1) Where by this Act or any Act passed after the commencement of this Act power to make, confirm or approve orders, rules, regulations or other subordinate legislation is conferred on His Majesty in Council or on any Minister of the Crown then, if the power is expressed—

(a) in the case of a power conferred on His Majesty, to be exercisable by Order in Council;
(b) in the case of a power conferred on a Minister of the Crown, to be exercisable by statutory instrument,

any document by which that power is exercised shall be known as a 'statutory instrument' and the provisions of this Act shall apply thereto accordingly....

2.—(1) Immediately after the making of any statutory instrument, it shall be sent to the King's printer of Acts of Parliament and numbered in accordance with regulations made under this Act, and except in such cases as may be provided by any Act passed after the commencement of this Act or prescribed by regulations made under this Act, copies thereof shall as soon as possible be printed and sold by the King's printer of Acts of Parliament....

3.—(1) Regulations made for the purposes of this Act shall make provision for the publication by His Majesty's Stationery Office of lists showing the date upon which every statutory instrument printed and sold by the King's printer of Acts of Parliament was first issued by that office; and in any legal proceedings a copy of any list so published purporting to bear the imprint of the King's printer shall be received in evidence as a true copy, and an entry therein shall be conclusive evidence of the date on which any statutory instrument was first issued by His Majesty's Stationery Office.

(2) In any proceedings against any person for an offence consisting of a contravention of any such statutory instrument, it shall be a defence to prove that the instrument had not been issued by His Majesty's Stationery Office at the date of the alleged contravention unless it is proved that at that date reasonable steps had been taken for the purpose of bringing the purport of the instrument to the notice of the public, or of persons likely to be affected by it, or of the person charged.

(3) Save as therein otherwise expressly provided, nothing in this section shall affect any enactment or rule of law relating to the time at which any statutory instrument comes into operation....

8.—(1) The Treasury may, with the concurrence of the Lord Chancellor and the Speaker of the House of Commons, by statutory instrument make regulations for the purposes of this Act, and such regulations may, in particular:—...

(c) provide with respect to any classes or descriptions of statutory instrument that they shall be exempt, either altogether or to such extent as may be determined by or under the regulations, from the requirement of being printed and of being sold by the King's printer of Acts of Parliament, or from either of those requirements:...

NOTE: Under the Statutory Instruments Regulations 1947, rr. 5–8 some regulations are exempted from the publication requirements of the 1946 Act. These are: local instruments and those otherwise published regularly (r. 5); temporary instruments (r. 6); schedules to rules which are too bulky and where other steps have been taken to bring them to the notice of the public (r. 7); cases in which it would be contrary to the public interest for publication to occur before the rules came into operation (r. 8). The Minister making rules subject to the exceptions in rr. 6–8 must certify that the conditions are satisfied.

R v *Sheer Metalcraft Ltd*

[1954] 1 QB 586, Kingston-upon-Thames Assizes

STREATFIELD J: ...This matter comes before the court in the form of an objection to the admissibility in evidence of a statutory instrument known as the Iron and Steel Prices Order, 1951. It appears that part and parcel of that instrument consisted of certain deposited schedules in which maximum prices for different commodities of steel were set out. The instrument is said to have been made by the Minister of Supply on February 16, 1951; laid before Parliament on February 20, 1951; and to have come into operation on February 21, 1951. It is under that statutory instrument that the present charges are made against the two defendants in this case.

The point which has been taken is that by reason of the deposited schedules not having been printed and not having been certified by the Minister as being exempt from printing, the instrument is not a valid instrument under the Statutory Instruments Act, 1946. That point was taken in *Simmonds* v *Newell* [1953] 1 WLR 826, but it was expressly left open in view of a certain admission then made by the Solicitor-General, which, however, does not apply to the present case. The point arises in this way: under regulation 55AB of the Defence (General) Regulations, 1939, as amended, a competent authority, which in this case is the Minister of Supply, may by statutory instrument provide for controlling the prices to be charged for goods of any description or the charges to be made for services of any description, and for any incidental and supplementary matters for which the competent authority thinks it expedient for the purposes of the instrument to provide. It is said in the statutory instrument here that it was made in exercise of the powers conferred upon the Minister by regulations 55AB and 98 of the Defence (General) Regulations, and other statutory authorities.

The contention is that the making of that instrument is governed by the provisions of the Statutory Instruments Act, 1946...

[His Lordship read sections 1 and 2 of the Act of 1946 and regulation 7 of the Statutory Instruments Regulations, 1947, and continued:] Section 1 visualizes the making of what is called a statutory instrument by a Minister of the Crown; section 2 visualizes that after the making of a statutory instrument it shall be sent to the King's Printer to be printed, except in so far as under regulations made under the Act it may be unnecessary to have it printed. It is said here that the Minister did not certify that the printing of these very bulky deposited schedules was unnecessary within the meaning of regulation 7. It is contended, therefore, that as he did not so certify it, it became an obligation under the Act that the deposited schedules as well as the instrument itself should be printed under section 2 of the Act of 1946, and in the absence of their having been printed as part of the instrument, the instrument cannot be regarded as being validly made.

To test that matter it is necessary to examine section 3 of the Act of 1946. By subsection (1) [see p. 340, sub section]... There does not appear to be any definition of what is meant by 'issue,' but presumably it does mean some act by the Queen's Printer of Acts of Parliament which follows the printing of the instrument. That section, therefore, requires that the Queen's Printer shall keep lists showing the date upon which statutory instruments are printed and issued.

Subsection (2) is important and provides [see p. 340, *ante*]... It seems to follow from the wording of this subsection that the making of an instrument is one thing and the issue of it is another. If it is made it can be contravened; if it has not been issued then that provides a defence to a person charged with its contravention. It is then upon the Crown to prove that, although it has not been issued, reasonable steps have been taken for the purpose of bringing the instrument to the notice of the public or persons likely to be affected by it.

I do not think that it can be said that to make a valid statutory instrument it is required that all of these stages should be gone through; namely, the making, the laying before Parliament, the printing and the certification of that part of it which it might be unnecessary to have printed. In my judgment the making of an instrument is complete when it is first of all made by the Minister concerned and after it has been laid before Parliament. When that has been done it then becomes a valid statutory instrument, totally made under the provisions of the Act.

The remaining provisions to which my attention has been drawn, in my view, are purely procedure for the issue of an instrument validly made—namely, that in the first instance it must be printed by the Queen's Printer unless it is certified to be unnecessary to print it; it must then be included in a list published by Her Majesty's Stationery Office showing the dates when it is issued and it may be issued by the Queen's Printer of Acts of Parliament. Those matters, in my judgment, are matters of procedure. If they were not and if they were stages in the perfection of a valid statutory instrument, I cannot see that section 3(2) would be necessary, because if each one of those stages were necessary to make a statutory instrument valid, it would follow that there could be no infringement of an unissued instrument and therefore it would be quite unnecessary to provide a defence to a contravention of any such instrument. In my view the very fact that subsection (2) of section 3 refers to a defence that the instrument has not been issued postulates that the instrument must have been validly made in the first place otherwise it could never have been contravened.

In those circumstances I hold that this instrument was validly made and approved and that it was made by or signed on behalf of the Minister on its being laid before Parliament; that so appears on the fact of the instrument itself. In my view, the fact that the Minister failed to certify under regulation 7 does not invalidate the instrument as an instrument but lays the burden upon the Crown to prove that at the date of the alleged contraventions reasonable steps had been taken for bringing the instrument to the notice of the public or persons likely to be affected by it. I, therefore, rule that this is admissible....

Verdict: Guilty on all counts.

NOTE: For a critical analysis of this case and s. 3 of the 1946 Act, see articles by Lanham at (1974) 37 *Modern Law Review* 510 and [1983] *Public Law* 395.

■ QUESTIONS

1. The publication requirements in the 1946 Act affect only statutory instruments in respect of which no exemption has been made. Should there be a general duty of publication?
2. With respect to publication of quasi-legislation:
   (a) should it only be required if it is reasonable and non-disclosure would prejudice the public; and
   (b) when would non-disclosure be reasonable?

(c) Parliamentary oversight

Public Information Office, House of Commons Sessional Information Digest

2007–08, 2008–09, and 2009–10 pp. 1, 2

Analysis of the time of the session

Types of Business	Total time spent (hours: minutes)		
	2007–08	2008–09	2009–10
Government Bills			
Second Reading debate (Bills committed to a Standing/ Public Bill Committee)	105:13	61:47	29:52
Second Reading debate (Bills committed to a Committee of the Whole House)	10:48	28:04	26:39
Committee of the Whole House	79:20	43:17	38:08
Consideration (Report stage)	116:06	77:53	42:04
Third Reading	15:40	9:04	9:10
Lords Amendments	38:29	28:38	5:49
Allocation of Time Orders	7:14	8:11	4:18
Committal & Carry-over Motions	0:00	0:56	0:00
Private Members' Bills			
Motions for the introduction of Ten Minute Rule Bills	10:51	8:42	3:43
Second Reading	51:22	48:23	18:28
Other stages	12:34	12:48	5:560
Money Resolutions	0:22	1:32	1:53
Ways and Means Resolutions (including Budget Debate)	24:31	22:44	25:22
Statutory Instruments Affirmative Statutory Instruments	24:56	12:30	16:31
Motions to annul or revoke Statutory Instruments	0:00	7:07	0:00

(a) Primary legislation

The Hansard Society, *Making the Law*

(1993), pp. 11–12

Volume of all Public General Acts, 1901–1991

Year	No. of Acts	Pages	No. of Sections and Schedules
1901	40	247	400
1911	58	584	701
1921	67	569	783
1931	34	375	440
1941	48	448	533
1951	66	675	803
1961	65	1048	1087
1971	81	2107	1963
1981	72	2276	2026
1991	69	2222*	1985

* Printed on A4 paper which was larger than the size previously used, so requiring fewer pages.

First Report from the Select Committee on Modernisation of the House of Commons

HC 1097 of 2005–06, p. 7

Table 1 Volume of primary legislation, 1992–2004

Year	No. of Acts	No. of pages of law
1992 (election year)	55	1,288
1993	65	2,041
1994	42	2,005
1995	48	2,290
1996	57	2,248
1997 (election year)	62	1,534
1998	47	2,357
1999	35	2,063
2000	45	3,610
2001 (election year)	25	1,232
2002	43	2,848
2003	44	3,435
2004	38	3,470

Source: Ev 77 and Acts & Statutory Instruments: volume of UK legislation 1950 to 2005, House of Commons Library Standard Note SN/SG/2911 (January 2006).

NOTE: Within the first month of the new Parliament elected in 1997, the House of Commons established a Select Committee to examine ways in which the House might be modernized. In its first report, it focused upon the legislative process in relation to primary legislation.

First Report from the Select Committee on Modernisation of the House of Commons

HC 190 of 1997–98, paras 4–17, 84–102

Perceived Defects in the Present System

4. Previous inquiries into the legislative process have consistently identified a number of defects in the way in which Parliament considers legislation. Criticisms are made not only of the procedures used but of the pattern and timing of legislative scrutiny during a typical parliamentary session.

5. The first criticism made is that there has hitherto been little, if any, consultation with Members or with the House as a whole before Bills are formally introduced. In recent years some draft Bills have been produced for prior consultation, and the present Government has specifically undertaken in the Queen's Speech to extend this process. The House itself has however made no attempt to undertake any systematic consideration of such draft Bills.

6. There has as a result been no formal channel to allow time and opportunity for Members to receive representations from interested parties. Consultations between Government and those outside Parliament with a legitimate concern in the legislation has also been criticised as patchy and spasmodic.

7. Once Bills are formally introduced they are largely set in concrete. There has been a distinct culture prevalent throughout Whitehall that the standing and reputation of Ministers have been dependent on their Bills getting through largely unchanged. As a result there has been an inevitable disposition to resist alteration, not only on the main issues of substance, but also on matters of detail.

8. The Committee stage of a Bill, which is meant to be the occasion when the details of the legislation are scrutinised, has often tended to be devoted to political partisan debate rather than constructive and systematic scrutiny. On Bills where policy differences are great, the role of Government backbenchers on a Standing Committee has been primarily to remain silent and to vote as directed. By contrast the Opposition has often set out to devise methods designed simply to extend debate. The Government has then been forced to bring in a guillotine which has often been draconian, as a result of which large sections of the Bill have not been considered.

9. Special Standing Committees, which were designed to encourage more informed discussion on Bills which were not highly politically controversial, have rarely been used. This has almost certainly been because of the perceived amount of extra time involved and the consequent pressure on the legislative timetable, although evidence from those concerned, including Ministers, suggests that such a perception is in fact misconceived.

10. Report stages have frequently been equally unconstructive. So far as the Opposition has been concerned, they have often been seen as an opportunity to debate on the floor of the House issues which they regard as of major political importance. Amendments and new clauses are tabled as a peg on which to hang a particular debate, not always closely related to the provisions of the Bill. By contrast the Government has frequently taken the opportunity to table literally hundreds of amendments, some very technical, some very long, possibly as a consequence of the Bill being, as First Parliamentary Counsel put it, 'produced too quickly to get the policy and drafting right'.

11. Turning to the pattern of legislation, critics regularly point to the marked imbalance in the legislative activity at different times in the session. Early on in a typical parliamentary year, the House is usually swamped with major Bills in Committee as Ministers seek to get a head start for their own measures. The recent change in the timing of the Budget and the subsequent Finance Bill has made this worse. By contrast the House of Lords is under extreme pressure at the latter end of the session as it receives the major Commons Bills.

12. This pattern, combined with the absolute cut-off imposed by prorogation, frequently makes the last few days of a session particularly chaotic as attempts are made to complete the Government's legislative programme. Bills go to and fro between the Houses, both of which are asked to agree (or disagree) usually with minimal notice to a large number of amendments. Few, if any Members, are able to know what is going on, and there is potential scope for error. The House has in the past even been asked to debate Lords Amendments of which there has been no available text.

The Essential Requirements of a Reformed System

13. We do not dissent from the general thrust of the criticisms outlined in the previous paragraphs. We do however note the considered view of the chairmen of standing committees, as conveyed to us by the Chairman of Ways and Means, that there has been a marked improvement in recent years, particularly since the adoption of the informal timetabling of bills following the Jopling reforms. The Chairman also suggested that the system also had some notable strengths: in particular, the system of appointing a committee with a separate membership for each bill, the fact that the process of detailed consideration and confrontation is carried out in public, and the tradition of impartial chairmanship.

14. Before considering ways in which the House's procedures and practices could be changed to meet the criticisms, we set out what in our view are the essential criteria which must be met in making any reforms. These may be summarised as follows:

(a) The Government of the day must be assured of getting its legislation through in reasonable time (provided that it obtains the approval of the House).
(b) The Opposition in particular and Members in general must have a full opportunity to discuss and seek to change provisions to which they attach importance.
(c) All parts of a Bill must be properly considered.
(d) The time and expertise of Members must be used to better effect.
(e) The House as a whole, and its legislative Committees in particular, must be given full and direct information on the meaning and effect of the proposed legislation from those most directly concerned, and full published explanations from the Government on the detailed provisions of its Bill.
(f) Throughout the legislative process there must be greater accessibility to the public, and legislation should, so far as possible, be readily understandable and in plain English.
(g) The legislative programme needs to be spread as evenly as possible throughout the session in both Houses.
(h) There must be sufficient flexibility in any procedures to cope with, for example, emergency legislation.
(i) Monitoring and, if necessary, amending legislation which has come into force should become a vital part of the role of Parliament.

Options for Improvement

15. Existing Standing Orders allow for considerable flexibility, as the attached flow chart demonstrates. There are several options already available which could lead to better scrutiny of legislation. With one or two notable exceptions, such as the creation of 'First Reading' Committees, the House could, if it so wished, do a great deal without a single amendment to Standing Orders. What is significant, however, is that it is the 'principal route of legislation' as shown in the attached diagram which is almost invariably used rather than the other options available. It is this inflexibility in practice which has led to the justifiable criticisms of the way in which legislation is scrutinised.

16. Much of this inflexibility arises because of the false perception that all Government bills merit broadly similar treatment. The reality is that each Bill is unique; and any categorisation risks obscuring this fact. The spectrum runs from long, politically controversial and complex Bills to short, wholly uncontentious and simple Bills. It would indeed be remarkable were one single principal route to be appropriate for such a complex array of types of Bill.

17. Another major factor in the largely inflexible approach to legislation adopted hitherto is essentially that of the culture of the House. There has been an inbuilt resistance to change of any sort on all sides. Governments have preferred the status quo largely because they perceive changes to threaten delay in their programmes. Oppositions have not been enthusiastic about any changes which might appear to prejudice their right to oppose and to seek to delay. We would be naive not to recognise that the House is and must be a place where major political differences exist and must be expressed. Nonetheless, if there is to be a real improvement in the quality of legislation, there must be a will in all parts of the House to achieve cooperation wherever it is possible.

...

Conclusions

84. There is general agreement that more thorough parliamentary scrutiny of legislation is necessary and long overdue. We have tried in this Report to begin to set out how best to achieve this end. We

have concluded that it would be wrong to prescribe a single approach for all types of legislation. We have stated some broad principles, in particular that the Government of the day must be assured of getting its legislation through in reasonable time (provided that it has the approval of the House), and that the Opposition and all Members must have a full opportunity to discuss and seek to change provisions to which they attach importance. Each bill will be different and its treatment should reflect this, with its passage to the statute book designed to recognise the broad principles to which we have referred. A higher quality of legislation must have substantial benefits for all.

85. There is much that can already be done by using to greater effect and with greater imagination the existing procedures and practices of the House. Beyond that, relatively minor changes could significantly improve the scrutiny of legislation. We recommend greater use in appropriate cases of more of the options already available and of others that could easily be brought forward. Fundamental to this is a willingness on the part of Government to experiment with such options. It equally entails some greater flexibility on the part of the House. If the new opportunities offered are wasted or abused, the chance will have been missed.

86. If significant changes are made to the scrutiny of legislation in the longer term, there would be consequences for the overall framework within which Parliament legislates. These could include in defined circumstances consideration of the 'rollover' of Bills from one parliamentary year to another, and the shape and form of that year. Such matters are in any event subject to alteration: for example, the Budget was moved in 1993 from March to November, whereas it has recently been announced that in 1998 there will be a spring Budget.

87. Flexibility is an inherent strength of our system, and any attempt to impose a straitjacket on it should be resisted.

88. The recommendations we make below are based on options either already available, or which would involve small changes in procedures.

Programming of legislation

89. We have explored the possibility of using arrangements for programming legislation which are more formal than the usual channels but more flexible than the guillotine. We believe that the spirit of these reforms requires co-operation from all sides of the House. We recommend to the House that, for a trial period, and in respect only of some bills, the House adopt an alternative approach as set out below—

(i) The Bills to be selected for programming during this trial period should be agreed through the usual channels, and should include some Bills of real substance, including at least one Bill against which the Opposition proposes to divide on Second Reading.

(ii) As soon as possible after formal presentation of such a Bill or its receipt from the House of Lords, discussions on a programme should take place between the usual channels, taking account of representations from all sides of the House, including backbenchers.

(iii) In the light of these discussions the Government should move an amendable programme motion directly after Second Reading, which could include—

  (a) the Committee option to be followed:
  (b) the date by which the Bill should be reported from committee. The Committee itself would then decide how its time should be used to consider all sections of the bill within this timetable:
  (c) the amount of time proposed for Report Stage and Third Reading:
  (d) in defined circumstances, provisions for carry-over to a subsequent session.

(iv) The questions necessary to dispose of proceedings on a programme motion shall be put not later than 45 minutes after the commencement of such proceedings.

(v) The question on any subsequent motion to modify the original programme should be put forthwith, provided that a motion proposing to reduce the time agreed in the original programme motion or to bring forward the date for reporting the bill from committee should be treated as a programme motion.

(vi) A Bill subject to the terms of a programme motion shall not subsequently be made subject to an allocation of time motion in respect of those stages referred to in the programme motion.

(vii) For any such Bill committed to a Standing Committee or Special Standing Committee a programming sub-committee would be appointed by the Committee of Selection, to be chaired by the Chairman of the Standing Committee.

(viii) Programming sub-committees would have power to meet before the first meeting of the Committee to agree a programme for consideration of the Bill within the limits agreed by the House.
(ix) In drawing up a programme the sub-committee should take into account the need for all parts of the Bill to receive proper consideration and the rights of the Opposition and other parties and Members to be given adequate time to discuss matters to which they attach particular importance.
(x) Sufficient time should also be allowed in the programme for consultation with those outside Parliament.
(xi) The conclusions of the sub-committee should be embodied in a committee programming motion to be moved at the beginning of the first sitting, and proceedings on that motion should be concluded no later than one hour after it is moved, together with any amendments selected: the question on any subsequent such motions should be put forthwith.
(xii) The Chairman of a Standing Committee on a Bill subject to a programme should be given discretion to extend the time for debate on a particular Question for up to one hour where it appears to him or her to be necessary to ensure that all parts of the Bill are properly considered, within the overall limits agreed by the House.

90. The recommendations and conclusions below apply in equal measure to programmed and unprogrammed bills.

Pre-legislative scrutiny

91. We welcome the Government's intention to publish 7 draft bills in the course of this Session, and recommend that some, or even all, be considered by the House, using one of the easily available avenues—

(i) an ad hoc Select Committee to consider a particular draft bill: or
(ii) following a discussion with the House of Lords, an ad hoc Joint Select Committee to consider a particular draft bill: or
(iii) consideration of a particular draft bill by the appropriate departmental select committee.

Presentation and First Reading

92. (i) We have invited First Parliamentary Counsel to explore as soon as possible ways in which the explanatory memorandum accompanying each bill can be made more user-friendly.

(ii) We recommend that the Government should also consider the production of a simpler explanatory guide, along the lines of that produced by the Chancellor of the Exchequer for the Budget, to be made available to interested parties, including via the Internet.

After First Reading

93. While we recognise that the first session of a new Parliament, with a new Government, constrains what can be achieved, we recommend that the Government seek an opportunity to appoint an ad hoc First Reading Select Committee to consider an appropriate bill, which had not previously been published in draft form.

Second Reading

94. We agree that the great majority of bills should be subject to a Second Reading debate on the floor of the House. We also consider however that greater use should be made of Second Reading Committees to consider 'non-controversial bills which do not raise substantial issues of principle', or those non-controversial Bills which may have been subject to previous committee scrutiny. To facilitate this the Government should bring forward proposals to amend Standing Order No. 90 so as to relax some of the provisions governing the procedures for sending bills to Second Reading Committees, and to permit all Members of the House to attend and speak.

Committee Stage

95. The committee stage of any bill should be handled in whatever way is most appropriate for that bill. Following the Second Reading of a bill, there is a range of committal options open to Government with decisions usually being taken following discussions. These options have been used very sparingly in the past, and we recommend greater use in future of:

(i) committal of appropriate bills to a Special Standing Committee, under Standing Order No. 91, which should be amended so as to give these committees greater flexibility in their operations; or
(ii) committal of appropriate bills to ad hoc Select Committees; or

(iii) splitting a bill on committal between the floor of the House and a Standing Committee, a procedure which we consider could be extended to make it possible, subject to agreement, to split bills between different sorts of committees, as deemed appropriate.

96. Where a pre-legislative or First Reading Committee has been used the Committee of Selection should so far as possible nominate the same core of Members to the subsequent committee stage, supplemented as necessary.

97. There are several changes to existing procedures and practices in Standing Committee which could lead to a more effective use of time, including:

(i) a sensible agreement to ensure that all parts of a Bill are discussed:

(ii) an amendment to Standing Orders so that the consideration of the existing Clauses of a bill can follow the practice currently used for new Clauses:

(iii) removal of many of the constraints and conventions on the times during which a committee may meet and the number of timings of sittings, including the extension to Standing Committees of the facility available to select committees to meet during recesses: and

(iv) the Chairman to be given powers similar to those given to the Speaker under Standing Order No. 47 to impose a limit on the length of speeches.

98. Notes on Clauses should be available to members of Standing Committees in time for them to be able to frame and table amendments which would be open to selection.

Report Stage

99. We recommend that, for a certain number of appropriate bills, the Standing Committee which had considered the bill should be reconvened to consider non-controversial Government amendments, such as those giving effect to assurances given at committee stage, with the reported Bill considered as at present on the floor of the House.

Lords Amendments

100. We recommend that the House should also explore the possibility of referring appropriate Lords Amendments to the Standing Committee which considered the bill. This would be followed by consideration in the House, normally on a formal motion to agree with the Committee's resolutions.

Post-legislative scrutiny

101. The Liaison Committee should encourage the monitoring by departmentally-related Select Committees of legislation newly in force. The option should remain open for the appointment of ad hoc Select Committees to consider and report on the operation of a particular piece of legislation causing concern which affects more than one Department.

The sessional cycle

102. (i) The Committee agrees the principle that, in defined circumstances and subject to certain safeguards, Government Bills may be carried over from one session to the next in the same way as hybrid and private Bills. Discussions should begin between the appropriate authorities in both Houses to determine how this might best be achieved, without infringing the constitutional implications of prorogation.

(ii) In drawing up detailed proposals the appropriate authorities should consider in particular the need to ensure (a) the identification by the Government as early as possible of any Bill it wished to be subject to a carry-over procedure (b) that the procedure should only be used for Bills which are either to be subject to select committee type scrutiny or are introduced after a certain period in the session and (c) that no Bill should be carried over more than once.

NOTE: A report by the Committee (HC 543 of 1997–98) led to agreement that in defined circumstances Government Bills not passed by the end of a session could be carried over in the next session. The first Government Bill to be carried over was the Financial Services and Markets Bill 1998–99. A new Order was agreed on carry-over on 22 October 2002 (HC Debs, Vol. 391, cols. 827–828, 29 October 2002).

The Modernisation Committee reported again on programming in 2003 (HC 1222 of 2002–03) discussing the benefits and drawbacks and giving good and bad examples of Bills which had been subjected to programming. It is the case that substantial parts of Bills may not be properly scrutinized despite programming. The committee made some suggestions on the timing of the different stages of a Bill and pointed out that programming should not be seen in isolation and that it could facilitate greater pre-legislative scrutiny of draft Bills (see pp. 245–247, *ante*, on scrutiny of draft Bills by select committees).

■ QUESTION

How far does the Modernisation Select Committee's report meet the concerns of the Hansard Society Commission's report?

The Committee revisited the legislative process with a view to improving the opportunities for the general public, lobbyists and stakeholders to influence Parliament's consideration of bills. The extracts concentrate on the pre-legislative stage, where it is feared that recent good progress has faltered, and on the committee stage.

First Report from the Select Committee on Modernisation of the House of Commons

HC 1097 of 2005–06, paras 16–35, 50–62, 67–77

Impact of pre-legislative scrutiny

16. The impact of pre-legislative scrutiny can be assessed against the three related purposes identified by the Modernisation Committee in 1997:

a) connecting with the public by involving outside bodies and individuals in the legislative process;
b) changing the bill to produce better law; and
c) achieving consensus so that the bill completes its passage through the House more smoothly.

Connecting with the public

17. A major theme of this inquiry has been the question of how to involve the public more closely in the legislative process. By 'the public', we mean not only individuals, but also the non-governmental organisations, lobby groups and interest groups who seek to influence the form and content of laws. It is an important matter of principle, in a democracy, that citizens should be able to make their views known to legislators, and an accessible legislative process provides access to the many thousands of smaller groups as well as to the larger, better-organised interests.

18. Pre-legislative scrutiny is an effective way of drawing all those who have a point of view to put across into the legislative process. Inquiries are usually well-publicised (though some are inevitably higher profile than others) and there are clear and well-understood routes for submitting evidence to committees considering draft bills. The Joint Committee on the draft Charities Bill, for example, received more than 360 written submissions and heard oral evidence from 34 individuals representing 28 organisations. This is also the only part of the legislative process in which innovative ways of connecting with the public, such as on-line consultation, can effectively be tried out.

19. Meetings where committees take evidence are, for a variety of reasons, generally more media-friendly than standing committee proceedings, so pre-legislative scrutiny also has the potential to stimulate and inform public debate in a way that other proceedings on a bill do not. It can therefore be effective in putting Parliament at the centre of the national debate on forthcoming legislation.

Improving the law

20. There is little doubt that pre-legislative scrutiny produces better laws. As the Law Society told us, 'it would probably be difficult to prove scientifically that more pre-legislative scrutiny has improved legislation, but it would seem unarguable in practice that it has.... Effective consultation procedures and processes such as publication and consideration of Bills in draft would appear to have greatly improved the text which is presented to Parliament or to have identified drawbacks in the draft text which require its rethinking'. This view was echoed by the Hansard Society, the Members of Parliament who gave evidence to us, and by academic witnesses. Witnesses from the CBI, the TUC and the Law Society all suggested that pre-legislative scrutiny could play a significant part in improving the quality of bills.

21. Examples of pre-legislative scrutiny having a major impact on a bill include the draft Communications Bill, where the Government accepted 120 of the Joint Committee's 148 recommendations and the Civil Contingencies Bill, which the Minister acknowledged at second reading was 'now stronger in a number of important ways' than the original draft, the Government having accepted in full 13 of the Joint Committee's 50 recommendations, including some key concessions and significant changes in policy. In the case of the Disability Discrimination Bill, the Government initially accepted 32 of the Committee's 75 recommendations at the pre-legislative stage, but by the time it had completed its passage in the Lords and reached the Commons, it had accepted a total of 61.

22. Even where there has been extensive consultation by Government and others during the production of a bill, pre-legislative scrutiny by Parliament can still make a valuable contribution to the process. A good example is the draft Corruption Bill, which was based on recommendations from the Royal Commission on Standards in Public Life in 1976 and further developed in a Law Commission Report of 1998. It had in the meantime been the subject of numerous reports and consultations of one kind or another. Despite the bill's leisurely journey in the direction of the statute book and the amount of expert interest that had been taken in it, the Joint Committee on the draft Bill was critical, noting 'many adverse comments on the approach adopted in the Bill and its drafting, clarity and comprehensibility'. They concluded that 'modifying the bill by trying to improve it marginally' would still leave it 'obscure and unsatisfactory' and recommend that it be completely re-drafted.

23. The Home Office accepted the Committee's recommendations and scrapped the bill, issuing a new consultation paper on bribery in December 2005, acknowledging that, in the light of the Joint Committee's Report, there 'no longer [seemed] to be broad consensus' on the approach proposed by the Law Commission.

24. In the case of the Company Law Reform Bill [*Lords*], the CBI argued that it should have been published in draft. The DTI had resisted this on the ground that the bill had been the product of a lengthy consultation exercise run by Government, but the bill as introduced contained some significant deviation from what had been agreed in that exercise, including important new material. Parliamentary scrutiny at the pre-legislative stage can play an important role in improving the law, even where there has already been lengthy and extensive external consultation by Government.

Smoothing the passage of legislation

25. Our predecessor Committee suggested that pre-legislative scrutiny should lead to less time being needed at later stages of the legislative process. If a consensus has been reached before a bill is introduced, and any points of disagreement or controversy have been resolved, then it would not seem unreasonable to assume that the subsequent passage of the bill through Parliament will be faster than it otherwise would have been. However, research into this question has failed to provide conclusive evidence of this. Jennifer Smookler, a Committee Specialist working with pre-legislative scrutiny committees in the House of Lords, argued that the process of pre-legislative scrutiny may cause a bill to be challenged on a greater number of issues precisely because of the level of knowledge gained by parliamentarians as a result of the inquiry. She cited the example of the Civil Contingencies Bill, which spent ten months in Parliament and saw two key amendments relating to the pre-legislative Committee's recommendations going to an exchange of Messages between the two Houses.

26. Whatever its impact on the passage of legislation, the purpose of pre-legislative scrutiny is not to secure an easy ride for the Government's legislative programme, it is to make better laws by improving the scrutiny of bills and drawing the wider public more effectively into the Parliamentary process. Some bills may enjoy a swifter progress through the two Houses as a result of pre-legislative scrutiny, whilst others may well take longer. If the result is a better Act, then that is a good thing. In an earlier Report, this Committee made the connection between pre-legislative scrutiny and carry-over of public bills. If a bill is to undergo an additional Parliamentary stage, without any guarantee that this will expedite the subsequent stages, then the one-Session time limit arguably becomes more of a burden than a safeguard.

27. The Law Society told us that carry-over had undoubtedly been useful in allowing greater and more considered attention to be given to bill, and getting legislation right, as opposed to getting it through within a given time-scale should be the priority for both sides of the House. Philip Cowley, Reader in Parliamentary Government at the University of Nottingham, went a step further: 'let us stop trying to legislate everything within a year and take instead the norm that we take two years for a run-of-the-mill

bill to pass through its legislative stages'. The House of Lords Constitution Committee has also recommended that carry-over should be the norm for bills that have been subject to pre-legislative scrutiny, a suggestion that was also put to us by David Kidney MP.

28. It is important to note that carry-over does not increase the House's overall capacity to deal with bills, since a bill which is carried over in one Session adds to the total volume of material to be considered in the next one. It does allow longer gaps to be left between stages, providing more time for consideration, reflection and informal discussions and negotiations during the bill's passage. It also allows greater flexibility in deciding how to divide the available Parliamentary time between bills.

29. The Sessional clock does not start ticking until a bill is formally presented in the first House, so pre-legislative scrutiny does not necessarily mean that a bill needs to be carried over if it is considered in draft in one Session and presented in the next. However, it is possible that the Sessional time-limit is placing some strain on the pre-legislative stage itself, as there is pressure for bills published in draft in the spring to have completed the pre-legislative stage and so be ready for presentation by the late Autumn, early in the following Session. Two chairmen of committees engaged in pre-legislative scrutiny of the draft Legal Services Bill and the draft Coroners Bill have expressed concern to us about the time available for their committees to complete their work. We recommend that, where a bill is introduced late in a Session because it has been subject to pre-legislative scrutiny, the assumption should be that it will be carried over to the next Session, subject to the same restrictions which currently apply, including the twelve-month time-limit. It is hoped and expected that this would be done with cross-party support. The purpose of carrying over these bills is to relieve pressure of time on both the pre-legislative and legislative stages. We would still expect to see them pass reasonably quickly from second reading to committee to report, with adequate time allowed at each stage.

Making pre-legislative scrutiny more effective

Volume of draft bills

30. The Government and Parliament are both committed to expanding the use of pre-legislative scrutiny. Publication of bills in draft rose from three in 1997–98, to a peak of 12 in 2003–04, equivalent to more than a third of the total number of Government bills that were passed in that Session, though a reduction in the number of draft Bills is to be expected in the Session following a general election, even where there has been no change of Government. It has more recently dropped off, to six in the pre-election 2004–05 Session and just two so far in the current Session, though a reduction in the number of draft Bills is to be expected in the Session following a general election, even where there has been no change of Government. Many witnesses have argued that pre-legislative scrutiny should be the norm for Government bills, with the exception of the Finance Bill and legislation which needs to be passed urgently. In 2003, this Committee said,

> 'We recognise that it will never be possible to have every Bill published in draft. There will always be occasions when new developments require urgent legislation. However, we hope eventually to see publication in draft become the norm. We recommend that the Government continue to increase with each Session the proportion of Bills published in draft'.

We welcome the Government's progress in increasing the proportion of legislation published in draft between 1997–98 and 2003–04. We are however concerned by the reduction in the number of draft bills since then, and we urge the Government to increase further the proportion of legislation published in draft. It will never be possible to produce all legislation in draft and there may be occasions, such as the Session following election of a new Government, when very little pre-legislative scrutiny is possible. But we believe that pre-legislative scrutiny should be the usual course for major Government bills.

31. Pre-legislative scrutiny has so far been used for bills which do not deal primarily with matters of party political controversy. That is not to say that the bills have all been uncontroversial—animal welfare, gambling and nuclear decommissioning, for example, are often the subject of lively public debate—only that they have not tended to deal with areas where there have been significant differences in the settled policies of the main political parties. Professor Robert Hazell of the Constitution Unit, UCL, has noted that pre-legislative scrutiny is rarely used for bills of constitutional significance, having been used in only three of the 55 constitutional bills he identifies in the last two Parliaments.

32. It might be that pre-legislative scrutiny is most useful for bills which are not controversial in the party-political sense but we would not like to see its use confined exclusively to bills of that kind. We

recommend that, in increasing the number of bills published in draft, the Government include bills that are likely to be the subject of party-political controversy.

Continuity of membership

33. In 1997, the Committee recommended that where a pre-legislative committee had been used the Committee of Selection should so far as possible nominate the same core of Members to the subsequent committee stage, supplemented as necessary. With a few exceptions, this recommendation has not been followed. Table 3 below shows the proportion of Commons members of pre-legislative committees who have been reappointed to the standing committee on the same bill.

Table 3 Members of pre-legislative committees appointed to standing committee on the same bill, 1997–98 to 2004–05

Proportion of Commons members of pre-legislative committee	Number of bills
None	5
A quarter or less	14
Half or less	9
Three-quarters or less	1
More than three-quarters	1

34. More than three-quarters of the pre-legislative committee members were appointed to the standing committee on the bill in only one case, the draft Financial Services and Markets Bill in 1998–99, where seven of eight Commons members of the Joint Committee were appointed to a standing committee of 25 members. The norm is that less than a quarter of the members of the pre-legislative committee are nominated to the standing committee, equivalent to one or two Members in most cases. Interestingly, all of the five bills where no members of the pre-legislative committee were included in the standing committee were considered in draft by permanent Commons select committees.

35. We recommend that Standing Order No. 86(2) be amended to make it clear that a Member's participation in the pre-legislative scrutiny of a bill is one of the qualifications to which the Committee of Selection shall have regard when nominating members of a standing committee. As a matter of practice, we suggest that the Committee aim to include at least four Members who were involved in the pre-legislative scrutiny of the bill (or half the members of the relevant pre-legislative committee, whichever is the fewer) on the standing committee considering the bill.

...

Committee Stage

50. Early in the inquiry, we decided to focus on the committee stage of bills. There were three main reasons for this:

a) First, the committee stage is where a great deal of the substance of the House's consideration of a bill takes place, and where most of the detail of the bill is settled.
b) Second, the committee stage permits of several variations—committal to a standing committee, a Committee of the whole House, and split committal between the two are all regularly used. Committal to a select committee is used every five years for the Armed Forces Bill and special standing committees have been used on a few occasions since 1980. We are therefore able to draw on the House's own experiences in evaluating different approaches to the committee stage.
c) Third, the work of standing committees has been one of the most criticised aspects of the legislative process. This criticism was summarised by the Hansard Society, who told us that standing committees 'fail to deliver genuine and analytical scrutiny of [bills], their political functions are neutered, dominated almost exclusively by government..., they fail to engage with the public and the media (in contrast to select committees) and they do not adequately utilise the evidence of experts or interested parties'.

51. Although some of this criticism of standing committees is valid, it is important not to over-state the weaknesses of the system. Partisan debates can be a useful way of testing the provisions of a bill,

of identifying its weaknesses and the case for change. Whilst it is unusual for the Government to accept back-bench or opposition amendments in standing committee, it is not unusual for the Government to table amendments at report stage which are intended to rectify problems identified in committee. We do believe that there is a strong case for introducing a more collaborative, evidence-based approach to the legislative process (see paragraphs 58–62, below), but it should supplement, rather than supplant, traditional standing committee debates.

52. We have considered two parallel sets of questions relating to standing committees: what are the alternatives to the traditional standing committee; and how might the existing standing committee system be improved? In order to address the first of these questions, we published a consultation paper in January this year, describing five alternative options which could be implemented with no or minimal changes to the existing Standing Orders of the House. The options were:

a) a special standing committee, which at present is able to hold three select-committee style evidence sessions before proceeding to consider the bill as a standing committee;
b) a select committee, or a joint committee of the two Houses, which has the power to take evidence, consider and amend the bill;
c) a first reading committee, as recommended by our predecessor committee in 1997, to conduct an inquiry into the bill before second reading;
d) committal to a select committee followed by re-committal to a standing committee, perhaps consisting of the select committee members plus another of others; and
e) split committal between committees of different types, as usually happens with the Finance Bill which is split between a Committee of the whole House (in respect of the more controversial parts) and a standing committee (in respect of the less controversial or technical aspects).

53. Most of our witnesses favoured those committee arrangements which provided for an evidence-taking, as well as a deliberative stage. There are several benefits that an evidence taking stage could provide. It is first and foremost a mechanism for ensuring that Members are informed about the subject of the bill and that there is some evidential basis for the debate on the bill. Evidence-gathering is also, by its nature, a more consensual and collective activity than debate, and there is evidence that those outside Parliament have a more positive view of select committee proceedings than of debate. So there is a reputational benefit to Parliament in being seen to engage in a more open, questioning and consensual style of law-making, before moving on to the necessary partisan debate.

54. An evidence-taking stage is also an effective way of engaging the wider public directly in the legislative process. The Law Society argued that it is important that the process for influencing a committee's thinking was as straightforward as possible and suggested that many organisations would value the opportunity to give evidence to a committee considering a bill, even if they had contributed to the Government's consultation exercise. A good example of this is the inquiry into the draft Corporate Manslaughter Bill by the Work and Pensions and Home Affairs Committees. They received over 150 submissions from organisations including victims' groups, trade unions, lawyers, and business representatives.

55. Witnesses from the CBI and the TUC, two organisations which are at the forefront of consultation and lobbying on proposed legislation, told us that they did not always find it easy to influence the standing committee process and that, as a consequence, they devoted more resources to trying to influence the process at other stages. Both organisations strongly favoured increasing the emphasis on formal evidence-taking as a way of improving the involvement of outside bodies in the process.

56. All these benefits, of course, are there to be had at the pre-legislative stage and pre-legislative committees usually (though not always) allow a rather longer inquiry than is possible once a bill has begun its passage through the House. But, as we have already noted, there is often a disjunction between the pre-legislative stage and the legislative stage, with few Members of pre-legislative committees finding their way onto the standing committee considering the bill. Furthermore, the bill which is presented is might differ significantly from the original draft, so that parts of it will not have been subject to the pre-legislative stage. Unlike the other stages of a bill, pre-legislative scrutiny is in the gift of the Government. As we have seen since the 2003–04 peak of draft bills, with the best will in the world, extensive pre-legislative scrutiny can never be guaranteed.

57. We do not wish to detract from the success of pre-legislative scrutiny, but we believe that, even with its further development, there is a compelling case for integrating evidence taking into the

legislative process itself. Both the Deputy Director-General of the CBI and the TUC's Head of Campaigns and Communications argued that introducing oral evidence into the standing committee process itself was the single most important change that they would like to see made to the primary legislative process.

Special standing committees

58. We recommend that special standing committees should, with some important modifications to the current Standing Order which we set out below, be the norm for Government bills which originate in the Commons. If they are to become the norm, then it is logical to drop the word 'special' from their title, and we recommend that this should be done in the context of broader changes to the nomenclature of standing committees set out in paragraphs 63 to 66 below. There will be cases where an evidence taking committee is not appropriate, such as the Finance and Consolidated Fund Bills and bills which, for whatever reason, have to be passed urgently. There may also be exceptions for bills which would usually go to a Committee of the whole House, such as bills of 'first class constitutional importance'. Even for bills outside these defined categories, there may be cases where a special standing committee is not appropriate: very short bills, for example, or those which are highly politically controversial. Some discretion might also be needed for bills which originate in the Lords.

59. There is a clear danger, as witnesses from the TUC pointed out, that over-use of special standing committees could lead to the process becoming ritualistic and unhelpful. But we believe that the single biggest improvement that could be made to the legislative process would be to adopt the committal of government bills to a special standing committee as the norm, deviating from it only when there was good reason to do so.

60. Special standing committees were first mooted in the early 1970s and established on an experimental basis in 1980. The temporary Order governing the procedure was made permanent in 1986, following a recommendation from the Procedure Committee. Including the experimental period from 1980 to 1986, there have only ever been nine special standing committees, listed in Table 6.

Table 6 Bills committed to a special standing committee

1980–81	Criminal Attempts Bill
1980–81	Education Bill
1980–81	Deep Sea Mining (Temporary Provisions) Bill [*Lords*]
1981–82	Mental Health (Amendment) Bill [*Lords*]
1983–84	Matrimonial and Family Proceedings Bill [*Lords*]
1994–95	Children (Scotland) Bill
1995–96	Licensing (Scotland) (Amendment) Bill
1998–99	Immigration and Asylum Bill
2001–02	Adoption and Children Bill

61. We would like to see the use of special standing committees entrenched in standing orders. A bill is automatically committed to a standing committee after second reading under Standing Order No. 63. However, in the case of most Government bills, this provision is superseded by the Programme Motion, which is defined as a motion, notice of which is given by a Minister of the Crown before the second reading of a bill, which provides

a) for committal of the bill, and
b) for any proceedings on the bill to be programmed.

62. We recommend that Standing Order No. 83A (Programme motions) be amended so that the definition of 'programme motion' includes a requirement that it provides for committal of the bill to a public bill committee with the power to take evidence, to a Committee of the whole House, or split committal between the two. Private Members' bills would continue to stand referred to an ordinary standing

committee under Standing Order No. 63, as would any Government bills which were not programmed (e.g. the Finance Bill).

. . .

Making public bill committees more flexible

67. Under the current Standing Order, a special standing committee considers a bill in two phases:

a) The evidence-taking phase. This must be completed within 28 days of the bill's committal, during which time the committee may hold one private deliberative, meeting (to decide when to meet, which witnesses to invite, etc.) and up to three public evidence sessions of not more than three hours each. The committee is chaired for this phase by the chairman of the relevant select committee and has the same powers as a select committee to call for evidence.
b) The standing committee phase. Having completed the evidence-taking phase, the committee proceeds to go through the bill in the normal way. This phase is chaired by a member of the Chairmen's Panel. The Minister in charge of the bill is a member of the committee, though he or she may also appear as a witness during the evidence-taking phase.

The evidence-taking phase

68. The time restrictions on the evidence-taking phase were proposed in the original Procedure Committee Report which recommended the establishment of such committees. The Committee was

> 'anxious that the House should proceed cautiously with this new and potentially most useful reform. If experience showed that the standard allocation of three sittings could be enlarged, this could be done later in the light of that experience... the addition of three morning sittings for the investigative stage of each bill would be offset by a reduction in the "amendment" stage whereas a longer allocation of investigative time would be bound to add considerably to the total time taken by each bill in committee'.

The requirement that the sittings be held in the morning was presumably to avoid clashing with the sittings of the House.

69. It is indeed likely that providing for evidence sessions on the bill will reduce the time needed and taken for debate on the bill. For example, many of the 'probing' amendments tabled in standing committee for the purpose of testing a particular piece of wording, most of which are in any event withdrawn, could be dispensed with if Members had an opportunity at the outset to question the Minister and officials on the bill. Direct questioning is perhaps a more efficient means for Members to examine the bill than the use of probing amendments, which often require officials to guess what the amendment might be getting at when preparing the Minister's brief, and then lead to debate on the technical merits of the proposed amendment rather than on the merits of the bill.

70. However, we are not confident that the right equilibrium between investigation and debate will always be reached with three evidence sessions. Some bills might require more evidence to do them justice. Others might require fewer, a single session with the Minister and officials being sufficient. The same applies to the length of the evidence sessions; and the requirement that they be held in the mornings, which was anyway waived in the most recent case of the Adoption and Children Bill, is out-of-date given the introduction of the new sitting hours of the House.

71. The simple purpose of these restrictions—to stop the evidence-taking phase of the committee from becoming unduly drawn-out and unnecessarily delaying the passage of the bill—can now adequately be met by a sensible programme order. We recommend that public bill committees should hold at least one evidence session, with the Minister and officials, in all cases. Beyond that, the general restrictions on the number, duration and timing of oral evidence sessions held by public bill committees should be lifted. Appropriate out-dates should be applied instead on a case-by-case basis in the programme order. The programming sub-committee of the public bill committee should decide on how the committee uses the time available to it, including the division of time between evidence-taking and debate.

Chairing public bill committees

72. As we have already noted, the evidence-taking phase of the special standing committee has usually been chaired by the chairman of the relevant departmental select committee. There are good reasons

for this practice, which provides a degree of continuity between select and standing committee work but, if all government bills are to go to a special standing committee, it could become an intolerable burden on some select committee chairmen. All departmental select committee chairmen should expect to chair the evidence-taking phase of a public bill committee from time to time but, in committees whose departments have a heavy legislative workload, we suggest that this work might be shared between the members of the committee. It might also be appropriate for the chairman of a non-departmental committee, such as Environmental Audit or Public Administration, to take the chair in some cases.

Public bill committees and pre-legislative scrutiny

73. The purpose of a public bill committee is not to replicate the pre-legislative inquiry, nor should it be seen as a substitute for a proper pre-legislative stage. The need to complete both the evidence-taking and the consideration of the bill in reasonable time means that these committees are not a suitable vehicle for exhaustive inquiries, nor are they a substitute for the consultation exercises undertaken by Government before a bill is presented. Where there has been a pre-legislative inquiry, we would expect the public bill committee to take the pre-legislative report as its starting point and not to re-examine the same witnesses on the same issues. In some cases, a more substantial series of evidence sessions will be appropriate but in many cases, it might be that only one investigative meeting is required.

Making public bill committees more effective

74. If the new public bill committees become the norm, bills will still be subject to detailed clause by clause consideration of the kind which is currently carried out in ordinary standing committees. We now consider ways in which this part of the process might be made more effective.

Committee papers

75. In its 2004 Report on *Connecting Parliament with the Public*, the Committee suggested that it might be possible to make standing committee papers more user-friendly. A participant in a standing committee on a bill typically needs to refer to four documents: the bill, the Explanatory Notes, the amendment paper and the Chairman's provisional selection list. There may also be other documents, such as the relevant House of Commons Library research paper, briefing notes provided by outside organisations and other background material. There is scope for improving standing committee papers in two ways: by consolidating existing documents for ease of reference, and by providing papers which are more readily understandable.

76. The draft Coroners Bill illustrates one way in which documents could usefully be combined, by printing the Explanatory Notes to each clause on the page facing the text of the clause itself. Though there are some technical issues which might need to be addressed, there is no reason why this practice should not routinely be adopted for all bills. Likewise, it would be possible to re-print clauses of the bill on the page facing the relevant amendments, for ease of reference.

77. A common complaint is that it is difficult to see exactly what effect an amendment will have on the text of the bill. It is often necessary to table several amendments to achieve a particular purpose, and working out exactly what a particular set of amendments is intended to achieve can sometimes be difficult. In order to overcome this problem, civil servants sometimes prepare for Ministers a text of the bill showing how it would look if the amendments were agreed to. We recommend that the Government aim to supply to members of the standing committee, and publish on the internet, copies of the pages of the ministerial briefing showing how the bill would look if particular sets of amendments were agreed to.

NOTES

1. Further recommendations on committee consideration of bills included improving the quality and format of information to committee members to enable them to keep track of amendments and their effect on the bill and it was suggested that IT could be used as is the case in the Scottish Parliament and National Assembly for Wales. It was also proposed that the public should have access to better information gateways to the legislation
2. The proposal that standing committees which consider public bills be renamed public bill committees was accepted. Government bills which are programmed (have a timetable for the various legislative stages) will be sent to these committees which will have the power to send 'for persons, papers and records'. Oral evidence shall be printed in the official report of the committee's debates and the committee shall have power to report written evidence to the House as if it were a select committee. It is expected that the committees will have around 17 members including

at least one minister from the relevant department and front benchers from the opposition parties. A pilot scheme on the publication of explanatory material on amendments to bills is to be conducted.

3. At para. 30 the Committee expressed concern about the Government's commitment to pre-legislative scrutiny, in relation to the number of draft bills. This has been reiterated by the House of Lords Constitution Committee which now reports on pre-legislative scrutiny. In its report on sessions 2008–09 and 2009–10 (HL 78 of 2009–10) it published this table:

Session	Goverment statistics		Ratio of draft bills to Government bills
	Number of Government bills introduced into at least one House	Number of draft bills published	
1997–98	53	3	1:18
1998–99	31	6	1:5
1999–2000	41	6	1:7
2000–01	28	2	1:14
2001–02	39	7	1:6
2002–03	36	9	1:4
2003–04	37	12	1:3
2004–05	34	5	1:7
2005–06	58	4	1:15
2006–07	36	4	1:9
2007–08	31	9	1:3
2008–09	27	4	1:7
2009–10	20	5	1:4

The committee was disappointed that the improvement the ratio of draft bills to Government bills in 2007–08 was not maintained in 2008–09. The committee was concerned at the time taken to establish committees so that they did not have a minimum of 12 weeks in which to conduct their scrutiny, and that the publication of draft bills tended to be concentrated around Easter. The committee understood that there were difficulties but repeated its recommendation for the Government to spread the publication of draft bills throughout the parliamentary year.

4. The House of Commons Modernisation Committee also thought that Parliament should conduct more post-legislative scrutiny but deferred for a report which was being carried out by the Law Commission. Its conclusions were:

Law Commission, *Post-Legislative Scrutiny*

Law Com 302 (2006) pp.46–47

6.2 For the purposes of this report, we understand post-legislative scrutiny to refer to a broad form of review the purpose of which is to address the effects of the legislation in terms of whether the intended policy objectives have been met by the legislation and, if so, how effectively. However, this does not preclude consideration of narrow questions of a purely legal or technical nature. [para 2.4]

6.3 The headline reasons for having more systematic post-legislative scrutiny are as follows:

- to see whether legislation is working out in practice as intended;
- to contribute to better regulation;
- to improve the focus on implementation and delivery of policy aims;
- to identify and disseminate good practice so that lessons may be drawn from the successes and failures revealed by the scrutiny work.

We recognise the real value of these arguments and are persuaded that together these reasons provide a strong case for more systematic post-legislative scrutiny. However, we also recognise the limitations. We acknowledge there are difficult challenges in relation to post-legislative scrutiny, namely: how to avoid a replay of policy arguments, how to make it workable within resource constraints and how to foster political will for it. [para 2.24]

6.4 We consider that the clarification of policy objectives is critical. RIAs provide a good place for the clarification of policy objectives and the setting out of criteria for monitoring and review. Therefore RIAs should be enhanced in order to incorporate these considerations more effectively. [para 3.16]

6.5 We consider that strengthened guidance from the centre of Government to departments will help to ensure that there is greater commitment from departments to post-enactment review work and that this would also strengthen the link between departmental review work and the Government's better regulation agenda. [para 3.29]

6.6 We recommend that consideration be given to the setting up of a new Parliamentary joint committee on post-legislative scrutiny. Select committees would retain the power to undertake post-legislative review, but, if they decided not to exercise that power, the potential for review would then pass to a dedicated committee. The committee, supported by the Scrutiny Unit, could be involved at pre-legislative as well as post-legislative stages in considering what should be reviewed, could undertake the review work itself or commission others to do so and would develop organically within its broad terms of reference. [para 3.47]

6.7 It already happens that legislation may provide for review by an external reviewer (for example in the Charities Bill). A new joint committee may wish to involve independent experts in its review work and in this context we do see a potential role for the National Audit Office. However, we do not see the need to create a new body independent of Parliament to carry out post-legislative scrutiny. [para 3.54]

6.8 Whether or not a Bill has formal pre-legislative scrutiny, we suggest that departments should give routine consideration to whether and if so how legislation will be monitored and reviewed. This can be addressed through strengthened guidance on RIAs. If there is a new joint committee on post-legislative scrutiny, it might also consider Bills and whether and if so how they should be reviewed post-enactment. The committee might recommend that, in certain cases, a carefully thought-out review clause would be appropriate. [para 3.59]

6.9 We believe that any system of post-legislative scrutiny should ensure that interested parties are able to channel their concerns about the operation of legislation to the reviewing body and play a part in any subsequent review through consultation or by giving evidence. [para 3.68]

6.10 For Parliamentary review, we consider that a new joint committee will be best placed to decide which legislation should be reviewed. For departmental review, the decision should be for the department in accordance with guidance from the centre of Government. [paras 3.72 and 3.81]

6.11 We remain of the opinion that the timescale for review should not be prescribed in order to allow for flexibility of approach depending on the type of legislation under review and the type of review. [para 3.75]

6.12 We invite the Government to consider whether departmental reviews should be published and possibly laid before Parliament. [para 3.77]

6.13 We suggest that in the light of experience of post-legislative scrutiny of primary legislation by a new committee serving this purpose, there is scope for the development of Parliamentary post-legislative scrutiny of secondary legislation. [para 4.7]

5. The Government broadly endorsed the Law Commission's proposals in the response made by the Leader of the House of Commons in 2008 (Cm 7320).

■ QUESTION

Do these proposals and initiatives in relation to both pre- and post-legislative scrutiny suggest a real change towards a more thorough approach to law-making and if so what might be the implications be for House of Lords reform, where the Lords has tended to conduct a more painstaking technical approach to scrutiny of legislation than the currents more politically driven approach in the Commons?

(b) Delegated legislation

NOTE: As we saw in section 2B of Chapter 6, one may divide the work of the House of Commons between that which takes place on the floor and that in committee. The most detailed scrutiny of a Bill or a statutory instrument will take place in committee.

There are various procedures by which statutory instruments are passed. The instrument may or may not be required to be laid before Parliament. If it is to be laid before Parliament, then there may or may not be provision for action by Parliament. The action to be taken by Parliament can be broadly divided into affirmative and negative procedures. Under the affirmative procedure Parliament must pass an affirmative resolution in order for the measure to become law or to continue as law. On the other hand, a measure will remain in force unless Parliament annuls it using the negative procedure. The negative resolution is by far the most frequently used procedure by which Parliament may supervise statutory instruments. In order to annul a statutory instrument the prayer for annulment must have been passed within 40 days of the laying of the instrument before Parliament.

The statute which enables the making of a statutory instrument will specify which procedure is to be used. Unlike the case with Bills, it is extremely rare for a statutory instrument to be amended as only a very few enabling statutes provide for amendment.

Specialist committees Parliament has created several specialist committees to examine delegated legislation and European Communities legislation. The committees dealing with delegated legislation are divided between those which deal with technical matters and those which deal with the merits. The technical committees are (i) the Joint Select Committee on Delegated Legislation; and (ii) the Commons Select Committee on Statutory Instruments, composed of the House of Commons members of the Joint Committee, which deals with instruments subject only to House of Commons oversight. The merits of an instrument may be referred to a House of Commons standing committee or be dealt with on the floor of the House.

Those committees dealing with the European Union are, in the House of Commons, the European Scrutiny Committee, and, in the House of Lords, the Select Committee on the European Communities. These committees consider both delegated legislation which is intended to implement EU legislation, and proposals from Brussels for future EU legislation.

The House of Commons Committee may refer matters to three European Standing Committees, two of which were established in 1990–91 and a third in 1998.

First Report from the Select Committee on Procedure

HC 48 of 1999–2000, paras 10–31, 40–59, pp. 26–27

Criticisms of the Existing System, and the 1996 Report's Recommendations

10. In devising an effective system of scrutiny of delegated legislation, the key question is how best to target Parliament's over-stretched resources of time and expertise. There is widespread agreement that at present those resources are ineffectively targeted. There are three major areas of criticism.

11. Firstly it is argued that instruments do not receive scrutiny in proportion to their merits. The current system, as outlined in paragraphs 5 to 9 above, rests on the assumption that affirmative instruments are intrinsically more significant and debate-worthy than negative ones. This may be true of a majority of instruments, but it is generally acknowledged that there is a significant minority of affirmatives which deal with matters too trivial or technical to merit debate, and negatives which deal with important or sensitive matters where there is demand for a debate. This mismatch between the level of scrutiny provided for in the parent legislation and the level which is actually appropriate may arise from a variety of factors. Ministers may have up-graded procedure from negative to affirmative as a political concession during committee stage of a bill; contrariwise, the conferral of significant powers may have 'slipped through' Parliament without provision for proper scrutiny; whilst in other cases, circumstances may have changed during the years or decades since the passage of the parent legislation, rendering issues once regarded as important less so, and vice versa. Nonetheless, in the words of the Clerk of the House, 'the House is locked into a procedural approach to an instrument by provisions made sometimes many, many years before in the parent act'. As a result, the time and expertise of Members is frequently wasted

in attendance at DL Committees to consider 'trivial affirmatives', often meeting for a few minutes only; whilst significant changes to the law may pass through Parliament unregarded and undebated because contained in negative instruments.

12. Our predecessors in 1996 [HC 152 of 1995–96] briefly considered the question of whether the existing distinction between affirmatives and negatives should be retained. They argued that 'there would in theory be something to be said for abolishing the distinction, and creating a uniform category of instruments, with a parliamentary mechanism for determining which required positive approval, based on their inherent significance rather than their statutory basis'. However, this would require primary legislation, 'and possibly wholesale amendment of much of statute law'. They therefore did not recommend such an approach, though they added that were their more modest proposals to prove ineffective, serious consideration should be given to the radical proposal of a uniform category and procedure for all delegated legislation.

13. Our predecessors proposed, as a more realistic and feasible way of tackling the problem, that the House should institute a process of systematic sift of negative instruments within Parliament. The possibility of using the existing Joint Committee on Statutory Instruments (JCSI) for this purpose was considered and ruled out, on the grounds that the sift would involve the application of political judgement and have a direct bearing on the business of the Commons, and was therefore not an appropriate task for a Joint Committee; that it would be a mistake to mix up the politics and the legal *vires* of instruments (the latter being the special concern of the JCSI); and that the sift would require a different set of advisers with different expertise. Our predecessors also considered the possibility of requiring departmental select committees to examine instruments made by the departments which they shadow. This option was also ruled out, largely on practical grounds (the workload involved would vary dramatically between committee and committee, and from week to week within each committee, whilst the level of enthusiasm for such work on the part of Members might also vary considerably between committees). The Liaison Committee, comprising chairmen of departmental and other select committees, endorsed the Procedure Committee's rejection of this option, whilst urging that departmental select committees should have the opportunity of making an input into the sifting process.

14. The 1996 report concluded that the most satisfactory way forward would be for the House to establish a single 'Sifting Committee' to consider and assess all SIs laid before Parliament. The committee would have power to call for further information from government departments where necessary. Its key task would be to make recommendations on which negative instruments merited debate. The recommendations would be put to the House by the chairman of the committee in the form of a motion which could be opposed and indeed defeated (thus enabling the Government to retain its ultimate control of the process). The committee would also have powers to identify affirmative instruments which did *not* merit debate, and on which the question could be put forthwith unless at least six Members had earlier indicated they wished for a debate. In order to allow a reasonable time for scrutiny, the report recommended that praying time against negative instruments should be extended from 40 to 60 days (this would require amendment of the Statutory Instruments Act 1946). The Sifting Committee would require specialist staff back-up.

15. The 1996 report also recommended that reference of a negative instrument to committee should be permitted to be moved by a Member where a prayer against it had been signed by at least 20 Members, with the ensuing Question being decided on a simple majority; and that minor affirmatives of 'broadly similar subject matter' should be grouped together for debate.

16. A further criticism of the existing system is that debate on instruments in committee is meaningless because it does not take place on a substantive motion. If a Delegated Legislation Committee votes against the motion, 'That the Committee has considered the instrument', the Chairman's report to the House is couched in the same terms as if the motion had been agreed to, and no procedural consequences follow from the Committee's vote.

17. The 1996 report recommended that motions in DL Committee should be substantive and amendable, and that where the Government's motion is defeated there should be up to an hour's further debate on the Floor. It also proposed that aspects of European Standing Committee procedure should be adopted for DL Committees, in particular that proceedings should begin with a Ministerial statement and questions, and that debate should last for up to two and a half hours, rather than one and a half as at present.

18. The 1996 report considered the question of whether statutory instruments themselves should be amendable during their passage. At present instruments cannot be amended unless the parent legislation allows for it, and virtually no legislation currently in force so allows. The Committee concluded that the complications that would ensue from any change in this position would greatly outweigh any likely benefits.

19. The report also looked at the existing differentiation between affirmatives and negatives in terms of the time allocated for debate when taken on the Floor. Under standing orders, affirmatives receive up to an hour and a half's debate without restriction, whilst negatives receive an hour and a half's debate subject to the restriction that debate must be concluded at 11.30 pm, even when it has commenced significantly after 10 pm (as may be the case if divisions have been held at 10 pm). The report concluded that this differentiation was illogical and that standing orders should be amended to repeal the 11.30 pm cut-off on debates on negative instruments.

20. The existing system of scrutiny has also been criticised for containing no provision for a higher level of scrutiny for a small number of very complex SIs. The 1996 Committee proposed a new category of 'super-affirmatives', whereby proposals for draft Orders would be laid for pre-legislative scrutiny by the relevant departmental select committee. This would be an adaptation of the existing procedure for considering draft Deregulation proposals.

21. The 1996 report contained a number of further recommendations. The most important of these was that a standing order should be passed to provide that no decision on a statutory instrument should be made by the House until the instrument had been considered by the Joint Committee on Statutory Instruments. A similar standing order already exists in the House of Lords. The report pointed out that it would always be open to the House to override the standing order by resolution if the Government could persuade it that this was justified in a particular case. This recommendation to create a 'scrutiny reserve' has been strongly supported by the Chairman and members of the present JCSI.

22. Other recommendations in the 1996 report related to such matters as improved documentation and identification of documents. A full list of the report's recommendations is given in the Annex to this report.

Developments since 1996

23. We have considered whether developments since publication of the 1996 report have affected the validity of its conclusions.

Statistical Trends

24. Printed with the report was a memorandum from the then Clerk of the House containing statistics on the numbers of statutory instruments made since 1950, and the numbers laid before Parliament under negative and affirmative procedure since 1980, with details of whether they were considered on the Floor or in committee. On the basis of this information, our predecessors concluded that 'the volume of delegated legislation has undoubtedly grown in recent years'. They pointed out that the number of instruments subject to parliamentary procedure had grown by around 50 per cent in the 15 years to 1996, from under 1,000 a year to around 1,500 a year. The number of negative instruments had almost doubled, from around 700 in the early 1980s to over 1,300 in 1994–95.

25. The present Clerk of the House has supplied us with updated versions of the statistical tables published with the 1996 report. These are set out in the evidence printed with this report. They show that the overall number of instruments laid before Parliament has remained fairly steady (though with individual annual fluctuations) at about 1,500 a year. The ratio between the two categories of instrument has also remained fairly constant: 174 affirmatives and 1,245 negatives were laid before Parliament in 1998–99, as against 175 affirmatives and 1,315 negatives in 1994–95 (the last Session for which figures were given in the 1996 report).

26. Thus there has been no significant change in the numbers of instruments laid over the past four years. However, this must be seen in the context of the increase over the previous 15 years to which our predecessors drew attention. We see no reason to dissent from their overall conclusion that 'there is…too great a readiness in Parliament to delegate wide legislative powers to Ministers, and no lack of enthusiasm on their part to take such powers. The result is an excessive volume of delegated legislation.' The Clerk of the House described the current position as 'on a high plateau in terms of numbers'.

27. The real change in recent years has not been in the overall number of instruments laid but in the manner of their scrutiny by Parliament. Table 3 in the Clerk of the House's evidence shows the number of instruments considered on the Floor and in committee, by Session. During the period for which details were given in the previous report, from 1980–81 to 1994–95, an average of 67 affirmatives per Session were considered on the Floor as against 84 in committee. During the subsequent four years, from 1995–96 to 1998–99, the respective averages per Session were 40 on the Floor and 149 in committee. Likewise, during the earlier period an average of 15 negatives per Session were considered on the Floor as against 16 in committee, whilst during each of the four most recent Sessions an average of 4 negatives were considered on the Floor as against 21 in committee. The statistics thus demonstrate a major shift from the Floor to committee, for both categories of instrument (this is no doubt attributable at least in part to the 'Jopling reforms', which sought to reduce the amount of business taken on the Floor); and a reduction in the overall number of negatives debated *either* on the Floor or in committee.

28. In our view the trends revealed by these statistics reinforce the case for the reform of the existing system of scrutiny. It is precisely the shift from the Floor to committee which has created the problem of 'trivial affirmatives': a DL Committee, with Minister, Opposition spokesman, other Members, Chairman, Clerk, Hansard reporter, doorkeeper, policeman and civil servants in attendance must assemble to consider an instrument which in earlier years would probably have been nodded through without debate on the Floor of the House. Likewise, the reduction in the overall number of negatives debated, at a time when there has been no decrease in the numbers laid or—it may confidently be assumed—in the complexity or importance of the instruments themselves, strengthens the supposition that existing arrangements for triggering debate on negatives are less than adequate.

Devolution

29. In our recent report on the procedural consequences of devolution we discussed the impact of devolution to Scotland, Wales and Northern Ireland in relation to delegated legislation. We supported what we described as the Government's 'pragmatic approach' to the procedures for dealing with such legislation. In terms of the effect on Westminster's workload, the Government estimated that the majority of SIs made by the Secretary of State for Scotland, estimated at 250 in an average year, would be dealt with by the Scottish Parliament and would not be dealt with at Westminster; however, this reduction would be offset by instruments to amend UK legislation affected by Acts of the Scottish Parliament. In the case of Wales, the Government expected a reduction of about 50 in the instruments at present made by the Secretary of State on his own. The Clerk of the House commented that 'reductions of this size would provide a welcome, though not major, lessening of the considerable burden on the JCSI, which considers some 1,700 instruments a year'.

30. Commenting in oral evidence in our present inquiry, the Clerk of the House told us that 'I think it is too early to say whether in a purely arithmetical sense devolution is a plus or a minus but, whatever, I should be surprised if it was a big plus or even a big minus'.

31. The extent of any changes in the pattern and quantity of delegated legislation arising from devolution is a matter which we will continue to monitor. However, there is no reason to think at this stage that changes attributable to devolution require any re-assessment of the conclusions and recommendations in the 1996 report.

...

40. We very much welcome the Royal Commission's support for the recommendations in the 1996 report. We note that the Lords vote on 22 February [when for the first time since 1968, the House of Lords disregarded its 'convention that [it] does not reject statutory instruments', by voting against the Greater London Authority Order 2000, and by approving a prayer that the Greater London Authority Election Rules 2000 be annulled] is further evidence that that House, as it evolves into a new role, is likely to give increasing attention to the scrutiny of statutory instruments. In our view this reinforces the Royal Commission's arguments for improving the quality of scrutiny given by *both* Houses.

41. With regard to the Royal Commission's proposal that the sifting of SIs should be entrusted to a Joint Committee, we consider that this might be a sensible way of avoiding duplication of effort, but measures would need to be taken to ensure that recommendations relating to Commons business were taken by the Commons members of any such committee alone.

Other Procedural Developments

42. Since 1996 there have been significant developments in the way the House of Commons operates. The Modernisation Committee has encouraged a greater emphasis on pre-legislative scrutiny of primary legislation, by way of draft bills referred to select or joint committees; and the House has been making greater use of Second Reading Committees and Special Standing Committees to examine bills once introduced.

43. Of equal, perhaps even greater, significance for our present purposes has been the extent to which other, permanent committees both of the Commons and the Lords have been developing techniques of scrutiny in recent years. Several deserve to be highlighted.

44. The *House of Lords Select Committee on Delegated Powers and Deregulation* was set up (as the Select Committee on Delegated Powers) on an experimental basis in 1992–93, and since 1993–94 has been routinely reappointed on a sessional basis. In 1994 it was given the additional role of scrutinising deregulation proposals. Its job in relation, the Committee commented that it 'operates in a non-partisan way' and noted that 'we have never needed to divide in the seven sessions of our existence'. It added that when it had advised the House that bills should be amended, this advice had 'almost always been accepted by the Government and the House'. The Government has undertaken to respond quickly to the Committee's reports, if practicable.

45. In the Commons, the *Deregulation Committee* was first set up in 1994, to consider proposals for orders and draft Orders laid under the Deregulation and Contracting Out Act 1994. In each case the Committee conducts its examination both at the pre-legislative stage (proposals for orders) and, if it is reached, the legislative stage (draft Orders). Within a fixed timetable the Committee can take written or oral evidence, and report to the House its opinion on whether or not the proposal should proceed or the draft Order be approved. What happens to draft Orders in the House depends on the nature of the Committee's report: if it has reported unanimously that the draft Order should be approved, a motion to that effect is put in the House and the Question put forthwith; if it has agreed on Division that the draft Order should be approved, a motion is moved and the Question put after a maximum of one and a half hours' debate; and if it has recommended that the draft Order should not be approved, the Government may move a motion to disagree with the Committee's report on which the Question can be put after a maximum of 3 hours' debate, with the Question on the draft Order put forthwith if that motion is agreed to.

46. Our predecessors in their 1996 report commented on the Deregulation Committee as follows:

> It should be recalled from the outset that Deregulation Orders are peculiar in that they all involve amendment of primary legislation, which would require further primary legislation to amend it, were it not for the terms of the Deregulation and Contracting Out Act 1994 and the parallel establishment of the Deregulation Committee with its special powers. The degree of scrutiny given by the Committee has demanded commitment of substantial resources, which could not conceivably be extended even to all affirmative orders. It is however in our view significant that the Committee has operated smoothly and effectively; that it has used its powers to persuade government to accept nearly all the amendments it has sought; that it and its House of Lords counterpart have effectively killed off one proposal; and that the end result to date is that 17 draft Orders have been agreed to by the House without any debate, but in the full confidence that they are generally acceptable.

47. The present Chairman of the Deregulation Committee, Mr Peter L. Pike, argued in his written submission that the deregulation procedure has the benefit of allowing public access and giving backbenchers a legislative role, that it is conducted in a bipartisan spirit, and that it need not require much time on the Floor. He urged that 'the techniques of the deregulation procedure could and should be extended to other delegated legislation'.

48. The *European Scrutiny Committee* (until 1998 the European Legislation Committee) is charged with the task of considering a range of EU documents, as defined in Standing Order No. 143. These include EU Regulations, Directives, Decisions of the Council, budgetary documents, Commission proposals, reports and recommendations, documents submitted to the European Central Bank, various inter-governmental proposals, and reports of the Court of Auditors. About 1,000 EU documents a year are deposited in

Parliament for scrutiny. The Committee's functions are to assess the political and/or legal importance of these documents and decide which merit further scrutiny, either in European Standing Committee or on the Floor; to report in detail on each document the Committee considers important (some 475 a year), taking written and oral evidence if necessary; to monitor business in the Council of Ministers and the negotiating position of UK Ministers; to review EU legal, procedural and institutional developments which may have implications for the UK and the House; and to police the scrutiny system.

49. When a document is referred by the Committee to one of the three *European Standing Committees*, that committee will meet to hear a Government Minister make a statement and answer questions put by Members for up to one hour (extendable by a further 30 minutes at the Chairman's discretion); this is followed by a debate on an amendable motion for up to a further one hour 30 minutes. The Chairman reports to the House any resolution to which the committee has come, or that it has come to no resolution. A Government motion couched in similar terms is usually moved in the House a few days later; the Question on this is put forthwith.

50. Some aspects of this European scrutiny process have potential implications for the House's consideration of delegated legislation. First, the European Scrutiny Committee acts as a 'filter' on behalf of the House. It assesses a large number of documents and reaches judgements on whether they merit further debate, either on the Floor of the House or in one of the European Standing Committees. This role would be similar to that envisaged in the 1996 report for the Sifting Committee on delegated legislation. The European Scrutiny Committee performs this role with the assistance of a comparatively large complement of staff and advisers. Second, the 1996 report recommended that certain aspects of European Standing Committee procedure be transferred to DL committees—in particular, beginning proceedings with a statement and questions, allowing debate on a substantive amendable motion, and extending the period of debate to two and a half hours from the present one and a half.

51. The 1996 report commented that 'the European Legislation Committee and the Deregulation Committee have demonstrated that scrutiny by committees can work, and can engage Members' attention and commitment'. We have taken evidence from the Chairman of both Committees, and are happy to endorse that view. The activities of the European Scrutiny Committee, European Standing Committees, the Deregulation Committee and the House of Lords Delegated Powers and Deregulation Committee have continued to develop during the four years since our predecessors reported, and form a valuable contribution to the effectiveness of Parliament. In particular, it has been demonstrated that committees working within the Westminster tradition can successfully develop modes of scrutiny involving the sifting of complex documents, the targeted use of specialist staff resources, the maintenance where appropriate of traditions of non-partisanship, and the holding of Ministers to account in public committee meetings through question-and-answer sessions as well as through debate on amendable and substantive motions. They have also demonstrated the ability of select committees, appropriately resourced, to combine the examination of technical detail which is characteristic of the Joint Committee on Statutory Instruments with the exercise of political judgement. In short, almost every element of the 1996 report's proposed reforms in the field of delegated legislation has been pioneered in one or other of these committees and shown to be eminently workable.

Conclusions

52. The package of proposals first put forward in 1996, which we endorse, was deliberately designed to be realistic, not Utopian. Taken as a whole, the proposals recognise the constraints imposed both by the Government's need to make progress with its legislative programme and the House's wish that minor business should not take up valuable time on the Floor. We recognise that it is in the nature of secondary legislation that it should receive less protracted and intensive scrutiny than primary legislation.

53. Nonetheless, the existing system of scrutinising delegated legislation is urgently in need of reform. We concur with our predecessors' description of that system as 'palpably unsatisfactory'. Some aspects of the system—for instance, the frequency with which DL Committees have to be summoned to consider instruments which no-one has any interest in discussing, or the fact that the only vote allowable in committee has no procedural consequences—can only be described as absurd, and tending to bring the House into disrepute. The failures of the current system are cast into even starker relief by the recent moves, which we welcome, to modernise the House's scrutiny of primary legislation and other aspects of the House's work. In our view this renders the task of modernising scrutiny of delegated legislation

even more pressing. We endorse the package of proposals put forward in the 1996 report. We have summarised the recommendations in paragraphs 13 to 22 above, and set them out in full in the Annex. The recommendations are aimed not at increasing the burden on the House but, by means of the sifting mechanism, at targeting the House's existing resources more effectively. As several of our witnesses pointed out, they do not represent a radical departure from the existing procedures of the House but rather seek to build on them (in particular, drawing on experience with the European Scrutiny Committee, European Standing Committees, the Deregulation procedure and the role of the JCSI).

54. Our inquiry has raised a number of major issues relating to Parliament's treatment of delegated legislation. Some of these remain to be explored more fully. For instance, the potential role of departmental select committees in the scrutiny of such legislation should be looked at in more detail. We may wish to return to this subject, along with others, following publication of the Liaison Committee's forthcoming report on the powers and functions of select committees. In addition, we propose to examine the Government's use of its powers under section 82 of the Welfare Reform and Pensions Act 1999 to place a report before the House seeking approval of expenditure on new services in advance of Royal Assent to the bill creating those services. The Social Security Committee has recently reported adversely on the Government's first proposed use of these powers, and has asked the Procedure Committee to investigate the way in which this new delegated power should be exercised in future.

55. In the interim, however, we believe that the most important thing is to make rapid progress in implementing the 1996 proposals.

56. In two respects those proposals, as originally advanced, would require primary legislation: (1) in order to extend praying time from 40 to 60 days, and (2) to establish a system of 'super-affirmatives'. We wish to make clear that, though we are fully supportive of both proposals, we do not believe that the implementation of the other, very important, changes which our predecessors proposed, and which we endorse, should be delayed while time is found for appropriate bills to be brought forward. With regard to praying time, we believe that experience in operating the new system for sifting SIs would in any case rapidly demonstrate the urgent need for such a bill.

57. With regard to super-affirmatives, we note that there is no reason for the Government to await primary legislation before initiating a 'super-affirmative' procedure, at least on experimental lines: just as the fairly widespread practice of presenting Government bills in draft has developed *ad hoc*, so it would be open now to individual Government departments to present to Parliament proposals for particularly complex or significant affirmative Orders (or, indeed, of instruments formally subject only to the negative procedure), with an indication of their intention to proceed with the formal instrument after an appropriate interval. It would be a relatively straightforward matter for the House to adopt temporary Standing Orders for the reference of such proposals for statutory instruments either to the relevant departmental select committee, or to the Deregulation Committee. An experimental arrangement on these lines would enable practical experience to be gained of how a permanent system for 'super-affirmatives' might work, and might ensure that any subsequent provisions in primary legislation were satisfactorily drafted. We recommend that such an experiment be conducted.

58. We support our predecessors' recommendation (never implemented) that there should be a full day's debate on those proposals. Much of the time of Members of the House is taken up with dealing with delegated legislation: it is clearly right and proper that opportunity should be given for the House to debate proposed changes to the system of such legislation.

59. The written and oral evidence we have received supported the 1996 proposals strongly. We note in particular the comment by the Chairman of Ways and Means, expressing the 'overwhelming view' of the Chairmen's Panel in support of a sifting mechanism, that the 'modernisation . . . of one of the more unsatisfactory procedures of the House . . . is very definitely long overdue'. The proposals have now been endorsed by the Procedure Committee under both a Conservative and a Labour Administration, as well as by the Royal Commission on House of Lords Reform and by the Chairman's Panel in the House of Commons. We believe they represent a significant contribution to the process of modernising Parliament, and we press the Government to accept them as a matter of urgency.

Memorandum from the Clerk of the House

UPDATED VERSION OF STATISTICS CONTAINED IN THE MEMORANDUM FROM THE CLERK OF THE HOUSE PRINTED WITH THE COMMITTEE'S FOURTH REPORT OF 1995/96. DELEGATED LEGISLATION (HC 152)

Table 1 Numbers of Statutory Instruments

Year	General	Local	Total
1950	1,211	933	2,144
1955	657	1,350	2,007
1960	733	1,762	2,495
1965	899	1,302	2,201
1970	1,040	1,004	2,044
1975	1,362	889	2,251
1980	1,197	854	2,051
1985	1,204	878	2,082
1990	1,408	1,256	2,664
1991	1,535	1,416	2,951
1992	1,693	1,667	3,360
1993	1,572	1,707	3,279
1994	1,688	1,646	3,334
1995	1,666	1,679	3,345
1996	1,832	1,459	3,291
1997	1,663	1,451	3,114
1998	1,576	1,747	3,323
1999 (to end October)	1,486	1,475	2,961

Table 2 Instruments subject to Parliamentary procedure

Session	Affirmatives[1]	Negatives[2]	All
1980–81	130	793	923
1981–82	121	721	842
1984–85	158	682	840
1985–86	158	861	1,019
1988–89	160	912	1,072
1989–90	164	965	1,129
1990–91	179	1,071	1,250
1993–94	155	1,225	1,380
1994–95	175	1,315	1,490
1995–96	188	1,308	1,596
1996–97[3]	139	899	1,308
1997–98[4]	208	1,591	1,799
1998–99	174	1,245	1,419

Table 3 Instruments considered in the House and in standing committee

Sessions	Floor	Committee	Floor	Committee
1980–81	94	55	15	7
1981–82	71	59	28	21
1984–85	91	72	15	27
1985–86	69	88	14	9
1988–89	53	99	15	18
1989–90	32	98	24	16
1990–91	35	121	13	18
1993–94	87	68	1	1
1994–95	73	99	8	27
1995–96	60	113	7	29
1996–97[5]	45	94	3	14
1997–98[6]	30	170	4	11
1998–99	23	149	1	28

1. Including instruments and draft instruments requiring approval, excluding those withdrawn.
2. Including instruments and draft instruments subject to attachment (including Northern Ireland Instruments), excluding those withdrawn.
3. Unusually short Session.
4. Unusually long Session.
5. Unusually short Session.
6. Unusually long Session.

NOTES

1. In relation to the proposal of sifting statutory instruments the House of Lords established a committee to do this but the House of Commons did not. The House of Lords appointed its Merits of Statutory Instruments Committee in December 2003 and began reporting weekly on SIs in April 2004. The Committee produced a report on its working methods (HL 73 of 2003–04) and it reported that it would focus primarily on negative instruments. Its terms of reference require it to bring an instrument to the special attention of the House on the following grounds: (a) that it is politically or legally important or gives rise to issues of public policy likely to be of interest to the House; (b) that it is inappropriate in view of the changed circumstances since the passage of the parent Act; (c) that it inappropriately implements European Union legislation; (d) that it imperfectly achieves its policy objectives. In the Commons the Procedure Committee proposed that a joint sifting committee should be created (HC 501 of 2002–03). The Government rejected this and the Committee was unimpressed with the reasons given: the increase in time spent on debating instruments, the desirability of considering the experience of the Lords' committee, and that the matter was one for the Modernisation Committee, arguing that the extra time would result in more systematic scrutiny; that the arguments for accepting sifting in the Lords were just as applicable in the Commons and working jointly would be more effective, and that the Modernisation Committee had agreed to the Procedure Committee taking the lead on this topic.
2. The Regulatory Reform Order is a type of delegated legislation which is unusual in that it (a) may amend primary legislation and (b) may itself be amended during its parliamentary passage if the super-affirmative procedure is used. This is provided for by the Legislative and Regulatory Reform Act 2006 which replaced the Regulatory Reform Act 2001. Its aim is to ease regulatory burdens but the initial proposals were thought to confer too much power on Ministers and met with strong opposition both inside and outside Parliament. Several select committees reported adversely. In the Commons the committees were: Regulatory Reform (HC 878 of 2005–06); Procedure (HC 894 of 2005–06); Public Administration (HC 1033 of 2005–06); and in the Lords, Delegated Powers and Regulatory Reform (HL 192 of 2005–06) and Constitution (HL 194 of 2005–06). A group of Cambridge Law professors wrote a letter to *The Times*, 16 February 2006, raising their concern about

the 'drastic power' and its 'weak limits'. Section 1 of the Regulatory Reform Act 2006 gives Ministers the power by order to remove or reduce burdens in legislation which are imposed directly or indirectly on any person. The burden may be (a) a financial cost; (b) an administrative inconvenience; (c) an obstacle to efficiency, productivity or profitability; or (d) a sanction, criminal or otherwise, which affects the carrying on of any lawful activity. The preconditions for such regulatory reform orders are (a) the policy objective intended to be secured by the provision could not be satisfactorily secured by non-legislative means; (b) the effect of the provision is proportionate to the policy objective; (c) the provision, taken as a whole, strikes a fair balance between the public interest and the interests of any person adversely affected by it; (d) the provision does not remove any necessary protection; (e) the provision does not prevent any person from continuing to exercise any right or freedom which that person might reasonably expect to continue to exercise; (f) the provision is not of constitutional significance. Before a Minister may make a regulatory reform order, there must a consultation process involving those affected by the proposals and others. If it is felt appropriate to proceed then a draft order with an explanatory document are to be laid before Parliament. The explanatory document as well as explaining the need for the order and the details and result of the consultation, including if any changes were made as a consequence of representations received, must make a reasoned recommendation as to which procedure should be following in making the order. The procedures are (a) the negative resolution procedure; (b) the affirmative resolution procedure; and (c) the super-affirmative procedure. Within 30 days of the laying of the draft order either House of Parliament can resolve that the procedure to be applied to a draft order can be 'upgraded' and thus require more Parliamentary control. The negative resolution procedure could be upgraded to either the affirmative or super-affirmative and the affirmative resolution procedure to the super-affirmative. The Commons' Regulatory Reform Committee and the Lords Delegated Powers and Regulatory Reform Committee will consider the draft order. Under the negative resolution procedure the Minister may make an order in the terms of the draft after 40 days from the laying of the draft order unless either House of Parliament resolves that it not be made. The committees which scrutinize the order may after 30 days and before 40 days from laying recommend that it not be made in the terms of the draft. This 'veto' may be overturned in the same session by a resolution of that committee's House. Under the affirmative resolution procedure the Minister makes the order in terms of the draft if it has been approved in a resolution by each House of Parliament. Under the super-affirmative procedure, the Minister is to have regard to any representations, any resolution of either House and the recommendation of any committee scrutinizing the draft made in the 60-day period following its laying. If the Minister seeks to make the order in terms of the draft, then a statement is to be laid which gives details of representations and recommendations made in the 60 days and the Minister may make the order if both Houses of Parliament so resolve. Either of the committees scrutinizing the order may recommend taking no further proceedings after the statement has been laid and this may be overturned in the same session by the relevant House. The Minister may after the 60-day period decide to revise the draft order, in which case this is laid with details of representations and the revisions. If this revised draft is approved by both Houses then the Minister may make it in those revised terms but a committee can recommend not proceeding with it and that can be overturned by resolution of the relevant House. Each House's Standing Orders specify the procedures to be followed when a committee has made a recommendation on a draft order.

■ QUESTIONS

1. Is Parliamentary oversight of law-making more illusory than real, given that the Government controls the passage of primary legislation, and that the scrutiny of delegated legislation is limited and non-existent for some quasi-legislation?
2. As there is so much pressure on parliamentary time, can consultation and publicity be improved so as to control quasi-legislation?
3. Could primary legislation contain standards and guidance about the content of legislative power which it delegates, thereby facilitating judicial review?

(d) Judicial review

Control of law-making by the courts through judicial review has increased beyond delegated legislation and quasi-legislation. The basis of this review is the doctrine of *ultra vires*. See generally Chapters 10 and 11 on judicial review.

R* v *Secretary of State for Employment, ex parte Equal Opportunities Commission
[1994] 2 WLR 409, House of Lords

The Equal Opportunities Commission (EOC) took the view that some provisions of the Employment Protection (Consolidation) Act 1978 were not in conformity with Community Law (Art. 119 (now 157 TFEU) of the EC Treaty and the Equal Pay (75/117) and Equal Treatment (76/207) Directives). This view was based on the discrimination between full-time and part-time employees in relation to the periods of continuous employment which were required to qualify for rights to redundancy pay and compensation for unfair dismissal. As the great majority of full-time employees were men and the great majority of part-time employees were women, the EOC felt that this amounted to indirect discrimination against women. The chief executive of the EOC wrote to the Secretary of State asking if steps would be taken to remove this discrimination. In a letter dated 23 April 1990 the Secretary of State replied that in the Department's view redundancy pay and compensation for unfair dismissal did not constitute pay within the terms of Art. 119 (now 141). The EOC obtained leave to apply for judicial review of the decision in the 23 April 1990 letter that the United Kingdom was not in breach of its Community law obligations, and sought declarations that the United Kingdom was breaching its obligations under (1) Art. 119 (now 141) and Directive 75/117; and (2) Directive 76/207, by providing less favourable treatment of part-time workers (most of whom were women) than full-time workers (most of whom were men) in relation to conditions of entitlement to redundancy pay and compensation for unfair dismissal. Subsequently another applicant, Ms Day, was joined to this application. Ms Day, a part-time cleaner, had been made redundant by her employer, but she did not qualify under the 1978 Act's provisions for redundancy pay. She sought further declarations and *mandamus* to compel the Secretary of State to introduce legislation to amend the 1978 statute.

The major point of substantive law at issue was whether the indirect discrimination against women in the 1978 Act was based on objectively justified grounds, a test derived from the ECJ in *Bilka-Kaufhaus GmbH* v *Weber von Hartz* (Case 170/84) [1986] ECR 1607.

The application was dismissed by the Divisional Court and this was affirmed by a majority in the Court of Appeal. The EOC and Ms Day appealed to the House of Lords.

LORD KEITH OF KINKEL: ...The next question is whether there exists any decision or justiciable issue susceptible of judicial review. The EOC's application sets out the Secretary of State's letter of 23 April 1990 as being the reviewable decision. In my opinion that letter does not constitute a decision. It does no more than state the Secretary of State's view that the threshold provisions of the Act of 1978 regarding redundancy pay and compensation for unfair dismissal are justifiable and in conformity with European Community law. The real object of the EOC's attack is these provisions themselves. The question is whether judicial review is available for the purpose of securing a declaration that certain United Kingdom primary legislation is incompatible with European Community law. It is argued for the Secretary of State that Ord. 53, r. 1(2), which gives the court power to make declarations in judicial review proceedings, is only applicable where one of the prerogative orders would be available under rule 1(1), and that if there is no decision in respect of which one of these writs might be issued a declaration cannot be made. I consider that to be too narrow an interpretation of the court's powers. It would mean that while a declaration that a statutory instrument is incompatible with European Community law could be made, since such an instrument is capable of being set aside by certiorari, no such declaration could be made as regards primary legislation. However, in the *Factortame* series of cases (*Reg.* v *Secretary of State for Transport, ex parte Factortame Ltd* [1990] 2 AC 85; *Reg.* v *Secretary of State for Transport, ex parte Factortame Ltd (No. 2)* (Case 213/89) [1991] 1 AC 603; *Reg.* v *Secretary of State for Transport, ex parte Factortame Ltd (No. 3)* (Case C 221/89) [1992] QB 680) the applicants for judicial review sought a declaration that the provisions of Part II of the Merchant Shipping Act 1988 should not apply to them on the ground that such application would be contrary to Community law, in particular articles 7 [now repealed] and 52 [now 43] of the EEC Treaty (principle of non-discrimination on the ground of nationality and right of establishment). The applicants were companies incorporated in England which were controlled by Spanish nationals and owned fishing vessels which on account of such control were denied registration in the register of British vessels by virtue of the restrictive conditions contained in Part II of the Act of 1988. The Divisional Court (*Reg.* v *Secretary of State for Transport, ex parte Factortame Ltd* [1989] 2 CMLR 353), under article 177 [now 234] of the Treaty, referred to the European Court of Justice a number of questions, including the question whether these restrictive conditions were compatible with articles 7 and 52 of the Treaty. The European Court [1992] QB 680 answered that question in the negative, and, although the final result is not reported, no doubt the Divisional Court in due course granted a declaration accordingly. The effect was that certain provisions of United Kingdom primary legislation were held to be invalid in their purported application to nationals of member states of the European Economic Community, but without any prerogative order being available to strike down the legislation in question, which of course remained valid as regards nationals of non-member states. At no stage in the course of the litigation, which included two visits to this House, was it suggested that judicial review was not available for the purpose of obtaining an adjudication upon the validity of the legislation in so far as it affected the applicants.

The *Factortame* case is thus a precedent in favour of the EOC's recourse to judicial review for the purpose of challenging as incompatible with European Community law the relevant provisions of the Act of 1978. It also provides an answer to the third procedural point taken by the Secretary of State, which maintains that the Divisional Court had no jurisdiction to declare that the United Kingdom or the Secretary of State is in breach of obligation under Community law. There is no need for any such declaration. A declaration that the threshold provisions of the Act of 1978 are incompatible with Community law would suffice for the purposes sought to be achieved by the EOC and is capable of being granted consistently with the precedent afforded by *Factortame*. This does not involve, as contended for the Secretary of State, any attempt by the EOC to enforce the international treaty obligations of the United Kingdom. The EOC is concerned simply to obtain a ruling which reflects the primacy of European Community law enshrined in section 2 of the Act of 1972 and determines whether the relevant United Kingdom law is compatible with the Equal Pay Directive and the Equal Treatment Directive.

Similar considerations provide the answer to the Secretary of State's fourth procedural point by which it is maintained that the Divisional Court is not the appropriate forum to decide the substantive issues at stake. The issues at stake are similar in character to those which were raised in *Factortame*. The Divisional Court is the only English forum in which the EOC, having the capacity and sufficient interest to do so, is in a position to secure the result which it desires. It is said that the incompatibility issue could be tested in proceedings before the European Court of Justice instituted by the European Commission against the United Kingdom under 169 [now 226] of the EEC Treaty. That may be true, but it affords no reason for concluding that the Divisional Court is an inappropriate forum for the application by the EOC designed towards a similar end and, indeed, there are grounds for the view that the Divisional Court is the more appropriate forum, since the European Court of Justice has said that it is for the national court to determine whether an indirectly discriminatory pay practice is founded on objectively justified economic grounds: see *Bilka-Kaufhaus GmbH* v *Weber Von Hartz* (Case 170/84) [1987] ICR 110, 126.

I turn now to the important substantive issue in the appeal, which is whether or not the threshold provisions in the Act of 1978 have been shown to be objectively justified, the onus of doing so being one which rests on the Secretary of State....

The original reason for the threshold provisions of the Act of 1978 appears to have been the view that part time workers were less committed than full-time workers to the undertaking which employed them. In his letter of 23 April 1990 the Secretary of State stated that their purpose was to ensure that a fair balance was struck between the interests of employers and employees. These grounds are not now founded on as objective justification for the thresholds. It is now claimed that the thresholds have the effect that more part-time employment is available than would be the case if employers were liable for redundancy pay and compensation for unfair dismissal to employees who worked for less than eight hours a week or between eight and 16 hours a week for under five years. It is contended that if employers were under that liability they would be inclined to employ less part-time workers and more full-time workers, to the disadvantage of the former.

The bringing about of an increase in the availability of part-time work is properly to be regarded as a beneficial social policy aim and it cannot be said that it is not a necessary aim. The question is whether the threshold provisions of the Act of 1978 have been shown, by reference to objective factors, to be suitable and requisite for achieving that aim. As regards suitability for achieving the aim in question, it is to be noted that the purpose of the thresholds is said to be to reduce the costs to employers of employing part-time workers. The same result, however, would follow from a situation where the basic rate of pay for part time workers was less than the basic rate for full-time workers. No distinction in principle can properly be made between direct and indirect labour costs. While in certain circumstances an employer might be justified in paying full-time workers a higher rate than part-time workers in order to secure the more efficient use of his machinery (see *Jenkins* v *Kingsgate (Clothing Productions) Ltd* [1981] 1 WLR 1485) that would be a special and limited state of affairs. Legislation which permitted a differential of that kind nationwide would present a very different aspect and considering that the great majority of part-time workers are women would surely constitute a gross breach of the principle of equal pay and could not possibly be regarded as a suitable means of achieving an increase in part-time employment. Similar considerations apply to legislation which reduces the indirect cost of employing part-time labour. Then as to the threshold provisions being requisite to achieve the stated aim, the question is whether on the evidence before the Divisional Court they have been proved actually to result in greater availability of part-time work than would be the case without them. In my opinion that question must be answered in the negative. The evidence for the Secretary of State consisted principally of an affidavit by an official in the Department of Employment which set out the views of the Department but did not contain anything capable of being regarded as factual evidence demonstrating the correctness of these views. One of the exhibits to the affidavit was a report with draft Directives prepared by the Social Affairs Commissioner of the European Commission in 1990 (COM(90) 228 final—SYN 280 and SYN 281, Brussels, 13 August 1990; Official Journal 1990 No. C 224, pp. 4–8). This covered a wide range of employment benefits and advantages, including redundancy pay and compensation for unfair dismissal, but proposed a qualifying threshold for those benefits of eight hours of work per week. The basis for that was stated to be the elimination of disproportionate administrative costs and regard to employers' economic needs. These are not the grounds of justification relied on by the Secretary of State. The evidence put in by the EOC consisted in large measure in a report of the House of Commons Employment Committee, 'Part-Time Work,' Vol. 1 in 1990 (HC 122–I, 10 January 1990) and a report of the House of Lords Select Committee on the European Communities, 'Part-Time and Temporary Employment,' in 1990 (HL Paper 7, 4 December 1990). These revealed a diversity of views upon the effect of the threshold provisions on part-time work, employers' organisations being of the opinion that their removal would reduce the amount available with trade union representatives and some employers and academics in the industrial relations field taking the opposite view. It also appeared that no other member state of the European Community, apart from the Republic of Ireland, had legislation providing for similar thresholds. The Republic of Ireland, where statute at one time provided for an 18-hour-per-week threshold, had recently introduced legislation reducing this to eight hours. In the Netherlands the proportion of the workforce in part-time employment was in 1988 29.4 per cent and in Denmark 25.5 per cent, neither country having any thresholds similar to those in the Act of 1978. In France legislation was introduced in 1982 providing for part-time workers to have the same rights as full-time, yet between 1983 and 1988 part-time work in that country increased by 36.6 per cent, compared with an increase of 26.1 per cent over the same period in the United Kingdom. While various explanations were suggested on behalf of the Secretary of State for these statistics, there is no means of ascertaining whether these explanations have any validity. The fact is, however, that the proportion of part-time employees in the national workforce is much less than the proportion of full-time employees, their weekly remuneration is necessarily much lower, and the number of them made redundant or unfairly dismissed in any year is not likely to be unduly large. The conclusion must be that no objective justification for the thresholds in the Act of 1978 has been established....

In the light of the foregoing I am of the opinion that the appeal by the EOC should be allowed and that declarations should be made in the following terms: (1) that the provisions of the Employment Protection (Consolidation) Act 1978 whereby employees who work for fewer than 16 hours per week are subject to different conditions in respect of qualification for redundancy pay from those which apply to employees who work for 16 hours per week or more are incompatible with article 119 [now 141] of the EEC Treaty and the Council Directive of 10 February 1975 (75/117/EEC); (2) that the provisions of the Employment Protection (Consolidation Act 1978 whereby employees who work for fewer than 16 hours per week are subject to different conditions in respect of the right to compensation for unfair dismissal from those which apply to employees who work for 16 hours per week or more are incompatible with the Council Directive of 9 February 1976 (76/207/EEC).

It remains to note that the EOC proposed that the House should grant a declaration to the effect that the Secretary of State is in breach of those provisions of the Equal Treatment Directive which require member states to introduce measures to abolish any laws contrary to the principle of equal treatment. The purpose of such a declaration was said to be to enable part-time workers who were employed otherwise than by the state or an emanation of the state, and who had been deprived of the right to obtain compensation for unfair dismissal by the restrictive thresholds in the Act of 1978, to take proceedings against the United Kingdom for compensation, founding upon the decision of the European Court of Justice in *Francovich* v *Italian Republic* (Cases C–6/90, C–9/90) [1991] ECR 1–5357. In my opinion it would be quite inappropriate to make any such declaration. If there is any individual who believes that he or she has a good claim to compensation under the *Francovich* principle, it is the Attorney-General who would be defendant in any proceedings directed to enforcing it, and the issues raised would not necessarily be identical with any of those which arise in the present appeal.

Lord Jauncey of Tullichettle dissented on the issue of the EOC's sufficient interest to seek judicial review, however, he concurred with the reasoning of his colleagues on the substance. EOC's appeal allowed, declarations made. Ms Day's appeal dismissed.

Council of Civil Service Unions v *Minister for the Civil Service*

[1985] AC 374, House of Lords

(For the facts of this case see p. 576, *post*.)

LORD FRASER OF TULLYBELTON: ...As *De Keyser's* case shows, the courts will inquire into whether a particular prerogative power exists or not, and, if it does exist, into its extent. But once the existence and the extent of a power are established to the satisfaction of the court, the court cannot inquire into the propriety of its exercise. That is undoubtedly the position as laid down in the authorities to which I have briefly referred and it is plainly reasonable in relation to many of the most important prerogative powers which are concerned with control of the armed forces and with foreign policy and with other matters which are unsuitable for discussion or review in the law courts. In the present case the prerogative power involved is power to regulate the Home Civil Service, and I recognise there is no obvious reason why the mode of exercise of that power should be immune from review by the courts. Nevertheless to permit such review would run counter to the great weight of authority to which I have briefly referred. Having regard to the opinion I have reached on Mr. Alexander's second proposition, it is unnecessary to decide whether his first proposition is sound or not and I prefer to leave that question open until it arises in a case where a decision upon it is necessary. I therefore assume, without deciding, that his first proposition is correct and that all powers exercised directly under the prerogative are immune from challenge in the courts. I pass to consider his second proposition....

LORD SCARMAN: ...My Lords, I would wish to add a few, very few, words on the reviewability of the exercise of the royal prerogative. Like my noble and learned friend Lord Diplock, I believe that the law relating to judicial review has now reached the stage where it can be said with confidence that, if the subject matter in respect of which prerogative power is exercised is justiciable, that is to say if it is a matter upon which the court can adjudicate, the exercise of the power is subject to review in accordance with the principles developed in respect of the review of the exercise of statutory power. Without usurping the role of legal historian, for which I claim no special qualification, I would observe that the royal prerogative has always been regarded as part of the common law, and that Sir Edward Coke had no doubt that it was subject to the common law: *Prohibitions del Roy* (1608) 12 Co Rep 63 and the *Proclamations Case* (1611) 12 Co Rep 74. In the latter case he declared, at p. 76, that 'the King hath no prerogative, but that which the law of the land allows him.' It is, of course, beyond doubt that in Coke's time and thereafter judicial review of the exercise of prerogative power was limited to inquiring into whether a particular power existed and, if it did, into its extent: *Attorney-General* v *De Keyser's Royal Hotel Ltd* [1920] AC 508. But this limitation has now gone, overwhelmed by the developing modern law of judicial review: *Reg.* v *Criminal Injuries Compensation Board, Ex parte Lain* [1967] 2 QB 864 (a landmark case comparable in its generation with the *Proclamations Case*, 12 Co Rep 74) and *Reg.* v *Secretary of State for Home Affairs, Ex parte Hosenball* [1977] 1 WLR 766. Just as ancient restrictions in the law relating to the prerogative writs and orders have not prevented the courts from extending the requirement of natural justice, namely the duty to act fairly, so that it is required of a purely administrative act, so also has the modern law, a vivid sketch of which my noble and learned friend Lord Diplock has included in his speech, extended the range of judicial review in respect of the exercise of prerogative power. Today, therefore, the controlling factor in determining whether the exercise of prerogative power is subject to judicial review is not its source but its subject matter....

LORD DIPLOCK: ...My Lords, that a decision of which the ultimate source of power to make it is not a statute but the common law (whether or not the common law is for this purpose given the label of 'the prerogative') may be the subject of judicial review on the ground of illegality is, I think, established by the cases cited by my noble and learned friend, Lord Roskill, and this extends to cases where the field of law to which the decision relates is national security, as the decision of this House itself in *Burmah Oil Co. Ltd* v *Lord Advocate*, 1964 SC (HL) 117 shows. While I see no *a priori* reason to rule out 'irrationality' as a ground for judicial review of a ministerial decision taken in the exercise of 'prerogative' powers, I find it difficult to envisage in any of the various fields in which the prerogative remains the only source of the relevant decision-making power a decision of a kind that would be open to attack through the judicial process upon this ground. Such decisions will generally involve the application of government policy. The reasons for the decision-maker taking one course rather than another do not normally involve questions to which, if disputed, the judicial process is adapted to provide the right answer, by which I mean that the kind of evidence that is admissible under judicial procedures and the way in which it has to be adduced tend to exclude from the attention of the court competing policy considerations which, if the executive discretion is to be wisely exercised, need to be weighed against one another—a balancing exercise which judges by their upbringing and experience are ill-qualified to perform. So I leave this as an open question to be dealt with on a case to case basis if, indeed, the case should ever arise.

As respects 'procedural propriety' I see no reason why it should not be a ground for judicial review of a decision made under powers of which the ultimate source is the prerogative. Such indeed was one of the grounds that formed the subject matter of judicial review in *Reg.* v *Criminal Injuries Compensation Board, Ex parte Lain* [1967] 2 QB 864. Indeed, where the decision is one which does not alter rights or obligations enforceable in private law but only deprives a person of legitimate expectations, 'procedural impropriety' will normally provide the only ground on which the decision is open to judicial review. But in any event what procedure will satisfy the public law requirement of procedural propriety depends upon the subject matter of the decision, the executive functions of the decision-maker (if the decision is not that of an administrative tribunal) and the particular circumstances in which the decision came to be made....

LORD ROSKILL: ...My Lords, the right of the executive to do a lawful act affecting the rights of the citizen, whether adversely or beneficially, is founded upon the giving to the executive of a power enabling it to do that act. The giving of such a power usually carries with it legal sanctions to enable that power if necessary to be enforced by the courts. In most cases that power is derived from statute though in some cases, as indeed in the present case, it may still be derived from the prerogative. In yet other cases, as the decisions show, the two powers may coexist or the statutory power may by necessary implication have replaced the former prerogative power. If the executive in pursuance of the statutory power does an act affecting the rights of the citizen, it is beyond question that in principle the manner of the exercise of that power may today be challenged on one or more of the three grounds which I have mentioned earlier in this speech. If the executive instead of acting under a statutory power acts under a prerogative power and in particular a prerogative power delegated to the respondent under article 4 of the Order in Council of 1982, so as to affect the rights of the citizen, I am unable to see, subject to what I shall say later, that there is any logical reason why the fact that the source of the power is the prerogative and not statute should today deprive the citizen of that right of challenge to the manner of its exercise which he would possess were the source of the power statutory. In either case the act in question is the act of the executive. To talk of that act as the act of the sovereign savours of the archaism of past centuries. In reaching this conclusion I find myself in agreement with my noble and learned friends Lord Scarman and Lord Diplock whose speeches I have had the advantage of reading in draft since completing the preparation of this speech.

But I do not think that that right of challenge can be unqualified. It must, I think, depend upon the subject matter of the prerogative power which is exercised. Many examples were given during the argument of prerogative powers which as at present advised I do not think could properly be made the subject of judicial review. Prerogative powers such as those relating to the making of treaties, the defence of the realm, the prerogative of mercy, the grant of honours, the dissolution of Parliament and the appointment of ministers as well as others are not, I think, susceptible to judicial review because their nature and subject matter are such as not to be amenable to the judicial process. The courts are not the place wherein to determine whether a treaty should be concluded or the armed forces disposed in a particular manner or Parliament dissolved on one date rather than another.

In my view the exercise of the prerogative which enabled the oral instructions of 22 December 1983 to be given does not by reason of its subject matter fall within what for want of a better phrase I would call the 'excluded categories' some of which I have just mentioned. It follows that in principle I can see no reason why those instructions should not be the subject of judicial review....

LORD BRIGHTMAN agreed with LORD FRASER on this point about the prerogative.

R v Secretary of State for the Home Department, ex parte Fire Brigades Union

[1995] 2 AC 513, House of Lords

The Criminal Injuries Compensation Scheme had been introduced under the prerogative. Under the Criminal Justice Act 1988, ss. 108–117, Scheds 6 and 7 the scheme was enacted and would come into force on 'such day as the Secretary of State may...appoint'—s. 171(1). No day was appointed and the non-statutory scheme continued. In 1993 the Secretary of State indicated that the enacted provisions would not be brought into force and that the existing scheme would be replaced by another non-statutory scheme under which the basis for the determination of compensation awards would be changed from common law principles to a tariff fixed according to particular categories of injury. The Appropriation Act 1994 approved supply estimates which contained an amount for criminal injury compensation under the tariff scheme. The applicants, representing people likely to be the victims of violent crime, sought declarations that the Secretary of State was in breach of a duty under the 1988 Act by (1) not bringing into force the enacted provisions, and (2) that the introduction of the tariff scheme was in breach of the duty and an abuse of prerogative power. The Divisional Court dismissed the application but the Court of Appeal allowed an appeal on the second declaration by a majority. On appeal their Lordships dismissed the cross-appeal that there was a legally enforceable duty to bring ss. 108–117 into force.

LORD BROWNE-WILKINSON: ...It does not follow that, because the Secretary of State is not under any duty to bring the section into effect, he has an absolute and unfettered discretion whether or not to do so. So to hold would lead to the conclusion that both Houses of Parliament had passed the Bill through all its stages and the Act received the Royal Assent merely to confer an enabling power on the executive to decide at will whether or not to make the parliamentary provisions a part of the law. Such a conclusion, drawn from a section to which the sidenote is 'Commencement,' is not only constitutionally dangerous but flies in the face of common sense. The provisions for bringing sections into force under section 171(1) apply not only to the statutory scheme but to many other provisions. For example, the provisions of Parts I, II and III relating to extradition, documentary evidence in criminal proceedings and other evidence in criminal proceedings are made subject to the same provisions. Surely, it cannot have been the intention of Parliament to leave it in the entire discretion of the Secretary of State whether or not to effect such important changes to the criminal law. In the absence of express provisions to the contrary in the Act, the plain intention of Parliament in conferring on the Secretary of State the power to bring certain sections into force is that such power is to be exercised so as to bring those sections into force when it is appropriate and unless there is a subsequent change of circumstances which would render it inappropriate to do so.

If, as I think, that is the clear purpose for which the power in section 171(1) was conferred on the Secretary of State, two things follow. First, the Secretary of State comes under a clear duty to keep under consideration from time to time the question whether or not to bring the sections (and therefore the statutory scheme) into force. In my judgment he cannot lawfully surrender or release the power contained in section 171(1) so as to purport to exclude its future exercise either by himself or by his successors. In the course of argument, the Lord Advocate accepted that this was the correct view of the legal position. It follows that the decision of the Secretary of State to give effect to the statement in paragraph 38 of the White Paper (Cm. 2434) that 'the provisions in the Act of 1988 will not now be implemented' was unlawful. The Lord Advocate contended, correctly, that the attempt by the Secretary of State to abandon or release the power conferred on him by section 171(1), being unlawful, did not bind either the present Secretary of State or any successor in that office. It was a nullity. But, in my judgment, that does not alter the fact that the Secretary of State made the attempt to bind himself not to exercise the power conferred by section 171(1) and such attempt was an unlawful act.

There is a second consequence of the power in section 171(1) being conferred for the purpose of bringing the sections into force. As I have said, in my view the Secretary of State is entitled to decide not to bring the sections into force if events subsequently occur which render it undesirable to do so. But if the power is conferred on the Secretary of State with a view to bringing the sections into force, in my judgment the Secretary of State cannot himself procure events to take place and rely on the occurrence of those events as the ground for not bringing the statutory scheme into force. In claiming that the introduction of the new tariff scheme renders it undesirable now to bring the statutory scheme into force, the Secretary of State is, in effect, claiming that the purpose of the statutory power has been frustrated by his own act in choosing to introduce a scheme inconsistent with the statutory scheme approved by Parliament.

The lawfulness of the decision to introduce the tariff scheme

The tariff scheme, if validly introduced under the Royal Prerogative, is both inconsistent with the statutory scheme contained in sections 108 to 117 of the Act and intended to be permanent. In practice, the tariff scheme renders it now either impossible or at least more expensive to reintroduce the old scheme or the statutory enactment of it contained in the Act of 1988. The tariff scheme involves the winding-up of the old Criminal Injuries Compensation Board together with its team of those skilled in assessing compensation on the common law basis and the creation of a new body, the Criminal Injuries Compensation Authority, set up to assess compensation on the tariff basis at figures which, in some cases, will be very substantially less than under the old scheme. All this at a time when Parliament has expressed its will that there should be a scheme based on the tortious measure of damages, such will being expressed in a statute which Parliament has neither repealed nor (for reasons which have not been disclosed) been invited to repeal.

My Lords, it would be most surprising if, at the present day, prerogative powers could be validly exercised by the executive so as to frustrate the will of Parliament expressed in a statute and, to an extent, to pre-empt the decision of Parliament whether or not to continue with the statutory scheme even though the old scheme has been abandoned. It is not for the executive, as the Lord Advocate accepted, to state as it did in the White Paper (paragraph 38) that the provisions in the Act of 1988 'will accordingly be repealed when a suitable legislative opportunity occurs.' It is for Parliament, not the executive, to repeal legislation. The constitutional history of this country is the history of the prerogative powers of the Crown being made subject to the overriding powers of the democratically elected legislature as the sovereign body. The prerogative powers of the Crown remain in existence to the extent that Parliament has not expressly or by implication extinguished them. But under the principle in *Attorney-General* v *De Keyser's Royal Hotel Ltd* [1920] AC 508, if Parliament has conferred on the executive statutory powers to do a particular act, that act can only thereafter be done under the statutory powers so conferred: any pre-existing prerogative power to do the same act is pro tanto excluded.

How then is it suggested that the executive has power in the present case to introduce under the prerogative power a scheme inconsistent with the statutory scheme? First, it is said that since sections 108 to 117 of the Act are not in force they confer no legal rights on the victims of crime and impose no duties on the Secretary of State. The *De Keyser* principle does not apply since it only operates to the extent that Parliament has conferred statutory powers which in fact replace pre-existing powers: unless and until the statutory provisions are brought into force, no statutory powers have been conferred and therefore the prerogative powers remain. Moreover, the abandonment of the old scheme and the introduction of the new tariff scheme does not involve any interference by the executive with private rights. The old scheme, being a scheme for ex gratia payments, conferred no legal rights on the victims of crime. The new tariff scheme, being also an ex gratia scheme, confers benefits not detriments on the victims of crime. How can it be lawful to confer benefits on the citizen, provided that Parliament has voted the necessary funds for that purpose?

In my judgment, these arguments overlook the fact that this case is concerned with public, not private, law. If this were an action in which some victim of crime were suing for the benefits to which he was entitled under the old scheme, the arguments which I have recited would have been fatal to his claim: such a victim has no legal right to any benefits. But these are proceedings for judicial review of the decisions of the Secretary of State in the discharge of his public functions. The well known passage in the speech of Lord Diplock in the G.C.H.Q. case, *Council of Civil Service Unions* v *Minister for the Civil Service* [1985] AC 374, 408–410, demonstrates two points relevant to the present case. First, an executive decision which affects the legitimate expectations of the applicant (even though it does not infringe his legal rights) is subject to judicial review. Second, judicial review is as applicable to decisions taken under prerogative powers as to decisions taken under statutory powers save to the extent that the legality of the exercise of certain prerogative powers (e.g. treaty-making) may not be justiciable.

The G.C.H.Q. case demonstrates that the argument based on the ex gratia and voluntary nature of the old scheme and the tariff scheme is erroneous. Although the victim of a crime committed immediately before the White Paper was published had no legal right to receive compensation in accordance with the old scheme, he certainly had a legitimate expectation that he would do so. Moreover, he had a legitimate expectation that, unless there were proper reasons for further delay in bringing sections 108 to 117 of the Act into force, his expectation would be converted into a statutory right. If those legitimate expectations were defeated by the composite decision of the Secretary of State to discontinue the old scheme and not to bring the statutory scheme into force and those decisions were unlawfully taken, he has locus standi in proceedings for judicial review to complain of such illegality.

Similar considerations apply when considering the legality of the minister's decisions. In his powerful dissenting judgment in the Court of Appeal Hobhouse LJ., ante, pp. 523c et seq., decided that, since the statutory provisions had not been brought into force, they had no legal significance of any kind. He held, in my judgment correctly, that the *De Keyser* principle did not apply to the present case: since the statutory provisions were not in force they could not have excluded the pre-existing prerogative powers. Therefore the prerogative powers remained. He then turned to consider whether it could be said that the Secretary of State had abused those prerogative powers and again approached the matter on the basis that since the sections were not in force they had no significance in deciding whether or not the Secretary of State had acted lawfully. I cannot agree with this last step. In public law the fact that a scheme approved by Parliament was on the statute book and would come into force as law if and when the Secretary of State so determined is in my judgment directly relevant to the question whether the Secretary of State could in the lawful exercise of prerogative powers both decide to bring in the tariff scheme and refuse properly to exercise his discretion under section 171(1) to bring the statutory provisions into force.

I turn to consider whether the Secretary of State's decisions were unlawful as being an abuse of power. In this case there are two powers under consideration: first, the statutory power conferred by section 171(1); second, the prerogative power. In order first to test the validity of the exercise of the prerogative power, I will assume that the Act of 1988, instead of conferring a discretion on the Secretary of State to bring the statutory scheme into effect, had specified that it was to come into force one year after that date of the Royal Assent. As Hobhouse LJ held, during that year the *De Keyser* principle would not apply and the prerogative powers would remain exercisable. But in my judgment it would plainly have been an improper use of the prerogative powers if, during that year, the Secretary of State had discontinued the old scheme and introduced the tariff scheme. It would have been improper because in exercising the prerogative power the Secretary of State would have had to have regard to the fact that the statutory scheme was about to come into force: to dismantle the machinery of the old scheme in the meantime would have given rise to further disruption and expense when, on the first anniversary, the statutory scheme had to be put into operation. This hypothetical case shows that, although during the suspension of the coming into force of the statutory provisions the old prerogative powers continue to exist, the existence of such legislation basically affects the mode in which such prerogative powers can be lawfully exercised.

Does it make any difference that the statutory provisions are to come into effect, not automatically at the end of the year as in the hypothetical case I have put, but on such day as the Secretary of State specifies under a power conferred on him by Parliament for the purpose of bringing the statutory provisions into force? In my judgment it does not. The Secretary of State could only validly exercise the prerogative power to abandon the old scheme and introduce the tariff scheme if, at the same time, he could validly resolve never to bring the statutory provisions and the inconsistent statutory scheme into effect. For the reasons I have already given, he could not validly so resolve to give up his statutory duty to consider from time to time whether to bring the statutory scheme into force. His attempt to do so, being a necessary part of the composite decision which he took, was itself unlawful. By introducing the tariff scheme he debars himself from exercising the statutory power for the purpose and on the basis which Parliament intended. For these reasons, in my judgment the decision to introduce the tariff scheme at a time when the statutory provisions and his power under section 171(1) were on the statute book was unlawful and an abuse of the prerogative power....

LORD MUSTILL: ...I turn to the second area of complaint, which relates to the implementation of the new scheme in a form which differs radically from that contained in Part VII of the Act. This complaint is advanced in two ways, first that the actions and statements of the Secretary of State were an abuse of the powers conferred by section 171(1), secondly, that the powers exercisable under the Royal Prerogative were limited by the presence in the background of the statutory scheme.

At first sight a negative answer to each of these averments seems inevitable, once given the premise that section 171(1) creates no duty to appoint a day. As regards the Act, in a perspective which may never yield a statutory scheme, the possibility of substituting one non-statutory scheme for another must have been just as much envisaged and tolerated as was the continuation of the existing non-statutory scheme, or indeed the termination of any scheme at all. The interval between the passing of the Act and the bringing into force of Part VII, if it ever happened, was simply a statutory blank.

So too, it would appear, as regards the argument based on the Royal Prerogative. The case does not fall within the principle of *Attorney-General* v *De Keyser's Royal Hotel* [1920] AC 508. There, in the words of Lord Dunedin, at p. 526, it was established that 'if the whole ground of something which could be done by the prerogative could be done by the statute, it is the statute that rules.' Thus, if in the present case Part VII had been brought into force there would have been no room left for the exercise of that aspect of the prerogative which had enabled the Secretary of State to establish and maintain the scheme. Once the superior power of Parliament has occupied the territory the prerogative must quit the field. In the present case, however, the territory is quite untouched. There is no Parliamentary dominion over compensation for criminal injuries, since Parliament has chosen to allow its control to be exercised today, or some day, or never, at the choice of the Secretary of State. Until he chooses to call the Parliamentary scheme into existence there is a legislative void, and the prerogative subsists untouched. The position is just the same as if Part VII had never been enacted, or had been repealed soon afterwards.

This is not to say that the decisions of the Secretary of State in the exercise of the prerogative power to continue, modify or abolish the scheme which his predecessor in the exercise of the same power had called into existence are immune from process. They can be called into question on the familiar grounds: *Reg.* v *Criminal Injuries Compensation Board, Ex parte Lain* [1976] 2 QB 864. But no question of irrationality arises here, and the decision to inaugurate a new scheme cannot be rendered unlawful simply because of its conflict on paper with a statutory scheme which is not part of the law.

VII

My Lords, I introduced the preceding discussion with the words 'At first sight' because the applicants have a further (and to my mind altogether more formidable) argument which challenges the implicit assumption that in the absence of a duty to appoint a day the Secretary of State's dealings with the compensation scheme are entirely free from statutory restraint. Contrary to this assumption, it is said, there is no statutory void; for although Part VII is not itself in force, section 171(1) is in force and must not be ignored. The continued existence of section 171(1) means that, even if there is no present duty to appoint a day, there is a continuing duty, which will subsist until either a day is appointed or the relevant provisions are repealed, to address in a rational manner the question whether the power created by section 171(1) should be exercised. This continuing duty overshadows the exercise by the Secretary of State of his powers under the Royal Prerogative.

To some degree this argument is uncontroversial. I accept, and indeed the Lord Advocate does not dispute, that the Secretary of State cannot simply put out of his mind the subsisting discretion under section 171(1). But I part company with the argument at the next stage. One must look at the practicalities, which Parliament must be taken to have envisaged. Pending the appointment of a day it is impossible for the Secretary of State to remain completely inactive. He has no choice but to do something about compensation for criminal injuries: whether wind up the existing scheme and put nothing in its place; or keep the existing scheme in force; or modify it; or copy the statutory scheme. It seems to me inevitable, once it is acknowledged that it may be proper at any given time for the Secretary of State to say, 'It is inappropriate at present to put the statutory scheme into force' that it can be proper for him to install something different from the statutory scheme. Otherwise there would be the absurdity that the Secretary of State is obliged to do something under the Royal Prerogative which he is not obliged to do under the statute. Thus, merely to introduce a cheaper scheme cannot in itself be an abuse of the prerogative powers which subsist in the interim. If the Secretary of State had made an announcement as follows: 'I have come to the conclusion after careful study that for the reasons which I have explained the Parliamentary scheme must now be seen as too expensive, slow and top-heavy; that its priority is not sufficiently high to justify the great expense when there are other calls on the country's resources; that the scheme which I propose will do substantial justice in a more efficient way; and that accordingly I shall run the scheme for a while to see how it works and if, as I confidently expect, it is a success I will ask Parliament to agree with me and repeal the statutory scheme...' it is hard to see what objection could have been taken. Does not the minister's actual stance, although perhaps more likely to provoke hostility, really come to the same thing?

The applicants reply that it does not, essentially for two reasons. First, they contend that the Secretary of State has renounced the statutory duty which still dominates the prerogative in this field: not the duty, as under the argument already discussed and rejected, to bring Part VII into force, but the duty to keep under review the powers conferred by section 171(1). I would reject this argument. Perhaps the Secretary of State has laid himself open to attack more than he need have done by the tone of his announcement, but I cannot read him as having said that however much circumstances may change he will never think again; and even if he had said this his statement would have been meaningless since, leaving aside questions arising from the doctrine of 'legitimate expectation' which do not arise here, nothing that he says on one day could bind him in law, or bind his successor, not to say and do the opposite the next day.

Furthermore, even if the argument were sound it would not yield any useful relief. The most that the court could do would be to grant a declaration that the Secretary of State is now and in the future obliged to keep the power under review in a spirit of good faith: something which the Lord Advocate on his behalf has not denied. To this declaration he could respond: 'As for the present, you can see that I have not only kept the appointment of a day under review but have examined it in depth, and have come to a conclusion which, even if you do not care for it, is undeniably rational. As for the future, I will continue to keep the power under review, although I cannot at present foresee circumstances which will impel me or my successors to a different view.' Such a reply would in practice be impregnable, and for my part I would not be prepared as a matter of discretion to grant relief so empty of content.

The applicants' second contention is that the Secretary of State has frustrated the intentions of Parliament by bringing in his own inconsistent scheme and hence nullifying any realistic possibility that he will perform his continuing duty to keep the implementation of the statutory scheme under review. I do not accept this. No doubt if Part VII had been the subject of section 171(1) and hence due to come into force inevitably on a fixed date the creation of any different scheme otherwise than purely as an interim measure would have been a breach of duty. It is also possible to imagine cases where the provisions to be brought into force on an appointed day are such as to become incapable of execution if irreversible changes have been made in the meantime, and it may be that to make such changes would be an abuse of the prerogative. But this is not so here. The new scheme is not in tablets of stone. Certainly, it would be an inconvenient, time-consuming and expensive business to dismantle the scheme and return to something on the former lines. But it would be feasible to do so, just as it proved feasible to pull down the original scheme which has been firmly established over many years. Nothing is certain in politics. Who is to say that a successor in office, under the present or some future administration, with wholly different ideas on social policy and financial means and priorities, might not decide that the present Secretary of State has taken a completely wrong turning and that after all the Parliamentary scheme is best? If he did so, and made an order under section 171(1), accompanied by the necessary regulations and by executive action to wind up the new scheme, there is nothing in what the present Secretary of State has done that could stand in his way. His words have no lasting effect; he has not put an end to the statutory scheme; only Parliament can do that. So long as he and his successors in office perform in good faith the duty to keep the implementation of Part VII under review there is in my opinion no ground for the court to interfere...

[Lords LLOYD OF BERWICK and NICHOLLS OF BIRKENHEAD gave speeches concurring with Lord BROWNE-WILKINSON, and Lord KEITH OF KINKEL concurred with Lord Mustill].

Appeal dismissed.

NOTE: See the discussion on this case at pp. 126–127, *ante*.

■ QUESTION

Are the majority buttressing legislative supremacy against improper executive intervention by way of the prerogative, or is their intervention improper?

The courts' general approach When the courts review delegated legislation the approach they take is to look at the purposes of the enabling statute in order to check if the delegated legislation is *intra vires* or not. The courts presume that certain things may not be done by delegated legislation without express authorization by the enabling statute. Thus delegated legislation has been found to be *ultra vires* where it purported to:

(a) impose taxation (*Attorney-General* v *Wilts United Dairies Ltd* (1921) 37 TLR 884);

(b) deny the citizen access to the courts to determine rights and obligations (*Customs & Excise Commissioners* v *Cure & Deely Ltd* [1962] 1 QB 340; *R* v *Lord Chancellor, ex parte Witham* [1998] QB 575);

(c) interfere with the liberty of the citizen (*Chester* v *Bateson* [1920] 1 KB 829).

Circumstances can change such a presumption, as in *Liversidge* v *Anderson* [1942] AC 206, in which a Defence of the Realm regulation was upheld which allowed a Minister to order detention of persons whom he had reasonable cause to believe to be of hostile origin or associations and in need of subjection to preventive control. The fact that this case was decided during the Second World War may explain its illiberality. See the powerful dissent by Lord Atkin, at pp. 225–46.

Procedural ultra vires Delegated legislation can be challenged on the ground that specified procedures were not followed in making the legislative measure. This is part of the procedural impropriety class of judicial review (see p. 557, *post*). For an example of this ground of review, see *R* v *Secretary of State for Social Services, ex parte Association of Metropolitan Authorities* [1986] 1 WLR 1, at p. 286, *ante*. An important distinction is whether the procedural requirement is mandatory or directory.

Substantive ultra vires See Chapter 10 on the illegality and irrationality grounds of review. Where irrationality or reasonableness is the ground of challenge, its chances of success would appear to be lower the more legislative in character the measure is. See *Nottinghamshire CC* v *Secretary of State for the Environment*, at p. 581, *post*. See also on the legislative/administrative distinction: *Bates* v *Lord Hailsham of St Marylebone*, at p. 285, *ante*. There also appears to be a distinction drawn between Parliamentary measures and local authority bye-laws, with bye-laws being less immune from challenge. There is still a presumption that bye-laws passed for general welfare will be benevolently construed (see *Kruse* v *Johnson* [1898] 2 QB 91).

The grounds of judicial review which seem to be most important with respect to quasi-legislation are legitimate expectations and unreasonableness. See G. Ganz, *Quasi-Legislation; Some Recent Developments in Secondary Legislation* (1987), pp. 41–46 and R. Baldwin and J. Houghton, 'Circular Arguments: The Status and Legitimacy of Administrative Rules' [1986] *Public Law* 239.

It seems that vagueness of regulations would, in a suitable case, be a ground of review.

McEldowney v *Forde*

[1971] AC 632, House of Lords

By the Civil Authorities (Special Powers) Act (Northern Ireland) 1922, s. 1:

> (1) The civil authority shall have power, in respect of persons, matters and things within the jurisdiction of the Government of Northern Ireland to take all such steps and issue all such orders as may be necessary for preserving the peace and maintaining order, according to and in the execution of this Act and the regulations contained in the Schedule thereto, or such regulations as may be made in accordance with the provisions of this Act (which regulations, whether contained in the said Schedule or made as aforesaid, are in this Act referred to as 'the regulations'): Provided that the ordinary course of law and avocations of life and the enjoyment of property shall be interfered with as little as may be permitted by the exigencies of the steps required to be taken under this Act.
>
> (2) For the purposes of this Act the civil authority shall be the Minister of Home Affairs for Northern Ireland....
>
> (3) The Minister of Home Affairs shall have power to make regulations—(*a*) for making further provision for the preservation of the peace and maintenance of order, and (*b*) for varying or revoking any provision of the regulations, and any regulations made as aforesaid shall, subject to the provisions of this Act, have effect and be enforced in like manner as regulations contained in the Schedule to this Act....

On 22 May 1922 the Minister of Home Affairs made a regulation under the powers conferred by s. 1(3) of the Act. This provided that:

> 24 A Any person who becomes or remains a member of an unlawful association or who does any act with a view to promoting or calculated to promote the objects of an unlawful association or seditious conspiracy shall be guilty of an offence against these regulations....
>
> The following organisations shall for the purposes of this regulation be deemed to be unlawful associations:

> The Irish Republican Brotherhood, The Irish Republican Army, The Irish Volunteers, The Cumann na m'Ban, The Fianna na h'Eireann.

The named organizations were existing organizations of a militant type and it was conceded before the House of Lords, as it had been before the Court of Appeal in Northern Ireland, that they were in fact unlawful organizations.

On 7 March 1967 the Minister of Home Affairs made a further regulation under s. 1(3) of the Act. After reciting that it was expedient to make further provision for the preservation of the peace and maintenance of order, this stated:

> 1. Regulation 24A of the principal regulations shall have effect as if the following organisations were added to the list of organisations which for the purpose of that regulation are deemed to be unlawful associations:
>
> 'The organisations at the date of this regulation or at any time thereafter describing themselves as "republican clubs" or any like organisation howsoever described.'

The appellant was charged in the magistrates' court with being a member of the Slaughtneil Republican Club contrary to reg. 24A as amended. The magistrates found that he was a member of the Club but that no evidence was given that he or the club was at any time a threat to peace, law, and order and that in so far as the police were aware there was nothing seditious in its pursuits or those of its members. The charge was dismissed but the Court of Appeal of Northern Ireland (Lord MacDermott CJ, dissenting) held that the amended regulation was *intra vires* the Act of 1922 and remitted the case to the magistrates. On appeal to the House of Lords:

> LORD HODSON: ... The proscription of present and future 'republican clubs' including 'any like organisations howsoever described' is said to be something outside the scope and meaning of the Act and so incapable of being related to the prescribed purposes of the Act. Accepting that the word 'republican' is an innocent word and need not connote anything contrary to law, I cannot escape the conclusion that in its context, added to the list of admittedly unlawful organisations of a militant type, the word 'republican' is capable of fitting the description of a club which in the opinion of the Minister should be proscribed as a subversive organisation of a type akin to those previously named in the list of admittedly unlawful organisations. The context in which the word is used shows the type of club which the Minister had in mind and there is no doubt that the mischief aimed at is an association which had subversive objects. On this matter, in my opinion, the court should not substitute its judgment for that of the Minister, on the ground that the banning of 'republican clubs' is too remote. I agree that the use of the words 'any like organisation howsoever described' lends some support to the contention that the regulation is vague and for that reason invalid, but on consideration I do not accept the argument based on vagueness. It is not difficult to see why the Minister, in order to avoid subterfuge, was not anxious to restrict himself to the description 'republican' seeing that there might be similar clubs which he might seek to proscribe whatever they called themselves. If and when any case based on the words 'any like organisation' arises it will have to be decided, but I do not, by reason of the use of those words, condemn the regulation as being too vague or uncertain to be supported. I would dismiss the appeal.
>
> LORD GUEST: ... The final argument for the appellant related to the third category of organisations which it is said the regulation covered, namely, 'or any like organisation howsoever described.' It was submitted that this would cover any club whatever its name and whatever its objects and that such an exercise of the Minister's power was unreasonable, arbitrary and capricious. In my view this argument is not well founded. The regulation first of all embraces republican clubs eo nomine and they are caught by their very description. If they do not bear the name 'republican,' it would be a question of interpretation after evidence whether any particular club was covered by the words 'any like organisation howsoever described.' It is indeed not necessary for the purposes of this case where the organisation bore the name 'republican club' to examine this question in any great detail. But my provisional view is that the regulation would cover any organisation having similar objects to those of a republican club or of any of the named organisations or of any organisation whose objects included the absorption of Northern Ireland in the Republic of Ireland.

Having regard to all these matters I cannot say that the class of 'like organisations' is either ambiguous or arbitrary so as to invalidate the regulation. In my view this ground of attack also fails.... I would therefore dismiss the appeal.

LORD PEARCE: ...Further, the 1967 regulation is too vague and ambiguous. A man may not be put in peril on an ambiguity under the criminal law. When the 1967 regulation was issued the citizen ought to have been able to know whether he could or could not remain a member of his club without being subject to a criminal prosecution. Yet I doubt if one could have said with certainty that any man or woman was safe in remaining a member of any club in Northern Ireland, however named or whatever its activities or objects.

Had the final phrase 'or any like organisation howsoever described' been absent, the regulation would have simply been an attack on the description 'republican,' however innocent the club's activities. Presumably the justification for it would have to be that the mere existence of the word republican in the name of a club was so inflammatory that its suppression was 'necessary for preserving the peace and maintaining order' and that the 'exigencies' of the need for its suppression did not permit the citizen's right in that respect to prevail. For the reasons given by the Lord Chief Justice I do not accept that such a justification could suffice. But be that as it may, the final phrase shows that this is more than an attack on nomenclature, since the club is deemed equally unlawful if it is a like organisation, whatever be the name under which it goes.

And what is the 'likeness' to a republican club which makes an organisation unlawful 'howsoever described'? Since a republican club is banned whatever may be its activities, the likeness cannot consist in its activities. And since the organisation is unlawful, howsoever described, the 'likeness' cannot consist in a likeness of nomenclature. The only possibility left seems to be that the 'likeness' may consist in the mere fact of being a club. In which case all clubs, however named, are unlawful—which is absurd.

One cannot disregard the final phrase, since that would wholly alter the meaning of the regulation. Without the final phrase it is simply an attack on nomenclature. But with the final phrase it cannot simply be an attack on nomenclature. One cannot sever the bad from the good by omitting a phrase when the omission must alter the meaning of the rest. One must take the whole sentence as it stands. And as it stands it is too vague and ambiguous to be valid.

I would therefore allow the appeal.

LORD PEARSON: ...There is one further argument against the validity of this regulation, and it is the most formidable one. It is that the regulation is too vague, because it includes the words 'or any like organisation howsoever described.' I have had doubts on this point, but in the end I think the argument against the validity of the regulation ought not to prevail. The Minister's intention evidently was (if I may use a convenient short phrase) to ban republican clubs. He had to exclude in advance two subterfuges which might defeat his intention. First, an existing republican club might be dissolved, and a new one created. The words 'or at any time thereafter' would exclude that subterfuge as well as applying to new republican clubs generally. Secondly, a new club, having the characteristic object of a republican club, might be created with some other title such as 'New Constitution Group' or 'Society for the alteration of the Constitution.' The words 'or any like organisation however described' would exclude that subterfuge.

In construing this regulation one has to bear in mind that it authorises very drastic interference with freedom of association, freedom of speech and in some circumstances the liberty of the subject. Therefore it should be narrowly interpreted. Also it should if possible be so construed as to have sufficient certainty to be valid—ut res magis valeat quam pereat.

In my opinion the proper construction of the regulation is that the organisations to be deemed unlawful are—

(i) any organisation describing itself as a 'republican club,' whatever its actual objects may be, and
(ii) any organisation which has the characteristic object of a republican club—namely, to introduce republican government into Northern Ireland—whatever its name may be.

I would dismiss the appeal.

LORD DIPLOCK: ...But there is another reason for rejecting this construction of the regulation which I find compelling. It is not, in my view, permissible to treat the regulation as severable in the way adopted by the majority of the Court of Appeal. To do so is to treat it as striking at more than one unrelated mischief whereas the inclusion in the description of the organisations deemed to be unlawful association of the words 'any like organisation' makes it plain that it is organisations possessing a common mischievous characteristic that are intended to be proscribed.

What then is that characteristic? Even if it were legitimate to infer that the Minister had knowledge of the objects of 'republican clubs' in existence at the date of the regulation he could not have knowledge of what would be the objects of clubs to be formed in the future which would describe themselves as 'republican clubs.' The characteristic struck at, therefore, cannot be the possession *in fact* of unlawful objects by the organisations proscribed. Nor for the reasons previously indicated can the common characteristic struck at be the use of the name 'republican club.' It is conceivable that the adoption of a particular name might of itself be so inflammatory in Northern Ireland as to endanger the preservation of peace and the maintenance of order, but the regulation proscribes 'like organisations' which do not adopt this name.

But there are no other ascertainable common characteristics of the organisations described in the regulation except that they are composed of members and possess objects of some kind or other and describe themselves by some name or other. If the Minister's intention was to proscribe all clubs and associations in Northern Ireland whatever their objects and name the regulation plainly falls outside the power delegated to him by section 1(3) of the Special Powers Act to make regulations 'for making further provision for the preservation of the peace and the maintenance of order.' It makes unlawful conduct which cannot have the effect of endangering the preservation of the peace or the maintenance of order. But if the Minister's intention was to proscribe some narrower category of organisations the suppression of which would have the effect of preserving the peace and maintaining order he has in my view failed to disclose in the regulation what the narrower category is. A regulation whose meaning is so vague that it cannot be ascertained with reasonable certainty cannot fall within the words of delegation.

It is possible to speculate that the Minister when he made the regulation now challenged bona fide believed that the sort of club which at that date described itself as a 'republican club' was likely to have unlawful objects which would endanger the preservation of the peace and the maintenance of order and by the words that he added he may have intended to do no more than to prevent such clubs from evading the regulation by dissolving and re-forming or by changing their names. If this was his intention he signally failed to express it in the regulation, for by no process of construction can it be given this limited effect. Or he may have thought it administratively convenient to insert in the regulation a description of proscribed organisations so wide as to include also those with lawful objects in order to be sure that none with unlawful objects should be omitted, and to rely upon the administrative discretion of the Attorney-General under section 3(2) of the Act not to enforce the regulation. But to do this, however, if administratively convenient, would be outside his delegated legislative powers.

But this is speculation not construction and your Lordships' function is limited to construing the words which the Minister has used. In my view the words used by the Minister in the regulation are either too wide to fall within the description of the regulations which he is empowered to make under section 1(3) of the Special Powers Act or are too vague and uncertain in their meaning to be enforceable.

I would allow this appeal.

Appeal dismissed.

NOTE: For criticism of this case, see MacCormick (1970) 86 *Law Quarterly Review* 171.

■ QUESTIONS

1. Do you think that the context of the 'troubles' in Northern Ireland helps explain the decision of the majority?
2. Is it not more important in that kind of situation for the courts to examine very carefully regulations which interfere with the liberty of the citizen?

Exclusion of judicial review

The exclusion of judicial review of delegated legislation has been the subject of a variety of decisions. On the one hand *Institute of Patent Agents* v *Lockwood* [1894] AC 347 indicated that it was possible, whilst *Minister of Health* v *R, ex parte Yaffe* [1931] AC 494 determined that judicial review was not excluded. See also p. 642, *post.*

Discretionary nature of judicial review

See *R* v *Secretary of State for Social Services, ex parte Association of Metropolitan Authorities* [1986] 1 WLR 1, at p. 286, *ante*.

See also p. 636, *post*, on the discretionary nature of judicial review.

■ QUESTIONS

1. Is it more likely that delegated legislation which has been in existence for a little time will not be struck down by the courts than is the case with the various types of quasi-legislation and administrative action?
2. What kinds of delegated legislation might be struck down even if they had been in existence for some time?
3. Is judicial wariness in striking down delegated legislation satisfactory given the lack of real parliamentary oversight?

Partial invalidity

DPP v *Hutchinson*

[1990] 2 AC 783, House of Lords

The Secretary of State was empowered to make bye-laws for land appropriated for military purposes under the Military Lands Act 1892, s. 14(1). The power allowed for bye-laws which could prohibit intrusion onto such land but did not permit any prejudicial effect on any right in common. The Secretary of State made the RAF Greenham Common Bye-laws 1985 in respect of common land which had been appropriated for military purposes. Bye-law 2(b) provided that no person could enter or remain in the protected area without the permission of an authorized person. Protestors against nuclear weapons who camped on the protected land were charged and convicted of infringing bye-law 2(b). The Crown Court allowed the appeal on the basis that it was *ultra vires* as it prejudiced the rights of commoners. This decision was overturned by the Divisional Court on an appeal by case stated. The defendants appealed to the House of Lords.

LORD BRIDGE: My Lords, these two appeals raise important questions as to the tests to be applied in determining whether delegated legislation which on its face exceeds the power conferred upon the legislator may nevertheless be upheld and enforced by the courts in part on the basis that the legislation is divisible into good and bad parts and that the good is independent of, and untainted by, the bad.

When a legislative instrument made by a law-maker with limited powers is challenged, the only function of the court is to determine whether there has been a valid exercise of that limited legislative power in relation to the matter which is the subject of disputed enforcement. If a law-maker has validly exercised his power, the court may give effect to the law validly made. But if the court sees only an invalid law made in excess of the law-maker's power, it has no jurisdiction to modify or adapt the law to bring it within the scope of the law-maker's power. These, I believe, are the basic principles which have always to be borne in mind in deciding whether legislative provisions which on their face exceed the law-maker's power may be severed so as to be upheld and enforced in part.

The application of these principles leads naturally and logically to what has traditionally been regarded as the test of severability. It is often referred to inelegantly as the 'blue pencil' test. Taking the simplest case of a single legislative instrument containing a number of separate clauses of which one exceeds the law-maker's power, if the remaining clauses enact free-standing provisions which were intended to operate and are capable of operating independently of the offending clause, there is no reason why those clauses should not be upheld and enforced. The law-maker has validly exercised his power by making the valid clauses. The invalid clause may be disregarded as unrelated to, and having no effect upon, the operation of the valid clauses, which accordingly may be allowed to take effect without the necessity of any modification or adaptation by the court. What is involved is in truth a double test. I shall refer to the two aspects of the test as textual severability and substantial severability. A legislative instrument is textually severable if a clause, a sentence, a phrase or a single word may be disregarded, as exceeding the law-maker's power, and what remains of the text is still grammatical and coherent. A legislative instrument is substantially severable if the substance of what remains after severance is essentially unchanged in its legislative purpose, operation and effect.

The early English authorities take it for granted, I think, that if byelaws are to be upheld as good in part notwithstanding that they are bad in part, they must be both textually and substantially severable....

Our attention has been drawn to a number of more recent English authorities on the severability of provisions contained in various documents of a public law character. I doubt if these throw much light on the specific problem of severance in legislative instruments. The modern authority most directly in point and that on which the Divisional Court relied is *Dunkley* v *Evans* [1981] 1 WLR 1522. The West Coast Herring (Prohibition of Fishing) Order 1978 (SI 1978 No. 930) prohibited fishing for herring in an area defined in the Schedule to the Order as within a line drawn by reference to coordinates and coastlines. The Order was made by the Minister of Agriculture, Fisheries and Food under the Sea Fish (Conservation) Act 1967. The prohibited area included a stretch of sea adjacent to the coast of Northern Ireland, representing 0.8 per cent of the total area covered by the Order, to which the enabling power in the Act of 1967 did not extend. The defendants admitted fishing in a part of the prohibited area to which the enabling power did extend but submitted that, by including the area to which the enabling power did not extend, the Minister had acted ultra vires and, since textual severance was not possible, the whole Order was invalid. The justices accepted this submission and dismissed the informations. The Divisional Court allowed the prosecutor's appeal. Delivering the judgment of the court, Ormrod LJ cited, at pp. 1524–1525, the following passage from the judgment of Cussen J in the Supreme Court of Victoria in *Olsen* v *City of Camberwell* [1926] VLR 58, 68:

> 'If the enactment, with the invalid portion omitted, is so radically or substantially different a law as to the subject matter dealt with by what remains from what it would be with the omitted portions forming part of it as to warrant a belief that the legislative body intended it as a whole only, or, in other words, to warrant a belief that if all could not be carried into effect the legislative body would not have enacted the remainder independently, then the whole must fail.'

It is to be noted that this quotation is from the judgment in a case where textual severance was possible. Following the quotation the judgment of Ormrod LJ continued:

> We respectfully agree with and adopt this statement of the law. It would be difficult to imagine a clearer example than the present case of a law which the legislative body would have enacted independently of the offending portion and which is so little affected by eliminating the invalid portion. This is clearly, therefore, an order which the court should not strive officiously to kill to any greater extent than it is compelled to do.... We can see no reason why the powers of the court to sever the invalid portion of a piece of subordinate legislation from the valid should be restricted to cases where the text of the legislation lends itself to judicial surgery, or textual emendation by excision. It would have been competent for the court in an action for a declaration that the provisions of the Order in this case did not apply to the area of the sea off Northern Ireland reserved by section 23(1) of the Act of 1967, as amended, to make the declaration sought, without in any way affecting the validity of the Order in relation to the remaining 99.2 per cent of the area referred to in the Schedule to the Order. Such an order was made, in effect, by the House of Lords in *Hotel and Catering Industry Training Board* v *Automobile Proprietary Ltd* [1969] 1 WLR 697, and by Donaldson J in *Agricultural, Horticultural and Forestry Industry Training Board* v *Aylesbury Mushrooms Ltd* [1972] 1 WLR 190....

The modern English authority to which I attach most significance is *Daymond* v *Plymouth City Council* [1976] AC 609, where severability was not in issue, but where it appears to have been taken for granted without question that severance was possible. Section 30(1) of the Water Act 1973 gave power to water authorities:

> to fix, and to demand, take and recover such charges for the services performed, facilities provided or rights made available by them (including separate charges for separate services, facilities or rights or combined charges for a number of services, facilities or rights) as they think fit.

The subsection was silent as to who was liable to pay the charges. The Water Authorities (Collection of Charges) Order 1974 (SI 1974 No. 448) embodied provisions which required a rating authority to collect on behalf of a water authority a 'general services charge' (article 7(2)) referable to sewerage services 'from every person who is liable to pay the general rate in respect of a hereditament....' (article 10(1)).

A householder whose property was not connected to a sewer, the nearest sewer being 400 yards away from his house, refused to pay the charge and brought an action for a declaration that the Order could not properly apply to him. This House held, by a majority of three to two, that on the true construction of the enabling legislation there was no power to impose a charge for sewerage services upon occupiers of property not connected to a sewer. As I have said, the question of severability was not raised, but there is no hint in the speeches that the invalidation of the charging provision in relation to properties not connected to sewers would affect their validity in relation to properties which were so connected.

The test of textual severability has the great merit of simplicity and certainty. When it is satisfied the court can readily see whether the omission from the legislative text of so much as exceeds the law-maker's power leaves in place a valid text which is capable of operating and was evidently intended to operate independently of the invalid text. But I have reached the conclusion, though not without hesitation, that a rigid insistence that the test of textual severability must always be satisfied if a provision is to be upheld and enforced as partially valid will in some cases, of which *Dunkley* v *Evans* and *Daymond* v *Plymouth City Council* are good examples, have the unreasonable consequence of defeating subordinate legislation of which the substantial purpose and effect was clearly within the law-maker's power when, by some oversight or misapprehension of the scope of that power, the text, as written, has a range of application which exceeds that scope. It is important, however, that in all cases an appropriate test of substantial severability should be applied. When textual severance is possible, the test of substantial severability will be satisfied when the valid text is unaffected by, and independent of, the invalid. The law which the court may then uphold and enforce is the very law which the legislator has enacted, not a different law. But when the court must modify the text in order to achieve severance, this can only be done when the court is satisfied that it is effecting no change in the substantial purpose and effect of the impugned provision. Thus, in *Dunkley* v *Evans*, the legislative purpose and effect of the prohibition of fishing in the large area of the sea in relation to which the minister was authorised to legislate was unaffected by the obviously inadvertent inclusion of the small area of sea to which his power did not extend. In *Daymond* v *Plymouth City Council* the draftsman of the Order had evidently construed the enabling provision as authorising the imposition of charges for sewerage services upon occupiers of property irrespective of whether or not they were connected to sewers. In this error he was in the good company of two members of your Lordships' House. But this extension of the scope of the charging power, which, as the majority held, exceeded its proper limit, in no way affected the legislative purpose and effect of the charging power as applied to occupiers of properties which were connected to sewers.

To appreciate the full extent of the problem presented by the Greenham byelaws it is necessary to set out the full text of the prohibitions imposed by byelaw 2 which provides:

> No person shall: (a) enter or leave or attempt to enter or leave the protected area except by way of an authorised entrance or exit. (b) enter, pass through or over or remain in or over the protected area without authority or permission given by or on behalf of one of the persons mentioned in byelaw 5(1). (c) cause or permit any vehicle, animal, aircraft or thing to enter into or upon or to pass through or over or to be or remain in or upon or over the protected area without authority or permission given by or on behalf of one of the persons mentioned in byelaw 5(1). (d) remain in the protected area after having been directed to leave by any of the persons mentioned in byelaw 4. (e) make any false statement, either orally or in writing, or employ any other form of misrepresentation in order to obtain entry to any part of the protected area or to any building or premises within the protected area. (f) obstruct any constable (including a constable under the control of the Defence Council) or any other person acting in the proper exercise or execution of his duty within the protected area. (g) enter any part of the protected area which is shown by a notice as being prohibited or restricted. (h) board, attempt to board, or interfere with, or interfere with the movement or passage, of any vehicle, aircraft or other installation in the protected area. (i) distribute or display any handbill, leaflet, sign, advertisement, circular, poster, bill, notice or object within the protected area or affix the same to either side of the perimeter fences without authority or permission given by or on behalf of one of the persons mentioned in byelaw 5(1). (j) interfere with or remove from the protected area any property under the control of the Crown or the service authorities of a visiting force or, in either case, their agents or contractors. (k) wilfully damage, destroy, deface or remove any notice board or sign within the protected area. (l) wilfully damage, soil, deface or mark any wall, fence, structure, floor, pavement, or other surface within the protected area.

It is at once apparent that paragraphs (a), (b), (c), (d), (g), (j) and (l) are ultra vires as they stand. Paragraphs (e), (f), (i) and (k) appear to be valid and paragraph (h) is probably good in part and bad in part, since the exercise by a commoner of his rights may well interfere with the movement or passage of vehicles. Textual severance can achieve nothing since it is apparent that the valid provisions are merely ancillary to the invalid provisions....

I think the proper test to be applied when textual severance is impossible, following in this respect the Australian authorities, is to abjure speculation as to what the maker of the law might have done if he had applied his mind to the relevant limitation on his powers and to ask whether the legislative instrument

> with the invalid portions omitted would be substantially a different law as to the subject matter dealt with by what remains from what it would be with the omitted portions forming part of it: *Rex v Commonwealth Court of Conciliation and Arbitration, Ex parte Whybrow & Co.* 11 CLR 1, 27.

In applying this test the purpose of the legislation can only be inferred from the text as applied to the factual situation to which its provisions relate. Considering the Greenham byelaws as a whole it is clear that the absolute prohibition which they impose upon all unauthorised access to the protected area is no less than is required to maintain the security of an establishment operated as a military airbase and wholly enclosed by a perimeter fence. Byelaws drawn in such a way as to permit free access to all parts of the base to persons exercising rights of common and their animals would be byelaws of a totally different character. They might serve some different legislative purpose in a different factual situation, as do some other byelaws to which our attention has been drawn relating to areas used as military exercise grounds or as military firing ranges. But they would be quite incapable of serving the legislative purpose which the Greenham byelaws, as drawn, are intended to serve.

For these reasons I conclude that the invalidity of byelaw 2(b) cannot be cured by severance. It follows that the appellants were wrongly convicted and I would allow their appeals, set aside the order of the Divisional Court and restore the order of the Crown Court at Reading.

[Lords Griffith, Goff and Oliver concurred with Lord Bridge.]

LORD LOWRY: ...My Lords, the accepted view in the common law jurisdictions has been that, when construing legislation the validity of which is under challenge, the first duty of the court, in obedience to the principle that a law should, whenever possible, be interpreted ut res magis valeat quam pereat, is to see whether the impugned provision can reasonably bear a construction which renders it valid. Failing that, the court's duty, subject always to any relevant statutory provision such as the Australian section 15A, is to decide whether the whole of the challenged legislation or only part of it must be held invalid and ineffective. That problem has traditionally been resolved by applying first the textual, and then the substantial, severability test. If the legislation failed the first test, it was condemned in its entirety. If it passed that test, it had to face the next hurdle. This approach, in my opinion, has a great deal in its favour.

The basic principle is that an ultra vires enactment, such as a byelaw, is void ab initio and of no effect. The so-called blue pencil test is a concession to practicality and ought not to be extended or weakened. In its traditional form it is acceptable because, once the offending words are ignored, no word or phrase needs to be given a meaning different from, or more restrictive than, its original meaning. Therefore the court has not legislated; it merely continues to apply that part of the existing legislation which is good.

It may be argued that a policy split has developed and that it is time to show common sense and bring our thinking up to date by a further application of the ut res magis valeat quam pereat principle. I am, however, chary of yielding to this temptation for a number of reasons.

1. The blue pencil test already represents a concession to the erring law-maker, the justification for which I have tried to explain.

2. When applying the blue pencil test (which actually means ignoring the offending words), the court cannot cause the text of the instrument to be altered. It will remain as the ostensible law of the land unless and until it is replaced by something else. It is too late now to think of abandoning the blue pencil method, which has much to commend it, but the disadvantage inherent in the method ought not to be enlarged.

3. It is up to the law-maker to keep within his powers and it is in the public interest that he should take care, in order that the public may be able to rely on the written word as representing the law. Further enlargement of the court's power to validate what is partially invalid will encourage the law-maker to enact what he pleases, or at least to enact what may or may not be valid, without having to fear any worse result than merely being brought back within bounds.

4. *Dunkley* v *Evans* [1981] 1 WLR 1522 and *Thames Water Authority* v *Elmbridge Borough Council* [1983] QB, 570 are very special cases. I recall in that regard what McNeill J said in *Reg.* v *Secretary of State for Transport, Ex parte Greater London Council* [1986] QB 556, 582D.

5. To liberalise the test would, in my view, be anarchic, not progressive. It would tend in the wrong direction, unlike some developments in the law of negligence, which have promoted justice for physically or economically injured persons, or the sounder aspects of judicial review, which have promoted freedom and have afforded protection from power.

6. The current of decisions and relevant authority has flowed in favour of the traditional doctrine.

This last observation brings me back to *Daymond* v *Plymouth City Council* [1976] AC 609, the case in which, as my noble and learned friend has said, it appears to have been taken for granted that severance was possible, and the question is, what significance should be attached to that fact when reviewing the doctrine of textual severability?

One cannot gainsay the authority of the Appellate Committee or that of the individual members of your Lordships' House of whom the committee was composed. Any indication, even if given obiter, that their Lordships, having considered the point, would have held that the Water Authorities (Collection of Charges) Order 1974 was valid and effective against occupiers of property who benefited directly from the water authority's services while inoperative against the occupiers who did not so benefit, could significantly erode the received doctrine of textual severability, since the blue pencil test could not have been used. But one must consider the way in which the case proceeded in your Lordships' House and also at first instance.

The remedy which the plaintiff sought was a declaration that the Plymouth City Council were not empowered to demand from him £4.89 or any sum on behalf of the South West Water Authority by way of a charge for sewerage and sewage disposal services. He contended that the water authority had power under section 30 of the Act of 1973 only to demand charges for services performed, facilities provided or rights made available and that, if the Order of 1974 purported to confer power to demand other charges, it was *to that extent* ultra vires. The words which I have emphasised set the stage for the argument and the decision. Phillips J made the declaration sought. On appeal direct to this House under section 12(1) of the Administration of Justice Act 1969 it was held, dismissing the appeal, Lord Wilberforce and Lord Diplock dissenting, that the plaintiff was entitled to the declaration made. The sole issue at each stage was whether section 30 empowered the water authority to charge occupiers of property who did not receive the benefit of the authority's services directly. No case was cited, and no argument was advanced, on the question whether the invalidity of the authority's demand against such occupiers as the plaintiff would nullify the Order of 1974 in relation to occupiers who were receiving the services, and both the initial judgment and their Lordships' speeches were entirely devoted to the complicated and strenuously contested issue concerning the scope of section 30. The minority took the view that section 30 authorised the proposed demand, and they had nothing to consider except the effect of the section on the plaintiff. And the majority, who reached the opposite conclusion, were concerned with the same point. The textual severability doctrine would have been of no help to either side.

It would therefore not be surprising if, having regard to the remedy sought and granted, the residual effect of the Order of 1974 on those who admittedly were liable for the charge was never mentioned.

I am therefore very reluctant to treat the case as an authority which by implication contradicts the established doctrine of textual severability for the purposes of the present appeal. Accordingly, I would allow this appeal on two grounds, (1) that there is no valid part of byelaw 2(b) which can be severed from the invalid part and stand by itself and (2) that the byelaw would not in any event survive the test of substantial severability.

Appeal allowed.

NOTE: In *The Confederation of Passenger Transport UK* v *The Humber Bridge Board and the Secretary of State for Transport, Local Government and the Regions* [2003] EWCA Civ 842, it was held that it was possible to correct a drafting error in delegated legislation applying the principles outlined by Lord Nicholls in interpreting primary legislation in *Inco Europe Limited* v *First Choice Distribution* [2000] 1 WLR 586, 592c–593a:

This power is confined to plain cases of drafting mistakes. The courts are ever mindful that their constitutional role in this field is interpretative. They must abstain from any course which might have the appearance of judicial legislation. A statute is expressed in language approved and enacted by the legislature. So the courts exercise considerable caution before adding or omitting or substituting words. Before interpreting a statute in this way the court must be abundantly sure of three matters: (1) the intended purpose of the statute or provision in question; (2) that by inadvertence the draftsman and Parliament failed to give effect to that purpose in the provision in question; and (3) the substance of the provision Parliament would have made, although not necessarily the precise words Parliament would have used, had the error in the bill been noticed. The third of these conditions is of crucial importance. Otherwise any attempt to determine the meaning of the enactment would cross the boundary between construction and legislation: see per Lord Diplock in *Jones* v *Wrotham Park Settled Estates* [1980] AC 74, 105–106.

■ QUESTIONS

1. Is the majority giving the courts a wide power to amend delegated legislation by severing invalid portions?
2. Is such a power to amend constitutional or desirable, given that Parliament can rarely amend delegated legislation?

SECTION 2: STANDARDS AND SELF-REGULATION

Scandals in 1994 and 2009 concerning the behaviour of MPs forced the House of Commons to reform its procedures using its powers of self-regulation. We will consider first the establishment of the regime for dealing with the standards and financial interests of MPs established in 1995. The House of Commons was responding to the report of the Committee on Standards in Public Life whose remit and first report also considered (a) the Executive: Ministers and officials and (b) Quangos. Next we will look at the reaction to the disclosure about MPs' expenses claims and the new arrangements for the payment of MPs allowances and finally the relationship of Parliamentary privilege, the basis for Parliament's self-regulation, with criminal law. We are focusing on the House of Commons as it implemented a system more quickly than the House of Lords, who had a similar system but only appointed an independent Commissioner for Standards in 2010.

A: Standards

The incident that triggered the establishment of a Standing Committee on Standards in Public Life in October 1994 was the exposure by a newspaper that two MPs accepted payment for putting Parliamentary Questions. The House of Commons' reaction to the Committee's first report was to vote for a new Select Committee on Standards and Privileges and a Parliamentary Commissioner for Standards. The extracts which follow deal with codes of conduct and Members' interests.

First Report of the Committee on Standards in Public Life

Cm 2850, 1995, pp. 32, 34–35

We recommend that the House should restate the 1947 resolution which places an absolute bar on Members entering into contracts or agreements which in any way restrict their freedom to act and speak as they wish, or which require them to act in Parliament as representatives of outside bodies.

We recommend that the House should prohibit Members from entering into any agreements in connection with their role as Parliamentarians to under-take services for or on behalf of organisations which provide paid Parliamentary services to multiple clients or from maintaining any direct or active connections with firms, or parts of larger firms, which provide such Parliamentary services.

We recommend that the House should set in hand without delay a broader consideration of the merits of Parliamentary consultancies generally, taking account of the financial and political funding implications of change.

We recommend that the House should:

- require agreements and remuneration relating to Parliamentary services to be disclosed;
- expand the guidance on avoiding conflicts of interest;
- introduce a new Code of Conduct for Members;
- appoint a Parliamentary Commissioner for Standards;
- establish a new procedure for investigating and adjudicating on complaints in this area about Members....

On disclosure we recommend:

- the Register should continue broadly in its present form, and should be published annually. However the detailed entry requirements should be improved to give a clearer description of the nature and scope of the interest declared;
- updating of the Register should be immediate. The current updated version should be made more widely available electronically;
- from the beginning of the 1995/96 session (expected in November) Members should be required to deposit in full with the Register any contracts relating to the provision of services in their capacity as Members, and such contracts should be available for public inspection;
- from the same time, Members should be required to declare in the Register their annual remuneration, or estimated annual remuneration, in respect of such agreements. It would be acceptable if this were done in bands: eg under £1,000; £1,000–5,000; £5,000–10,000; then in £5,000 bands. An estimate of the monetary value of benefits in kind, including support services, should also be made;
- Members should be reminded more frequently of their obligations to Register and disclose interests, and that Registration does not remove the need for declaration, and better guidance should be given, especially on first arrival in the House.

NOTES

1. The main elements of the arrangements are a Code of Conduct which prescribes and proscribes activities which MPs can carry out; requires them to register various interests and to revise them when they change; to have a Parliamentary Commissioner for Standards investigate allegations of breaches of the Code and report to a House's Standards and Privileges Committee which would decide if the breach had occurred and would recommend to the House a penalty.
2. The first Code was approved in 1995 and the current version was approved in 2009.

The Code of Conduct for Members of Parliament

HC 735 of 2008–09

Prepared pursuant to the Resolution of the House of 19th July 1995

I. Purpose of the Code

1. The purpose of this Code of Conduct is to assist Members in the discharge of their obligations to the House, their constituents and the public at large by:

a) Providing guidance on the standards of conduct expected of Members in discharging their parliamentary and public duties, and in so doing

b) Providing the openness and accountability necessary to reinforce public confidence in the way in which Members perform those duties.

II. Scope of the Code

2. The Code applies to Members in all aspects of their public life. It does not seek to regulate what Members do in their purely private and personal lives.

3. The obligations set out in this Code are complementary to those which apply to all Members by virtue of the procedural and other rules of the House and the rulings of the Chair, and to those which apply to Members falling within the scope of the Ministerial Code.

III. Public Duties of Members

4. By virtue of the oath, or affirmation, of allegiance taken by all Members when they are elected to the House, Members have a duty to be faithful and bear true allegiance to Her Majesty the Queen, her heirs and successors, according to law.

5. Members have a duty to uphold the law, including the general law against discrimination, and to act on all occasions in accordance with the public trust placed in them.

6. Members have a general duty to act in the interests of the nation as a whole; and a special duty to their constituents.

IV. General Principles of Conduct

7. In carrying out their parliamentary and public duties, Members will be expected to observe the following general principles of conduct identified by the Committee on Standards in Public Life in its First Report as applying to holders of public office.1 These principles will be taken into consideration when any complaint is received of breaches of the provisions in other sections of the Code.

"Selflessness

Holders of public office should take decisions solely in terms of the public interest. They should not do so in order to gain financial or other material benefits for themselves, their family, or their friends.

Integrity

Holders of public office should not place themselves under any financial or other obligation to outside individuals or organisations that might influence them in the performance of their official duties.

Objectivity

In carrying out public business, including making public appointments, awarding contracts, or recommending individuals for rewards and benefits, holders of public office should make choices on merit.

Accountability

Holders of public office are accountable for their decisions and actions to the public and must submit themselves to whatever scrutiny is appropriate to their office.

Openness

Holders of public office should be as open as possible about all the decisions and actions that they take. They should give reasons for their decisions and restrict information only when the wider public interest clearly demands.

Honesty

Holders of public office have a duty to declare any private interests relating to their public duties and to take steps to resolve any conflicts arising in a way that protects the public interest.

Leadership

Holders of public office should promote and support these principles by leadership and example."

V. Rules of Conduct

8. Members are expected in particular to observe the following rules and associated Resolutions of the House.

9. Members shall base their conduct on a consideration of the public interest, avoid conflict between personal interest and the public interest and resolve any conflict between the two, at once, and in favour of the public interest.

10. No Member shall act as a paid advocate in any proceeding of the House.

11. The acceptance by a Member of a bribe to influence his or her conduct as a Member, including any fee, compensation or reward in connection with the promotion of, or opposition to, any Bill, Motion, or other matter submitted, or intended to be submitted to the House, or to any Committee of the House, is contrary to the law of Parliament.

12. In any activities with, or on behalf of, an organisation with which a Member has a financial relationship, including activities which may not be a matter of public record such as informal meetings and functions, he or she must always bear in mind the need to be open and frank with Ministers, Members and officials.

13. Members must bear in mind that information which they receive in confidence in the course of their parliamentary duties should be used only in connection with those duties, and that such information must never be used for the purpose of financial gain.

14. Members shall at all times ensure that their use of expenses, allowances, facilities and services provided from the public purse is strictly in accordance with the rules laid down on these matters, and that they observe any limits placed by the House on the use of such expenses, allowances, facilities and services.

15. Members shall at all times conduct themselves in a manner which will tend to maintain and strengthen the public's trust and confidence in the integrity of Parliament and never undertake any action which would bring the House of Commons, or its Members generally, into disrepute.

VI. Registration and Declaration of Interests

16. Members shall fulfil conscientiously the requirements of the House in respect of the registration of interests in the Register of Members' Interests and shall always draw attention to any relevant interest in any proceeding of the House or its Committees, or in any communications with Ministers, Government Departments or Executive Agencies.

VII. Duties in respect of the Parliamentary Commissioner for Standards and the Committee on Standards and Privileges

17. The application of this Code shall be a matter for the House of Commons, and for the Committee on Standards and Privileges and the Parliamentary Commissioner for

Standards acting in accordance with Standing Orders Nos 149 and 150 respectively.

18. Members shall cooperate, at all stages, with any investigation into their conduct by or under the authority of the House.

19. No Member shall lobby a member of the Committee on Standards and Privileges in a manner calculated or intended to influence their consideration of a complaint of a breach of this Code.

NOTE: The main purpose of the Register is 'to provide information of any pecuniary interest or other material benefit which a Member receives which might reasonably be thought by others to influence his or her actions, speeches or votes in Parliament, or actions taken in his or her capacity as a Member of Parliament'. Members are required to keep that overall purpose in mind when registering their interests. The categories of registrable interests are:

1. Remunerated directorships
2. Remunerated employment, office, profession, etc.
3. Clients
4. Sponsorship or financial or material support
5. Gifts, benefits and hospitality (UK)
6. Overseas visits
7. Overseas benefits and gifts
8. Land and property
9. Registrable shareholdings
10. Controlled transactions within the meaning of Sched. 7A PPERA, not otherwise recorded in the Register
11. Miscellaneous and unremunerated interests
12. Family members employed and remunerated through parliamentary allowances

In the extracts from the Register the MPs selected are the leaders of the Conservative and Liberal Democrat parties who are, after the May 2010 General Election, the Prime Minister and Deputy Prime Minister, respectively.

The Register of Members' Financial Interests:

As at 6th September 2010

The Register of Members' Financial Interests is published soon after the beginning of a new Parliament, under the authority of the Committee on Standards and Privileges, and annually thereafter. Between publications the Register is regularly updated in a loose leaf form and, in that form, is available for public inspection in the Committee Office of the House of Commons. These amendments are also reflected in the Internet edition which is current as at 6th September 2010. Employment agreements deposited with the Registrar are available for personal inspection only.

CAMERON, Rt Hon David (Witney)

2. Remunerated employment, office, profession etc

Payment of £3089.06 from HarperCollins Publishers, via Ed Victor Ltd, 6 Bayley Street, Bedford Square, London WC1B 3HE, for publication advance for 'Cameron on Cameron: Conversations with Dylan Jones, ahead of paperback edition. Hours: Approximately 3 hrs on updated (paperback) edition. All payments relating to the book will be donated to charity. *(Registered 3 March 2010)*

4. Sponsorships

3 July 2009, I attended my local Principal Patrons Club Dinner which raised money for the West Oxfordshire Conservative Association. The following donations of over £1000 were received by the Association;

Name of donor: The Marquess of Headfort

Address of donor: Private

Amount of donation or nature and value if donation in kind: £1, 250 towards cost of dinner. £500 donation in kind for provision of venue.

Donor status: Individual

(Registered 21 July 2009)

Name of donor: Mr Nicholas Kaye

Address of donor: Private

Amount of donation or nature and value if donation in kind: £1,500 donation towards cost of dinner.

Donor status: Individual.

(Registered 21 July 2009)

Name of donor: News International Supply Company Ltd

Address of donor: 1 Virginia Street, London E98 1XY

Amount of donation or nature and value if donation in kind: Costs incurred from hosting the Leader of the Opposition's Combat Stress Summit at the House of Commons; total £1241.55 remitted directly to the relevant House of Commons Departments.

Date of receipt: 15 July 2009

Date of acceptance: £437 on 12 August 2009; £739 on 19 November 2009; £65 yet to be received.

Donor status: Company, registration number 01893198

(Registered 14 December 2009)

5. Gifts, benefits and hospitality (UK)

To facilitate my travel in my capacity as Leader of the Opposition I have received helicopter and private plane travel from the following:

JCB Research

Harris Ventures Ltd

IPGL Ltd

Henfield Lodge Aviation Ltd, London

William Cook Holdings, Sheffield

(The details of the travel provided by these sponsors have been provided to the office of the Parliamentary Commissioner for Standards for the period covered by this Register until 1 July 2009. Thereafter, itemised entries are shown below.)

In my capacity as Leader of the Conservative Party, I have accepted Honorary Membership for life of the Carlton Club.

Name of donor: Harris Ventures Ltd

Address of donor : Philip Harris House, 1A Spur Road, Orpington, Kent, BR6 OPH

Amount of donation or nature and value if donation in kind: £2,700 for private plane flight from Glasgow to Gatwick (5 passengers)

Date of receipt of donation: 16 October 2009

Date of acceptance of donation: 16 October 2009

Donor status: Company, registration number 02278367

(Registered 2 November 2009)

Name of donor: JCB Research

Address of donor : Rocester, Staffordshire, ST14 5JP

Amount of donation or nature and value if donation in kind: £5,875 for helicopter flight from Rhyl to London

Date of receipt of donation: 6 November 2009

Date of acceptance of donation: 6 November 2009

Donor status: Company, registration number 682651

(Registered 18 November 2009)

Name of donor: Lord Harris of Peckham

Address of donor: private

Amount of donation or nature and value if donation in kind: Christmas hamper and silver goblets; total value £3,500.

Date of receipt of donation: 24 December 2009

Date of acceptance of donation: 24 December 2009

Donor status: individual

(Registered 14 January 2010)

Name of donor: William Cook Holdings Ltd

Address of donor : Parkway Avenue, Sheffield S9 4UL

Amount of donation or nature and value if donation in kind: £4,355.06 for private plane flight from Manchester to Bristol on 8 January 2010 (4 passengers)

Date of receipt of donation: 8 January 2010

Date of acceptance of donation: 8 January 2010

Donor status: company, registration number 03283010

(Registered 25 January 2010)

Name of donor: IPGL Ltd.

Address of donor : Park House, 16 Finsbury Circus, London EC2M 7EB.

Amount of donation or nature and value if donation in kind: my wife and I received tickets to the Conservative Party's general election fundraising dinner. Value: £700. The donation will be reported to the Electoral Commission by the Conservative Party, as a donation to the Party.

Date of receipt of donation: 1 February 2010

Date of acceptance of donation: 1 February 2010

Donor status: company, registration number 02011009.

(Registered 16 February 2010)

Name of donor: IPGL Limited

Address of donor: Park House, 16 Finsbury Circus, London EC2M 7EB.

Amount of donation (or estimate of the probable value): one way flight from World Economic Forum, Davos (see Category 6 below), from Altenrhein, Switzerland to RAF Northolt, UK. There were six passengers on this flight. The total cost was £18.706.96. The individual benefit that I received was £3,117.83.

Date of receipt of donation: 30 January 2010

Date of acceptance of donation: 30 January 2010

Donor status: company, registration number 02011009

(Registered 2 March 2010)

Name of donor: William Cook Holdings Ltd

Address of donor: Parkway Avenue, Sheffield, S9 4UL.

Amount of donation or nature and value if donation in kind: two leg private flight from Wolverhampton to Edinburgh (11 February 2010) and Dundee to Oxford (12 February 2010). There were, including myself, four passengers on the first leg and seven on the second. The total value of both legs was £8,073.02.

Date of receipt of donation: 11 and 12 February 2010

Date of acceptance of donation: 11 and 12 February 2010

Donor status: company, registration number 03283010.

(Registered 16 March 2010)

Name of donor: Eastern Atlantic Helicopters Ltd

Address of donor: Unit 15B, Shoreham Airport, Shoreham-on-sea, West Sussex, BN43 5PA.

Amount of donation or nature and value if donation in kind: helicopter return flight from London to Llandudno. There were 3 passengers travelling return, including myself, and a further 3 who travelled one way. The total cost was £7,196.87, and the individual benefit I received was £1,599.30.

Date of receipt of donation: 6 March 2010

Date of acceptance of donation: 6 March 2010

Donor status: company, 04006527

(Registered 22 March 2010)

Name of donor: Noble Foods Ltd

Address of donor : Bridgeway House, Ickmeld Way, Tring, Herts. HP23 4JX

Amount of donation or nature and value if donation in kind: helicopter flight from Surrey to Staffordshire to Leeds to Holmfirth to London on 11 March 2010. There were 4 passengers on the flight and the total value was £6,301.97

Date of receipt of donation: 11 March 2010

Date of acceptance of donation: 11 March 2010

Donor status: company, registration number 05826545

(Registered 6 April 2010)

Name of donor: William Cook Holdings Ltd

Address of donor: Parkway Avenue, Sheffield, S9 4UL.

Amount of donation or nature and value if donation in kind: £7,067.33. The flight was from RAF Northolt to Exeter to Bristol to RAF Northolt. Although there were six passengers on the flight, the value reported here is the total value. It is this value that will be reported to the Electoral Commission. This benefit was provided to the Conservative Party and used by me in my role as Leader of the Party. The donation will be reported to the Electoral Commission by the Conservative Party, as a donation to the Party.

Date of receipt of donation: 25 March 2010

Date of acceptance of donation: 25 March 2010

Donor status: company, registration number 03283010

(Registered 22 April 2010)

Name of donor: Eastern Atlantic Helicopters Ltd

Address of donor: Unit 15B, Shoreham Airport, Shoreham-on-sea, West Sussex, BN43 5PA.

Amount of donation or nature and value if donation in kind: £12,780 on seven flights during the general election campaign: Wolverhampton to Oxfordshire, Oxfordshire to Birmingham, Berkshire to London, Essex to Oxfordshire, Berkshire to Yorkshire, Romsey to London, Essex to Oxfordshire. This value is the total for all seven flights. These benefits were provided to the Conservative Party and used by me in my role as Leader of the Party. The donations will be reported to the Electoral Commission by the Conservative Party, as donations to the Party.

Date of receipt of donation: 16 April 2010

Date of acceptance of donation: 16 April 2010

Donor status: company, registration number 04006527

(Registered 7 June 2010)

6. Overseas visits

Name of donor: World Economic Forum

Address of donor: 91–93 route de la Capite, CH-1223 Cologny/Geneva, Switzerland.

Amount of donation (or estimate of the probable value): estimated at £11,785.68 (conference pass, airport transfers and some hospitality)

Destination of visit: Davos, Switzerland.

Date of visit: 27–30 January 2010

Purpose of visit: to attend and speak at the World Economic Forum, Davos.

(Registered 23 February 2010)

7. Overseas benefits and gifts

Gift of a Christmas hamper from the Sultan of Brunei. *(Registered 13 January 2010)*

Painting by Abdul Rahim Salem, kindly given to me by His Highness, Sheikh Mohammed bin Rashid Al Maktoum, Vice President and Prime Minister of United Arab Emirates, and Ruler of Dubai. Address: The Ruler's Court, Bur Dubai, Dubai, United Arab Emirates. Given on 14 December 2009. I immediately gave this to Conservative Campaign Headquarters for all members of staff to enjoy. Value: £3,000-£4,000. *(Registered 13 January 2010)*

8. Land and Property

Residential property in London.

CLEGG, Rt Hon Nicholas (Sheffield, Hallam)

4. Sponsorship or financial or material support

(a) Donations to my constituency party or association, which have been or will be reported by my party to the Electoral Commission:

Name of donor: Mr Hugh Facey

Address of donor: private

Amount of donation or nature and value if donation in kind: £2,500, plus £100 per month as support for constituency office.

Donor status: individual

(Registered 10 June 2010)

Name of donor: Mr Duncan Greenland

Address of donor: private

Amount of donation or nature and value if donation in kind: £1,000 per quarter as support for constituency office

Donor status: individual

(Registered 10 June 2010)

(b) Support in the capacity as an MP:

The Liberal Democrat Leader's office has received additional donations, made through the Parliamentary Office of the Liberal Democrats, from:

Name of donor: Paul Strasburger

Address of donor: private

Amount of donation or nature and value if donation in kind: £2,600

Date of receipt: 2 September 2009

Date of acceptance: 9 September 2009

Donor status: individual

(Registered 17 September 2009)

Name of donor: Mr Richard Duncalf

Address of donor: private

Amount of donation or nature and value if donation in kind: £2,500

Date of receipt: 10 March 2010

Date of acceptance: 11 March 2010

Donor status: individual

(Registered 8 April 2010)

Name of donor: Mr Richard Duncalf

Address of donor: private

Amount of donation or nature and value if donation in kind: £2,263.50 (donation in kind; election tour goods).

Date of receipt: 26 March 2010

Date of acceptance: 29 March 2010

Donor status: individual

(Registered 8 April 2010)

Name of donor: Mr Oscar Pinto-Hervia

Address of donor: private

Amount of donation or nature and value if donation in kind: £2,500

Date of receipt: 10 March 2010
Date of acceptance: 11 March 2010
Donor status: individual
(Registered 8 April 2010)
Name of donor: Hervia Limited
Address of donor: 47 Spring Gardens, King Street, Manchester M2 2BG.
Amount of donation or nature and value if donation in kind: £10,000
Date of receipt: 10 March 2010
Date of acceptance: 11 March 2010
Donor status: company, registration number 02874245
(Registered 8 April 2010)

5. Gifts, benefits and hospitality (UK)

Name of donor: National Liberal Club
Address of donor : Whitehall Place, London SW1A 2HE
Amount of donation or nature and value if donation in kind: honorary life membership as Leader of the Liberal Democrat Party; value £560 pa plus £280 entrance fee.
Date of receipt of donation: 27 February 2008
Date of acceptance of donation: 27 February 2008
Donor status: friendly society
(Registered 10 June 2010)

NOTE: We now look at two of reports on investigation of breaches of the Code made by the Standards and Privileges Select Committee.

The first major case which the Commissioner and the Committee had to consider arose out of allegations by Mr Mohamed Al Fayed and *The Guardian* against Mr Neil Hamilton. It was quite protracted, given the amount of evidence which the Commissioner had to consider in his investigation. It was not completed before the General Election in 1997 in which Mr Hamilton lost his seat.

Eighth Report from the Select Committee on Standards and Privileges

HC 261 of 1997–98

COMPLAINTS FROM MR MOHAMED AL FAYED, THE GUARDIAN AND OTHERS AGAINST 25 MEMBERS AND FORMER MEMBERS: SECOND FURTHER REPORT: MR NEIL HAMILTON

The Committee on Standards and Privileges has agreed to the following Report:

1. On 3 July 1997 the Committee published its First Report, together with the report of the Parliamentary Commissioner for Standards on allegations made against twenty-five Members and former Members. On 1 August we published our Seventh Report containing our findings on twenty-four of those Members and former Members. We have now completed our proceedings in respect of Mr Neil Hamilton.

2. In our First Report we drew attention to the right of those Members criticised to submit a written statement to the Committee rebutting or challenging any findings of the Commissioner. Mr Hamilton's submission has already been published. We asked the Commissioner to provide us with briefing on the main points raised by Mr Hamilton. A written summary of the Commissioner's comments is appended. Mr Hamilton made an oral statement to the Committee on 14 October 1997, the text of which is published together with this Report. Also appended are representations from Mr Al Fayed's solicitors and from *The Guardian* seeking on behalf of witnesses, a comparable right of reply to Mr Hamilton's statement. After careful consideration the Committee concluded that these replies would not be necessary to enable it to reach its conclusions.

3. The procedures used by the Commissioner and the reasons for their adoption are published in the Committee's First Report. In his submission Mr Hamilton made a number of objections to the manner in which the Commissioner's inquiry had been conducted. We do not find Mr Hamilton's objections valid

in terms of our remit from the House. We accept the Commissioner's description of the approach he adopted:

> This was a parliamentary inquiry and there was no attempt to replicate the procedures of a court action. The proposed procedures were shown in advance to the previous Select Committee and to complainees. The approach was inquisitorial, not adversarial. Its sole purpose was to arrive at the truth, not to achieve a 'conviction'.

4. The Commissioner's findings on Mr Hamilton were as follows:

(i) *The evidence that Mr Hamilton received cash payments directly from Mr Al Fayed in return for lobbying services is compelling; and I so conclude. The amount received by him is unknown but is unlikely to have been less than the total amount received by Mr Smith. There is no evidence to indicate that Mr Hamilton received cash from Mr Al Fayed indirectly through Mr Greer.*

(ii) *The way in which these payments were received and concealed fell well below the standards expected of Members of Parliament.*

(iii) *There is insufficient evidence to show that Mr Hamilton received Harrods vouchers.*

(iv) *The hospitality Mr Hamilton received from Mr Al Fayed at the Ritz and elsewhere was intended, and accepted, as part of his reward for lobbying. It was not as it should have been, registered.*

(v) *Mr Hamilton failed to register two introduction payments from Mr Greer in relation to NNC (National Nuclear Corporation) and (United States Tobacco), some of which he look in kind. There is insufficient evidence to show that the UST payment was a disguised consultancy fee.*

(vi) *Mr Hamilton did not register hospitality received from UST in 1989; on balance, it would have been better had he done so.*

(vii) *Mr Hamilton deliberately misled the President of the Board of Trade about his financial relationship with Mr Greer.*

(viii) *Mr Hamilton failed to register a consultancy fee from Strategy Network International on the spurious grounds that an interest acquired and disposed of within four weeks was non-registrable.*

(ix) *Mr Hamilton persistently and deliberately failed to declare his interests in dealings with Ministers and officials on the issues of House of Fraser and Skoal Bandits and, in some cases, was positively misleading about the status of his representations.*

(x) *Mr Hamilton accepted a commission payment for introducing a constituent to Mr Greer, as well as a consultancy fee for representing that constituent's interests. Both these actions were unacceptable, the latter additionally so because it created a conflict of interest for Mr Hamilton in representing his other constituents.*

(xi) *The allegation that Mr Hamilton accepted a paid consultancy from Mobil Oil in return for asking Parliamentary questions is not substantiated.*

In his written statement Mr Hamilton apologised for his error of judgement in failing to register two commission payments and the SNI consultancy and for failing to register his hospitality at the Ritz hotel in Paris. He also apologised for his failure to declare the UST commission and the Ritz hospitality when making representations to Ministers. However, in both his written and his oral statement he contested many of the Commissioner's findings. In particular he has consistently denied that he received any cash payments from Mr Al Fayed.

5. We have carefully examined Mr Hamilton's representations. Essentially, these repeat the evidence he gave to the Commissioner for Standards. We do not consider that Mr Hamilton has brought forward relevant new evidence.

6. Our conclusions are as follows:

(i) When it investigated a complaint against Mr Hamilton's failure to register his stay at the Ritz Hotel in Paris in the previous Parliament, the Select Committee on Members' Interests did not elicit the detailed evidence on Mr Hamilton's relationship with Mr Al Fayed and the campaign managed by Ian Greer Associates which the Commissioner's inquiry has now established. The relationship was essentially a business relationship in which Mr Hamilton advocated Mr Al Fayed's cause. He received material benefits. The visit should have been registered and Mr Hamilton must have known that it should have been.

(ii) We examined the evidence relating to the information which Mr Hamilton gave to the then President of the Board of Trade, Mr Heseltine. Mr Hamilton never gave away more information about his relationship with Mr Greer than he had to. The Commissioner's finding that Mr Heseltine was 'deliberately misled' appears to us to be justified.

(iii) We accept the Commissioner's findings on Mr Hamilton's failures to declare his interests when dealing with Ministers and officials.

(iv) We recognise the force of the Commissioner's criticism of Mr Hamilton's acceptance of a commission payment for introducing a constituent to Mr Greer as well as a consultancy fee for representing that constituent's interests. Such actions do not appear to us to be contrary to the present rules of the House. We do not agree with the Commissioner's interpretation of the rules in this instance. We noted in our Seventh Report that we consider it to be inappropriate for a Member to receive a fee for introducing a constituency company to another company or organisation.

(v) The Commissioner found a variety of occasions, most of which are now admitted by Mr Hamilton, when he failed to register his interests. We draw attention to paragraph 813 of the Commissioner's report—

In addition to the stay at the Ritz (dealt with earlier) the main allegations against Mr Hamilton under this heading [alleged non-registration of interests] are considered below:

(i) In 1989 Mr and Mrs Hamilton spent a few days as guests of Mr Al Fayed on the estate of Balnagown Castle. This was clearly a benefit of substantial value and should, in my view, have been registered. Mr Hamilton regarded it as 'private hospitality': but this is a concept not recognised by the Register and, given the lobbying he was conducting at the time on Mr Al Fayed's behalf, the benefit could certainly have been thought to affect his conduct as a Member.

(ii) Mr Hamilton acknowledged receiving two Harrods hampers—one in 1988 and one in 1989. By today's standards these would be registrable, but I am inclined to think that this may not have been the accepted position at the time.

(iii) Unlike most, if not all, other lobbyists, IGA regularly paid commissions to Members who introduced new business. In 1987/88 Mr Hamilton received an introduction commission of £4,000 and a consultancy fee of £7,500 in relation to the National Nuclear Corporation. He registered the latter but not the former, on the grounds that the introduction payment was ex gratia and unexpected. In my view there is no doubt that the introduction commission should have been registered since it might have been thought to affect Mr Hamilton's conduct as a Member. This was also the view of the Select Committee on Members' Interests at the time and, although the Committee recognised that the categorisation of the Register was unsatisfactory, they did not see this as a justification for a failure to register such payments.

(iv) In 1989 Mr Hamilton received an introduction fee from IGA of £6,000, which had been agreed in 1988, in respect of US Tobacco (UST). Since this was his second such fee, it could no longer be argued that it was wholly unexpected. It should, in my judgement have been registered during 1989 and, in any event, in January 1990 after the Registrar had specifically reminded Members at the end of 1989 of their obligation to declare single payments.

(v) Also in 1989 Mr Hamilton enjoyed a three night stay at a hotel in New York at the invitation of UST. This, I think, was a marginal case, since he was on Select Committee business and his accommodation would have been paid for anyway. Nevertheless, the benefit could still have been thought to affect his conduct as a Member and would have been better registered.

(vi) It has been suggested that the payment relating to UST was, in fact, a consultancy fee and not an introduction payment. The evidence to the inquiry of Mr Walter, the former UST executive was not conclusive on this point. But this is not an important distinction if, as is the case, the payment was registrable in either event.

(vii) In 1990 Mr Hamilton received £667 from Strategy Network International for a month's consultancy work before becoming a Minister. He suggests that this would have been disregarded, as being *de minimis*, in 1990 and that, in any case, he resigned his appointment within the four-week period allowed for the registration of a new interest. In my view it is spurious to argue that an interest acquired and relinquished within four weeks is non-registrable; and the amount involved was far from negligible. I conclude that it should have been registered.

Cumulatively this list of omissions adds up to a casualness bordering on indifference or contempt towards the rules of the House on disclosure of interests.

7. Mr Hamilton's conduct fell seriously and persistently below the standards which the House is entitled to expect of its Members. Had Mr Hamilton still been a Member we would have recommended a substantial period of suspension from the service of the House. These conclusions are justified by paragraph 6 alone.

8. The most difficult issue is that of the alleged payments to Mr Hamilton by Mr Mohamed Al Fayed. Having regard to the nature of the alleged transactions and the conflict of evidence there can be no absolute proof that such payments were, or were not, made. The principal evidence upon which the Commissioner based his findings is contained in paragraph 789 of the Appendix to the First Report. There is no oral evidence independent of Mr Al Fayed and those who were working with him at the time. Mr Hamilton has consistently denied that he took 'cash for questions' or was paid for lobbying services. He questioned at length the credibility of witnesses who gave evidence on this matter. We have considered whether it is within our remit to carry out our own investigation. Such an investigation would have involved taking evidence from those witnesses who gave evidence to the Commissioner and also reassembling and reassessing a considerable body of material. The Committee would have become engaged in the details of inquiry which the appointment of the Commissioner was meant to avoid, with no certainty that we could take the matter any further than he had done. Detailed investigation was by the Commissioner. His terms of reference were:

> To enquire into allegations of misconduct against Mr Neil Hamilton and other Members of Parliament with a view to establishing whether there has been any breach of House of Commons rules, in the letter or in the spirit, and to report the findings to the Select Committee on Standards and Privileges.

We are satisfied that the Commissioner has carried out a thorough inquiry which took the evidence presented to him fully into account. The Committee did not arrive at a practicable way of reaching a judgement which adds to or subtracts from the Commissioner's findings.

9. As we have said in our Seventh Report,

> We recognise that, in practice, the powers of the House to punish non-Members are limited. In a future report we shall offer advice to the House on appropriate penalties and sanctions for Members, former Members and other persons involved in unacceptable behaviour.

10. This report is the final report dealing with allegations made in the media in the summer of 1996 on the conduct of Members. Its scale and scope were wholly unlike anything envisaged by the House when it created the new system for examining complaints against the conduct of Members and appointed a Commissioner for Standards. Indeed it is important to remember that the Commissioner's inquiry did not arise from a specific complaint but from a statement made to the House by the Speaker and from the request by our predecessors that he should 'investigate as a matter of urgency the serious allegations about the conduct of Members referred to by Madam Speaker in the House on 14 October'. Unlike our normal procedure where the onus is on a complainant to submit evidence supporting any complaint to the Commissioner, the Commissioner was given the task of defining the allegations and assembling the evidence. The amount of that evidence was very considerable. Over sixty witnesses provided evidence, thirteen oral hearings were held and some fourteen thousand pages of documents were submitted. The Commissioner was asked by the previous Committee not only to investigate but where possible to reach conclusions and then report to the Committee.

11. The scale and nature of this inquiry, analogous in some ways to that of a tribunal of inquiry, have highlighted the need for the Committee to assess its own role in relation to inquiries conducted by the Commissioner for Standards. Although some guidance was provided by the Select Committee on Standards in Public Life and by the Nolan Committee there is no agreement on whether there could be an appeal against the Commissioner's findings or conclusions by the Select Committee except in consideration by the House. The Committee will examine this matter further.

NOTES:

In his response to the Parliamentary Commissioner's report, Mr Hamilton complained about the investigation procedure used by the Commissioner. Mr Hamilton specifically mentioned the denial of a right to comment upon the Commissioner's findings before publication; that the burden of proof should have been placed squarely on the prosecution; that the standard of proof should have been 'beyond reasonable doubt'; that evidence was not taken on oath; that cross-examination was not allowed. The Commissioner's response to these points in the Annex was that the Standards and Privileges Committee had determined that Mr Hamilton should not be able to comment on the Commissioner's findings before publication; he had outlined his procedure in his report (HC 30 of 1997–98, paras. 69–73) and this inquiry was not meant to replicate a court action. The approach was inquisitorial, not adversarial; its purpose was to arrive at the truth, not secure a conviction. Thus there was no prosecution and no reversal of any burden of proof. The Commissioner had no power to take evidence on oath. Examination of witnesses was carried out by Counsel to the Inquiry and the Commissioner. Where witnesses were contradicted by later evidence they were given the opportunity to comment further (see articles by Doig and Woodhouse (1998) 51 *Parliamentary Affairs* at 36 and 51).

Second Report from the Select Committee on Standards and Privileges

HC 183 of 2008–09

Introduction

1. In our Fifth Report of Session 2007–08, published in February 2008, we informed the House that the Parliamentary Commissioner for Standards had submitted to us a memorandum on the progress of his investigation of complaints that the Rt Hon Peter Hain, the Member for Neath, had failed to register in the Register of Members' Interests within the required time limit all the donations he received in respect of his campaign for election as Deputy Leader of the Labour Party. The Commissioner informed us that, with the agreement of the Chairman of the Committee, he had suspended his inquiry pending the completion of police investigations into Mr Hain's failure to report the same donations to the Electoral Commission. The matter had been referred to the police by the Electoral Commission on 24 January. In line with our policy on such cases, we agreed with the decision of the Commissioner to suspend his inquiry.

2. The police completed their inquiries and passed a file to the Crown Prosecution Service in July 2008. It was not until December 2008 that the CPS announced there was insufficient evidence to charge Mr Hain with an offence under the Political Parties, Elections and Referendums Act 2000. The Commissioner informed us on 9 December that he was resuming his inquiry, a decision that we supported. We congratulate the Commissioner on completing his inquiry into this complaint within five weeks, notwithstanding that that period included the Christmas and New Year breaks.

3. A copy of the Commissioner's memorandum on this case is attached at Appendix 1. In accordance with our usual practice, we have shown the memorandum to Mr Hain. Mr Hain has informed us that he does not wish to add to what he has already told the Commissioner.

The complaint

4. The complaint against Mr Hain was brought by Mr David T C Davies, the Member for Monmouth. This was followed by complaints from Mr Bill Fry and from Mr Jeremy Wotherspoon. All three complaints related to Mr Hain's failure to declare to the Registrar of Members' Interests donations to his Labour party deputy leadership campaign totaling more than £100,000.

The Commissioner's findings

5. Mr Hain registered ten donations he received to his campaign in the period to May 2007 within the four-week deadline for registering such donations; these came to £77,000. He registered two further donations late, in November and December 2007, with a combined value of £10,000. He registered 17 further donations late in January 2008, the oldest of them dating back to April 2007 and the most recent to November. The donations registered in January 2008 totalled more than £103,000.

6. The Commissioner has accepted Mr Hain's assessment that a change of personnel in his campaign team was an important factor in his failure to register donations to the campaign between May and November 2007 (the campaign ended on 24 June). Another important factor was the disbandment of the campaign team while donations were still coming in, and before the large debts that were incurred during the campaign had come to light. A further important factor was Mr Hain's failure to identify any continuing need for registration after it ceased in May 2007, until prompted to do so by one of his donors in November.

7. At the time of the Labour leadership and deputy leadership elections, Mr Hain was Secretary of State for Northern Ireland and Secretary of State for Wales. Immediately after the elections, Mr Hain was made Secretary of State for Work and Pensions and Secretary of State for Wales. The Commissioner notes the pressures on Mr Hain as a senior member of the Government and that Mr Hain has accepted that he bore overall responsibility for ensuring that donations to his deputy leadership campaign were properly registered.

8. The Commissioner has upheld the complaints that Mr Hain failed to register in time all the donations he received for his campaign for election as Deputy Leader of the Labour Party. He has accepted Mr Hain's assurances that all the donations he received had been registered by 11 January 2008. He has also accepted that, once Mr Hain identified the oversight, he acted quickly and openly to address it, and that Mr Hain has both accepted responsibility for and rectified his errors. Finally, the Commissioner notes that Mr Hain apologised at the first opportunity.

9. However, the Commissioner also concludes that Mr Hain's breach of the rules "was both serious and substantial."

Conclusion

10. This is a case of an experienced Member, a Cabinet Minister at the time, failing in his duty as a Member of Parliament to register donations within the time required by the House. We understand that the pressures on Ministers and on front-benchers can be onerous, but we cannot accept—and we are sure that none of them would suggest—that this excuses them from their obligations under the rules of the House.

NOTE: The arrangements for the regulation of MPs' standards are under continuous review and the latest amendments will allow (a) the Parliamentary Commissioner for Standards to initiate a complaint into matters which have come to his attention, (not prompted by a complaint) but only if 'in his view there is sufficient evidence that the Code of Conduct or the rules relating to registration or declaration of interests may have been breached to justify taking the matter further' and (b) that three lay members should sit on the Standards and Privileges Select Committee (HC Deb Vol. 519, cols 995–1017, 2 December 2010). Both of these proposals originated in the Twelfth Report of the Committee on Standards in Public Life, *MPs Expenses and Allowances*, Cm 7724, 2009, and were accepted and proposed to the House by the Standards and Privileges committee (HC 67 of 2009–10).

B: MPs' expenses and allowances and Parliamentary privilege

The exposure in 2009 of the claims made by MPs under the House of Commons scheme for expenses and allowances, which included a practice known as 'flipping' in which some MPs changed the designation of their main home between their properties in London and their constituencies and thus secured substantial financial benefits in terms of mortgage relief, shocked and angered the public. The political parties recognized that something had to be done and rushed the Parliamentary Standards Act 2009 onto the statute book. In fact it was so rushed that it was substantially amended by the Constitutional Reform and Governance Act 2010. The Twelfth Report of Committee on Standards in Public Life was a major source of criticism of the 2009 Act and proposals for its reform. The Act, as amended creates the Independent Parliamentary Standards Authority (IPSA) which has the responsibility of determining and paying the salaries and allowances of MPs. IPSA is to review the allowances scheme and must refer to a list of statutory consultees. There were arrangements for investigation and enforcement with the 2009 Act officer whose original title of Commissioner for Parliamentary Investigations was renamed the Compliance Officer under the amendments in the 2010 Act and the powers and responsibilities were also amended. The Compliance Officer may investigate cases of suspected overpayment on his own initiative, on self-reference by a MP, on reference by IPSA or on receipt of a complaint. The investigation is a two-stage process with provisional and definitive findings. If the MP accepts the provisional finding then the investigation halts. The process will allow an MP to give oral evidence and to call and cross-examine witnesses. Enforcement may be carried out by recovery of overpayments. If IPSA was at fault then the Compliance Officer has a discretion whether or no to issue a repayment direction and if so the amount to be recovered; otherwise a repayment direction will be for the full amount of the overpayment. The repayment direction may also include interest on the amount overpaid, IPSA's costs in relation to the amount to be repaid and the costs of the Compliance Officer's investigation. A repayment direction may be appealed to the First-tier Tribunal. The Compliance Officer may impose a civil monetary penalty on an MPs who fails without reasonable excuse to provide information pursuant to an investigation. After giving IPSA a reasonable opportunity to review its decision to reject or pay in part a claim for an allowance, the Compliance Officer may conduct a review of IPSA's determination.

Seventh Report from the Justice Committee

HC 791 of 2008–09, EV 11

Written evidence

Memorandum submitted by Dr Malcolm Jack, Clerk and Chief Executive of the House of Commons

PRIVILEGE ASPECTS OF THE PARLIAMENTARY STANDARDS BILL

Introduction

1. This memorandum addresses privilege aspects of the Parliamentary Standards Bill. Since the Bill seeks to make statutory provision in relation to matters which fall within Parliament's exclusive cognisance or may affect proceedings in Parliament, it affects the established privileges of the House of Commons, thereby upsetting the essential comity established between Parliament and the Courts.

2. I should stress that I make no comment whatever on the merits of the Bill's policy proposals; it would be improper for me to do so. My concern is only with the constitutional implications for Parliamentary privilege (including the right of free speech) and the extent to which the courts are likely to come into conflict with Parliament thereby.

3. The principal provisions in issue are Clause 6 (MPs' code of conduct)... and Clause 10 (Proceedings in Parliament).

Clause 6

4. This Clause requires the House of Commons to maintain a code of conduct incorporating "the Nolan principles" (and such other principles as it may determine from time to time). The "Nolan principles" are defined as the seven general principles of public life set out in the First Report of the Committee on Standards in Public Life or "such other principles as may be adopted by the House from time to time".

5. The House already has a code of conduct based on the Nolan principles, originally adopted by resolution of the House on 19 July 1995 and most recently revised on 13 July 2005. The latest version of the Code and the Guidance to the rules relating to the conduct of Members was published on 23 June 2009 (HC 735).

6. Since the code of conduct is approved by resolution, the maintenance of such a resolution and the content of what it approves would become, by virtue of Clause 6, a matter which is justiciable in the courts. Questions would arise as to what was meant by "incorporating" the Nolan principles. If the exact words of the "Seven Principles of Public Life" as set out in the Nolan First Report were reproduced in the resolution, the duty would probably be satisfied in the eyes of the court, but if there were any re-stating of those principles in other words there would be room for legal argument as to whether the principles had been incorporated. By virtue of Clause 6(2) the House would be free to adopt other principles, but only such principles as were "similar". The question of whether those principles were "similar" would be a justiciable issue for the courts.

7. This might not come to court for some years—perhaps until some future addition to the Nolan principles became necessary in the light of events and on the recommendation of the Committee on Standards in Public Life. Equally, it might arise soon after enactment; in the present climate there might be no shortage of potential litigants trying to make a point.

8. The clause raises a constitutional issue by providing a basis for the judiciary to make determinations in respect of the proceedings of the House of Commons; in other words, to "question" proceedings in Parliament, notwithstanding the provisions of Article IX of the Bill of Rights. If a person (e.g. a taxpayer) is not satisfied that the code of conduct "incorporates" the Seven Principles, or does not do so in a way with which he agrees, or adopts principles which he does not consider to be "similar" to the Nolan principles, he could bring proceedings for judicial review and the courts will then determine the issue, if necessary by interpreting and construing resolutions as if they were law. This could lead to a finding by a court that the House of Commons was under a duty to adopt an amending resolution. Under the present law, the courts will not make such a finding, but Clause 6 would provide the courts with a justification for doing so.

9. It is not clear why this clause is in the Bill. If its effect would be minimal, then it cannot really be needed. If it would have a significant effect, then the risk of litigation affecting the boundaries of jurisdiction between the courts and Parliament is substantial...

Clause 10

17. Clause 10(c) allows any evidence of proceedings in Parliament to be admissible in proceedings for an offence under clause 9. This is a very wide qualification of the principle under Article IX of the Bill of Rights that such evidence is not admitted. It would mean that the words of Members generally, the evidence given by witnesses (including non-Members) before committees and advice given by House officials on questions, amendments and other House business could be admitted as evidence in criminal proceedings. This could have a chilling effect on the freedom of speech of Members and of witnesses before committees and would hamper the ability of House officials to give advice to Members.

18. It is for consideration whether the scope of this qualification could be narrowed—as in the current draft Bribery Bill—by confining the provision to the words or actions in Parliament of the Member concerned in the specific case. This reflects the compromise agreed to last time this issue was considered by a Parliamentary committee—the Joint Committee on the Draft Corruption Bill in 2003. At that time the Liaison Committee expressed concern that a wider provision might deter witnesses from speaking frankly before select committees.

19. However, even if the qualification were narrowed, the accused Member would be put in the position of having his words used against him, without being given the opportunity to adduce words spoken by other Members which might tend to exculpate him. This would create a very real risk of the trial being unfair and contrary to the requirements of Article 6 ECHR. [This prescribes as a minimum right the right to call and examine witnesses on his behalf on the same conditions as witnesses against him.] This demonstrates the difficulty caused by admitting evidence of proceedings in Parliament: either the admission is on such a wide basis that it has a chilling effect on Parliamentary proceedings (by prejudicing or effectively removing the right of free speech), or it is on such a narrow basis that the fairness of trials is put at risk.

20. I have argued in evidence to the current Joint Committee on the draft Bribery Bill that there is a case for not tinkering with parliamentary privilege on a piecemeal basis but implementing the recommendation of the Joint Committee on parliamentary privilege in 1999 that there should be a Parliamentary Privileges Act. Such an act would clarify the application of provisions of Article IX; define Parliament's control of its internal affairs and replace existing statute on the reporting of parliamentary proceedings.

The experience of the Defamation Act of 1996, intended to address one perceived anomaly of parliamentary privilege, has led to others. The provision of section 13 of the Act was later held to undermine the collective right of the House to immunity in respect of proceedings by allowing an individual Member to waive privilege. Other difficulties of a practical nature where more than one Member was involved led the Joint Committee to recommend repeal of the section. Other encroachments on parliamentary privilege suggest that a piecemeal approach to defining and defending the Houses' legitimate right to function effectively is no longer sufficient. The Australian model for a Parliamentary Privileges Act is at hand for adaptation to British circumstances.

NOTES

1. The government agreed to withdraw cl. 6, whereas cl. 10 was continued with but eventually defeated.
2. The relationship of the criminal law and Parliamentary privilege was considered by the Supreme Court in a case in which it was the basis for the defence of three MPs and a peer to the charge of false accounting under s. 17(1)(b) of the Theft Act 1968 in relation to their claims for allowances. Only the three MPs appealed to the Supreme Court, the peer was permitted to be an intervenor.

R v *Chaytor & Others*

[2010] UKSC 52, Supreme Court

LORD PHILLIPS:

15. It is now accepted in Parliament that the courts are not bound by any views expressed by parliamentary committees, by the Speaker or by the House of Commons itself as to the scope of parliamentary privilege. On 4 March 2010 the Clerk of the Parliaments wrote to the solicitor acting for Lord Hanningfield a letter that had received the approval of the Committee for Privileges. This stated:

> "Article 9 limits the application of parliamentary privilege to 'proceedings in Parliament.' The decision as to what constitutes a 'proceeding in Parliament', and therefore what is or is not admissible as evidence, is ultimately a matter for the court, not the House."

This statement was correct. It applies as much to the House of Commons as to the House of Lords, and to an issue as to the scope of the exclusive cognisance of Parliament as it does to an issue as to the application of article 9.

16. Although the extent of parliamentary privilege is ultimately a matter for the court, it is one on which the court will pay careful regard to any views expressed in Parliament by either House or by bodies or individuals in a position to speak on the matter with authority...

47. The jurisprudence to which I have referred is sparse and does not bear directly on the facts of these appeals. It supports the proposition, however, that the principal matter to which article 9 is directed is freedom of speech and debate in the Houses of Parliament and in parliamentary committees. This is where the core or essential business of Parliament takes place. In considering whether actions outside the Houses and committees fall within parliamentary proceedings because of their connection to them, it is necessary to consider the nature of that connection and whether, if such actions do not enjoy privilege, this is likely to impact adversely on the core or essential business of Parliament.

48. If this approach is adopted, the submission of claim forms for allowances and expenses does not qualify for the protection of privilege. Scrutiny of claims by the courts will have no adverse impact on the core or essential business of Parliament, it will not inhibit debate or freedom of speech. Indeed it will not inhibit any of the varied activities in which Members of Parliament indulge that bear in one way or another on their parliamentary duties. The only thing that it will inhibit is the making of dishonest claims...

59. None of these expressions of Parliamentary views lends support to the suggestion that submitting claims for allowances and expenses constitutes proceedings in Parliament for the purposes of article 9. On the contrary they all suggest, either expressly or by implication, that the submission of such claims falls outside the protection of that article. The recovery of allowances and expenses to defray the costs involved in attending Parliament, or travelling on Parliamentary business, has no closer nexus with proceedings in Parliament than incurring those expenses....

61. There are good reasons of policy for giving article 9 a narrow ambit that restricts it to the important purpose for which it was enacted—freedom for Parliament to conduct its legislative and deliberative business without interference from the Crown or the Crown's judges. The protection of article 9 is absolute. It is capable of variation by primary legislation, but not capable of waiver, even by Parliamentary resolution. Its effect where it applies is to prevent those injured by civil wrongdoing from obtaining redress and to prevent the prosecution of Members for conduct which is criminal. As to the latter, Parliament has no criminal jurisdiction. It has limited penal powers to treat criminal conduct as contempt. These once included imprisonment for a limited period. As to this Lord Denman CJ commented at p 114 in *Stockdale v Hansard:*

> "The privilege of committing for contempt is inherent in every deliberative body invested with authority by the Constitution. But, however flagrant the contempt, the House of Commons can only commit till the close of the existing session. Their privilege to commit is not better known than this limitation of it. Though the party should deserve the severest penalties, yet, his offences being committed the day before a prorogation, if the House ordered his imprisonment but for a week, every Court in Westminster Hall and every Judge of all the Courts would be bound to discharge him by habeas corpus."

Imprisonment has not been imposed in recent times and the same is true of the theoretical power to fine. Nor is it clear that Parliament is in a position to satisfy all the requirements of article 6 which apply when imposing penal sanctions—see *Demicoli v Malta* (1991) 14 EHRR 47.

62. Thus precedent, the views of Parliament and policy all point in the same direction. Submitting claims for allowances and expenses does not form part of, nor is it incidental to, the core or essential business of Parliament, which consists of collective deliberation and decision making. The submission of claims is an activity which is an incident of the administration of Parliament; it is not part of the proceedings in Parliament. I am satisfied that Saunders J and the Court of Appeal were right to reject the defendants' reliance on article 9.

72. The 1999 Report returns to this topic under the heading "Right of each House to administer its internal affairs within its precincts". It comments at para 240 that each House has the right to administer its internal affairs within the parliamentary precincts. It continues at para 241:

> "In one important respect this heading of privilege is unsatisfactory. 'Internal affairs' and equivalent phrases are loose and potentially extremely wide in their scope. On one interpretation they embrace, at one edge of the spectrum, the arrangement of parliamentary business and also, at the other extreme, the provision of basic supplies and services such as stationery and cleaning. This latter extreme would be going too far if it were to mean, for example, that a dispute over the supply of photocopy paper or dismissal of a cleaner could not be decided by a court or industrial tribunal in the ordinary way. Here, as elsewhere the purpose of parliamentary privilege is to ensure that Parliament can discharge its functions as a legislative and deliberative assembly without let or hindrance. This heading of privilege best serves Parliament if not carried to extreme lengths."

73. A little later the Report considers the dividing line between matters that fall

within this type of parliamentary privilege and those which fall outside it. This lies at the heart of these appeals and merits quotation in full:

> "246 Putting aside the activities of individuals, there is a need to distinguish between activities of the House which call for protection under this head of privilege and those which do not. The Palace of Westminster is a large building; it requires considerable maintenance; it provides an extensive range of services for members; it employs and caters for a large number of staff and visitors. These services require staff and supplies and contractors. For the most part, and rightly so, these services are not treated as protected by privilege. It is difficult to see any good reason why claims for breach of contract relating to catering or building services, for example, should be excluded from the jurisdiction of the courts, or why a person who sustains personal injury within the precincts of Parliament should not be able to mount a claim for damages for negligence. This has been formally recognised in the Parliamentary Corporate Bodies Act 1992. Under this Act each House established a corporate officer who can sign contracts on behalf of the House and sue or be sued.

247 The dividing line between privileged and non-privileged activities of each House is not easy to define. Perhaps the nearest approach to a definition is that the areas in which the courts ought not to intervene extend beyond proceedings in Parliament, but the privileged areas must be so closely and directly connected with proceedings in Parliament that intervention by the courts would be inconsistent with Parliament's sovereignty as a legislative and deliberative assembly. One example is the Speaker's decision on which facilities within the precincts of the House should be available to members who refuse to take the oath or affirmation of allegiance. Another example might be steps taken by the library of either House to keep members informed upon matters of significant political interest. Such steps, if authorised by the presiding officer of the House, would properly be within the scope of the principle and not amenable to orders of the court.

248 It follows that management functions relating to the provision of services in either House are only exceptionally subject to privilege. In particular, the activities of the House of Commons Commission, a statutory body appointed under the House of Commons (Administration) Act 1978, are not generally subject to privilege, nor are the management and administration of the House departments. The boundary is not tidy. Occasionally management in both Houses may deal with matters directly related to proceedings which come within the scope of article 9. For example, the members' pension fund of the House of Commons is regulated partly by resolutions of the House. So too are members' salaries and the appointment of additional members of the House of Commons Commission under section 1(2)(d) of the House of Commons (Administration) Act. These resolutions and orders are proceedings in Parliament, but their implementation is not."

76 .... The courts will respect the right of each House to reach its own decision in relation to the conduct of its affairs. Two examples will illustrate this. In *Re McGuinness's Application* [1997] NI 359 the applicant sought to challenge by judicial review the decision of the Speaker that those who had not complied with the requirements of the Parliamentary Oaths Act 1866 would be denied certain of the facilities of the House. Kerr J dismissed his application. He held at p 6:

"I am quite satisfied that, whether it qualifies as a proceeding in Parliament or not, the Speaker's action lies squarely within the realm of internal arrangements of the House of Commons and is not amenable to judicial review."

77. In *R v Parliamentary Commissioner for Standards, Ex p Al Fayed* [1998] 1 WLR 669 the Parliamentary Commissioner for Standards had published a report relating to a complaint by the applicant against a Member of Parliament. The applicant sought permission to challenge this by judicial review. The application was refused by Sedley J and renewed before the Court of Appeal. Lord Woolf MR gave a judgment with which the other members of the court agreed dismissing the application. He said, at p 673:

"The focus of the Parliamentary Commissioner for Standards is on the propriety of the workings and the activities of those engaged within Parliament. He is one of the means by which the select committee set up by the House carries out its functions, which are accepted to be part of the proceedings of the House. This being the role of the Parliamentary Commissioner for Standards, it would be inappropriate for this court to use its supervisory powers to control what the Parliamentary Commissioner for Standards does in relation to an investigation of this sort. The responsibility for supervising the Parliamentary Commissioner for Standards is placed by Parliament, through its standing orders, on the Committee of Standards and Privileges of the House, and it is for that body to perform that role and not the courts."

78. In summary, extensive inroads have been made into areas that previously fell within the exclusive cognisance of Parliament. Following *Ex p Herbert* there appears to have been a presumption in Parliament that statutes do not apply to activities within the Palace of Westminster unless they expressly provide to the contrary. That presumption is open to question. In 1984 three Law Lords, Lord Diplock, Lord Scarman and Lord Bridge of Harwich, on the Committee for Privileges expressed the view that sections 2–6 of the Mental Health Act 1983 applied to members of the House of Lords, although the Act did not expressly so state...

82. *Erskine May* records at pp 162–163 that in cases of breach of privilege which are also offences at law, where the punishment which the Commons has power to inflict would not be adequate to the offence, or where for any other reason the House has thought proceeding at law necessary, either as a substitute for, or in addition to, its own proceedings, the Attorney General has been directed to prosecute the offender. It is of note that in two of the cases cited the Attorney General was directed to prosecute witness to parliamentary committees for 'wilful and corrupt prejury'—CJ (1860) 258 and CJ (1866) 239. No instance is cited beyond the 19th century and a footnote records that on two ocassions in the 1970s the House authorities informally invited the police to consider prosecuting those responsible for gross misbehaviour in the gallery.

83. Thus the House does not assert an exclusive jurisdiction to deal with criminal conduct, even where this relates to or interferes with proceedings in committee or in the House. Where it is considered appropriate the police will be invited to intervene with a view to prosecution in the courts. Furthermore, criminal proceedings are unlikely to be possible without the cooperation of Parliament. Before a prosecution can take place it is necessary to investigate the facts and obtain evidence. The powers of the police in respect of these activities are contained in the Police and Criminal Evidence Act 1984. I am not aware that any court has had to consider the extent to which, if at all, the provisions of this Act apply within the Palace of Westminster. What occurs is that Parliament permits the police to carry out their investigations within the precincts.

92. Even if the House were not co-operating with the prosecuting authorities in these cases, I do not consider that the court would be prevented from exercising jurisdiction on the ground that they relate to matters within the exclusive cognisance of Parliament. If an applicant sought to attack by judicial review the scheme under which allowances and expenses are paid the court would no doubt refuse the application on the ground that this was a matter for the House. Examination of the manner in which the scheme is being implemented is not, however, a matter exclusively for Parliament. It was not suggested that Members have a contractual entitlement to allowances and expenses, but if they were to have such contractual rights, I see no reason why they should not sue for them. If a question were raised as to whether allowances and expenses were taxable, the court would be entitled to examine the circumstances in which they were paid. Equally there is no bar in principle to the Crown Court considering whether the claims made by the defendants were fraudulent. This is not to exclude the possibility that, in the course of a criminal prosecution, issues might arise involving areas of inquiry precluded by parliamentary privilege, although that seems unlikely having regard to the particulars of the charges in the cases before us.

93. For these reasons I am satisfied that neither article 9 nor the exclusive cognisance of the House of Commons poses any bar to the jurisdiction of the Crown Court to try these defendants. That is why I decided that each appeal should be dismissed.

Appeal dismissed

■ QUESTIONS

1. Does the inclusion of three lay people on the Standards and Privileges committee render more satisfactory the system of self-regulation of MP's standards?
2. How necessary is parliamentary privilege and is the current basis for deciding 'boundary disputes;' between it and the ordinary law of the land satisfactory?

8

The European Union

OVERVIEW

In this chapter we begin with a brief introduction to the European Union, moving on to the framework outlining the institutions, competences, legislative measures, and decision-making procedures following the changes to the founding treaties made by the Treaty of Lisbon. In the next section we examine the relationship between Union law and the law of the United Kingdom, focusing on the doctrines of supremacy of Union law and direct effect and directives.

NOTES

1. The European Union currently has 27 Member States whose relations with each other in a special legal order are founded on two treaties, the Treaty on European Union (TEU) and the Treaty on the Functioning of the European Union (TFEU) as amended by the Treaty of Lisbon, which came in to effect on 1 December 2009. These treaties were agreed in a process of development which had more modest origins starting with the original six Member States: Belgium, France, Germany, Italy, Luxembourg, and The Netherlands, creating an European Coal and Steel Community by the Treaty of Paris in 1952.
2. The next stage in the process occurred in 1957 when the original six developed their co-operation with the establishment of the European Economic Community (EEC) and the European Atomic Energy Community (EURATOM) under two Treaties signed in Rome. Subsequently other countries joined these Communities—Denmark, Ireland, and the United Kingdom in 1973, Greece in 1982, Portugal and Spain in 1986, Austria, Finland, and Sweden in 1995. In May 2004 the following countries joined: Cyprus, the Czech Republic, Estonia, Hungary, Latvia, Lithuania, Malta, Poland, Slovakia, and Slovenia. Bulgaria and Romania, joined in January 2007.
3. Initially the three Communities were separate entities with separate institutions. They merged the institutions and eventually created the European Community (EC) in which they sought to establish a single market in which there are (a) no barriers to trade amongst the Member States, and (b) freedom of movement of capital and of people, both as workers and as providers of services. This project is more than one of economic co-operation as it involves a degree of economic and political integration. This is demonstrated by the framework and practice of the EC by which Member States have agreed policies, the implementation of which is shared between Community institutions and themselves; and (b) the increasing scope of their partnership. Economic integration has been advanced by the Single European Act 1986 (SEA) and the TEU. Both of these treaties amended the founding treaties of the Communities. The TEU established the European Union within which was contained the EC. The SEA not only set a timetable for the completion of the single market, but also amended the decision-making process in respect of matters relating to the single market, while the TEU set out a timetable and process for a common currency, the Euro, and further revised the decision-making processes. Integration in political matters is not as advanced as in the economic sphere. The SEA introduced European Political Cooperation and the TEU elaborated upon this second pillar by replacing it with the Common Foreign and Security Policy, and added co-operation in home affairs and justice.
4. The Treaty of Amsterdam (1997) amended the TEU and the EC Treaty (TEC). The amendments to the TEC included border controls, visas, asylum, immigration, and other policies related to

the freedom of movement of persons. The United Kingdom and Ireland 'opted out' maintaining their border controls and their own common travel area.

5. The Treaty of Nice (2001) made changes to the institutional arrangements to enable the 15-member Union to cope with enlargement following the accession of the ten new members in May 2004.
6. A Convention on the Future of Europe was established to address making the Union more democratic, transparent and efficient and to prepare the way for a constitution for the citizens of Europe. Agreement on the Treaty was reached in the European Council held in Dublin in June 2004. The Constitutional Treaty was not ratified following rejection of ratification in referendums held in France and the Netherlands in 2005.
7. There then followed a fresh series of negotiations and the Treaty of Lisbon was signed in December 2007. During the negotiations Bulgaria and Romania became the 26th and 27th Member States in January 2007. The Lisbon Treaty amends the TEU and amends and renames the TEC as the TFEU. Changes brought about on the ratification of the Lisbon Treaty affect the institutions, competences, voting systems and working practices and do away with the confusion of the separate terms of Union and Community by the sole use of the Union term.

The Treaty of Amsterdam has renumbered the Articles of the TEU and Treaty of Rome, and in extracts from these Treaties the new number is given first, with the previous one in square brackets.

SECTION 1: THE FRAMEWORK OF THE UNION

In these extracts from the TEU and the TFEU, the framework for the Union is laid out. The treaties list objectives and create institutions which are to carry out specified tasks.

Treaty on European Union

TITLE I

COMMON PROVISIONS

Article 1 (ex Article 1 TEU) (1)

By this Treaty, the HIGH CONTRACTING PARTIES establish among themselves a EUROPEAN UNION, hereinafter called 'the Union', on which the Member States confer competences to attain objectives they have in common.

This Treaty marks a new stage in the process of creating an ever closer union among the peoples of Europe, in which decisions are taken as openly as possible and as closely as possible to the citizen.

The Union shall be founded on the present Treaty and on the Treaty on the Functioning of the European Union (hereinafter referred to as 'the Treaties'). Those two Treaties shall have the same legal value. The Union shall replace and succeed the European Community.

Article 2

The Union is founded on the values of respect for human dignity, freedom, democracy, equality, the rule of law and respect for human rights, including the rights of persons belonging to minorities. These values are common to the Member States in a society in which pluralism, non-discrimination, tolerance, justice, solidarity and equality between women and men prevail.

Article 3 (ex Article 2 TEU)

1. The Union's aim is to promote peace, its values and the well-being of its peoples.

2. The Union shall offer its citizens an area of freedom, security and justice without internal frontiers, in which the free movement of persons is ensured in conjunction with appropriate measures with respect to external border controls, asylum, immigration and the prevention and combating of crime.

3. The Union shall establish an internal market. It shall work for the sustainable development of Europe based on balanced economic growth and price stability, a highly competitive social market economy,

aiming at full employment and social progress, and a high level of protection and improvement of the quality of the environment. It shall promote scientific and technological advance.

It shall combat social exclusion and discrimination, and shall promote social justice and protection, equality between women and men, solidarity between generations and protection of the rights of the child.

It shall promote economic, social and territorial cohesion, and solidarity among Member States.

It shall respect its rich cultural and linguistic diversity, and shall ensure that Europe's cultural heritage is safeguarded and enhanced.

4. The Union shall establish an economic and monetary union whose currency is the euro.

5. In its relations with the wider world, the Union shall uphold and promote its values and interests and contribute to the protection of its citizens. It shall contribute to peace, security, the sustainable development of the Earth, solidarity and mutual respect among peoples, free and fair trade, eradication of poverty and the protection of human rights, in particular the rights of the child, as well as to the strict observance and the development of international law, including respect for the principles of the United Nations Charter.

6. The Union shall pursue its objectives by appropriate means commensurate with the competences which are conferred upon it in the Treaties.

Article 4

1. In accordance with Article 5, competences not conferred upon the Union in the Treaties remain with the Member States.

2. The Union shall respect the equality of Member States before the Treaties as well as their national identities, inherent in their fundamental structures, political and constitutional, inclusive of regional and local self-government. It shall respect their essential State functions, including ensuring the territorial integrity of the State, maintaining law and order and safeguarding national security. In particular, national security remains the sole responsibility of each Member State.

3. Pursuant to the principle of sincere cooperation, the Union and the Member States shall, in full mutual respect, assist each other in carrying out tasks which flow from the Treaties.

The Member States shall take any appropriate measure, general or particular, to ensure fulfilment of the obligations arising out of the Treaties or resulting from the acts of the institutions of the Union.

The Member States shall facilitate the achievement of the Union's tasks and refrain from any measure which could jeopardise the attainment of the Union's objectives.

Article 5 (ex Article 5 TEC)

1. The limits of Union competences are governed by the principle of conferral. The use of Union competences is governed by the principles of subsidiarity and proportionality.

2. Under the principle of conferral, the Union shall act only within the limits of the competences conferred upon it by the Member States in the Treaties to attain the objectives set out therein. Competences not conferred upon the Union in the Treaties remain with the Member States.

3. Under the principle of subsidiarity, in areas which do not fall within its exclusive competence, the Union shall act only if and in so far as the objectives of the proposed action cannot be sufficiently achieved by the Member States, either at central level or at regional and local level, but can rather, by reason of the scale or effects of the proposed action, be better achieved at Union level.

The institutions of the Union shall apply the principle of subsidiarity as laid down in the Protocol on the application of the principles of subsidiarity and proportionality. National Parliaments ensure compliance with the principle of subsidiarity in accordance with the procedure set out in that Protocol.

4. Under the principle of proportionality, the content and form of Union action shall not exceed what is necessary to achieve the objectives of the Treaties.

The institutions of the Union shall apply the principle of proportionality as laid down in the Protocol on the application of the principles of subsidiarity and proportionality.

Article 6 (ex Article 6 TEU)

1. The Union recognises the rights, freedoms and principles set out in the Charter of Fundamental Rights of the European Union of 7 December 2000, as adapted at Strasbourg, on 12 December 2007, which shall have the same legal value as the Treaties.

The provisions of the Charter shall not extend in any way the competences of the Union as defined in the Treaties.

The rights, freedoms and principles in the Charter shall be interpreted in accordance with the general provisions in Title VII of the Charter governing its interpretation and application and with due regard to the explanations referred to in the Charter, that set out the sources of those provisions.

2. The Union shall accede to the European Convention for the Protection of Human Rights and Fundamental Freedoms. Such accession shall not affect the Union's competences as defined in the Treaties.

3. Fundamental rights, as guaranteed by the European Convention for the Protection of Human Rights and Fundamental Freedoms and as they result from the constitutional traditions common to the Member States, shall constitute general principles of the Union's law.

Article 7 (ex Article 7 TEU)

1. On a reasoned proposal by one third of the Member States, by the European Parliament or by the European Commission, the Council, acting by a majority of four fifths of its members after obtaining the consent of the European Parliament, may determine that there is a clear risk of a serious breach by a Member State of the values referred to in Article 2. Before making such a determination, the Council shall hear the Member State in question and may address recommendations to it, acting in accordance with the same procedure.

The Council shall regularly verify that the grounds on which such a determination was made continue to apply.

2. The European Council, acting by unanimity on a proposal by one third of the Member States or by the Commission and after obtaining the consent of the European Parliament, may determine the existence of a serious and persistent breach by a Member State of the values referred to in Article 2, after inviting the Member State in question to submit its observations.

3. Where a determination under paragraph 2 has been made, the Council, acting by a qualified majority, may decide to suspend certain of the rights deriving from the application of the Treaties to the Member State in question, including the voting rights of the representative of the government of that Member State in the Council. In doing so, the Council shall take into account the possible consequences of such a suspension on the rights and obligations of natural and legal persons.

The obligations of the Member State in question under this Treaty shall in any case continue to be binding on that State.

4. The Council, acting by a qualified majority, may decide subsequently to vary or revoke measures taken under paragraph 3 in response to changes in the situation which led to their being imposed.

5. The voting arrangements applying to the European Parliament, the European Council and the Council for the purposes of this Article are laid down in Article 354 of the Treaty on the Functioning of the European Union.

TITLE II

PROVISIONS ON DEMOCRATIC PRINCIPLES

Article 9

In all its activities, the Union shall observe the principle of the equality of its citizens, who shall receive equal attention from its institutions, bodies, offices and agencies. Every national of a Member State shall be a citizen of the Union. Citizenship of the Union shall be additional to and not replace national citizenship.

Article 10

1. The functioning of the Union shall be founded on representative democracy.

2. Citizens are directly represented at Union level in the European Parliament.

Member States are represented in the European Council by their Heads of State or Government and in the Council by their governments, themselves democratically accountable either to their national Parliaments, or to their citizens.

3. Every citizen shall have the right to participate in the democratic life of the Union. Decisions shall be taken as openly and as closely as possible to the citizen.

4. Political parties at European level contribute to forming European political awareness and to expressing the will of citizens of the Union.

Article 11

1. The institutions shall, by appropriate means, give citizens and representative associations the opportunity to make known and publicly exchange their views in all areas of Union action.

2. The institutions shall maintain an open, transparent and regular dialogue with representative associations and civil society.

3. The European Commission shall carry out broad consultations with parties concerned in order to ensure that the Union's actions are coherent and transparent.

4. Not less than one million citizens who are nationals of a significant number of Member States may take the initiative of inviting the European Commission, within the framework of its powers, to submit any appropriate proposal on matters where citizens consider that a legal act of the Union is required for the purpose of implementing the Treaties.

The procedures and conditions required for such a citizens' initiative shall be determined in accordance with the first paragraph of Article 24 of the Treaty on the Functioning of the European Union.

Article 12

National Parliaments contribute actively to the good functioning of the Union:

(a) through being informed by the institutions of the Union and having draft legislative acts of the Union forwarded to them in accordance with the Protocol on the role of national Parliaments in the European Union;

(b) by seeing to it that the principle of subsidiarity is respected in accordance with the procedures provided for in the Protocol on the application of the principles of subsidiarity and proportionality;

(c) by taking part, within the framework of the area of freedom, security and justice, in the evaluation mechanisms for the implementation of the Union policies in that area, in accordance with Article 70 of the Treaty on the Functioning of the European Union, and through being involved in the political monitoring of Europol and the evaluation of Eurojust's activities in accordance with Articles 88 and 85 of that Treaty;

(d) by taking part in the revision procedures of the Treaties, in accordance with Article 48 of this Treaty;

(e) by being notified of applications for accession to the Union, in accordance with Article 49 of this Treaty;

(f) by taking part in the inter-parliamentary cooperation between national Parliaments and with the European Parliament, in accordance with the Protocol on the role of national Parliaments in the European Union.

TITLE III

PROVISIONS ON THE INSTITUTIONS

Article 13

1. The Union shall have an institutional framework which shall aim to promote its values, advance its objectives, serve its interests, those of its citizens and those of the Member States, and ensure the consistency, effectiveness and continuity of its policies and actions.

The Union's institutions shall be:

— the European Parliament,
— the European Council,
— the Council,
— the European Commission (hereinafter referred to as 'the Commission'),
— the Court of Justice of the European Union,
— the European Central Bank,
— the Court of Auditors.

2. Each institution shall act within the limits of the powers conferred on it in the Treaties, and in conformity with the procedures, conditions and objectives set out in them. The institutions shall practice mutual sincere cooperation.

3. The provisions relating to the European Central Bank and the Court of Auditors and detailed provisions on the other institutions are set out in the Treaty on the Functioning of the European Union.

4. The European Parliament, the Council and the Commission shall be assisted by an Economic and Social Committee and a Committee of the Regions acting in an advisory capacity.

Article 14

1. The European Parliament shall, jointly with the Council, exercise legislative and budgetary functions. It shall exercise functions of political control and consultation as laid down in the Treaties. It shall elect the President of the Commission.

2. The European Parliament shall be composed of representatives of the Union's citizens. They shall not exceed seven hundred and fifty in number, plus the President. Representation of citizens shall be degressively proportional, with a minimum threshold of six members per Member State. No Member State shall be allocated more than ninety-six seats.

The European Council shall adopt by unanimity, on the initiative of the European Parliament and with its consent, a decision establishing the composition of the European Parliament, respecting the principles referred to in the first subparagraph.

3. The members of the European Parliament shall be elected for a term of five years by direct universal suffrage in a free and secret ballot.

4. The European Parliament shall elect its President and its officers from among its members.

Article 15

1. The European Council shall provide the Union with the necessary impetus for its development and shall define the general political directions and priorities thereof. It shall not exercise legislative functions.

2. The European Council shall consist of the Heads of State or Government of the Member States, together with its President and the President of the Commission. The High Representative of the Union for Foreign Affairs and Security Policy shall take part in its work.

3. The European Council shall meet twice every six months, convened by its President. When the agenda so requires, the members of the European Council may decide each to be assisted by a minister and, in the case of the President of the Commission, by a member of the Commission. When the situation so requires, the President shall convene a special meeting of the European Council.

4. Except where the Treaties provide otherwise, decisions of the European Council shall be taken by consensus.

5. The European Council shall elect its President, by a qualified majority, for a term of two and a half years, renewable once. In the event of an impediment or serious misconduct, the European Council can end the President's term of office in accordance with the same procedure.

6. The President of the European Council:

(a) shall chair it and drive forward its work;

(b) shall ensure the preparation and continuity of the work of the European Council in cooperation with the President of the Commission, and on the basis of the work of the General Affairs Council;

(c) shall endeavour to facilitate cohesion and consensus within the European Council;

(d) shall present a report to the European Parliament after each of the meetings of the European Council.

The President of the European Council shall, at his level and in that capacity, ensure the external representation of the Union on issues concerning its common foreign and security policy, without prejudice to the powers of the High Representative of the Union for Foreign Affairs and Security Policy.

The President of the European Council shall not hold a national office.

Article 16

1. The Council shall, jointly with the European Parliament, exercise legislative and budgetary functions. It shall carry out policy-making and coordinating functions as laid down in the Treaties.

2. The Council shall consist of a representative of each Member State at ministerial level, who may commit the government of the Member State in question and cast its vote.

3. The Council shall act by a qualified majority except where the Treaties provide otherwise.

4. As from 1 November 2014, a qualified majority shall be defined as at least 55 % of the members of the Council, comprising at least fifteen of them and representing Member States comprising at least 65 % of the population of the Union.

A blocking minority must include at least four Council members, failing which the qualified majority shall be deemed attained.

The other arrangements governing the qualified majority are laid down in Article 238(2) of the Treaty on the Functioning of the European Union.

5. The transitional provisions relating to the definition of the qualified majority which shall be applicable until 31 October 2014 and those which shall be applicable from 1 November 2014 to 31 March 2017 are laid down in the Protocol on transitional provisions.

6. The Council shall meet in different configurations, the list of which shall be adopted in accordance with Article 236 of the Treaty on the Functioning of the European Union.

The General Affairs Council shall ensure consistency in the work of the different Council configurations. It shall prepare and ensure the follow-up to meetings of the European Council, in liaison with the President of the European Council and the Commission.

The Foreign Affairs Council shall elaborate the Union's external action on the basis of strategic guidelines laid down by the European Council and ensure that the Union's action is consistent.

7. A Committee of Permanent Representatives of the Governments of the Member States shall be responsible for preparing the work of the Council.

8. The Council shall meet in public when it deliberates and votes on a draft legislative act. To this end, each Council meeting shall be divided into two parts, dealing respectively with deliberations on Union legislative acts and non-legislative activities.

9. The Presidency of Council configurations, other than that of Foreign Affairs, shall be held by Member State representatives in the Council on the basis of equal rotation, in accordance with the conditions established in accordance with Article 236 of the Treaty on the Functioning of the European Union.

Article 17

1. The Commission shall promote the general interest of the Union and take appropriate initiatives to that end. It shall ensure the application of the Treaties, and of measures adopted by the institutions pursuant to them. It shall oversee the application of Union law under the control of the Court of Justice of the European Union. It shall execute the budget and manage programmes. It shall exercise coordinating, executive and management functions, as laid down in the Treaties. With the exception of the common foreign and security policy, and other cases provided for in the Treaties, it shall ensure the Union's external representation. It shall initiate the Union's annual and multiannual programming with a view to achieving interinstitutional agreements.

2. Union legislative acts may only be adopted on the basis of a Commission proposal, except where the Treaties provide otherwise. Other acts shall be adopted on the basis of a Commission proposal where the Treaties so provide.

3. The Commission's term of office shall be five years.

The members of the Commission shall be chosen on the ground of their general competence and European commitment from persons whose independence is beyond doubt.

In carrying out its responsibilities, the Commission shall be completely independent. Without prejudice to Article 18(2), the members of the Commission shall neither seek nor take instructions from any Government or other institution, body, office or entity. They shall refrain from any action incompatible with their duties or the performance of their tasks.

4. The Commission appointed between the date of entry into force of the Treaty of Lisbon and 31 October 2014, shall consist of one national of each Member State, including its President and the High Representative of the Union for Foreign Affairs and Security Policy who shall be one of its Vice-Presidents.

5. As from 1 November 2014, the Commission shall consist of a number of members, including its President and the High Representative of the Union for Foreign Affairs and Security Policy, corresponding to two thirds of the number of Member States, unless the European Council, acting unanimously, decides to alter this number.

The members of the Commission shall be chosen from among the nationals of the Member States on the basis of a system of strictly equal rotation between the Member States, reflecting the demographic and geographical range of all the Member States. This system shall be established unanimously by the European Council in accordance with Article 244 of the Treaty on the Functioning of the European Union.

6. The President of the Commission shall:

(a) lay down guidelines within which the Commission is to work;
(b) decide on the internal organisation of the Commission, ensuring that it acts consistently, efficiently and as a collegiate body;
(c) appoint Vice-Presidents, other than the High Representative of the Union for Foreign Affairs and Security Policy, from among the members of the Commission.

A member of the Commission shall resign if the President so requests. The High Representative of the Union for Foreign Affairs and Security Policy shall resign, in accordance with the procedure set out in Article 18(1), if the President so requests.

7. Taking into account the elections to the European Parliament and after having held the appropriate consultations, the European Council, acting by a qualified majority, shall propose to the European Parliament a candidate for President of the Commission. This candidate shall be elected by the European Parliament by a majority of its component members. If he does not obtain the required majority, the European Council, acting by a qualified majority, shall within one month propose a new candidate who shall be elected by the European Parliament following the same procedure.

The Council, by common accord with the President-elect, shall adopt the list of the other persons whom it proposes for appointment as members of the Commission. They shall be selected, on the basis of the suggestions made by Member States, in accordance with the criteria set out in paragraph 3, second subparagraph, and paragraph 5, second subparagraph.

The President, the High Representative of the Union for Foreign Affairs and Security Policy and the other members of the Commission shall be subject as a body to a vote of consent by the European Parliament. On the basis of this consent the Commission shall be appointed by the European Council, acting by a qualified majority.

8. The Commission, as a body, shall be responsible to the European Parliament. In accordance with Article 234 of the Treaty on the Functioning of the European Union, the European Parliament may vote on a motion of censure of the Commission. If such a motion is carried, the members of the Commission shall resign as a body and the High Representative of the Union for Foreign Affairs and Security Policy shall resign from the duties that he carries out in the Commission.

Article 18

1. The European Council, acting by a qualified majority, with the agreement of the President of the Commission, shall appoint the High Representative of the Union for Foreign Affairs and Security Policy. The European Council may end his term of office by the same procedure.

2. The High Representative shall conduct the Union's common foreign and security policy. He shall contribute by his proposals to the development of that policy, which he shall carry out as mandated by the Council. The same shall apply to the common security and defence policy.

3. The High Representative shall preside over the Foreign Affairs Council.

4. The High Representative shall be one of the Vice-Presidents of the Commission. He shall ensure the consistency of the Union's external action. He shall be responsible within the Commission for responsibilities incumbent on it in external relations and for coordinating other aspects of the Union's external action. In exercising these responsibilities within the Commission, and only for these responsibilities, the High Representative shall be bound by Commission procedures to the extent that this is consistent with paragraphs 2 and 3.

Article 19

1. The Court of Justice of the European Union shall include the Court of Justice, the General Court and specialised courts. It shall ensure that in the interpretation and application of the Treaties the law is observed.

Member States shall provide remedies sufficient to ensure effective legal protection in the fields covered by Union law.

2. The Court of Justice shall consist of one judge from each Member State. It shall be assisted by Advocates-General.

The General Court shall include at least one judge per Member State.

The Judges and the Advocates-General of the Court of Justice and the Judges of the General Court shall be chosen from persons whose independence is beyond doubt and who satisfy the conditions set out in Articles 253 and 254 of the Treaty on the Functioning of the European Union. They shall be appointed by common accord of the governments of the Member States for six years. Retiring Judges and Advocates-General may be reappointed.

3. The Court of Justice of the European Union shall, in accordance with the Treaties:

(a) rule on actions brought by a Member State, an institution or a natural or legal person;

(b) give preliminary rulings, at the request of courts or tribunals of the Member States, on the interpretation of Union law or the validity of acts adopted by the institutions;

(c) rule in other cases provided for in the Treaties. (c) appoint Vice-Presidents, other than the High Representative of the Union for Foreign Affairs and Security Policy, from among the members of the Commission.

NOTES

1. Art. 3 sets out the Union's competences and Art. 5 sets out the limits to those competences with definitions of the principles of subsidiarity and proportionality.
2. The Treaties seek to create a balance amongst the institutions. The Commission is required to take forward the Union view and so Commissioners are not meant to represent their home states (Art. 17(3)), whereas the Council and Parliament who together exercise legislative power can, and do put the interests of their home states first. The voting procedures in the Council provide for a specified majority (see Art. 16).
3. The Charter of Fundamental Rights becomes part of Union Law but Poland and the United Kingdom have a protocol which states that no court can declare laws or practices in Poland and the United Kingdom inconsistent with the rights and principles reaffirmed in the Charter and it does not create any justiciable rights unless they are provided for in the national law of Poland and the United Kingdom.
4. Other areas in which the United Kingdom has opted out include the common currency, the area of freedom, security and justice which relate to border controls immigration, asylum, and judicial and police co-operation. The United Kingdom may request to opt-in for particular matters and in October 2010 announced an intention to do in relation to a directive on the provision of information in criminal proceedings (HC Debs, vol. 517, 25 October 2010 6 WS). The draft directive would require a letter of rights to be given to suspects in their home language. The rights include: to be informed of the charge and, where appropriate, to have access to the case-file; to interpretation and translation for those who do not understand the language of the proceedings; to be brought promptly before a court following arrest. Such information is carried out by the police in the United Kingdom; opting in means that UK citizens who are suspects would receive such written information in the 15 Member States where it is not yet the practice.
5. Greater detail is spelt out in relation to the policies, institutions and decision-making procedures in TFEU. Extracts on legal acts and their procedures follow.

Treaty on the Functioning of the European Union

CHAPTER 2

LEGAL ACTS OF THE UNION, ADOPTION PROCEDURES AND OTHER PROVISIONS

SECTION 1

THE LEGAL ACTS OF THE UNION

Article 288 (ex Article 249 TEC)

To exercise the Union's competences, the institutions shall adopt regulations, directives, decisions, recommendations and opinions.

A regulation shall have general application. It shall be binding in its entirety and directly applicable in all Member States.

A directive shall be binding, as to the result to be achieved, upon each Member State to which it is addressed, but shall leave to the national authorities the choice of form and methods.

A decision shall be binding in its entirety. A decision which specifies those to whom it is addressed shall be binding only on them.

Recommendations and opinions shall have no binding force.

Article 289

1. The ordinary legislative procedure shall consist in the joint adoption by the European Parliament and the Council of a regulation, directive or decision on a proposal from the Commission. This procedure is defined in Article 294.

2. In the specific cases provided for by the Treaties, the adoption of a regulation, directive or decision by the European Parliament with the participation of the Council, or by the latter with the participation of the European Parliament, shall constitute a special legislative procedure.

3. Legal acts adopted by legislative procedure shall constitute legislative acts.

4. In the specific cases provided for by the Treaties, legislative acts may be adopted on the initiative of a group of Member States or of the European Parliament, on a recommendation from the European Central Bank or at the request of the Court of Justice or the European Investment Bank.

Article 290

1. A legislative act may delegate to the Commission the power to adopt non-legislative acts of general application to supplement or amend certain non-essential elements of the legislative act.

The objectives, content, scope and duration of the delegation of power shall be explicitly defined in the legislative acts. The essential elements of an area shall be reserved for the legislative act and accordingly shall not be the subject of a delegation of power.

2. Legislative acts shall explicitly lay down the conditions to which the delegation is subject; these conditions may be as follows:

(a) the European Parliament or the Council may decide to revoke the delegation;

(b) the delegated act may enter into force only if no objection has been expressed by the European Parliament or the Council within a period set by the legislative act.

For the purposes of (a) and (b), the European Parliament shall act by a majority of its component members, and the Council by a qualified majority.

3. The adjective 'delegated' shall be inserted in the title of delegated acts.

Article 291

1. Member States shall adopt all measures of national law necessary to implement legally binding Union acts.

2. Where uniform conditions for implementing legally binding Union acts are needed, those acts shall confer implementing powers on the Commission, or, in duly justified specific cases and in the cases provided for in Articles 24 and 26 of the Treaty on European Union, on the Council.

3. For the purposes of paragraph 2, the European Parliament and the Council, acting by means of regulations in accordance with the ordinary legislative procedure, shall lay down in advance the rules and general principles concerning mechanisms for control by Member States of the Commission's exercise of implementing powers.

4. The word 'implementing' shall be inserted in the title of implementing acts.

Article 292

The Council shall adopt recommendations. It shall act on a proposal from the Commission in all cases where the Treaties provide that it shall adopt acts on a proposal from the Commission. It shall act unanimously in those areas in which unanimity is required for the adoption of a Union act. The Commission, and the European Central Bank in the specific cases provided for in the Treaties, shall adopt recommendations.

SECTION 2

PROCEDURES FOR THE ADOPTION OF ACTS AND OTHER PROVISIONS

Article 293 (ex Article 250 TEC)

1. Where, pursuant to the Treaties, the Council acts on a proposal from the Commission, it may amend that proposal only by acting unanimously, except in the cases referred to in paragraphs 10 and 13 of Article 294, in Articles 310, 312 and 314 and in the second paragraph of Article 315.

2. As long as the Council has not acted, the Commission may alter its proposal at any time during the procedures leading to the adoption of a Union act.

Article 294 (ex Article 251 TEC)

1. Where reference is made in the Treaties to the ordinary legislative procedure for the adoption of an act, the following procedure shall apply.

2. The Commission shall submit a proposal to the European Parliament and the Council.

First reading

3. The European Parliament shall adopt its position at first reading and communicate it to the Council.

4. If the Council approves the European Parliament's position, the act concerned shall be adopted in the wording which corresponds to the position of the European Parliament.

5. If the Council does not approve the European Parliament's position, it shall adopt its position at first reading and communicate it to the European Parliament.

6. The Council shall inform the European Parliament fully of the reasons which led it to adopt its position at first reading. The Commission shall inform the European Parliament fully of its position.

Second reading

7. If, within three months of such communication, the European Parliament:

(a) approves the Council's position at first reading or has not taken a decision, the act concerned shall be deemed to have been adopted in the wording which corresponds to the position of the Council;
(b) rejects, by a majority of its component members, the Council's position at first reading, the proposed act shall be deemed not to have been adopted;
(c) proposes, by a majority of its component members, amendments to the Council's position at first reading, the text thus amended shall be forwarded to the Council and to the Commission, which shall deliver an opinion on those amendments.

8. If, within three months of receiving the European Parliament's amendments, the Council, acting by a qualified majority:
(a) approves all those amendments, the act in question shall be deemed to have been adopted;
(b) does not approve all the amendments, the President of the Council, in agreement with the

President of the European Parliament, shall within six weeks convene a meeting of the Conciliation Committee.

9. The Council shall act unanimously on the amendments on which the Commission has delivered a negative opinion.

Conciliation

10. The Conciliation Committee, which shall be composed of the members of the Council or their representatives and an equal number of members representing the European Parliament, shall have the task of reaching agreement on a joint text, by a qualified majority of the members of the Council or their representatives and by a majority of the members representing the European Parliament within six weeks of its being convened, on the basis of the positions of the European Parliament and the Council at second reading.

11. The Commission shall take part in the Conciliation Committee's proceedings and shall take all necessary initiatives with a view to reconciling the positions of the European Parliament and the Council.

12. If, within six weeks of its being convened, the Conciliation Committee does not approve the joint text, the proposed act shall be deemed not to have been adopted.

Third reading

13. If, within that period, the Conciliation Committee approves a joint text, the European Parliament, acting by a majority of the votes cast, and the Council, acting by a qualified majority, shall each have a period of six weeks from that approval in which to adopt the act in question in accordance with the joint text. If they fail to do so, the proposed act shall be deemed not to have been adopted.

14. The periods of three months and six weeks referred to in this Article shall be extended by a maximum of one month and two weeks respectively at the initiative of the European Parliament or the Council.

Special provisions

15. Where, in the cases provided for in the Treaties, a legislative act is submitted to the ordinary legislative procedure on the initiative of a group of Member States, on a recommendation by the European Central Bank, or at the request of the Court of Justice, paragraph 2, the second sentence of paragraph 6, and paragraph 9 shall not apply.

In such cases, the European Parliament and the Council shall communicate the proposed act to the Commission with their positions at first and second readings. The European Parliament or the Council may request the opinion of the Commission throughout the procedure, which the Commission may also deliver on its own initiative. It may also, if it deems it necessary, take part in the Conciliation Committee in accordance with paragraph 11.

Article 295

The European Parliament, the Council and the Commission shall consult each other and by common agreement make arrangements for their cooperation. To that end, they may, in compliance with the Treaties, conclude interinstitutional agreements which may be of a binding nature.

Article 296 (ex Article 253 TEC)

Where the Treaties do not specify the type of act to be adopted, the institutions shall select it on a case by-case basis, in compliance with the applicable procedures and with the principle of proportionality.

Legal acts shall state the reasons on which they are based and shall refer to any proposals, initiatives, recommendations, requests or opinions required by the Treaties.

When considering draft legislative acts, the European Parliament and the Council shall refrain from adopting acts not provided for by the relevant legislative procedure in the area in question.

Article 297 (ex Article 254 TEC)

1. Legislative acts adopted under the ordinary legislative procedure shall be signed by the President of the European Parliament and by the President of the Council.

Legislative acts adopted under a special legislative procedure shall be signed by the President of the institution which adopted them.

Legislative acts shall be published in the *Official Journal of the European Union*. They shall enter into force on the date specified in them or, in the absence thereof, on the twentieth day following that of their publication.

2. Non-legislative acts adopted in the form of regulations, directives or decisions, when the latter do not specify to whom they are addressed, shall be signed by the President of the institution which adopted them.

Regulations and directives which are addressed to all Member States, as well as decisions which do not specify to whom they are addressed, shall be published in the *Official Journal of the European Union*. They shall enter into force on the date specified in them or, in the absence thereof, on the twentieth day following that of their publication.

Other directives, and decisions which specify to whom they are addressed, shall be notified to those to whom they are addressed and shall take effect upon such notification.

Article 298

1. In carrying out their missions, the institutions, bodies, offices and agencies of the Union shall have the support of an open, efficient and independent European administration.

2. In compliance with the Staff Regulations and the Conditions of Employment adopted on the basis of Article 336, the European Parliament and the Council, acting by means of regulations in accordance with the ordinary legislative procedure, shall establish provisions to that end.

Article 299 (ex Article 256 TEC)

Acts of the Council, the Commission or the European Central Bank which impose a pecuniary obligation on persons other than States, shall be enforceable.

Enforcement shall be governed by the rules of civil procedure in force in the State in the territory of which it is carried out. The order for its enforcement shall be appended to the decision, without other formality than verification of the authenticity of the decision, by the national authority which the government of each Member State shall designate for this purpose and shall make known to the Commission and to the Court of Justice of the European Union.

When these formalities have been completed on application by the party concerned, the latter may proceed to enforcement in accordance with the national law, by bringing the matter directly before the competent authority.

Enforcement may be suspended only by a decision of the Court. However, the courts of the country concerned shall have jurisdiction over complaints that enforcement is being carried out in an irregular manner.

NOTES

1. Subsidiarity is a principle which seeks to devolve powers. Its application to the EU is set out in Art. 5 TEU. Some Member States are concerned about the powers which may be exercised at the Community level rather than at national level. For academic discussion of Art. 5, see Emiliou, 'Subsidiarity: An Effective Barrier against the Enterprises of Ambition?' (1992) 17 EL Rev 383; Toth, 'The Principle of Subsidiarity in the Maastricht Treaty' (1992) 29 CML Rev 1079; Cass, 'The Word That Saves Maastricht? The Principle of Subsidiarity and the Division of Powers within the European Community' (1992) 29, CML Rev 1107; Hartley, 'Constitutional and Institutional Aspects of the Maastricht Agreement' (1993) 42 ICLQ 213, at 214–218; Gonzalez, 'The Principle of Subsidiarity' (1995) 20 EL Rev 355, and Wyatt and Dashwood's *European Union Law* (2006), at 97–110. Opinion is divided on the justiciability of the principle of subsidiarity, but it may be that the political effect of the provision is such to ensure that there will be agreement between the Community institutions and the Member States, thereby obviating a challenge mounted on this principle before the European Court of Justice (ECJ).
2. The balance amongst the Union's institutions is quite different from that of organs of government in European States. The Commission is a permanent body and has important powers of proposal and supervision. It is required to act in the interests of the Union.

The Council will usually have the determinative say in the legislative processes and it represents the views of the Member States. Within the Council legislation can be made acting by qualified majority voting (QMV) and by unanimity. Before the SEA, despite provision for QMV, unanimity was the rule. It was agreed that the completion of the single market was both important and unlikely to be achieved through unanimity, so it was agreed that QMV was to apply to single market measures. The range of measures to which QMV can be applied has been increased over the years.

The European Parliament (EP) has limited powers. It is mainly a consultative body and its ability to hold the Commission to account by censure (Art. 201 TFEU) is too blunt to be useful. The EP did help to force the resignation of the Commission in March 1999, even though a motion of censure had not been passed. The issue was financial mismanagement, highlighted in a report by the Court of Auditors. The Commission resigned *en bloc* following the damning conclusions in a report of a committee of experts which had been appointed after the censure motion. (See A. Tomkins, 'Responsibility and Resignation in the European Commission' (1999) 62 *Modern Law Review* 744.)

The EP successfully flexed its muscles again in 2004 when objections, particularly to one of the nominated Commissioners, led to the withdrawal of the whole list for formal approval. Subsequently, the list was approved with two substitutions and a reshuffling of some nominees' responsibilities.

The EP tends to take a Union view. The EP has been given greater powers under Art. 251 (ex 189b) which has had its remit expanded. If it is minded to, the EP could veto an act, whereas under Art. 252 (ex 189c) the Council can override the EP's views if it acts unanimously.

The ECJ is of great importance and not just to lawyers. The ECJ as the final interpreter of the treaties and Union legislation has played a significant role in the development of the Union and shaped a new legal order with distinctive legal doctrines. Two of these are explored in Section 2 A and B.

3. Article 300 TFEU provides for two other institutions with members from each Member State, which are to be consulted for advice by the Commission and Council. They are (a) the Economic and Social Committee, which is comprised of representatives from economic and social activity, and (b) the Committee of the Regions, which is comprised of representatives from regional and local bodies.
4. The TEU amended Art. 228 (ex 171) so that there is now provision for the imposition of a financial sanction where a Member State has not taken the necessary measures to comply with a judgment by the ECJ that the Member State has failed to fulfil a Community obligation. This is now Art. 260 TFEU. See Art. 7 of the TEU for the sanctions which a Member State could be subjected to if it were in breach of the founding principles of the Union.
5. The TEU set out the timetable for the single currency, the Euro, and the economic convergence criteria which those Member States which wished to join would have to meet. In May 1998 it was agreed that the first wave of Member States participating in the single currency would number 11 out of the 15. Finland, Sweden, and the United Kingdom, despite meeting the convergence criteria, chose not to participate; while Greece did not meet the criteria. From 1999 the Euro has been able to be used in banking, and in 2002 the Euro notes and coins were issued and the national currencies of the participating Member States phased out.

   A decision by the United Kingdom Government and Parliament to join the single currency would have to be approved in a referendum.

SECTION 2: THE RELATIONSHIP BETWEEN UNION LAW AND UK LAW

The treaties have created a new legal order in which measures made by the Community institutions become part of the law of the Member States. Some measures, regulations, are directly applicable, i.e. they become part of the domestic law of the Member States without any implementing action being taken, whereas the Member States implement directives. In these circumstances it is possible that there could be confusion over, or conflict between, Union law and the domestic law of the Member States. Accordingly, the European Court of Justice (ECJ) has been given the jurisdiction of the final interpreter of Union law. Under Art. 267 TFEU (ex 234/177), national courts may seek preliminary rulings by asking questions on matters of Community law which are relevant points in cases before them. The decisions of the ECJ under this procedure have played an important part in the development of Union law.

A: Supremacy of Union law

One of the most important doctrines of Union law developed by the ECJ is that of its supremacy over inconsistent national law.

(a) The European Court of Justice's view

***Van Gend en Loos* v *Nederlandse Administratie der Belastingen* Case 26/62**

[1963] ECR 1, European Court of Justice

Article 12 of the European Economic Community (EEC) Treaty (now Art. 30) required Member States not to introduce new customs duties or charges having equivalent effect, nor to increase existing duties on trade between Member States. The plaintiff imported aminoplasts from West Germany into the Netherlands. Before the EEC Treaty came into force the duty was 3 per cent. Subsequently it was increased to 8 per cent under an international agreement. The claimant (formerly 'plaintiff') challenged this increase in the Dutch revenue courts. The Amsterdam *Tariefcommissie* sought a preliminary ruling on the interpretation of Art. 12 from the ECJ.

II—The first question

A—Jurisdiction of the Court

The Government of the Netherlands and the Belgian Government challenge the jurisdiction of the Court on the ground that the reference relates not to the interpretation but to the application of the Treaty in the context of the constitutional law of the Netherlands, and that in particular the Court has no jurisdiction to decide, should the occasion arise, whether the provisions of the EEC Treaty prevail over Netherlands legislation or over other agreements entered into by the Netherlands and incorporated into Dutch national law. The solution of such a problem, it is claimed, falls within the exclusive jurisdiction of the national courts, subject to an application in accordance with the provisions laid down by Articles 169 [now 258] and 170 [now 259] of the Treaty.

However in this case the Court is not asked to adjudicate upon the application of the Treaty according to the principles of the national law of the Netherlands, which remains the concern of the national courts, but is asked, in conformity with subparagraph (a) of the first paragraph of Article 177 [now 267] of the Treaty, only to interpret the scope of Article 12 [now 30] of the said Treaty within the context of Community law and with reference to its effect on individuals. This argument has therefore no legal foundation.

The Belgian Government further argues that the Court has no jurisdiction on the ground that no answer which the Court could give to the first question of the Tariefcommissie would have any bearing on the result of the proceedings brought in that court.

However, in order to confer jurisdiction on the Court in the present case it is necessary only that the question raised should clearly be concerned with the interpretation of the Treaty. The considerations which may have led a national court or tribunal to its choice of questions as well as the relevance which it attributes to such questions in the context of a case before it are excluded from review by the Court of Justice.

It appears from the wording of the questions referred that they relate to the interpretation of the Treaty. The Court therefore has the jurisdiction to answer them.

This argument, too, is therefore unfounded.

B—On the substance of the Case

The first question of the Tariefcommissie is whether Article 12 of the Treaty has direct application in national law in the sense that nationals of Member States may on the basis of this Article lay claim to rights which the national court must protect.

To ascertain whether the provisions of an international treaty extend so far in their effects it is necessary to consider the spirit, the general scheme and the wording of those provisions.

The objective of the EEC Treaty, which is to establish a Common Market, the functioning of which is of direct concern to interested parties in the Community, implies that this Treaty is more than an agreement which merely creates mutual obligations between the contracting states. This view is confirmed by the preamble to the Treaty which refers not only to governments but to peoples. It is also confirmed more specifically by the establishment of institutions endowed with sovereign rights, the exercise of which affects Member States and also their citizens. Furthermore, it must be noted that the nationals of the states brought together in the Community are called upon to cooperate in the functioning of this Community through the intermediary of the European Parliament and the Economic and Social Committee.

In addition the task assigned to the Court of Justice under Article 177 [now 267], the object of which is to secure uniform interpretation of the Treaty by national courts and tribunals, confirms that the states have acknowledged that Community law has an authority which can be invoked by their nationals before those courts and tribunals.

The conclusion to be drawn from this is that the Community constitutes a new legal order of international law for the benefit of which the states have limited their sovereign rights, albeit within limited fields, and the subjects of which comprise not only Member States but also their nationals. Independently of the legislation of Member States, Community law therefore not only imposes obligations on individuals but is also intended to confer upon them rights which become part of their legal heritage. These rights arise not only where they are expressly granted by the Treaty, but also by reason of obligations which the Treaty imposes in a clearly defined way upon individuals as well as upon the Member States and upon the institutions of the Community.

With regard to the general scheme of the Treaty as it relates to customs duties and charges having equivalent effect it must be emphasized that Article 9, which bases the Community upon a customs union, includes as an essential provision the prohibition of these customs duties and charges. This provision is found at the beginning of the part of the Treaty which defines the 'Foundations of the Community'. It is applied and explained by Article 12 [now 30].

The wording of Article 12 [now 30] contains a clear and unconditional prohibition which is not a positive but a negative obligation. This obligation, moreover, is not qualified by any reservation on the part of states which would make its implementation conditional upon a positive legislative measure enacted under national law. The very nature of this prohibition makes it ideally adapted to produce direct effects in the legal relationship between Member States and their subjects.

The implementation of Article 12 [now 30] does not require any legislative intervention on the part of the states. The fact that under this Article it is the Member States who are made the subject of the negative obligation does not imply that their nationals cannot benefit from this obligation.

In addition the argument based on Articles 169 [now 258] and 170 [now 259] of the Treaty put forward by the three Governments which have submitted observations to the Court in their statements of case is misconceived. The fact that these Articles of the Treaty enable the Commission and the Member States to bring before the Court a State which has not fulfilled its obligations does not mean that individuals cannot plead these obligations, should the occasion arise, before a national court, any more than the fact that the Treaty places at the disposal of the Commission ways of ensuring that obligations imposed upon those subject to the Treaty are observed, precludes the possibility, in actions between individuals before a national court, of pleading infringements of these obligations.

A restriction of the guarantees against an infringement of Article 12 [now 30] by Member States to the procedures under Articles 169 [now 258] and 170 [now 259] would remove all direct legal protection of the individual rights of their nationals. There is the risk that recourse to the procedure under these Articles would be ineffective if it were to occur after the implementation of a national decision taken contrary to the provisions of the Treaty.

The vigilance of individuals concerned to protect their rights amounts to an effective supervision in addition to the supervision entrusted by Articles 169 [now 258] and 170 [now 259] to the diligence of the Commission and of the Member States.

It follows from the foregoing considerations that, according to the spirit, the general scheme and the wording of the Treaty, Article 12 [now 30] must be interpreted as producing direct effects and creating individual rights which national courts must protect.

The ECJ ruled that Article 12 produced direct effects and created rights which national courts must protect and left it to the Tariefcommissie to determine if Article 12 had been breached by the Dutch revenue authorities.

NOTE: The style of judgment of the ECJ is somewhat different from that of a common law court. The ECJ uses consequentialist or purposive reasoning. The policy behind the creation of a Common Market is to remove trade barriers, and this will affect individuals. It would be counter to this policy to allow Member States to determine EU matters. The ECJ concludes that there is a new legal order created by the Treaties, and they provide that the ECJ is to be the final authority on the interpretation of the Treaties and EU law.

The case also makes clear that provisions of the Treaties which do not make explicit reference to individuals can, nevertheless, produce direct effects, that is create rights for individuals which national courts are to protect. The governments which filed briefs before the ECJ argued unsuccessfully that only the Commission and Member States could take legal action, under Arts 169, 170 of the EEC Treaty (now 259, 260 TFEU), against any Member State which was not honouring its EU obligations.

The nature of the new legal order was further developed in the following case.

Costa v *ENEL Case 6/64*

[1964] ECR 585, European Court of Justice

Mr Costa refused to pay an electricity bill. He was opposed to the nationalization of the Italian electricity industry which had occurred after the EEC Treaty had come into force. In defending his non-payment Mr Costa argued that the nationalization legislation breached Arts 102, 93, 53, and 37 of the EEC Treaty (now 117, 108, and 37 TFEU). The magistrate, the *Giudice Conciliatore*, sought a preliminary ruling from the ECJ.

The complaint is made that the Milan court has requested an interpretation of the Treaty which was not necessary for the solution of the dispute before it.

Since, however, Article 177 is based upon a clear separation of functions between national courts and the Court of Justice, it cannot empower the latter either to investigate the facts of the case or to criticize the grounds and purpose of the request for interpretation.

On the submission that the court was obliged to apply the national law

The Italian Government submits that the request of the Giudice Conciliatore is 'absolutely inadmissible', inasmuch as a national court which is obliged to apply a national law cannot avail itself of Article 177 [now 267].

By contrast with ordinary international treaties, the EEC Treaty has created its own legal system which, on the entry into force of the Treaty, became an integral part of the legal systems of the Member States and which their courts are bound to apply.

By creating a Community of unlimited duration, having its own institutions, its own personality, its own legal capacity and capacity of representation on the international plane and, more particularly, real powers stemming from a limitation of sovereignty or a transfer of powers from the States to the Community, the Member States have limited their sovereign rights, albeit within limited fields, and have thus created a body of law which binds both their nationals and themselves.

The integration into the laws of each Member State of provisions which derive from the Community, and more generally the terms and the spirit of the Treaty, make it impossible for the States, as a corollary, to accord precedence to a unilateral and subsequent measure over a legal system accepted by them on a basis of reciprocity. Such a measure cannot therefore be inconsistent with that legal system. The executive force of Community law cannot vary from one State to another in deference to subsequent domestic laws, without jeopardizing the attainment of the objectives of the Treaty set out in Article 5(2) [now 10(2)] and giving rise to the discrimination prohibited by Article 7 [now repealed].

The obligations undertaken under the Treaty establishing the Community would not be unconditional, but merely contingent, if they could be called in question by subsequent legislative acts of the signatories. Wherever the Treaty grants the States the right to act unilaterally, it does this by clear and precise provisions (for example Articles 15, 93(3), 223, 224 and 225 [now repealed, 108, 346, 347 and 348]). Applications, by Member States for authority to derogate from the Treaty are subject to a special authorization procedure (for example Articles 8(4), 17(4), 25, 26, 73 [now repealed], the third subparagraph of Article 93(2) [now 108(2)], and 226 [now repealed]) which would lose their purpose if the Member States could renounce their obligations by means of an ordinary law.

The precedence of Community law is confirmed by Article 189 [now 288], whereby a regulation 'shall be binding' and 'directly applicable in all Member States'. This provision, which is subject to no reservation, would be quite meaningless if a State could unilaterally nullify its effects by means of a legislative measure which could prevail over Community law.

It follows from all these observations that the law stemming from the Treaty, an independent source of law, could not, because of its special and original nature, be overridden by domestic legal provisions, however framed, without being deprived of its character as Community law and without the legal basis of the Community itself being called into question.

The transfer by the States from their domestic legal system to the Community legal system of the rights and obligations arising under the Treaty carries with it a permanent limitation of their sovereign rights, against which a subsequent unilateral act incompatible with the concept of the Community cannot prevail. Consequently Article 177 [now 267] is to be applied regardless of any domestic law, whenever questions relating to the interpretation of the Treaty arise.

The ECJ ruled that subsequent national measures cannot take precedence over EC law and that, whilst Articles 53 and 37(2) produced direct effects creating rights for individuals which national courts must protect, this was not so for Articles 102 and 93.

NOTE: The ECJ again showed that EU provisions which do not specifically mention individuals may still create rights for them. The ECJ also developed its views about the new legal order, and stated that the logic of EU law gives it supremacy over the municipal law of the Member States.

The full extent of this supremacy of EU law is revealed in the following case.

Internationale Handelsgesellschaft GmbH v Einfuhr und Vorratsstelle fur Getreide und Futtermittel Case 11/70

[1970] ECR 1125, European Court of Justice

The claimant (then called 'plaintiff'), a German company, had to obtain a licence to export corn flour. The EU provisions required a performance deposit, that is, if a licensee failed to export the full amount permitted in the licence then the deposit would be forfeit. The claimant failed to export the full amount specified in the licence and so forfeited the deposit. The claimant challenged this in the administrative court, the *verwaltungsgericht*. The German court sought a preliminary ruling on the EU provisions, as the court thought that they were in conflict with the basic rights guaranteed in the West German constitution.

[2] ...It appears from the grounds of the order referring the matter that the Verwaltungsgericht has until now refused to accept the validity of the provisions in question and that for this reason it considers it to be essential to put an end to the existing legal uncertainty. According to the evaluation of the Verwaltungsgericht, the system of deposits is contrary to certain structural principles of national constitutional law which must be protected within the framework of Community law, with the result that the primacy of supranational law must yield before the principles of the German Basic Law. More particularly, the system of deposits runs counter to the principles of freedom of action and of disposition, of economic liberty and of proportionality arising in particular from Articles 2 (1) and 14 of the Basic Law. The obligation to import or export resulting from the issue of the licences, together with the deposit attaching thereto, constitutes an excessive intervention in the freedom of disposition in trade, as the objective of the regulations could have been attained by methods of intervention having less serious consequences.

The protection of fundamental rights in the Community legal system

[3] Recourse to the legal rules or concepts of national law in order to judge the validity of measures adopted by the institutions of the Community would have an adverse effect on the uniformity and efficacy of Community law. The validity of such measures can only be judged in the light of Community law. In fact, the law stemming from the Treaty, an independent source of law, cannot because of its very nature be overridden by rules of national law, however framed, without being deprived of its character as Community law and without the legal basis of the Community itself being called in question. Therefore the validity of a Community measure or its effect within a Member State cannot be affected by allegations that it runs counter to either fundamental rights as formulated by the constitution of the State or the principles of a national constitutional structure.

[4] However, an examination should be made as to whether or not any analogous guarantee inherent in Community law has been disregarded. In fact, respect for fundamental rights forms an integral part of the general principles of law protected by the Court of Justice. The protection of such rights, whilst inspired by the constitutional traditions common to the Member States, must be ensured within the framework of the structure and objectives of the Community. It must therefore be ascertained, in the light of the doubts expressed by the Verwaltungsgericht, whether the system of deposits has infringed rights of a fundamental nature, respect for which must be ensured in the Community legal system.

The ECJ upheld the provisions creating the system of performance deposits.

NOTES

1. So far we have looked at conflicts between the municipal law of Member States and EU law where the ECJ, in its rulings, has affirmed the supremacy of the latter. The ECJ has taken this view further by declaring that EU law prevails over any conflicting provisions of Bills of Rights in Member States' constitutions. Again, this followed on from the logic of the Treaties that EU law applies uniformly throughout the Member States. The ECJ stated that it will protect fundamental rights. In *Nold* v *Commission* (Case 4/73) [1974] ECR 491 the ECJ reaffirmed that fundamental rights form part of the general principles of law protected by the court. It was also stated that the Court would draw inspiration from the constitutional traditions common to the Member States and from international treaties for the protection of human rights which Member States may have collaborated on or ratified.
2. The declaration of the supremacy of EU law by the ECJ creates a problem for national courts: they are supposed to protect the rights conferred by EU law even where they conflict with the law of Member States. How can this be done if a national court cannot strike down a municipal statute, as where, for example, only the Member State's Constitutional Court can carry out such action? Advice was offered in the following case.

Amministrazione delle Finanze dello Stato v *Simmenthal SpA Case 106/77*

[1978] ECR 629, European Court of Justice

Simmenthal imported beef into Italy. In an earlier case, *Simmenthal SpA* v *Italian Minister of Finance* (Case 35/76) [1976] ECR 1871, the ECJ had ruled that the Italian law requiring importers to pay for public health and veterinary checks at the border was contrary to Arts 30 and 12 of the EEC Treaty (now 34, 30 TFEU). The Italian court ordered the refund of these fees paid by Simmenthal, and the Ministry argued that until the Constitutional Court set aside the legislation it had a good defence. The Italian court sought a preliminary ruling.

[13] The main purpose of the first question is to ascertain what consequences flow from the direct applicability of a provision of Community law in the event of incompatibility with a subsequent legislative provision of a Member State.

[14] Direct applicability in such circumstances means that rules of Community law must be fully and uniformly applied in all the Member States from the date of their entry into force and for so long as they continue in force.

[15] These provisions are therefore a direct source of rights and duties for all those affected thereby, whether Member States or individuals, who are parties to legal relationships under Community law.

[16] This consequence also concerns any national court whose task it is as an organ of a Member State to protect, in a case within its jurisdiction, the rights conferred upon individuals by Community law.

[17] Furthermore, in accordance with the principle of the precedence of Community law, the relationship between provisions of the Treaty and directly applicable measures of the institutions on the one hand and the national law of the Member States on the other is such that those provisions and measures not only by their entry into force render automatically inapplicable any conflicting provision of current national law but—in so far as they are an integral part of, and take precedence in, the legal order applicable in the territory of each of the Member States—also preclude the valid adoption of new national legislative measures to the extent to which they would be incompatible with Community provisions.

[18] Indeed any recognition that national legislative measures which encroach upon the field within which the Community exercises its legislative power or which are otherwise incompatible with the provisions of Community law had any legal effect would amount to a corresponding denial of the effectiveness of obligations undertaken unconditionally and irrevocably by Member States pursuant to the Treaty and would thus imperil the very foundations of the Community.

[19] The same conclusion emerges from the structure of Article 177 [now 267] of the Treaty which provides that any court or tribunal of a Member State is entitled to make a reference to the Court whenever it considers that a preliminary ruling on a question of interpretation or validity relating to Community law is necessary to enable it to give judgment.

[20] The effectiveness of that provision would be impaired if the national court were prevented from forthwith applying Community law in accordance with the decision or the case-law of the Court.

[21] It follows from the foregoing that every national court must, in a case within its jurisdiction, apply Community law in its entirety and protect rights which the latter confers on individuals and must accordingly set aside any provision of national law which may conflict with it, whether prior or subsequent to the Community rule.

[22] Accordingly any provision of a national legal system and any legislative, administrative, or judicial practice which might impair the effectiveness of Community law by withholding from the national court having jurisdiction to apply such law the power to do everything necessary at the moment of its application to set aside national legislative provisions which might prevent Community rules from having full force and effect are incompatible with those requirements which are the very essence of Community law.

[23] This would be the case in the event of a conflict between a provision of Community law and a subsequent national law if the solution of the conflict were to be reserved for an authority with a discretion of its own, other than the court called upon to apply Community law, even if such an impediment to the full effectiveness of Community law were only temporary.

[24] The first question should therefore be answered to the effect that a national court which is called upon, within the limits of its jurisdiction, to apply provisions of Community law is under a duty to give full effect to those provisions, if necessary refusing of its own motion to apply any conflicting provision of national legislation, even if adopted subsequently, and it is not necessary for the court to request or await the prior setting aside of such provision by legislation or other constitutional means.

The ECJ ruled:

'A national court which is called upon, within the limits of its jurisdiction, to apply provisions of Community law is under a duty to give full effect to those provisions, if necessary refusing of its own motion to apply any conflicting provisions of national legislation, even if adopted subsequently, and it is not necessary for the court to request or await the prior setting aside of such provisions by legislation or other constitutional means.'

NOTE: While the ECJ states that any national court may set aside municipal legislation, this does not mean that such legislation is entirely void. It is only of no effect where there is a conflict between it and EU law.

■ QUESTIONS

1. The ECJ has declared that the Treaties have created a new legal order. Within this new legal order, what is the hierarchy of ranking amongst EU law, constitutional law, and ordinary municipal law?
2. What is the relationship between the ECJ and the national courts in this legal order?

(b) The United Kingdom courts' view

The traditional view of legislative supremacy explored in Chapter 2 would appear to conflict with the ECJ's rulings on the supremacy of Union law.

In order for Community law to become part of the United Kingdom's domestic law, it had to be incorporated by legislation. This was done by the following provisions.

The European Communities Act 1972

2.—(1) All such rights, powers, liabilities, obligations and restrictions from time to time created or arising by or under the Treaties, and all such remedies and procedures from time to time provided for by or under the Treaties, as in accordance with the Treaties are without further enactment to be given legal effect or used in the United Kingdom shall be recognised and available in law, and be enforced, allowed and followed accordingly; and the expression 'enforceable Community right' and similar expressions shall be read as referring to one to which this subsection applies.

(2) Subject to Schedule 2 of this Act, at any time after its passing Her Majesty may by Order in Council, and any designated Minister or department may by regulations, make provision—

(a) for the purpose of implementing any Community obligation of the United Kingdom, or enabling any such obligation to be implemented, or of enabling any rights enjoyed or to be enjoyed by the United Kingdom under or by virtue of the Treaties to be exercised; or

(b) for the purpose of dealing with matters arising out of or related to any such obligation or rights or the coming into force, or the operation from time to time, of subsection (1) above;

and in the exercise of any statutory power or duty, including any power to give directions or to legislate by means of orders, rules, regulations or other subordinate instrument, the person entrusted with the power or duty may have regard to the objects of the Communities and to any such obligation or rights as aforesaid.

In this subsection 'designated Minister or department' means such Minister of the Crown or government department as may from time to time be designated by Order in Council in relation to any matter or for any purpose, but subject to such restrictions or conditions (if any) as may be specified by the Order in Council.

...

(4) The provision that may be made under subsection (2) above includes, subject to Schedule 2 to this Act, any such provision (of any such extent) as might be made by Act of Parliament, and any enactment passed or to be passed, other than one contained in this Part of this Act, shall be construed and have effect subject to the foregoing provisions of this section; but, except as may be provided by any Act passed after this Act, Schedule 2 shall have effect in connection with the powers conferred by this and the following sections of this Act to make Orders in Council and regulations.

3.—(1) For the purposes of all legal proceedings any question as to the meaning or effect of any of the Treaties, or as to the validity, meaning or effect of any Community instrument, shall be treated as a question of law (and, if not referred to the European Court, be for determination as such in accordance with the principles laid down by and any relevant decision of the European Court).

(2) Judicial notice shall be taken of the Treaties, of the Official Journal of the Communities and of any decision of, or expression of opinion by, the European Court on any such question as aforesaid; and the Official Journal shall be admissible as evidence of any instrument or other act thereby communicated of any of the Communities or of any Community institution.

NOTE: Section 2(1) incorporates *some* EU law into United Kingdom law. This EU law is known as directly applicable EU law. Such law comes into effect in the UK without any further legislative action being taken by Parliament.

Section 2(2) provides for the making of delegated legislation in order to implement EU obligations. Schedule 2 specifies the limitations upon such legislative action, and some of these include the inability to increase taxation, or to introduce retrospective measures, or to create new criminal offences.

Section 2(4) provides that subsequent legislation is to be construed and to have effect subject to s. 2(1) and (2). Does this resolve any problems of conflict between EU and United Kingdom law subsequent to the passage of the European Communities Act 1972?

The courts have taken time to accustom themselves to Union law. There has been a variety of approaches taken on the issue of the supremacy of Union law. One approach is that of implied repeal, which is illustrated by a dictum from Lord Denning MR in *Felixstowe Dock and Railway Co* v *British Transport Docks Board* [1976] 2 CMLR 655. In this case the British Transport Docks Board (the Board) wished to take over the Felixstowe Dock and Railway Company (the Company). Terms were agreed between the parties but the Board, as a statutory body with limited powers, needed parliamentary approval for this action. In an unsuccessful challenge to the agreement by the Company, the ownership of which had changed, it was argued, *inter alia*, that the agreement was contrary to EU competition law and Art. 86 of the EEC Treaty (now 102 TFEU) in particular. Lord Denning MR said, at pp. 644–645:

> 'It seems to me that once the Bill is passed by Parliament and becomes a Statute that will dispose of all discussion about the Treaty. These courts will have to abide by the Statute without regard to the Treaty at all.'

Another approach would give priority to Union law over inconsistent United Kingdom law, unless the domestic legislation expressly repudiates Community obligations. This approach can also be illustrated by dicta from Lord Denning MR, on this occasion from *Macarthys* v *Smith* [1979] ICR 785. This case involved a claim of unlawful discrimination on grounds of sex in relation to equal pay. Ms Smith's contract of employment contained some minor differences from the contract of her male predecessor in the post. She received a smaller weekly wage than her male predecessor. The company's defence was that provisions of the Equal Pay Act 1970, as amended by the Sex Discrimination Act 1975, meant that Ms Smith was only entitled to compare her pay with that of a male employee engaged in 'like work' at the same time as her. Ms Smith argued that Art. 119 of the EEC (now 157 TFEU) Treaty permitted her to base a claim on a comparison with her male predecessor. In the Court of Appeal Lord Denning MR said, at p. 789:

> 'In construing our statute, we are entitled to look to the Treaty as an aid to its construction, and even more, not only as an aid but as an overriding force. If on close investigation it should appear that our legislation is deficient—or is inconsistent with Community law—by some oversight of our draftsmen—then it is our bounden duty to give priority to Community law. Such is the result of section 2(1) and (4) of the European Communities Act 1972.
>
> 1. I pause here, however, to make one observation on a constitutional point. Thus far I have assumed that our Parliament, whenever it passes legislation, intends to fulfil its obligations under the Treaty. If the time should come when our Parliament deliberately passes an Act—with the intention of repudiating the Treaty or any provision in it—or intentionally of acting inconsistently with it—and says so in express terms—then I should have thought that it would be the duty of our courts to follow the statute of our Parliament. I do not however envisage any such situation. As I said in *Blackburn* v *Attorney-General* [1971] WLR 1037, 1040: 'But, if Parliament should do so, then I say we will consider that event when it happens.' Unless there is such an intentional and express repudiation of the Treaty, it is our duty to give priority to the Treaty. In the present case I assume that the United Kingdom intended to fulfil its obligations under article 119.'

The House of Lords appears to have accepted that membership of the Union and the European Communities Act 1972 has altered the rules on legislative supremacy where there is inconsistency between Union law and domestic law.

R v *Secretary of State for Transport, ex parte Factortame Ltd and Others*

[1990] 2 AC 85, House of Lords

The applicants were companies which owned fishing vessels, the majority of which had first been registered as Spanish before being re-registered as British vessels. The United Kingdom Government was concerned that the operation of quotas under the Common Fisheries Policy would adversely affect the British fishing industry by the inclusion in the United Kingdom quotas of vessels fishing for the Spanish market. Parliament passed the Merchant Shipping Act 1988 and the Merchant Shipping (Registration of Fishing Vessels) Regulations 1988 (SI 1988 No. 1926) which would have the effect of ending the applicants' registration under the Merchant Shipping Act 1894 and precluding them from registration under the new regulations. The applicants claimed that the legislation was contrary to those provisions of EU law which (i) prohibited discrimination on grounds of nationality between Member States, (ii) prohibited restrictions on exports between Member States, (iii) created a common market in agricultural products, (iv) provided for the freedom of movement of workers and the freedom of establishment of companies, (v) required that nationals of Member States are to be treated equally with respect to participation in the capital of companies established in the EU. The Divisional Court decided to seek a preliminary ruling from the ECJ and decided to order as interim relief that, pending the ECJ's preliminary ruling on the compatibility of the United Kingdom law with EU law, Part II of the 1988 Act and the 1988 regulations be disapplied, and that the Secretary of State be restrained from applying them in respect of the applicants so as to enable the applicants' vessels to continue to be registered as British. On appeal the Court of Appeal reversed the decision on the granting of interim relief which involved the overriding of the United Kingdom legislation. This was appealed to the House of Lords. The relationship between domestic law and Community law was explained in a preliminary passage before dealing with the point about interim relief.

LORD BRIDGE: ...By virtue of section 2(4) of the Act of

1972 Part II of the Act of 1988 is to be construed and take effect subject to directly enforceable Community rights and those rights are, by section 2(1) of the Act of 1972, to be 'recognised and available in law, and...enforced, allowed and followed accordingly;...' This has precisely the same effect as if a section were incorporated in Part II of the Act of 1988 which in terms enacted that the provisions with respect to registration of British fishing vessels were to be without prejudice to the directly enforceable Community rights of nationals of any member state of the EEC. Thus it is common ground that, in so far as the applicants succeed before the ECJ in obtaining a ruling in support of the Community rights which they claim, those rights will prevail over the restrictions imposed on registration of British fishing vessels by Part II of the Act of 1988 and the Divisional Court will, in the final determination of the application for judicial review, be obliged to make appropriate declarations to give effect to those rights.

NOTES

1. Both the Court of Appeal and the House of Lords were of the view that domestic law did not allow, as interim relief, the disapplying of a statute where it had not been established that the statute was in breach of Union law. The House of Lords sought a preliminary ruling on this point from the ECJ which ruled that 'a national court which in a case before it concerning Union law considers itself that the sole obstacle which precludes it from granting interim relief is a rule of national law must set aside that rule' (*R* v *Secretary of State for Transport, ex parte Factortame Ltd* [1989] 3 CMLR 1). Subsequently the House of Lords considered the application for interim relief and decided to grant it (*R* v *Secretary of State for Transport, ex parte Factortame Ltd (No. 2)* [1991] 1 AC 603). The ECJ ruled on the Divisional Court's questions about the compatibility of the Merchant Shipping Act 1988 with Union law and ruled that Art. 52 (now 49 TFEU) had been infringed because of the local national and residence requirements for registration of owners of fishing vessels (*R* v *Secretary of State for Transport, ex parte Factortame Ltd (No. 3)* (Case C–221/89) [1991] 3 CMLR 589).

   Before the ECJ gave its rulings on the questions referred to it by the High Court and House of Lords, the European Commission brought a successful action for interim relief in an action under Art. 169 (now 258) against the United Kingdom, requiring that the nationality requirement of s. 14 of the Merchant Shipping Act 1988 be suspended (*Re Nationality of Fishermen: EC Commission* v *UK* (Case C–246/89R) [1989] 3 CMLR 601). This was implemented by the Merchant Shipping Act (Amendment) Order 1989 (SI 1989 No. 2006). Finally the ECJ upheld the Commission's challenge under Art. 169 (now Art. 258 TFEU) that the nationality requirements breached Arts 7, 52, and 221 of the EEC Treaty (now repealed, 49 and 55) (*Re Nationality of Fishermen: EC Commission* v *UK* (Case C–246/89) [1991] 3 CMLR 706).

2. See also *R* v *Secretary of State for Employment, ex parte Equal Opportunities Commission* [1994] 2 WLR 409, at p. 321, *ante*.
3. See pp. 86–88, *ante*, *Thoburn* v *Sunderland City Council*, [2002] EWHC (Admin) 195 [2003] QB 151.

B: Direct effect and directives

(a) Early development

In *Van Gend en Loos* (p. 373, *ante*), the ECJ ruled that Union law can confer rights upon individuals which national courts must protect. Thus Union law may have a direct effect in Member States' domestic law. In that case it was held that Art. 12 (now 30) of the Treaty of Rome (TFEU) had direct effect. Could a directive do this? A directive sets an objective which Member States are to implement, and in doing this they have a certain degree of discretion. The test for direct effect in *Van Gend en Loos* focused upon the unconditional nature of the prohibition in Article 12.

Van Duyn v Home Office Case 41/74

[1974] ECR 1337, European Court of Justice

Van Duyn, a Dutch woman, wished to take up employment with the Church of Scientology in the UK but was refused leave to enter by the Home Office. She sought to show that she could benefit from Community law on the freedom of movement of workers, particularly Art. 48 (now 45) and Directive 64/221/EEC. The Home Office contended that the public policy exemption to the freedom of movement of workers applied here as they claimed that the Church was socially undesirable. The High Court made an Art. 177 (now 267) reference, and one of the questions asked of the ECJ concerned the direct effect of directives.

[9] The second question asks the Court to say whether Council Directive No. 64/221 of 25 February 1984 on the coordination of special measures concerning the movement and residence of foreign nationals which are justified on grounds of public policy, public security or public health is directly applicable so as to confer on individuals rights enforceable by them in the courts of a Member State.

[10] It emerges from the order making the reference that the only provision of the Directive which is relevant is that contained in Article 3 (1) which provides that 'measures taken on grounds of public policy or public security shall be based exclusively on the personal conduct of the individual concerned.'

[11] The United Kingdom observes that, since Article 189 [now 288] of the Treaty distinguishes between the effect ascribed to regulations, directives and decisions, it must therefore be presumed that the Council, in issuing a directive rather than making a regulation, must have intended that the directive should have an effect other than that of a regulation and accordingly that the former should not be directly applicable.

[12] If, however, by virtue of the provisions of Article 189 [now 288] regulations are directly applicable and, consequently, may by their very nature have direct effects, it does not follow from this that other categories of acts mentioned in that Article can never have similar effects. It would be incompatible with the binding effect attributed to a directive by Article 189 [now 288] to exclude, in principle, the possibility that the obligation which it imposes may be invoked by those concerned. In particular, where the Community authorities have, by directive, imposed on Member States the obligation to pursue a particular course of conduct, the useful effect of such an act would be weakened if individuals were prevented from relying on it before their national courts and if the later were prevented from taking it into consideration as an element of Community law. Article 177 [now 267], which empowers national courts to refer to the Court questions concerning the validity and interpretation of all acts of the Community institutions, without distinction, implies furthermore that these acts may be invoked by individuals in the national courts. It is

necessary to examine, in every case, whether the nature, general scheme and wording of the provision in question are capable of having direct effects on the relations between Member States and individuals.

[13] By providing that measures taken on grounds of public policy shall be based exclusively on the personal conduct of the individual concerned, Article 3 (1) of Directive No. 64/221 is intended to limit the discretionary power which national laws generally confer on the authorities responsible for the entry and expulsion of foreign nationals. First, the provision lays down an obligation which is not subject to any exception or condition and which, by its very nature, does not require the intervention of any act on the part either of the institutions of the Community or of Member States. Secondly, because Member States are thereby obliged, in implementing a clause which derogates from one of the fundamental principles of the Treaty in favour of individuals, not to take account of factors extraneous to personal conduct, legal certainty for the persons concerned requires that they should be able to rely on this obligation even though it has been laid down in a legislative act which has no automatic direct effect in its entirety.

[14] If the meaning and exact scope of the provision raise questions of interpretation, these questions can be resolved by the courts, taking into account also the procedure under Article 177 [now 267] of the Treaty.

[15] Accordingly, in reply to the second question, Article 3 (1) of Council Directive No. 64/221 of 25 February 1964 confers on individuals rights which are enforceable by them in the courts of a Member State and which the national courts must protect.

NOTE: In para. 12 the ECJ partially bases the direct effect of a directive on the weakening of the useful effect of the measure if individuals could not rely upon it in their national courts.

Compare the requirement of unconditionality in *Van Gend en Loos* with the treatment of the Member State's discretion in implementing the directive in para. 13.

Pubblico Ministero v *Ratti Case 148/78*

[1979] ECR 1629, European Court of Justice

Ratti was charged with breaching certain Italian provisions although he had acted in conformity with Community law measures. These measures were directives made by the Council on the approximation of laws relating to the classification, packaging, and labelling of (a) solvents (No. 73/173/EEC), and (b) paints, varnishes, printing inks, adhesives, and similar products (No. 77/728/EEC). The period within which Directive 73/173/EEC should have been implemented had expired. If it had been implemented then the relevant Italian provisions should have been repealed. The period for the implementation of Directive 77/728/EEC had not yet expired. When implemented it would also have the effect of repealing the relevant Italian provisions. The *Pretura Penale* made an Art. 177 (now 267) reference.

[18] This question raises the general problem of the legal nature of the provisions of a directive adopted under Article 189 [now 288] of the Treaty.

[19] In this regard the settled case-law of the Court, last reaffirmed by the judgment of 1 February 1977 in Case 51/76 *Nederlandse Ondernemingen* [1977] 1 ECR 126, lays down that, whilst under Article 189 [now 288] regulations are directly applicable and consequently, by their nature capable of producing direct effects, that does not mean that other categories of acts covered by that article can never produce similar effects.

[20] It would be incompatible with the binding effect which Article 189 [now 288] ascribes to directives to exclude on principle the possibility of the obligations imposed by them being relied on by persons concerned.

[21] Particularly in cases in which the Community authorities have, by means of directive, placed Member States under a duty to adopt a certain course of action, the effectiveness of such an act would be weakened if persons were prevented from relying on it in legal proceedings and national courts prevented from taking it into consideration as an element of Community law.

[22] Consequently a Member State which has not adopted the implementing measures required by the directive in the prescribed periods may not rely, as against individuals, on its own failure to perform the obligation which the directive entails.

[23] It follows that a national court requested by a person who has complied with the provisions of a directive not to apply a national provision incompatible with the directive not incorporated into the internal legal order of a defaulting Member State, must uphold that request if the obligation in question is unconditional and sufficiently precise.

[24] Therefore the answer to the first question must be that after the expiration of the period fixed for the implementation of a directive a Member State may not apply its internal law—even if it is provided with penal sanctions—which has not yet been adapted in compliance with the directive, to a person who has complied with the requirements of the directive....

[39] In a fifth question the national court asks whether Council Directive No. 77/728 of 7 November 1977, in particular Article 9 thereof, is immediately and directly applicable with regard to the obligations imposed on Member States to refrain from action as from the date of notification of that directive in a case where a person, acting upon a legitimate expectation, has complied with the provisions of that directive before the expiry of the period within which the Member State must comply with the said directive.

[40] The objective of that directive is analogous to that of Directive No. 73/173 in that it lays down similar rules for preparations intended to be used as paints, varnishes, printing inks, adhesives and similar products, and containing dangerous substances.

[41] Article 12 of that directive provides that Member States must implement it within 24 months of its notification, which took place on 9 November 1977.

[42] That period has not yet expired and the States to which the directive was addressed have until 9 November 1979 to incorporate the provisions of Directive No. 77/728 into their internal legal orders.

[43] It follows that, for the reasons expounded in the grounds of the answer to the national court's first question, it is only at the end of the prescribed period and in the event of the Member State's default that the directive—and in particular Article 9 thereof—will be able to have the effects described in the answer to the first question.

NOTE: If directives are to have direct effect they must be precise and unconditional and the period for their implementation must have expired.

■ QUESTION

How does the ECJ justify holding that directives may have direct effect given the wording of Art. 288 (ex 189) (p. 368, *ante*)?

(b) Horizontal and vertical effect

Marshall v Southampton and South West Hampshire Area Health Authority (Teaching) Case 152/84

[1986] ECR 723, European Court of Justice

Marshall was dismissed by her employer when she reached the age of 62. She claimed that this was discrimination on grounds of sex as a male employee would not have been forced to retire at this age. Under the Sex Discrimination Act 1975 matters relating to retirement were excluded from the scope of sex discrimination. It was argued that the Equal Treatment Directive 76/207/EEC gave her a remedy for this situation; however, this directive had not been implemented in the United Kingdom although the period for implementation had expired. The Court of Appeal made an Art. 177 (now 267) reference. The ECJ first found that this situation constituted sex discrimination.

[39] Since the first question has been answered in the affirmative, it is necessary to consider whether Article 5(1) of Directive No. 76/207 may be relied upon by an individual before national courts and tribunals.

[40] The appellant and the Commission consider that the question must be answered in the affirmative. They contend in particular, with regard to Articles 2(1) and 5(1) of Directive No. 76/207, that those provisions are sufficiently clear to enable national courts to apply them without legislative intervention by the Member States, at least so far as overt discrimination is concerned.

[41] In support of that view, the appellant points out that directives are capable of conferring rights on individuals which may be relied upon directly before the courts of the Member States; national courts are obliged by virtue of the binding nature of a directive, in conjunction with Article 5 [now 4(3) TEU] of the EEC Treaty, to give effect to the provisions of directives where possible, in particular when construing or applying relevant provisions of national law (judgment of 10 April 1984 in Case 14/83 *Von Colson and Kamann* v *Land Nordrhein-Westfalen* [1984] ECR 1891). Where there is any inconsistency between national law and Community law which cannot be removed by means of such a construction, the appellant submits that a national court is obliged to declare that the provision of national law which is inconsistent with the directive is inapplicable.

[42] The Commission is of the opinion that the provisions of Article 5(1) of Directive No. 76/207 are sufficiently clear and unconditional to be relied upon before a national court. They may therefore be set up against section 6(4) of the Sex Discrimination Act, which, according to the decisions of the Court of Appeal, has been extended to the question of compulsory retirement and has therefore become ineffective to prevent dismissals based upon the difference in retirement ages for men and for women.

[43] The respondent and the United Kingdom propose, conversely, that the second question should be answered in the negative. They admit that a directive may, in certain specific circumstances, have direct effect as against a Member State in so far as the latter may not rely on its failure to perform its obligations under the directive. However, they maintain that a directive can never impose obligations directly on individuals and that it can only have direct effect against a Member State *qua* public authority and not against a Member State *qua* employer. As an employer a State is no different from a private employer. It would not therefore be proper to put persons employed by the State in a better position than those who are employed by a private employer.

[44] With regard to the legal position of the respondent's employees the United Kingdom states that they are in the same position as the employees of a private employer. Although according to United Kingdom constitutional law the health authorities, created by the National Health Service Act 1977, as amended by the Health Services Act 1980 and other legislation, are Crown bodies and their employees are Crown servants, nevertheless the administration of the National Health Service by the health authorities is regarded as being separate from the Government's central administration and its employees are not regarded as civil servants.

[45] Finally, both the respondent and the United Kingdom take the view that the provisions of Directive No. 76/207 are neither unconditional nor sufficiently clear and precise to give rise to direct effect. The directive provides for a number of possible exceptions, the details of which are to be laid down by the Member States. Furthermore, the wording of Article 5 is quite imprecise and requires the adoption of measures for its implementation.

[46] It is necessary to recall that, according to a long line of decisions of the Court (in particular its judgment of 19 January 1982 in Case 8/81 *Becker* v *Finanzamt Münster-Innenstadt* [1982] ECR 53), wherever the provisions of a directive appear, as far as their subject-matter is concerned, to be unconditional and sufficiently precise, those provisions may be relied upon by an individual against the State where that State fails to implement the directive in national law by the end of the period prescribed or where it fails to implement the directive correctly.

[47] That view is based on the consideration that it would be incompatible with the binding nature which Article 189 [now 288] confers on the directive to hold as a matter of principle that the obligation imposed thereby cannot be relied on by those concerned. From that the Court deduced that a Member State which has not adopted the implementing measures required by the directive within the prescribed period may not plead, as against individuals, its own failure to perform the obligations which the directive entails.

[48] With regard to the argument that a directive may not be relied upon against an individual, it must be emphasized that according to Article 189 [now 288] of the EEC Treaty the binding nature of a directive, which constitutes the basis for the possibility of relying on the directive before a national court, exists only in relation to 'each Member State to which it is addressed'. It follows that a directive may not of itself impose obligations on an individual and that a provision of a directive may not be relied upon as such against such a person. It must therefore be examined whether, in this case, the respondent must be regarded as having acted as an individual.

[49] In that respect it must be pointed out that where a person involved in legal proceedings is able to rely on a directive as against the State he may do so regardless of the capacity in which the latter is acting, whether employer or public authority. In either case it is necessary to prevent the State from taking advantage of its own failure to comply with Community law.

[50] It is for the national court to apply those considerations to the circumstances of each case; the Court of Appeal has, however, stated in the order for reference that the respondent, Southampton and South West Hampshire Area Health Authority (Teaching), is a public authority.

[51] The argument submitted by the United Kingdom that the possibility of relying on provisions of the directive against the respondent *qua* organ of the State would give rise to an arbitrary and unfair distinction between the rights of State employees and those of private employees does not justify any other conclusion. Such a distinction may easily be avoided if the Member State concerned has correctly implemented the directive in national law.

[52] Finally, with regard to the question whether the provision contained in Article 5 (1) of Directive No. 76/207, which implements the principle of equality of treatment set out in Article 2(1) of the directive, may be considered, as far as its contents are concerned, to be unconditional and sufficiently precise to be relied upon by an individual as against the State, it must be stated that the provision, taken by itself, prohibits any discrimination on grounds of sex with regard to working conditions, including the conditions governing dismissal, in a general manner and in unequivocal terms. The provision is therefore sufficiently precise to be relied on by an individual and to be applied by the national courts.

[53] It is necessary to consider next whether the prohibition of discrimination laid down by the directive may be regarded as unconditional, in the light of the exceptions contained therein and of the fact that according to Article 5(2) thereof the Member States are to take the measures necessary to ensure the application of the principle of equality of treatment in the context of national law.

[54] With regard, in the first place, to the reservation contained in Article 1(2) of Directive No. 76/207 concerning the application of the principle of equality of treatment in matters of social security, it must be observed that, although the reservation limits the scope of the directive *ratione materiae*, it does not lay down any condition on the application of that principle in its field of operation and in particular in relation to Article 5 of the directive. Similarly, the exceptions to Directive No. 76/207 provided for in Article 2 thereof are not relevant to this case.

[55] It follows that Article 5 of Directive No. 76/207 does not confer on the Member States the right to limit the application of the principle of equality of treatment in its field of operation or to subject it to conditions and that that provision is sufficiently precise and unconditional to be capable of being relied upon by an individual before a national court in order to avoid the application of any national provision which does not conform to Article 5 (1).

[56] Consequently, the answer to the second question must be that Article 5(1) of Council Directive No. 76/207 of 9 February 1976, which prohibits any discrimination on grounds of sex with regard to working conditions, including the conditions governing dismissal, may be relied upon against a State authority acting in its capacity as employer, in order to avoid the application of any national provision which does not conform to Article 5(1).

NOTES

1. The ECJ has limited the direct effect of directives to vertical effect, i.e. where an individual is seeking enforcement of rights against a State body. Enforcement of rights against another private individual, or horizontal effect, is not possible where a directive is the source of the rights.

2. In Case C–91/92 *Dori (Faccini)* v *Recreb* [1994] ECR I–3325, the ECJ reaffirmed that directives could not produce horizontal direct effect despite being urged to the contrary by the Advocate General. However, the Court has subsequently developed, in cases such as C–194/94 *CIA Security* [1996] ECR I–2201 and C–443/98 *Unilever Italia Spa* [2000] ECR I–7535, an exception so that 'a procedural rule in a directive can have horizontal direct effect to the extent that it renders a national provision inapplicable': see T.C. Hartley, *Foundations of European Union Law* (2010), p. 231.
3. It has been suggested that a reason for the ECJ changing the basis for giving direct effect to directives from 'useful effect' (*Van Gend en Loos*) to estoppel (*Ratti* and *Marshall*) was that it restricted the operation of direct effect, and this might lessen the opposition of national courts to the impact of Community law upon the legal systems of Member States.

(c) The scope of vertical effect

In order to benefit from vertical effect of directives an individual must be seeking enforcement against a State body. Guidance on what constitutes the State was given in the following case.

Foster v *British Gas Case C–188/89*

[1990] ECR I–3313, European Court of Justice

The applicant had been made to retire earlier than her male colleagues. She wished to rely upon the Equal Treatment Directive No. 76/207/EEC. The employer was the British Gas Corporation (BGC). The BGC was a statutory corporation and under the Gas Act 1972 it was responsible for developing and maintaining a system of gas supply in Great Britain and had a monopoly of the supply of gas. The Secretary of State appointed the members of the BGC and could issue directions on matters affecting the national interest. The BGC was required to submit reports to the Secretary of State and to run a balanced budget over two successive financial years. The House of Lords made an Art. 177 (now 267) reference.

[13] Before considering the question referred by the House of Lords, it must first be observed as a preliminary point that the United Kingdom has submitted that it is not a matter for the Court of Justice but for the national courts to determine, in the context of the national legal system, whether the provisions of a directive may be relied upon against a body such as the BGC.

[14] The question what effects measures adopted by Community institutions have and in particular whether those measures may be relied on against certain categories of persons necessarily involves interpretation of the articles of the Treaty concerning measures adopted by the institutions and the Community measure in issue.

[15] It follows that the Court of Justice has jurisdiction in proceedings for a preliminary ruling to determine the categories of persons against whom the provisions of a directive may be relied on. It is for the national courts, on the other hand, to decide whether a party to proceeding before them falls within one of the categories so defined.

Reliance on the provisions of the directive against a body such as the BGC

[16] As the Court has consistently held (see the judgment in Case 8/81 *Becker* v *Finanzamt Münster-Innenstadt* [1982] ECR 53, paragraphs 23 to 25), where the Community authorities have, by means of a directive, placed Member States under a duty to adopt a certain course of action, the effectiveness of such a measure would be diminished if persons were prevented from relying upon it in proceedings before a court and national courts were prevented from taking it into consideration as an element of Community law. Consequently, a Member State which has not adopted the implementing measures required by the directive within the prescribed period may not plead, as against individuals, its own failure to perform the obligations which the directive entails. Thus, wherever the provisions of a directive appear, as far as their subject-matter is concerned, to be unconditional and sufficiently precise, those provisions may, in the absence of implementing measures adopted within the prescribed period, be relied upon as against

any national provision which is incompatible with the directive or in so far as the provisions define rights which individuals are able to assert against the State.

[17] The Court further held in its judgment in Case 152/84 *Marshall*, paragraph 49, that where a person is able to rely on a directive as against the State he may do so regardless of the capacity in which the latter is acting, whether as employer or as public authority. In either case it is necessary to prevent the State from taking advantage of its own failure to comply with Community law.

[18] On the basis of those considerations, the Court has held in a series of cases that unconditional and sufficiently precise provisions of a directive could be relied on against organizations or bodies which were subject to the authority or control of the State or had special powers beyond those which result from the normal rules applicable to relations between individuals.

[19] The Court has accordingly held that provisions of a directive could be relied on against tax authorities (the judgments in Case 8/81 *Becker*, cited above, and in Case C–221/88 *ECSC* v *Acciaierie e Ferriere Busseni (in liquidation)* [1990] ECR I–495), local or regional authorities (judgment in Case 103/88 *Fratelli Constanzo* v *Comune di Milano* [1989] ECR 1839), constitutionally independent authorities responsible for the maintenance of public order and safety (judgment in Case 222/84 *Johnston* v *Chief Constable of the Royal Ulster Constabulary* [1986] ECR 1651), and public authorities providing public health services (judgment in Case 152/84 *Marshall*, cited above).

[20] It follows from the foregoing that a body, whatever its legal form, which has been made responsible, pursuant to a measure adopted by the State, for providing a public service under the control of the State and has for that purpose special powers beyond those which result from the normal rules applicable in relations between individuals is included in any event among the bodies against which the provisions of a directive capable of having direct effect may be relied upon.

[21] With regard to Article 5 (1) of Directive 76/207 it should be observed that in the judgment in Case 152/84 *Marshall*, cited above, paragraph 52, the Court held that that provision was unconditional and sufficiently precise to be relied on by an individual and to be applied by the national courts.

[22] The answer to the question referred by the House of Lords must therefore be that Article 5 (1) of Council Directive 76/207 of 9 February 1976 may be relied upon in a claim for damages against a body, whatever its legal form, which has been made responsible, pursuant to a measure adopted by the State, for providing a public service under the control of the State and has for that purpose special powers beyond those which result from the normal rules applicable in relations between individuals.

NOTE: In *Fratelli Constanzo* v *Comune di Milano* (Case 103/88) [1989] ECR 1839 the ECJ held that the State included local authorities.

(d) Indirect effect

It does seem unfair that direct effect of directives depends upon whether one is in conflict with a state body. A possible method of circumventing the vertical/horizontal distinction has been claimed as a result of the reasoning in the next case.

Von Colson and Kamann v *Land Nordrhein-Westfalen* Case 14/83

[1984] ECR 1891, European Court of Justice

The applicants had been rejected for jobs on the grounds of sex. The Hamm *Arbeitsgericht* held that there had been discrimination on grounds of sex, but that the only remedy available under German law was the reimbursement of their travel expenses. Von Colson argued that this was contrary to Art. 6 of the Equal Treatment Directive 76/207/EEC. Under this directive Member States were to introduce into their legal systems measures to enable victims of sex discrimination to pursue their claims by judicial process. Measures could include requiring employers to offer victims posts, or to receive adequate compensation. The directive left it to the discretion of Member States to choose the remedy which met the objectives of the directive. An Art. 177 (now 267) reference was made.

[22] It is impossible to establish real equality of opportunity without an appropriate system of sanctions. That follows not only from the actual purpose of the directive but more specifically from Article 6 thereof which, by granting applicants for a post who have been discriminated against recourse to the courts, acknowledges that those candidates have rights of which they may avail themselves before the courts.

[23] Although, as has been stated in the reply to Question 1, full implementation of the directive does not require any specific form of sanction for unlawful discrimination, it does entail that that sanction be such as to guarantee real and effective judicial protection. Moreover it must also have a real deterrent effect on the employer. It follows that where a Member State chooses to penalize the breach of the prohibition of discrimination by the award of compensation, that compensation must in any event be adequate in relation to the damage sustained.

[24] In consequence it appears that national provisions limiting the right to compensation of persons who have been discriminated against as regards access to employment to a purely nominal amount, such as, for example, the reimbursement of expenses incurred by them in submitting their application, would not satisfy the requirements of an effective transposition of the directive.

[25] The nature of the sanctions provided for in the Federal Republic of Germany in respect of discrimination regarding access to employment and in particular the question whether the rule in Paragraph 611a (2) of the Bürgerliches Gesetzbuch excludes the possibility of compensation on the basis of the general rules of law were the subject of lengthy discussion before the Court. The German Government maintained in the oral procedure that that provision did not necessarily exclude the application of the general rules of law regarding compensation. It is for the national court alone to rule on that question concerning the interpretation of its national law.

[26] However, the Member States' obligation arising from a directive to achieve the result envisaged by the directive and their duty under Article 5 [now 4(3) TFEU] of the Treaty to take all appropriate measures, whether general or particular, to ensure the fulfilment of that obligation, is binding on all the authorities of Member States including, for matters within their jurisdiction, the courts. It follows that, in applying the national law and in particular the provisions of a national law specifically introduced in order to implement Directive No. 76/207, national courts are required to interpret their national law in the light of the wording and the purpose of the directive in order to achieve the result referred to in the third paragraph of Article 189 [now 288].

[27] On the other hand, as the above considerations show, the directive does not include any unconditional and sufficiently precise obligation as regards sanctions for discrimination which, in the absence of implementing measures adopted in good time may be relied on by individuals in order to obtain specific compensation under the directive, where that is not provided for or permitted under national law.

[28] It should, however, be pointed out to the national court that although Directive No. 76/207/EEC, for the purpose of imposing a sanction for the breach of the prohibition of discrimination, leaves the Member States free to choose between the different solutions suitable for achieving its objective, it nevertheless requires that if a Member States chooses to penalize breaches of that prohibition by the award of compensation, then in order to ensure that it is effective and that it has a deterrent effect, that compensation must in any event be adequate in relation to the damage sustained and must therefore amount to more than purely nominal compensation such as, for example, the reimbursement only of the expenses incurred in connection with the application. It is for the national court to interpret and apply the legislation adopted for the implementation of the directive in conformity with the requirements of Community law, in so far as it is given discretion to do so under national law.

The Court ruled, in answer to the questions referred:

(1) Directive No. 76/207/EEC does not require discrimination on grounds of sex regarding access to employment to be made the subject of a sanction by way of an obligation imposed on the employer who is the author of the discrimination to conclude a contract of employment with the candidate discriminated against.

(2) As regards sanctions for any discrimination which may occur, the directive does not include any unconditional and sufficiently precise obligation which, in the absence of implementing measures adopted within the prescribed time-limits, may be relied on by an individual in order to obtain specific compensation under the directive, where that is not provided for or permitted under national law.

(3) Although Directive No. 76/207/EEC, for the purpose of imposing a sanction for the breach of the prohibition of discrimination, leaves the Member States free to choose between the different solutions suitable for achieving its objective, it nevertheless requires that if a Member State chooses to penalise breaches of that prohibition by the award of compensation, then in order to ensure that it is effective and that it has a deterrent effect, that compensation must in any event be adequate in relation to the damage sustained and must therefore amount to more than purely nominal compensation such as, for example, the reimbursement only of the expenses incurred in connection with the application. It is for the national court to interpret and apply the legislation adopted for the implementation of the directive in conformity with the requirements of Community law, in so far as it is given discretion to do so under national law.

NOTE: This approach is quite different from that used for direct effect. Using Art. 4(3) TEU (ex 5) (see p. 362, *ante*), the ECJ states that national courts must fulfil Community law obligations.

The ECJ has not settled the boundaries of this doctrine of 'indirect effect'. Compare the following two cases.

Marleasing SA v *La Commercial Internacional de Alimentacion SA* Case C–106/89

[1990] ECR I–4135, European Court of Justice

Marleasing wished to have the company, La Commercial, declared a nullity on the basis of Spanish law. Article 11 of Directive 68/151/EEC lists the exclusive grounds on which nullity may be ordered, and this did not include the ground sought by Marleasing. This directive had not been implemented by Spain and the deadline had expired. The *Juzgado de Primera Instancia e Instrucción* made an Art. 177 (now 267) reference on the status of the directive.

[6] With regard to the question whether an individual may rely on the directive against a national law, it should be observed that, as the Court has consistently held, a directive may not of itself impose obligations on an individual and, consequently, a provision of a directive may not be relied upon as such against such a person (judgment in Case 152/84 *Marshall* v *Southampton and South-West Hampshire Area Health Authority (Teaching)* [1986] ECR 723).

[7] However, it is apparent from the documents before the Court that the national court seeks in substance to ascertain whether a national court hearing a case which falls within the scope of Directive 68/151 is required to interpret its national law in the light of the wording and the purpose of that directive in order to preclude a declaration of nullity of a public limited company on a ground other than those listed in Article 11 of the directive.

[8] In order to reply to that question, it should be observed that, as the Court pointed out in its judgment in Case 14/83 *Von Colson and Kamann* v *Land Nordrhein-Westfalen* [1984] ECR 1891, paragraph 26, the Member States' obligation arising from a directive to achieve the result envisaged by the directive and their duty under Article 5 [now 4(3) TEU] of the Treaty to take all appropriate measures, whether general or particular, to ensure the fulfilment of that obligation, is binding on all the authorities of Member States including, for matters within their jurisdiction, the courts. It follows that, in applying national law, whether the provisions in question were adopted before or after the directive, the national court called upon to interpret it is required to do so, as far as possible, in the light of the wording and the purpose of the directive in order to achieve the result pursued by the latter and thereby comply with the third paragraph of Article 189 [now 288] of the Treaty.

[9] It follows that the requirement that national law must be interpreted in conformity with Article 11 of Directive 68/151 precludes the interpretation of provisions of national law relating to public limited companies in such a manner that the nullity of a public limited company may be ordered on grounds other than those exhaustively listed in Article 11 of the directive in question.

[10] With regard to the interpretation to be given to Article 11 of the directive, in particular Article 11(2)(b), it should be observed that that provision prohibits the laws of the Member States from providing for a judicial declaration of nullity on grounds other than those exhaustively listed in the directive, amongst which is the ground that the objects of the company are unlawful or contrary to public policy.

[11] According to the Commission, the expression 'objects of the company' must be interpreted as referring exclusively to the objects of the company as described in the instrument of incorporation or the articles of association. It follows, in the Commission's view, that a declaration of nullity of a company cannot be made on the basis of the activity actually pursued by it, for instance defrauding the founders' creditors.

[12] That argument must be upheld. As is clear from the preamble to Directive 68/151, its purpose was to limit the cases in which nullity can arise and the retroactive effect of a declaration of nullity in order to ensure 'certainty in the law as regards relations between the company and third parties, and also between Members' (sixth recital). Furthermore, the protection of third parties 'must be ensured by provisions which restrict to the greatest possible extent the grounds on which obligations entered into in the name of the company are not valid'. It follows, therefore, that each ground of nullity provided for in Article 11 of the directive must be interpreted strictly. In those circumstances the words 'objects of the company' must be understood as referring to the objects of the company as described in the instrument of incorporation or the articles of association.

[13] The answer to the question submitted must therefore be that a national court hearing a case which falls within the scope of Directive 68/151 is required to interpret its national law in the light of the wording and the purpose of that directive in order to preclude a declaration of nullity of a public limited company on a ground other than those listed in Article 11 of the directive.

Officier van Justitie v *Kolpinghuis Nijmegen* Case 80/86

[1987] ECR 3969, European Court of Justice

A café owner was prosecuted for stocking for sale and delivery mineral water which was, in fact, tap water with added carbon dioxide. As part of the prosecution's case reliance was placed on Directive 80/777/EEC, which, at the time of the alleged offence, had not been incorporated into Dutch law even though the implementation deadline had expired. The *Arrondismentsrechtbank* made an Art. 177 (now 267) reference.

[6] The first two questions concern the possibility whether the provisions of a directive which has not yet been implemented in national law in the Member State in question may be applied as such.

[7] In this regard it should be recalled that, according to the established case-law of the Court (in particular its judgment of 19 January 1982 in Case 8/81 *Becker* v *Finanzamt Münster-Innenstadt* [1982] ECR 53), wherever the provisions of a directive appear, as far as their subject-matter is concerned, to be unconditional and sufficiently precise, those provisions may be relied upon by an individual against the State where that State fails to implement the directive in national law by the end of the period prescribed or where it fails to implement the directive correctly.

[8] That view is based on the consideration that it would be incompatible with the binding nature which Article 189 [now 288] confers on the directive to hold as a matter of principle that the obligation imposed thereby cannot be relied on by those concerned. From that the Court deduced that a Member State which has not adopted the implementing measures required by the directive within the prescribed period may not plead, as against individuals, its own failure to perform the obligations which the directive entails.

[9] In its judgment of 26 February 1986 in Case 152/84 *Marshall* v *Southampton and South-West Hampshire Area Health Authority (Teaching)* [1986] ECR 723, the Court emphasized, however, that according to Article 189 [now 288] of the EEC Treaty the binding nature of a directive, which constitutes the basis for the possibility of relying on the directive before a national court, exists only in relation to 'each Member State to which it is addressed'. It follows that a directive may not of itself impose obligations on an individual and that a provision of a directive may not be relied upon as such against such a person before a national court.

[10] The answer to the first two questions should therefore be that a national authority may not rely, as against an individual, upon a provision of a directive whose necessary implementation in national law has not yet taken place.

The third question

[11] The third question is designed to ascertain how far the national court may or must take account of a directive as an aid to the interpretation of a rule of national law.

[12] As the Court stated in its judgment of 10 April 1984 in Case 14/83 *Von Colson and Kamann* v *Land Nordrhein-Westfalen* [1984] ECR 1891, the Member States' obligation arising from a directive to achieve the result envisaged by the directive and their duty under Article 5 [now 4(3)TEU] of the Treaty to take all appropriate measures, whether general or particular, to ensure the fulfilment of that obligation, is binding on all the authorities of Member States including, for matters within their jurisdiction, the courts. It follows that, in applying the national law and in particular the provisions of a national law specifically introduced in order to implement the directive, national courts are required to interpret their national law in the light of the wording and the purpose of the directive in order to achieve the result referred to in the third paragraph of Article 189 [now 288] of the Treaty.

[13] However, that obligation on the national court to refer to the content of the directive when interpreting the relevant rules of its national law is limited by the general principles of law which form part of Community law and in particular the principles of legal certainty and non-retroactivity. Thus the Court rules in its judgment of 11 June 1987 in Case 14/86 *Pretore di Salò* v *X* [1987] ECR 2545 that a directive cannot, of itself and independently of a national law adopted by a Member State for its implementation, have the effect of determining or aggravating the liability in criminal law of persons who act in contravention of the provisions of that directive.

[14] The answer to the third question should therefore be that in applying its national legislation a court of a Member State is required to interpret that legislation in the light of the wording and the purpose of the directive in order to achieve the result referred to in the third paragraph of Article 189 [now 288] of the Treaty, but a directive cannot, of itself and independently of a law adopted for its implementation, have the effect of determining or aggravating the liability in criminal law of persons who act in contravention of the provisions of that directive.

The fourth question

[15] The question whether the provisions of a directive may be relied upon as such before a national court arises only if the Member State concerned has not implemented the directive in national law within the prescribed period or has implemented the directive incorrectly. The first two questions were answered in the negative. However, it makes no difference to those answers if on the material date the period which the Member State had in which to adopt national law had not yet expired. As regards the third question concerning the limits which Community law might impose on the obligation or power of the national court to interpret the rules of its national law in the light of the directive, it makes no difference whether or not the period prescribed for implementation has expired.

[16] The answer to the fourth question must therefore be that it makes no difference to the answers set out above if on the material date the period which the Member State had in which to adapt national law had not yet expired.

NOTE: *Marleasing* seems to be very wide, covering national law made both before and after the directive (para. 8). Should it, like *Kolpinghuis Nijmegen*, be understood as subject to the general principles of Union law, including, for example, legal certainty and non-retroactivity?

(e) Damages for failure to implement a directive

Francovich v *Italian Republic Joined* Cases C–6/90 and C–9/90

[1991] ECR I–5357, European Court of Justice

Directive 80/987 was intended to guarantee employees a minimum level of protection under Community law in the event of the insolvency of their employer. Italy had not implemented the Directive before the period for doing so had expired. Employees who had not been paid by reason of their employers' insolvency sought the Directive's guarantee directly from the Italian State or, in the alternative, compensation. On Art. 177

(now 267) references the ECJ was asked if an individual who had been adversely affected by a Member State's failure to implement Directive 80/987 could directly invoke the legislation against that Member State to obtain the guarantees which the State should have provided. The ECJ held on the first part of the question that, even though the Directive's provisions relating to the content of the guarantee were sufficiently unconditional and precise, the Directive did not identify the person liable to provide the guarantee and the State could not be considered liable to pay those guarantees solely on the ground that it had failed to implement the directive. On the second part of the question:

Liability of the State for loss and damage resulting from breach of its obligations under Community law

[28] In the second part of the first question the national court seeks to determine whether a Member State is obliged to make good loss and damage suffered by individuals as a result of the failure to transpose Directive 80/987.

[29] The national court thus raises the issue of the existence and scope of a State's liability for loss and damage resulting from breach of its obligations under Community law.

[30] That issue must be considered in the light of the general system of the Treaty and its fundamental principles.

(a) The existence of State liability as a matter of principle

[31] It should be borne in mind at the outset that the EEC Treaty has created its own legal system, which is integrated into the legal systems of the Member States and which their courts are bound to apply. The subjects of that legal system are not only the Member States but also their nationals. Just as it imposes burdens on individuals, Community law is also intended to give rise to rights which become part of their legal patrimony. Those rights arise not only where they are expressly granted by the Treaty but also by virtue of obligations which the Treaty imposes in a clearly defined manner both on individuals and on the Member States and the Community institutions (see the judgments in Case 26/62 *Van Gend en Loos* [1963] ECR 1 and Case 6/64 *Costa* v *ENEL* [1964] ECR 585).

[32] Furthermore, it has been consistently held that the national courts whose task it is to apply the provisions of Community law in areas within their jurisdiction must ensure that those rules take full effect and must protect the rights which they confer on individuals (see in particular the judgments in Case 106/77 *Amministrazione delle Finanze dello Stato* v *Simmenthal* [1978] ECR 629, paragraph 16, and Case C–213/89 *Factortame* [1990] ECR I–2433, paragraph 19.

[33] The full effectiveness of Community rules would be impaired and the protection of the rights which they grant would be weakened if individuals were unable to obtain redress when their rights are infringed by a breach of Community law for which a Member State can be held responsible.

[34] The possibility of obtaining redress from the Member State is particularly indispensable where, as in this case, the full effectiveness of Community rules is subject to prior action on the part of the State and where, consequently, in the absence of such action, individuals cannot enforce before the national courts the rights conferred upon them by Community law.

[35] It follows that the principle whereby a State must be liable for loss and damage caused to individuals as a result of breaches of Community law for which the State can be held responsible is inherent in the system of the Treaty.

[36] A further basis for the obligation of Member States to make good such loss and damage is to be found in Article 5 [now 4(3) TEU] of the Treaty, under which the Member States are required to take all appropriate measures, whether general or particular, to ensure fulfilment of their obligations under Community law. Among these is the obligation to nullify the unlawful consequences of a breach of Community law (see, in relation to the analogous provision of Article 86 of the ECSC Treaty, the judgment in Case 6/60 *Humblet* v *Belgium* [1960] ECR 559).

[37] It follows from all the foregoing that it is a principle of Community law that the Member States are obliged to make good loss and damage caused to individuals by breaches of Community law for which they can be held responsible.

(b) The conditions for State liability

[38] Although State liability is thus required by Community law, the conditions under which that liability gives rise to a right to reparation depend on the nature of the breach of Community law giving rise to the loss and damage.

[39] Where, as in this case, a Member State fails to fulfil its obligation under the third paragraph of Article 189 [now 288] of the Treaty to take all the measures necessary to achieve the result prescribed by a directive, the full effectiveness of that rule of Community law requires that there should be a right to reparation provided that three conditions are fulfilled.

[40] The first of those conditions is that the result prescribed by the directive should entail the grant of rights to individuals. The second condition is that it should be possible to identify the content of those rights on the basis of the provisions of the directive. Finally, the third condition is the existence of a causal link between the breach of the State's obligation and the loss and damage suffered by the injured parties.

[41] Those conditions are sufficient to give rise to a right on the part of individuals to obtain reparation, a right founded directly on Community law.

[42] Subject to that reservation, it is on the basis of the rules of national law on liability that the State must make reparation for the consequences of the loss and damage caused. In the absence of Community legislation, it is for the internal legal order of each Member State to designate the competent courts and lay down the detailed procedural rules for legal proceedings intended fully to safeguard the rights which individuals derive from Community law (see the judgments in Case 60/75 *Russo* v *AIMA* [1976] ECR 45, Case 33/76 *Rewe* v *Landwirtschaftskammer für das Saarland* [1976] ECR 1989 and Case 158/80 *Rewe* v *Hauptzollamt Kiel* [1981] ECR 1805).

[43] Further, the substantive and procedural conditions for reparation of loss and damage laid down by the national law of the Member States must not be less favourable than those relating to similar domestic claims and must not be so framed as to make it virtually impossible or excessively difficult to obtain reparation (see, in relation to the analogous issue of the repayment of taxes levied in breach of Community law, *inter alia* the judgment in Case 199/82 *Amministrazione delle Finanze dello Stato* v *San Giorgio* [1983] ECR 3595).

[44] In this case, the breach of Community law by a Member State by virtue of its failure to transpose Directive 80/987 within the prescribed period has been confirmed by a judgment of the Court. The result required by that directive entails the grant to employees of a right to a guarantee of payment of their unpaid wage claims. As is clear from the examination of the first part of the first question, the content of that right can be identified on the basis of the provisions of the directive.

[45] Consequently, the national court must, in accordance with the national rules on liability, uphold the right of employees to obtain reparation of loss and damage caused to them as a result of failure to transpose the directive.

[46] The answer to be given to the national court must therefore be that a Member State is required to make good loss and damage caused to individuals by failure to transpose Directive 80/987.

NOTES

1. It seems that this liability on Member States includes failures to fulfil Union obligations other than a failure to implement a Directive within the specified period. See Ross, 'Beyond *Francovich*' (1993) 56 MLR 55; Steiner, 'From Direct Effect to *Francovich*: Shifting Means of Enforcement of Community Law' (1993) 18 EL Rev 3.
2. The principle in *Francovich* was developed in Joined Cases C–49/93 and C–48/93 *Brasserie du Pêcheur SA* v *Federal Republic of Germany, R* v *Secretary of State for Transport, ex parte Factortame* [1996] ECR I–1029, in which the ECJ ruled that where damage to an individual had been caused by a breach of Union law attributable to a national legislature acting in a field in which it has wide discretion to make legislative choices:

   'individuals suffering loss or injury thereby are entitled to reparation where the rule of Community law is intended to confer rights upon them, the breach is sufficiently serious and there is a direct

> causal link between the breach and the damage sustained by the individuals. Subject to that reservation, the state must make good the consequences of the loss or damage caused by the breach of Community law attributable to it, in accordance with its national law on liability. However the conditions laid down by the applicable national laws must not be less favourable than those relating to similar domestic claims or framed in such a way as in practice to make it impossible or excessively difficult to obtain compensation. Pursuant to the national legislation which it applies, reparation of loss or damage cannot be made conditional upon fault (intentional or negligent) on the part of the organ of the State responsible for the breach, going beyond that of a sufficiently serious breach of Community law'.

The Court was using the same basis for a Member State's liability as that under Art. 340 (ex 215) for liability of the Union for damage caused to individuals by unlawful legislative measures adopted by its institutions.

In Joined Cases C–178/94, C–179/94, C–188/94, C–189/94, and C–190/94 *Dillenkofer and others* v *Federal Republic of Germany* [1996] ECR I–4845, the ECJ held that failure to take any measures to implement a Directive to achieve its intended result within the prescribed period constitutes *per se* a serious breach of Union law for those individuals who can show a causal link between that failure and damage suffered.

(f) The United Kingdom courts' views on directives

The interpretation of directives by the House of Lords is somewhat confusing. Compare the following cases.

Duke v *GEC Reliance Ltd*

[1988] AC 618, House of Lords

The complainant had been dismissed in accordance with the employer's policy on different retirement ages for male and female employees. Whilst *Marshall* held that this constituted sex discrimination, it also held that directives did not have horizontal effect. The complainant argued that the Sex Discrimination Act 1975 ought to have been interpreted according to the guidance in *Von Colson* so that it conformed to Community law. An appeal was made to the House of Lords.

> LORD TEMPLEMAN: ... [I]t is now submitted that the appellant is entitled to damages from the respondent because Community law requires the Equal Pay Act enacted on 29 May 1970 and the Sex Discrimination Act enacted on 12 November 1975 to be construed in a manner which gives effect to the Equal Treatment Directive dated 9 February 1976 as construed by the European Court of Justice in *Marshall's* case published on 20 February 1986. Of course a British court will always be willing and anxious to conclude that United Kingdom law is consistent with Community law. Where an Act is passed for the purpose of giving effect to an obligation imposed by a directive or other instrument a British court will seldom encounter difficulty in concluding that the language of the Act is effective for the intended purpose. But the construction of a British Act of Parliament is a matter of judgment to be determined by British courts and to be derived from the language of the legislation considered in the light of the circumstances prevailing at the date of enactment. The circumstances in which the Equal Pay Act 1970 and the Sex Discrimination Act 1975 were enacted are set forth in the 1974 White Paper, in the judgment of Phillips J in *Roberts* v *Cleveland Area Health Authority* [1978] ICR 370, in the judgment of Browne-Wilkinson J in *Roberts* v *Tate & Lyle Food and Distribution Ltd* [1983] ICR 521 and in the submission of the United Kingdom Government in *Marshall's* case [1986] QB 401. The Acts were not passed to give effect to the Equal Treatment Directive and were intended to preserve discriminatory retirement ages. Proposals for the Equal Treatment Directive dated 9 February 1976 were in circulation when the Bill for the Sex Discrimination Act 1975 was under discussion but it does not appear that these proposals were understood by the British Government or the Parliament of the United Kingdom to involve the prohibition of differential retirement ages linked to differential pensionable ages.
>
> The appellant relied on the speech of Lord Diplock in *Garland* v *British Rail Engineering Ltd* [1983] 2 AC 751, 770–771. Lord Diplock expressed the view that section 6(4) of the Sex Discrimination Act 1975 could and should be construed in the manner consistent with article 119 [now 157] of the EEC Treaty, the Equal Pay Directive and the Equal Treatment Directive. In *Garland's* case, following a reference to the European

Court of Justice it was established that there had been discrimination contrary to article 119 [now 157] which has direct effect between individuals. It was thus unnecessary to consider the effect of the Equal Treatment Directive. Lord Diplock observed, at p. 771, that:

> 'even if the obligation to observe the provisions of article 119 were an obligation assumed by the United Kingdom under an ordinary international treaty or convention and there was no question of the Treaty obligation being directly applicable as part of the law to be applied by the courts in this country without need for any further enactment, it is a principle of construction of United Kingdom statutes, now too well established to call for citation of authority, that the words of a statute passed after the Treaty has been signed and dealing with the subject matter of the international obligation of the United Kingdom, are to be construed, if they are reasonably capable of bearing such a meaning, as intended to carry out the obligation, and not to be inconsistent with it.... The instant appeal does not present an appropriate occasion to consider whether, having regard to the express direction as to the construction of enactments 'to be passed' which is contained in section 2(4) anything short of an express positive statement in an Act of Parliament passed after 1 January 1973, that a particular provision is intended to be made in breach of an obligation assumed by the United Kingdom under a Community treaty, would justify an English court in construing that provision in a manner inconsistent with a Community treaty obligation of the United Kingdom, however wide a departure from the prima facie meaning of the language of the provision might be needed in order to achieve consistency.'

On the hearing of this appeal, your Lordships have had the advantage, not available to Lord Diplock, of full argument which has satisfied me that the Sex Discrimination Act 1975 was not intended to give effect to the Equal Treatment Directive as subsequently construed in the *Marshall* case [1986] QB 401 and that the words of section 6(4) are not reasonably capable of being limited to the meaning ascribed to them by the appellant. Section 2(4) of the European Communities Act 1972 does not in my opinion enable or constrain a British court to distort the meaning of a British statute in order to enforce against an individual a Community directive which has no direct effect between individuals. Section 2(4) applies and only applies where Community provisions are directly applicable.

The jurisdiction, composition and powers of the European Court of Justice are contained in articles 164 to 188 [now 251 and 281] of the EEC Treaty. Those sections include the following:

> '164. The Court of Justice shall ensure that in the interpretation and application of this Treaty the law is observed....
>
> 177. The Court of Justice shall have jurisdiction to give preliminary rulings concerning: (a) the interpretation of this Treaty; (b) the validity and interpretation of Act of the institutions of the Community; (c) the interpretation of the statutes of bodies established by an act of the council, where those statutes so provide.'

The submission that the Sex Discrimination Act 1975 must be construed in a manner which gives effect to the Equal Treatment Directive as construed by the European Court of Justice in *Marshall's* case is said to be derived from the decision of the European Court of Justice in *Von Colson and Kamann* v *Land Nordrhein-Westfalen* (Case 14/83) [1984] ECR 1891, delivered on 10 April 1984. In the *Von Colson* case the European Court of Justice ruled that the provisions of the Equal Treatment Directive which require equal treatment for men and women in access to employment do not require a member state to legislate so as to compel an employer to conclude a contract of employment with a woman who has been refused employment on the grounds of sex. The Directive does not specify the nature of the remedies which the member states must afford to a victim of discrimination. But the court also ruled, at p. 1910:

> '3. Although [the Equal Treatment Directive] 76/207/EEC for the purpose of imposing a sanction for the breach of discrimination, leaves the member states free to choose between the different solution suitable for achieving its object, it nevertheless requires that if a member state chooses to penalise breaches of that prohibition by the award of compensation, then in order to ensure that it is effective and that it has a deterrent effect, that compensation must in any event be adequate in relation to the damage sustained and must therefore amount to more than purely nominal compensation such as, for example, the reimbursement only of the expenses incurred in connection with the application. It is for the national court to interpret and apply the legislation adopted for the implementation of the Directive in conformity with the requirements of Community law, in so far as it is given discretion to do so under national law.'

In the *Von Colson* case the German court which submitted the case for a ruling asked whether it was acceptable that a woman who applied for a job and was refused because she was a woman, contrary to the intent of the Equal Treatment Directive, was only entitled under the German domestic law prohibiting such discrimination to the recovery of her expenses (if any) of her application. The German Government in making representations to the European Court expressed the view that under German law compensation for discrimination could include general damages for the loss of the job or of the opportunity to take up the job. The ruling of the European Court of Justice did not constrain the national court to construe German law in accordance with Community law but ruled that if under German law the German court possessed the power to award damages which were adequate and which fulfilled the objective of the Equal Treatment Directive then it was the duty of the German court to act accordingly.

The *Von Colson* case is no authority for the proposition that the German court was bound to invent a German law of adequate compensation if no such law existed and no authority for the proposition that a court of a member state must distort the meaning of a domestic statute so as to conform with Community law which is not directly applicable. If, following the *Von Colson* case, the German court adhered to the view that under German law it possessed no discretion to award adequate compensation, it would have been the duty of the German Government in fulfilment of its obligations under the Treaty of Rome to introduce legislation or evolve some other method which would enable adequate compensation to be obtained, just as the United Kingdom Government became bound to introduce legislation to amend the Equal Pay Act 1970 and the Sex Discrimination Act 1975 in the light of *Marshall's* case. Mrs Advocate-General Rozès in her opinion, delivered on 31 January 1984 in the *Von Colson* case, said, at p. 1919:

> 'In proceedings under article 177 it is not for me to express a view on questions which fall exclusively within the jurisdiction of the national courts inasmuch as they concern the application of national law.'

The EEC Treaty does not interfere and the European Court of Justice in the *Von Colson* case did not assert power to interfere with the method or result of the interpretation of national legislation by national courts.

It would be most unfair to the respondent to distort the construction of the 1975 Sex Discrimination Act in order to accommodate the 1976 Equal Treatment Directive as construed by the European Court of Justice in the 1986 *Marshall* case. As between the appellant and the respondent the Equal Treatment Directive did not have direct effect and the respondent could not reasonably be expected to reduce to precision the opaque language which constitutes both the strength and the difficulty of some Community legislation. The respondent could not reasonably be expected to appreciate the logic of Community legislators in permitting differential retirement pension ages but prohibiting differential retirement ages. The respondent is not liable to the appellant under Community law. I decline to hold that liability under British law attaches to the respondent or any other private employer to pay damages based on wages which women over 60 and under 65 did not earn before the amending Sex Discrimination Act 1986 for the first time and without retrospective effect introduced the statutory tort of operating differential retirement ages. I would dismiss this appeal.

Appeal dismissed.

Pickstone v *Freemans plc*

[1989] AC 66, House of Lords

The ECJ had ruled in *Commission of the European Communities* v *United Kingdom* (Case 61/81) [1982] ICR 578, that United Kingdom law did not meet Community law requirements on the principle that men and women should receive equal pay for work of equal value. Following this decision the Equal Pay Act 1970 was amended. Women who were employed as warehouse operatives were paid less than a man who was employed as a checker warehouse operative. The women contended that as the work of the two jobs was of equal value, then, under the amended Equal Pay Act 1970, s. 1(2)(c), they were entitled to the higher rate of pay. The Industrial Tribunal rejected the claim on the basis that their case came within s. 1(2)(a) of the 1970 Act, as there was a man who was employed at the same rate as the women in the post of warehouse operative. The Court of Appeal allowed the women's appeal on the basis of conformity with Art. 119 of the EEC (now 157 TFEU) Treaty. The employers appealed to the House of Lords.

LORD TEMPLEMAN: ... Section 1(2)(a) of the Act of 1970 as amended in 1975, was not further amended by the Regulations of 1983. Paragraph (a) enables any woman to claim equal pay with a man in the same employment engaged on like work. By section 1(4) like work is work of the same or a broadly similar nature where the differences in work are not of practical importance. The issue of 'like work' is decided by the industrial tribunal.

Section 1(2)(b) of the Act of 1970 as amended in 1975, was also not further amended by the Regulations of 1983. Paragraph (b) enables a woman to claim equal pay for work rated as equivalent to that of a man by a job evaluation study. By section 1(5) the issue of 'equivalent work' is decided by the job evaluation study. Such a study can only be carried out with the consent and cooperation of the employer.

In compliance with the ruling of the European Court of Justice in *Commission of the European Communities* v *United Kingdom of Great Britain and Northern Ireland* (Case 61/81) [1982] ICR 578, the Regulations of 1983 introduced into the Act of 1970 as amended in 1975, a provision which enables a woman to claim equal pay for work of equal value where the employer refuses to consent to a job evaluation study. The Regulations introduced into the Act section 1(2)(c) which modifies any term in a woman's contract which is less favourable than a term of a similar kind in the contract of a man

> '(c) where a woman is employed on work which, not being work in relation to which paragraph (a) or (b) above applies, is, in terms of the demands made on her (for instance under such headings as effort, skill and decision), of equal value to that of a man in the same employment.'

...

According to the employers in the present appeal, the Regulations of 1983 had the additional effect of depriving some women of the right to pursue their claims by judicial process or otherwise although they considered themselves wronged by failure to apply the principle of equal pay. The respondents may have a valid complaint in that they are not receiving equal pay with Mr Phillips for work of equal value. But if the respondents seek to remedy that discrimination under section 1(2)(c) of the Act of 1970 as amended by the Regulations, they will be debarred because they are employed on 'work in relation to which paragraph (a) or (b) above applies.' It is said that paragraph (a) operates, not because the respondents are employed on like work with Mr Phillips but because the respondents are employed on like work with some other man. Since paragraph (c) is expressed to apply only when a woman is employed on work which is not 'work in relation to which paragraph (a) or (b) above applies,' it follows, so it is said, that where a woman is employed on like work with any man or where a woman is employed on work rated as equivalent with any man, no claim can be made under paragraph (c) in respect of some other man who is engaged on work of equal value. In my opinion paragraph (a) or (b) only debars a claim under paragraph (c) where paragraph (a) or (b) applies to the man who is the subject of the complaint made by the woman. If the tribunal decides that the respondents are engaged 'on like work' with Mr Phillips then paragraph (a) applies and the respondents are not entitled to proceed under paragraph (c) and to obtain the report of an Acas expert. If there is a job evaluation study which covers the work of the respondents and the work of Mr Phillips then the respondents are debarred from proceeding under paragraph (c) unless the job evaluation study itself was discriminatory.

Whenever there is a claim for equal pay, the complainant, or the complainant's trade union representative supporting the claimant, may wish to obtain a report from an Acas expert under paragraph (c) to use for the purpose of general pay bargaining and in the hope of finding ammunition which will lead to a general increase in wage levels irrespective of discrimination. For this purpose the more Acas reports there are the better. It may be significant that in the present case a claim is made under paragraph (c) and not under paragraph (a) as well, or, in the alternative, although it is obvious that work of equal value in terms of the demands made on a woman under such headings as effort, skill and decision which may amount to discrimination under paragraph (c) may also be work of a broadly similar nature with differences of no practical importance which found a complaint under paragraph (a). If there is discrimination in pay the industrial tribunal must be able to grant a remedy. But the remedy available under paragraph (c) is not to be applied if the complainant has a remedy in respect of the male employee with whom she demands parity under paragraph (a) or if paragraph (b) applies to the woman and to that male employee. To prevent exploitation of paragraph (c) the tribunal must decide in the first instance whether the complainant and the man with whom she seeks parity are engaged on 'like work' under paragraph (a). If paragraph (a) applies, no Acas report is required. If paragraph (a) does not apply, then the tribunal considers whether paragraph (b) applies to the complainant and the man with whom she seeks parity; if so, the tribunal can only proceed under paragraph (c) if the job evaluation study obtained for the purposes of paragraph (b) is itself discriminatory. If paragraph (b) applies then, again, no Acas report is necessary. If paragraphs (a) and (b) do not apply, the tribunal must next consider whether there are reasonable grounds for determining that the work of the complainant and the work of the man with whom she seeks parity is of equal value. If the tribunal are not so satisfied, then no Acas report is required. The words in paragraph (c) on which the employers rely were not intended to create a new form of permitted discrimination. Paragraph (c) enables a claim to equal pay as against a specified man to be made without injustice to an employer. When a woman claims equal pay for work of equal value, she specifies the man with whom she demands parity. If the work of the woman is work in relation to which paragraph (a) or (b) applies in relation to that man, then the woman cannot proceed under paragraph (c) and cannot obtain a report from an Acas expert. In my opinion there must be implied in paragraph (c) after the word 'applies' the words 'as between the woman and the man with whom she claims equality.' This construction is consistent with Community law. The employers' construction is inconsistent with Community law and creates a permitted form of discrimination without rhyme or reason.

Under Community law, a woman is entitled to equal pay for work of equal value to that of a man in the same employment. That right is not dependent on there being no man who is employed on the same work as the woman. Under British law, namely the Equal Pay Act 1970 as amended in 1975, a woman was entitled to equal pay for work rated as equivalent with that of a man in the same employment. That right was not dependent on there being no man who was employed on the same work as the woman. Under the ruling of the European Court of Justice in *Commission of the European Communities* v *United Kingdom of Great Britain and Northern Ireland* (Case 61/81) [1982] ICR 578, the Equal Pay Act 1970 as amended in 1975 was held to be defective because the Act did not entitle every woman to claim before a competent authority that her work had the same value as other work, but only allowed a claim by a woman who succeeded in persuading her employer to consent to a job evaluation scheme. The Regulations of 1983 were intended to give full effect to Community law and to the ruling of the European Court of Justice which directed the United Kingdom Government to introduce legislation entitling any woman to equal pay with any man for work of equal value if the difference in pay is due to the difference in sex and is therefore discriminatory. I am of the opinion that the Regulations of 1983, upon their true construction, achieve the required result of affording a remedy to any woman who is not in receipt of equal pay for work equal in value to the work of a man in the same employment.

In *Murphy* v *Bord Telecom Eireann* (Case 157/86) [1988] ICR 445, 29 women were employed as factory workers engaged in such tasks as dismantling, cleaning, oiling and reassembling telephones and other equipment; they claimed the right to be paid at the same rate as a specified male worker employed in the same factory as a stores labourer engaged in cleaning, collecting and delivering equipment and components and in lending general assistance as required. The European Court of Justice in their judgment, at p. 449, paragraph 9, said that the principle of equal pay for men and women

> 'forbids workers of one sex engaged in work of equal value to that of workers of the opposite sex to be paid a lower wage than the latter on grounds of sex, it a fortiori prohibits such a difference in pay where the lower-paid category of workers is engaged in work of higher value.'

I cannot think that in Community law or in British law the result would be any different if instead of there being 29 women working on telephone maintenance and one male stores labourer, there were 28 women and one man working on telephone maintenance and one male stores labourer.

The draft of the Regulations of 1983 was not subject to any process of amendment by Parliament. In these circumstances the explanations of the Government and the criticisms voiced by Members of Parliament in the debates which led to approval of the draft Regulations provide some indications of the intentions of Parliament. The debate on the draft Regulations in the House of Commons which led to their approval by Resolution was initiated by the Under Secretary of State for Employment who, in the reports of the House of Commons for 20 July 1983 *Hansard*, column 479 et seq. said:

> 'The Equal Pay Act allows a woman to claim equal pay with a man... if she is doing the same or broadly similar work, or if her job and his have been rated equal through job evaluation in effort, skill and decision. However, if a woman is doing different work from a comparable man, or if the jobs are not covered by a job evaluation study, the woman has at present no right to make a claim for equal pay. This is the gap identified by the European Court, which we are closing....'

In the course of his speech at column 485, the Minister outlined the procedure which will apply if a claim is made under paragraph (c) in the following words:

'Under the amending Regulations which are the subject of this debate, an employee will be able to bring a claim for equal pay with an employee of the opposite sex working in the same employment on the ground that the work is of equal value. When this happens, conciliation will first be attempted, as in all equal pay claims. If conciliation is unsuccessful, the industrial tribunal will take the following steps. First, it will check that the work is not in fact so similar that the case can be heard under the current Act. Secondly, it will consider whether the jobs have already been covered by a job evaluation scheme and judged not to be of equal value. If this is the case, the claim may proceed only if the original job evaluation scheme is shown to have been sexually discriminatory. Having decided that the case should proceed, the tribunal will first invite the parties to see if they can settle the claim voluntarily. If not, the tribunal will consider whether to commission an independent expert to report on the value of the jobs. It will not commission an expert's report if it feels that it is unreasonable to determine the question of value—for example, if the two jobs are quite obviously of unequal value. Nor... will it commission an expert's report if the employer shows at this stage that inequality in pay is due to material factors other than sex discrimination...'.

Thus it is clear that the construction which I have placed upon the Regulations corresponds to the intentions of the Government in introducing the Regulations. In the course of the debate in the House of Commons, and in the corresponding debate in the House of Lords, no one suggested that a claim for equal pay for equal work might be defeated under the Regulations by an employer who proved that a man who was not the subject of the complaint was employed on the same or on similar work with the complainant. The Minister took the view, and Parliament accepted the view, that paragraph (c) will only apply if paragraphs (a) and (b) are first held by the tribunal not to apply in respect of the work of the woman and the work of the man with whom she seeks parity of pay. This is also the only view consistent with Community law.

In *von Colson and Kamann* v *Land Nordrhein-Westfalen* (Case 14/83) [1984] ECR 1891, 1910–1911, the European Court of Justice advised that in dealing with national legislation designed to give effect to a Directive:

'3.... It is for the national court to interpret and apply the legislation adopted for the implementation of the Directive in conformity with the requirements of Community law, in so far as it is given discretion to do so under national law.'

In *Duke* v *GEC Reliance Systems Ltd* [1988] AC 618 this House declined to distort the construction of an Act of Parliament which was not drafted to give effect to a Directive and which was not capable of complying with the Directive as subsequently construed by the European Court of Justice. In the present case I can see no difficulty in construing the Regulations of 1983 in a way which gives effect to the declared intention of the Government of the United Kingdom responsible for drafting the Regulations and is consistent with the objects of the EEC Treaty, the provisions of the Equal Pay Directive and the rulings of the European Court of Justice. I would dismiss the appeal.

Appeal dismissed.

NOTE: In *Pickstone* their Lordships referred to *Hansard* to determine the intention of Parliament in passing the amendments to the 1970 statute.

■ QUESTIONS

1. Why was it distortion in *Duke* to interpret the legislation as being in conformity with Union law but permissible in *Pickstone*?
2. If the interpretation of *Von Colson* in *Duke* is incompatible with *Marleasing*, is it in accordance with *Kolpinghuis Nijmegen*?

Litster v *Forth Dry Dock & Engineering Co Ltd*

[1990] 1 AC 546, House of Lords

A company had become insolvent and gone into receivership. An hour before the receiver transferred the business assets to a new owner, the employees were made redundant. Directive 77/187/EEC provides safeguards for employees where a business is transferred from one owner to another. Article 4(1) of the directive stops a new owner from evading the safeguards by prohibiting dismissal of employees by the old owner. The directive was implemented by the Transfer of Undertakings (Protection of Employment) Regulations 1981. Regulation 5(1) allows employees of the old owner to pursue claims against the new owner, but according to reg. 5(3), the employee must have been in employment immediately before the transfer. The employees succeeded in claims before the Industrial Tribunal and the Employment Appeal Tribunal. The appeal to the Court of Session was allowed on the basis that the employees were not employed immediately before the transfer. On appeal to the House of Lords.

LORD KEITH: ...In *Pickstone* v *Freemans Plc* [1989] AC 66 there had been laid before Parliament under paragraph 2 (2) of Schedule 2 to the European Communities Act 1972 the draft of certain Regulations designed, and presented by the responsible ministers as designed, to fill a lacuna in the equal pay legislation of the United Kingdom which had been identified by a decision of the European Court of Justice. On a literal reading the regulation particularly relevant did not succeed in completely filling the lacuna. Your Lordships' House, however, held that in order that the manifest purpose of the Regulations might be achieved and effect given to the clear but inadequately expressed intention of Parliament certain words must be read in by necessary implication.

In the present case the Transfer of Undertakings (Protection of Employment) Regulations 1981 were similarly laid before Parliament in draft and approved by resolutions of both Houses. They were so laid as designed to give effect to Council Directive (77/187/EEC) dated 14 February 1977. It is plain that if the words in regulation 5 (3) of the Regulations of 1981 'a person so employed immediately before the transfer' are read literally, as contended for by the second respondents, Forth Estuary Engineering Ltd, the provisions of regulation 5 (1) will be capable of ready evasion through the transferee arranging with the transferor for the latter to dismiss its employees a short time before the transfer becomes operative. In the event that the transferor is insolvent, a situation commonly forming the occasion for the transfer of an undertaking, the employees would be left with worthless claims for unfair dismissal against the transferor. In any event, whether or not the transferor is insolvent, the employees would be deprived of the remedy of reinstatement or re-engagement. The transferee would be under no liability towards the employees and a coach and four would have been driven through the provisions of regulation 5 (1).

A number of decisions of the European Court, in particular *P. Bork International A/S* v *Foreningen af Arbejdsledere i Danmark* (Case 101/87) [1989] IRLR 41 have had the result that where employees have been dismissed by the transferor for a reason connected with the transfer, at a time before the transfer takes effect, then for purposes of article 3 (1) of Council Directive (77/187/EEC) (which corresponds to regulation 5 (1)) the employees are to be treated as still employed by the undertaking at the time of the transfer.

In these circumstances it is the duty of the court to give to regulation 5 a construction which accords with the decisions of the European Court upon the corresponding provisions of the Directive to which the regulation was intended by Parliament to give effect. The precedent established by *Pickstone* v *Freemans Plc* indicates that this is to be done by implying the words necessary to achieve that result. So there must be implied in regulation 5 (3) words indicating that where a person has been unfairly dismissed in the circumstances described in regulation 8 (1) he is to be deemed to have been employed in the undertaking immediately before the transfer or any of a series of transactions whereby it was effected.

My Lords, I would allow the appeal.

LORD TEMPLEMAN: ...Thus, it is said, since the workforce of Forth Dry Dock were dismissed at 3.30 p.m., they were not employed 'immediately before the transfer' at 4.30 p.m. and therefore regulation 5 (1) did not transfer any liability for the workforce from Forth Dry Dock to Forth Estuary. The argument is inconsistent with the Directive. In *P. Bork International A/S* v *Foreningen af Arbejdsledere i Danmark* (Case 101/87) [1989] IRLR 41, 44 the European Court of Justice ruled that:

> 'the only workers who may invoke Directive [(77/187/EEC)] are those who have current employment relations or a contract of employment at the date of the transfer. The question whether or not a contract of employment or employment relationship exists at that date must be assessed under national law, subject, however, to the observance of the mandatory rules of the Directive concerning the protection of workers against dismissal by reason of the transfer. It follows that

> the workers employed by the undertaking whose contract of employment or employment relationship has been terminated with effect on a date before that of the transfer, in breach of article 4 (1) of the Directive, must be considered as still employed by the undertaking on the date of the transfer with the consequence, in particular, that the obligations of an employer towards them are fully transferred from the transferor to the transferee in accordance with article 3 (1) of the Directive.'

In *Von Colson and Kamann* v *Land Nordrhein-Westfalen* (Case 14/83) [1984] ECR 1891, 1909 the European Court of Justice dealing with Council Directive (76/207/EEC), forbidding discrimination on grounds of sex regarding access to employment, ruled that:

> 'the member states' obligation arising from a Directive to achieve the result envisaged by the Directive and their duty under article 5 of the Treaty [now 4(3) TEU] to take all appropriate measures, whether general or particular, to ensure the fulfilment of that obligation, is binding on all the authorities of member states including, for matters within their jurisdiction, the courts. It follows that, in applying the national law and in particular the provisions of a national law specifically introduced in order to implement Directive [(76/207/EEC)] national courts are required to interpret their national law in the light of the wording and the purpose of the Directive in order to achieve the result referred to in the third paragraph of article 189.'

Thus the courts of the United Kingdom are under a duty to follow the practice of the European Court of Justice by giving a purposive construction to Directives and to Regulations issued for the purpose of complying with Directives. In *Pickstone* v *Freemans Plc* [1989] AC 66, this House implied words in a regulation designed to give effect to Council Directive (75/117/EEC) dealing with equal pay for women doing work of equal value. If this House had not been able to make the necessary implication, the Equal Pay (Amendment) Regulations 1983 (SI 1983 No. 1794) would have failed their object and the United Kingdom would have been in breach of its treaty obligations to give effect to Directives. In the present case, in the light of Council Directive (77/187/EEC) and in the light of the ruling of the European Court of Justice in *Bork's* case [1989] IRLR 41, it seems to me, following the suggestion of my noble and learned friend, Lord Keith of Kinkel, that paragraph 5 (3) of the Regulations of 1981 was not intended and ought not to be construed so as to limit the operation of regulation 5 to persons employed immediately before the transfer in point of time. Regulation 5 (3) must be construed on the footing that it applies to a person employed immediately before the transfer or who would have been so employed if he had not been unfairly dismissed before the transfer for a reason connected with the transfer. . . .

LORD OLIVER: . . . The critical question, it seems to me, is whether, even allowing for the greater latitude in construction permissible in the case of legislation introduced to give effect to this country's Community obligations, it is possible to attribute to regulation 8 (1) when read in conjunction with regulation 5, the same result as that attributed to article 4 in the *Bork* case [1989] IRLR 41. Purely as a matter of language, it clearly is not. Regulation 8(1) does not follow literally the wording of article 4 (1). It provides only that if the reason for the dismissal of the employee is the transfer of the business, he has to be treated 'for the purposes of Part V of the 1978 Act' as unfairly dismissed so as to confer on him the remedies provided by sections 69 to 79 of the Act (including, where it is considered appropriate, an order for reinstatement or re-engagement). If this provision fell to be construed by reference to the ordinary rules of construction applicable to a purely domestic statute and without reference to Treaty obligations, it would, I think, be quite impermissible to regard it as having the same prohibitory effect as that attributed by the European Court to article 4 of the Directive. But it has always to be borne in mind that the purpose of the Directive and of the Regulations was and is to 'safeguard' the rights of employees on a transfer and that there is a mandatory obligation to provide remedies which are effective and not merely symbolic to which the Regulations were intended to give effect. The remedies provided by the Act of 1978 in the case of an insolvent transferor are largely illusory unless they can be exerted against the transferee as the Directive contemplates and I do not find it conceivable that, in framing Regulations intending to give effect to the Directive, the Secretary of State could have envisaged that its purpose should be capable of being avoided by the transparent device to which resort was had in the instant case. *Pickstone* v *Freemans Plc* [1989] AC 66, has established that the greater flexibility available to the court in applying a purposive construction to legislation designed to give effect to the United Kingdom's Treaty obligations to the Community enables the court, where necessary, to supply by implication words appropriate to comply with those obligations: see particularly the speech of Lord Templeman, at pp. 120–121. Having regard to the manifest purpose of the Regulations, I do not, for my part, feel inhibited from making such an implication in the instant case. The provision in regulation 8(1) that a dismissal by reason of a transfer is to be treated as an unfair dismissal, is merely a different way of saying that the transfer is not to 'constitute a ground for dismissal' as contemplated by article 4 of the Directive and there is no good reason for denying to it the same effect as that attributed to that article. In effect this involves reading regulation 5(3) as if there were inserted after the words 'immediately before the transfer' the words 'or would have been so employed if he had not been unfairly dismissed in the circumstances described in regulation 8(1).' For my part, I would make such an implication which is entirely consistent with the general scheme of the Regulations and which is necessary if they are effectively to fulfil the purpose for which they were made of giving effect to the provisions of the Directive.

Appeal dismissed.

Finnegan* v *Clowney Youth Training Programme Ltd

[1990] 2 AC 407, House of Lords

The facts of this case are similar to those in *Duke* (see p. 395)—the employer operated different retirement ages for male and female employees. The difference between the two cases lies in the fact that the parties to this case came from Northern Ireland, where the relevant legislation was the Sex Discrimination (Northern Ireland) Order 1976 which had been made after the Equal Treatment Directive 76/207/EEC. The relevant provisions of the 1976 Order were the same as those in the Sex Discrimination Act 1975. The employee was successful in arguing sex discrimination before the Industrial Tribunal, but the Court of Appeal of Northern Ireland held that Parliament intended the 1976 Order to have the same effect in Northern Ireland as the 1975 Act did in England. On appeal to the House of Lords.

LORD BRIDGE: ...[T]he relevant legislation by Order in Council applicable to Northern Ireland has been designed to reproduce precisely the substance of the legislation enacted by the Westminster Parliament. Thus, on turning to the Sex Discrimination (Northern Ireland) Order 1976, we find that article 8 reproduces precisely the provisions of section 6 of the English Act of 1975 and in the Equal Pay Act (Northern Ireland) 1970, set out in Schedule 1 to the Order of 1976 as amended by that Order, section 6 (1A) reproduces precisely the provisions of section 6 (1A) of the English Act of 1970. Similarly, following the *Marshall* case [1987] QB 401, appropriate amendments to the Order of 1976 were made by the Sex Discrimination (Northern Ireland) Order 1988 which precisely reproduced in article 4 the provisions of section 2 of the English Act of 1986.

On the face of it, therefore, the enactment applicable to the circumstances of the present employee's claim is indistinguishable from the enactment which fell to be applied in *Duke* v *GEC Reliance Systems Ltd* [1988] AC 618 and would appear, therefore, to dictate the inevitable result that the appeal must fail. This was the view of the Court of Appeal in Northern Ireland. Counsel for the employee submits, however, that a crucial distinction is to be derived from the chronology, in that the English Act of 1975 was passed before the Council of the European Communities adopted the Equal Treatment Directive, on 9 February 1976, whereas the Order of 1976 was not made until July of that year. He referred us to a familiar line of authority for the proposition that the national legislation of a member state of the European Community which is enacted for the purpose of implementing a European Council Directive must be construed in the light of the Directive and must, if at all possible, be applied in a sense which will effect the purpose of the Directive: see *Von Colson and Kamann* v *Land Nordrhein-Westfalen* (Case 14/83) [1984] ECR 1891; *Pickstone* v *Freemans Plc* [1989] AC 66; *Litster* v *Forth Dry Dock and Engineering Co. Ltd* [1990] 1 AC 546.

I entirely accept the validity of the proposition, but I do not accept that it has any application here. Before the decision in the *Marshall* case [1986] QB, 401 it is apparent from the history I have recounted that neither the United Kingdom Parliament nor the United Kingdom Government perceived any conflict between the provisions of section 6 (4) of the Sex Discrimination Act 1975 and section 6 (1A) of the Equal Pay Act 1970 on the one hand and the provisions of the European Equal Treatment Directive on the other hand, such as to call for amendment of the English statutes after the adoption of the Directive. Accordingly, it would appear to me to be wholly artificial to treat the Order of 1976 enacting identical provisions for Northern Ireland, because it was made after the Directive, as having been made with the purpose of implementing Community law in the same sense as the Regulations which fell to be construed in the *Pickstone* and *Litster* cases. The reality is that article 8 (4) of the Order of 1976 being in identical terms and in an identical context to section 6 (4) of the English Act of 1975, must have been intended to have the identical effect. To hold otherwise would be, as in *Duke* v *GEC Reliance Systems Ltd* [1988] AC 618, most unfair to the employers in that it would be giving retrospective operation to the amending Order of 1988 and effectively eliminating the distinction between Community law which is of direct effect between citizens of member states and Community law which only affects citizens of member states when it is implemented by national legislation.

Alternatively counsel for the employee invited us to depart from *Duke* v *GEC Reliance Systems Ltd* in pursuance of *Practice Statement (Judicial Precedent)* [1966] 1 WLR 1234. I need only say that, so far from being persuaded that the decision in that case was wrong, I entertain no doubt that it was right for the reasons so clearly set out in the speech of Lord Templeman.

We were further invited to make a reference to the European Court of Justice under article 177 [now 267] of the EEC Treaty. In my opinion, however, the determination of the appeal does not depend on any question of Community law. The interpretation of the Order of 1976 is for the United Kingdom courts and it is not suggested that the Equal Treatment Directive is of direct effect between citizens.

I would dismiss the appeal.

Appeal dismissed.

■ QUESTIONS

1. Has the House of Lords in these four cases simply been consistent in seeking to ascertain if the domestic legislation was intended to implement Community law?
2. Lord Bridge is correct in *Finnegan*, in that there was no question of horizontal effect, but should their Lordships not have asked the ECJ for advice on the application of *Von Colson*, given that the Northern Irish legislation was passed after the directive?

NOTE: See Szyszczak (1990) 15 EL Rev 480 for a critical review of these four cases.

Webb v EMO Air Cargo (UK) Ltd (No. 2)

[1995] 1 WLR 1454, House of Lords

The applicant was engaged by the employers initially with a view to her replacing, after a probationary period, a pregnant employee during the latter's maternity leave. Shortly after her appointment the applicant discovered that she too was pregnant and the employers dismissed her. Her claim that her dismissal was discrimination contrary to the Sex Discrimination Act 1975, s. 1, was rejected by an industrial tribunal, which held that the reason for her dismissal was her anticipated inability to carry out the primary task of covering for the absent employee. Appeals to the Employment Appeal Tribunal and the Court of Appeal were dismissed. On appeal to the House of Lords their Lordships sought a preliminary ruling from the ECJ on the implementation of the principle of the Equal Treatment Directive (76/207/EEC). The ECJ ruled that Art. 2(1), when read with Art. 5(1) of the directive, precluded dismissal of an employee who had been recruited for an unlimited term with a view to replacing another employee during the latter's maternity leave and who could not do so because shortly after her recruitment, she had herself been found to be pregnant.

LORD KEITH OF KINKEL: ...The provisions of the Act of 1975 which your Lordships must endeavour to construe, so as to accord if at all possible with the ruling of the European Court, are section 1(1)(a) and section 5(3).

Section 1(1)(a) provides:

> 'A person discriminates against a woman in any circumstances relevant for the purposes of any provision of this act if—(a) on the ground of her sex he treats her less favourably than he treats or would treat a man...'

Section 5(3) provides:

> 'A comparison of the cases of persons of different sex or marital status under section 1(1) or 3(1) must be such that the relevant circumstances in the one case are the same, or not materially different, in the other.'

The reasoning in my speech in the earlier proceedings [1993] 1 WLR 49, 53–55 was to the effect that the relevant circumstances which existed in the present case and which should be taken to be present in the case of the hypothetical man was unavailability for work at the time when the worker was particularly required, and that the reason for the unavailability was not a relevant circumstance. So it was not relevant that the reason for the woman's unavailability was pregnancy, a condition which could not be present in a man.

The ruling of the European Court proceeds on an interpretation of the broad principles dealt with in articles 2(1) and 5(1) of Council Directive (76/207/EEC). Sections 1(1)(a) and 5(3) of the Act of 1975 set out a more precise test of unlawful discrimination, and the problem is how to fit the terms of that test into the ruling. It seems to me that the only way of doing so is to hold that, in a case where a woman is engaged for an indefinite period, the fact that the reason why she will be temporarily unavailable for work at a time when to her knowledge her services will be particularly required is pregnancy is a circumstance relevant to her case, being a circumstance which could not be present in the case of the hypothetical man. It does not necessarily follow that pregnancy would be a relevant circumstance in the situation where the woman is denied employment for a fixed period in the future during the whole of which her pregnancy would make her unavailable for work, nor in the situation where after engagement for a such a period the discovery of her pregnancy leads to cancellation of the engagement.

Appeal allowed.

■ QUESTION

Did their Lordships here distort the construction of the Sex Discrimination Act 1975 so as to make it conform to the Equal Treatment Directive as interpreted by the ECJ?

9

Human Rights

OVERVIEW

In this chapter we consider first the former position on human rights, then the European Convention on Human Rights and its incorporation into domestic law by the Human Rights Act 1998. We look at the extent of its application to private bodies performing public functions, and between private parties; how it affects the interpretation of legislation, when courts may find legislation compatible with Convention rights and when they may issue a declaration of incompatibility, and end with a study of some House of Lords decisions on a key aspect of counter-terrorism policy.

SECTION 1: INTRODUCTION

The area of human rights is so large that it would merit a book on its own. Consequently, treatment of this topic in this chapter will be selective, seeking to highlight certain issues.

In most constitutions there are declarations of particular rights or liberties to be accorded to citizens and respected by Government, such as freedom of speech, freedom of the person, freedom of conscience, freedom of movement, the right to privacy, and the right to equal treatment. Often these freedoms or rights have an entrenched or protected status so that they may not easily be restricted or overridden by temporary political majorities in control of the legislature. These rights or freedoms are seen as essential to the existence and maintenance of a liberal democracy. The position in the United Kingdom was very different and owed much to Dicey. With the enactment of the Human Rights Act 1998 major changes have been introduced. These will be examined later in the chapter, but to understand the significance of these changes it is necessary to understand the way in which rights were protected prior to the enactment of the 1998 Act.

A. V. Dicey, *An Introduction to the Study of the Law of the Constitution*
(10th edn, 1969), p. 203

... [W]ith us the law of the constitution, the rules which in foreign countries naturally form part of a constitutional code, are not the source but the consequence of the rights of individuals, as defined and enforced by the courts; that, in short, the principles of private law have with us been by the action of the courts and Parliament so extended as to determine the position of the Crown and of its servants; thus the constitution is the result of the ordinary law of the land.

The former position in the United Kingdom was summarized as follows:

Legislation on Human Rights: A Discussion Document

(Home Office, 1976), paras 2.01–05

Our arrangements for the protection of human rights are different from those of most other countries. The differences are related to differences in our constitutional traditions. Although our present constitution may be regarded as deriving in part from the revolution settlement of 1688–89, consolidated by the Union of 1707, we, unlike our European neighbours and many Commonwealth countries, do not owe our present system of government either to a revolution or to a struggle for independence. The United Kingdom—

(a) has an omnicompetent Parliament, with absolute power to enact any law and change any previous law; the courts in England and Wales have not, since the seventeenth century, recognised even in theory any higher legal order by reference to which Acts of Parliament could be held void; in Scotland the courts, while reserving the right to treat an Act as void for breaching a fundamental term of the Treaty of Union [see *MacCormick* v *Lord Advocate* 1953 SC 396], have made it clear that they foresee no likely circumstances in which they would do so;

(b) unlike other modern democracies, has no written constitution;

(c) unlike countries in the civil law tradition, makes no fundamental distinction, as regards rights or remedies, between 'public law' governing the actions of the State and its agents, and 'private law' regulating the relationships of private citizens with one another; nor have we a coherent system of administrative law applied by specialised tribunals or courts and with its own appropriate remedies;

(d) has not generally codified its law, and our courts adopt a relatively narrow and literal approach to the interpretation of statutes;

(e) unlike the majority of EEC countries and the United States, does not, by ratifying a treaty or convention, make it automatically part of the domestic law (nor do we normally give effect to such an international agreement by incorporating the agreement itself into our law).

In other countries the rights of the citizen are usually (though not universally) to be found enunciated in general terms in a Bill of Rights or other constitutional document. The effectiveness of such instruments varies greatly. A Bill of Rights is not an automatic guarantee of liberty; its efficacy depends on the integrity of the institutions which apply it, and ultimately on the determination of the people that it should be maintained. The United Kingdom as such has no Bill of Rights of this kind. The Bill of Rights of 1688, though more concerned with the relationship between the English Parliament and the Crown, did contain some important safeguards for personal liberty—as did the Claim of Rights of 1689, its Scottish equivalent. Among the provisions common to both the Bill of Rights and the Claim of Rights are declarations that excessive bail is illegal and that it is the right of subjects to petition the Crown without incurring penalties. But the protection given by these instruments to the rights and liberties of the citizen is much narrower than the constitutional guarantees now afforded in many other democratic countries.

The effect of the United Kingdom system of law is to provide, through the development of the common law and by express statutory enactment, a diversity of specific rights with their accompanying remedies. Thus, to secure the individual's right to freedom from unlawful or arbitrary detention, our law provides specific and detailed remedies such as habeas corpus and the action for false imprisonment. The rights which have been afforded in this way are for the most part negative rights to be protected from interference from others, rather than positive rights to behave in a particular way. Those rights which have emerged in the common law can always be modified by Parliament. Parliament's role is all-pervasive—potentially, at least. It continually adapts existing rights and remedies and provides new ones, and no doubt this process would continue even if a comprehensive Bill of Rights were enacted.

The legal remedies provided for interference with the citizen's rights have in recent times been overlaid by procedures which are designed to afford not so much remedies in the strict sense of the term as facilities for obtaining independent and impartial scrutiny of action by public bodies about which an individual believes he has cause for complaint, even though the action may have been within the body's legal powers. For example, the actions of central government departments are open to scrutiny by the Parliamentary Commissioner for Administration; and complaints about the administration of the National Health Service are investigated by the Health Service Commissioners.

NOTES

1. Rights' and 'freedoms' were regarded negatively in the United Kingdom; they were the area of freedom which remained after legal restraints were subtracted. Thus a person was free to do anything subject to the provisions of the law. There was, however, no guarantee that the area of freedom would not be contracted by the incremental encroachment of legislation until little

freedom remained. In *Entick* v *Carrington* (1765) 19 St Tr 1030 [*ante*, p. 94], Lord Camden had made it clear that Government, if it is to be free to interfere with individual rights, must be able to point to specific statutory or common law powers. The problem with this was that if these powers did not exist, they could always be created by new legislation. Today, for example, the police and other officials, such as HM Revenue Inspectors and Officers, have considerable powers under various Acts to obtain warrants and enter and search premises and seize property. See, for example, Police and Criminal Evidence Act 1984, s. 8; Taxes Management Act 1970, s. 20C, inserted by Finance Act 1976; Customs and Excise Management Act 1979, s. 161; Official Secrets Act 1911, s. 9; Police Act 1997, ss. 92–108.

While some statutes may seek to limit rights, others may accord protection which did not exist at common law. For example, at common law discrimination on the grounds of race or sex was not generally prohibited. Parliament intervened by means of the Race Relations Act 1976 and the Sex Discrimination Act 1975 to prohibit discrimination in certain circumstances, such as employment, housing, education, and the provision of goods and services. This is not equivalent, however, to creating a general right to be free from discrimination. This kind of legislative intervention by Parliament is limited as each piece of legislation represents a limited response to a perceived mischief. Until the enactment of the Human Rights Act 1998 the practice was to provide limited remedies against particular abuses but to stop short of providing any general declaration of particular rights.

2. The UK's constitutional culture was not one in which there was widespread appreciation of, and concern for, the protection of human rights. Some thought that everything was fine and those who took the contrary view were divided in how to improve the situation, particularly in the role which should be given to the courts. It seemed that there were cycles in which the judiciary were and were not active in protecting civil liberties. A contrast may be drawn between the first half of the twentieth century and its final decade. Ewing and Gearty argued in *The Struggle for Civil Liberties: Political Freedom and the Rule of Law 1914–45* (2000) that the judicial record was decidedly unimpressive whereas in the 1990s there was a reawakening of judicial interest in constitutional rights and a much greater willingness to conceive of their existence as a brake on the power of the Executive. In *R* v *Lord Chancellor, ex parte Witham* [1998] QB 575, a litigant in person, who was unemployed and in receipt of income support and who wished to sue for defamation (for which legal aid was not available), sought judicial review of Art. 3 of the Supreme Court Fees (Amendment) Order 1996 made by the Lord Chancellor under s. 130 of the Supreme Court Act 1981. Article 3 imposed a minimum fee of £120 for the issuing of a writ and removed a provision under a previous Order of 1980 which relieved litigants in person who were in receipt of income support from the obligation to pay fees. The Divisional Court granted the application for a declaration that Art. 3 was unlawful. Laws J stated:

> [T]he right to a fair trial, which of necessity imports the right of access to the court, is as near to an absolute right as any which I can envisage.... Access to the courts is a constitutional right; it can only be denied by the government if it persuades Parliament to pass legislation which specifically—in effect by express provision—permits the executive to turn people away from the court door. That has not been done in this case.

There was nothing in s. 130 of the 1981 Act which provided expressly for the abrogation of this right.

This willingness to recognize the added importance of human rights began to have an impact on the way in which the *Wednesbury* unreasonableness test was applied in judicial review proceedings. In *R* v *Ministry of Defence, ex parte Smith* [1996] QB 517, the Court of Appeal adopted the approach that 'the more substantial the interference with human rights, the more the court will require by way of justification before it is satisfied that the decision is reasonable'. This involves 'anxious scrutiny' or 'high-intensity review' in human rights cases. In *Chesterfield Properties plc* v *Secretary of State for the Environment* [1998] JPL 568, at 579–580, Laws J expressed the operation of this process as follows:

> Where an administrative decision abrogates or diminishes a constitutional or fundamental right, *Wednesbury* requires that the decision-maker provide a substantial justification in the public interest for doing so.... The identification of any right as 'constitutional', however, means nothing in the absence of a written constitution unless it is defined by reference to some particular protection which the law affords it. The common law affords such protection by adopting, within *Wednesbury*, a variable standard of review. There is no question of the court exceeding the principle of reasonableness. It means only that reasonableness itself requires in such cases that in ordering

> the priorities which will drive his decision, the decision-maker must give a high place to the right in question. He cannot treat it merely as something to be taken into account, akin to any other relevant consideration; he must recognise it as a value to be kept, unless in his judgment there is a greater value which justifies its loss. In many arenas of public discretion, the force to be given to all and any factors which the decision-maker must confront is neutral in the eye of the law; he may make of each what he will, and the law will not interfere because the weight he attributes to any of them is for him and not the court. But where a constitutional right is involved, the law presumes it to carry substantial force. Only another interest, a public interest, of greater force may override it.

In *R* v *Lord Saville, ex parte A and Others* [1999] 4 All ER 860, the Court of Appeal applied the high-intensity review test. The Bloody Sunday Review Tribunal, chaired by Lord Saville of Newdigate, had denied anonymity to soldiers testifying before it although accepting that anonymity would not hamper it in finding the truth. The Tribunal concluded that anonymity would affect the openness of the inquiry. Seventeen soldiers applied for judicial review, claiming that disclosure of their identities would put them at risk and thus interfered with their right to life. Their application was allowed by the Divisional Court. The Tribunal appealed. Lord Woolf MR, delivering the judgment of the court, dismissing the appeal stated (at p. 872):

> [W]hen a fundamental right such as the right to life is engaged, the options available to the reasonable decision-maker are curtailed. They are curtailed because it is unreasonable to reach a decision which contravenes or could contravene human rights unless there are sufficiently significant countervailing considerations. In other words it is not open to the decision-maker to risk interfering with fundamental rights in the absence of compelling justification. Even the broadest discretion is constrained by the need for there to be countervailing circumstances justifying interference with human rights. The courts will anxiously scrutinise the strength of the countervailing circumstances and the degree of the interference with the human right involved and then apply the test accepted by Lord Bingham MR in *Smith*.

This judicial awakening to the existence of constitutional or fundamental rights ties in with the political developments of the late 1990s which resulted in the enactment of the Human Rights Act 1998, which incorporated the European Convention on Human Rights.

SECTION 2: THE EUROPEAN CONVENTION ON HUMAN RIGHTS

In 1950 Member States of the Council of Europe (which included the United Kingdom) drew up the European Convention on Human Rights and Fundamental Freedoms. This was based on the United Nations Declaration of Human Rights and is designed to provide basic protection for human rights. The Convention was ratified by the United Kingdom in 1951 and came into force in 1953, but it was not until 1966 that the United Kingdom accorded to its citizens the right to individual petition, whereby a victim of abuse could, upon exhausting all domestic remedies, pursue a complaint before the European Commission of Human Rights and ultimately, if found admissible, before the European Court on Human Rights.

In some States the Convention has been incorporated into municipal law and is enforceable before the domestic courts of those States; in others equivalent protection is afforded by a domestic Bill of Rights. In the United Kingdom the Convention was not initially incorporated into domestic law and thus could not be directly enforced before domestic courts. The success of the Convention in protecting human rights is very much dependent upon the goodwill of the signatory State in complying with its provisions initially, or in complying with the decisions of the Committee of Ministers or Court if it has acted in contravention of the Convention. If a government ignores these decisions there is no sanction which can be invoked. The only hope is that international diplomatic pressure will encourage compliance. The United Kingdom has been found to be in breach of the Convention on many occasions but has generally complied with decisions against it by taking the necessary steps to amend domestic law to comply with the Convention. This may, however, take time, as the Government's response is rarely immediate and the legislative process is slow. In the calendar year 2010, the European Court of Human Rights found the United Kingdom to have violated the Convention in 14 cases out of 21 judgments decided and 2,766 applications alleging breaches of the Convention by the United Kingdom were allocated to a judicial formation, 1,175 were declared inadmissible or struck off, 68 were referred to the Government and 27 declared admissible (see *European Court of Human Rights Annual Report 2009*).

Protocol No. 11 to the Convention for the Protection of Human Rights and Fundamental Freedoms, which entered into force on 1 November 1998, restructured the control machinery under the Convention. The pressure on the Commission and Court had increased greatly with the increase in the number of signatories to the Convention and the rising number of applications brought by individuals alleging a breach of the Convention. This led to a huge backlog of cases. The role of the European Commission in determining the admissibility of applications has ceased. In place of the previous procedure, all alleged violations of the rights of persons are referred directly to the new permanent Court. The number of judges in the Court is equivalent to the number of signatory States, which currently stands at 47. In the majority of cases, the Court will sit in Chambers of seven judges, but on occasions a Grand Chamber of 17 may be convened. The Court deals with individual and inter-State petitions. Initially a committee of three judges will determine admissibility, and by unanimous vote may declare manifestly ill-founded cases inadmissible. If the Court declares an application admissible, it will (in a Chamber of seven) pursue the examination of the case, together with the parties' representatives, and if necessary will undertake an investigation. The Court will also place itself at the disposal of the parties to seek to secure a friendly settlement on the basis of respect for human rights. (Where a case pending before a Chamber raises a serious question affecting the interpretation of the Convention or the protocols thereto, or where the resolution of a question before the Chamber might have a result inconsistent with a judgment previously delivered by the Court, the Chamber may, at any time before it has rendered its judgment, relinquish jurisdiction in favour of the Grand Chamber, unless one of the parties to the case objects.) If no friendly settlement has been arrived at the Court will deliver its judgment. Within a period of three months from the date of the judgment of the Chamber, any party to the case may, in exceptional cases (serious questions affecting the interpretation or application of the Convention or the protocols thereto, or serious issues of general importance), request that the case be referred to the Grand Chamber. If the request is accepted, the resulting judgment of the Grand Chamber will be final. Otherwise, judgments of Chambers will become final when the parties declare that they will not request that the case be referred to the Grand Chamber, or have made no request for reference three months after the date of the judgment; or, if such a request is made, when the panel of the Grand Chamber rejects the request to refer.

The changes brought about by the 11th Protocol have not been able to cope with the exponential increase in individual applications to the Court. Further work on reform on the control system culminated in the adoption of a 14th Protocol which entered into force on 1 June 2010. The new protocol seeks to manage the volume of cases by reinforcing the mechanisms which can filter out unmeritorious applications, applying new admissibility criteria in cases where the applicant has not suffered significant disadvantage, and dealing with repetitive cases. A single judge would be empowered to declare inadmissible or strike out an application, and it would be possible to declare inadmissible applications where the applicant has not suffered a significant disadvantage and which, in terms of respect for human rights, did not otherwise require an examination on the merits by the Court, this is subject to an explicit condition to ensure that it does not lead to rejection of cases which have not been duly considered by a domestic tribunal. The competence of committees of three judges would be extended to cover repetitive cases so they could rule, in a simplified procedure, not only on the admissibility but also on the merits of an application, if the underlying question in the case is already the subject of well-established case law of the Court.

European Convention for the Protection of Human Rights and Fundamental Freedoms

Article 1

The High Contracting Parties shall secure to everyone within their jurisdiction the rights and freedoms defined in section 1 of this Convention.

SECTION I

Article 2

1. Everyone's right to life shall be protected by law. No one shall be deprived of his life intentionally save in the execution of a sentence of a court following his conviction of a crime for which this penalty is provided by law.

2. Deprivation of life shall not be regarded as inflicted in contravention of this Article when it results from the use of force which is no more than absolutely necessary:
(a) in defence of any person from unlawful violence;
(b) in order to effect a lawful arrest or to prevent the escape of a person lawfully detained;
(c) in action lawfully taken for the purpose of quelling a riot or insurrection.

Article 3

No one shall be subjected to torture or to inhuman or degrading treatment or punishment.

Article 4

1. No one shall be held in slavery or servitude.

2. No one shall be required to perform forced or compulsory labour.

3. For the purpose of this Article the term 'forced or compulsory labour' shall not include:
(a) any work required to be done in the ordinary course of detention imposed according to the provisions of Article 5 of this Convention or during conditional release from such detention;
(b) any service of a military character or, in case of conscientious objectors in countries where they are recognized, service exacted instead of compulsory military service;
(c) any service exacted in case of an emergency or calamity threatening the life or well-being of the community;
(d) any work or service which forms part of normal civic obligations.

Article 5

1. Everyone has the right to liberty and security of person. No one shall be deprived of his liberty save in the following cases and in accordance with a procedure prescribed by law;
(a) the lawful detention of a person after conviction by a competent court;
(b) the lawful arrest or detention of a person for non-compliance with the lawful order of a court or in order to secure the fulfilment of any obligation prescribed by law;
(c) the lawful arrest or detention of a person effected for the purpose of bringing him before the competent legal authority on reasonable suspicion of having committed an offence or when it is reasonably considered necessary to prevent his committing an offence or fleeing after having done so;
(d) the detention of a minor by lawful order for the purpose of educational supervision or his lawful detention for the purpose of bringing him before the competent legal authority;
(e) the lawful detention of persons for the prevention of the spreading of infectious diseases, of persons of unsound mind, alcoholics or drug addicts, or vagrants;
(f) the lawful arrest or detention of a person to prevent his effecting an unauthorized entry into the country or of a person against whom action is being taken with a view to deportation or extradition.

2. Everyone who is arrested shall be informed promptly, in a language which he understands, of the reasons for his arrest and of any charge against him.

3. Everyone arrested or detained in accordance with the provisions of paragraph 1 (c) of this Article shall be brought promptly before a judge or other officer authorized by law to exercise judicial power and shall be entitled to trial within a reasonable time or to release pending trial. Release may be conditioned by guarantees to appear for trial.

4. Everyone who is deprived of his liberty by arrest or detention shall be entitled to take proceedings by which the lawfulness of his detention shall be decided speedily by a court and his release ordered if the detention is not lawful.

5. Everyone who has been the victim of arrest or detention in contravention of the provisions of this Article shall have an enforceable right to compensation.

Article 6

1. In the determination of his civil rights and obligations or of any criminal charge against him, everyone is entitled to a fair and public hearing within a reasonable time by an independent and impartial tribunal established by law. Judgment shall be pronounced publicly but the press and public may be excluded from all or part of the trial in the interest of morals, public order or national security in a democratic society, where the interest of juveniles or the protection of the private life of the parties so require, or to the extent strictly necessary in the opinion of the court in special circumstances where publicity would prejudice the interests of justice.

2. Everyone charged with a criminal offence shall be presumed innocent until proved guilty according to law.

3. Everyone charged with a criminal offence has the following minimum rights:
(a) to be informed promptly, in a language which he understands and in detail, of the nature and cause of the accusation against him;
(b) to have adequate time and facilities for the preparation of his defence;
(c) to defend himself in person or through legal assistance of his own choosing or, if he has not sufficient means to pay for legal assistance, to be given it free when the interests of justice so require;
(d) to examine or have examined witnesses against him and to obtain the attendance and examination of witnesses on his behalf under the same conditions as witnesses against him;
(e) to have the free assistance of an interpreter if he cannot understand or speak the language used in court.

Article 7

1. No one shall be held guilty of any criminal offence on account of any act or omission which did not constitute a criminal offence under national or international law at the time when it was committed. Nor shall a heavier penalty be imposed than the one that was applicable at the time the criminal offence was committed.

2. This Article shall not prejudice the trial and punishment of any person for any act or omission which, at the time when it was committed, was criminal according to the general principles of law recognized by civilized nations.

Article 8

1. Everyone has the right to respect for his private and family life, his home and his correspondence.

2. There shall be no interference by a public authority with the exercise of this right except such as is in accordance with the law and is necessary in a democratic society in the interests of national security, public safety or the economic well-being of the country, for the prevention of disorder or crime, for the protection of health or morals, or for the protection of the rights and freedoms of others.

Article 9

1. Everyone has the right to freedom of thought, conscience and religion; this right includes freedom to change his religion or belief, and freedom, either alone or in community with others and in public or private, to manifest his religion or belief, in worship, teaching, practice and observance.

2. Freedom to manifest one's religion or beliefs shall be subject only to such limitations as are prescribed by law and are necessary in a democratic society in the interests of public safety, for the protection of public order, health or morals, or for the protection of the rights and freedoms of others.

Article 10

1. Everyone has the right to freedom of expression. This right shall include freedom to hold opinions and to receive and impart information and ideas without interference by public authority and regardless of frontiers. This Article shall not prevent States from requiring the licensing of broadcasting, television or cinema enterprises.

2. The exercise of these freedoms, since it carries with it duties and responsibilities, may be subject to such formalities, conditions, restrictions or penalties as are prescribed by law and are necessary in a democratic society in the interests of national security, territorial integrity or public safety, for the prevention of disorder or crime, for the protection of health or morals, for the protection of the reputation or rights of others, for preventing the disclosure of information received in confidence, or for maintaining the authority and impartiality of the judiciary.

Article 11

1. Everyone has the right to freedom of peaceful assembly and to freedom of association with others, including the right to form and to join trade unions for the protection of his interests.

2. No restrictions shall be placed on the exercise of these rights other than such as are prescribed by law and are necessary in a democratic society in the interests of national security or public safety, for the prevention of disorder or crime, for the protection of health or morals or for the protection of the rights and freedoms of others. This Article shall not prevent the imposition of lawful restrictions on the exercise of these rights by members of the armed forces, of the police or of the administration of the State.

Article 12

Men and women of marriageable age have the right to marry and to found a family, according to the national laws governing the exercise of this right.

Article 13

Everyone whose rights and freedoms as set forth in this Convention are violated shall have an effective remedy before a national authority notwithstanding that the violation has been committed by persons acting in an official capacity.

Article 14

The enjoyment of the rights and freedoms set forth in this Convention shall be secured without discrimination on any ground such as sex, race, colour, language, religion, political or other opinion, national or social origin, association with a national minority, property, birth or other status.

Article 15

1. In time of war or other public emergency threatening the life of the nation any High Contracting Party may take measures derogating from its obligations under this Convention to the extent strictly required by the exigencies of the situation, provided that such measures are not inconsistent with its other obligations under international law.

2. No derogation from Article 2, except in respect of deaths resulting from lawful acts of war, or from Articles 3, 4 (paragraph 1) and 7 shall be made under this provision.

3. Any High Contracting Party availing itself of this right of derogation shall keep the Secretary-General of the Council of Europe fully informed of the measures which it has taken and the reasons therefore. It shall also inform the Secretary-General of the Council of Europe when such measures have ceased to operate and the provisions of the Convention are again being fully executed.

Article 16

Nothing in Articles 10, 11, and 14 shall be regarded as preventing the High Contracting Parties from imposing restrictions on the political activity of aliens.

Article 17

Nothing in this Convention may be interpreted as implying for any State, group or person any right to engage in any activity or perform any act aimed at the destruction of any of the rights and freedoms set forth herein or at their limitation to a greater extent than is provided for in the Convention.

Article 18

The restrictions permitted under this Convention to the said rights and freedoms shall not be applied for any purpose other than those for which they have been prescribed.

PROTOCOL 1—ENFORCEMENT OF CERTAIN RIGHTS AND FREEDOMS NOT INCLUDED IN SECTION I OF THE CONVENTION

Article 1

Every natural or legal person is entitled to the peaceful enjoyment of his possessions. No one shall be deprived of his possessions except in the public interest and subject to the conditions provided for by law and by the general principles of international law.

The preceding provisions shall not, however, in any way impair the right of a State to enforce such laws as it deems necessary to control the use of property in accordance with the general interest or to secure the payment of taxes or other contributions or penalties.

Article 2

No person shall be denied the right to education. In the exercise of any functions which it assumes in relation to education and to teaching, the State shall respect the right of parents to ensure such education and teaching in conformity with their own religious and philosophical convictions.

Article 3

The High Contracting Parties undertake to hold free elections at reasonable intervals by secret ballot, under conditions which will ensure the free expression of the opinion of the people in the choice of the legislature.

PROTOCOL 4—PROTECTING CERTAIN ADDITIONAL RIGHTS

Article 1

No one shall be deprived of his liberty merely on the ground of inability to fulfil a contractual obligation.

Article 2

1. Everyone lawfully within the territory of a State shall, within that territory, have the right to liberty of movement and freedom to choose his residence.

2. Everyone shall be free to leave any country, including his own.

3. No restrictions shall be placed on the exercise of these rights other than such as are in accordance with law and are necessary in a democratic society in the interests of national security or public safety, for the maintenance of 'order public', for the prevention of crime or for the protection of the rights and freedoms of others.

4. The rights set forth in paragraph 1 may also be subject, in particular areas, to restrictions imposed in accordance with law and justified by the public interest in a democratic society.

Article 3

1. No one shall be expelled, by means either of an individual or of a collective measure, from the territory of the State of which he is a national.

2. No one shall be deprived of the right to enter the territory of the State of which he is a national.

Article 4

Collective expulsion of aliens is prohibited.

PROTOCOL 6—CONCERNING THE ABOLITION OF THE DEATH PENALTY

Article 1

The death penalty shall be abolished. No one shall be condemned to such penalty or executed.

Article 2

A State may make provision in its law for the death penalty in respect of acts committed in time of war or of imminent threat of war; such penalty shall be applied only in the instances laid down in the law and in accordance with its provisions. The State shall communicate to the Secretary General of the Council of Europe the relevant provisions of that law.

Article 3

No derogation from the provisions of this Protocol shall be made under Article 15 of the Convention.

Article 4

No reservation may be made under Article 64 of the Convention in respect of the provisions of this Protocol.

PROTOCOL 7

Article 1

1. An alien lawfully resident in the territory of a State shall not be expelled therefrom except in pursuance of a decision reached in accordance with law and shall be allowed;

(a) to submit reasons against his expulsion;
(b) to have his case reviewed; and
(c) to be represented for these purposes before the competent authority or a person or persons designated by that authority.

2. An alien may be expelled before the exercise of his rights under paragraph 1(a), (b) and (c) of this article, when such expulsion is necessary in the interests of public order or is grounded on reasons of national security.

Article 2

1. Everyone convicted of a criminal offence by a tribunal shall have the right to have his conviction or sentence reviewed by a higher tribunal. The exercise of this right, including the grounds on which it may be exercised, shall be governed by law.

2. This right may be subject to exceptions in regard to offences of a minor character, as prescribed by law, or in cases in which the person concerned was tried in the first instance by the highest tribunal or was convicted following an appeal against acquittal.

Article 3

When a person has by a final decision been convicted of a criminal offence and when subsequently his conviction has been reversed, or he has been pardoned, on the ground that a new or newly discovered fact shows conclusively that there has been a miscarriage of justice, the person who has suffered punishment as a result of such conviction shall be compensated according to the law or the practice of the State concerned, unless it is proved that the non-disclosure of the unknown fact in time is wholly or partly attributable to him.

Article 4

1. No one shall be liable to be tried or punished again in criminal proceedings under the jurisdiction of the same State for an offence for which he has already been finally acquitted or convicted in accordance with the law and penal procedure of that State.

2. The provisions of the preceding paragraph shall not prevent the reopening of the case in accordance with the law and penal procedure of the State concerned, if there is evidence of new or newly discovered facts, or if there has been a fundamental defect in the previous proceedings, which could affect the outcome of the case.

3. No derogation from this article shall be made under Article 15 of the Convention.

Article 5

Spouses shall enjoy equality of rights and responsibilities of a private law character between them, and in their relations with their children, as to marriage, during marriage and in the event of its dissolution.

> This article shall not prevent States from taking such measures as are necessary in the interests of the children.

NOTE: The United Kingdom has made the following reservation to Article 2 to Protocol 1:

> ...in view of certain provisions of the Education Acts in force in the United Kingdom, the principle affirmed in the second sentence of Article 2 is accepted by the United Kingdom only so far as it is compatible with the provision of efficient instruction and training, and the avoidance of unreasonable expenditure.

The United Kingdom has not ratified Protocol 4 or 7. Articles 1 and 2 of Protocol 6 which abolish the death penalty in most circumstances are included in the list of 'convention rights' protected by the Human Rights Act, the Protocol being signed and ratified in 1999. Protocol 13 which abolished the death penalty in all circumstances has been ratified but not included in the Schedule to the Human Rights Act.

It should be noted that the rights are guaranteed in Art. 6 regarding the public nature of criminal trials) but that the rights guaranteed in Arts 8–12 are subject to a broad range of exceptions. In interpreting the Convention the Court adopts a teleological approach whereby it seeks to give effect to its 'object and purpose'. In *Soering* v *United Kingdom* Series A No. 161, (1989) 11 EHRR 439, the Court stated:

> 87. In interpreting the Convention regard must be had to its special character as a treaty for the collective enforcement of human rights and fundamental freedoms (see the *Ireland* v *The United Kingdom* judgment of 18 January 1978, Series A no. 25, p. 90, § 239). Thus, the object and purpose of the Convention as an instrument for the protection of individual human beings require that its provisions be interpreted and applied so as to make its safeguards practical and effective (see, *inter alia*, the *Artico* judgment of 13 May 1980, Series A no. 37, p. 16, § 33). In addition, any interpretation of the rights and freedoms guaranteed has to be consistent with 'the general spirit of the Convention, an instrument designed to maintain and promote the ideals and values of a democratic society' (see the *Kjeldsen, Busk Madsen and Pedersen* judgment of 7 December 1976, Series A No. 23, p. 27, § 53).

This also means that the interpretation of the Convention will develop over time just as conceptions of the 'ideals and values of a democratic society' will develop. This was emphasized by the Court in *Tyrer* v *UK*, Series A No. 26, (1978) 2 EHRR 1, where the practice of corporal punishment in the Isle of Man was challenged as amounting to degrading treatment. The Court stated at para. 31:

> The Court must...recall that the Convention is a living instrument which, as the Commission rightly stressed, must be interpreted in the light of present-day conditions. In the case now before it the Court cannot but be influenced by the developments and commonly accepted standards in the penal policy of Member States of the Council of Europe in this field.

When applying the Convention the Court also recognizes the open-textured nature of the language used; interpretation will always be required. In *Soering* at para. 89, the Court stated that 'inherent in the whole of the Convention is a search for a fair balance between the demands of the general interest of the community and the requirements of the protection of the individual's fundamental rights'. A principle which the Court has developed which flows from this is that of proportionality. This is particularly relevant where the Convention permits restrictions upon a right as in Articles 8–11. Any restrictions which a State places on these rights 'must be proportionate to the legitimate aim pursued' (see *Handyside* v *UK*, Series A, No. 24 (1976) 1 EHRR 737 para. 49).

When balancing individual claims against the needs of the community as a whole, a crucial qualification is that any limitation be 'necessary in a democratic society'. In *United Communist Party of Turkey* v *Turkey* (1998) 26 EHRR 121, the European Court of Human Rights emphasized (at p. 148) that democracy is the 'only political model contemplated by the Convention and, accordingly, the only one compatible with it'. The Court stated that freedom of expression and free elections are essential characteristics of a democracy and that political parties play an essential role in ensuring pluralism and the proper functioning of democracy. In *The Socialist Party* v *Turkey* (1998) 27 EHRR 51, the European Court of Human Rights stated (at pp. 84–85):

> [O]ne of the principal characteristics of democracy is the possibility it offers of resolving a country's problems through dialogue, without recourse to violence, even when they are irksome. Democracy thrives on freedom of expression.... It is the essence of democracy to allow diverse political programmes to be proposed and debated, even those that call into question the way a State is currently organised, provided that they do not harm democracy itself.

Diverse political parties, mass media which may freely criticize the *status quo*, and channels for public debate and participation are thus crucial to the existence of a democracy and at the centre of the values which the Convention is seeking to protect.

The Convention now applies in 47 countries, but these are far from homogeneous. The Court therefore tends to adopt an interpretative approach which recognizes differences and makes allowances for variations between States by means of the margin of appreciation doctrine. Harris, O'Boyle and Warbrick, *Law of the European Convention on Human Rights* (1995) state (at p. 12):

> In general terms, it means that the state is allowed a certain measure of discretion, subject to European supervision, when it takes legislative, administrative or judicial action in the area of a Convention right.

This doctrine was explained by the Court in the *Handyside* case which arose from a prosecution of the publisher of *The Little Red Schoolbook* under the Obscene Publications Act 1959 for possessing obscene books for publication for gain. The applicant complained that his conviction and the forfeiture and destruction of the books amounted to a breach of his Art. 10 rights. The volume had also been published in eight other European countries without giving rise to any prosecutions. It was also published in Northern Ireland and Scotland, where no proceedings against the publisher were taken as the 1959 Act did not apply to those countries. Despite this the Court found that Art. 10 had not been breached by the UK as the limitation on freedom of expression could be justified as being necessary for the 'protection of morals'. The Court stated:

> 48. The Court points out that the machinery of protection established by the Convention is subsidiary to the national systems safeguarding human rights. The Convention leaves to each Contracting State, in the first place, the task of securing the rights and freedoms it enshrines. The institutions created by it make their own contribution to this task but they become involved only through contentious proceedings and once all domestic remedies have been exhausted (Art. 26).
>
> These observations apply, notably, to Article 10(2). In particular, it is not possible to find in the domestic law of the various Contracting States a uniform European conception of morals. The view taken by their respective laws of the requirements of morals varies from time to time and from place to place, especially in our era which is characterised by a rapid and far-reaching evolution of opinions on the subject. By reason of their direct and continuous contact with the vital forces of their countries, State authorities are in principle in a better position than the international judge to give an opinion on the exact content of these requirements as well as on the 'necessity' of a 'restriction' or 'penalty' intended to meet them. The Court notes at this juncture that, whilst the adjective 'necessary', within the meaning of Article 10(2), is not synonymous with 'indispensable', neither has it the flexibility of such expressions as 'admissible', 'ordinary', 'useful', 'reasonable' or 'desirable'. Nevertheless, it is for the national authorities to make the initial assessment of the reality of the pressing social need implied by the notion of 'necessity' in this context.
>
> Consequently, Article 10(2) leaves to the Contracting States a margin of appreciation. This margin is given both to the domestic legislator ('prescribed by law') and to the bodies, judicial amongst others, that are called upon to interpret and apply the laws in force.

> 49. Nevertheless, Article 10(2) does not give the Contracting States an unlimited power of appreciation. The Court, which, with the Commission, is responsible for ensuring the observance of those States' engagements, is empowered to give the final ruling on whether a 'restriction' or 'penalty' is reconcilable with freedom of expression as protected by Article 10. The domestic margin of appreciation thus goes hand in hand with a European supervision. Such supervision concerns both the aim of the measure challenged and its 'necessity'; it covers not only the basic legislation but also the decision applying it, even one given by an independent court. In this respect, the Court refers to Article 50 of the Convention ('decision or... measure taken by a legal authority or any other authority') as well as to its own case-law.
>
> The Court's supervisory functions oblige it to pay the utmost attention to the principles characterising a 'democratic society'. Freedom of expression constitutes one of the essential foundations of such a society, one of the basic conditions for its progress and for the development of every man. Subject to Article 10(2), it is applicable not only to 'information' or 'ideas' that are favourably received or regarded as inoffensive or as a matter of indifference, but also to those that offend, shock or disturb the State or any sector of the population. Such are the demands of that pluralism, tolerance and broadmindedness without which there is no 'democratic society'. This means, amongst other things, that every 'formality', 'condition', 'restriction' or 'penalty' imposed in this sphere must be proportionate to the legitimate aim pursued.
>
> From another standpoint, whoever exercises his freedom of expression undertakes 'duties' and 'responsibilities' the scope of which depends on his situation and the technical means he uses. The Court cannot overlook such a person's 'duties' and 'responsibilities' when it enquires, as in this case; whether 'restrictions' or 'penalties' were conducive to the 'protection of morals' which made them 'necessary' in a 'democratic society'.

This doctrine of 'margin of appreciation' will be applied differentially depending upon the context, but generally it derives from the fact that the Court is exercising a supervisory jurisdiction and that the responsibility for ensuring that human rights are protected and respected within States lies with the contracting parties themselves. This can mean that widely varying practices amongst the contracting parties are tolerated depending on the degree of laxity the Court displays; this can vary with the context, namely the Article under consideration.

A: The Convention in British courts prior to the Human Rights Act coming into force

Prior to the Human Rights Act 1998, courts in the United Kingdom could pay only limited attention to the European Convention. The Convention was not incorporated into domestic law and thus could not be applied directly by courts to the cases before them. In *British Airways Board* v *Laker Airways Ltd* [1985] AC 58, Lord Diplock stated the general principle regarding treaties:

> The interpretation of treaties to which the United Kingdom is a party but the terms of which have not either expressly or by reference been incorporated in English domestic law by legislation is not a matter that falls within the interpretative jurisdiction of an English court of law.

In *Malone* v *MPC* [1979] Ch 344, where Malone sought declarations, *inter alia,* that tapping of his telephone by the police was unlawful and in breach of his Art. 8 rights, Megarry V-C held that the tapping was not unlawful and then addressed the Convention issue. He emphasized that the Convention was not law in the United Kingdom, as the obligation to secure to everyone in the jurisdiction the rights and freedoms defined in the Convention was 'an obligation under a treaty which is not justiciable in the courts of this country'. While the Convention might be used by a court to help it construe a piece of legislation, in which case the court would 'readily seek to construe the legislation in a way that would effectuate the Convention rather than frustrate it', the Court in the instant case was not faced with any legislation. Megarry V-C stated:

> It seems to me that where Parliament has abstained from legislating on a point that is plainly suitable for legislation, it is indeed difficult for the court to lay down new rules of common law or equity that will carry out the Crown's treaty obligations, or to discover for the first time that such rules have always existed.

Megarry V-C, referring to the decision of the European Court of Human Rights in *Klass* v *Germany* (1979) 2 EHRR 214, which examined the West German statutory scheme for controlling telephone tapping, concluded that the United Kingdom system which lacked any legal safeguards could not possibly satisfy the requirements of the Convention. But it was not his judicial function to regulate this activity, it being rather a matter for Parliament. Megarry V-C expressed the view that it was not possible to feel any pride in English law on this matter and that legislation was urgently required. He stated:

> However much the protection of the public against crime demands that in proper cases the police should have the assistance of telephone tapping, I would have thought that in any civilised system of law the claims of liberty and justice would require that telephone users should have effective and independent safeguards against possible abuses. The fact that a telephone user is suspected of crime increases rather than diminishes this requirement; suspicions, however reasonably held, may sometimes prove to be wholly unfounded.

There were some ways, however, in which the Convention did play a part in judicial decision-making. These were identified by Lord Bingham of Cornhill, the then Lord Chief Justice, in his first speech in the House of Lords.

House of Lords

HL Deb, Vol. 533, cols 1465–1467, 3 July 1996

> LORD BINGHAM OF CORNHILL: First, . . . where a United Kingdom statute is capable of two interpretations, one consistent with the convention and one inconsistent, then the courts will presume that Parliament intended to legislate in conformity with the convention and not in conflict with it. In other words, the courts will presume that Parliament did not intend to legislate in violation of international law. That may be thought by your Lordships to be a modest presumption.
>
> Secondly, if the common law is uncertain, unclear or incomplete, the courts have to make a choice; they cannot abdicate their power of decision. In declaring what the law is, they will rule, wherever possible, in a manner which conforms with the convention and does not conflict with it. Any other course would be futile since a rule laid down in defiance of the convention would be likely to prove short-lived.
>
> There is, of course, one field—freedom of expression—in which respected Members of this House have declared that they see no inconsistency between the common law and the convention. That is reassuring; it is also wholly unsurprising since we have a long record as a pioneer in the field of freedom of expression. But it means that the courts are encouraged to look to the convention and the jurisprudence of the European Court of Human Rights when resolving problems on the common law.
>
> Thirdly, when the courts are called upon to construe a domestic statute enacted to fulfil a convention obligation, the courts will ordinarily assume that the statute was intended to be effective to that end. That is mere common sense, but common sense is the stock-in-trade of much judicial decision-making.
>
> Fourthly, where the courts have a discretion to exercise—that is, they can act in one way or another—one or more of which violates the convention and another of which does not, they seek to act in a way which does not violate the convention. That again is usually common sense and requires no elaboration. However, it is not an invariable rule and your Lordships' House, sitting judicially, gave an important judgment only yesterday in which the convention right to privacy was held to be obliged to give way to the greater interests of justice.
>
> Fifthly, when, as sometimes happens, the courts are called upon to decide what, in a given situation, public policy demands, it has been held to be legitimate that we shall have regard to our international obligations enshrined in the convention as a source of guidance on what British public policy requires.

Sixthly and lastly, matters covered by the law of the European Community—that is, the law administered by the European Court of Justice in Luxembourg and not Strasbourg—on occasion give effect to matters covered by convention law. The Court of Justice takes the view that on matters subject to Community law, the law common to the member states is part of the law which applies. All member states are parties to the convention and it so happens from time to time that laws derived from the convention are incorporated as part of the law of the Community. That of course is a law which the courts in this country must apply since we are bound by Act of Parliament to do so, and that is a means by which, indirectly, convention rights find their way into domestic law.

NOTE: A difficulty which courts in the United Kingdom have faced is that even where a statute is clearly in breach of the Convention, they are still bound by it. This was clearly illustrated by the case of *R* v *Staines and Morrissey* [1997] 2 Cr App R 426. In *Saunders* v *United Kingdom* (1997) 23 EHRR 313, the European Court of Human Rights held that the applicant's right to freedom from self-incrimination under Art. 6(1) had been infringed by the use at his trial of statements which he had been compelled to give during an investigation by inspectors of the Department of Trade and Industry into allegations of fraud during the takeover of Distillers plc by Guinness plc. During the investigation Saunders had been required by law to answer questions put to him; failure to answer could lead to contempt proceedings which could result in a fine or imprisonment for up to two years (see ss. 432(2) and 436(3) of the Companies Act 1985). In *Staines and Morrissey* the appellants were prosecuted under s. 1(2) of the Company Securities (Insider Dealing) Act 1985. Statements made by the appellants under compulsion to inspectors of the Department of Trade and Industry exercising their powers under s. 177 of the Financial Services Act 1986 were admitted in evidence against them. On appeal the appellants argued that in light of the recent decision in *Saunders*, these statements should have been excluded by the trial judge in exercise of the discretion created by s. 78(1) of the Police and Criminal Evidence Act 1984 to exclude evidence which would have an adverse effect on the fairness of the proceedings. The Court of Appeal dismissed the appeal, Lord Bingham of Cornhill LCJ stating:

The difficulty, as it seems to us, which the appellants face is to show that the court should exercise its powers under section 78(1) to exclude, because of its adverse effect on the conduct of the proceedings, material which section 177(6) has expressly stipulated may be used in evidence against a defendant. No doubt the admission of evidence under section 177(b) is subject to the overriding discretion of the Court to exclude under section 78(1). But there is, so far as we can see, nothing which distinguishes this case from other similar cases. If the Court were to rule here that this evidence should be excluded, it would be obliged to exclude such evidence in all such cases. That would amount to a repeal, or a substantial repeal, of an English statutory provision which remains in force in deference to a ruling which does not have direct effect and which, as a matter of strict law, is irrelevant.

...[T]he section here expressly authorises the use of evidence so obtained and that, as we see it, amounts to a statutory presumption that what might otherwise be regarded as unfair is, for this purpose and in this context, to be treated as fair, at any rate in the absence of special features which would make the admission of the evidence unfair.

...[T]he present position is very unsatisfactory. It would appear that the appellants have or certainly may have grounds for complaining in Strasbourg and, if the penalty is enforced and they incur costs in seeking relief, they may have claims to compensation against Her Majesty's Government. That is not, however, something which the courts can remedy. Our domestic law remains as declared by this Court in *Saunders* (*supra*). The United Kingdom is subject to a Treaty obligation to give effect to the European Convention of Human Rights as interpreted by the Court of Human Rights, but that again is not something which this Court can enforce....

In 2001 the Court of Appeal considered the cases of Saunders, Lyons, Parnes, and Ronson again ([2001] EWCA 2860) following a reference back to them by the Criminal Cases Review Commission in light of the findings of the European Court of Human Rights in *Saunders* v *UK*. The grounds of appeal were, *inter alia*, (1) that the Human Rights Act 1998 was retrospective in effect so that on an appeal after it came into force, the appellants could rely on the breach of their right to a fair trial under Art. 6 by the prosecution's use in evidence against them of their answers given under compulsion to the DTI inspectors; and (2) that even if the HRA is not retrospective, the convictions were unsafe because: (i) the UK's treaty obligations, particularly under Art. 46, conferred on the appellants the right in domestic law to rely on the violation established by the ECtHR's conclusion that their trials were unfair and to seek reparation by the quashing of their convictions; (ii) it is not possible to uphold the convictions by reliance on evidence admitted in breach of Art. 6 because this would place the Court of Appeal in breach of the HRA s. 6(1) obligation to act compatibly with Convention rights; and (iii) contemporary standards of common law fairness required that the answers to the DTI inspectors should have been excluded by the trial judge in exercising his discretion under s. 78 of the Police and Criminal Evidence Act 1984.

On the first ground the Court of Appeal found against the appellants following the decision of the House of Lords in *R* v *Kansal (No. 2)* [2001] 3 WLR 1562 which held that a defendant whose trial took place before 2 October 2000 could not rely in an appeal after that date on an alleged breach of his Convention rights. *Kansal* was a case involving compulsory answers to questions under the Insolvency Act 1986. In *Kansal* the House of Lords had followed its earlier decision in *Lambert* [2001] 3 WLR 206 on retrospectivity even though three of their Lordships (Lord Lloyd of Berwick, Lord Steyn, and Lord Hope of Craighead) considered that *Lambert* had been wrongly decided!

On the second ground of appeal, the Court of Appeal, having examined the jurisprudence of the European Court of Human Rights, concluded that Art. 46, which provides that 'The high contracting parties undertake to abide by the final judgment of the court in any case to which they are parties', did not require a State to reopen a conviction. The European Court had made a declaration of violation in each case and awarded costs to the applicants. The jurisprudence of the Court indicated that a declaration (and award of costs and/or damages) amounted to sufficient just satisfaction. Furthermore, in light of the decision in *Staines and Morrissey* there was no unfairness at their trial, as the court had no power to exclude the evidence as to do so would have been to ignore the legislation.

SECTION 3: INCORPORATION OF THE EUROPEAN CONVENTION ON HUMAN RIGHTS INTO UK LAW

A: The Human Rights Act 1998

In October 1997 the Labour Government introduced the Human Rights Bill into Parliament and at the same time published the White Paper, *Rights Brought Home: The Human Rights Bill*, which explained the design of the Bill and the subsequent Act.

Rights Brought Home: The Human Rights Bill

(Cm 3782, 1997), cll. 1.14–1.16, 2. 1–3.12

CHAPTER 1—THE CASE FOR CHANGE

...

The case for incorporation

1.14 The effect of non-incorporation on the British people is a very practical one. The rights, originally developed with major help from the United Kingdom Government, are no longer actually seen as British rights. And enforcing them takes too long and costs too much. It takes on average five years to get an action into the European Court of Human Rights once all domestic remedies have been exhausted; and it costs an average of £30,000. Bringing these rights home will mean that the British people will be able to argue for their rights in the British courts—without this inordinate delay and cost. It will also mean that the rights will be brought much more fully into the jurisprudence of the courts throughout the United Kingdom, and their interpretation will thus be far more subtly and powerfully woven into our law. And there will be another distinct benefit. British judges will be enabled to make a distinctively British contribution to the development of the jurisprudence of human rights in Europe.

1.15 Moreover, in the Government's view, the approach which the United Kingdom has so far adopted towards the Convention does not sufficiently reflect its importance and has not stood the test of time.

1.16 ... It is plainly unsatisfactory that someone should be the victim of a breach of the Convention standards by the State yet cannot bring any case at all in the British courts, simply because British law does not recognise the right in the same terms as one contained in the Convention.

...

CHAPTER 2—THE GOVERNMENT'S PROPOSALS FOR ENFORCING THE CONVENTION RIGHTS

2.1 The essential feature of the Human Rights Bill is that the United Kingdom will not be bound to give effect to the Convention rights merely as a matter of international law, but will also give them further effect directly in our domestic law. But there is more than one way of achieving this. This Chapter explains the choices which the Government has made for the Bill.

A new requirement on public authorities

2.2 Although the United Kingdom has an international obligation to comply with the Convention, there at present is no requirement in our domestic law on central and local government, or others exercising similar executive powers, to exercise those powers in a way which is compatible with the Convention. This Bill will change that by making it unlawful for public authorities to act in a way which is incompatible with the Convention rights. The definition of what constitutes a public authority is in wide terms. Examples of persons or organisations whose acts or omissions it is intended should be able to be challenged include central government (including executive agencies); local government; the police; immigration officers; prisons; courts and tribunals themselves; and, to the extent that they are exercising public functions, companies responsible for areas of activity which were previously within the public sector, such as the privatised utilities. The actions of Parliament, however, are excluded.

2.3 A person who is aggrieved by an act or omission on the part of a public authority which is incompatible with the Convention rights will be able to challenge the act or omission in the courts. The effects will be wide-ranging. They will extend both to legal actions which a public authority pursues against individuals (for example, where a criminal prosecution is brought or where an administrative decision is being enforced through legal proceedings) and to cases which individuals pursue against a public authority (for example, for judicial review of an executive decision). Convention points will normally be taken in the context of proceedings instituted against individuals or already open to them, but, if none is available, it will be possible for people to bring cases on Convention grounds alone. Individuals or organisations seeking judicial review of decisions by public authorities on Convention grounds will need to show that they have been directly affected, as they must if they take a case to Strasbourg.

2.4 It is our intention that people or organisations should be able to argue that their Convention rights have been infringed by a public authority in our courts at any level. This will enable the Convention rights to be applied from the outset against the facts and background of a particular case, and the people concerned to obtain their remedy at the earliest possible moment. We think this is preferable to allowing cases to run their ordinary course but then referring them to some kind of separate constitutional court which, like the European Court of Human Rights, would simply review cases which had already passed through the regular legal machinery. In considering Convention points, our courts will be required to take account of relevant decisions of the European Commission and Court of Human Rights (although these will not be binding).

2.5 The Convention is often described as a 'living instrument' because it is interpreted by the European Court in the light of present day conditions and therefore reflects changing social attitudes and the changes in the circumstances of society. In future our judges will be able to contribute to this dynamic and evolving interpretation of the Convention. In particular, our courts will be required to balance the protection of individuals' fundamental rights against the demands of the general interest of the community, particularly in relation to Articles 8–11 where a State may restrict the protected right to the extent that this is 'necessary in a democratic society'.

Remedies for a failure to comply with the Convention

2.6 A public authority which is found to have acted unlawfully by failing to comply with the Convention will not be exposed to criminal penalties. But the court or tribunal will be able to grant the injured person any remedy which is within its normal powers to grant and which it considers appropriate and just in the circumstances. What remedy is appropriate will of course depend both on the facts of the case and on a proper balance between the rights of the individual and the public interest. In some cases, the right course may be for the decision of the public authority in the particular case to be quashed. In other cases, the only appropriate remedy may be an award of damages. The Bill provides that, in considering an award of damages on Convention grounds, the courts are to take into account the principles applied by the European Court of Human Rights in awarding compensation, so that people will be able to receive compensation from a domestic court equivalent to what they would have received in Strasbourg.

Interpretation of legislation

2.7 The Bill provides for legislation—both Acts of Parliament and secondary legislation—to be interpreted so far as possible so as to be compatible with the Convention. This goes far beyond the present rule which enables the courts to take the Convention into account in resolving any ambiguity in a legislative provision. The courts will be required to interpret legislation so as to uphold the Convention rights unless the legislation itself is so clearly incompatible with the Convention that it is impossible to do so.

2.8 This 'rule of construction' is to apply to past as well as to future legislation. To the extent that it affects the meaning of a legislative provision, the courts will not be bound by previous interpretations. They will be able to build a new body of case law, taking into account the Convention rights.

A declaration of incompatibility with the Convention rights

2.9 If the courts decide in any case that it is impossible to interpret an Act of Parliament in a way which is compatible with the Convention, the Bill enables a formal declaration to be made that its provisions are incompatible with the Convention. A declaration of incompatibility will be an important statement to make, and the power to make it will be reserved to the higher courts. They will be able to make a declaration in any proceedings before them, whether the case originated with them (as, in the High Court, on judicial review of an executive act) or in considering an appeal from a lower court or tribunal. The Government will have the right to intervene in any proceedings where such a declaration is a possible outcome. A decision by the High Court or Court of Appeal, determining whether or not such a declaration should be made, will itself be appealable.

Effect of court decisions on legislation

2.10 A declaration that legislation is incompatible with the Convention rights will not of itself have the effect of changing the law, which will continue to apply. But it will almost certainly prompt the Government and Parliament to change the law.

2.11 The Government has considered very carefully whether it would be right for the Bill to go further, and give to courts in the United Kingdom the power to set aside an Act of Parliament which they believe is incompatible with the Convention rights. In considering this question, we have looked at a number of models. The Canadian Charter of Rights and Freedoms 1982 enables the courts to strike down any legislation which is inconsistent with the Charter, unless the legislation contains an explicit statement that it is to apply 'notwithstanding' the provisions of the Charter. But legislation which has been struck down may be re-enacted with a 'notwithstanding' clause. In New Zealand, on the other hand, although there was an earlier proposal for legislation on lines similar to the Canadian Charter, the human rights legislation which was eventually enacted after wide consultation took a different form. The New Zealand Bill of Rights Act 1990 is an 'interpretative' statute which requires past and future legislation to be interpreted consistently with the rights contained in the Act as far as possible but provides that legislation stands if that is impossible. In Hong Kong, a middle course was adopted. The Hong Kong Bill of Rights Ordinance 1991 distinguishes between legislation enacted before and after the Ordinance took effect: previous legislation is subordinated to the provisions of the Ordinance, but subsequent legislation takes precedence over it.

2.12 The Government has also considered the European Communities Act 1972 which provides for European law, in cases where that law has 'direct effect', to take precedence over domestic law. There is, however, an essential difference between European Community law and the European Convention on Human Rights, because it is a requirement of membership of the European Union that member States give priority to directly effective EC law in their own legal systems. There is no such requirement in the Convention.

2.13 The Government has reached the conclusion that courts should not have the power to set aside primary legislation, past or future, on the ground of incompatibility with the Convention. This conclusion arises from the importance which the Government attaches to Parliamentary sovereignty. In this context, Parliamentary sovereignty means that Parliament is competent to make any law on any matter of its choosing and no court may question the validity of any Act that it passes. In enacting legislation, Parliament is making decisions about important matters of public policy. The authority to make those decisions derives from a democratic mandate. Members of Parliament in the House of Commons possess such a mandate because they are elected, accountable and representative. To make provision in the Bill for the courts to set aside Acts of Parliament would confer on the judiciary a general power over the decisions of Parliament which under our present constitutional arrangements they do not possess, and would be likely on occasions to draw the judiciary into serious conflict with Parliament. There is no evidence to suggest that they desire this power, nor that the public wish them to have it. Certainly, this Government has no mandate for any such change.

2.14 It has been suggested that the courts should be able to uphold the rights in the Human Rights Bill in preference to any provisions of earlier legislation which are incompatible with those rights. This is on the basis that a later Act of Parliament takes precedence over an earlier Act if there is a conflict. But the Human Rights Bill is intended to provide a new basis for judicial interpretation of all legislation, not a basis for striking down any part of it.

2.15 The courts will, however, be able to strike down or set aside secondary legislation which is incompatible with the Convention, unless the terms of the parent statute make this impossible. The courts can already strike down or set aside secondary legislation when they consider it to be outside the powers conferred by the statute under which it is made, and it is right that they should be able to do so when it is incompatible with the Convention rights and could have been framed differently.

Entrenchment

2.16 On one view, human rights legislation is so important that it should be given added protection from subsequent amendment or repeal. The Constitution of the United States of America, for example, guarantees rights which can be amended or repealed only by securing qualified majorities in both the House of Representatives and the Senate, and among the States themselves. But an arrangement of this kind could not be reconciled with our own constitutional traditions, which allow any Act of Parliament to be amended or repealed by a subsequent Act of Parliament. We do not believe that it is necessary or would be desirable to attempt to devise such a special arrangement for this Bill.

Amending legislation

2.17 Although the Bill does not allow the courts to set aside Acts of Parliament, it will nevertheless have a profound impact on the way that legislation is interpreted and applied, and it will have the effect of putting the issues squarely to the Government and Parliament for further consideration. It is important to ensure that the Government and Parliament, for their part, can respond quickly. In the normal way, primary legislation can be amended only by further primary legislation, and this can take a long time. Given the volume of Government business, an early opportunity to legislate may not arise; and the process of legislating is itself protracted. Emergency legislation can be enacted very quickly indeed, but it is introduced only in the most exceptional circumstances.

2.18 The Bill provides for a fast-track procedure for changing legislation in response either to a declaration of incompatibility by our own higher courts or to a finding of a violation of the Convention in Strasbourg. The appropriate Government Minister will be able to amend the legislation by Order so as to make it compatible with the Convention. The Order will be subject to approval by both Houses of Parliament before taking effect, except where the need to amend the legislation is particularly urgent, when the Order will take effect immediately but will expire after a short period if not approved by Parliament.

2.19 There are already precedents for using secondary legislation to amend primary legislation in some circumstances, and we think the use of such a procedure is acceptable in this context and would be welcome as a means of improving the observance of human rights. Plainly the Minister would have to exercise this power only in relation to the provisions which contravene the Convention, together with any necessary consequential amendments. In other words, Ministers would not have carte blanche to amend unrelated parts of the Act in which the breach is discovered.

Scotland

2.20 In Scotland, the position with regard to Acts of the Westminster Parliament will be the same as in England and Wales. All courts will be required to interpret the legislation in a way which is compatible with the Convention so far as possible. If a provision is found to be incompatible with the Convention, the Court of Session or the High Court will be able to make a declarator to that effect, but this will not affect the validity or continuing operation of the provision.

2.21 The position will be different, however, in relation to Acts of the Scottish Parliament when it is established. The Government has decided that the Scottish Parliament will have no power to legislate in a way which is incompatible with the Convention; and similarly that the Scottish Executive will have no power to make subordinate legislation or to take executive action which is incompatible with the Convention. It will accordingly be possible to challenge such legislation and actions in the Scottish courts on the ground that the Scottish Parliament or Executive has incorrectly applied its powers. If the challenge is successful then the legislation or action would be held to be unlawful. As with other issues concerning the powers of the Scottish Parliament, there will be a procedure for inferior courts to refer such issues to the superior Scottish courts; and those courts in turn will be able to refer the matter to the Judicial Committee of the Privy Council. If such issues are decided by the superior Scottish courts, an appeal from their decision will be to the Judicial Committee. These arrangements are in line with the Government's general approach to devolution.

Wales

2.22 Similarly, the Welsh Assembly will not have power to make subordinate legislation or take executive action which is incompatible with the Convention. It will be possible to challenge such legislation and action in the courts, and for them to be quashed, on the ground that the Assembly has exceeded its powers.

Northern Ireland

2.23 Acts of the Westminster Parliament will be treated in the same way in Northern Ireland as in the rest of the United Kingdom. But Orders in Council and other related legislation will be treated as subordinate legislation. In other words, they will be struck down by the courts if they are incompatible with the Convention. Most such legislation is a temporary means of enacting legislation which would otherwise be done by measures of a devolved Northern Ireland legislature.

CHAPTER 3—IMPROVING COMPLIANCE WITH THE CONVENTION RIGHTS

3.1 The enforcement of Convention rights will be a matter for the courts, whilst the Government and Parliament will have the different but equally important responsibility of revising legislation where necessary. But it is also highly desirable for the Government to ensure as far as possible that legislation which it places before Parliament in the normal way is compatible with the Convention rights, and for Parliament to ensure that the human rights implications of legislation are subject to proper consideration before the legislation is enacted.

Government legislation

3.2 The Human Rights Bill introduces a new procedure to make the human rights implications of proposed Government legislation more transparent. The responsible Minister will be required to provide a statement that in his or her view the proposed Bill is compatible with the Convention. The Government intends to include this statement alongside the Explanatory and Financial Memorandum which accompanies a Bill when it is introduced into each House of Parliament.

3.3 There may be occasions where such a statement cannot be provided, for example because it is essential to legislate on a particular issue but the policy in question requires a risk to be taken in relation to the Convention, or because the arguments in relation to the Convention issues raised are not clear-cut.

In such cases, the Minister will indicate that he or she cannot provide a positive statement but that the Government nevertheless wishes Parliament to proceed to consider the Bill. Parliament would expect the Minister to explain his or her reasons during the normal course of the proceedings on the Bill. This will ensure that the human rights implications are debated at the earliest opportunity.

Consideration of draft legislation within Government

3.4 The new requirement to make a statement about the compliance of draft legislation with the Convention will have a significant and beneficial impact on the preparation of draft legislation within Government before its introduction into Parliament. It will ensure that all Ministers, their departments and officials are fully seized of the gravity of the Convention's obligations in respect of human rights. But we also intend to strengthen collective Government procedures so as to ensure that a proper assessment is made of the human rights implications when collective approval is sought for a new policy, as well as when any draft Bill is considered by Ministers. Revised guidance to Departments on these procedures will, like the existing guidance, be publicly available.

3.5 Some central co-ordination will also be extremely desirable in considering the approach to be taken to Convention points in criminal or civil proceedings, or in proceedings for judicial review, to which a Government department is a party. This is likely to require an inter-departmental group of lawyers and administrators meeting on a regular basis to ensure that a consistent approach is taken and to ensure that developments in case law are well understood by all those in Government who are involved in proceedings on Convention points. We do not, however, see any need to make a particular Minister responsible for promoting human rights across Government, or to set up a separate new Unit for this purpose. The responsibility for complying with human rights requirements rests on the Government as a whole.

A Parliamentary Committee on Human Rights

3.6 *Rights Brought Home* suggested that 'Parliament itself should play a leading role in protecting the rights which are at the heart of a parliamentary democracy'. How this is achieved is a matter for Parliament to decide, but in the Government's view the best course would be to establish a new Parliamentary Committee with functions relating to human rights. This would not require legislation or any change in Parliamentary procedure. There could be a Joint Committee of both Houses of Parliament or each House could have its own Committee; or there could be a Committee which met jointly for some purposes and separately for others.

3.7 The new Committee might conduct enquiries on a range of human rights issues relating to the Convention, and produce reports so as to assist the Government and Parliament in deciding what action to take. It might also want to range more widely, and examine issues relating to the other international obligations of the United Kingdom such as proposals to accept new rights under other human rights treaties.

Should there be a Human Rights Commission?

3.8 *Rights Brought Home* canvassed views on the establishment of a Human Rights Commission, and this possibility has received a good deal of attention. No commitment to establish a Commission was, however, made in the Manifesto on which the Government was elected. The Government's priority is implementation of its Manifesto commitment to give further effect to the Convention rights in domestic law so that people can enforce those rights in United Kingdom courts. Establishment of a new Human Rights Commission is not central to that objective and does not need to form part of the current Bill.

3.9 Moreover, the idea of setting up a new human rights body is not universally acclaimed. Some reservations have been expressed, particularly from the point of view of the impact on existing bodies concerned with particular aspects of human rights, such as the Commission for Racial Equality and the Equal Opportunities Commission, whose primary concern is to protect the rights for which they were established. A quinquennial review is currently being conducted of the Equal Opportunities Commission, and the Government has also decided to establish a new Disability Rights Commission.

3.10 The Government's conclusion is that, before a Human Rights Commission could be established by legislation, more consideration needs to be given to how it would work in relation to such bodies, and to the new arrangements to be established for Parliamentary and Government scrutiny of human rights issues. This is necessary not only for the purposes of framing the legislation but also to justify the additional public expenditure needed to establish and run a new Commission. A range of organisational issues need more detailed consideration before the legislative and financial case for a new Commission is made, and there needs to be a greater degree of consensus on an appropriate model among existing human rights bodies.

3.11 However, the Government has not closed its mind to the idea of a new Human Rights Commission at some stage in the future in the light of practical experience of the working of the new legislation. If Parliament establishes a Committee on Human Rights, one of its main tasks might be to conduct an inquiry into whether a Human Rights Commission is needed and how it should operate. The Government would want to give full weight to the Committee's report in considering whether to create a statutory Human Rights Commission in future.

3.12 It has been suggested that a new Commission might be funded from non-Government sources. The Government would not wish to deter a move towards a non-statutory, privately-financed body if its role was limited to functions such as public education and advice to individuals. However, a non-statutory body could not absorb any of the functions of the existing statutory bodies concerned with aspects of human rights.

NOTE: See the Equality Act 2006 which established the Commission for Equality and Human Rights.

■ QUESTIONS

1. Does the existence of a democratic mandate entitle Parliament to pass laws which might threaten the very conditions essential to the existence of a democracy and which a Bill of Rights should protect (see cl. 2.13, p. 423, *ante*)? Does the fact that courts were unable to declare statutes unconstitutional necessarily mean that they should not be able to do so in the future? Would giving to judges the power to determine the constitutionality of statutes necessarily make them more political than they currently are?
2. Is the Human Rights Act unnecessarily weakened by preventing it from impliedly repealing pre-existing statutes which conflict with its provisions? Would permitting the doctrine of implied repeal (see pp. 423–424, *ante*) to operate have undermined the supremacy of Parliament?

THE HUMAN RIGHTS ACT 1998

Introduction

1. The Convention and the First Protocol

(1) In this Act, 'the Convention rights' means the rights and fundamental freedoms set out in—

(a) Articles 2 to 12 and 14 of the Convention,
(b) Articles 1 to 3 of the First Protocol, and
(c) Articles 1 and 2 of the Sixth Protocol,

as read with Articles 16 to 18 of the Convention.

(2) Those Articles are to have effect for the purposes of this Act subject to any designated derogation or reservation (as to which see sections 14 and 15).

(3) The Articles are set out in Schedule 1.

(4) The Lord Chancellor may by order make such amendments to this section or Schedule 1 as he considers appropriate to reflect the effect, in relation to the United Kingdom, of a protocol.

(5) In subsection (4) 'protocol' means a protocol to the Convention—

(a) which the United Kingdom has ratified; or
(b) which the United Kingdom has signed with a view to ratification.

(6) No amendment may be made by an order under subsection (4) so as to come into force before the protocol concerned is in force in relation to the United Kingdom.

2. Interpretation of Convention rights

(1) A court or tribunal determining a question which has arisen under this Act in connection with a Convention right must take into account any—

(a) judgment, decision, declaration or advisory opinion of the European Court of Human Rights,
(b) opinion of the Commission given in a report adopted under Article 31 of the Convention,
(c) decision of the Commission in connection with Article 26 or 27(2) of the Convention, or
(d) decision of the Committee of Ministers taken under Article 46 of the Convention,

whenever made or given, so far as, in the opinion of the court or tribunal, it is relevant to the proceedings in which that question has arisen.

(2)–(3)...

Interpretation of legislation

3. Legislation

(1) So far as it is possible to do so, primary legislation and subordinate legislation must be read and given effect in a way which is compatible with the Convention rights.

(2) This section—

(a) applies to primary legislation and subordinate legislation whenever enacted;
(b) does not affect the validity, continuing operation or enforcement of any incompatible primary legislation; and
(c) does not affect the validity, continuing operation or enforcement of any incompatible subordinate legislation if (disregarding any possibility of revocation) primary legislation prevents removal of the incompatibility.

4. Declaration of incompatibility

(1) Subsection (2) applies in any proceedings in which a court determines whether a provision of primary legislation is compatible with a Convention right.

(2) If the court is satisfied that the provision is incompatible with a Convention right, it may make a declaration of that incompatibility.

(3) Subsection (4) applies in any proceedings in which a court determines whether a provision of subordinate legislation, made in the exercise of a power conferred by primary legislation, is compatible with a Convention right.

(4) If the court is satisfied—

(a) that the provision is incompatible with a Convention right, and
(b) that (disregarding any possibility of revocation) the primary legislation concerned prevents removal of the incompatibility,

it may make a declaration of that incompatibility.

(5) In this section 'court' means—

(a) the House of Lords;
(b) the Judicial Committee of the Privy Council;
(c) the Courts-Martial Appeal Court;
(d) in Scotland, the High Court of Justiciary sitting otherwise than as a trial court or the Court of Session;
(e) in England and Wales or Northern Ireland, the High Court or the Court of Appeal.

(6) A declaration under this section ('a declaration of incompatibility')—

(a) does not affect the validity, continuing operation or enforcement of the provision in respect of which it is given; and
(b) is not binding on the parties to the proceedings in which it is made.

5. Right of Crown to intervene

(1) Where a court is considering whether to make a declaration of incompatibility, the Crown is entitled to notice in accordance with rules of court.

(2) In any case to which subsection (1) applies—

(a) a Minister of the Crown (or a person nominated by him);
(b) a member of the Scottish executive;
(c) a Northern Ireland Minister;
(d) a Northern Ireland department, is entitled, on giving notice in accordance with rules of court, to be joined as a party to the proceedings.

(3) Notice under subsection (2) may be made at any time during the proceedings.

(4) A person who has been made a party to criminal proceedings (other than in Scotland) as the result of a notice under subsection (2) may, with leave, appeal to the House of Lords against any declaration of incompatibility made in the proceedings.

(5) . . .

Public authoritieS

6. Acts of public authorities

(1) It is unlawful for a public authority to act in a way which is incompatible with a Convention right.

(2) Subsection (1) does not apply to an act if—

(a) as the result of one or more provisions of primary legislation, the authority could not have acted differently; or
(b) in the case of one or more provisions of, or made under, primary legislation which cannot be read or given effect in a way which is compatible with the Convention rights, the authority was acting so as to give effect to or enforce those provisions.

(3) In this section, 'public authority' includes—

(a) a court or tribunal, and
(b) any person certain of whose functions are functions of a public nature, but does not include either House of Parliament or a person exercising functions in connection with proceedings in Parliament.

(4) In subsection (3) 'Parliament' does not include the House of Lords in its judicial capacity.

(5) In relation to a particular act, a person is not a public authority by virtue only of subsection (3)(b) if the nature of the act is private.

(6) 'An act' includes a failure to act but does not include a failure to—

(a) introduce in, or lay before, Parliament a proposal for legislation; or
(b) make any primary legislation or remedial order.

7. Proceedings

(1) A person who claims that a public authority has acted (or proposes to act) in a way which is made unlawful by section 6(1) may—

(a) bring proceedings against the authority under this Act in the appropriate court or tribunal, or
(b) rely on the Convention right or rights concerned in any legal proceedings, but only if he is (or would be) a victim of the unlawful act.

(2) In subsection (1)(a) 'appropriate court or tribunal' means such court or tribunal as may be determined in accordance with rules; and proceedings against an authority includes a counterclaim or similar proceeding.

(3) If the proceedings are brought on an application for judicial review, the applicant is to be taken to have a sufficient interest in relation to the unlawful act only if he is, or would be, a victim of that act.

(4) If the proceedings are made by way of a petition for judicial review in Scotland, the applicant shall be taken to have title and interest to sue in relation to the unlawful act only if he is, or would be, a victim of that act.

(5) Proceedings under subsection (1)(a) must be brought before the end of—

(a) the period of one year beginning with the date on which the act complained of took place; or

(b) such longer period as the court or tribunal considers equitable having regard to all the circumstances,

but that is subject to any rule imposing a stricter time limit in relation to the procedure in question.

(6) In subsection (1)(b) 'legal proceedings' includes—

(a) proceedings brought by or at the instigation of a public authority; and
(b) an appeal against the decision of a court or tribunal.

(7) For the purposes of this section, a person is a victim of an unlawful act only if he would be a victim for the purposes of Article 34 of the Convention if proceedings were brought in the European Court of Human Rights in respect of that act.

(8) Nothing in this Act creates a criminal offence.

(9)–(11) . . .

8. Judicial remedies

(1) In relation to any act (or proposed act) of a public authority which the court finds is (or would be) unlawful, it may grant such relief or remedy, or make such order, within its jurisdiction as it considers just and appropriate.

(2) But damages may be awarded only by a court which has power to award damages, or to order the payment of compensation, in civil proceedings.

(3) No award of damages is to be made unless, taking account of all the circumstances of the case, including—

(a) any other relief or remedy granted, or order made, in relation to the act in question (by that or any other court), and
(b) the consequences of any decision (of that or any other court) in respect of that act,

the court is satisfied that the award is necessary to afford just satisfaction to the person in whose favour it is made.

(4) In determining—

(a) whether to award damages, or
(b) the amount of an award,

the court must take into account the principles applied by the European Court of Human Rights in relation to the award of compensation under Article 41 of the Convention.

(5) . . .

(6) In this section—

'court' includes a tribunal;

'damages' means damages for an unlawful act of a public authority; and

'unlawful' means unlawful under section 6(1).

9. Judicial acts

(1) Proceedings under section 7(1)(a) in respect of a judicial act may be brought only—

(a) by exercising a right of appeal;
(b) on an application (in Scotland a petition) for judicial review; or
(c) in such other forum as may be prescribed by rules.

(2) That does not affect any rule of law which prevents a court from being the subject of judicial review.

(3) In proceedings under this Act in respect of a judicial act done in good faith, damages may not be awarded otherwise than to compensate a person to the extent required by Article 5(5) of the Convention.

(4) An award of damages permitted by subsection (3) is to be made against the Crown; but no award may be made unless the appropriate person, if not a party to the proceedings, is joined.

(5) In this section—

'appropriate person' means the Minister responsible for the court concerned, or a person or government department nominated by him;

'court' includes a tribunal;

'judge' includes a member of a tribunal, a justice of the peace and a clerk or other officer entitled to exercise the jurisdiction of a court;

'Judicial act' means a judicial act of a court and includes an act done on the instructions, or on behalf, of a judge;

...

Remedial action

10. Power to take remedial action

(1) This section applies if—

(a) a provision of legislation has been declared under section 4 to be incompatible with a Convention right and, if an appeal lies—
 (i) all persons who may appeal have stated that they do not intend to do so;
 (ii) the time for bringing an appeal has expired and no appeal has been brought within that time; or
 (iii) an appeal brought within that time has been determined or abandoned;

(b) it appears to a Minister of the Crown or Her Majesty in Council that, having regard to a finding of the European Court of Human Rights made after the coming into force of this section in proceedings against the United Kingdom, a provision of legislation is incompatible with an obligation of the United Kingdom arising from the Convention.

(2) If a Minister of the Crown considers that there are compelling reasons for proceeding under this section, he may by order make such amendments to the legislation as he considers necessary to remove the incompatibility.

(3) If, in the case of subordinate legislation, a Minister of the Crown considers—

(a) that it is necessary to amend the primary legislation under which the subordinate legislation in question was made, in order to enable the incompatibility to be removed, and

(b) that there are compelling reasons for proceeding under this section, he may by order make such amendments to the primary legislation as he considers necessary.

(4) This section also applies where the provision in question is in subordinate legislation and has been quashed, or declared invalid, by reason of incompatibility with a Convention right and the Minister proposes to proceed under paragraph 2(b) of Schedule 2.

(5) If the legislation is an Order in Council, the power conferred by subsection (2) or (3) is exercisable by Her Majesty in Council.

(6) In this section 'legislation' does not include a Measure of the Church Assembly or of the General Synod of the Church of England.

(7)...

Other rights and proceedings

11. Safeguard for existing human rights

A person's reliance on a Convention right does not restrict—

(a) any other right or freedom conferred on him by or under any law having effect in any part of the United Kingdom, or

(b) his right to make any claim or bring any proceedings which he could make or bring apart from sections 7 to 9.

12. Freedom of expression

(1) This section applies if a court is considering whether to grant any relief which, if granted, might affect the exercise of the Convention right to freedom of expression.

(2) If the person against whom the application for relief is made ('the respondent') is neither present nor represented, no such relief is to be granted unless the court is satisfied—

(a) that the applicant has taken all practicable steps to notify the respondent; or

(b) that there are compelling reasons why the respondent should not be notified.

(3) No such relief is to be granted so as to restrain publication before trial unless the court is satisfied that the applicant is likely to establish that publication should not be allowed.

(4) The court must have particular regard to the importance of the Convention right to freedom of expression and, where the proceedings relate to material which the respondent claims, or which appears to the court, to be journalistic, literary or artistic material (or to conduct connected with such material), to—

(a) the extent to which—
  (i) the material has, or is about to, become available to the public; or
  (ii) it is, or would be, in the public interest for the material to be published;
(b) any relevant privacy code.

(5) In this section—
'court' includes a tribunal; and
'relief' includes any remedy or order (other than in criminal proceedings).

13. Freedom of thought, conscience and religion

(1) If a court's determination of any question arising under this Act might affect the exercise by a religious organisation (itself or its members collectively) of the Convention right to freedom of thought, conscience and religion, it must have particular regard to the importance of that right.

(2) In this section, 'court' includes a tribunal.

Derogations and reservations

14. Derogations

(1) In this Act, 'designated derogation' means any derogation by the United Kingdom from an Article of the Convention, or of any protocol to the Convention, which is designated for the purposes of this Act in an order made by the Lord Chancellor.

(2) [*repealed*].

(3) If a designated derogation is amended or replaced it ceases to be a designated derogation.

(4) But subsection (3) does not prevent the Lord Chancellor from exercising his power under subsection (1) to make a fresh designation order in respect of the Article concerned.

(5) The Lord Chancellor must by order make such amendments to Schedule 2 as he considers appropriate to reflect—

(a) any designation order; or
(b) the effect of subsection (3).

(6) A designation order may be made in anticipation of the making by the United Kingdom of a proposed derogation.

15. Reservations

(1) In this Act, 'designated reservation' means—

(a) the United Kingdom's reservation to Article 2 of the First Protocol to the Convention; and
(b) any other reservation by the United Kingdom to an Article of the Convention, or of any protocol to the Convention, which is designated for the purposes of this Act in an order made by the Lord Chancellor.

(2) The text of the reservation referred to in subsection (1)(a) is set out in Part II of Schedule 3.

(3) If a designated reservation is withdrawn wholly or in part it ceases to be a designated reservation.

(4) But subsection (3) does not prevent the Lord Chancellor from exercising his power under subsection (1)(b) to make a fresh designation order in respect of the Article concerned.

(5) The Lord Chancellor must by order make such amendments to this Act as he considers appropriate to reflect—

(a) any designation order; or
(b) the effect of subsection (3).

16. Period for which designated derogations have effect

(1) If it has not already been withdrawn by the United Kingdom, a designated derogation ceases to have effect for the purposes of this Act at the end of the period of five years beginning with the date on which the order designating it was made.

(2) At any time before the period—

(a) fixed by subsection (1), or
(b) extended by an order under this subsection,

comes to an end, the Lord Chancellor may by order extend it by a further period of five years.

(3) An order under section 14(1) ceases to have effect at the end of the period for consideration, unless a resolution has been passed by each House approving the order.

(4) Subsection (3) does not affect—

(a) anything done in reliance on the order; or
(b) the power to make a fresh order under section 14(1).

(5) In subsection (3) 'period for consideration' means the period of forty days beginning with the day on which the order was made.

(6) In calculating the period for consideration, no account is to be taken of any time during which—

(a) Parliament is dissolved or prorogued; or
(b) both Houses are adjourned for more than four days.

(7) If a designated derogation is withdrawn by the United Kingdom, the Lord Chancellor must by order make such amendments to this Act as he considers are required to reflect that withdrawal.

17. Periodic review of designated reservations

(1) The appropriate Minister must review the designated reservation referred to in section 15(1)(a)—

(a) before the end of the period of five years beginning with the date on which section 1(2) came into force; and
(b) if that designation is still in force, before the end of the period of five years beginning with the date on which the last report relating to it was laid under subsection (3).

(2) The appropriate Minister must review each of the other designated reservations (if any)—

(a) before the end of the period of five years beginning with the date on which the order designating the reservation first came into force; and
(b) if the designation is still in force, before the end of the period of five years beginning with the date on which the last report relating to it was laid under subsection (3).

(3) The Minister conducting a review under this section must prepare a report on the result of the review and lay a copy of it before each House of Parliament.

Judges of the European Court of Human Rights

18. Appointment to European Court of Human Rights

(1) In this section 'judicial office' means the office of—

(a) Lord Justice of Appeal, Justice of the High Court or Circuit judge, in England and Wales;
(b) judge of the Court of Session or sheriff, in Scotland;
(c) Lord Justice of Appeal, judge of the High Court or county court judge, in Northern Ireland.

(2) The holder of a judicial office may become a judge of the European Court of Human Rights ('the Court') without being required to relinquish his office.

(3) But he is not required to perform the duties of his judicial office while he is a judge of the Court.

(4)–(7) . . .

Parliamentary procedure

19. Statements of compatibility

(1) A Minister of the Crown in charge of a Bill in either House of Parliament must, before Second Reading of the Bill—

(a) make a statement to the effect that in his view the provisions of the Bill are compatible with the Convention rights ('a statement of compatibility'); or
(b) make a statement to the effect that although he is unable to make a statement of compatibility the government nevertheless wishes the House to proceed with the Bill.

(2) The statement must be in writing and be published in such manner as the Minister making it considers appropriate.

SUPPLEMENTAL

20. Orders under this Act

(1) Any power to make an order under this Act is exercisable by statutory instrument.

(2) The power to make rules (other than rules of court) under section 2(3) or 7(9) is exercisable by statutory instrument.

(3) Any statutory instrument made under section 14, 15 or 16(7) must be laid before Parliament.

(4) No order may be made under section 1(4), 7(11) or 16(2) unless a draft of the order has been laid before, and approved by, each House of Parliament.

(5) Any statutory instrument made under section 18(7) or Schedule 4, or to which subsection (2) applies, shall be subject to annulment in pursuance of a resolution of either House of Parliament.

(6)–(8) . . .

21. Interpretation, etc

(1) In this Act—

. . .

'the appropriate Minister' means the Minister of the Crown having charge of the appropri ate authorised government department (within the meaning of the Crown Proceedings Act 1947);

. . .

'primary legislation' means any—

(a) public general Act;
(b) local and personal Act;
(c) private Act;
(d) Measure of the Church Assembly;
(e) Measure of the General Synod of the Church of England;
(f) Order in Council—
    (i) made in exercise of Her Majesty's Royal Prerogative;
    (ii) made under section 38(1)(a) of the Northern Ireland Constitution Act 1973 or the corresponding provision of the Northern Ireland Act 1998; or
    (iii) amending an Act of a kind mentioned in paragraph (a), (b) or (c); and includes an order or other instrument made under primary legislation (otherwise than by the National Assembly for Wales, a member of the Scottish Executive, a Northern Ireland Minister or a Northern Ireland department) to the extent to which it operates to bring one or more provisions of that legislation into force or amends any primary legislation;

. . .

'remedial order' means an order under section 10;

'subordinate legislation' means any—

(a) Order in Council other than one—
    (i) made in exercise of Her Majesty's Royal Prerogative;
    (ii) made under section 38(1)(a) of the Northern Ireland Constitution Act 1973 or the corresponding provision of the Northern Ireland Act 1998; or

(iii) amending an Act of a kind mentioned in the definition of primary legislation;
(b) Act of the Scottish Parliament;
(c) Act of the Parliament of Northern Ireland;
(d) Measure of the Assembly established under section 1 of the Northern Ireland Assembly Act 1973;
(e) Act of the Northern Ireland Assembly;
(f) order, rules, regulations, scheme, warrant, byelaw or other instrument made under primary legislation (except to the extent to which it operates to bring one or more provisions of that legislation into force or amends any primary legislation);
(g) order, rules, regulations, scheme, warrant, byelaw or other instrument made under legislation mentioned in paragraph (b), (c), (d) or (e) or made under an Order in Council applying only to Northern Ireland;
(h) order, rules, regulations, scheme, warrant, byelaw or other instrument made by a member of the Scottish Executive, a Northern Ireland Minister or a Northern Ireland department in exercise of prerogative or other executive functions of Her Majesty which are exercisable by such a person on behalf of Her Majesty;

'transferred matters' has the same meaning as in the Northern Ireland Act 1998; and 'tribunal' means any tribunal in which legal proceedings may be brought.

...

22. Short title, commencement, application and extent

(1) This Act may be cited as the Human Rights Act 1998.

(2) Sections 18 and 20 and this section come into force on the passing of this Act.

(3) The other provisions of this Act come into force on such day as the Secretary of State may by order appoint; and different days may be appointed for different purposes.

(4) Paragraph (b) of subsection (1) of section 7 applies to proceedings brought by or at the instigation of a public authority whenever the act in question took place; but otherwise that subsection does not apply to an act committed before the coming into force of that section.

(5) This Act binds the Crown.

(6) This Act extends to Northern Ireland.

(7) Section 21(5), so far as it relates to any provision contained in the Army Act 1955, the Air Force Act 1955 or the Naval Discipline Act 1957, extends to any place to which that provision extends.

B: The implications of the Human Rights Act for human rights

Lord Irvine of Lairg LC, The Tom Sargant Memorial Lecture, 'The Development of Human Rights in Britain under an Incorporated Convention on Human Rights'

16 December 1997

...The traditional freedom of the individual under an unwritten constitution to do himself that which is not prohibited by law gives no protection from misuse of power by the State, nor any protection from acts or omissions by public bodies which harm individuals in a way that is incompatible with their human rights under the Convention.

The implications of the change

What then are the practical implications of this change to a rights based system within the field of civil liberties?

First, the Act will give to the courts the tools to uphold freedoms at the very time their infringement is threatened.... The courts will now have the power to give effect to the Convention rights in the course of proceedings when they arise in this country and to grant relief against an unlawful act of a public authority (a necessarily widely drawn concept). The courts will not be able to strike down primary legislation. But they will be able to make a declaration of incompatibility where a piece of primary legislation conflicts with a Convention right. This will trigger the ability to use in Parliament a special fast-track procedure to bring the law into line with the Convention.

This innovative technique will provide the right balance between the judiciary and Parliament. Parliament is the democratically elected representative of the people and must remain sovereign. The judiciary will be able to exercise to the full the power to scrutinise legislation rigorously against the fundamental freedoms guaranteed by the Convention but without becoming politicised. The ultimate decision to amend legislation to bring it into line with the Convention, however, will rest with Parliament. The ultimate responsibility for compliance with the Convention must be Parliament's alone.

That point illustrates the second important effect of our new approach. If there are to be differences or departures from the principles of the Convention they should be conscious and reasoned departures, and not the product of rashness, muddle or ignorance. This will be guaranteed both by the powers given to the courts but also by other provisions which will be enacted. In particular, Ministers and administrators will be obliged to do all their work keeping clearly and directly in mind its impact on human rights, as expressed in the Convention and the jurisprudence which attaches to it. For, where any Bill is introduced in either House, the Minister of the Crown, in whose charge it is, will be required to make a written statement that, either, in his view, the provisions of the Bill are compatible with the Convention rights; or that he cannot make that statement but the Government nonetheless wishes the House to proceed with the Bill. In the latter case the Bill would inevitably be subject to close and critical scrutiny by Parliament. Human rights will not be a matter of fudge. The responsible Minister will have to ensure that the legislation does not infringe guaranteed freedoms, or be prepared to justify his decision openly and in the full glare of Parliamentary and public opinion.

That will be particularly important whenever there comes under consideration those articles of the Convention which lay down what I call principled rights, subject to possible limitation. I have in mind Articles 8–11, dealing with respect for private life; freedom of religion; freedom of expression; and freedom of assembly and association; which confer those freedoms subject to possible limitations, such as, for instance in the case of Article 10 (freedom of expression):

> are prescribed by law and are necessary in a democratic society in the interests of national security, territorial integrity or public safety, for the prevention of disorder or crime, for the protection of health or morals, for the protection of the reputation or rights of others, for preventing the disclosure of information received in confidence, or for maintaining the authority and impartiality of the judiciary.

In such cases, administrators and legislators, will have to think clearly about whether what they propose really is necessary in a democratic society and for what object it is necessary. Quite apart from the concentration on the Convention and its jurisprudence this will require, the process should produce better thought-out, clearer and more transparent administration.

The important requirements of transparency on Convention issues that will accompany the introduction of all future legislation will ensure that Parliament knows exactly what it is doing in a human rights context. I regard this improvement in both the efficiency and the openness of our legislative process as one of the main benefits produced by incorporation of the Convention.

Substantive rights

Thirdly, the Convention will enable the Courts to reach results in cases which give full effect to the substantive rights guaranteed by the Convention. . . . But the courts have only had limited ability to give effect to those rights. . . .

It is moreover likely—although individual cases will be for the Courts to determine and I should not attempt to prejudge them—that the position will in at least some cases be different from what it would have been under the pre-incorporation practice. The reason for this lies in the techniques to be followed once the Act is in force. Unlike the old Diceyan approach where the Court would go straight to what restriction had been imposed, the focus will first be on the positive right and then on the justifiability of the exception. Moreover, the Act will require the Courts to read and give effect to the legislation in a way compatible with the Convention rights 'so far as it is possible to do so.' This, as the White Paper makes clear, goes far beyond the present rule. It will not be necessary to find an ambiguity. On the contrary the Courts will be required to interpret legislation so as to uphold the Convention rights unless the legislation itself is so clearly incompatible with the Convention that it is impossible to do so. Moreover, it should be clear from the Parliamentary history, and in particular the Ministerial statement of compatibility which will be required by the Act, that Parliament did not intend to cut across a Convention right. Ministerial statements of compatibility will inevitably be a strong spur to the courts to find means of construing statutes compatibly with the Convention. . . .

The Court will interpret as consistent with the Convention not only those provisions which are ambiguous in the sense that the *language* used is capable of two different meanings but also those provisions where there is *no* ambiguity in that sense, unless a *clear* limitation is expressed. In the latter category of case it will be 'possible' (to use the statutory language) to read the legislation in a conforming sense because there will be no clear indication that a limitation on the protected rights was intended so as to make it 'impossible' to read it as conforming.

The morality of decisions

The fourth point may be shortly stated but is of immense importance. The Courts' decisions will be based on a more overtly principled, indeed moral, basis. The Court will look at the positive right. It will only accept an interference with that right where a justification, allowed under the Convention, is made out. The scrutiny will not be limited to seeing if the *words* of an exception can be satisfied. The Court will need to be satisfied that the *spirit* of this exception is made out. It will need to be satisfied that the interference with the protected right *is* justified in the public interests in a free democratic society. Moreover, the Courts will in this area have to apply the Convention principle of proportionality. This means the Court will be looking *substantively* at that question. It will not be limited to a secondary review of the decision making process but at the primary question of the merits of the decision itself.

In reaching its judgment, therefore, the Court will need to expand and explain its own view of whether the conduct is legitimate. It will produce in short a decision on the *morality* of the conduct and not simply its compliance with the bare letter of the law.

The influence on other areas of law

I believe, moreover, that the effects of the incorporation of the Convention will be felt way beyond the sphere of the application of the rights guaranteed by the Convention alone. As we move from the traditional Diceyan model of the common law to a rights based system, the effects will be felt throughout the common law and in the very process of judicial decision-making. This will be a healthy and dynamic development in our law.

...

Although the legislative technique adopted under the Human Rights Bill is different from that under the European Communities Act, the effect on the general process of deciding cases will, I believe, be as influential. Courts will, from time to time be required to determine if primary or secondary legislation is incompatible with the Convention rights. They will decide if the acts of public authorities are unlawful through contravention, perhaps even conscious contravention, of those rights. They may have to award damages as a result.

These are all new remedies for our courts to apply and, as they begin to develop the tools and techniques to apply them, an influence on other areas of law and judicial decision making is, I believe, inevitable.

...

So too it is becoming increasingly hard not explicitly to recognise in English administrative law the Community law doctrine of proportionality.

That doctrine, drawn from German Administrative law principles, is a tool for judging the lawfulness of administrative action. It amounts to this. Excessive means are not to be used to attain permissible objects. Or, as it was more pithily put by Lord Diplock, 'a steam hammer should not be used to crack a nut'. There has been much argument whether this principle now forms a part of the criteria for review of public decisions generally since Lord Diplock opened that door in 1985 [see *Council of Civil Service Unions* v *Minister for the Civil Service* [1985] AC 374]. It seemed to have been slammed shut in *Brind* in 1991. This is not the occasion to trace those developments. Yet, by whatever name, it seems undeniable that the traditional common law concepts converge with their continental cousins. This is but another example of the inevitable incremental effects of introducing another system of law to be applied alongside traditional common law principles.

C: How does the Human Rights Act operate in practice?

NOTE: The introduction of the Human Rights Act is a major step forward in the protection of human rights. Gradually uncertainties as to how the Act will operate in practice are being resolved such as that the domestic system of precedent holds even though there is a subsequent inconsistent decision of the European Court of Human Rights (*Kay* v *Lambeth London Borough Council* [2006] UKHL 10 [2006] 2 AC 465), and that the Act extends beyond the territory of the UK where UK public authorities exercised control so that a military base in Iraq was within jurisdiction (*R (Al-Skeini)* v *Secretary of State for Defence* [2007] UKHL 26, [2007] 3 WLR 33).

Below some of the major questions are explored by means of extracts from academic and judicial writers and from decisions of the appellate courts.

(a) What is a 'public authority'?

Seventh Report from the Joint Committee on Human Rights

HL 39/HC 382 of 2003–2004, paras 3–7, 39–41, 138–47

3. The intention of Parliament was that a wide range of bodies performing public functions would fall within the obligation under section 6 to act in a manner compatible with the 'Convention rights' established under the Act.

4. However, while the Convention had been designed to protect the individual from abuse of power by the State, the Human Rights Act was enacted at a time when the map of the public sector had been redrawn, as privatisation and contracting-out had, over several decades, increased the role of the private and voluntary sectors in the provision of public services. This development was acknowledged and considered by those who drafted and debated the Act. In particular, it was clearly envisaged that the Act would apply beyond activities undertaken by purely State bodies, to those functions performed on behalf of the State by private or voluntary sector bodies, acting under either statute or under contract. The Act was therefore designed to apply human rights guarantees beyond the obvious governmental bodies. Section 6 identified two distinct categories of 'public authorities' which would have a duty to comply with the Convention rights.

5. First, under section 6(3)(a), ['core'] public authorities (such as government departments, local authorities, or the police) are required to comply with Convention rights in all their activities, both when discharging intrinsically public functions and also when performing functions which could be done by any private body. So, for example, a local authority must as a pure public authority comply with the non-discrimination standards imposed by Article 14 of the Convention not only in its provision of public housing but also in its dealings with building contractors [Courts and tribunals are specifically stated to be public authorities (in all their activities) under section 6(3)(a)].

6. Second, under section 6(3)(b), those who exercise some public functions but are not ['core'] public authorities are required to comply with Convention human rights when they are exercising a 'function of a public nature' but not when doing something where the nature of the act is private (section 6(5)). So, for example, a private security firm would be required to comply with Convention rights in its running of a prison, but not in its provision of security to a supermarket. These bodies to which section 6(3)(b) applies have been termed 'hybrid' or 'functional' public authorities.

7. The term 'hybrid' public authority is unhelpful—it is not the *intrinsic* nature of these bodies which brings them within the ambit of the Act, it is the nature of the *functions* they perform which is determinative. A body could be liable under the Act one day while delivering functions under contract to a 'pure' public authority; the next day, if the contract had ended, it might become again a purely private body without any alteration to its intrinsic nature. In the remainder of this report we will use the term 'functional public authority' to refer to a body to which section 6(3)(b) of the Act might apply.

...

39. It seems therefore that the courts are likely to interpret the category of 'pure' public authority (all of the actions of which would be required to be compatible with the Convention rights) narrowly. In particular, the courts consider that they must exclude bodies capable of enforcing their Convention rights. But when it comes to interpreting the definition of a 'functional' public authority, which can be held to account under the Human Rights Act only in respect of its 'public' functions, it is not clear that the approach of the House of Lords in *Aston Cantlow* [[2003] UKHL 37, [2003] 3 WLR 283], which stressed the importance of analysing the character of the function concerned rather than the character of the institutional arrangements of the body performing the function, is being applied in the lower courts. This may be because the clear principles set out by the House of Lords were stated without reference to, and

without express disapproval or overruling of, the earlier cases—including *Poplar Homes* [[2001] EWCA Civ 595, [2002] QB 48] and *Leonard Cheshire* [[2002] EWCA Civ 366, [2002] 2 All ER 936], which took a predominantly 'institutional' rather than 'functional' approach to the question...

41. The tests being applied by the courts to determine whether a function is a 'public function' within the meaning of section 6(3)(b) of the Human Rights Act are, in human rights terms, highly problematic. Their application results in many instances where an organisation 'stands in the shoes of the State' and yet does not have responsibilities under the Human Rights Act. It means that the protection of human rights is dependent not on the type of power being exercised, nor on its capacity to interfere with human rights, but on the relatively arbitrary (in human rights terms) criterion of the body's administrative links with institutions of the State. The European Convention on Human Rights provides no basis for such a limitation, which calls into question the capacity of the Human Rights Act to bring rights home to the full extent envisaged by those who designed, debated and agreed the Act.

42. In our view, the principles set out by Lord Hope of Craighead in *Aston Cantlow* [[2003] UKHL 37, at para. 31] would provide an effective basis for protection of the Convention rights. Although the House of Lords in that case did not expressly overrule the decisions in *Poplar* and in *Leonard Cheshire*, it appears that the principles set out by Lord Hope in *Aston Cantlow* are at odds with those earlier decisions of the lower courts. In our view, the approach in *Aston Cantlow* is to be preferred.

[The committee considered four potential solutions, rejecting amendment of the Human Rights Act, using contract to secure protection of convention rights, and the use of guidance but preferring the use of principles of interpretation to assist with the key terms of 'public' and 'function'.]

...

138. In our view, a function is a public one when government has taken responsibility for it. Very few services or acts are in themselves inherently public. There is no doubt that caring for the sick, or educating children, do not involve acts that are inherently public. Health and education services can be and are provided by the State; they can equally well be provided by commercial enterprises, or charitable organisations, or families. To limit the meaning of public functions to those functions which can only (legally) be carried out by the State would be to confine its meaning to a narrow category hardly extending beyond coercive powers. This would leave the Human Rights Act far short of fulfilling the UK's obligation to protect and secure Convention rights effectively, forcing the victims of violations to rely on the Strasbourg court for redress.

139. The range of functions which are generally considered to be public, in that they are generally expected to be performed directly or indirectly by the State, varies over time. The State has in the past used direct delivery by government-owned or controlled bodies to effect the enlargement of the scope of its activities, but in the last 25 years or so has moved significantly in the direction of indirect delivery of many of these same functions, and some new ones.

140. The key test of whether a function is public is whether it is one for which the government has taken responsibility in the public interest. For example, although the various activities involved in care for the sick may be performed by anyone, the State has chosen, through a comprehensive social programme, to provide healthcare to those who wish to receive healthcare from the State rather than privately. This programme is undertaken in the public interest to provide what the government considers to be an important social service. In our view, discharge of duties necessary for provision of the government programme of healthcare is a public function. Discharge of healthcare services, in itself, is not. It is the doing of this work as part of a government programme which denotes a public function, rather than the provision of healthcare in itself. In performing duties as part of the State programme of healthcare, a private organisation is assisting in performing what the State itself has identified as the State's responsibilities...

Public functions and statute

142. On the principles set out above, for a body to discharge a public function, it does not need to do so under direct statutory authority. A State programme or policy, with a basis in statute or otherwise, may

> delegate its powers or duties through contractual arrangements without changing the public nature of those powers or duties. Under section 6 of the Human Rights Act, there should be no distinction between a body providing housing because it itself is required to do so by statute, and a body providing housing because it has contracted with a local authority which is required by statute to provide the service. The loss of a single step in proximity to the statutory duty does not change the nature of the function, nor the nature of its capacity to interfere with Convention rights.
>
> **Public functions and public institutions**
>
> 143. Institutional links with a public body are not necessary to identifying a public function (although by contrast they are relevant to assessing whether a body as a whole is a 'pure public authority' under section 6, and to whether a body is amenable to judicial review). Although institutional proximity to the State may supply evidence that the organisation is delivering on a public or governmental programme, and is therefore performing a public function, it does not, in itself, determine the nature of the function being performed. An organisation could be closely administratively connected with a State authority, whilst performing only private functions, for example the recruitment of staff. Furthermore, the criterion of enmeshment or connection with a State authority has no basis in the jurisprudence of the European Court of Human Rights...

NOTE: This analysis was accepted and adopted by the successor committee in its report HL 77/HC 410 of 2006–07. In the intervening period the courts had not approached the interpretation of s. 6(3)(b) in its preferred manner and it had taken evidence to suggest that there was uncertainty. The Government did intervene in some cases arguing along the lines urged by the JCHR, however, by a three to two majority the House of Lords in *YL* v *Birmingham City Council* [2007] UKHL 27, [2007] 3 WLR 112, rejected this approach to interpretation. The case involved a resident of a care home, operated by Southern Cross a private company, whose place was paid for by the council. Lord Bingham and Baroness Hale did accept the point that this was a situation intended to be covered by s. 6(3)(b). The state has accepted the ultimate responsibility of providing and paying for care of the elderly and infirm who have no other source of assistance. The majority of Lords Scott, Mance and Neuberger, pointed to the fact that Southern Cross was a private company conducting a socially useful business for profit. Lord Mance and Baroness Hale differed in their interpretation of the Strasbourg case law on the State having a positive obligation. Lord Neuberger concluded his speech [171]:

> Finally, it is right to add this. It may well be thought to be desirable that residents in privately owned care homes should be given Convention rights against the proprietors. That is a subject on which there are no doubt opposing views, and I am in no position to express an opinion. However, if the legislature considers such a course appropriate, then it would be right to spell it out in terms, and, in the process, to make it clear whether the rights should be enjoyed by all residents of such care homes, or only certain classes (eg those whose care and accommodation is wholly or partly funded by a local authority).

The government was persuaded to pass legislation which specifically reversed the decision in *YL*. Section 145(1) of the Health and Social Care Act 2008:

> A person ("P") who provides accommodation, together with nursing or personal care, in a care home for an individual under arrangements made with P under the relevant statutory provisions is to be taken for the purposes of subsection (3)(b) of section 6 of the Human Rights Act 1998 ... to be exercising a function of a public nature in doing so.

This legislative provision only deals with the provision of accommodation and personal or nursing care under specific statutory powers. There are still difficulties in determining if a function is a public one or not as shown in the following majority decision by the Court of Appeal on the provision of subsidised housing to those in need by the Trust, a Registered Social Landlord (RSL), and if the termination of a tenancy is a private act. The Trust conceded that it was a hybrid authority.

London & Quadrant Housing Trust v *Weaver*

[2009] EWCA Civ 587

LORD JUSTICE ELIAS:..[41] First, the source of the power will be a relevant factor in determining whether the act in question is in the nature of a private act or not. Second, that will not be decisive, however, since the nature of the activities in issue in the proceedings is also important. This leads on to the third and related proposition, which is that the character of an act is likely to take its colour from the character of the function of which it forms part…

66. The essential question is whether the act of terminating the tenancy is a private act. When considering how to characterise the nature of the act, it is in my view important to focus on the context in which the act occurs; the act cannot be considered in isolation simply asking whether it involves the exercise of a private law power or not. As Lord Mance observed in *YL*, both the source and nature of the activities need to be considered when deciding whether a function is public or not, and in my view the same approach is required when determining whether an act is a private act or not within the meaning of section 6(5). Indeed, the difficulty of distinguishing between acts and functions reinforces that conclusion.

67. In this case there are a number of features which in my judgment bring the act of terminating a social tenancy within the purview of the Human Rights Act.

68. A useful starting point is to analyse the Trust's function of allocating and managing housing with respect to the four criteria identified by Lord Nicholls in paragraph 12 in the *Aston Cantlow* case, reproduced above. First, there is a significant reliance on public finance; there is a substantial public subsidy which enables the Trust to achieve its objectives. This does not involve, as in *YL*, the payment of money by reference to specific services provided but significant capital payments designed to enable the Trust to meet its publicly desirable objectives.

69. Second, although not directly taking the place of local government, the Trust in its allocation of social housing operates in very close harmony with it, assisting it to achieve the authority's statutory duties and objectives. In this context the allocation agreements play a particularly important role and in practice severely circumscribe the freedom of the Trust to allocate properties. This is not simply the exercise of choice by the RSL but is the result of a statutory duty to co-operate. That link is reinforced by the extent to which there has been a voluntary transfer of housing stock from local authorities to RSLs.

70. Third, the provision of subsidised housing, as opposed to the provision of housing itself, is, in my opinion a function which can properly be described as governmental. Almost by definition it is the antithesis of a private commercial activity. The provision of subsidy to meet the needs of the poorer section of the community is typically, although not necessarily, a function which government provides. The Trust, as one of the larger RSLs, makes a valuable contribution to achieving the government's objectives of providing subsidised housing. For similar reasons it seems to me that it can properly be described as providing a public service of a nature described in the Lord Nicholls' fourth factor.

71. Furthermore, these factors, which point in favour of treating its housing functions as public functions, are reinforced by the following considerations. First, the Trust is acting in the public interest and has charitable objectives. I agree with the Divisional Court that this at least places it outside the traditional area of private commercial activity. Second, the regulation to which it is subjected is not designed simply to render its activities more transparent, or to ensure proper standards of performance in the public interest. Rather the regulations over such matters as rent and eviction are designed, at least in part, to ensure that the objectives of government policy with respect to this vulnerable group in society are achieved and that low cost housing is effectively provided to those in need of it. Moreover, it is intrusive regulation on various aspects of allocation and management, and even restricts the power to dispose of land and property.

72. None of these factors taken in isolation would suffice to make the functions of the provision of housing public functions, but I am satisfied that when considered cumulatively, they establish sufficient public flavour to bring the provision of social housing by this particular RSL within that concept. That is particularly so given that their Lordships have emphasised the need to give a broad and generous construction to the concept of a hybrid authority.

Is termination of a tenancy a private act?

73. That still leaves the central question whether the act of termination itself can nonetheless be treated as a private act. Can it be said that since it involves the exercise of a contractual power, it is therefore to be characterised solely as a private act? It is true that in both *Aston Cantlow* and *YL* it is possible to find observations which appear to support an affirmative answer to that question. As I have said, in the *YL* case Lord Scott considered that the termination of the tenancy in that case was a private act, essentially because it involved the exercise of private rights. And in the *Aston Cantlow* case their Lordships focused on the private law source of the right being exercised in concluding that it was a private act.

74. Those decisions certainly lend force to the argument that the character of the act is related to and may be defined by the source of the power being exercised. Where it is essentially contractual, so the argument goes, it necessarily involves the exercise of private rights.

75. In my judgment, that would be a misreading of those decisions. The observations about private acts in *Aston Cantlow* and *YL* were in a context where it had already been determined that the function being exercised was not a public function. I do not consider that their Lordships would have reached the same conclusion if they had found that the nature of the functions in issue in those cases were public functions.

76. In my judgment, the act of termination is so bound up with the provision of social housing that once the latter is seen, in the context of this particular body, as the exercise of a public function, then acts which are necessarily involved in the regulation of the function must also be public acts. The grant of a tenancy and its subsequent termination are part and parcel of determining who should be allowed to take advantage of this public benefit. This is not an act which is purely incidental or supplementary to the principal function, such as contracting out the cleaning of the windows of the Trust's properties. That could readily be seen as a private function of a kind carried on by both public and private bodies. No doubt the termination of such a contract would be a private act (unless the body were a core public authority.)

77. In my opinion, if an act were necessarily a private act because it involved the exercise of rights conferred by private law, that would significantly undermine the protection which Parliament intended to afford to potential victims of hybrid authorities. Public bodies necessarily fulfil their functions by entering into contractual arrangements. It would severely limit the significance of identifying certain bodies as hybrid authorities if the fact that the act under consideration was a contractual act meant that it was a private act falling within section 6(5).

78. Assume, for example, that a local authority delegated some of its statutory functions to a private organisation, such as allocating housing to the homeless. As Lord Mance pointed out in *YL*, the express delegation of public functions in this way would certainly bring the delegatee within the range of bodies for whom the government would be liable under Strasbourg jurisprudence. It surely could not be said that the exercise of contractual powers necessarily involved in the performance of those functions and central to the concerns of the tenant, such as the termination of a tenancy, involved the exercise of private rights which thus escaped the purview of the Human Rights Act. In my judgment that would plainly be in breach of Convention principles.

79. It follows that in my view the act of terminating the tenancy of Mrs Weaver did not constitute an act of a private nature, and was in principle subject to human rights considerations. That may provide relatively limited protection in view of the decision of the House of Lords in *Doherty v Birmingham City Council* [2008] UKHL 57; [2008] 3 WLR 636, following *Kay v Lambeth London Borough Council* [2006] UKHL 10; [2006] 2 AC 465. But the claimant and others in a like situation are entitled to such protection as is available to them applying human rights principles.

80. A point which then arises is whether the protection afforded by the Human Rights Act will extend to all tenants of the Trust who are in social housing or only those in properties which were acquired as a result of state grants. I agree with the Divisional Court that it should be all those in social housing. The effect of the grant is not merely to assist the Trust (and other RSLs similarly placed) in being able to provide low cost housing to the tenants in the properties acquired by the grant; it necessarily has a wider impact, and bears upon its ability to provide social housing generally. Furthermore, it would be highly unsatisfactory if the protection of human rights' law depended upon the fortuitous fact whether a tenant happened to be allocated to housing acquired with a grant or not.

81. It does not follow, however, that all tenants of the Trust will receive the same protection... If the tenants are paying market rents in the normal way, then no question of subsidy arises. It is not obvious why the tenant should be in any different position to tenants in the private sector where human rights principles are inapplicable.

82. The effect of drawing this distinction does not lead to the unattractive consequence which would have resulted had the care home been held to have been a hybrid authority in *YL*, namely that two persons, each subject to the same level of care in the same care home, could be subject to different degrees of legal protection. Indeed, the distinction between those in social housing and those paying market rates merely mirrors the current distinction between those housed in local authority accommodation, who do have human rights protection with respect to evictions, and those housed in the private sector who do not...

LORD JUSTICE RIX: ... [147] ... I do not consider that the Trust's decision to terminate Mrs Weaver's tenancy by seeking possession from the court on mandatory ground 8 justified by her non-payment of rent is properly to be categorised as the exercise of a function of a public nature rather than a private act arising out of contract. In my judgment, although there may be strands based on a multi factorial approach to argue a conclusion to the contrary effect, the essential reasoning of our jurisprudence firmly supports the Trust's appeal.

148. First, Strasbourg jurisprudence does not suggest that the Trust is amenable to Convention liability or that the United Kingdom's liability can be invoked in respect of such an act.

149. Secondly, I cannot find in the decisions of domestic jurisprudence support for Mrs Weaver's case... As for *YL*, the statutory underpinnings there, for the reasons preferred by the minority, were much stronger than in the present case, for statute required the provision of care to a vulnerable person in need of welfare services. Lord Bingham himself emphasised the significance for him of the facts that statute required the *provision* of services and that the services concerned went beyond the accommodation and extended to *care* for the particularly vulnerable. In the present case, however, it is quite clear and common ground that statute does not require the provision of housing accommodation (see para [44]), and there is no question of Mrs Weaver being a particularly vulnerable person to whom care and medical services must also be provided. I am doubtful that even the minority view in *YL* would support the divisional court's declarations.

150. Thirdly, it seems to me that the argument in this case, reflected in the judgments of the divisional court, has been inappropriately influenced by the structure of the dispute in *YL*... it is clear that in our case a major issue ought to be whether, even on the assumption that allocation is a function of a public nature, termination under the terms of the tenancy is of the same nature or alternatively is of the nature of a private act.

151. Fourthly, under the influence of the structure of the argument in our case, submissions have proceeded from the concept that "management and allocation" is an all-embracing public function which includes termination... I do not accept that that is a satisfactory way to analyse the housing function... "Management" is a vast and undifferentiated area which, as it seems to me, inevitably includes functions and acts which are most unlikely to be of a public nature: such as the commercial acquisition or even development of property, or the financing of it (even on the basis that public subsidy plays an important role, as to which see below), or the maintenance and repair of it, or the daily grind of administering a very substantial portfolio of property of all kinds... the divisional court has proceeded on the basis that management is essentially a function of either a public or a private nature and chosen between these extremes in favour of the former. It has seemed to me that both sides of this dispute have had an interest in advancing an argument which would dispose, once and for all, of the issue whether an RSL is for all purposes a hybrid public authority or not. I very much doubt, however, that such an issue can be debated in this way.

152. Fifthly, my concern becomes increasingly acute when the proposition is that because management is a public function, then allocation is, or perhaps vice versa, and because allocation is, therefore termination is. *YL* is clear authority for the proposition that even where a public authority has a statutory duty both to arrange and to provide care and accommodation for the most vulnerable of our society, the fact that the arrangement may be of an inherently governmental or public nature does not mean

that their provision is. It seems to me that, as compared with the case of care and accommodation in a care home, a fortiori that is true of the case of housing, even social housing. Moreover, in as much as it is suggested that because allocation is a function of a public nature, therefore termination is, I would respectfully disagree. Allocation arises under arrangements made between an RSL and a local authority, where the local authority makes use of such arrangements to fulfil their statutory duty to have an allocation policy. However, once an allocation has been made and a prospective tenant has been accepted by an RSL as its tenant, the tenant then enters into a contractual tenancy with the RSL, and their relationship thenceforward is governed, just like any tenant's relationship with his or her landlord, by private law. That remains the case despite the relevance of regulation. Moreover, the statutes which govern the recovery of possession apply to an RSL's social housing tenancies and other landlords' tenancies alike. All the authorities I have considered stress the importance of private contractual rights. *Poplar's* decision was driven by very special factors.

153. While it is inevitable that core public authorities who enter into contractual tenancies are subject to the Convention, it seems to me to require special circumstances to impose Convention solutions on top of the working out of private law contracts of private bodies, even if such bodies are also in some respects hybrid public authorities.'. Where, however, as here, the contract concerned is one so well known to private/commercial life as a tenancy agreement, where such contracts are being entered into in almost identical or standard form with social housing tenants and non social housing tenants alike, it seems to me to be counter-intuitive to suppose that the working out of that contract as between a private (non-governmental) landlord and a tenant can depend on Convention rights. An exception might be where public functions fill the whole or a substantial space of that contract. I see no reason, however, for saying that that is the situation here. On the contrary, a contract like a tenancy contract, for all that it is hedged around by statutory provisions, is made for the specific purpose of determining the rights between the parties...

155. Seventhly, there is nothing about the nature of the Trust, or the typical RSL, to promote the concept that in the everyday administration of its tenancy agreements it is performing functions of a public nature. Although it is a charity, it has independent corporate status and is conducted by an independent board of directors and owned by its private shareholders. As a charity, it operates for the public benefit rather than for commercial profit, but its operations are essentially in the private and business world, rather than in the world of government, for all that. Richards LJ in the court below and Elias LJ in this court consider that the Trust's charitable status places it outside the sphere of commercial providers. In my judgment, however, the world of charity is essentially private, and, although a charity does not operate for profit in the ordinary way, nevertheless when its function is to provide a service such as housing in return for the payment of rent and to do so on a substantial scale (the Trust owns 33,000 dwellings), it has to operate according to (for want of a better word) business disciplines or else it is very likely to fail. It seems to me that what Lord Neuberger said about charities at para 135 of *YL* puts them into the private world rather than into the world of those performing functions of a public nature. ..

156. Eighthly, the majority of the Trust's capital finance comes from private lenders and the proceeds of housing sales, while a very substantial but decreasing minority comes from public grants... The Trust's revenues come from its rents. The typical ratio of private finance to public grant across the RSL sector as a whole is 2:1. Richards LJ and my Lords in this court see the substantial degree of public subsidy in the form of the public grants as a significant factor in determining that everything that an RSL does by way of social housing it does in exercise of a public function. I accept that public subsidy is a factor in the overall assessment; and that Lord Neuberger says in *YL* that a general subsidy is in this respect more telling than the defrayment by the public purse of the cost of individuals (whereas Baroness Hale took the opposite view). ..

157. ... Whereas I accept that public finance is an element in the equation, I would be sceptical about allowing it, or any particular form of it, to play a dominant role in the assessment.

158. Ninthly, there is the difficult question of public policy addressed by Lord Neuberger in *YL* at para 152 (see para [40] above). His prescription is that the competing views about policy render this factor neutral. As such, they do not strengthen the case for hybrid status. I would add this further consideration. Lord Neuberger spoke of the policy of contracting out as being to avoid the legal constraints and disadvantages of operating as a core governmental authority. I would diffidently suggest that there is another,

possibly even more significant, ambition of the policy of moving into the private sector what at some earlier period may have been carried on in the public sector. That is a recognition that, where large business operations have to be carried out, even when such operations are not governed purely by markets but have elements of social policy about them, they are better carried out by private expertise in the management of such operations, whose experience and efficiency nevertheless redound to the public interest.

159. Tenthly, and finally, the public welfare concern which all feel for those in need of social housing, and I mean to include government, the courts, the RSLs themselves and the public at large in that "all", is addressed or capable of being addressed in many different ways: in statutory provision, in regulation, in public subsidy, in the exercise of charitable status, in the contractual arrangements between local authorities and RSLs, in the form of tenancy agreements, in the expertise of RSLs, and in the ongoing duty of local authorities to assess and to allocate accommodation for those in need. It is, however, unnecessary to give to decisions, under contract, of an essentially private nature an artificial status as acts of a public nature or in performance of public functions, in order to ensure proper protection.

160. In sum, when I consider the various factors which the authorities teach us to consider, I can find insufficient to support the conclusion that in the exercise of its contractual rights under its tenancy agreement the Trust is acting in the public rather than in the private sphere, or in performance of a function of a public nature. While it is conceded by the Trust that in certain, limited but irrelevant respects the Trust is a hybrid public authority for the purpose of section 6(3)(b), I am sceptical how far the management of social housing by an RSL can be brought within the meaning of that sub-section. Even if allocation is to be brought within that subsection, that is not the same as provision of accommodation. In my judgment, however, for the purpose of section 6(5) the Trust's decision to exercise its contractual rights by invoking a claim for possession under ground 8 cannot be attacked in public law or by reference to the Convention.

■ QUESTION

Is it contrary to constitutional principle that the protections contained in the HRA should vary with the method of service delivery, whether it is directly provided by a core public authority, or under contract?

(b) Does the Convention apply between private litigants?

A major question relating to the impact which the Human Rights Act will have is whether it imposes an obligation on courts to apply the Convention in determining cases between private litigants. As s. 6(3)(a) includes a court or tribunal within the definition of a 'public authority', this has given rise to speculation whether the Human Rights Act has horizontal effect between private individuals and bodies. The extracts below give a flavour of the differing views which existed prior to the implementation of the Human Rights Act and are followed by extracts from an important case before the High Court, Family Division, involving arguments based on the Convention Art. 8 right to privacy.

I. Leigh and L. Lustgarten, 'Making Rights Real: the Courts, Remedies and the Human Rights Act'

(1999) 58 *Cambridge Law Journal* 509, 512–513

... One of the most contested provisions of the Act is the apparently innocuous section (s. 6(3)(a)) which includes a court or tribunal within the definition of a 'public authority'. Since 'public authorities' act unlawfully where they violate a person's Convention rights unless clearly required to do so by legislation, there is some debate about whether the effect of including courts is to require re-interpretation of the common law, even that applicable between private parties, or whether the section has more limited impact. Space precludes full discussion here of the arguments concerning full horizontal effect, but a straightforward case can be made that wherever a court has a procedural, evidential, or remedial discretion, whether under common law or statute and in criminal or civil litigation, a decision about how to use the discretion will constitute a judicial 'act' under section 6. Convention rights are therefore relevant to a number of judicial decisions affecting a person's liberties in the course of proceedings, quite apart from the substantive law to be applied. In the criminal sphere these might include: extensions of detention in police custody, delay before prosecution, decisions to prosecute, the adjournment of proceedings, the grant of legal aid, imposition of bail conditions, orders relating to pre-trial disclosure, the imposition of publication restrictions or bans, the treatment of vulnerable or protected witnesses, the mandatory or discretionary exclusion of evidence (under Police and Criminal Evidence Act, ss. 76 & 78), evidential inferences from silence, and the effect of conditions imposed on community sentences such as probation, community service orders, curfews and tagging orders. In the civil sphere examples would include discretions arising under the wardship jurisdiction and concerning the best interests of the child under the Children Act 1989 in other contexts such as custody, under the Contempt of Court Act 1981, s. 10 (identification of sources of information in limited circumstances), and in the grant of equitable orders. Prior to the Act, English courts have already recognised that the Convention may be relevant to a number of these discretionary decisions, and in others the failure to do so has resulted in adverse rulings from Strasbourg. The approach has, however, been somewhat haphazard. While the Convention has been taken into account on occasion, it has rarely been decisive. If our interpretation of the reach of section 6 is accepted a more rigorous approach will be needed in future: the test will be the *impact* of the discretionary decision on a person's Convention rights. There will be no possibility of balancing prejudice to those rights against other factors, except within the permitted restrictions of the Convention articles themselves. This approach is closer to that of the ECtHR which has held in a number of instances that member states are liable for infringements of the Convention resulting solely from the terms of court orders or, indeed, the failure of a court to grant effective protection of a right.

Lord Irvine of Lairg LC, Address to the Third Clifford Chance Conference on the Impact of a Bill of Rights on English Law

28 November 1997

Clause 6 makes it clear that 'public authority' includes a court and a tribunal which exercises functions in relation to legal proceedings. That inclusion, as this audience will recognise, does more than asking the courts to interpret legislation compatibly with the Convention. It imposes on them to a duty to act compatibly with the Convention.

We believe that it is right as a matter of principle for the courts to have the duty of acting compatibly with the Convention. They will be under this duty not only in cases involving other public authorities but also in developing the common law in deciding cases between individuals. It has been suggested that the courts should exclude Convention considerations altogether from cases between individuals. We do not think that that would be justifiable. Nor, indeed, do we think it would be practicable. The courts already bring Convention considerations to bear in cases before them. I have no doubt that they will continue to do so in developing the common law. Clause 3 makes this clear by requiring the courts to interpret legislation compatibly with the Convention rights and to the fullest extent possible in all cases coming before them.

You would not expect me to leave this subject without touching on privacy.

I would not agree with any proposition that the courts as public authorities will be obliged to fashion a law on privacy because of the terms of the Bill. That is simply not so. If it were so, whenever a law cannot be found either in the statute book or as a rule of common law to protect a Convention right, the courts would in effect be obliged to legislate by way of judicial decision to make one. That is not the true position. If it were—in my view, it is not—the courts would also have in effect to legislate where Parliament had acted, but incompatibly, with the Convention. Let us suppose that an Act of Parliament provides for detention on suspicion of drug trafficking but that the legislation goes too far and conflicts with Article 5. The court would so hold and would make a declaration of incompatibility. The scheme of the Bill is that Parliament may act to remedy a failure where the judges cannot.

In my opinion, the court is not obliged to remedy the failure by legislating via the common law either wherever a Convention right is infringed by incompatible legislation or wherever, because of the absence of legislation—say, privacy legislation—a Convention right is left unprotected.

In my view, the courts may not act as legislators and grant new remedies for infringement of Convention rights unless the common law itself enables them to develop new rights or remedies. I believe that the true view is that the courts will be able to adapt and develop the common law by relying on existing domestic principles in the laws of trespass, nuisance, copyright, confidence and the like, to fashion a common law right to privacy. I say this because members of the higher judiciary have already themselves said so.

The experience of continental countries shows that their cautious development of privacy law has been based on domestic law case by case, although they have also had regard to the Convention. My view is that any privacy law developed by the judges will be a better law after incorporation of the Convention because the judges will have to balance and have regard to Articles 10 and 8, giving Article 10 its due high value.

M. Hunt, 'The "Horizontal Effect" of the Human Rights Act'

[1998] *Public Law* 423, 438–442

It is clear beyond argument that *direct* horizontal application is not intended. This much is immediately apparent from the fact that the obligation to act compatibly with the Convention in section 6(1) of the Act is expressed to be binding only on public authorities, and that section 6 goes on to give examples of what is included in the definition of public authority. The clear implication is that there are persons who are *not* bound to act compatibly with the Convention at all; and indeed, by virtue of section 6(5), even the hybrid bodies made public authorities by section 6(3)(b), and therefore subject to the section 6(1) obligation, are not bound by the Convention in respect of those of their acts which are of a private nature. This inference, that the Act does not have direct horizontal effect, is further reinforced by the absence of any references to private individuals or organisations anywhere in the Act.

To put the matter beyond doubt, the Lord Chancellor, in his speech on Second Reading explaining the main provisions of the Bill, made clear that the Government had decided that:

> a provision of this kind [cl. 6(1)] should apply only to public authorities, however defined, and not to private individuals. That reflects the arrangements for taking cases to the Convention institutions in Strasbourg. The Convention had its origins in a desire to protect people from the misuse of power by the state, rather than from the actions of private individuals.... Clause 6 does not impose a liability on organisations which have no public functions at all.

Indeed, read in isolation, these explanatory comments about who is 'bound' by the Act might even be thought to give some sustenance to a vertical reading of the legislation's application. It is extremely important, however, that they are seen as precluding *direct* horizontal effect, rather than as endorsing a *vertical* approach. That this is the Government's intention is abundantly clear from the wider context provided not only by provisions in the rest of the Act, but by the parliamentary debates which preceded their adoption. In particular, the rejection of a purely vertical approach, and embrace of something more, is clear on the face of the provision that is without doubt the single most important feature of the legislation as far as determining the scope of its application is concerned: the express inclusion of courts and tribunals within the definition of public authorities obliged by section 6(1) to act compatibly with the Convention.

This inclusion of courts and tribunals in the definition of public authorities who are subject to the obligation in section 6(1) to act compatibly with the Convention is of great significance for the horizontality of Convention rights under the Human Rights Act.... [T]he effect of making courts expressly bound is to give a greater degree of horizontal effect to fundamental rights....

It is true that there is no clause in the UK's Human Rights Act expressly saying that the Convention rights 'apply to all law', or some phrase capable of making clear that the common law is subject to the Convention. It is also true that the interpretive obligation contained in section 3(1) relates only to legislation and not to the common law. But neither of these could he characterised as significant omissions in view of the clarity about the overall purpose of the Act and the unequivocal nature of the obligation imposed on courts and tribunals by section 6. The whole scheme of the Human Rights Act is premised on the proposition that the only domestic law which is not to be subjected to Convention rights is legislation which cannot possibly be given a meaning compatible with Convention rights. The nature of the section 6(1) obligation on courts and tribunals is in keeping with that purpose. Whereas section 3(1) of the Act imposes an *interpretive* obligation on courts in relation to statute law, requiring courts to read and give effect to legislation in a way which is compatible with Convention rights, but subject to the limitation that the legislative language must be capable of bearing the meaning necessary to make it compatible, section 6 goes further. By making courts and tribunals 'public authorities' it imposes a *duty* on them to act compatibly with the Convention, including when they decide purely private disputes between private parties governed solely by the common law.

That this is the intention behind the inclusion of courts and tribunals in section 6(1) was confirmed in the strongest possible terms by both the Lord Chancellor and Lord Williams of Mostyn during the Bill's Committee stage in the House of Lords. An amendment was proposed by Lord Wakeham, the head of the Press Complaints Commission, designed specifically to preclude the possibility of the legislation having *any* horizontal effect. The amendment proposed that the obligation to act compatibly with the Convention in section 6(1) not apply 'where the public authority is a court or tribunal and the parties to the proceedings before it do not include any public authority'. Its purpose was avowedly to confine the Convention right to having vertical effect only: to prevent them being used by the courts in disputes between private individuals, and in particular 'to stop the development of a common law of privacy'.

The Lord Chancellor, responding at the end of the debate on this proposed amendment, left no doubt about the intention behind the inclusion of courts in section 6(1):

> We...believe that it is right as a matter of principle for the courts to have the duty of acting compatibly with the Convention not only in cases involving other public authorities but also in developing the common law in deciding cases between individuals. Why should they not? In preparing this Bill, we have taken the view that it is the other course, that of excluding Convention considerations altogether from cases between individuals, which would have to be justified. We do not think that that would be justifiable; nor, indeed, do we think it would be practicable.

Lord Williams similarly made clear, in response to a different amendment, the Government's view that courts and tribunals 'are in a very similar position to obvious public authorities, such as government departments, in that all their acts are to be treated as being of such a public nature as to engage the Convention'.

The explanatory statements leave no room for doubt as to the intention behind the inclusion of courts and tribunals within the definition of 'public authority' for the purposes of section 6(1). It is to ensure that all law, other than unavoidably incompatible legislation, is to be subjected to Convention rights, which thereby attain the all-pervasive status of which the White Paper boasts. There it is made explicit that the Convention rights 'will be brought much more fully into the jurisprudence of the courts throughout the United Kingdom, and their interpretation...far more subtly and powerfully woven into our law'. That is consistent also with the clear policy decision not to have a special court or separate procedure for human rights cases, but for the questions to be dealt with as they arise by the ordinary courts in ordinary cases. As Lord Irvine made clear in his Tom Sargant Memorial Lecture, the Government's explicit purpose in choosing the model it has introduced is that 'the Convention rights must *pervade all law* and all court systems'.

That a degree of horizontal effect in purely private disputes between private parties is explicitly envisaged by the Government is therefore without doubt, but that leaves one important question unanswered: how far towards full horizontality does it go? In particular, does it go beyond the present position, in which UK courts are undoubtedly free to 'take the Convention into account' when interpreting or developing the common law, or beyond even the indirect horizontal effect of the Canadian (and German) approach, in which courts are under an obligation to take human rights 'values' into account in interpreting the common law?

It seems quite clear that the model which has been chosen goes considerably further in the direction of horizontality than either of these. When the Act comes into force, courts will not merely have a power to 'consider' the Convention when interpreting the common law in private disputes. nor will they merely have an obligation to take into account Convention 'values'. Rather they will be under an unequivocal duty to act compatibly with Convention rights. In some cases, this will undoubtedly require them actively to modify or develop the common law in order to achieve such compatibility. Precisely where the line is drawn between legitimate judicial development of the common law and illegitimate judicial 'legislation' is a matter of degree and, ultimately, a matter of legal and political philosophy. The Lord Chancellor in the course of the parliamentary debates sought to indicate that courts will not be empowered by the Human Rights Act to go beyond their legitimate function of incremental common law development, for example by creating entirely new causes of action, for that would be to tread on Parliament's toes. But it remains to be seen whether judges will be as cautious as the Lord Chancellor envisages or more adventurous in plugging the gaps in the common law's scheme of remedies by imaginative analogising from existing causes of action.

The most likely position, then, is that the Convention will be regarded as applying to all law, and therefore as potentially relevant in proceedings between private parties, but will fall short of being *directly* horizontally effective, because it will not confer any new private causes of action against individuals in respect of breach of Convention rights. This requires a distinction to be drawn between the evolution of existing causes of action over time and the creation of entirely new causes of action against private parties. It is beyond argument that the Human Rights Act does not do the latter, but the courts will undoubtedly develop over time causes of action such as trespass, confidence, and copyright, as the Lord Chancellor himself accepted in Parliament. Law which already exists and governs private relationships must be interpreted, applied and if necessary developed so as to achieve compatibility with the Convention. But where no cause of action exists, and there is therefore no law to apply, the courts cannot invent new causes of action, as that would be to embrace full horizontality which has clearly been precluded by Parliament.

NOTE: In the case which follows the Family Division confirmed that the doctrine of confidence had developed into a privacy remedy, placing emphasis on the relevance of the Convention rights.

Thompson and Venables v *News Group Newspapers Ltd*

[2001] 2 WLR 1038, Family Division

T and V had been convicted as children of the murder of two-year-old James Bulger and sentenced to detention during Her Majesty's pleasure in 1993. They were protected by injunctions issued by the trial judge for an unlimited period restricting publication of further information about them. In July 2000, four newspapers applied to the court for clarification of the injunctions in light of T's and V's impending majority. Subsequently T and V issued the present proceedings in which they sought injunctions against specific newspapers and all the world to protect all information about, *inter alia*, their whereabouts, movements, appearance, and their new identities on release on the basis that such injunctions were necessary to protect their rights of confidentiality and their rights to life and freedom from persecution and harassment conferred by the European Convention. Dame Elizabeth Butler-Sloss P granted permanent injunctions against all the world because of the disastrous consequences such disclosure might have for them, not least the serious possibility of physical harm or death.

DAME ELIZABETH BUTLER-SLOSS P:

...

C. The law: jurisdiction to grant an injunction

Application of the Convention

24 Before turning to the question of whether there is jurisdiction to grant injunctions, the preliminary issue is whether the Convention applies to this case. It is clear that, although operating in the public domain and fulfilling a public service, the defendant newspapers cannot sensibly be said to come within the definition of public authority in section 6(1) of the Human Rights Act 1998. Consequently, Convention rights are not directly enforceable against the defendants: see section 7(1) and section 8 of the 1998 Act. That is not, however, the end of the matter, since the court is a public authority (see section 6(3)) and must itself act in a way compatible with the Convention (see section 6(1)) and have regard to European jurisprudence: see section 2. In a private family law case, *Glaser* v *United Kingdom* [2000] 3 FCR 193, the European Court of Human Rights, sitting as a Chamber, declared admissible an application by a father seeking the enforcement of contact orders made in private law proceedings between him and the mother of his children. They considered the potential breach of the father's rights under article 8 and article 6. The court said, at pp 208–209, para 63:

> 'The essential object of article 8 is to protect the individual against arbitrary interference by public authorities. There may, however, be positive obligations inherent in an effective "respect" for family life. Those obligations may involve the adoption of measures designed to secure respect for family life even in the sphere of relations between individuals, including both the provision of a regulatory framework of adjudicatory and enforcement machinery protecting individuals' rights and the implementation, where appropriate, of specific steps (see among other authorities, *X and Y* v *The Netherlands* (1985) 8 EHRR 235 and mutatis mutandis, *Osman* v *United Kingdom* (1998) 29 EHRR 245). In both the negative and United Kingdom positive contexts, regard must be had to the fair balance which has to be struck between the competing interests of the individual and the

community, including other concerned third parties, and the state's margin of appreciation (see, among other authorities, *Keegan* v *Ireland* (1994) 18 EHRR 342, 362, para 49).'

25 The court held that, in that case, the authorities, including the courts, struck a fair balance between the competing interests and did not fail in their responsibilities to protect the father's right to respect for family life. This decision underlines the positive obligations of the courts including, where necessary, the provision of a regulatory framework of adjudicatory and enforcement machinery in order to protect the rights of the individual. The decisions of the European Court of Human Rights in *Glaser's* case and *X and Y* v *The Netherlands* (1985) 8 EHRR 235, seem to dispose of any argument that a court is not to have regard to the Convention in private law cases. In *Douglas* v *Hello! Ltd* [2001] 2 WLR 992, 1027, para 133, Sedley LJ held that section 12(4) of the Human Rights Act 1998 'puts beyond question the direct applicability of at least one article of the Convention as between one private party to litigation and another—in the jargon, its horizontal effect'.

26 In the light of the judgments in *Douglas's* case, I am satisfied that I have to apply article 10 directly to the present case.

27 That obligation on the court does not seem to me to encompass the creation of a free-standing cause of action based directly upon the articles of the Convention, although that proposition is advanced by Mr Fitzgerald as a fall-back position, if all else fails. The duty on the court, in my view, is to act compatibly with Convention rights in adjudicating upon existing common law causes of action, and that includes a positive as well as a negative obligation.

The jurisdictional basis for an injunction

28 ... The principal submission in favour of the existence of the court's power is based upon the law of confidence, taking into account the implementation of the Human Rights Act 1998....

The jurisdiction based on confidence

30 As I have already said, in my view, the claimants in private law proceedings cannot rely upon a free-standing application under the Convention. In their submissions, the claimants, supported by the Attorney General and the Official Solicitor, relied upon the common law right to confidence. The tort of breach of confidence is a recognised cause of action. Megarry J in *Coco* v *A N Clark (Engineers) Ltd* [1969] RPC 41, 47, identified three essentials of the tort of breach of confidence: (1) the evidence must have 'the necessary quality of confidence about it'; (2) the information 'must have been imparted in circumstances importing an obligation of confidence'; (3) there must be an 'unauthorised use of the information to the detriment of the party communicating it'.

31 In *Attorney General* v *Guardian Newspapers (No 2)* [1990] 1 AC 109, 281 Lord Goff of Chieveley said:

'I start with the broad general principle (which I do not intend in any way to be definitive) that a duty of confidence arises when confidential information comes to the knowledge of a person (the confidant) in circumstances where he has notice, or is held to have agreed, that the information is confidential, with the effect that it would be just in all the circumstances that he should be precluded from disclosing the information to others... in the vast majority of cases... the duty of confidence will arise from a transaction or relationship between the parties... But it is well settled that a duty of confidence may arise in equity independently of such cases...'

32 He raised three limiting principles, at p 282:

> 'that the principle of confidentiality only applies to information to the extent that it is confidential. In particular, once it has entered what is usually called the public domain (which means no more than that the information in question is so generally accessible that, in all the circumstances, it cannot be regarded as confidential) then, as a general rule, the principle of confidentiality can have no application to it... The second limiting principle is that the duty of confidence applies neither to useless information, nor to trivia. There is no need for me to develop this point. The third limiting principle is of far greater importance. It is that, although the basis of the law's protection of confidence is that there is a public interest that confidences should be preserved and protected by the law, nevertheless that public interest may be outweighed by some other countervailing public interest which favours disclosure... It is this limiting principle which may require a court to

carry out a balancing operation, weighing the public interest in maintaining confidence against a countervailing public interest favouring disclosure.'

33 The confidentiality sought to be protected in the present case is clearly not trivial. Lord Goff's third limiting principle cannot, I would respectfully suggest, now stand in the light of section 12 of the Human Rights Act 1998 and article 10(1) of the Convention, which together give an enhanced importance to freedom of expression and consequently to the right of the press to publish.

Article 10: freedom of expression

34 Article 10, as applied to the media, is central to this case....

35 In section 12 of the Human Rights Act 1998, special provisions are made in relation to applications to restrict freedom of expression. Section 12(4) states: 'The court must have particular regard to the importance of the Convention right to freedom of expression...'

36 There is no doubt, therefore, that Parliament has placed great emphasis upon the importance of article 10 and the protection of freedom of expression, inter alia for the press and for the media. The Human Rights Act 1998 and the Convention do not, however, establish new law. They reinforce and give greater weight to the principles already established in our case law. In *R* v *Secretary of State for the Home Department, Ex p Simms* [2000] 2 AC 115, 126, Lord Steyn said:

'Freedom of expression is, of course, intrinsically important: it is valued for its own sake. But it is well recognised that it is also instrumentally important. It serves a number of broad objectives. First, it promotes the self-fulfilment of individuals in society. Secondly, in the famous words of Holmes J (echoing John Stuart Mill), "the best test of truth is the power of the thought to get itself accepted in the competition of the market": *Abrams* v *United States* (1919) 250 US 616, 630 per Holmes J (dissenting). Thirdly, freedom of speech is the lifeblood of democracy. The free flow of information and ideas informs political debate. It is a safety valve: people are more ready to accept decisions that go against them if they can in principle seek to influence them. It acts as a brake on the abuse of power by public officials. It facilitates the exposure of errors in the governance and administration of justice of the country: see Stone, Seidman, Sunstein & Tushnet, *Constitutional Law*, 3rd ed (1996), pp 1078–1086.'

[Her Ladyship also quoted from the judgments of Hoffmann LJ in *R* v *Central Independent Television plc* [1994] Fam 192, 202–204 and Munby J in *Kelly* v *British Broadcasting Corpn* [2001] 2 WLR 253, 264 before continuing.]

39 In *Sunday Times* v *United Kingdom* (1979) 2 EHRR 245 the European Court of Human Rights said, at p. 281, para 65: 'The court is faced not with a choice between two conflicting principles, but with a principle of freedom of expression that is subject to a number of exceptions which must be narrowly interpreted.'

40 However, more recently, in *Douglas v Hello! Ltd* [2001] IP & T 391 at 426–427 (paras 136–137), Sedley LJ said:

'... by virtue of s 12(1) and (4) [of the 1998 Act] the qualifications set out in art 10(2) are as relevant as the right set out in art 10(1). This means, for example, the reputations and rights of others—not only but not least their convention rights—are as material as the defendant's right of free expression. So is the prohibition on the use of one party's convention rights to injure the convention rights of others. Any other approach to s 12 would in my judgment violate s 3 ... the much-quoted remark of Hoffmann J in *R v Central Independent Television plc* [1994] 3 All ER 641 at 652, [1994] Fam 192 at 203 that freedom of speech "is a trump card which always wins" came in a passage which expressly qualified the proposition as lying "outside the established exceptions (or any new ones which parliament may enact in accordance with its obligations under the convention)". If freedom of expression is to be impeded, in other words, it must be on a cogent ground recognised by law ... s 12 of the 1998 Act requires the court to have regard to art 10 ... this cannot ... give the art 10(1) right to freedom of expression a presumptive priority over other rights. What it does require the court to consider is art 10(2) along with 10(1), and by doing so bring into the frame the conflicting right to privacy. This right, contained in art 8 and reflected in English law, is in turn qualified in both contexts by the right of others to free expression. The outcome, which self evidently has to be the same under both articles, is determined principally by considerations of proportionality.'

41 In his Goodman Lecture on 22 May 1996, Lord Hoffmann referred to his judgment in *R* v *Central Television plc* [1994] Fam 192 and said:

> 'Some people have read that to mean that freedom of speech always trumps other rights and values. But that is not what I said. I said only that in order to be put [in] the balance against freedom of speech, another interest must fall within some established exception which could be justified under article 10 of the European Convention.'

42 Mr Desmond Browne [counsel for the defendants] submitted that it was not a balancing operation between the right to freedom of expression against any legitimate aim falling within article 10(2). It would seem to me however that, whether it is called a balancing process or any other description, the conflict that may arise between article 10(1) and article 10(2) has to be resolved and the legitimate aim in restricting freedom of expression within the exceptions in article 10(2) given appropriate weight according to the facts of the individual case. Sedley LJ said, in *Douglas*'s case, at p 1028G–H, para 136: 'the qualifications set out in article 10(2) are as relevant as the right set out in article 10(1)'.

43 There would not however be such a juggling act in a case which did not fall within the exceptions set out in article 10(2). It is clear however that, to obtain an injunction to restrain the media from publication of information, it requires a strong case. Brooke LJ said in *Douglas*'s case, at p 1006, para 49: 'Although the right to freedom of expression is not in every case the ace of trumps, it is a powerful card to which the courts of this country must always pay appropriate respect.' And Sedley LJ said, at p 1029, para 136: 'If freedom of expression is to be impeded... it must be on cogent grounds recognised by law.'

44 The onus of proving the case that freedom of expression must be restricted is firmly upon the applicant seeking the relief. The restrictions sought must, in the circumstances of the present case, be shown to be in accordance with the law, justifiable as necessary to satisfy a strong and pressing social need, convincingly demonstrated, to restrain the press in order to protect the rights of the claimants to confidentiality, and proportionate to the legitimate aim pursued. The right to confidence is, however, a recognised exception within article 10(2) and the tort of breach of confidence was the domestic remedy upon which the European Commission, in *Earl Spencer* v *United Kingdom* (1998) 25 EHRR CD 105, declared inadmissible an application by Lord and Lady Spencer on the basis that they had not exhausted their domestic remedies.

45 I turn to the three other articles of the Convention which are said by the claimants to be engaged in this case, and which clearly I must consider alongside article 10.

Article 2: right to life

46 If the claimants' case is made out, article 2 is clearly engaged. In *Osman* v *United Kingdom* (1998) 29 EHRR 245, the European Court of Human Rights held that the provisions of article 2 enjoined a positive obligation upon contracting states to take measures to secure the right to life. In that case it was the failure of the police to act to protect a family from criminal acts including murder. The European Court said, at p 305, paras 115–116:

> 'The court notes that the first sentence of article 2(1) enjoins the state not only to refrain from the intentional and unlawful taking of life, but also to take appropriate steps to safeguard the lives of those within its jurisdiction... it must be established to its satisfaction that the authorities knew or ought to have known at the time of the existence of a real and immediate risk to the life of an identified individual or individuals from the criminal acts of a third party and that they failed to take measures within the scope of their powers which, judged reasonably, might have been expected to avoid that risk.'

Article 3: prohibition of torture

47 Article 3 is equally potentially applicable, if I am satisfied as to the strength of the claimants' case. Other than in the specified exceptions in article 2, there is to be no derogation from the rights set out in these two articles.

Article 8: right to respect for private and family life

48 Article 8 is also potentially applicable....

49 In *X and Y* v *The Netherlands* (1985) 8 EHRR 235, the European Court of Human Rights held that, in a case where the prosecutor took no action on a complaint by a father of a sexual assault on his mentally

incapacitated daughter of 16, that the state had failed to protect a vulnerable individual from a criminal violation of her physical and moral integrity by another private individual. A violation of article 8 was found. The court said, at pp 239–240, para 23:

> 'The court recalls that although the object of article 8 is essentially that of protecting the individual against arbitrary interference by the public authorities, it does not merely compel the state to abstain from such interference: in addition to this primarily negative undertaking, there may be positive obligations inherent in an effective respect for private or family life. These obligations may involve the adoption of measures designed to secure respect for private life even in the sphere of the relations of individuals between themselves.'

50 Sedley LJ said in *Douglas v Hello! Ltd* [2001] IP & T 391 at 425–426 (paras 133–134):

> 'The other point, well made by Mr Tugendhat, is that it is "the convention right" to freedom of expression which both triggers the section (see s 12(1) [of the 1998 Act]) and to which particular regard is to be had. That convention right, when one turns to it, is qualified in favour of the reputation and rights of others and the protection of information received in confidence. In other words you cannot have particular regard to art 10 without having equally particular regard at the very least to art 8 ... [Mr Carr] balked at what Mr Tughendhat submitted, and I agree, was the necessary extension of the subsection's logic. A newspaper, say, intends to publish an article about an individual who learns of it and fears, on tenable grounds, that it will put his life in danger. The newspaper, also on tenable grounds, considers his fear unrealistic ... it seems to me inescapable that s 12(4) makes the right to life, which is protected by art 2 and implicitly recognised by art 10(2), as relevant as the right of free expression to the court's decision; and in so doing it also makes art 17 (which prohibits the abuse of rights) relevant.'

51 Although the Court of Appeal was concerned with an entirely different situation, the observations of Sedley LJ in *Douglas's* case are highly relevant to and helpful in the task facing me in the present case where I have to resolve a potential conflict between article 10 on the one hand and articles 2, 3 and 8 on the other hand.

[Her Ladyship went on to examine the evidence upon which the claimants relied in support of the applications for permanent injunctions and the evidence adduced by the defendant newspapers.]

E. Conclusions on jurisdiction

75 My conclusions on the application of the principles of English law to the facts of this case, are based on the assumption that the case put forward by the claimants has been established.

76 I am, of course, well aware that, until now, the courts have not granted injunctions in the circumstances which arise in this case. It is equally true that the claimants are uniquely notorious. On the basis of the evidence presented to me, their case is exceptional. I recognise also that the threats to the life and physical safety of the claimants do not come from those against whom the injunctions are sought. But the media are uniquely placed to provide the information that would lead to the risk that others would take the law into their own hands and commit crimes against the claimants.

77 The starting point is, however, the well-recognised position of the press, and their right and duty to be free to publish, even in circumstances described by Hoffmann LJ in *R* v *Central Independent Television plc* [1994] Fam 192. As Brooke LJ said in *Douglas* v *Hello! Ltd* [2001] 2 WLR 992, it is a powerful card to which I must pay appropriate respect. I am being asked to extend the domestic law of confidence to grant injunctions in this case. I am satisfied that I can only restrict the freedom of the media to publish if the need for those restrictions can be shown to fall within the exceptions set out in article 10(2). In considering the limits to the law of confidence, and whether a remedy is available to the claimants within those limits, I must interpret narrowly those exceptions. In so doing and having regard to articles 2, 3 and 8 it is important to have regard to the fact that the rights under articles 2 and 3 are not capable of derogation, and the consequences to the claimants if those rights were to be breached. It is clear that, on the basis that there is a real possibility that the claimants may be the objects of revenge attacks, the potential breaches of articles 2, 3 and 8 have to be evaluated with great care.

78 What is the information sought to be protected and how important is it to protect it? The single most important element of the information is the detection of the future identity of the claimants in the community. All the other matters sought to be protected for the present, and for the future, are bound up in the risk of identification, whether by photographs, or by descriptions of identifying features of their appearance as adults, and their new names, addresses and similar information. That risk is potentially extreme if it became known what they look like, and where they are. The risk might come from any quarter, strangers such as vigilante groups, as well as the parents, family and friends of the murdered child. In the present case, the public authority, the court, has knowledge of the risk to the claimants. Does the risk displace the right of the media to publish information about the claimants without any restriction imposed by the court?

79 As I have set out, article 10(2) recognises the express exception, 'for preventing the disclosure of information received in confidence'. None the less, in order for it to be used to restrict freedom of expression, all the criteria in article 10(2), narrowly interpreted, must be met. Taking each limb in turn:

'In accordance with the law'

80 I am satisfied that, taking into account the effect of the Convention on our law, the law of confidence can extend to cover the injunctions sought in this case and, therefore, the restrictions proposed are in accordance with the law. There is a well-established cause of action in the tort of breach of confidence in respect of which injunctions may be granted. The common law continues to evolve, as it has done for centuries, and it is being given considerable impetus to do so by the implementation of the Convention into our domestic law. I am encouraged in that view by the observations of Brooke LJ in *Douglas*'s case, at p. 1008, para 61:

> 'It is well known that this court in *Kaye* v *Robertson* [1991] FSR 62 said in uncompromising terms that there was no tort of privacy known to English law. In contrast, both academic commentary and extra-judicial commentary by judges over the last ten years have suggested from time to time that a development of the present frontiers of a breach of confidence action could fill the gap in English law which is filled by privacy law in other developed countries. This commentary was given a boost recently by the decision of the European Commission on Human Rights in *Earl Spencer* v *The United Kingdom* (1998) 25 EHRR CD 105, and by the coming into force of the Human Rights Act 1998.'

Keene LJ said at p. 1035, para 165: 'breach of confidence is a developing area of the law, the boundaries of which are not immutable but may change to reflect changes in society, technology and business practice.'

81 The duty of confidence may arise in equity independently of a transaction or relationship between parties. In this case it would be a duty placed upon the media. A duty of confidence does already arise when confidential information comes to the knowledge of the media, in circumstances in which the media have notice of its confidentiality. An example is the medical reports of a private individual which are recognised as being confidential. Indeed it is so well known that medical reports are confidential that Mr Desmond Browne submitted that it was not necessary to protect that information by an injunction. It is also recognised that it is just in all the circumstances that information known to be confidential should not be disclosed to others, in this case by publication in the press: see Lord Goff in *Attorney General* v *Guardian Newspapers Ltd (No 2)* [1990] 1 AC 109. The issue is whether the information leading to disclosure of the claimants' identity and location comes within the confidentiality brackets. In answering that crucial question, I can properly rely upon the European case law and the duty on the court, where necessary, to take appropriate steps to safeguard the physical safety of the claimants, including the adoption of measures even in the sphere of relations of individuals and/or private organisations between themselves. Under the umbrella of confidentiality there will be information which may require a special quality of protection. In the present case the reason for advancing that special quality is that, if the information was published, the publication would be likely to lead to grave and possibly fatal consequences. In my judgment, the court does have the jurisdiction, in exceptional cases, to extend the protection of confidentiality of information, even to impose restrictions on the press, where not to do so would be likely to lead to serious physical injury, or to the death, of the person seeking that confidentiality, and there is no other way to protect the applicants other than by seeking relief from the court.

'Necessary in a democratic society to satisfy a strong and pressing need'

82 It is a very strong possibility, if not, indeed, a probability, that on the release of these two young men there will be great efforts to find where they will be living and, if that information becomes public, they will be pursued. Among the pursuers may well be those intent on revenge. The requirement in the Convention that there can be no derogation from the rights under articles 2 and 3 provides exceptional support for the strong and pressing social need that their confidentiality be protected.

'Proportionate to the legitimate aim pursued'

83 Although injunctions have not been granted in such circumstances in the past, I am satisfied that, to protect information requiring a special quality of protection, injunctions can be granted. I gain support for that conclusion from the judgment of Lord Woolf MR in *Broadmoor Special Hospital Authority* v *Robinson* [2000] QB 775, and the fact that over the past 30 years or so the jurisdiction of the court to grant injunctions, where it has been demonstrated to be necessary and in accordance with general equitable principles, has been exercised. The provision of injunctions to achieve the object sought must be proportionate to the legitimate aim. In this case, it is to protect the claimants from serious and possibly irreparable harm, which would, in my judgment, clearly meet the requirement of proportionality. As I have already said above, there is a positive duty upon the court to take such steps as may be necessary to achieve that aim. In *Osman* v *United Kingdom* (1998) 29 EHRR 245, the European Court of Human Rights held that a breach of articles 2 and 3 would be established if the authorities knew, or ought to have known, of the existence of a real and immediate risk to the life of an identified individual, from criminal acts of a third party, and they failed to take measures, within the scope of their powers, which might have been expected to avoid that risk. In that case, the authority was the police. In the present case, the authority is this court. I know of the existence of a real risk, which may become immediate if confidentiality is breached.

84 Lord Woolf MR said in *R* v *Lord Saville of Newdigate, Ex p A* [2000] 1 WLR 1855, 1867, para 37:

> 'when a fundamental right such as the right to life is engaged, the options available to the reasonable decision-maker are curtailed. They are curtailed because it is unreasonable to reach a decision which contravenes or could contravene human rights unless there are sufficiently significant countervailing considerations. In other words it is not open to the decision-maker to risk interfering with fundamental rights in the absence of compelling justification.'

With that warning from Lord Woolf MR in mind, in my judgment, the appropriate measures to be taken, within the scope of my powers, would be to grant injunctions. This would have the effect of substantially reducing the risk to each of the claimants.

85 I do not see that this extension of the law of confidence, by the grant of relief in the exceptional circumstances of this case, as opening a door to the granting of general restrictions on the media in cases where anonymity would be desirable. In my judgment, that is where the strict application of article 10(2) bites. It will only be appropriate to grant injunctions to restrain the media where it can be convincingly demonstrated, within those exceptions, that it is strictly necessary.

86 I am uncertain, for instance, whether it would be appropriate to grant injunctions to restrict the press in this case if only article 8 were likely to be breached. Serious though the breach of the claimants' right to respect for family life and privacy would be, once the journalists and photographers discovered either of them, and despite the likely serious adverse effect on the efforts to rehabilitate them into society, it might not be sufficient to meet the importance of the preservation of the freedom of expression in article 10(1). It is not necessary, however, for me to come to a conclusion as to the weight of a breach of article 8, since I am entirely satisfied that there is a real and serious risk to the rights of the claimants under articles 2 and 3. Subject, therefore, to my assessment of the strength of the evidence presented to the court, and the possibility that some protection less than injunctions might be proportionate to the need for confidentiality, I find that, in principle, I have the jurisdiction to grant injunctions to protect the claimants in the present case.

F. Conclusions as to future risk

87 The test of future risk is not to be based upon a balance of probabilities. In *Davies* v *Taylor* [1974] AC 207, the House of Lords was considering the possibility of a future reconciliation between the deceased and his estranged wife in a fatal accident claim by her. They held that the issue was not whether it was more probable than not that there would have been a reconciliation, but whether there was a reasonable

probability or expectation, rather than a mere speculative possibility, of a reconciliation. There could be a reasonable expectation that something would come about even though the chance of it coming about was less than even.

88 In *In re H (Minors) (Sexual Abuse: Standard of Proof)* [1996] AC 563, the House of Lords considered the words 'likely to suffer significant harm' in section 31 of the Children Act 1989. Lord Nicholls of Birkenhead rejected the submission of counsel that likely in that context meant probable. He said, at p 585:

> 'In this context Parliament cannot have been using likely in the sense of more likely than not. If the word likely were given this meaning, it would have the effect of leaving outside the scope of care and supervision orders cases where the court is satisfied there is a real possibility of significant harm to the child in the future but that possibility falls short of being more likely than not... What is in issue is the prospect, or risk, of the child suffering *significant* harm... In my view therefore, the context shows that in section 31(2)(a) likely is being used in the sense of a real possibility, a possibility that cannot sensibly be ignored having regard to the nature and gravity of the feared harm in the particular case.' (Emphasis added.)

89 The decisions in *Davies* v *Taylor* [1974] AC 207 and in *In re H (Minors) (Sexual Abuse: Standard of Proof)*, although each made on facts far removed from the present, are in my view a helpful guide to the assessment I have to carry out in this case. Since the relief sought is to restrict the freedom of expression of the press, I approach the assessment of future risk to each of the claimants on the basis that the evidence supporting the case has to demonstrate convincingly the seriousness of the risk, but in order to assess the future, I cannot by the very nature of the task, have concrete facts upon which to rely, nor can I predict upon the basis of future probability.

90 The evidence, which I have set out above, demonstrates to me the huge and intense media interest in this case, to an almost unparalleled extent, not only over the time of the murder, during the trial and subsequent litigation, but also that media attention remains intense seven years later. Not only is the media interest intense, it also demonstrates continued hostility towards the claimants. I am satisfied from the extracts from the newspapers: (a) that the press have accurately reported the horror, moral outrage and indignation still felt by many members of the public; (b) that there are members of the public, other than the family of the murdered boy, who continue to feel such hatred and revulsion at the shocking crime and a desire for revenge that some at least of them might well engage in vigilante or revenge attacks if they knew where either claimant was living and could identify him. There also remains a serious risk from the Bulger family, and the father was quoted as recently as October 2000 saying that upon their release he would 'hunt the boys down'; (c) that some sections of the press support this feeling of revulsion and hatred to the degree of encouraging the public to deny anonymity to the claimants. The inevitable conclusion to which I am driven, in particular, by the editorial from the 'News of the World' (one of the newspapers in the defendant group), is that sections of the press would support, and might even initiate, efforts to find the claimants and to expose their identity and their addresses in their newspapers.

...

94 I consider it is a real possibility that someone, journalist or other, will, almost certainly, seek them out, and if they are found, as they may well be found, the media would, in the absence of injunctions, be likely to reveal that information in the newspapers and on television, radio, etc. If the identities of the claimants were revealed, journalists and photographers would be likely to descend upon them in droves, foreign as well as national and local, and there would be widespread dissemination of the new names, addresses and appearance of the claimants. From all the evidence provided to me, I have come to the clear conclusion that if the new identity of these claimants became public knowledge it would have disastrous consequences for the claimants, not only from intrusion and harassment but, far more important, the real possibility of serious physical harm and possible death from vengeful members of the public or from the Bulger family. If their new identities were discovered, I am satisfied that neither of them would have any chance of a normal life and that there is a real and strong possibility that their lives would be at risk.

95 The claimants seek injunctions effectively for the rest of their lives. Is the grant of injunctions proportionate to the risk which I have identified? Mr Desmond Browne argued that the editors of the newspapers that he represented could be trusted not to reveal information that would lead to the identity of

the claimants. Editorial judgment should be respected and trusted. That brings in the question whether it is necessary, in order to achieve anonymity, to require injunctions. Although I recognise that editors do exercise judgment and restraint in some of the stories they run, I do not consider that editorial restraint can be the answer here. I am prepared to believe that editors of some newspapers might well hesitate to reveal this information. I do not see how editorial judgment would be able to restrain all the newspapers, particularly those now calling for that information to be made available. I also find it difficult to accept the case of the newspapers that they should be trusted not to publish when, at the same time, their counsel submitted that it was wrong for the claimants to have the advantages of anonymity and to be allowed to live a lie. No offer has been made to the court not to publish. On the contrary, I am satisfied from the editorial in the 'News of the World' on 29 October 2000, that one newspaper at least would wish to publish information about identity or address if that information became available to them. Once one paper gives the information, all the papers will obviously be likely also to publish all the information they can obtain which remains live news. The judgment of editors cannot be an adequate protection to meet the risk I have identified.

96 The Press Code, as applied by the Press Complaints Commission, is not, in the exceptional situation of the claimants, sufficient protection. Criticism of, or indeed sanctions imposed upon, the offending newspaper after the information is published would, in the circumstances of this case, be too late. The information would be in the public domain and the damage would be done. The Press Code cannot adequately protect in advance. The risk is too great for the court to rely upon the voluntary Press Code. To do so would not be a sufficient response to the principles enunciated in *Osman* v *United Kingdom* 29 EHRR 245. I do not consider that the provisions of the Protection from Harassment Act 1997 would or could be adequate to protect the claimants if their identities became known. Recourse to the courts after the event would be too late—for example because they would have by then, almost certainly, been photographed, and would then be recognised everywhere.

97 These uniquely notorious young men are and will, on release, be in a most exceptional situation and the risks to them of identification are real and substantial. It is therefore necessary, in the exceptional circumstances of this case, to place the right to confidence above the right of the media to publish freely information about the claimants. Although the crime of these two young men was especially heinous, they did not thereby forfeit their rights under English law and under the European Convention for the Protection of Human Rights and Fundamental Freedoms. They have served their tariff period and when they are released, they have the right of all citizens to the protection of the law. In order to give them the protection they need and are entitled to receive, I am compelled to grant injunctions.

G. The scope of the injunctions

Orders contra mundum

98 The submission of the defendants was, that even if there was jurisdiction to grant injunctions against them in this case, there was no jurisdiction to grant those injunctions against the world at large. The general principle was stated by Lord Eldon in *Iveson* v *Harris* 7 Ves 251, 257 'you cannot have an injunction except against a party to the suit'. The injunctive relief granted by Balcombe J in *In re X (A Minor) (Wardship: Injunction)* [1984] 1 WLR 1422 (the Mary Bell case), was based on the exercise of the court's jurisdiction in wardship. Balcombe J, in relation to the power to grant an injunction contra mundum, said, at p 1425: 'Let me say at once that, if it were not an exercise of the wardship jurisdiction, I am satisfied that there would be no such power.' He held that not only would it not be fair to injunct one newspaper from publishing information which could identify the ward by her relationship to the mother, Mary Bell, but that the harm to the ward, which prohibition of publication is intended to prevent, would also be caused by publication in any other newspaper or medium. He referred to *Z Ltd* v *A-Z and AA-LL* [1982] QB 558, in which the Court of Appeal held that *Mareva* injunctions operated against the world at large, or at least against those members of the public who have notice of the existence of the order. He was satisfied that, at p 1427: 'If the court can protect proprietary interests in that way, as it clearly can, how much more should it be able to protect the interests of its wards if it is satisfied in a proper case that the interests of its wards require protection in this form?'

99 In the present case I have come to the conclusion that I am compelled to grant injunctive relief for the protection of the claimants in respect of a special category of confidential information. For that information to be revealed by a newspaper or television programme, not a party to these proceedings, would have an equally devastating effect as disclosure by one of the defendant groups. It would cause equal harm. It would also, as Balcombe J recognised in *In re X (A Minor) (Wardship: Injunction)* [1984] 1 WLR

1422, be most unjust to the defendants if they were the only newspaper groups to be so restricted. The granting of the injunctions would not, however, have that limited effect. Mr Desmond Browne submitted that, since the decision of the House of Lords in *Attorney General* v *Times Newspapers Ltd* [1992] 1 AC 191, publication of the injunctions against the newspapers would, in practice, act in a similar way, and have the same effect, as injunctions against the media generally. He argued that it was not, therefore, necessary for the injunctions to be made against the world at large. It seems to me that to accept that position would be to achieve through the back door, that which it is submitted I cannot do through the front. I agree with Mr Caldecott that this is somewhat of an academic exercise. There is a *positive* duty on the court as a public authority to take steps to protect individuals from the criminal acts of others: see *Osman* v *United Kingdom* 29 EHRR 245.

100 Although the dictum of Lord Eldon in *Iveson's* case 7 Ves 251 has been generally followed for nearly 200 years, in light of the implementation of the Human Rights Act 1998, we are entering a new era, and the requirement that the courts act in a way that is compatible with the Convention, and have regard to European jurisprudence, adds a new dimension to those principles. I am satisfied that the injunctive relief that I grant should, in this case, be granted openly against the world.

...

The information to be protected

104 In my judgment, there are compelling reasons to grant injunctions to protect, in the broadest terms, the following information. (i) Any information leading to the identity, or future whereabouts, of each claimant, which includes photographs, description of present appearance and so on. (ii) In order to protect the claimants on their release from detention, it is necessary to have injunctions to protect their present whereabouts, any information about their present appearance and similar information. That protection must include any efforts by the media to solicit information from past or present carers, staff or co-detainees at their secure units until the claimants' release from detention. (iii) In order further to protect their future identity and whereabouts, no information may be made public or solicited from their secure units that might lead to the identification of the units for a reasonable period after their release. It would seem to me that 12 months from the date of the release of each claimant would be a sufficient period to protect that information, subject to any further argument from counsel....

105 I am, of course, aware that injunctions may not be fully effective to protect the claimants from acts committed outside England and Wales resulting information about them being placed on the Internet. The injunctions can, however, prevent wider circulation of that information through the newspapers or television and radio. To that end, therefore, I would be disposed to add, in relation to information in the public domain, a further proviso, suitably limited, which would protect the special quality of the new identity, appearance and addresses of the claimants or information leading to that identification, even after that information had entered the public domain to the extent that it had been published on the Internet or elsewhere such as outside the United Kingdom. I am also aware that the Parole Board will soon be making inquiries and compiling a report for consideration at the Parole Board hearing. It is, in my view, essential that the nature of the inquiries, the content of the report and the hearing itself must be covered by the injunctions.

Injunctions accordingly.

NOTES

1. Case law suggests that in relation to privacy we have indirect horizontal effect which can develop existing rights.
2. In *Campbell* v *Mirror Group Newspapers* [2004] UKHL 22, [2004] 2 WLR 1232, the model Naomi Campbell brought an action over the publication of a story about her attending meetings of Narcotics Anonymous, which included details of her treatment and was accompanied by a photograph. It was a majority decision in the House of Lords and the possible impact upon Ms Campbell's struggle with addiction appeared to be a strong factor for members of the majority. Baroness Hale said [132]:

Neither party to this appeal has challenged the basic principles which have emerged from the Court of Appeal in the wake of the Human Rights Act 1998. The 1998 Act does not create any new cause of action between private persons. But if there is a relevant cause of action applicable, the court as a public authority must act compatibly with both parties' Convention rights. In a case such as this, the relevant vehicle will usually be the action for breach of confidence, as Lord Woolf CJ held in *A v B plc* [2002] EWCA Civ 337, [2003] QB 195] para. 4.

Convention privacy rights were expanded by the ECtHR in *von Hannover* v *Germany* 16 BHRC 545, which held that photographs of Princess Caroline of Monaco in public places published in German magazines infringed her Art. 8 rights.

3. Dame Elizabeth Butler-Sloss P granted another lifetime injunction in *X (Mary Bell) and another* v *News Group Newspapers and another* [2003] EWHC QB 1101, [2003] EMLR 37 which prohibited identifying the location of Mary Bell, who at the age of 11 had been found guilty of the murder of two young children. Unlike in the decision in *Venables and Thompson* v *News Group Newspapers*, the judge did not recognize any threat to the claimant's, or her daughter's, life but felt that the exceptional circumstances, which included the mental health of Mary Bell, justified the protection of their right to private and family life.
4. The House of Lords ruled against creating a new tort of invasion of privacy in *Wainwright* v *Home Office* [2003] UKHL 53, [2003] 3 WLR 1137, where the appellants complained about the strip searches carried out by prison officers.

■ QUESTION

PeJay, a famous pop star, has become the victim of a stalker who has issued threats against him. PeJay secretly moves home and stops making public appearances. Previously PeJay had courted publicity and had permitted various newspapers and magazines to have access to his previous home to photograph him and to do features on its design and décor. PeJay learns that *Pop Today*, a magazine, has discovered details about his new home and is planning a feature which will use photographs previously published in a property magazine and a photograph of PeJay in the grounds of the home. This photograph was taken by a birdwatcher using a telephoto lens from a position on a public right of way running next to the boundary of PeJay's property. The birdwatcher sold the photograph to *Pop Today*. PeJay applies to the High Court for an injunction against *Pop Today* and all the world forbidding publication of his address and any details or photographs of his home or grounds claiming that such would breach his right to privacy and put his life at risk. How might the Court decide the issue? Would your answer differ if there was no stalker and PeJay had simply decided to retire and withdraw from public life?

(c) How will the courts interpret legislation?

The task of interpreting legislation in actions brought under the Human Rights Act is a very sensitive one. Some of the factors are considered below:

NOTES

1. Section 2(1) of the 1998 Act requires a court or tribunal to 'take into account' the jurisprudence of the European Court of Human Rights and the decisions of other specified Strasbourg bodies.

   The jurisprudence of the European Court of Human Rights may be neither clear nor constant, or it may be subject to interpretation. In *Alconbury* the House of Lords differed in its interpretation of the jurisprudence of the European Court of Human Rights from the lower courts. The same occurred in *Brown* v *Stott (Procurator Fiscal, Dunfermline) and Another* [2001] 2 WLR 817 (p. 477, *post*), where the Privy Council differed in its interpretation of the Strasbourg jurisprudence from that adopted by the High Court of Justiciary. In *R* v *Horncastle* [2009] UKSC 14, Lord Philips said at [11]:

> ...The requirement to "take into account" the Strasbourg jurisprudence will normally result in this Court applying principles that are clearly established by the Strasbourg Court. There will, however, be rare occasions where this court has concerns as to whether a decision of the Strasbourg Court sufficiently appreciates or accommodates particular aspects of our domestic process. In such circumstances it is open to this court to decline to follow the Strasbourg decision, giving reasons for adopting this course. This is likely to give the Strasbourg Court the opportunity to reconsider the particular aspect of the decision that is in issue, so that there takes place what may prove to be a valuable dialogue between this court and the Strasbourg Court.

2. Section 3(1) of the 1998 Act requires courts to interpret all legislation, regardless of when it was enacted (and thus also of how it may have been interpreted previously), 'So far as it is possible to do so... in a way which is compatible with the Convention rights'. The New Zealand Bill of Rights Act 1990 contains a similar provision in s. 6, which reads: 'Wherever an enactment can be given a meaning that is consistent with the rights and freedoms contained in this Bill of Rights, that meaning shall be preferred to any other meaning.'

Lord Irvine of Lairg, 'Activism and Restraint: Human Rights and the Interpretative Process'

[1999] *European Human Rights Law Review* 350, 366–367

The Human Rights Legislation: A Constitutional Balancing Act

...The Human Rights Act is founded upon a division of functions between the different branches of government, which reflects the British conception of the separation of powers principle on which our constitution is based. Under the Act our courts have to interpret statutes 'so far as possible' to be compatible with Convention rights; if this is impossible they have been given a unique power to declare legislation to be incompatible, but then it is for the executive to initiate, and Parliament to enact, remedial legislation, with a fast track process available for that purpose. This balance which inheres in the text of the Act can be secured in practical terms only by a measured judicial response to the challenge of seeking, so far as is possible, to interpret national law consistently with the Convention.

If the courts were to adopt a very narrow view of this duty of consistent construction, their ability interpretatively to guarantee Convention rights would be severely curtailed. Instead of reading municipal law in a way which gave effect to individuals' rights, the courts would tend to discover irreconcilable conflicts between United Kingdom law and the Convention which would then require legislative correction. In contrast, a judiciary which took an extremely radical view of its interpretative duty would be likely to stretch legislative language, beyond breaking point, if necessary, in order to effect judicial vindication of Convention rights. Such an approach would yield virtually no declarations of incompatibility: the judges would, in effect, be taking it upon themselves to rewrite legislation in order to render it consistent with the Convention, and so excluding Parliament and the executive from the human rights enterprise.

Both of these approaches would be wrong. The constitutional theory on which the Human Rights Act rests is one of balance. It requires courts to recognise that they have a fundamental contribution to make in this area, while appreciating that the other elements of the constitution also have important roles to play in securing the effective protection of the Convention rights in domestic law. Thus the Act, while significantly changing the nature of the interpretative process, does not confer on the courts a licence to construe legislation in a way which is so radical and strained that it arrogates to the judges a power completely to rewrite existing law: that is a task for Parliament and the executive. The interpretative duty which the courts will soon begin to discharge in the human rights arena is therefore a strong one; but it is nevertheless subject to limits which the Act imposes, and which find still deeper resonance in the doctrine of the separation of powers on which the constitution is founded.

...A different, but related, challenge will arise once the Scottish Parliament begins to legislate. According to the Scotland Act 1998, s. 28(6), the courts must seek to avoid reaching the conclusion that Scottish legislation is invalid (on the ground of its being *ultra vires*) by construing it narrowly. Although this interpretative duty is different in nature from that which the Human Rights Act creates, the importance of balance will remain constant: the courts will have a fundamental contribution to make in seeking to ensure that the Scottish Parliament's legislation is effective (in the sense of being *intra vires*) while preserving the integrity of the distribution of legislative competence between Westminster and Edinburgh which the Scotland Act embodies. Thus, by utilising interpretative methodology to secure the protection of fundamental rights and the efficacy of Scottish legislation, both the Human Rights Act and the Scotland Act recognise that the interpretative process will be of central importance to the success of the constitutional reform programme.

R v Secretary of State for the Home Department, ex parte Simms and Another

[1999] 3 WLR 328, House of Lords

(For the facts of this case see p. 554, *post*.)

LORD HOFFMANN: ...Parliamentary sovereignty means that Parliament can, if it chooses, legislate contrary to fundamental principles of human rights. The Human Rights Act 1998 will not detract from this power. The constraints upon its exercise by Parliament are ultimately political, not legal. But the principle of legality means that Parliament must squarely confront what it is doing and accept the political cost. Fundamental rights cannot be overridden by general or ambiguous words. This is because there is too great a risk that the full implications of their unqualified meaning may have passed unnoticed in the democratic process. In the absence of express language or necessary implication to the contrary, the courts therefore presume that even the most general words were intended to be subject to the basic rights of the individual. In this way the courts of the United Kingdom, though acknowledging the sovereignty of Parliament, apply principles of constitutionality little different from those which exist in countries where the power of the legislature is expressly limited by a constitutional document.

The Human Rights Act 1998 will make three changes to this scheme of things. First, the principles of fundamental human rights which exist at common law will be supplemented by a specific text, namely the European Convention. But much of the Convention reflects the common law: see *Derbyshire County Council* v *Times Newspapers Ltd* [1993] AC 534, 551. That is why the United Kingdom government felt able in 1950 to accede to the Convention without domestic legislative change. So the adoption of the text as part of domestic law is unlikely to involve radical change in our notions of fundamental human rights. Secondly, the principle of legality will be expressly enacted as a rule of construction in section 3 and will gain further support from the obligation of the Minister in charge of a Bill to make a statement of compatibility under section 19. Thirdly, in those unusual cases in which the legislative infringement of fundamental human rights is so clearly expressed as not to yield to the principle of legality, the courts will be able to draw this to the attention of Parliament by making a declaration of incompatibility. It will then be for the sovereign Parliament to decide whether or not to remove the incompatibility.

NOTE: A number of appellate decisions have involved the courts in exploring the meaning of the interpretative obligation which s. 3 of the Human Rights Act 1998 places upon them. The impact of the section on the traditional approach to statutory interpretation is immense, as indicated by the following extract from the judgment of Lord Woolf CJ in *Poplar Housing Association Ltd* v *Donoghue* [2001] EWCA Civ 595:

75 It is difficult to overestimate the importance of section 3. It applies to legislation passed both before and after the Human Rights Act 1998 came into force. Subject to the section not requiring the court to go beyond that which is possible, it is mandatory in its terms. In the case of legislation predating the Human Rights Act 1998 where the legislation would otherwise conflict with the Convention, section 3 requires the court to now interpret legislation in a manner which it would not have done before the Human Rights Act 1998 came into force. When the court interprets legislation usually its primary task is to identify the intention of Parliament. Now, when section 3 applies, the courts have to adjust their traditional role in relation to interpretation so as to give effect to the direction contained in section 3. It is as though legislation which predates the Human Rights Act 1998 and conflicts with the Convention has to be treated as being subsequently amended to incorporate the language of section 3. However, the following points, which are probably self-evident, should be noted.

(a) Unless the legislation would otherwise be in breach of the Convention section 3 can be ignored (so courts should always first ascertain whether, absent section 3, there would be any breach of the Convention).
(b) If the court has to rely on section 3 it should limit the extent of the modified meaning to that which is necessary to achieve compatibility.
(c) Section 3 does not entitle the court to *legislate* (its task is still one of *interpretation*, but interpretation in accordance with the direction contained in section 3).
(d) The views of the parties and of the Crown as to whether a 'constructive' interpretation should be adopted cannot modify the task of the court (if section 3 applies the court is required to adopt the section 3 approach to interpretation).
(e) Where, despite the strong language of section 3, it is not possible to achieve a result which is compatible with the Convention, the court is not *required* to grant a declaration and presumably in exercising its discretion as to whether to grant a declaration or not it will be influenced by the usual considerations which apply to the grant of declarations.

The problem which courts confront, however, is determining where the line is to be drawn between interpreting the legislation and legislating themselves. The bolder the interpretative approach which the court adopts, the greater the risk that the line will be transgressed. Consider whether the House of Lords in the case which follows, by reading words into the statute in question to achieve compatibility, crossed the line.

Ghaidan v *Godin-Mendoza*

[2004] UKHL 30, [2004] 3 WLR 113, House of Lords

On the death of a protected tenant of a dwelling-house his or her surviving spouse, if then living in the house, becomes a statutory tenant by succession. But marriage is not essential for this purpose. A person who was living with the original tenant 'as his or her wife or husband' is treated as the spouse of the original tenant: see Rent Act 1977, Schedule 1, para. 2(2). In *Fitzpatrick* v *Sterling Housing Association Ltd* [2001] 1 AC 27, the House of Lords decided this provision did not include persons in a same-sex relationship. The question raised by this appeal is whether this reading of para. 2 can survive the coming into force of the Human Rights Act 1998. The county court held that it could, but this was overturned by the Court of Appeal. On appeal:

LORD STEYN: ... My Lords,

37. In my view the Court of Appeal came to the correct conclusion. I agree with the conclusions and reasons of my noble and learned friends Lord Nicholls of Birkenhead, Lord Rodger of Earlsferry and Baroness Hale of Richmond. In the light of those opinions, I will not comment on the case generally.

38. I confine my remarks to the question whether it is possible under section 3(1) of the Human Rights Act 1998 to read and give effect to paragraph 2(2) of Schedule 1 to the Rent Act 1977 in a way which is compatible with the European Convention on Human Rights. In my view the interpretation adopted by the Court of Appeal under section 3(1) was a classic illustration of the permissible use of this provision. But it became clear during oral argument, and from a subsequent study of the case law and academic discussion on the correct interpretation of section 3(1), that the role of that provision in the remedial scheme of the 1998 Act is not always correctly understood. I would therefore wish to examine the position in a general way.

39. I attach an appendix to this opinion [see pp. 525–528, *post*] which lists cases where a breach of an ECHR right was found established, and the courts proceeded to consider whether to exercise their interpretative power under section 3 or to make a declaration of incompatibility under section 4. For the first and second lists (A and B) I am indebted to the Constitutional Law Division of the Department of Constitutional Affairs but law report references and other information have been added. The third list (C) has been prepared by Laura Johnson, my judicial assistant, under my direction. It will be noted that in 10 cases the courts used their interpretative power under section 3 and in 15 cases the courts made declarations of incompatibility under section 4. In five cases in the second group the declarations of incompatibility were subsequently reversed on appeal: in four of those cases it was held that no breach was established and in the fifth case (*Hooper*) the exact basis for overturning the declaration of incompatibility may be a matter of debate. Given that under the 1998 Act the use of the interpretative power under section 3 is the principal remedial measure, and that the making of a declaration of incompatibility is a measure of last resort, these statistics by themselves raise a question about the proper implementation of the 1998 Act. A study of the case law reinforces the need to pose the question whether the law has taken a wrong turning.

40. My impression is that two factors are contributing to a misunderstanding of the remedial scheme of the 1998 Act. First, there is the constant refrain that a judicial reading down, or reading in, under section 3 would flout the will of Parliament as expressed in the statute under examination. This question cannot sensibly be considered without giving full weight to the countervailing will of Parliament as expressed in the 1998 Act.

41. The second factor may be an excessive concentration on linguistic features of the particular statute. Nowhere in our legal system is a literalistic approach more inappropriate than when considering

whether a breach of a Convention right may be removed by interpretation under section 3. Section 3 requires a broad approach concentrating, amongst other things, in a purposive way on the importance of the fundamental right involved.

42. In enacting the 1998 Act Parliament legislated "to bring rights home" from the European Court of Human Rights to be determined in the courts of the United Kingdom. That is what the White Paper said: see Rights Brought Home: The Human Rights Bill (1997) (Cm 3782), para 2.7. That is what Parliament was told. The mischief to be addressed was the fact that Convention rights as set out in the ECHR, which Britain ratified in 1951, could not be vindicated in our courts. Critical to this purpose was the enactment of effective remedial provisions.

43. The provisions adopted read as follows:

'3. Interpretation of legislation

(1) So far as it is possible to do so, primary legislation and subordinate legislation must be read and given effect in a way which is compatible with the Convention rights.

(2) This section—
  (a) applies to primary legislation and subordinate legislation whenever enacted;
  (b) does not affect the validity, continuing operation or enforcement of any incompatible primary legislation; and
  (c) does not affect the validity, continuing operation or enforcement of any incompatible subordinate legislation if (disregarding any possibility of revocation) primary legislation prevents removal of the incompatibility.

4. Declaration of incompatibility

(1) Subsection (2) applies in any proceedings in which a court determines whether a provision of primary legislation is compatible with a Convention right.

(2) If the court is satisfied that the provision is incompatible with a Convention right, it may make a declaration of that incompatibility.

(3)–(6).'

If Parliament disagrees with an interpretation by the courts under section 3(1), it is free to override it by amending the legislation and expressly reinstating the incompatibility.

44. It is necessary to state what section 3(1), and in particular the word 'possible', does not mean. First, section 3(1) applies even if there is no ambiguity in the language in the sense of it being capable of bearing two *possible* meanings. The word 'possible' in section 3(1) is used in a different and much stronger sense. Secondly, section 3(1) imposes a stronger and more radical obligation than to adopt a purposive interpretation in the light of the ECHR. Thirdly, the draftsman of the Act had before him the model of the New Zealand Bill of Rights Act which imposes a requirement that the interpretation to be adopted must be reasonable. Parliament specifically rejected the legislative model of requiring a reasonable interpretation.

45. Instead the draftsman had resort to the analogy of the obligation under the EEC Treaty on national courts, as far as possible, to interpret national legislation in the light of the wording and purpose of directives. In *Marleasing SA* v *La Comercial Internacional de Alimentación SA* (Case C–106/89) [1990] ECR I–4135, 4159 the European Court of Justice defined this obligation as follows:

> 'It follows that, in applying national law, whether the provisions in questions were adopted before or after the directive, the national court called upon to interpret it is required to do so, as far as possible, in light of the wording and the purpose of the directive in order to achieve the result pursued by the latter and thereby comply with the third paragraph of Article 189 of the Treaty'

Given the undoubted strength of this interpretative obligation under EEC law, this is a significant signpost to the meaning of section 3(1) in the 1998 Act.

46. Parliament had before it the mischief and objective sought to be addressed, viz the need 'to bring rights home'. The linch-pin of the legislative scheme to achieve this purpose was section 3(1). Rights could only be effectively brought home if section 3(1) was the prime remedial measure, and section 4 a measure of last resort. How the system modelled on the EEC interpretative obligation would work

was graphically illustrated for Parliament during the progress of the Bill through both Houses. The Lord Chancellor observed that 'in 99% of the cases that will arise, there will be no need for judicial declarations of incompatibility' and the Home Secretary said 'We expect that, in almost all cases, the courts will be able to interpret the legislation compatibly with the Convention': Hansard (HL Debates,) 5 February 1998, col 840 (3rd reading) and Hansard (HC Debates,) 16 February 1998, col 778 (2nd reading). It was envisaged that the duty of the court would be to strive to find (if possible) a meaning which would best accord with Convention rights. This is the remedial scheme which Parliament adopted.

47. Three decisions of the House can be cited to illustrate the strength of the interpretative obligation under section 3(1). The first is *R* v *A (No. 2)* [2002] 1 AC 45 which concerned the so-called rape shield legislation. The problem was the blanket exclusion of prior sexual history between the complainant and an accused in section 41(1) of the Youth Justice and Criminal Evidence Act 1999, subject to narrow specific categories in the remainder of section 41. In subsequent decisions, and in academic literature, there has been discussion about differences of emphasis in the various opinions in *A*. What has been largely overlooked is the unanimous conclusion of the House. The House unanimously agreed on an interpretation under section 3 which would ensure that section 41 would be compatible with the ECHR. The formulation was by agreement set out in paragraph 46 of my opinion in that case as follows:

> 'The effect of the decision today is that under section 41(3)(c) of the 1999 Act, construed where necessary by applying the interpretive obligation under section 3 of the Human Rights Act 1998, and due regard always being paid to the importance of seeking to protect the complainant from indignity and from humiliating questions, the test of admissibility is whether the evidence (and questioning in relation to it) is nevertheless so relevant to the issue of consent that to exclude it would endanger the fairness of the trial under article 6 of the Convention. If this test is satisfied the evidence should not be excluded.'

This formulation was endorsed by Lord Slynn of Hadley at p 56, para 13 of his opinion in identical wording. The other Law Lords sitting in the case expressly approved the formulation set out in para 46 of my opinion: Lord Hope of Craighead, at pp 87–88, para 110, Lord Clyde, at p 98, para 140; and Lord Hutton, at p 106, para 163. In so ruling the House rejected linguistic arguments in favour of a broader approach. In the subsequent decisions of the House in *In re S (Minors) (Care Order: Implementation of Case Plan)* [2002] 2 AC 291 and *Bellinger* v *Bellinger* [2003] 2 AC 467, which touched on the remedial structure of the 1998 Act, *the decision* of the House in the case of *A* was not questioned. And in the present case nobody suggested that *A* involved a heterodox exercise of the power under section 3.

48. The second and third decisions of the House are *Pickstone* v *Freemans plc* [1989] AC 66 and *Litster* v *Forth Dry Dock & Engineering Co Ltd* [1990] 1 AC 546 which involve the interpretative obligation under EEC law. *Pickstone* concerned section 1(2) of the Equal Pay Act 1970, (as amended by section 8 of the Sex Discrimination Act 1975 and regulation 2 of the Equal Pay (Amendment) Regulations 1983 (SI 1983/1794) which implied into any contract without an equality clause one that modifies any term in a woman's contract which is less favourable than a term of a similar kind in the contract of a man:

> '(a) where the woman is employed on like work with a man in the same employment...
> (b) where the woman is employed on work rated as equivalent with that of a man in the same employment...
> (c) where a woman is employed on work which, not being work in `relation to which paragraph (a) or (b) above applies, is, in terms of the demands made on her (for instance under such headings as effort, skill and decision), of equal value to that of a man in the same employment'.

Lord Templeman observed (at pp 120–121):

> 'In my opinion there must be implied in paragraph (c) after the word "applies" the words "as between the woman and the man with whom she claims equality." This construction is consistent with Community law. The employers' construction is inconsistent with Community law and creates a permitted form of discrimination without rhyme or reason.'

That was the ratio decidendi of the decision. *Litster* concerned regulations intended to implement an EC Directive, the purpose of which was to protect the workers in an undertaking when its ownership was transferred. However, the regulations only protected those who were employed 'immediately before' the transfer. Having enquired into the purpose of the Directive, the House of Lords interpreted the Regulations by reading in additional words to protect workers not only if they were employed 'immediately before' the time of transfer, but also when they would have been so employed if they had not been unfairly dismissed by reason of the transfer: see Lord Keith of Kinkel, at 554. In both cases the House eschewed linguistic arguments in favour of a broad approach. *Picksone* and *Litster* involved national legislation which implemented EC Directives. *Marleasing* extended the scope of the interpretative obligation to unimplemented Directives. *Pickstone* and *Litster* reinforce the approach to section 3(1) which prevailed in the House in the rape shield case.

49. A study of the case law listed in the Appendix to this judgment reveals that there has sometimes been a tendency to approach the interpretative task under section 3(1) in too literal and technical a way. In practice there has been too much emphasis on linguistic features. If the core remedial purpose of section 3(1) is not to be undermined a broader approach is required. That is, of course, not to gainsay the obvious proposition that inherent in the use of the word 'possible' in section 3(1) is the idea that there is a Rubicon which courts may not cross. If it is not possible, within the meaning of section 3, to read or give effect to legislation in a way which is compatible with Convention rights, the only alternative is to exercise, where appropriate, the power to make a declaration of incompatibility. Usually, such cases should not be too difficult to identify. An obvious example is *R (Anderson)* v *Secretary of State for the Home Department* [2003] 1 AC 837. The House held that the Home Secretary was not competent under article 6 of the ECHR to decide on the tariff to be served by mandatory life sentence prisoners. The House found a section 3(1) interpretation not 'possible' and made a declaration under section 4. Interpretation could not provide a substitute scheme. *Bellinger* is another obvious example. As Lord Rodger of Earlsferry observed '... in relation to the validity of marriage, Parliament regards gender as fixed and immutable': [2003] 2 WLR 1174, 1195, para 83. Section 3(1) of the 1998 Act could not be used.

50. Having had the opportunity to reconsider the matter in some depth, I am not disposed to try to formulate precise rules about where section 3 may not be used. Like the proverbial elephant such a case ought generally to be easily identifiable. What is necessary, however, is to emphasise that interpretation under section 3(1) is the prime remedial remedy and that resort to section 4 must always be an exceptional course. In practical effect there is a strong rebuttable presumption in favour of an interpretation consistent with Convention rights. Perhaps the opinions delivered in the House today will serve to ensure a balanced approach along such lines.

51. I now return to the circumstances of the case before the House. Applying section 3 the Court of Appeal interpreted 'as his or her wife or husband' in the statute to mean '*as if they were* his wife or husband'. While there has been some controversy about aspects of the reasoning of the Court of Appeal, I would endorse the reasoning of the Court of Appeal on the use of section 3(1) in this case. It was well within the power under this provision.

52. I would also dismiss the appeal.

LORD MILLETT:

55. I agree with all my noble and learned friends, whose speeches I have had the advantage of reading in draft, that such discriminatory treatment of homosexual couples is incompatible with their Convention rights and cannot be justified by any identifiable legitimate aim...

56. It follows that, unless the court can apply section 3 of the Human Rights Act 1998 to extend the reach of para 2(2) to the survivor of a couple of the same sex, it must consider making a declaration of incompatibility under section 4. The making of such a declaration is in the court's discretion (section 4 provides only that the court 'may' make one); and it may be a matter for debate whether it would be appropriate to do so at a time when not merely has the Government announced its intention to bring forward corrective legislation in due course (as in *Bellinger* v *Bellinger* [2003] 2 AC 467) but Parliament is currently engaged in enacting remedial legislation. It is, however, unnecessary to enter upon this question, for there is a clear majority in favour of the view that section 3 can be applied to interpret para 2(2) in a way which renders legislative intervention unnecessary.

57. I have the misfortune to be unable to agree with this conclusion. I have given long and anxious consideration to the question whether, in the interests of unanimity, I should suppress my dissent, but I have come to the conclusion that I should not. The question is of great constitutional importance, for it goes to the relationship between the legislature and the judiciary, and hence ultimately to the supremacy

of Parliament. Sections 3 and 4 of the Human Rights Act were carefully crafted to preserve the existing constitutional doctrine, and any application of the ambit of section 3 beyond its proper scope subverts it. This is not to say that the doctrine of Parliamentary supremacy is sacrosanct, but only that any change in a fundamental constitutional principle should be the consequence of deliberate legislative action and not judicial activism, however well meaning.

...

69. ... it may be helpful if I give some examples of the way in which I see section 3 as operating.

70. In the course of his helpful argument counsel for the Secretary of State, who did not resist the application of section 3, acknowledged that it could not be used to read 'black' as meaning 'white'. That must be correct. Words cannot *mean* their opposite; 'black' cannot *mean* 'not black'. But they may *include* their opposite. In some contexts it may be possible to read 'black' as meaning 'black or white'; in other contexts it may be impossible to do so. It all depends on whether 'blackness' is the essential feature of the statutory scheme; and while the court may look behind the words of the statute they cannot be disregarded or given no weight, for they are the medium by which Parliament expresses its intention.

71. Again, 'red, blue or green' cannot be read as meaning 'red, blue, green or yellow'; the specification of three only of the four primary colours indicates a deliberate omission of the fourth (unless, of course, this can be shown to be an error). Section 3 cannot be used to supply the missing colour, for this would be not to interpret the statutory language but to contradict it.

72. The limits on the application of section 3 may thus be in part at least linguistic, as in the examples I have given, but they may also be derived from a consideration of the legislative history of the offending statute. Thus, while it may be possible to read 'cats' as meaning 'cats or dogs' (on the footing that the essential concept is that of domestic pets generally rather than felines particularly), it would obviously not be possible to read 'Siamese cats' as meaning 'Siamese cats or dogs'. The particularity of the expression 'Siamese cats' would preclude its extension to other species of cat, let alone dogs. But suppose the statute merely said 'cats', and that this was the result of successive amendments to the statute as originally enacted. If this had said 'Siamese cats', and had twice been amended, first to read 'Siamese or Persian cats' and then to read simply 'cats', it would not, in my opinion, be possible to read the word 'cats' as including 'dogs'; the legislative history would demonstrate that, while Parliament had successively widened the scope of the statute, it had consistently legislated in relation to felines, and had left its possible extension to other domestic pets for future consideration. Reading the word 'cats' as meaning 'cats or dogs' in these circumstances would be to usurp the function of Parliament.

73. In *R* v *A* [2002] 1 AC 45 the offending statute had laid down an elaborate scheme to prevent the defendant to a charge of rape from adducing certain kinds of evidence at his trial. Read without qualification this could exclude logically relevant evidence favourable to the accused and deny him a fair trial contrary to article 6 of the Convention. The House read the statute as subject to the implied proviso that evidence or questioning which was required to ensure a fair trial should not be treated as inadmissible. The House supplied a missing qualification which significantly limited the operation of the statute but which did not contradict any of its fundamental features. As Lord Steyn observed (at p 68, para 45) it would be unrealistic to suppose that Parliament, if alerted to the problem, would have wished to deny an accused person the right to put forward a full and complete defence by advancing truly probative material.

74. For my own part, I have no difficulty with the conclusion which the House reached in that case. The qualification which it supplied glossed but did not contradict anything in the relevant statute. Neither expressly nor implicitly did the statute require logically probative evidence to be excluded if its exclusion would have the effect of denying the accused a fair trial. The meaning of the statute was not ambiguous, and in the absence of section 3 the proviso could not have been implied. But if it had been expressed it would not have made the statute self-contradictory or produced a nonsense.

75. Lord Hope of Craighead, who had more difficulty in the application of section 3, observed (*loc cit*) that compatibility was to be achieved only so far as this was possible, and that it would plainly not be possible if the legislation contained provisions which expressly contradicted the meaning which the enactment would have to be given to make it compatible. He added that the same result must follow if they did

so by necessary implication, as this too was a means of identifying the plain intention of Parliament. Lord Steyn said the same in *Anderson* [2003] 1 AC 837, p 894, para 59:

> 'Section 3(1) is not available where the suggested interpretation is contrary to express statutory words *or is by implication necessarily contradicted by the statute*' (emphasis added)

citing Lord Nicholls in *In re S (Minors)* [2002] 2 AC 291, 313–314, para 41 in support.

76. I respectfully agree with this approach, though I would add a caveat. I do not understand the word 'implication' as entitling the court to imply words which would render the statute incompatible with the Convention; that would be entirely contrary to the spirit of section 3. They mean only that the incompatibility need not be explicit; but if not then it must be implicit, that it to say manifest on the face of the statute.

[Lord Millet considered the legislative history.]

94. By 1988 Parliament, therefore, had successively widened the scope of paragraph 2(1). First applying only to the tenant's widow, it was extended first to his or her surviving spouse and later to a person who had lived with the tenant as his or her spouse though without actually contracting a legally binding marriage. The common feature of all these relationships is that they are open relationships between persons of the opposite sex. Persons who set up home together may be husband and wife or live together as husband and wife; they may be lovers; or brother and sister; or friends; or fellow students; or share a common economic interest; or one may be economically dependent on the other. But Parliament did not extend the right to persons who set up home together; but only to those who did so *as husband and wife*.

95. Couples of the same sex can no more live together as husband and wife than they can live together as brother and sister. To extend the paragraph to persons who set up home as lovers would have been a major category extension. It would have been highly controversial in 1988 and was not then required by the Convention. The practice of Contracting States was far from uniform; and Parliament was entitled to take the view that any further extension of paragraph (2) could wait for another day. One step at a time is a defensible legislative policy which the courts should respect. Housing Acts come before Parliament with some frequency; and Parliament was entitled to take the view that the question could be revisited without any great delay. It is just as important for legislatures not to proceed faster than society can accept as it is for judges; and under our constitutional arrangements the pace of change is for Parliament.

96. Parliament, as I have said, is now considering corrective legislation in the Civil Partnerships Bill currently before the House in its legislative capacity. The Bill creates a new legal relationship, called a civil partnership, which the persons of the same sex may enter into by registering themselves as civil partners. It inserts the words "or surviving civil partner" after the words 'surviving spouse' in paragraph 2(1), and adds a new paragraph (2)(b):

> '(b) a person who was living with the original tenant as if they were civil partners shall be treated as the civil partner of the original tenant.'

97. There will thus be four categories of relationship covered if the Bill becomes law: (i) spouses, ie married persons (necessarily being persons of the opposite sex); (ii) persons who live together as husband and wife who are to be treated as if they were married (and who must therefore also be of the opposite sex): (iii) civil partners (who must be of the same sex) who are given the same rights as but are not treated as if they were married persons; and (iv) persons who live together as if they were civil partners without having registered their relationship, who are treated as if they had done so. This is a rational and sensible scheme which does not involve pretending that couples of the same sex can marry or be treated as if they had done so.

98. Among the matters which Parliament will have had to consider in debating the Civil Partnerships Bill are: (i) which statutes to amend by extending their reach to civil partners and persons living together as civil partners: (ii) whether such statutes should extend to unregistered civil partnerships in every case or whether in some cases it would be appropriate to require the parties to register their relationship before taking the benefits of the statute: (iii) whether the Bill should be retrospective to any and what extent: and (iv) from what date should the new provisions come into force. Presumably some time must elapse before a system of registration can be established: should unregistered civil partners have to wait until it is? These, and no doubt other matters, are questions of policy for the legislature.

99. All this will be foreclosed by the majority. By what is claimed to be a process of interpretation of an existing statute framed in gender specific terms, and enacted at a time when homosexual relationships were not recognised by law, it is proposed to treat persons of the same sex living together as if they were living together as husband and wife and then to treat such persons as if they were lawfully married. It is to be left unclear as from what date this change in the law has taken place. If we were to decide this question we would be usurping the function of Parliament; and if we were to say that it was from the time when the European Court of Human Rights decided that such discrimination was unlawful we would be transferring the legislative power from Parliament to that court. It is, in my view, consonant with the Convention for the Contracting States to take time to consider its implications and to bring their laws into conformity with it. They do not demand retrospective legislation.

100. Worse still, in support of their conclusion that the existing discrimination is incompatible with the Convention, there is a tendency in some of the speeches of the majority to refer to loving, stable and long-lasting homosexual relationships. It is left wholly unclear whether qualification for the successive tenancy is confined to couples enjoying such a relationship or, consistently with the legislative policy which Parliament has hitherto adopted, is dependent on status and not merit.

101. In my opinion all these questions are essentially questions of social policy which should be left to Parliament. For the reasons I have endeavoured to state it is in my view not open to the courts to foreclose them by adopting an interpretation of the existing legislation which it not only does not bear but which is manifestly inconsistent with it.

102. I would allow the appeal....

LORD RODGER OF EARLSFERRY:

122.... the key to what it is possible for the courts to imply into legislation without crossing the border from interpretation to amendment does not lie in the number of words that have to be read in. The key lies in a careful consideration of the essential principles and scope of the legislation being interpreted. If the insertion of one word contradicts those principles or goes beyond the scope of the legislation, it amounts to impermissible amendment. On the other hand, if the implication of a dozen words leaves the essential principles and scope of the legislation intact but allows it to be read in a way which is compatible with Convention rights, the implication is a legitimate exercise of the powers conferred by section 3(1). Of course, the greater the extent of the proposed implication, the greater the need to make sure that the court is not going beyond the scheme of the legislation and embarking upon amendment. Nevertheless, what matters is not the number of words but their effect...

124. Sometimes it may be possible to isolate a particular phrase which causes the difficulty and to read in words that modify it so as to remove the incompatibility. Or else the court may read in words that qualify the provision as a whole. At other times the appropriate solution may be to read down the provision so that it falls to be given effect in a way that is compatible with the Convention rights in question. In other cases the easiest solution may be to put the offending part of the provision into different words which convey the meaning that will be compatible with those rights. The preferred technique will depend on the particular provision and also, in reality, on the person doing the interpreting. This does not matter since they are simply different means of achieving the same substantive result. However, precisely because section 3(1) is to be operated by many others besides the courts, and because it is concerned with interpreting and not with amending the offending provision, it respectfully seems to me that it would be going too far to insist that those using the section to interpret legislation should match the standards to be expected of a parliamentary draftsman amending the provision: cf *R v Lambert* [2002] 2 AC 545, 585, para 80 per Lord Hope of Craighead. It is enough that the interpretation placed on the provision should be clear, however it may be expressed and whatever the precise means adopted to achieve it.

Appeal disallowed.

NOTE: In *R* v *A (No. 2)* [2002] 1 AC 45, there was criticism that the Law Lords had gone too far and frustrated parliamentary intention, this may explain the justifications of it in *Ghaidan*. For an interesting defence of *R* v *A* see A. Kavanagh 'Unlocking the Human Rights Act: the Radical Approach to section 3(1) Revisited' (2005) 3 *European Human Rights Law Review* 259.

■ QUESTION

By interpreting 'as his or her wife or husband' to include same sex couples, have the majority gone beyond interpreting the legislation and, in effect, engaged in legislating, and, if yes, are the courts an appropriate institution to consider the various issues of policy?

(d) How do declarations of incompatibility operate?

Where there is a conflict between Convention rights and primary legislation which cannot be resolved by an interpretation which renders the legislation compatible with the Convention, a court at the level of the High Court or above may make a declaration of incompatibility (see s. 4(2) and (3)). Such a declaration has no impact, however, on the immediate proceedings; nor does it affect the validity or continuing enforcement of the impugned legislation (see s. 4(6)). As such the authority has not acted unlawfully and no remedies may be granted against it. The victim has, at best, a Pyrrhic victory. The declaration also casts the 'hot potato' into a politician's hands as the relevant Minister will then have to determine whether the incompatible legislation should be amended. He may use the fast-track procedure in s. 10 and Sched. 2 to amend the legislation by means of a 'remedial order' which must be approved in draft by positive resolution of each House of Parliament. Should the Minister decide not to act (and there may be pragmatic political reasons for such a decision), the victim will have to resort to seeking to enforce his or her rights under the Convention machinery.

Sir William Wade QC, 'The United Kingdom's Bill of Rights' in *Constitutional Reform in the United Kingdom: Practice and Principles*

(1998), pp. 66–67

... Under clause 4 a declaration of incompatibility may be made by the court if it is satisfied that there is an unavoidable conflict between Convention rights and primary legislation; and the same is to apply in the case of subordinate legislation if it cannot be made compatible because of primary legislation. The declaration is not to affect the validity, continuing operation or enforcement of the offending provision, nor is it to be binding on the parties. But it may lead to a 'remedial order' amending the offending legislation which may be made by a minister of the Crown and must be approved in draft by positive resolution of each House of Parliament. There are, however, certain escape clauses. In case of urgency the Parliamentary resolutions may be dispensed with for up to 40 days. Furthermore, a minister may make a remedial order without a declaration by the court if it appears to him that a finding of the European Court of Human Rights produces an incompatibility with the UK's Convention obligations—a provision comparable to that of the European Communities Act 1972 under which ministers may amend legislation by Order in Council or regulations for the purpose of reconciling it with EU law.

A remedial order, like the provision of the European Communities Act, is an exceptionally drastic form of Henry VIII clause, of the kind that has recently worried the House of Lords' Delegated Powers Scrutiny Committee. It may well be the most drastic example yet seen, since it is expressly made capable of operating retrospectively, subject only to a ban on retrospective criminal liability. There is wide power to include 'such incidental, supplemental, consequential and transitional provisions' as may be thought appropriate by the minister and it may amend or repeal legislation, whether primary or subordinate, other than that containing the incompatibility. These extraordinary powers were the subject of protests in the House of Lords, Lord Simon of Glaisdale saying 'we cannot have Henry VIII trampling through the statute book in this way'. But, inevitably, such powers have to be accepted, however grudgingly, as part of the mechanism for adopting an external system of law, and in default of new and speedy Parliamentary procedures.

Reverence for the sovereignty of Parliament was the motive behind this remarkable amalgam of judicial and executive powers. But the sovereignty of Parliament is not what it was, having suffered severe diminution by its subjection to EU law. Lord Lester's earlier private member's bill had provided for the Convention rights to prevail over inconsistent legislation without intervention by the executive, but now he declared a change of mind and accepted the government's plan as 'an ingenious and successful reconciliation of principles of Parliamentary sovereignty and the need for effective domestic remedies'—though only, he added, 'after a good deal of arm-twisting by some members of this place rather more noble and learned than myself'. It is not surprising if the government resorted to some degree of intellectual harassment in order to secure the support of Lord Lester, with his immense experience and authority in this field.

If, then, a declaration of incompatibility is granted in some case, what is the likely result? A litigant has established that he ought to win his case because of the infringement of his human rights, but yet he loses it since the declaration does not affect the validity of the offending statute or regulation, or its enforceability. The appropriate minister must then consider whether to make a remedial order. It would seem inevitable that the court would grant a stay of execution while the minister considers whether to make an order, and whether it should be retrospective. If he makes a retrospective order, he deprives the victorious party of the fruits of his judgment. If he does not, he leaves the other party to suffer a violation of his human rights; and it is the same if the minister makes no order at all. The minister's position between these two fires is far from enviable. There may be a lot of money at stake and the government itself may be a party, so that the minister is compelled to be judge in his own cause. In such cases there is certain to be trouble in Parliament and a risk that the positive resolution will be opposed. There may be very difficult questions about the effect on third parties, even though clause 11 allows different provision to be made for different cases. It is hard to think of a more invidious position for a minister. And what, finally, about Article 6 of the Convention, which entitles everyone to a fair and public hearing by an independent and impartial tribunal in the determination of his civil rights and obligations? Will the Strasbourg court allow civil rights, and especially human rights, to be decided by discretionary executive order in this way? It seems highly unlikely.

In the House of Lords' second reading and committee debates there was no mention, I think, of the rule of law. Yet to allow questions of personal legal right to be decided by executive discretion offends against the rule of law in its most basic sense: the rule of law as opposed to the rule of discretionary power. Remedial orders will, indeed, be subject to judicial review and the Bill makes no attempt to exempt them. But the taking of human rights cases so far out of the course of ordinary law does not seem to be an adequately constitutional solution.

G. Marshall, 'Patriating Rights—with Reservations: the Human Rights Bill 1998' in *Constitutional Reform in the United Kingdom: Practice and Principles*

(1998), pp. 81–82

Assessing Incompatibility

... [T]wo different questions can be distinguished. In the first place, all reviewing courts have to adopt some view of the relation of their function to that of the legislature. What standard of review or degree of deference, or presumption of constitutionality is appropriate? Should it be different for different kinds of legislation and so on? In this respect, how should United Kingdom courts take into account decisions of the European Court of Human Rights as the Bill requires? That court has applied to national legislatures a relatively low standard of scrutiny under the rubric of the margin of appreciation on the ground that state authorities are better able to judge national conditions and requirements than international judges. But that *rationale* does not apply within a state as between its legislature and judiciary. So in taking account of the decisions of the Strasbourg court, it would seem appropriate for British courts to subtract the effect of the margin of appreciation. In at least some cases this should lead to different and more activist decisions.

A second aspect of judicial review (or incompatibility assessment) relates to the substantive criteria that compatible legislation is required to meet. Here it can be seen that there are two analytically different, though sometimes confusingly related, reasons why a legislative provision might not contravene, or might not be incompatible, with the Convention. In the first place it might not be incompatible with an enumerated right because the Convention does not cover or relate to the disputed activity at all. A law restricting the use of firearms is not inconsistent with Convention rights, because nothing in the Convention guarantees the right to use firearms. In the second place, a legislative provision may be held to be compatible with the Convention because although the Convention is relevant and the disputed legislation appears to limit or impinge upon one or other of its rights, it is held to be a justified limitation in those cases where the Convention provides that limits may properly be imposed that are demonstrably justified by stated criteria or in a free and democratic society (the criterion found in some Convention rights and whose wording has been adopted in the general limitation sections of the Canadian and New Zealand rights legislation). Such limits may be said to place a restriction on, or involve a modification of, a right in its unqualified form, but they do not constitute a denial, negation, abridgement, curtailment, contravention, infringement or violation of a right.

...

A question for the future is the status of the Human Rights Bill when the European Convention is formally embodied in the law of the European Union. Within the area covered by the Treaties, United Kingdom courts may then find themselves obliged to disapply British statutes incompatible with Convention rights embodied in Community law whilst holding themselves unable to do so when the same provisions are alleged to conflict with the Convention rights included in the United Kingdom Human Rights legislation. At that point, the government's attitude to judicial review will appear even more bizarre and indefensible.

Sydney Kentridge QC, 'The Incorporation of the European Convention on Human Rights' in *Constitutional Reform in the United Kingdom: Practice and Principles*

(1998), p. 69

Some speakers regard the provision in the Bill for `declarations of incompatibility as an inadequate remedy against legislative infringements of fundamental rights. I regard it as a subtle compromise between the concepts of parliamentary sovereignty and fundamental rights. I believe, moreover, that declarations of incompatibility with primary legislation are likely to be rare, at least in relation to future legislation. There are two main reasons for this. The first, a very practical one, is that the individual litigant 'the victim' is likely to get little direct benefit from such a declaration. It is difficult to visualise a situation in which a lawyer will advise his client to go to court to seek a declaration of incompatibility. The second reason, a politico-legal one, is that Parliament, the executive and the courts will all strive to avoid the necessity for such declarations. The executive in introducing legislation, and Parliament in passing it, will do their utmost to ensure that there is no incompatibility with the Convention. The courts in compliance with clause 3 will, so far as it is possible to do so, read and give effect to legislation in a way which is compatible with the Convention rights. The executive, as litigant, will also in most instances prefer a 'reading down' of contested legislation to a declaration of incompatibility.

■ QUESTIONS

1. If Kentridge is correct that the individual litigant is likely to get little direct benefit from a declaration of incompatibility, is this not a cause for concern? Further, if a victim of a violation of the Convention is blocked from obtaining an effective remedy, is this not a further breach of the Convention, namely Art. 13? It should be noted that Art. 13 is excluded from those rights which are incorporated by the Human Rights Act.
2. If a declaration of incompatibility is made in respect of a particularly controversial issue on which political opinion and public opinion are strongly divided, will a Minister implement the fast-track procedure to amend the offending legislation; and, if he does so, will Parliament approve it? Would a government be acting unconstitutionally if it decided not to implement the fast-track procedure calculating that more political capital was to be made from inactivity?
3. What is the consequence of a statement by a Minister in charge of a Bill at Second Reading that although he is unable to make a 'statement of compatibility' the Government nevertheless wishes the House to proceed with the Bill (see s. 19(1)) if the Bill is ultimately enacted and challenged before a United Kingdom court resulting in a declaration of incompatibility?
4. Is Marshall correct when he states that 'the Human Rights Bill contains a major contradiction of purpose and is attempting to marry two inconsistent principles of action. The rights principle is in essence anti-majoritarian. You cannot success-

fully combine the effective protection of rights against the majority with unfettered Parliamentary supremacy'?

NOTE: For a summary of cases up to July 2010 where a declaration of incompatability was made under the Human Rights Act, see below.

Responding to human rights judgments

Government Response to the Joint Committee on Human Rights' Fifteenth Report of Session 2009–10

Cm 7982, 2010

Annex A: Declarations of incompatibility

Since the Human Rights Act 1998 came into force on 2 October 2000, 26 declarations of incompatibility have been made. Of these:

18 have become final (in whole or in part) and are not subject to further appeal;

8 have been overturned on appeal.

Of the 18 declarations of incompatibility that have become final:

10 have been remedied by later primary legislation

1 has been remedied by a remedial order under section 10 of the Human Rights Act;

4 relate to provisions that had already been remedied by primary legislation at the time of the declaration;

3 are under consideration as to how to remedy the incompatibility. ..

This information was last updated on 13 July 2010, and will not reflect any changes after that date.

(e) How will the Human Rights Act affect the way in which judges decide cases?

Lord Irvine of Lairg LC, The Tom Sargant Memorial Lecture, 'The Development of Human Rights in Britain under an Incorporated Convention on Human Rights'

16 December 1997

The Emergence of a new approach

I have referred to the effect the introduction of European Community law has had on the development of our own domestic law. I believe that incorporating into our own law the Convention rights will have an equally healthy effect.

Any court or tribunal determining any question relating to a Convention Right will be obliged to take into account the body of jurisprudence of the Court and Commission of Human rights and of the Council of Ministers. This is obviously right. it gives British courts both the benefit of 50 years careful analysis of the Convention rights and ensures British Courts interpret the Convention consistently with Strasbourg. The British courts will therefore need to apply the same techniques of interpretation and decision-making as the Strasbourg bodies. I have already mentioned recourse to Parliamentary materials such as Hansard—where we are now closer in line with our continental colleagues. I will mention three more aspects. As I do so, it should be remembered that the courts which will be applying these techniques will be the ordinary courts of the land; we have not considered it right to create some special human rights court alongside the ordinary system; the Convention rights must pervade all law and all the courts systems. Our courts will therefore learn these techniques and inevitably will consider their utility in deciding other non-Convention cases.

First there is the approach to statutory interpretation. The tools of construction in use in mainland Europe are known to be different from those the English courts have traditionally used. I will refer to just one: the so-called teleological approach which is concerned with giving the instrument its presumed legislative intent. It is less concerned with the textual analysis usual to the common law tradition of interpretation. It is a process of moulding the law to what the Court believes the law should be trying to achieve. It is undoubtedly the case that our own domestic approach to interpretation of statutes has become more purposive. Lord Diplock had already identified this trend 20 years ago when he noted that:

> If one looks back to the actual decisions of the [House of Lords] on questions of statutory construction over the last 30 years one cannot fail to be struck by the evidence of a trend away from the purely literal towards the purposive construction of statutory provisions.

This trend has not diminished since then, although there are cases where the Courts have declined to adopt what was in one case described as an 'over purposive' approach.

Yet as the Courts, through familiarity with the Convention jurisprudence, become more exposed to methods of interpretation which pay more heed to the purpose, and less to whether the words were felicitously chosen to achieve that end, the balance is likely to swing more firmly yet in the direction of the purposive approach.

Secondly, there is the doctrine of proportionality... This doctrine is applied by the European Court of Human Rights. Its application is to ensure that a measure imposes no greater restriction upon a Convention right than is absolutely necessary to achieve its objectives. Although not identical to the principle as applied in Luxembourg, it shares the feature that it raises questions foreign to the traditional *Wednesbury* approach to judicial review. Under the *Wednesbury* doctrine an administrative decision will only be struck down if it is so bad that no reasonable decision-maker could have taken it.

Closely allied with the doctrine of proportionality is the concept of the margin of appreciation. The Court of Human Rights has developed this doctrine which permits national courts a discretion in the application of the requirements of the Convention to their own national conditions. This discretion is not absolute, since the Court of Human Rights reserves the power to review any act of a national authority or court; and the discretion is more likely to be recognised in the application of those articles of the Convention which expressly include generally stated conditions or exceptions, such as Articles 8–11, rather than in the area of obligations which in any civilised society should be absolute, such as the rights to life, freedom from torture and freedom from slavery and forced labour that are provided by Articles 2–4.

This 'margin of appreciation', was first developed by the Court in a British case, *Handyside* v *UK*. It concerned whether a conviction for possessing an obscene article could be justified under Article 10(2) of the Convention as a limitation upon freedom of expression that was necessary for the 'protection of morals'. The court said:

> By reason of their direct and continuous contact with the vital forces of their countries, state authorities are in principle in a better position than the international judge to give an opinion on the exact content of those requirements [of morals] as well as on the 'necessity' of a 'restriction' or 'penalty' intended to meet them...

Although there is some encouragement in British decisions for the view that the margin of appreciation under the Convention is simply the *Wednesbury* test under another guise statements by the Court of Human Rights seem to draw a significant distinction. The Court of Human Rights has said in terms that its review is not limited to checking that the national authority 'exercised its discretion reasonably, carefully and in good faith'. It has to go further. It has to satisfy itself that the decision was based on an 'acceptable assessment of the relevant facts' and that the interference was no more than reasonably necessary to achieve the legitimate aim pursued.

That approach shows that there is a profound difference between the Convention margin of appreciation and the common law test of rationality. The latter would be satisfied by an exercise of discretion done 'reasonably, carefully and in good faith' although the passage I have cited indicates that the Court of Human Rights' review of action is not so restricted. In these cases a more rigorous scrutiny than traditional judicial review will be required. An illustration of the difference may be found in the speech of Simon Brown LJ in *ex p Smith* (the armed forces homosexual policy case)

> If the Convention for the Protection of Human Rights and Fundamental Freedoms were part of our law and we were accordingly entitled to ask whether the policy answers a pressing social need and whether the restriction on human rights involved can be shown proportionate to its benefits, then

> clearly the primary judgement (subject only to a limited 'margin of appreciation') would be for us and not for others; the constitutional balance would shift. But that is not the position. In exercising merely a secondary judgement, this court is bound, even though adjudicating in a human rights context, to act with some reticence.

The question I pose is how long the courts will restrict their review to a narrow *Wednesbury* approach in non-Convention cases, if used to inquiring more deeply in Convention cases? There will remain distinctions of importance between the two categories of case which should be respected. But some blurring of line may be inevitable.

I have expressed my views in my Administrative Law Bar Association Lecture in 1995 on how the Courts ought properly to regard the dividing line between their function and that of Parliament. But the process is not one way. British influence on the application of the Convention rights is likely to increase. British officials were closely involved in the drafting of the Convention. When our British courts make their own pronouncements on the Convention, their views will be studied in other Convention countries and in Strasbourg itself with great respect. I am sure that British judges' influence for the good of the Convention will be considerable. They will bring to the application of the Convention their great skills of analysis and interpretation. But they will also bring to it our proud British traditions of liberty.

The Shift from form to substance

So there is room to predict some decisive and far reaching changes in future judicial decision making. The major shift may be away from a concern with form to a concern with substance. Let me summarise the reasons.

In the field of review by judges of administrative action, the courts' decisions to date have been largely based on something akin to the application of a set of rules. If the rules are broken, the conduct will be condemned. But if the rules are obeyed, (the right factors are taken into account, no irrelevant factors taken into account, no misdirection of law and no out and out irrationality) the decision will be upheld, usually irrespective of the overall objective merits of the policy. In some cases much may turn—or at least appear to turn—on the form in which a decision is expressed rather than its substance. Does the decision as expressed show that the right reasons have been taken into account? Does it disclose potentially irrational reasoning? Might the court's review be different if the reasoning were expressed differently so as to avoid the court's *Wednesbury* scrutiny?

Now, in areas where the Convention applies, the Court will be less concerned whether there has been a failure in this sense but will inquire more closely into the merits of the decision to see for example that necessity justified the limitation of a positive right, and that it was no more... of a limitation than was needed. There is a discernible shift which may be seen in essence as a shift from form to substance. If, as I have suggested, there is a spillover into other areas of law, then that shift from form to substance will become more marked.

This may be seen as a progression of an existing and now long standing trend. In modern times, the emphasis on identifying the true substance at issue has been seen in diverse areas: in tax where new techniques have developed to view the substance of a transaction overall rather than to be mesmerised by the form of an isolated step, or in the areas of statutory control of leases, where the Courts are astute to prevent form being used to obscure the reality of the underlying transaction. In what may seem at first blush a very different area, that of interpretation of contracts, recent decisions also emphasise the need to cast away the baggage of older years where literal and semantic analysis was allowed to override the real intent of the parties.

In a very broad sense we can see here a similarity of approach: to get to the substance of the issue and not be distracted by the form.

These are trends already well developed but I believe they will gain impetus from incorporation of the Convention. In addition the Courts will be making decisions founded more explicitly and frequently on considerations of morality and justifiability.

This Bill will therefore create a more explicitly moral approach to decisions and decision making; will promote both a culture where positive rights and liberties become the focus and concern of legislators, administrators and judges alike; and a culture in judicial decision making where there will be a greater concentration on substance rather than form.

...

Peter Duffy QC, 'The European Convention on Human Rights, Issues Relating to its Interpretation in the Light of the Human Rights Bill' in *Constitutional Reform in the United Kingdom: Practice and Principles*

(1998), pp. 100–102

Several of the rights in the Convention, notably Article 8 (right to respect for private and family life, home and correspondence), Article 9 (freedom of thought, conscience and religion), Article 10 (freedom of expression) and Article 11 (freedom of assembly and association) are stated in general terms in a first paragraph and can be subject to restrictions in the interests of other legitimate interests provided such restriction is regulated by the law and is, in the language of the Convention, 'necessary in a democratic society'. The case law of the Court provides well established guidance on the approach to be taken.

First, a generous approach is to be taken when determining what comes within the scope of the protected fundamental rights. The Court has pointed out that to construe the scope of the rights protected broadly is consonant with the essential object and purpose of the ECHR [*Niemietz* v *Germany* 16 EHRR 97, para. 31] which, of course, is 'an instrument for the protection of individual human beings', accordingly 'its provisions [should] be interpreted and applied so as to make its safeguards practical and effective' [*Loizidou* v *Turkey*, 20 EHRR 99, para. 71]. Adopting a narrow construction of the rights protected risks denying Convention scrutiny in cases where a fundamental right may be affected, albeit indirectly. The Court has rightly stressed that giving a broad construction to the rights protected does not unduly hamper public bodies for they retain their entitlement to 'interfere' provided the conditions of the Convention are respected [*Niemietz*, para. 31].

The conditions under which restrictions are permitted vary somewhat from right to right but important underlying principles are well established in the Court's case law and practice. For an interference to be justified, four conditions must be fulfilled. These are that (i) the interference is 'lawful', (ii) it serves a legitimate purpose, (iii) it is 'necessary in a democratic society'; and (iv) it is not discriminatory. Each of these requirements is outlined in turn below.

First, the lawfulness requirement, this does not merely mean that interference with a fundamental right is permitted under domestic law. The Court has consistently stated that 'it [is] contrary to the rule of law for the legal discretion granted to the executive to be in the form of unfettered power':

> The law must indicate the scope of any such discretion conferred on the competent authorities and the manner of its exercise with sufficient clarity, having regard to the legitimate aim of the measure in question, to give the individual adequate protection against arbitrary interference [*Malone* v *United Kingdom* (1985) 7 EHRR 14, para. 68].

The condition of 'lawfulness' is unlikely to detain British courts much where legislation circumscribes the powers of public authorities. Where it will make a difference, once the Human Rights Act enters into force, is to the Diceyan rule of law concept that public bodies are permitted to do anything which is not specifically prohibited by law. This has led in a number of cases to British courts being unable to provide redress when intrusive powers were unregulated. In *Malone* v *Metropolitan Police Commissioner (No 2)* [[1979] 1 Ch 344 at 380], Sir Robert Megarry V-C described interception of communications as 'a subject which cries out for legislation' yet, without ECHR incorporation and under the old concept of the rule of law, he could not provide relief. The case proceeded to Strasbourg and the finding, as Sir Robert had predicted, that English law then failed to provide 'the minimum degree of legal protection to which citizens are entitled under the rule of law in a democratic society.'

The second condition is that the reason for an interference is a proper one. In very few cases under the ECHR has an improper purpose been shown. In the vast majority of cases, it is common ground that the public authority had a proper purpose. Forensic and judicial attention focuses instead on the third and fourth conditions, namely whether the interference for a proper purpose was 'necessary in a democratic society' and was done without any impermissible discrimination.

For an interference to be 'necessary in a democratic society', the courts must be satisfied that the public body can convincingly demonstrate the need for the interference and that the interference is 'fair'.

The fourth and final condition to mention is that any action undertaken by public bodies which gives effect to or interferes with Convention rights and freedoms must be done in a non-discriminatory manner. Not every difference of treatment amounts to discrimination. Discrimination occurs if 'the distinction has no objectives and reasonable justification' [*Belgian Linguistic* (1968) 1 EHRR 252, para. 10]. Checking this requirement also involves testing proportionality, similar to considering 'necessity in a democratic society'. This is not surprising as unjustified discrimination cannot sensibly be described as necessary in a democratic society. It is worth emphasising, however, that some grounds of distinction, particularly race or gender, cannot normally be accepted and that discriminatory treatment on such grounds is regarded as especially serious and that it can rarely be accepted and must be particularly closely scrutinised. This represents a significant change from the piece-meal protection against discrimination in existing British legislative schemes.

For incorporation to be effective, as Parliament intends, British courts will have to engage in an effective control of the reasons given for interference and their sufficiency. The courts have already emphasised that greater scrutiny is needed when fundamental rights are in play. In *R* v *Ministry of Defence, ex parte Smith* [[1996] QB 517], the case on dismissal of homosexuals and lesbians from the armed services, Sir Thomas Bingham MR (as he then was) stated [at p. 554] that:

> The court may not interfere with the exercise of an administrative discretion on substantive grounds save where the court is satisfied that the decision is unreasonable in the sense that it is beyond the range of responses open to a reasonable decision maker. But in judging whether the decision maker has exceeded this margin of appreciation the human rights context is important. The more substantial the interference with human rights, the more the court will require by way of justification before it is satisfied that the decision is reasonable in the sense outlined above.

For ECHR incorporation to be effective, the British courts in such cases will have to go beyond a heightened *Wednesbury* review, whilst still respecting the decision making discretion of the primary decision maker. The Lord Chancellor again explained this point with clarity in his 1997 Tom Sargant Lecture. In striking the balance, the Convention's case law uses phrases such as 'fair balance' and 'proportionate'. Domestic courts, of course, frequently exercise discretion that call for decisions on what is fair and reasonable in all circumstances. That experience, including that of applying principles of equity, can be drawn upon in ensuring that incorporation is made effective.

NOTE: Section 2(1) of the Human Rights Act 1998 requires a court when determining an issue relating to a Convention right to take into account any relevant jurisprudence from the European Court of Human Rights. Such decisions are not, however, binding—they simply have to be considered—but the Convention rights are binding. In arriving at their decisions the European Court of Human Rights has developed the doctrine of the margin of appreciation (see, p. 417, *ante*) to reflect diversity within Europe and also the fact that the Court is performing a supervisory function as the primary responsibility for ensuring that human rights are protected lies with the State. Could the courts within a state seek to apply or develop their own version of the doctrine of margin of appreciation? Sir John Laws, 'The Limitations of Human Rights' [1998] *Public Law* 254, at 258, states:

> The margin of appreciation...will necessarily be inapt to the administration of the Convention in the domestic courts for the very reason that they are domestic; they will not be subject to an objective inhibition generated by any cultural distance between themselves and the state organs whose decisions are impleaded before them.

There is a possibility, however, that Convention rights may be diluted if courts show undue deference to Parliament or the Executive or if they ignore the influence of the doctrine on decisions of the European Court of Human Rights when considering their relevance to the United Kingdom. That there is a notion of judicial deference is evidenced by dicta in several cases. In *R* v *Director of Public Prosecutions, ex parte Kebilene and Others* [2000] 2 AC 326, Lord Hope stated:

> [The doctrine of margin of appreciation] is an integral part of the supervisory jurisdiction which is exercised over state conduct by the international court. By conceding a margin of appreciation to each national system, the court has recognised that the Convention, as a living system, does not need to be applied uniformly by all states but may vary in its application according to local needs and conditions. This technique is not available to the national courts when they are considering Convention issues arising within their own countries. But in the hands of the national courts also the Convention should be seen as an expression of fundamental principles rather than as a set of mere rules. The question which the courts will have to decide in the application of these principles will involve questions of balance between competing interests and issues of proportionality.
>
> In this area difficult choices may have to be made by the executive or the legislature between the rights of the individual and the needs of society. In some circumstances it will be appropriate for the courts to recognise that there is an area of judgment within which the judiciary will defer, on democratic grounds, to the considered opinion of the elected body or person whose act or decision

> is said to be incompatible with the Convention. This point is well made at p. 74, para 3.21 of *Human Rights Law and Practice* (1999)... where the area in which these choices may arise is conveniently and appropriately described as the 'discretionary area of judgment'. It will be easier for such an area of judgment to be recognised where the Convention itself requires a balance to be struck, much less so where the right is stated in terms which are unqualified. It will be easier for it to be recognised where the issues involve questions of social or economic policy, much less so where the rights are of high constitutional importance or are of a kind where the courts are especially well placed to assess the need for protection.

In *R* v *Lambert, Ali and Jordan* [2001] 1 All ER 1014, Lord Woolf CJ stated (at para. 16):

> It is also important to have in mind that legislation is passed by a democratically elected Parliament and therefore the courts under the convention are entitled to and should, as a matter of constitutional principle, pay a degree of deference to the view of Parliament as to what is in the interest of the public generally when upholding the rights of the individual under the convention. The courts are required to balance the competing interests involved.

In according deference to Parliament or the Executive a key consideration will be the question of proportionality which featured in their Lordships' deliberations in the following two cases. In the second case a major shift in the test for judicial review, at least where Convention rights are involved, suggests that the proportionality principle may result in significantly less deference being accorded to the views of decision-makers than prior to the enactment of the Human Rights Act 1998, even under the 'anxious scrutiny' test adopted in *R* v *Ministry of Defence, ex parte Smith* [1996] QB 517 (p. 408, *ante*).

Brown v *Stott (Procurator Fiscal, Dunfermline) and Another*

[2001] 2 WLR 817, Privy Council

B was suspected of stealing a bottle of gin from a supermarket to which she had travelled by car. The police were called to the store. Her breath smelled of alcohol which prompted the police officer to ask her how she had travelled there. B replied that she had travelled by car and subsequently pointed out her car in the car park. By virtue of powers under s. 172(2)(a) of the Road Traffic Act 1988 she was required to say who had been driving the car. B admitted that she had. A breath test proved positive. B was charged both with theft and with driving her car after consuming an excess of alcohol contrary to s. 5(1)(a) of the 1988 Act. B sought to claim that use at her trial of the admission compulsorily obtained from her would be incompatible with her right to a fair hearing under Art. 6(1) of the Convention. The sheriff ruled against B but the High Court of Justiciary allowed her appeal declaring that the procurator fiscal had no power at her trial to lead evidence of, and rely on, the admission B had been compelled to make. The procurator fiscal and Advocate General appealed.

LORD BINGHAM OF CORNHILL: ...

Section 172 of the Road Traffic Act 1988

So far as material, s 172 of the 1988 Act at the relevant time provided:

> (2) Where the driver of a vehicle is alleged to be guilty of an offence to which this section applies—(a) the person keeping the vehicle shall give such information as to the identity of the driver as he may be required to give by or on behalf of a chief officer of police....
>
> (3) Subject to the following provisions, a person who fails to comply with a requirement under subsection (2) above shall be guilty of an offence.

It is evident that the power of the police to require information to be given as to the identity of the driver of a vehicle only arises where the driver is alleged to be guilty of an offence to which the section applies. Those offences include the most serious of driving offences, such as manslaughter or culpable homicide, causing death by dangerous driving, dangerous and careless driving, causing death by careless driving when under the influence of drugs or drink, and driving a vehicle after consuming alcohol above the prescribed limit. They also include the offence, in Scotland, of taking and driving away a vehicle without consent or lawful authority. The offences excluded are of a less serious and more regulatory nature. They include offences in relation to driving instruction, the holding of motoring events on public ways, the wearing of protective headgear, driving with uncorrected defective eyesight and offences pertaining to the testing, design, inspection and licensing of vehicles. The penalty for failing to comply with a requirement under sub-s (2) is a fine of (currently) not more than £1,000: in the case of an individual, disqualification from driving is discretionary but endorsement of the licence is mandatory. The requirement to supply information under sub-s (2) may be made of 'the person keeping the vehicle' or 'any other person', irrespective of whether either of them is suspected of being the driver alleged to have committed the relevant offence. In this case, it is clear that the respondent, when required to give information, was suspected of committing the offence for which she was later prosecuted....

Article 6 of the convention

Attention has often, and rightly, been drawn to contrasts between different articles of the convention. Some (such as arts 3 and 4) permit no restriction by national authorities. Others (such as arts 8, 9, 10 and 11) permit a measure of restriction if certain stringent and closely prescribed conditions are satisfied...

[Article 6] has more in common with the first group of articles mentioned above than the second. The only express qualification relates to the requirement of a 'public hearing'. But there is nothing to suggest that the fairness of the trial itself may be qualified, compromised or restricted in any way, whatever the circumstances and whatever the public interest in convicting the offender. If the trial as a whole is judged to be unfair, a conviction cannot stand.

What a fair trial requires cannot, however, be the subject of a single, unvarying rule or collection of rules. It is proper to take account of the facts and circumstances of particular cases, as the European Court has consistently done.

Conclusions

The convention is an international treaty by which the contracting states mutually undertake to secure to all within their respective jurisdictions certain rights and freedoms. The fundamental nature of these rights and freedoms is clear, not only from the full title and the content of the convention but from its preamble in which the signatory governments declared:

> their profound belief in those fundamental freedoms which are the foundation of justice and peace in the world and are best maintained on the one hand by an effective political democracy and on the other by a common understanding and observance of the human rights upon which they depend.

Judicial recognition and assertion of the human rights defined in the convention is not a substitute for the processes of democratic government but a complement to them. While a national court does not accord the margin of appreciation recognised by the European Court as a supra-national court, it will give weight to the decisions of a representative legislature and a democratic government within the discretionary area of judgment accorded to those bodies (see Lester and Pannick, *Human Rights Law and Practice* (1999) pp 73–76). The convention is concerned with rights and freedoms which are of real importance in a modern democracy governed by the rule of law. It does not, as is sometimes mistakenly thought, offer relief from 'The heart-ache and the thousand natural shocks That flesh is heir to'.

In interpreting the convention, as any other treaty, it is generally to be assumed that the parties have included the terms which they wished to include and on which they were able to agree, omitting other terms which they did not wish to include or on which they were not able to agree. Thus particular regard must be had and reliance placed on the express terms of the convention, which define the rights and freedoms which the contracting parties have undertaken to secure. This does not mean that nothing can be implied into the convention. The language of the convention is for the most part so general that some implication of terms is necessary, and the case law of the European Court shows that the court has been willing to imply terms into the convention when it was judged necessary or plainly right to do so. But the process of implication is one to be carried out with caution, if the risk is to be averted that the contracting parties may, by judicial interpretation, become bound by obligations which they did not expressly accept and might not have been willing to accept. As an important constitutional instrument the convention is to be seen as a 'living tree capable of growth and expansion within its natural limits'

(*Edwards* v *A-G for Canada* [1930] AC 124, 136 per Lord Sankey LC), but those limits will often call for very careful consideration.

Effect has been given to the right not to incriminate oneself in a variety of different ways.... [It] is an implied right. While it cannot be doubted that such a right must be implied, there is no treaty provision which expressly governs the effect or extent of what is to be implied.

The jurisprudence of the European Court very clearly establishes that while the overall fairness of a criminal trial cannot be compromised, the constituent rights comprised, whether expressly or implicitly, within article 6 are not themselves absolute. Limited qualification of these rights is acceptable if reasonably directed by national authorities towards a clear and proper public objective and if representing no greater qualification than the situation calls for. The general language of the convention could have led to the formulation of hard-edged and inflexible statements of principle from which no departure could be sanctioned whatever the background or the circumstances. But this approach has been consistently eschewed by the court throughout its history. The case law shows that the court has paid very close attention to the facts of particular cases coming before it, giving effect to factual differences and recognising differences of degree. Ex facto oritur jus. The court has also recognised the need for a fair balance between the general interest of the community and the personal rights of the individual, the search for which balance has been described as inherent in the whole of the convention (see *Sporrong* v *Sweden* (1982) 5 EHRR 35, 52, para 69; *Sheffield* v *UK* (1998) 27 EHRR 163, 191, para 52.

The high incidence of death and injury on the roads caused by the misuse of motor vehicles is a very serious problem common to almost all developed societies. The need to address it in an effective way, for the benefit of the public, cannot be doubted. Among other ways in which democratic governments have sought to address it is by subjecting the use of motor vehicles to a regime of regulation and making provision for enforcement by identifying, prosecuting and punishing offending drivers. Materials laid before the Board, incomplete though they are, reveal different responses to the problem of enforcement. Under some legal systems (Spain, Belgium and France are examples) the registered owner of a vehicle is assumed to be the driver guilty of minor traffic infractions unless he shows that some other person was driving at the relevant time or establishes some other ground of exoneration. There being a clear public interest in enforcement of road traffic legislation the crucial question in the present case is whether s 172 of the 1988 Act represents a disproportionate response, or one that undermines a defendant's right to a fair trial, if an admission of being the driver is relied on at trial.

I do not for my part consider that s 172, properly applied, does represent a disproportionate response to this serious social problem, nor do I think that reliance on the respondent's admission, in the present case, would undermine her right to a fair trial. I reach that conclusion for a number of reasons.

(1) Section 172 of the 1988 Act provides for the putting of a single, simple question. The answer cannot of itself incriminate the suspect, since it is not without more an offence to drive a car. An admission of driving may, of course, as here, provide proof of a fact necessary to convict, but the section does not sanction prolonged questioning about the facts alleged to give rise to criminal offences such as was understandably held to be objectionable in *Saunders* v *UK* [p. 425, *ante*], and the penalty for declining to answer under the section is moderate and non-custodial. There is in the present case no suggestion of improper coercion or oppression such as might give rise to unreliable admissions and so contribute to a miscarriage of justice, and if there were evidence of such conduct the trial judge would have ample power to exclude evidence of the admission.

(2) While the High Court was entitled to distinguish... between the giving of an answer under s 172 and the provision of physical samples, and had the authority of the European Court in *Saunders* 23 EHRR 313, 337–338, para 69, for doing so, this distinction should not in my opinion be pushed too far. It is true that the respondent's answer, whether given orally or in writing, would create new evidence which did not exist until she spoke or wrote. In contrast, it may be acknowledged, the percentage of alcohol in her breath was a fact, existing before she blew into the breathalyser machine. But the whole purpose of requiring her to blow into the machine (on pain of a criminal penalty if she refused) was to obtain evidence not available until she did so and the reading so obtained could, in all save exceptional circumstances, be enough to convict a driver of an offence. If one applies the language of *Wigmore on Evidence* (McNaughton revision 1961) vol 8, p 318, quoted by the High Court that an individual should 'not be conscripted by his opponent to defeat himself' it is not easy to see why a requirement to answer a question is objectionable and a requirement to undergo a breath test is not. Yet no criticism is made of the requirement that the respondent undergo a breath test.

(3) All who own or drive motor cars know that by doing so they subject themselves to a regulatory regime which does not apply to members of the public who do neither. Section 172 of the 1988 Act forms

part of that regulatory regime. This regime is imposed not because owning or driving cars is a privilege or indulgence granted by the state but because the possession and use of cars (like, for example, shotguns, the possession of which is very closely regulated) are recognised to have the potential to cause grave injury. It is true that s 172(2)(b) permits a question to be asked of 'any other person' who, if not the owner or driver, might not be said to have impliedly accepted the regulatory regime, but someone who was not the owner or the driver would not incriminate himself whatever answer he gave. If, viewing this situation in the round, one asks whether s 172 represents a disproportionate legislative response to the problem of maintaining road safety, whether the balance between the interests of the community at large and the interests of the individual is struck in a manner unduly prejudicial to the individual, whether (in short) the leading of this evidence would infringe a basic human right of the respondent, I would feel bound to give negative answers. If the present argument is a good one it has been available to British citizens since 1966, but no one in this country has to my knowledge, criticised the legislation as unfair at any time up to now.

... In the present case the High Court came very close to treating the right not to incriminate oneself as absolute, describing it as a 'central right' which permitted no gradations of fairness depending on the seriousness of the charge or the circumstances of the case. The High Court interpreted the decision in *Saunders* as laying down more absolute a standard than I think the European Court intended, and nowhere in the High Court judgments does one find any recognition of the need to balance the general interests of the community against the interests of the individual or to ask whether s 172 represents a proportionate response to what is undoubtedly a serious social problem.

In my opinion the procurator fiscal is entitled at the respondent's forthcoming trial to lead evidence of her answer given under s 172. I would allow the appeal and quash the declaration made by the High Court.

LORD STEYN: ...

II. The objectives of the convention

In the first real test of the Human Rights Act 1998 it is opportune to stand back and consider what the basic aims of the convention are. One finds the explanation in the very words of the preambles of the convention. There were two principal objectives. The first was to maintain and further realise human rights and fundamental freedoms. The framers of the convention recognised that it was not only morally right to promote the observance of human rights but that it was also the best way of achieving pluralistic and just societies in which all can peaceably go about their lives. The second aim was to foster effective political democracy. This aim necessarily involves the creation of conditions of stability and order under the rule of law, not for its own sake, but as the best way to ensuring the well being of the inhabitants of the European countries. After all, democratic government has only one raison d'être, namely to serve the interests of all the people. The inspirers of the convention, among whom Winston Churchill played an important role, and the framers of the convention, ably assisted by English draftsmen, realised that from time-to-time the fundamental right of one individual may conflict with the human right of another. Thus the principles of free speech and privacy may collide. They also realised only too well that a single-minded concentration on the pursuit of fundamental rights of individuals to the exclusion of the interests of the wider public might be subversive of the ideal of tolerant European liberal democracies. The fundamental rights of individuals are of supreme importance but those rights are not unlimited: we live in communities of individuals who also have rights. The direct lineage of this ancient idea is clear: the convention is the descendant of the Universal Declaration of Human Rights (Paris, 10 December 1948; UN TS 2 (1949); Cmd 7226) which in art 29 expressly recognised the duties of everyone to the community and the limitation on rights in order to secure and protect respect for the rights of others. It is also noteworthy that article 17 of the convention prohibits, among others, individuals from abusing their rights to the detriment of others. Thus, notwithstanding the danger of intolerance towards ideas, the convention system draws a line which does not accord the protection of free speech to those who propagate racial hatred against minorities: article 10; *Jersild* v *Denmark* (1995) 19 EHRR 1 at 25–26 (para 31). This is to be contrasted with the categorical language of the First Amendment to the United States Constitution which provides that 'Congress shall make no law ... abridging the freedom of speech'. The convention requires that where difficult questions arise a balance must be struck. Subject to a limited number of absolute guarantees, the scheme and structure of the convention reflects this balanced approach. It differs in material respects from other constitutional systems but as a European nation it represents our Bill of Rights. We must be guided by it. And it is a basic premise of the convention system that only an entirely neutral, impartial, and independent judiciary can carry out the primary task of securing and enforcing convention rights. This contextual scene is not only directly relevant to the issues arising on the present appeal but may be a matrix in which many challenges under the Human Rights Act should be considered.

III. Article 6 of the convention

The present case is concerned with art 6 of the convention which guarantees to every individual a fair trial in civil and criminal cases. The centrality of this principle in the convention system has repeatedly been emphasised by the European Court. But even in respect of this basic guarantee, there is a balance to be observed. First, it is well settled that the public interest may be taken into account in deciding what the right to a fair trial requires in a particular context. Thus in *Doorson* v *Netherlands* (1996) 22 EHRR 330 at 358 (para 70) it was held that 'principles of fair trial also require that in appropriate cases the interests of the defence are balanced against those of witnesses or victims called upon to testify'. Only one specific illustration of this balanced approach is necessary. Provided they are kept 'within reasonable limits' rebuttable presumptions of fact are permitted in criminal legislation (*Salabiaku* v *France* (1988) 13 EHRR 379). Secondly, once it has been determined that the guarantee of a fair trial has been breached, it is never possible to justify such breach by reference to the public interest or on any other ground. This is to be contrasted with cases where a trial has been affected by irregularities not amounting to denial of a fair trial. In such cases it is fair that a court of appeal should have the power, even when faced by the fact of irregularities in the trial procedure, to dismiss the appeal if in the view of the court of appeal the defendant's guilt is plain and beyond any doubt. However, it is a grave conclusion that a defendant has not had the substance of a fair trial. It means that the administration of justice has entirely failed. Subject to the possible exercise of a power to order a retrial where appropriate such a conviction can never be allowed to stand.

IV. The privilege against self-incrimination

It is well settled, although not expressed in the convention, that there is an implied privilege against self incrimination under art 6. Moreover, s 172(2) of the 1988 Act undoubtedly makes an inroad on this privilege. On the other hand, it is also clear that the privilege against self incrimination is not an absolute right....

V. Section 172(2) of the Road Traffic Act 1988

In considering whether an inroad on the privilege against self incrimination can be justified, it is necessary to concentrate on the particular context....

The effective prosecution of drivers causing serious offences is a matter of public interest. But such prosecutions are often hampered by the difficulty of identifying the drivers of the vehicles at the time of, say, an accident causing loss of life or serious injury or potential danger to others. The tackling of this social problem seems in principle a legitimate aim for a legislature to pursue.

The real question is whether the legislative remedy in fact adopted is necessary and proportionate to the aim sought to be achieved. There were legislative choices to be made. The legislature could have decided to do no more than to exhort the police and prosecuting authorities to redouble their efforts. It may, however, be that such a policy would have been regarded as inadequate. Secondly, the legislature could have introduced a reverse burden of proof clause which placed the burden on the registered owner to prove that he was not the driver of the vehicle at a given time when it is alleged that an offence was committed. Thirdly, and this was the course actually adopted, there was the possibility of requiring information about the identity of the driver to be revealed by the registered owner and others. As between the second and third techniques it may be said that the latter involves the securing of an admission of a constituent element of the offence. On the other hand, such an admission, if wrongly made, is not conclusive. And it must be measured against the alternative of a reverse burden clause which could without further investigation of the identity of the driver lead to a prosecution. In their impact on the citizen the two techniques are not widely different. And it is rightly conceded that a properly drafted reverse burden of proof provision would have been lawful.

It is also important to keep in mind the narrowness of the interference. Section 172(2) is directed at obtaining information in one category, namely the identity of the driver at the time when an offence was allegedly committed. The most important part of s 172(2) is para (a) since the relevant information is usually peculiarly within the knowledge of the owner... Section 172(2) does not authorise general questioning by the police to secure a confession of an offence. On the other hand, s 172(2) does, depending on the circumstances, in effect authorise the police officer to invite the owner to make an admission of one element in a driving offence. It would, however, be an abuse of the power under s 172(2) for the police officer to employ improper or overbearing methods of obtaining the information. He may go no further than to ask who the driver was at the given time. If the police officer strays beyond his power under s 172(2) a judge will have ample power at trial to exclude the evidence. It is therefore a relatively narrow interference with the privilege in one area which poses widespread and serious law enforcement problems.

VI. What deference may be accorded to the legislature?

Under the convention system the primary duty is placed on domestic courts to secure and protect convention rights. The function of the European Court is essential but supervisory. In that capacity it accords to domestic courts a margin of appreciation, which recognises that national institutions are in principle better placed than an international court to evaluate local needs and conditions. That principle is logically not applicable to domestic courts. On the other hand, national courts may accord to the decisions of national legislatures some deference where the context justifies it (see *R* v *DPP, ex p Kebilene* [1999] 4 All ER 801 at 844, [2000] 2 AC 326 at 381 per Lord Hope of Craighead...)

In my view this factor is of some relevance in the present case. Here s 172(2) addresses a pressing social problem, namely the difficulty of law enforcement in the face of statistics revealing a high accident rate resulting in death and serious injuries. The legislature was entitled to regard the figures of serious accidents as unacceptably high. It would also have been entitled to take into account that it was necessary to protect other convention rights, viz the right to life of members of the public exposed to the danger of accidents (see art 2(1)). On this aspect the legislature was in as good a position as a court to assess the gravity of the problem and the public interest in addressing it. It really then boils down to the question whether in adopting the procedure enshrined in s 172(2), rather than a reverse burden technique, it took more drastic action than was justified. While this is ultimately a question for the court, it is not unreasonable to regard both techniques as permissible in the field of the driving of vehicles. After all, the subject invites special regulation; objectively the interference is narrowly circumscribed; and it is qualitatively not very different from requiring, for example, a breath specimen from a driver. Moreover, it is less invasive than an essential modern tool of crime detection such as the taking of samples from a suspect for DNA profiling. If the matter was not covered by authority, I would have concluded that s 172(2) is compatible with art 6.

VII. *Saunders v UK*

The decision of the European Court in *Saunders* v *UK* 23 EHRR 313 gave some support to the view of the High Court of Justiciary. With due respect I have to say that the reasoning in *Saunders* v *UK* is unsatisfactory and less than clear. The European Court did not rule that the privilege against self incrimination is absolute. Surprisingly in view of its decision in *Murray* 22 EHRR 29 that the linked right of silence is not absolute it left the point open in respect of the privilege against self-incrimination. On the other hand, the substance of its reasoning treats both privileges as not absolute. The court observed, at p 373, para 68:

> The Court recalls that, although not specifically mentioned in article 6 of the convention, the right to silence and the right not to incriminate oneself are generally recognised international standards which lie at the heart of the notion of a fair procedure under article 6. Their rationale lies, inter alia, in the protection of the accused from improper compulsion by the authorities thereby contributing to the avoidance of miscarriages of justice and to the fulfilment of the aims of article 6...

The court emphasised the rationale of improper compulsion. It does not hold that *anything* said under compulsion of law is inadmissible. Admittedly, the court also observed, at para 68:

> The right not to incriminate oneself, in particular, presupposes that the prosecution in a criminal case seek to prove their case against the accused without resort to evidence obtained through methods of coercion or oppression in defiance of the will of the accused. In this sense the right is closely linked to the presumption of innocence contained in article 6(2) of the convention.

Again one finds the link with the non-absolute right of silence. In any event 'methods of coercion or oppression in defiance of the will of the accused' is probably another way of referring to improper compulsion. This is consistent with the following passage, at p 338, para 69:

> In the present case the Court is only called upon to decide whether the use made by the prosecution of the statements obtained from the applicant by the inspectors amounted to an unjustifiable infringement of the right. This question must be examined by the Court in the light of all the circumstances of the case. In particular, it must be determined whether the applicant has been subject to compulsion to give evidence and whether the use made of the resulting testimony at

his trial offended the basic principles of a fair procedure inherent in article 6(1) of which the right not to incriminate oneself is a constituent element.

The expression 'unjustifiable infringement of the right' implies that some infringements may be justified. In my view the observations in *Saunders* do not support an absolutist view of the privilege against self incrimination. It may be that the observations in *Saunders* will have to be clarified in a further case by the European Court. As things stand, however, I consider that the High Court of Justiciary put too great weight on these observations. In my view they were never intended to apply to a case such as the present.

VIII. Conclusion on art 6

That brings me back to the decision of the High Court of Justiciary. It treated the privilege against self incrimination as virtually absolute. That conclusion fits uneasily into the balanced convention system, and cannot be reconciled with art 6 of the convention in all its constituent parts and the spectrum of jurisprudence of the European Court on the various facets of art 6.

I would hold that the decision of the High Court of Justiciary on the merits was wrong. The procurator fiscal is entitled to lead the evidence of Miss Brown's admission under s 172(2) of the 1988 Act.

Appeal allowed.

■ QUESTION

Did the Privy Council strike the balance between the protection of individual rights and the interests of the community at large, in the right place?

Huang v *Secretary of State for the Home Department*, and *Kashmiri* v *Secretary of State for the Home Department*

[2007] UKHL 11 [2007] 2 AC 167

The two appeals raise the question as to what is the decision-making role or function of appellate immigration authorities (adjudicators, the Immigration Appeal Tribunal, immigration judges) when deciding appeals, on Convention grounds, against refusal of leave to enter or remain, under s. 65 of the Immigration and Asylum Act 1999 and Part III of Sched. 4 to that Act.

LORD BINGHAM of CORNHILL, LORD HOFFMANN, BARONESS HALE of RICHMOND, LORD CARSWELL and LORD BROWN of EATON-UNDER-HEYWOOD:...

11. These provisions, read purposively and in context, make it plain that the task of the appellate immigration authority, on an appeal on a Convention ground against a decision of the primary official decision-maker refusing leave to enter or remain in this country, is to decide whether the challenged decision is unlawful as incompatible with a Convention right or compatible and so lawful. It is not a secondary, reviewing, function dependent on establishing that the primary decision-maker misdirected himself or acted irrationally or was guilty of procedural impropriety. The appellate immigration authority must decide for itself whether the impugned decision is lawful and, if not, but only if not, reverse it. This is the decision reached by the Court of Appeal (Judge, Laws and Latham LJJ) in these conjoined appeals, and it is correct: [2005] EWCA Civ 105, [2006] QB 1...

13. In the course of his justly-celebrated and much-quoted opinion in *R (Daly) v Secretary of State for the Home Department* [2001] UKHL26, [2001] 2 AC 532, paras 26–28, Lord Steyn pointed out that neither the traditional approach to judicial review formulated in *Associated Provincial Picture Houses Ltd v Wednesbury Corporation* [1948] 1 KB 223 nor the heightened scrutiny approach adopted in *R v Ministry of Defence, Ex p Smith* [1996] QB 517 had provided adequate protection of Convention rights, as held by the Strasbourg court in *Smith and Grady v United Kingdom* (1999) 29 EHRR 493. Having referred to a material difference between the *Wednesbury* and *Smith* approach on the one hand and the proportionality approach applicable where Convention rights are at stake on the other, he said (para 28): "This does not mean that there has been a shift to merits review". This statement has, it seems, given rise to some misunderstanding. The policy attacked in *Daly* was held to be ultra vires the Prison Act 1952 (para 21) and also a breach of article 8. With both those conclusions Lord Steyn agreed (para 24). They depended on questions of pure legal principle, on which the House ruled. *Ex p Smith* was different. It raised a rationality

challenge to the recruitment policy adopted by the Ministry of Defence which both the Divisional Court and the Court of Appeal felt themselves bound to dismiss. The point which, as we understand, Lord Steyn wished to make was that, although the Convention calls for a more exacting standard of review, it remains the case that the judge is not the primary decision-maker. It is not for him to decide what the recruitment policy for the armed forces should be. In proceedings under the Human Rights Act, of course, the court would have to scrutinise the policy and any justification advanced for it to see whether there was sufficient justification for the discriminatory treatment. By contrast, the appellate immigration authority, deciding an appeal under section 65, is not reviewing the decision of another decision-maker. It is deciding whether or not it is unlawful to refuse leave to enter or remain, and it is doing so on the basis of up to date facts.

The task of the appellate immigration authority 14. Much argument was directed on the hearing of these appeals, and much authority cited, on the appellate immigration authority's proper approach to its task, due deference, discretionary areas of judgment, the margin of appreciation, democratic accountability, relative institutional competence, a distinction drawn by the Court of Appeal between decisions based on policy and decisions not so based, and so on. We think, with respect, that there has been a tendency, both in the arguments addressed to the courts and in the judgments of the courts, to complicate and mystify what is not, in principle, a hard task to define, however difficult the task is, in practice, to perform. In describing it, we continue to assume that the applicant does not qualify for leave to enter or remain under the Rules, and that reliance is placed on the family life component of article 8.

15. The first task of the appellate immigration authority is to establish the relevant facts. These may well have changed since the original decision was made. In any event, particularly where the applicant has not been interviewed, the authority will be much better placed to investigate the facts, test the evidence, assess the sincerity of the applicant's evidence and the genuineness of his or her concerns and evaluate the nature and strength of the family bond in the particular case. It is important that the facts are explored, and summarised in the decision, with care, since they will always be important and often decisive.

16. The authority will wish to consider and weigh all that tells in favour of the refusal of leave which is challenged, with particular reference to justification under article 8(2). There will, in almost any case, be certain general considerations to bear in mind: the general administrative desirability of applying known rules if a system of immigration control is to be workable, predictable, consistent and fair as between one applicant and another; the damage to good administration and effective control if a system is perceived by applicants internationally to be unduly porous, unpredictable or perfunctory; the need to discourage non-nationals admitted to the country temporarily from believing that they can commit serious crimes and yet be allowed to remain; the need to discourage fraud, deception and deliberate breaches of the law; and so on. In some cases much more particular reasons will be relied on to justify refusal, as in *Samaroo v Secretary of State for the Home Department* [2001] EWCA Civ 1139, [2002] INLR 55 where attention was paid to the Secretary of State's judgment that deportation was a valuable deterrent to actual or prospective drug traffickers, or *R (Farrakhan) v Secretary of State for the Home Department* [2002] EWCA Civ 606, [2002] QB 1391, an article 10 case, in which note was taken of the Home Secretary's judgment that the applicant posed a threat to community relations between Muslims and Jews and a potential threat to public order for that reason. The giving of weight to factors such as these is not, in our opinion, aptly described as deference: it is performance of the ordinary judicial task of weighing up the competing considerations on each side and according appropriate weight to the judgment of a person with responsibility for a given subject matter and access to special sources of knowledge and advice. That is how any rational judicial decision-maker is likely to proceed. It is to be noted that both *Samaroo* and *Farrakhan* (cases on which the Secretary of State seeks to place especial reliance as examples of the court attaching very considerable weight to decisions of his taken in an immigration context) were not merely challenges by way of judicial review rather than appeals but cases where Parliament had specifically excluded any right of appeal.

17. Counsel for the Secretary of State nevertheless put his case much higher even than that. She relied by analogy on the decision of the House in *Kay v Lambeth London Borough Council* [2006] UKHL 10, [2006] 2 AC 465, where the House considered the article 8 right to respect for the home. It held that the right of a public authority landlord to enforce a claim for possession under domestic law against an occupier whose right to occupy (if any) had ended and who was entitled to no protection in domestic law would in most cases automatically supply the justification required by article 8(2), and the courts would assume that domestic law struck the proper balance, at any rate unless the contrary were shown. So here, it was said, the appellate immigration authority should assume that the Immigration Rules and supplementary

instructions, made by the responsible minister and laid before Parliament, had the imprimatur of democratic approval and should be taken to strike the right balance between the interests of the individual and those of the community. The analogy is unpersuasive. Domestic housing policy has been a continuing subject of discussion and debate in Parliament over very many years, with the competing interests of landlords and tenants fully represented, as also the public interest in securing accommodation for the indigent, averting homelessness and making the best use of finite public resources. The outcome, changed from time to time, may truly be said to represent a considered democratic compromise. This cannot be said in the same way of the Immigration Rules and supplementary instructions, which are not the product of active debate in Parliament, where non-nationals seeking leave to enter or remain are not in any event represented. It must be remembered that if an applicant qualifies for the grant of leave to enter or remain under the Rules and is refused leave, the immigration appeal authority must allow such applicant's appeal by virtue of paragraph 21(1)(a) of Part III of Schedule 4 to the 1999 Act. It is a premise of the statutory scheme enacted by Parliament that an applicant may fail to qualify under the Rules and yet may have a valid claim by virtue of article 8.

18. The authority must of course take account, as enjoined by section 2 of the 1998 Act, of Strasbourg jurisprudence on the meaning and effect of article 8. While the case law of the Strasbourg court is not strictly binding, it has been held that domestic courts and tribunals should, in the absence of special circumstances, follow the clear and constant jurisprudence of that court: *R (Alconbury Developments Ltd) v Secretary of State for the Environment, Transport and the Regions* [2001] UKHL 23, [2003] 2 AC 295, para 26; *R (Ullah) v Special Adjudicator* [2004] UKHL 26, [2004] 2 AC 323, para 20. It is unnecessary for present purposes to attempt to summarise the Convention jurisprudence on article 8, save to record that the article imposes on member states not only a negative duty to refrain from unjustified interference with a person's right to respect for his or her family but also a positive duty to show respect for it. The reported cases are of value in showing where, in many different factual situations, the Strasbourg court, as the ultimate guardian of Convention rights, has drawn the line, thus guiding national authorities in making their own decisions. But the main importance of the case law is in illuminating the core value which article 8 exists to protect. This is not, perhaps, hard to recognise. Human beings are social animals. They depend on others. Their family, or extended family, is the group on which many people most heavily depend, socially, emotionally and often financially. There comes a point at which, for some, prolonged and unavoidable separation from this group seriously inhibits their ability to live full and fulfilling lives. Matters such as the age, health and vulnerability of the applicant, the closeness and previous history of the family, the applicant's dependence on the financial and emotional support of the family, the prevailing cultural tradition and conditions in the country of origin and many other factors may all be relevant. The Strasbourg court has repeatedly recognised the general right of states to control the entry and residence of non-nationals, and repeatedly acknowledged that the Convention confers no right on individuals or families to choose where they prefer to live. In most cases where the applicants complain of a violation of their article 8 rights, in a case where the impugned decision is authorised by law for a legitimate object and the interference (or lack of respect) is of sufficient seriousness to engage the operation of article 8, the crucial question is likely to be whether the interference (or lack of respect) complained of is proportionate to the legitimate end sought to be achieved. Proportionality is a subject of such importance as to require separate treatment.

Proportionality

19. In *de Freitas v Permanent Secretary of Ministry of Agriculture, Fisheries, Lands and Housing* [1999] 1 AC 69, 80, the Privy Council, drawing on South African, Canadian and Zimbabwean authority, defined the questions generally to be asked in deciding whether a measure is proportionate:

> "whether: (i) the legislative objective is sufficiently important to justify limiting a fundamental right; (ii) the measures designed to meet the legislative objective are rationally connected to it; and (iii) the means used to impair the right or freedom are no more than is necessary to accomplish the objective."

This formulation has been widely cited and applied. But counsel for the applicants (with the support of Liberty, in a valuable written intervention) suggested that the formulation was deficient in omitting reference to an overriding requirement which featured in the judgment of Dickson CJ in *R v Oakes* [1986] 1 SCR 103, from which this approach to proportionality derives. This feature is (p 139) the need to balance the interests of society with those of individuals and groups. This is indeed an aspect which should never be overlooked or discounted. The House recognised as much in *R (Razgar) v Secretary of State for the Home*

Department [2004] UKHL 27, [2004] 2 AC 368, paras 17–20, 26, 27, 60, 77, when, having suggested a series of questions which an adjudicator would have to ask and answer in deciding a Convention question, it said that the judgment on proportionality

must always involve the striking of a fair balance between the rights of the individual and the interests of the community which is inherent in the whole of the Convention. The severity and consequences of the interference will call for careful assessment at this stage" (see para 20).

If, as counsel suggest, insufficient attention has been paid to this requirement, the failure should be made good.

20. In an article 8 case where this question is reached, the ultimate question for the appellate immigration authority is whether the refusal of leave to enter or remain, in circumstances where the life of the family cannot reasonably be expected to be enjoyed elsewhere, taking full account of all considerations weighing in favour of the refusal, prejudices the family life of the applicant in a manner sufficiently serious to amount to a breach of the fundamental right protected by article 8. If the answer to this question is affirmative, the refusal is unlawful and the authority must so decide. It is not necessary that the appellate immigration authority, directing itself along the lines indicated in this opinion, need ask in addition whether the case meets a test of exceptionality. The suggestion that it should is based on an observation of Lord Bingham in *Razgar* above, para 20. He was there expressing an expectation, shared with the Immigration Appeal Tribunal, that the number of claimants not covered by the Rules and supplementary directions but entitled to succeed under article 8 would be a very small minority. That is still his expectation. But he was not purporting to lay down a legal test.

NOTES

1. The significance of *Huang* and *Kashmiri* may be recognized in its single unanimous opinion. The decision seeks to clarify two issues from Lord Steyn's speech in *Daly,* merits review and deference. On the first in [11] their Lordships say that human rights adjudication involves the immigration appellate authority deciding for itself if the primary decision-maker's decision is lawful (Convention-compatible) and, if it is not, to reverse it. This is neither merits review nor judicial review directed at illegality, irrationality or procedural irregularity. It is not merits review because the appellate authority is not the primary decision-maker and while the standard of review is different from that used in judicial review, this does not mean the determination of policy is being removed from the primary decision-maker, so as, to use the instance of *Smith*, to decide what the recruitment policy of the armed forces should be. On deference, their Lordships at [16] preferred to say this was the weighing-up of competing considerations with appropriate weight given to a person responsible for a subject matter with access to special sources of knowledge and advice.
2. Is the human rights adjudication discussed by their Lordships restricted to the immigration appellate authority considering a s. 65 appeal and not applicable to the courts hearing a human rights challenge brought by way of judicial review? M. Amos in 'Separating Human Rights Adjudication from Judicial Review—*Huang* v *Secretary of State for the Home Department* and *Kashmiri* v *Secretary of State for the Home Department*', (2007) 5 *European Human Rights Law Review* 679, argues that it is applicable on the basis of two House of Lords decisions where the approach of the Court of Appeal was criticized, *R.* v *(Begum) Headteacher and Governors of Denbigh High School* [2006] UKHL 15, [2007] 1 AC 100 and *Belfast City Council* v *Miss Behavin' Ltd* [2007] UKHL 19, [2007] 1WLR 1420. In the latter case Baroness Hale said at [31]:

   The first, and most straightforward, question is who decides whether or not a claimant's Convention rights have been infringed. The answer is that it is the court before which the issue is raised. The role of the court in human rights adjudication is quite different from the role of the court in an ordinary judicial review of administrative action. In human rights adjudication, the court is concerned with whether the human rights of the claimant have in fact been infringed, not with whether the administrative decision-maker properly took them into account. If it were otherwise, every policy decision taken before the Human Rights Act 1998 which came into force but which engaged a convention right would be open to challenge, no matter how obviously compliant with the right in question it was. That cannot be right.

3. Their Lordships' re-formulation of deference at [16], as taking into account the views of a person responsible with special access to knowledge and advice, could suggest that the courts give weight to primary decision-makers because of their institutional capacity and expertise,

however, the discussion at [17] about Parliamentary involvement in housing policy in relation to the House's decision *Kay* v *Lambeth London Borough Council* [2006] UKHL 10, [2006] 2 AC 465, compared with the Immigration Rules seems to suggest that the 'democratic compromise' in the housing policy is significant. Commentators including J. Jowell, 'Judicial Deference: Servility, Civility or Institutional Capacity' [2003] *Public Law* 592 and M. Hunt, 'Sovereignty's Blight: Why Contemporary Public Law Needs the Concept of "Due Deference"' in N. Bamforth and P. Leyland (eds), *Public Law in a Multi-Layered Constitution* (2003), p. 337; have taken issue with the idea that democratic arguments should pre-empt judicial involvement. The judiciary must not abdicate their responsibilities of deciding Convention rights, a view also shared by Lord Steyn, 'Deference: A Tangled Story' [2005] *Public Law* 346. Amos argues that it is implicit in their Lordships' arguments about *Kay* that weight is properly accorded to a primary decision-maker who had done its job properly in relation to Convention rights. Amos again draws on *Begum* and *Belfast City Council* for support. In *Begum* the Court of Appeal had found that the school had not followed a formal approach in devising its policy on uniform which specifically recognized that pupils' Art. 9 Convention right was engaged. Lord Bingham said at [34] in relation to the assessment of the proportionality of the interference with the claimant's Art. 9 right that it would be

> ...irresponsible of any court, lacking the experience, background and detailed knowledge of the head teacher, staff and governors, to overrule their judgment on a matter as sensitive as this.

In *Belfast City Council* the council in the exercise of its licensing powers had not explicitly or implicitly considered the proportionality of its interference with Convention rights, Baroness Hale said at [37]:

> ...the court has to decide whether the authority has violated the convention rights. In doing so, it is bound to acknowledge that the local authority is much better placed than the court to decide whether the right of sex shop owners to sell pornographic literature and images should be restricted—for the prevention of disorder or crime, for the protection of health or morals, of for the protection of the rights of others. But the views of the local authority are bound to carry less weight where the local authority has made no attempt to address that question. Had the Belfast City Council expressly set itself the task of balancing the rights of individuals to sell and buy pornographic literature and images against the interests of the wider community, a court would find it hard to upset the balance which the local authority had struck. But where there is no indication that this has been done, the court has no alternative but to strike the balance for itself, giving due weight to the judgments made by those who are in much closer touch with the people and the places involved that the court could ever be.

■ QUESTION

Does the *Huang* approach to deference set clear and appropriate boundaries to the courts' review function or does it seek to make palatable a significant shift in power to the judges?

R (Daly) v *Secretary of State for the Home Department*

[2001] UKHL 26, House of Lords

D, a prisoner, stored correspondence with his solicitor in his cell. He was subject to a standard cell searching policy under paras 17.69–17.74 of a Security Manual issued by the Secretary of State to prison governors under his power to make rules for the regulation and control of prisoners under s. 47(1) of the Prison Act 1952. The policy required prisoners to be excluded during cell searches to prevent intimidation and to prevent prisoners acquiring knowledge of the search techniques. Prison officers were to examine any legal correspondence to ensure it contained nothing likely to endanger prison security but they were not to read it. D sought judicial review of the decision that prisoners' legally privileged correspondence could be examined in their absence. The application was dismissed by the Court of Appeal. D appealed to the House of Lords. He did not contest the need for correspondence to be examined but contended that such examination should ordinarily take place in the presence of the prisoner.

LORD BINGHAM OF CORNHILL: ...

[His Lordship referred to the origins of the policy in the report of the Woodcock Inquiry following the escape of six dangerous prisoners from HMP Whitemoor in 1994. The report recommended that cells and property should be searched at frequent but irregular intervals. His Lordship examined the restrictions on rights which imprisonment involves and the case law relating thereto before quoting with approval from the speech by Lord Browne-Wilkinson in *R* v *Secretary of State for the Home Department, ex p Pierson* [1998] AC 539, 575:]

> From these authorities I think the following proposition is established. A power conferred by Parliament in general terms is not to be taken to authorise the doing of acts by the donee of the power which adversely affect the legal rights of the citizen or the basic principles on which the law of the United Kingdom is based unless the statute conferring the power makes it clear that such was the intention of Parliament.

The argument

...

15 It is necessary, first, to ask whether the policy infringes in a significant way Mr Daly's common law right that the confidentiality of privileged legal correspondence be maintained. He submits that it does for two related reasons: first, because knowledge that such correspondence may be looked at by prison officers in the absence of the prisoner inhibits the prisoner's willingness to communicate with his legal adviser in terms of unreserved candour; and secondly, because there must be a risk, if the prisoner is not present, that the officers will stray beyond their limited role in examining legal correspondence, particularly if, for instance, they see some name or reference familiar to them, as would be the case if the prisoner were bringing or contemplating bringing proceedings against officers in the prison. For the Home Secretary it is argued that the policy involves no infringement of a prisoner's common law right since his privileged correspondence is not read in his absence but only examined.

16 I have no doubt that the policy infringes Mr Daly's common law right to legal professional privilege. This was the view of two very experienced judges in *R* v *Secretary of State for the Home Department, Ex p Simms* [1999] QB 349, against which decision the present appeal is effectively brought. At p 366, Kennedy LJ said:

> In my judgment legal professional privilege does attach to correspondence with legal advisers which is stored by a prisoner in his cell, and accordingly such correspondence is to be protected from any unnecessary interference by prison staff. Even if the correspondence is only inspected to see that it is what it purports to be that is likely to impair the free flow of communication between a convicted or remand prisoner on the one hand and his legal adviser on the other, and therefore it constitutes an impairment of the privilege.

Judge LJ was of the same opinion. At p 373, he said:

> Prisoners whose cells are searched in their absence will find it difficult to believe that their correspondence has been searched but not read. The governor's order will sometimes be disobeyed. Accordingly I am prepared to accept the potential 'chilling effect' of such searches.

In an imperfect world there will necessarily be occasions when prison officers will do more than merely examine prisoners' legal documents, and apprehension that they may do so is bound to inhibit a prisoner's willingness to communicate freely with his legal adviser.

17 The next question is whether there can be any ground for infringing in any way a prisoner's right to maintain the confidentiality of his privileged legal correspondence. Plainly there can. Some examination may well be necessary to establish that privileged legal correspondence is what it appears to be and is not a hiding place for illicit materials or information prejudicial to security or good order.

18 It is then necessary to ask whether, to the extent that it infringes a prisoner's common law right to privilege, the policy can be justified as a necessary and proper response to the acknowledged need to maintain security, order and discipline in prisons and to prevent crime. Mr Daly's challenge at this point is directed to the blanket nature of the policy, applicable as it is to all prisoners of whatever category in all closed prisons in England and Wales, irrespective of a prisoner's past or present conduct and of any operational emergency or urgent intelligence. The Home Secretary's justification rests firmly on the

points already mentioned: the risk of intimidation, the risk that staff may be conditioned by prisoners to relax security and the danger of disclosing searching methods.

19 In considering these justifications, based as they are on the extensive experience of the prison service, it must be recognised that the prison population includes a core of dangerous, disruptive and manipulative prisoners, hostile to authority and ready to exploit for their own advantage any concession granted to them. Any search policy must accommodate this inescapable fact. I cannot however accept that the reasons put forward justify the policy in its present blanket form. Any prisoner who attempts to intimidate or disrupt a search of his cell, or whose past conduct shows that he is likely to do so, may properly be excluded even while his privileged correspondence is examined so as to ensure the efficacy of the search, but no justification is shown for routinely excluding all prisoners, whether intimidatory or disruptive or not, while that part of the search is conducted. Save in the extraordinary conditions prevailing at Whitemoor before September 1994, it is hard to regard the conditioning of staff as a problem which could not be met by employing dedicated search teams. It is not suggested that prison officers when examining legal correspondence employ any sophisticated technique which would be revealed to the prisoner if he were present, although he might no doubt be encouraged to secrete illicit materials among his legal papers if the examination were obviously very cursory. The policy cannot in my opinion be justified in its present blanket form. The infringement of prisoners' rights to maintain the confidentiality of their privileged legal correspondence is greater than is shown to be necessary to serve the legitimate public objectives already identified. I accept Mr Daly's submission on this point.

[His Lordship was fortified in reaching his view by four considerations, namely, (i) that the Prisons Ombudsman had upheld a similar complaint by another prisoner in 1996 resulting in Security Group (the company which ran the prison concerned) adopting revised procedures which permitted the prisoner to remain in his cell while his legal documents were searched; (ii) the Ombudsman's report also revealed a procedure adopted in HMP Full Sutton to accommodate a similar complaint from a prisoner there; (iii) the procedures in Scotland involved the prisoner being present during examination of his privileged legal correspondence; (iv) in only two cases have illicit items been found hidden in legally privileged documents.]

21 In *R* v *Secretary of State for the Home Department,` Ex p Simms* [1999] QB 349 and again in the present case, the Court of Appeal held that the policy represented the minimum intrusion into the rights of prisoners consistent with the need to maintain security, order and discipline in prisons. That is a conclusion which I respect but cannot share. In my opinion the policy provides for a degree of intrusion into the privileged legal correspondence of prisoners which is greater than is justified by the objectives the policy is intended to serve, and so violates the common law rights of prisoners. Section 47(1) of the 1952 Act does not authorise such excessive intrusion, and the Home Secretary accordingly had no power to lay down or implement the policy in its present form. I would accordingly declare paragraphs 17.69 to 17.74 of the Security Manual to be unlawful and void in so far as they provide that prisoners must always be absent when privileged legal correspondence held by them in their cells is examined by prison officers.

...

23 I have reached the conclusions so far expressed on an orthodox application of common law principles derived from the authorities and an orthodox domestic approach to judicial review. But the same result is achieved by reliance on the European Convention. Article 8(1) gives Mr Daly a right to respect for his correspondence. While interference with that right by a public authority may be permitted if in accordance with the law and necessary in a democratic society in the interests of national security, public safety, the prevention of disorder or crime or for protection of the rights and freedoms of others, the policy interferes with Mr Daly's exercise of his right under article 8(1) to an extent much greater than necessity requires. In this instance, therefore, the common law and the Convention yield the same result. But this need not always be so. In *Smith and Grady* v *United Kingdom* (1999) 29 EHRR 493, the European Court held that the orthodox domestic approach of the English courts had not given the applicants an effective remedy for the breach of their rights under article 8 of the Convention because the threshold of review had been set too high. Now, following the incorporation of the Convention by the Human Rights Act 1998 and the bringing of that Act fully into force, domestic courts must themselves form a judgment whether a Convention right has been breached (conducting such inquiry as is necessary to form that judgment) and, so far as permissible under the Act, grant an effective remedy. On this aspect of the case, I agree with and adopt the observations of my noble and learned friend Lord Steyn which I have had the opportunity of reading in draft.

LORD STEYN: . . .

24 My Lords, I am in complete agreement with the reasons given by Lord Bingham of Cornhill in his speech. For the reasons he gives I would also allow the appeal. Except on one narrow but important point I have nothing to add.

25 There was written and oral argument on the question whether certain observations of Lord Phillips of Worth Matravers MR in *R (Mahmood)* v *Secretary of State for the Home Department* [2001] 1 WLR 840 were correct. The context was an immigration case involving a decision of the Secretary of State made before the Human Rights Act 1998 came into effect. The Master of the Rolls nevertheless approached the case as if the Act had been in force when the Secretary of State reached his decision. He explained the new approach to be adopted. The Master of the Rolls concluded, at p 857, para 40:

> When anxiously scrutinising an executive decision that interferes with human rights, the court will ask the question, applying an objective test, whether the decision-maker could reasonably have concluded that the interference was necessary to achieve one or more of the legitimate aims recognised by the Convention. When considering the test of necessity in the relevant context, the court must take into account the European jurisprudence in accordance with section 2 of the 1998 Act.

. . .

26 The explanation of the Master of the Rolls in the first sentence of the cited passage requires clarification. It is couched in language reminiscent of the traditional *Wednesbury* ground of review (*Associated Provincial Picture Houses Ltd* v *Wednesbury Corpn* [1948] 1 KB 223), and in particular the adaptation of that test in terms of heightened scrutiny in cases involving fundamental rights as formulated in *R* v *Ministry of Defence, Ex p Smith* [1996] QB 517, 554E—G per Sir Thomas Bingham MR. There is a material difference between the *Wednesbury* and *Smith* grounds of review and the approach of proportionality applicable in respect of review where Convention rights are at stake.

27 The contours of the principle of proportionality are familiar. In *de Freitas* v *Permanent Secretary of Ministry of Agriculture, Fisheries, Lands and Housing* [1999] 1 AC 69 the Privy Council adopted a three-stage test. Lord Clyde observed, at p 80, that in determining whether a limitation (by an act, rule or decision) is arbitrary or excessive the court should ask itself:

> whether: (i) the legislative objective is sufficiently important to justify limiting a fundamental right; (ii) the measures designed to meet the legislative objective are rationally connected to it; and (iii) the means used to impair the right or freedom are no more than is necessary to accomplish the objective.

Clearly, these criteria are more precise and more sophisticated than the traditional grounds of review. What is the difference for the disposal of concrete cases? . . . The starting point is that there is an overlap between the traditional grounds of review and the approach of proportionality. Most cases would be decided in the same way whichever approach is adopted. But the intensity of review is somewhat greater under the proportionality approach. Making due allowance for important structural differences between various convention rights, which I do not propose to discuss, a few generalisations are perhaps permissible. I would mention three concrete differences without suggesting that my statement is exhaustive. First, the doctrine of proportionality may require the reviewing court to assess the balance which the decision maker has struck, not merely whether it is within the range of rational or reasonable decisions. Secondly, the proportionality test may go further than the traditional grounds of review inasmuch as it may require attention to be directed to the relative weight accorded to interests and considerations. Thirdly, even the heightened scrutiny test developed in *R* v *Ministry of Defence, Ex p Smith* [1996] QB 517, 554 is not necessarily appropriate to the protection of human rights. It will be recalled that in *Smith* the Court of Appeal reluctantly felt compelled to reject a limitation on homosexuals in the army. The challenge based on article 8 of the Convention for the Protection of Human Rights and Fundamental Freedoms (the right to respect for private and family life) foundered on the threshold required even by the anxious scrutiny test. The European Court of Human Rights came to the opposite conclusion: *Smith and Grady* v *United Kingdom* (1999) 29 EHRR 493. The court concluded, at p 543, para 138:

> the threshold at which the High Court and the Court of Appeal could find the Ministry of Defence policy irrational was placed so high that it effectively excluded any consideration by the domestic courts of the question of whether the interference with the applicants' rights answered a pressing social need or was proportionate to the national security and public order aims pursued, principles which lie at the heart of the court's analysis of complaints under article 8 of the Convention.

In other words, the intensity of the review, in similar cases, is guaranteed by the twin requirements that the limitation of the right was necessary in a democratic society, in the sense of meeting a pressing social need, and the question whether the interference was really proportionate to the legitimate aim being pursued.

28 The differences in approach between the traditional grounds of review and the proportionality approach may therefore sometimes yield different results. It is therefore important that cases involving Convention rights must be analysed in the correct way. This does not mean that there has been a shift to merits review. On the contrary, as Professor Jowell [2000] PL 671, 681 has pointed out the respective roles of judges and administrators are fundamentally distinct and will remain so. To this extent the general tenor of the observations in *Mahmood* [2001] 1 WLR 840 are correct. And Laws LJ rightly emphasised in *Mahmood*, at p 847, para 18, 'that the intensity of review in a public law case will depend on the subject matter in hand'. That is so even in cases involving Convention rights. In law context is everything.

Appeal allowed.

NOTE: In *Daly* their Lordships clearly accepted that in Human Rights Act cases, proportionality was the appropriate but different standard of review from unreasonableness or irrationality, see pp. 578–587, *post*. For development of the ECHR principles in a claim under the Human Rights Act to test if a restriction or condition to a qualified Convention right is lawful see this example of Art. 10 freedom of expression.

R v *Shayler*

[2002] UKHL 11; [2003] 1 AC 247

LORD HOPE OF CRAIGHEAD:...

54. Article 10(1) of the Convention states that the right to freedom of expression includes the right to impart information and ideas without interference by public authorities. Article 10(2) states, by way of qualification, that the exercise of this right,

> "...since it carries with it duties and responsibilities, may be subject to such formalities, conditions, restrictions or penalties as are prescribed by law and are necessary... in the interests of national security..."

55. The wording of article 10(2) as applied to this case indicates that any such restriction, if it is to be compatible with the Convention right, must satisfy two basic requirements. First, the restriction must be "prescribed by law". So it must satisfy the principle of legality. The second is that it must be such as is "necessary" in the interests of national security. This raises the question of proportionality. The jurisprudence of the European Court of Human Rights explains how these principles are to be understood and applied in the context of the facts of this case. As any restriction with the right to freedom of expression must be subjected to very close scrutiny, it is important to identify the requirements of that jurisprudence before undertaking that exercise.

56. The principle of legality requires the court to address itself to three distinct questions. The first is whether there is a legal basis in domestic law for the restriction. The second is whether the law or rule in question is sufficiently accessible to the individual who is affected by the restriction, and sufficiently precise to enable him to understand its scope and foresee the consequences of his actions so that he can regulate his conduct without breaking the law. The third is whether, assuming that these two requirements are satisfied, it is nevertheless open to the criticism on the Convention ground that it was applied in a way that is arbitrary because, for example, it has been resorted to in bad faith or in a way that is not

proportionate. I derive these principles, which have been mentioned many times in subsequent cases, from *The Sunday Times v United Kingdom* (1979–1980) 2 EHRR 245, para 49 and also from *Winterwerp v The Netherlands* (1979) 2 EHRR 387, 402–403, para 39 and *Engel v The Netherlands (No 1)* (1976) 1 EHRR 647, 669, paras 58–59 which were concerned with the principle of legality in the context of article 5(1): see also *A v The Scottish Ministers* 2001 SLT 1331, 1336L-1337B (PC).

57. The phrase "necessary ... in the interests of national security" has to be read in the light of article 18, which provides that the restrictions permitted under the Convention must not be applied for any purpose other than those for which they have been prescribed. The word "necessary" in article 10(2) introduces the principle of proportionality, although the word as such does not appear anywhere in the Convention: see *Handyside v United Kingdom* (1976) 1 EHRR 737, 753–755, paras 48–49. In para 49 of its judgment the court said:

> "The court's supervisory functions oblige it to pay the utmost attention to the principles characterising a 'democratic society'. Freedom of expression constitutes one of the essential foundations of such a society, one of the basic conditions for its progress and for the development of every man.... This means, amongst other things, that every 'formality', 'condition', 'restriction' or 'penalty' imposed in this sphere must be proportionate to the legitimate aim pursued."

58. Applied to the circumstances of this case, this means that a restriction on the disclosure of information cannot be said to be "necessary" in the interests of national security unless (a) "relevant and sufficient reasons" are given by the national authority to justify the restriction, (b) the restriction on disclosure corresponds to a "pressing social need" and (c) it is "proportionate to the legitimate aim pursued": *The Sunday Times v United Kingdom* (1979) 2 EHRR 245, para 62.

59. The principle involves a question of balance between competing interests. But it is important to appreciate that there is a process of analysis that must be carried through. The starting point is that an authority which seeks to justify a restriction on a fundamental right on the ground of a pressing social need has a burden to discharge. There is a burden on the state to show that the legislative means adopted were no greater than necessary: *R v Lambert* [2001] 3 WLR 206, 220H per Lord Steyn. As Sir Sydney Kentridge QC observed in his Tanner Lecture at Oxford, "Human Rights: A Sense of Proportion", 26 February 2001:

> "'Necessary' does not mean indispensable, but it does connote the existence of a pressing social need.... It is only on the showing of such need that the question of proportionality or 'balancing' should arise."

60. The European Court has not identified a consistent or uniform set of principles when considering the doctrine of proportionality: see Richard Clayton, "*Regaining a Sense of Proportion: The Human Rights Act* and *the Proportionality Principle*" [2001] EHRLR 504, 510. But there is a general international understanding as to the matters which should be considered where a question is raised as to whether an interference with a fundamental right is proportionate.

61. These matters were identified in the Privy Council case of *de Freitas v Permanent Secretary of Ministry of Agriculture, Fisheries, Lands and Housing* [1999] 1 AC 69 by Lord Clyde. He adopted the three stage test which is to be found in the analysis of Gubbay CJ in *Nyambirai v National Social Security Authority* [1996] 1 LRC 64, where he drew on jurisprudence from South Africa and Canada: see also *R (Daly) v Secretary of State for the Home Department* [2001] 2 WLR 1622, 1634H-1635A, per Lord Steyn; *R (Pretty) v Director of Public Prosecutions* [2001] 3 WLR 1598, 1637A-C. The first is whether the objective which is sought to be achieved—the pressing social need—is sufficiently important to justify limiting the fundamental right. The second is whether the means chosen to limit that right are rational, fair and not arbitrary. The third is whether the means used impair the right as minimally as is reasonably possible. As these propositions indicate, it is not enough to assert that the decision that was taken was a reasonable one. A close and penetrating examination of the factual justification for the restriction is needed if the fundamental rights enshrined in the Convention are to remain practical and effective for everyone who wishes to exercise them.

NOTE: In this case the restrictions on the former member of the Security Service's freedom of expression were lawful. There was a need to preserve secrecy of information relating to intelligence dealing with terrorism, criminal activity and subversion. The restrictions banned unauthorised disclosure and there were procedures in place to raise concerns, and if this did not result in disclosure about alleged impropriety by the Security Service, then it could be the subject of an application to make a disclosure which if not successful could be challenged by judicial review. These procedures provided safeguards to allow for reporting of impropriety and a former member of the Security Service should use them. It was not a defence to the making of an unauthorized disclosure to say that if they were used no notice would have been taken, or authorization to disclose refused.

■ QUESTION

Does the standard of review in the tests of 'prescribed by law' and 'necessary in a democratic society' take the judges outside their constitutional role and specialist knowledge?

D: Control Orders and Human Rights

The UK had enacted a Terrorism Act 2000 which put on permanent basis some of the features of previous temporary anti-terrorism laws which had been a response to terrorism, primarily related to Ireland, Prevention of Terrorism (Temporary Provisions) Act 1981, Northern Ireland (Emergency Provisions) Act 1996. The Terrorism Act 2000's definition of terrorism in s. 1 is very wide.

1 Terrorism: interpretation

(1) In this Act "terrorism" means the use or threat of action where—

(a) the action falls within subsection (2),
(b) the use or threat is designed to influence the government or to intimidate the public or a section of the public, and
(c) the use or threat is made for the purpose of advancing a political, religious or ideological cause.

(2) Action falls within this subsection if it—

(a) involves serious violence against a person,
(b) involves serious damage to property,
(c) endangers a person's life, other than that of the person committing the action,
(d) creates a serious risk to the health or safety of the public or a section of the public, or
(e) is designed seriously to interfere with or seriously to disrupt an electronic system.

(3) The use or threat of action falling within subsection (2) which involves the use of firearms or explosives is terrorism whether or not subsection (1)(b) is satisfied.

(4) In this section—

(a) "action" includes action outside the United Kingdom,
(b) a reference to any person or to property is a reference to any person, or to property, wherever situated,
(c) a reference to the public includes a reference to the public of a country other than the United Kingdom, and
(d) "the government" means the government of the United Kingdom, of a Part of the United Kingdom or of a country other than the United Kingdom.

(5) In this Act a reference to action taken for the purposes of terrorism includes a reference to action taken for the benefit of a proscribed organisation.

For an analysis of counter-terrorism law see H. Fenwick, *Civil Liberties and Human Rights* (4th edn, 2007), Chapter 14 and an analysis of the law and national insecurity, and public attitudes to civil liberties and terrorism see C. Gearty, *Civil Liberties* (2007), Chapter 3.

In the following extracts attention is directed to one aspect of the response to the September 2001 attacks in New York and Washington, detention without trial of suspected terrorists, and in turn the judicial response to that which provoked a legislative response which then had to be interpreted by the courts.

In looking at the following cases it may be helpful to consider models of legal responses to emergencies. T. Poole, in a paper, 'Courts and Conditions of Uncertainty in "Times of Crisis"' [2008] *Public Law* 234, focuses upon a selection of terrorism cases. They deal with a wider range of counter-terrorism provisions than in the cases extracted below and were decided earlier, however, one common case is *A* v *Secretary of State for the Home Department* [2004] UKHL 56, [2005] 2 AC 68. Poole draws on three models of legal responses to emergencies from O. Gross and F. Ní Aoláin, *Law in Times of Crisis: Emergency Powers in Theory and Practice* (2006). The first, *Accommodation,* affords some accommodation to the pressures on a state in an emergency but there is maintenance of normal principles and rules as much as possible. The second model, *Business as Usual* or *Holding the Line,* rejects such accommodation and denies a tension between protecting security and safeguarding basic values and rights. It has hard and soft types. The hard version stipulates that neither normal constitutional rules change nor does the result when they are applied to specific cases during an emergency. Whereas the soft variant agrees that the rules do not change but that the result may as the court adapts the meaning of what is reasonable in an emergency. The third model, *Extra-Legal Measures* accepts that a special response may be made but it is better that it is openly acknowledged that the response is different and separate from the ordinary law, thereby reducing its perversion in dealing with the hard cases in an emergency.

The idea of a democratic dialogue between the executive and legislative branches and the judicial branch of government should also be borne in mind. By this is meant that the legislation and its interpretation by the courts and the legislative reaction to interpretation, especially a declaration of incompatibility, is kind of conversation between these bodies. This idea began in Canada see 'Judicial Deference and "Democratic Dialogue": The Legitimacy of Judicial Intervention Under The HRA' Clayton [2004] *Public Law* 34 and the report of the House of Lords Constitution Committee 'Relations Between the Executive, the Judiciary and Parliament' (HL 151 of 2006–07, paras 88–111). Consider the 'deference' arguments discussed in *Huang* (see pp. 484–485, *ante*) and also the practical point raised by former Home Secretary, Charles Clarke MP, who wanted guidance from the Law Lords on legality of measures before they were enacted, and the principled rejection of this as compromising judicial independence (see p. 152, *ante*). The House of Lords Constitution Committee considered but rejected the idea of abstract review, where a bill or recently enacted statute is referred to a (constitutional) court for a ruling on its compatibility with the constitution. It was thought that there would be difficulties of delay, and, in the Human Rights Act context the right to pursue proceedings at the European Court of Human Right would remain, and there could be a discrepancy between consideration in the abstract and in a subsequent 'concrete' case, where the facts would play a crucial role in considering the provision's impact. The committee did point out that while it has not been used, there is provision in the devolution legislation for bills passed by the Scottish Parliament, and the Northern Ireland Assembly, before they are submitted for Royal Assent, to be referred to the Judicial Committee of the Privy Council by Law Officers for scrutiny that they are within those bodies' legislative competence (Scotland Act 1998, s. 33, and Northern Ireland Act 1998, s. 11). This jurisdiction transferred to the Supreme Court on its creation, and it will also have a similar jurisdiction in respect of the new Assembly measures which can be made by the National Assembly for Wales (Government of Wales Act 2006, s. 99).

The shock caused by the terrorist attacks on 11 September 2001 led in the United Kingdom to a legislative response which included special measures to deal with suspected foreign terrorists. The Anti-Terrorism, Crime and Security Act 2001 allowed for indefinite detention without charge or trial of suspected international terrorists (non-nationals) who cannot be deported to another country because there are substantial grounds for believing that removal to a state involves a real risk that the person would be subjected to torture, inhuman, or degrading treatment or punishment contrary to Art. 3 ECHR as decided in *Chahal* v *United Kingdom* (1996) 23 EHRR 413. In order to enact Part IV of the 2001 legislation, which breaches Art. 5(1) ECHR, in particular Art. 5(1)(f)) (see p. 411, *ante*) the United Kingdom Government entered a derogation under Article 15 ECHR and the Human Rights Act 1998, s. 14. The provisions in Part 4 of the 2001 Act included: a power to issue a certificate in relation to a person suspected of being an international terrorist whose presence in the United Kingdom is a risk to national security (s. 21); a power to take various actions in respect of a person certified under s. 21 whose removal is prevented by a point of law from an international agreement or for a practical consideration (s. 22); a power to detain a person certified under s. 21 whose removal is prevented by a point of law from an international agreement or for a practical consideration (s. 23); a certificate made under s. 21 may be appealed to the Special Immigration Appeals Commission (SIAC) (s. 25); SIAC will also conduct automatic reviews of certificates for the duration of a person's detention (s. 26); SIAC has also been given exclusive jurisdiction to deal with any legal proceedings which challenge the derogation from Art. 5 ECHR or the designation under the Human Rights Act 1998, s. 14; appeals may be made on a point of law to the Court of Appeal against decisions made by SIAC on appeals or reviews of s. 21 certificates (s. 28) and SIAC has been made a court of superior record and its decisions may only be challenged on appeal to the Court of Appeal (s. 35).

A and Others v *Secretary of State for the Home Department*

[2004] UKHL 56, [2005] 2 AC 68

A and other persons unsuccessfully challenged their detention under Part 4 of the Anti-Terrorism, Crime and Security Act 2001. On appeal to the House of Lords.

LORD BINGHAM OF CORNHILL: ...

Public emergency

16. The appellants repeated before the House a contention rejected by both SIAC and the Court of Appeal, that there neither was nor is a 'public emergency threatening the life of the nation' within the meaning of article 15(1). Thus, they contended, the threshold test for reliance on article 15 has not been satisfied.

17. The European Court considered the meaning of this provision in *Lawless v Ireland (No 3)* (1961) 1 EHRR 15, a case concerned with very low-level IRA terrorist activity in Ireland and Northern Ireland between 1954 and 1957... In para 22 of its judgment the Court held that it was for it to determine whether the conditions laid down in article 15 for the exercise of the exceptional right of derogation had been made out....

18. In the *Greek Case* (1969) 12 YB 1 the Government of Greece failed to persuade the Commission that there had been a public emergency threatening the life of the nation such as would justify derogation. In para 153 of its opinion the Commission described the features of such an emergency:

> 153. Such a public emergency may then be seen to have, in particular, the following characteristics:
>
> (1) It must be actual or imminent.
>
> (2) Its effects must involve the whole nation.

(3) The continuance of the organised life of the community must be threatened.

(4) The crisis or danger must be exceptional, in that the normal measures or restrictions, permitted by the Convention for the maintenance of public safety, health and order, are plainly inadequate.

In *Ireland v United Kingdom* (1978) 2 EHRR 25 the parties were agreed, as were the Commission and the Court, that the article 15 test was satisfied... [and] was accordingly not discussed, but the Court made valuable observations about its role where the application of the article is challenged:

(a) *The role of the Court*

207. The limits on the Court's powers of review are particularly apparent where Article 15 is concerned.

It falls in the first place to each Contracting State, with its responsibility for 'the life of [its] nation', to determine whether that life is threatened by a 'public emergency' and, if so, how far it is necessary to go in attempting to overcome the emergency. By reason of their direct and continuous contact with the pressing needs of the moment, the national authorities are in principle in a better position than the international judge to decide both on the presence of such an emergency and on the nature and scope of derogations necessary to avert it. In this matter, Article 15(1) leaves those authorities a wide margin of appreciation.

Nevertheless, the States do not enjoy an unlimited power in this respect. The Court, which, with the Commission, is responsible for ensuring the observance of the States' engagements (Art. 19), is empowered to rule on whether the States have gone beyond the 'extent strictly required by the exigencies' of the crisis. The domestic margin of appreciation is thus accompanied by a European supervision.

The Court repeated this account of its role in *Brannigan and McBride v United Kingdom* (1993) 17 EHRR 539, adding (para 43) that

in exercising its supervision the Court must give appropriate weight to such relevant factors as the nature of the rights affected by the derogation, the circumstances leading to, and the duration of, the emergency situation.

...

19. Article 4(1) of the ICCPR is expressed in terms very similar to those of article 15(1), and has led to the promulgation of 'The Siracusa Principles on the Limitation and Derogation Provisions in the International Covenant on Civil and Political Rights' (1985) 7 HRQ 3. In paras 39–40, under the heading 'Public Emergency which Threatens the Life of the Nation', it is said:

39. A state party may take measures derogating from its obligations under the International Covenant on Civil and Political Rights pursuant to Article 4 (hereinafter called 'derogation measures') only when faced with a situation of exceptional and actual or imminent danger which threatens the life of the nation. A threat to the life of the nation is one that:

(a) (a) affects the whole of the population and either the whole or part of the territory of the State, and

(b) (b) threatens the physical integrity of the population, the political independence or the territorial integrity of the State or the existence or basic functioning of institutions indispensable to ensure and protect the rights recognised in the Covenant.

40. Internal conflict and unrest that do not constitute a grave and imminent threat to the life of the nation cannot justify derogations under Article 4.

20. The appellants did not seek to play down the catastrophic nature of what had taken place on 11 September 2001 nor the threat posed to western democracies by international terrorism. But they argued that there had been no public emergency threatening the life of the British nation, for three main reasons: if the emergency was not (as in all the decided cases) actual, it must be shown to be imminent, which could not be shown here; the emergency must be of a temporary nature, which again could not be shown here; and the practice of other states, none of which had derogated from the European Convention, strongly suggested that there was no public emergency calling for derogation. All these points call for some explanation.

21. The requirement of imminence is not expressed in article 15 of the European Convention or article 4 of the ICCPR but it has, as already noted, been treated by the European Court as a necessary condition of a valid derogation...

In submitting that the test of imminence was not met, the appellants pointed to ministerial statements in October 2001 and March 2002: 'There is no immediate intelligence pointing to a specific threat to the United Kingdom, but we remain alert, domestically as well as internationally;' and '[I]t would be wrong to say that we have evidence of a particular threat'.

22. The requirement of temporariness is again not expressed in article 15 or article 4 unless it be inherent in the meaning of 'emergency'. But the UN Human Rights Committee on 24 July 2001, in General Comment No 29 on article 4 of the ICCPR, observed in para 2 that:

> Measures derogating from the provisions of the Covenant must be of an exceptional and temporary nature.

This view was also taken by the parliamentary Joint Committee on Human Rights, which in its Eighteenth Report of the Session 2003–2004 (HL paper 158, HC 713, 21 July 2004), in para 4, observed:

> Derogations from human rights obligations are permitted in order to deal with emergencies. They are intended to be temporary. According to the Government and the Security Service, the UK now faces a near-permanent emergency.

It is indeed true that official spokesmen have declined to suggest when, if ever, the present situation might change.

23. No state other than the United Kingdom has derogated from article 5. In Resolution 1271 adopted on 24 January 2002, the Parliamentary Assembly of the Council of Europe... called on all member states (para 12) to:

> refrain from using Article 15 of the European Convention on Human Rights (derogation in time of emergency) to limit the rights and liberties guaranteed under its Article 5 (right to liberty and security).

...In Opinion 1/2002 of the Council of Europe Commissioner for Human Rights (Comm DH (2002) 7, 28 August 2002), Mr Alvaro Gil-Robles observed, in para 33:

> ...[No other state had found it necessary to derogate] Detailed information pointing to a real and imminent danger to public safety in the United Kingdom will, therefore, have to be shown.

The Committee of Privy Counsellors established pursuant to section 122 of the 2001 Act under the chairmanship of Lord Newton of Braintree, which reported on 18 December 2003 (*Anti-terrorism, Crime and Security Act 2001 Review:* Report, HC 100) attached significance to this point:

> 189. *The UK is the only country to have found it necessary to derogate from the European Convention on Human Rights.* We found this puzzling, as it seems clear that other countries face considerable threats from terrorists within their borders.

It noted that France, Italy and Germany had all been threatened, as well as the UK.

24. The appellants submitted that detailed information pointing to a real and imminent danger to public safety in the United Kingdom had not been shown. In making this submission they were able to rely on a series of reports by the Joint Committee on Human Rights... its Second Report of the Session 2001–2002 (HL paper 37, HC 372)... its Fifth Report of the Session 2001–2002... its Fifth Report of the Session 2002–2003... its... Sixth Report of the Session 2003–2004, HL Paper 38, HC 381... in para 34:

> Insufficient evidence has been presented to Parliament to make it possible for us to accept that derogation under ECHR Article 15 is strictly required by the exigencies of the situation to deal with a public emergency threatening the life of the nation.

It adhered to this opinion in paras 15–19 of its Eighteenth Report of the Session 2003–2004 (HL Paper 158, HC 713), drawing attention (para 82) to the fact that the UK was the only country out of 45 countries in the Council of Europe which had found it necessary to derogate from article 5. The appellants relied on these doubts when contrasting the British derogation with the conduct of other Council of Europe member states which had not derogated, including even Spain which had actually experienced catastrophic violence inflicted by Al-Qaeda.

25. The Attorney General, representing the Home Secretary, answered these points. He submitted that an emergency could properly be regarded as imminent if an atrocity was credibly threatened by a body such as Al-Qaeda which had demonstrated its capacity and will to carry out such a threat, where the atrocity might be committed without warning at any time. The Government, responsible as it was and is for the safety of the British people, need not wait for disaster to strike before taking necessary steps to prevent it striking. As to the requirement that the emergency be temporary, the Attorney General did not suggest that an emergency could ever become the normal state of affairs, but he did resist the imposition of any artificial temporal limit to an emergency of the present kind, and pointed out that the emergency which had been held to justify derogation in Northern Ireland in 1988 had been accepted as continuing for a considerable number of years (see *Marshall v United Kingdom* (10 July 2001, Appn No 41571/98) para 18 above). Little help, it was suggested, could be gained by looking at the practice of other states. It was for each national government, as the guardian of its own people's safety, to make its own judgment on the basis of the facts known to it. Insofar as any difference of practice as between the United Kingdom and other Council of Europe members called for justification, it could be found in this country's prominent role as an enemy of Al-Qaeda and an ally of the United States. The Attorney General also made two more fundamental submissions. First, he submitted that there was no error of law in SIAC's approach to this issue and accordingly, since an appeal against its decision lay only on a point of law, there was no ground upon which any appellate court was entitled to disturb its conclusion. Secondly, he submitted that the judgment on this question was pre-eminently one within the discretionary area of judgment reserved to the Secretary of State and his colleagues, exercising their judgment with the benefit of official advice, and to Parliament.

26. The appellants have in my opinion raised an important and difficult question, as the continuing anxiety of the Joint Committee on Human Rights, the observations of the Commissioner for Human Rights and the warnings of the UN Human Rights Committee make clear. In the result, however, not without misgiving (fortified by reading the opinion of my noble and learned friend Lord Hoffmann), I would resolve this issue against the appellants, for three main reasons.

27. First, it is not shown that SIAC or the Court of Appeal misdirected themselves on this issue. SIAC considered a body of closed material, that is, secret material of a sensitive nature not shown to the parties. The Court of Appeal was not asked to read this material. The Attorney General expressly declined to ask the House to read it. From this I infer that while the closed material no doubt substantiates and strengthens the evidence in the public domain, it does not alter its essential character and effect. But this is in my view beside the point. It is not shown that SIAC misdirected itself in law on this issue, and the view which it accepted was one it could reach on the open evidence in the case.

28. My second reason is a legal one. The European Court decisions in *Ireland v United Kingdom* (1978) 2 EHRR 25; *Brannigan and McBride v United Kingdom* (1993) 17 EHRR 539; *Aksoy v Turkey* (1996) 23 EHRR 553 and *Marshall v United Kingdom* (10 July 2001, Appn. No. 41571/98) seem to me to be, with respect, clearly right. In each case the member state had actually experienced widespread loss of life caused by an armed body dedicated to destroying the territorial integrity of the state. To hold that the article 15 test was not satisfied in such circumstances, if a response beyond that provided by the ordinary course of law was required, would have been perverse. But these features were not, on the facts found, very clearly present in *Lawless v Ireland (No 3)* (1961) 1 EHRR 15. That was a relatively early decision of the European Court, but it has never to my knowledge been disavowed and the House is required by section 2(1) of the 1998 Act to take it into account. The decision may perhaps be explained as showing the breadth of the margin of appreciation accorded by the Court to national authorities. It may even have been influenced by the generous opportunity for release given to Mr Lawless and those in his position. If, however, it was open to the Irish Government in *Lawless* to conclude that there was a public emergency threatening the life of the Irish nation, the British Government could scarcely be faulted for reaching that conclusion in the much more dangerous situation which arose after 11 September.

29. Thirdly, I would accept that great weight should be given to the judgment of the Home Secretary, his colleagues and Parliament on this question, because they were called on to exercise a pre-eminently political judgment. It involved making a factual prediction of what various people around the world might or might not do, and when (if at all) they might do it, and what the consequences might be if they did. Any prediction about the future behaviour of human beings (as opposed to the phases of the moon or high water at London Bridge) is necessarily problematical. Reasonable and informed minds may differ, and a judgment is not shown to be wrong or unreasonable because that which is thought likely to happen

does not happen. It would have been irresponsible not to err, if at all, on the side of safety. As will become apparent, I do not accept the full breadth of the Attorney General's argument on what is generally called the deference owed by the courts to the political authorities. It is perhaps preferable to approach this question as one of demarcation of functions or what Liberty in its written case called 'relative institutional competence'. The more purely political (in a broad or narrow sense) a question is, the more appropriate it will be for political resolution and the less likely it is to be an appropriate matter for judicial decision. The smaller, therefore, will be the potential role of the court. It is the function of political and not judicial bodies to resolve political questions. Conversely, the greater the legal content of any issue, the greater the potential role of the court, because under our constitution and subject to the sovereign power of Parliament it is the function of the courts and not of political bodies to resolve legal questions. The present question seems to me to be very much at the political end of the spectrum: see *Secretary of State for the Home Department v Rehman* [2001] UKHL 47, [2003] 1 AC 153, para 62, per Lord Hoffmann. The appellants recognised this by acknowledging that the Home Secretary's decision on the present question was less readily open to challenge than his decision (as they argued) on some other questions. This reflects the unintrusive approach of the European Court to such a question. I conclude that the appellants have shown no ground strong enough to warrant displacing the Secretary of State's decision on this important threshold question.

Proportionality

30. Article 15 requires that any measures taken by a member state in derogation of its obligations under the Convention should not go beyond what is 'strictly required by the exigencies of the situation'. Thus the Convention imposes a test of strict necessity or, in Convention terminology, proportionality. The appellants founded on the principle adopted by the Privy Council in *de Freitas v Permanent Secretary of Ministry of Agriculture, Fisheries, Lands and Housing* [1999] 1 AC 69, 80. In determining whether a limitation is arbitrary or excessive, the court must ask itself:

> whether: (i) the legislative objective is sufficiently important to justify limiting a fundamental right; (ii) the measures designed to meet the legislative objective are rationally connected to it; and (iii) the means used to impair the right or freedom are no more than is necessary to accomplish the objective.

. . . [The appellants] submitted that even if it were accepted that the legislative objective of protecting the British people against the risk of catastrophic Al-Qaeda terrorism was sufficiently important to justify limiting the fundamental right to personal freedom of those facing no criminal accusation, the 2001 Act was not designed to meet that objective and was not rationally connected to it. Furthermore, the legislative objective could have been achieved by means which did not, or did not so severely, restrict the fundamental right to personal freedom.

31. The appellants' argument under this head can, I hope fairly, be summarised as involving the following steps:

(1) Part 4 of the 2001 Act reversed the effect of the decisions in *Hardial Singh* [1984] 1 WLR 704 and *Chahal* (1996) 23 EHRR 413 and was apt to address the problems of immigration control caused to the United Kingdom by article 5(1)(f) of the Convention read in the light of those decisions.
(2) The public emergency on which the United Kingdom relied to derogate from the Convention right to personal liberty was the threat to the security of the United Kingdom presented by Al-Qaeda terrorists and their supporters.
(3) While the threat to the security of the United Kingdom derived predominantly and most immediately from foreign nationals, some of whom could not be deported because they would face torture or inhuman or degrading treatment or punishment in their home countries and who could not be deported to any third country willing to receive them, the threat to the United Kingdom did not derive solely from such foreign nationals.
(4) Sections 21 and 23 did not rationally address the threat to the security of the United Kingdom presented by Al-Qaeda terrorists and their supporters because (a) it did not address the threat presented by UK nationals, (b) it permitted foreign nationals suspected of being Al-Qaeda terrorists or their supporters to pursue their activities abroad if there was any country to which they were able to go, and (c) the sections permitted the certification and detention of persons who were not suspected of presenting any threat to the security of the United Kingdom as Al-Qaeda terrorists or supporters.

(5) If the threat presented to the security of the United Kingdom by UK nationals suspected of being Al-Qaeda terrorists or their supporters could be addressed without infringing their right to personal liberty, it is not shown why similar measures could not adequately address the threat presented by foreign nationals.
(6) Since the right to personal liberty is among the most fundamental of the rights protected by the European Convention, any restriction of it must be closely scrutinised by the national court and such scrutiny involves no violation of democratic or constitutional principle.
(7) In the light of such scrutiny, neither the Derogation Order nor sections 21 and 23 of the 2001 Act can be justified.

32. It is unnecessary to linger on the first two steps of this argument, neither of which is controversial and both of which are clearly correct. The third step calls for closer examination. The evidence before SIAC was that the Home Secretary considered 'that the serious threats to the nation emanated predominantly (albeit not exclusively) and more immediately from the category of foreign nationals'. In para 95 of its judgment SIAC held:

> But the evidence before us demonstrates beyond argument that the threat is not so confined. [i.e. is not confined to the alien section of the population]. There are many British nationals already identified—mostly in detention abroad—who fall within the definition of 'suspected international terrorists', and it was clear from the submissions made to us that in the opinion of the [Home Secretary] there are others at liberty in the United Kingdom who could be similarly defined.

This finding has not been challenged, and since SIAC is the responsible fact-finding tribunal it is unnecessary to examine the basis of it. There was however evidence before SIAC that 'upwards of a thousand individuals from the UK are estimated on the basis of intelligence to have attended training camps in Afghanistan in the last five years', that some British citizens are said to have planned to return from Afghanistan to the United Kingdom and that 'The backgrounds of those detained show the high level of involvement of British citizens and those otherwise connected with the United Kingdom in the terrorist networks'. It seems plain that the threat to the United Kingdom did not derive solely from foreign nationals or from foreign nationals whom it was unlawful to deport. Later evidence, not before SIAC or the Court of Appeal, supports that conclusion. The Newton Committee recorded the Home Office argument that the threat from Al-Qaeda terrorism was predominantly from foreigners but drew attention (para 193) to

> accumulating evidence that this is not now the case. The British suicide bombers who attacked Tel Aviv in May 2003, Richard Reid ('the Shoe Bomber'), and recent arrests suggest that the threat from UK citizens is real. Almost 30% of Terrorism Act 2000 suspects in the past year have been British. We have been told that, of the people of interest to the authorities because of their suspected involvement in international terrorism, nearly half are British nationals.

33. The fourth step in the appellants' argument is of obvious importance to it. It is plain that sections 21 and 23 of the 2001 Act do not address the threat presented by UK nationals since they do not provide for the certification and detention of UK nationals. It is beside the point that other sections of the 2001 Act and the 2000 Act do apply to UK nationals, since they are not the subject of derogation, are not the subject of complaint and apply equally to foreign nationals. Yet the threat from UK nationals, if quantitatively smaller, is not said to be qualitatively different from that from foreign nationals. It is also plain that sections 21 and 23 do permit a person certified and detained to leave the United Kingdom and go to any other country willing to receive him, as two of the appellants did when they left for Morocco and France respectively (see para 2 above). Such freedom to leave is wholly explicable in terms of immigration control: if the British authorities wish to deport a foreign national but cannot deport him to country 'A' because of *Chahal* their purpose is as well served by his voluntary departure for country 'B'. But allowing a suspected international terrorist to leave our shores and depart to another country, perhaps a country as close as France, there to pursue his criminal designs, is hard to reconcile with a belief in his capacity to inflict serious injury to the people and interests of this country. It seems clear from the language of section 21 of the 2001 Act, read with the definition of terrorism in section 1 of the 2000 Act, that section 21 is capable of covering those who have no link at all with Al-Qaeda (they might, for example, be members of the Basque separatist organisation ETA), or who, although supporting the general aims of Al-Qaeda, reject its cult of violence. The Attorney General conceded that sections 21 and 23 could not lawfully be invoked in the case of suspected international terrorists other than those thought to be connected with Al-Qaeda, and undertook that the procedure would not be used in such cases. A restrictive reading of the

broad statutory language might in any event be indicated: *Padfield v Minister of Agriculture, Fisheries and Food* [1968] AC 997. The appellants were content to accept the Attorney General's concession and undertaking. It is not however acceptable that interpretation and application of a statutory provision bearing on the liberty of the subject should be governed by implication, concession and undertaking.

34. ... The Newton Committee, while expressing no opinion on the legality of Part 4 of the 2001 Act, echoed the [Council of Europe's Human Rights] Commissioner's criticisms:

> 185. The Part 4 detention powers present a number of problems that range from fundamental issues of principle to practical procedural difficulties. We are not persuaded that the powers are sufficient to meet the full extent of the threat from international terrorism. Nor are we persuaded that the risks of injustice are necessary or defensible.
>
> 186. Some of these problems arise because Part 4 is an adaptation of existing immigration and asylum legislation, rather than being designed expressly for the purpose of meeting the threat from international terrorism.
>
> ...
>
> 192. The Part 4 process *only tackles the threat from foreigners suspected of having links with al Qaeda or its associated networks*. It does not, therefore, address the threat:
>
> a. from British nationals with similar links; or from
> b. anyone in the UK with links to other foreign terrorist causes.
>
> ...
>
> 195. *Seeking to deport terrorist suspects does not seem to us to be a satisfactory response, given the risk of exporting terrorism*. If people in the UK are contributing to the terrorist effort here or abroad, they should be dealt with here. While deporting such people might free up British police, intelligence, security and prison service resources, it would not necessarily reduce the threat to British interests abroad, or make the world a safer place more generally. Indeed, there is a risk that the suspects might even return without the authorities being aware of it.
>
> ...
>
> 203. We consider the shortcomings described above to be sufficiently serious to strongly recommend that the Part 4 powers which allow foreign nationals to be detained potentially indefinitely should be replaced as a matter of urgency. New legislation should:
>
> a. deal with all terrorism, whatever its origin or the nationality of its suspected perpetrators; and
> b. not require a derogation from the European Convention on Human Rights.

35. The fifth step in the appellants' argument permits of little elaboration. But it seems reasonable to assume that those suspected international terrorists who are UK nationals are not simply ignored by the authorities. When G, one of the appellants, was released from prison by SIAC on bail (*G v Secretary of State for the Home Department* (SC/2/2002, Bail Application SCB/10, 20 May 2004), it was on condition (among other things) that he wear an electronic monitoring tag at all times; that he remain at his premises at all times; that he telephone a named security company five times each day at specified times; that he permit the company to install monitoring equipment at his premises; that he limit entry to his premises to his family, his solicitor, his medical attendants and other approved persons; that he make no contact with any other person; that he have on his premises no computer equipment, mobile telephone or other electronic communications device; that he cancel the existing telephone link to his premises; and that he install a dedicated telephone link permitting contact only with the security company. The appellants suggested that conditions of this kind, strictly enforced, would effectively inhibit terrorist activity. It is hard to see why this would not be so.

36. In urging the fundamental importance of the right to personal freedom, as the sixth step in their proportionality argument, the appellants were able to draw on the long libertarian tradition of English law, dating back to chapter 39 of Magna Carta 1215, given effect in the ancient remedy of habeas corpus, declared in the Petition of Right 1628, upheld in a series of landmark decisions down the centuries and

embodied in the substance and procedure of the law to our own day. Recent statements, not in themselves remarkable, may be found in *In re S-C (Mental Patient: Habeas Corpus)* [1996] QB 599, 603 and *In re Wasfi Suleman Mahmod* [1995] Imm A R 311, 314. In its treatment of article 5 of the European Convention, the European Court also has recognised the prime importance of personal freedom. In *Kurt v Turkey* (1998) 27 EHRR 373, para 122, it referred to 'the fundamental importance of the guarantees contained in Article 5 for securing the right of individuals in a democracy to be free from arbitrary detention at the hands of the authorities' and to the need to interpret narrowly any exception to 'a most basic guarantee of individual freedom'. In *Garcia Alva v Germany* (2001) 37 EHRR 335, para 39, it referred to 'the dramatic impact of deprivation of liberty on the fundamental rights of the person concerned'. The authors of the Siracusa Principles, although acknowledging that the protection against arbitrary detention (article 9 of the ICCPR) might be limited if strictly required by the exigencies of an emergency situation (article 4), were nonetheless of the opinion that some rights could never be denied in any conceivable emergency and, in particular (para 70 (b)),

> no person shall be detained for an indefinite period of time, whether detained pending judicial investigation or trial or detained without charge;...

37. While the Attorney General challenged and resisted the third, fourth and fifth steps in the appellants' argument, he directed the weight of his submission to challenging the standard of judicial review for which the appellants contended in this sixth step. He submitted that as it was for Parliament and the executive to assess the threat facing the nation, so it was for those bodies and not the courts to judge the response necessary to protect the security of the public. These were matters of a political character calling for an exercise of political and not judicial judgment. Just as the European Court allowed a generous margin of appreciation to member states, recognising that they were better placed to understand and address local problems, so should national courts recognise, for the same reason, that matters of the kind in issue here fall within the discretionary area of judgment properly belonging to the democratic organs of the state. It was not for the courts to usurp authority properly belonging elsewhere. The Attorney General drew attention to the dangers identified by Richard Ekins in 'Judicial Supremacy and the Rule of Law' (2003) 119 LQR 127. This is an important submission, properly made, and it calls for careful consideration.

38. Those conducting the business of democratic government have to make legislative choices which, notably in some fields, are very much a matter for them, particularly when (as is often the case) the interests of one individual or group have to be balanced against those of another individual or group or the interests of the community as a whole. The European Court has recognised this on many occasions: *Chassagnou v France* (1999) 29 EHRR 615, para 113, and *Hatton v United Kingdom* (2003) 37 EHRR 611, paras 97–98, may be cited as recent examples. In para 97 of *Hatton*, a case which concerned aircraft noise at Heathrow, the Court said:

> At the same time, the Court reiterates the fundamentally subsidiary role of the Convention. The national authorities have direct democratic legitimation and are, as the Court has held on many occasions, in principle better placed than an international court to evaluate local needs and conditions. In matters of general policy, on which opinions within a democratic society may reasonably differ widely, the role of the domestic policy maker should be given special weight.

Where the conduct of government is threatened by serious terrorism, difficult choices have to be made and the terrorist dimension cannot be overlooked. This also the European Commission and Court have recognised in cases such as *Brogan v United Kingdom* (1988) 11 EHRR 117, para 80; *Fox, Campbell & Hartley v United Kingdom* (1990) 13 EHRR 157, paras 32, 34; and *Murray v United Kingdom* (1994) 19 EHRR 193, para 47. The same recognition is found in domestic authority: see, for example, *Secretary of State for the Home Department v Rehman* [2003] 1 AC 153, paras 28, 62.

39. While any decision made by a representative democratic body must of course command respect, the degree of respect will be conditioned by the nature of the decision. As the European Court observed in *Fretté v France* (2002) 38 EHRR 438, para 40,

> ...the Contracting States enjoy a margin of appreciation in assessing whether and to what extent differences in otherwise similar situations justify a different treatment in law. The scope of the margin of appreciation will vary according to the circumstances, the subject-matter and its background; in this respect, one of the relevant factors may be the existence or non-existence of common ground between the laws of Contracting States.

A similar approach is found in domestic authority. In *R v Director of Public Prosecutions, Ex p Kebilene* [2000] 2 AC 326, 381, Lord Hope of Craighead said:

> It will be easier for such [a discretionary] area of judgment to be recognised where the Convention itself requires a balance to be struck, much less so where the right is stated in terms which are unqualified. It will be easier for it to be recognised where the issues involve questions of social or economic policy, much less so where the rights are of high constitutional importance or are of a kind where the courts are especially well placed to assess the need for protection.

Another area in which the court was held to be qualified to make its own judgment is the requirement of a fair trial: *R v A (No 2)* [2002] 1 AC 45, para 36. The Supreme Court of Canada took a similar view in *Libman v Attorney General of Quebec* (1997) 3 BHRC 269, para 59. In his dissenting judgment (cited with approval in *Libman*) in *RJR-MacDonald Inc v Attorney General of Canada* [1995] 3 SCR 199, para 68, La Forest J, sitting in the same court, said:

> Courts are specialists in the protection of liberty and the interpretation of legislation and are, accordingly, well placed to subject criminal justice legislation to careful scrutiny. However, courts are not specialists in the realm of policy-making, nor should they be....

40. The Convention regime for the international protection of human rights requires national authorities, including national courts, to exercise their authority to afford effective protection. The European Court made this clear in the early case of *Handyside v United Kingdom* (1976) 1 EHRR 737, para 48:

> The Court points out that the machinery of protection established by the Convention is subsidiary to the national systems safeguarding human rights. The Convention leaves to each Contracting State, in the first place, the task of securing the rights and freedoms it enshrines.

Thus the European Commissioner for Human Rights had authority for saying (Opinion 1/2002, para 9):

> It is furthermore, precisely because the Convention presupposes domestic controls in the form of a preventive parliamentary scrutiny and posterior judicial review that national authorities enjoy a large margin of appreciation in respect of derogations. This is, indeed, the essence of the principle of the subsidiarity of the protection of Convention rights.

In *Smith and Grady v United Kingdom* (1999) 29 EHRR 493 the traditional *Wednesbury* approach to judicial review was held to afford inadequate protection. It is now recognised that 'domestic courts must themselves form a judgment whether a Convention right has been breached' and that 'the intensity of review is somewhat greater under the proportionality approach': *R (Daly) v Secretary of State for the Home Department* [2001] UKHL 26, [2001] 2 AC 532, paras 23, 27.

41. Even in a terrorist situation the Convention organs have not been willing to relax their residual supervisory role: *Brogan v United Kingdom* above, para 80; *Fox, Campbell & Hartley v United Kingdom*, above, paras 32–34. In *Aksoy v Turkey* (1996) 23 EHRR 553, para 76, the Court, clearly referring to national courts as well as the Convention organs, held:

> The Court would stress the importance of Article 5 in the Convention system: it enshrines a fundamental human right, namely the protection of the individual against arbitrary interference by the State with his or her right to liberty. Judicial control of interferences by the executive with the individual's right to liberty is an essential feature of the guarantee embodied in Article 5(3), which is intended to minimise the risk of arbitrariness and to ensure the rule of law.

...

Simon Brown LJ in *International Transport Roth GmbH v Secretary of State for the Home Department* [2003] QB 728 observed, in para 27, that

> ...the court's role under the 1998 Act is as the guardian of human rights. It cannot abdicate this responsibility.

He went on to say, in para 54:

> But judges nowadays have no alternative but to apply the Human Rights Act 1998. Constitutional dangers exist no less in too little judicial activism as in too much. There are limits to the legitimacy of executive or legislative decision-making, just as there are to decision-making by the courts.

42. It follows from this analysis that the appellants are in my opinion entitled to invite the courts to review, on proportionality grounds, the Derogation Order and the compatibility with the Convention of

section 23 and the courts are not effectively precluded by any doctrine of deference from scrutinising the issues raised. It also follows that I do not accept the full breadth of the Attorney General's submissions. I do not in particular accept the distinction which he drew between democratic institutions and the courts. It is of course true that the judges in this country are not elected and are not answerable to Parliament. It is also of course true, as pointed out in para 29 above, that Parliament, the executive and the courts have different functions. But the function of independent judges charged to interpret and apply the law is universally recognised as a cardinal feature of the modern democratic state, a cornerstone of the rule of law itself. The Attorney General is fully entitled to insist on the proper limits of judicial authority, but he is wrong to stigmatise judicial decision-making as in some way undemocratic. It is particularly inappropriate in a case such as the present in which Parliament has expressly legislated in section 6 of the 1998 Act to render unlawful any act of a public authority, including a court, incompatible with a Convention right, has required courts (in section 2) to take account of relevant Strasbourg jurisprudence, has (in section 3) required courts, so far as possible, to give effect to Convention rights and has conferred a right of appeal on derogation issues. The effect is not, of course, to override the sovereign legislative authority of the Queen in Parliament, since if primary legislation is declared to be incompatible the validity of the legislation is unaffected (section 4(6)) and the remedy lies with the appropriate minister (section 10), who is answerable to Parliament. The 1998 Act gives the courts a very specific, wholly democratic, mandate. As Professor Jowell has put it

> The courts are charged by Parliament with delineating the boundaries of a rights-based democracy ('Judicial Deference: servility, civility or institutional capacity?' [2003] PL 592, 597).

See also Clayton, 'Judicial deference and "democratic dialogue": the legitimacy of judicial intervention under the Human Rights Act 1998' [2004] PL 33.

43. The appellants' proportionality challenge to the Order and section 23 is, in my opinion, sound, for all the reasons they gave and also for those given by the European Commissioner for Human Rights and the Newton Committee. The Attorney General could give no persuasive answer. In a discussion paper Counter-Terrorism Powers: Reconciling Security and Liberty in an Open Society (Cm 6147, February 2004) the Secretary of State replied to one of the Newton Committee's criticisms in this way:

> 32. It can be argued that as suspected international terrorists their departure for another country could amount to exporting terrorism: a point made in the Newton Report at paragraph 195. But that is a natural consequence of the fact that Part 4 powers are immigration powers: detention is permissible only pending deportation and there is no other power available to detain (other than for the purpose of police enquiries) if a foreign national chooses voluntarily to leave the UK. (Detention in those circumstances is limited to 14 days after which the person must be either charged or released.) Deportation has the advantage moreover of disrupting the activities of the suspected terrorist.

This answer, however, reflects the central complaint made by the appellants: that the choice of an immigration measure to address a security problem had the inevitable result of failing adequately to address that problem (by allowing non-UK suspected terrorists to leave the country with impunity and leaving British suspected terrorists at large) while imposing the severe penalty of indefinite detention on persons who, even if reasonably suspected of having links with Al-Qaeda, may harbour no hostile intentions towards the United Kingdom. The conclusion that the Order and section 23 are, in Convention terms, disproportionate is in my opinion irresistible.

44. Since, under section 7 of the Special Immigration Appeals Commission Act 1997 and section 30(5) of the 2001 Act, an appeal from SIAC lies only on a point of law, that is not the end of the matter. It is necessary to examine SIAC's reasons for rejecting this part of the appellants' challenge. They are given in para 51 of SIAC's judgment, and are fourfold:

(1) that there is an advantage to the UK in the removal of a potential terrorist from circulation in the UK because he cannot operate actively in the UK whilst he is either not in the country or not at liberty;
(2) that the removal of potential terrorists from their UK communities disrupts the organisation of terrorist activities;
(3) that the detainee's freedom to leave, far from showing that the measures are irrational, tends to show that they are to this extent properly tailored to the state of emergency; and

(4) that it is difficult to see how a power to detain a foreign national who had not been charged with a criminal offence and wished to leave the UK could readily be defended as tending to prevent him committing acts of terrorism aimed at the UK.

Assuming, as one must, that there is a public emergency threatening the life of the nation, measures which derogate from article 5 are permissible only to the extent strictly required by the exigencies of the situation, and it is for the derogating state to prove that that is so. The reasons given by SIAC do not warrant its conclusion. The first reason does not explain why the measures are directed only to foreign nationals. The second reason no doubt has some validity, but is subject to the same weakness. The third reason does not explain why a terrorist, if a serious threat to the UK, ceases to be so on the French side of the English Channel or elsewhere. The fourth reason is intelligible if the foreign national is not really thought to be a serious threat to the UK, but hard to understand if he is. I do not consider SIAC's conclusion as one to which it could properly come. In dismissing the appellants' appeal, Lord Woolf CJ broadly considered that it was sensible and appropriate for the Secretary of State to use immigration legislation, that deference was owed to his decisions (para 40) and that SIAC's conclusions depended on the evidence before it (para 43). Brooke LJ reached a similar conclusion (para 91), regarding SIAC's findings as unappealable findings of fact. Chadwick LJ also regarded SIAC's finding as one of fact (para 150). I cannot accept this analysis as correct. The European Court does not approach questions of proportionality as questions of pure fact: see, for example, *Smith and Grady v United Kingdom*, above. Nor should domestic courts do so. The greater intensity of review now required in determining questions of proportionality, and the duty of the courts to protect Convention rights, would in my view be emasculated if a judgment at first instance on such a question were conclusively to preclude any further review. So would excessive deference, in a field involving indefinite detention without charge or trial, to ministerial decision. In my opinion, SIAC erred in law and the Court of Appeal erred in failing to correct its error.

Appeal allowed. A quashing order in relation to the Human Rights Act (Designated Derogation) Order 2001 and a declaration of incompatibility between the Anti-terrorism, Crime and Security Act 2001, s. 23 and Articles 5, 14 ECHR.

NOTES

1. The decision was reached by a majority of 8–1 with Lord Walker dissenting.
2. Lord Steyn was not sitting on the panel because the Treasury Solicitor's Department had made a request to Lord Bingham, the Senior Law Lord, that Lord Steyn should not sit on this appeal because he had expressed the view that the suspension of Art. 5 ECHR 'is not in present circumstances justified' in a lecture given to the Holdsworth Club at the University of Birmingham in November 2001, entitled 'Human Rights—The Legacy of Mrs Roosevelt', which is reprinted in [2002] *Public Law* 473, 483–484 see *The Guardian*, 9 April 2004. The basis of the request was possible bias following *Locabail (UK) Ltd* v *Bayfield Properties Ltd* [2000] QB 451, para. 25, see p. 561, *post*.
3. The majority, with the exception of Lord Hoffmann, and Lord Walker agreed with Lord Bingham that there was a public emergency. Lord Hoffmann said in relation to the detention powers that 'The real threat to the life of the nation, in the sense of a people living in accordance with its traditional laws and political values, comes not from terrorism but from laws such as these. That is the true measure of what terrorism may achieve. It is for Parliament to decide whether to give the terrorists such a victory' (para. 97).
4. Lord Hoffmann did not express a view on the proportionality basis of the rest of the majority's reasoning nor on the additional discrimination ground which they held in favour of the appellants. Their Lordships did not find any basis in international law or in the ECHR which could justify the breach of Art. 14 through discrimination between British nationals and non-nationals suspected of involvement in terrorism. If the terrorist threat is so severe to be able to justify detention without trial, then it is not legitimate to lock up only the foreign nationals and not the British nationals who pose this threat.

■ QUESTIONS

1. Compare Lord Bingham's deference to the executive's assessment that the United Kingdom faces a public emergency in para. 29, with his proportionality assessment. Which proportionality test from *Daly* at p. 490, *ante*, is being used?

2. Does Lord Bingham's use of the opinions of the Council of Europe, the Joint Committee on Human Rights, and the Newton Committee of Privy Councillors buttress his decision on proportionality or demonstrate that this issue is more political than legal?

The Government accepted the decision and sought to legislate for a framework which would protect the public and meet the concerns about proportionality and discrimination. The Prevention of Terrorism Act 2005 provides for control orders which restrict the liberty of those, of whichever nationality, who are suspected of being terrorists. There is a distinction between a derogating and a non-derogating control order. If a derogating control order is made it will infringe Art. 5 and so will require a derogation to be made.

The Prevention of Terrorism Act 2005

1 Power to make control orders

(1) In this Act "control order" means an order against an individual that imposes obligations on him for purposes connected with protecting members of the public from a risk of terrorism.

(2) The power to make a control order against an individual shall be exercisable—

(a) except in the case of an order imposing obligations that are incompatible with the individual's right to liberty under Article 5 of the Human Rights Convention, by the Secretary of State; and
(b) in the case of an order imposing obligations that are or include derogating obligations, by the court on an application by the Secretary of State.

(3) The obligations that may be imposed by a control order made against an individual are any obligations that the Secretary of State or (as the case may be) the court considers necessary for purposes connected with preventing or restricting involvement by that individual in terrorism-related activity.

(4) Those obligations may include, in particular—

(a) a prohibition or restriction on his possession or use of specified articles or substances;
(b) a prohibition or restriction on his use of specified services or specified facilities, or on his carrying on specified activities;
(c) a restriction in respect of his work or other occupation, or in respect of his business;
(d) a restriction on his association or communications with specified persons or with other persons generally;
(e) a restriction in respect of his place of residence or on the persons to whom he gives access to his place of residence;
(f) a prohibition on his being at specified places or within a specified area at specified times or on specified days;
(g) a prohibition or restriction on his movements to, from or within the United Kingdom, a specified part of the United Kingdom or a specified place or area within the United Kingdom;
(h) a requirement on him to comply with such other prohibitions or restrictions on his movements as may be imposed, for a period not exceeding 24 hours, by directions given to him in the specified manner, by a specified person and for the purpose of securing compliance with other obligations imposed by or under the order;
(i) a requirement on him to surrender his passport, or anything in his possession to which a prohibition or restriction imposed by the order relates, to a specified person for a period not exceeding the period for which the order remains in force;
(j) a requirement on him to give access to specified persons to his place of residence or to other premises to which he has power to grant access;
(k) a requirement on him to allow specified persons to search that place or any such premises for the purpose of ascertaining whether obligations imposed by or under the order have been, are being or are about to be contravened;
(l) a requirement on him to allow specified persons, either for that purpose or for the purpose of securing that the order is complied with, to remove anything found in that place or on any such premises and

to subject it to tests or to retain it for a period not exceeding the period for which the order remains in force;

(m) a requirement on him to allow himself to be photographed;

(n) a requirement on him to co-operate with specified arrangements for enabling his movements, communications or other activities to be monitored by electronic or other means;

(o) a requirement on him to comply with a demand made in the specified manner to provide information to a specified person in accordance with the demand;

(p) a requirement on him to report to a specified person at specified times and places.

(5) Power by or under a control order to prohibit or restrict the controlled person's movements includes, in particular, power to impose a requirement on him to remain at or within a particular place or area (whether for a particular period or at particular times or generally).

(6) The reference in subsection (4)(n) to co-operating with specified arrangements for monitoring includes a reference to each of the following—

(a) submitting to procedures required by the arrangements;

(b) wearing or otherwise using apparatus approved by or in accordance with the arrangements;

(c) maintaining such apparatus in the specified manner;

(d) complying with directions given by persons carrying out functions for the purposes of those arrangements.

(7) The information that the controlled person may be required to provide under a control order includes, in particular, advance information about his proposed movements or other activities.

(8) A control order may provide for a prohibition, restriction or requirement imposed by or under the order to apply only where a specified person has not given his consent or approval to what would otherwise contravene the prohibition, restriction or requirement.

(9) For the purposes of this Act involvement in terrorism-related activity is any one or more of the following—

(a) the commission, preparation or instigation of acts of terrorism;

(b) conduct which facilitates the commission, preparation or instigation of such acts, or which is intended to do so;

(c) conduct which gives encouragement to the commission, preparation or instigation of such acts, or which is intended to do so;

(d) conduct which gives support or assistance to individuals who are known or believed to be involved in terrorism-related activity; and for the purposes of this subsection it is immaterial whether the acts of terrorism in question are specific acts of terrorism or acts of terrorism generally.

(10) In this Act—

"derogating obligation" means an obligation on an individual which—

(a) is incompatible with his right to liberty under Article 5 of the Human Rights Convention; but

(b) is of a description of obligations which, for the purposes of the designation of a designated derogation, is set out in the designation order;

(c) "designated derogation" has the same meaning as in the Human Rights Act 1998 (c. 42) (see section 14(1) of that Act);

(d) "designation order", in relation to a designated derogation, means the order under section 14(1) of the Human Rights Act 1998 by which the derogation is designated.

2 Making of non-derogating control orders

(1) The Secretary of State may make a control order against an individual if he—

(a) has reasonable grounds for suspecting that the individual is or has been involved in terrorism-related activity; and

(b) considers that it is necessary, for purposes connected with protecting members of the public from a risk of terrorism, to make a control order imposing obligations on that individual.

(2) The Secretary of State may make a control order against an individual who is or the time being bound by a control order made by the court only if he does so—

(a) after the court has determined that its order should be revoked; but
(b) while the effect of the revocation has been postponed for the purpose of giving the Secretary of State an opportunity to decide whether to exercise his own powers to make a control order against the individual.

(3) A control order made by the Secretary of State is called a non-derogating control order.
(4) A non-derogating control order—

(a) has effect for a period of 12 months beginning with the day on which it is made; but
(b) may be renewed on one or more occasions in accordance with this section.

(5) A non-derogating control order must specify when the period for which it is to have effect will end.
(6) The Secretary of State may renew a non-derogating control order (with or without modifications) for a period of 12 months if he—

(a) considers that it is necessary, for purposes connected with protecting members of the public from a risk of terrorism, for an order imposing obligations on the controlled person to continue in force; and
(b) considers that the obligations to be imposed by the renewed order are necessary for purposes connected with preventing or restricting involvement by that person in terrorism-related activity.

(7) Where the Secretary of State renews a non-derogating control order, the 12 month period of the renewal begins to run from whichever is the earlier of—

(a) the time when the order would otherwise have ceased to have effect; or
(b) the beginning of the seventh day after the date of renewal.

(8) The instrument renewing a non-derogating control order must specify when the period for which it is renewed will end.
(9) It shall be immaterial, for the purposes of determining what obligations may be imposed by a control order made by the Secretary of State, whether the involvement in terrorism-related activity to be prevented or restricted by the obligations is connected with matters to which the Secretary of State's grounds for suspicion relate.

3 Supervision by court of making of non-derogating control orders

(1) The Secretary of State must not make a non-derogating control order against an individual except where—

(a) having decided that there are grounds to make such an order against that individual, he has applied to the court for permission to make the order and has been granted that permission;
(b) the order contains a statement by the Secretary of State that, in his opinion, the urgency of the case requires the order to be made without such permission; or
(c) the order is made before 14th March 2005 against an individual who, at the time it is made, is an individual in respect of whom a certificate under section 21(1) of the Anti-terrorism, Crime and Security Act 2001 (c. 24) is in force.

(2) Where the Secretary of State makes an application for permission to make a non-derogating control order against an individual, the application must set out the order for which he seeks permission and—

(a) the function of the court is to consider whether the Secretary of State's decision that there are grounds to make that order is obviously flawed;
(b) the court may give that permission unless it determines that the decision is obviously flawed; and
(c) if it gives permission, the court must give directions for a hearing in relation to the order as soon as reasonably practicable after it is made.

(3) Where the Secretary of State makes a non-derogating control order against an individual without the permission of the court—

(a) he must immediately refer the order to the court; and
(b) the function of the court on the reference is to consider whether the decision of the Secretary of State to make the order he did was obviously flawed.

(4) The court's consideration on a reference under subsection (3)(a) must begin no more than 7 days after the day on which the control order in question was made.

(5) The court may consider an application for permission under subsection (1)(a) or a reference under subsection (3)(a)—

(a) in the absence of the individual in question;
(b) without his having been notified of the application or reference; and
(c) without his having been given an opportunity (if he was aware of the application or reference) of making any representations to the court; but this subsection is not to be construed as limiting the matters about which rules of court may be made in relation to the consideration of such an application or reference.

(6) On a reference under subsection (3)(a), the court—

(a) if it determines that the decision of the Secretary of State to make a non-derogating control order against the controlled person was obviously flawed, must quash the order;
(b) if it determines that that decision was not obviously flawed but that a decision of the Secretary of State to impose a particular obligation by that order was obviously flawed, must quash that obligation and (subject to that) confirm the order and give directions for a hearing in relation to the confirmed order; and
(c) in any other case, must confirm the order and give directions for a hearing in relation to the confirmed order.

(7) The directions given under subsection (2)(c) or (6)(b) or (c) must include arrangements for the individual in question to be given an opportunity within 7 days of the court's giving permission or (as the case may be) making its determination on the reference to make representations about—

(a) the directions already given; and
(b) the making of further directions.

(8) On a reference under subsection (3)(a), the court may quash a certificate contained in the order for the purposes of subsection (1)(b) if it determines that the Secretary of State's decision that the certificate should be contained in the order was flawed.

(9) The court must ensure that the controlled person is notified of its decision on a reference under subsection (3)(a).

(10) On a hearing in pursuance of directions under subsection (2)(c) or (6)(b) or (c), the function of the court is to determine whether any of the following decisions of the Secretary of State was flawed—

(a) his decision that the requirements of section 2(1)(a) and (b) were satisfied for the making of the order; and
(b) his decisions on the imposition of each of the obligations imposed by the order.

(11) In determining—

(a) what constitutes a flawed decision for the purposes of subsection (2), (6) or (8), or
(b) the matters mentioned in subsection (10), the court must apply the principles applicable on an application for judicial review.

(12) If the court determines, on a hearing in pursuance of directions under subsection (2)(c) or (6)(b) or (c), that a decision of the Secretary of State was flawed, its only powers are—

(a) power to quash the order;
(b) power to quash one or more obligations imposed by the order; and
(c) power to give directions to the Secretary of State for the revocation of the order or for the modification of the obligations it imposes.

(13) In every other case the court must decide that the control order is to continue in force.

(14) If requested to do so by the controlled person, the court must discontinue any hearing in pursuance of directions under subsection (2)(c) or (6)(b) or (c).

NOTES

1. If a derogating control order is to be made it will be made by a court and a derogation from Art. 5 would be required, whereas for a non-derogating control order the courts give permission for it to be made by the Secretary of State. In the usual case of a non-derogating order the court is involved in giving permission to make the order unless it is obviously flawed and permission having been given the court then considers if the Home Secretary's decisions were flawed in determining (a) that the criteria for making an order were met, and (b) the obligations imposed by the order. A special procedure may be followed in which closed material is used, that is material which is not disclosed to the person to be subjected to the order (the controlee) or to the controlee's lawyers, however, a special advocate may be appointed who does have access to the closed material but who may not discuss it with the controlee or the controllee's lawyers (see the Schedule to the Prevention of Terrorism Act 2005 and Part 76 of the Civil Procedure Rules).
2. In addition to the arrangements in ss. 2, 3 that limit control orders to 12 months but allow for their renewal and the involvement of the courts, s. 13 limits the control orders system to 12 months and both Houses of Parliament must approve its continuation for a further 12 months by making an order under the affirmative resolution procedure. Under s. 14(1) a quarterly report is to be made to Parliament by the Secretary of State on the exercise of control order powers during that period and s. 14(3) requires a report to Parliament on the operation of the Act by an independent reviewer. The reviewer is Lord Carlile QC and he sees the material which goes to the Home Secretary when it is considered appropriate to make a control order. He has supported the need for the system and each control order, although wondering if in some the terms are unduly restrictive.

Challenges have been made to control orders by controlees some of which were successful in the High Court. A number of cases were grouped together in three appeals which were heard together by the House of Lords.

Secretary of State for the Home Department v *JJ and Others*

[2007] UKHL 45, [2007] 3 WLR 642

The challenge by six controlees to their non-derogating control orders was upheld by Sullivan J who held that they breached Art. 5 and quashed them. The Court of Appeal dismissed the Minister's appeal and before the House of Lords the Minister's counsel argued that the terms of the control orders did not breach Art. 5 and if they did, then they should have been modified, not quashed.

LORD BINGHAM of CORNHILL: ... 13. It is, however, common ground between the parties that the prohibition in article 5 on depriving a person of his liberty has an autonomous meaning: that is, it has a Council of Europe-wide meaning for purposes of the Convention, whatever it might or might not be thought to mean in any member state. For guidance on the autonomous Convention meaning to be given to the expression, national courts must look to the jurisprudence of the Commission and the European Court in Strasbourg, which United Kingdom courts are required by section 2(1) of the Human Rights Act 1998 to take into account. But that jurisprudence must be used in the same way as other authority is to be used, as laying down principles and not mandating solutions to particular cases. It is, as observed in *R (Gillan) v Commissioner of Police of the Metropolis* [2006] UKHL 12, [2006] 2 AC 307, para 23, perilous to transpose the outcome of one case to another where the facts are different. The case law shows that the prohibition in article 5 has fallen to be considered in a very wide range of factual situations. It is to the principles laid down by the court in *Engel* [*v The Netherlands* (*No 1*) (1976) 1 EHRR 647] and *Guzzardi* [*v Italy* (1980) 3 EHRR 533], particularly, reiterated by the court on many occasions (see, for instance, *Ashingdane v United Kingdom* (1985) 7 EHRR 528, para 41, *Amuur v France* (1996) 22 EHRR 533, para 42), that national courts must look for guidance.

14. A series of Strasbourg decisions establishes that 24-hour house arrest has been regarded as tantamount to imprisonment and so as depriving the subject of his or her liberty: see, for example, *Mancini v Italy*, above, para 17; *Vachev v Bulgaria* (App no 42987/98, 8 October 2004), para 64; *NC v Italy* (App no 24952/94, 11 January 2001, para 33; *Nikolova v Bulgaria* (*No 2*) (App no 40896/98, 30 December 2004), para 60. In *Trijonis v Lithuania* (App no 2333/02, 17 March 2005) the applicant's complaint in relation to a

period of 24-hour home arrest was held to be admissible. In *Pekov v Bulgaria* (App no 50358/99, 30 June 2006), para 73, it was argued by the Government that the house arrest of the applicant did not deprive him of his liberty since the monitoring authorities were far away, so that he could leave his house with impunity, but this was not an argument which the court accepted. The decision of the High Court of Justiciary in *McDonald v Dickson* 2003 SLT 467, para 17, that the appellant had not been deprived of his liberty during six days of 22-hour house arrest because he had not been subject to any physical confinement or restraint, cannot, in my respectful opinion, be reconciled with this authority.

15. Continuous house arrest may reasonably be regarded as resembling, save as to the place of confinement, conventional modes of imprisonment or detention. But the court has made clear (*Guzzardi*, para 95) that deprivation of liberty may take numerous forms other than classic detention in prison or strict arrest. The variety of such forms is being increased by developments in legal standards and attitudes, and the Convention must be interpreted in the light of notions prevailing in democratic states (*ibid*). What has to be considered is the concrete situation of the particular individual (*Engel*, para 59; *Guzzardi*, para 92; *HL v United Kingdom* (2004) 40 EHRR 761, para 89). Thus the task of a court is to assess the impact of the measures in question on a person in the situation of the person subject to them. The Strasbourg court has been true to this guiding principle. Thus in *Engel*, para 59, the court recognised that "A disciplinary penalty or measure which on analysis would unquestionably be deemed a deprivation of liberty were it to be applied to a civilian may not possess this characteristic when imposed upon a serviceman."...

16. Thus the court has insisted that account should be taken of a whole range of factors such as the nature, duration, effects and manner of execution or implementation of the penalty or measure in question (*Engel*, para 59; *Guzzardi*, paras 92, 94). There may be no deprivation of liberty if a single feature of an individual's situation is taken on its own but the combination of measures considered together may have that result (*Guzzardi*, para 95). Consistently with this approach, account was taken in *Guzzardi* of a number of aspects of the applicant's stay on the island of Asinara: the locality; the possibilities of movement; his accommodation; the availability of medical attention; the presence of his family; the possibilities of attending worship; the possibilities of obtaining work; the possibilities for cultural and recreational activities; and communications with the outside (pp 342–345). In the result, the court on the facts attached weight (para 95) to the small area of the island open to him, the dilapidated accommodation, the lack of available social intercourse, the strictness of the almost constant supervision, a nine-hour overnight curfew, the obligation on him to report to the authorities twice a day and inform them of any person he wished to telephone, the need for consent to visit Sardinia on the mainland, the liability to punishment by arrest for breach of any obligation and the sixteen month period during which he was subject to these restrictions. Some of these matters plainly fall within the purview of other articles of the Convention. Because account must be taken of an individual's whole situation it seems to me inappropriate to draw a sharp distinction between a period of confinement which will, and one which will not, amount to a deprivation of liberty, important though the period of daily confinement will be in any overall assessment.

17. The Strasbourg court has realistically recognised that "The difference between deprivation of and restriction upon liberty is nonetheless merely one of degree or intensity, and not one of nature or substance" (*Guzzardi*, para 93). There is no bright line separating the two. The court acknowledges (*ibid*) the difficulty attending the process of classification in borderline cases, suggesting that in such cases the decision is one of pure opinion or what may, rather more aptly, be called judgment...

20. The obligations imposed on the controlled persons by the non-derogating control orders made by the Secretary of State in each of their respective cases were in more or less standard form....An obligation was imposed under almost all the heads specifically identified in the paragraphs of section 1(4) of the Act, and some under heads not so identified. The general effect of the obligations was helpfully summarised by the Court of Appeal in paragraph 4 of its judgment:

> 4. The obligations imposed by the control orders are set out in annex I to Sullivan J's judgment. They are essentially identical. Each respondent is required to remain within his 'residence' at all times, save for a period of six hours between 10 am and 4 pm. In the case of GG the specified residence is a one-bedroom flat provided by the local authority in which he lived before his detention. In the case of the other five respondents the specified residences are one-bedroom flats provided by the National Asylum Support Service. During the curfew period the respondents are confined in their small flats and are not even allowed into the common parts of the buildings in which these

> flats are situated. Visitors must be authorised by the Home Office, to which name, address, date of birth and photographic identity must be supplied. The residences are subject to spot searches by the police.
>
> During the six hours when they are permitted to leave their residences, the respondents are confined to restricted urban areas, the largest of which is 72 square kilometres. These deliberately do not extend, save in the case of GG, to any area in which they lived before. Each area contains a mosque, a hospital, primary health care facilities, shops and entertainment and sporting facilities. The respondents are prohibited from meeting anyone by pre-arrangement who has not been given the same Home Office clearance as a visitor to the residence.

It may be added that the controlled persons were required to wear an electronic tag and to report to a monitoring company on first leaving their flat after a curfew period and on returning to it before a curfew period. They were forbidden to use or possess any communications equipment of any kind save for one fixed telephone line in their flat maintained by the monitoring company. They could attend a mosque of their choice if it was in their permitted area and approved in advance by the Home Office. Some of the controlled persons are not permitted, because of their immigration status, to work; those who are permitted have not done so in the six hour period between 10am and 4pm. They received benefits of £30–£35 per week, mostly in vouchers, but in JJ's case £57.45. A request by JJ to study English at a college outside his area was refused.

21. In the course of a careful and detailed judgment Sullivan J reviewed the authorities mentioned above, and other authorities: in particular *Secretary of State for the Home Department v Mental Health Review Tribunal (PH)* [2002] EWCA Civ 1868 (Court of Appeal, 19 December 2002), where attention is drawn to the significance of the purpose for which restrictions are imposed, distinguishing between those which are for the benefit of the subject and those which are for some other purpose....

He expressed his conclusion in paragraph 73 of his judgment:

> 73. Drawing these threads together, and bearing in mind the type, duration, effects and manner of implementation of the obligations in these control orders, I am left in no doubt whatsoever that the cumulative effect of the obligations has been to deprive the respondents of their liberty in breach of Article 5 of the Convention. I do not consider that this is a borderline case. The collective impact of the obligations in Annex I could not sensibly be described as a mere restriction upon the respondents' liberty of movement. In terms of the length of the curfew period (18 hours), the extent of the obligations, and their intrusive impact on the respondents' ability to lead anything resembling a normal life, whether inside their residences within the curfew period, or for the 6-hour period outside it, these control orders go far beyond the restrictions in those cases where the European Court of Human Rights has concluded that there has been a restriction upon but not a deprivation of liberty.

He regarded the controlled persons' concrete situation (para 74) as the antithesis of liberty and more akin to detention in an open prison.

.... [22] ... He found reassurance for his conclusion in the observations of the House of Lords and House of Commons Joint Committee on Human Rights in their Twelfth Report of Session 2005–2006 (HL Paper 122, HC 915), para 38, addressing the proforma obligations without reference to any specific case :

> In our view, those obligations are so restrictive of liberty as to amount to a deprivation of liberty for the purposes of Article 5(1) ECHR. It therefore seems to us that the control order legislation itself is such as to make it likely that the power to impose non-derogating control orders will be exercised in a way which is incompatible with Article 5(1) in the absence of a derogation from that Article.

The judge also noted (para 82) the recognition by Mr Alvaro Gil-Robles, the Council of Europe Commissioner for Human Rights, in paragraph 17 his report (8 June 2005) of a visit to the United Kingdom, of the difficulty under the 2005 Act of distinguishing between derogating and non-derogating obligations:

> The Act does not, however, as noted, provide for any clear cut off point. This is understandable as it would be difficult to provide a clear limit, in particular where there might be many combinations of a variety of different restrictions which are imposable. House arrest would, for instance, clearly, fall within the scope of Article 5(1) ECHR. However, there might be, a strict combination of other restrictions on movement, contacts and residence, falling just short of this. The question of

whether the restrictions imposed by the non-derogating control order amount to a deprivation of liberty falling within the scope of Article 5(1) [ECHR] must inevitably be determined on a case-by-case basis...

23. On his appeal to the Court of Appeal the Secretary of State contended, as he was bound to do, that the judge had erred in law. He identified (para 7 of the Court of Appeal judgment) five errors of principle: that the judge had identified liberty too broadly, as freedom to do as one wishes; that he had wrongly had regard to the extent to which the obligations interfered with "normal life"; that he had wrongly had regard to restrictions on human rights protected by other specific articles of the Convention; that he had extended the meaning of liberty beyond that laid down in *Guzzardi*; and that he had concentrated excessively on the individual features of the idiosyncratic cases. The Court of Appeal reviewed these criticisms seriatim, but found no merit in any of them.

...[24]...No legal error in the reasoning of the judge or the Court of Appeal is shown, and it is not for the House to make a value judgment of its own. I would, however, add that on the agreed facts of these individual cases I would have reached the same conclusion...Their lives were wholly regulated by the Home Office, as a prisoner's would be, although breaches were much more severely punishable. The judge's analogy with detention in an open prison was apt, save that the controlled persons did not enjoy the association with others and the access to entertainment facilities which a prisoner in an open prison would expect to enjoy...

[27] ...section 1(2) of the Act provides that the court on the application of the Secretary of State has power to make an order imposing obligations that are or include derogating obligations, while the power to make a control order is exercisable by the Secretary of State "except in the case of an order imposing obligations that are incompatible with the individual's right to liberty under article 5" of the Convention. Thus the Secretary of State has no power to make an order that imposes any obligation incompatible with article 5. An administrative order made without power to make it is, on well-known principles, a nullity: see the recent decision of the Privy Council in *Dr Astley McLaughlin v Attorney General of the Cayman Islands* [2007] UKPC 50. The defects in the orders cannot be cured by amending specific obligations, since what the Secretary of State made was a series of orders, applicable to the individuals named, and these are what he had no power to make. It is true that, because public law remedies are generally discretionary, the court may in special circumstances decline to quash an order, despite finding it to be a nullity: *ibid*, para 16. But no such circumstances exist here, and it would be contrary to principle to decline to quash an order, made without power to make it, which had unlawfully deprived a person of his liberty.

LORD HOFFMANN: ...[45]. If one applies these principles to the facts of the present case, the answer seems to me to be clear. I find it impossible to say that a person in the position of LL is for practical purposes in prison. To describe him in such a way would be an extravagant metaphor. A person who lives in his own flat, has a telephone and whatever other conveniences he can afford, buys, prepares and cooks his own food, and is free on any day between 10 am and 4 pm to go at his own choice to walk the streets, visit the shops, places of entertainment, sports facilities and parks of a London borough, use public transport, mingle with the people and attend his place of worship, is not in prison or anything that can be called an approximation to prison. True, his freedom of movement, communication and association is greatly restricted compared with an ordinary person. But that is not the comparison which the law requires to be made. The question is rather whether he can be compared with someone in prison and in my opinion he cannot.

[46] ...The Lord Chief Justice said (at p 460) that "at the end of the day", Sullivan J had to make "a value judgment as to whether, having regard to 'the type, duration, effects and manner of implementation' of the control orders they effected a deprivation of liberty." But that formulation offers no guidance as to what would count as a deprivation of liberty. It simply says that the judge must take everything into account and decide the question, without saying what the question is. For these reasons I consider that the judge and the Court of Appeal not so much misdirected themselves as gave themselves no directions at all. If they had asked themselves whether the person in question could realistically be regarded as being for practical purposes in prison, I do not see how they could have arrived at the conclusion which they did.

BARONESS HALE OF RICHMOND: ...[62]...[the Judge] was not starting from a normal life and seeing how far the control order regime differed from this. He was starting from the 18 hour curfew and assessing how far they were nonetheless able to pursue a normal life. The reality is that every aspect of their lives was severely controlled. They were allowed out each day to go for a long and solitary walk, to attend prayers at their nominated mosques, and to buy such limited supplies as they could afford. This would not prevent detention in a psychiatric hospital under the Mental Health Act 1983 from being a deprivation of liberty: see *Ashingdane v United Kingdom* (1985) 7 EHRR 528. It is not surprising that the Judge concluded that "The respondents' 'concrete situation' is the antithesis of liberty, and is more akin to detention in an open prison, where the prisoner is 'likely to be released from prison regularly in order to work, take town visits and temporary release on resettlement or facility licence... Indeed, in several respects a prisoner might be better off: para 74...

LORD CARSWELL: ...73. It seems to me abundantly clear that Sullivan J's view of the case was governed by his comparison of the life led by the respondents in the case before him with a normal life. In this I consider that he was wrong. I think that the Court of Appeal also failed to consider the correct factors in upholding Sullivan J's judgment, as appears from paragraph 14 of its judgment, where it refers with apparent approval to his consideration of "the extent to which restrictions would prevent an individual from pursuing the life of his choice, whatever that choice might be."

...

79. The key in both judgments to the meaning of deprivation of liberty is, I think, to be found in the majority's comparison of Guzzardi's situation with detention in an open prison or committal to a disciplinary unit and in Judge Fitzmaurice's phrase "illegitimate imprisonment, or confinement so close as to amount to the same thing". It was in this context that the court referred to taking account of "a whole range of criteria such as the type, duration, effects and manner of implementation of the measure in question." In saying this the court was in my view doing no more than recognising that the situations in which a person may be confined or restricted may vary in many ways from the archetypical case of imprisonment in a cell, but still amount to deprivation of liberty. To take the phrase out its context and use it to reach the conclusion that a variety of restrictions which prevent the person from enjoying a normal life is not in my opinion legitimate.

[84] I am conscious of the concern which some of your Lordships have felt about the effect of a curfew as long as 18 hours per day, and I would not dismiss that concern lightly. I conclude, however, that on balance even that very long curfew does not take the cases of JJ and others over the line of deprivation of liberty. I am not disposed to enter into discussion of the length of time which would take a case over that line. A great deal depends on the overall factual matrix of any given case. Moreover, I feel that the House ought to focus more on the principles to be followed than in giving detailed directions.

LORD BROWN OF EATON-UNDER-HEYWOOD: ...[95]...[In Guzzardi the Court said]

> Deprivation of liberty may, however, take numerous other forms. Their variety is being increased by developments in legal standards and in attitudes; and the Convention is to be interpreted in the light of the notions currently prevailing in democratic States.

The Court also echoed (at para 92) what had been said in *Engel* as to the focus of article 5 being on physical liberty and the starting point [being the applicant's] concrete situation and account must be taken of a whole range of criteria such as the type, duration, effects and manner of implementation of the measure in question.

95. By "manner of implementation of the measure in question", the Court indicated (para 94), as indeed was already apparent from para 88, that it was concerned not with the Italian legislation authorising it.

96. *Guzzardi*, of course, was decided over a quarter of a century ago. But subsequent cases, whilst establishing certain parameters beyond which it is now clear one way or the other whether article 5 applies, afford little additional assistance. The borderline between deprivation of liberty and restriction upon liberty remains indistinct and around it decisions necessarily remain "a matter of pure opinion."

102. Ultimately, therefore, these appeals fall to be decided as "a matter of pure opinion" with little further guidance than that deprivation of liberty is concerned with "physical liberty", that it can take "numerous other forms", [other, that is, than "classic detention in prison or strict arrest imposed on a serviceman"], and that it is to be distinguished from mere restriction upon liberty as a question of "degree or intensity", starting with the applicants' "concrete situation" and then by reference to "a whole range of criteria such as the type, duration [and] effects" of that situation.

103. Plainly there must come a point at which a daily curfew (itself clearly a restriction upon liberty of movement) shades into a regime akin to house arrest, where so little genuine freedom is left that the line is crossed into deprivation of liberty. The 2005 Act itself recognises that control orders could be made that are so onerous as to cross that line and require derogation from article 5—and it recognises too that physical liberty is so important a freedom that not only must there then be derogation but also a substantially higher threshold for the imposition of such deprivation: proof that the person concerned actually is or has been involved in terrorist-related activity, rather merely than that there are reasonable grounds for suspecting this.

104. At what point, then, is the line crossed? The question plainly is one for the courts, not for the Secretary of State. She understandably wants to impose in these cases the longest curfews consistent with non derogation—doubtless to reduce so far as possible the need for surveillance (a scarce and now presumably over-stretched resource) and the suspects' opportunity to engage in terrorist-related activity. She contends for 18 hours. But there is no particular logic in this. Why not 20 hours, or 22? No useful comparison can be made with actual imprisonment. Indeed, conditions of imprisonment vary hugely. Some of those in open prisons daily go out to work unsupervised.

105. Taking account of all the other conditions and circumstances of these control orders—broadly similar not only in these six cases but in the other cases heard with them—and not least the length of time for which they are imposed, I have reached the clear conclusion that 18 hour curfews are simply too long to be consistent with the retention of physical liberty. In my opinion they breach article 5. I am equally clear, however, that 12 or 14-hour curfews (those at issue in two of the related appeals before the House) *are* consistent with physical liberty. Indeed, I would go further and, rather than leave the Secretary of State guessing as to the precise point at which control orders will be held vulnerable to article 5 challenges, state that for my part I would regard the acceptable limit to be 16 hours, leaving the suspect with 8 hours (admittedly in various respects controlled) liberty a day. Such a regime, in my opinion, can and should properly be characterised as one which restricts the suspect's liberty of movement rather than actually deprives him of his liberty. That, however, should be regarded as the absolute limit. Permanent home confinement beyond 16 hours a day on a long term basis necessarily to my mind involves the deprivation of physical liberty. And, although naturally I recognise that this cannot be the touchstone for the distinction, I think that any curfew regime exceeding 16 hours really *ought* not to be imposed unless the court can be satisfied of the suspect's actual involvement in terrorism, the higher threshold that would apply to the making of a derogating control order.

Appeal dismissed

NOTE: New, less restrictive control orders were made.

■ QUESTIONS

1. Is it a matter of opinion to determine if restrictions on liberty amount to a deprivation of liberty?
2. Should the Home Secretary be left to guess the duration of a curfew which would breach Art. 5?

Secretary of State for the Home Department v *E*

[2007] UKHL 47, [2007] 3 WLR 720

E had successfully challenged his control order in the High Court where Beatson J had quashed the order as breaching Art. 5 and because the Minister had not complied with the duty in s. 8 to consider a prosecution. The Court of Appeal upheld the Minister's appeal. On appeal to the House of Lords their Lordships agreed with the Court of Appeal that the control order did not breach Art. 5.

LORD BINGHAM of CORNHILL; ...13. Section 8 of the 2005 Act, so far as material for present purposes, provides:

8 *Criminal investigations after making of control order*

(1) This section applies where it appears to the Secretary of State–
  (a) that the involvement in terrorism–related activity of which an individual is suspected may have involved the commission of an offence relating to terrorism; and
  (b) that the commission of that offence is being or would fall to be investigated by a police force.

(2) Before making, or applying for the making of, a control order against the individual, the Secretary of State must consult the chief officer of the police force about whether there is evidence available that could realistically be used for the purposes of a prosecution of the individual for an offence relating to terrorism.

(3) If a control order is made against the individual the Secretary of State must inform the chief officer of the police force that the control order has been made and that subsection (4) applies.

(4) It shall then be the duty of the chief officer to secure that the investigation of the individual's conduct with a view to his prosecution for an offence relating to terrorism is kept under review throughout the period during which the control order has effect.

(5) In carrying out his functions by virtue of this section the chief officer must consult the relevant prosecuting authority, but only, in the case of the performance of his duty under subsection (4), to the extent that he considers it appropriate to do so.

(6) The requirements of subsection (5) may be satisfied by consultation that took place wholly or partly before the passing of this Act...

15. It was argued for E before the judge that compliance by the Secretary of State with his duty under section 8(2) was a condition precedent to his power to make a control order in a case falling within section 8(1) (see para 245 of Beatson J's judgment). The judge rejected this argument, holding that the conditions precedent to the making of a control order are set out in section 2(1), this condition could have been included but was not, and it was not necessary to construe section 8(2) as including this condition. The Court of Appeal also rejected it for very much the same reason (para 87 of the Court of Appeal judgment). I agree. Section 2(1) of the Act prescribes the circumstances in which the Secretary of State may make a non–derogating control order and compliance with the section 8(2) duty is not included as a qualifying condition. It is nonetheless true, as was urged for E, that section 8(2) is expressed in strong mandatory terms: "Before making, or applying for the making of, a control order against the individual, the Secretary of State must....". Plainly this duty is to be taken seriously. On the seeking by the Secretary of State of permission from the court to make a non–derogating control order under section 3(1)(a) of the Act or, where an order has been referred to the court under section 3(3)(a), I would expect the court, as a matter of strict routine, to seek to be satisfied that the section 8(2) duty has been complied with and, if it has not, to require very convincing reasons for that omission.

16. In submission to the House, it was argued for E that the absence of a realistic prospect of prosecution is a condition precedent to the making by the Secretary of State of a non–derogating control order. Thus the Secretary of State must not only consult under section 8(2), in a case falling within section 8(1), but must be given to understand that it is not feasible to prosecute with a reasonable prospect of success. Unless this was so, it was argued, it could not be "necessary" to impose obligations under a control order, since it would not be shown that the public could not be protected by arresting, charging and prosecuting the individual. This more ambitious submission must also fail, for the reason given in the last paragraph. But there are in my view strong practical reasons for rejecting it. The situation is, by definition, one in which the Secretary of State has reasonable grounds for suspecting that the individual is or has been involved in terrorism–related activity (section 2(1)(a)). He must consider that it is necessary, for purposes connected with protecting members of the public from a risk of terrorism, to make a control order imposing obligations on that individual (section 2(1)(b)). There may be a need to act with great urgency (section 3(1)(b)). The potential risk may be very great. It is one thing to require the Secretary of State to consult, as section 8(2) does in cases falling within section 8(1), which is the great majority of cases. But it is quite another to require him to obtain a clear answer: this is something the chief officer of police is unlikely to be in a position to give, he himself being subject to a duty (section 8(5)) to consult the relevant prosecuting authority which will in turn require time to consider the matter, and very probably to seek the advice of counsel. The condition precedent contended for would have the potential to emasculate what is clearly intended to be an effective procedure, and cannot be taken to represent the intention of Parliament...

18. The thrust of E's argument before the House was directed not to lack of consultation before the order was made on 12 March 2005 but on the Secretary of State's failure to take steps open to him to ensure that the possibility of prosecution was kept under effective review thereafter. Under section 8(4) of the Act the duty of keeping the prospect of prosecution under review is laid on the chief office of police, in conjunction (where he considers it appropriate: s.8(5)) with the relevant prosecuting authority. In its judgment in *MB*, however, in paragraph 44, the Court of Appeal held it to be implicit in the Act

> that it is the duty of the Secretary of State to keep the decision to impose a control order under review, so that the restrictions that it imposes, whether on civil rights or Convention rights, are no greater than necessary. A purposive approach to section 3(10) must enable the court to consider whether the continuing decision of the Secretary of State to keep the order in force is flawed.

Beatson J followed this ruling in the present case (para 282). It was argued for the Secretary of State in the Court of Appeal that the Secretary of State, having consulted the chief of police at the outset, need do no more thereafter than make periodic enquiry whether the prospect of prosecution had increased (Court of Appeal, para 96). But the Court of Appeal held (para 97) that more was called for:

> Once it is accepted that there is a continuing duty to review pursuant to *MB's* case, it is implicit in that duty that the Secretary of State must do what he reasonably can to ensure that the continuing review is meaningful…it was incumbent upon him to provide the police with material in his possession which was or might be relevant to any reconsideration of prosecution.

The Secretary of State, it is understood, now accepts the correctness of this approach, which I would respectfully endorse.

19. The materiality of this point arises in this way. On 30 September 2003 first instance judgments were given by a Belgian court, affirmed on appeal in Belgium on 21 February 2005. The effect of the judgments was to implicate E in terrorist-related activity. The Secretary of State learned of these judgments in September 2005, after the control order had been made against E but before it was renewed. He received copies of the judgments in November 2005, and English translations became available in January 2006. Before renewal of the order in March 2006 the chief officer of police informed the Secretary of State that there was insufficient evidence to prosecute. But neither the police nor the CPS has received copies of these judgments. They have, however, as the judge found (para 286), been part of the open evidence relied on by the Secretary of State since September 2006, and were now at the core of the Secretary of State's open national security case against E. It is pointed out on behalf of E that the Belgian judgments rested in part on intercept evidence which, because obtained abroad, would be admissible in an English court, that the availability of this evidence in the public domain could affect the judgment on whether it was in the public interest to prosecute, and that some of the Belgian material had already been relied on to prosecute defendants in this country.

20. The judge concluded (para 293) that the Secretary of State's failure to consider the impact of the Belgian judgments on the prospects of prosecuting E meant that his continuing decision to maintain the control order was flawed. The breach was not a technical one (para 293), and the judge would have quashed the order on this ground were he not already quashing it for incompatibility with article 5 (para 310). The Court of Appeal found (para 97) that the judge had been right to find a breach by the Secretary of State of his *MB* duty to keep the possibility of prosecution under review, even though the decision whether or not to prosecute was clearly not his. The breach (para 99) "arose from the omission of the Secretary of State himself to provide the police with the Belgian judgments so as to prompt and facilitate a reconsideration". But although tending to agree with the judge that the breach was not technical (para 102), the Court of Appeal differed from him on remedy. It was satisfied (para 103) that even if the Secretary of State had acted diligently and expeditiously in relation to the Belgian judgments they could not have given rise to a prosecution at any time material to this case. The question to be asked (para 105) was whether a particular breach had materially contributed to and vitiated the decision to make the control order, and the judge had erred in law in holding without further analysis that the breach justified the remedy of quashing the order.

21. Counsel for E criticised the Court of Appeal's reasoning on this point, but I do not think its approach was wrong in principle. It was certainly regrettable that the Belgian judgments were not made available promptly to the appropriate authorities, perhaps suggesting that the duty of continuing review by the Secretary of State was not appreciated before the Court of Appeal's judgment in *MB* in August 2006 or, if

appreciated, was not treated with the seriousness which its importance deserved. But I do not for my part think that the Court of Appeal's reasoning in this case can be faulted. If in any case it appeared that the duty to consult under section 8(2) or the duty to keep the prospect of prosecution under review had been breached, and also that but for the breach the individual could and should properly have been prosecuted with a reasonable prospect of success, there would be strong grounds for contending that the control order was not or was no longer necessary and that the Secretary of State's decision to make or maintain it was flawed. It might then be appropriate to quash the order. But the House cannot hold, on the material before it, that that condition was met in this case, and the order should not have been quashed.

Appeal dismissed.

■ QUESTION

Does this decision uphold the principle that control orders should be used as a last resort?

Secretary of State for the Home Department v *AF and Others*

[2009] UKHL 28

LORD PHILLIPS OF WORTH MATRAVERS: 1. The three appellants, AF, AN and AE, are subject to non-derogating control orders ("control orders") involving significant restriction of liberty... The issue raised by their appeals is whether, in each case, the procedure that resulted in the making of the control order satisfied the appellant's right to a fair hearing guaranteed by article 6 of the European Convention on Human Rights ("article 6") in conjunction with the Human Rights Act 1998 ("the HRA"). Each contends that this right was violated by reason of the reliance by the judge making the order upon material received in closed hearing the nature of which was not disclosed to the appellant.

[Lord Phillips outlined the history of control orders and of the appellants. He referred to the House of Lords' decision in *Secretary of State for the Home Department v MB* [2007] UKHL 46, [2008] AC 440, in which AF was a co-appellant seeking to reverse the Court of Appeal's overturning of Sullivan's J decision that the use of closed material even with the participation of special advocates, had breached Art. 6.]

...11. Lord Bingham did not share this view. He quoted a series of judicial dicta from sources of high standing to the effect that a fair hearing requires that a party must be informed of the case against him so that he can respond to it. Commenting on the decision of this House in *R (Roberts) v Parole Board* [2005] UKHL 45; [2005] 2 AC 738, he remarked at para 34:

> "I do not understand any of my noble and learned friends to have concluded that the requirements of procedural fairness under domestic law or under the Convention would be met if a person entitled to a fair hearing, in a situation where an adverse decision could have severe consequences, were denied such knowledge, in whatever form, of what was said against him as was necessary to enable him, with or without a special advocate, effectively to challenge or rebut the case against him."

12. Lord Bingham expressed the following conclusion at para 41 in respect of MB:

> "This is not a case (like *E*) in which the order can be justified on the strength of the open material alone. Nor is it a case in which the thrust of the case against the controlled person has been effectively conveyed to him by way of summary, redacted documents or anonymised statements. It is a case in which, on the judge's assessment which the Court of Appeal did not displace, MB was confronted by a bare, unsubstantiated assertion which he could do no more than deny. I have difficulty in accepting that MB has enjoyed a substantial measure of procedural justice, or that the very essence of the right to a fair hearing has not been impaired."

In relation to AF, Lord Bingham said this, as para 43:

> "This would seem to me an even stronger case than *MB*'s. If, as I understand the House to have accepted in *Roberts*, the concept of fairness imports a core, irreducible minimum of procedural protection, I have difficulty, on the judge's findings, in concluding that such protection has

been afforded to AF. The right to a fair hearing is fundamental. In the absence of a derogation (where that is permissible) it must be protected. In this case, as in *MB*'s, it seems to me that it was not."

13. Lord Hoffmann took a different view. He considered that the use of closed material, coupled with the protection afforded by special advocates, had been approved by the Strasbourg court:

"51. Thus a decision that article 6 does not allow the Secretary of State to rely on closed material would create a dilemma: either he must disclose material which the court considers that the public interest requires to be withheld, or he must risk being unable to justify to the court an order which he considers necessary to protect the public against terrorism. It was this dilemma, and the way in which it should be resolved, which the Strasbourg court recognized in *Chahal v United Kingdom* 23 EHRR 413, para 131: 'The court recognises that the use of confidential material may be unavoidable where national security is at stake. This does not mean, however, that the national authorities can be free from effective control by the domestic courts whenever they choose to assert that national security and terrorism are involved. The court attaches significance to the fact that, as the interveners pointed out in connection with article 13 (see para 144 below), in Canada a more effective form of judicial control has been developed in cases of this type. This example illustrates that there are techniques which can be employed which both accommodate legitimate security concerns about the nature and sources of intelligence information and yet accord the individual a substantial measure of procedural justice.'

52. The court described the Canadian procedure which they recommended as a model in para 144:

'[A] Federal Court judge holds an in camera hearing of all the evidence, at which the applicant is provided with a statement summarising, as far as possible, the case against him or her and has the right to be represented and to call evidence. The confidentiality of security material is maintained by requiring such evidence to be examined in the absence of both the applicant and his or her representative. However, in these circumstances, their place is taken by a security-cleared counsel instructed by the court, who cross- examines the witnesses and generally assists the court to test the strength of the state's case. A summary of the evidence obtained by this procedure, with necessary deletions, is given to the applicant.'"

14. Lord Hoffmann commented, at para 54:

"The Canadian model is precisely what has been adopted in the United Kingdom, first for cases of detention for the purposes of deportation on national security grounds (as in *Chahal*) and then for the judicial supervision of control orders. From the point of view of the individual seeking to challenge the order, it is of course imperfect. But the Strasbourg court has recognised that the right to be informed of the case against one, though important, may have to be qualified in the interests of others and the public interest. The weight to be given to these competing interests will depend upon the facts of the case, but there can in time of peace be no public interest which is more weighty than protecting the state against terrorism and, on the other hand, the Convention rights of the individual which may be affected by the orders are all themselves qualified by the requirements of national security. There is no Strasbourg or domestic authority which has gone to the lengths of saying that the Secretary of State cannot make a non-derogating control order (or anything of the same kind) without disclosing material which a judge considers it would be contrary to the public interest to disclose. I do not think that we should put the Secretary of State in such an impossible position and I therefore agree with the Court of Appeal that in principle the special advocate procedure provides sufficient safeguards to satisfy article 6."

15. The remaining three members of the committee reached conclusions which fell between those of Lord Bingham and Lord Hoffmann. They expressed the view that in some cases it would be possible for the controlee, with the assistance of the special advocate, to have a fair trial notwithstanding the admission of closed material and that in others it would not. The fair trial issue was fact specific and the trial judge was best placed to resolve it.

16. Baroness Hale of Richmond at para 66 expressed the view that one could not be confident that Strasbourg would hold that *every* control order hearing in which the special advocate procedure had been used would be sufficient to comply with article 6 but that, with strenuous efforts from all, it should usually be possible to accord the controlled person "a substantial measure of procedural justice"—the phrase used by the Strasbourg court in *Chahal.* Significantly, she was also inclined to accept the view of Ouseley J that this test had been satisfied in the case of AF, notwithstanding that the judge had observed that the essence of the case against him lay in the closed material.

17. In expressing her conclusions, Baroness Hale said this at para 74:

> "It follows that I cannot share the view of Lord Hoffmann, that the use of special advocates will always comply with article 6; nor do I have the same difficulty as Lord Bingham, in accepting that the procedure could comply with article 6 in the two cases before us. It is quite possible for the court to provide the controlled person with a sufficient measure of procedural protection even though the whole evidential basis for the basic allegation, which has been explained to him, is not disclosed."

The last sentence of this passage contains an ambiguity. "Even though the whole evidential basis . . . is not disclosed" could mean (i) "even though none of the evidential basis is disclosed" or (ii) "even though not all of the evidential basis is disclosed". It seems that some have read it in one way and some in another . . .

Submissions

39. Lengthy printed cases were submitted that indicated that there was to be a hard fought battle on the appeal to this House. The submissions made in the case on behalf of AF can be summarised as follows:

(i) Contrary to the decision of the Court of Appeal, the majority of the House decided in *MB* that article 6 of the Convention and the common law principle of fairness conferred on a controlee a core, irreducible entitlement to be told sufficient of the case against him to enable him to challenge that case unless, which was not the case so far as AF was concerned, the special advocates were able to defeat those allegations without such disclosure.
(ii) The House did not approve the "makes no difference" principle.
(iii) Alternatively, if the House held that there was no core, irreducible minimum that had to be disclosed, it should depart from that result and affirm the right of a controlee to know and respond to the case against him.

40. The joint case for AN and AE adopted the case for AF. It asserted that the common law right to a fair hearing, and the right to be aware of the case a person has to meet, was "a constitutional protection that is integral to the judicial function itself".

41. The case for the Secretary of State invited the House to depart from the approach of the majority in *MB* and to adopt instead the minority opinion of Lord Hoffmann. Alternatively it was submitted that the majority in *MB* had concluded correctly that article 6(1) did not guarantee a core, irreducible, minimum of disclosure. The relevant principle was whether, having regard to the proceedings as a whole, there had been significant injustice to the controlee or whether the controlee had been afforded "a substantial and sufficient measure of procedural justice". In answering that question it was permissible for the court to consider what difference further open disclosure would have made.

42. JUSTICE was granted permission to intervene and submitted a printed case that supported the appellants' cases. JUSTICE submitted that there was a "solid bedrock of a core legal principle" that the substance of the case upon which a control order was based should be disclosed to the controlee.

43. A decision was taken that the appeal should be heard by a committee of nine members. Application was made, both by the Secretary of State and by the appellants, with particular support from their special advocates, that the House should give directions for the consideration of the closed judgments below, and possibly other closed material, in closed session. Directions were given that the question

of whether to go into closed session would be taken after the parties had presented their cases in the open hearing.

44. On 19 February, a little over a week before the commencement of the appeal in the House, the Grand Chamber of the Strasbourg Court handed down its judgment in *A and others v United Kingdom* (Application No 3455/05). This addressed the extent to which the admission of closed material was compatible with the fair trial requirements of article 5(4). The Secretary of State recognised that the judgment cut the ground from under her feet in so far as she had hoped to persuade the House to adopt the approach of Lord Hoffmann in *MB*. An amended case was filed on her behalf. This contained a lengthy analysis of the decision in *A v United Kingdom*. It submitted that the decision was consistent with the decision of the majority of the House in *MB*, as correctly summarised by the Court of Appeal in the passage that I have set out above at paragraph 33. The Court of Appeal, applying the principles in that passage, had reached the appropriate conclusion in the case of each appellant.

45. The appellants also submitted amended cases that addressed the decision in *A v United Kingdom*. AF's amended case submitted that the Grand Chamber had made it clear that, regardless of the demands of national security, a person will not have a fair hearing for purposes of article 5(4) and article 6 unless they are told sufficient information about the case against them to enable them to give effective instructions to the special advocate who represents their interests. Accordingly, the decision of the majority of the Court of Appeal in relation to AF could not stand. The decision of Stanley Burnton J should be restored.

46. The amended case on behalf of AN and AE was to like effect. The Grand Chamber had established that a minimum requirement of procedural fairness was that a person had to be given the opportunity effectively to challenge the allegations against him. Where there was a closed hearing the special advocate could not do this on behalf of his client in any useful way unless provided with sufficient information about the allegations against him to enable him to give effective instructions to the special advocate. Mitting J had held that AN could not meet a substantial part of the case against him and did not know the gist of significant grounds of suspicion raised against him. Silber J had wrongly proceeded on the basis that the special advocate procedure could compensate for an absence of any evidence or of a relevant particularised allegation having been provided to AE. The Grand Chamber's decision demonstrated that in neither case were the requirements of article 6 satisfied.

47. In the light of the decision in *A v United Kingdom* counsel for the appellants no longer submitted that it was necessary or desirable for the House to consider closed material, albeit that the special advocates sought, as they candidly admitted, to have their cake and eat it by inviting the House to consider the closed material if otherwise minded to reject their submissions. In these circumstances the House decided that it would not have a closed hearing or look at closed material.

A v United Kingdom

48. There were referred to the Grand Chamber 11 applications. The applicants had been detained pursuant to the provisions of the ATCSA. They complained of violation of a number of their Convention rights, including their right to liberty under article 5(1), relying upon the findings in their favour by this House. The United Kingdom was permitted by the Court to challenge those findings, but did so without success. The relevant complaints were those brought in relation to article 5(4). The Court summarised the respective cases of the parties as follows:

> "The applicants complained about the procedure before SIAC for appeals under section 25 of the 2001 Act (see paragraph 91 above) and in particular the lack of disclosure of material evidence except to special advocates with whom the detained person was not permitted to consult. In their submission, Article 5 § 4 imported the fair trial guarantees of Article 6 § 1 commensurate with the gravity of the issue at stake. While in certain circumstances it might be permissible for a court to sanction non-disclosure of relevant evidence to an individual on grounds of national security, it could never be permissible for a court assessing the lawfulness of detention to rely on such material where it bore decisively on the case the detained person had to meet and where it had not been disclosed, even in gist or summary form, sufficiently to enable the individual to

> know the case against him and to respond. In all the applicants' appeals, except that of the tenth applicant, SIAC relied on closed material and recognised that the applicants were thereby put at a disadvantage.

On the applicants' second point, the Government submitted that there were valid public interest grounds for withholding the closed material. The right to disclosure of evidence, under Article 6 and also under Article 5 § 4, was not absolute. The Court's case-law from *Chahal* (cited above) onwards had indicated some support for a special advocate procedure in particularly sensitive fields. Moreover, in each applicant's case, the open material gave sufficient notice of the allegations against him to enable him to mount an effective defence."

49. In paragraph 4.54 of its Memorial to the Court the Government submitted that it would be highly desirable for the Grand Chamber to deal with the question of closed evidence in its proper place in the context of article 5(4), so that the law applicable in relation to the applicants should be properly and fully analysed by the Court. The Grand Chamber accepted that invitation.

50. The Government advanced in the Memorial a detailed defence of the use of closed material. At paragraph 4.77 it identified the critical issue in relation to this:

> "The Government submit that the result contended for by the applicants is wrong in principle. Their submission wrongly elevates the right of an individual to disclosure of relevant evidence under Article 5(4) (or Article 6) to an absolute right which necessarily overrides the rights of others, including the right to life under Article 2, and overrides the interests of the State in protecting secret sources of information so as to preserve the effectiveness of its intelligence, police and counter-terrorism services. Such an absolute right to disclosure would, if it existed, create a serious lacuna in the protection the State may offer its citizens and disregards the principle, inherent in the Convention as a whole, including Article 5(4) (and Article 6), that the general interests of the community must be balanced against the rights of an individual (see eg *Sporrong and Lönnroth v Sweden* (1982) 5 EHRR 35, at para 69; *Soering v United Kingdom* (1989) 11 EHRR 439, at para 89)."

This is the critical issue that arises on the present appeals. For the reasons that follow I consider that the Grand Chamber has provided the definitive resolution of it.

51. The Court cited at length from the decision of this House in *MB* and also quoted the passage in the decision of the majority of the Court of Appeal in *AF* that I have set out at paragraph 33. The conclusions of the Grand Chamber appear in the following section of its unanimous judgment:

> "215. The Court recalls that although the judges sitting as SIAC were able to consider both the "open" and "closed" material, neither the applicants nor their legal advisers could see the closed material. Instead, the closed material was disclosed to one or more special advocates, appointed by the Solicitor General to act on behalf of each applicant. During the closed sessions before SIAC, the special advocate could make submissions on behalf of the applicant, both as regards procedural matters, such as the need for further disclosure, and as to the substance of the case. However, from the point at which the special advocate first had sight of the closed material, he was not permitted to have any further contact with the applicant and his representatives, save with the permission of SIAC. In respect of each appeal against certification, SIAC issued both an open and a closed judgment.
>
> 216. The Court takes as its starting point that, as the national courts found and it has accepted, during the period of the applicants' detention the activities and aims of the al'Qaeda network had given rise to a 'public emergency threatening the life of the nation'. It must therefore be borne in mind that at the relevant time there was considered to be an urgent need to protect the population of the United Kingdom from terrorist attack and, although the United Kingdom did not derogate from Article 5 § 4, a strong public interest in obtaining information about al'Qaeda and its associates and in maintaining the secrecy of the sources of such information (see also, in this connection, *Fox, Campbell and Hartley*, cited above, (1990) 13 EHRR 157, para 39).

217. Balanced against these important public interests, however, was the applicants' right under Article 5 § 4 to procedural fairness. Although the Court has found that, with the exception of the second and fourth applicants, the applicants' detention did not fall within any of the categories listed in subparagraphs (a) to (f) of Article 5 § 1, it considers that the case-law relating to judicial control over detention on remand is relevant, since in such cases also the reasonableness of the suspicion against the detained person is a *sine qua non* (see paragraph 204 above). Moreover, in the circumstances of the present case, and in view of the dramatic impact of the lengthy -and what appeared at that time to be indefinite—deprivation of liberty on the applicants' fundamental rights, Article 5 § 4 must import substantially the same fair trial guarantees as Article 6 § 1 in its criminal aspect (*Garcia Alva v Germany* (2001) 37 EHRR 335, para 39, and see also *Chahal* (1996) 23 EHRR 413, paras 130—131).

218. Against this background, it was essential that as much information about the allegations and evidence against each applicant was disclosed as was possible without compromising national security or the safety of others. Where full disclosure was not possible, Article 5 § 4 required that the difficulties this caused were counterbalanced in such a way that each applicant still had the possibility effectively to challenge the allegations against him.

219. The Court considers that SIAC, which was a fully independent court (see paragraph 91 above) and which could examine all the relevant evidence, both closed and open, was best placed to ensure that no material was unnecessarily withheld from the detainee. In this connection, the special advocate could provide an important, additional safeguard through questioning the State's witnesses on the need for secrecy and through making submissions to the judge regarding the case for additional disclosure. On the material before it, the Court has no basis to find that excessive and unjustified secrecy was employed in respect of any of the applicants' appeals or that there were not compelling reasons for the lack of disclosure in each case.

220. The Court further considers that the special advocate could perform an important role in counterbalancing the lack of full disclosure and the lack of a full, open, adversarial hearing by testing the evidence and putting arguments on behalf of the detainee during the closed hearings. However, the special advocate could not perform this function in any useful way unless the detainee was provided with sufficient information about the allegations against him to enable him to give effective instructions to the special advocate. While this question must be decided on a case-by-case basis, the Court observes generally that, where the evidence was to a large extent disclosed and the open material played the predominant role in the determination, it could not be said that the applicant was denied an opportunity effectively to challenge the reasonableness of the Secretary of State's belief and suspicions about him. In other cases, even where all or most of the underlying evidence remained undisclosed, if the allegations contained in the open material were sufficiently specific, it should have been possible for the applicant to provide his representatives and the special advocate with information with which to refute them, if such information existed, without his having to know the detail or sources of the evidence which formed the basis of the allegations. An example would be the allegation made against several of the applicants that they had attended a terrorist training camp at a stated location between stated dates; given the precise nature of the allegation, it would have been possible for the applicant to provide the special advocate with exonerating evidence, for example of an alibi or of an alternative explanation for his presence there, sufficient to permit the advocate effectively to challenge the allegation. Where, however, the open material consisted purely of general assertions and SIAC's decision to uphold the certification and maintain the detention was based solely or to a decisive degree on closed material, the procedural requirements of Article 5 § 4 would not be satisfied."

... [59] ... I am satisfied that the essence of the Grand Chamber's decision lies in paragraph 220 and, in particular, in the last sentence of that paragraph. This establishes that the controlee must be given sufficient information about the allegations against him to enable him to give effective instructions in relation to those allegations. Provided that this requirement is satisfied there can be a fair trial notwithstanding that the controlee is not provided with the detail or the sources of the evidence forming the basis of the allegations. Where, however, the open material consists purely of general assertions and the case against the controlee is based solely or to a decisive degree on closed materials the requirements of a fair trial will not be satisfied, however cogent the case based on the closed materials may be.

LORD HOFFMANN:

My Lords,

70. I have had the advantage of reading in draft the speech of my noble and learned friend Lord Phillips of Worth Matravers and I agree that the judgment of the European Court of Human Rights (ECtHR) in *A v United Kingdom* (Application No 3455/05) requires these appeals to be allowed. I do so with very considerable regret, because I think that the decision of the ECtHR was wrong and that it may well destroy the system of control orders which is a significant part of this country's defences against terrorism. Nevertheless, I think that your Lordships have no choice but to submit. It is true that section 2(1)(a) of the Human Rights Act 1998 requires us only to "take into account" decisions of the ECtHR. As a matter of our domestic law, we could take the decision in *A v United Kingdom* into account but nevertheless prefer our own view. But the United Kingdom is bound by the Convention, as a matter of international law, to accept the decisions of the ECtHR on its interpretation. To reject such a decision would almost certainly put this country in breach of the international obligation which it accepted when it acceded to the Convention. I can see no advantage in your Lordships doing so...

74. There are practical limits to the extent to which one can devise a procedure which carries no risk of a wrong decision. It is sometimes said that it is better for ten guilty men to be acquitted than for one innocent man to be convicted. Sometimes it is a hundred guilty men. The figures matter. A system of justice which allowed a thousand guilty men to go free for fear of convicting one innocent man might not adequately protect the public. Likewise, the fact in theory there is always some chance that the applicant might have been able to contradict closed evidence is not in my opinion a sufficient reason for saying, in effect, that control orders can never be made against dangerous people if the case against them is based "to a decisive degree" upon material which cannot in the public interest be disclosed. This, however, is what we are now obliged to declare to be the law.

Appeal allowed

NOTES

In *AN* v *Secretary of State for the Home Department, Secretary of State for the Home Department* v *AE and AF* [2010] EWCA Civ 869, handed down on 28 July 2010, the Court of Appeal found that the appropriate remedy where the Secretary of State elects not to make sufficient disclosure to comply with Art. 6 of the ECHR is for the control order to be quashed from the date it was made and not for it to be revoked with effect from a date after the control order was served on the individual, as the Secretary of State had sought to argue. Two control orders had been revoked for this reason in 2009. As at 10 September 2010 there were nine control orders in force.

The Coalition Government announced on 20 May, in their Programme for Government, a review of counter-terrorism powers which included control orders. The previous Labour government had concluded that there was still a need for control orders and this was also the view in February 2010 of Lord Carlile of Berriew QC in his:

Fifth Report of the Independent Reviewer Pursuant to section 14(3) of the Prevention of Terrorism Act 2005

2010, p.1

The control orders system remains necessary, but only for a small number of cases where robust information is available to the effect that the suspected individual presents a considerable risk to national security, and conventional prosecution is not realistic.

He summarised the main arguments for and against them as follows:

For	Against
Provide public security and comfort where intelligence cannot be made admissible court evidence in criminal proceedings	Can change the rules of evidence, e. g. to allow intercept
Valuable safety net	Blunt instrument, offensive to human rights
Careful inquiry and advice given by CPS and prosecution occurs wherever possible	If rules of evidence were changed, more prosecutions would be advised
Protects UK as compared with foreign jurisdictions regarded as having no competent authority to deal with persons deported	As much protection could be provided without control orders, with 'normal' policing and surveillance
At least some persons discharged from control orders would resume terrorist activities	It would be known that they were subject to scrutiny, so their utility as terrorists would be very small
Capacity for necessary surveillance would mean significant moving of resources from other policing etc work	Not accepted
Excessive cost of alternatives	Cost not relevant in human rights context
System of law is ECHR compatible and special advocates have been effective	Special advocates complain that they cannot deal fully with cases because of limited assistance. Court disclosure requirements render control orders impracticable
Prevents foreign travel for training and insurgency	A very heavy-handed way of achieving a limited objective

NOTE

The Parliamentary Joint Committee on Human Rights (JCHR) has been critical in each of its reports published to coincide with the annual renewal of control orders sought by the government. Some of its concerns have been reflected in the court decisions and it does not believe that, in relation to closed material, the special advocates system can meet the required standard of procedural justice. In its February 2010 report HL 65/HC 395 of 2009–10 the committee said:

> Our conclusion is that the current control order regime is no longer sustainable. A heavy onus rests on the Government to explain to Parliament why alternatives, such as intensive surveillance of the very small number of suspects currently subject to a control order, and more vigorous pursuit of the possibility of prosecution, are not now to be preferred.

■ QUESTIONS

1. Does the standard for a fair trial in relation to closed material in control order cases draw an appropriate balance to protect society and the rights of suspected terrorists?
2. Should regimes such as that for control orders be enacted with a 'sunset clause' setting a specified date for their ending rather than providing for continuance subject to annual renewal by secondary legislation using the affirmative procedure?

10

Judicial Review: The Grounds

OVERVIEW

In this chapter the nature and constitutional role of judicial review is introduced before considering the various grounds of review which have been placed in three classes: illegality, procedural impropriety, and irrationality. The consideration of irrationality also looks at proportionality and substantive legitimate expectations.

SECTION 1: INTRODUCTION

A: The role of judicial review in the constitution

In some countries, for example in the United States, the judges are permitted to review legislation in order to establish whether it complies with the terms of the constitution. In the United Kingdom, the absence of a written constitution with the status of a higher law and the doctrine of parliamentary supremacy prevent the judges from exercising this role. They may, however, review the manner in which public authorities exercise the powers which have been conferred upon them by the legislature.

This power of judicial review may be defined as the jurisdiction of the superior courts (the High Court, the Court of Appeal, and the House of Lords) to review the acts, decisions, and omissions of public authorities in order to establish whether they have exceeded or abused their powers. The courts have developed a number of principles in order to establish whether there has been an excess or abuse of power. For example, a public authority must direct itself properly on the law, it must not use its powers for improper purposes, and it must not act in breach of the rules of natural justice.

What is the justification for permitting such judicial control? One theory, discussed in the following extract, is that the courts are simply giving effect to the intentions of Parliament.

P. Cane, *Administrative Law*

(2004), pp. 405–09

Most of the powers and duties of public functionaries are statutory. It follows from the first proposition about Parliamentary supremacy that courts are bound to apply statutes according to their terms. Although this does not follow from the first proposition, traditional theory also says that indeterminancy and ambiguities in the language of statutes should be resolved, and gaps in them filled, by reference to the intention of the legislature. Thus, it is often said that the enforcement of statutory duties and the control of the exercise of statutory powers by the courts is ultimately justifiable in terms of the doctrine of

Parliamentary supremacy: even though Parliament has not expressly authorized the courts to supervise governmental activity, it cannot have intended breaches of duty by governmental agencies to go unremedied (even if no remedy is provided in the statute itself), nor can it have intended to give administrative agencies the freedom to exceed or abuse their powers, or to act unreasonably. It is the task of the courts to interpret and enforce the provisions of statutes which impose duties and confer powers on public functionaries, in the light of the principles of legality embodied in the grounds of judicial review. In so doing they are giving effect to the will of Parliament.

There are three main weaknesses in this theory of the basis of judicial control of the exercise of public functions. The first is relevant to statutory interpretation generally: it is unrealistic to treat the process of interpreting statutes, resolving ambiguities, and filling gaps, as always being a matter of discerning and giving effect to the intentions of Parliament. Even assuming that we can make sense of the notion of intention when applied to a multi-member body following simple majoritarian voting procedures, there will be many cases in which Parliament did not think about the question relevant to resolving the indeterminacy or ambiguity or filling the gap. In such cases the courts must act creatively in deciding what the statute means. The weakness of the intention theory of statutory interpretation is made very clear by the notion of 'purposive interpretation'. Especially (but not only) in the context of interpreting statutes passed to give effect to EC law and of protecting Convention rights, courts may go beyond interpreting the words actually used in statutes and insert (or 'imply') into legislative provisions words or phrases needed to give effect to what the court perceives to be the true purpose or aim of the provision in question. It makes little sense to describe this process in terms of giving effect to what Parliament actually intended all along.

A technique for giving some meaning to the idea of the intention of the legislature is for courts to pay attention to what are called '*travaux préparatoires*', that is policy documents and statements that preceded the enactment of the relevant legislation and might throw some light on its intended meaning or, at least, the purpose for which it was enacted. In *Pepper* v *Hart* [[1995] AC 593] the House of Lords held that where a statutory provision is ambiguous or obscure or leads to an absurdity, a court required to interpret the provision can refer to clear statements, made in Parliament by a Minister or promoter of the bill, as to its intended meaning and effect, and to other Parliamentary material that might be necessary to understand such statements. This decision was of considerable constitutional significance because it implied that the relevant intention was not that of Parliament in enacting the legislation but rather that of the government in promoting it. It seemed to acknowledge the effective reality that Parliament does not legislate but rather legitimizes the government's legislation. In so doing, it further undermined the notion that in interpreting legislation, the courts were giving effect to the intention of Parliament. In an influential article critical of the decision in *Pepper* v *Hart*, Lord Steyn made these implications explicit; [(2001) 21 *OJLS* 59] and in its wake the House of Lords has embarked on a process of re-interpreting *Pepper* v *Hart* so that it does not undermine the principles that the job of interpreting legislation belongs ultimately to the courts, not to the government, and that the question for the court is what the statutory words mean, not what the government or anyone else thinks they mean.

A second weakness of the 'intention-of-Parliament' justification of judicial control of the performance of public functions is that it is at variance with the actual conduct of the courts. The mechanism, grounds, and remedies of judicial review were created and developed by the courts as means of controlling public power. The courts have shown themselves prepared to go a very long way to preserve their jurisdiction to supervise the exercise of public power by applying these principles. Perhaps the most striking modern example of this is the case of *Anisminic Ltd* v *Foreign Compensation Commission* [[1969] [2 AC 147]. The main question in this case was whether a section in the Foreign Compensation Act, purporting to oust the jurisdiction of the court to review 'determinations' of the Commission, was effective to that end. The House of Lords held that the word 'determination' must be read so as to exclude *ultra vires* determinations. It then went on to extend considerably the notion of *ultra vires* as it applied to decisions on questions of law, the final result being to reduce the application of the ouster clause almost to vanishing point, despite the fact that it had arguably been meant to have wide effect.

A second example is provided by the attitude of the courts to the exclusion by statute of the rules of natural justice. In the face of legislative silence on the question of whether an applicant before an administrative body is entitled to the protection of these procedural rules, two approaches are possible. It could be said that the rules of natural justice will apply only if there is evidence of a legislative intention that they should; alternatively, it could be argued that silence should be construed as an invitation to the courts to apply common law procedural standards of natural justice. On the whole the courts, especially in recent years, have tended to the latter view, thus asserting the independent force of the rules of natural justice.

A third example is provided by cases, concerning powers given to a Minister, for example, 'to act as he sees…'. Such phraseology appears to give the Minister unfettered discretion, but it has been held that such powers must be exercised reasonably in the light of the aims and purposes of the legislation conferring the power and of the relevant facts. In reality, the terms of the legislation may give very little guidance as to the way the power was meant to be exercised, even assuming that the Minister was not meant to be free to exercise his or her own best judgment. In effect, the courts are imposing standards of reasonable conduct on the Minister, irrespective of the question of legislative intent.

A third weakness in the statutory interpretation approach to judicial control of public power is that it does not justify judicial control of the performance of non-statutory functions. As we have seen…, in the *GCHQ* case the House of Lords rejected the proposition that the common law (prerogative) powers of central government are immune from judicial review in favour of the proposition that the exercise of a common law power can be challenged provided only that the power or the circumstances of its exercise do not raise non-justiciable issues of policy. We have also seen…that the courts have extended the scope of judicial review to embrace the exercise, for public purposes, of *de facto* power which has no identifiable legal source either in common law or statute. Whatever the criteria that the courts will apply in reviewing the exercise of non-statutory powers, they cannot, by definition, be derived from a power-conferring statute.

If judicial control of governmental action cannot adequately be explained in terms of Parliamentary intention, how is it to be justified? Two lines of argument suggest themselves. First, despite the second proposition of Parliamentary supremacy stated above, it can be argued that there are certain features of our constitutional and political arrangements that are so basic to our system of government that it is not seriously thought that they could ever be subject to the whim of Parliament—for example, the right to vote in free elections. Parliament could, of course, pass legislation inimical to this right, but attempts to enforce it, whether in the courts or outside would, no doubt, either simply fail or else precipitate a constitutional crisis. Similarly, we might say, the right to seek judicial review of the exercise of public powers and to receive a fair hearing are of fundamental importance in a democratic society, and it is vital that these rights be protected from any but the most limited statutory abridgement. A second line of argument that might support the refusal of the courts to be too deferential to Parliament is this: a vital underpinning assumption of Parliamentary supremacy is that Parliament is the most democratic governmental institution in our system. The political reality is that when the party in government has a comfortable majority in the House of Commons, Parliament is almost as much under the control of the government as is the day-to-day conduct of government business. The implications of this line of argument will be considered more later….

The autonomy of judicial review has an important implication that ought to be made explicit, namely that in controlling the performance of public functions, the courts are asserting and exercising, in their own right and in their own name, a power to limit and define the powers of other public functionaries. Parliament allocates decision-making powers to public functionaries by virtue of its almost unlimited legislative power. The courts, by virtue of their inherent (i.e. self-conferred) common law power of judicial review of public functions, decide the legal limits of those allocations of power. In so doing they can not only castigate public functionaries for abuses or excesses of power but, equally importantly, they can legitimize controversial exercises of power by holding them to have been lawful. The courts, in short, perform an indirect power-allocation function. Once this is realized, it can be seen how important it is to understand the nature of this function and the justification for it, since it is clear that the courts are not detached umpires in the governmental process but that they play an integral part in deciding how it will operate.

NOTES

1. Cane refers to the view that the independent attitude of the courts may be justified because a vital underpinning of the assumption of parliamentary supremacy—that Parliament is the most democratic governmental institution in our system—is not borne out in practice. In considering the implications of this argument later in the chapter, he states, at p. 354, 'although judicial and parliamentary control of government activity are directed to different ends, it can be argued that the popularity and importance of judicial review is likely to bear an inverse relationship

to the strength of parliamentary and other non-legal means of controlling government'. (See Chapter 6, *ante*, for a discussion of the mechanisms of political accountability.)

The links between judicial review and democracy are also explored by T. R. S. Allan in 'Legislative Supremacy and the Rule of Law' (1985) 44 *Cambridge Law Journal*, 111–43 at 129–33. In this extract Allan argues that judicial review is not inconsistent with the legislative supremacy of Parliament because the courts will give effect to the clear and unambiguous words of statutes. He also argues that judicial review functions to protect the democratic principle of the political sovereignty of the people. Unless prevented from doing so by the clear and unambiguous words of statutes, the courts in judicial review proceedings will give effect to common standards of morality and the natural expectations of the citizen. Allan thus differs from Cane in that he claims that ultimately judicial review poses no threat to the doctrine of parliamentary supremacy. Further, while Cane raises the possibility that judicial review may be more justifiable because of the inadequacies of other means of scrutinizing the Executive, he does not claim, as Allan does, that judicial review actually promotes democracy because it gives effect to common standards of morality and the natural expectations of the citizen.

2. Cane's discussion is concerned with judicial review of statutory powers, but we shall see below that the courts have reviewed the exercise of powers conferred by the royal prerogative (see *Council of Civil Service Unions* v *Minister for the Civil Service* [1985] AC 374). Recently, it has been clearly established that, in certain circumstances, the courts may review the exercise of powers which are not conferred by either statute or the royal prerogative but which depend on the consent of those who are subject to them (see *R* v *Panel on Take-overs and Mergers, ex parte Datafin Plc* [1987] QB 815 at p. 630, *post*). Can any of the justifications which have been put forward for judicial review of statutory powers be used to justify judicial review of powers derived from other sources?

B: The distinction between review and appeal

The courts have been concerned to emphasize that, in judicial review proceedings, they are exercising a supervisory, not an appellate, jurisdiction. Where statute provides for an appeal and the grounds of appeal are not restricted by the statute itself, the court is generally required to decide whether the decision under appeal was right or wrong. If it decides that the decision was wrong, the court hearing the appeal is generally permitted to substitute its decision for that of the authority which first determined the matter in question. What is the position in judicial review proceedings?

Chief Constable of the North Wales Police v *Evans*

[1982] 1 WLR 1155, House of Lords

The Chief Constable of North Wales decided that Evans, a probationer constable in the force, should be required to resign or, if he refused, be discharged from the force. Evans resigned but subsequently challenged the decision on the ground that it was taken in breach of natural justice because he was not told of the allegations which had led to the decision and had not been given an opportunity to offer any explanation. The House of Lords agreed with the decision of the Court of Appeal that there had been a breach of natural justice, but in the light of comments made in the Court of Appeal, felt it necessary to make some general comments on the scope of judicial review.

LORD HAILSHAM: The first observation I wish to make is by way of criticism of some remarks of Lord Denning MR which seem to me to be capable of an erroneous construction of the purpose and the remedy by way of judicial review under RSC Ord 53. This remedy, vastly increased in extent, and rendered, over a long period in recent years, of infinitely more convenient access than that provided by the old prerogative writs and actions for a declaration, is intended to protect the individual against the abuse of power by a wide range of authorities, judicial, quasi-judicial, and, as would originally have been thought when I first practised at the Bar, administrative. It is not intended to take away from those authorities the powers and discretions properly vested in them by law and to substitute the courts as the bodies making the decisions. It is intended to see that the relevant authorities use their powers in a proper manner.

Since the range of authorities, and the circumstances of the use of their power, are almost infinitely various, it is of course unwise to lay down rules for the application of the remedy which appear to be of universal validity in every type of case. But it is important to remember in every case that the purpose of the remedies is to ensure that the individual is given fair treatment by the authority to which he has been subjected and that it is no part of that purpose to substitute the opinion of the judiciary or of individual judges for that of the authority constituted by law to decide the matters in question. The function of the court is to see the lawful authority is not abused by unfair treatment and not to attempt itself the task entrusted to that authority by the law. There are passages in the judgment of Lord Denning MR (and perhaps in the other judgments of the Court of Appeal) in the instant case and quoted by my noble and learned friend which might be read as giving the courts carte blanche to review the decision of the authority on the basis of what the courts themselves consider fair and reasonable on the merits. I am not sure whether the Master of the Rolls really intended his remarks to be construed in such a way as to permit the courts to examine, as for instance in the present case, the reasoning of the subordinate body with a view to substituting its own opinion. If so, I do not think this is a correct statement of principle. The purpose of judicial review is to ensure that the individual receives fair treatment, and not to ensure that the authority, after according fair treatment, reaches on a matter which it is authorised by law to decide for itself a conclusion which is correct in the eyes of the court....

LORD BRIGHTMAN: ...I turn secondly to the proper purpose of the remedy of judicial review, what it is and what it is not. In my opinion the law was correctly stated in the speech of Lord Evershed [in *Ridge* v *Baldwin* [1964] AC 40], at p. 96. His was a dissenting judgment but the dissent was not concerned with this point. Lord Evershed referred to 'a danger of usurpation of power on the part of the courts... under the pretext of having regard to the principles of natural justice.' He added:

> I do observe again that it is not the decision as such which is liable to review; it is only the circumstances in which the decision was reached, and particularly in such a case as the present the need for giving the party dismissed an opportunity for putting his case.

Judicial review is concerned, not with the decision, but with the decision-making process. Unless that restriction on the power of the court is observed, the court will in my view, under the guise of preventing the abuse of power, be itself guilty of usurping power....

■ QUESTIONS

1. What, then, are the differences between appeal and review?
2. This case concerned the principles of natural justice. The other grounds for judicial review are summarized, at pp. 534–535, *post*. Do you think they could all be said to be concerned not with 'the decision but with the decision-making process'? Do you think their Lordships intended their remarks to apply to all the grounds for judicial review?

C: The use of judicial review

Judicial and Court Statistics 2009

2010, p.173

Table 7.12 High Court—Administrative Court[1]

Summary statistics on Judicial Review applications 2009[2]

							Number of applications
				Applications for Judicial Review disposed of, by result			
	Applications for permission to apply for judicial Review			Determined by Single Judge			
	Received	Granted	Refused	Allowed	Dismissed	Withdrawn	Total
Nature of Review							
Immigration/ Asylum	6,660	344	2,501	52	77	10	139
Criminal	305	66	172	33	21	4	58
Others	2,132	452	937	107	184	7	293
Total	**9,097**	**862**	**3,610**	**192**	**282**	**21**	**495**

Source: High Court–Administrative Court

Notes:
1. Includes Regional Offices of the Administrative Court
2. 93% of cases received In 2009 were issued in London

NOTES

1. For a period homelessness cases provided the second largest group of judicial review applications. However, the fall in homelessness cases is mainly due to a right of appeal to the county court introduced in 1997.
2. For an earlier study, see L. Bridges and G. Mészáros, in M. Sunkin, *Judicial Review in Perspective* (2nd edn, 1995).

SECTION 2: THE GROUNDS FOR JUDICIAL REVIEW

This chapter is concerned with the grounds for judicial review. The extracts which are included do, however, contain a number of references to the remedies which are available where there is a breach of the principles of judicial review. Before reading the cases, students should acquaint themselves with the following terms.

Subject to certain qualifications, which will be examined in further detail in Chapter 11, the normal method of seeking review is through making a claim for judicial review. In the claim for judicial review the court may grant one or more of the following remedies which have been renamed by the Civil Procedure Rules Part 54, p. 607, *post*.

A: The prerogative orders

These are:

(1) Quashing order, formerly *certiorari*: this remedy quashes an unlawful decision of a public authority.

(2) Prohibiting order, formerly prohibition: this remedy prohibits an unlawful act which a public authority is proposing to perform.

(3) Mandatory order, formerly *mandamus*: this remedy compels a public authority to perform a public duty.

Prerogative orders may not be granted against the Crown, although they may be granted against individual ministers of the Crown. They may not be used to challenge delegated legislation.

Injunctions Injunctions may be prohibitory (restraining unlawful action) or mandatory (compelling the performance of a duty). An interim injunction is one granted before trial in order to preserve the status quo until the issues have been determined. In an emergency an injunction may be granted without hearing the defendant. Note, however, that s. 21 of the Crown Proceedings Act 1947 prevents the grant of injunctions against the Crown. So far as Ministers of the Crown are concerned, injunctions can be granted against them, both in matters of European Community law (see *R* v *Secretary of State for Transport, ex parte Factortame (No. 2)* [1990] 1 AC 603) and in domestic law (see *In re M* [1993] 3 WLR 433, p. 117, *ante*).

Declarations Declarations are a very flexible remedy. They may, for instance, simply state the parties' rights, set out the true construction of a statute, or state that an administrative act is invalid.

Damages Damages may be awarded in an application for judicial review provided the applicant has claimed one or more of the remedies specified above. Damages are not available simply because one of the principles of judicial review has been breached. The applicant must show, in addition, that the authority has breached a right of his for which damages are available (e.g. that the authority has committed a tort or breach of contract).

There has been an exchange of views on the basis and justification of judicial review between broadly those who argue for a common law basis and those who advocate *ultra vires* and legislative intent. In the common law group are D. Oliver, 'Is the Ultra Vires Rules the Basis of Judicial Review?' [1987] *Public Law* 543; Sir John Laws 'Illegality: The Problem of Jurisdiction' in M. Supperstone and J. Goudie (eds), *Judicial Review* (1997); P. Craig, 'Ultra Vires and the Foundations of Judicial Review' [1998] CLJ 63 and 'Competing Models of Judicial Review' [1999] *Public Law* 428; and J. Jowell, 'Of Vires and Vacuums: The Constitutional Context of Judicial Review' [1999] *Public Law* 448*. The defenders of *ultra vires* are C. Forsyth, 'Of Fig Leaves and Fairy Tales: The *Ultra Vires* Doctrine, the Sovereignty of Parliament and Judicial Review' [1996] *Cambridge Law Journal* 122 and M. Elliott, 'The Demise of Parliamentary Sovereignty? The Implications for Justifying Judicial Review' (1999) 115 *Law Quarterly Review* 119* and 'The *Ultra Vires* Doctrine in A Constitutional Setting: Still the Central Principle of Administrative Law' [1999] *Cambridge Law Journal* 129. All of these extracts, except for those asterisked, are reprinted in C. Forsyth (ed.), *Judicial Review and the Constitution* (2000). The debate has continued with M. Elliott, *The Constitutional Foundations of Judicial Review* (2001); P. Craig and N. Bamforth, 'Constitutional Analysis, Constitutional Principle and Judicial Review' [2001] *Public Law* 763; T. Allan, 'The Constitutional Foundations of Judicial Review, Conceptual Conundrum or Interpretative Inquiry?' [2002] *Cambridge*

Law Journal 87; P. Craig, 'Constitutional Foundations, The Rule of Law and Supremacy' [2003] *Public Law* 92, C. Forsyth & M. Elliott, 'The Legitimacy of Judicial Review' [2003] *Public Law* 286.

Council of Civil Service Unions v *Minister for the Civil Service*

[1985] AC 374, House of Lords

The facts are stated at p. 576, *post*.

LORD DIPLOCK: ...Judicial review has I think developed to a state today when, without reiterating any analysis of the steps by which the development has come about, one can conveniently classify under three heads the grounds on which administrative action is subject to control by judicial review. The first ground I would call 'illegality', the second 'irrationality' and the third 'procedural impropriety'. That is not to say that further development on a case by case basis may not in course of time add further grounds. I have in mind particularly the possible adoption in the future of the principle of 'proportionality' which is recognised in the administrative law of several of our fellow members of the European Economic Community; but to dispose of the instant case the three already well-established heads that I have mentioned will suffice.

By illegality as a ground for judicial review I mean that the decision-maker must understand correctly the law that regulates his decision-making power and must give effect to it. Whether he has or not is par excellence a justiciable question to be decided in the event of dispute, by those persons, the judges, by whom the judicial power of the state is exercisable.

By irrationality I mean what can by now be succinctly referred to as '*Wednesbury* unreasonableness' (see *Associated Provincial Picture Houses Ltd* v *Wednesbury Corp* [1948] 1 KB 223). It applies to a decision which is so outrageous in its defiance of logic or accepted moral standards that no sensible person who had applied his mind to the question to be decided could have arrived at it. Whether a decision falls within the category is a question that judges by their training and experience should be well-equipped to answer, or else there would be something badly wrong with our judicial system. To justify the court's exercise of this role, resort I think today is no longer needed to Viscount Radcliffe's ingenious explanation in *Edwards* v *Bairstow* [1956] AC 14 of irrationality as a ground for a court's reversal of a decision by ascribing it to an inferred though identifiable mistake of law by the decision-maker. 'Irrationality' by now can stand on its own feet as an accepted ground on which a decision may be attacked by judicial review.

I have described the third head as 'procedural impropriety' rather than failure to observe basic rules of natural justice or failure to act with procedural fairness towards the person who will be affected by the decision. This is because susceptibility to judicial review under this head covers also failure by an administrative tribunal to observe procedural rules that are expressly laid down in the legislative instrument by which its jurisdiction is conferred, even where such failure does not involve any denial of natural justice.

NOTE: Lord Diplock's threefold classification of the grounds for judicial review has been cited in many subsequent cases. The classification will be followed in this chapter, where each of the three categories will be examined in more detail. Proportionality will be considered in the section on irrationality, p. 578, *post*.

B: Illegality

Lord Diplock used this phrase to cover a number of different grounds which are frequently treated separately. The most important are:

(1) An authority must not exceed its jurisdiction by purporting to exercise powers which it does not possess.

(2) An authority must direct itself properly on the law.

(3) An authority must not use its power for an improper purpose.
(4) An authority must take into account all relevant considerations and disregard all irrelevant considerations.
(5) An authority to which the exercise of a discretion has been entrusted cannot delegate the exercise of its discretion to another unless clearly authorized to do so.
(6) An authority must not fetter its discretion.
(7) An authority acts unlawfully if it fails to fulfil a statutory duty.
(8) An authority must not make a mistake of fact.
(9) An authority must not excessively interfere with fundamental rights.

It should be noted that this list is not exhaustive and that the grounds clearly overlap to some extent. Consider the following cases.

Anisminic Ltd v *Foreign Compensation Commission*

[1969] 2 AC 147, House of Lords

Anisminic Ltd owned property in Egypt which was sequestrated in 1956 by the Egyptian government. In 1957 Anisminic sold the property, for substantially less than its real value, to TEDO, an Egyptian organization.

Under a treaty, the United Arab Republic paid to the United Kingdom £27.5 million as compensation for property confiscated in Egypt in 1956. Responsibility for distributing the compensation money was vested in the Foreign Compensation Commission (FCC). Anisminic Ltd submitted a claim for compensation to the FCC.

Article 4 of the Foreign Compensation (Egypt) (Determination and Registration of Claims) Order 1962 provided that the Commission shall treat a claim as established if satisfied of the following matters:

(a) the applicant is the person referred to in the relevant part of Annex E of the Order as 'the owner of the property or is the successor in title of such a person';
(b) the person referred to in the relevant part of Annex E 'and any person who became successor in title of such person on or before February 28, 1959, were British nationals on October 31, 1956, and February 28, 1959.'

The Commission's provisional determination was that Anisminic Ltd had failed to establish its claim because TEDO, its successor in title, was not a British national.

Anisminic Ltd sought a declaration that the Commission had misconstrued the Order.

LORD REID: It has sometimes been said that it is only where a tribunal acts without jurisdiction that its decision is a nullity. But in such cases the word 'jurisdiction' has been used in a very wide sense, and I have come to the conclusion that it is better not to use the term except in the narrow and original sense of the tribunal being entitled to enter on the inquiry in question. But there are many cases where, although the tribunal had jurisdiction to enter on the inquiry, it has done or failed to do something in the course of inquiry which is of such nature that its decision is a nullity. It may have given its decision in bad faith. It may have made a decision which it had no power to make. It may have failed in the course of the inquiry to comply with the requirements of natural justice. It may in perfect good faith have misconstrued the provisions giving it power to act so that it failed to deal with the question remitted to it and decided some question which was not remitted to it. It may have refused to take into account something which it was required to take into account. Or it may have based its decision on some matter which, under the provisions setting it up, it had no right to take into account. I do not intend this list to be exhaustive. But if it decides a question remitted to it for decision without committing any of these errors it is as much entitled to decide that question wrongly as it is to decide it rightly. I understand that some confusion has been caused by my having said in *Reg* v *Governor of Brixton Prison, Ex parte Armah* [1968] AC 192, 234 that if a tribunal has jurisdiction to go right it has jurisdiction to go wrong. So it has, if one uses 'jurisdiction' in the narrow original sense. If it is entitled to enter on the inquiry and does not do any of those things which I have mentioned in the course of the proceedings, then its decision is equally valid whether it is right or wrong subject only to the power of the court in certain circumstances to correct an error of law. I think that, if these views are correct, the only case cited which was plainly wrongly decided is *Davies* v *Price* [1958] 1 WLR 434. But in a number of other cases some of the grounds of judgment are questionable.

I can now turn to the provisions of the Order under which the commission acted, and to the way in which the commission reached their decision. It was said in the Court of Appeal that publication of their reasons was unnecessary and perhaps undesirable. Whether or not they could have been required to publish their reasons, I dissent emphatically from the view that publication may have been undesirable. In my view, the commission acted with complete propriety, as one would expect looking to its membership.

The meaning of the important parts of this Order is extremely difficult to discover, and, in my view, a main cause of this is the deplorable modern drafting practice of compressing to the point of obscurity provisions which would not be difficult to understand if written out at rather greater length. . . .

The main difficulty in this case springs from the fact that the draftsman did not state separately what conditions have to be satisfied (1) where the applicant is the original owner and (2) where the applicant claims as the successor in title of the original owner. It is clear that where the applicant is the original owner he must prove that he was a British national on the dates stated. And it is equally clear that where the applicant claims as being the original owner's successor in title he must prove that both he and the original owner were British nationals on those dates, subject to later provisions in the article about persons who had died or had been born within the relevant period. What is left in obscurity is whether the provisions with regard to successors in title have any application at all in cases where the applicant is himself the original owner. If this provision had been split up as it should have been, and the conditions, to be satisfied where the original owner is the applicant had been set out, there could have been no such obscurity.

This is the crucial question in this case. It appears from the commission's reasons that they construed this provision as requiring them to inquire, when the applicant is himself the original owner, whether he had a successor in title. So they made that inquiry in this case and held that TEDO was the applicant's successor in title. As TEDO was not a British national they rejected the appellants' claim. But if, on a true construction of the Order, a claimant who is an original owner does not have to prove anything about successors in title, then the commission made an inquiry which the Order did not empower them to make, and they based their decision on a matter which they had no right to take into account. If one uses the word 'jurisdiction' in its wider sense, they went beyond their jurisdiction in considering this matter. It was argued that the whole matter of construing the Order was something remitted to the commission for their decision. I cannot accept that argument. I find nothing in the Order to support it. The Order requires the commission to consider whether they are satisfied with regard to the prescribed matters. That is all they have to do. It cannot be for the commission to determine the limits of its powers. Of course if one party submits to a tribunal that its powers are wider than in fact they are, then the tribunal must deal with that submission. But if they reach a wrong conclusion as to the width of their powers, the court must be able to correct that—not because the tribunal has made an error of law, but because as a result of making an error of law they have dealt with and based their decision on a matter with which, on a true construction of their powers, they had no right to deal. If they base their decision on some matter which is not prescribed for their adjudication, they are doing something which they have no right to do and, if the view which I expressed earlier is right, their decision is a nullity. So the question is whether on a true construction of the Order the applicants did or did not have to prove anything with regard to successors in title. If the commission were entitled to enter on the inquiry whether the applicants had a successor in title, then their decision as to whether TEDO was their successor in title would I think be unassailable whether it was right or wrong: it would be a decision on a matter remitted to them for their decision. The question I have to consider is not whether they made a wrong decision but whether they inquired into and decided a matter which they had no right to consider.

I have great difficulty in seeing how in the circumstances there could be a successor in title of a person who is still in existence. This provision is dealing with the period before the Order was made when the original owner had no title to anything: he had nothing but a hope that some day somehow he might get some compensation. The rest of the article makes it clear that the phrase (though inaccurate) must apply to a person who can be regarded as having inherited in some way the hope which a deceased original owner had that he would get some compensation. But 'successor in title' must I think mean some person who could come forward and make a claim in his own right. There can only be a successor in title where the title of its original possessor has passed to another person, his successor, so that the original possessor of the title can no longer make a claim, but his successor can make the claim which the original possessor of the title could have made if his title had not passed to his successor. The 'successor' of a deceased person can do that. But how could any 'successor' do this while the original owner is still in existence? One can imagine the improbable case of the original owner agreeing with someone that, for a consideration immediately paid to him, he would pay over to the other party any compensation which he might ultimately receive. But that would not create a 'successor in title' in any true sense. And I can think of no other way in which the original owner could transfer inter vivos his expectation of receiving compensation. If there were anything in the rest of the Order to indicate that such a case was intended to be covered, we might have to attribute to the phrase 'successor in title' some unusual and inaccurate meaning which would cover it. But there is nothing of that kind. In themselves the words 'successor in title' are, in my opinion, inappropriate in the circumstances of this Order to denote any person while the original owner is still in existence, and I think it most improbable that they were ever intended to denote any such person. There is no necessity to stretch them to cover any such person. I would therefore hold that the words 'and any person who became successor in title to such person' in article 4(1)(b)(ii) have no application to a case where the applicant is the original owner. It follows that the commission rejected the appellants' claim on a ground which they had no right to take into account and that their decision was a nullity. I would allow this appeal.

LORD PEARCE: Lack of jurisdiction may arise in various ways. There may be an absence of those formalities or things which are conditions precedent to the tribunal having any jurisdiction to embark on an inquiry. Or the tribunal may at the end make an order that it has no jurisdiction to make. Or in the intervening stage, while engaged on a proper inquiry, the tribunal may depart from the rules of natural justice; or it may ask itself the wrong questions; or it may take into account matters which it was not directed to take into account. Thereby it would step outside its jurisdiction. It would turn its inquiry into something not directed by Parliament and fail to make the inquiry which Parliament did direct. Any of these things would cause its purported decision to be a nullity....

LORD WILBERFORCE: In every case, whatever the character of a tribunal, however wide the range of questions remitted to it, however great the permissible margin of mistakes, the essential point remains that the tribunal has a derived authority, derived, that is, from statute: at some point, and to be found from a consideration of the legislation, the field within which it operates is marked out and limited. There is always an area, narrow or wide, which is the tribunal's area; a residual area, wide or narrow, in which the legislature has previously expressed its will and into which the tribunal may not enter. Equally, though this is not something that arises in the present case, there are certain fundamental assumptions, which without explicit restatement in every case, necessarily underlie the remission of power to decide such as (I do not attempt more than a general reference, since the strength and shade of these matters will depend upon the nature of the tribunal and the kind of question it has to decide) the requirement that a decision must be made in accordance with principles of natural justice and good faith. The principle that failure to fulfil these assumptions may be equivalent to a departure from the remitted area must be taken to follow from the decision of this House in *Ridge* v *Baldwin* [1964] AC 40. Although, in theory perhaps, it may be possible for Parliament to set up a tribunal which has full and autonomous powers to fix its own area of operation, that has, so far, not been done in this country. The question, what is the tribunal's proper area, is one which it has always been permissible to ask and to answer, and it must follow that examination of its extent is not precluded by a clause conferring conclusiveness, finality, or unquestionability upon its decisions. These clauses in their nature can only relate to decisions given within the field of operation entrusted to the tribunal. They may, according to the width and emphasis of their formulation, help to ascertain the extent of that field, to narrow it or to enlarge it, but unless one is to deny the statutory origin of the tribunal and of its powers, they cannot preclude examination of that extent....

The extent of the interpretatory power conferred upon the tribunal may sometimes be difficult to ascertain and argument may be possible whether this or that question of construction has been left to the tribunal, that is, is within the tribunal's field, or whether, because it pertains to the delimitation of the tribunal's area by the legislature, it is reserved for decision by the courts. Sometimes it will be possible to form a conclusion from the form and subject-matter of the legislation. In one case it may be seen that the legislature, while stating general objectives, is prepared to concede a wide area to the authority it establishes: this will often be the case where the decision involves a degree of policy-making rather than

> fact-finding, especially if the authority is a department of government or the Minister at its head. I think that we have reached a stage in our administrative law when we can view this question quite objectively, without any necessary predisposition towards one that questions of law, or questions of construction, are necessarily for the courts. In the kind of case I have mentioned there is no need to make this assumption. In another type of case it may be apparent that Parliament is itself directly and closely concerned with the definition and delimitation of certain matters of comparative detail and has marked by its language the intention that these shall accurately be observed.... The present case, by contrast, as examination of the relevant Order in Council will show, is clearly of the latter category....
>
> *Lord Pearce and Lord Wilberforce also agreed with Lord Reid's interpretation of the Order.*
>
> *Lord Morris and Lord Pearson dissented.*

■ QUESTION

On what ground or grounds did the court grant judicial review?

NOTES

1. The Foreign Compensation Act 1950 purported to oust the jurisdiction of the courts to question any determination of the Commission. This aspect of the case is considered, at p. 642, *post*.
2. Since *Anisminic*, there has been considerable dispute as to whether all errors of law take a public authority outside its jurisdiction. In *Re Racal Communications Ltd* [1981] AC 374 Lord Diplock stated, at p. 383:

> The break-through made by *Anisminic* [1969] 2 AC 147 was that, as respects administrative tribunals and authorities, the old distinction between errors of law that went to jurisdiction and errors of law that did not, was for practical purposes abolished. Any error of law that could be shown to have been made by them in the course of reaching their decision on matters of fact or of administrative policy would result in their having asked themselves the wrong question with the result that the decision they reached would be a nullity....
>
> But there is no similar presumption that where a decision-making power is conferred by statute upon a court of law, Parliament did not intend to confer upon it power to decide questions of law as well as questions of fact. Whether it did or did not and, in the case of inferior courts, what limits are imposed on the kinds of questions of law they are empowered to decide, depends upon the construction of the statute unencumbered by any such presumption. In the case of inferior courts where the decision of the court is made final and conclusive by the statute, this may involve the survival of those subtle distinctions formerly drawn between errors of law which go to jurisdiction and errors of law which do not that did so much to confuse English administrative law before *Anisminic* [1969] 2 AC 147; but upon any application for judicial review of a decision of an inferior court in a matter which involves, as so many do, interrelated questions of law, fact and degree the superior court conducting the review should not be astute to hold that Parliament did not intend the inferior court to have jurisdiction to decide for itself the meaning of the ordinary words used in the statute to define the question which it has to decide.

In *O'Reilly* v *Mackman* [1983] 2 AC 237, at p. 278, Lord Diplock referred to the *Anisminic* case as liberating English public law 'from the fetters that the courts had theretofore imposed upon themselves so far as determinations of inferior courts and statutory tribunals were concerned by drawing esoteric distinctions between errors of law committed by such tribunals that went to their jurisdiction, and errors of law committed by them within their jurisdiction'.

There is division of opinion on the point as to whether inferior courts, but not administrative tribunals, may be immune from judicial review for errors of law within jurisdiction. In *R* v *Lord President of the Privy Council, ex parte Page* [1993] AC 682 (a case concerning the jurisdiction of a university visitor), the majority of Lords Keith, Griffiths, and Browne-Wilkinson affirmed Lord Diplock's dicta in *Re Racal Communications* on inferior courts.

■ QUESTION

What light is thrown on judicial thinking on the boundaries and basis of judicial review by:

(a) the erosion of the difference between jurisdictional errors and errors of law within jurisdiction; and

(b) the exception to this for inferior courts and visitors but not administrative tribunals, even those staffed by lawyers?

Wheeler* v *Leicester City Council

[1985] AC 1054, House of Lords

Leicester Football Club had a licence to use a recreation ground administered by the local council. Under s. 10 of the Open Spaces Act the council held and administered the recreation ground in trust to allow, and with a view to, its enjoyment by the public as an open space. Section 76 of the Public Health (Amendment) Act 1907 gave the council power to set apart pitches for the purpose of playing football. Section 56 of the Public Health Act 1925 gave the council power to permit the exclusive use by any club of such a pitch, subject to such charges and conditions as the local authority thought fit.

In April 1984 three members of the club were invited to join the English rugby football team selected to tour South Africa. The council supported a Commonwealth Agreement to withhold support for and discourage sporting links with South Africa. It put four questions to the club and indicated that only an affirmative answer to each of them would be acceptable:

(a) Does the Leicester Football Club support the Government opposition to the tour?

(b) Does the Leicester Football Club agree that the tour is an insult to a large proportion of the Leicester population?

(c) Will the Leicester Football Club press the Rugby Football Union to call off the tour?

(d) Will the Leicester Football Club press the players to pull out of the tour?

The club stated that, while it agreed with the council in condemning apartheid in South Africa, it was not unlawful for members to participate in the tour, nor was it contrary to the rules of the Rugby Football Union or the club. The club's role was purely advisory and it had asked the members to consider the memorandum to the Rugby Football Union prepared by the anti-apartheid movement. The three members subsequently took part in the tour. In August 1984 the council passed a resolution banning the club and its members from using the recreation ground for 12 months. The club applied for an order of *certiorari* to quash the decision. The judge refused the application and his decision was upheld by the Court of Appeal.

ACKNER LJ: ...[Counsel], for the council, has submitted, and I entirely accept, that in exercising their discretion the council are entitled to take into account the effect that such an exercise would have on the performance of their other statutory functions. He gave us instances where the use of the pitch might potentially contravene the council's policies under the Town and Country Planning Acts, or interfere with their obligations under the Housing Acts, or contravene the Public Health Acts. In all such cases obviously the council, in considering how to exercise its discretion in relation to the recreation ground, would be entitled to and indeed be under a duty to have regard to their other statutory functions and duties.

The statutory function which [counsel] submits the council were fully entitled to take into account in exercising their discretionary powers in relation to this recreation ground, is to be found in section 71 of the Race Relations Act 1976.... The relevant words of the section read as follows:

> ...it shall be the duty of every local authority to make appropriate arrangements with a view to securing that their various functions are carried out with due regard to the need...(b) to promote...good relations, between different persons of different racial groups.

[Counsel] for the club accepts that a local authority are, vis a vis race relations, in a very special position. It is the local authority that provides many of the social services, they are a substantial employer of labour and are thus capable of setting an example in regard to race relations conduct and policies which is likely to be followed. Notwithstanding this concession, [counsel] submits that this section is what he describes as an 'inward-looking' section, directed to requiring that the local authority themselves maintain the standards laid down by the Act, that is to say their codes of practice in regard to their own internal behaviour so as to comply with the requirements of the Act. It is a section whose function is limited to ensuring that the local authority put their own house in order.

I consider this to be too narrow a construction. To my mind the section is imposing an obligation on the local authority, when they consider discharging any of their functions which might have a race relations content, to do so in such a manner as would tend to promote good relations between persons of different racial groups. Accordingly, in my judgment, the council were fully entitled when exercising their discretionary powers in relation to this recreation ground to have regard to the purposes expressed in section 71....

If I am right so far, this leaves only one final question to consider. Can it be said in the circumstances of this case that no reasonable local authority could properly conclude that temporarily banning from the use of their recreational ground an important local rugger club, which declined to condemn a South African tour and declined actively to discourage its members from participating therein, could promote good relations between persons of different racial groups? (see the well-known Wednesbury test: *Associated Provincial Picture Houses Ltd* v *Wednesbury Corp* [1948] 1 KB 223).

Ackner LJ decided that the answer to this question was no. Sir George Waller also dismissed the club's appeal, but Browne-Wilkinson LJ dissented. The club then appealed to the House of Lords.

LORD TEMPLEMAN: ... My Lords, the laws of this country are not like the laws of Nazi Germany. A private individual or a private organisation cannot be obliged to display zeal in the pursuit of an object sought by a public authority and cannot be obliged to publish views dictated by a public authority.

The club having committed no wrong, the council could not use their statutory powers in the management of their property or any other statutory powers in order to punish the club. There is no doubt that the council intended to punish and have punished the club. When the club were presented by the council with four questions it was made clear that the club's response would only be acceptable if, in effect, all four questions were answered in the affirmative. When the club committee made their dignified and responsible response to these questions, a response which the council find unsatisfactory to the council, the council commissioned a report on possible sanctions that might be taken against the club. That report suggested that delaying tactics could be used to hold up the grant of a lease then being negotiated by the club. It suggested that land could be excluded from the lease as it was 'thought that this could embarrass the club because it had apparently granted sub-leases...' It was suggested that the council's consent, which had already been given for advertisements by the club's sponsors, could be withdrawn although according to the report 'the actual effect of this measure on the club is difficult to assess.' It was suggested that 'a further course is to insist upon strict observance of the tenant's covenants in the lease. However, the city estate's surveyor, having inspected the premises, is of the opinion that the tenant's covenants are all being complied with.' Finally, it was suggested that 'the council could terminate the club's use of the recreation ground.' This might cause some financial loss to the council and might 'form the basis of a legal challenge to the council's decision. The club may contend that the council has taken an unreasonable action against the club in response to personal decisions of members of its team over which it had no control.' Notwithstanding this warning, the council accepted the last suggestion and terminated the club's use of the recreation ground. In my opinion, this use by the council of its statutory powers was a misuse of power. The council could not properly seek to use its statutory powers of management or any other statutory powers for the purposes of punishing the club when the club had done no wrong.

In *Congreve* v *Home Office* [1976] 1 QB 629 the Home Secretary had a statutory power to revoke television licences. In exercise of that statutory power he revoked the television licences of individuals who had lawfully surrendered an existing licence and taken out a new licence before an increase in the licence fee was due to take effect. Lord Denning MR said at p. 651:

> If the licence is to be revoked—and his money forfeited—the Minister would have to give good reasons to justify it. Of course, if the licensee had done anything wrong—if he had given a cheque for £12 which was dishonoured, or if he had broken the conditions of the licence—the Minister

could revoke it. But when the licensee has done nothing wrong at all, I do not think the Minister can lawfully revoke the licence, at any rate, not without offering him his money back, and not even then except for good cause. If he should revoke it without giving reasons, or for no good reason, the courts can set aside the revocation and restore the licence. It would be a misuse of the power conferred on him by Parliament: and these courts have the authority—and I would add the duty—to correct a misuse of power by a Minister or his department, no matter how much he may resent it or warn us of the consequences if we do.

Similar considerations apply, in my opinion, to the present case. Of course this does not mean that the council is bound to allow its property to be used by a racist organisation or by any organisation which, by its actions or its words, infringes the letter or the spirit of the Race Relations Act 1976. But the attitude of the club and of the committee of the club was a perfectly proper attitude, caught as they were in a political controversy which was not of their making.

For these reasons and the reasons given by my noble and learned friend Lord Roskill I would allow this appeal.

Lord Roskill decided that the council had made a decision which was so unreasonable that no reasonable authority could have come to it. The other Law Lords agreed with both Lord Templeman and Lord Roskill.

■ QUESTIONS

1. On which ground(s) for judicial review did each of the judges base his decision?
2. How did (a) Ackner LJ and (b) Lord Templeman decide which purposes the council was/was not entitled to pursue? Did they find assistance in the statutes under which the council managed the recreation ground or in the Race Relations Act 1976? What other matters did they refer to in determining this issue?
3. How did they decide which purposes the club had pursued?
4. Would it have made any difference to the decision of Lord Templeman if the club had espoused racist views in its reply to the council's request?
5. Does this case provide support for Allan's view that in judicial review proceedings the judges are furthering the political sovereignty of the people by giving effect to common standards of morality or the natural expectations of citizens?

NOTE: Lord Templeman based his decision on the ground that the council had acted for an improper purpose. Difficulties may arise when an authority acts for more than one purpose, some of which are lawful and others unlawful. The courts have not always been consistent in deciding how to deal with this conflict. Consider the approach adopted in the following extract.

R v *ILEA, ex parte Westminster City Council*

[1986] 1 WLR 28, High Court

The Inner London Education Authority (ILEA) determined the rates for education spending precepted on rating authorities in Inner London, including Westminster City Council. ILEA was opposed to the Government's policies, announced in 1983, of limiting the amount of rates levied by local authorities, a process known as rate-capping. By s. 142(2) of the Local Government Act 1972 ILEA was empowered to incur expenditure on arranging for the publication within their area of information on matters relating to local government. In July 1983 an education sub-committee of ILEA agreed to retain an advertising agency, referred to in the extract below as AMV, at a cost of £651,000, to mount a media and poster campaign to 'gain awareness of the authority's views of the needs of the education service and to alter the basis of the public debate about the effect of... Government actions.' Westminster City Council sought a declaration that the decision of the sub-committee was *ultra vires* because ILEA sought to persuade the public to support ILEA's views on rate-capping. ILEA accepted that the decision was made with the dual purpose of informing and persuading.

GLIDEWELL LJ: . . .

Two purposes

This brings me to what I regard as being the most difficult point in the case, namely, if a local authority resolves to expend its ratepayers' money in order to achieve two purposes, one of which it is authorised to achieve by statute but for the other of which it has no authority, is that decision invalid?

I was referred to the following authorities.

(i) *Westminster Corp* v *London and North Western Rly Co* [1905] AC 426. Westminster City Council had power to provide public lavatories under the Public Health (London) Act 1891, section 44. They constructed public lavatories underground, under the centre of the south end of Whitehall. The lavatories were approached from each side of the street by a subway, which could also be used as a pedestrian subway for people who wished to cross the street and not to use the lavatories. The London and North Western Railway Co., who owned the land at the east end of the subway, challenged the construction of the lavatories and subway, alleging that the main purpose of the Corporation was to construct a pedestrian subway which did not fall within the power of the Act. The Court of Appeal found for the railway company. By a majority, the House of Lords allowed the appeal, but did so on the facts, i.e., by holding that the Court of Appeal had drawn a wrong inference from the affidavits and documents before the court. In his speech, the Earl of Halsbury LC said at p. 428:

> I quite agree that if the power to make one kind of building was fraudulently used for the purpose of making another kind of building, the power given by the legislature for one purpose could not be used for another.

Lord Macnaghten said at p. 433:

> I entirely agree with Joyce J at first instance that the primary object of the council was the construction of the conveniences with the requisite and proper means of approach thereto and exit therefrom.

This suggests that a test for answering the question is, if the authorised purpose is the primary purpose, the resolution is within the power.

(ii) . . . . [is omitted]

(iii) More recently in *Hanks* v *Minister of Housing and Local Government* [1963] 1 QB 999, Megaw J did have to deal with a case in which it was alleged that a compulsory purchase order had been made for two purposes, one of which did not fall within the empowering Act. . . . [He stated] at [1963] 1 QB 999 at 1020–1021:

> I confess that I think confusion can arise from the multiplicity of words which have been used in this case as suggested criteria for the testing of the validity of the exercise of a statutory power. The words have included 'objects', 'purposes', 'motives', 'motivation', 'reasons', 'grounds' and 'considerations'. In the end, it seems to me, the simplest and clearest way to state the matter is by reference to 'considerations'. A 'consideration', I apprehend, is something which one takes into account as a factor in arriving at a decision. I am prepared to assume, for the purposes of the case, that, if it be shown that an authority exercising a power has taken into account as a relevant factor something which it could not properly take into account in deciding whether or not to exercise the power, then the exercise of the power, normally at least, is bad. Similarly, if the authority fails to take into account as a relevant factor something which is relevant, and which is or ought to be known to it, and which it ought to have taken into account, the exercise of that power is normally bad. I say 'normally', because I can conceive that there may be cases where the factor wrongly taken into account, or omitted, is insignificant, or where the wrong taking-into-account, or omission, actually operated in favour of the person who later claims to be aggrieved by the decision.

. . . I have considered also the views of the learned authors of the textbooks on this. Professor Wade in his book *Administrative Law* 5th edn (1982) under the heading Duality of Purpose says at p. 388:

> Sometimes an act may serve two or more purposes, some authorised and some not, and it may be a question whether the public authority may kill two birds with one stone. The general rule is that its action will be unlawful provided the permitted purpose is the true and dominant purpose behind the act, even though some secondary or incidental advantage may be gained for some purpose which is outside the authority's powers.

Professor Evans, in *de Smith's Judicial Review of Administrative Action* 4th edn (1980) p. 329, comforts me by describing the general problem of plurality of purpose as 'a legal porcupine which bristles with difficulties as soon as it is touched.' He distils from the decisions of the courts five different tests on which reliance has been placed at one time or another, including, at pp. 330–332:

> (1) What was the *true purpose* for which the power was exercised? If the actor has in truth used his power for the purposes for which it was conferred, it is immaterial that he was thus enabled to achieve a subsidiary object… (5) Was any of the purposes pursued an unauthorised purpose? If so, and if the unauthorised purpose has materially influenced the actor's conduct, the power has been invalidly exercised because irrelevant considerations have been taken into account.

These two tests, and Professor Evans's comment on them, seem to me to achieve much the same result and to be similar to that put forward by Megaw J in *Hanks* v *Minister of Housing and Local Government* [1963] 1 QB 999 in the first paragraph of the passage I have quoted from his judgment. That is the part that includes the sentence: 'In the end, it seems to me, the simplest and clearest way to state the matter is by reference to considerations.' I gratefully adopt the guidance of Megaw J and the two tests I have referred to from *de Smith's Judicial Review of Administrative Action*.

It thus becomes a question of fact for me to decide, on the material before me, whether, in reaching its decision of 23 July 1984, the staff and general sub-committee of ILEA was pursuing an unauthorised purpose, namely that of persuasion, which has materially influenced the making of its decision. I have already said that I find that one of the sub-committee's purposes was the giving of information. But I also find that it had the purpose of seeking to persuade members of the public to a view identical with that of the authority itself, and indeed I believe that this was a, if not the, major purpose of the decision. In reaching this decision of fact, I have taken into account in particular the material to which I have referred above in AMV's 'presentation' of 18 July 1984, the passages I have quoted from the report of the Education Officer to the sub-committee, particularly the reference to changing 'the basis of public debate', and the various documents which have been published by AMV since 23 July with the approval of ILEA. I accept that some of the documents do inform, but in my view some of them contain little or no information and are designed only to persuade. This is true in particular, in my view, of the poster slogan 'Education Cuts Never Heal' (skilful though I think it is) and it is also true of the advertisement 'What do you get if you subtract £75 million from London's education budget?'

Adopting the test referred to above, I thus hold that ILEA's sub-committee did, when making its decision of 23 July 1984, take into account an irrelevant consideration, and thus that decision was not validly reached.

■ QUESTIONS

1. On which of the grounds for judicial review did the Court base its decision?
2. Glidewell LJ quoted part of a passage from de Smith. Do you agree with his comment that the two tests set out in this passage achieve much the same result? On the facts of *Westminster Corporation* v *London and North Western Railway Co* [1905] AC 426, might it have been possible to say that, although the construction of a subway was not a primary object, the desire to provide such a subway was a material influence on the council's decision?

NOTE: In *R* v *Greenwich London Borough Council, ex parte Lovelace* [1991] 3 All ER 511, Staughton LJ in the Court of Appeal stated that, in cases of 'mixed motives', the question was whether the improper motive had exercised a 'substantial influence' on the decision.

Although *R* v *ILEA, ex parte Westminster City Council* was argued on the basis that the authority had acted for an improper purpose, Glidewell LJ stated that he felt the case was best approached on the basis of whether the authority had been materially influenced by an irrelevant consideration. This ground for judicial review is dealt with in more detail in the following extract.

Padfield v *Minister for Agriculture, Fisheries and Food*

[1968] AC 997, House of Lords

The Agricultural Marketing Act 1958 regulated the marketing of various agricultural products, including milk. Section 19(3) provided: 'A committee of investigation shall...(b) be charged with the duty, if the Minister in any case so directs, of considering and reporting to the Minister...any complaint made to the Minister as to the operation of any scheme which, in the opinion of the Minister, could not be considered by a consumers' committee...'. The south-eastern dairy farmers complained to the Minister about the operation of a scheme involving the fixing of price differentials by the Milk Marketing Board, but the Minister refused to refer the complaint to a committee of investigation. They accordingly applied for an order of *mandamus*.

The Divisional Court made an order against the Minister which was set aside by the Court of Appeal.

LORD REID: ...The question at issue in this appeal is the nature and extent of the Minister's duty under section 19(3)(b) of the Act of 1958 in deciding whether to refer to the committee of investigation a complaint as to the operation of any scheme made by persons adversely affected by the scheme. The respondent contends that his only duty is to consider a complaint fairly and that he is given an unfettered discretion with regard to every complaint either to refer it or not to refer it to the committee as he may think fit. The appellants contend that it is his duty to refer every genuine and substantial complaint, or alternatively that his discretion is not unfettered and that in this case he failed to exercise his discretion according to law because his refusal was caused or influenced by his having misdirected himself in law or by his having taken into account extraneous or irrelevant considerations.

In my view, the appellants' first contention goes too far. There are a number of reasons which would justify the Minister in refusing to refer a complaint. For example, he might consider it more suitable for arbitration, or he might consider that in an earlier case the committee of investigation had already rejected a substantially similar complaint or he might think the complaint to be frivolous or vexatious. So he must have at least some measure of discretion. But is it unfettered?

It is implicit in the argument for the Minister that there are only two possible interpretations of this provision—either he must refer every complaint or he has an unfettered discretion to refuse to refer in any case. I do not think that is right. Parliament must have conferred the discretion with the intention that it should be used to promote the policy and objects of the Act; the policy and objects of the Act must be determined by construing the Act as a whole and construction is always a matter of law for the court. In a matter of this kind it is not possible to draw a hard and fast line, but if the Minister, by reason of his having misconstrued the Act or for any other reason, so uses his discretion so as to thwart or run counter to the policy and objects of the Act, then our law would be very defective if persons aggrieved were not entitled to the protection of the court. So it is first necessary to construe the Act....

The approval of Parliament shows that this scheme was thought to be in the public interest, and in so far as it necessarily involved detriment to some persons, it must have been thought to be in the public interest that they should suffer it. But in sections 19 and 20 Parliament drew a line. They provide machinery for investigating and determining whether the scheme is operating or the board is acting in a manner contrary to the public interest.

The effect of these sections is that if, but only if, the Minister and the committee of investigation concur in the view that something is being done contrary to the public interest the Minister can step in. Section 20 enables the Minister to take the initiative. Section 19 deals with complaints by individuals who are aggrieved. I need not deal with the provisions which apply to consumers. We are concerned with other persons who may be distributors or producers. If the Minister directs that a complaint by any of them shall be referred to the committee of investigation, that committee will make a report which must be published. If they report that any provision of this scheme or any act or omission of the Board is contrary to interests of the complainers *and* is not in the public interest, then the Minister is empowered to take action but not otherwise. He may disagree with the view of the committee as to public interest, and, if he thinks that there are other public interests which outweigh the public interest that justice should be done to the complainers, he would be not only entitled but bound to refuse to take action. Whether he takes action or not, he may be criticised and held accountable in Parliament but the court cannot interfere.

I must now examine the Minister's reasons for refusing to refer the appellant's complaint to the committee. I have already set out the letters of March 23 and May 3, 1965. I think it is right also to refer to a letter sent from the Ministry on May 1 1964, because in his affidavit the Minister says he has read this letter and there is no indication that he disagrees with any part of it.

[Lord Reid read the letter and continued.] The first reason which the Minister gave in his letter of March 23, 1965, was that this complaint was unsuitable for investigation because it raised wide issues. Here it appears to me that the Minister has clearly misdirected himself. Section 19(6) contemplates the raising of issues so wide that it may be necessary for the Minister to amend a scheme or even to revoke it. Narrower issues may be suitable for arbitration but section 19 affords the only method of investigating wide issues. In my view it is plainly the intention of the Act that even the widest issues should be investigated if the complaint is genuine and substantial, as this complaint certainly is.

Then it is said that the issue should be 'resolved through the arrangements available to producers and the board within the framework of the scheme itself.' This re-states in a condensed form the reasons given in paragraph 4 of the letter of May 1, 1964, where it is said 'the Minister owes no duty to producers in any particular region,' and reference is made to the 'status of the Milk Marketing Scheme as an instrument for the self-government of the industry,' and to the Minister 'assuming an inappropriate degree of responsibility.' But as I have already pointed out, the Act imposes on the Minister a responsibility whenever there is a relevant and substantial complaint that the board are acting in a manner inconsistent with the public interest, and that has been relevantly alleged in this case. I can find nothing in the Act to limit this responsibility or to justify the statement that the Minister owes no duty to producers in a particular region. The Minister is, I think, correct in saying that the board is an instrument of the self-government of the industry. So long as it does not act contrary to the public interest the Minister cannot interefere. But if it does act contrary to what both the committee of investigation and the Minister hold to be the public interest the Minister has a duty to act. And if a complaint relevantly alleges that the board has so acted, as this complaint does, then it appears to me that the Act does impose a duty on the Minister to have it investigated. If he does not do that he is rendering nugatory a safeguard provided by the Act and depriving complainers of a remedy which I am satisfied that Parliament intended them to have....

The House of Lords by a majority allowed the appeal and granted an order of mandamus (Lord Morris of Borth-y-Gest dissenting).

NOTE: The aftermath of this case provides a good illustration of the point that success in a judicial review application does not require that the authority whose actions have been challenged must reach a decision which is favourable to the applicant. After this case the Minister submitted a complaint for investigation to the investigative committee. The Minister then rejected the committee's advice. Commenting on this Carol Harlow stated that 'The remedy had proved illusory; the same decision could be reached with only nominal deference to the court, and the waste of time and money entailed is a deterrent to future complainants' (C. Harlow, 'Administrative Reaction to Judicial Review' [1976] *Public Law* 116). Do you agree?

■ QUESTIONS

1. How did the House of Lords decide which considerations were relevant and which were irrelevant?
2. How did the House of Lords decide which considerations had been taken into account?
3. Are there any circumstances in which the taking into account of an irrelevant consideration will not render the decision unlawful. Does *R* v *Inner London Education Authority* (p. 551, *ante*) suggest an answer? (See also *R* v *BBC, ex parte Owen* [1985] 2 All ER 522.)

NOTES

1. Public bodies will have various duties and powers and responsibilities. Are they entitled to take into account their own financial resources in making decisions involving expenditure? In *R* v *Gloucestershire County Council, ex parte Barry* [1997] AC 584, the removal of cleaning and laundry services by the council on the ground of lack of resources was challenged. The House of Lords by a 3:2 majority held that it was a relevant consideration for a council to take into account the resources it had available when carrying out its statutory duty under the Chronically Sick and Disabled Persons Act 1970, s. 2(1), to consider the needs of chronically sick and disabled persons in its area. Lord Nicholls said that 'needs for services cannot be sensibly assessed without having some regard to the cost of providing them. A person's need for a particular type or level of service cannot

be decided in a vacuum from which all considerations of cost have been expelled'. In a subsequent decision the Court of Appeal held in *R* v *Sefton Metropolitan Borough Council, ex parte Help the Aged* [1997] 4 All ER 532, that a council making decisions under National Assistance Act 1948, s. 21(1) as to whether an elderly person was in need of care and attention, was entitled to have regard to its own resources. Where it was decided that a person was in such need then a lack of resources was no excuse if arrangements were not made to provide for the identified needs. Subsequently *ex parte Barry* has been distinguished by the House of Lords in *R* v *East Sussex County Council, ex parte Tandy* [1998] 2 All ER 769, where it was held that a local education authority's resources were an irrelevant consideration in determining what constituted suitable education for the purposes of the Education Act 1993, s. 298. This section imposed a duty to make arrangements for suitable education for children in specified circumstances. Their Lordships also held that if there was more than one way of providing suitable education, then it would be permissible for a local education authority to have regard to its resources in choosing between different ways of making such provision. See E. Palmer, 'Resource Allocation, Welfare Rights—Mapping the Boundaries of Judicial Control in Public Administrative Law' (2000) 20 *Oxford Journal of Legal Studies* 63, and J. A. King 'The Justiciability of Resource Allocation' (2007) 70 *Modern Law Review* 197.

A Chief Constable may have regard to available resources when determining policing priorities: see *R* v *Chief Constable of Sussex, ex parte International Trader's Ferry Ltd* [1999] 2 AC 418, p. 585, *post*.

2. Failure to consider a legitimate expectation is a failure to consider a relevant consideration: see p. 596, *post*, *R (Bibi)* v *Newham London Borough Council* [2001] EWCA Civ 607, [2002] 1 WLR 237.
3. It has been held to be an irrelevant consideration for the Home Secretary to take into account a public campaign urging a long period of minimum detention for boys who had murdered a younger child. The majority of the House of Lords held in *R* v *Secretary of State for the Home Department, ex parte Venables* [1997] 3 WLR 23, that in this position of determining the minimum period of detention or tariff, it was permissible to take into account general considerations of public confidence in the administration of justice. In making this decision the Home Secretary was acting like a judge determining sentence. It was further held that the consideration of the public campaign in a particular case would also amount to a breach of natural justice.
4. It will be clear that the court is required to address some difficult issues in deciding upon the legality of an authority's decisions. For example, how do the courts decide what considerations were taken into account? How do they decide whether an irrelevant consideration has had only an insignificant or insubstantial influence on a decision?

   Two points in particular should be noted. First, the burden of proof in an application for judicial review generally falls on the applicant. Hence, for example, the onus was on the complainants in *Padfield* to prove that irrelevant consideration(s) were taken into account.

   Secondly, there is no general requirement that the authority should give reasons for its decision. In the course of argument in *Padfield* it was submitted that the Minister may properly refuse to act on a complaint without giving any reasons, and that in such a case a complainant would have no remedy and the decision could not be questioned. Lord Pearce stated at pp. 1053–1054:

> CSI do not regard a Minister's failure or refusal to give any reasons as a sufficient exclusion of the court's surveillance. If all the prima facie reasons seem to point in favour of his taking a certain course to carry out the intention of Parliament in respect of a power which it has been given to him in that regard, and he gives no reason whatever for taking a contrary course, the court may infer that he has no good reason and that he is not using the power given by Parliament to carry out its intentions. In the present case, however, the Minister has given reasons which show that he was not exercising his discretion in accordance with the intentions of the Act.

   (See also the comments of Lord Reid, at pp. 1032(G)–1033(A) and Lord Upjohn, at pp. 1061(G)–62(A).)

After citing this passage in the case of *Lonrho plc* v *Secretary of State* [1989] 2 All ER 609, at p. 620, Lord Keith, with whom the other Law Lords agreed, stated:

> The absence of reasons for a decision where there is no duty to give them cannot of itself provide any support for the suggested irrationality of the decision. The only significance of the absence of reasons is that if all other known facts and circumstances appear to point overwhelmingly in favour of a different decision, the decision-maker who has given no reasons cannot complain if the court draws the inference that he had no rational reason for his decision.

While there is no general duty to provide reasons authorities are sometimes obliged by statute to provide them (see, in particular, s. 10 of the Tribunal and Inquiries Act 1992). It has also been recently accepted that natural justice could, in exceptional cases, require the provision of reasons (see *R* v *Civil Service Appeal Board, ex parte Cunningham* [1991] 4 All ER 310, discussed at [1991] *Public Law*, 340–346). In *Doody* v *Secretary of State for the Home Department* [1993] 3 All ER 92 the House of Lords held that the Secretary of State was obliged to give reasons to prisoners when he proposed to depart from the periods recommended by the judiciary for the purposes of retribution and deterrence. Yet in *R* v *Higher Education Funding Council, ex parte Institute of Dental Surgery* [1994] 1 All ER 651, although the council's reasons for refusing to give reasons for its decision to lower the institute's research rating were not well grounded, this was not a case in which the law might require reasons. In *R* v *Ministry of Defence, ex parte Murray* [1998] COD 134 the principles from those three cases were drawn together by Hooper J. While there was as yet no general duty to give reasons, the courts will seek to ensure that bodies given power to make decisions affecting individuals act fairly and it may be that a procedure of not giving reasons is unfair, even if there is no requirement to do so. Particular concern will arise if a tribunal's decisions affect personal liberty. In deciding if fairness requires a tribunal to give reasons, then regard will be had to the initial hearing but also to the availability of any appeal or judicial review and the absence of such a remedy could be a point in favour of requiring reasons. Reasons will not be required where considerations of public interest would outweigh the advantages of requiring reasons or if the procedures of a particular decision-maker would be frustrated if required to give reasons, even short reasons. In summary, factors in favour of requiring reasons are: 'the giving of reasons may among other things concentrate the decision-maker's mind on the right questions; demonstrate to the recipient that this is so; show that the issues have been conscientiously addressed and how the result has been reached; or alternatively alert the recipient to a justiciable flaw in the process'. On the other hand factors not requiring the giving of reasons include where: 'it may place an undue burden on decision-makers; demand an appearance of unanimity where there is diversity; call for articulation of sometimes inexpressible value judgments; and offer an invitation to the captious to comb the reasons for previously unsuspected grounds of challenge'.

In *R* v *Secretary of State for the Home Department, ex parte Fayed* [1997] 1 All ER 228, British Nationality Act 1981, s. 44(2) allowed the Home Secretary not to give reasons when deciding applications for naturalization as British citizens. By a majority the Court of Appeal held that the Minister had to be fair and that an applicant should be given sufficient information about the Minister's concerns to allow the applicant to make representations. If that would involve disclosing matters not in the public interest then this should be indicated so that the applicant could challenge the justification for the refusal to give reasons in the courts. Note that the section did not ban the giving of reasons.

British Oxygen Co Ltd v *Minister of Technology*

[1971] AC 610, House of Lords

British Oxygen Co Ltd used metal cylinders to store pressurized gases which it manufactured. It applied for a grant in respect of the cylinders under s. 1(1) of the Industrial Development Act 1966, which provided that the Board of Trade 'may make to any person carrying on a business in Great Britain a grant towards approved capital expenditure incurred by that person in providing new machinery or plant'. The Board had a policy of denying grants for any item of plant costing less than £25 and, in pursuance of that policy, rejected British Oxygen's application as the gas cylinders cost just under

£20 each. British Oxygen sought declarations that (*inter alia*) the cylinders were eligible for grant.

LORD REID: Section 1 of the Act provides that the Board of Trade 'may' make grants. It was not argued that 'may' in this context means 'shall', and it seems to me clear the Board were intended to have a discretion. But how were the Board intended to operate that discretion? Does the Act read as a whole indicate any policy which the Board is to follow or even give any guidance to the Board? If it does then the Board must exercise its discretion in accordance with such policy or guidance (*Padfield* v *Minister of Agriculture, Fisheries and Food* [1986] AC 997). One generally expects to find that Parliament has given some indication as to how public money is to be distributed. In this Act Parliament has clearly laid down the conditions for eligibility for grants and it has clearly given to the Board a discretion so that the Board is not bound to pay to every person who is eligible to receive such a grant. But I can find nothing to guide the Board as to the circumstances in which they should pay or the circumstances in which they should not pay grants to such persons....

There are two general grounds on which the exercise of an unqualified discretion can be attacked. It must not be exercised in bad faith, and it must not be so unreasonably exercised as to show that there cannot have been any real or genuine exercise of the discretion. But, apart from that, if the Minister thinks that policy or good administration requires the operation of some limiting rule, I find nothing to stop him.

It was argued on the authority of *Rex* v *Port of London Authority ex parte Kynoch* [1919] 1 KB 176 that the Minister is not entitled to make a rule for himself as to how he will in future exercise his discretion. In that case Kynoch owned land adjoining the Thames and wished to construct a deep water wharf. For this they had to get the permission of the authority. Permission was refused on the ground that Parliament had charged the authority with the duty of providing such facilities. It appeared that before reaching their decision the authority had fully considered the case on its merits and in relation to the public interest. So their decision was upheld.

Bankes LJ said at p. 184:

> There are on the one hand cases where a tribunal in the honest exercise of its discretion has adopted a policy, and, without refusing to hear an applicant, intimates to him what its policy is, and that after hearing him it will in accordance with its policy decide against him, unless there is something exceptional in his case. I think counsel for the applicants would admit that, if the policy has been adopted for reasons which the tribunal may legitimately entertain, no objection could be taken to such a course. On the other hand there are cases where a tribunal has passed a rule, or come to a determination, not to hear any application of a particular character by whomsoever made. There is a wide distinction to be drawn between these two classes.

I see nothing wrong with that. But the circumstances in which discretions are exercised vary enormously and that passage cannot be applied literally in every case. The general rule is that anyone who has to exercise a statutory discretion must not 'shut his ears to an application' (to adapt from Bankes LJ on p. 183). I do not think there is any great difference between a policy and a rule. There may be cases where an officer or authority ought to listen to a substantial argument reasonably presented urging a change of policy. What the authority must not do is to refuse to listen at all. But a ministry or large authority may have had to deal already with a multitude of similar applications and then they will almost certainly have evolved a policy so precise that it could well be called a rule. There can be no objection to that, provided the authority is always willing to listen to anyone with something new to say—of course I do not mean to say that there need be an oral hearing. In the present case the respondent's officers have carefully considered all that the appellants have had to say and I have no doubt that they will continue to do so....

VISCOUNT DILHORNE: ...[T]he distinction between a policy decision and a rule may not be easy to draw. In this case it was not challenged that it was within the power of the Board to adopt a policy not to make a grant in respect of such an item. The policy might equally well be described as a rule. It was both reasonable and right that the Board should make known to those interested the policy it was going to follow. By doing so fruitless applications involving expense and expenditure of time might be avoided. The Board says that it has not refused to consider any application. It considered the appellants'. In these circumstances it is not necessary to decide in this case whether, if it had refused to consider an application on the ground that it related to an item costing less than £25, it would have acted wrongly.

I must confess that I feel some doubt whether the words used by Bankes LJ in the passage cited above [see p. 548, *ante*] are really applicable to a case of this kind. It seems somewhat pointless and a waste of time that the Board should have to consider applications which are bound as a result of its policy decision to fail. Representations could of course be made that the policy should be changed. . . .

Lord Morris of Borth-y-gest, Lord Wilberforce and Lord Diplock agreed with Lord Reid.

■ QUESTIONS

1. On which ground(s) was the decision of the House of Lords based?
2. Under the Children Act 1989 local authorities have a duty to safeguard and promote the welfare of children within their area who are in need 'by providing a range and level of services appropriate to those children's needs' (s. 17). The services may include giving assistance in kind or, in exceptional circumstances, in cash. Assume that a local authority has made certain policies to govern the provision of such assistance. An applicant for assistance in cash is told that her application will be refused under the general policies operated by the council (of which she is aware) unless she wishes to make representations that the policies should be altered and the authority is prepared to accept the representations. Would the applicant be able to challenge this decision? (See *Attorney-General ex relator Tilley* v *Wandsworth LBC* [1981] 1 WLR 854.)

NOTES

1. In *R (P)* v *Secretary of State for the Home Department* and *R (Q)* v *Secretary of State for the Home Department* [2001] EWCA Civ 1151, [2001] 1 WLR 2002 the Court of Appeal demonstrated how to deal with a rigid or blanket policy when human rights were engaged. In these cases the Prison Service's policy requiring babies to be separated from their prisoner mothers on reaching 18 months of age was considered in the light of the mother's, and particularly the child's, right to family life. The Prison Service was required to consider whether the interference with the right was justified by the legitimate aims in Art. 8(2). Factors to be taken into account include necessary limitations upon the mother's rights because of her imprisonment, how relaxation of the policy might affect the good order and discipline of the prison, the length of the mother's sentence, the welfare of the child including the extent of harm likely to be caused by separation, the extent of harm likely to be caused by remaining in prison, and the quality of alternative arrangements. The Court concluded that in most cases separation before 18 months would be justified but there could be cases in which the interests of mother and child outweighed other factors. In the case of P the application of the policy would be lawful but so far as Q was concerned there were factors which led to the court to remit the case to the Prison Service for reconsideration. On the application of this test with pressing social need see p. 455, *ante*, and for its relationship with *Wednesbury* unreasonableness/irrationality and proportionality see p. 490, *ante*.
2. See C. Hilson, 'Judicial Review, Polices and the Fettering of Discretion' [2002] *Public Law* 111 for a thorough examination of the 'no fettering' doctrine in which the doctrine and its application by the courts are criticized and an argument is made for a more nuanced approach which allows for justifiable rigid policies and also for more individualized decision-making where required and, where human rights are engaged, for a relationship in which the newer human rights approach can be combined with the older doctrine.
3. The application of a policy may result in breaches of the duty to be fair (see p. 557, *post*). For example, in *R* v *Secretary of State for the Environment, ex parte Brent LBC* [1982] QB 593 the Secretary of State failed to consider any of the representations made to him to change his policy on reducing the rate support grant to certain authorities. The Divisional Court held that he had both unlawfully fettered his discretion and failed to discharge the duty of fairness.

E v Secretary of State for the Home Department

[2004] EWCA Civ 49, [2004] 2 WLR 1351, Court of Appeal

Two asylum cases were joined in the appeal. The asylum claims had been rejected by the Secretary of State and the appeals to the Adjudicator and Immigration Appeal Tribunal (IAT) had been unsuccessful, however, new evidence had come to light between the hearing and the promulgation of the decision by the IAT and the appellants had not been able to persuade the IAT to hear appeals based on this evidence which would show the mistake, as the IAT took the view it could not take the new evidence into account. On appeal on a point of law to the Court of Appeal.

CARNWATH LJ: ...

37. We will consider first the question of error of fact as a ground for review in administrative law. The appellants' case is that the new evidence shows that the basis of the IAT's decision in each case was mistaken, and that such a mistake can provide grounds for an appeal even where it is limited to questions of law.

38. It is convenient to start from a summary in a recent case in this Court of the principles applicable to an appeal on a point of law from a specialist tribunal, in that case the Lands Tribunal (*Railtrack plc v Guinness Ltd* [2003] RVR 280, [2003] EWCA Civ 188). Having referred to another Lands Tribunal case, in which an appeal had been allowed because the Tribunal had failed to take account of the "whole of the evidence" on a particular point (*Aslam v South Bedfordshire DC* [2001] RVR 65, [2001] EWCA Civ 514), Carnwath LJ (with whom the other members of the Court agreed) said (para 51):

> This case is no more than an illustration of the point that issues of 'law' in this context are not narrowly understood. The Court can correct 'all kinds of error of law, including errors which might otherwise be the subject of judicial review proceedings' (*R v IRC ex p Preston* [1985] 1 AC 835, 862 per Lord Templeman; see also De Smith, Woolf and Jowell, Judicial Review 5th Ed para 15–076). Thus, for example, a material breach of the rules of natural justice will be treated as an error of law. Furthermore, judicial review (and therefore an appeal on law) may in appropriate cases be available where the decision is reached 'upon an incorrect basis of fact', due to misunderstanding or ignorance (see *R (Alconbury Ltd) v Secretary of State* [2001] 2 WLR 1389, 2001 UKHL 23, para 53, per Lord Slynn). A failure of reasoning may not in itself establish an error of law, but it may 'indicate that the tribunal had never properly considered the matter... and that the proper thought processes have not been gone through' (*Crake v Supplementary Benefits Commission* [1982] 1 All ER 498. 508).

39. Two aspects of that summary require elaboration in the context of the present case: first, the relationship of this form of appeal with judicial review; and secondly the availability of appeal "upon an incorrect basis of fact".

Appeal on law, and judicial review

40. There was some discussion in the present case as to whether the grounds upon which the Court may question a decision of the IAT differ materially, depending on whether the case comes before the Court as an application for judicial review, or as an appeal on a point of law. It would certainly be surprising if the grounds for judicial review were more generous than those for an appeal. In practice, such cases only come by way of judicial review because the IAT has refused leave to appeal, and its refusal can only be challenged in that way. There is certainly no logical reason why the grounds of challenge should be wider in such cases.

41. More generally, the history of remedies in administrative law has seen the gradual assimilation of the various forms of review, common law and statutory. The history was discussed by the Law Commission in its Consultation Paper *Administrative Law: Judicial Review and Statutory Appeals* CP 126, Parts 17 to 18. The appeal "on a point of law" became a standard model (supplanting in many contexts the appeal by "case stated") following the Franks Committee report on *Administrative Tribunals and Inquiries* (1957 Cmnd 218), which was given effect in the Tribunals and Inquiries Act 1958 (now Tribunals and Inquiries Act 1992 s11). In other statutory contexts (notably, planning, housing and the like), a typical model was the statutory application to quash on the grounds that the decision was "not within the powers of the

Act" (see e.g. *Ashbridge Investments Ltd v Minister of Housing and Local Government* [1965] 1 WLR 1320). Meanwhile the prerogative writ procedures were remodelled into the modern judicial review procedure. In *R v Hull University Visitor ex p Page* [1993] AC 682, the House of Lords acknowledged the evolution of a common set of principles "to ensure that the powers of public decision-making bodies are exercised lawfully" (p. 701, per Lord Browne-Wilkinson).

42. Thus, in spite of the differences in history and wording, the various procedures have evolved to the point where it has become a generally safe working rule that the substantive grounds for intervention are identical. (The conceptual justifications are another matter; see, for example, the illuminating discussion in Craig *Administrative Law* 5th Ed pp 476ff). The main practical dividing line is between appeals (or review procedures) on both fact and law, and those confined to law. The latter are treated as encompassing the traditional judicial review grounds of excess of power, irrationality, and procedural irregularity. This position was confirmed in *R v IRC ex p Preston* [1985] AC 835, 862E–F (a tax case), where Lord Templeman said:

> Appeals from the General Commissioners or the Special Commissioners lie, but only on questions of law, to the High Court by means of a case stated and the High Court can then correct all kinds of errors of law including error which might otherwise be the subject of judicial review proceedings...

43. Of course the application of these principles will vary according to the power or duty under review; and, in particular, according to whether it is a duty to decide a finite dispute (such as that of a tribunal), or a continuing responsibility (such as that of a minister or local authority). As will be seen, this distinction is important in analysing some of the cases cited in this appeal. Furthermore, some decisions reflect the relative procedural flexibility of judicial review. While a statutory appeal is normally confined by the terms of the statute to consideration of the decision appealed against, judicial review is not so confined. An application for a judicial review of a particular decision may, subject to the Court's discretion, be expanded by amendment to include review of subsequent decisions of the same agency (see e.g. *Turgut* below), or even related decisions of other agencies.

Incorrect basis of fact

44. Can a decision reached on an incorrect basis of fact be challenged on an appeal limited to points of law? This apparently paradoxical question has a long history in academic discussion, but has never received a decisive answer from the courts. The answer is not made easier by the notorious difficulty of drawing a clear distinction between issues of law and fact (see, Craig *op cit* p488; *Moyna v Secretary of State for Work and Pensions* [2003] UKHL 44 para 22 ff, per Lord Hoffmann).

45. The debate received new life following the affirmative answer given by Lord Slynn in *R v Criminal Injuries Compensation Board ex parte A* [1999] 2AC 330. In that case the claimant had claimed compensation on the basis that in the course of a burglary she had been the victim of rape and buggery. She was examined five days after the burglary by a police doctor who reported that her findings were consistent with the allegation of buggery. However, at the hearing of her claim that report was not included in the evidence, and the Board was given the impression by the police witnesses that there was nothing in the medical evidence to support her case. The claimant did not ask for the report, but, in Lord Slynn's words:

> "...having been told that she should not ask for police statements as they would be produced by the police, it would not be surprising that she assumed that if there was a report from the police doctor, it would be made available with the police report" (p 343F).

46. One of the issues discussed in detail in argument was whether the decision could be quashed on the basis of a mistake, in relation to material which was or ought to have been within the knowledge of the decision maker (see p 333–336). Lord Slynn thought it could. He said:

> Your Lordships have been asked to say that there is jurisdiction to quash the Board's decision because that decision was reached on a material error of fact. Reference has been made to "*Administrative Law*" (*Wade and Forsyth* (7th edition)) in which it is said at pp. 316–318 that:
>
> > Mere factual mistake has become a ground of judicial review, described as 'misunderstanding or ignorance of an established and relevant fact,' [*Secretary of State for Education v Tameside MBC* [1977] AC 1014, 1030] or acting 'upon an incorrect basis of fact.'... This

> ground of review has long been familiar in French law and it has been adopted by statute in Australia. It is no less needed in this country, since decisions based upon wrong fact are a cause of injustice which the courts should be able to remedy. If a 'wrong factual basis' doctrine should become established, it would apparently be a new branch of the ultra vires doctrine, analogous to finding facts based upon no evidence or acting upon a misapprehension of law.

De Smith, Woolf and Jowell *Judicial Review of Administrative Action* 5th ed., at p. 288

> The taking into account of a mistaken fact can just as easily be absorbed into a traditional legal ground of review by referring to the taking into account of an irrelevant consideration, or the failure to provide reasons that are adequate or intelligible, or the failure to base the decision on any evidence. In this limited context material error of fact has always been a recognised ground for judicial intervention.

For my part, I would accept that there is jurisdiction to quash on that ground in this case..." (p 344G–345E).

47. However, Lord Slynn "preferred" to decide the instant case on the alternative basis that there had been a breach of the rules of natural justice amounting to "unfairness." As to that he said:

> It does not seem to me to be necessary to find that anyone was at fault in order to arrive at this result. It is sufficient if objectively there is unfairness. Thus I would accept that it is in the ordinary way for the applicant to produce the necessary evidence. There is no onus on the Board to go out to look for evidence, nor does the Board have a duty to adjourn the case for further enquiries if the applicant does not ask for one.... Nor is it necessarily the duty of the police to go out to look for evidence on a particular matter.

Nonetheless, he considered that the police do have a special position in these cases, and he noted the evidence that the Board is very dependent on the assistance of and the co-operation of the police who have investigated these alleged crimes of violence. He said:

> In the present case, the police and the Board knew that A had been taken by the police to see a Police Doctor. It was not sufficient for the police officer simply to give her oral statement without further inquiry when it was obvious that the doctor was likely to have made notes and probably a written report."(p 345F–346B).

He concluded:

> I consider therefore, on the special facts of this case and in the light of the importance of the role of the police in co-operating with the Board in the obtaining of the evidence, that there was unfairness in the failure to put the doctor's evidence before the board and if necessary to grant an adjournment for that purpose. I do not think it possible to say here that justice was done or seen to be done. (p 347B).

48. The other members of the House agreed with Lord Slynn's reasoning, thereby (as I read the speeches) endorsing his "preferred" basis of unfairness. Only Lord Hobhouse made any direct reference to the question of review for "error of fact", specifically reserving that issue for consideration in the future (p 348E).

49. The same statement on that question was repeated by Lord Slynn, in another context, in *R v Secretary of State for the Environment ex p Alconbury* [2003] 2AC 295, [2001] UKHL 23 para. 53. He referred to the jurisdiction to quash for "misunderstanding or ignorance of an established and relevant fact", as part of his reasons for holding that the court's powers of review (under a statutory procedure to quash for excess of power) met the requirements of the European Convention on Human Rights. This part of his reasoning was not in terms adopted by the other members of the House of Lords. The point was mentioned by Lord Nolan and Lord Clyde. Lord Nolan put it in somewhat narrower terms; he said:

> But a review of the merits of the decision-making process is fundamental to the Court's jurisdiction. The power of review may even extend to a decision on a question of fact. As long ago as 1955 your Lordships' House, in *Edwards v Bairstow* [1956] AC 14, a case in which an appeal (from General Commissioners of Income Tax) could only be brought on a question of law, upheld the right and duty of the appellate court to reverse a finding of fact which had no justifiable basis. (para. 61).

He saw *Edwards v Bairstow* as an illustration of "the generosity" with which the Courts have interpreted the power to review questions of law, corresponding to "a similarly broad and generous" approach in the development of judicial review (para 62). Lord Clyde referred to Lord Slynn's statement on this issue in *CICB*, commenting that it was:

> ...sufficient to note...the extent to which the factual areas of a decision may be penetrated by a review of the account taken by a decision-maker of facts which are irrelevant or even mistaken. (para. 169)

50. In the present case the appellants rely on Lord Slynn's statement as representing the law. Mr Kovats, for the Secretary of State, contents himself with the observation that the *CICB* case is "not in point" because it was a judicial review case, and Lord Slynn's statement was *obiter*. For the reasons already given, we do not think the fact that *CICB* was a judicial review case is an adequate ground of distinction. Indeed, Lord Slynn himself (and Lord Clyde) treated it as no less relevant to a statutory review procedure in *Alconbury*. The fact that the statement was *obiter* means of course that it is not binding on us, but does not detract from its persuasive force, bearing in mind also the authority of the textbooks cited by him.

51. Although none of the parties found it necessary to examine in any detail the authorities referred to in argument in the *CICB* case or in the textbooks, it seems to us difficult to avoid such examination, if we are to address properly the issue in these appeals. Fortunately the ground is very well-covered, not only in the textbooks, but also in two excellent articles: by Timothy Jones, "Mistake of fact in Administrative Law" [1990] PL 507; and by Michael Kent QC (no doubt stimulated by his unsuccessful advocacy in *CICB* itself) "Widening the scope of review for error of fact" [1999] JR 239. The authorities are helpfully summarised in Michael Fordham's invaluable *Judicial Review Handbook* 3rd Ed pp 730–2 (see also Demetriou and Houseman *Review for Error of fact—a brief guide* [1997] JR 27). Michael Kent includes a useful comparison with the concept of "manifest error" as applied by the European Court of Justice. He concludes:

> A cautious extension of the power of the court on judicial review to reopen the facts might now be appropriate. This would need to be limited to cases where the error is manifest (not requiring a prolonged or heavily contested inquiry), is decisive (on which the decision turned) and not susceptible of correction by alternative means... (*op cit* p. 243).

52. That is not dissimilar to the formulation approved by Lord Slynn, although he required that the error should be "material", rather than "decisive". Before reaching a conclusion that mistake of fact is now a ground for judicial review in its own right, it is necessary to review briefly the authorities mentioned in those articles. Two main points emerge: first, that widely differing views have been expressed as to the existence or scope of this ground of review; but, secondly, that, in practice, this uncertainty has not deterred administrative court judges from setting aside decisions on the grounds of mistake of fact, when justice required it...

63. In our view, the *CICB* case points the way to a separate ground of review, based on the principle of fairness. It is true that Lord Slynn distinguished between "ignorance of fact" and "unfairness" as grounds of review. However, we doubt if there is a real distinction. The decision turned, not on issues of fault or lack of fault on either side; it was sufficient that "objectively" there was unfairness. On analysis, the "unfairness" arose from the combination of five factors:

i) An erroneous impression created by a mistake as to, or ignorance of, a relevant fact (the availability of reliable evidence to support her case);
ii) The fact was "established", in the sense that, if attention had been drawn to the point, the correct position could have been shown by objective and uncontentious evidence;
iii) The claimant could not fairly be held responsible for the error;
iv) Although there was no duty on the Board itself, or the police, to do the claimant's work of proving her case, all the participants had a shared interest in co-operating to achieve the correct result;
v) The mistaken impression played a material part in the reasoning.

64. If that is the correct analysis, then it provides a convincing explanation of the cases where decisions have been set aside on grounds of mistake of fact. Although planning inquiries are also adversarial, the planning authority has a public interest, shared with the Secretary of State through his inspector, in ensuring that development control is carried out on the correct factual basis. Similarly, in *Tameside*, the

Council and the Secretary of State, notwithstanding their policy differences, had a shared interest in decisions being made on correct information as to practicalities. The same thinking can be applied to asylum cases. Although the Secretary of State has no general duty to assist the appellant by providing information about conditions in other countries (see *Abdi and Gawe v Secretary of State* [1996] 1 WLR 298, he has a shared interest with the appellant and the Tribunal in ensuring that decisions are reached on the best information. It is in the interest of all parties that decisions should be made on the best available information (see the comments of Sedley LJ in *Batayav*, quoted above).

(We have also taken account of the judgment of Maurice Kay J in *R (Cindo) v Secretary of State* [2002] EWHC 246 para 8–11, drawn to our attention since the hearing by Mr Gill, in which some of these issues were discussed.)

65. The apparent unfairness in *CICB* was accentuated because the police had in their possession the relevant information and failed to produce it. But, as we read the speeches, "fault" on their part was not essential to the reasoning of the House. What mattered was that, because of their failure, and through no fault of her own, the claimant had not had "a fair crack of the whip". (See *Fairmount Investments v Secretary of State* [1976] 1 WLR 1255, 1266A, per Lord Russell.) If it is said that this is taking "fairness" beyond its traditional role as an aspect of procedural irregularity, it is no further than its use in cases such as *HTV Ltd v Price Commission* [1976] ICR 170, approved by the House of Lords in *R v IRC ex p Preston* [1985] AC 835, 865–6.)

66. In our view, the time has now come to accept that a mistake of fact giving rise to unfairness is a separate head of challenge in an appeal on a point of law, at least in those statutory contexts where the parties share an interest in co-operating to achieve the correct result. Asylum law is undoubtedly such an area. Without seeking to lay down a precise code, the ordinary requirements for a finding of unfairness are apparent from the above analysis of *CICB*. First, there must have been a mistake as to an existing fact, including a mistake as to the availability of evidence on a particular matter. Secondly, the fact or evidence must have been "established", in the sense that it was uncontentious and objectively verifiable. Thirdly, the appellant (or his advisers) must not been have been responsible for the mistake. Fourthly, the mistake must have played a material (not necessarily decisive) part in the Tribunal's reasoning.

67. Accordingly, we would accept the submissions of each of the present appellants, that, if the new evidence is admitted, the Court will be entitled to consider whether it gives rise to an error of law in the sense outlined above.

Appeals allowed

NOTE: The court was seeking to show that mistake of fact was a ground of challenge available both in an appeal on a point of law and in a claim for judicial review and this required that it be regarded as an error of law. The chosen rationale is that the mistake of fact leads to unfairness which can amount to an error of law. See P. Craig 'Judicial Review, Appeal and Factual Error' [2004] *Public Law* 788.

R v Secretary of State for the Home Department, ex parte Simms

[1999] 3 WLR 328, House of Lords

The applicants were prisoners who were convicted of murder and who continued to protest their innocence after they had been refused permission to appeal against their convictions. On becoming aware that some of the applicants' visitors were journalists who were interested in publicizing the applicants' stories, the prison authorities refused to allow journalists to visit the prisoners unless they signed an undertaking that no material obtained in the visits would be used for professional purposes. The authority for this was para. 37 of section A of the Prison Service Standing Order No. 5 of 1996. The journalists did not seek permission under para. 37A where, exceptionally, professional visits could be permitted conditionally. The Home Secretary had a blanket policy excluding professional visits on the basis that they tended to undermine proper control and discipline. The applicants successfully sought judicial review arguing that the blanket ban on the use of information was an excessive interference with the right of free speech. The Court of Appeal reversed this decision. On appeal to the House of Lords.

LORD STEYN: ...Two important inferences can and should be drawn. First, until the Home Secretary imposed a blanket ban on oral interviews between prisoners and journalists in or about 1995, such interviews had taken place from time to time and had served to identify and undo a substantial number of miscarriages of justice. There is no evidence that any of these interviews had resulted in any adverse impact on prison discipline. Secondly, the evidence establishes clearly that without oral interviews it is now virtually impossible under the Home Secretary's blanket ban for a journalist to take up the case of a prisoner who alleges a miscarriage of justice. In the process a means of correcting errors in the functioning of the criminal justice system has been lost.

(c) The counter-arguments on behalf of the Home Secretary

For my part I am reasonably confident that once it is accepted that oral interviews with prisoners serve a useful purpose in exposing potential miscarriages of justice the Home Secretary would not wish his present policy to be maintained. But, if I am mistaken in that supposition, my view is that investigative journalism, based on oral interviews with prisoners, fulfils an important corrective role, with wider implications than the undoing of particular miscarriages of justice. Nevertheless. I must directly address the counter arguments advance by the Home Secretary.

Latham J was unimpressed with the reasons advanced in opposition to the applicants' limited claim in the first affidavit of Audrey Wickington. In my judgment the judge was right. The two new affidavits make a case that any oral interviews between prisoners and journalist will tend to disrupt discipline and order in prisons. In my view these affidavits do not take sufficient account of the limited nature of the applicants' claims, viz to have interviews for the purpose of obtaining a thorough investigation of their cases as a first step to possibly gaining access through the Criminal Cases Review Commission to the Court of Appeal (Criminal Division). The affidavits do not refute the case that until 1995 such interviews enabled a substantial number of miscarriages to be undone. Moreover, they do not establish that interviews confined to such limited purposes caused disruption to prison life. In any event, the affidavits do not establish a case of pressing need which might prevail over the prisoners' attempt to gain access to justice: see decision of the Court of Appeal in *Reg.* v *Secretary of State for the Home Department, Ex parte Leech* [1994] QB 198, the correctness of which was expressly accepted by counsel for the Home Secretary.

Counsel for the Home Secretary relied on the decision of the United States Supreme Court in *Pell* v *Procunier* (1974) 417 US 817. The case involved a ban by prison authorities of face to face interviews between journalists and inmates. The background was a relatively small number of inmates who as a result of press attention became virtual 'public figures' within prison society and gained a disproportionate notoriety and influence among their fellow inmates. The evidence showed that the interviews caused severe disciplinary problems. By a majority of five to four the Supreme Court held the ban to be constitutional. The majority enunciated an approach of a 'measure of judicial deference owed to corrections officials'. This approach was followed in *Turner* v *Safley* (1987) 482 US 78 where the Supreme Court upheld restrictions on correspondence between inmates. In *Pell* v *Procunier* the Supreme Court was faced with a very particular and intolerable situation in the Californian prison service where there had been virtually unlimited access by journalists to inmates. Nobody suggests anything of the kind in the present case. While the inmates in *Pell* v *Procunier* no doubt wished to air their general grievances, there is nothing in the report to indicate that the prisoners wanted interviews with journalists for the specific purpose of obtaining access to an appeal process to challenge their convictions. And, in any event, the approach of judicial deference to the views of prison authorities enunciated in *Pell* v *Procunier* does not accord with the approach under English law. It is at variance with the principle that only a pressing social need can defeat freedom of expression as explained in the *Derbyshire* case [*Derbyshire County Council* v *Times Newspapers*] [1993] AC 534, 550H–551A, the *Leech* case [1994] QB 198, 212 E–F, and *Silver* v *United Kingdom* (1980) 3 EHRR 475, 514–515, paras 372–375 (the commission): (1983) 5 EHRR 347, 377, para. 99(e) (the court). It is also inconsistent with the principle that the more substantial the interference with fundamental rights the more the court will require by way of justification before it can be satisfied that the interference is reasonable in a public law sense: *Reg.* v *Ministry of Defence, Ex parte Smith* [1996] QB 517, 554E–F. In my view *Pell* v *Procunier* does not assist.

(d) Conclusion

On the assumption that paragraphs 37 and 37A should be construed as the Home Secretary contends, I have no doubt that these provisions are exorbitant in width in so far as they would undermine the fundamental rights invoked by the applicants in the present proceedings and are therefore ultra vires.

2. The interpretation of paragraphs 37 and 37A

It is now necessary to examine the correctness of the interpretation of paragraphs 37 and 37A, involving a blanket ban on interviews, as advanced by the Home Secretary. Literally construed there is force in the extensive construction put forward. But one cannot lose sight that there is at stake a fundamental or basic right, namely the right of a prisoner to seek through oral interviews to persuade a journalist to investigate the safety of the prisoner's conviction and to publicise his findings in an effort to gain access to justice for the prisoner. In these circumstances even in the absence of an ambiguity there comes into play a presumption of general application operating as a constitutional principle as Sir Rupert Cross explained in successive editions of his classic work: *Statutory Interpretation*, 3rd ed. (1995), pp. 165–166. This is called 'the principle of legality': *Halsbury's Laws of England*, 4th ed. reissue, Vol. 8(2) (1996), pp. 13–14, para. 6. Ample illustrations of the application of this principle are given in the speech of Lord Browne-Wilkinson, and in my speech, in *Reg.* v *Secretary of State for the Home Department, Ex parte Pierson* [1998] AC 539, 573G–575D, 587C–590A. Applying this principle I would hold that paragraphs 37 and 37A leave untouched the fundamental and basic rights asserted by the applicants in the present case.

The only relevant issue in the present proceedings is whether paragraphs 37 and 37A are ultra vires because they are in conflict with the fundamental and basic rights claimed by the applicants. The principle of legality justifies the conclusion that paragraphs 37 and 37A have not been demonstrated to be ultra vires in the cases under consideration.

3. The disposal of the appeal

My Lords, my judgment does not involve tearing up the rule book governing prisons. On the contrary I have taken full account of the essential public interest in maintaining order and discipline in prisons. But, I am satisfied that consistently with order and discipline in prisons it is administratively workable to allow prisoners to be interviewed for the narrow purposes here at stake notably if a proper foundation is laid in correspondence for the requested interview or interviews. One has to recognise that oral interviews with journalists are not in the same category as visits by relatives and friends and require more careful control and regulation. That is achievable. This view is supported by the favourable judgment of past experience. Moreover, in reality an oral interview is simply a necessary and practical extension of the right of a prisoner to correspond to journalists about his conviction: compare *Silver* v *United Kingdom* (1980) 3 EHRR 475 (the commission): 5 EHRR, 347 (the court) and Livingstone & Owen, *Prison Law*, 2nd ed. (1999), pp. 228–230, paras 7.30–7.33.

The criminal justice system has been shown to be fallible. Yet the effect of the judgment of the Court of Appeal is to outlaw the safety valve of effective investigative journalism. In my judgment the conclusions and reasoning of the Court of Appeal were wrong.

Declarations should be granted in both cases to the effect that the Home Secretary's current policy is unlawful, and that the governors' administrative decisions pursuant to that policy were also unlawful. I would allow both appeals.

While the rules were *intra vires*, the policy was unlawful.

NOTES

1. The decision is based on common law and not the Human Rights Act 1998, the entry into force of which it pre-dated by some 14 months.
2. In *R (Daly)* v *Secretary of State for the Home Department* [2001] UKHL 26, [2001] 2 AC 532, p. 487, *ante*, and p. 584, *post*, their Lordships accepted that there were some fundamental rights recognized by the common law which included access to a court; access to legal advice; and the right to communicate confidentially with a legal adviser under the seal of legal professional privilege, which only the express words of a statute could restrict. Accordingly the policy on searching cells including papers covered by legal professional privilege without the prisoner being present was unlawful under both the common law and the Human Rights Acts 1998.

C: Procedural impropriety

In *CCSU* v *Minister for the Civil Service* (p. 534, *ante*) Lord Diplock used this phrase specifically to include a breach both of express statutory procedural requirements and the common law rules of natural justice. Express statutory requirements include, for example, a requirement to give notice or to consult certain persons before a decision is made. Whether or not a breach of a statutory requirement will render the resulting decision invalid depends on a number of circumstances, including the importance of the provision which has been disregarded in the light of the objects of the statute, whether there was total or only partial breach of the requirement, and whether or not the breach caused any prejudice (see, for example, *Coney* v *Choyce* [1975] 1 All ER 979; *Bradbury* v *London Borough of Enfield* [1967] 3 All ER 434; *London and Clydeside Estates Ltd* v *Aberdeen DC* [1979] 2 All ER 876). This section will focus on the common law rules of natural justice.

Council of Civil Service Unions v *Minister for the Civil Service*

[1985] AC 374, House of Lords

The facts are set out, *post*, at p. 576.

LORD ROSKILL: ...the use of this phrase [natural justice] is no doubt hallowed by time and much judicial repetition, but it is a phrase often widely misunderstood and therefore as often misused. The phrase perhaps might now be allowed to find a permanent resting place and be better replaced by speaking of a duty to act fairly. But the latter phrase must not in its turn be misunderstood or misused. It is not for the courts to determine whether a particular policy or particular decisions taken in fulfilment of that policy are fair. They are only concerned with the manner in which those decision have been taken and the extent of the duty to act fairly will vary greatly from case to case as indeed the decided cases since 1950 consistently show. Many features will come into play including the nature of the decision and the relationship of those involved on either side before the decision was taken.

NOTE: The use of the phrase 'duty to act fairly' rather than 'natural justice' is frequently traced to the decision in *Re HK* [1967] 2 QB 617 where it was held that, although immigration officers were not obliged to hold a hearing before determining an immigrant's status, they were obliged to act fairly. Since then there has been a difference of opinion on the correct use of the two phrases. In *McInnes* v *Onslow Fane* [1978] 1 WLR 1520 Megarry V-C stated that 'the further the situation is away from anything that resembles a judicial or quasi-judicial decision, and the further the question is removed from what may reasonably be called a justiciable question, the more appropriate it is to reject an expression which includes the word justice and to use instead terms such as "fairness" or "the duty to act fairly".' Other judges have used the phrases interchangeably. What did Lord Roskill state on this point and why?

A related difficulty is whether there is any difference between the content of natural justice and the content of the duty to be fair. On one view, which appears to be that of both Lord Roskill and Megarry V-C, there is no difference: the content of natural justice and the content of the duty to be fair are both flexible and depend on all the circumstances of the case. Another view, however, is that the duty to be fair might include requirements which were not part of the traditional concept of natural justice, for example a duty to act on evidence (see *R* v *Deputy Industrial Injuries Commissioner, ex parte Moore* [1965] 1 QB 456).

In the notes and questions which follow, reference will be made to the duty to be fair. The cases cited will, however, contain references to both concepts for the reasons explained above.

What then is required of the duty to be fair? As Lord Fraser indicated in *CCSU* v *Minister for the Civil Service*, the requirements of fairness depend on all the circumstances of the case. In an earlier case, *Russell* v *Duke of Norfolk* [1949] 1 All ER 109, in which the term natural justice was used, Tucker LJ stated, at p. 118:

> ...There are, in my view, no words which are of universal application to every kind of inquiry and every kind of domestic tribunal. The requirements of natural justice must depend on the circumstances of the case, the nature of the inquiry, the rules under which the tribunal is acting, the subject matter which is being dealt with and so forth. Accordingly, I do not derive much assistance from the definitions of natural justice which have been from time to time used....

The requirements of the duty to be fair are generally divided into two general principles, the rule against bias and the right to a fair hearing.

(a) The rule against bias

R v *Bow Street Metropolitan Stipendiary Magistrate, ex parte Pinochet Ugarte (No. 2)*

[2000] 1 AC 119, House of Lords

The applicant was the former head of state of Chile. Extradition proceedings were brought at the request of a Spanish judge in respect of allegations of crimes against humanity committed when the applicant was President of Chile. Two arrest warrants had been issued by the magistrate, but they had been quashed in an application for judicial review; however, the quashing of the second was stayed so that an appeal could be heard by the House of Lords on the scope of immunity of a former head of state from arrest and extradition proceedings in the United Kingdom in respect of acts committed while he was head of state. Amnesty International (AI) was permitted to act as a third-party intervenor in these proceedings. By a 3:2 majority the appeal was allowed on 25 November 1998 and the second warrant was restored. Afterwards the applicant learnt that Lord Hoffmann, who was a member of the majority in the appeal before the House of Lords, was a member and chairman of Amnesty International Charity Ltd (AICL), a body which carried out AI's charitable purposes. The applicant petitioned the House to set aside the order of 25 November.

> LORD BROWNE-WILKINSON: ...The contention is that there was a real danger or reasonable apprehension or suspicion that Lord Hoffmann might have been biased, that is to say, it is alleged that there is an appearance of bias not actual bias.
>
> The fundamental principle is that a man may not be a judge in his own cause. This principle, as developed by the courts, has two very similar but not identical implications. First it may be applied literally: if a judge is in fact a party to the litigation or has a financial or proprietary interest in its outcome then he is indeed sitting as a judge in his own cause. In that case, the mere fact that he is a party to the action or has a financial or proprietary interest in its outcome is sufficient to cause his automatic disqualification. The second application of the principle is where a judge is not a party to the suit and does not have a financial interest in its outcome, but in some other way his conduct or behaviour may give rise to a suspicion that he is not impartial, for example because of his friendship with a party. This second type of case is not strictly speaking an application of the principle that a man must not be judge in his own cause, since the judge will not normally be himself benefiting, but providing a benefit for another by failing to be impartial.
>
> In my judgment, this case falls within the first category of case, viz. where the judge is disqualified because he is a judge in his own cause. In such a case, once it is shown that the judge is himself a party to the cause, or has a relevant interest in its subject matter, he is disqualified without any investigation into whether there was a likelihood or suspicion of bias. The mere fact of his interest is sufficient to disqualify him unless he has made sufficient disclosure: see Shetreet, *Judges on Trial* (1976), p. 303; De Smith,

Woolf and Jowell, *Judicial Review of Administrative Action*, 5th ed. (1995) p. 525, I will call this 'automatic disqualification'.

In *Dimes* v *Proprietors of Grand Junction Canal* (1852) 3 HL Cas 759, the then Lord Chancellor, Lord Cottenham, owned a substantial shareholding in the defendant canal which was an incorporated body. In the action the Lord Chancellor sat on appeal from the Vice-Chancellor, whose judgment in favour of the company he affirmed. There was an appeal to your Lordships' House on the grounds that the Lord Chancellor was disqualified. Their Lordships consulted the judges who advised, at p. 786, that Lord Cottenham was disqualified from sitting as a judge in the cause because he had an interest in the suit. This advice was unanimously accepted by their Lordships. There was no inquiry by the court as to whether a reasonable man would consider Lord Cottenham to be biased and no inquiry as to the circumstances which led to Lord Cottenham sitting. Lord Campbell said, at p. 793:

> No one can suppose that Lord Cottenham could be, in the remotest degree, influenced by the interest he had in this concern: but, my Lords, it is of the last importance that the maxim that no man is to be a judge in his own cause should be held sacred. And that is not to be confined to a cause *in which he a party*, but applies to a cause in which he has an interest. (Emphasis added.)

On occasion, this proposition is elided so as to omit all references to the disqualification of a judge who is a party to the suit: see, for example, *Reg.* v *Rand* (1866) LR 1 QB 230; *Reg.* v *Gough* [1993] AC 646, 661. This does not mean that a judge who is a party to a suit is not disqualified just because the suit does not involve a financial interest. The authorities cited in the *Dimes* case show how the principle developed. The starting-point was the case in which a judge was indeed purporting to decide a case in which he was a party. This was held to be absolutely prohibited. That absolute prohibition was then extended to cases where, although not nominally a party, the judge had an interest in the outcome.

The importance of this point in the present ease is this. Neither AI, nor AICL have any financial interest in the outcome of this litigation. We are here confronted, as was Lord Hoffmann, with a novel situation where the outcome of the litigation did not lead to financial benefit to anyone. The interest of AI in the litigation was not financial: it was its interest in achieving the trial and possible conviction of Senator Pinochet for crimes against humanity.

By seeking to intervene in this appeal and being allowed so to intervene, in practice AI became a party to the appeal. Therefore if, in the circumstances, it is right to treat Lord Hoffmann as being the alter ego of AI and therefore a judge in his own cause, then he must have been automatically disqualified on the grounds that he was a party to the appeal. Alternatively, even if it be not right to say that Lord Hoffmann was a party to the appeal as such, the question then arises whether, in non-financial litigation, anything other than a financial or proprietary interest in the outcome is sufficient automatically to disqualify a man from sitting as judge in the cause.

Are the facts such as to require Lord Hoffmann to be treated as being himself a party to this appeal? The facts are striking and unusual. One of the parties to the appeal is an unincorporated association, AI. One of the constituent parts of that unincorporated association is AICL. AICL was established, for tax purposes, to carry out part of the functions of AI those parts which were charitable which had previously been carried on either by AI itself or by AIL. Lord Hoffmann is a director and chairman of ALCL, which is wholly controlled by AI, since its members (who ultimately control it) are all the members of the international executive committee of AI. A large part of the work of AI is as a matter of strict law, carried on by AICL which instructs AIL, to do the work on its behalf. In reality, AI, AICL and AIL are a close-knit group carrying on the work of AI.

However, close as these links are, I do not think it would be right to identify Lord Hoffmann personally as being a party to the appeal. He is closely linked to AI but he is not in fact AI. Although this is an area in which legal technicality is particularly to be avoided, it cannot be ignored that Lord Hoffmann took no part in running AI. Lord Hoffmann, AICL and the executive committee of AI are in law separate people.

Then is this a case in which it can be said that Lord Hoffmann had an 'interest' which must lead to his automatic disqualification? Hitherto only pecuniary and proprietary interests have led to automatic disqualification. But, as I have indicated, this litigation is most unusual. It is not civil litigation but criminal litigation. Most unusually, by allowing AI to intervene, there is a party to a criminal cause or matter who is neither prosecutor nor accused. That party, AI, shares with the government of Spain and the CPS, not a financial interest but an interest to establish that there is no immunity for ex-heads of state in relation to crimes against humanity. The interest of these parties is to procure Senator Pinochet's extradition and trial a non-pecuniary interest. So far as AICL is concerned, clause 3(c) of its memorandum provides that one of its objects is 'to procure the abolition of torture, extra-judicial execution and disappearance'. AI has, amongst other objects, the same objects. Although AICL, as a charity, cannot campaign to change the law, it is concerned by other means to procure the abolition of these crimes against humanity. In my opinion, therefore, AICL plainly had a non-pecuniary interest, to establish that Senator Pinochet was not immune.

That being the case, the question is whether in the very unusual circumstances of this case a non-pecuniary interest to achieve a particular result is sufficient to give rise to automatic disqualification and, if so, whether the fact that AICL had such an interest necessarily leads to the conclusion that Lord Hoffmann, as a director of AICL, was automatically disqualified from sitting on the appeal? My Lords, in my judgment, although the cases have all dealt with automatic disqualification on the grounds of pecuniary interest, there is no good reason in principle for so limiting automatic disqualification. The rationale of the whole rule is that a man cannot be a judge in his own cause. In civil litigation the matters in issue will normally have an economic impact; therefore a judge is automatically disqualified if he stands to make a financial gain as a consequence of his own decision of the case. But if, as in the present case, the matter at issue does not relate to money or economic advantage but is concerned with the promotion of the cause, the rationale disqualifying a judge applies just as much if the judge's decision will lead to the promotion of a cause in which the judge is involved together with one of the parties. Thus in my opinion if Lord Hoffmann had been at member of AI he would have been automatically disqualified because of his non-pecuniary interest in establishing that Senator Pinochet was not entitled to immunity. Indeed, so much I understood to have been conceded by Mr Duffy.

Can it make any difference that, instead of being a direct member of AI Lord Hoffmann is a director of AICL, that is of a company which is wholly controlled by AI and is carrying on much of its work? Surely not. The substance of the matter is that AI, AIL and AICL are all various parts of an entity or movement working in different fields towards the same goals. If the absolute impartiality of the judiciary is to be maintained, there must be a rule which automatically disqualifies a judge who is involved, whether personally or as a director of a company, in promoting the same causes in the same organisation as is a party to the suit. There is no room for fine distinctions if Lord Hewart CJ's famous dictum is to be observed: it is 'of fundamental importance that justice should not only be done, but should manifestly and undoubtedly be seen to be done': see *Rex* v *Sussex Justices, Ex parte McCarthy* [1924] 1 KB 256, 259.

...

It is important not to overstate what is being decided. It was suggested in argument that a decision setting aside the order of 25 November 1998 would lead to a position where judges would be unable to sit on cases involving charities in whose work they are involved. It is suggested that, because of such involvement, a judge would be disqualified. That is not correct. The facts of this present case are exceptional. The critical elements are (1) that AI was a party to the appeal; (2) that AI was joined in order to argue for a particular result; (3) the judge was a director of a charity closely allied to AI and sharing, in this respect, AI's objects. Only in cases where a judge is taking an active role as trustee or director of a charity which is closely allied to and acting with a party to the litigation should a judge normally be concerned either to recuse himself or disclose the position to the parties. However, there may well be other exceptional cases in which the judge would be well advised to disclose a possible interest.

Finally on this aspect of the case, we were asked to state in giving judgment what had been said and done within the Appellate Committee in relation to Amnesty International during the hearing leading to the order of 25 November. As is apparent from what I have said, such matters are irrelevant to what we have to decide: in the absence of any disclosure to the parties of Lord Hoffmann's involvement with AI such involvement either did or did not in law disqualify him regardless of what happened within the Appellate Committee. We therefore did not investigate those matters and make no findings as to them.

Election, waiver, abuse of process

Mr Alun Jones submitted that by raising with the Home Secretary the possible bias of Lord Hoffmann as a ground for not authorising the extradition to proceed, Senator Pinochet had elected to choose the Home Secretary rather than your Lordships' House as the arbiter as to whether such bias did or did not exist. Consequently, he submitted, Senator Pinochet had waived his right to petition your Lordships and, by doing so immediately after the Home Secretary had rejected the submission, was committing an abuse of the process of the House.

This submission is bound to fail on a number of different grounds, of which I need mention only two. First, Senator Pinochet would only be put to his election as between two alternative courses to adopt. I cannot see that there are two such courses in the present case, since the Home Secretary had no power in the matter. He could not set aside the order of 25 November and as long as such order stood, the Home Secretary was bound to accept it as stating the law. Secondly, all three concepts—election, waiver and abuse of process require that the person said to have elected etc. has acted freely and in full knowledge of the facts. Not until 8 December 1998 did Senator Pinochet's solicitors know anything of Lord Hoffmann's position as a director and chairman of AICL. Even then they did not know anything about AICL and its constitution. To say that by hurriedly notifying the Home Secretary of the contents of the letter from AI's solicitors Senator Pinochet had elected to pursue the point solely before the Home Secretary is unrealistic. Senator Pinochet had not yet had time to find out anything about the circumstances beyond the bare facts disclosed in the letter.

...

LORD HOPE: ...As for the facts of the present case, it seems to me that the conclusion is inescapable that Amnesty International has associated itself in these proceedings with the position of the prosecutor. The prosecution is not being brought in its name, but its interest in the case is to achieve the same result because it also seeks to bring Senator Pinochet to justice. This distinguishes its position fundamentally from that of other bodies which seek to uphold human rights without extending their objects to issues concerning personal responsibility. It has for many years conducted an international campaign against those individuals whom it has identified as having been responsible for torture, extra-judicial executions and disappearances. Its aim is that they should be made to suffer criminal penalties for such gross violations of human rights. It has chosen, by its intervention in these proceedings, to bring itself face to face with one of those individuals against whom it has for so long campaigned.

But everyone whom the prosecutor seeks to bring to justice is entitled to the protection of the law, however grave the offence or offences with which he is being prosecuted. Senator Pinochet is entitled to the judgment of an impartial and independent tribunal on the question which has been raised here as to his immunity. I think that the connections which existed between Lord Hoffmann and Amnesty International were of such a character, in view of their duration and proximity, as to disqualify him on this ground. In view of his links with Amnesty International as the chairman and a director of Amnesty International Charity Ltd. he could not be seen to be impartial. There has been no suggestion that he was actually biased. He had no financial or pecuniary interest in the outcome. But his relationship with Amnesty International was such that he was, in effect, acting as a judge in his own cause. I consider that his failure to disclose these connections leads inevitably to the conclusion that the decision to which he was a party must be set aside.

...

Petition granted.

Locabail (UK) Ltd* v *Bayfield Properties Ltd

[2000] QB 451, Court of Appeal

LORD BINGHAM of CORNHILL CJ, LORD WOOLF MR and SIR RICHARD SCOTT V-C: ...

18. When applying the test of real danger or possibility (as opposed to the test of automatic disqualification under *Dimes'* case and *Ex p Pinochet (No. 2)* it will very often be appropriate to inquire whether the judge knew of the matter relied on as appearing to undermine his impartiality, because if it is shown that he did not know of it the danger of its having influenced his judgment is eliminated and the appearance of possible bias is dispelled. As the Court of Appeal of New Zealand observed in *Auckland Casino Ltd* v *Casino Control Authority* [1995] 1 NZLR 142 at 148, if the judge were ignorant of the allegedly disqualifying interest: '...there would be no real danger of bias, as no one could suppose that the Judge could be unconsciously affected by that of which he knew nothing...'

19. It is noteworthy that in *R* v *Gough* evidence was received from the juror whose impartiality was in issue (see pp. 651E and 658D), and reliance was placed on that evidence (see p. 652F); both in the Court of Appeal and the House of Lords it was accepted that if the correct test was the real danger or possibility test the appeal could not succeed, since the allegedly disqualifying association had admittedly not been known to the juror at the time when the verdict had been returned, and therefore there was no possibility that it could have affected her decision (see pp. 652D, 660G and 670G). While a reviewing court may

receive a written statement from any judge, lay justice or juror specifying what he or she knew at any relevant time, the court is not necessarily bound to accept such statement at its face value. Much will depend on the nature of the fact of which ignorance is asserted, the source of the statement, the effect of any corroborative or contradictory statement, the inherent probabilities and all the circumstances of the case in question. Often the court will have no hesitation in accepting the reliability of such a statement; occasionally, if rarely, it may doubt the reliability of the statement; sometimes, although inclined to accept the statement, it may recognise the possibility of doubt and the likelihood of public scepticism. All will turn on the facts of the particular case. There can, however, be no question of cross-examining or seeking disclosure from the judge. Nor will the reviewing court pay attention to any statement by the judge concerning the impact of any knowledge on his mind or his decision: the insidious nature of bias makes such a statement of little value, and it is for the reviewing court and not the judge whose impartiality is challenged to assess the risk that some illegitimate extraneous consideration may have influenced the decision.

20. When members of the Bar are appointed to sit judicially, whether full-time or part-time, they may ordinarily be expected to know of any past or continuing professional or personal association which might impair or be thought to impair their judicial impartiality. They will know of their own affairs, and the independent, self-employed status of barristers practising in chambers will relieve them of any responsibility for, and (usually) any detailed knowledge of, the affairs of other members of the same chambers. The position of solicitors is somewhat different, for a solicitor who is a partner in a firm of solicitors is legally responsible for the professional acts of his partners and does as a partner owe a duty to clients of the firm for whom he or she personally may never have acted and of whose affairs he or she personally may know nothing. While it is vital to safeguard the integrity of court proceedings, it is also important to ensure that the rules are not applied in such a way as to inhibit the increasingly valuable contribution which solicitors are making to the discharge of judicial functions. Problems are, we apprehend, very much more likely to arise when a solicitor is sitting in a part-time capacity, and in civil rather than criminal proceedings. But we think that problems can usually be overcome if, before embarking on the trial of any assigned civil case, the solicitor (whether sitting as deputy district judge, assistant recorder, recorder or s. 9 judge) conducts a careful conflict search within the firm of which he is a partner. Such a search, however carefully conducted and however sophisticated the firm's internal systems, is unlikely to be omission-proof. While parties for and against whom the firm has acted, and parties closely associated, would (we hope) be identified, the possibility must exist that individuals involved in such parties, and parties more remotely associated, may not be identified. When in the course of a trial properly embarked upon some such association comes to light (as could equally happen with a barrister-judge), the association should be disclosed and addressed, bearing in mind the test laid down in *Reg.* v *Gough*. The proper resolution of any such problem will, again, depend on the facts of the case.

21. In any case giving rise to automatic disqualification on the authority of *Dimes'* case 3 H.L. Cas and *Ex parte Pinochet (No. 2)* [2000] 1 AC 119, the judge should recuse himself from the case before any objection is raised. The same course should be followed if, for solid reasons, the judge feels personally embarrassed in hearing the case. In either event it is highly desirable, if extra cost, delay and inconvenience are to be avoided, that the judge should stand down at the earliest possible stage, not waiting until the eve or the day of the hearing. Parties should not be confronted with a last-minute choice between adjournment and waiver of an otherwise valid objection. If, in any case not giving rise to automatic disqualification and not causing personal embarrassment to the judge, he or she is or becomes aware of any matter which could arguably be said to give rise to a real danger of bias, it is generally desirable that disclosure should be made to the parties in advance of the hearing. If objection is then made, it will be the duty of the judge to consider the objection and exercise his judgment upon it. He would be as wrong to yield to a tenuous or frivolous objection as he would to ignore an objection of substance. We find force in observations of the Constitutional Court of South Africa in *President of the Republic of South Africa* v *South African Rugby Football Union* 1999 (4) SA 147 at 177, even though these observations were directed to the reasonable suspicion test:

> It follows from the foregoing that the correct approach to this application for the recusal of members of this Court is objective and the *onus* of establishing it rests upon the applicant. The question is whether a reasonable, objective and informed person would on the correct facts reasonably apprehend that the Judge has not or will not bring an impartial mind to bear on the adjudication of the case, that is a mind open to persuasion by the evidence and the submissions of counsel. The

> reasonableness of the apprehension must be assessed in the light of the oath of office taken by the Judges to administer justice without fear or favour; and their ability to carry out that oath by reason of their training and experience. It must be assumed that they can disabuse their minds of any irrelevant personal beliefs or predispositions. They must take into account the fact that they have a duty to sit in any case in which they are not obliged to recuse themselves. At the same time, it must never be forgotten that an impartial judge is a fundamental prerequisite for a fair trial and a judicial officer should not hesitate to recuse herself or himself if there are reasonable grounds on the part of a litigant for apprehending that the judicial officer, for whatever reasons, was not or will not be impartial.

22. We also find great persuasive force in three extracts from Australian authority. In *Re JRL, ex p CJL*, (1986) 161 CLR 342 at 352 Mason J, sitting in the High Court of Australia, said:

> Although it is important that justice must be seen to be done, it is equally important that judicial officers discharge their duty to sit and do not, by acceding too readily to suggestions of appearance of bias, encourage parties to believe that by seeking the disqualification of a judge, they will have their case tried by someone thought to be more likely to decide the case in their favour.

23. In *Re Ebner, Ebner* v *Official Trustee in Bankruptcy* (1999) 161 ALR 557 at 568 (para. 37) the Federal Court asked:

> Why is it to be assumed that the confidence of fair-minded people in the administration of justice would be shaken by the existence of a direct pecuniary interest of no tangible value, but not by the waste of resources and the delays brought about by setting aside a judgment on the ground that the judge is disqualified for having such an interest?

24. In the *Clenae* case [1999] VSCA 35 Callaway JA observed (para. 89(e)):

> As a general rule, it is the duty of a judicial officer to hear and determine the cases allocated to him or her by his or her head of jurisdiction. Subject to certain limited exceptions, a judge or magistrate should not accede to an unfounded disqualification application.

25. It would be dangerous and futile to attempt to define or list the factors which may or may not give rise to a real danger of bias. Everything will depend on the facts, which may include the nature of the issue to be decided. We cannot, however, conceive of circumstances in which an objection could be soundly based on the religion, ethnic or national origin, gender, age, class, means or sexual orientation of the judge. Nor, at any rate ordinarily, could an objection be soundly based on the judge's social or educational or service or employment background or history, nor that of any member of the judge's family; or previous political associations; or membership of social or sporting or charitable bodies; or Masonic associations; or previous judicial decisions; or extra-curricular utterances (whether in textbooks, lectures, speeches, articles, interviews, reports or responses to consultation papers); or previous receipt of instructions to act for or against any party, solicitor or advocate engaged in a case before him; or membership of the same Inn, circuit, local Law Society or chambers (*KFTCIC* v *Icori Estero SpA* (Court of Appeal of Paris, 28 June 1991, International Arbitration Report, vol 6, 8/91)). By contrast, a real danger of bias might well be thought to arise if there were personal friendship or animosity between the judge and any member of the public involved in the case; or if the judge were closely acquainted with any member of the public involved in the case, particularly if the credibility of that individual could be significant in the decision of the case; or if, in a case where the credibility of any individual were an issue to be decided by the judge, he had in a previous case rejected the evidence of that person in such outspoken terms as to throw doubt on his ability to approach such person's evidence with an open mind on any later occasion; or if on any question at issue in the proceedings before him the judge had expressed views, particularly in the course of the hearing, in such extreme and unbalanced terms as to throw doubt on his ability to try the issue with an objective judicial mind (see *Vakauta* v *Kelly* (1989) 167 CLR 568); or if, for any other reason, there were real ground for doubting the ability of the judge to ignore extraneous considerations, prejudices and predilections and bring an objective judgment to bear on the issues before him. The mere fact that a judge, earlier in the same case or in a previous case, had commented adversely on a party or witness, or found the evidence of a party or witness to be unreliable, would not without more found a sustainable objection. In most cases, we think, the answer, one way or the other, will be obvious. But if in any case there is real ground for doubt, that doubt should be resolved in favour of recusal. We repeat:

every application must be decided on the facts and circumstances of the individual case. The greater the passage of time between the event relied on as showing a danger of bias and the case in which the objection is raised, the weaker (other things being equal) the objection will be.

26. We do not consider that waiver, in this context, raises special problems (*Shrager* v *Basil Dighton Ltd* [1924] 1 KB 274 at 293; *R* v *Essex Justices, ex p Perkins* [1927] 2 KB 475 at 489; *Ex parte Pinochet (No. 2)* [2000] 1 AC 119, 136–137, the *Auckland Casino* case [1995] 1 NZLR 142 at 150–151 and *Vakauta* v *Kelly* (1989) 167 CLR 568 at 572, 577). If, appropriate disclosure having been made by the judge, a party raises no objection to the judge hearing or continuing to hear a case, that party cannot thereafter complain of the matter disclosed as giving rise to a real danger of bias. It would be unjust to the other party and undermine both the reality and the appearance of justice to allow him to do so. What disclosure is appropriate depends in large measure on the stage that the matter has reached. If, before a hearing has begun, the judge is alerted to some matter which might, depending on the full facts, throw doubt on his fitness to sit, the judge should in our view inquire into the full facts, so far as they are ascertainable, in order to make disclosure in the light of them. But if a judge has embarked on a hearing in ignorance of a matter which emerges during the hearing, it is in our view enough if the judge discloses what he then knows. He has no obligation to disclose what he does not know. Nor is he bound to fill any gaps in his knowledge which, if filled, might provide stronger grounds for objection to his hearing or continuing to hear the case. If, of course, he does make further inquiry and learn additional facts not known to him before, then he must make disclosure of those facts also. It is, however, generally undesirable that hearings should be aborted unless the reality or the appearance of justice requires that they should.

NOTES

1. The specially staffed Court of Appeal was here dealing with five applications for permission to appeal on the ground of bias of the judge. The listing and hearing together of these applications enabled the court to give this guidance. In *Locabail (UK) Ltd* v *Bayfield Properties Ltd, Locabail (UK) Ltd* v *Waldorf Investment Corp; Williams* v *HM Inspector of Taxes,* and *R* v *Bristol Betting and Gaming Licensing Committee, ex parte O'Callaghan,* permission to appeal was not granted. In *Timmins* v *Gormley,* the defendant in a personal injuries case successfully argued that the articles in legal publications written by the recorder who heard the case, in which he expressed pronounced pro-claimant anti-insurer views, allowed for the possibility that the recorder might lean in favour of the claimant and against the defendant. The Court held that it was not wrong for the recorder to be engaged in writing but that it is 'inappropriate for a judge to use intemperate language about subjects on which he has adjudicated or will have to adjudicate'.
2. There has been debate over what is the appropriate test for apparent bias.

Porter v *Magill*

[2001] UKHL 67, [2002] 2 AC 357, House of Lords

LORD HOPE OF CRAIGHEAD: ...

101. The English courts have been reluctant, for obvious reasons, to depart from the test which Lord Goff of Chieveley so carefully formulated in *R v Gough.* In *R v Bow Street Metropolitan Stipendiary Magistrate, Ex p Pinochet Ugarte (No 2)* [2000] 1 AC 119, 136A–C Lord Browne-Wilkinson said that it was unnecessary in that case to determine whether it needed to be reviewed in the light of subsequent decisions in Canada, New Zealand and Australia. I said, at p 142F–G, that, although the tests in Scotland and England were described differently, their application was likely in practice to lead to results that were so similar as to be indistinguishable. The Court of Appeal, having examined the question whether the "real danger" test might lead to a different result from that which the informed observer would reach on the same facts, concluded in *Locabail (UK) Ltd v Bayfield Properties Ltd* [2000] QB 451, 477 that in the overwhelming majority of cases the application of the two tests would lead to the same outcome.

102. In my opinion however it is now possible to set this debate to rest. The Court of Appeal took the opportunity in *In re Medicaments and Related Classes of Goods (No 2)* [2001] 1 WLR 700 to reconsider the whole question. Lord Phillips of Worth Matravers MR, giving the judgment of the court, observed, at p 711A–B, that the precise test to be applied when determining whether a decision should be set aside on account of bias had given rise to difficulty, reflected in judicial decisions that had appeared in conflict, and

that the attempt to resolve that conflict in *R v Gough* had not commanded universal approval. At p 711B–C he said that, as the alternative test had been thought to be more closely in line with Strasbourg jurisprudence which since 2 October 2000 the English courts were required to take into account, the occasion should now be taken to review *R v Gough* to see whether the test it lays down is, indeed, in conflict with Strasbourg jurisprudence. Having conducted that review he summarised the court's conclusions, at pp 726H–727C:

> 85 When the Strasbourg jurisprudence is taken into account, we believe that a modest adjustment of the test in *R v Gough* is called for, which makes it plain that it is, in effect, no different from the test applied in most of the Commonwealth and in Scotland. The court must first ascertain all the circumstances which have a bearing on the suggestion that the judge was biased. It must then ask whether those circumstances would lead a fair-minded and informed observer to conclude that there was a real possibility, or a real danger, the two being the same, that the tribunal was biased.

103. I respectfully suggest that your Lordships should now approve the modest adjustment of the test in *R v Gough* set out in that paragraph. It expresses in clear and simple language a test which is in harmony with the objective test which the Strasbourg court applies when it is considering whether the circumstances give rise to a reasonable apprehension of bias. It removes any possible conflict with the test which is now applied in most Commonwealth countries and in Scotland. I would however delete from it the reference to "a real danger". Those words no longer serve a useful purpose here, and they are not used in the jurisprudence of the Strasbourg court. The question is whether the fair-minded and informed observer, having considered the facts, would conclude that there was a real possibility that the tribunal was biased.

R v Abdroikov, R v Green, R v Williamson

[2007] UKHL 37, [2007] 1 WLR 2679, House of Lords

Bias was raised to challenge convictions where a member of the jury in criminal trials was a police officer in the first two cases, and a solicitor in the Crown Prosecution Service in the third.

LORD BINGHAM OF CORNHILL: . . . 25 In the case of the first appellant, it was unfortunate that the identity of the officer became known at such a late stage in the trial, and on very short notice to the judge and defence counsel. But had the matter been ventilated at the outset of the trial, it is difficult to see what argument defence counsel could have urged other than the general undesirability of police officers serving on juries, a difficult argument to advance in face of the parliamentary enactment. It was not a case which turned on a contest between the evidence of the police and that of the appellant, and it would have been hard to suggest that the case was one in which unconscious prejudice, even if present, would have been likely to operate to the disadvantage of the appellant, and it makes no difference that the officer was the foreman of the jury. In the event, confronted with this question at very short notice, defence counsel raised no objection. I conclude, not without unease, that having regard to the parliamentary enactment the Court of Appeal reached the right conclusion in this case, and I would dismiss the appeal.

26. The second appellant's case is different. Here, there was a crucial dispute on the evidence between the appellant and the police sergeant, and the sergeant and the juror, although not personally known to each other, shared the same local service background. In this context the instinct (however unconscious) of a police officer on the jury to prefer the evidence of a brother officer to that of a drug-addicted defendant would be judged by the fair-minded and informed observer to be a real and possible source of unfairness, beyond the reach of standard judicial warnings and directions. The second appellant was not tried by a tribunal which was and appeared to be impartial. It cannot be supposed that Parliament intended to infringe the rule in the *Sussex Justices* case, still less to do so without express language. I would allow this appeal, and quash the second appellant's conviction.

27. In the case of the third appellant, no possible criticism is to be made of Mr McKay-Smith, who acted in strict compliance with the guidance given to him and left the matter to the judge. But the judge gave no serious consideration to the objection of defence counsel, who himself had little opportunity to review

the law on this subject. It must, perhaps, be doubted whether Lord Justice Auld or Parliament contemplated that employed Crown prosecutors would sit as jurors in prosecutions brought by their own authority. It is in my opinion clear that justice is not seen to be done if one discharging the very important neutral role of juror is a full-time, salaried, long-serving employee of the prosecutor. This is a much stronger case than *Pullar v United Kingdom* (1996) 22 EHRR 391 (see para 17 above): it is as if, on the facts of that case, F had been employed in the department of the procurator fiscal. Had that been so, one may be sure the court would have agreed with the commission. The third appellant was entitled to be tried by a tribunal that was and appeared to be impartial, and in my opinion he was not. The consequence is that his convictions must be quashed. This is a most unfortunate outcome, since the third appellant was accused of very grave crimes, of which he may have been guilty. But even a guilty defendant is entitled to be tried by an impartial tribunal and the consequence is inescapable. I would allow the appeal and remit the case to the Court of Appeal with an invitation to quash the convictions and rule on any application which may be made for a retrial.

NOTE: Lords Rodger and Carswell dissented on the second and third appeals arguing that the Criminal Justice Act 2003 in amending the qualifications on jurors had added to the existing risk that people of similar backgrounds to parties in a trial might unconsciously favour them and that the fair-minded and informed observer would have realized that given there are 12 members of a jury, while there is a possible risk of one juror being partial this does not meant that there is a real possibility that the jury is incapable of reaching an impartial verdict.

(b) Right to a fair hearing

Ridge v *Baldwin*

[1964] AC 40, House of Lords

Following his arrest and charge for conspiracy to obstruct the course of justice, Ridge, the Chief Constable of Brighton, was suspended from duty. At his trial Ridge was acquitted but the judge was critical of his leadership of the force. A further charge of corruption was brought against Ridge and the judge repeated these comments when directing Ridge's acquittal.

Under the Municipal Corporations Act 1882, s. 191(4) a watch committee could dismiss 'any borough constable whom they think negligent in the discharge of his duty, or otherwise unfit for the same'. After Ridge's acquittal the watch committee met and decided that Ridge should be dismissed. Ridge was not asked to attend the meeting, but at the request of his solicitor the watch committee reconvened some days later and decided not to change its original decision. Before this second meeting Ridge gave notice of appeal to the Home Secretary against the original decision under the Police (Appeals) Act 1927. He also stated, however, that this was without prejudice to his right to argue that the procedure adopted by the committee was in breach of the relevant statutory provisions and of the rules of natural justice. The Home Secretary dismissed his appeal and Ridge appealed to the courts, seeking a declaration that the purported dismissal was *ultra vires*. Ridge, whose case failed before Streatfield J and the Court of Appeal, appealed to the House of Lords. The following extract deals with his claim that there was a breach of natural justice.

LORD REID: The appellant's case is that in proceeding under the Act of 1882 the watch committee were bound to observe what are commonly called the principles of natural justice. Before attempting to reach any decision they were bound to inform him of the grounds on which they proposed to act and give him a fair opportunity of being heard in his own defence. The authorities on the applicability of the principles of natural justice are in some confusion, and so I find it necessary to examine this matter in some detail. The principle audi alteram partem goes back many centuries in our law and appears in a multitude of judgments of judges of the highest authority. In modern times opinions have sometimes been expressed to the effect that natural justice is so vague as to be almost meaningless. But I would regard these as tainted by the perennial fallacy that because something cannot be cut and dried or nicely weighed and measured therefore it does not exist. . . . It appears to me that one reason why the authorities on natural justice have been found difficult to reconcile is that insufficient attention has been paid to the great difference between various kinds of cases in which it has been sought to apply the principle. What a minister ought to do in considering objections to a scheme may be very different from what a watch committee ought to do in considering whether to dismiss a chief constable. So I shall deal first with cases of dismissal. These appear to fall into three classes: dismissal of a servant by his master, dismissal from an office held during pleasure, and dismissal from an office where there must be something against a man to warrant his dismissal.

Lord Reid then went on to consider the three different cases and concluded that, in the case of the third category (into which *Ridge* fell), there was an unbroken line of authority to the effect that an officer cannot lawfully be dismissed without first telling him what is alleged against him and hearing his defence or explanation.

Stopping there, I would think that authority was wholly in favour of the appellant, but the respondent's argument was mainly based on what has been said in a number of fairly recent cases dealing with different subject-matter. Those cases deal with decisions by ministers, officials and bodies of various kinds which adversely affected property rights or privileges of persons who had no opportunity or no proper opportunity of presenting their cases before the decisions were given. And it is necessary to examine those cases for another reason. The question which was or ought to have been considered by the watch committee on March 7, 1958, was not a simple question whether or not the appellant should be dismissed. There were three possible courses open to the watch committee—reinstating the appellant as chief constable, dismissing him, or requiring him to resign. The difference between the latter two is that dismissal involved forfeiture of pension rights, whereas requiring him to resign did not. Indeed, it is now clear that the appellant's real interest in this appeal is to try to save his pension rights. . . .

I would start an examination of the authorities dealing with property rights and privileges with *Cooper* v *Wandsworth Board of Works* (1863) 14 CBNS 180. Where an owner had failed to give proper notice to the Board they had under an Act of 1855 authority to demolish any building he had erected and recover the cost from him. This action was brought against the board because they had used that power without giving the owner an opportunity of being heard. The board maintained that their discretion to order demolition was not a judicial discretion and that any appeal should have been to the Metropolitan Board of Works. But the Court decided unanimously in favour of the owner. . . .

[Lord Reid examined a number of other authorities and continued.] . . . It appears to me that if the present case had arisen thirty or forty years ago the court would have had no difficulty in deciding this issue in favour of the appellant on these authorities which I have cited. So far as I am aware none of these authorities has ever been disapproved or even doubted. Yet the Court of Appeal have decided this issue against the appellant on more recent authorities which apparently justify that result. How has this come about?

At least three things appear to have contributed. In the first place there have been many cases where it has been sought to apply the principles of natural justice to the wider duties imposed on Ministers and other organs of government by modern legislation. For reasons which I shall attempt to state, it has been held that those principles have a limited application in such cases and those limitations have tended to be reflected in other decisions on matters to which in principle they do not appear to me to apply. Secondly, again for reasons which I shall attempt to state, those principles have been held to have a limited application in cases arising out of war-time legislation; and again such limitations have tended to be reflected in other cases. And, thirdly, there has, I think, been a misunderstanding of the judgment of Atkin LJ in *Rex* v *Electricity Commissioners ex parte London Electricity Joint Committee Co.* [1924] 1 KB 171.

In cases of the kind I have been dealing with the Board of Works or the Governor of the club committee was dealing with a single isolated case. It was not deciding, like a judge in a lawsuit, what were the rights of the person before it. But it was deciding how he should be treated—something analogous to a judge's duty in imposing a penalty. No doubt policy would play some part in the decision—but so it might when a judge is imposing a sentence. So it was easy to say that such a body is performing a quasi-judicial task in considering and deciding such a matter, and to require it to observe the essentials of all proceedings of a judicial character—the principles of natural justice.

Sometimes the functions of a minister or department may also be of that character, and then the rules of natural justice can apply in much the same way. But more often their functions are of a very different character. If a minister is considering whether to make such a scheme for, say, an important new road, his primary concern will not be with the damage which its construction will do to the rights of individual owners of land. He will have to consider all manner of questions of public interest and, it may be, a number of alternative schemes. He cannot be prevented from attaching more importance to the fulfilment of his policy than to the fate of individual objectors, and it would be quite wrong for the courts to say that the minister should or could act in the same kind of way as a board of works deciding whether a house should be pulled down. And there is another important difference. As explained in *Local Government Board* v *Arlidge* [1915] AC 120 a minister cannot do everything himself. His officers will have to gather and sift all the facts, including objections by individuals, and no individual can complain if the ordinary accepted methods of carrying on public business do not give him as good protection as would be given by the principles of natural justice in a different kind of case.

Lord Reid continued to discuss cases decided under the Defence Regulations made in wartime and concluded that the fact that the rules of natural justice were not applied should not be regarded as of any great weight in cases arising under the 1882 Act because it was a reasonable inference in the former case that it was Parliament's intention to exclude the application of the rules of natural justice....

The matter has been further complicated by what I believe to be a misunderstanding of a much-quoted passage in the judgment of Atkin LJ in *Rex* v *Electricity Commissioners, ex parte London Electricity Joint Committee Co.* [1925] 1 KB 171. He said '... the operation of the writs [of prohibition and certiorari] has extended to control the proceedings of bodies which do not claim to be, and would not be recognised as courts of justice. Wherever any body of persons having legal authority to determine questions affecting the rights of subjects, and having the duty to act judicially, act in excess of their legal authority, they are subject to the controlling jurisdiction of the King's Bench Division exercised in these writs.'

A gloss was put on this by Lord Hewart CJ in *Rex* v *Legislative Committee of the Church Assembly, ex parte Haynes-Smith* [1928] 1 KB 411.... Lord Hewart said, having quoted the passage from Atkin LJ's judgment: '... It is to be observed that in the last sentence which I have quoted... the word is not "or", but "and". In order that a body may satisfy the required test it is not enough that it should have legal authority to determine questions affecting the rights of subjects; there must be superadded to that characteristic the further characteristic that the body has the duty to act judicially. The duty to act judicially is an ingredient which, if the test is to be satisfied, must be present. As these writs in the earlier days were issued only to bodies which without any harshness of construction could be called, and naturally would be called courts, so also today these writs do not issue except to bodies which act or are under a duty to act in a judicial capacity.'

...If Lord Hewart meant that it is never enough that a body simply has a duty to determine what the rights of an individual should be, but that there must always be something more to impose on it a duty to act judicially before it can be found to observe the principles of natural justice, then that appears to me impossible to reconcile with the earlier authorities....

There is not a word in Atkin LJ's judgment to suggest disapproval of the earlier line of authority which I have cited. On the contrary, he goes further than those authorities. I have already stated my view that it is more difficult for the courts to control an exercise of power on a large scale where the treatment to be meted out to a particular individual is only one of many matters to be considered. This was a case of that kind, and, if Atkin LJ was prepared to infer a judicial element from the nature of the power in this case, he could hardly disapprove such an inference when the power relates solely to the treatment of a particular individual.

I would sum up my opinion in this way. Between 1882 and the making of police regulations in 1920, section 191(4) had to be applied to every kind of case. The respondents' contention is that, even where there was a doubtful question whether a constable was guilty of a particular act of misconduct, the watch committee were under no obligation to hear his defence before dismissing him. In my judgment it is abundantly clear from the authorities I have quoted that at that time the courts would have rejected any such contention. In later cases dealing with different subject-matter opinions have been expressed in wide terms so as to appear to conflict with those earlier authorities. But learned judges who expressed those opinions generally had no power to overrule those authorities, and in any event it is a salutary rule that a judge is not to be assumed to have intended to overrule or disapprove of an authority which has not been cited to him and which he does not even mention. So I would hold that the power of dismissal in the Act of 1882 could not then have been exercised and cannot now be exercised until the watch committee have informed the constable of the grounds on which they propose to proceed and given him a proper opportunity to present his case in defence....

Lord Reid decided that this failure was not made good by the reconvening of the watch committee because this did not provide for a full rehearing and granted a declaration that the dismissal was unlawful. Lord Morris, Lord Hodson, and Lord Devlin delivered judgments in favour of allowing the appeal. Lord Evershed delivered a speech in favour of dismissing the appeal.

NOTES

1. The significance of *Ridge* v *Baldwin* is that it helped to free the rules of natural justice from strict limitations which had been imposed in earlier decisions, in particular from the requirement that the decision-making body must be under a duty to act judicially. The decision in the case may be compared with that in *Nakkuda Ali* v *Jayaratne* [1951] AC 66 which was disapproved in *Ridge* v *Baldwin*.
2. The requirements of a fair hearing depend on all the circumstances. They may include:
   (a) the right to notice, but restrictions may be placed on this where the public interest so requires (see, for example, *R* v *Gaming Board of Great Britain, ex parte Benaim and Khaida* [1970] 2 QB 417);
   (b) the right to make representations, whether in writing or orally; oral hearings are not required in all circumstances where the rules of natural justice apply (see, for example, *Lloyd* v *McMahon* [1987] 1 All ER 1118);
   (c) where an oral hearing is held—
      (i) the right to comment on any evidence presented,
      (ii) where evidence is given orally by witnesses, the right to put questions to those witnesses (see, for example, *R* v *Deputy Industrial Injuries Commissioner, ex parte Moore* [1965] 1 QB 456);
   (d) legal representation (see, at p. 575, *post*).

In order to understand the flexibility of the principles, consider the following cases.

R v *Board of Visitors of Hull Prison, ex parte St Germain (No. 2)*

[1979] 1 WLR 1401, Divisional Court

Following a riot in Hull Prison in 1976, numerous charges of breaches of the Prison Rules 1964 were heard by the prison's board of visitors. During the hearing reference was made to a number of statements by prison officers, who were not available to give evidence, to support the evidence given by a witness. Seven of the prisoners who were found guilty of offences against prison discipline sought an order of *certiorari* on the grounds that the proceedings before the prison's board of visitors breached the rules of natural justice. The following extracts relate to the prisoners' complaint that hearsay evidence was taken into account.

GEOFFREY LANE LJ: ...[W]e now turn to the suggestion that hearsay evidence is not permissible in a hearing before a board of visitors. It is of course common ground that the board of visitors must base their decisions on evidence. But must such evidence be restricted to that which would be admissible in a criminal court of law? Viscount Simon LC in *General Medical Council* v *Spackman* [1943] AC 627, 634, considered there was no such restriction. That was also clearly the view of the Privy Council in *Ceylon University* v *Fernando* [1960] 1 WLR 223, 234. The matter was dealt with in more detail by Diplock LJ in *Reg.* v *Deputy Industrial Injuries Commissioner ex parte Moore* [1965] 1 QB 456, 488:

> These technical rules of evidence, however, form no part of the rules of natural justice. The requirement that a person exercising quasi-judicial functions must base his decision on evidence means

> no more than it must be based upon material which tends logically to show the existence or non-existence of facts relevant to the issue to be determined, or to show the likelihood or unlikelihood of the occurrence of some future event the occurrence of which would be relevant. It means that he must not spin a coin or consult an astrologer, but he may take into account any material which, as a matter of reason, has some probative value in the sense mentioned above. If it is capable of having any probative value, the weight to be attached to it is a matter for the person to whom Parliament has entrusted the responsibility of deciding the issue. The supervisory jurisdiction of the High Court does not entitle it to usurp this responsibility and to substitute its own view for his.

However, it is clear that the entitlement of the board to admit hearsay evidence is subject to the overriding obligation to provide the accused with a fair hearing. Depending upon the facts of the particular case and the nature of the hearsay evidence provided to the board, the obligation to give the accused a fair chance to exculpate himself, or a fair opportunity to controvert the charge—to quote the phrases used in the passages cited above—or a proper or full opportunity of presenting his case—to quote the language of section 47 or rule 49—may oblige the board not only to inform the accused of the hearsay evidence but also to give the accused a sufficient opportunity to deal with that evidence. Again, depending upon the nature of that evidence and the particular circumstances of the case, a sufficient opportunity to deal with the hearsay evidence may well involve the cross-examination of the witness whose evidence is initially before the board in the form of hearsay.

We again take by way of example the case in which the defence is an alibi. The prisoner contends that he was not the man identified on the roof. He, the prisoner, was at the material time elsewhere. In short the prisoner has been mistakenly identified. The evidence of identification given by way of hearsay may be of the 'fleeting glance' type as exemplified by the well-known case of *Reg* v *Turnbull* [1977] QB 224. The prisoner may well wish to elicit by way of questions all manner of detail, e.g. the poorness of the light, the state of the confusion, the brevity of the observation, the absence of any contemporaneous record, etc., all designed to show the unreliability of the witness. To deprive him of the opportunity of cross-examination would be tantamount to depriving him of a fair hearing.

We appreciate that there may well be occasions when the burden of calling the witness whose hearsay evidence is readily available may impose a near impossible burden upon the board. However, it has not been suggested that hearsay evidence should be resorted to in the total absence of any first-hand evidence. In the instant cases hearsay evidence was only resorted to supplement the first-hand evidence and this is the usual practice. Accordingly where a prisoner desires to dispute the hearsay evidence and for this purpose to question the witness, and where there are insuperable or very grave difficulties in arranging for his attendance, the board should refuse to admit that evidence, or, if it has already come to their notice, should expressly dismiss it from their consideration. . . .

The findings of guilt which were based on hearsay evidence were quashed by orders of certiorari.

R v *Commissioner for Racial Equality, ex parte Cottrell and Rothon*

[1980] 1 WLR 1580, Court of Appeal

The Commission for Racial Equality received a complaint that a firm of estate agents, Messrs Cottrell & Rothon, was committing acts of unlawful discrimination in the course of its business as an estate agent. Under s. 48 of the Race Relations Act 1976, the Commission nominated two of its members to conduct an investigation. When the Commission were minded to issue a non-discrimination notice, they notified the firm under s. 58(5) of the Act of their intention, and gave the firm an opportunity to make written and oral representations to the nominated commissioners. The firm took the opportunity to make both oral and written representations. At the hearing before the commissioners, no witnesses were available to give evidence to sustain the complaint or be cross-examined on behalf of the firm. The Commission decided to issue the notice. The firm applied for an order of *certiorari* on the ground, *inter alia,* that witnesses ought to have been available for cross-examination.

LORD LANE CJ: Of course there is a wealth of authority on what are and what are not the rules of natural justice. The rules have been described in various ways, as an 'unruly horse,' I think, in one decision, and there is no doubt that what may be the rules of natural justice in one case may well not be the rules of natural justice in another. As has frequently been said, and there is no harm in repeating it, all that the rules of natural justice mean is that the proceedings must be conducted in a way which is fair to the firm in this case, fair in all the circumstances. All the circumstances include a number of different considerations: first of all, the penalties, if any. There are no penalties under the Race Relations Act in the form of fines or imprisonment or anything like that, but what [counsel for the firm] has drawn to our attention, quite correctly, is that under the terms of the Estate Agents Act 1979 (and no one has been able to discover whether that has come into operation yet or not) there is no doubt that a person on whom a non-discriminatory notice has been served may, if he is an estate agent, suffer, if certain procedural steps are taken, grave disadvantages because it is open, under a number of safeguards into which I do not propose to go, for the Director General of Fair Trading to take steps to see that a person against whom this action had been taken under the Race Relations Act 1976 does not practise in business as an estate agent. Of course it is a very long call from saying that a person who has this non-discriminatory notice served on him is necessarily going to suffer in his business by the action of the Director General of Fair Trading. Many procedures have to be gone through before that can take place, but there is a danger there, and that is one of the matters which is a circumstance to be taken into account.

The next matter, and possibly the most important matter, is the nature of the provisions of the Race Relations Act 1976 itself. I have read sufficient of the contents of section 58 of that Act to indicate that there is no mention in that section, or indeed in any other section, of any right to cross-examine any of the witnesses. That perhaps is a surprising omission if it was the intention of Parliament to allow a person in the position of the firm in this case the full panoply of legal rights which would take place at a judicial hearing.

It seems to me that there are degrees of judicial hearing, and those degrees run from the borders of pure administration to the borders of the full hearing of a criminal cause or matter in the Crown Court. It does not profit one to try to pigeon-hole the particular set of circumstances either into the administrative pigeon-hole or into the judicial pigeon-hole. Each case will inevitably differ, and one must ask oneself what is the basic nature of the proceeding which was going on here. It seems to me that, basically, this was an investigation being carried out by the commission. It is true that in the course of the investigation the commission may form a view, but it does not seem to me that is a proceeding which requires, in the name of fairness, any right in the firm in this case to be able to cross-examine witnesses whom the commission have seen and from whom they have taken statements. . . .

[Counsel for the firms] sought to derive assistance from some of the passages of the decision of this court in *Reg v Hull Prison Board of Visitors ex parte St Germain* [1979] QB 425, but it seems to me that the decision there was based on facts widely differing from those in the present case. That was truly a judicial proceeding carried out by the prison visitors and the complaint there was that there had been no opportunity to cross-examine prison officers in hotly disputed questions of identity. Speaking for myself, I derive little assistance from any dicta in that case.

. . . It seems to me for the reasons I have endeavoured to set out that in this case there was no breach of the rules of fairness in that cross-examination was not permitted or that the witnesses did not attend. . . .

Woolf J agreed with Lord Lane LJ.

R v Army Board of the Defence Council, ex parte Anderson

[1991] 3 WLR 42, Divisional Court

In this case the court had to scrutinize the procedures adopted by the Army Board in deciding upon complaints of racial discrimination by soldiers under the Race Relations Act 1976. (Complaints of racial discrimination in employment are normally dealt with by industrial tribunals but special procedures apply to complaints by soldiers.) The applicant was a former soldier who alleged that he had been subjected to forms of racial abuse which caused him to go absent without leave. The papers relating to the complaint were seen separately by two members of the Army Board who reached individual conclusions that, although there was some truth in the applicant's claim, there was no basis for making an apology to him or awarding him compensation. The applicant's requests for disclosure of documents relating to investigations into his complaints were refused, as was his request for an oral hearing. He applied for judicial review of the Board's decision.

TAYLOR LJ: . . .

Procedural requirements

What procedural requirements are necessary to achieve fairness when the Army Board considers a complaint of this kind? In addressing this issue, counsel made much of the distinction between judicial and administrative functions. Were it necessary to decide in those terms the functions of the Army Board when considering a race discrimination complaint, I would characterise it as judicial rather than administrative. The board is required to adjudicate on an alleged breach of a soldier's rights under the 1976 Act and, if it be proved, to take any necessary steps by way of redress. It is accepted that the board has the power, inter alia, to award compensation. A body required to consider and adjudicate upon an alleged breach of statutory rights and to grant redress when necessary seems to me to be exercising an essentially judicial function. It matters not that the body has other functions which are non-judicial: see *R* v *Secretary of State for the Home Dept, ex p Tarrant* [1985] QB 251, 268.

However, to label the board's function either 'judicial' or 'administrative' for the purpose of determining the appropriate procedural regime is to adopt too inflexible an approach. . . .

What, then, are the criteria by which to decide the requirements of fairness in any given proceeding? Authoritative guidance as to this was given by Lord Bridge in *Lloyd* v *McMahon* [1987] AC 625, 702. He said:

> My Lords, the so-called rules of natural justice are not engraved on tablets of stone. To use the phrase which better expresses the underlying concept, what the requirements of fairness demand when any body, domestic, administrative or judicial, has to make a decision which will affect the rights of individuals depends on the character of the decision-making body, the kind of decision it has to make and the statutory or other framework in which it operates. In particular, it is well established that when a statute has conferred on any body the power to make decisions affecting individuals, the courts will not only require the procedure prescribed by the statute to be followed, but will readily imply so much and no more to be introduced by way of additional procedural safeguards as will ensure the attainment of fairness.

Applying these principles to the present case, the character of the Army Board and its role in this context have already been described. It is pertinent, however, to note that its decision is final apart from the possibility of judicial review. There is no appeal from its findings. The kind of decision it has to make has also been described. [Mr Sedley, counsel for the applicant] argues from that and from the statutory framework that all the procedural features to be found in a court trial are required—full discovery of documents, an oral hearing and cross-examination. As to the statutory framework, he points out that complaints of racial discrimination under Pt III of the 1976 Act relating to goods and services go before the county court with all the incidents of court procedure. Most civilian complaints of racial discrimination contrary to s. 4 of the 1976 Act go to an industrial tribunal under s. 54(1). There they are subject to rules requiring the procedures Mr Sedley claims here. Thus, if Mr Anderson had been seeking entry to the army, and had been turned down on allegedly racial grounds, his case could have been presented to the industrial tribunal under s. 4(1)(c), and he would have enjoyed all the procedures claimed here. Why should he be worse off simply because he is actually in the army and s. 54(2) requires his complaint to be considered by a different body?

Against this, [Mr Pannick, counsel for the Army Board] contends that Parliament has expressly provided that a soldier's complaint shall not go before an industrial tribunal but shall instead be subject to the army procedures pursuant to s. 181 of the 1955 Act. Parliament must, he submits, have been aware of the procedures normally followed in regard to other complaints under that section. Moreover, had Parliament wished to impose a more rigid and rigorous procedure, still in an army context, it could have directed that complaints of racial discrimination should be subject to s. 135 (board of inquiry), s. 137 (regimental inquiry) or even ss. 92 to 103 (court-martial). Process under each of those sections would have afforded the complainant the procedural formalities contended for here.

I should say that the existence of those forms of inquiry and their procedure undercuts [the] suggestion that exigencies of the service would make oral hearings impracticable.

In my judgment, there is force in Mr Pannick's argument. Since Parliament has deliberately excluded soldiers' complaints from industrial tribunals and thus from the procedures laid down for such tribunals, it cannot be axiomatic that by analogy all those procedures must be made available by the Army Board. Had Parliament wished to impose those detailed procedures on the Army Board, it could have done so.

However, Mr Pannick went on to contend that the Army Board's duty of fairness required no more than that it should act bona fide, not capriciously or in a biased manner, and that it should afford the complainant a chance to respond to the basic points put against him. In my judgment, this does not go far enough. The Army Board as the forum of last resort, dealing with an individual's fundamental statutory rights, must by its procedures achieve a high standard of fairness. I would list the principles as follows.

(1) There must be a proper hearing of the complaint in the sense that the board must consider, as a single adjudicating body, all the relevant evidence and contentions before reaching its conclusions. This means, in my view, that the members of the board must meet. It is unsatisfactory that the members should consider the papers and reach their individual conclusions in isolation and, perhaps as here, having received the concluded views of another member. Since there are ten members of the Army Board and any two can exercise the board's powers to consider a complaint of this kind, there should be no difficulty in achieving a meeting for the purpose.

(2) The hearing does not necessarily have to be an oral hearing in all cases. There is ample authority that decision-making bodies other than courts and bodies whose procedures are laid down by statute are masters of their own procedure. Provided that they achieve the degree of fairness appropriate to their task it is for them to decide how they will proceed and there is no rule that fairness always requires an oral hearing: see *Local Government Board* v *Arlidge* [1915] AC 120, 132–133, *Selvarajan* v *Race Relations Board* [1975] 1 WLR 1686, 1694 and *R* v *Immigration Appeal Tribunal, ex parte Jones* [1988] 1 WLR 477, 481. Whether an oral hearing is necessary will depend upon the subject matter and circumstances of the particular case and upon the nature of the decision to be made. It will also depend upon whether there are substantial issues of fact which cannot be satisfactorily resolved on the available written evidence. This does not mean that, whenever there is a conflict of evidence in the statements taken, an oral hearing must be held to resolve it. Sometimes such a conflict can be resolved merely by the inherent unlikelihood of one version or the other. Sometimes the conflict is not central to the issue for determination and would not justify an oral hearing. Even when such a hearing is necessary, it may only require one or two witnesses to be called and cross-examined.

Mr Sedley submits that, whatever the position regarding other complaints under s. 181, an oral hearing should be obligatory where the complaint is of race discrimination. He submits that experience shows proof of discrimination to be elusive. Discriminatory motivation can be innocent and subconscious. Without cross-examination at an oral hearing it may not emerge. I recognise the difficulties of proving discrimination in many cases, but I do not accept that a general rule requiring oral hearings must be applied by the Army Board to all complaints of discrimination. In the present case, for example, the direct and crude nature of the alleged racial abuse hardly raises any specially subtle possibility of subconscious motivation. Either the racial attacks, oral and physical, took place or they did not. Whether, when the Army Board sees all the statements and transcripts, it considers it necessary to hold an oral hearing to decide that issue or whether it can resolve it on the written material will be for it to decide in its discretion. What it cannot do, at the other extreme from Mr Sedley's submission, is to have an inflexible policy not to hold oral hearings. The findings of the two members in this case suggest that is what they did....

[T]he board fettered its discretion and failed to consider the request for an oral hearing in the present case on its own merits.

(3) The opportunity to have the evidence tested by cross-examination is again within the Army Board's discretion. The decision whether to allow it will usually be inseparable from the decision whether to have an oral hearing. The object of the latter will usually be to enable witnesses to be tested in cross-examination, although it would be possible to have an oral hearing simply to hear submissions.

(4) Whether oral or not, there must be what amounts to a hearing of any complaint under the 1976 Act. This means that the Army Board must have such a complaint investigated, consider all the material gathered in the investigation, give the complainant an opportunity to respond to it and consider his response.

But what is the board obliged to disclose to the complainant to obtain his response? Is it sufficient to indicate the gist of any material adverse to his case or should he be shown all the material seen by the board?

Mr Pannick submits that there is no obligation to show all to the complainant. He relies upon three authorities, *R* v *Secretary of State, ex parte Mughal* [1974] QB 313 *R* v *Secretary of State, ex parte Santillo* [1981] QB 778 and *R* v *Monopolies and Mergers Commission, ex parte Matthew Brown plc* [1987] 1 WLR 1235. However, in each of those cases, the function of the decision-making body was towards the administrative end of the spectrum. Because of the nature of the Army Board's function pursuant to the 1976 Act, already analysed above, I consider that a soldier complainant under that Act should be shown all the material seen by the board, apart from any documents for which public interest immunity can properly be claimed. The board is not simply making an administrative decision requiring it to consult interested parties and hear their representations. It has a duty to adjudicate on a specific complaint of breach of a statutory right. Except where public interest immunity is established, I see no reason why on such an adjudication the board should consider material withheld from the complainant.

In the present case it is true that Mr Anderson was shown a summary of the SIB report, though not the report itself. He also received the commanding officer's letter of 20 July which summarised points made against him, but he did not see the statements of other soldiers. Nor was he shown the information obtained individually by each of the board members. Thus, the response he made to the commanding officer's letter was hampered by a lack of full information....

The Divisional Court granted an order of certiorari to quash the Board's decision.

NOTES

1. A commentary on the use of judicial review in the context of racial discrimination in the public sector may be found at [1991] *Public Law,* at pp. 317–325.
2. *Ex parte St Germain (No. 2)* and *ex parte Cottrell and Rothon* have been used by H. F. Rawlings to illustrate a particular criticism of the rules of natural justice.

H. F. Rawlings, 'Judicial Review and the Control of Government'

(1986) 64 *Public Administration* 135–145, at 140–141

...It has long been the concern of many academic administrative lawyers that our system of judicial review is for various reasons not adequate to ensure protection of the citizen against government excess.... In contrast, the adequacy of our administrative law principles from the point of view of the civil or public servant has rarely been considered. I suggest that the principles which have been developed by the courts over the last twenty years are quite simply not sufficiently precise to offer any meaningful guidance to administrators in their day-to-day decision-making, even if those administrators are aware of the existence of administrative law....

What, then, are those principles? In essence there are two (I leave out of account here the question of illegality, which is not germane to the present discussion). First, there is the obligation to observe the rules of natural justice. Here we may return to *Ridge* v *Baldwin* [1964] AC 40. That case establishes that in a far wider category of situations than had previously been thought true, a public authority had, in exercising statutory functions, to observe the natural justice requirement. But what is that requirement? It must be remembered that the content of the natural justice rule derives from the court proceedings paradigm—judges must be unbiased, and parties must be given an opportunity to present their cases. How might these rules be applied in the infinite variety of administrative practices to which *Ridge* v *Baldwin* now extends them?

Two possibilities were open to the courts, given this new activist approach to the applicability of natural justice.... [W]e might characterise these as the 'formal activist' and the 'informal activist' approaches. Under the former, the courts could seek, by firm application of the rules, to force the administrative process into a more judicial mould, to follow the formal procedures of the courts so far as possible. Under the latter, the courts could permit administrators a greater degree of latitude in their procedures and allow the applicability of the rules of natural justice in particular circumstances to be determined by the realities of administration, while all the time insisting that compliance with the rules was necessary. As is now well-known, the courts adopted the latter approach—natural justice was to be flexibly applied, to fit the circumstances of the case. In the result, observation of the rules of natural justice came to mean that the procedure required of the administrator had to be, in all the circumstances of the case, 'fair' (see, for example *Re HK* [1967] 2 QB 617 and *R* v *Commission for Racial Equality ex parte Cottrell and Rothon* [1980] 1 WLR 1580).

Now it may be that this was an inevitable result, although potentially pregnant with danger for the individual citizen asserting a right to be heard. It seems to me, however, that in their understandable desire to avoid over-judicialising administrative procedures, the courts have thrown out the baby with the bath-water. Flexible natural justice, or 'fairness', has come to have no fixed or settled content that an administrator should know must be observed in exercising decision-making powers. All he knows... is that he must be 'fair'—and what 'fairness' requires in the particular circumstances he can only ultimately find out when the court, on judicial review, tells him that he has, or has not, been fair. Is this an adequate administrative law principle, from the point of view of the administrator?

The point may briefly be illustrated by considering a specific issue in natural justice. It is sometimes said that, before any administrative decision is taken, a party who is likely to be affected by it shall have the right to hear what evidence against his interests has been given by someone else, and shall have the opportunity to question that person on the assertions contained therein... Decided cases, tell us, to take just two examples, that in the context of prison disciplinary proceedings, 'fairness' requires that such cross-examination is permitted (*R* v *Hull Prison Visitors ex parte St Germain (No. 2)* [1979] 1 WLR 1401), whereas in the context of issuance of a non-discrimination notice against a private estate agency under the Race Relations Act, 'fairness' does not require that such cross-examination is permitted (*R* v *CRE ex parte Cottrell and Rothon* [1980] 1 WLR 1580).

Now these results can be defended, because as Lord Lane CJ says in the *Cottrell and Rothon case*, there are 'degrees of judicial hearing, and those degrees run from the borders of pure administration to the borders of a full hearing of a criminal cause or matter'. The precise requirements of fairness depend upon how far along that continuum is the particular administrative process to be placed—the closer to 'pure administration' it is, the less onerous will be the procedural requirements imposed on administrators. This, as I have said, is defensible as a matter of theory, but I suggest that as guidance to administrative practice it is hopelessly imprecise from the point of view of those who want to know what procedural requirements the law lays down for them to observe.

■ QUESTIONS

1. What distinctions did Lord Lane CJ draw between the circumstances in *ex parte St Germain* and those in *ex parte Cottrell and Rothon*? Do you consider that the distinctions justify the different decisions reached in each case?
2. Cane, in the extract at pp. 528–529, *ante*, has suggested that there are two possible approaches which the court might adopt in the face of legislative silence on the precise content of the rules of natural justice. 'It could be said that the rules of natural justice will apply only if there is evidence of a legislative intention that they should; alternatively it could be argued that silence should be construed as an invitation by the courts to apply common law procedural standards of natural justice.' Which approach did the courts adopt in *ex parte St Germain, ex parte Cottrell and Rothon*, and *ex parte Anderson*?
3. Write a paragraph to guide public administrators on the circumstances in which public authorities should be willing (a) to permit oral hearings and (b) to permit the cross-examination of witnesses.
4. Is there any solution to the problems identified by Rawlings?
5. Can there be a breach of the rules of natural justice where an applicant has been deprived of an opportunity to present his case, not through the fault of the decision-making body, but through the fault of his own advisers? (See *Al-Mehdawi* v *Secretary of State for the Home Department* [1990] AC 876, noted at [1990] *Public Law* 467–475.)

NOTE: One problem which has been discussed in a number of recent cases is that of legal representation. In *R* v *Board of Visitors of HM Prison, The Maze, ex parte Hone* [1988] 2 WLR 177 the House of Lords rejected the argument that a prisoner facing a disciplinary charge before a prison board of visitors had a right to legal representation. The House of Lords did, however, approve the decision in *R* v *Secretary of State for the Home Department, ex parte Tarrant* [1985] QB 251 that a board of visitors still has a discretion to allow legal representation and that in certain circumstances it would be wrong not to allow it. Webster J specified a number of points which are to be taken into account, including the seriousness of the charge and potential penalty, whether points of law are likely to arise, the particular prisoner's ability to present his case and the need for reasonable speed in reaching a decision.

The rules governing hearings before the prison board of visitors did not state that legal representation was prohibited. What is the position where the rules governing a particular hearing *do* prohibit legal representation? In *Enderby Town Football Club Ltd* v *Football Association Ltd* [1971] Ch 591, Lord Denning MR stated, at p. 607:

> Seeing that the courts can inquire into the validity of the rule, I turn to the next question: Is it lawful for a body to stipulate in its rules that its domestic tribunal shall not permit legal representation? Such a stipulation is, I think, clearly valid so long as it is construed as directory and not imperative: for that leaves it open to the tribunal to permit legal representation in an exceptional case when the justice of the case so requires. But I have some doubt whether it is legitimate to make a rule which is so imperative in its terms as to exclude legal representation altogether, without giving the tribunal any discretion to admit it, even when the justice of the case so requires.

Lord Denning has repeated this view on other occasions (see e.g. *Edwards* v *SOGAT* [1971] Ch 354). In *Enderby Town* itself, however, Cairns LJ took a contrary view.

> In *Maynard* v *Osmond* [1977] QB 240 Lord Denning was a member of the Court of Appeal which was required to consider the validity of police discipline regulations prohibiting legal representation. The regulations were made under statutory powers. It was held unanimously that the regulations were not *ultra vires*, and in particular that they were not in breach of natural justice. In this case Lord Denning stated, obiter, that it is permissible for a domestic tribunal to adopt a rule forbidding legal representation, and Orr LJ endorsed the view of Cairns LJ in *Enderby Town*.

The two principles so far discussed have been concerned with procedural fairness. In recent years the courts have begun to develop a principle of fairness which may require public authorities to reach a particular decision rather than simply to follow a fair procedure. The concept of legitimate expectation, which is explained in *CCSU* v *Minister for the Civil Service*, has been important in the development of this principle.

Council of the Civil Service Unions v *Minister for the Civil Service*

[1985] AC 374, House of Lords

Government Communications Headquarters, a branch of the civil service, is responsible for the security of the United Kingdom military and official communications and the provision of signals intelligence for the Government. Since the formation of GCHQ in 1947, all the staff had been permitted to belong to trade unions. There was an established practice of consultation between the management and the civil service unions at GCHQ. Following incidents of industrial action at GCHQ the Minister for the Civil Service, the Prime Minister, issued an oral instruction to the effect that the terms and conditions of civil servants at GCHQ should be revised to exclude membership of any trade union other than a departmental staff association approved by the Minister. The instruction was issued under art. 4 of the Civil Service Order in Council 1982 'to give instructions...for controlling the conduct of the Service, and providing for the...conditions of service', the Order itself having been made under the royal prerogative. The union applied for judicial review, seeking a declaration that the Minister had acted unfairly in removing their fundamental right to belong to a trade union without consultation. The Court of Appeal allowed the Minister's appeal against the judge's decision that the Minister had acted unlawfully. The appellants appealed to the House of Lords. Having held that the courts could review the exercise of a power delegated to the decision-maker under the royal prerogative, Lord Fraser went on to consider whether there was a duty to consult the unions.

LORD FRASER:

The duty to consult

[Counsel for the appellants] submitted that the Minister had a duty to consult the CCSU, on behalf of employees at GCHQ, before giving the instruction on 22 December 1983 for making an important change in their conditions of service. His main reason for so submitting was that the employees had a legitimate, or reasonable, expectation that there would be such prior consultation before any important change was made in their conditions.

It is clear that the employees did not have a legal right to prior consultation. The Order in Council confers no such right and article 4 makes no reference at all to consultation.... But even where a person claiming some benefit or privilege has no legal right to it, as a matter of private law, he may have a legitimate expectation of receiving the benefit or privilege, and, if so, the courts will protect his expectation by judicial review as a matter of public law. This subject has been fully explained by Lord Diplock, in *O'Reilly* v *Mackman* [1983] 2 AC 237 and I need not repeat what he has so recently said. Legitimate, or reasonable, expectation may arise either from an express promise given on behalf of a public authority or from the existence of a regular practice which the claimant can reasonably expect to continue. Examples of the former type of expectation are *Reg* v *Liverpool Corporation, ex parte Liverpool Taxi Fleet Operators Association* [1972] 2 QB 299 and *A-G of Hong Kong* v *Ng Yuen Shiu* [1983] 2 AC 629. (I agree with Lord Diplock's view, expressed in the speech in this appeal, that 'legitimate' is to be preferred to the word 'reasonable' in this context. I was responsible for using the word 'reasonable' for the reason explained in *Ng Yuen Shiu*, but it was intended only to be exegetical of 'legitimate'.) An example of the latter is *Reg* v *Hull Prison Board of Visitors ex parte St Germain* [1979] 1 All ER 701, [1979] QB 425, approved by this House in *O'Reilly* v *Mackman* [1982] 3 All ER 1124 at 1126, [1983] 2 AC 237 at 274. The submission on behalf of the appellants is that the present case is of the latter type. The test of that is whether the practice of prior consultation of the staff on significant changes in their conditions of service was so well established by 1983 that it would be unfair or inconsistent with good administration for the Government to depart from the practice in this case. Legitimate expectations such as are now under consideration will always relate to a benefit or privilege to which the claimant has no right in private law, and it may even be to one which conflicts with his private law rights. In the present case the evidence shows that, ever since GCHQ began in 1947, prior consultation has been the invariable rule when conditions of service were to be significantly altered. Accordingly in my opinion if there had been no question of national security involved, the appellants would have had a legitimate expectation that the Minister would consult them before issuing the instruction of 22 December 1983.

NOTES

1. A majority of their Lordships held that the exercise of prerogative powers could be challenged in judicial review proceedings provided that the subject matter was justiciable. (On the issue of justiciability, see p. 633, *post*.) Lord Fraser and Lord Brightman left open the question whether a direct exercise of the prerogative powers could be subject to judicial review, but they did accept that powers which had been delegated to decision-makers by an Order in Council made under prerogative powers were subject to judicial review. All their Lordships agreed that, had issues of national security not been involved, the unions would have been entitled to consultation. (On the issues of national security which arose in this case, see p. 634, *post*.) This was applied to the making of Orders in Council for a colony as well as to the exercise of the powers thus conferred in *R (Bancoult) Secretary of State for Foreign and Commonwealth Affairs (No. 2)* v *The Queen* [2008] UKHL 61, [2009] 1 AC 453.
2. There have been various cases on consultations. One high profile case was *R (Greenpeace)* v *Secretary of State for Trade and Industry* [2007] EWHC 311 (Admin), [2007] in which Greenpeace successfully challenged the policy on building new nuclear power stations as it did not met their expectation of being the fullest public consultation. The consultation exercise had a paper which was adequate as an issues paper but not as a consultation paper because it contained no proposals as such, the information provided was wholly insufficient to enable an intelligent response and contained nothing on two issues which had been identified as being of critical

importance, the economics of new nuclear build and the disposal of nuclear waste. Indeed on the latter point it was wholly misleading about the position of the Committee on Radioactive Waste Management. Material on these two issues was produced after the close of the consultation period so it was procedural unfairness to make a decision on this material when consultees did not have a chance to respond to it. The decision was given in February 2007 and in May the Government launched a new Energy White paper and consultation process which ran from May until October (see *Meeting the Energy Challenge: A White Paper on Energy*, Cm 7124, and *The Future of Nuclear Power: The Role of Nuclear Power in A Low Carbon UK Economy, A Consultation Paper*, Department of Trade and Industry). In January 2008 the result of the consultation and the new policy were announced. Nuclear power had a place in the energy policy and invitations were being made to energy companies to produce plans for building and operating new nuclear power stations (see *Meeting the Energy Challenge: A White Paper on Nuclear Power*, Cm 7296, and *The Future of Nuclear Power: An Analysis of Consultation Responses*, Department for Business Enterprise and Regulatory Reform). Therefore Greenpeace's challenge brought about a fuller consultation process but did not prevent new nuclear build.

3. The concept of legitimate expectation has been discussed by a number of writers (see, for example, C. Forsyth, 'The Provenance and Protection of Legitimate Expectations' (1988) 47 CLJ 238–260; B. Hadfield, 'Judicial Review and the Concept of Legitimate Expectation' (1988) 39 *Northern Ireland Legal Quarterly* 103–119; Ganz, 'Legitimate Expectation' in C. Harlow (ed.), *Public Law and Politics* (1986), 145; P. Craig, 'Legitimate Expectations: A Conceptual Analysis', (1992) 108 *Law Quarterly Review* 79), P. Sales and K. Steyn, 'Legitimate Expectations in English Public Law: An Analysis' [2004] *Public Law* 564. They have highlighted the different ways in which the concept is used by the courts. Predominantly, the legitimate expectation has related to fair procedures but see p. 587, *post*, for substantive legitimate expectations.

D: Irrationality

Prior to the decision in *CCSU* v *Minister for the Civil Service* this ground was often expressed in the principle that an authority must not reach a decision which is so unreasonable that no reasonable body could have come to it. After *CCSU* the use of the term 'irrationality' has become more common, but in *R* v *Devon CC, ex parte G* [1988] 3 WLR 49, at p. 51, the Master of the Rolls stated that he preferred the older test because the term 'irrationality' could be widely misunderstood as casting doubt on the mental capacity of the decision-maker. Subsequent cases have used both terms.

Wheeler* v *Leicester City Council

[1985] AC 1054, House of Lords

The facts are set out at p. 539, *ante*.

LORD ROSKILL: It is important to emphasise that there was nothing illegal in the action of the three members in joining the tour. The government policy recorded in the well-known Gleneagles agreement has never been given the force of law at the instance of any government, whatever its political complexion, and a person who acts otherwise than in accordance with the principles of that agreement, commits no offence even though he may by his action earn the moral disapprobation of large numbers of his fellow citizens. That the club condemns apartheid, as does the council, admits of no doubt. But the council's actions against the club were not taken, as already pointed out, because the club took no action against its three members. They were taken, according to Mr Soulsby, because the club failed to condemn the tour and to discourage its members from playing. The same point was put more succinctly by Mr Sullivan QC, who appeared for the council—'The club failed to align themselves whole-heartedly with the council on a controversial issue.' The club did not condemn the tour. They did not give specific affirmative answers to the first two questions. Thus, so the argument ran, the council, legitimately bitterly hostile to the policy of apartheid, were justified in exercising their statutory discretion to determine by whom the recreation ground should be used so as to exclude those, such as the club, who would not support the council's policy on the council's terms. The club had, however, circulated to those involved the powerfully reasoned and impressive memorandum which had been sent to the RFU [the Rugby Football Union] on 12 March 1984 by the anti-apartheid movement. Of the club's own opposition to apartheid as expressed in its memorandum which was given to Mr Soulsby, there is no doubt. But the club recognised that those views, like those of the council, however passionately held by some, were by no means universally held, especially by those who sincerely believed that the evils of apartheid were enhanced rather than diminished by a total prohibition of all sporting links with South Africa.

The council's main defence rested on section 71 of the Race Relations Act 1976. That section appears as the first section in Part X of the Act under the cross-heading 'Supplemental.' For ease of reference I will set out the section in full:

> Without prejudice to their obligation to comply with any other provision of this Act, it shall be the duty of every local authority to make appropriate arrangements with a view to securing that their various functions are carried out with due regard to the need—(a) to eliminate unlawful racial discrimination; and (b) to promote equality of opportunity, and good relations, between persons of different racial groups.

My Lords, it was strenuously argued on behalf of the club that this section should be given what was called a 'narrow' construction. It was suggested that the section was only concerned with the actions of the council as regards its own internal behaviour and was what was described as 'inward looking.' The section had no relevance to the general exercise by the council or indeed of any local authority of their statutory functions, as for example in relation to the control of open spaces or in determining who should be entitled to use a recreation ground and on what terms. It was said that the section was expressed in terms of a 'duty.' But it did not impose any duty so as to compel the exercise by a local authority of other statutory functions in order to achieve the objectives of the Act of 1976.

My Lords, in respectful agreement with the courts below, I unhesitatingly reject this argument. I think the whole purpose of the section is to see that in employment, and in Part III, education, local authorities must in relation to 'their various functions' make 'appropriate arrangements' to secure that those functions are carried out 'with due regard to the need' mentioned in the section.

It follows that I do not doubt that the council were fully entitled in exercising their statutory discretion under, for example, the Open Spaces Act 1906 and the various Public Health Acts, which are all referred to in the judgments below, to pay regard to what they thought to be in the best interests of race relations.

The only question is, therefore, whether the action of the council of which the club complains is susceptible of attack by way of judicial review. It was forcibly argued by Mr Sullivan QC for the council, that once it was accepted, as I do accept, that section 71 bears the construction for which the council contended, the matter became one of political judgment only, and that by interfering the courts would be trespassing across that line which divides a proper exercise of a statutory discretion based on a political judgment, in relation to which the courts will not interfere, from an improper exercise of such a discretion in relation to which the courts will interfere.

Lord Roskill referred to the judgment in *Council of the Civil Service Unions* v *Minister for the Civil Service* (p. 534, *ante*) and continued.

To my mind the crucial question is whether the conduct of the council in trying by their four questions, whether taken individually or collectively, to force acceptance by the club of their own policy (however proper that policy may be) on their own terms, as for example, by forcing them to lend their considerable prestige to a public condemnation of the tour, can be said either to be so 'unreasonable' as to give rise to '*Wednesbury* unreasonableness' (*Associated Provincial Picture Houses Ltd* v *Wednesbury Corporation* [1948] 1 KB 223) or to be so fundamental a breach of the duty to act fairly which rests upon every local authority in matters of this kind and thus to justify interference by the courts.

I do not doubt for one moment the great importance which the council attach to the presence in its midst of a 25 per cent population of persons who are either Asian or of Afro-Caribbean origin. Nor do I doubt for one moment the sincerity of the view expressed in Mr Soulsby's affidavit regarding the need for the council to distance itself from bodies who hold important positions and who do not actively discourage sporting contacts with South Africa. Persuasion, even powerful persuasion, is always a permissible way of seeking to obtain an objective. But in a field where other views can equally legitimately be held, persuasion, however powerful, must not be allowed to cross that line where it moves into the field of illegitimate pressure coupled with the threat of sanctions. The four questions, coupled with the insistence that only affirmative answers to all four would be acceptable, are suggestive of more than powerful persuasion. The second question is to my mind open to particular criticism. What, in the context, is meant by the 'club?' The committee? 90 playing members? 4,300 non-playing members? It by no means follows that the committee would all have agreed on an affirmative answer to the question and still less that a majority of their members, playing or non-playing, would have done so. Nor would any of these groups of members necessarily have known whether 'the large proportion,' whatever that phrase may mean in the context, of the Leicester population would have regarded the tour as 'an insult' to them.

None of the learned judges in the court below have felt able to hold that the action of the club was unreasonable or perverse in the *Wednesbury* sense. They do not appear to have been invited to consider whether those actions, even if not unreasonable on *Wednesbury* principles, were assailable on the grounds of procedural impropriety or unfairness by the council in the manner in which, in the light of the facts I have outlined, they took their decision to suspend for 12 months the use by the club of the Welford Road recreation ground.

I greatly hesitate to differ from four learned judges on the *Wednesbury* issue but for myself I would have been disposed respectfully to do this and to say that the actions of the council were unreasonable in the *Wednesbury* sense. But even if I am wrong in this view, I am clearly of the opinion that the manner in which the council took that decision was in all the circumstances of the case unfair within the third of the principles stated in *Council for the Civil Service Unions* v *Minister for the Civil Service* [1985] AC 374. The council formulated those four questions in the manner of which I have spoken and indicated that only such affirmative answers would be acceptable. They received reasoned and reasonable answers which went a long way in support of the policy which the council had accepted and desired to see accepted. The views expressed in these reasoned and reasonable answers were lawful views and the views which, as the evidence shows, many people sincerely hold and believe to be correct. If the club had adopted a different and hostile attitude, different considerations might well have arisen. But the club did not adopt any such attitude....

I would therefore allow the appeal.

NOTE: The judgment of Lord Roskill may be compared to that of Ackner LJ in the Court of Appeal in *Wheeler*. Having decided that the council were lawfully entitled to take into account the purposes expressed in s. 71 of the Race Relations Act 1976, Ackner LJ continued:

If I am right so far, this leaves only one final question to consider. Can it be said in the circumstances of the case that no reasonable local authority could properly conclude that temporarily banning from the use of its recreation grounds an important local rugger club, which declined to condemn a South African tour and declined actively to discourage its members from participating therein, could promote good relations between persons of different racial groups? (The well-known *Wednesbury* test: see *Associated Provincial Picture Houses Ltd* v *Wednesbury Corp.* [1947] 2 All ER 680, [1948] 1 KB 223.) Forbes J was at pains to point out, as I certainly would wish also to do, that courts are not concerned with the merits of the two rival views, no doubt equally honestly held, as to the value of severing sporting links with South Africa. I am fully prepared to accept that, even amongst those who feel strongly that sporting links should be severed, there may be some who could take the view that the club acted wholly reasonably in the action it took and should not have been expected to go further. But to accept the mere existence of such a school of thought does not establish that the council's decision was perverse and this is what the club is obliged to do to succeed under this head. Nor is the club's case advanced by emphasising that the council were imposing a sanction against members of the club for refusing publicly to endorse the reasonable views of the council and thereby interfering with the club's freedom of speech. The view which the council held as to the importance of severing sporting links with South Africa had clearly been fully considered by the council well before the events of 1984, and in view of the make-up of the population of the city it was a view which understandably was very strongly supported. It represented no more than that clearly recorded in the Gleneagles Agreement. In my judgment it would be quite wrong to categorise as perverse the council's decision to give an outward and visible manifestation of their disapproval of the club's failure, indeed refusal, 'to take every practical step to discourage' the tour, and in particular the participation of its members.

I would accordingly dismiss this appeal.

■ QUESTIONS

1. On the question of whether the council had acted in a way in which no reasonable council could have acted, do you find the reasoning of Lord Roskill or that of Ackner LJ more convincing?
2. Does Lord Roskill explain which of the particular aspects of Lord Diplock's third category, procedural impropriety, he considered to have been breached?

Nottinghamshire CC v *Secretary of State for the Environment*

[1986] 1 AC 240, House of Lords

In 1984 the Secretary of State issued a report containing the guidance for expenditure by local authorities for 1985–86. The guidance was based on the 1984–85 budgets of local authorities and an amount known as 'grant-related expenditure' (GRE). Grant-related expenditure is the notional expenditure which an authority might incur if all authorities provided the same standard of service with the same degree of efficiency at a level consistent with the Government's aggregate spending plans for local authorities. The guidance for 1985–86 stated that authorities which had budgeted to spend at or below the GRE expenditure in 1984–85 could budget in 1985–86 for the 1984/85 GRE plus 3.75 per cent. Those which had budgeted at above their GRE for 1984/85 could budget for the figure in the 1984–85 guidance plus 3.75 per cent. Under the scheme established by the Local Government Planning and Land Act 1980, if a local authority's expenditure exceeded that set in the guidance to it, the Secretary of State was empowered to reduce the amount of the rate support grant made by central government to the authority.

The report was laid before the House of Commons pursuant to s. 60 of the Act, and was approved by an affirmative resolution of the House. Nottinghamshire CC and the City of Bradford MC applied for an order of *certiorari* to quash the decision of the Secretary of State contained in the report and for declarations that the expenditure guidance contained in the report was invalid. They based their application on two grounds. First, the Secretary of State's guidance did not comply with the requirement in s. 59(11A) of the 1980 Act that 'any guidance issued...be framed by reference to principles applicable to all local authorities...' because it differentiated between authorities budgeting to spend above or below the GRE. Secondly, they argued that the decision of the Secretary was unreasonable because the guidance was disproportionately disadvantageous to a small group of public authorities whose 1984–85 guidance was below GRE and who were budgeting to spend above GRE.

At first instance, the application was dismissed but the Court of Appeal allowed the authority's appeal. On appeal to the House of Lords the first ground was rejected; it was held that, on the true construction of the Act, while there had to be one set of principles applicable to all local authorities, it was permissible for those principles to identify and reflect differences between local authorities, including their past expenditure records. The following extracts deal with the second ground.

LORD SCARMAN: ...Their second submission is that, even if the guidance complies with the words of the statute, it offends a principle of public law in that the burden which the guidance imposes on some authorities, including Nottingham and Bradford, is so disproportionately disadvantageous when compared with its effect upon others that it is a perversely unreasonable exercise of the power conferred by the statute upon the Secretary of State. The respondents rely on what has become known to lawyers as the 'Wednesbury principles'—by which is meant the judgment of Lord Greene MR in *Associated Provincial Picture House Ltd* v *Wednesbury Corporation* [1948] 1 KB 223, 229....

The submission raises an important question as to the limits of judicial review. We are in the field of public financial administration and we are being asked to review the exercise by the Secretary of State of an administrative discretion which inevitably requires a political judgment on his part and which cannot lead to action by him against a local authority unless that action is first approved by the House of Commons.

...My Lords, I think the courts below were absolutely right to decline the invitation to intervene. I can understand that there may well be a justiciable issue as to the true construction of the words of the statute and that, if the Secretary of State has issued guidance which fails to comply with the requirement of subsection (11 A) of section 59 of the Act of 1980 the guidance can be quashed. But I cannot accept that it is constitutionally appropriate, save in very exceptionable circumstances, for the courts to intervene on the ground of 'unreasonableness' to quash guidance framed by the Secretary of State and by necessary implication approved by the House of Commons, the guidance being concerned with the limits of public expenditure by local authorities and the incidence of the tax burden as between taxpayers and ratepayers. Unless and until a statute provides otherwise, or it is established that the Secretary of State has abused his power, these are matters of political judgment for him and for the House of Commons. They are not for the judges or your Lordships' House in its judicial capacity.

For myself, I refuse in this case to examine the detail of the guidance or its consequences. My reasons are these. Such an examination by a court would be justified only if a prima facie case were to be shown for holding that the Secretary of State has acted in bad faith, or for an improper motive, or that the consequences of his guidance were so absurd that he must have taken leave of his senses. The evidence comes nowhere near establishing any of these propositions. Nobody in the case has ever suggested bad faith on the part of the Secretary of State. Nobody suggests, nor could it be suggested in the light of the evidence as to the matters he considered before reaching his decision, that he had acted for an improper motive. Nobody now suggests that the Secretary of State failed to consult local authorities in the manner required by statute. It is plain that the timetable, to which the Secretary of State in the preparation of the guidance was required by statute and compelled by circumstances to adhere, involved him necessarily in framing guidance on the basis of the past spending record of authorities. It is recognised that the Secretary of State and his advisers were well aware that there would be inequalities in the distribution of the burden between local authorities but believed the guidance upon which he decided would by discouraging the high spending and encouraging the low spending be the best course of action in the circumstances. And as my noble and learned friend, Lord Bridge of Harwich, demonstrates, it was guidance which complied with the terms of the statute. This view of the language of the statute has inevitably a significant bearing upon the conclusion of 'unreasonableness' in the *Wednesbury* sense. If, as your Lordships are holding, the guidance was based on principles applicable to all authorities, the principles would have to be either a pattern of perversity or an absurdity of such proportions that the guidance could not have been framed by a bona fide exercise of political judgment on the part of the Secretary of State. And it would be necessary to find as a fact that the House of Commons had been misled: for their approval was necessary and was obtained to the action that he proposed to take to implement the guidance.

...The present case raises in acute form the constitutional problem of the separation of powers between Parliament, the executive, and the courts. In this case, Parliament has enacted that an executive power is not to be exercised save with the consent and approval of one of its Houses. It is true that the framing of the guidance is for the Secretary of State alone after consultation with local authorities; but he cannot act on the guidance so as to discriminate between local authorities without reporting to, and obtaining the approval of, the House of Commons. That House has, therefore, a role and responsibility not only at the legislative stage when the Act was passed but in the action to be taken by the Secretary of State in the exercise of the power conferred upon him by the legislation.

To sum it up, the levels of public expenditure and the incidence and distribution of taxation are matters for Parliament and, within Parliament, especially for the House of Commons. If Parliament legislates, the courts have their interpretative role: they must, if called upon to do so, construe the statute. If a minister exercises a power conferred on him by the legislation, the courts can investigate whether he has abused his power. But if, as in this case, effect cannot be given to the Secretary of State's determination without the consent of the House of Commons and the House of Commons has consented, it is not open to the courts to intervene unless the minister and the House must have misconstrued the statute or the minister has—to put it bluntly—deceived the House. The courts can properly rule that a minister has acted unlawfully if he has erred in law as to the limits of his power even when his action has the approval of the House of Commons, itself acting not legislatively but within the limits set by a statute. But, if a statute, as in this case, requires the House of Commons to approve a minister's decision before he can lawfully enforce it, and if the action proposed complies with the terms of the statute (as your Lordships, I understand, are convinced that it does in the present case), it is not for the judges to say that the action has such unreasonable consequences that the guidance upon which the action is based and on which the House of Commons had notice was perverse and must be set aside. For that is a question of policy for the minister and the Commons, unless there has been bad faith or misconduct by the minister. Where Parliament has legislated that the action to be taken by the Secretary of State must, before it is taken, be approved by the House of Commons, it is no part of the judge's role to declare that the action proposed is unfair, unless it constitutes an abuse of power in the sense which I have explained; for Parliament has enacted that one of its Houses is responsible. Judicial review is a great weapon in the hands of the judges: but the judges must observe the constitutional limits set by our parliamentary system upon their exercise of this beneficent power....

Lord Bridge and Lord Templeman delivered judgments in which they agreed with Lord Scarman. Lord Roskill and Lord Griffiths agreed with Lord Scarman.

NOTE: Lord Scarman's judgment was discussed and followed by the House of Lords in *R* v *Secretary of State for the Environment, ex parte Hammersmith and Fulham LBC* [1990] 3 All ER 589, a case which also involved a dispute between central and local government over finances. The House of Lords held that the Secretary of State had acted lawfully in setting a maximum amount for the budgets of a number of authorities under the Local Government Finance Act 1988.

■ QUESTIONS

1. Do you interpret Lord Scarman's judgment as stating that judicial review of a decision of this nature on the ground of unreasonableness is excluded?
2. Would judicial review be available on any other grounds, for example that the Minister had acted for an improper purpose or on the basis of irrelevant considerations?
3. Which constitutional theory did his Lordship rely on in this case?
4. Commenting on this decision in (1986) 45 *Cambridge Law Journal* (169–173), Colin Reid sees it, at p. 171:

   ...as an affirmation of our traditional constitutional theory. There may be no formal separation of powers in this country, but the basic notions of our constitution, such as parliamentary sovereignty, the rule of law and responsibility of the Executive to Parliament, do create a fundamental distribution of powers and functions between the various elements of the state. It is to Parliament that one must look to control the executive on matters of policy and principle, *a fortiori* in cases where it has been enacted that the Executive must seek parliamentary approval for the exercise of the powers conferred on it....

   The question must be asked, though, how well this structure serves us in the political realities of today. Can we rely on Parliament to provide an adequate check on the powers of the executive?

   If the answer is no, can judicial review provide a solution? Note that Reid's view is that it cannot; 'the way to achieve greater control over the Executive must lie in far-reaching reforms to our constitutional structure, rather than to a continued extension, or rather distortion, of judicial review to embrace issues and arguments not suited to judicial resolution.' Compare this with the view expressed by Cane (pp. 527–29, *ante*).

NOTE: The *Nottinghamshire* and *Hammersmith & Fulham* cases have been described as being super-*Wednesbury* because their approach imposes a higher threshold. The appropriate standard of *Wednesbury* review was at issue in the next case.

R (Daly) v *Secretary of State for the Home Department*

[2001] UKHL 26, [2001] 2 AC 532, House of Lords

LORD STEYN: …

My Lords,

24. I am in complete agreement with the reasons given by Lord Bingham of Cornhill in his speech. For the reasons he gives I would also allow the appeal. Except on one narrow but important point I have nothing to add.

25. There was written and oral argument on the question whether certain observations of Lord Phillips of Worth Matravers MR in *R (Mahmood)* v *Secretary of State for the Home Department* [2001] 1 WLR 840 were correct. The context was an immigration case involving a decision of the Secretary of State made before the Human Rights Act 1998 came into effect. The Master of the Rolls nevertheless approached the case as if the Act had been in force when the Secretary of State reached his decision. He explained the new approach to be adopted. The Master of the Rolls concluded, at p 857, para 40:

> When anxiously scrutinising an executive decision that interferes with human rights, the court will ask the question, applying an objective test, whether the decision-maker could reasonably have concluded that the interference was necessary to achieve one or more of the legitimate aims recognised by the Convention. When considering the test of necessity in the relevant context, the court must take into account the European jurisprudence in accordance with section 2 of the 1998 Act.

These observations have been followed by the Court of Appeal in *R* v *Secretary of State for the Home Department, Ex p Isiko* (unreported), 20 December 2000 and by Thomas J in *R* v *Secretary of State for the Home Department, Ex p Samaroo* (unreported), 20 December 2000.

26. The explanation of the Master of the Rolls in the first sentence of the cited passage requires clarification. It is couched in language reminiscent of the traditional *Wednesbury* ground of review *(Associated Provincial Picture Houses Ltd* v *Wednesbury Corporation* [1948] 1 KB 223), and in particular the adaptation of that test in terms of heightened scrutiny in cases involving fundamental rights as formulated in *R* v *Ministry of Defence, Ex p Smith* [1996] QB 517, 554E–G per Sir Thomas Bingham MR. There is a material difference between the *Wednesbury* and *Smith* grounds of review and the approach of proportionality applicable in respect of review where convention rights are at stake.

27. The contours of the principle of proportionality are familiar. In *de Freitas* v *Permanent Secretary of Ministry of Agriculture, Fisheries, Lands and Housing* [1999] 1 AC 69 the Privy Council adopted a three stage test. Lord Clyde observed, at p 80, that in determining whether a limitation (by an act, rule or decision) is arbitrary or excessive the court should ask itself:

> whether: (i) the legislative objective is sufficiently important to justify limiting a fundamental right; (ii) the measures designed to meet the legislative objective are rationally connected to it; and (iii) the means used to impair the right or freedom are no more than is necessary to accomplish the objective.

Clearly, these criteria are more precise and more sophisticated than the traditional grounds of review. What is the difference for the disposal of concrete cases? Academic public lawyers have in remarkably similar terms elucidated the difference between the traditional grounds of review and the proportionality approach: see Professor Jeffrey Jowell QC, 'Beyond the Rule of Law: Towards Constitutional Judicial Review' [2000] PL 671; Craig, *Administrative Law*, 4th ed (1999), 561–563; Professor David Feldman, 'Proportionality and the Human Rights Act 1998', essay in *The Principle of Proportionality in the Laws of Europe* (1999), pp 117, 127 et seq. The starting point is that there is an overlap between the traditional grounds of review and the approach of proportionality. Most cases would be decided in the same way whichever approach is adopted. But the intensity of review is somewhat greater under the proportionality approach. Making due allowance for important structural differences between various convention rights, which I do not propose to discuss, a few generalisations are perhaps permissible. I would mention three concrete differences without suggesting that my statement is exhaustive. First, the doctrine of proportionality may require the reviewing court to assess the balance which the decision maker has struck, not merely whether it is within the range of rational or reasonable decisions. Secondly, the proportionality test may go further than the traditional grounds of review inasmuch as it may require attention to be directed to the relative weight accorded to interests and considerations. Thirdly, even the heightened scrutiny test developed in *R* v *Ministry of Defence, Ex p Smith* [1996] QB 517, 554 is not necessarily appropriate to the protection of human rights. It will be recalled that in *Smith* the Court of Appeal reluctantly felt compelled to reject a limitation on homosexuals in the army. The challenge based on article 8 of the Convention for the Protection of Human Rights and Fundamental Freedoms (the right to respect for private and family life) foundered on the threshold required even by the anxious scrutiny test. The European Court of Human Rights came to the opposite conclusion: *Smith and Grady* v *United Kingdom* (1999) 29 EHRR 493. The court concluded, at p 543, para. 138:

> the threshold at which the High Court and the Court of Appeal could find the Ministry of Defence policy irrational was placed so high that it effectively excluded any consideration by the domestic courts of the question of whether the interference with the applicants' rights answered a pressing social need or was proportionate to the national security and public order aims pursued, principles which lie at the heart of the court's analysis of complaints under article 8 of the Convention.

In other words, the intensity of the review, in similar cases, is guaranteed by the twin requirements that the limitation of the right was necessary in a democratic society, in the sense of meeting a pressing social need, and the question whether the interference was really proportionate to the legitimate aim being pursued.

28. The differences in approach between the traditional grounds of review and the proportionality approach may therefore sometimes yield different results. It is therefore important that cases involving convention rights must be analysed in the correct way. This does not mean that there has been a shift to merits review. On the contrary, as Professor Jowell [2000] PL 671, 681 has pointed out the respective roles of judges and administrators are fundamentally distinct and will remain so. To this extent the general tenor of the observations in *Mahmood* [2001] 1 WLR 840 are correct. And Laws LJ rightly emphasised in *Mahmood*, at p 847, para 18, 'that the intensity of review in a public law case will depend on the subject matter in hand'. That is so even in cases involving Convention rights. In law context is everything.

NOTE: We appear to have ordinary *Wednesbury* unreasonableness, super-*Wednesbury*, which is less intensive, and when human rights are at issue, a more searching scrutiny by the courts based on proportionality. It has been argued that this variability in *Wednesbury* unreasonableness moves domestic law closer to the proportionality standard of review found in European law, in Community law, and the jurisprudence of the European Court of Human Rights. It is suggested that proportionality is a clearer and more honest basis for substantive review. It has been applied in three types of situation in relation to penalties, to human rights and other exercises of administrative discretion. The case law indicates that the following tests are used:

(a) *balancing*: where the ends sought to be achieved are measured against the means applied and the impact upon affected individuals;
(b) *necessity*: where more than one means is available, was the action taken the least restrictive way of achieving the aim;
(c) *suitability*: where the means are appropriate, e.g., capable of implementation, lawful.

See Craig, *Administrative Law* (2008) pp. 622–635; Wade and Forsyth, *Administrative Law* (2009) pp. 305–314; Ellis (ed.), *The Principle of Proportionality in the Laws of Europe* (1999); and Wong, 'Towards the Nutcracker Principle: Reconsidering the Objections to Proportionality' [2000] *Public Law* 92.

In *Brind*, some members of the House of Lords were clear that proportionality was very different from *Wednesbury* unreasonableness and might overstep the legality/merits boundary. This view is changing, in part because the judges have more experience in applying it in cases involving European Union law.

R v *Chief Constable of Sussex, ex parte International Trader's Ferry Ltd*

[1999] 2 AC 418, House of Lords

The applicant company (ITF) was engaged in exporting live animals. People who were opposed to this demonstrated at ports seeking to stop the transport of the livestock. The police operations enabled five sailings a week to be operated out of Shoreham. The Chief Constable reviewed the situation and, after taking into account his resources, decided to deploy officers at Shoreham on two consecutive days a week, or four consecutive days a fortnight. The applicants challenged this decision by judicial review. In the Divisional Court the Chief Constable's decision was quashed on the basis that it breached Art. 34 (now 35 TFEU) of the EC Treaty, as it was a measure having equivalent effect to a quantitative restriction on exports. In domestic law it was a lawful exercise of his discretion. On appeal the Court of Appeal held that if this decision was within the scope of Art. 34 (now 35 TFEU) it was covered by Art. 36 (now 36 TFEU) and was justified on grounds of public policy, the pursuit of effective policing. The applicants appealed.

LORD SLYNN: ...What is required in a case like the present where the Chief Constable has statutory and common law duties to perform is to ask whether he did all that proportionately and reasonably he could be expected to do with the resources available to him. He is after all dealing with an emergency situation and there is no question of funds being deliberately withheld by the state to hamper his work. The budget for the authority was a very large one and it was for him to decide how he would use the moneys apportioned to him. These decisions have to be taken on the information available at the time. It is not right, in my view, that there should be an ex post facto examination of accounts to see whether, in some way or another, in the event moneys did prove to be available which perhaps could have been used. Thus, in the present case, I do not consider that the fact that the amount attributed to reserves in the final accounts in the 1995–96 year (£13.13m.) meant that, at the time he had to take his decision, the Chief Constable should have assumed that the police authorities would allocate more money to this particular task than appeared as reserves in the budget (£7.25m.). It seems to me that at the end of the day it is all a question of considering whether 'appropriate measures' have been taken. That in turn involves an inquiry as to whether the steps taken were proportionate.

In *Reg.* v *Secretary of State for the Home Department, Ex parte Brind* [1991] 1 AC 696 the House treated *Wednesbury* reasonableness and proportionality as being different. So in some ways they are though the distinction between the two tests in practice is in any event much less than is sometimes suggested. The cautious way in which the European Court usually applies this test, recognising the importance of respecting the national authority's margin of appreciation, may mean that whichever test is adopted, and even allowing for a difference in onus, the result is the same.

I am satisfied, as was the Court of Appeal, that the Chief Constable has shown here that what he did in providing police assistance was proportionate to what was required. To protect the lorries, in the way he did, was a suitable and necessary way of dealing with potentially violent demonstrators. To limit the occasions when sufficient police could be made available was, in the light of the resources available to him to deal with immediate and foreseeable events at the port, and at the same time to carry out all his other police duties, necessary and in no way disproportionate to the restrictions which were involved. Unlike the authorities in *Commission of the European Communities* v *French Republic* (Case C–265/95) [1997] ECR I–6959 he was controlling and arresting violent offenders. He was, moreover, not dealing with a situation where no other way of exporting the animals was available. Dover was available and there were and might be other occasions when the lorries could get through. Far from failing to protect the applicant's trade he was seeking to do it in the most effective way available to him with his finite resources. It was only on rare and necessary, even dangerous, occasions that lorries were turned back. In the light of article 36 [now 36] it is not open to ITF to say, as they at times seem to be saying, that they had an absolute right to export animals on seven days a week and there is no suggestion that with such a short Channel crossing their claim was necessarily limited to one sailing a day. This case is quite different from *Commission of the European Communities* v *French Republic* where 'manifest and persistent failure' to control those interfering with imports was shown and where there was no evidence to show that those responsible could have acted. Since this case involves the application of the principles laid down in the *French Republic* case, where clearly the European Court left a considerable discretion to national authorities in dealing with issues of this sort, I do not find it necessary, nor are your Lordships obliged, to refer a question concerning article 36 [now 30] to the European Court of Justice under article 177 [now 267] of the EC Treaty.

I am satisfied that here the Chief Constable has shown that the steps that he took were justified on grounds of public order and I would dismiss this appeal.

NOTES

1. Lord Cooke was also of the view that in this case 'the European concepts of proportionality and margin of appreciation produce the same result as what are commonly called *Wednesbury* principles'. He seemed to prefer a simpler test than the twice used tautologous formula in *Wednesbury*—'so unreasonable that no reasonable authority could ever have come to it'—'whether the decision in question was one which a reasonable authority could reach'.
2. Wong [2000] *Public Law* 92, at 109 suggests that Lord Slynn was implicitly *actually* using proportionality, not *Wednesbury*, see his use of suitable and necessary.

■ QUESTION

Which do you think is a better approach to irrationality, adopting Lord Cooke's simpler test or adopting proportionality with its structured tests?

E: Substantive legitimate expectations

NOTE: Earlier we saw how the concept of legitimate expectations had initially been concerned with procedure. It has been held to have a substantive aspect, but there has been doubt about the test which should be used—*Wednesbury* unreasonableness or proportionality. Consider the following case.

R v *North and East Devon Health Authority, ex parte Coughlan*

[2000] 2 WLR 622, Court of Appeal

The applicant was severely disabled in a road accident. In 1993 she and other disabled patients had been moved from a hospital to Mardon House. The health authority had promised that this would be their home for life. Following the issue of criteria by the Department of Health, the authority concluded that the applicant did not qualify for specialist nursing services to be provided by the authority but for general nursing care to be purchased by local authorities. Subsequently the health authority, following a public consultation, decided to close Mardon House and to transfer the applicant to the local authority for long-term general nursing care. In a successful application for judicial review of the decision to close Mardon House, it was held that the applicant and others had received a clear promise that Mardon House would be their home for life; that no overriding public interest had been established to justify breaking that promise; that the closure decision was flawed as no alternative placement for the applicant had been identified; that all nursing care was an NHS responsibility and that it was not open to the health authority to transfer general nursing care responsibility to a local authority, and that the health authority's eligibility criteria for long-term health care were flawed. On appeal to the Court of Appeal.

LORD WOOLF MR, MUMMERY and SEDLEY LJJ: . . .

56. What is still the subject of some controversy is the court's role when a member of the public, as a result of a promise or other conduct, has a legitimate expectation that he will be treated in one way and the public body wishes to treat him or her in a different way. Here the starting point has to be to ask what in the circumstances the member of the public could legitimately expect. In the words of Lord Scarman in *In re Findlay* [1985] AC 318, 338, 'But what was their *legitimate* expectation?' Where there is a dispute as to this, the dispute has to be determined by the court, as happened in *In re Findlay*. This can involve a detailed examination of the precise terms of the promise or representation made, the circumstances in which the promise was made and the nature of the statutory or other discretion.

57. There are at least three possible outcomes. (a) The court may decide that the public authority is only required to bear in mind its previous policy or other representation, giving it the weight it thinks right, but no more, before deciding whether to change course. Here the court is confined to reviewing the

decision on *Wednesbury* grounds (*Associated Provincial Picture Houses Ltd* v *Wednesbury Corporation* [1948] 1 KB 223). This has been held to be the effect of changes of policy in cases involving the early release of prisoners: see *In re Findlay* [1985] AC 318; *Reg.* v *Secretary of State for the Home Department, Ex parte Hargreaves* [1997] 1 WLR 906. (b) On the other hand the court may decide that the promise or practice induces a legitimate expectation of, for example, being consulted before a particular decision is taken. Here it is uncontentious that the court itself will require *the opportunity for consultation* to be given unless there is an overriding reason to resile from it (see *Attorney-General of Hong Kong* v *Ng Yuen Shiu* [1983] 2 AC 629) in which case the court will itself judge the adequacy of the reason advanced for the change of policy, taking into account what fairness requires. (c) Where the court considers that a lawful promise or practice has induced a legitimate expectation of a *benefit which is substantive*, not simply procedural, authority now establishes that here too the court will in a proper case decide whether to frustrate the expectation is so unfair that to take a new and different course will amount to an abuse of power. Here, once the legitimacy of the expectation is established, the court will have the task of weighing the requirements of fairness against any overriding interest relied upon for the change of policy.

58. The court having decided which of the categories is appropriate, the court's role in the case of the second and third categories is different from that in the first. In the case of the first, the court is restricted to reviewing the decision on conventional grounds. The test will be rationality and whether the public body has given proper weight to the implications of not fulfilling the promise. In the case of the second category the court's task is the conventional one of determining whether the decision was procedurally fair. In the case of the third, the court has when necessary to determine whether there is a sufficient overriding interest to justify a departure from what has been previously promised.

59. In many cases the difficult task will be to decide into which category the decision should be allotted. In what is still a developing field of law, attention will have to be given to what it is in the first category of case which limits the applicant's legitimate expectation (in Lord Scarman's words in *In re Findlay* [1985] AC 318) to an expectation that whatever policy is in force at the time will be applied to him. As to the second and third categories, the difficulty of segregating the procedural from the substantive is illustrated by the line of cases arising out of decisions of justices not to commit a defendant to the Crown Court for sentence, or assurances given to a defendant by the court: here to resile from such a decision or assurance may involve the breach of legitimate expectation: see *Reg.* v *Grice* (1977) 66 Cr App R 167; cf. *Reg.* v *Reilly* [1982] QB 1208, *Reg.* v *Dover Magistrates' Court, Ex parte Pamment* (1994) 15 Cr App R (S) 778, 782. No attempt is made in those cases, rightly in our view, to draw the distinction. Nevertheless, most cases of an enforceable expectation of a substantive benefit (the third category) are likely in the nature of things to be cases where the expectation is confined to one person or a few people, giving the promise or representation the character of a contract. We recognise that the courts' role in relation to the third category is still controversial; but, as we hope to show, it is now clarified by authority.

60. We consider that Mr Goudie and Mr Gordon are correct, as was the judge, in regarding the facts of this case as coming into the third category. (Even if this were not correct because of the nature of the promise, and even if the case fell within the second category, the health authority in exercising its discretion and in due course the court would have to take into account that only an overriding public interest would justify resiling from the promise.) Our reasons are as follow. First, the importance of what was promised to Miss Coughlan (as we will explain later, this is a matter underlined by the Human Rights Act 1998); second, the fact that promise was limited to a few individuals, and the fact that the consequences to the health authority of requiring it to honour its promise are likely to be financial only.

The authorities

61. Whether to frustrate a legitimate expectation can amount to an abuse of power is the question which was posed by the House of Lords in *Reg.* v *Inland Revenue Commissioners, Ex parte Preston* [1985] AC 835 and addressed more recently by this court in *Reg.* v *Inland Revenue Commissioners, Ex parte Unilever Plc* [1996] S.T.C. 681. In each case it was in relation to a decision by a public authority (the Crown) to resile from a representation about how it would treat a member of the public (the taxpayer). It cannot be suggested that special principles of public law apply to the Inland Revenue or to taxpayers. Yet this is an area of law which has been a site of recent controversy, because while *Ex parte Preston* has been followed in tax cases, using the vocabulary of abuse of power, in other fields of public law analogous challenges, couched in the language of legitimate expectation, have not all been approached in the same way.

62. There has never been any question that the propriety of a breach by a public authority of a legitimate expectation of the second category, of a *procedural* benefit—typically a promise of being heard or consulted—is a matter for full review by the court. The court has, in other words, to examine the relevant circumstances and to decide for itself whether what happened was fair. This is of a piece with the historic jurisdiction of the courts over issues of procedural justice. But in relation to a legitimate expectation of a substantive benefit (such as a promise of a home for life) doubt has been cast upon whether the same standard of review applies. Instead it is suggested that the proper standard is the so-called *Wednesbury* standard which is applied to the generality of executive decisions. This touches the intrinsic quality of the decision, as opposed to the means by which it has been reached, only where the decision is irrational or (*per* Lord Diplock in *Council of Civil Service Unions* v *Minister for the Civil Service* [1985] AC 374, 410) immoral.

63. This is not a live issue in the common law of the European Union, where a uniform standard of full review for fairness is well established: see Schwarze, *European Administrative Law* (1992), pp. 1134–1135 and the European Court of Justice cases reviewed in *Reg.* v *Ministry of Agriculture, Fisheries' and Food, Ex parte Hamble (Offshore) Fisheries Ltd* [1995] 2 All ER 714, 726–728. It is, however, something on which the Human Rights Act 1998, when it comes into force, may have a bearing.

64. It is axiomatic that a public authority which derives its existence and its powers from statute cannot validly act outside those powers. This is the familiar ultra vires doctrine adopted by public law from company law (*Colman* v *Eastern Counties Railway Co.* (1846) 10 Beav 1). Since such powers will ordinarily include anything fairly incidental to the express remit, a statutory body may lawfully adopt and follow policies (*British Oxygen Co. Ltd* v *Board of Trade* [1971] AC 610) and enter into formal undertakings. But since it cannot abdicate its general remit, not only must it remain free to change policy; its undertakings are correspondingly open to modification or abandonment. The recurrent question is when and where and how the courts are to intervene to protect the public from unwarranted harm in this process. The problem can readily be seen to go wider than the exercise of statutory powers. It may equally arise in relation to the exercise of the prerogative power, which at least since *Reg.* v *Criminal Injuries Compensation Board, Ex parte Lain* [1967] 2 QB 864, has been subject to judicial review, and in relation to private monopoly powers: *Reg.* v *Panel on Take-overs and Mergers, Ex parte Datafin Plc* [1987] QB 815.

65. The court's task in all these cases is not to impede executive activity but to reconcile its continuing need to initiate or respond to change with the legitimate interests or expectations of citizens or strangers who have relied, and have been justified in relying, on a current policy or an extant promise. The critical question is by what standard the court is to resolve such conflicts. It is when one examines the implications for a case like the present of the proposition that, so long as the decision-making process has been lawful, the court's only ground of intervention is the intrinsic rationality of the decision, that the problem becomes apparent. Rationality, as it has developed in modern public law, has two faces: one is the barely known decision which simply defies comprehension; the other is a decision which can be seen to have proceeded by flawed logic (though this can often be equally well allocated to the intrusion of an irrelevant factor). The present decision may well pass a rationality test; the health authority knew of the promise and its seriousness; it was aware of its new policies and the reasons for them; it knew that one had to yield, and it made a choice which, whatever else can be said of it, may not easily be challenged as irrational. As Lord Diplock said in *Secretary of State for Education and Science* v *Tameside Metropolitan Borough Council* [1977] AC 1014, 1064:

> The very concept of administrative discretion involves a right to choose between more than one possible course of action upon which there is room for reasonable people to hold differing opinions as to which is to he preferred.

But to limit the court's power of supervision to this is to exclude from consideration another aspect of the decision which is equally the concern of the law.

66. In the ordinary case there is no space for intervention on grounds of abuse of power once a rational decision directed to a proper purpose has been reached by lawful process. The present class of case is visibly different. It involves not one but two lawful exercises of power (the promise and the policy change) by the same public authority, with consequences for individuals trapped between the two. The policy decision may well, and often does, make as many exceptions as are proper and feasible to protect individual expectations. The departmental decision in *Ex parte Hamble (Offshore) Fisheries Ltd* [1995] 2 All ER 714 is a good example. If it does not, as in *Ex parte Unilever Plc* [1996] STC 681, the court is there to ensure

that the power to make and alter policy has not been abused by unfairly frustrating legitimate individual expectations. In such a situation a bare rationality test would constitute the public authority judge in its own cause, for a decision to prioritise a policy change over legitimate expectations will almost always be rational from where the authority stands, even if objectively it is arbitrary or unfair. It is in response to this dilemma that two distinct but related approaches have developed in the modern cases.

67. One approach is to ask not whether the decision is ultra vires in the restricted *Wednesbury* sense but whether, for example through unfairness or arbitrariness it amounts to an abuse of power. The leading case on the existence of this principle is *Ex parte Preston* [1985] AC 835. It concerned an allegation, not in the event made out, that the Inland Revenue Commissioners had gone back impermissibly on their promise not to reinvestigate certain aspects of an individual taxpayer's affairs. Lord Scarman, expressing his agreement with the single fully reasoned speech (that of Lord Templeman) advanced a number of important general propositions. First, he said, at p. 851:

> ... I must make clear my view that the principle of fairness has an important place in the law of judicial review: and that in an appropriate case it is a ground upon which the court can intervene to quash a decision made by a public officer or authority in purported exercise of a power conferred by law.

Second, Lord Scarman reiterated, citing the decision of the House of Lords in *Reg.* v *Inland Revenue Commissioners, Ex parte National Federation of Self-Employed and Small Businesses Ltd* [1982] AC 617, that a claim for judicial review may arise where the Commissioners have failed to discharge their statutory duty to an individual or 'have abused their powers or acted outside them'. Third, that 'unfairness in the purported exercise of a power can be such that it is an abuse or excess of power.'

68. It is evident from these passages and from Lord Scarman's further explanation of them that, in his view, at least, it is unimportant whether the unfairness is analytically within or beyond the power conferred by law: on either view public law today reaches it. The same approach was taken by Lord Templeman, at p. 862:

> Judicial review is available where a decision-making authority exceeds its powers, commits an error of law, commits a breach of natural justice, reaches a decision which no reasonable tribunal could have reached, or abuses its powers.

69. Abuses of power may take many forms. One, not considered in the *Wednesbury* case [1948] 1 KB 223 (even though it was arguably what the case was about), was the use of a power for a collateral purpose. Another, as cases like *Ex parte Preston* [1985] AC 835 now make clear, is reneging without adequate justification, by an otherwise lawful decision, on a lawful promise or practice adopted towards a limited number of individuals.

There is no suggestion in *Ex parte Preston* or elsewhere that the final arbiter of justification, rationality apart, is the decision-maker rather than the court. Lord Templeman, at pp. 864–866, reviewed the law in extenso, including the classic decisions in *Laker Airways Ltd* v *Department of Trade* [1977] QB 643; *Padfield* v *Minister of Agriculture, Fisheries and Food* [1968] AC 997; *Congreve* v *Home Office* [1976] QB 629 and *H.T.V. Ltd* v *Price Commission* [1976] ICR 170 ('It is a commonplace of modern law that such bodies must act fairly... and that the courts have power to redress unfairness:' Scarman LJ at p. 189.) He reached this conclusion, at pp. 866–867:

> In principle I see no reason why the [taxpayer] should not be entitled to judicial review of a decision taken by the commissioners if that decision is unfair to the [taxpayer] because the conduct of the commissioners is equivalent to a breach of contract or a breach of representation. Such a decision falls within the ambit of an abuse of power for which in the present case judicial review is the sole remedy and an appropriate remedy. There may be cases in which conduct which savours of breach of [contract] or breach of representation does not constitute an abuse of power; there may be circumstances in which the court in its discretion might not grant relief by judicial review notwithstanding conduct which savours of breach of contract or breach of representation. In the present case, however, I consider that the [taxpayer] is entitled to relief by way of judicial review for 'unfairness' amounting to abuse of power if the commissioners have been guilty of conduct equivalent to a breach of contract or breach of representations on their part.

The entire passage, too long to set out here, merits close attention. It may be observed that Lord Templeman's final formulation, taken by itself, would allow no room for a test of overriding public interest.

This, it is clear, is because of the facts then before the House. In a case such as the present the question posed in the *H.T.V.* case [1976] ICR 170 remains live.

70. This approach, in our view, embraces all the principles of public law which we have been considering. It recognises the primacy of the public authority both in administration and in policy development but it insists, where these functions come into tension, upon the adjudicative role of the court to ensure fairness to the individual. It does not overlook the passage in the speech of Lord Browne-Wilkinson in *Reg.* v *Hull University Visitor, Ex parte Page* [1993] AC 682, 701, that the basis of the 'fundamental principle...that the courts will intervene to ensure that the powers of public decision-making bodies are exercised lawfully' is the *Wednesbury* limit on the exercise of powers; but it follows the authority not only of *Ex parte Preston* [1985] AC 835 but of Lord Scarman's speech in *Reg.* v *Secretary of State for the Environment, Ex parte Nottinghamshire County Council* [1986] AC 240, 249, in treating a power which is abused as a power which has not been lawfully exercised.

71. Fairness in such a situation, if it is to mean anything, must for the reasons we have considered include fairness of outcome. This in turn is why the doctrine of legitimate expectation has emerged as a distinct application of the concept of abuse of power in relation to substantive as well as procedural benefits, representing a second approach to the same problem. If this is the position in the case of the third category, why is it not also the position in relation to the first category? May it be (though this was not considered in *In re Findlay* [1985] AC 318 or *Ex parte Hargreaves* [1997] 1 WLR 906) that, when a promise is made to a category of individuals who have the same interest, it is more likely to be considered to have binding effect than a promise which is made generally or to a diverse class, when the interests of those to whom the promise is made may differ or, indeed, may be in conflict? Legitimate expectation may play different parts in different aspects of public law. The limits to its role have yet to be finally determined by the courts. Its application is still being developed on a case by case basis. Even where it reflects procedural expectations, for example concerning consultation, it may be affected by an overriding public interest. It may operate as an aspect of good administration, qualifying the intrinsic rationality of policy choices. And without injury to the *Wednesbury* doctrine it may furnish a proper basis for the application of the now established concept of abuse of power.

72. A full century ago in the seminal case of *Kruse* v *Johnson* [1898] 2 QB 91 Lord Russell of Killowen CJ set the limits of the courts' benevolence towards local government byelaws at those which were manifestly unjust, partial, made in bad faith or so gratuitous and oppressive that no reasonable person could think them justified. While it is the latter two classes which reappear in the decision of this court in the *Wednesbury* case [1948] 1 KB 223, the first two are equally part of the law. Thus in *Reg.* v *Inland Revenue Commissioners, Ex parte M.F.K. Underwriting Agents Ltd* [1990] 1 WLR 1545 a Divisional Court (Bingham LJ and Judge J) rejected on the facts a claim for the enforcement of a legitimate expectation in the face of a change of practice by the Inland Revenue. But having set out the need for certainty of representation, Bingham LJ went on, at pp. 1569–1570:

> In so stating these requirements I do not, I hope, diminish or emasculate the valuable, developing doctrine of legitimate expectation. If a public authority so conducts itself as to create a legitimate expectation that a certain course will be followed it would often be unfair if the authority were permitted to follow a different course to the detriment of one who entertained the expectation, particularly if he acted on it. If in private law a body would be in breach of contract in so acting or estopped from so acting a public authority should generally be in no better position. The doctrine of legitimate expectation is rooted in fairness.

73. This approach, which makes no formal distinction between procedural and substantive unfairness, was expanded by reference to the extant body of authority by Simon Brown LJ in *Reg.* v *Devon County Council, Ex parte Baker* [1995] 1 All ER 73, 88–89. He identified two categories of substantive legitimate expectation recognised by modern authority:

> (1) Sometimes the phrase is used to denote a substantive right: an entitlement that the claimant asserts cannot be denied him. It was used in this sense and the assertion upheld in cases such as *Reg.* v *Secretary of State for the Home Department, Ex parte Asif Mahmood Khan* [1984] 1 WLR 1337 and *Reg.* v *Secretary of State for the Home Department, Ex parte Ruddock* [1987] 1 WLR 1482. It was used in the same sense but unsuccessfully in, for instance, *Reg.* v *Inland Revenue Commissioners, Ex parte M.F.K. Underwriting Agents Ltd* [1990] 1 WLR 1545 and *Reg.* v *Jockey*

> *Club, Ex parte R.A.M. Racecourses Ltd* [1993] 2 All ER 225. These various authorities show that the claimant's right will only be found established when there is a clear and unambiguous representation upon which it was reasonable for him to rely. Then the administrator or other public body will be held bound in fairness by the representation made unless only its promise or undertaking as to how its power would be exercised is inconsistent with the statutory duties imposed upon it. The doctrine employed in this sense is akin to an estoppel. In so far as the public body's representation is communicated by way of a stated policy, this type of legitimate expectation falls into two distinct sub-categories: cases in which the authority are held entitled to change their policy even so as to affect the claimant, and those in which they are not. An illustration of the former is *Reg.* v *Torbay Borough Council, Ex parte Cleasby* [1991] COD 142, of the latter *Ex parte Asif Mahmood Khan*. (2) Perhaps more conventionally the concept of legitimate expectation is used to refer to the claimant's interest in some ultimate benefit which he hopes to retain (or, some would argue, attain). Here, therefore, it is the interest itself rather than the benefit that is the substance of the expectation. In other words the expectation arises not because the claimant asserts any specific right to a benefit but rather because his interest in it is one that the law holds protected by the requirements of procedural fairness; the law recognises that the interest cannot properly be withdrawn (or denied) without the claimant being given an opportunity to comment and without the authority communicating rational grounds for any adverse decision. Of the various authorities drawn to our attention, *Schmidt* v *Secretary of State for Home Affairs* [1969] 2 Ch 149, *O'Reilly* v *Mackman* [1983] 2 AC 237 and the recent decision of Roch J in *Reg.* v *Rochdale Metropolitan Borough Council, Ex parte Schemet* [1993] 1 FCR 306 are clear examples of this head of legitimate expectation.

Simon Brown LJ has not in that passage referred expressly to the situation where the individual can claim no higher expectation than to have his individual circumstances considered by the decision-maker in the light of the policy then in force. This is not surprising because this entitlement, which can also be said to be rooted in fairness, adds little to the standard requirements of any exercise of discretion: namely that the decision will take into account all relevant matters which here will include the promise or other conduct giving rise to the expectation and that if the decision-maker does so the courts will not interfere except on the basis that the decision is wholly unreasonable. It is the classic *Wednesbury* situation, not because the expectation is substantive but because it lacks legitimacy.

74. Nowhere in this body of authority, nor in *Ex parte Preston* [1985] AC 835, nor in *In re Findlay* [1985] AC 318, is there any suggestion that judicial review of a decision which frustrates a substantive legitimate expectation is confined to the rationality of the decision. But in *Ex parte Hargreaves* [1997] 1 WLR 906, 921, 925 Hirst LJ (with whom Peter Gibson LJ agreed) was persuaded to reject the notion of scrutiny for fairness as heretical, and Pill LJ to reject it as 'wrong in principle.'

75. *Ex parte Hargreaves* concerned prisoners whose expectations of home leave and early release were not to be fulfilled by reason of a change of policy. Following *In re Findlay* [1985] AC 318 this court held that such prisoners' only legitimate expectation was that their applications would be considered individually in the light of whatever policy was in force at the time: in other words the case came into the first category. This conclusion was dispositive of the case. What Hirst LJ went on to say at p. 919, under the head of 'The proper approach for the court to the Secretary of State's decision' was therefore obiter. However Hirst LJ accepted in terms the submission of leading counsel for the Home Secretary that, beyond review on *Wednesbury* grounds, the law recognised no enforceable legitimate expectation of a substantive benefit. In relation to the decision in *Ex parte Hamble (Offshore) Fisheries Ltd* [1995] 2 All ER 714, he said [1997] 1 WLR 906, 921:

> Mr Beloff characterised Sedley J's approach as heresy, and in my judgment he was right to do so. On matters of substance (as contrasted with procedure) *Wednesbury* provides the correct test.

A number of learned commentators have questioned this conclusion (see e.g. P.P. Craig, 'Substantive legitimate expectations and the principles of judicial review' in *English Public Law and the Common Law of Europe*, ed. M. Andenas (1998); T.R.S. Allan, 'Procedure and substance in judicial review' [1997] CLJ 246; Steve Foster, 'Legitimate expectations and prisoners' rights' (1997) 60 MLR 727).

Ex parte Hargreaves [1997] 1 WLR 906 can, in any event, be distinguished from the present case. Mr Gordon has sought to distinguish it on the ground that the present case involves an abuse of power. On one view all cases where proper effect is not given to a legitimate expectation involve an abuse of power.

Abuse of power can be said to be but another name for acting contrary to law. But the real distinction between *Ex parte Hargreaves* and this case is that in this case it is contended that fairness in the statutory context required more of the decision-maker than in *Ex parte Hargreaves* where the sole legitimate expectation possessed by the prisoners had been met. It required the health authority, as a matter of fairness, not to resile from their promise unless there was an overriding justification for doing so. Another way of expressing the same thing is to talk of the unwarranted frustration of a legitimate expectation and thus an abuse of power or a failure of substantive fairness. Again the labels are not important except that they all distinguish the issue here from that in *Ex parte Hargreaves*. They identify a different task for the court from that where what is in issue is a conventional application of policy or exercise of discretion. Here the decision can only be justified if there is an overriding public interest. Whether there is an overriding public interest is a question for the court.

77. The cases decided in the European Court of Justice cited in *Ex parte Hamble (Offshore) Fisheries Ltd* [1995] 2 All ER 714 all concern policies or practices conferring substantive benefits from which member states were not allowed to resile when the policy or practice was altered. In this country *Reg.* v *Secretary of State for the Home Department, Ex parte Ruddock* [1987] 1 WLR 1482 and *Reg.* v *Secretary of State for the Home Department, Ex parte Asif Mahmood Khan* [1984] 1 WLR 1337 were cited as instances of substantive legitimate expectations to which the courts were if appropriate prepared to give effect. Reliance was also placed, as we would place it, on Lord Diplock's carefully worded summary in *Council of Civil Service Unions* v *Minister for the Civil Service* [1985] AC 374, 408–409 of the contemporary heads of judicial review. They included benefits or advantages which the applicant can legitimately expect to be permitted to continue to enjoy. Not only did Lord Diplock not limit these to procedural benefits or advantages; he referred expressly to *In re Findlay* [1985] AC 318 (a decision in which he had participated) as an example of a case concerning a claim to a legitimate expectation—plainly a substantive one, albeit that the claim failed. One can readily see why: Lord Scarman's speech in *In re Findlay* is predicated on the assumption that the courts will protect a substantive legitimate expectation if one is established; and Taylor J so interpreted it in *Ex parte Ruddock* [1987] 1 WLR 1482. None of these cases suggests that the standard of review is always limited to bare rationality, though none developed it as the revenue cases have done.

78. It is from the revenue cases that, in relation to the third category, the proper test emerges. Thus in *Ex parte Unilever Plc* [1996] STC 681 this court concluded that for the Crown to enforce a time limit which for years it had not insisted upon would be so unfair as to amount to an abuse of power. As in other tax cases, there was no question of the court's deferring to the Inland Revenue's view of what was fair. The court also concluded that the Inland Revenue's conduct passed the 'notoriously high' threshold of irrationality; but the finding of abuse through unfairness was not dependent on this.

79. It is worth observing that this was how the leading textbook writers by the mid-1990s saw the law developing. In the (still current) seventh edition of *Wade & Forsyth's Administrative Law* (1994) the authors reviewed a series of modern cases and commented, at p. 419:

> These are revealing decisions. They show that the courts now expect government departments to honour their statements of policy or intention or else to treat the citizen with the fullest personal consideration. Unfairness in the form of unreasonableness is clearly allied to unfairness by violation of natural justice. It was in the latter context that the doctrine of legitimate expectation was invented, but it is now proving to be a source of substantive as well as of procedural rights. Lord Scarman [in *Ex parte Preston* [1985] AC 835] has stated emphatically that unfairness in the purported exercise of power can amount to an abuse or excess of power, and this may become an important general doctrine.

To similar effect is De Smith, Woolf & Jowell, *Judicial Review of Administrative Action*, 5th edn (1995), pp. 575–576, para. 13–035. Craig, *Administrative Law*, 3rd edn (1994), pp. 672–675, links the issue, as Schwarze does (*European Administrative Law* (1992)), to the fundamental principle of legal certainty.

80. In *Ex parte Unilever Plc* [1996] STC 681, 695 Simon Brown LJ proposed a valuable reconciliation of the existing strands of public law:

> 'Unfairness amounting to an abuse of power' as...in *Preston* and the other revenue cases is unlawful not because it involves conduct such as would offend some equivalent private law principle, not principally indeed because it breaches a legitimate expectation that some different

substantive decision will be taken, but rather because it is illogical or immoral or both for a public authority to act with conspicuous unfairness and in that sense abuse its power. As Lord Donaldson MR said in *Reg.* v *Independent Television Commission, Ex parte T.S.W. Broadcasting Ltd, The Times*, 7 February 1992: 'The test in public law is fairness, not an adaption of the law of contract or estoppel.' In short, I regard the *M.F.K.* category of legitimate expectation as essentially but a head of *Wednesbury* unreasonableness, not necessarily exhaustive of the grounds upon which a successful substantive unfairness challenge may be based.

81. For our part, in relation to this category of legitimate expectation, we do not consider it necessary to explain the modern doctrine in *Wednesbury* terms, helpful though this is in terms of received jurisprudence (cf. Dunn LJ in *Reg.* v *Secretary of State for the Home Department, Ex parte Asif Mahmood Khan* [1984] 1 WLR 1337, 1352: 'an unfair action can seldom be a reasonable one'). We would prefer to regard the *Wednesbury* categories themselves as the major instances (not necessarily the sole ones: see *Council of Civil Service Unions* v *Minister for the Civil Service* [1985] AC 374, 410, *per* Lord Diplock) of how public power may be misused. Once it is recognised that conduct which is an abuse of power is contrary to law its existence must be for the court to determine.

82. The fact that the court will only give effect to a legitimate expectation within the statutory context in which it has arisen should avoid jeopardising the important principle that the executive's policy-making powers should not be trammelled by the courts: see *Hughes* v *Department of Health and Social Security* [1985] AC 766, 788 *per* Lord Diplock. Policy being (within the law) for the public authority alone, both it and the reasons for adopting or changing it will be accepted by the courts as part of the factual data—in other words, as not ordinarily open to judicial review. The court's task—and this is not always understood is then limited to asking whether the application of the policy to an individual who has been led to expect something different is a just exercise of power. In many cases the authority will already have considered this and made appropriate exceptions (as was envisaged in *British Oxygen Co. Ltd* v *Board of Trade* [1971] AC 610 and as had happened in *Ex parte Hamble (Offshore) Fisheries Ltd* [1995] 2 All ER 714), or resolved to pay compensation where money alone will suffice. But where no such accommodation is made, it is for the court to say whether the consequent frustration of the individual's expectation is so unfair as to be a misuse of the authority's power.

Fairness and the decision to close

83. How are fairness and the overriding public interest in this particular context to be judged? The question arises concretely in the present case. Mr Goudie argued, with detailed references, that all the indicators, apart from the promise itself, pointed to an overriding public interest, so that the court ought to endorse the health authority's decision. Mr Gordon contended, likewise with detailed references, that the data before the health authority were far from uniform. But this is not what matters. What matters is that, having taken it all into account, the health authority voted for closure in spite of the promise. The propriety of such an exercise of power should be tested by asking whether the need which the health authority judged to exist to move Miss Coughlan to a local authority facility was such as to outweigh its promise that Mardon House would be her home for life.

84. That a promise was made is confirmed by the evidence of the health authority that:

> the applicant and her fellow residents were justified in treating certain statements made by the health authority's predecessor, coupled with the way in which the authority's predecessor conducted itself at the time of the residents' move from Newcourt Hospital, as amounting to an assurance that, having moved to Mardon House, Mardon House would be a permanent home for them.

And the letter of 7 June 1994 sent to the residents by Mr Peter Jackson, the then general manager of the predecessor of the health authority, following the withdrawal of John Grooms stated:

> During the course of a meeting yesterday with Ross Bentley's father, it was suggested that each of the former Newcourt residents now living at Mardon House would appreciate a further letter of reassurance from me. I am writing to confirm therefore, that the health authority has made it clear to the community trust that it expects the trust to continue to provide good quality care for you at Mardon House for as long as you choose to live there. I hope that this will dispel any anxieties you may have arising from the forthcoming change in management arrangements, about which I wrote to you recently.

As has been pointed out by the health authority, the letter did not actually use the expression 'home for life.'

85. The health authority had, according to its evidence, formed the view that it should give considerable weight to the assurances given to Miss Coughlan; that those assurances had given rise to expectations which should not, in the ordinary course of things, be disappointed; but that it should not treat those assurances as giving rise to an absolute and unqualified entitlement on the part of the Miss Coughlan and her co-residents since that would be unreasonable and unrealistic; and that:

> If there were compelling reasons which indicated overwhelmingly that closure was the reasonable and—other things being equal—the right course to take, provided that steps could be taken to meet the applicant's (and her fellow residents') expectations to the greatest degree possible following closure, it was open to the authority, weighing up all these matters with care and sensitivity, to decide in favour of the option of closure.

Although the first consultation paper made no reference to the 'home for life' promise, it was referred to in the second consultation paper as set out above.

86. It is denied in the health authority's evidence that there was any misrepresentation at the meeting of the board on 7 October 1998 of the terms of the 'home for life' promise. It is asserted that the board had taken the promise into account; that members of the board had previously seen a copy of Mr Jackson's letter of 7 June 1994, which, they were reminded, had not used the word 'home'; and that every board member was well aware that, in terms of its fresh decision-making, the starting point was that the Newcourt patients had moved to Mardon on the strength of an assurance that Mardon would be their home as long as they chose to live there. This was an express promise or representation made on a number of occasions in precise terms. It was made to a small group of severely disabled individuals who had been housed and cared for over a substantial period in the health authority's predecessor's premises at Newcourt. It specifically related to identified premises which it was represented would be their home for as long as they chose. It was in unqualified terms. It was repeated and confirmed to reassure the residents. It was made by the health authority's predecessor for its own purposes, namely to encourage Miss Coughlan and her fellow residents to move out of Newcourt and into Mardon House, a specially built substitute home in which they would continue to receive nursing care. The promise was relied on by Miss Coughlan. Strong reasons are required to justify resiling from a promise given in those circumstances. This is not a case where the health authority would, in keeping the promise, be acting inconsistently with its statutory or other public law duties. A decision not to honour it would be equivalent to a breach of contract in private law.

87. The health authority treated the promise as the 'starting point' from which the consultation process and the deliberations proceeded. It was a factor which should be given 'considerable weight', but it could be outweighed by 'compelling reasons which indicated overwhelmingly that closure was the reasonable and the right course to take'. The health authority, though 'mindful of the history behind the residents' move to Mardon House and their understandable expectation that it would be their permanent home', formed the view that there were 'overriding reasons' why closure should nonetheless proceed. The health authority wanted to improve the provision of reablement services and considered that the mix of a long stay residential service and a reablement service at Mardon House was inappropriate and detrimental to the interests of both users of the service. The acute reablement service could not be supported there without an uneconomic investment which would have produced a second class reablement service. It was argued that there was a compelling public interest which justified the health authority's prioritisation of the reablement service.

88. It is, however, clear from the health authority's evidence and submissions that it did not consider that it had a legal responsibility or commitment to provide a *home*, as distinct from care or funding of care, for the applicant and her fellow residents. It considered that, following the withdrawal of the John Grooms Association, the provision of care services to the current residents had become 'excessively expensive', having regard to the needs of the majority of disabled people in the authority's area and the 'insuperable problems' involved in the mix of long-term residential care and reablement services at Mardon House. Mardon House had, contrary to earlier expectations, become:

> a prohibitively expensive white elephant. The unit was not financially viable. Its continued operation was dependent upon the authority supporting it at an excessively high cost. This did not represent value for money and left fewer resources for other services.

The health authority's attitude was that:

> It was because of our appreciation of the residents' expectation that they would remain at Mardon House for the rest of their lives that the board agreed that the authority should accept a continuing commitment to finance the care of the residents of Mardon for whom it was responsible.

But the cheaper option favoured by the health authority misses the essential point of the promise which had been given. The fact is that the health authority has not offered to the applicant an equivalent facility to replace what was promised to her. The health authority's undertaking to fund her care for the remainder of her life is substantially different in nature and effect from the earlier promise that care for her would be provided *at Mardon House*. That place would be her home for as long as she chose to live there.

89. We have no hesitation in concluding that the decision to move Miss Coughlan against her will and in breach of the health authority's own promise was in the circumstances unfair. It was unfair because it frustrated her legitimate expectation of having a home for life in Mardon House. There was no overriding public interest which justified it. In drawing the balance of conflicting interests the court will not only accept the policy change without demur but will pay the closest attention to the assessment made by the public body itself. Here, however, as we have already indicated, the health authority failed to weigh the conflicting interests correctly. Furthermore, we do not know (for reasons we will explain later) the quality of the alternative accommodation and services which will be offered to Miss Coughlan. We cannot prejudge what would be the result if there was on offer accommodation which could be said to be reasonably equivalent to Mardon House and the health authority made a properly considered decision in favour of closure in the light of that offer. However, absent such an offer, here there was unfairness amounting to an abuse of power by the health authority.

...

Appeal dismissed.

NOTES

1. The Court also held that the closure decision amounted to an unlawful interference with the right to respect for one's home under Art. 8, ECHR.
2. The use of the term 'abuse of power', like 'unreasonable' or 'irrational', is conclusionary and does not articulate its basis. In substantive legitimate expectations one must establish that an expectation is legitimate and that there is no overriding public interest which justifies frustrating it. See comments: Elliott [2000] *Judicial Review* 27, Craig and Schønberg [2000] *Public Law* 684.

■ QUESTIONS

1. If the health authority had found cheaper accommodation for the applicant, would this have overridden the promise made to her?
2. Did the court move from considering legality to the merits in this case?

R (Bibi) v Newham London Borough Council

[2001] EWCA Civ 607, [2002] 1 WLR 237, Court of Appeal

The applicants had been given a promise that, as unintentionally homeless persons in priority need of accommodation, they would be provided with accommodation with security of tenure. Whilst they were provided with accommodation, this did not have security of tenure. They successfully sought judicial review that the accommodation provided did not discharge the housing authority's obligations to them. The court found that the obligation was founded on a legitimate expectation and not a statutory duty, as the promise was made on a misunderstanding of what the statute (then the Housing (Homeless Persons) Act 1977) required. The authority appealed.

SCHIEMANN LJ: ....

19. In all legitimate expectation cases, whether substantive or procedural, three practical questions arise. The first question is to what has the public authority, whether by practice or by promise, committed

itself; the second is whether the authority has acted or proposes to act unlawfully in relation to its commitment; the third is what the court should do....

To what has the authority committed itself?

20. The answer to the first is a question of analysing the evidence—it poses no jurisprudential problems.

21. Sometimes, as in the first category of outcome analysed in *Ex parte Coughlan* [2000] 2 WLR 622 (para. 57) the answer to this first question is dispositive of the case. It seems to us that the present authorities in that group of cases (in particular *In re Findlay* [1985] AC 318, 338) make it generally appropriate to allocate the issue of legitimacy to this initial question. In other words, if the public body has done nothing and said nothing which can legitimately have generated the expectation that is advanced to the court, the case ends there. It seems likely that a representation made without lawful power will be in this class. In the present case the answer to the first question is not in dispute and is in favour of the applicants.

The interrelation of the second and third questions

22. Two problems face a court in answering these questions. The first is to find one or more measuring rods by which it can be objectively determined whether a certain action or inaction is an abuse of power. The second is what order to make once an abuse of power has been discerned—can the court come to a substantive decision itself or should it send the matter back to the decision taker to decide afresh according to law?

23. To a degree the answer to the second depends on the approach one takes to the first. As Laws LJ pointed out in *R* v *Secretary of State for Education and Employment, ex parte Begbie* [2000] 1 WLR 1115 at page 1131C

> The more the decision challenged lies in what may inelegantly be called the macro-political field, the less intrusive will be the court's supervision. More than this: in that field, true abuse of power is less likely to be found, since within it changes of policy, fuelled by broad conceptions of the public interest, may more readily be accepted as taking precedence over the interests of groups which enjoyed expectations generated by an earlier policy.

Has the authority acted unlawfully? Introduction

24. As Professor Craig makes clear in his perceptive discussion of this topic in Craig, *Administrative Law*, 4th ed, (1999), chp 19, it is important to recognise that there is often a tension between several values in these cases. A choice may need to be made as to which good we attain and which we forego. There are administrative and democratic gains in preserving for the authority the possibility in the future of coming to different conclusions as to the allocation of resources from those to which it is currently wedded. On the other hand there is value in holding authorities to promises which they have made, thus upholding responsible public administration and allowing people to plan their lives sensibly. The task for the law in this area is to establish who makes the choice of priorities and what principles are to be followed.

25. Several attempts have been made to find a formulation which will provide a test for all cases. However, history shows that wide-ranging formulations, while capable of producing a just result in the individual case, are seen later to have needlessly constricted the development of the law. Thus it was the view of this court in *Coughlan* that a principle, apparently earlier embraced by this court in *R* v *Secretary of State for the Home Department, ex parte Hargreaves* [1997] 1 WLR 906, to the effect that the court would only enforce expectations as to procedure as opposed to expectations of a substantive benefit, *was wrongly* framed.

Has the authority acted unlawfully? The relevance of reliance on the promise

26. Mr Matthias submits that, in cases where the expectation which has been generated is of a substantive as opposed to a procedural benefit, authority limits the court to enforcing it only if (a) the motive for resiling from it was improper, or (b) there has been detrimental reliance on it. Only then, he submits, can the departure be said to amount, as it must, to an abuse of power. Founding on the distinction between procedural and substantive expectations identified in *Coughlan* para. 57, on the reasoning in *Ex parte Preston* [1985] AC 835, 866–7 and on the cases reported to date, he argues that (absent bad faith) a substantive legitimate expectation can only arise where a situation analogous to a private law wrong, and therefore involving detrimental reliance, exists.

27. We would not accept this formulation. As Sir Thomas Bingham MR observed in *R* v *Inland Revenue Commissioners, ex p. Unilever plc* [1996] STC p. 681 at page 690f:

> The categories of unfairness are not closed, and precedent should act as a guide and not as a cage.

28. As indicated in *R* v *Secretary of State for Education and Employment, ex parte Begbie* [2000] 1 WLR 1115 reliance, though potentially relevant in most cases, is not essential. In that case a letter sent to the parents of one child affected by legislative and policy changes concerning assisted school places came to the knowledge of another child's parent, who relied on it in judicial review proceedings. Peter Gibson LJ, giving the leading judgment, said at page 1123H:

> Mr. Beloff submits... (v) it is not necessary for a person to have changed his position as a result of such representations for an obligation to fulfil a legitimate expectation to subsist; the principle of good administration prima facie requires adherence by public authorities to their promises. He cites authority in support of all these submissions and for my part I am prepared to accept them as correct, so far as they go. I would however add a few words by way of comment on his fifth proposition, as in my judgment it would be wrong to understate the significance of reliance in this area of the law. It is very much the exception, rather than the rule, that detrimental reliance will not be present when the court finds unfairness in the defeating of a legitimate expectation.

29. In the light of this, we respectfully adopt what Professor Craig has proposed in this regard in Craig, *Administrative Law* at p. 619:

> Detrimental reliance will normally be required in order for the claimant to show that it would be unlawful to go back on a representation. This is in accord with policy, since if the individual has suffered no hardship there is no reason based on legal certainty to hold the agency to its representation. It should not, however, be necessary to show any monetary loss, or anything equivalent thereto.

30. But he gives the following instance of a case where reliance is not essential—

> Where an agency seeks to depart from an established policy in relation to a particular person detrimental reliance should not be required. Consistency of treatment and equality are at stake in such cases, and these values should be protected irrespective of whether there has been any reliance as such.

31. In our judgment the significance of reliance and of consequent detriment is factual, not legal. In *Begbie* both aspects were in the event critical: there had been no true reliance on the misrepresentation of policy and therefore no detriment suffered specifically in consequence of it. In a strong case, no doubt, there will be both reliance and detriment; but it does not follow that reliance (that is, credence) without measurable detriment cannot render it unfair to thwart a legitimate expectation....

Has the authority acted unlawfully? 'So unfair as to amount to an abuse of power'

33. The traditional view has been that the *Wednesbury* categories were exhaustive of what was an abuse of power. However in *Coughlan* the court preferred 'to regard the Wednesbury categories as the major instances (not necessarily the sole ones...), of how public power may be misused' (para. 81).

34. In *Coughlan* the court followed *R* v *Inland Revenue Commissioners, ex parte Unilever* [1996] STC 681, in asking itself whether the reneging by an authority on its promise was 'so unfair as to amount to an abuse of power' (para. 78). It concluded that it was. However, without refinement, the question whether the reneging on a promise would be so unfair as to amount to an abuse of power is an uncertain guide.

35. Where one is dealing with a promise made by an authority a major part of the problem is that it is often not adequate to look at the situation purely from the point of view of the disappointed promisee who comes to the court with a perfectly natural grievance.

36. Sometimes many promises have been made to many different persons each of which has induced a reasonable expectation of a substantive benefit for that person but all of which promises cannot be fulfilled. This situation is not uncommon in central and local Government. Decision takers promise and find themselves unable to deliver that which they have promised. As Bacon, perhaps cynically, remarked 400 years ago 'it is a certain sign of wise government and proceeding that it can hold men's hearts by

hopes when it can not by satisfaction'. Seen from the point of view of administrators focusing on the problem immediately before their eyes a promise seems reasonable or will at least reduce the need to worry further in the immediate future about the promisee. But when they, or their superiors, focus on a wider background it appears that the making of the promise was unwise or that, in any event, its fulfilment seems too difficult.

37. Thus in cases such as those before the court, the family with the highest points on the Authority's scale can be regarded as having a legitimate expectation that the next five bedroom flat would go to them. So can the applicant who was promised a five bedroom flat within 18 months which have elapsed. So can all the other persons who have been promised suitable accommodation within 18 months. Yet the Authority does not possess enough housing for them all.

38. The suggestion was made in argument that this problem can be avoided by the authority which is short of housing giving every family enough money to provide its own housing. But this is not always an escape from the problem because the money can often not be found without depriving others of money which they expected to retain or of benefits which they expected to receive.

39. But on any view, if an authority, without even considering the fact that it is in breach of a promise which has given rise to a legitimate expectation that it will be honoured, makes a decision to adopt a course of action at variance with that promise then the authority is abusing its powers.

The role of the court

40. The court has two functions—assessing the legality of actions by administrators and, if it finds unlawfulness on the administrators' part, deciding what relief it should give. It is in our judgment a mistake to isolate from the rest of administrative law cases those which turn on representations made by authorities. The same constitutional principles apply to the exercise by the court of each of these two functions.

41. The court, even where it finds that the applicant has a legitimate expectation of some benefit, will not order the authority to honour its promise where to do so would be to assume the powers of the executive. Once the court has established such an abuse it may ask the decision taker to take the legitimate expectation properly into account in the decision making process.

42. Only part of the relevant material upon consideration of which any decision must be made is before the court. Because of the need to bear in mind more than the interests of the individual before the court, relevant facts are always changing. As Lord Bingham said in *R v Cambridge Health Authority, ex parte B* [1995] 2 All ER 129:

> ... it would be totally unrealistic to require the authority to come to the court with its accounts and seek to demonstrate that if this treatment were provided for B then there would be a patient, C, who would have to go without treatment. No major authority could run its financial affairs in a way which would permit such a demonstration.

43. While in some cases there can be only one lawful ultimate answer to the question whether the authority should honour its promise, at any rate in cases involving a legitimate expectation of a substantive benefit, this will not invariably be the case.

The present case

...

48. We proceed therefore on the basis that the Authority has lawfully committed itself to providing the applicants with suitable accommodation with secure tenure.

Has the authority acted unlawfully?

...

51. The law requires that any legitimate expectation be properly taken into account in the decision making process. It has not been in the present case and therefore the Authority has acted unlawfully.

52. It was submitted that neither applicant has changed his or her position on the strength of the expectation and therefore no weight ought to be given to the fact that the promises have not been

fulfilled. We have already said that this factor does not rank as a legal inhibition on giving effect to the legitimate expectation. But what weight ought to be given to the lack of change of position?

53. The fact that someone has not changed his position after a promise has been made to him does not mean that he has not relied on the promise. An actor in a play where another actor points a gun at him may refrain from changing his position just because he has been given a promise that the gun only contains blanks.

54. A refugee such as Mr Al-Nashed might, had he been told the true situation, have gone to one of the bodies which assist refugees for advice as to where in England and Wales he might have better prospects; or have tried to find the deposit on an assured tenancy, with the possibility thereafter of housing benefit to help with the rent.

55. The present case is one of reliance without concrete detriment. We use this phrase because there is moral detriment, which should not be dismissed lightly, in the prolonged disappointment which has ensued; and potential detriment in the deflection of the possibility, for a refugee family, of seeking at the start to settle somewhere in the United Kingdom where secure housing was less hard to come by. In our view these things matter in public law, even though they might not found an estoppel or actionable misrepresentation in private law, because they go to fairness and through fairness to possible abuse of power. To disregard the legitimate expectation because no concrete detriment can be shown would be to place the weakest in society at a particular disadvantage. It would mean that those who have a choice and the means to exercise it in reliance on some official practice or promise would gain a legal toehold inaccessible to those who, lacking any means of escape, are compelled simply to place their trust in what has been represented to them.

A further element for the Authority to bear in mind is the possibility of monetary compensation or assistance. As this court indicated in *Coughlan* (*ante*) para 82, a legitimate expectation may in some cases be appropriately taken into account by such a payment.

57. An element which may tell against giving effect to the legitimate expectation is the effect on others on the housing list of giving the present applicants special preference. Mr Matthias understandably relies on this both as a reason why Newham's stance is not unfair and, in the alternative, as an overriding policy reason why effect should not be given to the representation. Ostensibly powerful as this is it faces the obstacle, as Mr Luba has argued, that nothing unlawful would necessarily be involved in allocating secure housing to the applicants. For example, the Authority could change the allocation scheme to give weight to its representation to the applicants and the 115 others in their situation. Changing the scheme might not in truth be so simple—but it does not seem to have been considered by the Authority.

58. When considering the legitimate expectations which it has created, the Authority is entitled to take into account the current statutory framework, the allocation scheme, the legitimate expectations of other people, its assets both in terms of what housing it has at its disposal and in terms of what assets it has or could have available. It should consider whether, if it considers it inappropriate to grant the applicants secure tenancies of a council house, it should adopt any other way of helping the applicants to obtain secure housing whether by cash or other aid or by amending the allocation scheme so as to give some weight to legitimate expectations in cases similar to the present, of which we understand there to be a number.

59. But when the Authority looks at the matter again it must take into account the legitimate expectations. Unless there are reasons recognised by law for not giving effect to those legitimate expectations then effect should be given to them. In circumstances such as the present where the conduct of the Authority has given rise to a legitimate expectation then fairness requires that, if the Authority decides not to give effect to that expectation, the Authority articulate its reasons so that their propriety may be tested by the court if that is what the disappointed person requires.

What should the court do?

60. *Coughlan* emphasised the importance of considering these questions in their statutory context....

61. In the context of housing Lord Brightman said of the Act of 1977 in *R* v *Hillingdon LBC, ex parte Puhlhofer* [1986] AC484, p. 517,

> It is an Act to assist persons who are homeless, not an act to provide them with homes... It is intended to provide for the homeless a lifeline of last resort; not to enable them to make inroads into the local authority's waiting list of applicants for housing. Some inroads there are probably bound to be, but in the end the local authority will have to balance the priority needs of the homeless on the one hand and the legitimate aspirations of those on their housing waiting list on the other hand....

63. The present case illustrates a potential conflict between the 'legitimate aspirations' of those who have been told where they are on the housing waiting list and what the Authority's allocation scheme is on the one hand and the 'legitimate expectations' of those to whom promises have been made by the Authority the fulfilment of which conflicts with the priorities contained in the allocation scheme on the other.

64. In an area such as the provision of housing at public expense where decisions are informed by social and political value judgments as to priorities of expenditure the court will start with a recognition that such invidious choices are essentially political rather than judicial. In our judgment the appropriate body to make that choice in the context of the present case is the authority. However, it must do so in the light of the legitimate expectations of the respondents.

65. Turner J declared that the Authority were 'bound to treat the duties originally owed by them to both applicants under section 65(2) as not discharged until the applicants be provided by them with suitable accommodation on a secure tenancy'. Rightly, he did not direct that they be given priority over everyone else who was on the housing register and was seeking the same type of accommodation. The applicants' counsel have not suggested that he should have so directed. They wish merely to hold the declaration which was made.

66. The Judge accepted that the applicants each have a legitimate expectation that they would be provided with suitable accommodation on a secure tenancy. We agree. However, we consider that the Judge went too far in the form of declaration which he made since it seems implicit in his declaration that there cannot be factors which inhibit the fulfilment of the legitimate expectations, even where the Authority has never so concluded.

67. We consider that it would be better simply to declare that the Authority is under a duty to consider the applicants' applications for suitable housing on the basis that they have a legitimate expectation that they will be provided by the Authority with suitable accommodation on a secure tenancy.

Appeal allowed in part.

Nadarajah v *Secretary of State for the Home Department*

[2005] EWCA Civ 1363, Court of Appeal

The appellant's claim for asylum had been rejected. In a subsequent unsuccessful challenge in the High Court it was held that the Secretary of State had misconstrued his 'family links' policy. The policy had been revised between the rejection of asylum and the court's decision. On appeal it was argued that the misconstruction of the original policy and the failure to apply it to the appellant amounted to an error of law and so the appellant then had an expectation that this would lead to the mistake being corrected by the application of the original policy rather than a reconsideration of the case applying the current policy which is unfavourable to the appellant.

LAWS LJ: ...

67. For my part I would accept Mr Underwood's contention that there is no abuse of power here, and therefore nothing, in terms of legitimate expectation, to entitle the appellant to a judgment compelling the Secretary of State to apply the unrevised Family Links Policy in his case. I would so conclude on the

simple ground that the merits of the Secretary of State's case press harder than the appellant's, given the way the points on either side were respectively developed by counsel. If my Lords agree, that disposes of the appeal. But I find it very unsatisfactory to leave the case there. The conclusion is not merely simple, but simplistic. It is little distance from a purely subjective adjudication. So far as it appears to rest on principle, with respect to Mr Underwood I think it superficial to hold that for a legitimate expectation to bite there must be something more than failure to honour the promise in question, and then to list a range of possible additional factors which might make the difference. It is superficial because in truth it reveals no principle. Principle is not in my judgment supplied by the call to arms of abuse of power. Abuse of power is a name for any act of a public authority that is not legally justified. It is a useful name, for it catches the moral impetus of the rule of law. It may be, as I ventured to put it in *Begbie*, "the root concept which governs and conditions our general principles of public law". But it goes no distance to tell you, case by case, what is lawful and what is not. I accept, of course, that there is no formula which tells you that; if there were, the law would be nothing but a checklist. Legal principle lies between the overarching rubric of abuse of power and the concrete imperatives of a rule-book. In *Coughlan* (paragraph 71, cited above) Lord Woolf said of legitimate expectation, "[t]he limits to its role have yet to be finally determined by the courts. Its application is still being developed on a case by case basis." I do not begin to suggest that what follows fulfils the task. But although as I have said I would conclude the case in the Secretary of State's favour on the arguments as they stand, I would venture to offer some suggestions—no doubt *obiter*—to see if we may move the law's development a little further down the road, not least so as to perceive, if we can, how legitimate expectation fits with other areas of English public law.

68. The search for principle surely starts with the theme that is current through the legitimate expectation cases. It may be expressed thus. Where a public authority has issued a promise or adopted a practice which represents how it proposes to act in a given area, the law will require the promise or practice to be honoured unless there is good reason not to do so. What is the principle behind this proposition? It is not far to seek. It is said to be grounded in fairness, and no doubt in general terms that is so. I would prefer to express it rather more broadly as a requirement of good administration, by which public bodies ought to deal straightforwardly and consistently with the public. In my judgment this is a legal standard which, although not found in terms in the European Convention on Human Rights, takes its place alongside such rights as fair trial, and no punishment without law. That being so there is every reason to articulate the limits of this requirement—to describe what may count as good reason to depart from it—as we have come to articulate the limits of other constitutional principles overtly found in the European Convention. Accordingly a public body's promise or practice as to future conduct may only be denied, and thus the standard I have expressed may only be departed from, in circumstances where to do so is the public body's legal duty, or is otherwise, to use a now familiar vocabulary, a proportionate response (of which the court is the judge, or the last judge) having regard to a legitimate aim pursued by the public body in the public interest. The principle that good administration requires public authorities to be held to their promises would be undermined if the law did not insist that any failure or refusal to comply is objectively justified as a proportionate measure in the circumstances.

69. This approach makes no distinction between procedural and substantive expectations. Nor should it. The dichotomy between procedure and substance has nothing to say about the reach of the duty of good administration. Of course there will be cases where the public body in question justifiably concludes that its statutory duty (it will be statutory in nearly every case) requires it to override an expectation of substantive benefit which it has itself generated. So also there will be cases where a procedural benefit may justifiably be overridden. The difference between the two is not a difference of principle. Statutory duty may perhaps more often dictate the frustration of a substantive expectation. Otherwise the question in either case will be whether denial of the expectation is in the circumstances proportionate to a legitimate aim pursued. Proportionality will be judged, as it is generally to be judged, by the respective force of the competing interests arising in the case. Thus where the representation relied on amounts to an unambiguous promise; where there is detrimental reliance; where the promise is made to an individual or specific group; these are instances where denial of the expectation is likely to be harder to justify as a proportionate measure. They are included in Mr Underwood's list of factors, all of which will be material, where they arise, to the assessment of proportionality. On the other hand where the government decision-maker is concerned to raise wide-ranging or "macro-political" issues of policy, the expectation's enforcement in the courts will encounter a steeper climb. All these considerations, whatever their direction, are pointers not rules. The balance between an individual's fair treatment in

particular circumstances, and the vindication of other ends having a proper claim on the public interest (which is the essential dilemma posed by the law of legitimate expectation) is not precisely calculable, its measurement not exact. It is no surprise that, as I ventured to suggest in *Begbie*, "the first and third categories explained in the *Coughlan* case... are not hermetically sealed". These cases have to be judged in the round.

70. There is nothing original in my description of the operative principle as a requirement of good administration. The expression was used in this context at least as long ago as the *Ng Yuen Shiu* case, in which Lord Fraser of Tullybelton, delivering the judgment of the Privy Council, said this (638F):

> It is in the interest of good administration that [a public authority] should act fairly and should implement its promise, so long as implementation does not interfere with its statutory duty.

My aim in outlining this approach has been to see if we can conform the shape of the law of legitimate expectations with that of other constitutional principles; and also to go some small distance in providing a synthesis, or at least a backdrop, within or against which the authorities in this area may be related to each other. I would make these observations on the learning I have summarised earlier. First, there are some cases where, on a proper apprehension of the facts, there is in truth no promise for the future: *Ex p. Hargreaves*; see also *In re Findlay* [1985] AC 318. Then in *Ng Yuen Shiu* and *Ex p. Khan* the breach of legitimate expectations—of the standard of good administration—could not be justified as a proportionate response to any dictate of the public interest; indeed I think it may be said that there was no public interest to compete with the expectation. In *Coughlan* the promise's denial could not be justified as a proportionate measure. The three categories of case there described by Lord Woolf represent, I would respectfully suggest, varying scenarios in which the question whether denial of the expectation was proportionate to the public interest aim in view may call for different answers. In *Begbie*, the legitimate expectation was frustrated by the operation of statute. *Bibi* went off essentially on the basis that the authority had "simply not acknowledged that the promises were a relevant consideration in coming to a conclusion as to whether they should be honoured". Its primary importance arises from the court's comments on reliance, including its citation of Professor Craig. That there is no hard and fast rule about reliance to my mind illustrates the fact, which I have already sought to emphasise, that it is in principle no more than a factor to be considered in weighing the question whether denial of the expectation is justified—justified, as I would suggest, as a proportionate act or measure.

71. Applying this approach to the present case, I would arrive at the same result as I have reached on the arguments as they were presented. I am clear that the Secretary of State was entitled to decline to apply the original policy, construed as Stanley Burnton J construed it, in the appellant's case. I have already said that the Secretary of State acted consistently throughout. The appellant knew nothing of the Family Links Policy at the time of the February 2002 decision. He seeks the benefit, not of a government policy intended to apply to persons in his position but unfairly denied him, but the windfall of the Secretary of State's misinterpretation. There is nothing disproportionate, or unfair, in his being refused it. Nothing in Mr Husain's points seems to me to shift that position.

Appeal dismissed.

NOTES

1. In *Bibi* the Court has identified the range of factors which the authority has to take into account when reconsidering these cases.
2. There is a right to good administration in the Charter of Fundamental Rights of the European Union, Art. 41.
3. The development of legitimate expectations has led the House of Lords to say that estoppel should be confined to private law (*R (Reprotech (Pebsham) Ltd)* v *East Sussex CC* [2002] UKHL 8, [2003] 1 WLR 348). There is a problem where a body makes an *ultra vires* representation, can a legitimate expectation be based on it? The position in common law was that the lack of legal capacity by the public body would frustrate the enforcement of the expectation against it, but where an ECHR right is concerned, it is less clear. In *Stretch* v *UK* (2004) 38 EHRR 12, which concerned an option to renew a lease, the ECtHR held that the option was a factor which could attach to property rights arising under the lease and be protected by Art 1, Protocol 1. Unlike the Court of Appeal who found that the lack of legal capacity to grant the option was conclusive, the ECtHR held that this was a factor which would be included in the balancing exercise the court conducts when

deciding if the expectation should be enforced or frustrated. It decided that damages could be awarded as the unlawful grant of the option did not prejudice the authority's statutory functions or third parties. Subsequently a different approach was used in *Rowland* v *Environment Agency* [2003] EWCA Civ 1885, a case about a stretch of the River Thames and the incorrect representations by the Agency that it did not have a public right of navigation. At common law, the Agency could not be required to act on its representations, but as Art. 1, Protocol 1 was engaged, the Court felt that the Agency could 'alleviate any injustice by benevolent exercise of its powers' by, as the Agency had offered, not promoting public use of the stretch of river. Damages were not sought, and some argue that it is a better method to reconcile the competing public and private interests: e.g. H. W. R. Wade and C. F. Forsyth, *Administrative Law* (2004), p. 314, whereas May LJ in *Rowland* thought that if, after conducting the balancing exercise, it was appropriate to enforce an unlawfully generated expectation, this was preferable to compensation from the public purse. Elliott argues that in principle there is no reason why the approach adopted in *Rowland* could not be adopted where Convention rights are not engaged (2004) 63 *CLJ* 261 (see also Craig (1999), at 611–649; (2008), at 675–691, whose 1999 discussion was considered by Peter Gibson and May LJJ in *Rowland*).

■ QUESTION

Does the test of proportionality offer clearer guidance in determining if it would be an abuse of power to deny a legitimate expectation than does the *Wednesbury* test or its reformulation by Lord Cooke in *ex parte International Trader's Ferry* when determining irrationality?

11

The Availability of Judicial Review

OVERVIEW

In this chapter we consider some questions in order to determine the availability of judicial review and its significance in the constitution. What is the nature of the procedure to seek judicial review and is it exclusive? Who can apply for judicial review? Against whom and in respect of what matters may judicial review be sought? Then comes a consideration of the discretionary nature of the remedies available in judicial review proceedings and the manner in which the courts exercise this discretion. We end with an examination of the courts' approach to legislative attempts to exclude judicial review.

SECTION 1: THE CLAIM FOR JUDICIAL REVIEW

In 1969 the Law Commission was asked to 'review the existing remedies for the judicial control of administrative acts or omissions with a view to evolving a simpler and more effective procedure'. At that time litigants seeking to challenge administrative acts or omissions had a choice of two procedures. They could begin an action by writ or originating summons seeking an injunction, declaration, and, if appropriate, damages. This is the normal way of commencing an action to establish a breach of a private law right, but the courts also allowed it to be used to challenge the decisions of public authorities on the ground that they had acted beyond their powers. Alternatively, litigants could use a special procedure to seek one or more of the prerogative orders, *certiorari*, prohibition, or *mandamus*. The difficulties surrounding the old prerogative order procedure are set out in the judgment of Lord Diplock in *O'Reilly* v *Mackman* (p. 615, *post*).

The result of the review was the Report on Remedies in Administrative Law (Law Com. No. 73, Cmnd 6407) which made a number of recommendations. It was assumed that implementation of the recommendations would require legislation, but the bulk of the changes contained in the proposals were in fact made by an amendment in 1977 to Ord. 53 of the Rules of the Supreme Court (SI 1977 No. 1955). Some of these provisions were themselves amended in 1980 by SI 1980 No. 2000. A number of provisions relevant to the application for judicial review were subsequently enacted in the Supreme Court Act 1981, which was renamed the Senior Courts Act 1981 by the Constitutional Reform Act 2005, s. 59, Sched. 11. Following Lord Woolf's review of civil justice, new Civil Procedure Rules were made, but judicial review was not initially reformed according to the new philosophy. A subsequent review of the Crown Office List chaired by Sir Jeffery Bowman led to various changes. The judicial review procedure was amended, becoming a claim for judicial review under Part 54 of the Civil

Procedure Rules (CPR Part 54). The Crown Office List was renamed the Administrative Court, which was a recognition that the great bulk of cases assigned to it involved issues of public law. These changes took effect on 2 October 2000, the day the Human Rights Act 1998 came into force. A pre-action protocol for CPR Part 54 came into force on 4 March 2002.

SENIOR COURTS ACT 1981

31.—(1) An application to the High Court for one or more of the following forms of relief, namely—

(a) an order of mandamus, prohibition or certiorari;
(b) a declaration or injunction under subsection (2); . . .

shall be made in accordance with rules of court by a procedure to be known as an application for judicial review.

(2) A declaration may be made or an injunction granted under this subsection in any case where an application for judicial review, seeking that relief, has been made and the High Court considers that, having regard to—

(a) the nature of the matters in respect of which relief may be granted by orders of mandamus, prohibition or certiorari;
(b) the nature of the persons and bodies against whom relief may be granted by such orders; and
(c) all the circumstances of the case, it would be just and convenient for the declaration to be made or the injunction to be granted, as the case may be.

(3) No application for judicial review shall be made unless the leave of the High Court has been obtained in accordance with rules of court; and the court shall not grant leave to make such an application unless it considers that the applicant has a sufficient interest in the matter to which the application relates.

(4) On an application for judicial review the High Court may award damages to the applicant if—

(a) he has joined with his application a claim for damages arising from any matter to which the application relates; and
(b) the court is satisfied that, if the claim had been made in an action begun by the applicant at the time of making his application, he would have been awarded damages.

(5) If, on an application for judicial review, the High Court quashes the decision to which the application relates, it may in addition—

(a) remit the matter to the court, tribunal or authority which made the decision, with a direction to reconsider the matter and reach a decision in accordance with the findings of the High Court, or
(b) substitute its own decision for the decision in question.

(5A) But the power conferred by subsection (5)(b) is exercisable only if—

(a) the decision in question was made by a court or tribunal,
(b) the decision is quashed on the ground that there has been an error of law, and
(c) without the error, there would have been only one decision which the court or tribunal could have reached.

(5B) Unless the High Court otherwise directs, a decision substituted by it under subsection (5)(b) has effect as if it were a decision of the relevant court or tribunal.

(6) Where the High Court considers that there has been undue delay in making an application for judicial review, the court may refuse to grant—

(a) leave for the making of the application; or
(b) any relief sought on the application,

if it considers that the granting of the relief sought would be likely to cause substantial hardship to, or substantially prejudice the rights of, any person or would be detrimental to good administration.

(7) Subsection (6) is without prejudice to any enactment or rule of court which has the effect of limiting the time within which an application for judicial review may be made.

CIVIL PROCEDURE RULES

Schedule to The Civil Procedure (Amendment No. 4) Rules 2000, SI 2000 No. 2092

Also at <www.justice.gov.uk/civil/procrules_fin/menus/rules.htm>.

Note source still refers to Supreme Court Act 1981 and not Senior Courts Act 1981.

Part 54

I JUDICIAL REVIEW

SCOPE AND INTERPRETATION

54.1 (1) This Part contains rules about judicial review.

(2) In this Section—

- (a) a 'claim for judicial review' means a claim to review the lawfulness of—
  - (i) an enactment; or
  - (ii) a decision, action or failure to act in relation to the exercise of a public function;
- (b) [*revoked*]
- (c) [*revoked*]
- (d) [*revoked*]
- (e) 'the judicial review procedure' means the Part 8 procedure as modified by this Part;
- (f) 'interested party' means any person (other than the claimant and defendant) who is directly affected by the claim; and
- (g) 'court' means the High Court, unless otherwise stated.

(Rule 8.1(6)(b) provides that a rule or practice direction may, in relation to a specified type of proceedings, disapply or modify any of the rules set out in Part 8 as they apply to those proceedings)

WHEN THIS SECTION MUST BE USED

54.2 The judicial review procedure must be used in a claim for judicial review where the claimant is seeking—

- (a) a mandatory order;
- (b) a prohibiting order;
- (c) a quashing order; or
- (d) an injunction under section 30 of the Supreme Court Act 1981 (restraining a person from acting in any office in which he is not entitled to act).

WHEN THIS SECTION MAY BE USED

54.3 (1) The judicial review procedure may be used in a claim for judicial review where the claimant is seeking—

- (a) a declaration; or
- (b) an injunction.

(Section 31(2) of the Supreme Court Act 1981 sets out the circumstances in which the court may grant a declaration or injunction in a claim for judicial review)

(Where the claimant is seeking a declaration or injunction in addition to one of the remedies listed in rule 54.2, the judicial review procedure must be used)

(2) A claim for judicial review may include a claim for damages, restitution or the recovery of a sum due but may not seek such a remedy, alone.

(Section 31(4) of the Supreme Court Act sets out the circumstances in which the court may award damages, restitution or the recovery of a sum due on a claim for judicial review)

PERMISSION REQUIRED

54.4 The court's permission to proceed is required in a claim for judicial review whether started under this Part or transferred to the Administrative Court.

TIME LIMIT FOR FILING CLAIM FORM

54.5 (1) The claim form must be filed—

(a) promptly; and
(b) in any event not later than 3 months after the grounds to make the claim first arose.

(2) The time limit in this rule may not be extended by agreement between the parties.

(3) This rule does not apply when any other enactment specifies a shorter time limit for making the claim for judicial review.

CLAIM FORM

54.6 (1) In addition to the matters set out in rule 8.2 (contents of the claim form) the claimant must also state—

(a) the name and address of any person he considers to be an interested party;
(b) that he is requesting permission to proceed with a claim for judicial review; and
(c) any remedy (including any interim remedy) he is claiming.

(Part 25 sets out how to apply for an interim remedy)

(2) The claim form must be accompanied by the documents required by Practice Direction 54A.

SERVICE OF CLAIM FORM

54.7 The claim form must be served on—

(a) the defendant; and
(b) unless the court otherwise directs, any person the claimant considers to be an interested party, within 7 days after the date of issue.

ACKNOWLEDGMENT OF SERVICE

54.8 (1) Any person served with the claim form who wishes to take part in the judicial review must file an acknowledgment of service in the relevant practice form in accordance with the following provisions of this rule.

(2) Any acknowledgment of service must be—

(a) filed not more than 21 days after service of the claim form; and
(b) served on—
   (i) the claimant; and
   (ii) subject to any direction under rule 54.7(b), any other person named in the claim form,

as soon as practicable and, in any event, not later than 7 days after it is filed.

(3) The time limits under this rule may not be extended by agreement between the parties.

(4) The acknowledgment of service—

(a) must—
   (i) where the person filing it intends to contest the claim, set out a summary of his grounds for doing so; and
   (ii) state the name and address of any person the person filing it considers to be an interested party; and
(b) may include or be accompanied by an application for directions.

(5) Rule 10.3(2) does not apply.

FAILURE TO FILE ACKNOWLEDGMENT OF SERVICE

54.9 (1) Where a person served with the claim form has failed to file an acknowledgment of service in accordance with rule 54.8, he—

(a) may not take part in a hearing to decide whether permission should be given unless the court allows him to do so; but

(b) provided he complies with rule 54.14 or any other direction of the court regarding the filing and service of—
  (i) detailed grounds for contesting the claim or supporting it on additional grounds; and
  (ii) any written evidence,

may take part in the hearing of the judicial review.

(2) Where that person takes part in the hearing of the judicial review, the court may take his failure to file an acknowledgment of service into account when deciding what order to make about costs.

(3) Rule 8.4 does not apply.

PERMISSION GIVEN

54.10 (1) Where permission to proceed is given the court may also give directions.

(2) Directions under paragraph (1) may include—

(a) a stay of proceedings to which the claim relates;
(b) directions requiring the proceedings to be heard by a Divisional Court.

(Rule 3.7 provides a sanction for the non-payment of the fee payable when permission to proceed has been given)

SERVICE OF ORDER GIVING OR REFUSING PERMISSION

54.11 The court will serve—

(a) the order giving or refusing permission; and
(b) any directions,

on—
  (i) the claimant;
  (ii) the defendant; and
  (iii) any other person who filed an acknowledgment of service.

PERMISSION DECISION WITHOUT A HEARING

54.12 (1) This rule applies where the court, without a hearing—

(a) refuses permission to proceed; or
(b) gives permission to proceed—
  (i) subject to conditions; or
  (ii) on certain grounds only.

(2) The court will serve its reasons for making the decision when it serves the order giving or refusing permission in accordance with rule 54.11.

(3) The claimant may not appeal but may request the decision to be reconsidered at a hearing.

(4) A request under paragraph (3) must be filed within 7 days after service of the reasons under paragraph (2).

(5) The claimant, defendant and any other person who has filed an acknowledgment of service will be given at least 2 days' notice of the hearing date.

(6) The court may give directions requiring the proceedings to be heard by a Divisional Court.

DEFENDANT ETC. MAY NOT APPLY TO SET ASIDE

54.13 Neither the defendant nor any other person served with the claim form may apply to set aside an order giving permission to proceed.

RESPONSE

54.14 (1) A defendant and any other person served with the claim form who wishes to contest the claim or support it on additional grounds must file and serve—

(a) detailed grounds for contesting the claim or supporting it on additional grounds; and
(b) any written evidence,

within 35 days after service of the order giving permission.

(2) The following rules do not apply—

(a) rule 8.5 (3) and 8.5 (4) (defendant to file and serve written evidence at the same time as acknowledgment of service); and
(b) rule 8.5 (5) and 8.5 (6) (claimant to file and serve any reply within 14 days).

WHERE CLAIMANT SEEKS TO RELY ON ADDITIONAL GROUNDS

54.15 The court's permission is required if a claimant seeks to rely on grounds other than those for which he has been given permission to proceed.

EVIDENCE

54.16 (1) Rule 8.6 does not apply.

(2) No written evidence may be relied on unless—

(a) it has been served in accordance with any—
   (i) rule under this Part; or
   (ii) direction of the court; or
(b) the court gives permission.

COURT'S POWERS TO HEAR ANY PERSON

54.17 (1) Any person may apply for permission—

(a) to file evidence; or
(b) make representations at the hearing of the judicial review.

(2) An application under paragraph (1) should be made promptly.

JUDICIAL REVIEW MAY BE DECIDED WITHOUT A HEARING

54.18 The court may decide the claim for judicial review without a hearing where all the parties agree.

COURT'S POWERS IN RESPECT OF QUASHING ORDERS

54.19 (1) This rule applies where the court makes a quashing order in respect of the decision to which the claim relates.

(2) The court may—

(a) (i) remit the matter to the decision-maker; and
   (ii) direct it to reconsider the matter and reach a decision in accordance with the Judgment of the court; or
(b) in so far as any enactment permits, substitute its own decision for the decision to which the claim relates.

(Section 31 of the Supreme Court Act 1981 enables the High Court, subject to certain conditions, to substitute its own decision for the decision in question.)

TRANSFER

54.20 The court may

(a) order a claim to continue as if it had not been started under this Section; and
(b) where it does so, give directions about the future management of the claim.

(Part 30 (transfer) applies to transfers to and from the Administrative Court)

Pre-Action Protocol for Judicial Review

INTRODUCTION

This protocol applies to proceedings within England and Wales only. It does not affect the time limit specified by Rule 54.5(1) of the Civil Procedure Rules which requires that any claim form in an application for judicial review must be filed promptly and in any event not later than 3 months after the grounds to make the claim first arose.

1 Judicial review allows people with a sufficient interest in a decision or action by a public body to ask a judge to review the lawfulness of:

- an enactment; or
- a decision, action or failure to act in relation to the exercise of a public function.

2 Judicial review may be used where there is no right of appeal or where all avenues of appeal have been exhausted.

Alternative Dispute Resolution

3.1 The parties should consider whether some form of alternative dispute resolution procedure would be more suitable than litigation, and if so, endeavour to agree which form to adopt. Both the Claimant and Defendant may be required by the Court to provide evidence that alternative means of resolving their dispute were considered. The Courts take the view that litigation should be a last resort, and that claims should not be issued prematurely when a settlement is still actively being explored. Parties are warned that if the protocol is not followed (including this paragraph) then the Court must have regard to such conduct when determining costs. However, parties should also note that a claim for judicial review 'must be filed promptly and in any event not later than 3 months after the grounds to make the claim first arose'.

3.2 It is not practicable in this protocol to address in detail how the parties might decide which method to adopt to resolve their particular dispute. However, summarised below are some of the options for resolving disputes without litigation:

- Discussion and negotiation.
- Ombudsmen—the Parliamentary and Health Service and the Local Government Ombudsmen have discretion to deal with complaints relating to maladministration. The British and Irish Ombudsman Association provide information about Ombudsman schemes and other complaint handling bodies and this is available from their website at www.bioa.org.uk . Parties may wish to note that the Ombudsmen are not able to look into a complaint once court action has been commenced.
- Early neutral evaluation by an independent third party (for example, a lawyer experienced in the field of administrative law or an individual experienced in the subject matter of the claim).
- Mediation—a form of facilitated negotiation assisted by an independent neutral party.

3.3 The Legal Services Commission has published a booklet on 'Alternatives to Court', CLS Direct Information Leaflet 23 (www.clsdirect.org.uk/), which lists a number of organisations that provide alternative dispute resolution services.

3.4 *It is expressly recognised that no party can or should be forced to mediate or enter into any form of ADR*

4 Judicial review may not be appropriate in every instance.
Claimants are strongly advised to seek appropriate legal advice when considering such proceedings and, in particular, before adopting this protocol or making a claim. Although the Legal Services Commission will not normally grant full representation before a letter before claim has been sent and the proposed defendant given a reasonable time to respond, initial funding may be available, for eligible claimants, to cover the work necessary to write this. (See Annex C for more information.)

5 This protocol sets out a code of good practice and contains the steps which parties should generally follow before making a claim for judicial review.

6 This protocol does not impose a greater obligation on a public body to disclose documents or give reasons for its decision than that already provided for in statute or common law. However, where the court considers that a public body should have provided relevant documents and/or information, particularly where this failure is a breach of a statutory or common law requirement, it may impose sanctions.

This protocol will not be appropriate where the defendant does not have the legal power to change the decision being challenged, for example decisions issued by tribunals such as the Immigration Appeal Authorities.

This protocol will not be appropriate in urgent cases, for example, when directions have been set, or are in force, for the claimant's removal from the UK, or where there is an urgent need for an interim order to compel a public body to act where it has unlawfully refused to do so (for example, the failure of a local housing authority to secure interim accommodation for a homeless claimant) a claim should be made immediately. A letter before claim will not stop the implementation of a disputed decision in all instances.

7 All claimants will need to satisfy themselves whether they should follow the protocol, depending upon the circumstances of his or her case. Where the use of the protocol is appropriate, the court will normally expect all parties to have complied with it and will take into account compliance or non-compliance when giving directions for case management of proceedings or when making orders for costs [Civil Procedure Rules Costs Practice Direction]. However, even in emergency cases, it is good practice to fax to the defendant the draft Claim Form which the claimant intends to issue. A claimant is also normally required to notify a defendant when an interim mandatory order is being sought.

The letter before claim

8 Before making a claim, the claimant should send a letter to the defendant. The purpose of this letter is to identify the issues in dispute and establish whether litigation can be avoided.

9 Claimants should normally use the suggested standard format for the letter outlined at Annex A.

10 The letter should contain the date and details of the decision, act or omission being challenged and a clear summary of the facts on which the claim is based. It should also contain the details of any relevant information that the claimant is seeking and an explanation of why this is considered relevant.

11 The letter should normally contain the details of any interested parties known to the claimant. They should be sent a copy of the letter before claim for information. Claimants are strongly advised to seek appropriate legal advice when considering such proceedings and, in particular, before sending the letter before claim to other interested parties or making a claim.

12 A claim should not normally be made until the proposed reply date given in the letter before claim has passed, unless the circumstances of the case require more immediate action to be taken.

The letter of response

13 Defendants should normally respond within 14 days using the standard format at Annex B. Failure to do so will be taken into account by the court and sanctions may be imposed unless there are good reasons.

14 Where it is not possible to reply within the proposed time limit the defendant should send an interim reply and propose a reasonable extension. Where an extension is sought, reasons should be given and, where required, additional information requested. This will not affect the time limit for making a claim for judicial review [See Civil Procedure Rule 54.5(1)] nor will it bind the claimant where he or she considers this to be unreasonable. However, where the court considers that a subsequent claim is made prematurely it may impose sanctions.

15 If the claim is being conceded in full, the reply should say so in clear and unambiguous terms.

16 If the claim is being conceded in part or not being conceded at all, the reply should say so in clear and unambiguous terms, and:

(a) where appropriate, contain a new decision, clearly identifying what aspects of the claim are being conceded and what are not, or, give a clear timescale within which the new decision will be issued;
(b) provide a fuller explanation for the decision, if considered appropriate to do so;
(c) address any points of dispute, or explain why they cannot be addressed;
(d) enclose any relevant documentation requested by the claimant, or explain why the documents are not being enclosed; and
(e) where appropriate, confirm whether or not they will oppose any application for an interim remedy.

17 The response should be sent to all interested parties identified by the claimant and contain details of any other parties who the defendant considers also have an interest.

Practice Direction 54D Administrative Court (Venue)

This Practice Direction supplements Part 54

SCOPE AND PURPOSE

1.1 This Practice Direction concerns the place in which a claim before the Administrative Court should be started and administered and the venue at which it will be determined.

1.2 This Practice Direction is intended to facilitate access to justice by enabling cases to be administered and determined in the most appropriate location. To achieve this purpose it provides flexibility in relation to where claims are to be administered and enables claims to be transferred to different venues.

VENUE—GENERAL PROVISIONS

2.1 The claim form in proceedings in the Administrative Court may be issued at the Administrative Court Office of the High Court at –

(1) the Royal Courts of Justice in London; or

(2) at the District Registry of the High Court at Birmingham, Cardiff, Leeds, or Manchester unless the claim is one of the excepted classes of claim set out in paragraph 3 of this Practice Direction which may only be started and determined at the Royal Courts of Justice in London.

2.2 Any claim started in Birmingham will normally be determined at a court in the Midland region (geographically covering the area of the Midland Circuit); in Cardiff in Wales; in Leeds in the North-Eastern Region (geographically covering the area of the North Eastern Circuit); in London at the Royal Courts of Justice; and in Manchester, in the North-Western Region (geographically covering the Northern Circuit).

EXCEPTED CLASSES OF CLAIM

3.1 The excepted classes of claim referred to in paragraph 2.1(2) are –

(1) proceedings to which Part 76 or Part 79 applies, and for the avoidance of doubt –

(a) proceedings relating to control orders (within the meaning of Part 76);
(b) financial restrictions proceedings (within the meaning of Part 79);
(c) proceedings relating to terrorism or alleged terrorists (where that is a relevant feature of the claim); and
(d) proceedings in which a special advocate is or is to be instructed;

(2) proceedings to which RSC Order 115 applies;
(3) proceedings under the Proceeds of Crime Act 2002;
(4) appeals to the Administrative Court under the Extradition Act 2003;
(5) proceedings which must be heard by a Divisional Court; and
(6) proceedings relating to the discipline of solicitors.

3.2 If a claim form is issued at an Administrative Court office other than in London and includes one of the excepted classes of claim, the proceedings will be transferred to London.

URGENT APPLICATIONS

4.1 During the hours when the court is open, where an urgent application needs to be made to the Administrative Court outside London, the application must be made to the judge designated to deal with such applications in the relevant District Registry.

4.2 Any urgent application to the Administrative Court during the hours when the court is closed, must be made to the duty out of hours High Court judge by telephoning 020 7947 6000.

ASSIGNMENT TO ANOTHER VENUE

5.1 The proceedings may be transferred from the office at which the claim form was issued to another office. Such transfer is a judicial act.

5.2 The general expectation is that proceedings will be administered and determined in the region with which the claimant has the closest connection, subject to the following considerations as applicable –

(1) any reason expressed by any party for preferring a particular venue;

(2) the region in which the defendant, or any relevant office or department of the defendant, is based;

(3) the region in which the claimant's legal representatives are based;

(4) the ease and cost of travel to a hearing;

(5) the availability and suitability of alternative means of attending a hearing (for example, by videolink);

(6) the extent and nature of media interest in the proceedings in any particular locality;

(7) the time within which it is appropriate for the proceedings to be determined;

(8) whether it is desirable to administer or determine the claim in another region in the light of the volume of claims issued at, and the capacity, resources and workload of, the court at which it is issued;

(9) whether the claim raises issues sufficiently similar to those in another outstanding claim to make it desirable that it should be determined together with, or immediately following, that other claim; and

(10) whether the claim raises devolution issues and for that reason whether it should more appropriately be determined in London or Cardiff.

5.3 (1) When an urgent application is made under paragraph 4.1 or 4.2, this will not by itself decide the venue for the further administration or determination of the claim.

(2) The court dealing with the urgent application may direct that the case be assigned to a particular venue.

(3) When an urgent application is made under paragraph 4.2, and the court does not make a direction under sub-paragraph (2), the claim will be assigned in the first place to London but may be reassigned to another venue at a later date.

5.4 The court may on an application by a party or of its own initiative direct that the claim be determined in a region other than that of the venue in which the claim is currently assigned. The considerations in paragraph 5.2 apply.

5.5 Once assigned to a venue, the proceedings will be both administered from that venue and determined by a judge of the Administrative Court at a suitable court within that region, or, if the venue is in London, at the Royal Courts of Justice. The choice of which court (of those within the region which are identified by the Presiding Judge of the circuit suitable for such hearing) will be decided, subject to availability, by the considerations in paragraph 5.2.

5.6 When giving directions under rule 54.10, the court may direct that proceedings be reassigned to another region for hearing (applying the considerations in paragraph 5.2). If no such direction is given, the claim will be heard in the same region as that in which the permission application was determined (whether on paper or at a hearing).

NOTES

1. The objectives of the pre-action protocols are '(1) to encourage the exchange of early and full information about the prospective legal claim, (2) to enable parties to avoid litigation by agreeing a settlement of the claim before the commencement of proceedings, and (3) to support the efficient management of proceedings where litigation cannot be avoided.' As we shall see later point (2) is a very important consideration (p. 636, *post*).
2. Where the use of the protocol is considered appropriate, then failure to follow it can result in the application of sanctions provided for in the CPR Pre-Action Protocol Practice Direction. Thus, failure to send the letters or not to provide sufficient information could result in an order that the party at fault pay the costs of the proceedings, or part of those costs, of the other party or parties if, in the opinion of the court, non-compliance has led to the commencement of proceedings which might otherwise not have needed to be commenced, or has led to costs being incurred in the proceedings that might otherwise not have been incurred (para. 2.3).
3. Practice Direction 54D on the venue followed a report by a judicial working group entitled, *Justice Outside London,* (2007) chaired by Lord Justice May. The direction came into effect on 6 April

2009. Some initial research on the new arrangements has been published: S. Nason, D. Hardy, and M. Sunkin, 'Regionalisation of the Administrative Court and Access to Justice' [2010] 15(3) *Judicial Review* 220. They found that the waiting times were substantially shorter in the four regional centres than in London and in a survey 66 per cent of regional solicitors felt that it was reducing client costs and 75 per cent thought that client convenience had improved. In the survey of London based solicitors 66 per cent thought that their clients had increased costs and inconvenience. This may be explained by the fact that regional solicitors are more likely to be acting for claimants, and London solicitors are likely to be acting for both claimants and defendants. The new arrangements are designed to be claimant friendly so that the claimant's choice of venue is more likely to be preferred. They report that around 9 per cent of all claims including asylum and immigration reconsideration cases were listed in the regional centres. As these reconsideration cases since February 2010 are now considered by the First-tier and Upper Tribunals (see pp. 696–699 *post*) it is estimated that the regions are generating about 25 per cent of Administrative Court claims having excluded the reconsideration cases. Using a different timescale *Judicial and Court Statistics 2009* records that 93 per cent of judicial review cases received were issued in London.

4. As we shall see, aspects of the CPR Part 54 procedure have been criticized. See D. Oliver, 'Public Law Procedures and Remedies—Do We Need Them?' [2002] *Public Law* 91, who argues that judicial review could be regarded as an ordinary claim inside the CPR without the need for this special Part 54 procedure.

SECTION 2: THE EXCLUSIVITY PRINCIPLE

As stated above, prior to the introduction of the revised Ord. 53, the courts frequently permitted litigants to commence an action by way of a claim for a declaration or injunction as an alternative to using the special procedure for obtaining orders of *certiorari*, *mandamus*, and prohibition. Would the courts continue to offer litigants this choice following the introduction of the reformed procedure in 1977?

O'Reilly v *Mackman*

[1983] 2 AC 237, House of Lords

A number of prisoners at Hull Prison wished to challenge decisions reached by the prison's board of visitors on the ground that they were in breach of the rules of natural justice. They did not make use of Ord. 53, but instead began proceedings by writ or originating summons, asking for a declaration that the findings and subsequent penalties were null and void. The application was refused by the judge at first instance but the Court of Appeal allowed an appeal by the board. On appeal to the House of Lords:

LORD DIPLOCK: ...All that is at issue in the instant appeal is the procedure by which such relief ought to be sought. Put in a single sentence the question for your Lordships is: whether in 1980 after RSC Ord. 53 in its new form, adopted in 1977, had come into operation it was an abuse of the process of the court to apply for such declarations by using the procedure laid down in the Rules for proceedings begun by writ or by originating summons instead of using the procedure laid down by Ord. 53 for an application for judicial review of the awards of forfeiture of remission of sentence made against them by the board which the appellants are seeking to impugn?

In their respective actions, the appellants claim only declaratory relief. It is conceded on their behalf that, for reasons into which the concession makes it unnecessary to enter, no claim for damages would lie against the members of the board of visitors by whom the awards were made. The only claim was for a form of relief which it lies within the discretion of the court to grant or withhold. So the first thing to note is that the relief sought in the action is discretionary only.

It is not, and it could not be, contended that the decision of the board awarding him forfeiture of remission had infringed or threatened to infringe any right of the appellant derived from private law, whether a common law right or one created by statute. Under the Prison Rules remission of sentence is not a matter of right but of indulgence. So far as private law is concerned all that each appellant had was a legitimate expectation, based upon his knowledge of what is the general practice, that he would be granted the maximum remission permitted by rule 5(2) of the Prison Rules, of one third of his sentence if by that time no disciplinary award of forfeiture of remission had been made against him. So the second thing to be noted is that none of the appellants had any remedy in private law.

In public law, as distinguished from private law, however, such legitimate expectation gave to each appellant a sufficient interest to challenge the legality of the adverse disciplinary award made against him by the board on the ground that in one way or another the board in reaching its decision had acted without the powers conferred upon it by the legislation under which it was acting; and such grounds would include the board's failure to observe the rules of natural justice: which means no more than to act fairly towards him in carrying out their decision-making process, and I prefer so to put it.

Lord Diplock went on to outline the disadvantages of the procedure for applying for prerogative orders prior to 1977. These were:

(1) the absence of any provision for discovery;
(2) the absence of any express provision for cross-examination.

His Lordship continued to outline, on the other hand, the protections which the procedure for applying for prerogative orders afforded to public bodies:

(1) the requirement to obtain leave;
(2) the time-limits on the grant of certiorari.

His Lordship continued:

. . . I accept that having regard to disadvantages . . . [of the prerogative order procedure], it could not be regarded as an abuse of the process of the court, before the amendments made to Order 53 in 1977, to proceed against the authority by an action for a declaration of nullity of the impugned decision with an injunction to prevent the authority from acting on it, instead of applying for an order of certiorari; and this despite the fact that, by adopting this course, the plaintiff evaded the safeguards imposed in the public interest against groundless, unmeritorious or tardy attacks upon the validity of decisions made by public authorities in the field of public law.

Those disadvantages, which formerly might have resulted in an applicant's being unable to obtain justice in an application for certiorari under Order 53, have all been removed by the new Order introduced in 1977. . . .

Lord Diplock discussed the provisions of the new Order which allow for interlocutory applications for discovery and cross-examination. He also discussed the provisions which permit claims for damages and applications for declarations and injunctions to be included in applications under the Order.

His Lordship continued:

So Order 53 since 1977 has provided a procedure by which every type of remedy for infringement of the rights of individuals that are entitled to protection in public law can be obtained in one and the same proceeding by way of an application for judicial review, and whichever remedy is found to be the most appropriate in the light of what has emerged upon the hearing of the application, can be granted to him. If what should emerge is that his complaint is not of an infringement of any of his rights that are entitled to protection in public law, but may be an infringement of his rights in private law and thus not a proper subject for judicial review, the court has power under rule 9(5), instead of refusing the application, to order the proceedings to continue as if they had begun by writ. There is no such converse power under the RSC to permit an action begun by writ to continue as if it were an application for judicial review; and I respectfully disagree with that part of the judgment of Lord Denning MR which suggests that such a power may exist; nor do I see the need to amend the rules in order to create one.

My Lords, Order 53 does not expressly provide that procedure by application for judicial review shall be the exclusive procedure available by which the remedy of a declaration or injunction may be obtained for infringement of rights that are entitled to protection under public law; nor does section 31 of the Supreme Court Act 1981. There is great variation between individual cases that fall within Order 53 and the Rules Committee and subsequently the legislature were, I think, for this reason content to rely upon the express and the inherent power of the High Court, exercised upon a case to case basis, to prevent abuse of its process whatever might be the form taken by that abuse. Accordingly, I do not think that your Lordships would be wise to use this as an occasion to lay down categories of cases in which it would necessarily always be an abuse to seek in an action begun by writ or originating summons a remedy against infringement of rights of the individual that are entitled to protection in public law....

Now that those disadvantages to applicants have been removed and all remedies for infringements of rights protected by public law can be obtained upon an application for judicial review, as can also remedies for infringements of rights under private law if such infringements should also be involved, it would in my view as a general rule be contrary to public policy and, as such an abuse of the process of the court, to permit a person seeking to establish that a decision of a public authority infringed rights to which he was entitled to protection under public law to proceed by way of an ordinary action and by this means to evade the provisions of Order 53 for the protection of such authorities.

My Lords, I have described this as a general rule; for though it may normally be appropriate to apply it by the summary process of striking out the action, there may be exceptions, particularly where the invalidity of the decision arises as a collateral issue in a claim for infringement of a right of the plaintiff arising under private law, or where none of the parties objects to the adoption of the procedure by writ or originating summons. Whether there should be other exceptions should, in my view, at this stage in the development of procedural public law, be left to be decided on a case to case basis—a process that your Lordships will be continuing in the next case in which judgment is to be delivered today [*Cocks* v *Thanet District Council* [1983] 2 AC 286].

In the instant cases where the only relief sought is a declaration of nullity of the decisions of a statutory tribunal, the Board of Visitors of Hull Prison, as in any other case in which a similar declaration of nullity in public law is the only relief claimed, I have no hesitation, in agreement with the Court of Appeal, in holding that to allow the actions to proceed would be an abuse of the process of the court. They are blatant attempts to avoid the protections for the defendants for which Order 53 provides.

The other Law Lords agreed with Lord Diplock.

■ QUESTION

The Law Commission's Report on Administrative Law Remedies, Law Com. No. 73, Cmnd 6407, stated in para. 34 that 'we are clearly of the opinion that the new procedure we envisage in respect of applications to the Divisional Court should not be exclusive in the sense that it would become the only way by which issues relating to the acts or omissions of public authorities should come before the courts'.

The *JUSTICE–All Souls Report on Administrative Law* (1988) criticizes the decision in *O'Reilly* v *Mackman* on the ground 'that it has all the appearance of judicial legislation without the benefit of the consultation and debating process normally associated with legislation' (para. 6.19).

Do you agree?

NOTES

The procedural safeguards referred to in *O'Reilly* v *Mackman* and which are to be found in CPR Part 54 require some further explanation.

1. *Permission* (see Senior Courts Act 1981, s. 31(3); and now CPR r. 54.4, p. 607, *ante*). The requirement that an applicant for judicial review must obtain permission has been criticized. The *JUSTICE–All Souls Report* recommended that it should be abolished for several reasons:
   (a) Permission is not required in private law proceedings. A particular category of litigants, namely those seeking judicial review, should not be subjected to an impediment which is not placed before litigants generally.

(b) The administration can be protected from 'groundless, unmeritorious or tardy harassment' by the procedure which allows parties to apply to strike out a case. A statement of case may be struck out under the rules CPR r. 34 if they disclose no reasonable cause of action, are likely to obstruct the just disposed of proceedings or if they otherwise constitute an abuse of the process of the courts, and the claim may be dismissed.

(c) Issues of standing are no longer conclusively determined at the stage of the application for leave (see *IRC* v *National Federation of Self-Employed and Small Businesses Ltd* [1982] AC 617, p. 626, *post*).

2. Despite criticism from academics (e.g. A. Le Sueur and M. Sunkin, 'Applications for Judicial Review: The Requirement of Leave' [1992] *Public Law* 102), the requirement for permission was retained in CPR Part 54 but it was changed from an *ex parte* (without notice) to an *inter partes* (with notice) proceeding decided by the judge on the papers. The thinking behind this was that because of the significant number of cases which, after obtaining permission, were either settled or withdrawn, it would be better to allow defendants to make an initial outline of their defence so that weak cases would be recognized and claimants ejected at this early stage. In two articles, V. Bondy and M. Sunkin reported on their research on the dynamics of judicial review litigation 'Accessing Judicial Review' [2008] *Public Law* 647, and 'Settlement in Judicial Review Proceedings' [2009] *Public Law* 237. They found that while the success rate of claims for permission for judicial review had declined, there was an increasing number of claimants achieving successful outcomes without the need to have an adjudication in the Administrative Court. It would seem that the reforms have assisted in changing the culture to increase early dialogue between the parties and encourage timely settlement. They found that there were still barriers to early dialogue which included, in some public bodies, structural, procedural and policy factors delaying the involvement of their lawyers. It would also seem that there was a significant degree of variability amongst the judges deciding permission.

3. *Time-limits* Problems have arisen as to the relationship between the provisions in the Senior Courts Act 1981, s. 31(6) and the RSC Ord. 53, r. 4, now CPR r. 54.5 (see p. 608, *ante*). The House of Lords dealt with time-limits in *R* v *Dairy Produce Quota Tribunal, ex parte Caswell* [1990] 2 AC 738.

(a) At the stage of the application for permission the court considers whether the application has been made promptly. The fact that an application has been made within three months does not necessarily mean that it has been made promptly.

(b) If the application has not been made promptly or within three months the court will have to consider whether there is good reason for the delay.

(c) Where there is a finding of promptness at the permission stage, this does not preclude a finding of undue delay at the substantive hearing.

(d) Whenever there is a failure to act promptly or within three months there is undue delay, and the court may either refuse to grant permission for the making of the application or, at the hearing, refuse to grant relief if it considers that the granting of the relief sought would be likely to cause substantial hardship to, or substantially prejudice the rights of, any person or would be detrimental to good administration.

It is open to the court to deliberate upon undue delay under s. 31(6) at the substantive hearing even where promptness under CPR r. 54.5 was considered at the permission stage if new relevant material is brought forward or a relevant point was overlooked (*R* v *Lichfield DC, ex p. Lichfield Securities Ltd* [2001] 3 LGLR 35).

4. The *JUSTICE—All Souls Report* (1988), criticized the three-month period as too short, and recommended that Ord. 53, r. 4 (now CPR r. 54.5) be removed, thus leaving the question of delay to be dealt with by reference to the statutory test in s. 31(6) of the 1981 Act (see paras 6.28–6.31). The Law Commission concluded that certainty was desirable and recommended the continuance of the three-month time-limit. A case could move to a substantive hearing if the reason for the delay in making the application for permission was the pursuit of an alternative remedy—*R* v *Rochdale Metropolitan Borough Council, ex parte Cromer Ring Mill Ltd* [1982] 3 All ER 761.

5. Lords Steyn and Hope have wondered whether the use of the term 'promptly' in CPR 54.5(1)(a) is sufficiently certain to comply with both EC law and Art 6(1) ECHR (*R* v *London Borough of Hammersmith and Fulham and Others, ex parte Burkett* [2002] UKHL 23, [2002] 1 WLR 593). Lord Clyde went on to point out that in Scotland there is no statutory time-limit for judicial review but that it is regulated by the common law concepts of delay, acquiescence, and personal bar.

■ QUESTION

Do the criticisms made of the procedural safeguards in the CPR Part 54 procedure undermine the basis of the decision in *O'Reilly* v *Mackman*?

NOTES

Lord Diplock mentioned that there may be certain exceptions to the general exclusivity principle. The courts have been required to consider the scope of the exclusivity rule, and the exceptions to it, in a number of cases.

1. In *Wandsworth London Borough Council* v *Winder* [1985] AC 461 it was held that a council tenant could, in defending proceedings for rent arrears, seek a declaration that the rent increases were *ultra vires*. It was subsequently held that the rent increases were in fact valid and an appeal to the Court of Appeal was dismissed (see *London Borough of Wandsworth* v *Winder (No. 2)* (1987) 19 HLR 204, (1988) 20 HLR 400).
2. The principle of raising a public law issue as a defence in civil litigation has been applied to criminal prosecution. Such a collateral challenge to the validity of a bye-law or administrative action was approved in the House of Lords in *Boddington* v *British Transport Police* [1997] 2 AC 143. Their Lordships overruled *Bugg* v *DPP* [1993] QB 473, which allowed a collateral challenge of a bye-law for substantive but not procedural invalidity. There is an exception, in that if legislation specified an appeal process then collateral challenge is not permitted (see *R* v *Wicks* [1998] AC 92—enforcement notices under the planning legislation).

Roy v *Kensington and Chelsea FPC*

[1992] 2 WLR 239, House of Lords

The Kensington and Chelsea and Westminster Family Practitioner Committee (FPC) was responsible, under the National Health Service (General Medical and Pharmaceutical Services) Regulations 1974, for making payments to general practitioners undertaking National Health Service work within its area. Dr Roy was on the list of doctors undertaking National Health Service work within the FPC's area. The FPC decided to use its powers under the Regulations to reduce Dr Roy's basic practice allowance by 20 per cent on the basis that he was not devoting a substantial amount of time to general practice under the National Health Service. Dr Roy issued a writ claiming the full amount of the basic practice allowance. In the same writ he also claimed repayment of sums due to him in relation to the employment of ancillary staff. The FPC argued that the inclusion of the claim relating to the basic practice allowance was an abuse of the process of the court. The judge decided that, as the committee's decision was clearly a public law decision, it could only be challenged by judicial review. His decision was reversed by the Court of Appeal and the FPC appealed to the House of Lords. (In the meantime Dr Roy proceeded with his claim in relation to the employment of ancillary staff and obtained an order for repayment.)

LORD BRIDGE OF HARWICH: My Lords, the circumstances from which this appeal arises are fully set out in the speech of my learned and noble friend, Lord Lowry, in which he has also undertaken a comprehensive review of the relevant authorities. Agreeing, as I do, with the conclusion he reaches, I shall state my own reasons briefly.

The decisions of this House in *O'Reilly* v *Mackman* [1983] 2 AC 237 and *Cocks* v *Thanet District Council* [1983] 2 AC 286, have been the subject of much academic criticism. Although I appreciate the cogency of some of the arguments advanced in support of that criticism, I have not been persuaded that the essential principle embodied in the decisions requires to be significantly modified, let alone overturned. But if it is important, as I believe, to maintain the principle, it is certainly no less important that its application should be confined within proper limits. It is appropriate that an issue which depends exclusively on the existence of a purely public law right should be determined in judicial review proceedings and not otherwise. But where a litigant asserts his entitlement to a subsisting right in private law, whether by way of claim or defence, the circumstance that the existence and extent of the private right asserted may incidentally involve the examination of a public law issue cannot prevent the litigant from seeking to establish his right by action commenced by writ or originating summons, any more than it can prevent him from setting up his private law right in proceedings brought against him. I think this proposition necessarily follows from the decisions of this House in *Davy* v *Spelthorne Borough Council* [1984] AC 262 and *Wandsworth London Borough Council* v *Winder* [1985] AC 461. In the latter case Robert Goff LJ in the Court of Appeal, commenting on a passage from the speech of Lord Fraser of Tullybelton in the former case, said, at p. 480:

> I read this passage in Lord Fraser of Tullybelton's speech as expressing the opinion that the principle in *O'Reilly* v *Mackman* should not be extended to require a litigant to proceed by way of judicial review in circumstances where his claim for damages for negligence might in consequence be adversely affected. I can for my part see no reason why the same consideration should not apply in respect of any private law right which a litigant seeks to invoke, whether by way of action or by way of defence. For my part, I find it difficult to conceive of a case where a citizen's invocation of the ordinary procedure of the courts in order to enforce his private law rights, or his reliance on his private law rights by way of defence in an action brought against him, could, as such, amount to an abuse of the process of the court.

I entirely agree with this....

I do not think the issue in the appeal turns on whether the doctor provides services pursuant to a contract with the family practitioner committee. I doubt if he does and am content to assume that there is no contract. Nevertheless, the terms which govern the obligations of the doctor on the one hand, as to the services he is to provide, and of the family practitioner committee on the other hand, as to the payments which it is required to make to the doctor, are all prescribed in the relevant legislation and it seems to me that the statutory terms are just as effective as they would be if they were contractual to confer upon the doctor an enforceable right in private law to receive the remuneration to which the terms entitle him. It must follow, in my view, that in any case of dispute the doctor is entitled to claim and recover in an action commenced by writ the amount of remuneration which he is able to prove as being due to him. Whatever remuneration he is entitled to under the statement is remuneration he has duly earned by the services he has rendered. The circumstance that the quantum of that remuneration, in the case of a particular dispute, is affected by the discretionary decision made by the committee cannot deny the doctor his private law right of recovery or subject him to the constraints which the necessity to seek judicial review would impose upon that right.

LORD LOWRY: [Lord Lowry reviewed a number of authorities including *Wandsworth Borough Council* v *Winder* [1985] AC 461 and *Cocks* v *Thanet DC* [1983] 2 AC 286 and continued.]...

[T]he actual or possible absence of a contract is not decisive against Dr Roy. He has in my opinion a bundle of rights which should be regarded as his individual private law rights against the committee, arising from the statute and regulations and including the very important private law right to be paid for the work that he has done. As Judge White put it [1989] 1 Med LR 10, 12:

> The rights and duties are no less real or effective for the individual practitioner. Private law rights flow from the statutory provisions and are enforceable, as such, in the courts but no contractual relations come into existence.

The judge, however, held that, *even if the doctor's rights to full payments under the scheme were contractually based*, the committee's duty was a public law duty and could be challenged only on judicial review. Mr Collins admitted that, if the doctor had a *contractual* right, he could... vindicate it by action. But, my Lords, I go further: if Dr Roy has any kind of *private law right*, even though not contractual, he can sue for its alleged breach. In this case it has been suggested that Dr Roy could have gone by judicial review, because there is no issue of fact, but that would not always hold good in a similar type of case.... In any event, a successful application by judicial review could not lead directly, as it would in an action, to an order for payment of the full basic practice allowance. Other proceedings would be needed.

An important point is that the court clearly has *jurisdiction* to entertain the doctor's action. Furthermore, even if one accepts the full rigour of *O'Reilly* v *Mackman*, there is ample room to hold that this case comes within the exceptions allowed for by Lord Diplock. It is concerned with a private law right, it involves a question which *could* in some circumstances give rise to a dispute of fact and one object of the plaintiff is to obtain an order for the payment (not by way of damages) of an ascertained or ascertainable sum of money. If it is wrong to allow such a claim to be litigated by action, what is to be said of other disputed claims for remuneration? I think it is right to consider the whole spectrum of claims which a doctor might make against the committee. The existence of any dispute as to entitlement means that he will be alleging a breach of his private law rights through a failure by the committee to perform their public duty. If the committee's argument prevails, the doctor must in all these cases go by judicial review, even when the facts are not clear. I scarcely think that this can be the right answer....

The judgments [in the Court of Appeal] to which I have referred effectively dispose of an argument pressed by the committee that Dr Roy had no right to be paid a basic practice allowance until the committee had carried out their public duty of forming an opinion under paragraph 12.1(b) [of the National Health Service Regulations 1974] with the supposed consequence that, until that had happened, the doctor had *no private law right* which he could enforce. The answer is that Dr Roy had a right to a fair and legally correct consideration of his claim. Failing that, his private law right has been infringed and he can sue the committee.

Mr Collins [counsel for the FPC] sought to equate the committee's task under paragraph 12.1(b) with the council's duty in phase 1 of *Cocks* v *Thanet District Council* and the committee's duty to pay with the council's duty in phase 2. For an answer to that argument I refer to the judgments in the Court of Appeal and would also point out that Mr Cocks was simply a homeless member of the public in phase 1, whereas Dr Roy had already an established relationship with the committee when his claim... fell to be considered.

Dr Roy's printed case contained detailed arguments in favour of a contract between him and the committee, but before your Lordships Mr Lightman simply argued that the doctor had a private law right, whether contractual or statutory. With regard to *O'Reilly* v *Mackman* [1983] 2 AC 237 he argued in the alternative. The 'broad approach' was that the rule in *O'Reilly* v *Mackman* did not apply generally against bringing actions to vindicate private rights in all circumstances in which those actions involved a challenge to a public law act or decision, but that it merely required the aggrieved person to proceed by judicial review only when private law rights were not at stake. The 'narrow approach' assumed that the rule applied generally to *all* proceedings in which public law acts or decisions were challenged, subject to some exceptions when private law rights were involved. There was no need in *O'Reilly* v *Mackman* to choose between these approaches, but it seems clear that Lord Diplock considered himself to be stating a general rule with exceptions. For my part, I much prefer the broad approach, which is both traditionally orthodox and consistent with the *Pyx Granite* principle [1960] AC 260, 286, as applied in *Davy* v *Spelthorne Borough Council* [1984] AC 262, 274 and in *Wandsworth London Borough Council* v *Winder* [1985] AC 461, 510. It would also, if adopted, have the practical merit of getting rid of a procedural minefield. I shall, however, be content for the purpose of this appeal to adopt the narrow approach, which avoids the need to discuss the proper scope of the rule, a point which has not been argued before your Lordships and has hitherto been seriously discussed only by the academic writers.

Whichever approach one adopts, the arguments for excluding the present case from the ambit of the rule or, in the alternative, making an exception of it are similar and to my mind convincing.

(1) Dr Roy has either a contractual or a statutory private law right to his remuneration in accordance with his statutory terms of service.

(2) Although he seeks to enforce performance of a public law duty... his private law rights dominate the proceedings.

(3) The type of claim and other claims for remuneration (although not this particular claim) may involve disputed issues of fact.

(4) The order sought (for the payment of money due) could not be granted on judicial review.

(5) The claim is joined with another claim which is fit to be brought in an action (and has already been successfully prosecuted).

(6) When individual rights are claimed, there should not be a need for leave or a special time limit, nor should the relief be discretionary.

(7) The action should be allowed to proceed unless it is plainly an abuse of process.

(8) The cases I have cited show that the rule in *O'Reilly* v *Mackman* [1983] 2 AC 237, assuming it to be a rule of general application, is subject to many exceptions based on the nature of the claim and on the undesirability of erecting procedural barriers.

My Lords, I have already disclaimed the intention of discussing the scope of the rule in *O'Reilly* v *Mackman* but, even if I treat it as a general rule, there are many indications in favour of a liberal attitude towards the exceptions contemplated but not spelt out by Lord Diplock. For example: first, the Law Commission, when recommending the new judicial review procedure, contemplated the continued coexistence of judicial review proceedings and actions for a declaration with regard to public law issues. *Associated Provincial Picture Houses Ltd* v *Wednesbury Corporation* [1948] 1 KB 223 is a famous prototype of the latter. Secondly, this House has expressly approved actions for a declaration of nullity as alternative to applications for certiorari to quash, where private law rights were concerned: *Wandsworth London Borough Council* v *Winder* [1985] AC 461, 477 *per* Robert Goff LJ. Thirdly:

> 'The principle remains intact that public authorities and public servants are, unless clearly exempted, answerable in the ordinary courts for wrongs done to individuals. But by an extension of remedies and a flexible procedure it can be said that something resembling a system of public law is being developed. Before the expression "public law" can be used to deny a subject a right of action in the court of his choice it must be related to a positive prescription of law, by statute or by statutory rules. We have not yet reached the point at which mere characterisation of a claim as a claim in public law is sufficient to exclude it from consideration by the ordinary courts: to permit this would be to create a dual system of law with the rigidity and procedural hardship for plaintiffs which it was the purpose of the recent reforms to remove': *Davy* v *Spelthorne Borough Council* [1984] AC 262, 276, *per* Lord Wilberforce.

In conclusion, my Lords, it seems to me that, unless the procedure adopted by the moving party is ill suited to dispose of the question at issue, there is much to be said in favour of the proposition that a court having jurisdiction ought to let a case be heard rather than entertain a debate concerning the form of the proceedings.

For the reasons already given I would dismiss this appeal.

The other Law Lords agreed with Lord Bridge and Lord Lowry.

Clarke v *University of Lincolnshire and Humberside*

[2000] 1 WLR 1988, Court of Appeal

A student was in dispute over an examination matter with her university, which as a new university under the Education Reform Act 1988 had neither a charter nor visitor. She attended the university from 1992–95 and in 1998 began proceedings alleging breach of contract. The claim was struck out on the grounds that such disputes between students and universities were not justiciable but on appeal she was allowed to amend her pleadings. The university contended that the student should have proceeded by judicial review and so it was an abuse of process to bring an action outside the three-month time limit.

Sedley LJ, with whom Ward LJ and Lord Woolf agreed, ruled that there were issues of academic judgment which would not be justiciable but the amended pleadings did not fall into that category and involved contractual issues which the courts were capable of adjudicating.

LORD WOOLF MR:

The effect of the Civil Procedure Rules on O'Reilly v Mackman

22. It is over eighteen years ago that Lord Diplock made his speech in *O'Reilly* v *Mackman* [1983] 2 AC 237, which has had such a strong influence on the development of public law in this jurisdiction. Generally, since that time, the courts have continued to follow the statement as to the practice which should be adopted when bringing a claim against a public body that Lord Diplock made in that case. Lord Diplock indicated, at p 285, that in his view it would:

> as a general rule be contrary to public policy, and as such an abuse of the process of the court, to permit a person seeking to establish that a decision of a public authority to infringe rights of which he was entitled to protection under public law to proceed by way of an ordinary action and by this means to evade the provisions of Order 53 for the protection of such authorities.

23. Although the speech of Lord Diplock is extremely well known it is important to place the passage just cited from his speech in its context. First it is to be noted that counsel for the plaintiffs had:

> conceded that the fact that by adopting the procedure of an action begun by writ or by originating summons instead of an application for judicial review under Order 53...the plaintiffs had thereby been able to evade those protections against groundless, unmeritorious or tardy harassment that were afforded to statutory tribunals or decision making public authorities by Order 53. (p. 284)

Lord Diplock also pointed out that an advantage of Order 53 was that the court had an opportunity to exercise its discretion at the outset of the proceedings rather than would have happened at that time in proceedings begun by originating summons at the end of the proceedings. This was an important protection in the interests of good administration and for third parties who may be indirectly affected by the proceedings. As Lord Diplock said at p. 284:

> Unless such an action can be struck out summarily at the outset as an abuse of the process of the court the whole purpose of the public policy to which the change in Order 53 was directed would be defeated.

24. Lord Diplock went on to indicate that why Order 53 was not made an exclusive procedure was because he considered that the Rules Committee and the Legislature were content to rely upon the inherent power of the High Court to prevent abuse of its process whatever might be the form taken by that abuse: at pp. 285 A–D.

25. Lord Diplock was however at pains to point out that what he had said with regard to the exclusivity of Order 53 was a *general* rule. He recognised that there could be exceptions. He identified an exception in the case of collateral issues and went on to say that other exceptions should in his view be developed on a case by case basis. This is what has since happened.

26. Pending the report of Sir Jeffrey Bowman's Committee on the Crown Office Proceedings, Order 53 has not been subject to detailed amendment by the Rules Committee, but it is included in Schedule 1 to the CPR. The proceedings now have to be initiated by use of a 'claim form', maintaining the principle that all proceedings under the CPR are to be commenced in the same way (see Ord. 53 r5 (2)(A). In relation to the protection of the public and the interests of the administration which it provides, Order 53 has not been amended. However already Order 53 is part of the new code of civil procedure created by the CPR. It is subject to the general over-riding principles contained in Part 1.

27. In addition, if proceedings involving public law issues are commenced by an ordinary action under Part 7 or Part 8 they are now subject to Part 24. Part 24 is important because it enables the court, either on its own motion or on the application of a party, if it considers that a claimant has no real prospect of succeeding on a claim or an issue, to give summary judgment on the claim or issue. This is a markedly different position from that which existed when *O'Reilly* v *Mackman* [1983] 2 AC 237 was decided. If a defendant public body or an interested person considers that a claim has no real prospect of success an application can now be made under Part 24. This restricts the inconvenience to third parties and the administration of public bodies caused by a hopeless claim to which Lord Diplock referred.

28. The distinction between proceedings under Order 53 and an ordinary claim are now limited. Under Order 53 the claimant has to obtain permission to bring the proceedings so the onus is upon him to establish he has a real prospect of success. In the case of ordinary proceedings the defendant has to establish that the proceedings do not have a real prospect of success.

29. A university is a public body. This is not in issue on this appeal. Court proceedings would, therefore, normally be expected to be commenced under Order 53. If the university is subject to the supervision of a visitor there is little scope for those proceedings (*Page* v *Hull University Visitor* [1993] AC 682). Where a claim is brought against a university by one of its students, if because the university is a 'new university' created by statute, it does not have a visitor, the role of the court will frequently amount to performing the reviewing role which would otherwise be performed by the visitor. The court, for reasons which have been explained, will not involve itself with issues that involve making academic judgments. Summary judgment dismissing a claim, which if it were to be entertained, would require the court to make academic judgments should be capable of being obtained in the majority of situations. Similarly, the court has now power to stay the proceedings if it came to the conclusion that, in accordance with the over-

riding objective, it would be desirable for a student to use an internal disciplinary process before coming to the court: see CPR 1.4(1)(e).

30. One of Lord Diplock's reasons which he gave in *O'Reilly* v *Mackman* [1983] 2 AC 237 for his concern about an ordinary civil action being commenced against public bodies when a more appropriate procedure was under Order 53 was the fact that in ordinary civil proceedings the claimant could defer commencing the proceedings until the last day of the limitation period. This compares unfavourably with the requirement, that subject to the court's discretion to extend time, under Order 53 proceedings have to be commenced promptly and in any event within three months. If a student could bypass this requirement to bring proceedings promptly by issuing civil proceedings based on a contract, this could have a very adverse affect on administration of universities.

31. This is a matter of considerable importance in relation to litigation by dissatisfied students against universities. Grievances against universities are preferably resolved within the grievance procedure which universities have today. If they cannot be resolved in that way, where there is a visitor, they then have (except in exceptional circumstances) to be resolved by the visitor. The courts will not usually intervene.

32. While the courts will intervene where there is no visitor normally this should happen after the student has made use of the domestic procedures for resolving the dispute. If it is not possible to resolve the dispute internally, and there is no visitor, then the courts may have no alternative but to become involved. If they do so, the preferable procedure would usually be by way of judicial review. If, on the other hand, the proceedings are based on the contract between the student and the university then they do not have to be brought by way of judicial review.

33. The courts today will be flexible in their approach. Already, prior to the introduction of the CPR the courts were prepared to prevent abuse of their process where there had been an inordinate delay even if the limitation period had not expired. In such a situation, the court could, in appropriate circumstances, stay subsequent proceedings. This is despite the fact that a litigant normally was regarded as having a legal right to commence proceedings at any time prior to the expiry of the limitation period. (See *Birkett* v *James* [1978] AC 297)

34. The courts' approach to what is an abuse of process has to be considered today in the light of the changes brought about by the CPR. Those changes include a requirement that a party to proceedings should behave reasonably both before and after they have commenced proceedings. Parties are now under an obligation to help the court further the over-riding objectives which include ensuring that cases are dealt with expeditiously and fairly. (CPR 1.1(2)(d) and 1.3) They should not allow the choice of procedure to achieve procedural advantages. The CPR are as Part 1.1(1) states a new procedural code. Parliament recognised that the CPR would fundamentally change the approach to the manner in which litigation would be required to be conducted. That is why the Civil Procedure Act 1997 (Section 4(1) and (2)) gives the Lord Chancellor a very wide power to amend, repeal or revoke any enactment to the extent he considers necessary or desirable in consequence of the CPR.

35. While in the past, it would not be appropriate to look at delay of a party commencing proceedings other than by judicial review within the limitation period in deciding whether the proceedings are abusive this is no longer the position. While to commence proceedings within a limitation period is not in itself an abuse, delay in commencing proceedings is a factor which can be taken into account in deciding whether the proceedings are abusive. If proceedings of a type which would normally be brought by judicial review are instead brought by bringing an ordinary claim, the court in deciding whether the commencement of the proceedings is an abuse of process can take into account whether there has been unjustified delay in initiating the proceedings.

36. When considering whether proceedings can continue the nature of the claim can be relevant. If the court is required to perform a reviewing role or what is being claimed is a discretionary remedy, whether it be a prerogative remedy or an injunction or a declaration the position is different from when the claim is for damages or a sum of money for breach of contract or a tort irrespective of the procedure adopted. Delay in bringing proceedings for a discretionary remedy has always been a factor which a court could take into account in deciding whether it should grant that remedy. Delay can now be taken into account on an application for summary judgment under CPR Part 24 if its effect means that the claim has no real prospect of success.

37. Similarly if what is being claimed could affect the public generally the approach of the court will be stricter than if the proceedings only affect the immediate parties. It must not be forgotten that a court can extend time to bring proceedings under Order 53. The intention of the CPR is to harmonise procedures as far as possible and to avoid barren procedural disputes which generate satellite litigation.

38. Where a student has, as here, a claim in contract, the court will not strike out a claim which could more appropriately be made under Order 53 solely because of the procedure which has been adopted. It may however do so, if it comes to the conclusion that in all the circumstances, including the delay in initiating the proceedings, there has been an abuse of the process of the court under the CPR. The same approach will be adopted on an application under Part 24.

39. The emphasis can therefore be said to have changed since *O'Reilly* v *Mackman* [1983] 2 AC 237. What is likely to be important when proceedings are not brought by a student against a new university under Order 53, will not be whether the right procedure has been adopted but whether the protection provided by Order 53 has been flouted in circumstances which are inconsistent with the proceedings being able to be conducted justly in accordance with the general principles contained in Part 1. Those principles are now central to determining what is due process. A visitor is not required to entertain a complaint when there has been undue delay and a court in the absence of a visitor should exercise its jurisdiction in a similar way. The courts are far from being the ideal forum in which to resolve the great majority of disputes between a student and his or her university. The courts should be vigilant to ensure their procedures are not misused. The courts must be equally vigilant to discourage summary applications which have no real prospect of success.

Appeal allowed.

NOTE: Cornford [2000] 5 Web JCLI, <webjcli.ncl.ac.uk/2000/issue5/cornford5.html> argues that the logic of having a special procedure for judicial review means that (predominantly) public law issues should be brought under it and that Lord Woolf's views on how the CPR can protect public authorities from abuse still leave the problem that some claimants may wrongly identify their claim as a private one and not use CPR Part 54. They will not be able to transfer to Part 54 if they are outside the time limit.

■ QUESTION

Why do public authorities need safeguards in litigation involving public law issues but not private law ones?

SECTION 3: WHO MAY APPLY FOR JUDICIAL REVIEW?

The principles of standing or sufficient interest determine *who* is entitled to bring a particular dispute before the courts. They can thus be distinguished from the principles which determine whether a particular matter is suitable for adjudication in the courts (see the section on justiciability at p. 633, *post*), whether a particular matter is one of public law (see p. 633, *post*), and what proceedings may be used to challenge the decision (see p. 615, *ante*).

There are many people who may consider that they are affected or have an interest in an administrative decision. Consider, for example, the range of persons who might be said to have an interest in a decision to close a school because of falling numbers. The list will obviously include persons whose children will have to start a new school, but it could also include a number of others, for example persons who are opposed in principle to the closure of small schools and persons who are concerned about the financial implications of the closure for the local education authority. The principles of standing have the function of determining which interests merit access to the courts.

What arguments might be put forward in favour of the courts' power to select the interests which merit access to the courts? Cane (2004) suggests a number of possible functions.

P. Cane, *Administrative Law*

(2004), pp. 78–79

What is the function of standing rules? In general terms it is to restrict access to judicial review. But why restrict access? One suggested reason is to protect public bodies from vexatious litigants with no real interest in the outcome of the case but just a desire to make things difficult for the government. But it is highly doubtful that many such litigants exist in real life, and if they do, the requirement of leave to apply for judicial review should be adequate to deal with them. Other reasons for restricting access have been suggested: to prevent the conduct of government business being unduly hampered and delayed by 'excessive' litigation; to reduce the risk that civil servants will behave in over-cautious and unhelpful ways in dealing with citizens for fear of being sued if things go wrong; to ration scarce judicial resources; to ensure that the argument on the merits is presented in the best possible way, by a person with a real interest in presenting it (but quality of presentation and personal interest do not always go together); to ensure that people do not meddle paternalistically in the affairs of others.

What, then, are the principles of standing in judicial review proceedings?

Inland Revenue Commissioners v *National Federation of Self-Employed and Small Businesses Ltd (NFSESB)*

[1982] AC 617, House of Lords

The NFSESB sought an order of *mandamus* requiring the Inland Revenue Commissioners to assess and collect arrears of income tax due from a number of workers in the printing industry, known as the Fleet Street Casuals. This group had for some years been engaged in practices which deprived the Revenue of tax due in respect of their casual earnings. The Inland Revenue, on becoming aware of this, made an arrangement under which the workers were required to register in respect of their casual employment, so that in future tax could be collected in the normal way. Arrears of tax from 1977–78 were to be paid and current investigations to proceed, but investigations in respect of earlier years were not to take place. The House of Lords considered whether the Federation had *locus standi*. At that time the relevant rule was r. 3(5) of the Rules of the Supreme Court. Section 31(3) of the Supreme Court Act 1981 (now Senior Courts Act 1981 p. 606, *ante*) and r. 3(7) now repeat the provisions that used to be contained in this rule.

LORD WILBERFORCE: ...There may be simple cases in which it can be seen at the earliest stage that the person applying for judicial review has no interest at all or no sufficient interest to support the application: then it would be quite correct at the threshold to refuse him leave to apply. The right to do so is an important safeguard against the courts being flooded and public bodies being harassed by irresponsible applications. But in other cases this will not be so. In these it will be necessary to consider the powers or the duties in law of those against whom the relief is asked, the position of the applicant in relation to those powers or duties, and to the breach of those said to have been committed. In other words, the question of sufficient interest cannot, in such cases, be considered in the abstract, or as an isolated point: it must be taken together with legal and factual context. The rule requires sufficient interest in the matter to which the application relates. This, in the present case, necessarily involves the whole question of the duties of the Inland Revenue and the breaches for failure of those duties of which the respondents complain....

[After examining the relevant statutory provisions, his Lordship continued.]

From this summary analysis it is clear that the Inland Revenue Commissioners are not immune from the process of judicial review. They are an administrative body with statutory duties, which the courts, in principle, can supervise... It must follow from these cases and from principle that a taxpayer would not be excluded from seeking judicial review if he could show that the revenue had either failed in its statutory duty toward him or had been guilty of some action which was an abuse of their powers or outside their powers altogether. Such a collateral attack—as contrasted with a direct appeal on law to the courts—would no doubt be rare, but the possibility certainly exists.

The position of other taxpayers—other than the taxpayers whose assessment is in question—and their right to challenge the revenue's assessment or non-assessment of that taxpayer, must be judged according to whether, consistently with the legislation, they can be considered as having sufficient interest to complain of what has been done or omitted. I proceed therefore to examine the revenue's duties in that light.

These duties are expressed in very general terms and it is necessary to take account also of the framework of the income tax legislation. This established that the commissioners must assess each individual taxpayer in relation to his circumstances. Such assessments and all information regarding a taxpayer's affairs are strictly confidential. There is no list or record of assessments which can be inspected by other taxpayers nor is there any common fund of the produce of income tax in which income taxpayers as a whole can be said to have any interest. The produce of income tax, together with that of other inland revenue taxes, is paid into the consolidated fund which is at the disposal of Parliament for any purposes that Parliament thinks fit.

The position of taxpayers is therefore very different from that of ratepayers. As explained in *Arsenal Football Club Ltd* v *Ende* [1979] AC 1, the amount of rates assessed upon ratepayers is ascertainable by the public through the valuation list. The produce of rates goes into a common fund applicable for the benefit of the ratepayers. Thus any ratepayer has an interest, direct and sufficient, in the rates levied upon other ratepayers; for this reason his right as a 'person aggrieved' to challenge assessments upon them has long been recognised and is so now in section 69 of the General Rate Act 1967. This right was given effect to in the *Arsenal* case.

The structure of the legislation relating to income tax, on the other hand, makes clear that no corresponding right is intended to be conferred upon taxpayers. Not only is there no express or implied provision in the legislation upon which such a right could be claimed, but to allow it would be subversive of the whole system, which involves that the commissioners' duties are to the Crown, and that matters relating to income tax are between the commissioners and the taxpayer concerned. No other person is given any right to make proposals about the tax payable by any individual: he cannot even inquire as to such tax. The total confidentiality of assessments and of negotiations between individuals and the revenue is a vital element in the working of the system. As a matter of general principle I would hold that one taxpayer has no sufficient interest in asking the court to investigate the tax affairs of another taxpayer or to complain that the latter has been under-assessed or over-assessed: indeed, there is a strong public interest that he should not. And this principle applies equally to groups of taxpayers: an aggregate of individuals each of whom has no interest cannot of itself have an interest.

That a case can never arise in which the acts or abstentions of the revenue can be brought before the court I am certainly not prepared to assert, nor that, in a case of sufficient gravity, the court might not be able to hold that another taxpayer or other taxpayers could challenge them. Whether this situation has been reached or not must depend upon an examination, upon evidence, of what breach of duty or illegality is alleged. Upon this, and relating it to the position of the complainant, the court has to make its decision....

[After considering the evidence his Lordship decided that the Federation had no sufficient interest.]

LORD DIPLOCK: For my part I should prefer to allow the appeal and dismiss the Federation's application under RSC Ord. 53, not upon the specific ground of no sufficient interest but upon the more general ground that it has not been shown that in the matter of which complaint was made, the treatment of the tax liabilities of the Fleet Street casuals, the board did anything that was *ultra vires* or unlawful. They acted in the bona fide exercise of the wide managerial discretion which is conferred on them by statute....

[His Lordship nonetheless went on to consider the question of *locus standi*.]

The procedure under the new Order 53 involves two stages: (1) the application for leave to apply for judicial review, and (2) if leave is granted, the hearing of the application itself. The former, or 'threshold' stage is regulated by rule 3. The application for leave to apply for judicial review is made ex parte, but may be adjourned for the persons or bodies against whom relief is sought to be represented. This did not happen in the instant case. Rule 3(5) specifically requires the court to consider at this stage whether 'it considers that the applicant has a sufficient interest in the matter to which the application relates.' So this is a 'threshold' question in the sense that the court must direct its mind to it and form a prima facie view about it upon the material that is available at the first stage. The prima facie view so formed, if favourable to the applicant, may alter on further consideration in the light of further evidence that may be before the court at the second stage, the hearing of the application for judicial review itself.

The need for leave to start proceedings for remedies in public law is not new. It applied previously to applications for prerogative orders, though not to civil actions for injunctions or declarations. Its purpose is to prevent the time of the court being wasted by busybodies with misguided or trivial complaints of administrative error, and to remove the uncertainty in which public officers and authorities might be left as to whether they could safely proceed with administrative action while proceedings for judicial review of it were actually pending even though misconceived....

My Lords, at the threshold stage, for the Federation to make out a prima facie case of reasonable suspicion that the board in showing a discriminatory leniency to a substantial class of taxpayers had done so for ulterior reasons extraneous to good management, and thereby deprived the national exchequer of considerable sums of money, constituted what was in my view reason enough for the Divisional Court to consider that the Federation or, for that matter, any taxpayer, had a sufficient interest to apply to have the question whether the board was acting *ultra vires* reviewed by the court. The whole purpose of requiring that leave should first be obtained to make the application for judicial review would be defeated if the court were to go into the matter in any depth at that stage. If, on a quick perusal of the material then available, the court thinks that it discloses what might on further consideration turn out to be an arguable case in favour of granting to the applicant the relief claimed, it ought, in the exercise of a judicial discretion, to give him leave to apply for that relief. The discretion that the court is exercising at this stage is not the same as that which it is called upon to exercise when all the evidence is in and the matter has been fully argued at the hearing of the application....

The analyses to which, on the invitation of the Lord Advocate, the relevant legislation has been subjected by some of your Lordships, and particularly the requirement of confidentiality which would be broken if one taxpayer could complain that another taxpayer was being treated by the revenue more favourably than himself, mean that occasions will be very rare on which an individual taxpayer (or pressure group of taxpayers) will be able to show a sufficient interest to justify an application for judicial review of the way in which the revenue has dealt with the tax affairs of any taxpayer other than the applicant himself.

Rare though they may be, however, if, in the instant case, what at the threshold stage was suspicion only had been proved at the hearing of the application for judicial review to be true in fact (instead of being utterly destroyed), I would have held that this was a matter in which the federation had a sufficient interest in obtaining an appropriate order, whether by way of declaration or mandamus, to require performance by the board of statutory duties which for reasons shown to be *ultra vires* it was failing to perform.

It would, in my view, be a grave lacuna in our system of public law if a pressure group, like the Federation, or even a single public-spirited taxpayer, were prevented by outdated technical rules of *locus standi* from bringing the matter to the attention of the court to vindicate the rule of law and get the unlawful conduct stopped. The Attorney-General, although he occasionally applies for prerogative orders against public authorities that do not form part of central government, in practice never does so against government departments. It is not, in my view, a sufficient answer to say that judicial review of the actions of officers or departments of central government is unnecessary because they are accountable to Parliament for the way in which they carry out their functions. They are accountable to Parliament for what they do so far as regards efficiency and policy, and of that Parliament is the only judge; they are responsible to a court of justice for the lawfulness of what they do, and of that the court is the only judge.

Lord Fraser and Lord Roskill delivered judgments in which they agreed with Lord Wilberforce. Lord Scarman delivered a judgment which agreed in general with that of Lord Diplock.

NOTE: Lord Diplock refers in his judgment to the role of the Attorney-General. The Attorney-General has a discretion to institute legal proceedings in the public interest. He may do so on his own initiative or upon the request of an individual or organization. Where the Attorney-General institutes litigation at the request of an individual or organization, this is known as a relator action. The Attorney-General's decision whether to bring a relator action cannot be challenged (see *Gouriet* v *Union of Post Office Workers* [1978] AC 435).

■ QUESTIONS

1. What are the differences, if any, between the approaches of Lord Diplock and Lord Wilberforce ?

2. Do the judgments suggest what their Lordships perceived to be the justification for standing rules (see Cane, p. 626, *ante*)?
3. Do the judgments suggest that the function of judicial review is:
   (a) to protect the individual who is specially affected by the decision;
   (b) to protect the public interest in rooting out administrative illegality?

NOTES

1. In *R* v *The Attorney-General, ex parte ICI plc* [1987] 1 CMLR 72 the applicant, ICI, was held to have standing to question the validity of the Inland Revenue's assessment of the tax payable by one of its competitors. The fact that ICI was challenging the assessment of a competitor was held to distinguish the application from that of the NFSESB in the *National Federation* case. Furthermore, the issue of confidentiality did not arise because the Revenue had already agreed voluntarily to disclose the basis of its assessment.
2. The Law Commission in its 1994 report favoured the broadly liberal approach of the courts on sufficient interest. They were concerned about the effect of *R* v *Secretary of State for the Environment, ex parte Rose Theatre Trust* [1990] 1 QB 504 on challenges brought by people who were concerned about, but not directly affected by, the administrative action. The Law Commission recommended that public interest applications be treated as having sufficient interest. Subsequently the courts have taken this approach. In *R* v *HM Inspector of Pollution, ex parte Greenpeace Ltd (No. 2)* [1994] 4 All ER 329 Otton J declined to follow *Rose Theatre Trust*. Greenpeace, an environmental pressure group, not only had a genuine interest in the issues involved (disposal of radioactive waste) but it had some 2,500 supporters in the area where the plant was situated and it if was not permitted to seek judicial review, then those who Greenpeace represents, who would have sufficient interest, e.g. neighbours, would not be able to command the expertise which Greenpeace has. A less well-informed challenge would not render the court the assistance which it needs in order to do justice between the parties. In *R* v *Secretary of State for Foreign Affairs, ex parte World Development Movement Ltd* [1995] 1 WLR 386 the applicant pressure group was regarded as having sufficient interest to challenge the decision by the Foreign Secretary to make a payment of aid under the Overseas Development and Co-operation Act 1980 to the Malaysian Government towards the construction of the Pergau dam and hydro-electric scheme. This was despite the fact that, unlike Greenpeace, it was unlikely that any of the applicant's individual members had a direct interest in the issue. The significant factors listed by Rose LJ were that the issue was important; it involved the vindication of the rule of law; there appeared to be no other responsible challenger; the nature of the breach of duty against which relief was sought, and the prominent role of these applications in giving advice, guidance, and assistance with regard to aid. See S. Chakrabati, J. Stephens and C. Gallagher [2003] *Public Law* 697 on costs and groups litigating in the public interest.

SECTION 4: AGAINST WHOM AND IN RESPECT OF WHAT ACTIVITIES MAY JUDICIAL REVIEW BE SOUGHT?

O'Reilly v *Mackman* was a case in which the litigants attempted to use the procedure by way of writ instead of the application for judicial review. Conversely, there have been a number of cases in which the courts have held that litigants are not entitled to use the procedure for judicial review because their cases do not raise issues of 'public law'.

In *R* v *BBC, ex parte Lavelle* [1983] 1 WLR 23, the applicant sought to challenge a decision of a disciplinary board within the BBC suspending her from her employment. Woolf LJ considered that the scope of Ord. 53 was not necessarily confined to that of the old prerogative orders but depended solely on the criteria set out in Ord. 53, r. 1(2) (now Part 54.3(1) (p. 607, *ante*)). He did, however, hold that Ord. 53 could not be used to challenge the decisions of purely private or domestic tribunals such as the disciplinary body within the BBC which derived its power solely from the contract between Miss Lavelle and the BBC.

In the case which follows, the applicants sought to use judicial review to challenge the decision of an unincorporated association which exercised no statutory or prerogative powers.

R v Panel on Take-overs and Mergers, ex parte Datafin plc

[1987] QB 815, Court of Appeal

The Take-over Panel is an unincorporated association which represents a wide range of institutional bodies operating in the financial market, for example, the Stock Exchange. It has a regulatory function concerning take-overs and mergers. In this role it makes, administers, and enforces a code of conduct known as the City Code.

The applicants, Datafin plc, were involved in a competitive take-over and complained to the Panel that their rivals, Norton Opax plc, had breached the City Code. The Panel dismissed the complaint and Datafin unsuccessfully sought leave in the High Court to apply for judicial review, seeking *certiorari*, prohibition, *mandamus*, and an injunction. Leave was granted on appeal by the Court of Appeal. The Court of Appeal considered three main issues:

(a) the susceptibility of the Panel's decisions to judicial review;

(b) the manner in which any jurisdiction was to be exercised; and

(c) whether, if there was jurisdiction, relief should be granted in the present case.

The following extracts are concerned only with the first question.

SIR JOHN DONALDSON MR: The Panel on Take-overs and Mergers is a truly remarkable body. Perched on the 20th floor of the Stock Exchange building in the City of London, both literally and metaphorically it oversees and regulates a very important part of the United Kingdom financial market. Yet it performs this function without any visible means of legal support.... 'Self-regulation' is an emotive term. It is also ambiguous. An individual who voluntarily regulates his life in accordance with stated principles, because he believes that this is morally right and also, perhaps, in his own long-term interests, or a group of individuals who do so, are practising self-regulation. But it can mean something quite different. It can connote a system whereby a group of people, acting in concert, use their collective power to force themselves and others to comply with a code of conduct of their own devising. This is not necessarily morally wrong or contrary to the public interest, unlawful or even undesirable. But it is very different.

The panel is a self-regulating body in the latter sense. Lacking any authority de jure, it exercises immense power de facto by devising, promulgating, amending and interpreting the City Code on Take-overs and Mergers, by waiving or modifying the application of the code in particular circumstances, by investigating and reporting on alleged breaches of the code and by the application or threat of sanctions. The sanctions are no less effective because they are applied indirectly and lack a legally enforceable base...

The unspoken assumption, which I do not doubt is a reality, is that the Department of Trade and Industry or, as the case may be, the Stock Exchange or other appropriate body would in fact exercise statutory or contractual powers to penalise the transgressors....

The principal issue in this appeal, and the only issue which may matter in the long term is whether this remarkable body is above the law. Its respectability is beyond question. So is its bona fides. I do not doubt for one moment that it is intended to and does operate in the public interest and that the enormously wide discretion which it arrogates to itself is necessary if it is to function efficiently and effectively. Whilst not wishing to become involved in the political controversy on the relative merits of self-regulation and governmental or statutory regulation, I am content to assume for the purposes of this appeal that self-regulation is preferable in the public interest. But that said, what is to happen if the panel goes off the rails? Suppose, perish the thought, that it were to use its powers in a way which was manifestly unfair. What then? [Counsel for the panel] submits that the panel would lose the support of public opinion in the financial markets and would be unable to operate. Further or alternatively, Parliament could and would intervene. Maybe, but how long would that take and who in the meantime could or would come to the assistance of those who were being oppressed by such conduct?...

The jurisdictional issue

...The picture which emerges is clear. As an act of government it was decided that, in relation to take-overs, there should be a central self-regulatory body which would be supported and sustained by a periphery of statutory powers and penalties wherever non-statutory powers and penalties were insufficient or non-existent or where EEC requirements called for statutory provisions....

The issue is whether the historic supervisory jurisdiction of the Queen's courts extends to such a body discharging such functions, including some which are quasi-judicial in their nature, as part of such a system. [Counsel] for the panel, submits that it does not. He says that this jurisdiction only extends to bodies whose power is derived from legislation or the exercise of the prerogative. [Counsel for the applicants] submits that this is too narrow a view and that regard has to be had not only to the source of the body's power, but also to whether it operates as an integral part of a system which has a public law character, is supported by public law in that public law sanctions are applied if its edicts are ignored and performs what might be described as public law functions.

After discussing a number of cases, *R* v *Criminal Injuries Compensation Board, ex parte Lain* [1967] 2 QB 864, *O'Reilly* v *Mackman* [1983] 2 AC 237, *Council for the Civil Service Unions* v *Minister for the Civil Service* [1985] AC 374 and *Gillick* v *West Norfolk and Wisbech Area Health Authority* [1986] AC 112, the Master of Rolls continued:

In all the reports it is possible to find enumerations of factors giving rise to the jurisdiction, but it is a fatal error to regard the presence of all those factors as essential or as being exclusive of other factors. Possibly the only essential elements are what can be described as a public element, which can take many different forms, and the exclusion from the jurisdiction of bodies whose sole source of power is a consensual submission to its jurisdiction.

In fact, given its novelty, the panel fits surprisingly well into the format which this court had in mind in the *Criminal Injuries Compensation Board* case. It is without doubt performing a public duty and an important one. This is clear from the expressed willingness of the Secretary of State for Trade and Industry to limit legislation in the field of take-overs and mergers and to use the panel as the centrepiece of his regulation of that market. The rights of citizens are indirectly affected by its decisions, some, but by no means all of whom, may in a technical sense be said to have assented to this situation, e.g. the members of the Stock Exchange. At least in its determination of whether there has been a breach of the code it has a duty to act judicially and it asserts that its raison d'être is to do equity between one shareholder and another. Its source of power is only partly based upon moral persuasion and the assent of institutions and their members, the bottom line being the statutory powers exercised by the Department of Trade and Industry and the Bank of England. In this context I should be very disappointed if the courts could not recognise the realities of executive power and allowed their vision to be clouded by the subtlety and sometimes the complexity of the way in which it can be exerted.

Given that it is really unthinkable that, in the absence of legislation such as affects trade unions, the panel should go on its way cocooned from the attention of the courts in defence of the citizenry, we sought to investigate whether it could conveniently be controlled by established forms of private law, e.g. torts such as actionable combinations in restraint of trade, and, to this end, pressed [counsel for the applicants] to draft a writ. Suffice it to say that the result was wholly unconvincing and, not surprisingly, [counsel for the panel] did not admit that it would be in the least effective....

LLOYD LJ: ...I add only a few words on the important question whether the Panel on Take-overs and Mergers is a body which is subject to judicial review. In my judgment it is....

On this part of the case counsel for the panel has advanced arguments on two levels. On the level of pure policy he submits that it is undesirable for decisions or rulings of the panel to be reviewable. The intervention of the court would at best impede, at worst frustrate, the purposes for which the panel exists. Secondly, on a more technical level, he submits that to hold that the panel is subject to the supervisory jurisdiction of the High Court would be to extend that jurisdiction further than it has ever been extended before.

On the policy level, I find myself unpersuaded. Counsel for the panel made much of the word 'self-regulating'. No doubt self-regulation has many advantages. But I was unable to see why the mere fact that a body is self-regulating makes it less appropriate for judicial review. The committee of an ordinary club affords an obvious example. But the reason why a club is not subject to judicial review is not just because it is self-regulating. The panel wields enormous power. It has a giant's strength. The fact that it is self-regulating, which means, presumably, that it is not subject to regulation by others, and in particular the Department of Trade and Industry, makes it not less but more appropriate that it should be subject to judicial review by the courts....

So long as there is a possibility, however remote, of the panel abusing its great powers, then it would be wrong for the courts to abdicate responsibility. The courts must remain ready, willing and able to hear a legitimate complaint in this as in any other field of our national life. I am not persuaded that this particular field is one in which the courts do not belong, or from which they should retire, on grounds of policy. And if the courts are to remain in the field, then it is clearly better, as a matter of policy, that legal proceedings should remain in the realm of public law rather than private law, not only because they are quicker, but also because the requirement of leave under Ord. 53 will exclude claims which are clearly unmeritorious.

So I turn to [counsel for the panel's] more technical argument....

After referring to Lord Diplock's speech in *Council of Civil Service Unions* v *Minister for the Civil Service* [1985] AC 374 Lloyd LJ continued:

I do not agree that the source of the power is the sole test whether a body is subject to judicial review, nor do I so read Lord Diplock's speech. Of course the source of power will often, perhaps usually, be decisive. If the source of power is a statute, or subordinate legislation under a statute, then clearly the body in question will be subject to judicial review. If, at the other end of the scale, the source of power is contractual, as in the case of private arbitration, then clearly the arbitrator is not subject to judicial review: see *R* v *National Joint Council for the Craft of Dental Technicians (Disputes Committee), ex parte Neate* [1953] 1 QB 704.

But in between these extremes there is an area in which it is helpful to look not just at the source of the power but at the nature of the power. If the body in question is exercising public law functions, or if the exercise of its functions have public law consequences, then that may, as counsel for the applicants submitted, be sufficient to bring the body within the reach of judicial review....

But suppose I am wrong: suppose that the courts are indeed confined to looking at the source of the power, as [counsel for the panel] submits. Then I would accept the submission of counsel for the applicants that the source of the power in the present case is indeed governmental, at least in part. [Counsel for the panel] argued that, so far from the source of the power being governmental, this is a case where the government has deliberately abstained from exercising power. I do not take that view. I agree with [counsel for the applicants] when he says there has been an implied devolution of power. Power exercised behind the scenes is power nonetheless. The express powers conferred on inferior tribunals were of critical importance in the early days when the sole or main ground for intervention by the courts was that the inferior tribunal had exceeded its powers. But those days are long since past. Having regard to the way in which the panel came to be established, the fact that the Governor of the Bank of England appoints both the chairman and the deputy chairman, and the other matters to which Sir John Donaldson MR has referred, I am persuaded that the panel was established under the authority of the government, to use the language of Diplock LJ in *Lain's* case. If in addition to looking at the source of the power we are entitled to look at the nature of the power, as I believe we are, then the case is all the stronger....

NICHOLLS LJ:...

Jurisdiction

I take as my starting point *Reg* v *Criminal Injuries Compensation Board, ex parte Lain* [1967] 2 QB 864, 882, where Lord Parker CJ noted that the only constant limits on the ancient remedy of certiorari were that the tribunal in question was performing a public duty. He contrasted private or domestic tribunals whose authority is derived solely from the agreement of the parties concerned....

In my view, and quite apart from any other factors which point in the same direction, given the leading and continuing role played by the Bank of England in the affairs of the panel, the statutory source of the powers and duties of the Council of the Stock Exchange, the wide-ranging nature and importance of the matters covered by the code, and the public law consequences of non-compliance, the panel is performing a public duty in prescribing and operating the code (including ruling on complaints).

■ QUESTIONS

1. Is it correct to say, after *Datafin*, that the only criterion for deciding whether an authority is subject to judicial review is whether it performs a public function?
2. Would judicial review be available to challenge the decisions of the following:
   (a) the Advertising Standards Authority (see *R* v *Advertising Standards Authority Limited, ex parte The Insurance Service* (1989) 133 SJ 1545);
   (b) the National Greyhound Racing Club (see *Law* v *National Greyhound Racing Club* [1983] 1 WLR 1302, but note that this case was decided before *ex parte Datafin*. Do you think it would be decided any differently after *ex parte Datafin*?);
   (c) the Jockey Club (see *R* v *Disciplinary Committee of the Jockey Club, ex parte Aga Khan* [1993] 1 WLR 909);
   (d) the Association of the British Pharmaceutical Industry (see *R* v *Code of Practice Committee of the Association of the British Pharmaceutical Industry, The Times*, 7 November 1990);
   (e) a university (see *Page* v *Hull University Visitor* [1993] AC 682).

NOTE: There have been a number of cases in which the courts considered whether the decisions of statutory bodies to dismiss an employee/employees could be challenged under Ord. 53. In *R* v *East Berkshire Health Authority, ex parte Walsh* [1985] QB 152 the Court of Appeal held that this question depended on whether the employment had sufficient 'statutory underpinning'. The health authority was required by statute to contract with its employees on terms which included the conditions agreed by the Whitley Council for the Health Service and approved by the Secretary of State. The Court of Appeal decided that this did not provide a sufficient statutory underpinning. On the other hand, in *R* v *Secretary of State for the Home Department, ex parte Benwell* [1985] QB 152 Hodgson J granted judicial review of a decision to dismiss a prison officer. Benwell was not in a contractual relationship with his employers and Hodgson J considered that, because his employment was governed by a code of discipline issued under statutory authority, there was sufficient statutory underpinning to provide a public law element. See also *Roy* v *Kensington and Chelsea FPC* p. 619, *ante*. Ordinary civil servants have now been held to have contracts of employment (*R* v *Lord Chancellor's Department, ex parte Nangle* [1992] 1 All ER 897).

For further discussion of the distinction between public law and private law, see J. Beatson, '"Public" and "Private" in English Administrative Law' (1987) 103 *Law Quarterly Review*, 34–65.

Although the courts might decide that the claim for judicial review is not available because the dispute does not raise issues of public law, this does not mean that the principles of judicial review are irrelevant. The rules of natural justice are frequently applied to bodies (such as sporting clubs) which could not be challenged under the application for judicial review procedure (see, for example, *R* v *BBC, ex parte Lavelle* [1983] 1 WLR 23). In such cases the judges may describe their role as one of exercising judicial review. This means that it is important to bear in mind that there may be a distinction between the scope of judicial review at the substantive level (that is, the scope of the principles of judicial review) and the scope of judicial review at the procedural level (the scope of the application for judicial review).

SECTION 5: JUSTICIABILITY

Even if a matter raises an issue of public law, the courts may nonetheless refuse to review it on the ground that the matter is not justiciable. This generally means that the courts consider judicial procedures are unsuitable to control the exercise of discretion. This may be for a variety of reasons, for example because of lack of expertise on the part of the court or because of the constitutional inappropriateness of judicial intervention.

Council of Civil Service Unions v *Minister for the Civil Service*

[1985] AC 374, House of Lords

The facts of this case are at p. 576, *ante*. In it, the court accepted that prerogative powers were subject to judicial review. The question of whether public powers are subject to judicial review was not therefore to be established on the basis of whether the source of the powers was statute or the prerogative (see further *R* v *Panel on Take-overs and Mergers*). Review of the exercise of powers might, however, be denied if the subject matter of the dispute raised issues which were not justiciable.

LORD FRASER OF TULLYBELTON: ...The respondent's case is that she deliberately made the decision without prior consultation because prior consultation 'would involve a real risk that it would occasion the very kind of disruption [at GCHQ] which was a threat to national security and which it was intended to avoid.'...

The question is one of evidence. The decision on whether the requirements of national security outweigh the duty of fairness in any particular case is for the Government and not for the courts; the Government alone has access to the necessary information, and in any event the judicial process is unsuitable for reaching decisions on national security. But if the decision is successfully challenged, on the ground that it has been reached by a process which is unfair, then the Government is under an obligation to produce evidence that the decision was in fact based on grounds of national security....

[After considering *The Zamora* [1916] 2 AC 77 and the speeches of Lord Reid and Viscount Radcliffe in *Chandler* v *Director of Public Prosecutions* [1964] AC 763 his Lordship concluded that]...The affidavit [of Sir Robert Armstrong], read as a whole, does in my opinion undoubtedly constitute evidence that the Minister did indeed consider that prior consultation would have involved a risk of precipitating disruption at GCHQ. I am accordingly of opinion that the respondent has shown that her decision was one which not only could reasonably have been based, but was in fact based, on considerations of national security, which outweighed what would otherwise have been the reasonable expectation on the part of the appellants for prior consultation....

LORD SCARMAN: My Lords, I would dismiss this appeal for one reason only. I am satisfied that the respondent has made out a case on the ground of national security. Notwithstanding the criticisms which can be made of the evidence and despite the fact that the point was not raised, or, if it was, was not clearly made before the case reached the Court of Appeal, I have no doubt that the respondent refused to consult the unions before issuing her instruction of the 22 December 1983 because she feared that, if she did, union-organised disruption of the monitoring services of GCHQ could well result. I am further satisfied that the fear was one which a reasonable minister in the circumstances in which she found herself could reasonably entertain. I am also satisfied that a reasonable minister could reasonably consider such disruption to constitute a threat to national security. I would, therefore, deny relief to the appellants upon their application for judicial review of the instruction, the effect of which was that staff at GCHQ would no longer be permitted to belong to a national trade union.

The point of principle in the appeal is as to the duty of the court when in proceedings properly brought before it a question arises as to what is required in the interest of national security. The question may arise in ordinary litigation between private persons as to their private rights and obligations: and it can arise, as in this case, in proceedings for judicial review of a decision by a public authority. The question can take one of several forms. It may be a question of fact which Parliament has left to the court to determine: see for an example section 10 of the Contempt of Court Act 1981. It may arise for consideration as a factor in the exercise of an executive discretionary power. But, however it arises, it is a matter to be considered by the court in the circumstances and context of the case. Though there are limits dictated by law and common sense which the court must observe in dealing with the question, the court does not abdicate its judicial function. If the question arises as a matter of fact, the court requires evidence to be given. If it arises as a factor to be considered in reviewing the exercise of a discretionary power, evidence is also needed so that the court may determine whether it should intervene to correct excess or abuse of the power....

Lord Scarman, after discussing *The Zamora, Chandler* v *Director of Public Prosecutions,* and *Secretary of State for Defence* v *Guardian Newspapers Ltd* [1985] AC 339, continued:

My Lords, I conclude, therefore, that where a question as to the interests of national security arises in judicial proceedings the court has to act on evidence. In some cases a judge or jury is required by law to be satisfied that the interest is proved to exist: in others, the interest is a factor to be considered in the review of the exercise of an executive discretionary power. Once the factual basis is established by evidence so that the court is satisfied that the interest of national security is a relevant factor to be considered in the determination of the case, the court will accept the opinion of the Crown or its responsible officer as to what is required to meet it, unless it is possible to show that the opinion was one which no reasonable minister advising the Crown could in the circumstances reasonably have held. There is no abdication of the judicial function, but there is a common sense limitation recognised by the judges as to what is justiciable: and the limitation is entirely consistent with the general development of the modern case law of judicial review....

LORD ROSKILL: My Lords, the conflict between private rights and the rights of the state is not novel either in our political history or in our courts. Historically, at least since 1688, the courts have sought to present a barrier to inordinate claims by the executive. But they have also been obliged to recognise that in some fields that barrier must be lowered and that on occasions, albeit with reluctance, the courts must accept that the claims of executive power must take precedence over those of the individual. One such field is that of national security. The courts have long shown themselves sensitive to the assertion by the executive that considerations of national security must preclude judicial investigation of a particular individual grievance. But even in that field the courts will not act on a mere assertion that questions of national security are involved. Evidence is required that the decision under challenge was in fact founded on those grounds. That that principle exists is I think beyond doubt. In a famous passage in *The Zamora* [1916] 2 AC 77, 107 Lord Parker of Waddington, delivering the opinion of the Judicial Committee, said:

> Those who are responsible for the national security must be the sole judges of what the national security requires. It would be obviously undesirable that such matters should be the subject of evidence in a court of law or otherwise discussed in public.

The Judicial Committee were there asserting what I have already sought to say, namely that some matters, of which national security is one, are not amenable to the judicial process....

Lord Diplock and Lord Brightman delivered judgments in favour of dismissing the appeals.

■ QUESTION

What differences, if any, are there between the speeches of Lord Fraser and Lord Roskill on the one hand, and Lord Scarman on the other?

NOTES

1. In *R* v *Secretary of State for the Home Department, ex parte Ruddock* [1987] 1 WLR 1482, at p. 1490 it was said that 'credible evidence' was required in support of a plea of national security before judicial investigation of a factual issue (in this case whether a warrant had been issued to tap Mrs Ruddock's telephone) is precluded. Taylor J rejected the argument that the court should decline jurisdiction because a Minister states that to do so would be detrimental to national security. He did, however, accept that in an extreme case where there was 'cogent', 'very strong and specific' evidence of potential damage to national security flowing from the trial of the issues a court might have to decline to try factual issues.
2. In other cases the courts have held that certain decisions cannot be challenged on particular grounds (see *Nottinghamshire CC* v *Secretary of State for the Environment* [1986] AC 240, p. 581, *ante*).
3. In *R* v *Secretary of State for the Home Department, ex parte Bentley* [1994] QB 349 the exercise of the prerogative of mercy was successfully challenged, albeit on a narrow ground. The court held the Minister approached the question of a posthumous pardon on the wrong basis that a grant of a free pardon required moral and technical innocence, rather than considering whether, in all the circumstances, the appropriate punishment had been suffered.

   The challenge to the Treaty on European Union was not successful (*R* v *Secretary of State for Foreign and Commonwealth Affairs, ex parte Rees-Mogg* [1994] QB 552).
4. In *Clark* v *University of Lincolnshire and Humberside* (p. 622, *ante*) Sedley LJ said that issues of academic or pastoral judgement were ones which universities were better placed to judge than the

courts and instanced the particular mark or class a student ought to be awarded or whether an aegrotat is justified. He also said that religious or aesthetic matters might fall within such a class of non-justiciable matters (para. 12).

■ QUESTION

Consider whether you think each of the following issues is justiciable and why/why not? Then read the cases cited to establish the views of the courts. What reasons did the courts give?

(a) A British citizen residing in Spain applied for a British passport. The application was refused, and he was told that the reason for this was that a warrant for his arrest had been issued in the United Kingdom and the Secretary of State would not issue a passport in such circumstances (see *R* v *Secretary of State for Foreign and Commonwealth Affairs, ex parte Everett* [1989] 2 WLR 224).

(b) The Attorney-General has power to stop or institute prosecutions and to issue directions to the Director of Public Prosecutions to take over the conduct of prosecutions. He or she may also give, or refuse to give, consent to the institution of relator actions (actions brought at the instance of a relator by the Attorney-General to restrain infringements of public rights). (See *Gouriet* v *UPOW* [1978] AC 435.)

SECTION 6: JUDICIAL REVIEW AS A DISCRETIONARY REMEDY

NOTE: It is important to remember that judicial review is a discretionary remedy. Hence, the effective scope of the principles of judicial review will depend on how the court chooses to exercise its discretion.

There are a number of factors which are relevant to the exercise of the court's discretion: the availability of alternative remedies and the question whether the applicant has suffered injustice have been particularly important in recent years.

A: The availability of alternative remedies

In the Practice Statement (Administrative Court: Listing and Urgent Cases) the then Lead judge of the Administrative Court Scott Baker J stated at para. 5:

Use of alternative means of resolution

I draw the attention of litigants and their advisers to the decision of the Court of Appeal in *R (Cowl)* v *Plymouth City Council (Practice Note)* [2001] EWCA Civ 1935, [2002] 1 WLR 803. The nominated judges are fully committed to resolving disputes by alternative means where appropriate and are exploring ways of promoting this.

R (Cowl) v *Plymouth City Council (Practice Note)*

[2001] EWCA Civ 1935, [2002] 1WLR 803, Court of Appeal

The claimants, who were residents of a residential home, appealed the refusal of permission to grant judicial review of the decision by the council to confirm its social services committee's decision to close the residential home. The council had offered to convene a complaints panel under Local Authority Social Services Act, s. 7B as inserted by National Health Service and Community Care Act 1990, s. 50.

LORD WOOLF CJ:

1 The importance of this appeal is that it illustrates that, even in disputes between public authorities and the members of the public for whom they are responsible, insufficient attention is paid to the paramount importance of avoiding litigation whenever this is possible. Particularly in the case of these disputes both sides must by now be acutely conscious of the contribution alternative dispute resolution can make to resolving disputes in a manner which both meets the needs of the parties and the public and saves time, expense and stress.

2 The appeal also demonstrates that courts should scrutinise extremely carefully applications for judicial review in the case of applications of the class with which this appeal is concerned. The courts should then make appropriate use of their ample powers under the Civil Procedure Rules to ensure that the parties try to resolve the dispute with the minimum involvement of the courts. The legal aid authorities should co-operate in support of this approach.

3 To achieve this objective the court may have to hold, on its own initiative, an inter partes hearing at which the parties can explain what steps they have taken to resolve the dispute without the involvement of the courts. In particular the parties should be asked why a complaints procedure or some other form of alternative dispute resolution has not been used or adapted to resolve or reduce the issues which are in dispute. If litigation is necessary the courts should deter the parties from adopting an unnecessarily confrontational approach to the litigation. If this had happened in this case many thousands of pounds in costs could have been saved and considerable stress to the parties could have been avoided.

...

14 It appears that one reason why the wheels of the litigation may have continued to roll is that both parties were under the impression that unless they agreed otherwise the claimants were *entitled* to proceed with their application for judicial review unless the complaints procedure on offer technically constituted an 'alternative remedy' which would fulfil all the functions of judicial review. This is too narrow an approach to adopt when considering whether an application to judicial review should be stayed. The parties do not today, under the Civil Procedure Rules, have a right to have a resolution of their respective contentions by judicial review in the absence of an alternative procedure which would cover exactly the same ground as judicial review. The courts should not permit, except for good reason, proceedings for judicial review to proceed if a significant part of the issues between the parties could be resolved outside the litigation process. The disadvantages of doing so are limited. If subsequently it becomes apparent that there is a legal issue to be resolved, that can thereafter be examined by the courts which may be considerably assisted by the findings made by the complaints panel.

...

21 Having read the numerous witness statements placed before us and the substantial skeleton arguments prior to the hearing, the members of this court came to the clear conclusion that the appeal raised no point of legal principle. However, while this was the position, the claimants were intent on examining in detail the previous decisions of courts, primarily at first instance, involving the closure of care homes in order to erect a series of legal hoops which it was contended Plymouth had to proceed through before it could close Granby Way. In reality, however, there was no legal principle which divided the parties. It was common ground that there has to be the fullest assessment of the effect of a possible move on the claimants before a decision whether to move the claimants could be reached. Plymouth were perfectly prepared to carry out such an assessment, and recognise that as yet it has not been carried out and that it has to be carried out. This does not satisfy the claimants. They contend that as a matter of law the assessment is required to take place before closure. But absent any statutory requirement what is important is that an assessment takes place, not the time at which it takes place.

22 We understand the reason why the claimants attach such importance to the assessment being carried out before the decision to close. They do not want an assessment as to the propriety of moving the individual claimants to be taken against a decision that the home is to be closed as that could, they fear, prejudge the outcome. This is why they submit that the full assessment should take place before the decision to close the home is taken. The position of Plymouth now, whatever may have been the position in the past, is clearly to regard the decision to close as merely a decision in principle; that is, to close Granby Way subject to the full assessment of the impact upon the residents of their having to move. This approach on the part of Plymouth is understandable. Plymouth needed to make financial savings. The

closure of Granby Way and another home would produce the required financial saving. From Plymouth's point of view therefore the first step was to consider whether closure would be a viable option. For this purpose they needed a limited assessment of the impact on the residents and of the practicality of their being rehoused, but no more than this. This exercise was carried out. The decision was made to proceed with this option. Detailed examination of what is involved in rehousing was then required so that a final decision could be made. The final decision would only be made after the full assessment of the impact upon the residents. Such an approach could be beneficial to the residents because, if the closure option was not viable, there was no need to subject them to the stress which would be involved in determining what would happen to them if they had to move.

23 Unfortunately Plymouth failed to make their strategy clear. They should have done this at the outset. Initially, therefore, there was justification for the claimants' concern that they were to be moved without any proper assessment being made before a final decision to close had taken place.

24 Nonetheless the decision which was taken did not have the technicality the claimants attached to it. There was nothing wrong with Plymouth adopting a two-stage process, with the detailed assessment being part of the second process. However, if this was what they were doing, it is regrettable that far from explaining it they obscured the fact that this was their intention. On the other hand, those who were acting on behalf of the claimants adopted a far too technical approach. Their treatment in their skeleton argument of the authorities on which they rely make this abundantly clear.

25 We do not single out either side's lawyers for particular criticism. What followed was due to the unfortunate culture in litigation of this nature of over-judicialising the processes which are involved. It is indeed unfortunate that, that process having started, instead of the parties focusing on the future they insisted on arguing about what had occurred in the past. So far as the claimants were concerned, that was of no value since Plymouth were prepared, as they ultimately made clear was their position, to reconsider the whole issue. Without the need for the vast costs which must have been incurred in this case already being incurred, the parties should have been able to come to a sensible conclusion as to how to dispose the issues which divided them. If they could not do this without help, then an independent mediator should have been recruited to assist. That would have been a far cheaper course to adopt. Today sufficient should be known about alternative dispute resolution to make the failure to adopt it, in particular when public money is involved, indefensible.

26 The disadvantages of what happened instead were apparent to the trial judge. They were also apparent to this court. At the opening of the hearing we therefore insisted on the parties focusing on what mattered, which was the future well-being of the claimants. Having made clear our views, building on the proposal which had been made in the 23 May letter, the parties had no difficulty in coming to a sensible agreement in the terms which are annexed to this judgment and will form part of the order of the court. The terms go beyond what Plymouth was required to do under the statutory complaint procedure. This does not however, matter because it is always open to the parties to agree to go beyond their statutory obligations. For example, sensibly the claimants are to have the benefit of representatives to appear on their behalf, who may well be non-lawyers who can be extremely experienced in handling issues of the nature of those which are involved. We trust that the parties will now draw a line under what has happened in the past and focus instead on what should happen in the future.

27 This case will have served some purpose if it makes it clear that the lawyers acting on both sides of a dispute of this sort are under a heavy obligation to resort to litigation only if it is really unavoidable. If they cannot resolve the whole of the dispute by the use of the complaints procedure they should resolve the dispute so far as is practicable without involving litigation. At least in this way some of the expense and delay will be avoided. We hope that the highly skilled and caring practitioners who practise in this area will learn from what we regard as the very unfortunate history of this case.

Appeal dismissed.

NOTES

1. *Cowl* and the Practice Statement seem, at least, to be reiterating in the strongest terms the case law which requires exhaustion of alternative remedies. The actual facts of *Cowl* suggest that review was premature and Beatson argues that many of the cases on exhaustion of alternatives are not really concerned with the tests of adequacy and relative expertise of the alternative remedies,

but rather the prematurity of review proceedings ('Prematurity and Ripeness for Review' in C. Forsyth and I. Hare (eds), *The Golden Metwand and the Crooked Cord* (1998), 221 at 234). See *R* v *Inland Revenue Commissioners, ex parte Preston,* [1985] AC 835 for a presumption that appellate procedures should be used and see pp. 659–660, *post,* for the Law Commission's proposal on the relationship between public services ombudsmen and the courts.

2. The previous case law on exhaustion did allow for exceptions. In *R* v *Chief Constable of Merseyside Police, ex parte Calvely* [1986] 2 WLR 144 some police officers had been found guilty of disciplinary offences by their Chief Constable. They had initiated a statutory appeal to the Home Secretary but also sought judicial review on the basis that there had been a breach of reg. 7, Police (Discipline) Regulations. Sir John Donaldson MR said:

[Counsel] for the Chief Constable, submits that the application for judicial review was rightly dismissed, not upon the ground that it was premature, but because judicial review is not an available remedy when another avenue of appeal is open. In this context he referred to *Reg* v *Epping and Harlow General Commissioners, ex parte Goldstraw* [1983] 3 All ER 257 where, with the agreement of Purchas LJ, I said, at p. 262:

> it is a cardinal principle that, save in the most exceptionable circumstances, [the judicial review] jurisdiction will not be exercised where other remedies were available and have not been used.

This, like other judicial pronouncements on the interrelationship between remedies by way of judicial review on the one hand and appeal procedures on the other, is not to be regarded or construed as a statute. It does not support the proposition that judicial review is not available where there is an alternative remedy by way of appeal. It asserts simply that the court, in the exercise of its discretion, will very rarely make this remedy available in these circumstances.

In other cases courts have asserted the existence of this discretion, albeit with varying emphasis on the reluctance to grant judicial review. Thus in *Reg* v *Paddington Valuation Officer, ex parte Peachey Property Corporation Ltd* [1966] 1 QB 380, 400, Lord Denning MR, with the agreement of Danckwerts and Salmon LJJ, held that certiorari and mandamus were available where the alternative statutory remedy was 'nowhere near so convenient, beneficial and effectual.' In *Reg* v *Hillingdon London Borough Council, ex parte Royco Homes Ltd* [1974] QB 720, 728 Lord Widgery CJ said: 'it has always been a principle that certiorari will go only where there is no other equally effective and convenient remedy.' In *Ex parte Waldron* [1985] 3 WLR 1090, 1108, Glidewell LJ, after referring to this passage, said:

> Whether the alternative statutory remedy will resolve the question at issue fully and directly; whether the statutory procedure would be quicker, or slower, than procedure by way of judicial review; whether the matter depends on some particular or technical knowledge which is more readily available to the alternative appellate body; these are amongst the matters which a court should take into account when deciding whether to grant relief by judicial review when an alternative remedy is available.

Finally, this approach is, I think, consistent with *Reg* v *Inland Revenue Commissioners, ex parte Preston* [1985] AC 835....

The statutory scheme for police discipline contained in the Police (Discipline) Regulations 1977 and the Police (Appeals) Rules 1977 (SI 1977 No. 759) contemplates a right of appeal to the Secretary of State from a determination by the Chief Constable.... However, it is not speedy and, even if there had been no application for judicial review, it is not certain that the appeal would have been determined much before the present time. The application for judicial review in fact caused the appeal to be stayed and, on the most optimistic view, it could not be determined in less than five to six months from now.

Mr Livesey submits that the applicants' complaint of delay in serving the regulation 7 notices and of consequential prejudice should be determined by the appeal procedure provided by Parliament. The appeal tribunal would have a specialised expertise rendering it better able than a court to assess the prejudice. Furthermore, the applicants would be able to raise new points and call fresh evidence directed to the disciplinary charges themselves.

I acknowledge the specialised expertise of such a tribunal, but I think Mr Livesey's submission overlooks the fact that a police officer's submission to police disciplinary procedures is not unconditional. He agrees and is bound by these procedures taking them as a whole. Just as his right of appeal is constrained by the requirement that he give prompt notice of appeal, so he is not to be put in peril in respect of disciplinary, as contrasted with criminal, proceedings unless there is substantial compliance with the police disciplinary regulations. That has not occurred in this case. Whether in all the circumstances the Chief Constable, and the Secretary of State on appeal, is to be regarded as being without jurisdiction to hear and determine the charges which are not processed in accordance with the statutory scheme or whether, in natural justice, the Chief Constable and the Secretary of State would, if they directed themselves correctly in law, be bound to rule in favour of the applicants on the preliminary point, is perhaps only of academic interest. The substance of the matter is that, against the background of the requirement of regulation 7 that the applicants be informed of the complaint and given an opportunity to reply within days rather than weeks, the applicants had no formal notice of the complaints for well over two years. This is so serious a departure from the police disciplinary procedure that, in my judgment, the court should, in the exercise of its discretion, grant judicial review and set aside the determination of the Chief Constable.

I would allow the appeal accordingly.

■ QUESTIONS

1. In *Calvely* how important was the length of time of the statutory appeal to the decision of the court?
2. Is the convenience of the alternative remedy compatible with *Cowl*?

B: Needs of good administration

R v *Monopolies and Mergers Commission, ex parte Argyll Group plc*

[1986] 1 WLR 763, Court of Appeal

Argyll Group plc and Guinness plc were rivals in a bid to take over another company, Distillers. The Secretary of State for Trade and Industry referred the Guinness proposal to the Monopolies and Mergers Commission for inquiry and report. One week later the Chairman of the Monopolies and Mergers Commission sought and obtained the consent of the Secretary of State for Trade and Industry to the withdrawal of the reference on the ground that the proposal to make the arrangements had been abandoned. Argyll sought judicial review of this decision, seeking an order of *certiorari*. The Court of Appeal accepted that the Chairman of the Commission did not have the power to act alone in the matter. The following extracts relate to the court's discretion whether to grant a remedy.

SIR JOHN DONALDSON MR: ...

Discretion

The judge accepted that the chairman derives authority to act as he did from paragraph 10 of schedule 3 to the Act, read with section 75(5). He did not, therefore, have to consider the issue of discretion. As I respectfully disagree with the judge on this aspect, I do, therefore, have to consider how discretion should be exercised.

We are sitting as a public law court concerned to review an administrative decision, albeit one which has to be reached by the application of judicial or quasi-judicial principles. We have to approach our duties with a proper awareness of the needs of public administration. I cannot catalogue them all, but, in the present context, would draw attention to a few which are relevant.

Good public administration is concerned with substance rather than form. Difficult although the decision upon the fact of abandonment may or my not have been, I have little doubt that the commission, or a group of members charged with the conduct of the reference, would have reached and would now reach the same conclusion as did their experienced chairman.

Good public administration is concerned with speed of decision, particularly in the financial field. The decision to lay aside the reference was reached on 20 February 1986. If relief is granted, it must be some days before a new decision is reached.

Good public administration requires a proper consideration of the public interest. In this context, the Secretary of State is the guardian of the public interest. He consented to the reference being laid aside, although he need not have done so if he considered it to be in the public interest that the original proposals be further investigated. He could have made a further reference of the new proposals, if such they be, but has not done so.

Good public administration requires a proper consideration of the legitimate interests of individual citizens, however rich and powerful they may be and whether they are natural or juridical persons. But in judging the relevance of an interest, however legitimate, regard has to be had to the purpose of the administrative process concerned. Argyll has a strong and legitimate interest in putting Guinness in baulk, but that is not the purpose of the administrative process under the Fair Trading Act 1973. To that extent their interest is not therefore of any great, or possibly any, weight.

Lastly good public administration requires decisiveness and finality unless there are compelling reasons to the contrary. The financial public has been entitled to rely upon the finality of the announced decision to set aside the reference and upon the consequence that, subject to any further reference, Guinness were back in the ring, from 20 February until at least 25 February when leave to apply for judicial review was granted, and possibly longer in the light of the judge's decision. This is a very long time in terms of a volatile market and account must be taken of the probability that deals have been done in reliance upon the validity of the decisions now impugned.

Taking account of all these factors, I do not consider that this is a case in which judicial review should be granted. Accordingly, I would dismiss the appeal.

Dillon LJ and Neill LJ delivered judgments in favour of dismissing the appeal.

NOTE: *R* v *Panel on Take-overs and Mergers, ex parte Datafin plc* [1987] QB 815 also illustrates the use of discretion in the grant of remedies. Sir John Donaldson MR stated (at p. 841) that the court would decide what order, if any, needed to be made, bearing in mind 'the likely outcome of the proceedings which will depend partly upon the facts as they appear from the information available to the court, but also in part upon the public administrative purpose which the panel is designed to serve'.

■ QUESTIONS

1. Commenting on the factors referred to by Sir John Donaldson, S. Lee writes in (1987) 103 *Law Quarterly Review*, 166–168, at 167 that:

> If these are only a few of the possible reasons for judicial restraint, then their discretion is indeed very wide. There are obvious dangers to good public administration, let alone to aggrieved citizens, in such broad judicial discretion. Firstly, there is the danger that administrators will come to believe that they can get away with a breach of the principles of administrative action. Secondly, the prospect of winning the argument on abuse of administrative discretion but failing to secure a remedy through the exercise of judicial discretion may well act as a disincentive to bring applications for judicial review.

Do you agree that decisions such as *R* v *Monopolies and Mergers Commission* carry such risks?

2. Contrast the approach adopted in this case to arguments based on the interests of good administration with *O'Reilly* v *Mackman* (p. 615, *ante*) and *Wandsworth Borough Council* v *Winder* (p. 619, *ante*).

NOTE: The relevance of the argument that a fair hearing would make no difference has been considered by the courts in recent years. There are, in fact, a number of contrasting cases. Of these, *Glynn* v *Keele University* [1971] 1 WLR 487 provides an example of a case which accepts, as in *R* v *Monopolies and Mergers Commission, ex parte Argyll Group plc*, that a remedy may be denied where a fair hearing 'would make no difference'. In that case the claimant had been fined and excluded from residence on a university campus for a particular period. Pennycuick V-C found that there had been a breach of the rules of natural justice, but he refused to grant an injunction since he thought that the claimant had only lost a chance to make a plea in mitigation, and this was not a sufficient reason to set aside a decision which he believed to be perfectly proper. In contrast Megarry J in *John* v *Rees* [1970] Ch 345, at 402 stated:

> It may be that there are some who would decry the importance which the courts attach to the observance of the rules of natural justice. 'When something is obvious,' they may say, 'why force

everybody to go through the tiresome waste of time involved in framing charges and giving an opportunity to be heard? The result is obvious from the start.' Those who take this view do not, I think, do themselves justice. As everybody who has anything to do with the law well knows, the path of the law is strewn with open and shut cases which, somehow, were not; of unanswerable charges which, in the event, were completely answered; of inexplicable conduct which was fully explained; of fixed and unalterable determinations that, by discussion, suffered a change. Nor are those with any knowledge of human nature who pause to think for a moment likely to underestimate the feelings of resentment of those who find that a decision against them has been made without their being afforded any opportunity to influence the course of events.

SECTION 7: EXCLUSION OF JUDICIAL REVIEW

The legislature has sometimes attempted to protect public authorities from judicial review by inserting clauses which appear to be intended to exclude the jurisdiction of the court. For example, in *Anisminic Ltd* v *Foreign Compensation Commission* [1969] 2 AC 147, Anisminic Ltd wished to challenge a decision of the Foreign Compensation Commission that it was not entitled to compensation in respect of the sequestration of property which it had owned in Egypt, and accordingly applied for a declaration (see p. 535, *ante*). The legislation, however, provided that any determination by the Commission of an application 'shall not be called in question in any court of law' (Foreign Compensation Act 1950, s. 4(4)). The House of Lords considered the effect of this clause.

Anisminic Ltd v *Foreign Compensation Commission*

[1969] 2 AC 147, House of Lords

LORD REID: ...The next argument was that, by reason of the provisions of section 4(4) of the 1950 Act, the courts are precluded from considering whether the respondent's determination was a nullity, and therefore it must be treated as valid whether or not inquiry would disclose that it was a nullity....

The respondent maintains that these are plain words only capable of having one meaning. Here is a determination which is apparently valid: there is nothing on the face of the document to cast any doubt on its validity. If it is a nullity, that could only be established by raising some kind of proceedings in court. But that would be calling the determination in question, and that is expressly prohibited by statute. The appellants maintain that this is not the meaning of the words of this provision. They say that 'determination' means a real determination and does not include an apparent or purported determination which in the eyes of the law has no existence because it is a nullity. Or, putting it another way, if you seek to show that a determination is a nullity you are not questioning the purported determination—you are maintaining that it does not exist as a determination. It is one thing to question a determination which does not exist: it is quite another to say that there is nothing to be questioned.

Let me illustrate the matter by supposing a simple case. A statute provides that a certain order may be made by a person who holds a specified qualification or appointment, and it contains a provision similar to section 4(4), that such an order made by such a person shall not be questioned in any court of law. A person aggrieved by an order alleges that it is a forgery or that the person who made the order did not hold that qualification or appointment. Does such a provision require the court to treat that order as a valid order? It is a well-established principle that a provision ousting the ordinary jurisdiction of the court must be construed strictly—meaning, I think, that, if such provision is reasonably capable of having two meanings, that meaning shall be taken which preserves the ordinary jurisdiction of the court.

Statutory provisions which seek to limit the ordinary jurisdiction of the court have a long history. No case has been cited in which any other form of words limiting the jurisdiction of the court has been held to protect a nullity. If the draftsman or Parliament had intended to introduce a new kind of ouster clause so as to prevent any inquiry as to whether the document relied on was a forgery, I would have expected to find something much more specific than the bald statement that a determination shall not be called in question in any court of law. Undoubtedly such a provision protects every determination which is not a nullity. But I do not think that it is necessary or even reasonable to construe the word 'determination' as including everything which purports to be a determination but which is in fact no determination at all....

The other Law Lords delivered speeches in which they agreed that the ouster clause would not protect a decision from challenge if the FCC had acted outside its jurisdiction. A majority of their Lordships also held that Anisminic Ltd was entitled to the declaration which it sought because the FCC had made an error of law which took it outside its jurisdiction [p. 537, ante].

NOTE: After the decision in *Anisminic* the Foreign Compensation Act 1969 was passed. Section 3 provided that a person aggrieved by a determination of the Commission on any question of law had a right to require the Commission to state and sign a case for the Court of Appeal. It was provided, however, that there was to be no appeal to the House of Lords from a decision of the Court of Appeal. Section 3(9) stated that, except as provided by the section and in respect of claims that the Commission had breached the rules of natural justice, no determination by the Commission on any claim under the Foreign Compensation Act 1950 shall be called in question in any court of law. Determination was defined as including a purported determination.

■ QUESTION

If these provisions had been in force at the time of the decision in *Anisminic*, do you think the House of Lords would have granted the declaration sought?

NOTE: The Tribunals and Inquiries Act 1992, s. 12(1) (formerly s. 11 of the Tribunal and Inquiries Act 1958) provides that, as respects England and Wales:

> any provision in an Act passed before 1 August 1958 that any order or determination shall not be called in question in any court, or any provision in such an Act which by similar words excludes any of the powers of the High Court, shall not have effect so as to prevent the removal of the proceedings into the High Court by order of certiorari or to prejudice the powers of the High Court to make orders of mandamus.

(Section 11 of the 1958 Act expressly excluded orders or determinations of the Foreign Compensation Commission from this general provision; in *Anisminic*, however, Lord Pearce specifically stated that s. 11 had no bearing on the issue which the court was required to consider.)

■ QUESTION

Why do you think this provision was confined to Acts passed before 1 August 1958?

NOTES

1. *Anisminic* concerned an absolute ouster clause. Partial or limited ouster clauses sometimes appear in certain statutory provisions. For example, in planning law persons aggrieved by a compulsory purchase order are permitted to appeal to the High Court on certain grounds within six weeks of publication of the order. Apart from this it is provided that a compulsory purchase order 'shall not...be questioned in any legal proceedings whatsoever' (see Acquisition of Land Act 1981, ss. 23–25). The courts have upheld the validity of the partial or limited ouster clauses which attempt to protect decisions from challenge after the expiry of a time-limit (see *R* v *Secretary of State for the Environment, ex parte Ostler* [1977] QB 122).
2. Where a legislative provision stipulates that the issuing of a certificate 'shall be conclusive evidence' that the conditions for the issue of the certificate had been satisfied, it seems that this can exclude review of the decision to issue the certificate—*R* v *Registrar of Companies, ex parte Central Bank of India* [1986] QB 1114.
3. An example of a relatively recent ouster clause is the Security Services Act 1989, s. 5(4) 'decisions of the Tribunal...(including any decisions as to their jurisdiction) shall not be subject to appeal or liable to be questioned in any court'.
4. The inclusion of an ouster clause in the Asylum and Immigration (Treatment of Claimants) Bill might, if it had been preserved in the 2004 Act, have led to a constitutional crisis. The Government was concerned that the two tiers of tribunal appeals followed by claims for judicial review were being abused, and so sought to create a single tribunal and severely restrict judicial review of the tribunal's determinations. Part of the ouster clause stipulated:

(3) Subsections (1) and (2)—

(a) prevent a court, in particular, from entertaining proceedings to determine whether a purported determination, decision or action of the Tribunal was a nullity by reason of—

(i) lack of jurisdiction,
(ii) irregularity,
(iii) error of law,
(iv) breach of natural justice, or
(v) any other matter....

The clause was comprehensive. In the view of the Commons Constitutional Affairs Select Committee its extensiveness was without precedent (HC 211 of 2003–04, para. 70). This was achieved according to Lord Woolf CJ, in a speech given to the Faculty of Law at the University of Cambridge, as a result of the Government's consultations with him and other members of the judiciary, so that 'the clause was extended to close the loopholes we had identified instead of being abandoned as we had argued' ([2004] *Cambridge Law Journal*, 317, at 328). Another parliamentary committee, the Joint Committee on Human Rights (JCHR), also criticized the ouster clause, along with other provisions in the Bill, on human rights grounds. All of the critics argued that the ouster clause's degree of restriction of access to the courts was a serious breach of the rule of law. The Government decided to withdraw the clause and amendments were enacted. The JCHR's opinion of the amendments was that they could lead to violations of ECHR Arts 2, 3, 8 and 13, and 14 in conjunction with 2, 3, 6(1), 8, and 13 (HL 102/HC 240 of 2003–04). See R. Rawlings 'Review, Revenge and Retreat' (2005) 68 *Modern Law Review* 378 who doubts that the courts would have disapplied the ouster clause had it been enacted, a suggestion proposed by M Fordham that Parliament would have been trespassing on the separation of powers and the courts' constitutional function of controlling administrative action (see 'Common Law Illegality of Ousting Judicial Review' [2004] *Judicial Review* 86, 93, and also Lord Woolf at p. 48 *ante*). Despite the amendments a great deal of the Administrative Court's time was spent on asylum and immigration matters and a review by judges and administrators led to the proposal that Immigration and Asylum Chambers should be created in the First-tier and Upper Tribunals. This return to a two-stage tribunal process came into effect in February 2010: see pp. 697–699, *post*.

■ QUESTIONS

1. Do you think that the decision in *Anisminic* reflected the intention of Parliament?
2. Cane, in the extracts set out in p. 527, *ante*, uses this case to support a particular argument which he wishes to make. What was the argument, and do you agree that the decision in *Anisminic* supports it?

12

Ombudsmen

OVERVIEW

In this chapter we look at the institution of the ombudsman, its origins, the conditions of access and the range of matters within the jurisdiction of the parliamentary and local government ombudsmen, a consideration of the key terms of maladministration and injustice with which the ombudsmen are concerned, how they investigate and resolve complaints and seek improvements and the outcome of the investigations and remedies recommended by the ombudsman. We end with their arrangements for dealing with dissatisfied complainants.

SECTION 1: INTRODUCTION

In 1961 an influential report by the JUSTICE organization recommended that an impartial officer, to be known as a Parliamentary Commissioner, should be established and report on complaints of maladministration in central government. It argued that:

> there appears to be a continuous flow of relatively minor complaints, not sufficient in themselves to attract public interest but nevertheless of great importance to the individuals concerned, which give rise to feelings of frustration and resentment because of the inadequacy of the existing means of seeking redress. (JUSTICE, *The Citizen and the Administration* (1961), para. 76.)

The report outlined the weaknesses in the parliamentary question procedure and in adjournment debates as mechanisms for the investigation of complaints (on parliamentary questions and adjournment debates, see pp. 256–261, *ante*). The report envisaged that the Parliamentary Commissioner would be independent of the Executive and responsible only to Parliament. He would conduct investigations informally, in order to ensure that there would be no serious interference with the working of a department, and have access to departmental files. A Select Committee would be established to consider the annual reports of the Parliamentary Commissioner and any special reports which he might issue on particular issues. On the controversial question of whether the establishment of a Parliamentary Commissioner would have any implications for the doctrine of ministerial responsibility, the Report stated, at para. 155:

> It is a principle of such fundamental importance in our constitution that we think it would be wrong to make any proposal which might seem to qualify it and therefore we have suggested that a Minister should have the power to veto any proposed investigation by the Parliamentary Commissioner against his Department. We would expect, however, that as so often has happened in our constitutional history, a convention would grow up that the Minister would not exercise his power of veto unreasonably.

The report was also careful to stress that 'any additional procedure should not disturb the basic position of Parliament as a channel for complaint against the Executive and should not even appear to interfere with the relations between individual members and their constituents' (para. 156). With this in mind it recommended that, during an initial testing period, complaints should only be considered on reference from a Member of either House of Parliament. It did, however, anticipate that, after a period of about five years, the Commissioner should be empowered to receive complaints direct from the public. 'The ultimate object', according to the report, 'should be to establish a channel by which the investigation of administrative grievances should take place initially outside the political sphere. Parliament would, however, always be able to take up grievances in the last resort if the Commissioner's investigation failed to procure justice' (para. 157).

Following the publication of *The Citizen and the Administration*, the Conservative Lord Chancellor, Lord Dilhorne, argued that 'a Parliamentary Commissioner would seriously interfere with the prompt and efficient dispatch of public business' (HL Deb., Vol. 244, cols 384–385). Subsequently, however, a new government accepted, with certain modifications, the introduction of the Parliamentary Commissioner as a development and reinforcement of 'our existing constitutional arrangements for the protection of the individual' (see *The Parliamentary Commissioner for Administration*, Cmnd 2767 (1965)). On the introduction of the ombudsman system in the United Kingdom, see further, R. Gregory and P. Giddings, *The Ombudsman, the Citizen and Parliament* (2002).

The office of the Parliamentary Commissioner for Administration (or Parliamentary Ombudsman PO) was thus created in 1967. Since then there has been a proliferation of ombudsmen in the United Kingdom. In 1969 the offices of PCA for Northern Ireland and the Commissioner for Complaints for Northern Ireland were established; both offices are held by the same person. The offices of Health Service Commissioners of England, Wales, and Scotland were created by legislation in 1972 and 1973; and before devolution all three posts were held by the person who was the PO. In 1974 Local Commissioners were established to deal with maladministration in local government in England and Wales. The office of Local Ombudsman for Scotland was established in 1975; the work of the Scottish Local Ombudsman has been studied by J. Logie and P. Watchman, *The Local Ombudsman* (1990). The establishment of the Scottish Parliament and the National Assembly for Wales has also led to the creation of new Public Services Ombudsmen. When the Scottish Public Services Ombudsman Act 2002 and Public Services Ombudsman (Wales) Act 2005 came into force one-stop shops were created for complaints about devolved and local government, public/social housing and the National Health Service in Scotland and Wales. Similar amalgamating arrangements had initially been proposed for England but instead the separate ombudsmen operating in England can now work in collaboration (see p. 670, *post*).

In addition to central and local government and the health service, public sector ombudsmen now include part of the police with the Police Ombudsman for Northern Ireland (Police (Northern Ireland) Act 1998, s. 51). There is a Prisons & Probation Ombudsman, but unlike all of the aforementioned ombudsmen this officer does not have the same status of independence of the Executive and is more like the Adjudicator in HM Revenue and Customs or the Independent Case Examiner in the various agencies in the Department of Work and Pensions, being above the internal departmental procedure and below the Parliamentary Commissioner in the complaints-handling chain.

In the private sector some ombudsmen dealing with aspects of financial services such as (a) banking, building societies, and insurance; and (b) legal services have statutory frameworks (respectively (a) Financial Services and Markets Act 2000; and (b) Legal Services Act 2007).

This chapter focuses on the PO and the Local Commissioners or LO.

The main legislative provisions governing the PO are contained in the Parliamentary Commissioner Act 1967. The provisions governing the LO are set out in the Local Government Act 1974. Both pieces of legislation have been amended on a number of occasions.

The following extracts from the reports of the PO and the LO provide some indication of the work which they carry out.

Parliamentary & Health Service Ombudsman, *Making an Impact: Annual Report 2009–10*

HC 274 of 2009–10, pp. 13–15

Investigation

The most complex and difficult complaints, which are not suitable for resolution by intervention, are referred for a full investigation. The scope of each investigation is carefully defined and involves the gathering and in-depth consideration of detailed evidence.

Recovery of unpaid tax caused worry and stress

Mrs N, a retired woman who worked part time and received a widow's pension, found herself owing HM Revenue & Customs (HMRC) over £2,500 in unpaid tax, the recovery of which was causing her hardship. She complained to the Adjudicator's Office, who did not uphold her complaint.

Our investigation found that HMRC had made mistakes over Mrs N's tax code and had then not properly applied the concession that allows them to waive tax that is legally due. The Adjudicator's Office failed to identify this, causing Mrs N avoidable worry and stress. At our recommendation, HMRC reviewed her case, as a result of which they waived all but £480 of the unpaid tax, and refunded everything she had paid over and above that. They also paid her compensation of £150; agreed to circulate our findings internally and to tell us what action they had taken, or planned to take, to help retired people engage with HMRC. The Adjudicator's Office apologised to Mrs N and circulated our findings to relevant staff.

Persistent mishandling led to loss of maintenance and distress

Mrs B's application for child support maintenance was mishandled by the Child Support Agency (the Agency) over a number of years. For example, they incorrectly closed down her case, and wrongly asked her to make a further application which they then delayed processing. There were also significant delays in taking enforcement action against the non-resident parent. The stress of all this, over several years, affected Mrs B's health, but when she took her complaint to the Independent Case Examiner (ICE) they compounded her distress by not considering the full extent of the injustice she had suffered.

During our investigation, the Agency made Mrs B an advance payment of maintenance of nearly £17,000 plus interest, to make good the maintenance she had forgone because of their mistakes. At our recommendation they also apologised to Mrs B and paid her £3,000 to recognise the impact of their errors on her health, employment and finances. ICE apologised to Mrs B as well and paid her £250…

Resolution through intervention

These cases involve us identifying, and then asking the body to provide, a remedy which resolves the complaint in question. We attempt this approach where appropriate as it provides a faster resolution for the complainant and does not require an in-depth investigation. These cases can result in a variety of outcomes. For example, we might ask that an apology and/or an explanation is given to the complainant, that a delayed claim, appeal or application is progressed or that financial compensation is awarded.

Failure to act following successful benefits appeal

Mr A complained directly to us in mid-May 2009 that the Independent Case Examiner had not sorted out his underlying problem, which was that Jobcentre Plus had not implemented a tribunal decision about his jobseeker's allowance entitlement. We were unable to consider Mr A's complaint initially as it had not been referred by an MP, but once we had received the referral from his MP (in early July) we contacted Jobcentre Plus about the case. As a result of our intervention, Jobcentre Plus paid Mr A the two days benefit he was owed and awarded him nine months National Insurance credits.

Delayed handling of an application

Mrs P complained directly to us in August 2009 that her husband had still not received the European Economic Area residence card he had applied to the UK Border Agency (the Agency) for in October 2008. The Agency should have dealt with the application within six months, as required by the legislation. We could not consider Mrs P's complaint initially without a referral from an MP, but once we had received the referral from her MP in November we contacted the Agency. Our intervention prompted them to process Mr P's application and to issue his residence card...

Decisions not to investigate

We may decide not to investigate complaints for a number of reasons. Some may be outside our jurisdiction, for example, if the body complained about is not one we can investigate or has not yet completed its own consideration of the complaint in question. However, in many cases we decide not to investigate following a detailed further assessment of the complaint. The following case studies are examples of those.

Problems with a boiler installation

Ms K complained to us about the problems she was having with a new boiler installed under the Warm Front scheme (overseen by the Department of Energy and Climate Change). Among other things, the boiler had never worked properly and needed constant attention, and Ms K was expected to increase the boiler pressure herself, something she found difficult to do because of her health. Our enquiries established that the Department were willing to deal with the problems arising from what was a poor installation, and that they had already offered a number of solutions to remedy Ms K's complaint which we encouraged her to consider.

Impact of a mishandled complaint

Mr F complained to us about the way the Consumer Council for Water (the Council) had mishandled his grievance about a water company. We saw that the Council had already apologised to Mr F for the poor service they had given him (among other things they had lost his complaint when moving to a computer-based system); had tightened their procedures; and had retrained their complaint handling staff on their complaint systems. The Council also reimbursed Mr F the £20 he had spent pursuing his grievance. Satisfied that the Council had taken appropriate steps to put things right and to prevent a recurrence, we took no further action.

Local Government Ombudsman, *Annual Report 09–10 Delivering Public Value*

(2010) pp. 7, 9, 11, 13

Homelessness

Mrs K was eight months pregnant, and left privately-rented accommodation following an incident of domestic violence. She applied to the council for help.

Housing officers encouraged her to find accommodation in the private sector through the Direct Lettings Scheme, but they

- applied too strict a test when deciding whether to provide Mrs K with temporary accommodation by insisting she provide proof of homelessness first
- did not tell her that she could apply for housing as a homeless person
- did not refer her to specialist support for victims of domestic violence.

Mrs K said that, later, she spent four nights sleeping rough in a park.

The Ombudsman's investigation was hindered by the council's very poor records. He concluded that Mrs K suffered injustice because the council had not provided her with the level of support and assistance she should have had as a homeless person in priority need.

The council apologised to Mrs K, paid her £750 compensation and improved its practices.

Case reference 09 001 262...

Environmental health and planning enforcement

From 2000 to 2007, thousands of tonnes of rubbish were illegally burned and processed on farmland a few metres from Mrs D's home, enough to fill three Olympic-sized swimming pools.

The area was a beauty spot in the green belt noted for its biological and archaeological heritage. Mrs D and her son made many complaints. Three public bodies knew about the extent of the problem and the damage being caused to the environment, but failed to take effective action.

A national protocol between the Environment Agency and the Local Government Association clearly required a co-ordinated joint approach on waste management but it was not applied.

The complaint was investigated jointly by the Local Government Ombudsman and the Parliamentary Ombudsman.

The Ombudsmen said: "Anyone seeing the evidence of what happened on that land and of the devastation wrought on this beauty spot should be justifiably shocked and outraged that despite all the legal safeguards in place, such events could actually happen.

The three bodies agreed to apologise and pay Mrs D and her son a total of £95,000 to reflect years of extreme distress, aggravation and financial loss and determine whether any other action was required to prevent a recurrence of such events.

Case references 05C11620 and 05C09690…

School admissions

M had an undiagnosed hearing problem when he sat the entrance tests for a selective grammar school. He misheard some important instructions, so part of his work was not marked and he did not pass.

His parents appealed twice against the refusal of a place, producing medical evidence of M's hearing problem, which had been diagnosed by then. Both appeals failed. The parents complained that the appeal panels failed to properly consider the effect of the Disability Discrimination Act.

The Ombudsman found that the panel should have concluded that M had a disadvantage as defined in the legislation and that he had been disadvantaged in his test. Had this happened, it was likely that the panel would have concluded that M's case outweighed any prejudice that would arise by admitting an extra child.

In accordance with the Ombudsman's recommendation, the school's governing body:

- offered M a place at the school
- apologised
- paid £250 compensation, and
- ensured that future admission appeal hearings take into account a claim that a child suffers from a disability.

Case reference 08 011 742

Disabled facilities grants

Mrs M complained about long and unreasonable delay before a council provided housing appropriate to her family's needs. Two of her five children were seriously disabled by a rare muscle-wasting condition. They needed 24 hour care and assistance with feeding, dressing, bathing and toileting.

Mrs M could only keep her disabled children clean by hosing them down in the garden, strip-washing them in a downstairs toilet, or risking injury by getting upstairs to a small and inadequately-equipped bathroom. The council knew the family needed a home with ground floor bathroom and bedrooms. The family was moved to a four-bedroomed house with the intention of building a ground floor extension, but the council did not check feasibility and planning permission was refused.

The Ombudsman said "The underlying cause was ineffective management that can fairly be described as 'institutionalised indifference'…"

Eventually a purpose-built property was provided for the family, but in the meantime the council failed to provide adequate interim adaptations.

The family spent three years in unsuitable accommodation as a result of the council failures. The Ombudsman recommended the council to:

- apologise to Mrs M and her family
- pay £36,000 to Mrs M and her older disabled child over three years
- create a fund of £5,000 for the other children, and
- review its procedures and leadership capacity in the relevant services.

Case reference 07C03887

SECTION 2: ACCESS TO THE OMBUDSMAN

PARLIAMENTARY COMMISSIONER ACT 1967

5.—(1) Subject to the provisions of this section, the Commissioner may investigate any action taken by or on behalf of a government department or other authority to which this Act applies, being action taken in the exercise of administrative functions of that department or authority, in any case where—

(a) a written complaint is duly made to a member of the House of Commons by a member of the public who claims to have sustained injustice in consequence of maladministration in connection with the action so taken; and

(b) the complaint is referred to the Commissioner, with the consent of the person who made it, by a member of that House with a request to conduct an investigation thereon.

6.—...

(3) A complaint shall not be entertained under this Act unless it is made to a member of the House of Commons not later than twelve months from the day on which the person aggrieved first had notice of the matters alleged in the complaint; but the Commissioner may conduct an investigation pursuant to a complaint not made within that period if he considers that there are special circumstances which make it proper to do so.

LOCAL GOVERNMENT ACT 1974

26.—(5) Before proceeding to investigate a complaint, a Local Commissioner shall satisfy himself that

(a) a matter has been brought, by or on behalf of the person affected, to the notice of the authority to which it relates and that that authority has been afforded a reasonable opportunity to investigate, the matter and to respond; or

(b) in the particular circumstances, it is not reasonable to expect the matter to be brought to the notice of that authority or for that authority to be afforded a reasonable opportunity to investigate the matter and to respond.

26A Who can complain

(1) Under this Part of this Act, a complaint about a matter may only be made—

(a) by a member of the public who claims to have sustained injustice in consequence of the matter,
(b) by a person authorised in writing by such a member of the public to act on his behalf, or
(c) in accordance with subsection (2).

(2) Where a member of the public by whom a complaint about a matter might have been made under this Part of this Act has died or is otherwise unable to authorise a person to act on his behalf, the complaint may be made—

(a) by his personal representative (if any), or
(b) by a person who appears to a Local Commissioner to be suitable to represent him.

26B Procedure for making complaints

(1) Subject to subsection (3), a complaint about a matter under this Part of this Act must be made—

(a) in writing, and
(b) before the end of the permitted period.

(2) In subsection (1)(b), "the permitted period" means the period of 12 months beginning with—

(a) the day on which the person affected first had notice of the matter, or
(b) if the person affected has died without having notice of the matter—
  (i) the day on which the personal representatives of the person affected first had notice of the matter, or
  (ii) if earlier, the day on which the complainant first had notice of the matter.

(3) A Local Commissioner may disapply either or both of the requirements in subsection (1)(a) and (b) in relation to a particular complaint.

26C Referral of complaints by authorities

(1) This section applies where a complaint about a matter is made to a member of an authority to which this Part of this Act applies.

(2) If the complainant consents, the complaint may be referred to a Local Commissioner by—

(a) the member of the authority to whom the complaint was made,

(b) any other member of that authority, or

(c) a member of any other authority to which this Part of this Act applies which is alleged in the complaint to have taken or authorised the action complained of.

(3) Subject to subsection (4), a referral under this section must be made in writing.

(4) A Local Commissioner may disapply the requirement in subsection (3) in relation to a particular referral.

(5) If a Local Commissioner is satisfied that the complainant asked a member of an authority mentioned in subsection (2) to refer the complaint to a Local Commissioner, he may treat the complaint as if it had been referred to him under this section. . . .

26D Matters coming to attention of Local Commissioner

(1) This section applies to a matter which has come to the attention of a Local Commissioner if—

(a) the matter came to his attention during the course of an investigation under this Part of this Act,

(b) (subject to subsection (3)) the matter came to his attention—

(i) before the person affected or his personal representatives had notice of the matter, or

(ii) in any other case, before the end of the permitted period, and

(c) it appears to the Local Commissioner that a member of the public has, or may have, suffered injustice in consequence of the matter.

(2) In subsection (1)(b)(ii), "the permitted period" means the period of 12 months beginning with—

(a) the day on which the person affected first had notice of the matter, or

(b) if the person affected has died without having notice of the matter, the day on which the personal representatives of the person affected first had notice of the matter.

(3) A Local Commissioner may disapply the requirement in subsection (1)(b) in relation to a particular matter.

NOTE: There has been concern about the public's awareness of ombudsmen. Survey research conducted for the ombudsmen indicates that poorer people, the young and those in ethnic minority groups are the least aware of ombudsmen. In the 2006–07 Annual Report the PO stated:

> Moreover, the multitude of complaints systems in force across the public services can make it difficult for potential complainants to know where to turn. For these reasons, we consider it a priority to improve awareness of our service and make putting a complaint to the Ombudsman as simple and straightforward as possible. Since we cannot reach all the people who might want to use our service directly, we have developed close contacts with advocacy and advice bodies. These include Citizens' Advice and the Independent Complaints Advocacy Service of the NHS. We intend to strengthen our contacts with these bodies, and are developing an outreach strategy to help us achieve this.

■ QUESTION

Can you think of any ways of publicizing the work of the ombudsmen?

The Law Commission, *Administrative Redress: Public Bodies and the Citizen: A Consultation Paper*

(2008) Law Com CP 186, paras 5.76–5.87

The MP filter

5.76 As noted in Part 3, the Parliamentary Ombudsman cannot accept a complaint directly from a member of the public. All complaints must be channelled through a Member of Parliament. The Public Services Ombudsman of Wales and the Local Government Ombudsman do not have an equivalent filter.

5.77 The MP filter was introduced in response to concerns raised about the office when it was established in 1967: first, that it would undermine the role of MPs acting on behalf of and looking after their constituents, thereby undermining the role of Parliament; second, that the new office would be overwhelmed by complaints. The office was consequently conceived of as an adjunct to Parliament, "rather than the citizens' defender" with the filter introduced to preserve MPs' constitutional role. In addition it was intended to be a mechanism by which only suitable complaints would be passed on to the ombudsman, that is, cases in which there was a strong prima facie case and over which the ombudsman had jurisdiction. The filter was "seen as experimental" and it was recommended that consideration should be given to a right of direct access after a period of five years. The review never materialised.

5.78 The filter has since attracted much criticism. It has been considered an unnecessary barrier to access, particularly for certain groups such as ethnic minorities, younger people and those from deprived backgrounds who might find it more difficult and demanding to approach their MP. Moreover, many see the filter's underlying rationale as no longer applicable. The Collcutt review argued that the principle that MPs should represent constituents in seeking redress was no longer applicable in light of the modernisation of government and the new, more diverse methods by which citizens can obtain redress from public bodies.

5.79 In contrast, other commentators take the view that MPs still have an important role to play in channelling complaints to the ombudsman. It has been suggested that the filter keeps MPs in touch with the problems and concerns of their constituents and in turn this "informs MPs' contributions to larger debates... on legislation and otherwise".

5.80 The MP filter has, it has been claimed, been "proved remarkably successful" at preventing an onslaught of complaints to the ombudsman. But if this is true, it is not clear whether this means that the filter is an effective method of screening out unmeritorious claims, or an arbitrary bar to access to the ombudsman. Indeed, there is now concern that the Parliamentary Ombudsman is underused and that this is at least partly attributable to the lack of direct access. The experience of the Local Government Ombudsman and other ombudsmen suggest a strong correlation between the provision of direct access and increased recourse to ombudsmen. There was a 44% increase in complaints to the Local Government Ombudsman in the year following the removal of the "councillor filter".

5.81 There has been a concern that the Parliamentary Ombudsman would not be able to cope with the increased workload that direct access would bring, although the Ombudsman has indicated recently that that would not be the case. It is true that the Local Government Ombudsman faced some difficulty in determining complaints speedily in the period following removal of the filter but it has since adjusted. In addition, direct access to the Health Commissioner has been long established and complaints are dealt with relatively easily and speedily.

5.82 The removal of the filter has considerable support. Direct access has been recommended by Justice, the Collcutt Review and the Public Administration Select Committee, amongst others. The Parliamentary Ombudsman herself and the majority of Parliamentarians support abolition of the filter. Others have advocated dual access. This was the approach taken in a recent Private Members Bill, which created a right of direct access but retained the option of making a complaint through an MP. It was an attempt to improve access, while assuaging the concerns of those who wished to see the filter retained. The Bill passed successfully through the Lords but was not taken up in the Commons. The Government nevertheless recognised that it was an important issue.

Suggested options for reform

5.83 Given the concerns that the MP filter is limiting access to the Parliamentary Ombudsman—and in light of our view that the role of the ombudsmen should be strengthened—our preliminary view is that there is a strong case for abolition of the MP filter. There are four reasons in support of this view.

5.84 First, it no longer appears necessary to use the filter to control the flow of complaints to the ombudsman. The ombudsman is not obliged to accept every complaint received but has a broad discretion whether or not to investigate. The ombudsman is free to exercise this discretion to refuse those complaints that are vexatious, misconceived or more appropriately dealt with by other means. In our view, this "internal filter mechanism" is sufficient to exclude unsuitable cases. We feel it likely that the MP filter significantly reduces the volume of complaints not because MPs have exercised their judgment that the complaints should not be passed on to the ombudsman but rather because complainants fail to make the initial approach to an MP. If this is right, it is likely to be an inaccurate way of weeding out weak cases. The point has also been made that the need for the ombudsman to be protected by a filter mechanism has reduced over time:

The wider complaints system that now exists is more developed than the one in place when the 1967 Act was first introduced and the Parliamentary Ombudsman normally expects complaints to be put before second-tier complaint handlers before she considers them.

5.85 Secondly, removing the MP filter will help facilitate the movement of cases between the courts and ombudsmen. Under our suggested options, a court would be unlikely to order a stay of proceedings to refer a matter to the ombudsman unless it considered the case was suitable for investigation by the ombudsman. The MP filter, as an additional mechanism to weed out unsuitable cases, would, in our provisional view, be superfluous and likely to create delay.

5.86 Thirdly, the argument that the filter allows MPs to keep in touch with constituents' concerns can be addressed adequately by a notification requirement. Once the ombudsman has accepted jurisdiction, the constituent MP or any nominated MP could be notified of the complaint and given the option of having continued involvement with the progress of the claim. Furthermore, there may be merit in allowing a complainant to have the option of making a complaint through an MP in addition to direct access—the "dual access" approach recently put forward in the Parliamentary Commissioner (Amendment) Bill and operated by the European Ombudsman.

5.87 Finally, the abolition of the filter would bring the Parliamentary Ombudsman in line with other public sector ombudsmen in the UK and ombudsmen in most other parliamentary democracies. Their experience shows that the institution is able to operate effectively without the filter.

NOTE The majority view is in favour of abolition of the MP filter with the Public Administration Select Committee renewing its call for it in HC 107 of 2009–10; however, the government declines to instigate legislation itself or to support the initiatives of others. The select committee highlighted at para. 5 the evidence from the PO that while Parliament was dissolved for the 2010 general election, no complaints could be referred to her as there were no MPs. The Law Commission in its latest consultation paper *Public Services Ombudsmen* (2010, Law Com CP 196) now proposes dual access instead of simple abolition of the MP filter, which the select committee and the PO support.

■ QUESTION

Apart from discontinuing the MP filter, by what other means can access to the PO be strengthened and enlarged?

SECTION 3: JURISDICTION OF THE OMBUDSMAN

PARLIAMENTARY COMMISSIONER ACT 1967

4.—(1) Subject to the provisions of this section and to the notes contained in Schedule 2 to this Act, this Act applies to the government departments, corporations and unincorporated bodies listed in that Schedule; and references in this Act to an authority to which this Act applies are references to any such corporation or body.

(2) Her Majesty may by Order in Council amend Schedule 2 to this Act by the alteration of any entry or note, the removal of any entry or note or the insertion of any additional entry or note.

(3) An Order in Council may only insert an entry if—

(a) it relates—

(i) to a government department; or

(ii) to a corporation or body whose functions are exercised on behalf of the Crown; or

(b) it relates to a corporation or body—

(i) which is established by virtue of Her Majesty's prerogative or by an Act of Parliament or an Order in Council or order made under an Act of Parliament or which is established in any other way by a Minister of the Crown in his capacity as a Minister or by a government department;

(ii) at least half of whose revenues derive directly from money provided by Parliament, a levy authorised by an enactment, a fee or charge of any other description so authorised or more than one of those sources; and

(iii) which is wholly or partly constituted by appointment made by Her Majesty or a Minister of the Crown or government department.

(3A) No entry shall be made if the result of making it would be that the Parliamentary Commissioner could investigate action which can be investigated by the Public Services Ombudsman for Wales under the Public Services Ombudsman (Wales) Act 2007.

(3B) No entry shall be made in respect of—

(a) the Scottish Administration or any part of it;

(b) any Scottish public authority with mixed functions or no reserved functions within the meaning of the Scotland Act 1998; or

(c) the Scottish Parliamentary Corporate Body.

(4) No entry shall be made in respect of a corporation or body whose sole activity is, or whose main activities are, included among the activities specified in subsection (5) below.

(5) The activities mentioned in subsection (4) above are—

(a) the provision of education, or the provision of training otherwise than under the Industrial Training Act 1982;

(b) the development of curricula, the conduct of examinations or the validation of educational courses;

(c) the control of entry to any profession or the regulation of the conduct of members of any profession;

(d) the investigation of complaints by members of the public regarding the actions of any person or body, or the supervision or review of such investigations or of steps taken following them.

(6) No entry shall be made in respect of a corporation or body operating in an exclusively or predominantly commercial manner or a corporation carrying on under national ownership an industry or undertaking or part of an industry or undertaking.

(7) Any statutory instrument made by virtue of this section shall be subject to annulment in pursuance of a resolution of either House of Parliament...

5.—...

(2) Except as hereinafter provided, the Commissioner shall not conduct an investigation under this Act in respect of any of the following matters, that is to say—

(a) any action in respect of which the person aggrieved has or had a right of appeal, reference or review to or before a tribunal constituted by or under any enactment or by virtue of Her Majesty's prerogative;

(b) any action in respect of which the person aggrieved has or had a remedy by way of proceedings in any court of law:

Provided that the Commissioner may conduct an investigation notwithstanding that the person aggrieved has or had such a right or remedy if satisfied that in the particular circumstances it is not reasonable to expect him to resort or have resorted to it.

(3) Without prejudice to subsection (2) of this section, the Commissioner shall not conduct an investigation under this Act in respect of any such action or matter as is described in Schedule 3 to this Act.

(4) Her Majesty may by Order in Council amend the said Schedule 3 so as to exclude from the provisions of that Schedule such actions or matters as may be described in the Order; and any statutory instrument made by virtue of this subsection shall be subject to annulment in pursuance of a resolution of either House of Parliament.

(5) In determining whether to initiate, continue or discontinue an investigation under this Act, the Commissioner shall, subject to the foregoing provisions of this section, act in accordance with his own

discretion; and any question whether a complaint is duly made under this Act shall be determined by the Commissioner.

(5A) For the purposes of this section, administrative functions of a government department to which this Act applies include functions exercised by the department on behalf of the Scottish Ministers by virtue of section 93 of the Scotland Act 1998.

(5B) The Commissioner shall not conduct an investigation under this Act in respect of any action concerning Scotland and not relating to reserved matters which is taken by or on behalf of a cross-border public authority within the meaning of the Scotland Act 1998.

(6) For the purposes of this section, the administrative functions exercisable by any person appointed by the Lord Chancellor as a member of the administrative staff of any court or tribunal shall be taken to be administrative functions of the Lord Chancellor's Department...

SCHEDULE 3 MATTERS NOT SUBJECT TO INVESTIGATION

1. Action taken in matters certified by a Secretary of State or other Minister of the Crown to affect relations or dealings between the Government of the United Kingdom and any other Government or any international organisation of States or Governments.

2. Action taken, in any country or territory outside the United Kingdom, by or on behalf of any officer representing or acting under the authority of Her Majesty in respect of the United Kingdom, or any other officer of the Government of the United Kingdom other than

(a) action which is taken by an officer (not being an honorary consular officer) in the exercise of a consular function on behalf of the Government of the United Kingdom;
(b) action which is taken by an officer within a control zone or a supplementary control zone; or
(c) action which is taken by a British sea-fishery officer.

3. Action taken in connection with the administration of the government of any country or territory outside the United Kingdom which forms part of Her Majesty's dominions or in which Her Majesty has jurisdiction.

4. Action taken by the Secretary of State under the Extradition Act 2003.

5. Action taken by or with the authority of the Secretary of State for the purposes of investigating crime or of protecting the security of the State, including action so taken with respect to passports.

6. The commencement or conduct of civil or criminal proceedings before any court of law in the United Kingdom, of proceedings at any place under the Naval Discipline Act 1957, the Army Act 1955 or the Air Force Act 1955, or of proceedings before any international court or tribunal.

6A. Action taken by any person appointed by the Lord Chancellor as a member of the administrative staff of any court or tribunal, so far as that action is taken at the direction, or on the authority (whether express or implied) of any person acting in a judicial capacity or in his capacity as a member of the tribunal.

6B.—(1) Action taken by any member of the administrative staff of a relevant tribunal, so far as that action is taken at the direction, or on the authority (whether express or implied), of any person acting in his capacity as a member of the tribunal.

(2) In this paragraph, 'relevant tribunal' has the meaning given by section 5(8) of this Act.

6C. Action taken by any person appointed under section 5(3)(c) of the Criminal Injuries Compensation Act 1995, so far as that action is taken at the direction, or on the authority (whether express or implied), of any person acting in his capacity as an adjudicator appointed under section 5 of that Act to determine appeals.

7. Any exercise of the prerogative of mercy or of the power of a Secretary of State to make a reference in respect of any person to the High Court of Justiciary or the Courts-Martial Appeal Court.

8.—(1) Action taken on behalf of the Minister of Health or the Secretary of State by a Health Authority, a Primary Care Trust, a Special Health Authority except the Rampton Hospital Review Board...the Rampton Hospital Board, the Broadmoor Hospital Board or the Moss Side and Park Lane Hospitals Board, a Health

Board or the Common Services Agency for the Scottish Health Service, by the Dental Practice Board or the Scottish Dental Practice Board or by the Public Health Laboratory Service Board.

(2) For the purposes of this paragraph, action taken by a Health Authority, Special Health Authority or Primary Care Trust in the exercise of functions of the Secretary of State shall be regarded as action taken on his behalf.

9. Action taken in matters relating to contractual or other commercial transactions, whether within the United Kingdom or elsewhere, being transactions of a government department or authority to which this Act applies or of any such authority or body as is mentioned in paragraph (a) or (b) of subsection (1) of section 6 of this Act and not being transactions for or relating to—

(a) the acquisition of land compulsorily or in circumstances in which it could be acquired compulsorily;
(b) the disposal as surplus of land acquired compulsorily or in such circumstances as aforesaid.

10. (1) Action taken in respect of appointments or removals, pay, discipline, superannuation or other personnel matters, in relation to—

(a) service in any of the armed forces of the Crown, including reserve and auxiliary and cadet forces;
(b) service in any office or employment under the Crown or under any authority to which this Act applies; or
(c) service in any office or employment, or under any contract for services, in respect of which power to take action, or to determine or approve the action to be taken, in such matters is vested in Her Majesty, any Minister of the Crown or any such authority as aforesaid....

11. The grant of honours, awards or privileges within the gift of the Crown, including the grant of Royal Charters.

LOCAL GOVERNMENT ACT 1974

25.—(1) This Part of this Act applies to the following authorities—

[these include councils, National Park Authorities, fire and rescue authorities, police authorities]

(2) Her Majesty may by Order in Council provide that this Part of this Act shall also apply, subject to any modifications or exceptions specified in the Order, to any authority specified in the Order, being an authority which is established by or under an Act of Parliament, and which has power to levy a rate, or to issue a precept.

(3) An Order made by virtue of subsection (2) above may be varied or revoked by a subsequent Order so made and shall be subject to annulment in pursuance of a resolution of either House of Parliament.

(4) Any reference to an authority to which this Part of this Act applies includes a reference—

(a) to the members and officers of that authority, and
(b) to any person or body of persons acting for the authority under section 101, or
(c) any committee mentioned in section 101(9) of the said Act.

(4A) Any reference to an authority to which this Part of this Act applies also includes, in the case of the Greater London Authority, a reference to each of the following—

(a) the London Assembly;
(b) any committee of the London Assembly;
(c) any body or person exercising functions on behalf of the Greater London Authority.

(4B) Any reference to an authority to which this Part of this Act applies also includes, in the case of the London Transport Users' Committee, a reference to a sub-committee of that Committee.

(5) Any reference to an authority to which this Part of this Act applies also includes a reference to—

(a) a school organisation committee constituted in accordance with section 24 of the School Standards and Framework Act 1998,
(b) an exclusion appeals panel constituted in accordance with Schedule 18 to that Act,
(c) an admission appeals panel constituted in accordance with Schedule 24 or paragraph 3 of Schedule 25 to that Act, and

(d) the governing body of any community, foundation or voluntary school so far as acting in connection with the admission of pupils to the school or otherwise performing any of their functions under Chapter I of Part III of that Act.

...

26.—...

(6) A Local Commissioner shall not conduct an investigation under this Part of this Act in respect of any of the following matters, that is to say:

(a) any action in respect of which the person affected has or had a right of appeal, reference or review to or before a tribunal constituted by or under any enactment;
(b) any action in respect of which the person affected has or had a right of appeal to a Minister of the Crown or the National Assembly for Wales; or
(c) any action in respect of which the person affected has or had a remedy by way of proceedings in any court of law:

Provided that a Local Commissioner may conduct an investigation notwithstanding the existence of such a right or remedy if satisfied that in the particular circumstances it is not reasonable to expect the person aggrieved to resort or have resorted to it.

(7) A Local Commissioner shall not conduct an investigation in respect of any action which in his opinion affects all or most of the inhabitants of the... area of the authority concerned.

(8) Without prejudice to the preceding provisions of this section, a Local Commissioner shall not conduct an investigation under this Part of this Act in respect of any such action or matter as is described in Schedule 5 to this Act.

(9) Her Majesty may by Order in Council amend the said Schedule 5 so as to add to or exclude from the provisions of that Schedule... such actions or matters as may be described in the Order;

[Schedule 5 contains a number of exclusions, including in particular: legal proceedings; investigation or prevention of crime, contractual or commercial transactions (but the acquisition or disposal of land and the procurement of goods and services are within jurisdiction); personnel matters, and some educational matters.]

(10) In determining whether to initiate, continue or discontinue an investigation, a Local Commissioner shall, subject to the preceding provisions of this section, act at discretion; and any questions whether a complaint is duly made under this Part of this Act shall be determined by the Local Commissioner.

NOTE: See how these jurisdictional conditions are applied by the PO process shown below and how for both the PO and LO these checks exclude a significant proportion of complaints.

Parliamentary & Health Service Ombudsman, *Making an Impact: Annual Report 2009–10*

HC 274 of 2009–10, p.11

The PHSO received 24,240 enquiries in 2009–10 (8,543 were parliamentary).

In the year decisions were made on 24,240 enquiries;

9,856 were not properly made; (health complaints not in writng, no MP referral);

4,756 were premature (not raised first at local level or that process not completed);

4,293 were discretionary (for example, the body has acted correctly, reasonably or, where there have been errors, that the complainant has already been offered appropriate redress);

1,661 were withdrawn by the complainant

356 accepted for investigation (52 parliamentary).

In 2009–10 the LO Advice Team received a total of 18,020 complaints and enquiries compared with 21,012 in 2008/09. These include telephone enquiries that were not pursued any further at the time beyond giving the caller advice. In the year 10,309 decisions were made in respect of case forwarded by the Advice Team. Of these

1,520 were assessed as outside jurisdiction; 4,065 had no or insufficient evidence of maladministration and 2,284 were closed following the exercise of discretion.

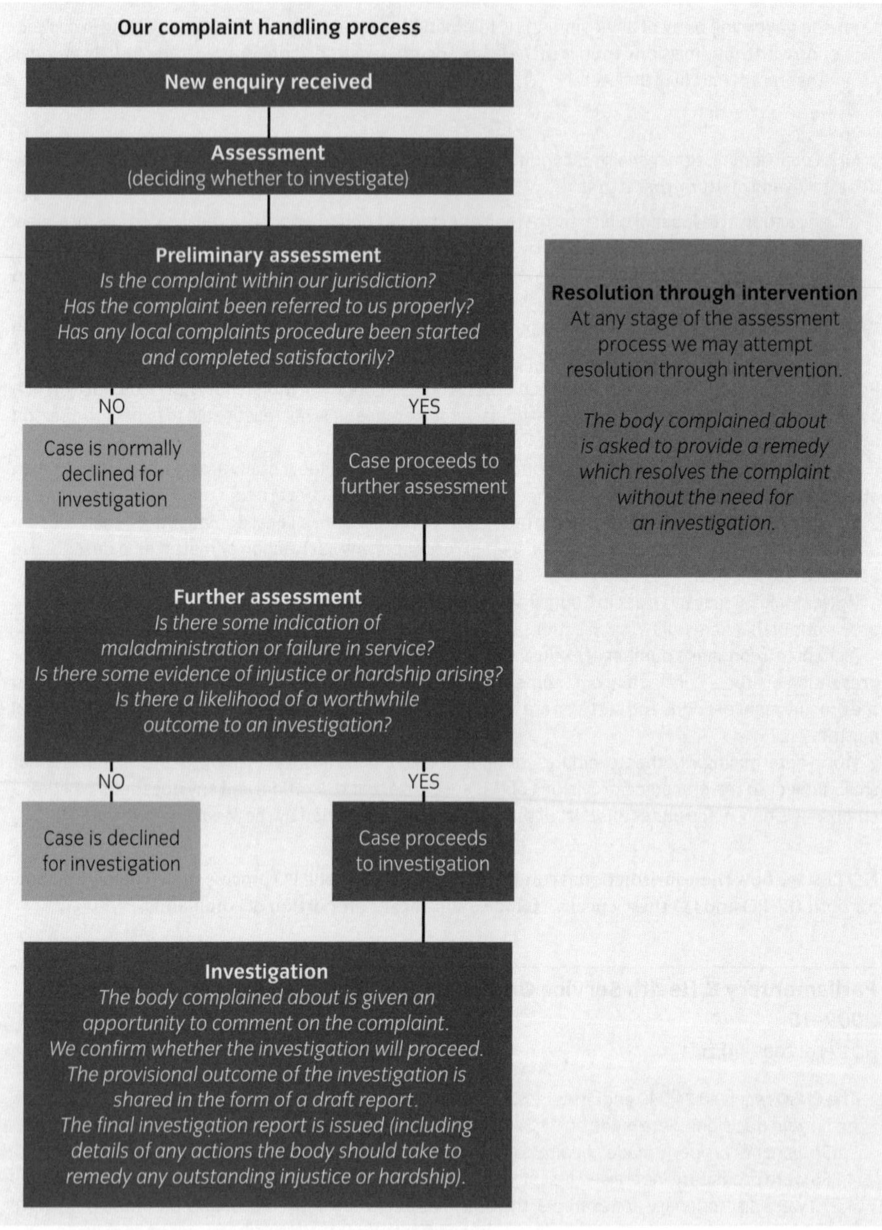
Our complaint handling process
New enquiry received
Assessment
(deciding whether to investigate)
Preliminary assessment
Is the complaint within our jurisdiction?
Has the complaint been referred to us properly?
Has any local complaints procedure been started and completed satisfactorily?
NO
YES
Case is normally declined for investigation
Case proceeds to further assessment
Resolution through intervention
At any stage of the assessment process we may attempt resolution through intervention.
The body complained about is asked to provide a remedy which resolves the complaint without the need for an investigation.
Further assessment
Is there some indication of maladministration or failure in service?
Is there some evidence of injustice or hardship arising?
Is there a likelihood of a worthwhile outcome to an investigation?
NO
YES
Case is declined for investigation
Case proceeds to investigation
Investigation
The body complained about is given an opportunity to comment on the complaint.
We confirm whether the investigation will proceed.
The provisional outcome of the investigation is shared in the form of a draft report.
The final investigation report is issued (including details of any actions the body should take to remedy any outstanding injustice or hardship).

NOTES

1. It is not always easy to identify that a complaint is outside jurisdiction, so that it may require a detailed, and sometimes lengthy, assessment to produce that advice to the complainant.
2. Where a complaint is outside jurisdiction the ombudsmen staff may be able to redirect the complainant to a more appropriate source of assistance. The LO in the 2009–10 Annual Report gave details on the work of their Advice Team:

Advice given in 2009/10

A. Complain to council 29%
B. Go to advice agency 3%
C. Go to another organisation 11%
D. Outside jurisdiction 7%
E. Insufficient data to be able to advise/make complaint 48%
F. Complainant decides not to proceed 2%.

3. Where the complaint is premature because it has not first been raised with the body concerned, there is a risk that the complainant will not pursue the complaint.

The jurisdiction of the LO has been extended beyond local government services.

Complaints about privately arranged or funded adult social care came within jurisdiction in October 2010: see Part 3A of the 1974 Act as inserted by the Health Act 2009. Under the Apprenticeships, Skills, Children and Learning Act 2009, ss. 206–224, complaints about acts of governing bodies or prescribed functions of headteachers in a qualifying school (community, foundation or voluntary school, a community or foundation special school, a maintained nursery school, or a short stay school) but not about the admissions process can be made from October 2011. The LO is phasing this jurisdiction in following pilots in four areas.

A: Overlap with alternative remedies

The Law Commission, *Public Services Ombudsman: A Consultation Paper*

(2010) Law Com CP 196, paras. 4.11, 4.17- 4.26, 4.38–46

4.11 In all of the governing statutes for the ombudsmen there are provisions which have the aim of preventing an ombudsman opening a complaint, where the complainant has previously had recourse to another institution for administrative justice. [see s. 5(2)(b) of the Parliamentary Commissioner Act 1967 at p. 654, *ante* and s. 26(6) of Local Government Act 1974 at p. 657, *ante*.].

4.17 The existence of these provisions is an acknowledgment that there are overlapping jurisdictions. In broad terms overlaps can exist because of the definition of maladministration. The area of overlap has therefore been enlarged as the grounds for review in judicial review have expanded in recent years. Maladministration, as we set out in Part 2, was left deliberately undefined in the governing statutes of the public services ombudsmen, so that the ombudsmen would define it on the basis of their own case law.

4.18 Subsequently, maladministration has been taken to include—amongst many other things:

(1) corruption;
(2) bias and unfair discrimination; and
(3) making the decision on the basis of faulty information which should have been properly ascertained and assembled.

4.19 These would also be grounds for judicial review. Consequently, at a fundamental level, there is a significant potential for overlap between the administrative justice institutions.

4.20 The effect of these provisions is to give a preference for the courts in those circumstances. Where there is an overlap then section 5(2)(b) of the Parliamentary Commissioner Act 1967, and similar provisions in the statutes of the other public services ombudsmen apply. These require the ombudsmen to decline jurisdiction unless it is not reasonable to expect the complainant to have resorted to an alternative path– be that the Administrative Court, tribunal or other appeal body.

Recent case law suggests that the discretion to accept a complaint does not extend to cases where an action for judicial review has been commenced. In *Umo*, the Administrative Court stated that:

In a case where legal proceedings have in fact been instituted, the wording of the proviso precludes there being discretion in the local ombudsman to proceed thereafter. [*R (Umo)* v *Commissioner for Local Administration in England* [2003] EWHC 3202 (Admin) at [17]].

4.22 This case law concerns the Local Government Ombudsman. Whether the same principle applies to the Parliamentary Commissioner is not clear but the provisions for the Parliamentary Commissioner are identical to those for the Local Government Ombudsman.

4.23 One potential corollary of this preference is to place pressure on complainants to move towards confrontational litigation at an early date. This preference in favour of judicial review is reinforced by the limitation period of judicial review. This requires that an action should be commenced as soon as practicable, and in any event within three months of the decision objected to. In contrast a claimant has twelve months in which to bring a complaint to the ombudsman.

4.24 Given recent developments in administrative justice and the acceptance of the importance of ombudsmen—as demonstrated by their creation for the devolved administrations of Wales, Scotland and Northern Ireland—we do not think that the default position in favour of judicial review is sustainable.

Consultation responses

4.25 In our consultation paper Administrative Redress: Public Bodies and the Citizen

we suggested that the current statutory bar should be reformed such that:

An ombudsman may conduct an investigation, notwithstanding that the person aggrieved has or had a legal remedy, if in all the circumstances it is in the interests of justice to investigate.

4.26 We listed four factors to be taken into account when taking a decision to investigate:

(1) The availability of statutory procedures.
(2) The nature of the complaint.
(3) The characteristics of the parties.
(4) The claimant's objectives....

Conclusions and provisional proposals

4.38 Consultation responses to our original proposals were generally favourable and suggested that the abolition of the statutory bar is a useful course to pursue further. 4.39 We think that Government concerns in relation to any change causing the extra delay in administrative processes—such as deportation—are over-stated. There are no powers in the governing statutes that would prevent the process continuing—where this felt to be necessary by the public body.

4.40 On reflection and after consultation, we suggest that the question of whether it is appropriate for an ombudsman to investigate a matter should be entrusted to the ombudsmen—though with the normal oversight of the Administrative Court.

4.41 In 1967, there was a single, young and untested institution. There is now a family of experienced public services ombudsmen. The statutory provisions, though, are those of 1967. We suggest that the current rules that dictate particular conclusions to the ombudsmen and contain a preference in favour of courts are inappropriate within the current landscape of administrative justice.

4.42 Having conducted initial consultation, we remain of the opinion that the statutory bars for the public services ombudsmen should be reformed. However, on reflection, we would like to strengthen and simplify our initial approach. Therefore, we provisionally propose that the existing statutory bars be reformed. We provisionally propose that there is a general presumption in favour of a public services ombudsman being able to open a complaint.

4.43 Our original proposal was based around a mechanism that the public services ombudsmen should have to consider whether it is "in the interests of justice" to open an investigation—with reference to the four factors we listed above. However, we now think that if the ombudsman has jurisdiction, then there is, on the face of it, a good argument for opening an investigation.

4.44 By reversing the current bar the public services ombudsmen must consider the fact that a complainant has had, or may have, recourse to another mechanism for administrative redress.

4.45 We think this would be a suitable change as it would remove a troublesome barrier to jurisdiction. However, it would not create a new set of factors or procedures for the ombudsmen to consider—rather it would leave them with a simplified jurisdictional question.

4.46 We suggest that our proposed reform to the statutory bar and the creation of a dedicated power to stay and transfer cases to the ombudsmen—as detailed in the next section—emphasise the role of the Administrative Court as a mechanism of last resort. Reform of the statutory bars in their current form would remove a preference in favour of the Administrative Court where the public services ombudsmen are an equally viable option.

NOTES

1. There is less of a problem if the complainant has a possible choice between pursuing a remedy in the court or with the ombudsman as the complainant's desired outcome may only be achieved in one. The Court of Appeal in *R* v *Local Commissioner for Administration in North and North East England, ex parte Liverpool City Council* [2001] All ER 462, held that it was permissible to take into account that complaining to the LO is free whereas going to court is not. The Court said that this case was one better suited to the LO, as her powers of investigation were better equipped for gathering facts than the judicial review process and so she was more likely to provide a just remedy.
2. The principle in *Umo* is clearly unfair if it stops a complaint to the ombudsman if the complainant has unsuccessfully attempted another remedy. It could be unfair even if the complainant had been successful but the full injustice had not been remedied. For example a judicial review could lead to the quashing of an unlawful decision but not provide compensation for past losses; however, a complaint to the ombudsman could result in a recommendation for financial redress to cover that injustice.

SECTION 4: MEANING OF INJUSTICE IN CONSEQUENCE OF MALADMINISTRATION

PARLIAMENTARY COMMISSIONER ACT 1967

[See s. 5(1) at pp. 650, *ante*.]

12.—(3) It is hereby declared that nothing in this Act authorises or requires the Commissioner to question the merits of a decision taken without maladministration by a government department or other authority in the exercise of a discretion vested in that department or authority....

LOCAL GOVERNMENT ACT 1974

26. For the purposes of section 24A(1)(b), in relation to an authority to which this Part of this Act applies, the following matters are subject to investigation by a Local Commissioner under this Part of this Act—

(a) alleged or apparent maladministration in connection with the exercise of the authority's administrative functions;

(b) an alleged or apparent failure in a service which it was the authority's function to provide;

(c) an alleged or apparent failure to provide such a service.

...

34.—(3) It is hereby declared that nothing in this Part of this Act authorises or requires a Local Commissioner to question the merits of a decision taken without maladministration by an authority in the exercise of a discretion vested in that authority.

Debate on the Second Reading of the Parliamentary Commissioner Bill, House of Commons, House of Commons Debates, Vol. 734 (18 October 1966), col. 51

MR CROSSMAN: We might have made an attempt...to define, by catalogue, all of the qualities which make up maladministration by a civil servant. It would be a wonderful exercise—bias, neglect, inattention, delay, incompetence, inaptitude, perversity, turpitude, arbitrariness and so on. It would be a long and interesting list.

In the following case note the different approach to considering the legality of the ombudsman's finding of maladministration and injustice between the majority and Lord Donaldson, who is much more accommodating to the ombudsman's analysis and expression of findings.

R v *Local Commissioner, ex parte Eastleigh Borough Council*

[1988] 3 WLR 116, Court of Appeal

Eastleigh Borough Council challenged an adverse report of the LO on the basis that it sought to challenge a decision taken without maladministration by an authority in the exercise of a discretion vested in the authority. Nolan J held that the ombudsman had indeed exceeded its jurisdiction, but that it would be wrong to make a declaration to that effect. The authority appealed to the Court of Appeal and the Local Commissioner cross-appealed. There were three main issues in the appeal:

(a) Had the Commissioner acted contrary to law in concluding that the council had been guilty of maladministration?

(b) Had the Commissioner acted contrary to law in concluding that such maladministration, if it had occurred, had caused injustice to the complainant?

(c) If the Commissioner had acted contrary to law in one or both of these respects, should the court grant a remedy?

LORD DONALDSON OF LYMINGTON MR: This appeal is about drains and an ombudsman. Most of the time the drains served six houses in Hampshire. However, on occasion they backed up to the discomfiture of the householders. The ombudsman was, to give him his proper title, a Local Commissioner of the Commission for Local Administration in England whose territory included the borough of Eastleigh. On the complaint of one of the householders, he investigated and concluded that the continued existence of the defect in the drains was caused by maladministration upon the part of the Eastleigh Borough Council. The council was not amused and sought judicial review of the ombudsman's report.

Nolan J held that the council had cause for complaint on two grounds. First, the ombudsman had acted contrary to section 34(3) of the Local Government Act 1974, in that he had questioned 'a decision taken without maladministration by an authority in the exercise of a discretion vested in that authority.' Second, the ombudsman had acted contrary to section 26(1) of the Act in that he had made a report on a complaint when it had not been established that the complainant had suffered injustice in consequence of the maladministration which was the subject of that complaint. However the judge refused to quash the report or to grant the council a declaration that the ombudsman had exceeded his jurisdiction. The council now appeals against this refusal and the ombudsman cross-appeals against the finding that he exceeded his powers.

Although this might be dismissed as a storm in a sewer, in fact it raises issues of some importance concerning the relationship between the courts and the local ombudsmen. But before considering those issues, I must say a word about the facts. These I take from the ombudsman's report, because for the purposes of judicial review proceedings he, and he alone, is the tribunal of fact.

The six houses were built in 1977 within the area of the Eastleigh Borough Council. It was accordingly the function of that council to enforce the Building Regulations 1976 (SI 1976 No. 1676): see section 4(3) of the Public Health Act 1961. It was for the council to decide on the scale of resources which it could make available to carry out this function. In doing so it had to strike a balance between the claims of efficiency and thrift, being answerable for that balance to the electorate through the ballot box rather than to the courts: *per* Lord Wilberforce in *Anns* v *Merton London Borough Council* [1978] AC 728, 754.

The ombudsman has found that the building control staff processed, on average, 210 applications per officer, which was 50 per cent higher per officer than in the remainder of Hampshire. This placed considerable demands on the staff and was achieved by limiting inspection to four of the more important of the nine stages requiring statutory notice of inspection to be submitted by builders. These four stages were the excavations for foundations, the oversite concrete, the damp proof course and the drains. The reason for limiting the inspections to these four stages was that the council had always been 'lean on members of staff' and it was thought appropriate to concentrate resources on inspections at the 'critical stages' of building work, on the basis that defects at these stages were likely to prove the most difficult to correct at a later date. The council operated a 'demand' system for inspection, meaning thereby that the council did not indulge in random inspections, but only inspected when notified that the appropriate stages had been reached. This was the policy of the council. It is now necessary to look at the practice.

It is now known that the problem experienced by the householders stemmed from the fact that the sewer over part of its length had a very shallow gradient of 1 in 140 and that there were undulations in it such that in places it was flat or had a reverse fall. The relevant code of practice called for a minimum gradient of 1 in 80 and the plans showed a gradient of 1 in 27 in one section and 1 in 70 in another. A gradient of 1 in 140 would not have been approved....

The ombudsman's conclusions are stated in paragraphs 30 and 31 of his report:

> 30. In my view good administration dictates that the council should carry out an inspection under the Building Regulations in respect of all stage inspections for which they have received notice from the owner or builder as the case may be. Where inspections have not been made at a particular stage I consider that special attention should be given on the final inspection to remedy the omission. In the case of drains it is a relatively easy matter to carry out a full test, such as a ball test or its equivalent, at the final inspection stage and I consider that a council have a duty to ensure that this is done because a final inspection should mean that, so far as the council are concerned, they have with reasonable diligence and expenditure of officer time found no defect under the Building Regulations. I am satisfied that in this case the private foul sewer in question was not fully or thoroughly inspected. The defects in piping discovered as a result of the soil and vent pipe test should have alerted officers to the possibility of other defects in the pipe work.
>
> 31. I find, therefore, that the complainant has sustained injustice as a result of the council's maladministration. However, I cannot say, categorically, whether had the council carried out the final inspection in accordance with the dictates of good administration the trouble at the centre of this complaint would not have arisen. Equally, I have taken account of the argument that with synthetic piping of the sort employed in this case soil compaction can cause undulation at a later date. I have also considered the fact that the original fault was the builder's and that that (and the council's fault) occurred some years ago. On the other hand the final inspection was, in my view, incomplete and the council could have become aware of the problem at an early stage because of the difficulties experienced by the owner of house 3. Having considered these factors I feel on balance it would be inequitable to ask the council to defray the whole cost of the necessary remedial work. Accordingly, upon the residents' agreement to pay a proportion of the reasonable cost, I consider that the council themselves should take the action which the Assistant Director of Technical Services commended to the residents (see paragraph 29, above).

The action referred to in paragraph 29 consisted of exposing that part of the sewer which lay between two manholes and adjusting the pipe work to eliminate the undulation.

The ombudsman's cross-appeal

Section 34(3)

This subsection is in the following terms:

> It is hereby declared that nothing in this Part of this Act authorises or requires a Local Commissioner to question the merits of a decision taken without maladministration by an authority in the exercise of a discretion vested in that authority.

'Maladministration' is not defined in the Act, but its meaning was considered in *Reg* v *Local Commissioner for Administration for the North and East Area of England, Ex parte Bradford Metropolitan City Council* [1979] QB 287. All three judges (Lord Denning MR, at p. 311, Eveleigh LJ, at p. 314, and Sir David Cairns, at p. 319) expressed themselves differently, but in substance each was saying the same thing, namely, that administration and maladministration in the context of the work of a local authority is concerned with the *manner* in which decisions by the authority are reached and the *manner* in which they are or are not implemented. Administration and maladministration have nothing to do with the nature, quality or reasonableness of the decision itself.

The key to this part of the cross-appeal lies in identifying the policy decision of the council in relation to the inspection of drains. This was, as I have stated, to inspect at four of the more important of nine stages of construction. I did not condescend to the nature of the inspections. These houses were built in 1977 and that was the policy in that year. In 1980 and 1984 the policy was modified, so that not all houses were inspected, but that is immaterial for present purposes. That being the 1977 policy of the council, it was for its building control officers to implement that policy as a matter of administration.

Nolan J read paragraph 30 of the ombudsman's report, which I have set out in full, as questioning the merits of that policy. I do not so read it. I can best illustrate my understanding of that paragraph by adding words which render explicit what, in my judgment, is implicit [the words in square brackets are the words added by Sir John Donaldson MR to the report of the ombudsman]:

> In my view good administration dictates that the council should carry out an inspection under the Building Regulations in respect of all stage inspections for which they have received notice from the owner or builder as the case may be. [However I recognise that, on the authority of *Anns'* case [1978] AC 728 to which I have referred at length earlier in this report, it was open to the council in the exercise of their discretion and taking account of the competing claims of efficiency and thrift to decide to inspect on fewer occasions. This the council has done and I accept its decisions. That said] Where inspections have not been made at a particular stage I consider that special attention should be given on the final inspection to remedying the omission. [In saying this I am not calling for an expenditure of time and effort which would nullify the council's discretionary decision on the resources to be devoted to building regulation inspections.] In the case of drains it is a relatively easy matter to carry out a full test, such as a ball test or its equivalent, at the final inspection stage... [The choice of test must be a matter for the council's officers and I would not criticise them for not using the ball test, if they had used some equivalent test. However an air pressure test, such as the council's officers used, is not such an equivalent, because it only reveals whether or not the sewer is watertight. It tells the inspector nothing about its gradient or its ability to self-clear and efficiently carry away matter discharged into it as required by regulation N10.] I consider that [this is of considerable importance and that] a council have a duty to ensure that this is done because a final inspection [if the council decide to make one, as this council did] should mean that, so far as the council are concerned, they have with reasonable diligence and expenditure of officer time found no defect under the Building Regulations. I am satisfied that in this case the private foul sewer in question was not fully or thoroughly inspected [in terms of the council's own 1977 policy. Even if in other circumstances a lesser inspection might have been justified in terms of that policy] the defects in piping discovered as a result of the soil and vent pipe tests should have alerted officers to the possibility of other defects in the pipe work.

So read, and I do so read it, paragraph 30 loyally accepts the council's discretionary decision on the inspection of drains. It simply criticises the way in which that decision was implemented. I do not, therefore, think that this complaint by the council is made out.

Section 26(1)

This subsection is in the following terms:

> Subject to the provisions of this Part of this Act where a written complaint is made by or on behalf of a member of the public who claims to have sustained injustice in consequence of maladministration in connection with action taken by or on behalf of an authority to which this Part of this Act applies, being action taken in the exercise of administrative functions of that authority, a Local Commissioner may investigate that complaint.

Clearly this subsection does not prevent the ombudsman from investigating a complaint of maladministration which prima facie may have led the complainant to sustain consequential injustice (see the *Bradford Council* case [1979] QB 287), but it does mean that he cannot report adversely upon an authority unless his investigation reveals not only maladministration, but injustice to the complainant sustained as a consequence of that maladministration.

The mischief at which this subsection is directed is not difficult to detect. Every local authority has living within its boundaries a small cadre of citizens who would like nothing better than to spend their spare time complaining of maladministration. The subsection limits the extent to which they can involve the ombudsman by requiring, as a condition precedent to his involvement, that the complainant shall personally have been adversely affected by the alleged maladministration. If he was not so affected, he did not himself suffer injustice. If he was, he did....

Like Nolan J, I am loath to criticise a busy Local Commissioner on merely semantic grounds, but I think that he laid himself open to criticism by finding maladministration in paragraph 30 and then proceeding, without any explanation, to his conclusion of consequential injustice. The words 'I find, therefore...' without further ado might suggest that, having found maladministration, injustice to the complainant followed as a matter of course.

This is not the case and I do not understand the ombudsman to be suggesting that it was. The facts, as found by him, were that the inspection by the council's officers was designed to detect defects in the drains, it was inadequate and it failed to detect the defects which in fact caused substantial inconvenience to the complainant. If the matter had stopped there, his finding of a causal connection would have been clear and not open to attack. It is his reference in paragraph 31 to the fact that he could not affirm categorically that a proper inspection would have revealed the defects and to the argument that the synthetic piping soil compaction can cause undulation at a later date which has cast doubt on his finding. This point has given me some concern, but in the end I have come to the conclusion that the ombudsman was intending to say that, whilst there could be no absolute certainty that a proper inspection would have revealed the defects and it was a possibility that the undulation occurred after the date of the inspection, on the balance of probabilities he was satisfied that the defects were present at the time of the inspection, that a proper inspection would have revealed them and that he was therefore satisfied that the complainant had suffered injustice in consequence of the maladministration.

An ombudsman's report is neither a statute nor a judgment. It is a report to the council and to the ratepayers of the area. It has to be written in everyday language and convey a message. This report has been subjected to a microscopic and somewhat legalistic analysis which it was not intended to undergo. Valid criticisms have been made, particularly of paragraph 31, but in my judgment they go to form rather than substance and, notwithstanding occasional dicta to the contrary, judicial review is concerned with substance. I would therefore allow the ombudsman's cross-appeal.

The council's appeal

As Parker and Taylor LJJ are minded to dismiss the ombudsman's appeal, it is necessary to consider the council's appeal. I would allow it.

Nolan J considered that there was no need for any declaration that the ombudsman had exceeded his remit by contravening the limits upon his jurisdiction set by section 34(3). He said that this was a free country and that there was nothing to prevent the council responding to the report with equal publicity. He concluded by saying that, since Parliament had not thought it necessary to create a right of appeal against the findings in the Local Commissioner's report, and in the absence of impropriety, it seemed to him that the courts ought not to provide the equivalent of such a right by judicial review.

I have to say that I profoundly disagree with this approach. Let me start with the fact that Parliament has not created a right of appeal against the findings in a Local Commissioner's report. It is this very fact, coupled with the public law character of the ombudsman's office and powers, which is the foundation of the right to relief by way of judicial review.

Next there is the suggestion that the council should issue a statement disputing the right of the ombudsman to make his findings and that this would provide the council with an adequate remedy. Such an action would wholly undermine the system of ombudsman's reports and would, in effect, provide for an appeal to the media against his findings. The Parliamentary intention was that reports by ombudsmen should be loyally accepted by the local authorities concerned. This is clear from section 30(4) and (5), which require the local authority to make the report available for inspection by the public and to advertise this fact, from section 31(1), which requires the local authority to notify the ombudsman of the action which it has taken and proposes to take in the light of his report and from section 31(2), which entitles the ombudsman to make a further report if the local authority's response is not satisfactory.

Whilst I am very far from encouraging councils to seek judicial review of an ombudsman's report, which, bearing in mind the nature of his office and duties and the qualification of those who hold that office, is inherently unlikely to succeed, in the absence of a successful application for judicial review and the giving of relief by the court, local authorities should not dispute an ombudsman's report and should carry out their statutory duties in relation to it.

If Nolan J thought that the publication of his judgment in favour of the council was itself an adequate remedy, he did not say so, and, in any event, I think that he would have been mistaken, because this by itself does not relieve the council of its obligations to respond to the report in accordance with section 31(1) and, assuming that the report should never have been made, it is wrong that the council should be expected to respond.

I would grant a declaration in terms which reflect the decision of this court on the ombudsman's appeal against the decision of Nolan J.

PARKER LJ: The only question of difficulty arises on the cross-appeal of the ombudsman. If the cross-appeal is dismissed, I agree that the appeal must be allowed for the reasons given by Lord Donaldson of Lymington MR. On that matter I have nothing to add. I turn therefore to the cross-appeal.

The first question thereby raised is whether, as Nolan J held, the ombudsman has in his report acted contrary to section 34(3) of the Local Government Act 1974, the terms of which have been set out by Lord Donaldson MR. I do not therefore repeat them. Whether he has or not depends upon the interpretation of paragraph 30 of his report, read of course in its context. This context includes amongst other things an early paragraph in which the ombudsman specifically refers to and quotes the relevant passage from the speech of Lord Wilberforce in *Anns v Merton London Borough Council* [1978] AC 728. It must therefore be taken that he correctly directed himself as to the law. Accordingly I approach paragraph 30 on the basis that it is inherently unlikely that, having so directed himself, he would in the vital paragraph have intended to act contrary to his own direction. I also approach the paragraph on the basis that it should not be interpreted to lead to such a result if on a fair reading such a result can be avoided.

Before turning to the paragraph itself I should mention two further matters. The first is that the terms of section 34(3) do not preclude the ombudsman from questioning the merits of all discretionary policy decisions, but only those taken without maladministration. He can therefore examine or investigate a decision, as Eveleigh LJ said in *Reg.* v *Local Commissioner for Administration for the North and East Area of England, Ex parte Bradford Metropolitan City Council* [1979] QB 287, 316–317:

> If the commissioner carries out his investigation and in the course of it comes personally to the conclusion that a decision was wrongly taken, but is unable to point to any maladministration other than the decision itself, he is prevented by section 34(3) from questioning the decision.

The second matter to which attention may be usefully directed is that section 26(1) of the Act of 1974, which provides for complaints to a Local Commissioner, specifies that the complaint must be made by a member of the public

> who claims to have sustained injustice in consequence of maladministration in connection with action taken by or on behalf of an authority... *being action taken in the exercise of administrative functions* of that authority... (My emphasis.)

It appears to me to be plain from the report that the council had failed to carry out their own policy, and indeed it was made plain by Mr Sullivan on their behalf that, had the report so found, the council would have had no objection. The objection taken is that the report goes further than this and questions the merits of the policy decision to inspect only 'at the four more important of the nine stages requiring statutory notice of inspection to be submitted by builders.' The council's case depends entirely upon the wording of paragraph 30, and particularly the opening words thereof:

> In my view good administration dictates that the council should carry out an inspection under the Building Regulations in respect of all stage inspections for which they have received notice from the owner or builder as the case may be.

This, it is submitted, clearly questions the merits of the decision to inspect at the four more important stages only and, there being no suggestion of any maladministration in arriving at that decision, clearly exceeds the powers of the ombudsman.

I can see no answer to that submission, but it does not follow that the conclusion reached is vitiated. On a fair reading of the whole of paragraph 30 it appears to me that the ombudsman is not concluding that there was maladministration because there was no inspection at all nine stages, but merely that the inspections of the sewer which were called for by the policy of inspecting at the four most important stages were not fully or thoroughly carried out. This conclusion was not dependent upon the view expressed in the opening sentence and indeed it could not have been because the policy did call for drain inspections, indeed two drain inspections. The policy was silent as to the nature of such inspections, but, since the regulations (see regulation N10(1)(e)) call for a drain or private sewer to be 'so designed and constructed, of such size and... laid at such a gradient as to ensure that it is self-cleansing and efficiently carries away the maximum volume of matter which may be discharged into it,' it appears to me that inspections which were not directed at all to checking whether the private sewer was so designed, constructed and laid were rightly found to constitute maladministration by the council in its administrative functions.

I conclude therefore that the ombudsman's conclusion in paragraph 30 was valid, but if the council felt it necessary to seek some declaratory relief with regard to the opening words of the paragraph I would be prepared to consider granting it.

I turn to the second question raised on the cross-appeal, namely, whether the conclusion that the complainant had suffered injustice as a result of the maladministration can be sustained. This depends upon paragraph 31 of the report. Had the ombudsman stopped at the first sentence, I should have had no doubt that the decision was sustainable. It seems to me abundantly clear that the complainant had suffered injustice if the failure to inspect properly led to the subsequent expenditure and the ombudsman could in my view easily have determined that it had. It is submitted however that, having stated his conclusion in the opening sentence, he proceeds to negate it and that the paragraph read as a whole really amounts to this: 'I cannot say whether the failure to inspect led to the expenditure, but as the council were at fault it would be fair that they should contribute to the cost of remedial measures.' For the ombudsman it is submitted that this is not so and that on a fair reading the paragraph says no more than: 'I cannot be absolutely sure, but on the balance of probabilities I conclude...'.

I regret to say that, unlike Lord Donaldson MR I cannot accept this construction. It appears to me that to do so involves applying legal concepts of differing standards of proof in order to uphold a paragraph which, like its predecessor, must be broadly considered. I have, despite its opening words, been able, by a broad reading and the correctness of the ombudsman's directions to himself on the law, to uphold the conclusion in paragraph 30. In the case of paragraph 31 I am unable to do so.

I would therefore dismiss the cross-appeal and allow the appeal.

TAYLOR LJ: I agree that the council's appeal must be allowed if the ombudsman's cross-appeal fails. The council should not be denied a remedy if the ombudsman's finding was ultra vires or otherwise unlawful. I agree that for the reasons given by Lord Donaldson MR, Nolan J's grounds for refusing a declaration cannot be sustained.

The crucial issue therefore is whether the ombudsman's findings in both paragraphs 30 and 31 of his report can be upheld and his cross-appeal thus allowed. I agree with Nolan J that both paragraphs contain findings which cannot be justified.

As to paragraph 30, the conclusion adverse to the council is contained in the penultimate sentence. Its rationale is said to be that, in terms of the council's own 1977 policy, the foul sewer was not fully or thoroughly inspected because no gradient test was applied such as the ball test or its equivalent. It is accepted to be a matter for the council's discretion whether, with their available resources, they could and should have inspected at all stages or only at the four most important stages. But in my judgment, it was equally a matter for the council's discretion as to what tests they could and should carry out having regard to those resources. The ombudsman's finding in paragraph 30 is that at the final inspection, if not before, the council:

> have a duty to insure that [a gradient test] is done because a final inspection should mean that, so far as the council are concerned, they have with reasonable diligence and expenditure of officer time found no defect under the Building Regulations.

This begs the question whether 'reasonable diligence and expenditure of officer time' permits and requires a gradient test to be made of every drain and sewer. It was not the policy of this council that they did. That is a matter of discretion for the council. I do not accept Mr Beloff's suggestion that what precedes the penultimate sentence in paragraph 30 should be regarded as obiter dicta. The paragraph is headed 'Conclusions' and should be read as a whole. It culminates in, and is explanatory of, the finding. In my judgment its tenor shows the ombudsman to be trespassing into the field of discretion by laying down what policy as to inspections the dictates of good administration require, and what tests the council ought to ensure are carried out. That is quite different from finding that a test specifically required by the council's policy has not been carried out or has been carried out inefficiently. I therefore agree with Nolan J that the ombudsman was in breach of section 34(3) of the Local Government Act 1974 in his conclusion that maladministration was established.

As to paragraph 31, I agree with Parker LJ. Only by straining the language used by the ombudsman and attributing to him speculatively considerations as to the burden of proof, could one render his finding on causation sound. I do not think such straining and speculation is justified.

Accordingly I conclude that in respect of both paragraphs 30 and 31 of the report, Nolan J reached the correct conclusions. I would therefore dismiss the cross-appeal and allow the council's appeal.

■ QUESTIONS

1. How did each of the three judges answer the questions raised in the appeal?
2. Is there any difference between the interpretation placed on s. 34(3) by Lord Donaldson MR and that by Parker LJ?
3. What advice would you give to Commissioners on the drawing up of their reports after this case?

NOTES

1. In its *Second Report for the Session 1967–68* (HC 350) the Select Committee encouraged the PO to investigate complaints relating to 'bad decisions' and 'bad rules'. In respect of the 'bad decision' the Select Committee (at para. 14) stated that if the PO

> finds a decision which, judged by its effect upon the aggrieved person, appears to him to be thoroughly bad in quality, he might infer from the quality of the decision itself that there had been an element of maladministration in the taking of it and ask for its review.

In respect of the 'bad rule', where an administrative rule, despite being applied properly, has caused hardship and injustice, the PO was urged

> to enquire whether, given the effect of the rule in the case under his investigation, the Department had taken any action to review the rule. If found defective and revised, what action had been taken to remedy the hardship sustained by the complainant? If not revised, whether there had been due consideration by the Department of the grounds for maintaining the rule?

The PO accepted these suggestions, but it has been argued that they have had little impact on the number of cases in which he has been willing to find maladministration. In relation to the 'bad rule', Gregory in 'The Select Committee on the PCA 1967–80' [1982] *Public Law* 49, at p. 69 points out that 'only an extraordinarily inept department might be expected to conduct its review of a rule [so] that the Commissioner would find defects in the process subsequently described to him'.

2. A number of the cases considered by the PO and LOs have involved allegations that authorities have failed to give proper advice; for a discussion of the Parliamentary Commissioner's approach to such cases, see A. Mowbray, 'A Right to Official Advice: The Parliamentary Commissioner's Perspective' [1990] *Public Law* 68–69.
3. In *Our Fettered Ombudsman* (1977), ch. VII, JUSTICE suggested that, following the New Zealand model, the jurisdiction of the PO should be extended to allow him to investigate any action which is 'unreasonable, unjust or oppressive...instead of maladministration'. The PO responded to this suggestion in his *Annual Report for 1977* (HC 157 of 1977–78) by stating that he believed he already had power to investigate complaints that actions by Government Departments are unjust or oppressive. He continued:

> 21. What the Act certainly does exclude from my jurisdiction are complaints about discretionary decisions taken 'without maladministration'. I believe this to be right. It is no part of my function to substitute my judgment for that of a Minister or one of his officials if I see no evidence of 'maladministration' either in the way the decision was taken or in the nature of the decision itself.
>
> 22. I believe therefore that the difficulty which has been detected in the limitation of my investigation powers to cases of 'maladministration' is more theoretical than practical. But if there is thought to be some semantic difficulty which confuses members of the public or members of parliament than I should see no objection to seeing my powers redefined in the sort of language suggested by JUSTICE. I think that in practice it would make very little difference.

Subsequently JUSTICE adopted the view that the definition of maladministration was not a source of much difficulty, bearing in mind the approach which the Commissioner took to his jurisdiction (see the reference to this in the *Fourth Report from the Select Committee*, HC 615 of 1977–78). The *JUSTICE–All Souls Report on Administrative Law* (1988) did not recommend any change in the definition (see pp. 92–93 and 133–134).

■ QUESTION

In the light of the decision in *ex parte Eastleigh Borough Council* (p. 662, *ante*), do you think the PO was correct in the extract from the Annual Report for 1977?

NOTE: Sir Cecil Clothier, who was PO from 1979 to 1985, stated that he did not wish to be dragged into a review of political decision-making; and he suggested that a complaint is political if it has been debated in Parliament or where a very large proportion of the population is affected as well as the person making the complaint (see Clothier (1984) 81 *Law Society's Gazette* 3108–3109). On this ground he refused to investigate complaints relating to the Inland Revenue's agreement concerning Fleet Street casual workers who evaded their tax arrangements. This agreement subsequently gave rise to *Inland Revenue Commissioners* v *National Federation of Self-Employed and Small Businesses Ltd* [1982] AC 617 (see p. 626, *ante*).

Section 26(7) of the Local Government Act 1974 specifically provides that a local commissioner shall not conduct an investigation in respect of any action which in his opinion affects all or most of the inhabitants in the area of the authority concerned.

NOTE: One of the areas in which the ombudsmen can assist is in human rights, and the Health Service Ombudsman and the LO have conducted joint investigations in which they found that a failure to take into account human rights issues was maladministration: for example, the 2009 report *Six Lives the provision of public services to people with learning disabilities* (HC 203 of 2008–09).

The PO has suggested that as the concept of maladministration and remedy by the ombudsman has enabled people to have more convenient redress from public bodies the same can also be true in human rights. In A. Abraham, 'The Ombudsman and Individual Rights,' (2008) 61 *Parliamentary Affairs*, 370, at pp. 377–378:

> If a human rights culture is to be realised on the ground, public servants can reasonably expect to be judged against standards that expressly acknowledge the place that human rights principles should play in public administration. Good administration will invariably show signs of a human rights culture. For the Ombudsman, as protector on behalf of Parliament of those features of good administration, the task of making findings of maladministration is unavoidably implicated with human rights considerations, and in a way that is far less feasible for the High Court, which will find many of the relevant disputes well beneath its elevated horizon.

See also on the suitability of the ombudsman approach to the protection of rights and social rights, N. O'Brien, 'Ombudsmen and Social rights Adjudication' [2009] *Public Law,* 466 and N. O'Brien and B. Thompson, 'Human Rights Accountability in the UK: Deliberative Democracy and the Role of the Ombudsman' (2010) *European Human Rights Law Review* 504.

SECTION 5: INVESTIGATION, RESOLUTION, AND IMPROVEMENT

A: Investigation and resolution

PARLIAMENTARY COMMISSIONER ACT 1967

7.—(1) Where the Commissioner proposes to conduct an investigation pursuant to a complaint under this Act, he shall afford to the principal officer of the department or authority concerned, and to any other person who is alleged in the complaint to have taken or authorised the action complained of, an opportunity to comment on any allegations contained in the complaint.

(2) Every such investigation shall be conducted in private, but except as aforesaid the procedure for conducting an investigation shall be such as the Commissioner considers appropriate in the circumstances of the case; and without prejudice to the generality of the foregoing provision the Commissioner may obtain information from such persons and in such manner, and make such inquiries, as he thinks fit, and may determine whether any person may be represented, by counsel or solicitor or otherwise, in the investigation.

(3) The Commissioner may, if he thinks fit, pay to the person by whom the complaint was made and to any other person who attends or furnishes information for the purposes of an investigation under this Act—

(a) sums in respect of expenses properly incurred by them;

(b) allowances by way of compensation for the loss of their time, in accordance with such scales and subject to such conditions as may be determined by the Treasury.

(4) The conduct of an investigation under this Act shall not affect any action taken by the department or authority concerned, or any power or duty of that department or authority to take further action with respect to any matters subject to the investigation...

8.—(1) For the purposes of an investigation under this Act the Commissioner may require any Minister, officer or member of the department or authority concerned or any other person who in his opinion is able to furnish information or produce documents relevant to the investigation to furnish any such information or produce any such document.

(2) For the purposes of any such investigation the Commissioner shall have the same powers as the Court in respect of the attendance and examination of witnesses (including the administration of oaths or affirmations and the examination of witnesses abroad) and in respect of the production of documents.

(3) No obligation to maintain secrecy or other restriction upon the disclosure of information obtained by or furnished to persons in Her Majesty's service, whether imposed by any enactment or by any rule of law, shall apply to the disclosure of information for the purposes of an investigation under this Act; and the Crown shall not be entitled in relation to any such investigation to any such privilege in respect of the production of documents or the giving of evidence as is allowed by law in legal proceedings.

(4) No person shall be required or authorised by virtue of this Act to furnish any information or answer any question relating to proceedings of the Cabinet or of any committee of the Cabinet or to produce so much of any document as relates to such proceedings; and for the purposes of this subsection a certificate issued by the Secretary of the Cabinet with the approval of the Prime Minister and certifying that any information, question, document or part of a document so relates shall be conclusive.

(5) Subject to subsection (3) of this section, no person shall be compelled for the purposes of any investigation under this Act to give any evidence or produce any document which he could not be compelled to give or produce in civil proceedings before the Court.

9.—(1) If any person without lawful excuse obstructs the Commissioner or any officer of the Commissioner in the performance of his functions under this Act, or is guilty of any act or omission in relation to an investigation under this Act which, if that investigation were a proceeding in the Court, would constitute contempt of court, the Commissioner may certify the offence to the Court....

NOTES

1. Similar provisions regarding the conduct of investigations by the LOs are set out in the Local Government Act 1974, ss. 26(5), 28–29.
2. The Regulatory Reform (Collaboration etc Between Ombudsmen) Reform Order 2007 amends the principal statutes of the PO, LO and HSO in England to allow them to work together, with the consent of the complainant, where a complaint has elements which overlap their separate jurisdictions e.g. the PO could deal with social security issues and the LO with social care. The amendments also allow delegation to, and the sharing of information amongst, the officers of the various ombudsmen.
3. Investigation was the method by which ombudsmen dealt with citizens' complaints to determine if there was injustice caused by maladministration and, if there was, to recommend redress. This was thorough but lengthy. In 1979–80 the LO was the first ombudsman to interpret its statutory powers not to initiate or to discontinue an investigation so as to facilitate a local settlement of the case, rather than issuing a statutory investigation report. The PO did not introduce a similar change to its working practices until April 2000, prompted by a desire to achieve resolution, but also to speed up the average time taken to dispose of cases and reduce a burgeoning backlog. The Collcutt *Review of Public Sector Ombudsmen in England* (2000) was keen to see increased emphasis on resolving complaints more quickly and informally at para. 6.16:

> The elements of the new approach are therefore:
>
> - a focus on outcomes and in particular on complaints resolution;
> - clear recognition of when intervention is required;
> - a positive attitude to assisting complainants in progressing their complaint whether with the ombudsman or by other means;
> - initially an informal approach aiming to achieve co-operation and perhaps using a conciliatory approach;
> - investigation in the old sense to be used if informal methods do not work.
>
> It would be wrong to imply that the ombudsmen are not using these methods—often they will but this concept of their role is not sufficiently reflected in their legislation.

4. The Regulatory Reform (Collaboration etc Between Ombudsmen) Order 2007 also allows the PO, HSO, and LOs to appoint mediators in the conduct of their investigations. This type of resolution seems to differ from Scotland where the Scottish Public Service Ombudsmen Act 2002 provides:

> S.2 (4) The Ombudsman may take such action in connection with the complaint or request as the Ombudsman thinks may be of assistance in reaching any such decision.
>
> (5) Such action may, in particular, include action with a view to resolving the complaint or request.

This approach was extended by the Public Services Ombudsman (Wales) Act 2005:

3 Alternative resolution of complaints

(1) The Ombudsman may take any action he thinks appropriate with a view to resolving a complaint which he has power to investigate under section 2.

(2) The Ombudsman may take action under this section in addition to or instead of conducting an investigation into the complaint.

(3) Any action under this section must be taken in private.

Parliamentary & Health Service Ombudsman, *Making an Impact: Annual Report 2009–10*

HC 274 of 2009–10, p.20.

We accepted 52 parliamentary enquiries for investigation during the year. Wherever possible, we will try to resolve as many complaints as we can through intervention, avoiding the need for a full investigation. In 2009-10 we resolved 105 parliamentary cases in this way. Intervention often means a quicker resolution for complainants, and it also emphasises the importance we attach to a body's own responsibility for resolving complaints. The majority of the complaints we receive are generated by relatively few government departments. We have been able to establish good lines of communication with these bodies in order to make our expectations clear (such as the application of the Ombudsman's Principles), achieve interventions, and feed back learning from the cases we have considered, at a case level and more widely through our case digests and special reports. This means that we only need to accept the most complex and intractable complaints for a full investigation. The fact that 80 per cent of the parliamentary complaints we investigated were upheld or partly upheld indicates that we are making the right decisions about what cases to take forward for investigation.

In 2009–10 the LO report that they obtained or recommended redress in 2,435 cases of which 2,366 were local settlements which they define as:

the outcome of a complaint where, during the course of our consideration of the complaint, the council takes, or agrees to take, some action that the Ombudsman considers is a satisfactory response to the complaint and the investigation is discontinued. This may occur, for example, in any of the following circumstances:

- the council on its own initiative says that there was fault that caused injustice, and proposes a remedy which the Ombudsman accepts is satisfactory;
- the council accepts the suggestion by the Ombudsman, as an independent person, that there was fault which caused injustice, and agrees a remedy which the Ombudsman accepts is satisfactory;
- the council does not consider that there was fault but is able to take some action which the Ombudsman accepts is a satisfactory outcome;
- the council and the complainant themselves agree upon a course of action and the Ombudsman sees no reason to suggest any different outcome; or
- the Ombudsman considers that, even if the investigation were to continue, no better outcome would be likely to be achieved for the complainant than the action the council has already taken or agreed.

Local Government Ombudsman, *Annual Report 09–10 Delivering Public Value*

(2010), p. 18

Table 2 : Analysis of outcome of complaints 2009/10

Outcome	Number of complaints	Percentage of total (excluding those outside jurisdiction)
Local settlements	2,366	26.92
Maladministration causing injustice (issued report)	69	0.78
Maladministration, no injustice (issued report)	2	0.02
No maladministration (issued report)	3	0.03
No or insufficient evidence of maladministration (without report)	4,065	46.25
Ombudsman's discretion	2,284	26.00
Outside jurisdiction	1,520	
Total	**10,309**	

See the ***Glossary of terminology*** for an explanation of terms used.

NOTES

1. The Law Commission in its *Public Services Ombudsmen Consultation Paper,* (2010, paras. 4.84–85) has proposed that the PO and LO be given specific powers to allow them to dispose of complaints in ways other than by conducting an investigation and they have a preference for the more broadly drawn power in s. 3 of the Public Services Ombudsman (Wales) Act 2005.
2. There is a concern that emphasizing resolving complaints rather than investigating them fully, carries the possibility that wider administrative issues raised by a case are not pursued. The ombudsmen all say that they are aware of this and do seek to continue work on cases where they think there may be systemic issues even though the parties are happy to resolve them.

■ QUESTION

Are the possible problems associated with resolution of complaints worse than the problem of the time taken to conduct formal investigations?

B: Improvement

A. Abraham, 'The Ombudsman as Part of the UK Constitution: A Contested Role?'

(2008) 61 *Parliamentary Affairs*, 206, 209–212

There is, though, another essential aspect of my role that transcends the limitations that are common both to ADR and to conventional litigation: the ability to codify good practice and to recommend systemic change. The contemporary fluorescence of codification in the public sector can be traced back at least to John Major's experiment with the Citizens' Charter as a device for re-articulating the social contract between state and citizen, between the provider and the consumer of services. The Human Rights Act 1998 itself on one construction of its import represents the culmination of such an approach. Rightly characterised as more mission statement than reforming legislation of the usual black-letter sort, the Human Rights Act seeks to make explicit those fundamental and generic principles that must inform the most basic encounter between citizen and state, from which all other particular standards, codes and charters must derive their authority and to which they must be subservient.

In the sphere of public administration there are, of course, many recent and concrete manifestations of this phenomenon: the Committee on Standards in Public Life is currently reviewing its Seven Principles of Public Life; the British and Irish Ombudsman Association in April 2007 published its Guide to Principles of Good Complaint Handling; and the Civil Service Code, revised in June 2006, describes the values and behaviours which the Civil Service is expected to espouse. For my own part, the Principles of Good Administration that I published in March 2007 were intended not as a checklist but as a broad statement of what I believe public authorities within my jurisdiction should be doing to deliver good administration and customer service. The production of such principles (getting it right; being customer focused; being open and accountable; acting fairly and proportionately; putting things right; seeking continuous improvement) is entirely symbiotic with my function of investigating complaints, the one effortlessly informing the other. The grievances that citizens bring to my Office put me on notice of where things are going wrong and of where improvement is most needed; they make it possible for me to prescribe values and behaviours that will reduce the likelihood of repetition; and they also enable me to tackle future breaches. In this way a virtuous circle is established, the ultimate objective being not so much the retrospective eradication of maladministration but the prospective promotion of good administration, prevention rather than cure.

This codifying function, albeit derived from and closely implicated with my core complaint-investigating function, marks out a very distinctive role that sets me apart from either the courts and tribunals or other forms of ADR. It is a function that is also complementary to my ability to issue 'special reports', concerned not so much with individual grievances but rather with the underlying and systemic defects that have given rise to an entire cluster of complaints. It is the sort of function to which the common law mentality with its inherent individualism is a stranger, constrained from looking beyond the facts of the particular case, compelled invariably to resort to a simplistic 'rotten apple' theory of organisational malfunction instead of a more realistic analysis that makes room for systemic and institutional failure. It is this ability of the Ombudsman to transcend the individualism of the common law, to get behind the camouflage of apparently esoteric detail so often presented by an individual complaint and instead penetrate to the underlying structure of what has really gone wrong that makes most acute the question of where the Ombudsman's authentic identity resides: in the ability to deliver tangible benefit to individuals or in the ability to serve a much broader public benefit remit? The ability to deliver meaningful redress to individuals, albeit through a process significantly different from that of the courts and tribunals, certainly casts the Ombudsman in the role of servant of the people (or more particularly of individual citizens) and establishes the Ombudsman's credentials as a system of justice....

The founding legislation of 1967 in effect established the Ombudsman as an aid to Parliament in its constitutional scrutiny of the Executive. That role has evolved to comprise the distinct but inter-related functions of dispute resolution, guardian of good public administration, and of systemic check on the Executive's effectiveness. It is the core activity of investigating complaints that makes operational those strategic priorities and makes possible the broader public interest remit that so characterises the role of Ombudsman. It does so in three ways in particular.

First, there is the ability of the Ombudsman... to codify and share expertise on good administrative practice and on good complaint handling. This is my special territory, the field of expertise to which I lay special claim. In addition to recommending ways in which the particular complaint might be avoided in future, I have the capacity to identify patterns of maladministration disclosed by an entire sequence of complaints and so to propose principles of practice that will bring about substantive future improvement of administration and complaint handling, either within a particular organisation or even a whole sector. In other cases, an individual complaint will itself exemplify how a particular policy, system or statutory framework is being administered, pointing without further ado towards the need for systemic change. Secondly, there is my wider-reaching ability to influence and contribute to the improvement, not just of administration and complaint handling, but of public service delivery itself. In part, this ability is the natural concomitant of improving internal administration: there is a necessary link between good administration and the improvement of service delivery. Yet beyond that, there is also scope to extract the lessons yielded by a comprehensive 'database' of complaints in such a way that I can present a compelling narrative of ineffective service delivery and so bring about insight, a shift in awareness and, if necessary, a change of 'culture' within the public sector. This 'influencing' work is no doubt more remote from the resolution of individual complaints than a more conventional 'system of justice' role might entail, but it is nevertheless part and parcel of the remedial action available to me and ultimately rooted in the core activity of complaint handling. Thirdly, and most ambitiously, there is the prospect of drawing upon the experience of complaint handling not just to improve administration and change culture, but to inform policy debate on aspects of a particular case or sequence of cases is greater still. Yet it still finds its origins in the bedrock of complaints handling, whilst nevertheless having as its target the highest level of policy direction and of sustainable impact. This is in effect the gilt-edged Ombudsman 'dividend' that can transcend the limits of individual redress and effect real and sustainable change for the entire citizen body, the users of public services at large.

A recent example suggests how this cumulative remedial action can work in practice to the public benefit. In June 2005, I completed a special report into the UK Government's then new system for operating tax credits. That report focused in particular on the social group intended to benefit from the reform: low-income families with children, and low-income earners. Drawing directly on the experience of the individual complaints referred to me, I identified an underlying pattern of dissatisfaction that stemmed to a large extent from the Government having adopted a 'one size fits all' system, a system designed to require minimum human intervention and relying instead on IT. In short, I found that this 'blanket' approach took no account of the very different circumstances and needs within the target group. The result was that the new system often had harsh and unintended consequences for the most vulnerable users of the system, frequently leading to debt recovery action by the Government to retrieve overpayments caused by the malfunctioning of its own reforms and, irony of ironies, casting into debt those most in need of financial support and intended to benefit from the reform in the first place.

On top of investigating individual complaints (which at one stage accounted for a quarter of all complaints referred to my Office), I made twelve detailed recommendations aimed at improving the administration of the system in its entirety. But I did not stop there: instead, I felt compelled to ask the bigger policy question of whether a financial support system that included a degree of inbuilt financial insecurity could ever in practice meet the needs of very low-income families and earners. Now, two years later, in a second follow-up report published on 9 October 2007, I have drawn attention to the impact of that financial insecurity on that especially vulnerable client group and to how it is leading to confusion and hardship, and in some cases even to a desire to opt out of the tax credits system altogether. The picture that emerges is one of a tax credits system that, even when working as intended, in some respects runs counter to the key policy objectives of helping tackle child poverty and of encouraging more people to work by 'making work pay'.

As I said in my 2005 report, the design of the tax credits system is, in the end, a matter for Government and Parliament, not for me. It is certainly not the place of the Ombudsman to usurp the function of the legislature and the Executive. It is, however, very much the role of the Ombudsman, as the purveyor of public benefit, to invite further public service delivery. Here the degree of abstraction from the facts of reflection on the empirical evidence disclosed by complaints that these unintended, but nonetheless adverse, consequences continue to occur and must be recognised in future policy development.

Parliamentary and Health Service Ombudsman, *Principles of Good Administration*

(2009), pp. 2–3

Good administration by public bodies means:

1. Getting it right

- Acting in accordance with the law and with regard for the rights of those concerned.
- Acting in accordance with the public body's policy and guidance (published or internal).
- Taking proper account of established good practice.
- Providing effective services, using appropriately trained and competent staff.
- Taking reasonable decisions, based on all relevant considerations.

2. Being customer focused

- Ensuring people can access services easily.
- Informing customers what they can expect and what the public body expects of them.
- Keeping to its commitments, including any published service standards
- Dealing with people helpfully, promptly and sensitively, bearing in mind their individual circumstances
- Responding to customers' needs flexibly, including, where appropriate, co-ordinating a response with other service providers

3. Being open and accountable

- Being open and clear about policies and procedures and ensuring that information, and any advice provided, is clear, accurate and complete.
- Stating its criteria for decision making and giving reasons for decisions
- Handling information properly and appropriately.
- Keeping proper and appropriate records
- Taking responsibility for its actions.

4. Acting fairly and proportionately

- Treating people impartially, with respect and courtesy.
- Treating people without unlawful discrimination or prejudice, and ensuring no conflict of interests.
- Dealing with people and issues objectively and consistently.
- Ensuring that decisions and actions are proportionate, appropriate and fair.

5. Putting things right

- Acknowledging mistakes and apologising where appropriate.
- Putting mistakes right quickly and effectively.
- Providing clear and timely information on how and when to appeal or complain.
- Operating an effective complaints procedure, which includes offering a fair and appropriate remedy when a complaint is upheld.

6. Seeking continuous improvement

- Reviewing policies and procedures regularly to ensure they are effective.
- Asking for feedback and using it to improve services and performance.
- Ensuring that the public body learns lessons from complaints and uses these to improve services and performance.

Parliamentary and Health Service Ombudsman, *Principles of Good Complaint Handling*

(2009), pp. 2–3.

Good complaint handling by public bodies means:

1. Getting it right

- Acting in accordance with the law and relevant guidance, and with regard for the rights of those concerned.
- Ensuring that those at the top of the public body provide leadership to support good complaint management and develop an organisational culture that values complaints.
- Having clear governance arrangements, which set out roles and responsibilities, and ensure lessons are learnt from complaints.
- Including complaint management as an integral part of service design.
- Ensuring that staff are equipped and empowered to act decisively to resolve complaints.
- Focusing on the outcomes for the complainant and the public body.
- Signposting to the next stage of the complaints procedure, in the right way and at the right time.

2. Being customer focused

- Having clear and simple procedures.
- Ensuring that complainants can easily access the service dealing with complaints, and informing them about advice and advocacy services where appropriate.
- Dealing with complainants promptly and sensitively, bearing in mind their individual circumstances.
- Listening to complainants to understand the complaint and the outcome they are seeking.
- Responding flexibly, including co-ordinating responses with any other bodies involved in the same complaint, where appropriate.

3. Being open and accountable

- Publishing clear, accurate and complete information about how to complain, and how and when to take complaints further.
- Publishing service standards for handling complaints.
- Providing honest, evidence-based explanations and giving reasons for decisions.
- Keeping full and accurate records.

4. Acting fairly and proportionately

- Treating the complainant impartially, and without unlawful discrimination or prejudice.
- Ensuring that complaints are investigated thoroughly and fairly to establish the facts of the case.
- Ensuring that decisions are proportionate, appropriate and fair.
- Ensuring that complaints are reviewed by someone not involved in the events leading to the complaint.
- Acting fairly towards staff complained about as well as towards complainants.

5. Putting things right

- Acknowledging mistakes and apologising where appropriate.
- Providing prompt, appropriate and proportionate remedies.
- Considering all the relevant factors of the case when offering remedies.
- Taking account of any injustice or hardship that results from pursuing the complaint as well as from the original dispute.

6. Seeking continuous improvement

- Using all feedback and the lessons learnt from complaints to improve service design and delivery.
- Having systems in place to record, analyse and report on the learning from complaints.

- Regularly reviewing the lessons to be learnt from complaints.
- Where appropriate, telling the complainant about the lessons learnt and changes made to services, guidance or policy.

Parliamentary and Health Service Ombudsman, *Principles for Remedy*

(2009), pp. 2–3

Good practice with regard to remedies means:

1. Getting it right
   - Quickly acknowledging and putting right cases of maladministration or poor service that have led to injustice or hardship.
   - Considering all relevant factors when deciding the appropriate remedy, ensuring fairness for the complainant and, where appropriate, for others who have suffered injustice or hardship as a result of the same maladministration or poor service.

2. Being customer focused
   - Apologising for and explaining the maladministration or poor service.
   - Understanding and managing people's expectations and needs.
   - Dealing with people professionally and sensitively.
   - Providing remedies that take account of people's individual circumstances.

3. Being open and accountable
   - Being open and clear about how public bodies decide remedies.
   - Operating a proper system of accountability and delegation in providing remedies.
   - Keeping a clear record of what public bodies have decided on remedies and why.

4. Acting fairly and proportionately
   - Offering remedies that are fair and proportionate to the complainant's injustice or hardship.
   - Providing remedies to others who have suffered injustice or hardship as a result of the same maladministration or poor service, where appropriate.
   - Treating people without bias, unlawful discrimination or prejudice.

5. Putting things right
   - If possible, returning the complainant and, where appropriate, others who have suffered similar injustice or hardship, to the position they would have been in if the maladministration or poor service had not occurred.
   - If that is not possible, compensating the complainant and such others appropriately.
   - Considering fully and seriously all forms of remedy (such as an apology, an explanation, remedial action, or financial compensation).
   - Providing the appropriate remedy in each case.

6. Seeking continuous improvement
   - Using the lessons learned from complaints to ensure that maladministration or poor service is not repeated.
   - Recording and using information on the outcome of complaints to improve services.

NOTE: Each set of principles has advice to the effect that they are not a checklist to be applied mechanically. Public bodies should use their judgement in applying them to produce reasonable, fair and proportionate results or remedies in all the circumstances of the case. The ombudsman will adopt a similar approach when deciding if maladministration or service failure has occurred and when considering the standard of complaint handling by public bodies in her jurisdiction and when recommending remedies.

Local Government Ombudsman, *Annual Report 09–10 Delivering Public Value*

(2010), pp. 27–28,

Giving advice and guidance

We published our 13th annual *Digest of cases* on our website only in October. This summarises important decisions we have made in cases during the year, from which councils and advisers can draw general lessons. During the year we also gave individual local authorities and other bodies ad hoc advice on administrative practice at their request. We sent out annual reviews to every council in the country. These summarise our experience of handling their complaints and may make suggestions for improvements where relevant. The reviews are published on our website. We published three issues of the electronic newsletter for local authorities—LGO Link—in 2009/10. These alert local authorities to changes in our processes, including the introduction of the 'Council First' changes; Government initiatives that have an impact on our work, such as *Making Experiences Count* (the new arrangements for dealing with complaints about health and adult social care); consultation with local authorities on changes that will affect them, such as the introduction of 'statements of reasons' on complaints; new publications, including our revised *Guidance on running a complaints system*; and information about our training courses for local authorities . . . We ran *Making Experiences Count* seminars in each office for complaints managers to discuss initial experiences of health and adult social care complaints arrangements and to help identify training needs. A seminar for advisers, organised with the Public Law Project and held jointly with the Housing Ombudsman, took place in April 2009 and another in March 2010.

Our programme of training in complaints handling and investigation for all levels of local authority staff continued, and we delivered 118 courses in 2009/10 against a target of 120 for the year. These continue to get excellent feedback—over 90 per cent of delegates were satisfied with all aspects of the training. The overall number included three open courses for groups of staff from smaller authorities held at our offices at Millbank Tower and at venues in Coventry and Leeds. All three courses were fully booked and 40 per cent of delegates were from district councils. We aim to run more regional courses in 2010/11 in different locations. Our new Effective Complaint Handling course in Adult Social Care proved very popular. We also offer customised courses to meet councils' specific requirements. We played an active part in the work of a number of groups and forums set up to review the mechanisms for dealing with complaints about councils and bodies covered by the LGO's extended jurisdiction.

■ QUESTION

How can we measure the ombudsmen's success in seeking to improve administration?

SECTION 6: OUTCOME OF INVESTIGATIONS AND REMEDIES

PARLIAMENTARY COMMISSIONER ACT 1967

10.—(1) In any case where the Commissioner conducts an investigation under this Act or decides not to conduct such an investigation, he shall send to the member of the House of Commons by whom the request for investigation was made (or if he is no longer a member of that House, to such member of that House as the Commissioner thinks appropriate) a report of the results of the investigation or, as the case may be, a statement of his reasons for not conducting an investigation.

(2) In any case where the Commissioner conducts an investigation under this Act, he shall also send a report of the results of the investigation to the principal officer of the department or authority concerned and to any other person who is alleged in the relevant complaint to have taken or authorised the action complained of.

(3) [see p. 681, *post*]

(4) The Commissioner shall annually lay before each House of Parliament a general report on the performance of his functions under this Act and may from time to time lay before each House of Parliament such other reports with respect to those functions as he thinks fit.

11.—(2) Information obtained by the Commissioner or his officers in the course of or for the purposes of an investigation under this Act shall not be disclosed except—

(a) for the purposes of the investigation and of any report to be made thereon under this Act;
(b) for the purposes of any proceedings for an offence under the Official Secrets Acts 1911 to 1939 alleged to have been committed in respect of information obtained by the Commissioner or any of his officers by virtue of this Act or for an offence of perjury alleged to have been committed in the course of an investigation under this Act or for the purposes of an inquiry with a view to the taking of such proceedings; or
(c) for the purposes of any proceedings under section 9 of this Act; and the Commissioner and his officers shall not be called upon to give evidence in any proceedings (other than such proceedings as aforesaid) of matters coming to his or their knowledge in the course of an investigation under this Act.

(3) A Minister of the Crown may give notice in writing to the Commissioner, with respect to any document or information specified in the notice, or any class of documents or information so specified, that in the opinion of the Minister the disclosure of that document or information, or of documents or information of that class, would be prejudicial to the safety of the State or otherwise contrary to the public interest; and where such a notice is given nothing in this Act shall be construed as authorising or requiring the Commissioner or any officer of the Commissioner to communicate to any person or for any purpose any document or information specified in the notice, or any document or information of a class so specified.

Local Government Act 1974

30 Reports on investigations

(1) If a Local Commissioner completes an investigation of a matter under this Part of this Act, he shall prepare a report of the results of the investigation and send a copy to each of the persons concerned (subject to subsection (1B)).

(1A) A Local Commissioner may include in a report on a matter under subsection (1) any recommendations that he could include in a further report on the matter by virtue of section 31(2A) to (is completed, the Local Commissioner decides—

(a) that he is satisfied with action which the authority concerned have taken or propose to take, and
(b) that it is not appropriate to prepare and send a copy of a report under subsection (1),

he may instead prepare a statement of his reasons for the decision and send a copy to each of the persons concerned.

(1C) If a Local Commissioner decides—

(a) not to investigate a matter, or
(b) to discontinue an investigation of a matter,

he shall prepare a statement of his reasons for the decision and send a copy to each of the persons concerned.

(1D) For the purposes of subsections (1) to (1C), the persons concerned are—

(a) the complainant (if any),
(b) any person who referred the matter under section 26C(2),
(c) the authority concerned, and
(d) any other authority or person who is alleged in the complaint, or who otherwise appears to the Local Commissioner, to have taken or authorised the action which is or would be the subject of the investigation.

Parliamentary & Health Service Ombudsman, *Making an Impact: Annual Report 2009–10*

HC 274 of 2009–10, pp. 48, 26

Figure 11: Top five government departments by number of complaints received (with agency breakdown)

Department for Work and Pensions	
Jobcentre Plus:	1,274
Child Support Agency	805
The Pension. Disability and Carers Service	475
Independent Case Examiner	230
Department for Work and Pensions	81
Medical Services ATOS Healthcare*	34
Debt Management Unit	30
Health and Safety Executive	26
Pensions Ombudsman	26
Independent Review Service for the Social Fund	9
Independent Living Funds	4
The Pensions Regulator	4
Health and Safety Commission	1
Pension Protection Fund	1
Department for Work and Pensions Total	3,000

HM/ Revenue & Customs	
HM Revenue & Customs	1,369
The Adjudicator's Office	323
Child Benefit Office	181
National Insurance Contributions Office	23
HM Revenue & Customs Total	1,896

Home Office	
UK Border Agency	688
Criminal Records Bureau	85
Home Office**	63
Identity and Passport Service	50
Security Industry Authority	44
Police (Victims' Code)	11
Independent Safeguarding Authority	6
Independent Complaints Mediator (Criminal Records Bureau)	3
National Policing Improvement Agency	1
Serious Organised Crime Agency	1
Home Office Total	952

Ministry of Justice	
HM Courts Service	275
Tribunals Service	135
Legal Services Commission	114
Information Commissioner	80
HM Prison Service	67
Land Registry	48
Criminal Injuries Compensation Authority	46
Office of the Public Guardian	44
Ministry of Justice	43
Prisons and Probation Ombudsman for England and Wales	27
Independent Complaints Reviewer (Land Registry)	17
Adjudicator to HM Land Registry	6
Official Solicitor	6
Legal Complaints Service	5
Parole Board	5
Crown Prosecution Service (Victims' Code)	4
Court Funds Office	3
Judicial Appointments and Conduct Ombudsman	2
National Probation Service (Victims' Code)	1
Legal Services Complaints Commissioner	1
National Archives	1
Ministry of Justice Total	931

Department for Transport	
Driver and Vehicle Licensing Agency	248
Driving Standards Agency	43
Highways Agency	27
Department for Transport	21
Vehicle and Operator Service Agency	11
Independent Complaints Assessor (Driver and Vehicle Licensing Agency)	2
Rail Accident Investigation Branch	1
Department for Transport Total	353

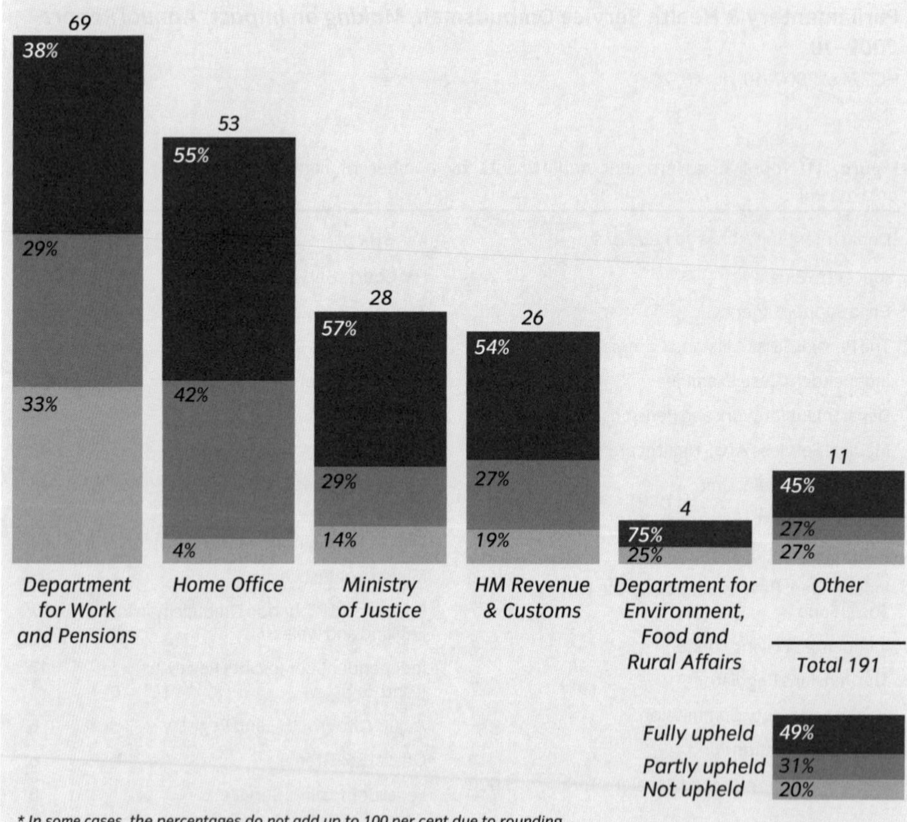

Figure 6: Top five government departments by number of complaints reports reported on*

Local Government Ombudsman, *Annual Report 09–10 Delivering Public Value* (2010), pp. 18, 20

Table 2 : Analysis of Outcome of Complaints 2009/10

Outcome	Number of complaints	Percentage of total (excluding those outside jurisdiction)
Local settlements	2,366	26.92
Maladministration causing injustice (issued report)	69	0.78
Maladministration, no injustice (issued report)	2	0.02
No maladministration (issued report)	3	0.03
No or insufficient evidence of maladministration (without report)	4,065	46.25
Ombudsman's discretion	2,284	26.00
Outside jurisdiction	1,520	
Total	10,309	

Table 3: Type of remedy or settlement obtained

Type of remedy/settlement	2007/08	2008/09	2009/10
Apology	815	640	585
Take action:			
New hearing/appeal	130	170	
Offer of new accommodation	34	24	15
Revise publication/published information	29	24	38
Consider others in similar situation	13	15	5
Make inspection and take appropriate action	106	99	57
Other	1,485	1,507	1,224
Review policies and/or procedures	309	272	220
Make payment:			
'Before and after' valuation	15	17	18
Other payment	1,812	1,577	1,379
Total number of remedies/settlements recorded*	4,748	4,345	3,764
Total number of complaints where a remedy/settlement was recorded	**3,057**	**2,857**	**2,435**

Some complaints have more than one remedy description recorded against them so the number of remedies recorded is greater than the number of complaints remedied

NOTE: The range of remedies offered by ombudsmen is much wider than could be obtained in the courts.

A: Compliance with ombudsmen's reports

Usually reports by the PO are accepted and the recommendations are to a greater or lesser extent implemented.

PARLIAMENTARY COMMISSIONER ACT 1967

10. (3) If, after conducting an investigation under this Act, it appears to the Commissioner that injustice has been caused to the person aggrieved in consequence of maladministration and that the injustice has not been, or will not be, remedied, he may, if he thinks fit, lay before each House of Parliament a special report upon the case.

There have been six reports produced under this power (see summary) with four of them published in the period 2005–09. In the Foreword to the 2003–04 Annual Report (HC 702 of 2003–04) the PO stated:

> ... there is a clear reluctance among some government departments and agencies to accept my findings and recommendations for redress. I will be looking for significant changes in mindset among such government bodies and, as a result, an improvement in their response in the coming year.

After the fourth one had been published in 2006, the second in consecutive years, the Public Administration Select Committee produced a report, *The Ombudsman in*

Question: the Ombudsman's report on pensions and its constitutional implications, (HC1081 of 2005–6). In its conclusions the select committee stated:

> **8.** It is not unprecedented for the Government to contest an Ombudsman's finding of maladministration. It is, however, unprecedented for there to be so many problems, in such a short space of time. Our scrutiny leads us to conclude that the fault lies with the Government, not the Ombudsman. (Paragraph 70)
>
> **9.** We share the Ombudsman's concern that the Government has been far too ready to dismiss her findings of maladministration. Our investigations have shown that these findings were sound. It would be extremely damaging if government became accustomed simply to reject findings of maladministration, especially if an investigation by this Committee proved there was indeed a case to answer. It would raise fundamental constitutional issues about the position of the Ombudsman and the relationship between Parliament and the Executive. (Paragraph 78)
>
> **10.** We trust that this Report will act as a warning to the Government. We will continue to monitor the Government's responses to the Parliamentary Commissioner's reports. If necessary we will seek a debate on the floor of the House, so that all Members can discuss these issues, and re-establish the Parliamentary Commissioner's role. The Parliamentary Commissioner is Parliament's Ombudsman: Government must respect her. (Paragraph 79)

Normal relations were restored but only for three years as two more s. 10(3) reports were published, the fifth and sixth, within seven months of each other in 2009. The response to every s. 10(3) report is that the select committee which oversees the PO produces a report. In all six cases the select committee, after conducting its own inquiry, has supported the PO and the political process has led to an outcome which has satisfied the PO. In the fifth case, however, *Equitable Life*, action has to be taken to implement the commitment given in the *Programme for Government* by the Coalition Government to provide more compensation. See the table summarizing the PO's s. 10(3) reports at pp. 683–684, *post*.

The trend in compliance has been different in LO cases. Historically, there had been difficulties and the Widdicombe Report (*The Conduct of Local Authority Business* Cmnd 9797, 1986) had suggested enacting provisions similar to those relating to the Commissioner for Complaints in Northern Ireland (see *post*). This recommendation was not accepted instead the Local Government Act 1974 was amended by the Local Government and Housing Act 1989, ss. 26 and 28, to provide that authorities must notify the Local Ombudsman of the action which they propose to take within three months from the date of an adverse report (Local Government Act 1974, s. 31(2), as amended). Similar time-limits apply in respect of the consideration of a further report (s. 31(2)–(2c)). If an authority proposes not to accept the recommendation of the LO in a further report, the report must generally be considered by the authority as a whole (s. 31A(1)). If, in considering the report, the authority take into account a report by a person or body with an interest in the LO's report, they must also take into account a report by a person or body without an interest in the report (s. 31A(4)). No member of the council is entitled to vote on any question with respect to a report or a further report in which he is named and criticized (s. 31A(5)). If the authority do not satisfy the LO with respect to a further report, he may require the authority to publish a statement, in a form agreed between the local authority and the Ombudsman, consisting of the details of the action recommended by the Local Ombudsman, such supporting material as he may require, and, if the authority so require, a statement of the reasons for non-compliance with the LO's recommendations. The statement must be published in two editions of a local newspaper within a fortnight, the first publication to be as soon as possible. If the authority do not arrange for publication, the LO may do so at their expense (s. 31(2D)–(2H)).

It would seem that the number of occasions in which the LO has been dissatisfied and required a statement to be published following a further report have reduced. The Annual Report until 2006–07 included a table on compliance with recommendations,

T. Buck, R. Kirkham, B. Thompson, *The Ombudsman Enterprise and Administrative Justice*
(2011), pp. 252–253

Appendix 7 Parliamentary Ombudsman's section 10(3) reports

Name/Issue/Year/Dept	Disputed PO Findings and/or Recommendations	Governmental Objections	Select Committee View	Outcome/Reason
Rochester Way, Road Administration of complensaion, 1978 Dept of Transport	Defective arrangements for publicizing details of compensation scheme led to applications being rejected as out of time	To make *ex gratia* payments would override the will of Parliament	The commitment to inform people about the compensation scheme was not met	Amendments made to the legislation authorizing payments for late claims
Channel Tunnel Rail Link, planning blight, 1994 Dept of Transport	There was exceptional uncertainty about an unusual project which gave rise to general blight but this caused exceptional hardship for some people	The project, the uncertainty and the hardship were not so exceptional as to override policy of not compensating for general blight	dept had not considered identifying those who were inequitably affected by rigid adherence to the letter of law	Ombudsman satisfied as government indicated it was prepared to discuss terms of compensation but nothing done until change of government in 1997
Wartime Detainees, Administration of Compensation, 2005 Ministry of Defence	Both the scheme's terms and its announcement were unclear; new criterion not reviewed to check for equal treatment; no information provided to applicants on clarification of criteria; no review undertaken	Challenged PO's decision to investigate new 'bloodlink' criterion given an unsuccessful judicial review; complainant's case should not have been accepted	in preparing for select committee appearance, new evidence found suggesting unequal treatment; committee hoped MOD would pay	Ombudsman satisfied following the subsequent ministerial statement
Occupational Pensions, Compensation for poor regulation, 2006 Dept for Work and Pensions, Treasury, National Insurance Contributions Office (HMRC), Occupational Pensions Regulatory Authority	Misleading information on degree of protection; maladministration in not following advice on disclosing risks; maladmin in changing Minimum Funding Requirement and so contributed to losses in winding-up process	Rejected findings which were not substantiated; leaflets not comprehensive guide and no causal link to loss in the winding-up of companies	Agreed that maladmin had occurred, govt should engage properly with PO's recommendations rather than assuming too large a burden on the public purse	Ombudsman satisfied as Government actuary department (GAD) review found ways to improve Financial Assistance Scheme

(Continued)

Appendix 7 Continued

Name/Issue/Year/Dept	Disputed PO Findings and/or Recommendations	Governmental Objections	Select Committee View	Outcome/Reason
Equitable Life, Compensation for poor regulation, 2009 HM Treasury	PO found a total of 10 instances of maladmin by DTI, GAD, FSA and recommended apology and compensation scheme. In s.10(3) report the terms of reference for the judge's advice will restrict those eligible for compensation and the likely amount will not be adequate	Accepted most findings, not accepting proposed compensation but asking judge to advise on a narrower *ex gratia* scheme for those who had suffered disproportionate impact	Select Committee supported PO's initial report before govt response report; their reaction to it made before s.10(3) report; disliked disproportionate impact test, not simple or quick	Ombudsman satisfied as following 2010 election new coalition proposed better terms
Single Payments Scheme and Rural Land Register, 2009 Department for Environment, Food and Rural Affairs (Defra)	Maladmin by not determining issues in stipulated period; did not react appropriately following indications of problems which led to delay and these two cases were representative, so apply recommendations to 22 others similarly placed	Dept concerned that indications on targets for decisions had become legitimate expectations; compensation had been paid, which was adequate and to provide the recommended compensation for other cases was a distraction	Following its evidence session with permanent secretary, the chair wrote to minister advising the dept had misunderstood basis for PO's decisions on targets; compensation for other 22 cases within Treasury guidance	Ombudsman satisfied as minister completely accepted recommendations following select committee chair's letter

Note: * See also Appendix 1, col. 2, which lists the principal Acts in each jurisdiction showing the number of cases in which reports recommending remedies for injustice had resulted in an outcome unsatisfactory to the LO. Perhaps it can be inferred from t the absence of this table on compliance from the annual report indicates that it is no longer a problem.

Where the Commissioner for Complaints in Northern Ireland makes a finding that an individual has sustained injustice in consequence of maladministration, the individual may apply to the county court, and the court may award 'such damages as the court may think just in all the circumstances to compensate' the applicant for loss or injury suffered on account of (a) expenses reasonably incurred, and (b) lost opportunity of acquiring benefit (Commissioner for Complaints Order (Northern Ireland) 1996, art. 16(2)). If it appears to the court that justice can only be done by ordering that body to take or refrain from taking some action, then the court may, if satisfied that in all the circumstances it is reasonable so to do, grant a mandatory or other injunction (art. 16(5)). In addition, where maladministration coupled with injustice has been found, and it appears to the Commissioner for Complaints that the body concerned has previously engaged in conduct of the same kind and is likely to continue to engage in future in conduct of the type which he has condemned, he may request the Attorney-General to apply to the High Court for appropriate relief, such as an injunction to restrain the continuation of the maladministration (art. 17). From 1978–88 there were on average three applications each year to the county court by successful complainants. The Attorney-General has, however, never been asked to make an application (see the *JUSTICE–All Souls Report on Administrative Law* (1988), pp. 123–125, for a discussion of the role of the Commissioner for Complaints in Northern Ireland and C. White (1994) 45 *NILQ* 395 on the Northern Ireland enforcement provision).

No action has been brought by a dissatisfied claimant in 26 years and in the consultation paper on proposed legislation, issued by a committee of the Northern Ireland Assembly in September 2010, it is asked if this 'enforcement provision' should be retained.

Both the Scottish Public Services Ombudsman Act 2002 and the Public Services Ombudsman (Wales) Act 2005 continue the tradition of non-binding investigation reports, and allow the Ombudsmen to issue special reports if dissatisfied with the remedy taken or proposed. During the passage of the Welsh statute there was concern about non-compliance which led to an amendment which became s. 20. This provision would allow the Ombudsman to issue a certificate to the High Court if of the view that a listed authority had without lawful excuse wilfully disregarded a report which upheld a complaint. This provision has not been brought into force by the commencement order made by the National Assembly for Wales (SI 2005 No. 2800 (W.119)).

B: Findings and recommendations

Although the fourth and fifth cases involving s. 10(3) reports (*Occupational Pensions* and *Equitable Life*) were settled in the political arena, the complainants sought judicial review of the government's rejection of the PO's reports. In the *Occupational Pensions* case *R (Bradley)* v *Secretary of State for Work & Pensions* it was conceded that recommendations for remedy could not be binding upon the government. However, in the Administrative Court Bean J held that it was irrational for the Minister to reject the first finding of maladministration ([2007] EWHC 242 (Admin) at [66]). On appeal the Court of Appeal accepted ([2008] EWCA Civ 36 at [72]) the argument that:

> The question is not whether the defendant himself considers that there was maladministration, but whether in the circumstances his rejection of the ombudsman's finding to this effect is based on cogent reasons

The Court of Appeal held that the position in relation to findings was different for the LO whose findings would be binding unless successfully challenged in a judicial review.

The reason for the distinction was the difference between the ombudsmen's respective statutes, the Parliamentary Commissioner Act 1967 and the Local Government Act 1974 ([2008] EWCA Civ 36 at [40]):

> The purpose for which the legislation was introduced was to give Members of Parliament—in particular, Members of the House of Commons—access to the services of an independent and authoritative investigator as "a better instrument which they can use to protect the citizen".

In *R (Equitable Members Action Group)* v *HM Treasury* [2009] EWHC 2495 (Admin), the Administrative Court held that no cogent reasons had been put forward to reject some of the PO's findings of maladministration and injustice, but that there were cogent reasons for departing from other findings, and reaffirmed that the enforcement of the PO's recommendations was a matter for Parliament.

The requirement of cogent reasons for a Minister to reject the PO's finding of maladministration is an extension of the irrationality ground of judicial review. It has been attacked as inappropriate by J. Varuhas, 'Governmental rejections of ombudsman findings: what role for the courts?' (2009) 72 *Modern Law Review* 102, and T. Endicott, *Administrative Law* (2009), pp. 495–496 and has been defended by R. Kirkham, T. Buck and B. Thompson, *The Ombudsman Enterprise and Administrative Justice* (2011), pp. 217–219.

The Law Commission has considered ombudsmen findings and recommendations, proposing that these terms should be used and that findings should be statutorily defined. They agree that enforcing recommendations should be part of the political process.

Law Commission, Public Services *Ombudsmen, A Consultation Paper*

(2010) Law Com CP 196, paras 6.96 -6.107

> 6.96 Concerning findings, however, we think that the position is slightly different. The finding of maladministration should be, primarily, the role of ombudsmen and a judgment that Parliament has entrusted to them through their governing statutes. Obviously, whatever the position, a decision which is illegal in administrative law terms would be susceptible to judicial review. However, this is different from the current situation. The mere necessity to find "cogent reasons" before being able to reject the findings of the ombudsmen does not really protect the core competence of the Parliamentary Commissioner.
>
> 6.97 We suggest that *Bradley* and *Equitable Members Action Group* did not go far enough in respect of this matter. The argument in both *Bradley* and *Equitable Members Action Group* was that this would be placed better in terms of the relationship that the Parliamentary Commissioner has with Parliament. However, past practice shows that it is in fact quite likely that the Government will be able to reject the Parliamentary Commissioner's finding of maladministration and that Parliament will be unable to force the Government, which through its majority effectively controls the House of Commons, to accept the ombudsman's view.
>
> 6.98 In all of the examples given above, where the findings were not accepted the involvement of the Select Committee (now the Public Administration Select Committee), though supportive, did not change the position of the Government. *Court Line* gives probably the starkest example of how the relationship plays out, as this led to a vote in the House of Commons. The Commons divided on party lines and the then Government won.
>
> 6.99 The effect of the current relationship is that the Government can be the judge in its own cause, which—it seems to us—goes against the allocation of competences inherent in the Parliamentary Commissioner Act 1967.
>
> 6.100 We accept that in the cases considered in this Part, the Government went on to take some form of remedial action, as happened with *Sachsenhausen*, *Court Line* and *Barlow Clowes*, as well as the most recent cases—*Occupational Pensions* and *Equitable Life*. In the case of the latter, the Coalition Agreement of 2010 states that the Government will pay compensation.

6.101 In the next Part we detail how recent developments within the House of Commons may have strengthened the position of the Select Committee—if the Select Committee supports the ombudsman. However, these developments do not change our initial view that a finding of maladministration is primarily the province of the relevant ombudsman, including the Parliamentary Commissioner, and that this should be protected.

6.102 Consequently, our provisional conclusion is that the current case law does not go far enough to protect the findings of the Parliamentary Commissioner. 6.103 We prefer the position in *ex parte Eastleigh*, which essentially protects the preserve of the ombudsman unless illegality in an administrative law sense can be shown—which would include coming to a conclusion that no rational ombudsman could come to.

6.104 Commenting on the effect that *Bradley* may have on the other ombudsmen, Kirkham and others thought it likely that the courts would follow the same line for the Health Service Ombudsman and the Public Services Ombudsman for Wales. This was on the basis of their having a relationship with an elected body.

6.105 In respect of the Housing Ombudsman, its relationship with members of an approved scheme is very different to those that the other ombudsmen have with the bodies within their jurisdiction. There is also no formal relationship between the Housing Ombudsman and an elected body. It is, therefore, impossible to predict what would develop in the future as to the status of its determinations.

6.106 We think that this could lead, potentially, to courts adopting a position on findings that we do not favour. Therefore, we suggest that the situation in relation to these public services ombudsmen should also be clarified in statutory provisions.

6.107 We provisionally propose that a public body should only be able to reject the findings in a report of a public services ombudsman following the successful judicial review of that report.

■ QUESTION

Do you agree with the Law Commission's proposals that (a) ombudsmen's findings of maladministration and injustice should be binding unless successfully challenged by way of judicial review, and (b) that the enforcement of recommendations for remedying injustice should be confined to the political arena?

SECTION 7: ARRANGEMENTS FOR DISSATISIFIED COMPLAINANTS

The ombudsmen's legislation does not provide arrangements for complainants who are dissatisfied with the treatment of their complaints. The ombudsmen have developed a non-statutory process.

Parliamentary & Health Service Ombudsman, *Making an Impact: Annual Report 2009–10*

HC 274 of 2009–10, p. 35

Complaints about us

Anyone who is unhappy with a decision made by us or with the service they have received from us can ask for a review under our Complaints About Us policy. Such reviews are undertaken by a separate Review Team and are signed off by a senior member of staff.

We take the complaints we receive very seriously and use learning from them to develop and improve the service we provide. Complaints not only help us identify individual training needs but can also flag up organisational issues and concerns we may need to address. For example, the complaints we received about delays in our handling of cases has led us to reduce the turnaround time for obtaining papers from bodies being complained about, increase the number of caseworkers we have and raise our operational targets for 2010-11.

During 2009-10:

- We received 1,208 new complaints about us
- We resolved 1,280 complaints about us

Of the 1,280 reviews completed during 2009-10:

- 1,115 were about our handling of enquiries
- 88 were about health investigations
- 42 were about parliamentary investigations
- 35 were about our responses to requests for information under the Freedom of Information Act 2000 or Data Protection Act 1998

Of these, 12 per cent were either fully or partly upheld. The largest proportion of upheld complaints related to complaints about our service, particularly delays in the handling of cases or issues relating to our communication with complainants.

Judicial review

Judicial review is the procedure through which a person can challenge the lawfulness of a decision or action (or failure to act) taken by a public body by making an application to the High Court. Our decisions can be subject to judicial review. There were nine applications for judicial review of our decisions (seven in 2008-09) and one county court claim (none in 2008–09). Of the judicial review applications, seven were initially refused permission to proceed and we are awaiting the court's initial decision on the other two. Of the seven refused permission, all renewed their application and five were then refused again; one of those five has now been granted a hearing in the Court of Appeal. We are awaiting a decision on the other two. The county court claim was settled.

Local Government Ombudsman, *Annual Report 09–10 Delivering Public Value*

(2010), p.22

Table 4 : Customer complaints in 2008/09–2009/10

	2008/09	2009/10
Review request: decision confirmed	1,108	977
Review request: decision correct, but wrongly justified	14	3
Review request: decision correct, but further explanation provided	47	30
Review request: investigation relaunched because of new information	50	27
Review request: investigation relaunched because of procedural error	23	20
Non-substantive response sent*	22	23
Service complaint: not upheld	24	37
Service complaint: upheld in part or in full	34	18
Total	**1,322**	**1,135**

* These are cases were the complaint did not go through the review process, mostly because the review was not requested quickly enough (within three months of the decision on the case).

We measure the level of complaints about us, dealt with in accordance with our complaints procedure. Customer complaints cover both cases where complainants question our decisions on local authority complaints we have dealt with (review requests) and complaints about our staff or service. Table 4 above shows a breakdown of these complaints. Cases questioning our decisions on complaints are reviewed by a senior member of staff not previously involved in the case to see if the concerns are justified. In 2009/10, 20 review requests were upheld. We aim that this figure should be less than 1 per cent of all decisions taken, excluding decisions on premature complaints. This year the percentage is 0.2 per cent. We analyse all those service complaints that are upheld to learn lessons for improvement in our performance. We recognise that there could be errors that do not get picked up because the complainant does not request a review of our decision, so we also check a sample of files from each investigator as part of our quality control process. We pass on any learning points from the file examination back to our staff—both individually and where there are general lessons to use them in staff workshops and written guidance.

We aim to ensure all our offices have a common and proactive approach to the identification of maladministration arising from councils' failures relating to their equalities duties and their responsibilities under the Human Rights Act. We are continuing to consider these matters on a case by case basis; we await developments from the new Equalities and Human Rights Commission, and the new Government, before developing further our staff guidance and training in this area.

The ultimate challenge to the Ombudsmen's decisions is judicial review. Our aim is that no judicial reviews of our decisions are successful. There are two stages in the judicial review process. The applicant has to apply for permission for judicial review of a decision and, only if permission is granted, is there a second stage hearing in the Administrative Court. In 2009/10 there were 13 applications for permission to apply for judicial review. Eight applications were refused by the court; one application was granted permission to apply for judicial review but was subsequently withdrawn; and four are awaiting the court's decision. (In 2008/09 there were nine applications for permission to apply for judicial review of which seven were refused by the court and two were withdrawn.)

NOTE: Most judicial reviews against the ombudsmen are unsuccessful but one complainant was successful in three successive judicial reviews as first the initial PO report was challenged and then the subsequent reconsiderations were found to be flawed.

■ QUESTION

Is it appropriate that the ombudsmen should reconsider dissatisfied complainants' cases with judicial review as the final possibility for challenge?

13

Statutory Tribunals

OVERVIEW

In this chapter we consider the rationale for giving the task of resolving disputes to statutory tribunals rather than courts, the new structure and organization for most tribunals, how they conduct dispute resolution and the arrangements for oversight of not only tribunals, but the administrative justice system.

SECTION 1: INTRODUCTION: THE RATIONALE FOR TRIBUNALS

Concern about the growth of tribunals and their functions and procedures prompted the formation of the Committee on Administrative Tribunals and Inquiries in 1955. The Committee reported in 1957, and its recommendations led to important reforms in the Tribunal and Inquiries Act 1958 and there were amendments to this framework in the Tribunals and Inquiries Act 1971 and the Tribunals and Inquiries Act 1992. The Committee addressed the question of the reasons why tribunals are created.

Report of the Committee on Administrative Tribunals and Enquiries

Cmnd 218 (1957), paras 20–22, 26–27, 29–32

20. It is noteworthy that Parliament, having decided that the decisions with which we are concerned should not be remitted to the ordinary courts, should also have decided that they should not be left to be reached in the normal course of administration. Parliament has considered it essential to lay down special procedures for them.

Good administration

21. This must have been to promote good administration. Administration must not only be efficient in the sense that the objectives of policy are securely attained without delay. It must also satisfy the general body of citizens that it is proceeding with reasonable regard to the balance between the public interest which it promotes and the private interest which it disturbs. Parliament has, we infer, intended in relation to the subject-matter of our terms of reference that the further decisions or, as they may rightly be termed in this context, adjudications must be acceptable as having been properly made.

22. It is natural that Parliament should have taken this view of what constitutes good administration. In this country government rests fundamentally upon the consent of the governed. The general acceptability of these adjudications is one of the vital elements in sustaining that consent.

...

26. At this stage another question naturally arises. On what principle has it been decided that some adjudications should be made by tribunals and some by Ministers? If from a study of the history of the subject we could discover such a principle, we should have a criterion which would be a guide for any future allocation of these decisions between tribunals and Ministers.

27. The search for this principle has usually involved the application of one or both notions, each with its antithesis. Both notions are famous and have long histories. They are the notion of what is judicial, its antithesis being what is administrative, and the notion of what is according to the rule of law, its antithesis being what is arbitrary.

...

29. The rule of law stands for the view that decisions should be made by the application of known principles or laws. In general such decisions will be predictable, and the citizen will know where he is. On the other hand there is what is arbitrary. A decision may be without principle, without any rules. It is therefore unpredictable, the antithesis of a decision taken in accordance with the rule of law.

30. Nothing that we say diminishes the importance of these pairs of antitheses. But it must be confessed that neither pair yields a valid principle on which one can decide whether the duty of making a certain decision should be laid upon a tribunal or upon a Minister or whether the existing allocation of decisions between tribunals and Ministers is appropriate. But even if there is no such principle and we cannot explain all the facts, we can at least start with them. An empirical approach may be the most useful.

31. Starting with the facts, we observe that the methods of adjudication by tribunals are in general not the same as those of adjudication by Ministers. All or nearly all tribunals apply rules. No ministerial decision of the kind denoted by the second part of our terms of reference is reached in this way. Many matters remitted to tribunals and Ministers appear to have, as it were, a natural affinity with one or other method of adjudication. Sometimes the policy of the legislation can be embodied in a system of detailed regulations. Particular decisions cannot, single case by single case, alter the Minister's policy. Where this is so, it is natural to entrust the decisions to a tribunal, if not to the courts. On the other hand it is sometimes desirable to preserve flexibility of decision in the pursuance of public policy. Then a wise expediency is the proper basis of right adjudication, and the decision must be left with a Minister.

32. But in other instances there seems to be no such natural affinity. For example, there seems to be no natural affinity which makes it clearly appropriate for appeals in goods vehicles cases to be decided by the Transport Tribunal when appeals in a number of road passenger cases are decided by the Minister.

NOTE: The authors of the report have candidly confessed that the principles they cite do not yield an explanation for why a particular decision should be laid upon a tribunal rather than upon a Minister. Other factors which may come into play are explored by Keith Hendry in the following article.

K. H. Hendry, 'The Tasks of Tribunals: Some Thoughts'

(1982) 1 *Civil Justice Quarterly* 253, 256–259

Tribunals as components of administration schemes

A peremptory glance at the governmental picture in a modern welfare state such as the United Kingdom, will show a multiplicity of tribunals each operating within the bounds of a confined jurisdiction and each directed toward disposing of claims and arguments arising out of a particular statutory scheme. So, for example, Supplementary Benefits Appeal Tribunals constituted under Schedule 4 of the Supplementary Benefits Act 1976 deal with the many disputes that arise from the grant or withholding of supplementary benefit; similarly under section 40 of the Finance Act 1972 (as amended) Value Added Tax Tribunals hear disagreements between tax officials and those liable to pay VAT. Many more examples could be given.

Parliament's enactment of various schemes and the inclusion within these schemes of specialist tribunals recognises firstly the social need for that scheme and secondly a social need for having machinery to dispose of disputes arising under that scheme. It is insufficiently stressed that as such tribunals have a task as essential parts of the machinery of administrative government.

So we see in particular the Council on Tribunals stressing that 'tribunals are bodies set up to *adjudicate* between the State and the individual . . .' with little mention of a tribunal's role in the administrative field. This is not to belittle their role as adjudicatory machinery, but at the same time their responsibilities to their schemes will be vitally important to administration. To take an example: under section 3 of the Mental Health Act 1959, 14 Mental Health Review Tribunals are constituted. They disposed of 696 cases in 1978. The gravity of these tribunals should not be underestimated—they are empowered to determine whether a patient shall be compulsorily detained, and so lose his personal liberty. As such they are vital to the administration of a particular social necessity recognised by legislation.

The Franks Report expressly recognises this factor, albeit in a somewhat guarded way. Having noted that 'Parliament' decided that certain decisions should not be dealt with by the ordinary courts, nor in the normal course of administration, the Report sees tribunals existing so as to 'promote good administration,' that is 'efficient in the sense that the objectives of policy are securely attained without delay,' but at the same time 'with reasonable regard to the balance between the public interest... and the private interest' '... adjudications must be acceptable as having been properly made.' Already we can see the emergence of the Franks bias, carried on today by its offspring, the Council on Tribunals, namely that what was important was the *correctness* of administration to the detriment of *administration* itself. Had more attention been paid to this task of tribunals one might have seen a greater recognition of its central importance and a consequent appreciation of tribunals as instruments of government. Having devised special procedures as essential elements of administration it can be inferred that tribunals have two further linked, but not quite so obvious, tasks. These are to avoid Ministerial Responsibility and to ease the workload of Governmental Departments.

Under the United Kingdom constitution, a Minister is primarily responsible to Parliament for his and his department's activities. Ultimately he is responsible to public opinion. Under a new legislative scheme it is a matter of choice as to whether decisions will be left to the Minister personally or to his Department. In both cases he remains responsible. However, if a dispute is to be decided outside the Department, for present purposes by a tribunal, the Minister will be able to disclaim responsibility for it. Furthermore, it will not be possible to bring political pressure to bear in order to affect that decision. The creation of a tribunal may therefore have as one of its purposes the evasion of Ministerial responsibility and the easing of Departmental workloads. So under section 12 of the Immigration Act 1971, one sees a two-tier appeal system; at first instance, adjudicators, and above them Immigration Tribunals. The volume of work done by these tribunals indicates the extent to which particularly the Home Office's workload is eased, and how a very politically sensitive decision is hived off to tribunals.

The decision to retain a decision within Departmental/Ministerial hands or to turn it over to a tribunal will, of course, be motivated by a number of factors: a 1980 Council on Tribunals Special Report felt that 'Parliament's' selection of subjects to be referred to tribunals does not form a regular pattern although basic guidelines and various factors included the nature of the decision, historical accidents, Departmental preferences and political consideration. The last-mentioned consideration could operate in both ways—one could give a matter which is potentially sensitive to a tribunal to desensitise it (the system of Immigration Tribunals is an example), or alternatively retain it for that reason within Departmental/Ministerial hands. Other factors would include the likely number of disputes, national interest, the level of discretion involved and so on, but one is forced to agree with the Council on Tribunals that there is no application of a set of coherent principles.

It seems, therefore, that the use of tribunals is a convenient means for affording Ministers immunity from responsibility to Parliament and public opinion for certain kinds of decision. It might even be argued that it is an aspect of 'good administration' for Departments to be denied and/or relieved of certain kinds of decisions which could expose them to pressures of many kinds—not least political.

The Franks Committee stressed that tribunals were not to be seen as 'appendages of Government Departments'...'Parliament has deliberately provided for a decision outside and independent of the Department concerned'...'the intention of Parliament to provide for the independence of tribunals is clear and unmistakable.' With respect, there seems to be a rather large degree of unadulterated constitutional fiction here. John Griffith argues strongly that it is completely wrong to refer to some theoretic notion of Parliamentary intention; tribunals he says are instituted in reality by the Government of the day and in effect it is the relevant Department which will make the rules. The Council on Tribunals expressly cited Departmental preferences as one of the factors relevant to the creation of a tribunal. In their Annual Report for 1975–76 the Council states specifically that the detailed arrangements for tribunals remains the responsibility of Departments. To say, therefore, that tribunals are created to ensure that decisions should be made independently of Departments is simply not valid. Griffith suggests that Departments simply do not want to be bothered with the sorts of decisions tribunals will make: the policy is settled; it only has to be administered and disputes sorted out.

I introduce all this merely to stress the important role of tribunals as rudimentary but nevertheless vital components of administration. Writers today still insist on taking issue with the term '*administrative* tribunals' as giving too much emphasis to the administrative associations that tribunals have: ever since Franks the 'machinery for adjudication' theme has been predominant. In particular the Council of

Tribunals has seen its most important contribution as being 'our constant effort to translate the general ideals of the Franks Committee into workable codes of principle and practice...' As I have suggested it is my view that the Franks Report seriously underplayed the task of tribunals to be instruments of their respective administrative schemes. Be that as it may the Council on Tribunals continues the ideals of Franks with some zeal despite the fact that the Tribunals and Enquiries Act simply asks that they keep under review the constitution and working of Schedule 1 tribunals, report thereon and consider and report on matters as may be referred to them in respect of any tribunals other than courts of law. Is there not here some leeway for a more expansive notion of what tribunals are supposed to be doing?

NOTES

1. On the role of the Council on Tribunals and its successor, see p. 721, *post*.
2. A controversial example of apparent governmental disenchantment with a tribunal arose in the field of social security. Until 1986 there was an appeal from all claims concerning supplementary benefit, a means-tested benefit available to unemployed persons on low incomes. Such appeals were made to Supplementary Benefit Appeal Tribunals until 1984, when tribunals concerned with social security benefits were re-organized, and thereafter to Social Security Appeal Tribunals (SSATs). In 1986 changes were made under which supplementary benefit was replaced by income support, and a Social Fund was established to consider claims for specific items, such as furniture and clothing. Prior to this such claims had been made under the Single Payments regulations and appeals concerning single payments were dealt with by SSATs. The amended scheme did not, however, provide for any appeal from the Social Fund to an independent tribunal.

   The reasoning of the Government was explained in the White Paper on *The Reform of Social Security*, Cmnd 9518 (1985), paras 2.107–2.112.

The Reform of Social Security

Cmnd 9518 (1985), paras 2.107–2.112

How the social fund will be run

2.107 The fund will be run from DHSS local offices by a group of specialist officers. Special expertise will be needed, based on specific training in relevant skills, such as interviewing, counselling, and knowledge of help available from other sources. Decision-making will rest more on casework, liaison with other bodies and discussion with claimants. There will need to be clear links with the work of social service and health professionals who may also be involved in helping the same person. The views of outside professionals may have a part to play in helping officers reach judgments on individual cases.

2.108 Such expertise is to an extent already possessed by special case officers who since 1980 have had a remit to help claimants whose cases present special difficulty. Special case officers' concerns include: claimants with difficulties in adjusting to major changes in their circumstances (such as marital breakdown or discharge after a long stay in hospital); cases where there are doubts about claimants' ability to care for themselves or their children; those who have problems in managing essential living expenses; and others whose characteristics may create tension in dealing with staff. The Government believe it is right to develop existing good practice in this area and to expand the responsibilities of special case officers.

2.109 Specialist staff will exercise their judgment in reaching decisions on individual cases. The basis of deciding social fund payments is rather different from traditional benefit decision-making. There is widespread recognition that the present adjudication arrangements for handling special needs have not worked satisfactorily. There is also widespread agreement that, in handling the special difficulties of a minority of claimants, the scheme needs a degree of flexibility that is only possible with discretion.

2.110 The Government recognise that people who have asked for help with particular pressures should have an effective means of questioning the outcome. In all organisations, management has the first responsibility to see that services are well handled. This basic principle applies just as much to the administration of benefits as it does to other areas. It is however clear that the present appeal arrangements in special needs areas can have a sledgehammer effect. The full weight of legal consideration can be brought to bear on matters which may involve small sums of money for particular items with considerable delays between initial decision and formal review. We do not believe that the present system of appeals has best served the claimant's prime interest of a quick and effective reconsideration of decisions. The result is too slow, too cumbersome, and too inflexible.

2.111 The first safeguard for claimants under the new arrangements will be a professional approach to the administration of the social fund. That is the reason for using specialist officers. Reviews which turn on judgment in difficult individual circumstances are best handled as near to the point of decision as possible. The further the review gets from the initial judgment both in terms of formality and time, the less equipped the reviewing authority is to judge whether the outcome is sensible. The Government therefore intend to provide for review by management as near as possible to where responsibility for the original decision rests. Just as social service and health care decisions are best taken locally by those directly responsible, so should the social fund be seen as an important responsibility of those administering it in local offices. The arrangements proposed by the Government involve judgment—local people are best placed to make that judgment.

2.112 The fund will work successfully only if there is a clear limit to its role; that is, if it concentrates on the special needs of a limited number of claimants. The fund will have a fixed annual budget. Some form of budgeting is the reality in most areas of social provision. The Government do not consider that this specialist part of the new arrangements should be any different.

NOTE: In the absence of a right of appeal, judicial review proceedings have been used to challenge the operation of the Social Fund (see, e.g. *R* v *Secretary of State for Social Services, ex parte Stitt, The Times*, 5 July 1990, and the study by M. Sunkin and K. Pick, 'The Changing Impact of Judicial Review: The Independent Review Service of the Social Fund' [2001] *PL* 736).

■ QUESTION

Does either the Franks Report or Hendry's article provide an explanation for these developments?

NOTES

1. The removal of the right of appeal was criticized by the Council on Tribunals (see p. 721, *post*, for its role and subsequent developments).
2. The Franks Report referred to the natural affinity between, on the one hand, cases where the policy of legislation can be set out in detailed regulations and adjudication by tribunals and, on the other hand, cases where it is necessary to preserve flexibility in the pursuance of policy and ministerial decision-making. There are, however, tribunals which operate largely for the purposes of developing and applying policy (see, for example, the Independent Television Commission and the Competition Commission). This has led some commentators to draw a distinction between court-substitute and policy-oriented tribunals (on this distinction see further, B. Abel-Smith and R. Stevens, *In Search of Justice* (1968), pp. 20–21 and J. A. Farmer, *Tribunals and Government* (1974), Chapter 8).
3. The extracts from the Franks Report at pp. 690–691 have been concerned with the choice between providing an appeal to a Minister and providing an appeal to a tribunal. Assuming, then, that a decision has been made to establish a form of adjudication independently of the Department, what explains the decision to establish a tribunal rather than provide a statutory right of appeal to the courts?

Report of the Committee on Administrative Tribunals and Enquiries

Cmnd 218 (1957), paras 38–39

The choice between tribunals and courts of law

38. We agree with the Donoughmore Committee that tribunals have certain characteristics which often give them advantages over the courts. These are cheapness, accessibility, freedom from technicality, expedition and expert knowledge of their particular subject... But as a matter of general principle we are firmly of the opinion that a decision should be entrusted to a court rather than to a tribunal in the absence of special considerations which make a tribunal more suitable.

39. Moreover, if all decisions arising from new legislation were automatically vested in the ordinary courts the judiciary would by now have been grossly overburdened...We agree with the Permanent Secretary to the Lord Chancellor that any wholesale transfer to the courts of the work of tribunals would be undesirable.

Tribunals for Users: One System, One Service

The Stationery Office (2001), paras 1.11–13

Tribunals or courts

1.10 It is important to be clear what work should be done by tribunals, rather than by courts. Franks did not consider in detail what principles should guide the allocation of cases to tribunals, accepting that the already large number of cases decided by tribunals in 1957 made the amalgamation of tribunals and courts impracticable. As the areas in which some kind of appeal is required proliferate, Parliament, policymakers and users should have principles to guide that allocation. We suggest that there should be three tests of whether tribunals rather than courts should decide cases.

Participation

1.11 First, the widest common theme in current tribunals is the aim that users should be able to prepare and present their own cases effectively, if helped by good-quality, imaginatively presented information, and by expert procedural help from tribunal staff and substantive assistance from advice services. We think the element of direct participation is particularly important in the field of disputes between the citizen and the state.... The use of tribunals to decide disputes should be considered when the factual and legal issues raised by the majority of cases to be brought under proposed legislation are unlikely to be so complex as to prevent users from preparing their own cases and presenting them to the tribunal themselves, if properly helped.

The need for special expertise

1.12 Where the civil courts require expert opinion on the facts of the case, they generally rely on the evidence produced by the parties—increasingly jointly—or on a court-appointed assessor. Tribunals offer a different opportunity, by permitting decisions to be reached by a panel of people with a range of qualifications and expertise. A larger decision-taking body is obviously likely to be more expensive. But users clearly feel that the greater expertise makes for better decisions. They also say that having more members, and non-lawyers, on the panel makes it easier for at least some users to present their cases. The second reason why cases should be considered for allocation to a tribunal is if expertise, or accessibility to users, is a major issue in the resolution of the relevant disputes.

Expertise in administrative law

1.13 Thirdly, tribunals can be particularly effective in dealing with the mixture of fact and law often required to consider decisions taken by administrative or regulatory authorities. Our recommendations for a more coherent system will increase that effectiveness. Where any legislation establishes a statutory scheme involving decisions by an arm of government, the responsible minister should explicitly consider whether a right of appeal is required, on the basis that there should be strong specific arguments if an appeal route is not to be created, and that a tribunal route, rather than redress in the courts, should be the normal option in the interests of accessibility. It should not be regarded as satisfactory to leave judicial review as the citizen's only recourse, since that is expensive and difficult for the unassisted.

NOTE: The Donoughmore Committee produced a *Report on Ministers' Powers*, Cmd 4060 in 1932 which concerned delegated legislation and tribunals and inquiries.

■ QUESTIONS

1. Are the two reports consistent with each other? Is the objective of not overburdening the judiciary a special consideration in favour of establishing a tribunal?
2. What do these passages indicate about the desirable qualities of tribunals and, in particular, how those qualities should differ from those of the courts? See further, at pp. 709–715, *post*.

SECTION 2: THE STRUCTURE AND ORGANIZATION OF TRIBUNALS

Tribunals were now well established but their proliferation caused problems. In May 2000 a former Lord Justice of Appeal Sir Andrew Leggatt was commissioned to chair a review of tribunals. The terms of reference required the review 'to look at the administrative justice system as a whole: its coherence, its accessibility, its organisation...'. Their report *Tribunals for Users: One System, One Service* was published in 2001 along with a consultation paper by the Lord Chancellor's Department (LCD, now the Ministry of Justice). As the title of the report suggests, the review's recommendations proposed bringing the various tribunals together, to be supported administratively by an executive agency and for judicial leadership to be provided by a Senior President of Tribunals, who would be assisted by presidents responsible for various tribunals grouped into nine divisions. The benefits to users would be a clearly independent and more efficient tribunals system which was more focused on the users' needs with better information, advice and support. The hotchpotch of appeal and review routes would be streamlined to an appellate tribunal.

The Government accepted the main thrust of the Leggatt recommendations and in a White Paper *Transforming Public Services: Complaints, Redress and Tribunals*, Cm 6243 (July 2004) expanded its coverage beyond tribunals to the whole of administrative justice. A graduated programme of incorporating tribunals into the Tribunals Service was begun. It was formally launched in 2006 and did not require legislation; however, statutory authority was needed to create a two-tier structure with judicial leadership and the rationalization of procedure and onward appeals and judicial review.

A: The two-tier structure

TRIBUNALS, COURTS AND ENFORCEMENT ACT 2007

3 The First-tier Tribunal and the Upper Tribunal

(1) There is to be a tribunal, known as the First-tier Tribunal, for the purpose of exercising the functions conferred on it under or by virtue of this Act or any other Act.

(2) There is to be a tribunal, known as the Upper Tribunal, for the purpose of exercising the functions conferred on it under or by virtue of this Act or any other Act.

(3) Each of the First-tier Tribunal, and the Upper Tribunal, is to consist of its judges and other members.

(4) The Senior President of Tribunals is to preside over both of the First-tier Tribunal and the Upper Tribunal.

(5) The Upper Tribunal is to be a superior court of record.

...

7 Chambers: jurisdiction and Presidents

(1) The Lord Chancellor may, with the concurrence of the Senior President of Tribunals, by order make provision for the organisation of each of the First-tier Tribunal and the Upper Tribunal into a number of chambers.

(2) There is—

(a) for each chamber of the First-tier Tribunal, and

(b) for each chamber of the Upper Tribunal, to be a person, or two persons, to preside over that chamber.

(3) A person may not at any particular time preside over more than one chamber of the First-tier Tribunal and may not at any particular time preside over more than one chamber of the Upper Tribunal (but may

at the same time preside over one chamber of the First-tier Tribunal and over one chamber of the Upper Tribunal).

(4) A person appointed under this section to preside over a chamber is to be known as a Chamber President.

(5) Where two persons are appointed under this section to preside over the same chamber, any reference in an enactment to the Chamber President of the chamber is a reference to a person appointed under this section to preside over the chamber.

(6) The Senior President of Tribunals may (consistently with subsections (2) and (3)) appoint a person who is the Chamber President of a chamber to preside instead, or to preside also, over another chamber.

(7) The Lord Chancellor may (consistently with subsections (2) and (3)) appoint a person who is not a Chamber President to preside over a chamber.

(8) Schedule 4 (eligibility for appointment under subsection (7), appointment of Deputy Chamber Presidents and Acting Chamber Presidents, assignment of judges and other members of the First-tier Tribunal and Upper Tribunal, and further provision about Chamber Presidents and chambers) has effect.

(9) Each of the Lord Chancellor and the Senior President of Tribunals may, with the concurrence of the other, by order—

(a) make provision for the allocation of the First-tier Tribunal's functions between its chambers;
(b) make provision for the allocation of the Upper Tribunal's functions between its chambers;
(c) amend or revoke any order made under this subsection.

NOTES

1. The chart on p. 698 shows the two tribunal tiers and their chambers and the tribunal jurisdictions in those chambers. It is an evolving process, because it was planned in phases and it is a structure which is designed to accommodate additions. It is expected that in the future the first-tier Tribunal will have a Land, property and Housing Chamber. Currently the residential property tribunal service, which could be transferred to it, is administered by the department for Communities and Local Government. The general regulatory chamber is expected to expand with the implementation of the regulatory enforcement and sanctions act 2008.
2. Not all tribunals are included within the new structure. The largest omission is employment, which has its own two-tier structure with Employment Tribunals and the Employment Appeal Tribunal. It was not felt appropriate to include these tribunals, in part because they determine disputes between private parties (party and party) rather than between the state and individuals (party and state). Some other tribunals including those dealing with appeals concerning admission to and exclusion from schools and parking in London and the rest of the country are administered by local councils. Leggatt recommended that they be included (para. 3.15) but the Government decided to exclude them initially from the Tribunal Service and then to review the position (Cm 6243).
3. The biggest change was the addition of two Immigration and Asylum Chambers in 2010. This amounted to a complete reversal of policy which had been intended to streamline challenges by having only one appeal instead of two and a limited reconsideration in the Administrative Court. This had not worked and resulted in the Administrative Court being overwhelmed with asylum and immigration cases causing backlogs across the whole range of judicial review cases in the court.

The Senior President of Tribunals Annual Report: Tribunals Transformed

(2010), para.45

45. The Transfer of Functions of the Asylum and Immigration Tribunal Order 2010 comes into force on 15 February 2010, abolishing the Asylum and Immigration Tribunal and transferring its functions to the First-tier Tribunal. Also on that day, the Upper Tribunal assumes jurisdiction in respect of appeals against decisions of the First-tier Tribunal in immigration and asylum cases. What was a single tier jurisdiction thus becomes a two tier one, in common with other tribunal jurisdictions.

This is perhaps an appropriate moment to reflect on how the decision came about to bring the AIT wholly within the scheme of the TCEA. By 2007, the volume of immigration and asylum work in the

Tribunals Srtucture Chart

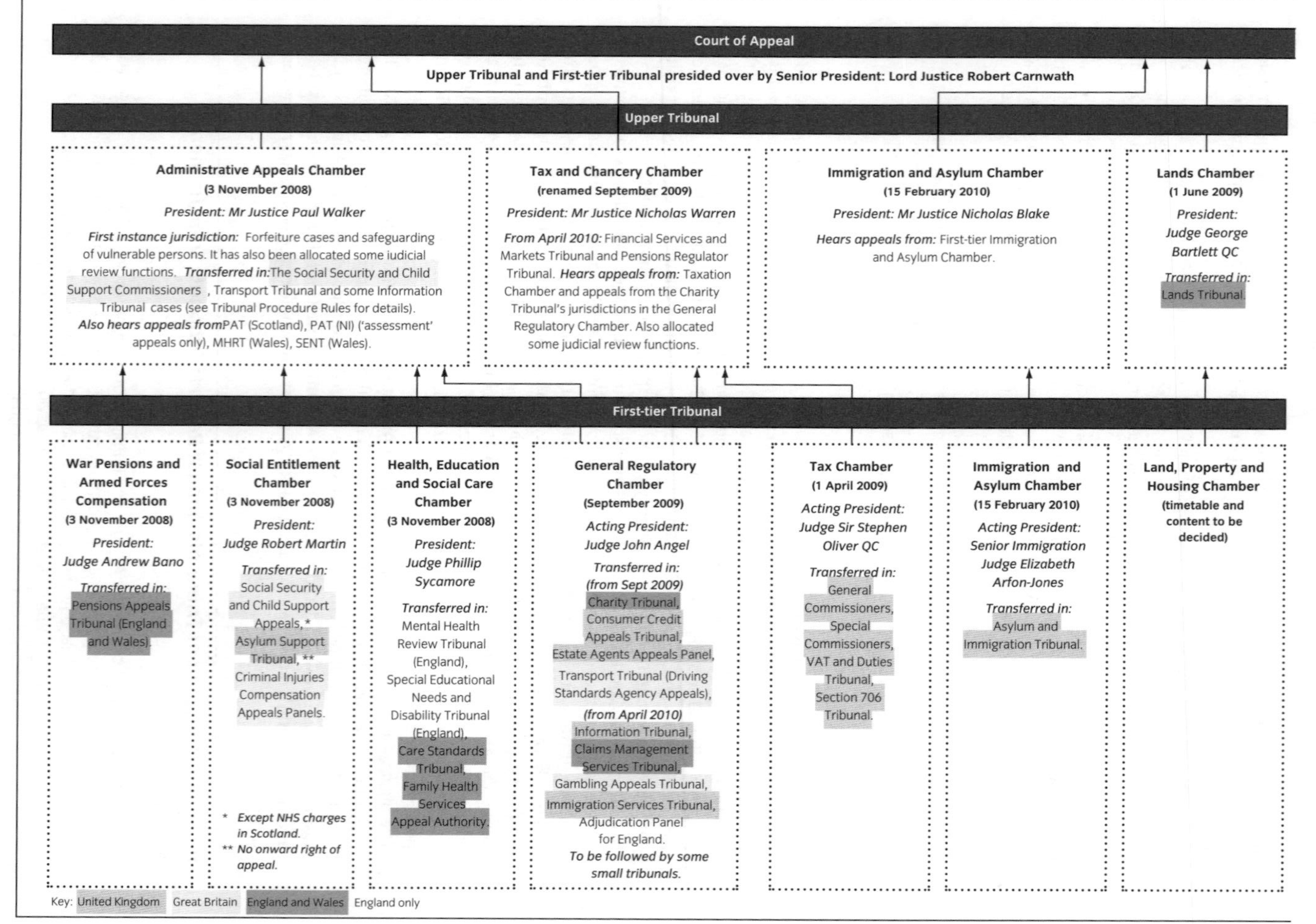
Court of Appeal
Upper Tribunal and First-tier Tribunal presided over by Senior President: Lord Justice Robert Carnwath
Upper Tribunal
Administrative Appeals Chamber
(3 November 2008)
President: Mr Justice Paul Walker
First instance jurisdiction: Forfeiture cases and safeguarding of vulnerable persons. It has also been allocated some judicial review functions. Transferred in: The Social Security and Child Support Commissioners, Transport Tribunal and some Information Tribunal cases (see Tribunal Procedure Rules for details).
Also hears appeals from PAT (Scotland), PAT (NI) ('assessment' appeals only), MHRT (Wales), SENT (Wales).
Tax and Chancery Chamber
(renamed September 2009)
President: Mr Justice Nicholas Warren
From April 2010: Financial Services and Markets Tribunal and Pensions Regulator Tribunal. Hears appeals from: Taxation Chamber and appeals from the Charity Tribunal's jurisdictions in the General Regulatory Chamber. Also allocated some judicial review functions.
Immigration and Asylum Chamber
(15 February 2010)
President: Mr Justice Nicholas Blake
Hears appeals from: First-tier Immigration and Asylum Chamber.
Lands Chamber
(1 June 2009)
President: Judge George Bartlett QC
Transferred in: Lands Tribunal.
First-tier Tribunal
War Pensions and Armed Forces Compensation
(3 November 2008)
President: Judge Andrew Bano
Transferred in: Pensions Appeals Tribunal (England and Wales).
Social Entitlement Chamber
(3 November 2008)
President: Judge Robert Martin
Transferred in: Social Security and Child Support Appeals,* Asylum Support Tribunal,** Criminal Injuries Compensation Appeals Panels.
* Except NHS charges in Scotland.
** No onward right of appeal.
Health, Education and Social Care Chamber
(3 November 2008)
President: Judge Phillip Sycamore
Transferred in: Mental Health Review Tribunal (England), Special Educational Needs and Disability Tribunal (England), Care Standards Tribunal, Family Health Services Appeal Authority.
General Regulatory Chamber
(September 2009)
Acting President: Judge John Angel
Transferred in: (from Sept 2009) Charity Tribunal, Consumer Credit Appeals Tribunal, Estate Agents Appeals Panel, Transport Tribunal (Driving Standards Agency Appeals), (from April 2010) Information Tribunal, Claims Management Services Tribunal, Gambling Appeals Tribunal, Immigration Services Tribunal, Adjudication Panel for England.
To be followed by some small tribunals.
Tax Chamber
(1 April 2009)
Acting President: Judge Sir Stephen Oliver QC
Transferred in: General Commissioners, Special Commissioners, VAT and Duties Tribunal, Section 706 Tribunal.
Immigration and Asylum Chamber
(15 February 2010)
Acting President: Senior Immigration Judge Elizabeth Arfon-Jones
Transferred in: Asylum and Immigration Tribunal.
Land, Property and Housing Chamber
(timetable and content to be decided)
Key: United Kingdom Great Britain England and Wales England only

Administrative Court was causing serious concern, particularly as regards the number of applications to that Court for reconsideration of AIT decisions, following initial refusal by that tribunal under s. 103A of the Nationality, Immigration and Asylum Act 2002. A small working group, jointly chaired by Richards LJ and Lin Homer, was formed in order to examine (amongst other things) how best to handle applications that sought to challenge first instance decisions of immigration judges.

The working group concluded that there would be advantages in replacing the system of reconsideration of single-tier decisions with a two-tier appellate process, whereby initial judicial decisions in immigration and asylum cases could be appealed (with permission) to the Upper Tribunal. As well as having the benefit of placing ultimate responsibility for permission applications with a specialist tribunal (which would nevertheless be able to call on High Court input, where appropriate), the creation of a two-tier system was seen to have the advantage of enabling initially legally erroneous decisions to be remade in the Upper Tribunal, thereby leading to a reduction in the immigration and asylum workload of the Court of Appeal, which had also increased to levels that were causing concern.

The Government welcomed the working group's recommendations, which it saw as leading to a more efficient but nevertheless fair and expert system. In August 2008 a consultation paper was published, inviting responses on the proposal to transfer the jurisdiction of the AIT in the manner just described. Following what was seen as a generally favourable response, the government announced in May 2009 that the necessary legislation would be brought forward. The Transfer Order is a key part of that legislative package; but other legislation also creates dedicated Immigration and Asylum Chambers in both the First-tier Tribunal and the Upper Tribunal, and provides the necessary procedure rules for both tiers.

B: Judicial leadership and tribunal composition

The Leggatt recommendations sought to ensure that the tribunals were independent of the departments whose decisions were under challenge and judicial leadership which, in the larger tribunal systems had been provided by presidents, was to be carried into the new structure. This leadership would be responsible for tribunal composition and thus ensuring that the classic tribunal characteristic of expertise, both legal and specialist in relation to the work which the tribunal carries out, would be available.

TRIBUNALS, COURTS AND ENFORCEMENT ACT 2007

1 Independence of tribunal judiciary

In section 3 of the Constitutional Reform Act 2005 (c. 4) (guarantee of continued judicial independence), after subsection (7) insert—

'(7A) In this section "the judiciary" also includes every person who—

(a) holds an office listed in Schedule 14 or holds an office listed in subsection (7B), and
(b) but for this subsection would not be a member of the judiciary

for the purposes of this section.

(7B) The offices are those of—

(a) Senior President of Tribunals;
(b) President of Employment Tribunals (Scotland);
(c) Vice President of Employment Tribunals (Scotland);
(d) member of a panel of chairmen of Employment Tribunals (Scotland);
(e) member of a panel of members of employment tribunals that is not a panel of chairmen;
(f) adjudicator appointed under section 5 of the Criminal Injuries Compensation Act 1995.'

2 Senior President of Tribunals

(1) Her Majesty may, on the recommendation of the Lord Chancellor, appoint a person to the office of Senior President of Tribunals.

(2) Schedule 1 makes further provision about the Senior President of Tribunals and about recommendations for appointment under subsection (1).

(3) A holder of the office of Senior President of Tribunals must, in carrying out the functions of that office, have regard to—

(a) the need for tribunals to be accessible,
(b) the need for proceedings before tribunals—
  (i) to be fair, and
  (ii) to be handled quickly and efficiently,
(c) the need for members of tribunals to be experts in the subject-matter of, or the law to be applied in, cases in which they decide matters, and
(d) the need to develop innovative methods of resolving disputes that are of a type that may be brought before tribunals.

(4) In subsection (3) "tribunals" means—

(a) the First-tier Tribunal,
(b) the Upper Tribunal,
(c) employment tribunals,
(d) the Employment Appeal Tribunal, and
(e) the Asylum and Immigration Tribunal.

...

7 Chambers: jurisdiction and Presidents

(1) The Lord Chancellor may, with the concurrence of the Senior President of Tribunals, by order make provision for the organisation of each of the First-tier Tribunal and the Upper Tribunal into a number of chambers.

(2) There is—

(a) for each chamber of the First-tier Tribunal, and
(b) for each chamber of the Upper Tribunal,

to be a person, or two persons, to preside over that chamber.

(3) A person may not at any particular time preside over more than one chamber of the First-tier Tribunal and may not at any particular time preside over more than one chamber of the Upper Tribunal (but may at the same time preside over one chamber of the First-tier Tribunal and over one chamber of the Upper Tribunal).

(4) A person appointed under this section to preside over a chamber is to be known as a Chamber President.

(5) Where two persons are appointed under this section to preside over the same chamber, any reference in an enactment to the Chamber President of the chamber is a reference to a person appointed under this section to preside over the chamber.

(6) The Senior President of Tribunals may (consistently with subsections (2) and (3)) appoint a person who is the Chamber President of a chamber to preside instead, or to preside also, over another chamber.

(7) The Lord Chancellor may (consistently with subsections (2) and (3)) appoint a person who is not a Chamber President to preside over a chamber.

(8) Schedule 4 (eligibility for appointment under subsection (7), appointment of Deputy Chamber Presidents and Acting Chamber Presidents, assignment of judges and other members of the First-tier Tribunal and Upper Tribunal, and further provision about Chamber Presidents and chambers) has effect.

(9) Each of the Lord Chancellor and the Senior President of Tribunals may, with the concurrence of the other, by order—

(a) make provision for the allocation of the First-tier Tribunal's functions between its chambers;

(b) make provision for the allocation of the Upper Tribunal's functions between its chambers;
(c) amend or revoke any order made under this subsection.

8 Senior President of Tribunals: power to delegate

(1) The Senior President of Tribunals may delegate any function he has in his capacity as Senior President of Tribunals—

(a) to any judge, or other member, of the Upper Tribunal or First-tier Tribunal;
(b) to staff appointed under section 40(1).

(2) Subsection (1) does not apply to functions of the Senior President of Tribunals under section 7(9).

(3) A delegation under subsection (1) is not revoked by the delegator's becoming incapacitated.

(4) Any delegation under subsection (1) that is in force immediately before a person ceases to be Senior President of Tribunals continues in force until varied or revoked by a subsequent holder of the office of Senior President of Tribunals.

(5) The delegation under this section of a function shall not prevent the exercise of the function by the Senior President of Tribunals.

Transforming Tribunals: Implementing Part 1 of the Tribunals, Courts and Enforcement Act 2007

Ministry of Justice (2007), paras 141–146, 157–164, 227–239

The Senior President's Functions

141 The functions of the Senior President are set out in the 2007 Act. These will be commenced when the new tribunal structures are populated with judges, members and jurisdictions. The principal functions will include:

- responsibility for representing the views of tribunal judiciary to Parliament and Ministers
- responsibility, within the resources provided by the Lord Chancellor, for the maintenance of appropriate arrangements for the training; guidance and welfare of judges and other members of the First-tier and Upper Tribunals as well as those of the AIT, ET and EAT (for which purpose he shares mutual duties of co-operation with the Lord Chief Justices of England and Wales, and of Northern Ireland, and the Lord President
- concurrence (with the Lord Chancellor) in relation to the chambers structure for the First-tier Tribunal and the Upper Tribunal, the allocation of functions between chambers, and the making of orders prescribing the qualifications required for appointment of members of the First-tier Tribunal and the Upper Tribunal
- assigning judges and members to chambers, for which purpose he is required to publish a policy agreed with the Lord Chancellor
- reporting to the Lord Chancellor in relation to tribunal cases on matters which the Senior President wishes to bring to the attention of the Lord Chancellor and matters which the Lord Chancellor has asked the Senior President to cover
- requesting court judges (with the agreement of the relevant chief justice) to act as a judge of the First-tier or Upper Tribunal
- taking oaths of allegiance and judicial oaths (or nominating someone to do so) from tribunal judges and other members, and
- acting as (or nominating) a member of the Tribunal Procedure Committee (it is expected that the Senior President or his nominee will chair the Committee).

142 Many of the responsibilities described above are completely new (for example those in relation to the organisation of the First-tier and Upper Tribunals), but judicial heads of the existing tribunal jurisdictions may already undertake many of these functions. The 2007 Act brings them together under the Senior President (subject to a power to delegate), but gives them a statutory basis and imposes an obligation on the Lord Chancellor to provide the necessary resources.

143 As the Senior President, Lord Justice Carnwath is a Lord Justice of Appeal and the Lord Chief Justice can already delegate to him certain functions in relation to judicial discipline and complaints under the CRA and the Judicial Discipline (Prescribed Procedures) Regulations 2006. The provisions in the 2007

Act make those functions delegable to the Senior President of Tribunals. The Lord Chief Justice's role in relation to tribunal appointments under the CRA remains unchanged.

144 Lord Justice Carnwath has been supported in his work by a small team to date. In the short term, that team will expand to create a Tribunals Judicial Office that can support the Senior President in his statutory and leadership functions. Where administrative staff within that office provide support to the Senior President and the other tribunals judiciary, the staff will be answerable to them. The Tribunals Judicial Office will work closely with the Judicial Office, to ensure a common approach on issues of joint concern, and to enable support services to be shared between courts and tribunals judiciary where it is sensible and practicable to do so.

145 In time the Tribunals Judicial Office will also provide support to Chamber Presidents and extend the existing pockets of judicial support that exist within some tribunals to benefit all those falling within their remit. For example, within the Commissioners' Office there are legal officers who undertake case specific research; in AIT there are legal officers who prepare comprehensive country specific advice, and in SSCSA there is a periodic Judicial Information Bulletin which includes case reports relevant to their jurisdictions. It is anticipated that case specific research will be extended across the Upper Tribunal and also that more comprehensive legal information services will be provided to both Tribunals.

Training

146 The Senior President is responsible for maintaining appropriate arrangements for judicial training. His Judicial Office, the Tribunals Service and the Judicial Studies Board will work together to devise and maintain these arrangements, having particular regard to the value of shared training where there is sufficient in common, such as with general tribunal practice and judicial leadership. Common proposals for appraisal of judicial members will also be developed.

...

Deployment of Judges and Non-Legal Members

157 The deployment of judges is a judicial matter. Under the 2007 Act the Senior President will have oversight of the process and, with Chamber Presidents, will determine the role of individual judges and members within the tribunal system.

158 Legally qualified and non-legal members of existing tribunals will be transferred into the new generic offices of 'judge of the First-tier Tribunal' and 'member of the First-tier Tribunal'. Judges and members will initially be assigned to Chambers on the basis of their previous tribunal-specific appointments. This may mean that those who held several tribunal appointments may be assigned to more than one Chamber.

159 Under the 2007 Act, judges and members may sit in any of the jurisdictions within the Chamber or Chambers to which they are assigned. There is, however, no expectation that every judge and member will sit in all of a Chamber's jurisdictions immediately. Initially most judges and members are likely to deal with the types of cases with which they were previously dealing.

'Ticketing'

160 It will be for the Chamber Presidents to decide how best to use the judges and members *within* a Chamber in order to match their experience and expertise to the needs of the Chamber.

161 Judges and members will be given a 'ticket' by the Chamber President indicating their suitability to sit in a particular jurisdiction. This will be subject to business need, and before being allowed to sit in additional jurisdictions within the Chamber, judges and members will require training and induction in areas with which they are unfamiliar (this may, for example, include training to enable them to deal effectively with cultural differences, where these are relevant to the decisions they have to take). There will be some jurisdictions which generate comparatively few cases and where it will be necessary for cases to be dealt with by a more limited number of judges and members. But as Chambers will group similar subject matter and skills together there is an expectation that, over time, judges and members will increase the number of 'tickets' they hold, widening the pool of expertise within their Chambers.

Assignment

162 A decision as to whether a judge or member should sit in a *different* Chamber follows a different process, known as assignment. It is important to bear in mind that the 2007 Act introduces the concept of appointment to a generic office of judge or member. This is different to the historical position of appointment to a particular jurisdiction. The assignment process will thus allow those judges and members appointed through the JAC [Judicial Appointments Commission] to be deployed to a number of Chambers where the need arises.

163 Assignment will only take place with the consent of the Chamber President and the individual judge or member. The actual process for assignment may depend on whether the assignment is to meet a long or short term need.

164 Under the 2007 Act the Senior President is required to publish a document, to which the Lord Chancellor has to agree, setting out his policy on assignment. The overriding principles will be:

- that the judge or member has the necessary skills and ability to hear cases within the Chamber to which they are assigned
- that the assignment process is open and transparent
- that assignment will be based on merit, with a link to judicial appraisal where appropriate
- that the assignment process will not be used for promotion. Promotion opportunities will be advertised and subject to the JAC processes, and
- that, subject to business need, the process must also balance opportunities for judges and members to develop their judicial careers while at the same time retaining their skills and expertise.

Appointments and Tribunal Composition

227 In future, members of the First-tier Tribunal will be appointed under paragraph 2(1) of Schedule 2 to the 2007 Act, and to the Upper Tribunal under paragraph 2(1) of Schedule 3. Members of the Asylum and Immigration Tribunal and the Employment Tribunals will become *ex officio* members of the First-tier Tribunal by virtue of sections 4(3)(c) and (d) and 5(2)(d). Similarly, members of the Employment Appeal Tribunal and the AIT will become *ex officio* members of the Upper Tribunal (by virtue of section 5(2)(c) and (d)). It is these provisions that will allow members to be pooled together and deployed across jurisdictions in the same way as tribunal judges. However, there is no general expectation that *ex officio* members will automatically sit on cases—they will only sit if requested to do so by the Senior President.

228 Under the 2007 Act the general rules on composition of tribunals for hearings will be laid down by an order or orders made by the Lord Chancellor, with the concurrence of the Senior President and subject to Parliamentary approval. The 2007 Act also allows the Lord Chancellor to delegate his duty in relation to regulating tribunal composition to the Senior President or to a Chamber President. The government considers it important to identify what principles should underlie tribunal composition and the orders to be made.

229 Whatever may have been the policies that led to existing statutory rules on tribunal composition, the government's approach is centred on the user. In a number of tribunals, cases are routinely heard by more than one member. Generally, there are good reasons for that, and there is some evidence that users prefer this approach. However, it may not be necessary in all cases. It must be acknowledged that most tribunal users simply want to have their cases disposed of quickly, rigorously and fairly, with the right kind of expertise brought to bear. It is reasonable to note that all civil trial courts and many existing tribunals (particularly the Social Security Commissioners, the AIT, the VAT and Duties Tribunal and the Lands Tribunal) rarely have more than one member sitting on a case, and in other tribunals much of the work is dealt with by one judge or member sitting alone. There is no evident dissatisfaction from tribunal users. The government considers that the reputation of tribunal justice is high enough not to need to be buttressed by rigid rules on composition.

230 The government intends to map existing tribunal non-legal members into the new roles in a way which maximises the opportunity for their flexible use in appeals. The overriding principle will be that the use of non-legal members on a particular hearing should bring to the table skills, experience or knowledge that tribunal judges cannot provide (in certain employment tribunal cases, for example, there can arguably be circumstances in which little value is added by their presence. However, there is a clear body of opinion in support of their use in more complex cases).

231 To put that overriding principle into practice the government intends that the order stipulating tribunal composition will reflect the following:

- The maximum number hearing a case is three.
- Hearings with more than one judge are appropriate only where there is a significant question of law to be considered, or for training purposes.
- In tribunals of two the Chair has the deciding vote.
- Non-legal members are there to provide expertise. They should therefore be deployed selectively on the basis of the needs of the case following the Leggatt principle set out above. The needs of the case include the likely skills and understanding of the parties.
- Expertise comes in many forms: it is not confined to those with professional qualifications.
- Analytical and chairing skills are not confined to judges, so non-legal members may be able to chair hearings or conduct cases alone.
- Non-legal experts can and should be used outside formal hearings, such as by providing reports or chairing meetings of expert witnesses or advising generally, subject always to the rules of natural justice.
- Tribunal composition is not to change during a hearing except with the consent of the parties.
- Case management arrangements need to be in place to ensure that composition is geared to the needs of the individual case.

232 The government intends that the order will set a default position close to the present rules for the composition of existing tribunals but, in line with the principles above, it will also provide for a general discretion to order a tribunal to be composed in a different way for a particular hearing. It may also provide for non-legal expertise to be brought to bear in ways other than sitting in a hearing—for instance, by providing an independent examination and report or by leading a discussion between expert witnesses. If expertise is being provided in this way it would be open to the judiciary to conclude that the presence of the expert at a hearing was not always necessary.

Categories of Non-Legal Member

233 Non legal members will be mapped into Chambers on the basis of the subject matter of the cases they currently adjudicate. Within their Chamber they will then be 'ticketed' (as will tribunal judges) to hear those cases for which they have the appropriate skills, expertise and training. The Lord Chancellor, with the concurrence of the Senior President, will in orders specify the qualifications of different categories of non-legal members. The government proposes three categories.

Healthcare Qualified Professional

234 A single order could encompass doctors; nurses; psychologists and allied professionals. This would help to overcome some of the difficulties in recruitment highlighted by the review. The government is also thinking of supplementing the existing groups of fee paid medical members with a limited number of salaried clinically qualified members who might combine sitting for a substantial proportion of their time on tribunals with ordinary clinical practice. This would help them to maintain their levels of expertise and ensure that they meet professional requirements for revalidation.

235 Up to now medical membership of a tribunal has been limited to doctors. Some tribunals are used to all their medical members being consultants. In the changing world of health care, and with increasing demands from tribunals for some clinical specialisations, the government has it in mind to use a wider range of health care professionals in tribunals, according to the needs of the cases. This would be particularly appropriate if the role of the clinical expert member is more varied than simply sitting as a 'wing' member with a judge.

236 With an effective case management system in place and proper control of these different health care specialisations the government favours a 'healthcare qualified professionals' member category which is not confined to doctors. An alternative would be to have a number of medical/clinical groupings, based on the different health care professions. That might also include a separate category for psychiatrists in view of the particular demand for their services in cases of the type dealt with by the MHRT (although mental health cases form a significant proportion of the work of some other tribunals).

Other Qualified Professionals

237 There is a variety of other qualified professionals who are called upon across jurisdictions—these include surveyors; accountants; pharmacologists; social workers and vets. Their unifying feature is an independently and professionally validated qualification.

Other Experts

238 The government does not believe that there is a place for a purely lay category. All tribunal judges and members should have their place at the hearing table by virtue of their expertise. The government does recognise that there are experts who provide valuable assistance in the decision making process but whose expertise cannot be described in terms of a professional qualification. These experts include those who have experience in delivering specialist services (for example for people with mental health or disability problems) and those whose work experience has given them a particular insight (for example in the armed services or in a particular trade such as the hotel and catering industries). The users of certain services may also acquire relevant experience and expertise. In the mental health field, there are a number of people who either have used or still do use mental health services who can legitimately be described as 'experts by experience'. The SSCSA currently has some members who are themselves disabled.

239 A member could satisfy the requirements for more than one category. Although the AIT non-legal members will be members of the Upper Tribunal, they will be eligible to sit in the First-tier tribunal. In practice their expertise is more likely to be of use in First-tier cases rather than appellate cases, as the latter are generally confined to points of law. Again, there is no general expectation that they will automatically sit on cases—they will only sit when invited to do so by the Senior President.

NOTES

1. The Senior President has a crucial role and this is reflected in the arrangements for appointment which can be either by (a) agreement amongst the Lord Chancellor, the Lord Chief Justice of England and Wales, the Lord President of the Court of Session and the Lord Chief Justice of Northern Ireland on a Lord or Lady Justice of Appeal or a member of the Inner House of the Court of Session, or (b) in the absence of such agreement the Lord Chancellor asks the JAC to select someone for recommendation for appointment. The eligibility criteria for the Senior President are the same as those for a Lord or Lady Justice of Appeal and the JAC process to be followed is that which would be used to appoint a Head of Division of the High Court with appropriate modifications.
2. Similarly Chamber Presidents have an important role, and it appears that the Senior President will rely on them to manage the work of their chambers. The appointment process, as with that for the Senior President, may be one in which there is consensus about a person from a defined group of judges, or be a recommendation following a selection process organized by the JAC. If the former, a candidate is a member of the High Court or the Court of Session, or in Northern Ireland the High Court and the Court of Appeal, who would be nominated by the relevant Chief Justice and the Senior President would be consulted by the Lord Chancellor.
3. The involvement of the Lord Chancellor in various functions alongside the Senior President provides for accountability, as in the policy for assigning tribunal judges and members to chambers other than the one to which they were appointed, but the allocation of tribunal members to hear particular cases is a matter solely for judicial leadership.

C: Appeals and judicial review

Transforming Tribunals: Implementing Part 1 of the Tribunals, Courts and Enforcement Act 2007

Ministry of Justice (2007), paras 177–179

177 The creation of the Upper Tribunal is probably the most significant innovation in the tribunal system. The need to rationalise the hotchpotch of appeal routes from administrative tribunals has

been highlighted by a number of reports, including the Law Commission report on Administrative Law, the Woolf report on Civil Justice, and the Leggatt report. The present arrangements are illogical and incoherent, reflecting the piecemeal historical development of the tribunal system. Appeals routes from first instance tribunals in England and Wales vary between specialised tribunals, the High Court (Administrative Court or Chancery Division), and the Court of Appeal. In some cases there is no statutory right of appeal, but judicial review provides an alternative remedy in the Administrative Court; or judicial review may be required to fill the gaps in a restricted statutory scheme. There are similar variations in the form and nature of the appeal, for example: whether on law only, or on law and fact; whether leave is required; and whether the procedure is primarily oral or written.

178 The creation of the Upper Tribunal provides the opportunity not only to rationalise the procedures, but also to establish a strong and dedicated appellate body at the head of the new system. Its authority will derive from its specialist skills, and its status as a superior court of record, with judicial review powers, presided over by the Senior President. It is expected that the Upper Tribunal will come to play a central, innovative and defining role in the new system, enjoying a position in the judicial hierarchy at least equivalent to that of the Administrative Court in England and Wales. The government expects it to benefit from the participation of senior judges from the courts in all parts of the United Kingdom. Appeal from the Upper Tribunal will be to the Court of Appeal with permission. The Lord Chancellor intends to exercise his power to prescribe that such appeals in England and Wales will only be permitted in cases of general importance or for other special reason (as for second appeals from the courts).

179 The structure of the Upper Tribunal will need to reflect the variety of jurisdictions within its remit. It will work alongside the existing dedicated appeal systems, respectively, for asylum and immigration and for employment. These will continue as separate pillars of the new structure, each presided over by a High Court judge, but under the general supervision of the Senior President.

TRIBUNALS, COURTS AND ENFORCEMENT ACT 2007

18 Limits of jurisdiction under section 15(1)

(1) This section applies where an application made to the Upper Tribunal seeks (whether or not alone)—

(a) relief under section 15(1), or
(b) permission (or, in a case arising under the law of Northern Ireland, leave) to apply for relief under section 15(1).

(2) If Conditions 1 to 4 are met, the tribunal has the function of deciding the application.

(3) If the tribunal does not have the function of deciding the application, it must by order transfer the application to the High Court.

(4) Condition 1 is that the application does not seek anything other than—

(a) relief under section 15(1);
(b) permission (or, in a case arising under the law of Northern Ireland, leave) to apply for relief under section 15(1);
(c) an award under section 16(6);
(d) interest;
(e) costs.

(5) Condition 2 is that the application does not call into question anything done by the Crown Court.

(6) Condition 3 is that the application falls within a class specified for the purposes of this subsection in a direction given in accordance with Part 1 of Schedule 2 to the Constitutional Reform Act 2005 (c. 4).

(7) The power to give directions under subsection (6) includes—

(a) power to vary or revoke directions made in exercise of the power, and
(b) power to make different provision for different purposes.

(8) Condition 4 is that the judge presiding at the hearing of the application is either—

(a) a judge of the High Court or the Court of Appeal in England and Wales or Northern Ireland, or a judge of the Court of Session, or

(b) such other persons as may be agreed from time to time between the Lord Chief Justice, the Lord President, or the Lord Chief Justice of Northern Ireland, as the case may be, and the Senior President of Tribunals.

(9) Where the application is transferred to the High Court under subsection (3)—

(a) the application is to be treated for all purposes as if it—
 (i) had been made to the High Court, and
 (ii) sought things corresponding to those sought from the tribunal, and
(b) any steps taken, permission (or leave) given or orders made by the tribunal in relation to the application are to be treated as taken, given or made by the High Court.

(10) Rules of court may make provision for the purpose of supplementing subsection (9).

...

19 Transfer of judicial review applications from High Court

(1) In the Supreme Court Act 1981 (c. 54), after section 31 insert—

"31A Transfer of judicial review applications to Upper Tribunal

(1) This section applies where an application is made to the High Court—
 (a) for judicial review, or
 (b) for permission to apply for judicial review.

(2) If Conditions 1, 2, 3 and 4 are met, the High Court must by order transfer the application to the Upper Tribunal.

(3) If Conditions 1, 2 and 4 are met, but Condition 3 is not, the High Court may by order transfer the application to the Upper Tribunal if it appears to the High Court to be just and convenient to do so.

(4) Condition 1 is that the application does not seek anything other than—
 (a) relief under section 31(1)(a) and (b);
 (b) permission to apply for relief under section 31(1)(a) and (b);
 (c) an award under section 31(4);
 (d) interest;
 (e) costs.

(5) Condition 2 is that the application does not call into question anything done by the Crown Court.

(6) Condition 3 is that the application falls within a class specified under section 18(6) of the Tribunals, Courts and Enforcement Act 2007.

(7) Condition 4 is that the application does not call into question any decision made under—
 (a) the Immigration Acts,
 (b) the British Nationality Act 1981 (c. 61),
 (c) any instrument having effect under an enactment within paragraph (a) or (b), or
 (d) any other provision of law for the time being in force which determines British citizenship, British overseas territories citizenship, the status of a British National (Overseas) or British Overseas citizenship."

...

(3) Where an application is transferred to the Upper Tribunal under 31A of the Supreme Court Act 1981 (c. 54) or section 25A of the Judicature (Northern Ireland) Act 1978 (transfer from the High Court of judicial review applications)—

(a) the application is to be treated for all purposes as if it—
 (i) had been made to the tribunal, and
 (ii) sought things corresponding to those sought from the High Court,

(4) Where—

(a) an application for permission is transferred to the Upper Tribunal under section 31A of the Supreme Court Act 1981 (c. 54) and the tribunal grants permission, or

(b) an application for leave is transferred to the Upper Tribunal under section 25A of the Judicature (Northern Ireland) Act 1978 (c. 23) and the tribunal grants leave, the tribunal has the function of deciding any subsequent application brought under the permission or leave, even if the subsequent application does not fall within a class specified under section 18(6).

(5) Tribunal Procedure Rules may make further provision for the purposes of supplementing subsections (3) and (4).

NOTES

1. Sections 9 and 10 allow for the First-tier and Upper Tribunals to review their own decisions without the need for an appeal. If the tribunals decide that there was an accidental error in the record or the reasoning then this may be corrected or the decision may be set aside. If a decision is set aside the tribunal may re-decide the matter or if it is the First-tier Tribunal it may refer it to the Upper Tribunal. Review may be instigated by the tribunal itself or by a party who has a right of appeal.
2. A party has under s. 11 a right to an appeal on a point of law from the First-tier Tribunal to the Upper Tribunal. Permission to appeal is required from either the First-tier Tribunal or the Upper Tribunal. Some decisions are excluded from appeal under s. 11(5) and include: appeals against decisions on reviews in relation to criminal injuries compensation; appeals against national security certificates under the Data Protection Act 1998 and the Freedom of Information Act 2000; a decision by the First-tier Tribunal under s. 9 to review or not to review, to take or not take any action in the light of an earlier review, or to refer or not to refer a decision to the Upper Tribunal; and any decision of the First-tier Tribunal of a description specified in an order made by the Lord Chancellor.
3. On appeal the Upper Tribunal must set aside the decision if it finds an error of law and may remit to the First-tier Tribunal with directions for reconsideration, or make the decision which should have been made. If the Upper Tribunal finds that the error does not invalidate the decision then it may let the decision stand.
4. Under s. 13 there may be an appeal to the relevant appellate court, Court of Appeal, Court of Session, Court of Appeal of Northern Ireland. Permission is required from the Upper Tribunal or the relevant appellate court specified by the Upper Tribunal. Some decisions are excluded from appeal replicating those in s. 11(5) substituting Upper for First-tier Tribunal (see note 2, *ante*).
5. The 'revolutionary' jurisdiction conferred on the Upper Tribunal is that of judicial review. Section 15 confers this jurisdiction on the Upper Tribunal and s. 19 allows for the transfer of judicial review applications from the High Court (s. 21 from the Court of Session). The Upper Tribunal, where it has jurisdiction, will be able to grant the same relief as if it were the High Court (Court of Session in Scotland) applying the same principles of judicial review in relation to permission, sufficient interest in the matter, delay in applying and grant of remedy. Where the Upper Tribunal makes a quashing order under s. 15(1) it may remit the matter to body which made the decision or substitute its own decision. The power to substitute its own decision is conditional on the decision in question having been made by a court of tribunal, the decision was quashed on the ground of error of law and, without the error, there is only one decision the court or tribunal could have made.
6. In England and Wales the Lord Chief Justice has made an order specifying two classes of judicial review cases which should be transferred from the Administrative Court to the Upper Tribunal. They are (1) any decision of the First-tier Tribunal concerning criminal injuries compensation, in respect of which there is no right of appeal to the Upper Tribunal and (2) any decision of the First-tier Tribunal for which there is no right of appeal.
7. The Court of Appeal has held that the Upper Tribunal is itself amenable to judicial review on limited grounds, those of outright excess of jurisdiction and denial of a fair hearing: *R (Cart)* v *Upper Tribunal* [2010] EWCA Civ 859; however, in Scotland the Inner House of the Court of Session has held in *Eba* v *Advocate General for Scotland* [2010] ScotCS CSIH 78, that the Upper Tribunal is amenable to judicial review on the normal basis in Scots law. The Supreme Court may be able to resolve this, or legislation may be required.

SECTION 3: TRIBUNALS AND DISPUTE RESOLUTION

A: Tribunal characteristics

Tribunals as 'court substitutes' were thought to have some advantages over the courts because of their characteristics. These were identified in the Franks Report.

Report of the Committee on Administrative Tribunals and Enquiries

Cmnd 218 (1957), paras 40–42, 62–64, 71–72, 76–77, 90

[See also paras. 38–39, p. 694, *ante*].

40. Tribunals are not ordinary courts, but neither are they appendages of Government Departments. Much of the official evidence, including that of the Joint Permanent Secretary to the Treasury, appeared to reflect the view that tribunals should properly be regarded as part of the machinery of administration, for which the Government must retain a close and continuing responsibility. Thus, for example, tribunals in the social services field would be regarded as adjuncts to the administration of the services themselves. We do not accept this view. We consider that tribunals should be regarded as machinery provided by Parliament for adjudication rather than as part of the machinery for administration. The essential point is that in all these cases Parliament has deliberately provided for a decision outside and independent of the Department concerned, either at first instance (for example, in the case of Rent Tribunals and the Licensing Authorities for Public Service and Goods Vehicles) or on appeal from a decision of a Minister or of an official in a special statutory position (for example a valuation officer or an insurance officer). Although the relevant statutes do not in all cases expressly enact that tribunals are to consist entirely of persons outside the Government service, the use of the term 'tribunal' in legislation undoubtedly bears this connotation, and the intention of Parliament to provide for the independence of tribunals is clear and unmistakeable.

The application of the principle of openness, fairness and impartiality

41. We have already expressed our belief, in Part 1, that Parliament in deciding that certain decisions should be reached only after a special procedure must have intended that they should manifest three basic characteristics: openness, fairness and impartiality. The choice of a tribunal rather than a Minister as the deciding authority is itself a considerable step towards the realisation of these objectives, particularly the third. But in some cases the statutory provisions and the regulations thereunder fall short of what is required to secure these objectives...

42. In the field of tribunals openness appears to us to require the publicity of proceedings and knowledge of the essential reasoning underlying the decisions; fairness to require the adoption of a clear procedure which enables parties to know their rights, to present their case fully and to know the case which they have to meet; and impartiality to require the freedom of tribunals from the influence, real or apparent, of Departments concerned with the subject-matter of their decisions.

Codes of procedure

62. Most of the evidence we have received concerning tribunals has placed great emphasis upon procedure, not only at the hearing itself but also before and after it. There has been general agreement on the broad essentials which the procedure, in this wider sense, should contain, for example provision for notice of the right to apply to a tribunal, notice of the case which the applicant has to meet, a reasoned decision by the tribunal and notice of any further right of appeal.

63. We agree that procedure is of the greatest importance and that it should be clearly laid down in a statute or statutory instrument. Because of the great variety of the purposes for which tribunals are established, however, we do not think it would be appropriate to rely upon either a single code or a small number of codes. We think that there is a case for greater procedural differentiation and prefer that the detailed procedure for each type of tribunal should be designed to meet the particular circumstances....

Informality of atmosphere

64. There has been considerable emphasis, in much of the evidence we have received, upon the importance of preserving informality of atmosphere in hearings before tribunals, though it is generally conceded that in some tribunals, for example the Lands Tribunal, informality is not an over-riding necessity. We endorse this view, but we are convinced that an attempt which has been made to secure informality in the general run of tribunals has in some instances been at the expense of an orderly procedure. Informality without rules of procedure may be positively inimical to right adjudication, since the proceedings may well assume an unordered character which makes it difficult, if not impossible, for the tribunal properly to sift the facts and weigh the evidence. It should be remembered that by their very nature tribunals may be less skilled in adjudication than courts of law. None of our witnesses would seek to make tribunals in all respects like courts of law, but there is a wide measure of agreement that in many instances their procedure could be made more orderly without impairing the desired informality of atmosphere. The object to be aimed at in most tribunals is the combination of a formal procedure with an informal atmosphere. We see no reason why this cannot be achieved. On the one hand it means a manifestly sympathetic attitude on the part of the tribunal and the absence of the trappings of a court, but on the other hand such prescription of procedure as makes the proceedings clear and orderly.

Knowledge of the case to be met

71. The second most important requirement before the hearing is that citizens should know in good time the case which they will have to meet....

72. We do not suggest that the procedure should be formalised to the extent of requiring documents in the nature of legal pleadings. What is needed is that the citizen should receive in good time beforehand a document setting out the main points of the opposing case. It should not be necessary and indeed in view of the type of person frequently appearing before tribunals it would in many cases be positively undesirable, to require the parties to adhere rigidly at the hearing to the case previously set out, provided always that the interests of another party are not prejudiced by such flexibility.

Public hearings

76. We have already said that we regard openness as one of the three essential features of the satisfactory working of tribunals. Openness includes the promulgation of reasoned decisions, but its most important constituent is that the proceedings should be in public. The consensus of opinion in the evidence received is that hearings before tribunals should take place in public except in special circumstances.

77. We are in no doubt that if adjudicating bodies, whether courts or tribunals, are to inspire that confidence in the administration of justice which is a condition of civil liberty they should, in general, sit in public. But just as on occasion the courts are prepared to try certain types of case wholly or partly *in camera* so, in the wide field covered by tribunals, there are occasions on which we think that justice may be better done, and the interests of the citizen better served, by privacy.

The Committee went on to outline three types of case: where considerations of public security are involved, where intimate personal or financial circumstances have to be disclosed, and where there are preliminary hearings involving professional capacity and reputation.

Evidence

90. Tribunals are so varied that it is impossible to lay down any general guidance on the requirement of evidence at hearings. In the more formal tribunals, for example, the Lands Tribunal, there seems no good reason why some of the rules of evidence as in courts of law should not apply. In the majority of tribunals, however, we think it would be a mistake to introduce the strict rules of evidence of the courts. The presence of a legally qualified chairman should enable the tribunal to attach the proper weight to such matters as hearsay and written evidence.

■ QUESTION

Are the Franks Committee's recommendations on the characteristics of tribunals consistent with its statement of the reasons for adjudication by tribunals rather than by the courts (p. 694, *ante*)?

The Franks view of tribunals as part of the machinery of justice and not of the machinery of administration has been soundly criticized (see for example K. H. Hendry, 'The Tasks of Tribunals: Some Thoughts' (1982) 1 *Civil Justice Quarterly* 253) and as we shall see the Government's conception of dispute resolution views tribunals not solely as a means of securing justice but also of improving administration. The supposed advantages of the characteristics identified have also been challenged.

H. Genn, 'Tribunal Review of Administrative Decision-Making' in G. Richardson and H. Genn (eds), *Administrative Law and Government Action*

(1994), pp. 284–286

This chapter has attempted to show that there are considerable limits to the effectiveness of tribunals as a check on administrative decision-making and that these limitations stem at least in part from the design of tribunals and the low levels of representation at tribunals. In order for tribunals to act as an *effective* means of review they must be capable of conducting an accurate and fair review of administrative decisions. This requires time, expertise, and full information. It also requires that those who appear before tribunals are capable of understanding the relevance of regulations and the basis of their entitlement, and can provide relevant information and evidence of facts, largely without the benefit of advice or representation.

Given the weakness of first-line administrative decision-making, tribunals theoretically represent an important means of minimizing administrative injustice. However, evidence collected from recipients of adverse administrative decisions, although not conclusive, suggests that even when a relatively straightforward mechanism exists for review of decisions the opportunity is not taken because those affected may assume that the original decision was 'correct' or that it is unlikely to be changed. Thus, even if tribunal hearings provided perfect conditions for effective review of administrative decisions, they could only every afford a partial corrective to poor decision-making and administrative injustice. In practice, however, from the perspective of tribunal applicants, the conditions that operate in many tribunals are far from perfect. Despite their conventional characterization as informal, accessible, and non-technical, frequently tribunals are not particularly quick, there is considerable variation in the degrees of informality, and the issues dealt with are highly complex in terms of both the regulations to be applied and the factual situations of applicants. This study of tribunal processes and decision-making has highlighted the complexity of many areas of law with which tribunals must deal and the impact of this complexity on decision-making. Although tribunal procedures are generally more flexible and straightforward than court hearings, the nature of tribunal adjudication means that those who appear before tribunals without representation are often at a disadvantage. The short-comings of tribunals as effective checks on administrative decisions are the result of misdescription of procedures as informal and misconceptions about simple decision-making and the scope for unrepresented applicants to prepare, present, and advocate convincing cases.

The analysis of factors influencing the outcome of tribunal hearings suggests that increased advice and representation for applicants, and improved training and monitoring of tribunals, would be likely to increase the rate at which cases reviewed at tribunal hearings were allowed. This may not, of course, be the desired objective. It has been argued that tribunals were never intended to act as 'effective review mechanisms' and that their primary role is to provide a cloak of legitimacy for unpopular social regulation. If, however, there is a genuine intention that tribunals should provide a check on administrative decision-making, rather than merely providing a forum in which disappointed and disgruntled applicants can let off steam, their deficiencies must be addressed. It is not sufficient to assume or to assert that tribunals operate well. In order to achieve their theoretical objectives and to attain the qualities claimed for tribunals, consideration must be given to their procedures and to standards of tribunal adjudication. Finally, and most importantly, explicit attention must be paid to the means by which a balance can be struck between the conflicting demands of procedural simplicity and legal precision, in order to achieve substantive justice.

In the two extracts below conclusions are drawn from research on the users of tribunals. In the first extract Adler and Gulland have reviewed the research literature and in the second extract Genn et al's later study focuses upon the users of three tribunals: the Appeals Service (TAS) which dealt with social security and child support appeals; the Criminal Injuries Compensation Appeals Panel (CICAP); and the Special Educational Needs and Disability Tribunal (SENDIST).

M. Adler, J Gulland, *Tribunal Users' Experiences, Perceptions and Expectations: A Literature Review*

(available at <www.council-on-tribunals.gov.uk/publications/577.htm>) (2003), pp. 24–28

Practical barriers that prevent potential users from accessing tribunals

Most of the research on users' experiences looks at appellants rather than those who do not appeal. This means that most research is based on those who were *not* deterred by barriers that can prevent users from accessing the tribunal system and makes it difficult to gauge the full extent of these potential barriers.

Ignorance of rights or procedures

There are two types of ignorance which can prevent an appellant from making an appeal—ignorance of the fact that there may be grounds for appealing against the original decision and ignorance of the procedures which need to be followed. The general conclusion, supported by much of the research evidence, is that ignorance of the possible grounds of appeal is often more important than ignorance of procedures. Most appellants appear to have little understanding of the appeals procedure or the powers of tribunals but this does not, in itself, appear to be a barrier to appealing, since the procedures for appealing to most tribunals are fairly straight forward. Many researchers found that people appeal because they think the original decision s unjust, without necessarily understanding the legal basis for the decision or what their chances of success would be. There is, however, some variation between different tribunals.

Cost

There are five types of cost which can act as a deterrent for users: tribunal fees, the cost of advice and/or representation, the cost of obtaining independent assessments, the cost of attending a hearing and the risk of having costs awarded against them if they lose. Although cost is currently not an issue in most tribunals, a number of recent developments involving fees and awards of costs suggest that it may become more of an issue in future. There is little evidence from the research about whether the cost of representation acts as a barrier because most research has studied those who did appeal rather than those who did not. Non-financial costs (for example stress and time commitment) are also a concern for some appellants.

The complexity of the appeal process and absence of appropriate help

Research on many different tribunals makes it clear that many appellants are confused by the appeal process and have little idea of what will happen at a tribunal hearing. In some cases, they do not even realise that there will be a hearing and they are often confused by the paperwork they are sent. There are frequent references to the difficulties people find in obtaining advice about their appeals—this problem is especially acute in areas like child support and special educational needs where there is a shortage of specialist agencies that are able to provide representation. In addition, there is evidence that people often experience difficulties in accessing free sources of advice (such as Citizens Advice Bureaux) due to limited opening hours which necessitate taking time off work, waiting times for appointments, and difficulties in making telephone contact to arrange appointments. These are likely to disadvantage members of the public with 'low levels of competence in terms of education, income, confidence, verbal skills literacy skills and emotional fortitude'...

Physical barriers

There are a number of references to the difficulties faced by physically disabled appellants in accessing tribunal venues. Most of the research refers to the Appeals Service, i.e. to social security appeals but this is because there has been a good deal of research on appeals relating to disability benefits that has involved a high proportion of disabled appellants. On the other hand, there were favourable references to the use by the SENT of local hotels as venues since they can provide easy access for people with disabilities. Most other research on appeals has not looked specifically at appellants with disabilities, who, in most cases, constitute only a relatively small proportion of appellants.

...

The balance between speed, quality and cost

There are many references in the literature to long delays before hearings are held and to the problems they cause, especially in social security appeals where people may have had their benefit stopped or reduced, in educational appeals where a delay can constitute a significant proportion of a child's school education and in mental health reviews where civil liberties are at stake. Even where appellants may appear to benefit from a delay, for example, in social security overpayments and asylum appeals, they may suffer because of the stress involved in waiting for a tribunal hearing. There does not appear to have been any research which has examined users' views about the optimum balance between speed, quality and cost.

Informality of hearings

There are many references to the fact that users find tribunals more formal than they had expected and to the problems that this sometimes causes. However, there are clearly substantial variations in formality, not only between different types of tribunal but also between different sittings (with different chairs) of the same tribunal. Some appellants confuse the formality of tribunal hearings with the fact that they are bound by legislation.

The value of representation

Most of the research concludes that appellants find it difficult to represent themselves. When people have the opportunity to be represented (because they are able to afford legal representation, because they are able to obtain legal aid, or because free lay representation is available) they tend to make use of it. Although some appellants choose to represent themselves, they often find that the process is more complex and legalistic than they had imagined and regret their decision afterwards. There is little research-based support for one of the central tenets of the Leggatt Report, namely that 'a combination of good quality information and advice, effective procedures and well-conducted hearings, and competent and well-trained tribunal members' would make it possible for 'the vast majority of appellants to put their cases properly themselves', i.e. without representation.

...

Users' views on the independence and impartiality of tribunals

There is little research evidence to suggest that users question the independence or impartiality of tribunal proceedings. However, there are some exceptions to this general finding. Although the existence of strong 'outcome effects' confuses the issue, research indicates that some appellants feel that Employment tribunals are biased in favour of employers, that Rent Assessment Panels are biased in favour of landlords, that Exclusion Appeal Panels pre-judge cases and that Mental Health Review Tribunals are too dependent on the evidence of the RMO. Research also indicates that some appellants (particularly in social security and child support appeals) confuse the 'independence and impartiality' of tribunals with their duty to apply the law.

H. Genn, B. Lever and L. Gray, *Tribunals For Diverse Users*

DCA Research Series 1/06, pp. ii–iii

Motivation and preparedness for tribunal hearings

A waiting room survey of tribunal users revealed that, across all ethnic groups, the principal motivation for appealing to tribunals was a sense of unfairness. Few users had known about the possibility of seeking redress from their general knowledge and in most cases information about the possibility of appealing to the tribunal had come from the initial decision letter sent by the Department or Authority.

Users' expectations of proceedings were relatively vague, with an unacceptably high proportion of users in TAS and CICAP not knowing what to expect. Some anticipated a judge and jury, others a friendly and informal chat. This presents a challenge to the new Tribunal Service in helping to prepare users for hearings so that they can present their cases effectively. In SENDIST, the practice of sending a video to users prior to their hearing appears to have been effective in framing users' expectations.

About half of the users interviewed at hearings were attending without representation, generally because it had not occurred to them to seek representation, or because they had tried and been unable to obtain representation. Unrepresented Minority Ethnic users attending hearings were more likely than White users to have tried and failed to obtain representation.

Delivering fair hearings

Observation of tribunal hearings revealed generally high levels of professionalism among tribunal judiciary, with most being able to combine authority with approachability. There were few examples of insensitive language and with rare exceptions tribunals treated users from all ethnic backgrounds with courtesy and respect. Tribunals used a wide range of techniques to enable users to participate effectively in hearings and to convey that they were listening to, and taking seriously, the user's case. Although, with the assistance of tribunals, most users were able to present their cases reasonably well, observation of users during hearings revealed deep and fundamental differences in language, literacy, culture, education, confidence and fluency, which traverse ethnic boundaries. These differences significantly affect users' ability to present their case. Even with the benefit of training, there are limits to the ability of tribunals to compensate for users' difficulties in presenting their case. In some circumstances, an advocate is not only helpful to the user and to the tribunal, but may be crucial to procedural and substantive fairness.

Users' assessments of hearings and outcome

Most users, interviewed after their hearing and before receiving their decision, made generally positive assessments of treatment during hearings and of their own ability to participate. Where dissatisfaction occurred, it tended to result from tribunals communicating the impression that they had already made up their mind or that they were not listening attentively to the user. This underlines the significance that users attach to feeling that they have been heard, that their arguments have been taken seriously and weighed by the tribunal. Lack of preparedness affected users' responses to the hearing and those startled by the relative formality of hearings tended to feel less comfortable and to express greater dissatisfaction. Despite users' generally positive assessments of hearings, about one in five, when prompted, raised concerns about perceived unfairness or lack of respect during the hearing. South Asian users and some other non-European users were consistently more negative than other groups in their assessments of hearings and were the most likely to perceive unfairness. Importantly, however, there was evidence that those Minority Ethnic groups most likely to perceive unfairness at hearings were less likely to do so when the tribunal was itself ethnically diverse. This suggests that increasing the ethnic diversity of tribunal panels might have a positive effect on perceptions of fairness among Minority Ethnic users.

Post-decision interviews revealed that about one-quarter of unsuccessful users had not understood the reason for the decision and this was more often the case among Minority Ethnic than White users. This presents a significant challenge to tribunals.

The outcome of tribunal hearings

Modelling the outcome of hearings in the three tribunals revealed that in TAS case type, representation and ethnic group independently influenced the outcome of hearings. Controlling for other factors, unrepresented TAS users were less likely to succeed at their hearing than represented TAS users and Minority Ethnic TAS users were slightly less likely to be successful at their hearing than White TAS users. By contrast, in CICAP and SENDIST only case type had a significant impact on the outcome of hearings, although the number of Minority Ethnic users in SENDIST is very small. Once case type had been controlled for, neither representation nor ethnic group appeared to affect outcome in either CICAP or SENDIST. The TAS outcome findings regarding representation and ethnicity raise some important questions.

Identifying the source of disadvantage that seems to flow from lack of representation and ethnicity would be valuable not only for TAS, but also more broadly for discussion about procedures and judicial training in other tribunals and in the courts. One clue may be that users' observed ability to argue their case was significantly associated with outcome at hearings. TAS users, who often come from among the most disadvantaged groups in society, were significantly less likely than CICAP or SENDIST users to present their cases well. This constitutes a general challenge to the enabling skills of TAS judiciary during relatively brief hearings, but in the case of some Minority Ethnic groups, language and cultural differences may present additional complications in enabling users to make the best of their case.

B: Alternative dispute resolution

These findings demonstrate that users did not find that some of the supposed advantages of tribunals over courts were realized. Despite the evidence suggesting that represented users are more successful than unrepresented users, Leggatt had recommended that users should normally be expected to present their cases themselves (para. 4.21). The Government took the view that users found oral hearings stressful and expounded a different strategy for people dealing with legal problems and disputes.

Transforming Public Services: Complaints, Redress and Tribunals

Cm 6243, paras 2.3–2.4

2.3 ...The aim is to develop a range of policies and services that, so far as possible, will help people to avoid problems and legal disputes in the first place; and where they cannot, provides tailored solutions to resolve the dispute as quickly and cost effectively as possible. It can be summed up as 'Proportionate Dispute Resolution'.

2.3 We want to:

- minimise the risk of people facing legal problems by ensuring that the framework of law defining people's rights and responsibilities is as fair, simple and clear as possible, and that State agencies, administering systems like tax and benefits, make better decisions and give clearer explanations;
- improve people's understanding of their rights and responsibilities, and the information available to them about what they can do and where they can go for help when problems do arise. This will help people to decide how to deal with the problem themselves if they can, and ensure they get the advice and other services they need if they cannot;
- ensure that people have ready access to early and appropriate advice and assistance when they need it, so that problems can be solved and potential disputes nipped in the bud long before they escalate into formal legal proceedings;
- promote the development of a range of tailored dispute resolution services, so that different types of dispute can be resolved fairly, quickly, efficiently and effectively, without recourse to the expense and formality of courts and tribunals where this is not necessary;
- but also deliver cost-effective court and tribunal services, that are better targeted on those cases where a hearing is the best option for resolving the dispute or enforcing the outcome.

[One of the features of this new approach is the use of alternative dispute resolution methods.]

2.11 There are a number of alternative dispute resolution (ADR) processes:

- adjudication involves an impartial, independent third party hearing the claims of both sides and issuing a decision to resolve the dispute. The outcome is determined by the adjudicator, not by the parties. Determinations are usually made on the basis of fairness, and the process used and means of decision-making are not bound by law. It can involve a hearing or be based on documents only;
- arbitration involves an impartial, independent third party hearing the claims of both sides and issuing a binding decision to resolve the dispute. The outcome is determined by the arbitrator, is final and legally binding, with limited grounds for appeal. It requires both parties' willing and informed consent to participate. It can involve a hearing or be based on documents only;

- conciliation involves an impartial third party helping the parties to resolve their dispute by hearing both sides and offering an opinion on settlement. It requires both parties' willing and informed consent to participate. The parties determine the outcome, usually with advice from the conciliator. An example is Acas conciliation;
- early neutral evaluation involves an independent person assessing the claims made by each side and giving an opinion on (a) the likely outcome in court or tribunal, (b) a fair outcome, and/or (c) a technical or legal point. It is non-binding, and the parties decide how to use the opinion in their negotiations. It requires both parties' willing and informed consent to participate. It can be useful to help moderate a party's unrealistic claims;
- mediation involves an independent third party helping parties to reach a voluntary, mutually agreed resolution. A key principle is that the parties, not the mediator, decide the outcome. It requires both parties' willing and informed consent to participate. It requires mediating skills, and it has a structured format;
- negotiation involves dealing directly with the person or the organisation in dispute. It is non-binding and can be done by the person in dispute or by a representative ('assisted negotiation'). The negotiator is not impartial but instead represents a party's interests. An example of negotiation is settlement discussions between solicitors; and
- ombudsmen are impartial, independent 'referees' who consider, investigate and resolve complaints about public and private organisations. Their decisions are made on the basis of what is fair and reasonable. They also have a role in influencing good practice in complaints handling.

M. Adler, 'Tribunal Reform: Proportionate Dispute Resolution and the Pursuit of Administrative Justice'

(2006) 69 *Modern Law Review* 958, 983–985

The ... White Paper is an ambitious document in that it sets out to turn on its head the Government's traditional emphasis on courts, judges and court procedure, and on legal aid to pay for litigation lawyers; to develop a range of policies and services that will help people to avoid problems and disputes in the first place; and to provide 'tailored solutions' to resolve disputes without necessarily seeking redress from a tribunal. In order to achieve these ends, it develops the principle of 'proportionate dispute resolution' and notes that, in order to put this principle into practice, the types of problems and disputes people have; the outcomes they wish to achieve; the various options available and the extent to which these options will promote administrative justice need to be considered. I have considered a number of policy options, each of which holds out the prospect of enhancing administrative justice, and my conclusions are summarised below.

As far as the types of problems and disputes people have are concerned, what is at issue is frequently contested by the parties in dispute—so called 'experts' think the issue about one thing while those who experienced the problem think it is about something else. However, I have pointed out that the distinctions invoked by the experts, e.g. between fact and law, rule and discretion, process and out come, and law and policy, are more relevant to deciding how problems and disputes should be handled than the accounts of what is at issue that are given by those with grievances. It follows that more work needs to be done on refining a typology based on these 'top-down' distinctions. As far as the outcomes people wish to achieve are concerned, I have argued that it is by no means clear that it is always in the public interest that people's preferences should prevail. This is because those who just want an apology may have a strong legal case while those who seek a legal remedy may have a very weak case or no case at all. Thus, although there is a case for considering the remedies that people want, it may be in the public interest that cases are considered by a tribunal (or by a court or an ombudsman) so that there can be a clear and authoritative ruling on the issue in question. This outcome might be achieved if a 'one-door' approach, in which everyone who is dissatisfied with a decision or the way in which it was reached puts their concerns to an official who would then decide what kind of problem they have and directs them to the appropriate dispute resolution procedure.

I do not believe that effective external forms of accountability on their own will be sufficient to raise standards of first-instance decision making to acceptable levels and argue that effective internal forms of accountability, such as internal quality controls and quality assurance systems, are also required. I support the introduction of a 'one-door' approach, in which everyone who is dissatisfied with a decision, or with the way in which it is reached, would put their concerns to an official who would then decide what kind of problem they had and direct them to the appropriate dispute resolution procedure. This procedure ought to reduce the number of errors that individuals currently make when they select redress procedures for themselves.

It is my view that, if initial decisions were reviewed as a matter of routine by the line manager of the first-instance decision maker or by a specialist reviewing officer, many cases could probably be resolved at an early stage and I conclude that there is a very strong case for making departmental reviews mandatory. Although this would add to administrative costs, there would be administrative savings because, in the case of tribunals, there would be a reduction in the number of cases proceeding to a tribunal hearing. I argue that, providing the staff are of sufficient calibre, early-neutral evaluation would result in the identification of 'weak' cases on both sides and that, together with mandatory reviews of decisions that are complained about or appealed against, it would result in the 'filltering out' of a substantial proportion of the weak cases that are currently heard by tribunals. The costs of compulsory departmental review and early-neutral evaluation could be set against the savings, for government department or public bodies and the new Tribunals Service, which would result from a smaller number of tribunal hearings.

Because, in administrative disputes, citizens may settle for less than they are entitled to, I am somewhat skeptical about the contribution of mediation and conciliation (and likewise of negotiation) to the resolution of administrative disputes and I argue that tribunal hearings may be needed to protect the interests of the citizen. I am also, for different reasons, rather skeptical about the extent to which ombudsman techniques are transferable to many of the citizen versus state disputes that tribunals deal with and doubtful about whether the substitution of one mode of dispute resolution for another could be achieved in a smooth and orderly way. Thus, I conclude that the potential for mediation and conciliation, and for ombudsman techniques, in a tribunal system is rather limited. However, I do favour the provision of publicly-funded representation for appellants in second-tier appeal tribunals. I point out that, to the extent that cases are diverted from tribunals, the tribunal caseload should be smaller but argue that the need for representation in the smaller number of cases that still proceed to a tribunal hearing may actually be greater. Since this applies, in particular, to second-tier appeal tribunals, which will require leave and be limited to points of law, I conclude that there is a strong case for providing publicly-funded representation (not necessarily by lawyers) in such cases.

NOTES

1. Adler supports the use of internal review and early neutral evaluation. The Tribunals Service has undertaken two pilot projects in early dispute resolution. The first was conducted in three employment tribunal offices from August 2006–July 2007. It involved a trained judicial member offering facilitative mediation with the aim of assisting the parties to resolve their dispute without the need for a hearing. Participation in this mediation was voluntary. There was a national roll out of judicial mediation before the publication of the evaluation which had not found it to be cost-effective and had not recommended a national roll out. See P. Urwin et al, *Evaluation of Early Neutral Evaluation Alternative Dispute Resolution in the Social Security and Child Support Tribunal* (Ministry of Justice Research Series 7/10, 2010).

   The second pilot is examining whether a form of Early Neutral Evaluation can be effective as a means of dealing with some Disability Living Allowance and Attendance Allowance appeals. Here a designated judicial member assesses the case papers of appellants who have agreed to participate. The assessor forms a view on the likely outcome at hearing. The District Chairman then contacts the party who is assessed as the likely loser. If that is the Disability and Carers Service, they would be invited to reconsider the case. If it is the appellant then he or she is warned that the appeal is likely to fail. Contact with the appellant might suggest that if the appellant has other evidence then it should be submitted, or seek advice, or focus on the specific issues which the tribunal will need to consider. Thus it is hoped weak cases will be discouraged or action taken to strengthen them. If the assessment is that the case is finely balanced then no contact is made with either party. The evaluation of this pilot found that 'Overall, therefore, there was evidence to conclude that ADR had achieved more proportionate resolution of cases to an extent but that it had impacted negatively on the speed of resolution of cases across the pilot as a whole'. This led to a recommendation to conduct a limited roll out and to adjust the procedure and monitor it. There has been no further action.

See C. Hay, K. McKennna & T. Buck, *Evaluation of Early Neutral Evaluation Alternative Dispute Resolution in the Social Security and Child Support Tribunal* (Ministry of Justice Research Series 2/10, 2010).

2. Concern about the rise of ADR has been expressed. One commentator notes the rise of informality and fears that it could create a transparency gap, 'There is a public, not merely a private interest in challenges brought by citizens against public authorities' (A Le Sueur Courts, 'Tribunals Ombudsmen, ADR; Administrative Justice Constitutionalism and Informality' in J. Jowell, and D. Oliver, *The Changing Constitution* (6th edn, 2007), p. 317 at 333). He is also concerned that parties might be compelled to use ADR.
3. Adler thinks that internal accountability mechanisms in administrative bodies such as quality assurance have to be supported by external mechanisms. Leggatt recommended that review should be developed and supplemented by feedback from tribunals on systemic aspects of decision-making within departments (Ch 9). The Government accepted this proposal, including it in the new approach to dispute resolution which would help departments to get decisions 'right first time' (Cm 6243, para. 6.32). The Senior President is required under s. 43 to report annually to the Lord Chancellor on matters which he wishes to bring to the Lord Chancellor's attention and on matters which the Lord Chancellor has asked to covered.

■ QUESTION

Bearing in mind the reservations of Adler and Le Sueur do you think there is (a) much scope for the use of the ADR in public law cases generally and tribunals in particular and (b) would the use of ADR be desirable?

C: Oral hearings

While ADR may be encouraged it is recognized that oral hearings will still be used. What might be the cases where oral hearings are to be preferred as the method of dispute resolution? This question was addressed in a consultation exercise by the Council on Tribunals which produced a report *Consultation on the Use and Value of Oral Hearings in the Administrative Justice System, Summary of Responses* (2006): <www.council-on-tribunals.gov.uk/publications/628.htm>. This and other research was considered by Richardson and Genn (see *post*) who noted there were instrumental reasons supporting oral hearings in both the law (common law and the jurisprudence on Art. 6(1) of the European Convention on Human Rights) and the research literature, to the effect that oral hearings could improve the accuracy of decisions, enhance transparency and improve public confidence. There are other factors independent of the outcome of the decision, such as the dignity of the individual, democratic legitimacy and participation. They also referred to the research on tribunal users' experiences, (including Genn et al, see p. 713, *ante*) highlighting T. Tyler, 'Social Justice: Outcome and Procedure' (2000) 35 *International Journal of Psychology* 117, who identified four primary factors: 'opportunities for participation (voice), the neutrality of the forum, the trustworthiness of the authorities, and the degree to which people receive treatment with dignity and respect'. In the extract they draw on case law on due process from the US and on the guidance on what procedure is due in relation to a protected interest in *Mathews* v *Eldridge* 424 U.S. 319 (1976). In this case about the timing of a hearing on the termination of a benefit, the United States Supreme Court identified three factors which had to be balanced: 'the private interest affected, the risk of error, and the state's interest in minimising costs and additional burdens'.

G. Richardson, H. Genn, 'Tribunals in Transition: Resolution or Adjudication?'

[2007] *Public Law* 116, pp. 135–140

Fundamental rights cases

A small minority of tribunals deal directly with the fundamental rights of individuals. The Asylum and Immigration Tribunal (AIT) and the Mental Health Review Tribunal (MHRT) are the most obvious examples. An appeal against the refusal of asylum before the AIT can raise questions of an individual's right to liberty of the person, the right to be free from torture and even his or her right to life, while a case before the MHRT can involve both compulsory detention in hospital and the imposition of compulsory treatment. Issues of such weight to the individuals concerned might be thought automatically to demand immediate determination by way of independent adjudication and an oral hearing, particularly where the political background is highly sensitive. There might be legitimate reasons for determining preliminary matters in advance by way of case management reviews, some aspects of which might be conducted on paper, but speedy access to adjudication by way of an oral hearing might properly be regarded as non-negotiable. It is certainly not the intention here to argue against this conclusion, rather to place it in context.

These cases can correctly be described as involving fundamental rights but such rights have to be carefully articulated before they can be accurately applied to individual circumstances. In relation to asylum the AIT (previously the IAT) has to decide when the feared mistreatment would amount to "torture" or "inhuman or degrading treatment or punishment" under Art.3 ECHR. As Thomas has explained, the tribunal has distinguished between mere hardship on the one hand and persecution or ill-treatment on the other, because "it is simply not possible for this country to take in all who might suffer hardship". But the tribunal has been unable to state how these are to be distinguished other than by identifying "some particular reason in an individual case" which establishes that the treatment will contravene Art.3. In the context of compulsory detention and treatment under mental health legislation, although the MHRT is policing a legal boundary between lawful and unlawful detention, the statutory criteria for lawfulness are couched in medical terms. The ambiguities and difficulties to which this gives rise for both tribunal members and, to some extent, the reviewing courts have been discussed elsewhere. Here it is relevant simply to note that in policing the individual's fundamental legal rights the tribunal has to rely heavily on its understanding of the medical implications.

Thus the AIT and the MHRT both possess an extensive interpretative role. They are doing more than simply striving for an accurate application of an individual's legal rights, however fundamental; they are directly determining the boundaries of those rights. And they are occasionally doing so in a highly charged political atmosphere, or in a context where proper communication between disciplines is key. In these circumstances the use of adjudication rather than resolution through negotiation is essential. The rights at stake are so fundamental that their precise boundaries must be established through an independent and authoritative procedure and once established they cannot be susceptible to negotiation. In addition there is a powerful case for arguing that this adjudication should be conducted by way of an oral hearing, because such hearings would promote the interests of all parties. To return to the three factors listed in *Mathews v Eldridge*: the individual interests are exceptionally high, the notions of accuracy or even error are themselves contentious and need to be aired publicly, and the benefits accruing to government from such openness should outweigh any additional financial costs incurred through the provision of an oral rather than a paper hearing. The literature has long recognised that the creation of a tribunal can serve to distance the government from the implementation of unpopular policies. In the same spirit, the maintenance of oral hearings where the application of difficult legal boundaries can be seen to take place at arm's length from government and to be subject to public scrutiny must help to enhance the apparent legitimacy of public policy.

Entitlements to a material benefit

Secondly, there are entitlement cases. The citizen claims a material entitlement falling short of a private law right which is denied by the state agency. Appeals to the Social Security and Child Support Appeals Service or to the Criminal Injuries Compensation Appeals Panel would fall into this category. Are such cases appropriate for and amenable to settlement negotiations or do they require adjudication? In answering the question it might be helpful to distinguish between eligibility cases and those concerned primarily with questions of quantum where eligibility is accepted and the dispute concerns the appropriate level of award. On pure eligibility issues, the outcome to which the redress process should be directed is the accurate determination of the citizen's claim, as in *Mathews v Eldridge* itself, and this might suggest determination by adjudication rather than resolution via negotiation. Either the entitlement is made out and owed to the citizen or it is not. It might be acceptable for the tribunal to check the facts and approach the agency for reconsideration if relevant, or even to explain to the citizen that the claim had no legal merit. But if either party remained adamant an adjudication would be required. In such cases the concept of dispute "resolution" seems inappropriate. There is not an unlimited range of alternative outcomes that the parties can explore in order to "resolve" a difference of view. Entitlement is based on the factual situation of the claimant in relation to the relevant regulation. The claimant may believe that her situation satisfies the requirements while the agency takes a different view. The role of the tribunal is to decide which view will prevail and award or deny the benefit on that basis.

In the second category of case, where the dispute concerns the quantum of entitlement rather than eligibility, there might, at first glance, be a stronger argument in favour of seeking a negotiated resolution before resorting to adjudication. However, even though negotiation might assist in clarifying the factual situation and pinpointing areas of conflict, there is in fact little scope for compromise. Either the claimant is entitled to the specified level of benefit or award on the strength of her factual situation, or she is not. Only very rarely will either the agency or tribunal have the freedom to "split the difference" or to offer an alternative to the disputed benefit. In so far as the tribunal has discretion, it resides in the interpretation and meaning attributed to the facts presented, not in the remedy contingent on that interpretation and meaning. It is therefore apparent that when early intervention fails to achieve agreement, disputes as to the level of entitlement may also demand an accurate determination of the merits and require adjudication.

On the question of oral hearings more specifically it is necessary to return again to the three factors in *Mathews v Eldridge*. In both eligibility and quantum cases the citizen's interest, the acquisition of the material benefit claimed, will be significant but, unlike the fundamental rights cases, it may not be determinative either for or against orality. Similarly, the risk of error is present in both eligibility and quantum cases where an accurate determination of the merits will turn on an accurate determination of facts: how far can the claimant walk, for example. In such cases a proper testing of evidence is required in order to establish whether or not the claimant has a "right" to the award or benefit and at a particular level. While the clarification and testing of evidence might be more effectively achieved via some form of oral hearing rather than on paper, this does not point inevitably to the use of traditional tribunal hearings on purely instrumental grounds. The full oral hearing might not be essential to achieve accuracy.

Finally in terms of the state's interests in minimising costs there may be little to distinguish eligibility and quantum cases. Ideally a form of process should be adopted which will lead to an accurate outcome as economically as possible. There is no conflict here between the state's interests and those of the individual provided the state does not seek to reduce the process to the point where accuracy is compromised. However, the adjudication process does not occur in isolation. From the citizen's point of view it would be preferable to receive an accurate decision at the first tier and not to face the necessity of appealing. On the other hand the provision of high quality decision-making at the first tier might cost the agency more than the provision of an effective appeal. There will be a complex web of government priorities at play here, particularly now the DCA has become responsible for the major appeal systems but not the initial decisions. Perhaps all that can be done is to remain vigilant on the need to maintain procedural standards but reasonably flexible as to their precise form.

Entitlements to an assessment or to a consideration

In certain circumstances children with special educational needs are entitled to special educational provision. Parents who wish to appeal against decisions of their Local Education Authority (LEA) regarding such provision may do so to the Special Educational Needs and Disability Tribunal (SENDIST). As the term is being used in this paper, an entitlement describes the claim to a government or state benefit which falls short of the assertion of a private law right. These entitlements can be to a material benefit, as in the cases considered above, or to an assessment and/or consideration. Both forms of entitlement are common within modern developed states and will often arise in the context of a social right, such as the right to education. According to Harris, social rights and the public law duties from which they are derived "tend to be difficult to enforce ... and highly conditional". They are resource-constrained and vulnerable to economic and political fluctuations. The education of children with special educational needs is an area of social policy where such "rights" abound.

Before a child can access special educational provision he or she must be assessed by the LEA as having special educational needs and the LEA may issue a statement detailing the special help required. Parents may appeal to SENDIST about the failure either to assess or to issue a statement or, if a statement is provided, about the contents of that statement. In 2004–05 SENDIST upheld 87 per cent of all such "contents" appeals. This extremely high success rate does not, however, imply that the needs articulated in the statement will immediately be met. SENDIST has no means of enforcing its decisions. It also makes it clear in its advice to parents that they cannot appeal "about how the LEA is arranging to provide the help set out in your child's statement". As Deans suggests, parents have "a right to have their needs assessed, but not necessarily to command the resources necessary to satisfy their needs". It is an entitlement to assessment rather than to the material benefit itself. The conditional nature of these entitlements is further illustrated in relation to the choice of school. Parents have the right to express a preference for a particular maintained school but that preference can be denied if the placement would not be compatible with efficient education or "the efficient use of resources".

Thus while the entitlement either to an assessment or to the expression of a preference might be susceptible to determination through adjudication by SENDIST, the extent of the material benefits lying at the heart of the dispute can be highly contentious and resource dependent. There is often no single accurate outcome to be identified and imposed through adjudication by one tribunal. The issues raised may also involve complex questions of educational and psychological theory and practice where, as King has argued, the reliance on a legal process of decision-making may "simplify, reduce, distort and filter psychological and educational information". Further, and most significantly, these disputes tend to arise in the context of an ongoing relationship. Unless the family moves the parents will be negotiating with the same LEA throughout their child's school career. In such circumstances it is relevant to ask whether other forms of resolution should be attempted before resort to adjudication. LEAs are already required to provide "arrangements to prevent or sort out disagreements", but it may be appropriate to introduce something more systematic. In terms of the analysis in *Mathews* v *Eldridge*, the desired outcome at this stage might not be an accurate determination of the entitlements directly at stake. The limited nature of these entitlements already reflects the need to achieve a balance between the interests of the individual child in having the best possible educational provision and the public interest in the fair allocation of limited resources between all eligible children. And in these circumstances the interests of all parties might be better served by a procedure designed to penetrate below the formal entitlement and to seek an allocation of resources which appears fair and achievable to all sides. Of course there will always be cases where parents who feel driven to strive for the very best outcome on behalf of their child may be very reluctant to compromise. In such cases, and in others where attempts to identify an agreed resolution have failed, it would still be necessary to turn to the tribunal to adjudicate on the relevant entitlements.

In these intractable cases an oral hearing is likely to be indicated by reference to all three of the *Mathews* v *Eldridge* criteria. Here the issues are of considerable importance to the parents and the child and possibly to future potential beneficiaries of the LEA's special needs budget. Even if the crucial outcome is not simply the accurate determination of the merits but the transparent explanation of that determination, the risks of error or failure are considerable. In these circumstances, if the provision of an oral hearing before the tribunal helps to avoid the need for onward appeal or judicial review, the additional costs incurred would be well spent.

SECTION 4: REVIEWING THE ADMINISTRATIVE JUSTICE SYSTEM

TRIBUNALS, COURTS AND ENFORCEMENT ACT 2007

44 The Administrative Justice and Tribunals Council

(1) There is to be a council to be known as the Administrative Justice and Tribunals Council.

...

SCHEDULE 7

Membership

1 (1) The Council is to consist of—

(a) the Parliamentary Commissioner for Administration, and

(b) not more than fifteen nor fewer than ten appointed members.

(2) Of the appointed members—

(a) either two or three are to be appointed by the Scottish Ministers with the concurrence of the Lord Chancellor and the Welsh Ministers,
(b) either one or two are to be appointed by the Welsh Ministers with the concurrence of the Lord Chancellor and the Scottish Ministers, and
(c) the others are to be appointed by the Lord Chancellor with the concurrence of the Scottish Ministers and the Welsh Ministers.

Chairman of the Council

2 (1) After consultation with the Scottish Ministers and the Welsh Ministers, the Lord Chancellor must nominate one of the appointed members to be chairman of the Council.

(2) The chairman of the Council is to hold and vacate that office in accordance with the terms of his nomination, but—

(a) may resign that office by giving written notice to the Lord Chancellor, and
(b) ceases to be chairman if he ceases to be a person who is a member of the Council by virtue of appointment under paragraph 1(2).

Scottish Committee

4 (1) There is to be a Scottish Committee of the Council (referred to in this Schedule as "the Scottish Committee") for the purpose of exercising the functions conferred on it by any statutory provision.

(2) The Scottish Committee is to consist of—

(a) the Parliamentary Commissioner for Administration,
(b) the Scottish Public Services Ombudsman,
(c) the members of the Council appointed under paragraph 1(2)(a), and
(d) either three or four other persons, not being members of the Council, appointed by the Scottish Ministers.

Welsh Committee

7 (1) There is to be a Welsh Committee of the Council (referred to in this Schedule as "the Welsh Committee") for the purpose of exercising the functions conferred on it by any statutory provision.

(2) The Welsh Committee is to consist of—

(a) the Parliamentary Commissioner for Administration,
(b) the Public Services Ombudsman for Wales,
(c) the members of the Council appointed under paragraph 1(2)(b), and
(d) either two or three other persons, not being members of the Council, appointed by the Welsh Ministers.

Transforming Tribunals: Implementing Part 1 of the Tribunals, Courts and Enforcement Act 2007

Ministry of Justice (2007), paras 115–118

115 The new landscape of justice which the government is seeking to develop has at its core two fundamental assumptions about the provision of justice. The first is that justice, while an all-encompassing concept, can usefully be sub-divided: criminal, civil, administrative, family, employment, housing and so on. There is room for debate about how many "justice systems" there are, the precise boundaries between them, and the extent to which they inevitably overlap. But the essential point is that justice, within each of these systems, is provided not just by courts or tribunals but by a range of interlocking institutions and mechanisms.

116 The second fundamental assumption is that the institutions will pursue the common goal in different ways. They are not intended just to respond or process, although they must of course be responsive and efficient: each, in their own way, seeks to improve the lot of those going through the system. Thus the

Tribunals Service has been set up to play an active role in reforming and improving the system of administrative justice of which it is part.

A New Body and a New Remit

117 Administrative justice and tribunals are complex and diverse worlds. The government—following Leggatt—concluded that in the new landscape created by its reforms there was a need for an institution independent of government, tribunals and the other participants. This institution would have a focus on the whole administrative justice system and an important role to play in setting standards and championing the interests of the user.

118 The result is the Administrative Justice and Tribunals Council (AJTC). In addition to taking on the Council of Tribunals' existing role in respect of tribunals and inquiries, its remit is to:

- keep the administrative justice system under review
- consider ways to make the system accessible, fair and efficient
- advise Ministers and the Senior President on the development of the system and refer proposals for change to them, and
- make proposals for research into the system.

The AJTC retains the abolished Council on Tribunals' remit of keeping under review and reporting on tribunals and inquiries illustrated by this extract from its last annual report on social security and criminal injuries compensation.

Administrative Justice and Tribunals Council, Annual Report 2009–10

(2010), pp. 21–25

4. Exploiting opportunities for our voice to be heard on behalf of users

WORK AND PENSIONS SELECT COMMITTEE INQUIRY: DECISION MAKING AND APPEALS IN THE BENEFITS SYSTEM

1. The House of Commons Work and Pensions Committee announced an inquiry into decision making and appeals in the benefits system, with particular regard to its effectiveness and how it could be improved. In respect of appeals, the Committee was interested in how the system operated from the users' perspective and whether there was sufficient support available to those people bringing appeals.

2. We submitted evidence to the Committee highlighting a number of user concerns, including:

- The need for greater drive by the Department for Work and Pensions (DWP) to reduce the level of complexity in the benefit rules;
- More needing to be done by the decision making Agencies to analyse systematically the outcomes of tribunal hearings in order to provide better guidance to decision makers;
- Presenting Officers should attend tribunal hearings as a matter of course in order to assist tribunals and to provide a feedback link to decision makers;
- The DWP should consider rolling out the Professionalism in Decision Making and Appeals training initiative across all its decision making Agencies;
- Appeals should be lodged with the Tribunals Service rather than with the original decision making Agencies;
- A uniform statutory time limit for responding to appeals should be introduced for the decision making Agencies;
- Greater efforts are needed to reduce appeal delays and to provide meaningful information for tribunal users about how long appeals take to get to a hearing.

3. We were pleased to note that many of the issues we raised were highlighted in the Committee's final report. In particular, the Committee recognised the need to reduce delay in the appeals process and shared our view of the need for a statutory time limit for the DWP to respond to appeals, recommending a one month time limit from the date an appeal is lodged.

4. The response by the previous government, which was published just before the announcement of the general election, was largely disappointing in its failure to address seriously many of the report's recommendations. The response dismissed the recommendation for a one month time limit on grounds that it would not improve the situation, without any explanation of the reason for taking that view.

5. Our Chairman has written to the new Secretary of State outlining our ongoing concerns and highlighting the potential financial benefits that would accrue from streamlining the decision making and appeals processes and getting more decisions "right first time".

TRAINING FOR ADMISSION APPEAL PANEL MEMBERS AND CLERKS

6. In our 2007–08 Report we reported that the then Department for Children, Schools and Families had agreed to legislate to make provision for mandatory training for appeal panel members and clerks. This was achieved through the Education (Admission Appeals Arrangements) (England) (Amendment) Regulations 2007, which provides for all panel members and clerks to have received prescribed training within the previous two years as a requirement to being allowed to hear appeals. In order to avoid a burdensome training requirement for existing members and clerks, the regulations provided that the training requirement was deemed to be satisfied for all those who had served as a member or clerk from 1 March 2007 until 29 February 2008. This provision, however, ceased to apply from 1 March 2010, from which time all members and clerks are required to satisfy the new training requirement. We were concerned that many clerks and members may not be aware of this and that appeals for this year's admission round might be compromised as a result.

7. Our Chairman wrote to the then Secretary of State raising this and noting that the AJTC had begun receiving enquiries from appeals clerks enquiring where they might obtain assistance in accessing good quality training for themselves and their panel members. This was an issue we had raised with the department in our response to consultation on the draft 2007 regulations. We highlighted the lack of access to good quality training, particularly in respect of the clerks to the panels serving voluntary-aided and foundation schools, which are their own admission authorities. We invited the department to consider updating the training material produced by the organisation *'Information for School and College Governors'*, which they had funded a few years earlier.

8. In her response the Parliamentary Under Secretary of State at that time confirmed that departmental officials were considering ways of disseminating good practice training provision for panel members and clerks, including updating the existing material, combined with good practice training guidance from local authorities, which could be made more widely available. However, her reply did not fully address the more crucial point about the need to ensure that panel members and clerks were aware of the universal application of the mandatory training requirement. We intend to monitor this issue closely at our forthcoming visits to hearings and have also brought it to the attention of the local government ombudsman as an issue to bear in mind in dealing with complaints about admission appeal panels.

JOINT COMMITTEE ON HUMAN RIGHTS: ENHANCING PARLIAMENT'S ROLE IN RELATION TO HUMAN RIGHTS JUDGMENTS

9. In 2008, the former Council on Tribunals had expressed concern as to whether the limited appeal provisions in the Safeguarding Vulnerable Groups Act 2006 were compliant with Article 6 of the European Convention on Human Rights (ECHR). We were therefore interested in the judgment of the Court of Appeal in Governors of X School v R (on the application of G) & Ors [2010] EWCA Civ 1. In this case, the Court held that in any proceedings leading up to a person being placed on a list barring them from working with children or vulnerable adults, Article 6 of the ECHR is engaged, since the claimants' civil right to practise his profession is affected. The Court concluded that this result could not be dislodged by the existence of a limited right of appeal on a point of law to the Upper Tribunal from a decision of the Independent Safeguarding Authority (ISA), since the merits of the ISA's decision lay beyond the Upper Tribunal's jurisdiction.

10. Our Chairman decided to raise this matter with the Chair of the Joint Select Committee on Human Rights in connection with its review of Parliament's role in relation to human rights judgments. Our continuing concern is that an individual who is found by the ISA to be unsuitable to work with children or vulnerable adults, and thereby potentially deprived of their livelihood, should have access to a full right of appeal on the merits of the ISA's decision and not just on the limited ground of error of law or fact. The

Select Committee's report included our Chairman's letter, acknowledging the seriousness of our concerns and recommending that the government respond directly to the issues raised, including its analysis of the compatibility of the appeal provisions in the Safeguarding Vulnerable Groups Act 2006 (SVGA). Our Chairman subsequently wrote to the Home Secretary providing further background information about our concerns, which have been well documented in previous annual reports. However, his letter arrived after the preelection period prior to the beginning of the general election.

8[sic]. On 15 June 2010 the new Home Secretary announced that registration with the vetting and barring scheme was being halted to enable the government to undertake a review of the scheme, which was widely believed to be disproportionate and overly burdensome in its operation. Following the announcement of this review our Chairman wrote to the new Home Secretary inviting her to take the opportunity to consider whether the associated SVGA appeal provisions are fair, open and accessible.

...

FIRST-TIER TRIBUNAL (MENTAL HEALTH)

12. Our concerns about the former Mental Health Review Tribunal, now the First-tier Tribunal (Mental Health), have been well documented in past annual reports. The Mental Health Tribunals Stakeholder Group continues to provide a useful forum for stakeholders to exchange views with tribunal administrators and judiciary about the operation of the tribunal. Nevertheless, we became aware of a growing perception of renewed concern about the tribunal, which unfortunately coincided with a hiatus in appointing a new Head of Administration following the departure of the previous post-holder who had been successful in establishing real momentum for change following the move of the administration from London to Leicester. Some members of the tribunal contacted us expressing the view that, having been encouraged by signs of real improvement, matters seemed to be slipping back again. These views were reinforced in discussion with members of the tribunal at a number of mental health conferences which we attended. The areas of concern included:

- Ongoing concerns about late booking of tribunal members;
- Lack of up-to-date medical reports for hearings;
- Hearing papers not arriving until the day of the hearing, or the day before;
- Delays in cases getting to hearing;
- Lack of clerking support for tribunals;
- Breakdown in communication links between tribunal judges and administrators, particularly with regard to the promulgation of decision letters.

13. Our Chairman raised these matters with Kevin Sadler, the Chief Executive of the Tribunals Service who acknowledged the seriousness of the issues and set out details of the actions that were being taken to remedy the situation. Among the most noteworthy actions were the establishment of a tribunal members' focus group to provide advice on current issues to the new Secretariat Head and give feedback on proposals for organisational change; and the setting up of a dedicated feedback 'in-box' for members to provide views on general tribunal related issues. Both of these initiatives should go some way to resolving the difficulties which arise through poor channels of communication between members and administrators. Later in the year, Kevin Sadler provided a helpful update of the progress being made in resolving many of these areas of concern and in seeking to address the unique difficulties faced in this jurisdiction and the "whole system" issues which need to be solved to enable sustained improvement in tribunal performance.

NOTES

1. This report could be the last or the penultimate one which the AJTC produced as the chair noted in his foreword to this report:

> However, as the text of this foreword was being finalised we learned that the AJTC is to be included among the MoJ sponsored Arms Length Bodies to be abolished through the Public Bodies Reform Bill, due to be introduced in Parliament in the autumn. Whilst recognising the absolute prerogative of Ministers and Parliament to take such a decision, the outcome is disappointing and it is unfortunate that we were not included in the discussions leading to this decision. However we look forward to contributing to the debate about how our functions are to be discharged in the future. The AJTC and the former Council on Tribunals have been valued for playing a leading role in the development of tribunals and administrative justice for over 50 years. Even if the life of the AJTC itself is to be cut short, we firmly believe that our functions of monitoring, influencing and improving the administrative justice system as a whole, particularly from the perspective of the

> users, will continue to be vital. This is especially so at a time when simultaneously we see a wish to reinforce the power of the citizen against the state, massive pressures upon public services and a mushrooming in the volumes of complaints and appeals.
>
> The administrative justice system is not well understood and, historically, has not been given a high priority, either within the Ministry of Justice or across government as a whole. Notwithstanding the establishment of the Tribunals Service, whose own operations continue to benefit from our oversight, there are still many important tribunal systems operating outside the unified system, and likely to remain so for the foreseeable future. The AJTC was also established to take a unique perspective of how the various components of the administrative justice system—i.e. decision makers, tribunals, ombudsmen, complaint handlers and the courts—fit together. It will be a great pity if this wider perspective were to be lost completely.
>
> I also hope that one or more other bodies, whether inside or outside the public sector, will be able to take on the AJTC's role as the "voice of the user". The recently announced Courts and Tribunals Integration Programme provides a pertinent example of where the AJTC's influence has encouraged policy makers in the MoJ to give proper consideration to the particular needs of tribunal users in taking this work forward. Who will do this in the future?

2. The AJTC's remit of keeping under review 'the administrative justice system' is rather wide. The Tribunals, Courts and Enforcement Act 2007, Sched. 7, para. 13(4) defines it as:

> ...the overall system by which decisions of an administrative or executive nature are made in relation to particular persons, including:
>
> (a) the procedures for making such decisions
> (b) the law under which such decisions are made, and
> (c) the systems for resolving disputes and airing grievances in relation to such decisions.

The Parliamentary Ombudsman, who is an ex officio member of the AJTC, in a speech at the AJTC's launch said:

> ...the role of the AJTC spans the entire spectrum, from awareness of the small places of first-instance decision-making; to strategic oversight of the construction of an integrated administrative justice system in the round, embracing not just courts and tribunals but Ombudsmen too; and finally to the larger task of stimulating public education, both of citizens and of administrators, about the benefits of good administration and the perils of bad.

She said the AJTC had to be aware of realities for citizens faced with officialdom who get things wrong and the complexity of the redress systems as well the fact that through ignorance many people suffer from legal problems which they have not identified as such and so do not seek to remedy them.

The AJTC's approach to administrative justice as a system led to their producing *Principles for Administrative Justice* (2010):

A good administrative justice system should:

1. make users and their needs central, treating them with fairness and respect at all times;
2. enable people to challenge decisions and seek redress using procedures that are independent, open and appropriate for the matter involved;
3. keep people fully informed and empower them to resolve their problems as quickly and comprehensively as possible;
4. lead to well-reasoned, lawful and timely outcomes;
5. be coherent and consistent;
6. work proportionately and efficiently;
7. adopt the highest standards of behaviour, seek to learn from experience and continuously improve.

These principles not only apply to initial decision-makers but also the providers of methods of redress. The AJTC was also keen to ensure that lessons are learnt so as to improve administration. It hoped that more feedback could be provided, as illustrated by this diagram from their publication *The Developing Administrative Justice Landscape* (2009):

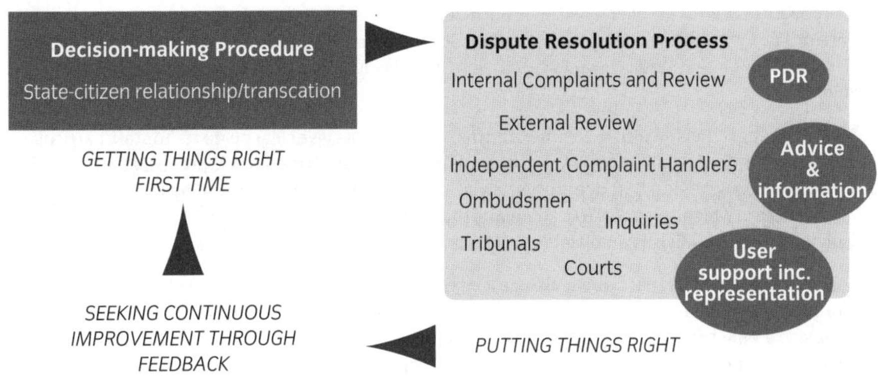

3. The AJTC's concern for the user is substantiated by this research.

H. Genn, B. Lever, and L. Gray, *Tribunals For Diverse Users*

(2006 DCA Research Series 1/06) pp. i–ii

Public knowledge about and access to systems of redress

Discussion groups with Black, South Asian and White members of the public revealed generally weak levels of understanding about avenues of redress for administrative grievances and limited awareness of tribunals. There was little consistent variation between ethnic groups in attitudes to seeking redress or expectations of tribunal proceedings, but language and cultural barriers, coupled with poor information about systems of redress, were seen as critical obstacles in accessing tribunals. Public awareness of advice sources was rather variable. Reported experiences of difficulty in accessing free advice services demonstrates the continuing need to improve the availability of information and advice about seeking redress and for more information to be produced in community languages. Those who take the step of challenging administrative decisions tend to be the most determined and confident, or those who are successful in obtaining advice and support.

There was evidence of reluctance to become involved in legal proceedings because of anticipated expense and complexity. The dominance of criminal justice in the public imagination of courts and tribunals also deters people from seeking redress. There is a considerable job to be done in educating the public about the difference between the criminal courts and those parts of the legal system where rights or entitlements can be made effective. Discussions revealed nagging apprehensions among Black and Minority Ethnic groups about their likely treatment within the legal system. Although concerns tended to be more acute among those who associated legal processes with criminal courts, these concerns, and in some case fears, need to be taken seriously. Tribunals and other legal institutions should seek to reinforce the message that all users are treated fairly and that citizens are equal in the eyes of the law.

The Government, since it commissioned this research is therefore aware of this lack of knowledge. Indeed it is something which the new strategy to legal problems had taken into account.

Transforming Public Services: Complaints, Redress and Tribunals

Cm 6243, paras 107–10.11

10.7 So the individual needs information but also often needs realistic advice about options open to them and the prospects of success. There is an important distinction between the two needs, with implications for the services which are available. It is a responsibility of departments to explain their decisions clearly and fully. It is a joint responsibility between departments and tribunals to explain what the options and procedures are for obtaining redress. Both departments and tribunals should strive to provide a service of a quality which makes assistance at this stage unnecessary. However, at present, this information is not always integrated in a way which helps the individual to chart a way through their particular problem.

10.8 The Leggatt Review also recommended that departments give clear guidance to staff, particularly those involved in departmental review, on the kinds of case for which the various processes are appropriate. The Review suggested that departments give clear information in their leaflets to users about the circumstances in which an appeal to a tribunal is the route to follow and, by explaining the differences in jurisdiction, those in which a complaint to an ombudsman or adjudicator is more appropriate.

10.9 We agree with all that but we also believe that many users want and would benefit from advice from a source independent of government about what they should do in relation to their case. Some need clear advice on whether they have a case at all in any forum. So while departments should always provide information on appeal and grievance routes it may be more appropriate for government to support external providers, particularly the voluntary and charitable sector, in providing diagnostic tools and advice. Staff at the new tribunal organisation will be able to provide advice on procedure and may be allowed to offer a view on prospects or merits but they have to be neutral, in a way that an advisor does not. They do have a role in assisting independent advisors to give accurate information about procedural options. Because the independent advisor can advise both on the options and the merits it may make more sense from the user's point of view for both types of advice to come from the same source.

10.10 The voluntary and charitable sector has always played an important role in advice and assistance in administrative justice and tribunal cases. We want that to continue and expand, although the private sector will always have a role in assisting the users of some tribunals and may be able to take on an expanded role in others. Likewise, we see a continuing role for public funding in tribunals where the right to asylum and the right to liberty are involved and in the Employment Appeal Tribunal. Within those parameters, we accept that there is a need in some cases to provide assistance in, for instance, gathering information and evidence and filling in paperwork, and in advising on merits and presentation. We intend to provide resources and work with potential providers to pilot innovative schemes to do this. This will be called the Enhanced Advice Project. We do not want to be prescriptive at this stage about what those schemes might be: our intention is to work together with the Legal Services Commission and the voluntary and charitable sector within the resources available. Much will depend on the nature of the innovative dispute resolution methods which the new service succeeds in establishing. Our work together will be as much focused on making procedures more accessible as on devising new ways of assisting people through procedures.

10.11 Our aim is to reduce the need for hearings before tribunals through better decisions and innovative proportionate dispute resolution methods. But some cases will require oral hearings and the extent to which publicly funded advocacy is necessary or desirable in tribunals remains a matter of debate. Tribunals bear many similarities to courts but the hearings are intended to be less formal and adversarial in nature which ought in time to reduce the need for representation. The relevant law may also be simpler than in many court cases and even where it is not in many tribunals there will rarely be a need for a party to concern themselves with technical evidential issues or to deploy the traditional lawyer skill of cross-examination of witnesses.

NOTES

1. The Enhanced Advice Project has not yet been implemented but see *Making Legal Rights A Reality: The Legal Services Commission's Strategy for the Community Legal Service 2006–2011* which proposed commissioning centres and networks that provide access to a service which ranges from basic advice to legal representation in the full range of social welfare problems as well as children and

family legal problems, expanding the free telephone service CLS Direct (renamed Community Legal Advice) to provide readily accessible specialist advice, and reaching out to provide legal advice and representation to the most disadvantaged in society. The AJTC will no doubt be very interested in monitoring such schemes and working with the Legal Services Commission on their policy for funding legal advice, assistance and representation in the administrative justice system.

2. The Public Legal Education and Support (PLEAS) Task Force produced its report *Developing capable citizens: the role of public legal education* in July 2007 which recommended a more coherent approach to public legal education to be pursued by a specialist agency. It was welcomed by the Minister for Legal Aid who said that public legal education is vital in providing access to justice by making people aware of their rights and responsibilities and that he would now discuss with colleagues in government how best we can overcome the obstacles to effective public legal education.

■ QUESTIONS

1. If the Government's strategy on administrative justice can be compared to medicine, (a) how much preventative medicine in the form of public legal education, advice and support will be needed to prevent or 'nip in the bud' problems thus reducing the need for the curative medicine of complaints systems, ombudsmen, tribunals and courts; (b) who will provide it; and (c) who will pay for it?
2. To what extent are the Government's arguments about a lesser need for representation in tribunals in para. 10.11 consistent with the research evidence on users' needs and experiences?
3. Is it desirable to view administrative justice as a system, considering together both 'putting it right' and 'getting it right'?

INDEX